# The Blackwell Companion to the Sociology of Families

# BLACKWELL COMPANIONS TO SOCIOLOGY

The *Blackwell Companions to Sociology* provide introductions to emerging topics and theoretical orientations in sociology as well as presenting the scope and quality of the discipline as it is currently configured. Essays in the Companions tackle broad themes or central puzzles within the field and are authored by key scholars who have spent considerable time in research and reflection on the questions and controversies that have activated interest in their area. This authoritative series will interest those studying sociology at advanced undergraduate or graduate level as well as scholars in the social sciences and informed readers in applied disciplines.

*Series List:*

1 *The Blackwell Companion to Social Theory*, Second Edition
Edited by Bryan S. Turner

2 *The Blackwell Companion to Major Social Theorists*
Edited by George Ritzer

3 *The Blackwell Companion to Political Sociology*
Edited by Kate Nash and Alan Scott

4 *The Blackwell Companion to Medical Sociology*
Edited by William C. Cockerham

5 *The Blackwell Companion to Sociology*
Edited by Judith R. Blau

6 *The Blackwell Companion to Major Classical Social Theorists*
Edited by George Ritzer

7 *The Blackwell Companion to Major Contemporary Social Theorists*
Edited by George Ritzer

8 *The Blackwell Companion to Criminology*
Edited by Colin Sumner

9 *The Blackwell Companion to the Sociology of Families*
Edited by Jacqueline Scott, Judith Treas, and Martin Richards

10 *The Blackwell Companion to Social Movements*
Edited by David A. Snow, Sarah A. Soule, and Hanspeter Kriesi

11 *The Blackwell Companion to Law and Society*
Edited by Austin Sarat

12 *The Blackwell Companion to the Sociology of Culture*
Edited by Mark Jacobs and Nancy Hanrahan

13 *The Blackwell Companion to Social Inequalities*
Edited by Mary Romero and Eric Margolis

# The Blackwell Companion to the Sociology of Families

*Edited by*

Jacqueline Scott, Judith Treas,
and
Martin Richards

BLACKWELL PUBLISHING
350 Main Street, Malden, MA 02148-5020, USA
9600 Garsington Road, Oxford OX4 2DQ, UK
550 Swanston Street, Carlton, Victoria 3053, Australia



First published 2004 by Blackwell Publishing Ltd
First published in paperback 2007 by Blackwell Publishing Ltd

1 2007

*Library of Congress Cataloging-in-Publication Data*

The Blackwell companion to the sociology of families / edited by Jacqueline Scott,
Judith Treas, and Martin Richards.
p. cm. – (Blackwell companions to sociology)
Includes bibliographical references and index.
ISBN 978-0-631-22158-6 (hardcover: alk. paper) ISBN 978-1-4051-7563-0 (paperback: alk. paper)
1. Family–Research. 2. Sociology. I. Scott, Jacqueline II. Treas, Judith.
III. Richards, Martin. IV. Series.
HQ519.B53 2004
306.85′072–dc21

2003004166

A catalogue record for this title is available from the British Library.

Set in 10/12pt Sabon
by Kolam Information Services Pvt. Ltd, Pondicherry, India
Printed and bound in Great Britain
by TJ International Ltd, Padstow, Cornwall

The publisher's policy is to use permanent paper from mills that operate a sustainable forestry policy, and which has been manufactured from pulp processed using acid-free and elementary chlorine-free practices. Furthermore, the publisher ensures that the text paper and cover board used have met acceptable environmental accreditation standards.

For further information on
Blackwell Publishing, visit our website:
www.blackwellpublishing.com

# Contents

# Contributors

**Graham Allan** is Professor of Social Relations at Keele University. His research mainly focuses on aspects of informal social relationships. He is particularly interested in the sociology of friendship, family and domestic life, kinship, and community, and has written widely on these subjects. His current research includes projects on stepfamily kinship and on marital affairs.

**Duane F. Alwin** is the McCourtney Professor of Sociology, Demography, and Human Development at Pennsylvania State University. He is completing work on a research monograph related to his contribution in this volume on the impact of changes in the American family over the past century entitled *The Disciplined Self: Transformations of Child-Rearing in American Society Over the Twentieth Century.* In addition to families and children, the focus of his teaching and research includes the study of aging and the life-course, the development and change in social and political attitudes over the life span, and the linkages between historical events, socialization processes, and social change.

**Ronald J. Angel** is Professor of Sociology at the University of Texas, Austin and one of the nation's leading Hispanic social scientists. For over 25 years his research and writing have focused on the social situation and health-care needs of minority populations, with a special focus on Hispanics. This work documents serious inequities in income, wealth, and health-care access among Hispanic subgroups and relates those to structural factors, particularly those that result from labor market disadvantages. His recent research focuses on the role of non-governmental organizations in providing health and social services to poor Americans and extends this research to the study of the poor in Latin America. With Laura Lein and Jane Henrici he is author of *Poor Families in America's Health Care Crisis* (2006), and with his wife, Jacqueline Angel, he is author of *Painful Inheritance: Health and the New Generation of Fatherless Families* (1993) and *Who Will Care For Us? Aging and Long-Term Care in Multicultural America* (1997). Professor Angel served as

Editor of the *Journal of Health and Social Behavior* from 1994 to 1997, and he has served on the editorial boards of numerous other journals. He has administered several large grants from NIA, NIMH, NICHD, and several private foundations. He is currently involved in a large multi-method national study of the impact of welfare reform on poor families. For more information see: http://www.jhu.edu/~welfare/. In 1996 he was elected Fellow of the American Association for the advancement of Science.

**Jacqueline L. Angel** is a Professor of Public Affairs and Sociology and a Faculty Affiliate at the Population Research Center at The University of Texas at Austin. Her research addresses the relationships linking family structures, inequality, and health across the life course. She is particularly interested in public policies influencing the well-being of the Hispanic population. Her books include: *The Health of Aging Hispanics: The Mexican-Origin Population* (2007), co-edited with Keith Whitfield; *Who Will care for Us? Aging and Long-Term Care in Multicultural America* (1997); *Painful Inheritance: Health and the New Generation of Fatherless Families* (1993), with Ronald Angel; and *Health and Living Arrangements of the Elderly* (1991).

**Nicholas M. Bala** has been a Professor at the Faculty of Law at Queen's University, Kingston, Ontario, since 1980 and has been a visiting professor at the University of Calgary and McGill and Duke Universities. His primary area of teaching and research interest is family and children's law, focusing on such issues as juvenile justice, child abuse and child witnesses, domestic violence, parental rights and responsibilities after divorce, spousal support obligations, and the legal definition of the family. He is a member of the Board of Directors of the Canadian Research Institute for Law and the Family.

**Ulrich Beck** is Professor for Sociology at the University of Munich, and the *British Journal of Sociology* Visiting Centennial Professor at the London School of Economics and Political Science. He is chief-editor of *Soziale Welt* and editor of *Zweite Moderne* at Suhrkamp (Frankfurt am Main). His interests focus on "risk society," "individualization," "reflexive modernization," and "cosmopolitan society and sociology." He is the director of a research center at the University of Munich (in cooperation with four other universities in the area) – Reflexive Modernization – financed since 1999 by the DFG (German Research Society).

**Elisabeth Beck-Gernsheim** is Professor for Sociology at the University of Erlangen-Nuremberg. Her research areas are the family, reproductive technology, migration, and ethnicity. Her latest publications in English are *Reinventing the Family. In Search of New Lifestyles* and (with Ulrich Beck) *Individualization. Institutionalized Individualism and its Social and Political Consequences* (both 2002).

**Vern L. Bengtson** is Professor of Sociology and AARP/University Professor of Gerontology at the University of Southern California. He has published 12 books and over 200 articles in the areas of family sociology and aging. A past president of the Gerontological Society of America, he started the Longitudinal Study of Generations, a 31-year investigation of multigenerational families, aging, and social change. His most recent book is *How Families Still Matter: A Longitudinal Study of Youth in Two Generations* (2002). He has received numerous awards, including the Reuben Hill Award (1980 and 1986) and the Ernest W. Burgess Award (1998) from the National Council of Family Relations; the Distinguished Scholar Award from the American Sociological Association (1995); and the Robert W. Kleemeier Award from the Gerontological Society of America (1996).

**Lorne D. Bertrand** is Senior Research Associate at the Canadian Research Institute for Law and the Family at the University of Calgary. He holds a BA, an MA, and a Ph.D. in Social Psychology from Carleton University, Ottawa. Since joining the Institute in 1993, he has conducted research projects and published in the areas of adolescent substance use, youth delinquency and justice, the victimization of adults, child support, and child custody and access.

**Michelle J. Budig** is an Associate Professor of Sociology and the Associate Director of the Social and Demographic Research Institute at the University of Massachusetts. Her research interests are gender and employment, work and family conflict, inequality, and social policy. Her recent publications investigate cross-national differences in the wage penalty for motherhood, gender differences in self-employment participation and earnings, and the effects of feminization of academic fields. In 2003, she was awarded the Rosabeth Moss Kanter Award for Research Excellence in Families and Work, presented by the Center for Families at Purdue University and the Boston College Center for Work and Family. Her current research examines motherhood wage penalties in a comparative perspective, racial/ethnic discrepancies in the effects of human capital on wages, and racial/ethnic differences in the rising trends of childlessness and only-child families.

**Philip N. Cohen** is Associate Professor of Sociology, University of North Carolina at Chapel Hill, where he teaches in the areas of social inequality, sociological theory, and demography. His research concerns the relationship between family structure and inequality within and between families – over time and across various social contexts. He also studies micro–macro linkages in social inequality, including the effects of labor market racial/ethnic composition on inequality by race and gender, and the determinants of inequality within and between jobs across labor markets.

**Claire Collins** was a research intern and undergraduate student in the School of Sociology and Social Policy, University of Nottingham.

**Graham Crow** is Professor of Sociology at the University of Southampton and Deputy Director of the ESRC National Centre for Research Methods. His publications have contributed to debates in the sociology of families and households, the sociology of communities, comparative sociology, sociological theory and research methods.

**Shirley Dex** is Professor of Longitudinal Social Research at the Institute of Education, London University, and formerly (1998–2004) Research Advisor to the Joseph Rowntree Foundation's Work and Family Life research program. She has published widely on the topics of families and labor markets, women's employment in Britain and in cross-national comparisons, equal opportunities, and family-friendly employment policies in organizations. Two recent publications are *The Nature and Patterns of Family-friendly Employment Policies in Britain* (with Colin Smith, 2002) and *SMEs and Flexible Working Arrangements* (with Fiona Scheibl, 2002).

**Catherine Donovan** is a Senior Lecturer in Sociology at the University of Sunderland. Her research interests include families of choice; assisted conception, especially donor insemination; and domestic violence. She is co-author (with Jeffrey Weeks and

Brian Heaphy) of *Same Sex Intimacies: Families of Choice and other Life Experiments* (2001).

**Don Edgar** was foundation Director of the Australian Institute of Family Studies and is now an international policy consultant and writer on work–family programs, early childhood development, community building, and aging. He has held senior positions at the universities of Chicago, Monash, and La Trobe. His most recent books are *Men, Mateship, Marriage* (1997) and *The Patchwork Nation: Rethinking Government, Rebuilding Community* (2001).

**Sinikka Elliott** is a Doctoral Candidate of Sociology at the University of Texas, Austin. In a recent publication, she examines family communication and interaction patterns. Current projects focus on stressful life events and chronic strains over the life course and how these may affect marital quality over time, negotiating group identities, and relationship dynamics over the life course.

**Frank F. Furstenberg** is the Zellerbach Family Professor of Sociology and Research Associate in the Population Studies Center at the University of Pennsylvania. His interest in the American family began at Columbia University, where he received his Ph.D. in 1967. His current research projects focus on the family in the context of disadvantaged urban neighborhoods, adolescent sexual behavior, cross-national research on children's well-being, urban education, and the transition to adulthood. He is current Chair of the MacArthur Foundation Research Network on the Transitions to Adulthood.

**Jonathan Gershuny** is Professor of Sociology and the Director of the Institute for Social and Economic Research at Essex University. He is the Principal Investigator of the British Household Panel Survey, and the originator and director of the Multinational Time Use Study, which now includes more than 50 time-use surveys from 25 countries in a harmonized format. His research concerns the interrelations between patterns of daily activity at the individual level, and the determination of social position through the life course. He is a Fellow of the British Academy.

**Roseann Giarrusso** is a Research Associate Professor of Gerontology and Sociology at the University of Southern California, and the Project Director of the Longitudinal Study of Generations. Her research interests include intergenerational family relations, social psychology, and the sociology of aging and the life course. Her most recent publications include an examination of reciprocity in parent–child relations over the life course, cross-ethnic differences in grandparent–adult grandchild solidarity, and how the self-concept changes across two decades.

**Lisa Glennon** is a Lecturer in Law at Queen's University, Belfast. Her main research interest is family law and her recent publications examine the legal definition of the family in light of contemporary societal trends, the rights of same-sex couples, the viability of same-sex marriage as a strategy for reform, and the distribution of property and income on relationship breakdown. As well as being an Executive Committee member of the Socio-Legal Studies Association, she is a member of the Editorial Advisory Committee of the multidisciplinary journal *Child Care in Practice* and is Northern Ireland Editor of the *Irish Journal of Family Law*. She has also acted as consultant to the Law Reform Advisory Committee for Northern Ireland.

**Brian Heaphy** is Senior Lecturer in Sociology at Nottingham Trent University. His recent publications have focused on the everyday politics of living with HIV, and on same-sex relating. He has recently coauthored *Same Sex Intimacies: Families of Choice and other Life Experiments* (with Jeffrey Weeks and Catherine Donovan, 2001). His current research is concerned with the social and policy implications of lesbian, gay, and bisexual aging.

**Sarah B. Kaplan** is a Ph.D. candidate in sociology at the University of Pennsylvania and she received her BA from Brown University. Her interests include parenting, childhood, work and families. Her current research project looks at how families view the after-school hours and how they arrange care and activities for this time period.

**Catherine Kenney** is an Assistant Professor of Sociology and Women's Studies at the University of Illinois at Urbana-Champaign. Her current research includes work on cohabiting-parent families, money management and resource allocation within households, and domestic violence in different family forms.

**Kathleen Kiernan** is Professor of Social Policy and Demography at York University. She has conducted research on a wide range of issues pertaining to family life, including teenage parenthood, divorce, cohabitation, nonmarital childbearing, lone motherhood, and the demography of disadvantage. Much of her research uses longitudinal data from the British birth cohort studies and, more recently, comparative data from a range of European countries and the USA.

**Hilary Land** is Professor Emerita of Family Policy and Child Welfare at the University of Bristol, where she was head of the School for Policy Studies from 1997 to 2000. She has had a long-standing interest in family policies from both historical and comparative perspectives. Her recent research focuses on child-care, grandparenting, and pensions. Recent publications include *Lone Motherhood in Twentieth Century Britain* (with Kathleen Kiernan and Jane Lewis, 1998). She is currently a member of the Elizabeth Nuffield Educational Fund committee and is president of the Social Policy Association.

**J. Beth Mabry** is Assistant Professor of Sociology at Indiana University of Pennsylvania, and a past National Institute on Aging Postdoctoral Fellow in Sociology at the University of Southern California's Andrus Gerontology Center. Her research interests include intergenerational exchanges in adulthood, adult child – parent relationships across the life-course, and social structure and emotional experience.

**Danielle MacCartney** is an Assistant Professor at Webster University, where she conducts research and teaches on social inequality in labor markets and the family. Her most recent research is about the effects of gender transgression at work by race, gender, and sexual orientation.

**Dr Catherine Maclean** was previously a Lecturer in Sociology in the School of Social and Political Studies at the University of Edinburgh. Her research interests and publications are in the areas of community, childhood, work – family balance, social change and migration in remote rural areas, and qualitative research methodology.

**David H. J. Morgan** is Professor Emeritus in Sociology at the University of Manchester and a Visiting Professor at Keele University. He has worked in family studies and gender studies (with particular reference to issues of men and masculinities) for about 30 years. His latest book is, in collaboration with Clare Holdsworth, *Transitions in Context: Leaving Home, Independence and Adulthood* (2005).

**Joanne J. Paetsch** is the Administrator/Research Associate with the Canadian Research Institute for Law and the Family, which is a nonprofit, independent institute that undertakes and promotes interdisciplinary research, education, and publication on issues related to law and the family. Her recent publications examine issues such as juvenile justice, victimization, legal aid, child abuse, child custody and access, and child support.

**Chris Phillipson** is Director of the Centre for Social Gerontology at Keele University. He has published extensively in the field of aging studies, especially in relation to retirement, family life, and social theory and aging. He is currently co-directing a study on social exclusion in old age (as part of the ESRC Growing Older Programme), and has also been directing a project exploring the lives of women from Bangladesh living in London's East End. His recent publications include a report for the Joseph Rowntree Foundation on changing transitions from work to retirement, and articles on the impact of globalization on the lives of older people.

**Jan Pryor** is the Director of the Roy McKenzie Centre for the Study of Families at the Victoria University of Wellington, in New Zealand. Her research includes the study of transitions in families, and dynamics in stepfamilies. She is co-author with Bryan Rodgers of *Children in Changing Families. Life After Parents Separate* (Blackwell, 2001).

**Karen Pyke** is an Associate Professor of Sociology at the University of California, Riverside. She is a qualitative researcher who studies Asian Americans, families, gender, race, and internalized racial oppression. Her recent publications focus on second-generation Asian Americans and racialized femininities, racism, and the formation of sub-ethnic identities; the way narrow cultural notions of an ideal family shape the perceptions of immigrant children, and acculturative differences among siblings in immigrant families. She is currently involved in two new projects on multiracial and biracial Asian Americans and East Asian "parachute" children who live in the US without their parents. Her article "Asian American Women and Racialized Femininities: 'Doing' Gender Across Cultural Worlds," *Gender & Society*, recently received the Best Article Award from the Sex and Gender Section of American Sociological Association. She is deputy editor of *Journal of Family Issues*.

**Martin Richards** is Professor of Family Research and Director of the Centre for Family Research at the University of Cambridge. His research has ranged over a number of aspects of family life, but in recent years has focused on parents and children and divorce, and the family aspects of new genetic and reproductive technologies. The latter work includes both investigations of contemporary issues and historical work on human selective breeding and eugenics.

**Jacqueline Scott** is a Reader in Sociology at the University of Cambridge. Her former positions include Director of Research at the ESRC Centre for Micro-social Change at the University of Essex and Director of the Detroit Area Study at the University of Michigan. She is Co-Director of the Cambridge Interdisciplinary Research Centre on Ageing and her current interests include life-course research and gender inequalities. Her recent publications examine youth and disadvantage, intergenerational attitudinal change, and cross-national comparisons of family and demographic change.

**Alison Shaw** is a Senior Research Fellow in the Department of Public Health at the University of Oxford and was previously a lecturer in Social Anthropology at Brunel University. She has conducted field research in Pakistan and with British Pakistanis and directed an adult education project teaching Urdu. Her current research investigates British Pakistani interpretations of genetic diagnosis. Her recent publications include an updated monograph on Pakistani families in Britain, and analyses of Pakistani marriage trends, the lives of the elderly without children, Pakistani attitudes to genetic risk and disability, and the clinical processes that shape genetic diagnosis.

**Wendy Sigle-Rushton** is a lecturer in Social Policy at the London School of Economics and Political Science An economic demographer, she has worked on a variety of issues related to child fostering, child health, and single parenthood in both historical and contemporary societies. Her recent publications have focused on the potential impact of proposed welfare reform policies in the US and the living arrangements of new parents. Her current research interests include the social networks and social isolation of young adults who have been in care as children or who became young parents – with a particular emphasis on the differences between men and women.

**Judith Treas** is Professor of Sociology at the University of California, Irvine. A Fellow of the Gerontological Society of America, she is recognized for research on the life course and aging, family, sexuality, inequality, and population. Her recent publications investigate cross-national differences in gender beliefs and family behavior, the lives of elderly immigrants, and the determinants of change in sexual attitudes.

**Liz Trinder** is Director of Newcastle Centre for Family Studies, Newcastle University. She has a longstanding interest in post-divorce family relationships. She has recently completed a study on contact after divorce for the Joseph Rowntree Foundation and is currently undertaking a study on the process and outcomes of in court conciliation for the Lord Chancellor's Department.

**Bryan S. Turner** is Professor of Sociology in the Asia Research Institute, National University of Singapore. He edited the *Cambridge Dictionary of Sociology* (2006) and published *Vulnerability and Human Rights* (2006). He is the founding editor of the journals *Citizenship Studies*, *Body & Society* (with Mike Featherstone), and *Journal of Classical Sociology* (with John O'Neill). His current research interests include women and piety, and state responses to religious diversity in Southeast Asia.

**Debra Umberson** is Professor and Chair of Sociology at the University of Texas. Her research focuses on structural determinants of physical and mental health, with a specific focus on gender and life-course variation. Her latest work, on domestic violence, shows how the effects of relationship dynamics on mental health differ for violent and nonviolent men. Her current research, funded by the National Institute on Aging (NIA #AG17455), examines change in marital quality and the effect of marital quality on health over the life course.

**Robert Walker** is Professor of Social Policy and Fellow of Green College, University of Oxford. He is Fellow of the Royal Society of Arts and a Research Affiliate of the National Poverty Center, University of Michigan. His research interests include poverty dynamics, social exclusion, unemployment and employment progression, children's aspirations, family dynamics, and household budgeting strategies. He has published 18 books and over 50 research reports.

**Jeffrey Weeks** is Professor of Sociology and Dean of Humanities and Social Science at London South Bank University. He has written widely on the history and social organization of sexuality, intimacy, and family life. Recent books include *Invented Moralities: Sexual Values in an Age of Uncertainty* (1995), *Sexual Cultures* (with Janet Holland, 1996), *Making Sexual History* (2000), *Same Sex Intimacies: Families of Choice and other Life Experiments* (with Brian Heaphy and Catherine Donovan, 2001), and *Sexualities and Society: A Reader* (with Janet Holland and Matthew Waites, 2003).

**Eric Widmer** is at the Sociology Department of Geneva University. His long-term interests include family relations, life-course research, and social networks. His most recent publications empirically investigate the diversity of contemporary conjugal relationships and their social determinants.

# Preface

The sociology of families has moved from being at the fringes of the discipline to being one of the key areas for understanding the structural and life-course transformations that are taking place across the globe. The upheavals of the late twentieth century have left social researchers keen to understand how individuals are responding to and shaping the rapid changes that are occurring in economic, political, and cultural spheres. For examining the impact of globalization and the ramifications of individualization, there is no better test-bed than the family setting. As the social theorist Anthony Giddens notes:

> Among all the changes going on today, none are more important than those happening in our personal lives – in sexuality, relationships, marriage and the family. There is a global revolution going on in how we think of ourselves and how we form ties and connections with others. It is a revolution advancing unevenly in different regions and cultures, with many resistances. (1999: 51)

In this *Companion to the Sociology of Families* we examine both changing family forms and relationships and the changing social context – globalization, technological innovation, state policy, religion, employment, and community – that shape family life today. While the book has a deliberate comparative focus, families in Europe and North America are given special attention, with discussion of previously neglected groups, including immigrant families, gays, and lesbians. Globalization and upheavals of the "risk" society provide the backdrop for issues ranging from new reproductive technologies to the changing family role of men. The *Companion* shows how revolutionary changes in sexual behavior, aging, and longevity have radically affected the experiences of children and parents over the life-course and have shifted the ties that bind across the generations.

The *Companion to the Sociology of Families* tackles a range of questions that are relevant to family life today and looks ahead to changes to come. How is family life shaped by social inequality? How have parenting practices changed? Why has children's work been neglected in family sociology? What implications do the new reproductive technologies and genetic technologies have for family relations? What effects will changing patterns of citizenship have on family life? What challenges confront families in multicultural societies? The authors are experts in their fields and provide a selective overview of empirical research and address emerging issues. Together, the chapters of this volume show why the study of social change in families is a necessary key for understanding the transformations in individual and social life taking place across the globe.

While the focus of this *Companion* is on the *sociology* of families, the subject matter is inherently interdisciplinary. The boundaries between sociology and psychology become blurred in research concerned with parent and child relations. Sociology crosses with economics in discussions of rational choice and the inter- and intra-generational transmission of human, material, social, and cultural capital. Insights from biology are crucial to understanding the impact of genetics and new reproductive technologies. Sociology interlinks with medicine in the study of aging and family health. Thus, while sociological theories and concepts are central throughout this *Companion*, many chapters explicitly draw on a diverse range of theoretical and empirical approaches to inform the analyses of family change. These include the life-course perspective, feminism, inequality and stratification, kinship, and social networks. We attempt to break down what were once rigid boundaries between the sociology of families and other specialist domains such as the sociology of work and the sociology of health.

The metaphor of the kaleidoscope is an apt one to describe the complexities and overlaps between areas such as gender, work, kinship, economy, health, time use, communications, and community. In his book *Family Connections*, David Morgan expressed this well when he suggested:

> With one turn we see a blending of the distinctions between home and work, family and economy, and the idea of household comes into focus. With another turn, the apparently solid boundaries of the household dissolve and we see family and kinship, and possibly other relationships spreading out across these fainter boundaries. With each twist of the kaleidoscope we see these patterns are differently coloured according to gender, age and generation and other social divisions. (1996: 33).

This *Companion* shows these crucial intersections, with individuals interlinked with other family members, and families interlinked with other institutions, including education, citizenship, and religion, and the whole blending process stretching across time.

The overlap of family and gender is now so taken for granted that it is sometimes overlooked that the feminist influence on the sociology of families has occurred only in the last three or four decades. In this *Companion*, we highlight the intellectual debt owed to feminist scholars and review current and future directions of feminist research. There is still a tension between feminism and family (see Budig, chapter 24 in this volume). Debates on family patriarchalism and whether or not patriarchalism is in global decline are only briefly touched on in this *Companion* (interested readers should see Castells, 1997). However, there is a related, but more general, ongoing debate of "family decline" and family diversity. This is sometimes framed in terms of gender inequalities, but also, more generally, in terms of individual well-being, particularly of children's welfare. This broader debate is referred to in many chapters in this volume.

No one can read this *Companion* and remain unaware of family change and the increasing diversity of family forms. Indeed, the very title *Sociology of Families* deliberately avoids the static and universal terminology of "the Family." Our title acknowledges the plurality of family forms and, by implication, the dynamic processes of family formation and dissolution across time. The family concept of "marriage" illustrates this complexity. Marriage has a very different meaning for someone growing up in Europe or North America today than it had for previous generations, when cohabitation and divorce were relatively rare. Patterns of cohabitation vary enormously across different cultures, in part reflecting different religious traditions. For some cultures cohabitation is an acceptable prelude or alternative to marriage, for others it is still seen as a sin. Similarly, in some cultures childbirth is still predominantly within the marital union, whereas in others, notably Scandinavia, reproduction and marriage are becoming increasingly distinct.

Crosscultural variations in family life pose a huge challenge for research. However, even within one family there is much to unravel before we can begin to understand family forms and relationships. Family life is very different from the perspective of each different family member. Home is a tangle of conventions and totally incommensurable rights and duties, as Douglas (1993) pointed out. Family life runs on a gift, not a money, economy, with every service and transfer a part of a comprehensive system of exchanges within and between the generations. Being a parent and being a child are very different roles that can be closer or more distant at different points in time. Whatever the relationship, the bond has ramifications across the life-course and beyond to the next generation.

Family life is also very different from the perspective of gender. Too often in the past, the study of families has been undertaken, almost exclusively, from the viewpoint of women. Feminists were right to express concern that women were "imprisoned" in families (conceptually speaking) and needed to be liberated to give them voice. If women were seen only in terms of family, this clearly misrepresents the multidimensional nature of women's lives. Similarly, the gender bias in family sociology has been a problem for understanding the complex lives of men as partners, fathers, and carers. The gender, generational, ethnic, and cultural biases of family sociology have also, in the past, hindered efforts to understand the rich variety of family forms and experiences.

To understand lives in the modern era, reproductive and productive spheres must be seen as interlinked – the divide between "sociology of work" and "sociology of families" is an untenable one. A focus on working families brings recognition of new questions concerning children's work, the complex relationship between marketable work skills and family care, and the reciprocal exchanges that flow between generations. The changing relationship between paid work and family life has huge ramifications for inequality, citizenship, and public policy. Many chapters in this volume review this complex, interdependent domain and discuss the emerging debates and policy relevance.

The *Companion* takes as axiomatic the importance of bringing time and space to the fore in reviewing key areas of family research. Historical research has exposed many of the myths concerning previous eras and has helped uncover the complex interweaving of continuities and change in family life. For example, the early findings of Louis Henry and the Annales group in France, the Cambridge Group for the History of Population and Social Structure, and the historians of colonial North America – that preindustrial populations resided in small, predominantly nuclear households, married later than previously assumed, and practiced some form of family limitation – have led to a drastic revision of generalizations about the impact of industrialization on family and demographic behavior (Laslett, 1965; Wrigley, 1966, Henry, 1968; Laslett and Wall, 1972; Hareven, 2000).

A complementary strand of research has been the continuing focus on community studies that provide insight into the specificity of the influence of time and space on family living, as well as the more diffuse class, religious, and ethnic differences in family forms. Repeated community studies have given insights into the changes and continuities over time (e.g., see Lynd and Lynd 1929, 1937; Caplow et al., 1982; Young and Wilmott, 1957, 1973; Crow and Maclean, chapter 5 in this volume; Phillipson and Allan, chapter 8 in this volume). One profound consequence of contemporary globalization – with its migration streams, instant communication, and transnational interdependence – is that many families, especially immigrant families, now reside in communities bounded not by geography, but rather by identity.

Advances in longitudinal analysis and comparative methodologies are posing new opportunities for family life-course research. In addition, the expanding use of cross-national research has been invaluable for identifying the common and distinctive features of family forms in different cultural contexts. Comparison is important for assessing the uniqueness of family life in a particular culture, an ongoing concern of family sociology associated with particular nations (e.g., for Britain see Allan, 1999; and for the US see Caspi and Bianchi, 2002). It is also important for understanding how similar social forces affect people in various societies differentially, as they encounter the transformations of urbanization, industrialization, and globalization. This *Companion* has not, in the main, focused on new methodologies, in part because these tend to be geared toward quite specialist audiences (e.g., Giele and Elder, 1998), but exceptions include Gershuny, chapter 10 in this volume.

## Organization and Overview

The contributing authors were asked not only to provide an appraisal and synthesis of the major lines of inquiry that have dominated their field, but also to forecast new theoretical and empirical debates that are emerging in response to the changing circumstances of the contemporary world. In particular, authors were encouraged (1) to ensure that their chapters make clear the major theoretical ideas and empirical studies that have helped shape the best current work of the area; (2) to explain how current concerns have responded to the changing circumstances of contemporary society; (3) to consider the implications that recent developments in the field have for further study; and (4) to review how controversies and debates can contribute to advancing sociological understanding and knowledge, including possible policy relevance.

We have organized the chapters in this volume to address five broad domains. The first five chapters examine families in the context of a global world. This *Companion*, while explicitly adopting a global perspective, does give greater emphasis to European and North American research than to the family sociology of the developing world. In part, this restricted focus is due to space constraints. To do justice to the wealth of family research from Asia, Africa, and other parts of the globe would require another volume, at least.

Don Edgar (chapter 1) examines issues of globalization and Western bias in family sociology. He suggests that Western sociology has placed considerable emphasis on the rise of individualism. Individualism has been closely tied with stress on the risk society and with the need for individuals to negotiate their own life course. Edgar challenges the applicability of this emphasis, suggesting instead that sociologists should be examining the nature of those family resources and family processes that open up or limit the options available to each individual. In his emphasis on family agency, Edgar sets the scene for later chapters that stress the role of interlinked lives in shaping the modern life course.

Kathleen Kiernan (chapter 2) and Sinikka Elliott and Debra Umberson (chapter 3) examine the patterns of family change in Europe and the US. Kiernan's chapter documents how major demographic changes are directly influencing the relationship between the family and public policy and shows how changes in partnership and parenthood behavior vary widely across Europe. Despite the predominance of the traditional one-family household in Europe, the "family norm" of a married couple is gradually being replaced with other living arrangements, including cohabitation, lone parents, and reconstituted families. Kiernan anticipates policy questions that are picked up in later chapters, including "What should the contribution of families and the state be to the rearing of children, and who should pay?" Elliott and Umberson document the demographic changes that are going on in the US, focusing on how these trends are associated with the health and well-being of individuals. They emphasize that it is not merely the existence of family relationships that affect individual well-being, but the quality of these relationships as well.

Hilary Land (chapter 4) explores some of the key challenges which the new international framework governing children's rights poses for the private world of families and the public worlds of civil society, international agencies, and corporations in the twenty-first century. She draws attention to the tension between treating children independently of their families and invoking parental responsibilities. With 13 million children orphaned through AIDS and 20 million displaced as refugees, the question of society's responsibility for children is not something that can be confined within national boundaries. Land questions whether the international community has the will to turn platitudes about children's rights into the social and economic investment needed for a just society. Globalization has, as many commentators have noted, the rather paradoxical consequence of both enlarging the international arena and revitalizing concern with local identities and community. Graham Crow and Catherine Maclean (chapter 5) point to varied solutions to the problems posed by geographic distance for supportive family networks. Despite greater dispersion of families, the positive value of local community clearly persists, and increasing globalization is accompanied by the reconstruction, not the dissolution, of local communities.

Part II is explicitly framed around the life-course perspective on families. A key insight of the life-course perspective is the way early experiences help shape later opportunities and outcomes across the interrelated sectors of people's lives, including education, family, work, and leisure. A second insight is that lives are interdependent both within and across the generations and that agency is a relational, not an individual, concept. Family strategies, for example, in allocating time between paid and unpaid labor, have immediate and incremental consequences for all members that can persist from one generation to the next. According to J. Beth Mabry, Roseanne Giarrusso, and Vern Bengtson (chapter 6), despite the changing structure and interactions of intergenerational families over the last century, around the world, families still serve as the principal site of the socialization and rearing of children and of support and care for the aged. Discussing diverse intergenerational roles associated with different intergenerational structures, including nonmarital childbearing, gay parenting, step(grand)parenting, acculturation of immigrant families, and childlessness, the authors explore how "boundary ambiguities" (underdefined roles) and "generational asymmetries" (in the flow of affection and resources) are played out in different structural and cultural contexts. Jacqueline Scott discusses children's families (chapter 7), using both the new sociology of childhood, with its emphasis on children as agents, and the life-course perspective, with its emphasis on children's development. She argues that both perspectives are important. She suggests that we need to "deconstruct" the literature on children's families to examine how ideals of childhood have limited the questions asked and biased the answers found. Chris Phillipson and Graham Allan (chapter 8) focus on key changes affecting family commitments and solidarities in later life. In particular they explore the nature of partnerships and domestic organization, generational ties, and relationships beyond the immediate family. They point to the questions posed by the globalization of family life for the maintenance of family networks within and across nation-states. Duane Alwin (chapter 9) demonstrates why parenting practices must be studied in their historical, economic, demographic, cultural, ecological, and structural contexts. Raising the possibility that parenting practices may only serve to moderate the more basic genetic and environmental opportunities and constraints that families bestow on their children, Alwin argues that parenting practices have considerable sociological interest because they provide a key to understanding crucial aspects of social and cultural change.

Jonathan Gershuny (chapter 10) empirically demonstrates how men and women's time-use differs according to family changes through the life-course. Identifying the crucial turning points for men and women's patterns of unpaid and paid work, Gershuny shows how time allocation in families is central to the processes of social structuration. Time-use alone can explain why, if a partnership dissolves, the man ends up with high human capital and income, while the woman ends up with domestic skills and children. Marketable work skills have a payoff in life chances and, put simply, he wins, she loses.

Part III is pivotal, dealing as it does with inequality and diversity. The inequalities of generation, gender, and birth order long served as basic principles of family governance. Indeed, many of the changes in contemporary family life can be seen as struggles for more egalitarian, democratic, or companionate forms of family organization. International immigration has added to the diversity of families and to the complexity of these issues. If there are inequalities within families, there are also inequalities between families. Understanding the family transmission of advantage and disadvantage has challenged generations of sociologists. This challenge is made only more acute by changes in state welfare policies, the nature of employment, and the linkages between work and family.

While crediting families as a resource against hardship, Philip Cohen and Danielle MacCartney (chapter 11) examine how societal inequality constrains the family forms to which various individuals can aspire, even as the different family forms lead to very different socioeconomic outcomes for their members. Regarding gender inequalities, Cohen and MacCartney look explicitly at the role of power, authority, and violence within families. They contend that cultural and economic inequalities permeate families, which then contribute in turn to the reproduction of wider forms of social inequality. Focusing on the most disadvantaged families, Robert Walker and Claire Collins (chapter 12) provide cross-national analyses of what triggers poverty, what types of families are chronically poor, and how effective state intervention is. The chapter moves us forward from the more familiar discussions of poverty based on income shortfall, to evidence of dynamics that point to the differing experiences of poor people. Despite the emerging literature that documents the worlds of the poor as described and experienced by poor people themselves, there is a dearth of knowledge about the social and psychological consequences of different forms of poverty. The possibility that social capital can help ameliorate the consequences of deprivation is taken up by Frank Furstenberg and Sarah Kaplan (chapter 13). Taking aim at the diffuse concept of social capital, the authors critically evaluate the argument that weaker family ties and poorer integration of families in their communities have deprived children of the family-based social capital that contributes to their welfare. They also raise issues about trade-off within families in the management and deployment of social capital. While concurring with the belief that social capital theory has great potential for helping in understanding how the kinship system functions to reproduce social advantage and disadvantage, Furstenberg and Kaplan insist that we need a more systematic and sophisticated approach to examining production, distribution, and effects of social capital both within families and communities.

Moving from the local to the global, Ronald and Jacqueline Angel (chapter 14) show the increasing globalization of social and health problems. Demonstrating how differences by race, citizenship, and income translate into inequality in access to medical care, the authors point to the need to know more about how families in different cultural and political contexts cope with the illness of family members, particularly elderly ones. They also suggest that international migration has given scholars a new opportunity to study how family culture and family support systems may protect health care of immigrant groups in the local environments of their new host countries. The US is a prime site for studying the challenge to racial and cultural hegemony that results from immigration. Locating immigrant families in the context of current theorizing about the processes of incorporation, Pyke (chapter 15) points to the new attention being given to gender relations, children, and elderly people in America's immigrant families. Pyke points to the twin poles of harmony and conflict that characterize much research on immigrant families, suggesting that both have truth. As Karen Pyke observes, the more assimilated show weaker familism norms. Focusing on Britain, Alison Shaw (chapter 16) cautions against placing undue emphasis on how second- and third-generation immigrants have assimilated the values of the host society. As she suggests, similarities in form can mask distinctive patterns of kinship, authority, and gender that vary with ethnicity and are likely to persist.

Parts IV and V examine family forms and relationships in the context of changing social contexts. In many ways, these parts blend together. The separation of family relationships from social context is not one that the editors would wish to defend on theoretical or empirical grounds. It is a question of emphasis. Part IV allows us to zoom in on individuals, their partnerships and separations, ideologies of romance, how couples form and function, and the ways family relationships differ by gender, sexual orientation, ethnicity, and age. Part V takes a wide-angle perspective, showing how the changing social contexts provide the backcloth against which family relationships are enacted. This part examines changing attitudes, beliefs, and behaviors concerning sex and gender. It also looks at policy priorities concerning family relationships and forms, new gender and intergenerational policy initiatives, changes in the labor market, the promotion of better work–family balance, and medical advances and new technologies. These all have far-reaching consequences for the opportunities and constraints that mold the dynamic pathways that reflect the unfolding life experiences of individuals and families.

The importance of religion for understanding families can not be overstated, as Bryan Turner (chapter 17) demonstrates. Focusing on the role of religion and the impact of secularization on marriage and romantic love, Turner's review is wide-ranging. He examines how Christian and Islamic fundamentalism have influenced the struggle between the state and the status of women, and considers the role of religion in the governance of reproductive citizenship. In chapter 18, Joanne Paetsch, Nicholas Bala, Lorne Bertrand, and Lisa Glennon continue the theme of partnerships, by examining recent trends in the formation and dissolution of couples in modern industrialized countries. The chapter considers both heterosexual and same sex couples, and for the latter, points to the uneven progress across nations in the move from discrimination to legal recognition. Accompanying the trends that point to greater instability and diversity of partnerships is the concern that children will suffer. The clear message of Jan Pryor and Liz Trinder's chapter on children, families, and divorce (chapter 19) is that chronic instability and multiple transitions put children at significantly increased risk. Pryor and Trinder call for more focus on the process of family change, irrespective of family structure, in order to identify aspects of families that can promote resilience and adaptability among all family members, but especially children.

How are families of choice – lesbian and gay families – reinventing intimate life? Jeffrey Weeks, Brian Heaphy, and Catherine Donovan (chapter 20) consider what it means for same sex couples to "do families," and how such family practices, whether or not children are present, are bound up with gender, sexuality, work, and caring. Eric Widmer, by contrast, focuses on conjugal networks and conjugal dyads (chapter 21). Noting that conjugality is dominant and brittle in contemporary Western societies, Widmer suggests that future studies may have more to learn by focusing on the more persistent parent–child dyad, that is, the backbone of extended family relationships. David Morgan, however, takes issue with the notion that fatherhood is the key to understanding men in families and households (chapter 22). He argues that the parent–child dimension is only one of the many complex, unfolding relationships that underlie transitions from boyhood through to advanced old age. Analyzing issues as diverse as domestic violence and caring, Morgan reinserts men into the discussion of how the private sphere intersects with gender identities. Morgan suggests that tensions and ambiguities are to be expected when old gender inequalities coexist with new forms of openness and experimentation.

The final part, *Changing Social Contexts*, aptly begins with consideration of the sexual revolution, which has transformed intimate relations and has provoked extensive (approving and disapproving) commentary on the moral condition of modern Western societies. Looking at the changes and challenges of sex and family, Judith Treas (chapter 23) examines the consistency and change in public opinion and private behaviors that shape the sex lives of young and old, married and single, heterosexual and nonheterosexual individuals. Treas notes how most of the life course is sexualized, but paradoxically, as heterosexual unions became sexier – at least in terms of enlargement of sexual scripts and practices – same-sex ones have come to be seen as struggling with domestic concerns such as partnering and parenting, that have long taken their toll on the sex lives of married heterosexuals. The theme of sexuality is continued in Michelle Budig's discussion of feminism and the family (chapter 24). Compulsory heterosexuality, for some, has been equated with the family's patriarchal oppression of women. However, the impact of radical feminism on the family is far more diffuse, pushing for contraception and abortion rights, domestic and sexual violence legislation, and legitimization of a plurality of family forms: single-parent, lesbian, gay, and childless families. But not all feminists agree that the family or motherhood is the source of women's oppression. Budig points to how new feminist questions involve dismantling the legacy of the separation of public and private spheres. She poses the highly contentious question of the reward for child-rearing. Who pays? Should those opting to remain childless be allowed to free-ride on the men and, more often, women who rear the next generation of workers?

The complex question of the relation between work and families is the focus of chapter 25. Shirley Dex points out that the reproduction of the workforce is a matter of critical public interest. Her chapter discusses how there is still much work to be done to understand the complex, fourfold framework that governs cross-national differences in work and family relations: countries' industrial structures; the labor-market conditions; the work-related regulations and organization policies; and the political economy of social reproduction embodied in the welfare system. Picking up on the issue of public policy and families, Wendy Sigle-Rushton and Catherine Kenney provide a comparative overview of governmental responses to parent's work-care conflicts in the European Union. They highlight the role of the father as a matter where there is urgent need for action, but where there has been relatively little progress in bringing about a more equal gender allocation of paid and unpaid work.

The penultimate chapter moves the focus from production to reproduction. Martin Richards discusses some of the ways in which genetic and reproductive technologies are being used, how they may influence family life, and how attitudes and assumptions about the family may in turn shape their development and use. Assisted reproduction has a very long history, but the implications of modern DNA technologies for families are only just starting to be debated. It is a field in which family researchers face a rapidly changing future.

In the final chapter, Ulrich Beck and Elisabeth Beck-Gernsheim review what reflexive modernization means in regard to the family. They argue that, as far as family is concerned, there has been a normalization of diversity, in family law, in the self-images of family members, and the observational viewpoint of sociology. They suggest that it becomes unclear what "objectively" constitutes the reference unit of family research, how it can be circumscribed, what should be ascertained or investigated, and how and from what perspective. How does a researcher order, count, and classify family relationships and forms when the boundaries keep changing and when different boundaries come into play for different members, at different points of time? If family relations are so ambivalent, then sociological research is faced with a twofold challenge. On the one hand, it becomes ever more important to consciously listen to subjects and deliberately open up interpretations. On the other, continual effort is needed to resist slipping back into "White-think, middle-class-think, men-think, hetero-think, or some combination of these," whereby the erasure of key components of the everyday experience of people in nondominant family relationships are inevitable.

Beck and Beck-Gernsheim's chapter emphasizes one of the key points made throughout the *Companion*: that a crucial part of good practice in the sociology of families is to evaluate critically the questions that sociologists ask. The family domain poses a particularly difficult challenge for research, because all researchers have vested interests and ideology can displace or distort evidence. Yet the research challenge is of unique importance because, in our global world, individualization is not the same as atomization. Individuals are continually re-creating and reshaping families, and families are the key to all our futures.

## Tribute to Tamara Hareven

It is with great sadness that we note the death of Tamara Hareven (1937–2002). Tamara was Professor of Family Studies and History at the University of Delaware, and had been commissioned to write a chapter for this volume on "the contribution of history to family sociology." The chapter was to appear in the life-course section – an approach she helped pioneer. Described in an obituary in *Le Monde* as "missionnaire infatigable des recherches sur la famille," Hareven would have welcomed the challenge to identify important future directions for family research. Fortunately, before her untimely death, she published a collection of her essays in her book *Families, History and Social Change* (2000). In this work she reiterates the huge challenge for scholars in reconstructing the multilayered reality – the lives of individual families and their interactions with major social, economic, and political forces, pointing out how the enterprise is complicated by our increasing appreciation of the changing and diverse nature of "the family," rendered fluid by shifts in internal age and gender configurations across regions and time. The formidable goal she sets is to understand the interrelationship between "individual time," "family time," and "historical time" (Hareven, 1977; Elder, 1978, 1981).

Her challenge to future research, however, did not stop there. She identified two interrelated future directions for research in family history. The first is to pursue established topics that are underresearched, including how families relate to social space, and to engage with a more systematic study of families in relation to religion, the state, and the legal system. She also pointed to the need for more work on kinship, particularly as it relates to friendship, family transitions over the life course, generational relations, especially in the later years of life, and family strategies, especially where the family's interaction with other institutions is concerned. A second future direction is the forging of more systematic linkages between interrelated family patterns and processes: these include a closer linkage of demographic patterns with household structure and internal family dynamics; a closer integration of the study of household with nonresident kin; and a more careful linkage of kinship and household patterns with various processes such as work and migration, and cultural dimensions including rituals.

*The Blackwell Companion to the Sociology of Families* makes a start in addressing some of the challenges Hareven issued, but the editors acutely feel the loss of her input. Her meticulous cross-national research anticipated the comparative emphasis that informs the *Companion*. Hareven's legacy is felt in the chapters in this volume that address how families are the arenas in which the relations between individuals and social change are acted out, and how families act as broker between individuals, institutions, and social change. Her pioneering contributions to the development of the life-course perspective make it impossible to ignore the intersection of individual lives and history, even as we struggle to make sense of the latest contemporary developments. Just as she inspired so many of us, the brilliant and stimulating books and articles that she wrote, the journals she helped establish, and the example of research she set will inspire future generations of family sociologists.

## References

Allan, G. (1999) *The Sociology of the Family: A Reader.* Oxford: Blackwell.

Caplow, T., Bahr, H., Chadwick, B., Hill, R., and Holmes Williamson, M. (1982) *Middletown Families: Fifty Years of Continuity and Change.* Toronto: Bantam.

Caspi, L., and Bianchi, S. (2002) *Continuity and Change in the American Family.* London: Sage.

Castells, M. (1997) *The Power of Identity.* Vol. 2 of *The Information Age: Economy, Society and Culture.* Oxford: Blackwell.

Douglas, M. (1993) The idea of a home: a kind of space. In A. Mack (ed.), *Home: A Place in the World.* New York: New York University Press.

Elder, G., Jr. (1978) Family history and the life course. In T. Hareven (ed.), *Transitions: The Family and Life Course in Historical Perspective.* New York: Academic Press.

Elder, G., Jr. (1981) History and the family: the discovery of complexity. *Journal of Marriage and the Family,* 43, 489–519.

Giddens, A. (1999) *Runaway World: How Globalization Is Reshaping Our Lives.* London: Profile Books.

Giele, J., and Elder, G., Jr. (1998) *Methods of Life Course Research: Qualitative and Quantitative Approaches.* London: Sage.

Hareven, T. (1977) Family time and historical time. *Daedalus,* 106, 57–70.

Hareven, T. (2000) *Families, History and Social Change; Life Course and Cross-Cultural Perspectives.* Oxford: Westview.

Henry, L. (1968) Historical demography. *Daedalus,* 97, 385–96.

Laslett, P. (1965) *The World We Have Lost.* London: Methuen.

Laslett, P., and Wall, R. (eds.) (1972) *Household and Family in Time Past: Comparative Studies in the Size and Structure of the Domestic Group over the Last Three Centuries in England, France, Serbia, Japan and Colonial America.* Cambridge: Cambridge University Press.

Lynd, R., and Lynd, H. (1929) *Middletown: A Study in American Culture.* New York: Harcourt & Brace.

Lynd, R., and Lynd, H. (1937) *Middletown in Transition: A Study in Cultural Conflicts.* New York: Harcourt & Brace.

Morgan, D. (1996) *Family Connections: An Introduction to Family Studies.* Cambridge: Polity.

Wrigley, E. (1966) Family limitation in pre-industrial England. *Economic History Review,* 2nd Ser., 19, 82–109.

Young, M., and Wilmott, P. (1957) *Family and Kinship in East London.* Glencoe, IL: Free Press.

Young, M., and Wilmott, P. (1973) *The Symmetrical Family.* London: Penguin.

# I

# Families in a Global World

# 1

# Globalization and Western Bias in Family Sociology

Don Edgar

Sociology of the family has always been caught between a rock and a hard place. On the one hand, an emphasis on family structures, traditions, and their unequal social and financial capital tended to reify the institution and its powerful effects on an individual's life course. We studied family roles, especially gender roles, and assumed a direct influence from expectations to behavior, leaving little room for individual agency or initiative. On the other hand, a more psychological focus on the way "self" emerged from interaction with significant others, and on the active, interpretive part played by every individual in adapting to or resisting family pressures, led us away from any sensible definition of the family as a unit of analysis and into a welter of apparently unfettered individualism. There was talk of the "over-socialized conception of man," and a move away from structural analysis of the family as an institution within its wider (and very diverse) social settings (see Wrong, 1961; Edgar, 1992a, 1992b).

As the phenomenon of globalization has emerged, built in part on the immediacy and universality of communication and knowledge networks, in part on the expanding division of labor, expertise, and range of "choice" for individuals in the postmodern world, the balance has swung even more toward what I regard as an unsociological, nonstructural view which bedevils family sociology.

I will argue here that this arises from a Western bias in the literature, one based on the dominant ideology of individualism and free-market liberalism, and arising from the triumph of individualistic psychology over sociology as a discipline. It is difficult to find good data, even harder to find good theory, based on non-Western societies where life chances are still very much constrained by family background, family networks and values, and by wider structural influences such as religion or the law, and structural inequalities in education and financial and social status (for some Asia-Pacific information, see Ariffin and Louis, 2001). If we look at how globalization affects people differently according to their social circumstances, we may gain a better perspective on the significance of family (as opposed to individual agency) in our rapidly changing world.

## Globalization and the Place of Family versus Individual

Indeed, globalization itself has led family sociology into a theoretical contradiction. At one level, globalization is blamed for a massive shift away from the authority of traditional institutions and the rise of an individualism based on risk, reflexivity, and the need to negotiate one's own life course. Individual agency rises supreme and personal psychology overwhelms the social. At another level, globalization is seen as an uncontrollable force, largely economic, but also cultural and therefore political, beyond the control not just of individual actors, but also of any family, group, or nation-state. Reification and passive reaction thus inform our perceptions of family and the individual's role in reality construction.

This chapter urges a reassessment of the centrality of family as a mediating structure, as a structure increasingly crucial to the development of individual human capital, to the potential of social capital to influence life chances, and to the way individuals are unequally able to make "choices" in a globalized world. It is not the individual who acts reflexively; it is the family (increasingly varied as it is) which mediates the impact of globalization, community resources, and government action for and with individuals acting as parts of a sharing, interactive unit. Rarely does any individual make decisions outside of the resources and emotional attachments of family. It is the family as agent, *familia faber,* that requires urgent research attention (Boulding, 1983). Moreover, we need to reassess our theories of family change in light of evidence about families in non-Western countries.

Globalization as a phenomenon of the postmodern world seems to be diametrically the opposite of "family" as an institution. It is the anonymity and freedom of the World Wide Web versus the intimacy and close control of the family unit. It is the unfamiliar world of diverse and indifferent others versus the familiar world of the primary group. It is a network of strangers versus the more closed networks of families and their local communities. Just as the Industrial Revolution and urbanization were built on the breaking of extended family ties and the rise of the separate nuclear family, so too is the Information Age reliant on individual skill portfolios and the freedom of the footloose worker to move as the new "turbo-capitalism" requires (Hutton and Giddens, 2001).

Marriage as an institution traditionally linked to family seems to be being replaced by the couple relationship, an inherently volatile and constantly negotiated state, and by the institution of parenthood, perhaps the last enclave of social control over the "public consequences of private decisions." The age of risk, innovation, and flexibility (what Schumpeter called "creative destruction") is indifferent to inequality, social justice, or family impacts, and gives new power to that minority of knowledge workers, symbolic analysts, shareholders, and owners whose so-called rationality or reflexivity rides roughshod over family and community interests. An ironic corollary of an increasingly networked society (Castells, 1997) is the rise and rise of negotiated individuality. Indeed, most theorists do not talk of the agency of families, or even couples; they speak as if the individual and his/her search for personal satisfaction and fulfillment were the key driving force behind social change.

We are told also (and there is clear evidence for this) that globalization undermines the ability of nation-states and the families within them to control their own economy, the very nature of their jobs, and the income they derive for family maintenance.

Monetary control via industry regulation and taxation is more difficult with free-flowing global capital, so governments are forced to rethink the nature of welfare payments and family support services. The individual's personally accumulated and owned human capital is supposedly now more useful than social status. The arbitrariness with which corporations shift whole industries (or the International Monetary Fund dictates financial policy) can destroy whole regions (even nations), leaving those family links impotent and exacerbating inequality within increasingly "patchwork" nations and an increasingly unequal world (Edgar, 2001).

## New Forms of State and Family Agency

Globalization thus alters the role of family as mediator between private and public (Berger and Berger, 1983). As a result, and in contradiction to declining national economic autonomy, globalization places new demands upon the state to carry the burden of those left behind by free-market capitalism. Family policy takes on a new face as governments talk about business–community partnerships, corporate philanthropy, and community-building as a euphemism for cutting costs, and tighten eligibility criteria for welfare benefits. The state could become in this process even more of a "policer" of family life (Donzelot, 1979), certainly as that involves sources of income and the treatment of children. But the key factor to examine is the way in which families are forced to become more self-reliant despite their lack of control over global economic forces. It is this process of rethinking family agency that needs to be given more attention in family sociology.

In terms of personal relationships, globalization is indifferent to gender or race, though its many critics argue that US values dominate the communications revolution and thus homogenize the global family and the norms of intimacy. In any event, globalization has run parallel to an unprecedented rise in the education levels of women, the number of two-income households, and the capacity of women (through birth control and separate earning capacity) to throw off their dependence on men. Rising divorce rates, postponed and abandoned decisions to marry or have children, the flight from commitment of both men and women, and the prolonged life expectancy of women are all correlated to that new autonomy and women's power to exercise choice. Such trends clearly alter the ways in which family units (however constituted) operate as mediating agents.

As Giddens puts it, one's personal life course and one's sense of self now have to be created actively by the individual, and women are staking a claim to those areas of decision making that were once the domain of men. People can no longer rely on tradition and authority, and the undermining of public authority that began with the Enlightenment has now moved into the arena of private, everyday life. The family becomes democratized as couples in a "pure relationship" find they have to engage in an active dialogue of mutual disclosure if personal satisfaction is to be achieved. In Giddens's optimistic view, the rise of democracy has been a major component of the global communications revolution, undermining the monopoly of information, authoritarian power, and the resistance of elite and fundamentalist groups. It has built tolerance via a "democracy of the emotions," as much in the private world of family life as across and within nations. While he notes the parallel rise of localism, religious fundamentalism, ethnic cleansing, and the paradoxical place of children in a world of chaotic uncoupling and pure relationships, he is basically hopeful that this new form of democratic family negotiation will lead to a cosmopolitan society where family, work, and nation are mere shell institutions and reality is forged by increasingly reflexive individuals (Giddens, 1992; Hutton and Giddens, 2001). These are important factors in rethinking family sociology.

## The Importance of Family, Locality, and New Identity Networks

We should be careful, however, not to overgeneralize about the impact of globalization, because it has another face. Several writers have noted the parallel rise in importance of the local, the increase in ethnic group solidarity, and an expanding number of interest groups working against the forces of Americanization and corporate control. As Castells (1997: 11) puts it, a life open to reflection and personal planning is impossible "except for the elite inhabiting the timeless space of flows of global networks and their ancillary locales." Most people do not have the skills or resources to operate in such an autonomous and fearless fashion, so they construct defensive identities around communal or tribal principles. This form of "project identity" grows from communal resistance, and takes a variety of forms. It stands in stark contrast to the isolated self-construction that Giddens suggests typifies modern lifestyles, and it relies on active family and community togetherness, not free-floating individualism.

Some project-identity social movements are large-scale, such as the resurgence of Islamic fundamentalism and ethnic/national rebellions in once-unified countries such as the USSR or Yugoslavia. Other identity-seeking movements are smaller but no less dramatic, such as the Aum Shinrikyo cult in Japan which formed a sort of "family" for those wanting to start the apocalypse. Many are based on shared opposition to global forces: the American Christian fundamentalists who oppose the inroads of feminism, godlessness, and permissiveness; the Basque movement in Spain struggling to preserve its own language and culture; the American Militia and Patriot movements taking up arms against central government; and the more recent coalitions of protesters at Seattle, Davos, and Melbourne against the World Trade Organization/World Economic Forum and the impact of global corporations on poverty in the developing world.

At a more local level, we see the growth of community building as an ethos, a demand for more responsive, less top-down government, of regional economic development as a way of protecting people against the winds of global change (OECD, 2001). Not all these movements are localized, however, and they point to a new form of tribalism that may have a positive effect on globalization processes (and which transcend traditional family structures), a form of project identity-formation that is not inward-looking but, rather, transformative of society. There is, for example, increasing political activity via the Internet, directed against such firms as Shell, Nike, McDonald's, and Microsoft. Nongovernmental organizations act as vast lobby groups on behalf of family well-being, the environment, and human rights, and they are neither elected by nor answerable to the wider polity. All of these trends alter the conditions under which families, and individual men, women, and children are able to make, or are prevented from making, decisions affecting their own "autonomous" lives. They are all, in my view, probably more significant to an understanding of the family's place in a global society than any examination of individualized self-construction.

## Giddens and the Place of Individual Agency

Giddens's concept of reflexivity, in particular, appears to rely on an unduly psychological analysis of what is essentially a sociological and economic phenomenon. By reflexivity, he means both the capacity of an individual to know and justify his or her own actions and therefore also the capacity of people and societies to reflexively produce and reproduce their social life. While Giddens acknowledges and analyses carefully how societies are structured, his emphasis is on what he calls "practical consciousness," an awareness of why we do things and thus an ability to change social structures as we see fit (see the extended critique of Giddens by Tucker, 1998).

This is a peculiarly Western view, both of what is happening to families worldwide and of the values underpinning current political and religious conflicts. Even within Western, developed nations one must ask whether what Giddens describes is so much a growth of individualization and autonomy, of "reflexivity," as it is of risk and the importance of risk management. The former are terms of privatization and personal psychology, whereas risk management implies the interplay between personal human resources and the altered economic and political contexts in which such reflexivity is played out. To be fair, Giddens does distinguish between free-floating individualism and what he calls "individualization," a situation where traditional social categories no longer serve as a framework for moral decision-making or social interaction. But both he and Beck seem too dismissive of the still-important collective contexts in which the risks of biography are mastered (Beck, 1998: 35; see also Beck, 2001).

Though traditional forms of authority have doubtless weakened, and individuals increasingly have to negotiate their own moral stance (Smart and Neale, 1999), plus their relationships and their personal work and family biographies (Pryor and Rodgers, 2001), they do not (one might say, sociologically cannot) engage in a process of "re-embedding" whereby "individuals must produce, stage and cobble together their biographies for themselves" (Beck, 1998: 33).

## The Continued Centrality of Family

Personal human resources, human capital, develop in and through family resources, the emotional and marketable skills a child learns within this primary group, the networks within which the family is embedded, and the family's access to financial and other social resources within its own community and national context (Edgar, 1999). Moreover, the decisions to marry, remain single, have children, leave the parental home, or take a particular job, are never totally disembedded, they are developed in a social context with significant others and in the light of social as well as individual resources. Negotiation is itself an essentially social process, no matter how much internalized introspection it involves. We must question the dominance of an individualized, psychological theoretical framework to explain what is essentially a social process, a process in which the family unit (whatever its form) is a central agent (Edgar and Glezer, 1994).

Not everyone can manage personal and family risk if a global corporation has withdrawn employment from an entire region or the World Bank has demanded a complete restructuring of the nation's economy. Nor can one negotiate a pure relationship if the choices are limited by poverty, religious fundamentalism, ethnic persecution, or a socialized lack of emotional competence.

The stereotype of men lacking both self-perception and empathy, compared with women, is an apt, if glib, illustration of the limits of such an analysis. Men develop such flaws within a context of gender-based power and discrimination, socially structured pressures to be "real men," the expectation that their skills will focus on work, money-making, and emotional self-control, and an entire set of social institutions which develop and reinforce their emotional and interactional differences from women. Male power can be challenged through legislation, but it is the new power of women within (mostly Western) families (via contraception, earnings, time in public work settings) which alters internal family dynamics and challenges the taken-for-granted reality of sexism (Edgar, 1997b). Women living under fundamentalist religious constraints have less to work with, but the agent of change is the family, not just the individual.

Notwithstanding the existence of many forms of masculinity, historically and anthropologically, and current pressures for men to behave differently if they are to achieve a satisfactory relationship with an intimate other, the applicability of such an individualized theory of change is severely limited by its cultural assumptions and by the realities faced by millions of individuals worldwide whose options are not as negotiable as those of some in the West.

## Globalization and Its Impacts on Family Life

Globalization also underpins several new demographic trends which alter forever the life course and interpersonal relationships of those millions. It creates greater mobility in the search for work or refuge from conflict (there were 12 million refugees worldwide in 1999). It is usually whole families that move, their entire motivation to forge a new life, as families, elsewhere. Immigrant nations such as Australia, the US, and Israel have very strong "family values" precisely because families in a new land are important sources of emotional and financial security, strong motivators to succeed and forge a new life (Edgar, 1997a). Prolonged education is now a prerequisite for gainful employment, and the consequent delays in age of independence from parents, age at marriage, and age of first childbearing make the family of orientation even more important to young people's life chances and lifestyles. Too often sociologists ignore the evidence that flows of support (both financial and emotional) are more often from older parents to young adults than the reverse (Milward, 1992, 1995; de Jong Gierveld, 1998). These young adults may appear to be acting autonomously, and forging pure relationships reflexively, but it is family action, and differential resources, not self-directed choice-making, that explains their current status (Commaille, 1998: 26).

The family as primal shelter is central to the creation of meaning and identity-formation, drawing on its own membership, networks, and community and, most significantly, central to the task of forging an accommodation between social integration and individual autonomy as an adult (Kellerhals, 1998; Donati, 1998). As I put it in relation to the development of child competence: "Life situations change and bring new challenges and problems (over the life course)." But the child whose family and social support systems have provided both the equipment for competence and some sense of the competent self will be better able to adapt to those new challenges and construct effective coping strategies. There will be what Hobfoll (1988) calls a "caravan of resources," or what Bruner (1988) calls a "toolkit for managing your world," as well as some moderate stability in the child's style of coping (Compas, 1995; Frydenberg and Lewis, 1997), "guiding the child's attempts to reduce stress and shape the environment to his or her own purposes" (Edgar, 1999: 123). The best research about divorce effects on children supports this view of the way parental resources and management processes link the individual and the social (Amato, 1987; Amato and Booth, 1997).

## Non-Western Family Realities

And we must keep in mind the reality within which most of the world's families have to forge their lives, before we assert too readily either individual agency or the decline of the family as an institution of importance.

Barely two percent of the world's population now works in agriculture. The drift to cities creates new problems in nations such as China because the conditions of industry are not the same as during the labor-hungry Industrial Revolution. The World Bank calculates that a quarter of the population of the developing world – about 1.2 billion people – is living in poverty, on under $1 a day (UNO, 2001: 17). And there are huge regional variations (Settles, 1998; Otero, 1994). In Europe and Central Asia the number in poverty soared (1987–8) from 1.1 million to 24 million, and South Asia and sub-Saharan Africa accounted for 70 percent of those living on $1 a day. Life expectancy in those regions is a full generation less than the OECD average. Within Europe, that part of the population living on less than $2 a day varies from below 5 percent in Hungary and Poland to 19 percent in Russia and 68 percent in Tajikistan. Pakistan and Sri Lanka made little progress in poverty reduction during the 1990s, and in countries such as Zambia and Mexico rural poverty fell while urban poverty rose.

Extremes of affluence and poverty characterize not only West versus the rest, but also marked regional differences within all nation-states. Global competition makes regional and local capacities more significant than ever, and the twenty-first century is likely to see a reinforcement of class segregation through ecological mechanisms and create an increasingly violent society (OECD, 2001).

We cannot ignore such socially variable constraints on the sorts of family and relationship negotiations individuals can make. In particular, we need to remember that Western progress in the capacity of women to negotiate a new deal for themselves is not matched elsewhere. The gap between male and female school enrolment rates varies from 20 percent in countries such as Pakistan to almost zero in Brazil or the Philippines. Wealthy families in India have less of a gender education gap than poorer families. Births to mothers under the age of 20 are as low as 1.3 percent in Japan and 2.9 in Norway, but as high as 19.9 percent in Venezuela, 15.7 in Mexico, and 16.5 in Romania. The adult illiteracy rate in non-Western countries is higher for women than men, despite some progress in the last decade. For example, in Ethiopia it is 57 percent for men, 68 percent for women; in Egypt it is 34 percent for men, 57 percent for women; in Turkey it is 7 percent for men, 24 percent for women; in the Indian sub-continent it is 32 percent for men, 56 percent for women (UNDP, 1999; UNICEF, 1997, 2001; UNO, 2001). Such women enjoy none of the autonomy, self-reflexivity, individualism, and freedom to negotiate life choices that Western sociologists see as the distinguishing features of modern family life. Nor, for that matter, do men with such low education, income-earning capacity, and life expectancy.

Given that marriage and family are institutions structured round human sexuality and social reproduction, we need to be reminded that life is not the same elsewhere as in affluent Western nations in that regard either. The majority of women worldwide are still severely discriminated against, their choices limited by religious rules, extended family decision-making about marriage partners, and the impact of male sexuality on their life chances. The UNDP Human Development Report (1999) estimates that 340 million women will not survive to age 40, 880 million lack access to basic health services, and the proportion of infant deaths due to AIDS by the year 2010 will reach 61 percent in Botswana, 58 percent in Zimbabwe, 41 percent in Kenya, and 5 percent in Thailand.

Moreover, the number of HIV infections clearly varies by gender in different regions of the world, reflecting huge cultural and religious variations in the treatment of women. Whereas in major Western countries it is males more than females who become infected, largely because of greater prevalence and tolerance of male homosexuality, the figures are low overall (0.1 percent for Australian males, 0 percent for women; 0.2 percent for Netherlands males, 0.1 percent for women) because of better education and medical treatment. On the African continent and in some Asian countries, more women than men are infected with HIV, because of male myths about sex with virgins, rape, prostitution and male promiscuity, government inaction, and religious taboos. For example, in Botswana the male HIV rate is 15.8 percent compared with 34.3 percent for women; in South Africa it is 11.3 percent for men, 24.8 percent for women; in Cambodia the male HIV rate is 2.4 percent, female 3.5 percent; in Thailand the male rate is 1.2 percent, female 2.3 percent). In South America, HIV rates are again higher for males than females, though the numbers are relatively low (Argentina 0.9 percent male, 0.3 percent female; Brazil 0.7 percent male, 0.3 percent female). No analysis of family trends can ignore the dramatic effect of AIDS and inadequate health services on the lives of men, women, and children in such countries.

One of the more obvious impacts is on the relative composition of young and old. Many African populations have a majority aged below 25, and the high incidence of HIV/AIDS means they have little prospect of marrying or having a family of their own. High fertility rates "suggest an exclusively reproductive role for women and limited participation by women in economic and political activities" (ESCAP, 1998: 3). Unlike the dominant discourse about aging in Western nations (based on reduced fertility rates and increasing longevity), early death combined with high fertility result in an increasing proportion of young people in a population, often in a situation of growing unemployment. In countries such as Pakistan, Afghanistan, and Cambodia the fertility rate is above 5, whereas in Iran (which has encouraged contraceptive use since 1989, especially among rural families) the slogan "small families are healthy families" has dramatically reduced the birthrate. Age at first marriage has increased (now 21.1 In Iran) and the proportion of never-married women has grown (31.4 percent in Iran; 48.0 percent in Thailand). This may improve life choices for women, though most are still involved in agriculture, with little landownership by women, and older women are less able to remarry than men, resulting in increasing numbers of female-headed households and the feminization of poverty.

In China, the problem of population imbalance is different, in that their long-standing "one-child" policy has led to an imbalance of young males to young females. Over the next two decades, as many as 40 million young Chinese men will be unable to find marriage partners or to form a family of procreation (there is already a boom in kidnapping eligible females), and the entire structure of traditional family life, kinship, respect for elders, and the submergence of individuality to an authoritarian social order comes under threat. There are fears of an unruly cohort of young males causing social problems, such as increased prostitution, homosexuality and rising crime rates, and there is pressure to distract them through military service and future wars (Wiseman, 2002). Western sociology can ill afford to ignore the close connections between sexuality, family forms, and social order.

## Globalization's Differential Impact on Family Life

Put this together with the globalization of employment and we have a very different prospect for future family life. There are several levels of such globalization. One is the rise, in Western post-industrial societies (and, for IT specialists, India) of the Solos, Generation-S, the well-educated symbolic analysts who are unattached, mobile, and can sell their skills to the highest bidder worldwide or readily move to another company location when required. Their relationships are likely to be very fluid, similar to the sailors of old with a friend in every port. They are also likely to be instrumental (that is, based on sexual gratification and the comfort of temporary intimacy) rather than on an angst-ridden pure relationship of endless negotiation and mutual disclosure.

At the other level is the impetus to seek work in a foreign country because job prospects at home are low. ESCAP (1998) describes this as "the feminization of labor" or "the globalization of female employment" (p. 10), with women in Asian-Pacific countries making up 40 percent of the industrial labor force and as many as 75–90 percent of workers in the leading export industries – textiles, footwear, processed food, and electronics. Wage rates for women are half the male rate and women are underrepresented at professional and managerial levels. The withering away of the public administrative and services sector reduces job opportunities for women and they become migratory in search of any wage-paying job, often leaving their families behind. Women wage-workers are very mobile across national borders and regions, with dramatic effects on family relationships. And we must remember that these are not individual decisions about forging one's own biography; they are life and death choices which have ripple effects across generations, gender relations, and whole nations.

Arlie Hochschild writes about "global care chains and emotional surplus value" (2001), pointing out that roughly two percent of the world's population migrate each year, of which half are women. Female care workers and housekeepers in the US are largely women from Mexico, the Philippines, and South America, the US thus "importing maternal love" as American women stay in full employment, while the migrant carers try to maintain their own families at a distance by sending money home to their own substitute child-carers and providing "virtual care" as they displace their emotions onto the American children they now are paid to look after. As Hochschild puts it: "such chains often connect three sets of care-takers.... Poorer women raise children for wealthier women while still poorer – or older or more rural – women raise their children.... As mothering is passed down the race/class/nation hierarchy, each woman becomes a provider and hires a wife" (2001: 136–7).

In the UK there is contrasting evidence of sustained family contacts, despite distance. Cheap airfares have made it possible for most UK-born Pakistani 7-year-olds to visit relatives in Pakistan: the Khojas diaspora (which covers America, Europe, South Africa and beyond) has a number of its own community websites, with family and religious news, health education material, and other information resources.

Men, in this global workplace scenario, leave childrearing to women, and many themselves migrate (to the Arabian Peninsula and Northern European industrial countries) as "guest-workers," now under threat of deportation as Europe tries to cope with its own refugee and population–welfare overload. Those men who do return after several years working elsewhere find themselves displaced both as fathers and as dominant family members. Family sociology needs to know more about such trends before it generalizes about the rise and rise of the individual and the decline of family life.

## Gender Differences and Work–Family Links

The male career pattern, both in the countries we have just described and in Western countries, is remarkably resistant to change, with fathers unlikely to take a larger share of either child-care or elder care, resulting in a reduction in the value of caring work, and a continued under-valuation of the social reproduction side of family life.

If we look at the Western evidence on work–family relationships, the "work–family" discourse arose largely out of the post-World War II movement of women into the paid labor force, based on higher education levels, better contraceptive control, and legislation for equal opportunity and an end to sex discrimination (Haas et al., 2000). Most employers saw it as a "women's issue," not something relevant to men, and that is still the case, with a slowing down of work–family initiatives as governments leave policy to private companies, and focus on child-care payments for women, and paid maternity leave rather than parental leave, instead of serious attempts to alter the culture of the workplace. The globalization of time via the Internet and e-mail, notions of just-in-time production, pressures to improve productivity through downsizing, computerization, and more flexible hours (that is, longer hours for most workers and 24/7 round-the-clock schedules) have made a mockery of many discussions about balancing work and family life, notwithstanding some outstanding examples to the contrary. So too, has the increase in nonstandard work schedules and shift work, and its negative impact on marital relationships and instability (Presser, 2000; Glass and Estee, 1997; Kinnear, 2002).

In this context, industrial relations "flexibility" is of more benefit to corporate productivity than to employees struggling to "balance" their increasingly conflicting work and family responsibilities, and policy solutions will have to involve structural change in workplace conditions. Demographers increasingly assert that declining birthrates can only be changed if workplace conditions, public child-care, parental leave payments, and a greater sharing of the domestic workload by men become the norm. Yet the reality is, in the industrialized economies, a retreat from public welfare expenditure and a privatized ideology of parenthood, which suggests the individual should accept the cost and time consequences of their own decisions. Simplistic dichotomies between women who want babies and those who do not will not help in this policy debate about family life (see Hakim, 2000). Nor does a theoretical framework which suggests every individual is the agent of his or her own destiny, engaged in self-reflexivity, individual choice, praxis, or agency of a psychologized kind.

Structurally, the impetus for employers to be more "family-friendly" will come from a reduced labor supply, competition for the best workers, driving them to become and stay the "employer of choice," not from policy exhortations or internal efforts at workplace culture change. Necessity may eventually drive culture change, but work structures are still male-oriented, work times not in synchrony with family responsibilities.

Schools are still run at fixed times which assume a carer at home; there are no systems for time-out "sabbaticals" at peak family demand periods such as infancy, adolescence, or caring for elderly parents; unions and employers still talk about full-time work as the ideal and about part-time workers as the uncommitted "Mummy Track" or even "Daddy Track"; and women are still seen as nuisance invaders of a safely male workplace, with wage discrimination and the glass ceiling driving many women into self-employment or casual and intermittent work. Nor do government or nongovernment services for families respond to the diversity of family circumstances and needs, usually being categorical and top-down, paternalistic and managerial in style, oriented to "problem" families and responding to family crises rather than to supporting every family in ways that resource them so they can better function in their own chosen ways (Edgar, 2001).

## Restoring Family Resources and Agency to the Debate

It may therefore be instructive to revisit Elise Boulding's (1983) concept of *familia faber*, in order to restore the centrality of family life to our theories of society. Boulding refers to the active role families play in entering a new urban community – they actively seek out the best child-care, schools, clubs, and community contacts in order to maximize their own resources on behalf of their children and their own quality of life. This is the same process by which families (not just individuals) build communities and the facilities they need. The better their networks, the greater their connectedness (what is being called "social capital"), the better their life chances (Putnam, 1993a, 1993b; Winter, 2000).

It must be noted that most voluntarism is not pure altruism on behalf of the wider community; it is time given to enhance the interests of special interest groups, especially family groups. In all the discussion of our supposedly declining civil society, social capital, and the selfish individualism of Western consumer societies (Putnam, 1993a, 1993b; Winter, 2000), the evidence shows a remarkable level of time-giving by adults with children, and by grandparents. They work on school committees, sports clubs, and church and cultural associations because it is in their (joint) family interests. The quality of life of the wider community certainly benefits, and much altruism is involved, but it is family units that are the driving force, not isolated individuals acting for the common good.

Most political activity, especially voting, is also motivated by ensuring that jobs, family incomes, family-related services, and the quality of schools, health care and other community services are safeguarded, not by party ideology or national vision. Local issues often override broader national appeals precisely because family interests are central concerns. The family is the filter through which issues such as border protection, terrorism, public transport, and education are interpreted. Moreover, public interest in issues changes as cohorts change – care for the aged being the most obvious now that the Baby Boom generation is itself aging and many face the dual tasks of the Sandwich Generation, caring for still-dependent adult offspring and for aging parents. Kinship is still more important than citizenship, and for most people citizenship only has practical meaning through kinship.

Even looking at the statistics on family forms, one has to wonder at the persistence of marriage and the family as core units of society. Certainly there is more normative acceptance (in most Western societies, though even there in a fragmented and contested way) of new types – single-parent, stepparent, single-sex, separated, divorced, even the "un-family" of friendship groups (which hardly meet the usual criteria of long-term relationships between people related by blood, adoption, or marriage and linking the generations preceding and/or succeeding). There is growing evidence that divorced and reconstituted families are emerging as a new form (the "Lattice Family") as couples ensure ongoing contacts with children and other relatives, their new partners and offspring being incorporated in a cooperative lattice of networks which potentially add to the resources of everyone involved (Kuczynski, 2001). There are increasing numbers of couple-only families, maintaining intergenerational links with their forebears and relatives but without procreating for the future. Couples who survive both marriage and childrearing form a rising new tribe of "Renewed Oldies," their lives not always centered around offspring and grandchildren but entering a new phase of exploration and self-fulfillment. And there are the almost 28 percent of Solos, mostly young adults, who will never marry and never have children. They may be individuals, but they are still tied intergenerationally and they have relationships that are, at least temporarily and spasmodically, family-like.

But the statistics still show that the nuclear couple with children is the dominant form. Coupling can be casual and multiple, but the majority of human beings prefer to forge a longer-lasting relationship with one other who is exclusively committed to them. And though the formality of marriage has become less important as a public declaration of commitment and exclusivity, de facto, "common-law" marriage is still the norm. Even in the US, the most recent Census shows that only 27 percent are "never-married," with 56 percent now married, 10 percent divorced, and 7 percent widowed. The figures for 1950 (before the so-called divorce revolution) were 23 percent never-married, 67 percent then married, and 2 percent then divorced. Similarly, in Australia, intact couple families still comprise 72 percent of all families and the majority of children live with their natural parents.

My point is not to deny significant shifts in the nature and composition of families, rather to suggest that the family (whether two-parent, one-parent, step, or lattice) is still the central agency of childhood socialization, social integration, the marshaling of resources, human capital, social capital, and cultural values. It is not individualization that matters in a globalized world, so much as the nature of those family resources and family processes, insofar as they open up or limit the options available to each individual.

Sociology of the family must eschew its domination by personalistic psychology and theories based on a Western lifestyle. It must adopt a more informed reality-construction approach, look more closely at family and locational differences in opportunity structures, and examine more systematically the processes by which family agency translates into effective versus ineffective attempts by individuals embedded in new social contexts to negotiate their social (not merely their psychological) self.

## References

Amato, P. (1987) *Children in Australian Families: The Growth of Competence*. Sydney: Prentice Hall.

Amato, P., and Booth, A. (1997) *A Generation at Risk: Growing Up in an Era of Family Upheaval*. Cambridge, MA: Harvard University Press.

Ariffin, J., and Louis, A. (eds.) (2001) *Family Well-Being: Learning From the Past for the Betterment in the Future*. Johor, Malaysia: Institute Sultan Iskandar (ISI) Publications.

Beck, U. (1998) *Democracy Without Enemies*. Cambridge: Polity.

Beck, U. (2001) Living your own life in a runaway world: individualization, globalisation and politics. In W. Hutton and A. Giddens (eds.), *On the Edge: Living with Global Capitalism*. London: Vintage.

Berger, P., and Berger, B. (1983) *The War Over the Family*. London: Hutchinson.

Boulding, E. (1983) Familia faber: The family as maker of the future. *Journal of Marriage and the Family*, May, 257–66.

Bruner, J. (1994) *Four Ways to Make a Meaning*. Paper presented at the Annual Meeting of the American Educational Research Association, New Orleans, April 4–8.

Castells, M. (1997) *The Power of Identity*. Vol. 2 of *The Information Age: Economy, Society & Culture*, Oxford: Blackwell.

Commaille, J. (1998) Family and democracy. In K. Matthijs (ed.), *The Family: Contemporary Perspectives and Challenges*. Leuven: Leuven University Press.

Compas, B. E. (1995) Promoting successful coping during adolescence. In M. Rutter (ed.), *Psychological Disturbances in Young People: Challenges for Prevention*. New York: Cambridge University Press.

de Jong Gierveld, J. (1998) Intergenerational relationships and solidarity within the family. In K. Matthijs (ed.), *The Family: Contemporary Perspectives and Challenges*. Leuven: Leuven University Press.

Donati, P. (1998) The new citizenship of the family. In K. Matthijs (ed.), *The Family: Contemporary Perspectives and Challenges*. Leuven: Leuven University Press.

Donzelot, J. (1979) *The Policing of Families*. London: Hutchinson.

Edgar, D. (1992a) Childhood in its social context: The under-socialised child. *Family Matters*, 33, 32–6, Melbourne: Australian Institute of Family Studies.

Edgar, D. (1992b) Conceptualising family life and family policy. *Family Matters*, 32, 28–37, Melbourne: Australian Institute of Family Studies.

Edgar, D. (1997a) La famille Australienne comme expression de la modernité. In J. Commaille and F. de Singly (eds.), *La Question Familiale en Europe*. Paris: L'Harmattan.

Edgar, D. (1997b) *Men, Mateship, Marriage*. Sydney: HarperCollins.

Edgar, D. (1999) Families as the crucible of competence in a changing social ecology. In E. Frydenberg (ed.), *Learning to Cope: Developing as a Person in Complex Societies*. Oxford: Oxford University Press.

Edgar, D. (2001) *The Patchwork Nation: Rethinking Government, Rebuilding Community*. Sydney: HarperCollins.

Edgar, D., and Glezer, H. (1994) Family and intimacy: family careers and the reconstruction of private life. *International Social Science Journal*, 46, 117–39.

ESCAP (1998) *Asia and the Pacific into the 21st Century: Prospects for Social Development*. Kuala Lumpur: ESCAP.

Frydenberg, E., and Lewis, R. (1997) *Coping Scale for Adults*. Melbourne: Australian Council for Educational Research.

Giddens, A. (1992) *The Transformation of Intimacy: Sexuality, Love and Eroticism in Modern Societies*. Cambridge: Polity.

Glass, J. L., and Estee, S. B. (1997) The family-responsive workplace. *Annual Review of Sociology*, 23, 289–304.

Haas, L., Hwang, P., and Russell, G. (eds.) (2000) *Organisational Change and Gender Equity: International Perspectives on Fathers and Mothers at the Workplace*. Thousand Oaks, CA: Sage.

Hakim, C. (2000) *Work-Lifestyle Choices in the 21st Century: Preference Theory*. Oxford: Oxford University Press.

Hobfoll, S. E. (1988) *The Ecology of Stress*. New York: Hemisphere.

Hochschild, A. (2001) Global care chains and emotional surplus value. In W. Hutton and A. Giddens (eds.), *On the Edge: Living with Global Capitalism*. London: Vintage.

Hutton, W., and Giddens, A. (eds.) (2001) *On the Edge: Living with Global Capitalism*. London: Vintage.

Kellerhals, J. (1998) The family and the construction of adult identity. In K. Matthijs (ed.), *The Family: Contemporary Perspectives and Challenges*. Leuven: Leuven University Press.

Kinnear, P. (2002) *New Families for Changing Times*. Canberra: Australia Institute.

Kuczynski, A. (2001) Guess who's coming to dinner? *New York Times*, December 23, Section 9.

Milward, C. (1992) Keeping in touch: extended family networks. *Family Matters*, 32, 14–19, Melbourne: Australian Institute of Family Studies.

Milward, C. (1995) Family networks in rural and urban settings. *Family Matters*, 41, 10–14, Melbourne: Australian Institute of Family Studies.

OECD (2001) *Cities and Regions in the New Learning Economy*. Paris: Organization for Economic Cooperation and Development.

Otero, L. L. (1994) *Nature, Plurality and the Future of the Family Phenomenon*. New York: United Nations Organization, IYF94 Report.

Presser, H. B. (2000) Non-standard work schedules and marital instability. *Journal of Marriage and the Family*, 62, 93.

Pryor, J., and Rodgers, B. (2001) *Children in Changing Families: Life after Parents Separate*. Oxford: Blackwell.

Putnam, R. (1993a) *Making Democracy Work: Civic Traditions in Italy*. Princeton, NJ: Princeton University Press.

Putnam, R. (1993b) Bowling alone: America's declining social capital. *Journal of Democracy*, 6, 65–78.

Settles, B. (1998) Putting families in family policy and programs: local, regional, national and international options. In K. Matthijs (ed.), *The Family: Contemporary Perspectives and Challenges*. Leuven: Leuven University Press.

Smart, C., and Neale, B. (1999) *Family Fragments?* Cambridge: Polity and Blackwell.

Tucker, K. H. (1998), *Anthony Giddens and Modern Social Theory*. London: Sage.

UNDP (1999) *Human Development Report*. New York: United Nations Organization and Oxford University Press.

UNICEF (1997) *The Progress of Nations*. Paris: United Nations Children's Fund.

UNICEF (2001) *The State of the World's Children: Early Childhood*. New York: United Nations Organization.

UNO (2001) *The Nature and Evolution of Poverty, World Development Report*. New York: United Nations Organization.

Winter, I. (ed.) (2000) *Social Capital and Public Policy in Australia*. Melbourne: Australian Institute of Family Studies.

Wiseman, P. (2002) China's future is awry as boys outnumber girls. *USA Today*, June 19, 1–2.

Wrong, D. H. (1961) The oversocialised conception of man. *American Sociological Review*, 26,183–93; reprinted in P. I. Rose (ed.), *The Study of Society*. New York: Random House, 1970.

# 2

# Changing European Families: Trends and Issues

Kathleen Kiernan

## Introduction

In many European countries the family has been featuring in political and policy discussions due to the developing pattern of family change that has occurred in many European countries over the last few decades. Among these changes in family patterns are major demographic changes that directly influence the relationship between the family and public policy. These demographic changes include: fewer marriages, more cohabitation and more births outside marriage; increases in divorce, remarriage and reconstituted families; an increase in the proportion of lone-parent families; falling birthrates; and smaller families. Although the traditional one-family household still predominates throughout the European Union (EU), the "family norm" of a married couple is gradually being replaced by other living arrangements. This chapter will examine these trends across the EU, highlighting the similarities and differences across nations as well as discussing the implications of these novel developments.

## The Transformation of Marriage

In the recent past marriage heralded the start of a first union for most couples in Europe. There were identifiable stages in the development of a relationship: courtship, engagement, and, ultimately, the marriage ceremony that was followed by the couple setting up home together. Marriage was also popular and youthful. Nowadays, there is much more flexibility in becoming a couple and whether they co-reside; and young people are marrying less and are doing so at older ages.

## Declining marriage rates

After World War II the general trend in European marriage rates had been to a younger and more universal marriage pattern that reached its zenith during the 1960s and the early part of the 1970s, since when marriage rates have declined and the mean age at marriage has risen. In broad outline, the decline in marriage rates began in Sweden and Denmark in the late 1960s, spread through most of Western Europe in the early part of the 1970s, and became evident in the southern European countries (Spain, Italy, Portugal, and Greece) around the mid-1970s. Since the 1980s, the decline in marriage rates has continued in most European countries but at a slower pace.

To illustrate some of these changes we can compare the mean age at first marriage amongst women in 1975, which is generally close to the lowest average age observed in the twentieth century for many countries, with the most recently available data (Council of Europe, 2001). It is noticeable from table 2.1 that in many countries the average age at marriage has increased by between two and four years, regardless of the starting position. In the mid-1970s the average ages of first-time brides in most West European nations were clustered in the 22–24 age range, whereas by the year 2000 they are clustered in the later twenties, predominantly at age 27.

## The rise of cohabitation

One of the important engines behind the decline in marriage rates and a movement to a later age at marriage is the rise in cohabitation that has occurred, particularly since the beginning of the 1980s, in many European countries. However, it should be emphasized that men and women living together outside marriage is not new. Prior to the 1970s it was largely statistically invisible and probably socially

**Table 2.1** Average age at first marriage among women marrying in 1975 and 2000, European nations

| *Average age* | *Countries 1975* | *Countries 2000* |
|---|---|---|
| 30 | | Sweden |
| 29 | | Denmark |
| 28 | | Finland, Norway |
| 27 | | Austria, France, Germany, Ireland, Italy, Luxembourg, Netherlands, Spain, Switzerland, UK |
| 26 | | Belgium, Greece |
| 25 | Sweden | Portugal |
| 24 | Denmark, Ireland, Portugal, Spain, Switzerland | |
| 23 | Austria, Finland, West Germany, Greece, Italy, Luxembourg, Netherlands, Norway, UK | |
| 22 | Belgium, France | |

*Source*: Council of Europe (2001).

invisible outside of the local community or social milieu. In some European countries there were subgroups that were probably more prone to cohabitation than others: the very poor; those whose marriages had broken up but were unable to obtain a divorce, as there was no such legislation, or it was more stringent than nowadays or it was very expensive to obtain a divorce; certain groups of rural dwellers; and groups ideologically opposed to marriage. It is a new type of cohabitation that is implicated in the marriage declines that have occurred across European nations in recent decades. A form of cohabitation that came to the fore in the 1970s escalated during the 1980s and 1990s and continues unabated, whereby young people live together as a prelude to, or as an alternative to, marriage.

To provide a perspective on the incidence of cohabitation and the popularity of marriage and singlehood across European nations we used data from a series of Eurobarometer Surveys carried out in the 15 member states of the EU in 1998, 1999, and 2000 (European Commission, 1998, 1999, 2000). In an attempt to reduce variation due to small sample sizes we have used the combined data from these three years. Eurobarometer Surveys are primarily opinion surveys carried out under the auspices of the administration of the EU, and we should bear in mind that data from such surveys are unlikely to be as accurate as those obtained in dedicated family and fertility surveys, but they probably reflect the relative position of different European countries in these developments.

Figure 2.1 shows the combined proportions of men and women aged 25–34 in the 15 European Community (EC) countries who were currently cohabiting, married, single, or separated/divorced/widowed at the time of the surveys in 1998, 1999, and 2000. It is clear from figure 2.1 that there is a good deal of diversity across European states in the incidence of cohabitation. Three broad groupings can be seen. Cohabitation is strikingly common in the Nordic countries of Denmark, Sweden, and Finland, and France also has relatively high proportions cohabiting. There is a middle group of countries, including the Benelux countries (the Netherlands, Belgium, and Luxembourg), Great Britain, West and East Germany, and Austria,

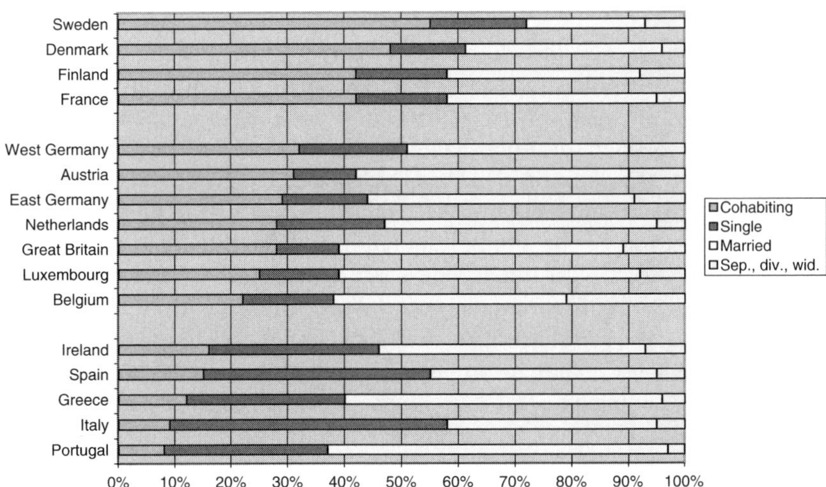


**Figure 2.1** Marital status distributions among 25–34-year-olds: European nations combined data, 1998–2000

with intermediate levels of cohabitation. At the other extreme is the set of southern European countries and Ireland, where cohabitation is less common than in other European nations.

It is also clear from these data that there is a good deal of variation in the proportions of women in marital unions. Marriage is most popular in the southern European countries of Greece and Portugal, but this is much less the case in the other southern European countries of Italy and Spain, which have low proportions in marital unions and the highest proportions single. It would seem that not only are men and women in Spain and Italy avoiding parenthood (as we will see later), they are also not forming partnerships either, at least in their late twenties and early thirties. In the Nordic countries, as well as in France, cohabitation is more popular than marriage at these ages, whereas marriage is seemingly more popular in countries such as Austria, the Netherlands Great Britain, and Luxembourg.

There is also evidence from analyses of data from the United Nations Economic Commission for Europe Fertility and Family Surveys (UNECE FFS) (United Nations, 1992; United Nations Economic Commission for Europe,1996–2001), carried out in the first half of the 1990s, that cohabitation has eclipsed marriage as the marker for entry into first union in many European countries and that overtime there have been noteworthy increases in proportions of young people cohabiting (Kiernan, 1999a). But how durable are such unions? Analyses of the FFS data (Kiernan, 2002) showed that after five years, only a minority of cohabiting unions remain intact: they have either converted into marriages or dissolved. Sweden was the only country where there was evidence of longer-term cohabitation. The comparative data that we have on union behavior show that cohabitation tends to be a short-lived affair in many countries, but this may well be changing. Existing data relate in the main to the behavior of cohorts forming partnerships in the early 1990s, and since then there is evidence from individual country surveys of further increases in the level and duration of cohabitation (Toulemon, 1997; Haskey, 1999; Murphy, 2000; Bumpass and Lu, 2000).

## A partnership transition?

It has been suggested by several scholars that many European societies may be going through a transition in the way that men and women become couples or partners (see Prinz, 1995 for a review). Most scholars draw on the experience of the Swedish population, which is the nation that has gone furthest in these developments, from which a number of stages can be identified (Hoem and Hoem, 1988). Simplifying, in the first stage cohabitation emerges as a deviant or *avant-garde* phenomenon practiced by a small group of the single population, whilst the great majority of the population marry directly. In the second stage cohabitation functions as either a prelude to marriage or a probationary period where the strength of the relationship may be tested prior to committing to marriage, and is predominantly a childless phase. In the third stage cohabitation becomes socially acceptable as an alternative to marriage and becoming a parent is no longer restricted to marriage. Finally, in the fourth stage, cohabitation and marriage become indistinguishable, with children being born and reared within both, and the partnership transition could be said to be complete. Sweden and Denmark are countries that have made the transition to this fourth stage. These stages may vary in duration, but once a society has reached a particular stage it is unlikely that there will be a return to an earlier stage. Also, once a certain stage has been reached all the previous types of cohabiting unions can coexist. Such stages also have parallels at the level of the individual. At any given time cohabitation may have different meanings for the men and women involved (Manting, 1996). For example, it may be viewed as an alternative to being single, or as a precursor to marriage, or a substitute for marriage. Moreover, how a couple perceives their cohabitation may change over time and the perception may also vary between the partners. Dissecting cohabitation in this way highlights the diversity of the phenomenon and suggests that, more so than marriage, it is a process rather than an event. Moreover, the inconstancy of cohabitation poses challenges at the both the macro and micro levels for understanding this development in family life.

In sum, the major themes in marriage behavior in recent decades across European nations is that formal marriage is on the decline, and cohabitation has become increasingly popular, but there is little evidence that the propensity to form partnerships has declined. However, there remains marked variation across nations in the extent to which these changes have occurred.

## Becoming a Parent

Becoming a parent arguably involves one of the most profound changes in an individual's life course. The adjustment in adapting to responsibility for a totally dependent being is substantial, and the biggest change in lifestyle usually occurs with the advent of the first child. In modern, low-fertility societies the few births that couples or individuals have are usually tightly clustered in a period of a very few years, so the two most crucial decisions are when to become a parent and how many children to have (Hobcraft and Kiernan, 1995). Across Europe parenthood is being entered into at increasingly older ages, higher proportions of men and women are remaining childless, and an increasing proportion of children are being born outside of marriage.

### A birth dearth

As a consequence of later and less parenthood at the close of the old millennium European states had the lowest levels of fertility in the world. Table 2.2 shows the total fertility rates (TFRs) for a range of Western European nations for the years 1970, 1980, 1990, and 2000. These rates provide a guide to the average number of children that would be born to a woman during her lifetime if the prevailing fertility rates were to continue. Over time across Europe there has been a downward trend in fertility (with some oscillations) and it is clear that the timing and the extent of the decline vary substantially from one country to another. Currently, the lowest rates are to be seen in the southern European countries of Spain and Italy and the highest rates in Ireland, France, and several of the Nordic countries. These rates are much lower than the US, which had a rate of just over 2 in 1999, and also most Third World countries, which have rates in excess of 3 children per woman.

### Older parenthood

In most Western European countries in recent decades there has been a movement to a later age at entry into motherhood. Data on entry into fatherhood are rare but we

**Table 2.2** Total period fertility rates, 1970–2000, European nations

| *Country* | *1970* | *1980* | *1990* | *2000* |
|---|---|---|---|---|
| Ireland | 3.93 | 3.25 | 2.11 | 1.89 |
| France | 2.47 | 1.95 | 1.78 | 1.89 |
| Norway | 2.50 | 1.72 | 1.93 | 1.85 |
| Luxembourg | 1.98 | 1.49 | 1.60 | 1.79 |
| Denmark | 1.95 | 1.55 | 1.67 | 1.77 |
| Finland | 1.83 | 1.63 | 1.78 | 1.73 |
| Netherlands | 2.57 | 1.60 | 1.62 | 1.72 |
| Belgium | 2.25 | 1.68 | 1.62 | 1.66 |
| UK | 2.45 | 1.90 | 1.83 | 1.65 |
| Sweden | 1.92 | 1.68 | 2.13 | 1.54 |
| Portugal | 3.02 | 2.18 | 1.57 | 1.52 |
| Switzerland | 2.10 | 1.55 | 1.58 | 1.50 |
| Germany | 2.03 | 1.56 | 1.45 | 1.36 |
| Austria | 2.29 | 1.62 | 1.45 | 1.34 |
| Greece | 2.39 | 2.21 | 1.39 | 1.29 |
| Spain | 2.88 | 2.20 | 1.36 | 1.24 |
| Italy | 2.42 | 1.64 | 1.33 | 1.23 |

*Source*: Council of Europe (2001).

assume that trends have followed the same general direction as that observed for motherhood. In 1970, across Western European nations average ages at first birth amongst women were predominantly in the 23–24 age range; in 2000 the average was typically in the 27–28 age range (Council of Europe, 2001). As yet, there are only few signs of stabilization in the movement to a later age pattern of childbearing.

## Childlessness

The movement to older parenthood and the growth in childlessness have both contributed to the decline in European fertility rates. Very few couples expect to remain childless. For example, in 1989, fewer than 5 percent of EC citizens regarded being childless as ideal: the only country where the proportion exceeded 5 percent was West Germany, at 7 percent (Eurobarometer, 1991). Other insights on the salience of children in people's lives come from a more recent Eurobarometer survey (European Commission, 1998). The Eurobarometer 50.1 survey carried out in late 1998 had a special section on family issues in which survey respondents were asked how important it was to have children: very important, fairly important, fairly unimportant, and very unimportant. We examined the responses of men and women aged 25–34, as these ages are those of prime family formation, as well as being ages when men and women are likely to be considering the issue of parenthood. Across the EU 15, 55 percent reported that having a child was very important, 30 percent that it was fairly important, 9 percent that it was fairly unimportant, only 3 percent that it was very unimportant, and a further 3 percent that they did not know. Overall, 14 percent of the men and 10 percent of the women in the age range 25–34 responded that children were unimportant. For our comparison of responses across nations we combined the responses of fairly and very important/unimportant.

**Table 2.3** The proportions of 25–34-year-olds reporting on the importance of children in their lives, 1998 (%), European Union

| *Country* | *Important* | *Unimportant* | *Don't know* |
|---|---|---|---|
| Great Britain | 70 | 24 | 6 |
| Ireland | 74 | 18 | 8 |
| Belgium | 80 | 18 | 2 |
| West Germany | 79 | 16 | 4 |
| Netherlands | 81 | 16 | 3 |
| Luxembourg | 83 | 15 | 2 |
| Finland | 82 | 14 | 4 |
| Denmark | 85 | 14 | 1 |
| Sweden | 86 | 12 | 2 |
| Spain | 86 | 10 | 4 |
| France | 89 | 10 | 1 |
| Austria | 86 | 9 | 5 |
| East Germany | 89 | 7 | 4 |
| Italy | 92 | 6 | 2 |
| Portugal | 95 | 4 | 1 |
| Greece | 98 | 2 | – |
| Total | 84 | 12 | 3 |

*Source*: Analysis of *Eurobarometer No.50.1* (European Commission, 1998).

Table 2.3 shows the responses including a "don't know" category for the 15 nations of the EU (with East and West Germany separately identified). The table is graded from countries with the highest level of negativity toward children to the lowest. Great Britain tops the league, with almost 1 in 4 reporting that children were unimportant to them. Then there is a cluster of countries in the 14–18 percent range, including the geographically close Benelux (Belgium, Luxembourg, and the Netherlands) countries, West Germany, and Ireland. The Nordic countries of Sweden, Finland, and Denmark have similar levels (12–14 percent) and the lowest levels are to be seen in the southern European countries of Portugal, Italy, and Greece.

It is clear that most Europeans think that having a child is important for them, notwithstanding that discrepancies between espoused attitudes and behavior are not uncommon. This is clearly apparent amongst the southern Europeans, who report that children are very important in their lives but exhibit the lowest fertility rates in the EU. It is estimated that levels of childlessness will increase to over 20 percent in many European countries, which is in sharp contrast to the levels of 10 percent amongst most recent generations of women to have reached the end of their reproductive years (Eurostat, 1994).

How do people decide not to have children? The consensus on this issue is that men and women delay having their first child and then, after a number of years, decide not to have children. Childlessness emerges from a series of decisions to postpone having children (Veevers, 1980) – in Lee's (1980) formulation of fertility behavior, "aiming at a moving target" rather than a fixed one. That is not to say that some couples or individuals may decide at a young age never to have children and actively pursue that goal, although it is always possible for such couples to change their minds. As couples grow older opportunities to engage in work, community, and leisure activities may compete with parenthood. An interesting and unexplored question is who is in the driving seat in this development: women or men, or is there dual control by the couple? Much of the current literature assumes that women are in the driving seat and, in the main, argues that, as women have become increasingly attached to the labor market, the potential incompatibilities between motherhood and work have become more apparent. Undoubtedly, whatever the mechanism behind the growth in childlessness, the perceived advantages of remaining childless have increased since the 1970s, while the perceived disadvantages have declined.

## The separation of marriage and reproduction

The other major development in fertility behavior across most European states is the noteworthy increases in the proportions of births occurring outside of legal marriage, which in most countries, at least in the twentieth century, has been the conventional setting for having children.

Figure 2.2 shows the proportions of births outside of marriage in 1975, 1985, and 1999. It is clearly apparent that across all nations there have been increases but there is also a good deal of variation in the level of childbearing outside of marriage. At one extreme are the Nordic countries, where in 1999 well over 40 percent of births were outside of marriage, and at the other extreme are the southern European countries of Italy and Greece where, along with Switzerland, 10 percent or fewer births occurred outside of marriage. Between these two extremes two broad groupings can be discerned. A set of countries with ratios between 15 and 25 percent, including the Benelux countries, West Germany, and Portugal and a set with 30 percent or more, which encompasses Ireland (which has experienced one of the most notable changes – up from 8 percent in 1985 to 31 percent in 1999), the UK, and France (with remarkably similar trends), and Austria and Finland. The US falls into this group. In 1975, only 7 of the 20 countries represented here had nonmarital birth ratios of

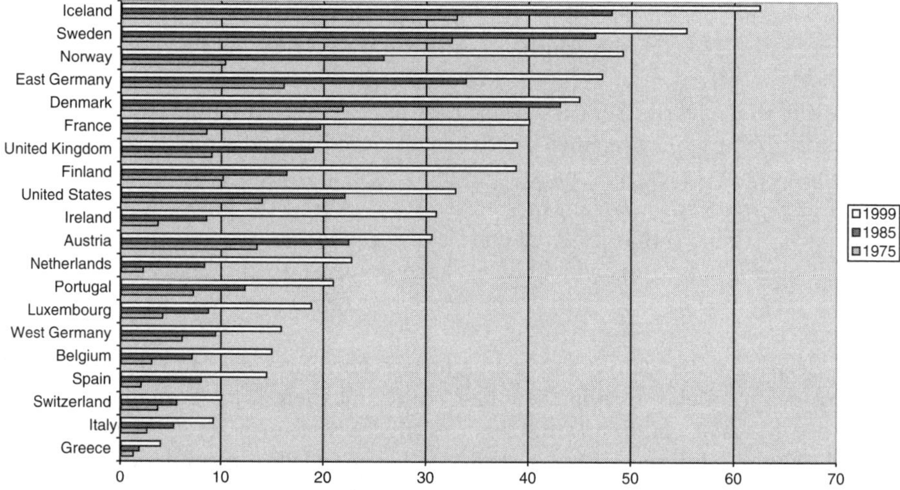


**Figure 2.2** Percentage of births outside of marriage, 1975–1999, Western Europe

more than 10 percent: in 1985 this had increased to 11, and by 1999 stood at 17. In 1975, Sweden and Iceland were dramatic outliers, with 1 in 3 births already occurring outside of marriage. This is much less the case today.

So, over the last few decades we have witnessed the increased severance of marriage and parenthood. However, it should be emphasized that we have not witnessed the separation of partnership and parenthood; as most of the rise in births outside of marriage emanates from cohabiting couples. Analyses of the FFS show that in most Western European countries there is little evidence of a growth in the proportions of women having babies on their own, Great Britain being an exception to this as is the US (Kiernan, 1999b; Raley, 2001 ). It is still the case that the current generation of first-born Europeans are born to parents who are in a union, and typically in their first union. However, it is also important to stress, as vividly portrayed in figure 2.2, that in the realm of extramarital childbearing there is still a good deal of intra-European variation in the level of childbearing outside of marriage.

A question one might ask is whether it matters whether children are born within or outside of marriage. Children born to a solo mother are likely to be living in more impoverished circumstances than children born into a couple-family, but does it matter whether a child is born within a cohabiting union or marital union? On a day-to-day basis, from a child's perspective there may be little to distinguish between the two types of union. But there is evidence that cohabiting unions are more fragile than marital unions. In an earlier analysis (Kiernan, 1999b) we showed that children born within marriage were less likely to see their parents separate than those born in a cohabiting union. Within the set of cohabiting unions those that had not been converted into marriages were the most fragile, with at least 1 in 5 of these unions having dissolved by the time the child was 5 years old. This held across all the European nations included in the analysis. However, there were cross-national differences in the fragility of cohabiting unions that converted to marriages after the birth of the child. Among children born within marriage or cohabiting unions that subsequently converted to marriages there was little difference in the chances of them seeing the break-up of their parents' marriage by their fifth birthday in Sweden, Norway, Austria, and West Germany; with less than one in ten of these children having experienced parental separation. However, in France, Switzerland, the US, and most noticeably Great Britain, children born into marital unions were more likely to see their parents remain together until their fifth birthday than those children born into a cohabiting union that converted into a marriage (Kiernan, 1999b, forthcoming).

## Family Dissolution

Alongside the increasing separation of marriage and childbearing there has also been, with the rise in divorce, the increasing separation of childbearing and child-rearing for at least one of the parents, typically the father. It is still the case that the majority of European marriages are only terminated by death. However, marriages are increasingly being dissolved by divorce at a stage in marriage before death has made any significant inroad and at a stage in the marriage when there are likely to be dependent children.

## The rise of divorce

In most European countries divorce has increased since the mid-1960s, following a period of very stable divorce rates throughout the 1950s and the early part of the 1960s. Figure 2.3 shows trends since the early 1970s in the extent of divorce as measured by the number of divorces per 1,000 population for a range of Western countries. At the beginning of the 1970s the highest divorce rates were to be found in the US, and in Denmark and Sweden in Europe. Divorce rates increased during the 1980s in most countries, since when rates have stabilized in many. Between 1960 and the mid-1980s divorce policy was either completely revised or substantially reformed in almost all Western countries (Phillips, 1988). Most countries liberalized their divorce laws, moving from fault-based divorce to no-fault divorce laws whereby fault, responsibility, or offense were no longer attributed by the law to either spouse. After the liberalization of divorce laws, divorce rates in many countries continued their upward trend, frequently at a faster pace than in the years preceding legislative changes, followed by a period of stabilization from the mid- to late 1980s.

In the mid-1990s there was still a good deal of variation in the level of divorce across European nations. In 1995 the total divorce rate in the EU was 0.30, whereas in 1970 it had stood at 0.11 (Eurostat, 1997). This indicator is an estimate of the mean number of divorces per marriage for a notional cohort subjected to current divorce rates at each marriage duration. It can broadly be interpreted to mean that if the propensity to divorce remained unchanged over time then 30 percent of marriages would end in divorce. If current rates were to prevail then nearly one in three marriages in the EU would dissolve. This is a lower level than in Canada with 44 percent, and the US, where the total divorce rate has been above 50 percent since the late 1970s. Within Europe there is also a good deal of diversity in the level of

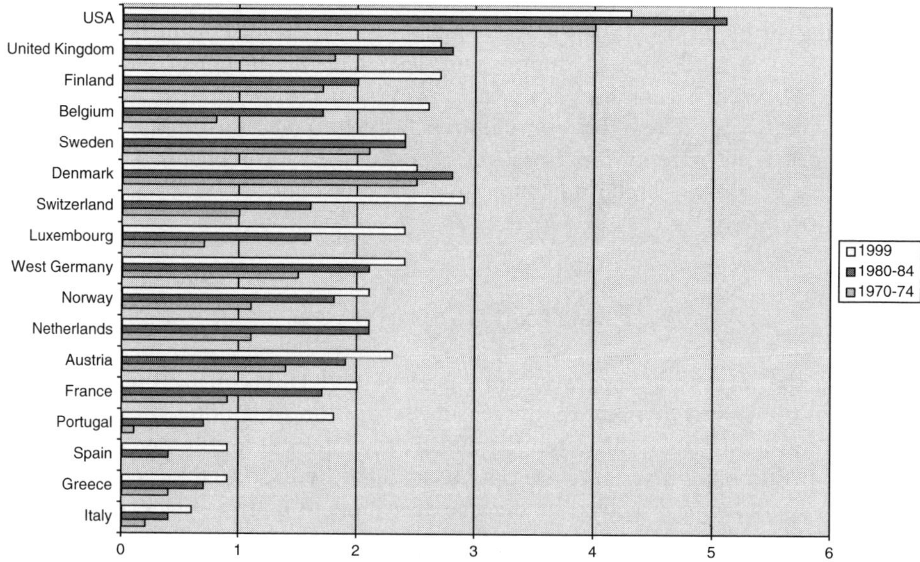


**Figure 2.3** Crude divorce rates per 1,000 population, 1970–1999, Western Europe

divorce. During the 1990s three distinct divorce regions could be distinguished: the Nordic countries, England, and Wales, where the total divorce rate had been consistently above the 0.40 level; Western and Central European nations (Austria, Switzerland, Germany, France, Belgium, the Netherlands, Iceland, and Luxembourg), where the indicator lay between 0.30 and 0.40; and the southern European countries (Greece, Portugal, Spain, and Italy), where it was below 0.20.

Divorce statistics have invariably underestimated the totality of marital dissolutions, and with the rise of cohabitation even fewer partnership dissolutions are captured by divorce registration data. In countries where divorce is more longstanding and more prevalent, there has been a tendency for marriages to break up sooner. As a consequence more couples are likely to be childless, and among couples with children the children are likely to be younger. Rising divorce has led to a growth in lone-parent families and the residential separation of fathers from their children, as well as remarried couples and stepfamilies.

## Lone-parent families

The prevalence of lone parenthood varies considerably between countries and the proportion of families headed by a lone parent has been increasing just about everywhere, as can be seen from table 2.4. As yet, no Western European country has matched the US, where more than one in four families with children are lone-parent families. Various reports made for the EU (e.g., Bradshaw et al., 1996) show that the great majority of lone-parent families are headed by a woman (80–90 percent). The largest group of lone parents are those who have experienced a marital breakdown; the next largest group comprises widows, while lone mothers who had never been married (but not necessarily never partnered) were the smallest category. In many countries where there have been marked increases in childbearing outside of

**Table 2.4** Lone-parent families as a percentage of all families with dependent children, selected years, Western Europe

| *Country* | *1980/1*[a] | *1990/1*[a] | *1996*[b] |
|---|---|---|---|
| United Kingdom | 14 | 16 | 23 |
| Denmark | 18 | 21 | – |
| Finland | – | – | 17 |
| France | 8 | 11 | 15 |
| Belgium | 9 | 15 | 15 |
| Germany | 10 | 15 | 13 |
| Ireland | 7 | 11 | 13 |
| Portugal | 12 | 12 | 12 |
| Luxembourg | 9 | 12 | 11 |
| Netherlands | 8 | 12 | 11 |
| Italy | 7 | 6 | 11 |
| Spain | 5 | 8 | 8 |
| Greece | 4 | 6 | 7 |

*Sources*: Bradshaw et al. (1996). *a*. Eurostat, *Labour Force Surveys Social Europe 1/94 – The European Union and the Family* and *b*. Eurostat, *Statistics in Focus: Population and Social Conditions 1998/12*. Additional data in *b* come from Labour Force Surveys.

marriage (but again not necessarily outside a partnership), this ordering may well have changed, such that never-married women with children may now constitute the second largest group of lone-mother families. Overall, the majority of lone-parent families emanate from the break-up of partnerships, either marital or cohabiting ones.

There is a good deal of evidence that children who experience the break-up of their parents' marriage or nonmarital union are more likely to experience poverty or reduced economic circumstances than children who grow up with both natural parents, but that the depth of poverty varies across nations (Bradshaw et al., 1996, Bradbury and Jantti, 1999). For example, children living in lone-parent families in Sweden and Denmark are much less likely to be living in impoverished circumstances than their contemporaries in Germany, Ireland, and the UK. The financial exigencies associated with marital breakdown arise from the precarious economic position of lone mothers, with whom most children reside, and the diseconomies of scale associated with the maintenance of two households when fathers live apart from their children. The low incomes of lone-mother families are due to a combination of factors: low earnings from employment, lack of or low levels of child support from the natural father, or inadequate state support.

### Remarriage

Being reared by a lone parent is frequently not a long-term arrangement as a substantial proportion of divorced persons eventually remarry. Men are even more likely than women to remarry and are also more likely to remarry more quickly after a divorce. As well as being more likely to remarry, divorced men are more likely to cohabit than are divorced women. Remarriages are also at greater risk of dissolving than are first marriages. After an initial upsurge in remarriage rates in the early years following the enactment of more lenient divorce legislation, which occurred in most European countries in recent decades, remarriage has taken a downturn due to some extent to postmarital cohabitation becoming more common.

## Family Circumstances of Children

As a consequence of these demographic changes children are increasingly experiencing a variety of family settings as they pass through childhood and adolescence. A recent study by Andersson (2001) provides us with insights into the complex living arrangements of children.

This study collated the events occurring to children in the UNECE FFS surveys. It used the experiences of a synthetic cohort based on mapping the events occurring to all children of different ages in a period six years prior to the survey to build a picture derived from life-table estimates of lifetime experiences. Table 2.5 shows the estimated cumulative percentage of children who have spent time not living in couple families at different ages. There are some striking findings in this table. Compared with the European countries, the US has noticeably higher proportions of children commencing life with a mother living on their own (17 percent compared with 10 percent or less in the other countries), and the highest proportion of children experiencing a period without both parents (an estimated 50 per cent by age 15). Andersson did not include Britain in his analyses. But it is likely that Britain, with its

**Table 2.5** Cumulative percentage of children not living with both parents at a given age, selected years and countries

| *Country* | *Period* | *At birth* | *Age 1* | *Age 3* | *Age 9* | *Age 15* |
|---|---|---|---|---|---|---|
| Sweden | (1987–93) | 5 | 7 | 13 | 24 | 34 |
| Norway | (1983–89) | 7 | 9 | 13 | 21 | 26 |
| Finland | (1983–89) | 3 | 4 | 8 | 16 | 22 |
| France | (1988–94) | 10 | 12 | 15 | 24 | 31 |
| United States | (1989–95) | 17 | 21 | 28 | 41 | 50 |
| Austria | (1990–96) | 10 | 12 | 15 | 26 | 34 |
| West Germany | (1986–92) | 6 | 8 | 12 | 21 | 34 |
| East Germany | (1984–89) | 18 | 19 | 25 | 37 | 46 |
| Italy | (1990–95) | 2 | 2 | 3 | 6 | 9 |
| Spain | (1989–95) | 2 | 3 | 5 | 9 | 13 |

*Source*: Andersson (2001).

high divorce rates alongside the growth in solo motherhood, is likely to be closer to the US in these matters than any other Western European nation. In most other European nations the proportions of children not having lived with their parents throughout childhood are quite similar at around three in ten. We also observe that the vast majority of Italian and Spanish children grow up with both their parents.

Andersson also provided us with estimates of the extent to which children see the repartnering of their parents. Table 2.6 shows the proportions of children who have in effect become part of a *de facto* or *de jure* stepfamily by the length of time since their parents separated. Repartnering is more popular in the US than in any of the other countries, with two-thirds being in a stepfamily within six years, and is least common in Italy, Spain, and France, with around one-third having become part of a stepfamily within six years. In the remainder of the countries about one in two of the children were in a stepfamily six years after the separation of their parents. These data suggest that a significant minority of children are experiencing several transitions in quick succession; the separation of their parents and the repartnering of their mothers, with all the adjustments that this implies on both the part of the child, the parents, and the partners.

As a consequence of these demographic changes children are increasingly experiencing a variety of family settings as they pass through childhood and adolescence. Other chapters discuss the implications of these changing circumstances for the welfare and development of children both in the short and longer terms (see Scott, chapter 7, this volume; Pryor and Trinder, chapter 19, this volume).

## Discussion

Our review has shown that across Europe in recent decades men and women have been marrying and having children less and at older ages than their recent predecessors, as well as cohabiting and divorcing more. These are the broad trends, but it is also apparent that there is variation across nations in the extent to which these developments have taken hold. In my discussion I am going to focus mainly on

**Table 2.6** Cumulative percentage of children experiencing a repartnership of a their parent, by time since union disruption, amongst children experiencing parental separation, selected years and countries

| | | *Duration* | | | |
|---|---|---|---|---|---|
| *Country* | *Period* | *1 year* | *3 years* | *6 years* | *10 years* |
| Sweden | (1987–93) | 11 | 32 | 51 | 62 |
| Norway | (1983–89) | 17 | 41 | 57 | – |
| Finland | (1983–89) | 15 | 31 | 45 | 64 |
| France | (1988–94) | 10 | 23 | 35 | 47 |
| United States | (1989–95) | 21 | 47 | 67 | 78 |
| Austria | (1990–96) | 18 | 30 | 47 | 54 |
| West Germany | (1986–92) | 8 | 29 | 50 | – |
| East Germany | (1984–89) | 28 | 55 | 65 | – |
| Italy | (1990–95) | 2 | 8 | 28 | – |
| Spain | (1989–95) | 5 | 25 | 37 | 47 |

*Source*: Andersson (2001).

parenthood and cohabitation issues, as the ramifications of parental separation and divorce are covered in other chapters.

European men and women are having children later in their lives because they have more life choices combined with highly effective means of controlling their fertility (Hobcraft and Kiernan, 1995). Spending longer together as a dual-earner couple before becoming parents generally improves a couple's position in terms of housing and consumer goods as well as allowing time for career development and leisure activities. Moreover, the increased participation in higher education and training that has occurred in most European nations (United Nations Economic Commission for Europe, 2000), as well as accrual of qualifications to meet the demands of modern economies, have led to an extension of the period of dependency into the third decade of life. Consequently, the time span of the transition to adulthood, from leaving education, entering the labor market and marrying and becoming parents has become more protracted. There has been a noticeable upward shift in the social and economic timetables of young European men and women which has knock-on effects for their marriage, and perhaps more importantly, their parenthood behavior. Once men and women become parents decisions have to be made about combining family life and work: including the care of children, whether both parents should continue in paid employment, and the renegotiation of the domestic division of labor. Difficulties in resolving these issues may lead to reductions in the number of children that a couple will have. The growth in childlessness leads to disparities in incomes and lifestyles between couples with and without children. This raises questions as to who should pay for children if they are both public and private goods. What should be the contribution of families and the state to the rearing of children, given that society benefits (*in extremis* would cease to exist) from the production of children and the fact that positive externalities accrue to members of society who do not have children (Folbre, 1994, 2001)? For further discussion of the contribution that different governments make to families see Land, chapter 4, this volume, and Sigle-Rushton and Kenney, chapter 26, this volume.

The role of fertility control also should not be underestimated in changing fertility behavior. Since the 1960s we have seen widespread availability and use made of the contraceptive pill, the IUD, surgical sterilization, and safe, legal abortion. The breaking of the intimate connection between sex and reproduction (Lewis and Kiernan, 1996) had asymmetrical gender consequences. Women were more likely to bear the consequences of unwanted birth than men, and the ability to avoid this allowed women to better explore their sexuality and reduce the number of bridal pregnancies and to delay becoming a parent. The emergence of safe and effective means of birth control was probably also an important precondition for the emergence of cohabitation (Kiernan, 1989; van de Kaa, 1987).

Undoubtedly, with increasing resort to divorce, marriage has become a more fragile institution. Rising divorce rates are likely to have increased the perceived risks of investing in marriage, and the emergence of cohabitation may be a logical response to this kind of uncertainty. At the individual level there is robust evidence for a range of European nations that men and women who experienced divorce during childhood are more likely to cohabit and to have children outside of marriage (Kiernan, 2000, 2001).

In many European countries and the US, the recent marked rises in cohabitation and having children outside of marriage show little sign of abatement, which raises questions about the hegemony of legal marriage and many of the assumptions on which public policies and even social scientific theories are built. In the past, ties between spouses were deemed to be sufficiently important that marriages and divorces were included within the scope of vital registration systems. With the rise in cohabitation this public acknowledgment has been eroded and consequently raises policy questions about the links between partners, unmarried parents, and their children with respect to the public domains of life. Many European countries are recognizing that changes in union behavior are underway and marriage law, practices, and values, as well as the regulation of cohabitation, are being discussed and evaluated (see *International Journal of Law, Policy and Family*, 2001).

Why are people excluding themselves from formal marriage, and does it matter? The anxiety expressed in the literature, in the main by US authors (see Waite and Gallagher, 2000), stems largely from the fact that at the present time cohabiting unions are more fragile than marital unions. However, this difference between the two types of unions may be largely due to the stronger and more committed partnerships being selected into marriage. Moreover, if the general trend and future course of cohabitation is for parents who live together to eschew marriage, then cohabitations, other things being equal, will become more durable alternatives to marriage.

In conclusion, our review has shown that the demographics of family life in Europe have been transformed in recent decades, but there continues to be marked variation across nations in the extent to which the changes in partnership and parenthood behavior have taken hold.


## Acknowledgments

The Economic and Social Research Council UK provided the funding for this project with a grant to the ESRC Centre for the Analysis of Social Exclusion at the London School of Economics. The UK Data Archive at Essex University supplied the Eurobarometer data. Thanks also to Gunnar Andersson of the Max Planck Demographic Institute at Rostock for permission to use his tables.

## References

Andersson, G. (2001) Children's experience of family disruption and family formation: evidence from 16 FFS countries. *Paper presented at XXIV IUSSP General Population Conference, Session on Family Demography from a Children's Perspective*, Salvador, Brazil, August. Available online at www.demogr.mpg.de

Bradbury, B., and Jantti, M. (1999) *Child Poverty across Industrialised Nations*. Innocenti Occasional Papers: Economic and Social Policy Series, no. 71.

Bradshaw, J., Kennedy, S., Kilkey, M., Hutton, S., Corden, A., Eardley, T., Holmes, H., and Neale, J. (1996) *The Employment of Lone Parents: A Comparison of Policy in Twenty Countries*. London: Family Policy Studies Centre/Joseph Rowntree Foundation.

Bumpass, L., and Lu, H-H. (2000) Trends in cohabitation and implications for children's family contexts in the United States. *Population Studies*, 54, 29–41.

Council of Europe. (2001) *Recent demographic developments in Europe*. Strasbourg: Council of Europe.

Eurobarometer (1991) *Desire for Children*. Eurobarometer, No. 32.

European Commission (1998) *Eurobarometer No. 50.1*. ESRC Data Archive, Essex, England.

European Commission (1999) *Eurobarometer No. 51*. ESRC Data Archive, Essex, England.

European Commission (2000) *Eurobarometer No. 53*. ESRC Data Archive, Essex, England.

Eurostat (1994) *Demographic Statistics 1994*. Luxembourg.

Eurostat (1997) *Statistics in Focus: Population and Social Conditions No. 14*. Luxembourg: Office for Official Publications of the European Communities.

Folbre, N. (1994) *Who Pays for the Kids? Gender and Structures of Constraint*. London: Routledge.

Folbre, N. (2001) *The Invisible Heart: Economics and Family Values*. New York: The New Press.

Haskey, J. (1999) Cohabitational and marital histories of adults in Great Britain. *Population Trends*, 96, 13–24.

Hobcraft, J. N., and Kiernan, K. (1995) Becoming a Parent in Europe. Plenary paper for European Population Conference. In EAPS/*IUSSP Proceedings of European Population Conference* Milan, September, 27–65. Also available as LSE STICERD Discussion Paper No. 116, 58pp.

Hoem, J., and Hoem, B. (1988) The Swedish family: Aspects of contemporary developments. *Journal of Family Issues*, 9, 397–424.

*International Journal of Law, Policy and Family* (2001) special issue, *Unmarried Cohabitation in Europe,* 15, 1.

Kiernan, K. (1989) The family: Fission or fusion. In H. Joshi (ed.), *The Changing Population of Britain*. Oxford: Basil Blackwell.

Kiernan, K. (1999a) Cohabitation in Western Europe. *Population Trends*, 96, 25–32.

Kiernan, K. (1999b) Childbearing outside marriage in Western Europe. *Population Trends*, 98, 11–20.

Kiernan, K. (2000) European perspectives on union formation. In L. Waite, C. Bachrach, M. Hindin, E. Thomson, and A. Thornton (eds.), *Ties that Bind: Perspectives on Marriage and* Cohabitation. Hawthorne, NY: Aldine de Gruyter.

Kiernan, K. (2001) Non-marital childbearing: A European perspective In L. Wu and B. Wolfe (eds.), *Out of Wedlock: Causes and Consequences of Nonmarital Fertility*. New York: Russell Sage Foundation.

Kiernan, K. (2002) Cohabitation in Western Europe: Trends, issues and implications. In A. Booth and A. Crouter (eds.), *Just Living Together: Implications of Cohabitation on Families, Children and Social Policy*. Mahwah, NJ: Lawrence Erlbaum.

Kiernan, K. (forthcoming) Divorce and cohabitation across nations and generations. In P. L. Chase-Lansdale, K. Kiernan, and R. Friedman (eds.), *Potential for Change across Lives and Generations: Multidisciplinary Perspectives*. Cambridge: Cambridge University Press.

Lee, R. D. (1980) Aiming at a moving target: Period fertility and changing reproductive goals. *Population Studies,* 34, 205–26.

Lewis, J., and Kiernan, K. (1996) The boundaries between marriage, non-marriage and parenthood: Changes in behaviour and policy in post-war Britain. *Journal of Family History,* 20, 372–87.

Manting, D. (1996) The changing meaning of cohabitation. *European Sociological Review,* 12, 53–65.

Murphy, M. (2000) The evolution of cohabitation in Britain 1960–1995. *Population Studies,* 54, 43–56.

Phillips, R. (1988) *Putting Asunder: A History of Divorce in Western Society.* Cambridge: Cambridge University Press.

Prinz, C. (1995) *Cohabiting, Married, or Single.* Aldershot: Ashgate.

Raley, R. K. (2001) Increasing fertility in cohabiting unions: Evidence for the second demographic transition in the United States? *Demography,* 38, 59–66.

Toulemon, L. (1997) Cohabitation is here to stay. *Population: An English Selection*, 9, 11–46.

United Nations (1992) *Questionnaire and Codebook: Fertility and Family Surveys in Countries of the ECE Region.* New York: United Nations.

United Nations Economic Commission for Europe (2000) *Women and Men in Europe and North America 2000.* New York and Geneva: United Nations.

United Nations Economic Commission for Europe 1996–2001 (2001) *Fertility and Family Surveys in Countries of the ECE Region.* Geneva: United Nations.

van de Kaa, D. (1987) Europe's second demographic transition. *Population Bulletin*, 42.

Veevers, J. E. (1980) *Childless by Choice.* Toronto: Butterworth.

Waite, L., and Gallagher, M. (2000) *The Case for Marriage.* New York: Doubleday.

# 3

# Recent Demographic Trends in the US and Implications for Well-Being

Sinikka Elliott and Debra Umberson

## Introduction

This chapter examines contemporary demographic trends and debates surrounding the family in the US. We begin by describing current trends in marital status, cohabitation, same-sex relationships, and parenting. We then focus on how these trends are associated with the health and well-being of individuals and emphasize that it is not merely the existence of family relationships that affect individual well-being, but the quality of these relationships as well.

## Defining the Family

The US Census Bureau defines a family as two or more persons related by birth, marriage, or adoption and residing together (US Bureau of the Census, 1998b). According to this definition, family households in 2000 comprised 69 percent of all American households, down from 81 percent in 1970 (US Bureau of the Census, 2001). However, while the Census Bureau's definition reveals the legal, biological, and spatial arrangements that constitute a family, it does not capture the myriad meanings attached to the term *family*. When individuals speak of family, it may mean their long-dead ancestors, divorced people who live apart, unmarried partners, or friends who are so close they are "like family." In fact, research in the US confirms that there has never been one distinct *family*; rather what emerges when we refer to the American family is a vast array of possible *families*. Yet, despite the historical prevalence of different family forms, the social recognition and support of diverse family structures remains highly contested.

## Demographic Trends

### Marriage

In 1970, married couples comprised 71 percent of households in the US. By 2000, only 52 percent of American households consisted of married couples (US Bureau of the Census 2001). The probability of marriage in the US varies by race and gender. In 2000, less than one half of African American family households were married-couple households. In marked contrast, in the same year, nearly 70 percent of Hispanic family households, 80 percent of Asian and Pacific Islander family households, and 83 percent of white family households consisted of married couples (US Bureau of the Census, 2001).

Currently, 40 percent of American women aged 15–44 are in their first marriage and almost 40 percent have never married (Chadwick and Heaton, 1999). Recent research suggests that nearly one in three African American women may never marry (Teachman, Tedrow, and Crowder, 2000). Correspondingly, between 1970 and 2000, the average age at first marriage increased by about four years for both men and women. In 2000, the average age at first marriage was 25 for women and just under 27 for men (US Bureau of the Census, 2001). Marital status also varies by age, and is an important predictor of economic hardship among the elderly. Studies show that women are more likely than men to live alone after the age of 65 (Mirowsky, 1996), and that older individuals living alone are more likely to be in poverty than those living with a spouse (US Bureau of the Census, 1999). In 1998, roughly 7 percent of men aged 65 or older were living in poverty, compared to nearly 13 percent of their female counterparts (Federal Interagency Forum on Aging-Related Statistics, 2000).

### Divorce

By 1990, 50 percent of all American marriages ended in divorce. The divorce rate was almost twice as high in the US as in Canada, Japan, and most Western European nations (Sorrentino, 1990). However, data show that divorce rates in most Western industrialized countries continued to rise throughout the 1990s while the US divorce rate declined somewhat over that decade, so that presently about four out of ten American marriages end in divorce (US Bureau of the Census, 1997b).

Most divorces in the US happen within the first 10 years of marriage, usually around the sixth year (US Bureau of the Census, 1992). By the tenth year of marriage, two-thirds of those who are going to divorce have done so. Only 10 percent of marriages that last beyond the twentieth anniversary end in divorce (ibid.).

The majority of individuals who divorce remarry (Ahlburg and DeVita, 1992), although the rate of remarriage has declined somewhat since the 1970s (Teachman, Tedrow, and Crowder, 2000). Women in the US are somewhat less likely to remarry than men (Waite and Nielsen, 2001), and rates of remarriage are higher for the young (Teachman and Heckert, 1985). Race/ethnicity also affects the probability of remarriage. Two-thirds of white women who divorce remarry, but only half of African American and Hispanic women remarry following a divorce (Teachman, Tedrow, and Crowder, 2000).

### Widowhood

Women live longer than men – 79.5 years compared to 74.1 (Minino and Smith, 2001) – and are far more likely to be widowed. In 1998, roughly 45 percent of women aged 65 or older were widowed, compared to 15 percent of men in the same age group. Moreover, while 75 percent of men aged 65 or older were married, only 43 percent of women of the same age were married. This gender gap widens among those 75 and older (Federal Interagency Forum on Aging-Related Statistics, 2000). Thus, women spend more time both unmarried and in old age than do men, and both are associated with reduced access to emotional and economic support, as well as to caregivers.

At older ages, men consistently have higher rates of labor-force participation than do women (Minino and Smith, 2001). And while this gender gap in labor-force participation among the aged has narrowed considerably since the 1960s (Federal Interagency Forum on Aging-Related Statistics, 2000), older women are still more likely to be widowed, unmarried, and/or economically strained.

### Cohabitation

Cohabitation is defined as a family formed outside of marriage by co-residence. Between 1960 and 1998, the number of cohabiting couples in the US increased by nearly 1,000 percent (National Marriage Project, 2000). However, cohabitation is still a relatively new family type in the US and generally culminates in either marriage or separation (Bumpass, Raley, and Sweet, 1994), suggesting that cohabitation may be the modern-day version of a marital engagement.

Eleven percent of all cohabiting couples are gay and lesbian (US Bureau of the Census 2001). As in most other nations, US law does not recognize marriages between same-sex couples (Patterson, 2000). Recently, a few states have considered legislation legalizing same-sex marriages, while other states have introduced, and some have passed, bills that ban the performance or recognition of same-sex marriage (National Gay and Lesbian Task Force, 2001). Nevertheless, gay and lesbian couples in the US are increasingly celebrating their relationships in commitment ceremonies (Butler, 1997) and referring to themselves as married (Sherman, 1992).

## Implications for Health and Well-Being

### Marriage

Since the 1960s, when many feminists and other activists decried the traditional family as patriarchal and oppressive, academics have debated the benefits of marriage for American adults. A substantial body of work on marital status and physical health finds that, compared to the unmarried, the married are at lower risk for mortality and exhibit better physical health and fewer negative health behaviors (Gove, 1973; Zick and Smith, 1991). Moreover, the apparent benefits of marriage seem to be greater for men than women. Studies on the physical health benefits of marriage identify several mechanisms through which marriage confers health benefits. These mechanisms include social support (Wyke and Ford, 1992), financial support (Zick and Smith, 1991), social control of health behavior (Umberson, 1992a), and immunologic protection (House, Landis, and Umberson, 1988; Seeman et al., 1994).

Similarly, most studies on marital status and mental health find that the married exhibit lower rates of mental illness than the unmarried (Umberson and Williams, 1999). And while this advantage is greater for men than women, it is the case that married men *and* women have a mental health advantage compared to their unmarried peers (Marks and Lambert, 1998). However, recent research indicates that the effects of marriage on health and well-being are more nuanced and complicated than previously understood. In their longitudinal study on the effects of marital status on the psychological well-being of individuals, Marks and Lambert (1998) distinguish between the newly married and continuously married and find a significant "honeymoon effect" that inflates mean levels of psychological well-being for the married in most cross-sectional studies. Also, Marks and Lambert (1998: 676) find that unmarried individuals score higher than the married on certain dimensions of psychological well-being, such as autonomy and personal growth, indicating "that marriage is not a universal beneficial determinant of all dimensions of psychological well-being."

Research also reveals that it is not the case that any marriage is better than no marriage when it comes to health benefits. The *quality* of marital relationships is linked to mental and physical health. Among the married, those in distressed marriages are in poorer health than those in nondistressed marriages (Burman and Margolin, 1992; Wickrama et al., 2001). Aseltine and Kessler (1993) find that individuals in low-quality marriages are at an even greater risk for health problems than are divorced individuals. Recent studies also suggest that the social context and meaning of marriage may differ by race. In turn, marital disruption through separation, divorce, or widowhood may be less predictive of psychiatric disturbance for African Americans than for Whites (Williams, Takeuchi, and Adair, 1992).

Despite general consensus regarding the benefits of marriage, recent research indicates that conclusions about family status and health are highly dependent on measurement and method (Umberson and Williams, 1999). For example, most studies of marriage and mental health are cross-sectional, which is problematic since this sampling method does not address the possibility of selection effects. A selection effect would occur if, for example, individuals with better mental health were more likely to get and stay married than those who are psychologically disturbed or physically unhealthy. In an attempt to address the issue of selectivity, some researchers use longitudinal data or include controls for selection effects, such as personality traits. Most find that, even with controls, being married is associated with better mental and physical health (Hemstrom, 1996; Marks, 1996), suggesting that something more than selectivity is operative.

## Cohabitation

A few studies suggest that cohabitation provides mental health benefits that are very similar to those provided by marriage (Ross, 1995). However, the effect of cohabitation on individual health and well-being may depend on whether individuals view their cohabiting lifestyle as an end in itself or whether they view it as a precursor to marriage. Recent longitudinal research demonstrates that, net of sociodemographic characteristics, cohabitors have significantly higher levels of depression than the married, largely due to higher rates of relationship instability (Brown, 2000). Yet three-fourths of cohabitors plan to eventually marry, and studies find that cohabitors planning marriage do not differ from the married in the quality of their intimate relationships (Brown and Booth, 1996).

Studies on the physical health benefits of cohabitation yield inconsistent findings. One study reports that illness rates of cohabitors are very similar to those of the married (Murphy, Glaser, and Grundy, 1997). Other researchers conclude that, compared to married couples, cohabiting couples are less likely to attempt to influence one another's health behaviors (Bachman et al., 1997; Clarkberg, Stolzenber, and Waite, 1995). This has led some researchers to speculate that moving in together does not seem to motivate young people to reduce unhealthy behavior as much as getting married does (Waite and Gallagher, 2000).

Those who cohabit prior to marriage are statistically more likely to eventually divorce (National Marriage Project, 2000). However, due to the difficulty of separating selection from causation effects, researchers have not yet determined whether marital instability post-cohabitation is due to innate characteristics of people who cohabit, or if the experience of cohabitation leads to marital instability (ibid.).

Very few studies examine the link between gay and lesbian relationships and health and well-being. Due to the relative absence of national data on gay and lesbian relationships, comparisons to heterosexual couples remain largely speculative. National, longitudinal data are needed to make generalizations and comparisons about these different groups.

## Divorce

Across studies, compared to the married, the divorced exhibit significantly higher levels of psychological distress and alcohol consumption (Umberson and Williams, 1999), along with greater suicide risk (Stack and Wasserman, 1993) and increased mortality generally (Trovato and Lauris, 1989; Hemstrom 1996; Lillard and Panis, 1996; Lillard and Waite, 1995). However, researchers usually note that some of the deleterious effects of divorce may be due to selection effects. For example, in a study using longitudinal data Horwitz, White, and Howell-White (1996) find that depressed women are less likely to get married and more likely to have their marriages dissolve if they do marry.

Are the detrimental effects of divorce greater for women or men? Previous studies provide inconsistent answers to this question. For example, Aseltine and Kessler (1993) report that women's mental health is more adversely affected than men's by divorce, whereas Booth and Amato (1991) find no gender difference in the mental health effect of divorce.

Social scientists also disagree about the most important factors that lead to psychological distress following divorce. According to Aseltine and Kessler (1993), financial pressures and role changes do not explain postdivorce depressive symptoms in either men or women, while Hope, Power, and Rodgers (1999) find that economic circumstances and parental role are important moderators of change in *women's* distress following separation, but not men's. In short, Hope, Power, and Rodgers find that women who have no ongoing parental responsibilities after divorce are not as likely to experience an increase in depression. Similarly, they observe that upwardly mobile divorced women's levels of distress are akin to women who remain in intact marriages. Age may also shape the gendered effects of divorce. Among the elderly in the US, women are more likely than men to experience diminished financial resources and enduring economic hardship resulting from divorce (Mirowsky, 1996).

The gendered effects of divorce on physical health and mortality may be less than previously thought. In the past, studies on the impact of divorce on physical health consistently found higher mortality rates for divorced men relative to divorced women, suggesting that men are more negatively affected by marital dissolution than are women (Gove, 1973). However, using a number of statistical controls for variables that may explain gender differences in mortality following divorce – such as socioeconomic status, labor-force participation, and number of children in the household – Hemstrom (1996) finds much smaller gender differences in mortality following marital dissolution than has been reported in previous studies.

Marital status differences in mental health may be largely attributed to the *strains* associated with marital dissolution. For example, Booth and Amato (1991) find that divorced individuals, both male and female, experience elevated distress, but only for approximately two years following the divorce. After this period of time, the divorced do not significantly differ from the married on psychological distress. Hence, the transition to divorce may be more conducive to distress than is being divorced, per se.

## Health Implications of Relationship Status: Key Debates

Theoretical explanations for the apparent health benefits of marriage focus on the higher levels of social integration and social support, the lower levels of financial strain, and the enhanced sense of meaning that may accompany marriage (e.g., Waite and Gallagher, 2000). Social scientists who support this theoretical perspective emphasize that the benefits of marriage are largely responsible for marital status differences in health (Lillard and Waite, 1995; Waite and Gallagher, 2000).

For example, in their controversial book, *The Case for Marriage: Why Married People Are Happier, Healthier, and Better Off Financially*, Waite and Gallagher (2000) offer an array of evidence for the positive mental and physical health benefits of marriage. Waite and Gallagher contend that nonmarital unions, such as cohabitation, have some, but not all, the characteristics of marriage and thus provide some, but not all, of the benefits. In particular, they argue, marriage entails a greater commitment and emotional investment than does cohabitation, and thus leads to enhanced mental and physical health. This argument is also explored by Kiernan in chapter 2 of this volume.

Alternative explanations for the apparent health benefits of marriage focus on the stress of marital dissolution, the quality of marriage, processes of selectivity as opposed to causation, and methods of measurement used by researchers (see review in Umberson and Williams, 1999). This approach tends to emphasize that, due to concerns with selection effects and methodology, researchers are unable to unequivocally establish that marriage is uniquely important to the health and well-being of individuals. For example, Ross (1995) finds that it is the attachment to a significant person, rather than marriage per se, that contributes to mental health.

Some scholars argue that it is more appropriate to focus on the adverse mental and physical health consequences of exits from marriage through divorce or widowhood than to focus on the benefits of marriage. This viewpoint is buttressed by emerging research that raises questions about the processes underlying marital status differences in health and well-being. For example, a cross-sectional study by Williams, Takeuchi, and Adair (1992) reveals few significant differences in the mental health of the married compared to the never-married. The advantages of marriage emerge only when the married are compared to the divorced or widowed (Williams et al., 1992). Similarly, a recent study on the effects of divorce and widowhood on self-assessed health finds the never-married and those divorced more than five years do not report worse health than their married counterparts (Williams and Umberson, 2001).

In sum, a growing body of research on the stress of marital transitions leads increasingly to the view that the stress associated with marital dissolution is primarily responsible for marital status differences in health and well-being, and that the adverse effects of marital dissolution are ephemeral, typically lasting about two years (Booth and Amato, 1991; Williams, Takeuchi, and Adair, 1992; see review in Umberson and Williams, 1999).

## Demographic Trends: Parenting

As noted by Kiernan (chapter 2, this volume), American women continue to have more children than women in most developed European countries. In 2000, the average number of children born to an American woman over her lifetime was 2.1. Total fertility rates vary somewhat by race/ethnicity. White, Asian/Pacific Islander and American Indian women have total fertility rates of 2.1, while African American women have a total fertility rate of 2.2. Among Hispanic women, the total fertility rate (3.1) is higher than the national rate, with the highest rates for Mexican women (3.3) and Puerto Rican women (2.6), and the lowest for Cuban women (1.9) (US Department of Health and Human Services, 2002).

Today, only half of US children live in a traditional nuclear family, defined by the US Census Bureau as a married couple living with their biological children and no one else (Erera, 2002). The likelihood of children living with two parents varies by race. In 1998, 74 percent of white children, 64 percent of Hispanic children, and 36 percent of African American children resided with two parents (biological, adopted or step) (Teachman, Tedrow, and Crowder, 2000).

Increasingly American women are bearing a child, or children, outside of conventional marriage. One of three births now occurs to a woman who is not married (US Bureau of the Census, 2001). Race differences in nonmarital childbirth mirror race differences in marital behavior (Teachman, Tedrow, and Crowder., 2000). In 1995, approximately 25 percent of white births, 41 percent of Hispanic births, and 70 percent of African American births occurred outside of marriage (US Bureau of the Census, 1998c). For all racial groups, births occurring outside of marriage have increased by 10 to 12 percent since the mid-1980s (US Bureau of the Census, 1998c). Nonmarital childbirth generally results in single parenting or parenting within a cohabiting union.

### Single-parent households

Most single-parent households (5 of 6) are headed by a mother (US Bureau of the Census, 1998a). The proportion of single mother families more than doubled in the decades between 1970 and 2000 – from 12 percent to 26 percent, respectively. The proportion of single-father families, while still relatively small, increased from 1 percent of all families in 1970 to 5 percent in 2000 (US Bureau of the Census, 2001). The majority of single-parent households are white, although statistically, African American households have a higher proportion of single-parent households

(Amato, 2000a). Among households of Hispanic origin, single parenthood is most common among Puerto Ricans, least common among Cubans, and intermediate among Mexican Americans (ibid.).

Although many single-parent families are created as a result of unwed motherhood, far more result from divorce. Of 18.6 million children in the US living with only one parent, approximately two-thirds are with divorced or separated parents (US Bureau of the Census, 1997a). Divorced parents are on average older, have more education, and have higher incomes than parents who never marry (ibid.). Fifty percent of white single mothers are divorced, compared to 17 percent of African American single mothers (US Bureau of the Census, 2001).

### Cohabiting-parent households

Forty-one percent of cohabiting households in 2000 included children under 18 (ibid.). According to some estimates, 25–40 percent of children will live in a cohabiting household at some time during childhood (Graefe and Lichter, 1999). Fertility within cohabiting unions is also on the rise. About two-thirds of children born to Latino women outside of marriage are born into two-parent cohabiting unions, compared with 57 percent for white women and 26 percent for African American women (Bachu, 1999).

### Same-sex parent households

It is difficult to estimate the number of children being raised in lesbian or gay households since the US Census Bureau does not address this household status. In the 1994 National Lesbian Health Care Survey, 16 percent of participants reported bearing children and another 5 percent said they had another woman's children living with them (Bradford, Ryan, and Rothblum, 1994). Ninety-nine percent of children being raised in gay or lesbian families are born within marriage and live with a parent who "came out" after a divorce (Flaks et al., 1995). However, in recent years a growing number of lesbian women and gay men are becoming parents after coming out (Patterson, 1992), either through pregnancy or adoption (Ricketts and Achtenberg, 1990).

## Parenting: Implications for Health and Well-Being

Studies find that parents of minor children exhibit higher levels of psychological distress than do nonparents and parents of adult children. Parenting of minor children seems to be more detrimental to the well-being of women than men (Kandel, Davies, and Raveis, 1985; Umberson and Gove, 1989), but mothers also seem to experience more psychological benefits from having adult children than do fathers (Umberson, 1992b). Recent research suggests that the influence of children on parental well-being varies depending on relationship status. A longitudinal study finds that cohabitors have higher levels of depression than their married counterparts and that cohabitors' levels of depression are further exacerbated by the presence of both biological and step children, whereas levels of depression among marrieds, in contrast, are not appreciably affected by the presence of children (Brown, 2000).

Family scholars typically conclude that the birth of a child diminishes marital quality (McLanahan and Adams, 1989), but recent longitudinal research on newly married couples shows that *all* couples tend to experience a decline in marital satisfaction – whether they have a baby or not (Adelman, Chadwick, and Baerger, 1996). Similarly, while some researchers using cross-sectional data report an upturn in marital happiness after children grow up (Orbuch et al., 1996), a recent longitudinal study does not support this finding (VanLaningham, Johnson, and Amato, 2001).

While parenting is associated with higher levels of psychological distress, some studies suggest that other dimensions of well-being may actually benefit from parenthood. Compared to nonparents, parents, especially those with minor children, are less likely to take health risks and more likely to engage in preventive health behaviors (Umberson, 1987). Parents also have lower mortality rates (Kobrin and Hendershot, 1977) than do nonparents and report a greater sense of meaningfulness and purpose in life (Umberson and Gove, 1989).

In general, studies find that children contribute to parental distress through the demands of child-care and increased economic hardship (see review in Ross and Van Willigen, 1996). Researchers note three factors that significantly contribute to mothers' health and well-being: employment, a more equitable division of household labor, and access to affordable childcare (see review in Ross, Mirowsky, and Goldstein, 1990). However, the effects of each of these factors on well-being requires some qualification, as they vary in degree and direction, depending on sociodemographic characteristics of individuals as well as social contextual factors (e.g., supportive ties, financial strain).

A married woman's paid work is positively associated with mental and physical health, but depends on the type of employment, childcare arrangements, and husband's participation in childcare (Ross et al., 1990). Similarly, while studies find that a more equitable division of household labor improves the health and well-being of parents, especially mothers (Ross and Van Willigen, 1996; Walzer, 1998), researchers observe race and gender differences in the interplay between marital satisfaction and the domestic division of labor. For example, findings from a cross-sectional study reveal that African American women are less satisfied with their marriage than white women, regardless of how much housework they do (Dillaway and Broman, 2001). In contrast, Dillaway and Broman find that African American men who perform considerable amounts of work around the house are *less* likely than white men to report high marital satisfaction.

Access to quality child-care contributes to parental well-being, but in the absence of social policy initiatives to assist with the strains of dual-parent employment or single parenthood, affordable, quality child-care is not available for most American families (United Nations Children's Fund, 1994). Many single mothers find that the high cost of child-care, combined with a lack of flexibility and health care in available jobs, make working and caring for young children incompatible (Harris, 1996; Edin and Lein, 1997). Relying on family and other network members for financial support and child-care may strain these close relationships, ultimately undermining social support and heightening vulnerability to a number of stressors (Edin and Lein, 1997).

Since the 1970s, women's housework contributions have declined while men's have slowly increased (Coltrane, 2000). As a result, women now do about twice the amount of housework as the men they live with, compared to six times the amount in 1965 (Coltrane, 2000). However, housework is typically fraught and stress-provoking (Bird, 1997; Ross and Van Willigen, 1996) and women continue to perform the "core" tasks, such as cooking and cleaning. Thus, although employment tends to benefit the psychological well-being of women, the double burden of housework and childcare can impose strains that undermine well-being (Ross and Van Willigen, 1996).

The experience of being a single parent varies dramatically, depending on such factors as gender, race, education, marital status (e.g., never-married, divorced), age, and kin residence (Amato, 2000a). To date, however, how mental and physical health varies among single parents is not well understood (ibid.). Some evidence suggests that divorce creates fewer negative consequences among African American mothers than white mothers (Fine et al., 1992). In one study, no differences in psychological well-being and health were found between divorced and never-married mothers (Acock and Demo, 1994). Both Hispanic and African American single mothers are more likely than white single mothers to live in an extended family household (US Bureau of the Census, 2001), but findings on the impact of kin support are inconsistent. Wilson (1989) finds that single parents who live with other adult relatives report greater happiness and physical health and fewer symptoms of depression than those living alone. In contrast, some studies show that relatives can be a source of friction for single parents and that tension can outweigh benefits (Milardo, 1987).

Recently, gay and lesbian parents have received a great deal of legal and media attention in the US – primarily concerning their legal right to adopt children. In order to gain legal parental status, some same-sex couples turn to the adoption system, but it is often difficult, time-consuming, and costly for a gay or lesbian couple to adopt a child together in the US. Only seven states expressly permit gay and lesbian couples to adopt their partners' children, while one state prohibits such adoptions and two effectively ban them (Goode, 2002). The difficulty most lesbian and gay couples encounter gaining legal recognition as co-parents has a number of potentially negative consequences, especially in terms of financial status and psychological distress (Patterson, 2000). Recently, the American Academy of Pediatrics (2002) has endorsed legalizing second-parent adoptions, citing numerous benefits for the health and well-being of parents and children.

To date, little research explores the transition to parenthood among gay men or lesbian-headed households and no published studies focus on the psychological adjustment of gay fathers (Patterson, 2000). Research on the psychological adjustment of lesbian mothers stems largely from questions raised in child custody disputes and is not generalizable to the larger population of lesbian parents.

An emerging issue in the study of parenting is the strain that parents experience in balancing the demands of parenthood while providing care for their own aging parents. Families of the twenty-first century are becoming more "vertical," with smaller generations but more generations alive concurrently (Himes, 2001). Predominantly middle-aged women caregivers face the challenge of balancing the competing intergenerational responsibilities of work, elder care, and childrearing and have been referred to as the "sandwich generation" (Bengtson, Rosenthal, and Burton, 1996; Himes, 2001). Current studies show that caregiving stress has negative effects on the well-being of adult daughters who experience incompatible pressures of these multiple roles (Stephens et al., 2001).

## Parenting: Key Debates

In assessing health and well-being, family researchers sometimes combine all single-parent families into one category and two-parent families into another. However, this method tends to obscure variability in resources and outcomes within different family types (Demo and Cox 2000). Noticeable differences in parenting practices, values, and situations within and across racial groups and different family structures indicate that researchers "need to move beyond a preoccupation with conventional classifications of family structure to explore the rich variety of family members, kin support networks, and neighborhood resources" (Demo and Cox, 2000: 889) and the impact of, or interaction with, these factors and the health and well-being of family members. Using the two-parent structure as the benchmark against which all other family arrangements are compared also masks the importance of the quality of relationships.

Some family scholars argue that by emphasizing deficiency and deficit in focusing on the deleterious effects of "nontraditional" parenting, researchers highlight their own negative stereotypes about these family structures (Smith, 1997; Demo and Cox, 2000). Family researchers are beginning to focus less on comparisons between various parent-headed households and more on the differences and similarities among parents. For example, research finds racial differences among single-parent families. African American nonresident fathers are more involved in their children's rearing than white nonresident fathers (Mott, 1990) and African American mothers are less negatively affected by divorce (Fine et al., 1992) and receive more informal support following divorce (Friedman, Chiriboga, and Catron, 1991) than white mothers. Other studies note that social-psychological factors, such as values and normative orientations, contribute to the quality of parenting and mental health. One exploratory study of urban, economically disadvantaged African American mothers finds that variation in parenting and values regarding children accounts for more than 40 percent of variation in depression among these mothers (Roxburgh et al., 2001).

Longitudinal research on parenting in the last decade has substantially contributed to an understanding of how the transition to parenthood affects parental health and well-being by focusing on variation in parents' adjustment to parenthood and the factors associated with that variability. In the past, however, family researchers tended to focus primarily on motherhood, neglecting to examine how men are changed by becoming parents and how their behaviors and attitudes affect their families (Demo and Cox, 2000). The efforts of researchers in the 1990s to expand the area of family study to include fathers have contributed to a growing body of literature on diverse forms of fatherhood and father involvement (see review in Marsiglio et al., 2000).

## Family Structure: Implications for Child Health and Well-Being

Over the past several decades, researchers have attempted to identify family environments that facilitate or impair child development and well-being. However, some researchers argue that family structure per se illuminates little about children's adjustment (Demo and Cox, 2000). For example, examining data from the first wave of the National Survey of Families and Households, Acock and Demo (1994) find few statistical differences in mothers' reports of children's well-being across first-married, divorced, remarried, and continuously single-parent families.

Recent studies highlight the deleterious effects on children's well-being of multiple family transitions (Kurdek, Fine, and Sinclair, 1995; Amato and Sobolewski, 2001). Researchers find that stable dual- and single-parent living arrangements benefit children's socioemotional adjustment and global well-being (Acock and Demo, 1994), while children's psychological well-being declines in relation to the number of family transitions they experience (Amato and Sobolewski, 2001). Although few studies to date examine the impact of cohabitation on child health and well-being, some studies suggest that children in cohabiting households are disadvantaged, and that this may be partly due to the higher break-up rate among cohabitors in comparison to the married since this results in multiple family transitions (National Marriage Project, 2000).

However, marriage does not guarantee stability. It is estimated that one million children experience their parents' divorce each year (Hetherington and Stanley-Hagan, 2000). One of the most often cited findings is that divorce adversely affects child well-being. Divorce has been linked to teen-age pregnancy, lower levels of achievement, and poorer life outcomes, including increased health risks and psychological disorders (McLanahan and Sandefur, 1994; Waite and Gallagher, 2000; Wallerstein et al., 2000). Yet recent research suggests a much more complex and less dismal picture. In particular, it seems that family resources, father involvement, a relatively conflict-free relationship between the parents after divorce, and the absence of additional transitions (e.g., changing schools and neighborhoods, additional divorces), can all serve to protect child well-being following divorce (Hetherington and Kelly, 2002; Seltzer, 1998).

The available evidence suggests that divorce should be conceptualized as a lengthy sequence involving numerous pre- and post-divorce experiences (Furstenberg and Kiernan, 2001). The *conflict* associated with marital distress, rather than the actual divorce, may be primarily responsible for the problems found in children whose parents divorce (Forehand et al., 1986; Cherlin, Chase-Lansdale, and McRae, 1998; Furstenberg and Kiernan, 2001; Sun, 2001). Researchers are only just beginning to understand the complex ways in which marital conflict and divorce affect children. For example, in a study using national, longitudinal data, Booth and Amato (2001) find that the level of marital conflict that precedes divorce moderates the effects of divorce on child well-being. Their evidence suggests that the dissolution of low-conflict marriages has a strong negative influence on offspring, whereas divorce among high-conflict couples has a relatively benign or even beneficial effect.

About half the children whose parents divorce will experience the transition into stepfamilies within four years of the separation (Hetherington and Stanley-Hagan, 2000). Research suggests that children in stepfamilies, compared to those in first-married families, are more likely to experience a broad range of adjustment problems (Acock and Demo, 1994), but that these usually diminish with time (Amato, 2000b; Hetherington and Stanley-Hagan, 2000). However, remarried couples are statistically more likely to divorce than first married couples (Hetherington and Stanley-Hagan, 2000). Hence, children in stepfamilies face the risk of multiple family transitions with little opportunity for stabilization, and this poses challenges for child well-being (Amato and Sobolewski, 2001).

Very little research evidence exists about the well-being of children living in same-sex family households compared to other children. In a recent study, Tasker and

Golombok (1997) analyze longitudinal data to compare children living with lesbian mothers with children living with heterosexual single mothers. They find little difference in child development, emotional adjustment, behavioral problems, or peer relations between these two groups. In order to truly understand the effect, if any, of same-sex family households on child well-being, more longitudinal studies, employing rigorous methodologies, are needed.

In sum, research suggests that the quality of the parent–child relationship is a pivotal aspect of the family environment for children in intact, separated, remarried, single, and cohabiting heterosexual and same-sex family households. Although family transitions, such as divorce, remarriage, or separation, may undermine the skills that parents need to buttress child well-being in the short term (Cherlin et al., 1991; Cherlin, 1992), studies suggest that children of divorced families fare at least as well as, if not better than, children raised in conflict-ridden two-parent families. Recent findings that parental discord and divorce affect children into adulthood (Amato and Sobolewski, 2001) support the notion that parents and children's lives are linked throughout the life course (Elder, 1994) and suggest that child health and well-being are not predicted by family status alone.

## Children in Families: Key Debates

A growing number of family scholars emphasize family diversity and the multiplicity of children's responses to family transitions. These researchers question the value of a deficit-comparison approach and the related concentration on finding differences in children's adjustment as a function of parents' sexual orientation or marital status (Demo and Cox, 2000). Taken as a whole, the research on children in families shows that race, class, and ethnicity all affect family formation and functioning. Moreover, the child's own age, gender, individual temperament, and interaction with siblings also play a role in shaping the experience of children in families (Coontz, 1997), as well as the effects of family experiences on children.

Nevertheless, family researchers continue to disagree about the benefits of the two-parent structure over other types of family structures for child well-being. Among certain family scholars in the US, there is a marked ideological divide that may be loosely described as the "families in distress" theory versus the "families in transition" argument.

Researchers who favor the "families in distress" argument emphasize that changes in childhood living arrangements are detrimental to the well-being of children (Popenoe, 1993; Waite and Gallagher, 2000; Wallerstein, Lewis, and Blakeslee, 2000). Sociologist David Popenoe (1988; 1993), a major proponent of this position, argues that family decline is associated with serious social consequences for child well-being. In Popenoe's terminology, family decline refers to the weakening of the family institution as family systems become more nontraditional. In other words, for Popenoe, family *change* represents family decline. Similarly, based on qualitative data collected over nearly three decades, Wallerstein, Lewis, and Blakeslee (2000) argue that children whose parents divorce are unhappier compared to children whose parents remain married, regardless of the quality of the marriage. And Waite and Gallagher (2000) cite numerous studies supporting their stance that married parents make better parents. These researchers tend to call for policies that support the "traditional" family, such as a pro-marriage tax (Waite and Gallagher, 2000).

Others, most prominently Judith Stacey (1996, 1998), make the "families in transition" argument that embraces changing family patterns because of their implication for expanding the definition of the family to encompass a diversity of forms and memberships. This view holds that divorce and other family changes are not disastrous for children, but rather should be conceptualized as family challenges that most children adapt to over time. For example, Hetherington and Kelly's (2002) recent longitudinal research findings emphasize the resilience of children following their parents' divorce. Hetherington and Kelly find that, although children encounter a number of stressors associated with divorce, most of these children become happy, competent adults much like their peers who grew up in intact families.

According to Stacey (1996), the process of legitimizing diverse family structures, coupled with governmental support, demythologizes marriage and the nuclear family and thus enables children to blossom in a variety of family structures. In support of this theory, a cross-national study by Houseknecht and Sastry (1996) compares the well-being of children in four industrialized countries – Sweden, the US, the former West Germany, and Italy – and finds that a shift toward family nontraditionalism – or family decline, using Popenoe's terminology – is not necessarily associated with negative consequences for child well-being.

Houseknecht and Sastry observe that while Sweden has the most nontraditional family system of the four countries, with the US a close second, Sweden nevertheless ranks higher on most measures of child well-being. In contrast, the US ranks the lowest on overall child well-being (Houseknecht and Sastry, 1996). The authors conclude that societies with nontraditional family structures can positively influence child well-being through the support of social policies that "help alleviate the stress of family nontraditionalism and the social problems that go with it" (ibid.: 737).

The scholars involved in these debates typically take an extreme position, yet it is unlikely that either generalization is completely accurate. Certainly, for example, divorce is difficult for parents and for children. It is a significant life transition that involves many changes and, often, some sense of loss. Yet it is also the case that many factors can serve to ameliorate the impact of this loss (financial support, continuing father involvement), and recent evidence suggests that the negative effects of divorce on both adults and children may be transitory (although the transitional difficulties should not be minimized).

## Conclusion

The definition and reality of "family" have changed throughout history (Stacey, 1996, 1998; Coontz, 1997). Yet public debate in the US continues to center around what "family" means and which "family" is best for adults and for children. As this chapter has shown, families in the US take many different forms and the prevalence and dominance of any particular family structure are constantly changing.

Certainly, involvement in family relationships can have substantial effects on the physical and psychological well-being of family members. Family relationships have the potential to offer emotional support and sustenance to individuals and this can enhance well-being. But as well, family relationships can be stressful and this can undermine well-being. All family relationships exist in a social context and this context strongly influences how sustaining or stressful those relationships might be. For example, some family forms are more likely than others to be characterized by financial hardship, and financial strain is difficult for families. Some family forms are more likely to be protected by law, and this protects the individuals in those families. Some family forms are more likely to threaten the existing social order, and this poses challenges for individuals in such families.

Yet the evidence suggests that, within any particular family form, the quality of the relationships therein determines the value or the risk of that family form for adults and children. Of course, certain social contexts make it easier to experience high-quality relationships. For example, financial resources and access to high-quality and affordable child-care benefit all families in ways that can enhance family relationships. And some family forms – for example, single-parent families – are more likely to exist in social contexts that are characterized by stress and hardship. The challenge then, is to create a social and political context that recognizes, equalizes, enriches, and supports diverse family forms.

## References

Acock, A. C., and Demo, D. H. (1994) *Family Diversity and Well-Being*. Thousand Oaks, CA: Sage.

Adelman, P. K., Chadwick, K., and Baerger, D. R. (1996) Marital quality of Black and White adults over the life course. *Journal of Social and Personal Relationships*, 13, 361–84.

Ahlburg, D. A., and DeVita, C. J. (1992) *New Realities of the American Family*. Population Bulletin 47. Washington, DC: Population Reference Bureau.

Amato, P. R. (2000a) Diversity within single-parent families. In D. H. Demo, K. R. Allen, and M.A. Fine (eds.), *Handbook of Family Diversity*. New York and Oxford: Oxford University Press.

Amato, P. R. (2000b) The consequences of divorce for adults and children. *Journal of Marriage and the Family*, 62, 1269–87.

Amato, P. R., and Booth, A. (1991) Consequences of parental divorce and marital unhappiness for adult well-being. *Social Forces*, 69, 895–914.

Amato, P. R., and Sobolewski, J. M. (2001) The effects of divorce and marital discord on adult children's psychological well-being. *American Sociological Review*, 66, 900–21.

American Academy of Pediatrics (2002) Coparent or second-parent adoption by same-sex parents. *Pediatrics*, 109, 339–40.

Aseltine, R. H., Jr., and Kessler, R. C. (1993) Marital disruption and depression in a community sample. *Journal of Health and Social Behavior*, 34, 237–51.

Bachman, J. G., Wadsworth, K. N., O'Malley, P. M., Johnson, L. D., and Schulenberg, J. E. (1997) *Smoking, Drinking, and Drug Use in Young Adulthood*. Mahwah, NJ: Lawrence Erlbaum.

Bachu, A. (1999) Trends in premarital childbearing: 1930–1994. *Current Population Reports, P23-197*. Washington, DC: US Census Bureau.

Bengtson, V. L., Rosenthal, C. J, and Burton, L. M. (1996) Paradoxes of families and aging. In R. H. Binstock and L. K. George (eds.), *Handbook of Aging and the Social Sciences*. 4th ed. San Diego: Academic Press.

Bird, C. E. (1997) Gender differences in the social and economic burdens of parenting and psychological distress. *Journal of Health and Social Behavior*, 33, 809–23.

Booth, A., and Amato, P. R. (1991) Divorce and psychological stress. *Journal of Health and Social Behavior*, 32, 396–407.

Booth, A., and Amato, P. R. (2001) Parental predivorce relations and offspring postdivorce well-being. *Journal of Marriage and the Family*, 63, 197–212.

Bradford, J., Ryan, C., and Rothblum, E. D. (1994) National Lesbian Health Care Survey: Implications for mental health. *Journal of Consulting and Clinical Psychology*, 62, 228–42.

Brown, S. (2000) The effect of union type on psychological well-being: Depression among cohabitors versus marrieds. *Journal of Health and Social Behavior*, 41, 241–55.

Brown, S. L., and Booth, A. (1996) Cohabitation versus marriage: A comparison of relationship quality. *Journal of Marriage and the Family*, 58, 667–8.

Bumpass, L. L., Raley, R. K., and Sweet, J. A. (1994) *The changing character of stepfamilies: Implications of cohabitation and nonmarital childbearing*. NSFH working paper No. 63.

Burman, B., and Margolin, G. (1992) Analysis of the association between marital relationships and health problems: An interactional perspective. *Psychological Bulletin*, 112, 39–63.

Butler, B. (ed.) (1997) *Ceremonies of the Heart: Celebrating Lesbian Unions*. Seattle: Seal Press.

Chadwick, B. A., and Heaton, T. B. (eds.) (1999) *Statistical Handbook on the American Family*. 2nd ed. Phoenix, AZ: Oryx Press.

Cherlin, A. J. (1992) *Marriage, Divorce, Remarriage*. Cambridge, MA: Harvard University Press.

Cherlin, A. J., Chase-Lansdale, P. L., and McRae, C. (1998) Effects of divorce on mental health throughout the life course. *American Sociological Review*, 63, 239–9.

Cherlin, A. J., Furstenberg, F. F., Jr., Chase-Lansdale, L. P., Kiernan, K. E., Robins, P. K., Morrison, D. R., and Teitler, J. O. (1991) Longitudinal effects of divorce in Great Britain and the United States. *Science*, 252, 1386–9.

Clarkberg, M., Stolzenber, R. M., and Waite, L. J. (1995) Attitudes, values and entrance into cohabitational versus marital unions. *Social Forces*, 74, 609–32.

Coltrane, S. (2000) Research on household labor: Modeling and measuring the social embeddedness of routine family work. *Journal of Marriage and the Family*, 62, 1208–33.

Coontz, S. (1997) *The Way We Really Are: Coming to Terms with America's Changing Families*. New York: Basic Books.

Demo, D. H., and Cox, M. J. (2000) Families with young children: A review of research in the 1990s. *Journal of Marriage and the Family*, 62, 876–95.

Dillaway, H., and Broman, C. (2001) Race, class, and gender differences in marital satisfaction and divisions of household labor among dual-earner couples: A case for intersectional analysis. *Journal of Family Issues*, 22, 309–27.

Edin, K., and Lein, L. (1997) Work, welfare, and single mothers' economic survival strategies. *American Sociological Review*, 62, 253–66.

Elder, G. H. Jr. (1994) Time, agency, and social change: Perspectives on the life course. *Social Psychology Quarterly*, 57, 5–15.

Erera, P. I. (2002) *Family Diversity: Continuity and Change in the Contemporary Family*. Thousand Oaks, CA: Sage.

Federal Interagency Forum on Aging-Related Statistics (2000) *Older Americans 2000: Key Indicators of Well-Being. Federal Interagency Forum on Aging-Related Statistics*. Washington, DC: US Government Printing Office, August.

Fine, M. A., McKenry, P. C., Donnelly, B. W., and Voydanoff, P. (1992) Perceived adjustment of parents and children: Variations by family structure, race, and gender. *Journal of Marriage and the Family*, 54, 118–28.

Flaks, D. K., Fischer, I., Masterpasqua, F., and Joseph, G. (1995) Lesbians choosing motherhood: A comparative study of lesbian and heterosexual parents and their children. *Developmental Psychology*, 31, 105–14.

Forehand, R., Bordy, G., Long, N., Slotkin, J., and Fauber, R. (1986) Divorce/divorce potential and interparental conflict: The relationship to early adolescent social and cognitive functioning. *Journal of Adolescence Research*, 1, 389–97.

Friedman, L., Chiriboga, D. A., and Catron, L. S. (1991) Social supports in the context of divorce. In D. A. Chiriboga and L. S. Catron (eds.), *Divorce: Crisis, Challenge, or Relief?* New York: New York University Press.

Furstenberg, F. F., and Kiernan, K. E. (2001) Delayed parental divorce: How much do children benefit? *Journal of Marriage and the Family*, 63, 446–57.

Goode, E. (2002) Group backs gays who seek to adopt a partner's child. *New York Times*, February 4, pp. A1, A21.

Gove, W. R. (1973) Sex, marital status and mortality. *American Journal of Sociology*, 79, 45–67.

Harris, K. M. (1996) Life after welfare: Women, work, and repeat dependency. American *Sociological Review*, 61, 407–26.

Graefe, D., and Lichter, D. (1999) Life course transitions of American children: Parental cohabitation, marriage, and single motherhood. *Demography*, 36, 205–18.

Hemstrom, O. (1996) Is marriage dissolution linked to differences in mortality risks for men and women? *Journal of Marriage and the Family*, 58, 366–78.

Hetherington, E. M., and Kelly, J. (2002) *For Better or For Worse: Divorce Reconsidered*. New York: Norton.

Hetherington, E. M., and Stanley-Hagan, M. (2000) Diversity among stepfamilies. In D. H. Demo, K. R. Allen and M. A. Fine (eds.), *Handbook of Family Diversity*. New York: Oxford University Press.

Himes, C. L. (2001) Elderly Americans. *Population Bulletin*, 56(4). Washington, DC: Population Reference Bureau, December. Retrieved from: http://www.prb.org/Content/NavigationMenu/PRB/AboutPRB/Population_Bulletin2/Elderly_Americans.htm

Hope, S., Power, C., and Rodgers, B. (1999) Does financial hardship account for elevated psychological distress in lone mothers? *Social Science and Medicine*, 49, 1637–49.

Horwitz, A. V., White, H. R., and Howell-White, S. (1996) Becoming married and mental health: A longitudinal study of a cohort of young adults. *Journal of Marriage and the Family*, 58, 895–907.

House, J. S., Landis, K., and Umberson, D. (1988) Social relationships and health. *Science*, 241, 540–5.

Houseknecht, S. K., and Sastry, J. (1996) Family "decline" and child well-being: A comparative assessment. *Journal of Marriage and the Family*, 58, 726–39.

Kandel, D. B., Davies, M., and Raveis, V. H. (1985) The stressfulness of daily social roles for women. *Journal of Health and Social Behavior*, 26, 64–78.

Kobrin, F. E., and Hendershot, G. E. (1977) Do family ties reduce mortality? Evidence from the United States, 1966–1968. *Journal of Marriage and the Family*, 39, 737–45.

Kurdek, L. A., Fine, M. A., and Sinclair, R. J. (1995) School adjustment in sixth graders: Parenting transitions, family climate, and peer norm effects. *Child Development*, 66, 430–45.

Lillard, L. A., and Panis, C. (1996) Marital status and mortality: The role of health. *Demography*, 33, 313–27.

Lillard, L. A., and Waite, L. J. (1995) Till death do us part: Marital disruption and mortality. *American Journal of Sociology*, 100, 1131–56.

Marks, N. F. (1996) Flying solo at midlife: Gender, marital status and psychological well-being. *Journal of Family Issues*, 9, 917–33.

Marks, N. F., and Lambert, J. D. (1998) Marital status continuity and change among young and midlife adults. *Journal of Family Issues*, 19, 652–86.

Marsiglio, W., Amato, P., Day, R. D., and Lamb, M. E. (2000) Scholarship on fatherhood in the 1990s and beyond. *Journal of Marriage and the Family*, 62, 1173–91.

McLanahan, S., and Adams, J. (1989) The effects of children on parents' psychological well-being: 1957–1976. *Social Forces*, 68, 1124–46.

McLanahan, S., and Sandefur, G. (1994) *Growing Up with a Single Parent: What Hurts, What Helps?* Cambridge, MA: Harvard University Press.

Milardo, R. M. (1987) Changes in social networks of women and men following divorce: A review. *Journal of Family Issues*, 8, 78–96.

Minino, A. M., and Smith, B. L.(2001) Deaths: Preliminary data for 2000. *National Vital Statistics Reports*, 49(12). Hyattsville, MD: National Center for Health Statistics, October, 1–40. Retrieved from http://www.cdc.gov/nchs/data/nvsr/nvsr49/nvsr49_12.pdf

Mirowsky, J. (1996) Age and the gender gap in depression. *Journal of Health and Social Behavior*, 37, 362–80.
Mott, F. K. (1990) When is a father really gone? Paternal–child contact in father-absent homes. *Demography*, 27, 499–517.
Murphy, M., Glaser, K., and Grundy, E. (1997) Marital status and long-term illness in Great Britain. *Journal of Marriage and the Family*, 59, 156–64.
National Gay and Lesbian Task Force (2001) *Issues: Same-Sex Marriage*. Washington, DC: 2001. Retrieved from: http://www.ngltf.org/issues/issue.cfm?issueID=10
National Marriage Project (2000) *The state of our unions, 2000: The social health of marriage in America*. New Brunswick, NJ: Rutgers University Press.
Orbuch, T. L., House, J. S., Mero, R. P., and Webster, P. S. (1996) Marital quality over the life course. *Social Psychology Quarterly*, 59, 162–71.
Patterson, C. J. (1992) Children of lesbian and gay parents. *Child Development*, 63, 1025–42.
Patterson, C. J. (2000) Family relationships of lesbians and gay men. *Journal of Marriage and the Family*, 62, 1052–69.
Popenoe, D. (1988) *Disturbing the Nest: Family Change and Decline in Modern Societies*. New York: Aldine De Gruyter.
Popenoe, D. (1993) American family decline, 1960-1990: A review and appraisal. *Journal of Marriage and the Family*, 55, 527–42.
Ricketts, W., and Achtenberg, R. (1990) Adoption and foster parenting for lesbian and gay men: creating new traditions in family. In F. W. Bozett and M. B. Sussman (eds.), *Homosexuality and Family Relations*. New York: Praeger.
Ross, C. E. (1995) Reconceptualizing marital status as a continuum of social attachment. *Journal of Marriage and the Family*, 57, 129–40.
Ross, C. E., Mirowsky, J., and Goldsteen, K. (1990) The impact of the family on health: The decade in review. *Journal of Marriage and the Family*, 52, 1059–78.
Ross, C. E., and Van Willigen, M. (1996) Gender, parenthood, and anger. *Journal of Marriage and the Family*, 58, 572–84.
Roxburgh, S., Stephens, R. C., Toltzis, P., and Adkins, I. (2001) The value of children, parenting strains, and depression among urban African American mothers. *Sociological Forum*, 16, 55–72.
Seeman, T. E., Berkman, L. F., Blazer, D., and Rowe, J. W. (1994) Social ties and support and neuroendocrine function: The MacArthur studies of successful aging. *Annals of Behavioral Medicine*, 16, 95–106.
Seltzer, J. A. (1998) Men's contributions to children and social policy. In A. Booth and A. C. Crouter (eds.), *Men in Families: When do They Get Involved? What Difference Does it Make?* Mahwah, NJ: Lawrence Erlbaum.
Sherman, S. (ed.) (1992) *Lesbian and Gay Marriage: Private Commitments, Public Ceremonies*. Philadelphia: Temple University Press.
Smith, M. (1997) Psychology's under-valuation of single motherhood. *Feminism and Psychology*, 7, 529–32.
Sorrentino, C. (1990) The Changing Family in International Perspective. *Monthly Labor Review*, 113, 41–58.
Stacey, J. (1996) *In the Name of the Family: Rethinking Family Values in the Postmodern Age*. Boston: Beacon.
Stacey, J. (1998) *Brave New Families: Stories of Domestic Upheaval in Late Twentieth Century America*, Revised ed. New York: Basic Books.
Stack, S., and Wasserman, I. (1993) Marital status, alcohol consumption, and suicide: An analysis of national data. *Journal of Marriage and the Family*, 55, 1018–24.
Stephens, M. A. P., Townsend, A. L., Martire, L. M., and Druley, J. A. (2001) Balancing parent care with other roles: Interrole conflict of adult daughter caregivers. *Journal of Gerontology: Psychological Sciences*, 56B, P24–34.

Sun, Y. (2001) Family environment and adolescents' well-being before and after parents' marital disruption: A longitudinal analysis. *Journal of Marriage and the Family*, 63, 697–713.

Tasker, F. L., and Golombok, S. (1997) *Growing Up in a Lesbian Family: Effects on Child Development*. New York: Guilford.

Teachman, J. D., and Heckert, A. (1985) The impact of age and children on remarriage. *Journal of Family Issues*, 6, 185–203.

Teachman, J. D., Tedrow, L. M., and Crowder, K. D. (2000) The changing demography of America's families. *Journal of Marriage and the Family*, 62, 1234–46.

Trovato, F., and Lauris, G. (1989) Marital status and mortality in Canada: 1951–1981. *Journal of Marriage and the Family*, 51, 907–22.

Umberson, D. (1987) Family status and health behaviors: Social control as a dimension of social integration. *Journal of Health and Social Behavior*, 28, 306–19.

Umberson, D. (1992a) Gender, marital status, and the social control of health behavior. *Social Science and Medicine*, 34, 907–17.

Umberson, D. (1992b) Relationships between adult children and their parents: Psychological consequences for both generations. *Journal of Marriage and the Family*, 54, 664–74.

Umberson, D., and Gove, W. R. (1989) Parenthood and psychological well-being: Theory, measurement and stage in the family life course. *Journal of Family Issues*, 10, 440–62.

Umberson, D., and Williams, K. (1999) Family status and mental health. In C. S. Aneshensel and J. C. Phelan (eds.), *Handbook of the Sociology of Mental Health*. New York: Kluwer Academic/Plenum.

United Nations Children's Fund (1994) *The Progress of Nations*. New York.

US Bureau of the Census (1992) Marriage, divorce, and remarriage in the 1990s. *Current Population Reports, Series P23-180*. Washington, DC: US Government Printing Office.

US Bureau of the Census (1997a) Marital status and living arrangements: March (Update). *Current Population Reports*, Series P20–506. Washington, DC: US Government Printing Office.

US Bureau of the Census (1997b) *Statistical Abstract of the United States: 1997*, 117th ed. Washington, DC.

US Bureau of the Census (1998a) *Household and Family Characteristics: March, 1997*. Washington, DC, pp. 20–509.

US Bureau of the Census (1998b) Marital status and living arrangements: March, 1998. *Current Population Reports*, Series P20–514. Washington, DC: US Government Printing Office.

US Bureau of the Census (1998c) *Statistical Abstract of the United States: 1998*, 118th ed. Washington, DC: US Government Printing Office.

US Bureau of the Census (1999) Poverty in the United States: 1998. Table 2. *Current Population Reports*, Series P60–207. Washington, DC: US Government Printing Office.

US Bureau of the Census (2001) America's families and living arrangements: Population characteristics 2000. *Current Population Reports*, Series P20–537. Washington, DC: US Government Printing Office.

US Department of Health and Human Services (2002) *Women are having more children, new report shows, teen birth rate continues to decline*, Vol. 50. Washington, DC. Retrieved from: http://www.hhs.gov/news/press/2002pres/20020212.html

VanLaningham, J., Johnson, D. R., and Amato, P. (2001) Marital happiness, marital duration, and the U-shaped curve: Evidence from a five-wave panel study. *Social Forces*, 79, 1313–41.

Waite, L. J., and Gallagher, M. (2000) *The Case for Marriage: Why Married People are Happier, Healthier, and Better Off Financially*. New York: Broadway Books.

Waite, L. J., and Nielsen, M. (2001) The rise of the dual-earner family, 1963–1997. In R. Hertz and N. L. Marshall (eds.), *Working Families: The Transformation of the American Home*. Berkeley and Los Angeles: University of California Press.

Wallerstein, J., Lewis, J. M., and Blakeslee, S. (2000) *The Unexpected Legacy of Divorce: A 25-Year Landmark Study*. New York: Hyperion.

Walzer, S. (1998) *Thinking About the Baby: Gender and Transitions into Parenthood*. Philadelphia: Temple University Press.

Wickrama, K. A. S., Lorenz, F. O., Wallace, L. E., Peiris, L., Conger, R. D., and Elder, G. H. (2001) Family influence on physical health during the middle years: The case of onset of hypertension. *Journal of Marriage and the Family*, 63, 527–39.

Williams, D. R., Takeuchi, D. T., and Adair, R. K. (1992) Marital status and psychiatric disorders among blacks and whites. *Journal of Health and Social Behavior*, 33, 140–57.

Williams, K., and Umberson, D. (2001) Marital status stability, marital transitions, and physical health status: A life course perspective. Presented at the Annual Meeting of the Population Association of America, Washington, DC.

Wilson, M. N. (1989) Child development in the context of the Black extended family. *American Psychologist*, 44, 380–5.

Wyke, S., and Ford, G. (1992) Competing explanations for associations between marital status and health. *Social Science and Medicine*, 34, 523–32.

Zick, C. D., and Smith, K. R. (1991) Marital transitions, poverty, and gender differences in mortality. *Journal of Marriage and the Family*, 53, 327–36.

# 4

# Children, Families, States, and Changing Citizenship

Hilary Land

> There is no trust more sacred than the one the world holds with children. There is no duty more important than ensuring that their rights are respected, that their welfare is protected, that their lives are free from fear and want and that they grow up in peace.
>
> *The State of the World's Children 2000* is a rallying cry to us all. It is a call to governments, civil society, the private sector and the whole international community to renew our commitment to children's rights by advancing a new vision for the 21st century: a vision in which every infant has a healthy beginning, every child a quality education and every adolescent the opportunity to develop his or her unique abilities. It is a call to families and communities – and to children and adolescents themselves – to make their voices heard in helping translate this lexicon to reality in their daily lives.
>
> – Kofi Annan, Secretary-General of the United Nations, 2000

During the twentieth century, citizenship and the rights arising from citizenship were not only matters of debate across the world as they had been from the seventeenth century in Europe, but also had become encoded in both national and international law. In the aftermath of World War II the Universal Declaration of Human Rights was passed by the United Nations. At the same time, in Western industrialized societies, the rights of citizenship were expanded to include rights to social welfare as well as political and civil rights. The welfare states which were based on the principles of universality no longer treated those who relied on state-funded health and welfare services as dependants and second-class citizens.

This chapter will examine the changing definitions of citizenship both in law and in practice as they have been broadened to include not only women but also children. It will explore some of the key challenges which the new international framework governing children's rights poses for the private world of families and the public worlds of civil society and international agencies and corporations in the twenty-first century. First, the concept of rights will be described, and the particular issues raised when it is applied to children will be discussed.

## The Language of Rights and Reason

Historically the language of rights or "justified claims" (Ladd, 1996) has been used to challenge absolute monarchs or undemocratic and oppressive institutions by appealing directly to the powerless to demand their rights and reject their dependence. As Onora O'Neill says: "The rhetoric of rights disputes established powers and their categories and seeks to empower the powerless: it is the rhetoric of those who lack power but do not accept the status quo" (1996: 36)

The treatment of the rights of children compared with other oppressed groups is different however. As Carolyn Steedman wrote in her biography of Margaret McMillan, who a hundred years ago campaigned for children to have nurseries, school meals, and medical services, as well as a healthy and pleasant environment:

> Children present a particular problem within the broad humanitarian struggle to make their groups part of the commonweal, for whilst not everyone has been a slave or a woman, all people have experienced childhood. Developments in scientific thought in the nineteenth century showed that childhood was a stage of growth and development common to all of us, abandoned and left behind, but at the same time a core of the individual's psychic life, always immanent, waiting there to be drawn on in various ways. (1990: 64)

Onora O'Neill argues that although those who denied women, slaves, and other groups their rights often used familial analogies (monarchs claimed to be acting as supreme fathers, colonial powers kept their colonies subordinate to "the mother country," and women and slaves were described as childlike), the dependency of children on their families cannot be regarded entirely in the same way. It is not artificially produced, although it may be prolonged. Moreover, childhood is a stage of life from which children normally emerge "and are helped and urged to emerge by those who have most power over them. Those with power over children's lives usually have an interest in ending childish dependence. Oppressors usually have an interest in maintaining the oppression of social groups" (1996: 38).

However, that rather depends on whether children are an economic liability or an economic asset to their parents. Looking at the treatment of children in Victorian England, or in some developing countries today, there can be compelling reasons for parents, particularly if they are very poor, to deny that children have any rights or interests distinct from their own. Parents may indeed by dependent upon their children's services and labor.

Aristotle's view that "the slave has absolutely no deliberative faculty; the woman has but its authority is imperfect, so has the child, but in this case it is immature" (quoted in Hughes, 1996: 17), cast a long shadow over ideas about citizenship in Western countries for centuries. Those who have challenged their oppressors have demanded recognition of their capacity for rational and independent life. This meant they were competent to judge for themselves what was in their best interests. In the seventeenth century, when in Western Europe the idea that monarchs ruled by Divine Right was seriously challenged, Locke argued that human relations should be based on consent. Men (*sic*) were rational beings and the only justifiable authority was that to which they consented. That, however, only applied in the public world. Relationships within the private world of the family were different both for women and for children because both needed the protection of husbands and fathers in law and in practice. Women in many countries over the past two hundred years have, with varying degrees of success, challenged many of the oppressive aspects of the "protection" husbands and fathers purported to offer them but the position of children remains more firmly embedded within the family.

Locke argued that the authority of parents over children was not based on consent but on trust in parental responsibility for their children's welfare. This created a duty on parents to care for their children and to make sure that they grew up to become reasonable adults. This required education for, as Mary Wollstonecraft wrote a century later, "children cannot be taught too early to submit to reason." She therefore advocated "public education of every denomination should be directed to form citizens" (1992: 285). Agreeing with Locke, she wrote: "A slavish bondage to parents cramps every faculty of the mind and Mr Locke very judiciously observes that 'if the mind be curbed or humbled too much in children; if their spirits be abused and broken much by too strict a hand over them, they lose all their vigour and industry'" (ibid.: 276).

However, unlike the male moral philosophers at the time, she not only argued that girls as well as boys should be educated but that they should be educated together. She understood very well, however, that much had to change both within the private world of the family and the public world of civil society before this could happen. She continued:

> till esteem and love are blended together in the first duty, morality will stumble at the threshold. But till society is very differently constituted, parents I fear will still insist on being obeyed, because they will be obeyed, and constantly endeavour to settle that power on a Divine Right which will not bear the investigation of reason. (ibid.: 278)

The arguments surrounding children's rights therefore have had to address the question of how these relate to parental rights and responsibilities. These arguments have always been gendered and applied differentially on the basis of class, "race," ethnicity, and religion.

When Wollstonecraft was writing, children had very few rights. From early times the role of law both in England, governed by Anglo-Saxon law, and in countries governed by Roman law, was to protect the parent or guardian against the loss of the property or the services which the minor represented. The parent or guardian in question was invariably the father, for women as wives and mothers also had few rights of their own, let alone over their children. Fathers had the right to the custody of their children, they could inflict reasonable chastisement, and could refuse permission for a minor child to marry. Property was only an issue in a minority of families, although this minority grew substantially in England with the growth of the middle classes and professions in the nineteenth century. However, the services children owed their fathers included the right to the proceeds of their labor. This became an issue when education became more widespread and was made compulsory in 1870. Children's earnings were necessary to many poor families where the father did not earn a "family wage."

Although overall the demand for child labor had fallen in the second half of the century, many employers, particularly in textile and agricultural areas, were reluctant to lose this source of cheap and flexible labor. The compromise was to allow children to study "half-time" and it was not until after World War I that the meaning of working-class childhood changed and the children of the poor were no longer seen as primarily workers belonging to an adult and dangerous world, but as children who belonged in school. This change in perception owes as much to the threat that deformed and diseased working-class children posed to the maintenance of the British Empire and fears of the lawless children of the "residuum" in the cities as to changing ideas about the distinct differences between childhood and adulthood (see Steedman, 1990). The conflicts around child labor are very real in many countries in the twenty-first century. In the UK it is estimated that in the 1990s about one and a half million 11–15-year-olds were employed, about three-quarters of them illegally (Hobbs and McKechnie, 1998: 11). The International Labour Organization (ILO) estimates that some 50–60 million children between the ages of 5 and 11 work in hazardous circumstances (Bellamy, 2000: 24).

## Children's Rights and Adults' Obligations

> In essence, an assertion of children's rights changes the child from the subject of policies directed towards his or her wellbeing, development and protection, to the child as an active participant in constructing those goals and the means of achieving them. (Funder, 1997: 2)

Children's rights can take various forms. Welfare rights involve protection from neglect or abuse by the adults entrusted with their care. Conversely, they may involve protection from state power, thus reinforcing the authority of parents. They can include the right to education and to health care, but alongside these have gone limits on the child's right, for example, to work, to refuse education, or to refuse medical care. Freedom rights involve the assertion of a child's autonomy, i.e., acknowledging that a child is competent to judge what is in their own best interests and, like an adult, should be free to make a mistake. Rights may therefore involve opposition to the power of the state, opposition to the power of parents, and the child's right to choose for themselves. However, as Minow writes: "State and parental interests in controlling and guiding children counter or constrict notions of individual rights for children" (1996: 49).

Children's liberationists (Holt, 1974; Harris, 1982) argue therefore that the only way forward is to remove these constraints by giving children a broad range of civil and legal rights, including being able to choose guardians other than their own family, as well as having the right to vote, manage their own financial affairs, and direct their education. However, as Hughes points out, adult citizens have rights but they also have duties and responsibilities: "He may not exercise his rights or he may shirk his duties, but he cannot forego them. They are not just available to him, they are his. That is what being a citizen involves" (1996: 20).

Holt, however, would allow the child "to pick and choose" (1974: 16, cited in Hughes, 1996). Minow proposes a different way forward. Rather than see children's rights as caught between the principle of individual rights and the principle of parental interest in, and indeed obligation to control and guide, children, we should widen our focus and engage in "a richer debate over the rights for children – a debate joining goals of autonomy and goals of affiliation – would challenge social patterns that permit public neglect, assign private responsibility for children, and also perpetuate public failure to develop the preconditions for that responsibility" (1996: 56) Onora

O'Neill also believes that a narrow focus on children's rights is unhelpful: "Why does so much current discussion of fundamental ethical issues focus on children's rights and not on obligations to children?" (1996: 35). Distinguishing between *fundamental* rights, which include moral, natural, and human rights, and *positive* rights, meaning legal, institutional, and autonomy rights, she argues that: "Children's fundamental rights are best grounded by embedding them in a wider account of fundamental obligations, which can also be used to justify positive rights and obligations." (ibid.: 29–30). In her view, unless this is done the Declaration of the Rights of the Child will remain little more than "manifesto" rights which cannot be effectively claimed. Children's rights therefore raise questions which go beyond the relationship and balance between parents' rights and individual children's rights. There are public responsibilities for children because societies have an interest in and responsibility for their future citizens and workers. On the other hand, it is argued that individual parents have responsibilities because they choose to have children. Children, however, do not consent to be born, and neither do they choose their parents.

## Childhood and Child Welfare

The concept of children's rights also has to be understood in the context of beliefs about the capacity of children to judge what is in their best interests, as well as what creates responsible and intelligent adults. These have changed over time. Locke believed children were born tabula rasa, so their development depended entirely on parents, their experience, and in particular, their education. When he was writing there was a growing interest in children as objects of scientific enquiry. Sixteenth- and seventeenth-century Calvinists in Britain argued that children would be sinful and evil unless controlled strictly by their parents. Pat Thane argues that "this historically new conception was important because it introduced the notion that children were psychologically and morally different from adults" (1981: 20). What these differences are perceived to be, changes over time. For example, Rousseau, writing a little later than Locke, took the view that children were innocent and innately good but unless protected would be corrupted by society. Children must therefore be helped to retain this goodness. Wollstonecraft's views reflected the eighteenth-century Enlightenment view that children should not be allowed to remain ignorant but could be educated to become rational and loving adults. Protestantism in the nineteenth century emphasized the importance of control by parents and in school. Later in that century Darwinism encouraged the perception of children as incomplete and different from adults: childhood was a distinct stage in human development. Earlier educationalists like Froebel had based their teaching practices on an elaboration of the stages in the journey from childhood to adulthood. He linked the growth and activities of the body with the development of the mind. Margaret McMillan later drew on his theories and believed firmly that "our mental life is conditioned by our physical life" (Steedman, 1990: 112). Moreover, unlike many of her contemporaries, who were influenced by eugenic ideas, she did not believe that the poor working-class child was inherently inferior to the middle- or upper-class child: "McMillan was quite clear... that child development followed the same order and sequence in poor children as it did in more favoured ones. The child in the Deptford slum was certainly cheated out of her rights as a human being, but was not perceived as *inadequate* for this reason" (ibid.: 208, emphasis in the original).

During the twentieth century the emotional development of children became as much an object of concern as their physical and intellectual development. The new professionals – child psychologists, psychoanalysts, and psychiatrists – not only regarded childhood as different from adulthood but also held parents, particularly mothers, responsible for the physical health and welfare of their children and for their attainment of maturity as well-adjusted, responsible, and law-abiding adults. A glance at advice manuals on child-care over the past century in the United States and Britain illustrates very vividly how opinions on how this is best achieved. They have been contradictory as well as changing over time (see Ehrenreich and English, 1979). (At the beginning of the century employed mothers in Britain were blamed for high infant mortality rates. By the middle of the century they were being blamed for high rates of juvenile delinquency.) The relationship of the young child to his or her mother was of key concern and this became one of the reasons in the early decades of the century for beginning to revise the policies for protecting children from abusive or neglectful parents (Parker, 1988). Rescuing children by removing them permanently from their parents or from the streets and placing them in institutions was gradually reconsidered and placements more closely resembling a family were sought, even if these foster parents were on the other side of the world in Canada or Australia. Significantly, both these countries were short of labor at this time. It also altered judges' views in favor of giving mothers custody of their children, particularly when very young.

By the end of the nineteenth century fathers' rights over their children had begun to be curbed in the name of protecting children. In 1889 a child subjected to cruel treatment could be committed to the care of a "fit person." The 1889 Act made cruelty and neglect of children a criminal offense. This Act was described by a contemporary as indicating "The great awakening of the nation to a true and full recognition of the rights of children, rights as subjects (sic) to the Crown, and as sentient beings capable of misery and of happiness" (Waugh, 1897: Foreword).

The state had started at the beginning of that century by specifying the age at which children could be employed and by limiting the working hours of orphans in the care of the Poor Law. In the following decades further restrictions were placed on children's and women's working hours and they were prohibited from working in certain dangerous occupations. From 1859, magistrates could send children caught begging to industrial schools. By the middle of the century the Factory Inspectorate was systematically collecting evidence of the state of a substantial proportion of the working population. This, together with the regular census and requirements to register births, marriages, and deaths, meant that both reformers and politicians had a much clearer picture of the state of the nation. The picture was a disturbing one, particularly in relation to the children. Compulsory education in 1870 made children even more visible. The children of the urban poor who were not in school were visible on the streets, apparently free from parental control. It was true then as now that "Good statistics enable us to look more closely, see more clearly and act more conscientiously. Improved statistics are vital to changing the world for and with children" (UNICEF, 2001: 1). The moral as well as the social welfare of children had become an issue and it was no longer believed that the responsibility for either could be safely left entirely with parents.

In the early years of the twentieth century school meals and medical inspections were introduced in France, Germany, and Great Britain. In England, the fathers whose children received them did not have *their* rights as citizens restricted (at that time receipt of assistance from the Poor Law lost a man his right to vote, if he had it). Politicians on the Left and on the Right of the political spectrum were concerned about eroding the responsibility of fathers to maintain their children (Bosanquet, 1905). Others argued that school meals should be provided to *all* children rather than only to poor children, because children should go to the common table by virtue of their citizenship, not by virtue of their poverty (see Land, 1975; Steedman, 1990). However, this was a minority view. There were those, too, who argued that feeding children was as much to do with imperialism as socialism (see Land, 1975). When in the 1920s children's rights were codified for the first time by the Save the Child Fund International Union, the principles were exclusively concerned with the needs of children for welfare and protection rather than with their rights as citizens. The first attempt to codify children's rights, *Codifying Children's Rights*, was endorsed by the League of Nations in 1924. The Declaration describes what should be done *for* children but children had no rights to any services, although one of its drafters believed that "we should claim certain rights for the children and labour for their universal recognition" (the founder of the Save the Children Fund, cited in Bellamy, 2000: 14).

In 1959 the successor of the League of Nations, the United Nations (UN), adopted the Declaration on the Rights of the Child. It did contain a commitment to children's civil and political rights but only in relation to the right to a home and nationality from birth. Twenty years later the UN started work on the Convention on the Rights of the Child, which was adopted by the General Assembly in 1989. This was significantly different from the earlier Declaration because it not only addressed children's need for care, protection, *and* adequate provision, but also for participation. Moreover, a Convention, unlike a Declaration, is binding on those states who ratify it for, under international law, governments are obliged to comply with its provisions. Governments can enter reservations over particular articles but they have a duty to ensure its implementation, to make its principles known both to adults and to children, and to make reports on progress toward implementation widely available. The UN Committee on the Rights of the Child reviews individual countries' progress every five years and publishes a report. All but two countries, the US and Somalia, had ratified the Convention by the year 2000.

The Convention is wide-ranging and applies to everyone under age 18. It is based on the general principles of nondiscrimination, the best interests of the child; the right to life, survival, and development; and respect for the views of the child. Its articles set out children's civil rights and freedoms, including the right to a name and nationality; the preservation of identity and access to appropriate information, freedom of thought, conscience, and religion; as well as freedom of expression, of association, and of peaceful assembly; and the right not to be subjected to violence, abuse, neglect, torture, or cruel and inhuman treatment. Articles concerning children's family environment spell out parental responsibilities, the rights of children separated from their parents and deprived of a family environment, as well as adoption procedures and the rights to contact with and to be reunified with their families.

Rights to basic health and welfare include the right to access to health care, including preventative health care: this includes the provision of clean drinking water and consideration of the issue of environmental pollution. Article 27 asserts "the right of every child to a standard of living adequate for a child's physical, mental, spiritual, moral and social development." In other words, governments have a duty to tackle poverty not just in terms of a low income but in relation to acceptable standards within a particular society. The articles concerning the rights to education, play, leisure, and cultural activities involve access to education for all on the basis of equality of opportunity. This includes the rights of disabled children and children with special needs to education and training. Finally, there are a group of articles covering children in need of special measures of protection because they are in situations of emergency, e.g., refugee children and children caught up in armed conflict. These articles also cover children in situations of exploitation, e.g., economic exploitation, drug abuse, sexual exploitation and abuse, sale, trafficking and abduction. The rights of children in conflict with the law are also included and these involve the administration of justice and the sentencing and treatment of children and juveniles deprived of their liberty. Article 30 concerns the rights of children belonging to a minority or indigenous group to respect for their culture, language, and religion.

This is a formidable list of rights, many of which are "claims based on ideals regarding how children should be treated" (Fortin, 1998: 14). They also go "far beyond the scope of what is recognisable as law" (King, 1997: 171). Before looking at the Convention's influence and its impact on the key issue or paradox of children's need for protection as well as rights, other changes in international law will be described.

## The European Convention on Human Rights

The European Convention on Human Rights, dating from 1951, includes four articles of particular significance to family law (Eekalaar, 2000). Article 14 requires that the rights and freedoms of the Convention are based on the principle of nondiscrimination and Article 6 states that "everyone is entitled to a fair and public hearing within a reasonable time by an independent and impartial tribunal established by law." Article 8 concerns the right to respect to everyone's private and family life, home, and correspondence, and Article 12 concerns the right of men and women of marriageable age to marry. Eekalaar (2000) gives some examples of the impact rulings by the European Court of Human Rights have had on English family law, in particular those concerning the rights of parents and the rights of children "looked after" by local authorities.

Corporal punishment is an interesting example of where different cultures draw the line between parents' rights and children's rights and welfare. Physical punishment of children by parents has been illegal in Sweden for over twenty years and is now illegal in at least nine countries in Europe. While Scotland is seriously considering proposals to make it illegal it is widely accepted and practiced in England. Indeed the Prime Minister and the previous Archbishop of Canterbury recently admitted using corporal punishment (Boushel, Fawcett, and Selwyn, 2000: 97). The government has resisted acting on the views of the European Court, and the latest report (UN Committee on the Rights of the Child, 2002) of the Committee monitoring the UN Convention on the Rights of the Child emphasized again that it constitutes inhumane and degrading treatment. Corporal punishment in state schools was abolished as a result of the European Court's ruling on *Campbell and Cozens v. UK* in 1989. Ten years later, following further appeals to the European Court, it was abolished in private schools. However, the government's response to the European court's ruling on a case involving the acquittal in the English courts of a stepfather who had severely beaten a 9-year-old child with a garden cane was to produce *Protecting Children, Supporting Parents: A consultation document on the physical punishment of children* (Department of Health, 2000). This only proposed to define "reasonable chastisement" more carefully. Michael Freeman comments: "The refusal by the Labour Government even to contemplate making corporal punishment unlawful is in part recognition that even the "nanny state" has some limits" (2000: 470). He does, however, go on to say: "But we have long accepted that its tentacles can intrude further into the deviant and the dysfunctional and governments may push on despite resistance" (ibid.).

Certainly, child curfews and imprisoning parents who fail to get their children to attend school seem rather more intrusive. However, it is interesting to note that at the same time the government refused to ban childminders from smacking children (or smoking in front of them) if parents had given permission for them to do so. As the Minister explained: "The government should not have to regulate on what people can and cannot do in their own homes" (Department for Education and Employment, 2000).

Another important case decided by the European courts, *Gaskin v. UK* (1989), dealt with the disclosure of confidential records of children in state care. As a result adults who spent their childhood in care have successfully won compensation for the ill treatment and abuse they suffered. The immunity from liability in negligence which local authorities had in relation to their child's protection policies and practices can only be granted after an analysis of each case, following the court's decision relating to police liability in negligence in 1999. Judith Masson concludes: "There is a possibility that compensation proceedings will hold local authorities accountable for the care they provide and systems to ensure adequate care will be imposed by insurers to minimise the risk of future claims" (2000: 579).

Whether "defensive social work" will be in the interests of children's welfare any more than defensive medicine is in the interests of patients' health remains to be seen – one result is a massive increase in insurance premiums. Accountability to children is important, but is this the best way forward? Eekalaar believes that the European Convention will have greater potential for guiding English law than the UN Convention, because the Human Rights Act 1998 incorporated it into domestic law from October 2000 (2000: 654).

## The Hague Conventions

There are three Hague Conventions concerning inter-country administrative and judicial cooperation on matters involving children. The first, adopted in 1980 and by 2000 ratified by over sixty countries, concerns child abduction. The second concerns inter-country adoption and arose from worries about the trafficking of children and the buying of babies. These worries became more widespread and visible after the fall of the Ceauçescu regime in 1989 when the press was full of stories of children being offered for cash, not just from Romanian orphanages, but by their parents on the streets. The third, adopted in 1996, recognizes measures and enforces international custody decrees across transnational borders. Its primary objective is to resolve conflicts of jurisdiction. By 2000 only two countries had ratified it and at the time of writing it is not in force. Nevertheless: "It symbolises an important international effort in achieving co-operation among the countries of the world to better protect the interests of children everywhere and, it is hoped, will be widely adopted and used to that end." (Silberman, 2000: 606).

Assessing the value of these three Conventions overall, Linda Silberman concludes that they have been important in developing norms to be used in resolving child-centered disputes. Together, she suggests, they signify an internationalization of "child law" and an attempt to operationalize what she calls "the aspirational goals" of the UN Convention on the Rights of the Child (ibid.: 616).

## Children's Rights and the US Constitution

Although the US has not ratified the UN Convention on the Rights of the Child, children's rights have changed under the US Constitution during the twentieth century. The US Supreme Court has played an important part in recognizing children as persons separate from their parents. Barbara Bennet Woodhouse states that:

> The Court's focus on tradition as the touchstone of rights, and on the individual as the entity in which rights are vested, tends to cast children's emerging rights as a contest between children and parents. Our involvement model of rights . . . makes it difficult to recognise children's rights while still protecting children's relationships within family systems. (2000: 426)

Nevertheless, there have been some important changes recognizing that children do have the "status" as constitutional persons. Woodhouse describes the Supreme Court's opinion on *Brown v. Board of Education* in the 1950s, which held that school segregation on racial lines was indefensible, even if school facilities were of equal quality. Black children should have equal protection of the laws guaranteed by the Fourteenth Amendment. "This case is widely recognised as the most important American civil rights case of the twentieth century" (ibid.: 427). Since the 1960s there has been a trend toward treating children equally, regardless of their parents' marital status, as there has been in English law. Giving rights to public education to children of illegal immigrants is also an example of respecting children's rights separately from their parents, although at the time of writing some states are considering reversing this policy. The principle of the child's best interest has become a standard used in most custody cases, although it is not without its critics (ibid.: 33). Children's voices are heard in courtrooms to an extent unthought-of even twenty years ago. Woodhouse concludes her review of change over the second half of the twentieth century in the US as follows: "The twentieth-century shift that defines parental powers not as rights in and of themselves, but as a means to advancing children's welfare, is consistent with the human rights generally, and with the children's rights revolution taking place around the globe" (ibid.: 439).

## The UN Convention on the Rights of the Child: Ten Years Later

> The 1990s was a decade of great promise and modest achievements. – UN Special Session, 2002

The first World Summit for Children at the UN took place the year after the adoption of the Convention on the Rights of the Child. Following this summit 155 countries prepared national programs or plans of actions for children. These included a number of specific goals to be achieved by the year 2000. Seven were identified as the most important and included the reduction of mortality and malnutrition rates for children under five, reduction of maternal mortality rates and of adult illiteracy rates, provision of universal access to basic education as well as to safe drinking water and sanitary conditions, and improved protection of children in especially difficult circumstances, e.g., in armed conflicts. In 1999 the UN agreed that progress toward meeting these plans and agreed objectives would be reviewed in a special session of the UN General Assembly in September 2001. This session was postponed to May 2002 because of events on September 11. Meanwhile, UNICEF worked with the preparatory committee evaluating progress both in general and in particular and identifying the key challenges facing children at the beginning of the twenty-first century. A brief analysis of the key UN and UNICEF reports of the Summit reveals how the concept of children's citizenship has been operationalized in specific national and international policies and legal frameworks, as well as how much the context within which children's rights are now considered and discussed, has widened – controversially – since the 1990s.

Some progress has been made. First, polio is almost eradicated, death from measles and neonatal tetanus has been reduced by 85 percent and 25 percent, respectively, in ten years and 12 million children are now free from the risk of mental retardation due to iodine deficiency. Blindness from vitamin A deficiency has been reduced. Seventy-one percent of the world's population has access to clean drinking water, up from 61 percent in 1990. Mortality rates among under-5s have been decreasing since the 1960s, but in many countries the AIDS pandemic is reversing these trends. There are more children in primary school, as enrolment rates have increased since 1980 but more than 130 million children of school age in the developing world still do not have access to basic education. Sixty percent of those not in school are girls, and in many countries the proportion of girls not in secondary school is even higher. There are 960 million illiterate people, 700 million of whom are women.

Second, the rights of children to be protected from dangerous and abusive situations have been incorporated in other international legal frameworks. In 1999 the ILO agreed a Convention in the Elimination of the Worst Forms of Child Labour. These include forced recruitment into armed conflict, prostitution, pornography, and drug trafficking, as well as debt bondage. A supplementary protocol on trafficking in persons, especially women and children, has been included in a draft Convention against Transnational Organised Crime. An optional protocol, which raises the minimum age of recruitment into the armed forces from 15 to 18, was adopted at the World Summit 2002.

Third, the UN and UNICEF reports draw attention to the many different ways in which children are being seen and heard, both by making room for them in government structures and procedures in many countries and by children themselves seizing initiatives. For example, in Colombia the Children's Movement for Peace mobilized a third of those aged between 7 and 18 to vote for the rights to survival, peace, family, and freedom from abuse.

Fourth, children are also becoming more visible in the statistics. In 1994 and 1998 UNICEF sponsored international meetings to further the development of indicators for the global monitoring of children's rights. Internationally agreed indicators for monitoring children's health, nutrition, and schooling have existed for some time. "The challenge is how to chart *practical* progress on many of the newer principles laid down in the Conventions such as children's rights to play a full part in the decisions affecting their lives" (UNICEF, 1998: Preface). The World Summit 2002 agreed to "strengthen our national statistical capacity... and support a wide range of child-focused research" (UN Special Session, 2002: 27).

Fifth, most recent reports acknowledge to a far greater extent than earlier reports, the importance of empowering girls and women: "The achievement of goals for children, particularly for girls, will be advanced if women fully enjoy all human rights and fundamental freedoms, including the right to development, and are empowered to participate fully and equally in all spheres of society" (ibid.: 9).

This has been stimulated in part by the women's movement and other movements to end discrimination and to protect other vulnerable groups. It is two hundred years since Mary Wollstonecraft wrote: "the weakness of the mother will be visited on the children." She continued: "Make women rational creatures and free citizens and they will quickly become good wives and mothers – that is if men do not neglect their duties of husbands and fathers" (1992 [1792]: 305–6).

## The Challenges and Controversies

> Chronic poverty remains the single biggest obstacle to meeting the needs, protecting and promoting the rights of children. – UN Special Session, 2002

The picture of child poverty both within and between countries is a deeply shocking one. At the end of the 1990s there were 1.2 billion people living on less than $1 a day, and over half were children. This represents 40 percent of all children in developing countries. There are big variations between these countries, so high rates are not necessarily inevitable. However, poverty rates are high in industrialized countries too. Altogether 10 percent of children in OECD are in poverty – defined as half average income – but in some countries like the UK and the US it is over 20 percent. In the UK a third of all children were poor in 1999 compared with 10 percent in 1979. Meanwhile, the rich are getting richer. In the 1960s the income of the richest fifth of the world's population was 30 times that of the income of the poorest fifth. By 1997 this had increased to 74 times (Townsend, 2002). Some developing countries are spending more on debt repayments than on basic education and health services. Others spend more on arms. "The world is marked by deepening poverty and a widening gap between rich and poor... Children are hardest hit by poverty which cannot be measured by economic indicators alone" (UNICEF, 2001).

All the reports, including the agreed text of the World Summit, stress the importance of including access to basic health and social services, clean water, and sanitation in any measure of poverty. The World Summit restated a commitment to access to free basic education for all children but was much more vague about access to free health and other social services. Inadequate sanitation, unsafe drinking water and food, and a number of environmental problems were all identified as needing to be addressed in a sustainable way, but the explicit commitment to the provision of universal services, found in the first report to the Preparatory Committee two years earlier, was missing. Indeed, they stated that "targeted interventions that achieve rapid successes need to be pursued." The first report had recognized that "vertical approaches and targetted interventions often achieved rapid success, but that sustainability of this success is often more difficult to assure" (UN Preparatory Committee, 2000: 8). They therefore considered "universal access to basic social services to be a public sector priority" (ibid.). This is an example of the inroads that neoliberalism is making into commitments to universal welfare rights. The latest General Agreement on Trade in Services will exacerbate and hasten these trends.

The Preparatory Committee's report had also drawn attention to the expanding role of the multinational corporations in global markets and global decision-making at the same time as the influence of many national governments has weakened (ibid.: 8). Fifty-one of the world's largest economies are now corporations and the rest nation-states. One hundred of the largest corporations control about 20 percent of foreign assets (Townsend, 2002). Onora O'Neill warned that the UN Convention on the Rights of the Child will remain a manifesto, "Unless or until practices and institutions are established that determine against whom claims on behalf of a particular child may be lodged" (1996: 6).

But these corporations are accountable to shareholders rather than to citizens or even to national governments. The World Summit, however, only "*appealed* to the private sector and corporations to adopt and adhere to practices that demonstrate social responsibility to provide resources" (UN Special Session, 2002: 12, emphasis added). The Bretton Woods Institutions and other multilateral agencies "should be *encouraged* to collaborate and plan a key role in accelerating and achieving progress for children" (ibid., emphasis added). UNICEF and the nongovernmental organizations at the World Summit were as disappointed as they were three months later at the Johannesburg Summit (Bellamy, 2002; NGO Human Rights Watch, 2002).

## Parents' Rights and Children's Rights

> The right of children, including adolescents, to express themselves freely must be respected and promoted and their views taken into account in all matters affecting them, the views of the child being given due weight in accordance with the age and maturity of the child . . . . Parents, families, legal guardians and other caregivers have the primary role and responsibility for the wellbeing of children, and must be supported in the performance of their child-rearing responsibilities" (UN Special Session, 2002: 11)

The fundamental tension between children's and parents' rights and responsibilities and the question of how the maturity of a child is assessed and by whom, remains. This tension was revealed at the World Summit in the controversy over the rights of adolescents to sexual and reproductive health education, information, and services. Despite placing the promotion and protection of this right in the context of "the rights, duties and responsibilities of parents and in a manner consistent with the evolving capacities of the adolescent" (UN Preparatory Committee, 2001: 10), the paragraph spelling out these rights was deleted. There was very strong pressure from the US, who argued only for teaching girls to say "no." The US has subsequently withdrawn funds from overseas organizations providing this information.

There is also a tension between treating children independently of their families and invoking parental responsibilities. This includes, for example, the possibility of permanently removing children from poor or inadequate parents, as occurred as a result of legislation at the end of the nineteenth century in England, and the more recent American Adoption and Safe Families Act 1997, instead of ensuring that parents are adequately supported to provide for their children themselves. As the principle and practice of universal rights to health, welfare, and basic utilities based on citizenship are increasingly being challenged and denied by the international financial institutions and corporations, this is a very important issue. On the other hand, as Eekalaar (2000) asks, is the emphasis on parental responsibilities a means of strengthening governance through families and avoiding radical reform of existing institutions?

There is also the growing problem of children living without or apart from their parents. In the 1990s 13 million children were orphans as a result of AIDS and 20 million children had been internally displaced or driven from their countries as refugees. The question of society's wider responsibility for children is not confined to individuals and organizations within national boundaries. Children have certainly become more visible and have moved closer to center stage of national and international debates on economic and social policies since the UN Convention on the Rights of the Child was agreed. The implications of treating children as citizens with rights have been clearly spelt out. There has been some progress made but there is still a long way to go before it is fully recognized and accepted that "Investments in children are extraordinarily productive if they are sustained over the medium to long term. Investing in children and respecting their rights lays the foundation for a just society, a strong economy and a world free of poverty" (UN Special Session, 2002: 25).

## References

Bellamy, C. (2000) *The State of the World's Children*. New York: UNICEF.

Bellamy, C. (2002) Speech to the World Summit on Sustainable Development. Johannesburg: UNICEF Press Centre, August 30.

Bosanquet, H. (1905) *The Family*. London: Macmillan.

Boushel, M., Fawcett, M., and Selwyn, J. (eds.) (2000) *Focus on Early Childhood, Principles and Realities*. Oxford: Blackwell.

Children's Rights Development Unit (1994) *UK Agenda for Children*. London: Children's Rights Development Unit.

Department for Education and Employment (2000) Press release, September 14.

Department of Health (2000) *Protecting Children, Supporting Parents: A consultation document on the physical punishment of children*. London: Department of Health.

Eekalaar, J. (2000) The end of an era? In S. Katz, J. Eekalaar, and M. Maclean (eds.), *Cross Currents: Family Law in the US and England*. Oxford: Oxford University Press.

Ehrenreich, B., and English, D. (1979) *For Her Own Good: 150 Years of the Experts' Advice to Women*. London: Pluto.

Fortin, J. (1998) *Children's Rights and the Developing Law*. London: Butterworth.

Freeman, M. (2000) Disputing children. In S. Katz, J. Eekalaar, and M. Maclean (eds.), *Cross Currents: Family Law in the US and England*. Oxford: Oxford University Press.

Funder, K. (1997) Children's rights: Setting the scene. In K. Funder (ed.), *Citizen Child, Australian Law and Children's Rights*. Melbourne: Australian Institute of Family Studies.

Harris, J. (1982) The political status of children. In K. Graham (ed.), *Contemporary Political Philosophy*. Cambridge: Cambridge University Press.

Hobbs, S., and McKechnie, J. (1998) Children and work in the UK: the evidence. In B. Pettit (ed.), *Children and Work in the UK: Reassessing the Issues*. London: Child Poverty Action Group.

Holt, J. (1974) *Escape from Childhood: the Needs and Rights of Children.* Harmondsworth: Penguin.

Hughes, J. (1996) The philosopher's child. In R. Ladd (ed.), *Children's Rights Revisioned, Philosophical Readings.* London, New York, and Belmont: Wadsworth.

King, M. (1997) *A Better World for Children: Explorations in Morality and Authority.* London: Routledge.

Ladd, R. E. (1996) *Children's Rights Re-visioned.* London, New York, and Belmont: Wadsworth.

Land, H. (1975) The introduction of family allowances: an act of historic justice? In P. Hall, H. Land, R. Parker, and A. Webb (eds.), *Change, Choice and Conflict in Social Policy.* London: Heinemann.

Masson, J. (2000) From Curtis to Waterhouse: state care and child protection in the UK 1945-2000. In S. Katz, J. Eekalaar, and M. Maclean (eds.), *Cross Currents: Family Law in the US and England.* Oxford: Oxford University Press.

Minow, M. (1996) Rights for the next generation: a feminist approach to children's rights. In R. Ladd (ed.), *Children's Rights Revisioned, Philosophical Readings.* London, New York, and Belmont: Wadsworth.

NGO Human Rights Watch (2002) Retrieved from http:www.hrw.wg/press/2002/05/UNchildren qa 0502.html

O'Neill, O. (1996) Children's rights and children's lives. In R. Ladd (ed.), *Children's Rights Revisioned, Philosophical Readings.* London, New York, and Belmont: Wadsworth.

Parker, R. (1988) An historical background. In I. Sinclair (ed.), *Residential Care: The Research Reviewed.* London: HMSO.

Silberman, L. (2000) The Hague children's conventions: The internationalisation of child law. In S. Katz, J. Eekalaar, and M. Maclean (eds.), *Cross Currents: Family Law in the US and England.* Oxford: Oxford University Press.

Steedman, C. (1990) *Childhood, Culture and Class in Britain: Margaret McMillan 1860–1931.* London: Virago.

Thane, P. (1981) Childhood in history. In M. King (ed.), *Childhood, Welfare and Justice.* London: Batsford.

Townsend, A. (2002) Human rights, transnational corporations and the World Bank. In P. Townsend and D. Gordon (eds.), *World Poverty: New Policies to Defeat an Old Enemy.* Bristol: Policy Press.

UN Committee on the Rights of the Child (2002) Press Release HR/4624, 04/10/2002.New York: UN.

UN Preparatory Committee for the Special Session of the General Assembly for the Follow-up to the World Summit for Children in 2001 (2000) *Emerging Issues for Children in the Twenty-first Century,* A/AC.256/3. New York: UN.

UN Preparatory Committee for the Special Session of the General Assembly on Children (2001) *A World Fit for Children,* A/AC.256/CRP.6/Rev.3. New York: UN.

UN Special Session of the General Assembly (2002) Agreed Text, A/S – 27/19/Rev.1. New York: UN.

UNICEF (1998) *Indicators for Global Monitoring of Child Rights.* New York: UNICEF.

UNICEF (2001) *Children's Rights: A Second Chance.* New York: UNICEF.

Waugh, B. (1897) Introduction to W. Clarke-Hall, *The Queen's Reign for Children.* London: Fisher Unwin.

Wollstonecraft, M. (1992) [1792] *A Vindication of the Rights of Women.* Harmondsworth: Penguin.

Woodhouse, B. (2000) The status of children, a story of emerging rights. In S. Katz, J. Eekalaar, and M. Maclean (eds.), *Cross-Currents: Family Law in the US and England.* Oxford: Oxford University Press.

# 5

# Families and Local Communities

Graham Crow and Catherine Maclean

## Introduction

This chapter explores the interconnections between families and local communities. In it, we argue that local community context continues to be important for understanding how families operate, even though several processes such as globalization and individualization may be identified as tending to weaken the connection. This is because these processes are counteracted by the need for connectedness to others that, we suggest, helps to explain the continuing importance of local community influences on family life. In the second part, we discuss the significance of local community context for family relationships, both past and present; "family communities" and social order are the focus of Section III; and Section IV deals with social change in family and community life. The penultimate section elaborates on the theoretical and methodological developments in the field that have underpinned the advances in understanding that are discussed in the chapter. Throughout the chapter, we draw on a wide range of research, conducted in various countries, to examine the themes of each section. We conclude with a summary of key issues and an assessment of the ongoing relevance for family research of sociological accounts of community. It is useful for the reader to be aware of several general points about community studies and the connections between community and family before engaging with the specifics of each section, so we outline these in the rest of this introductory section.

It is an established axiom of research into people's family lives that their relationships with other household members and with wider kin need to be placed in context. The local setting within which family relationships take place is a crucial part of this context. Community studies are particularly important in this respect because they encourage readers "to think about family relationships in a wider context of overlapping ties of family, kindred, friends and neighbours" (Morgan, 1996: 5). The message of community studies is not that individuals and their families are inevitably embedded in dense networks of social support. On the contrary, numerous studies have shown that the connection between families and local communities varies considerably, both historically and currently. Nevertheless, we are skeptical of the conventional wisdom that the linkage between families and local communities is subject to progressive and relentless erosion by the growth of geographical mobility, the rise of more affluent and individualistic lifestyles, and the development of new technologies that allow social relationships to be maintained from a distance. In developing the argument that community relationships have been "liberated" from dependence on specific places, writers like Wellman and his colleagues (1988) have successfully challenged the idea that there is a given, fixed link between family and local community. It thus becomes an empirical question precisely how this link is developing. Our view is that place communities continue to be an important component of what provides many people's "sense of security and belonging" (Jasper, 2000: 185), and that this is quite compatible with the high levels of mobility that characterize the contemporary world.

Several related issues add to the complexity of examining family ties and physical location. First, the definition of "community" is notoriously problematical and contested (Hoggett, 1997). It is important to separate out the meaning of community as "shared place" from the analytically distinct meanings of "shared interests" or "shared identity," even though in practice these different dimensions overlap more often than not. The difficulties of defining precisely what constitutes a family relationship and deciding how far into wider kin networks it is appropriate to extend one's focus compound this problem. Secondly, there is the propensity of writers to operate with distorted perceptions of the past that are deployed in support of particular interpretations of the present. Difficulties arise from the uncritical use of romanticized images of former patterns of family and community life that are said to have subsequently been "lost." Gender inequality, conflict, diversity and change all tend to be overlooked in favorable accounts of "traditional" arrangements that highlight their cohesiveness and supportiveness (Crow and Allan, 1994: ch. 2). Giddens takes a somewhat different view, contrasting the emergent pattern of "the democratic family" (1998: 89) with the shortcomings of "traditional" family relationships that rested on the restriction of individual family members' rights. Both the positive and the negative characterizations rely on a picture of the past that is selective and overgeneralized.

A third issue concerns the causal processes that structure the connections between family and community. Conventional accounts have tended to be framed in terms of large-scale trends such as industrialization and urbanization working themselves out more or less inexorably. The implication of these approaches, that family and community forms are shaped by macro-level forces beyond the control of their members, is far from satisfactory. The family is more than "a dependent variable" (Harris, 1980: 402). Both families and communities influence as well as respond to macro-level changes; for example, through local resistance to globalization (Castells, 1997), and family responses to welfare policies adopted in different states (Duncan and Edwards, 1997).

Finally, the influence of local context on processes of change raises the issue of the typicality of locations chosen for research. Certainly, the study of unusual places can be valuable. For example, Goldthorpe and his colleagues deliberately chose Luton, an atypical town in southern Britain, for their celebrated study of affluent workers. They argued that if privatization was not found in the highly favorable conditions of

Luton, then "it was unlikely to be occurring to any significant extent within British society at large" (1969: 31). Every location has its unique features and it is possible to take advantage of these, but it is hazardous to monitor and forecast patterns of change on the basis of information gleaned from particular people in one particular place such as Muncie, Indiana, better known as "Middletown" (Caccamo, 2000). Despite these risks, continuing with community-based research is justified: without it, theories of family change in an age of globalization and individualization are left literally ungrounded and speculative.

## The Significance of Local Community Context for Family Relationships

Closer inspection of community networks often reveals them to be composed to a significant degree of family relationships. Rees's classic account of community life in rural Wales in the 1940s found the kinship connections between households in the parish to be so dense and complex that they resembled "a pig's entrails" (1951: 74), in the words of a local saying. Intermarriage among populations characterized by limited geographical mobility meant that similar patterns emerged in many traditional rural communities, and the bonds of kinship consequently also tied individuals to particular places. An early recognition of this point is captured in Tönnies's concept of *Gemeinschaft*, about which he remarked that communities "can be considered as large families" (1955 [1887]: 267) because of the way in which kinship ties were central to them. Tönnies did not regard such extended family networks as limited to village locations, and subsequent research such as Gans's (1962) *The Urban Villagers* has confirmed the potential that exists for kin-based communities to thrive in urban as well as rural settings. The Italian Americans living in the West End of Boston studied by Gans had features of both nuclear and extended family patterns, and community ties between them were reinforced by the fact that "[m]arried daughters often retain close ties with their mothers and try to settle near them" (1962: 45). The propensity for urban environments to generate ethnic enclaves founded on kinship links had also been noted earlier in the twentieth century, in the writings of the Chicago School, that described in great detail the settlement of successive waves of immigrants in that city's various neighborhoods. The transferability of the cultures that these immigrants brought with them was illustrated by the area of Chicago known as "Little Sicily," where migrants originating from the Palermo district "seemed to have continued in almost every respect the mores of the village areas from which they had migrated' (Madge, 1970: 105). Contrary to spatially deterministic theories, such cases demonstrated that "[i]t is not helpful to identify a particular way of life with a particular ecological space" (Bell and Newby, 1971: 100–1) and by doing so caused researchers to look elsewhere for the bases of the continued importance of family and kinship ties in modern communities.

One key reason why family and kinship relationships prove durable in the context of geographical mobility is that relatives are a useful resource for migrants to draw upon. During the Industrial Revolution, people migrating from the countryside to the towns chose destinations where kin could provide them with points of entry into local housing and labor markets, as Hareven's research findings about "kinship clusters" (1982: 90) in the mills of New England revealed. Anderson's parallel finding for nineteenth-century Lancashire, England that "*positive* efforts were being made by migrants to build up and maintain kinship bonds" (1971: 152, emphasis in original) continues to hold true in more established urban and industrial contexts, as is illustrated by Baumann's (1996) study of migrants from the New Commonwealth to the Southall district of London, and Grieco's (1987) study of Scottish migrants to Corby in the English Midlands. Baumann's Southall study demonstrates that migration across continents is compatible with a situation in which "[w]hole clusters of kin may reside in close proximity" (1996: 45). Grieco's findings show that chain migration is by no means restricted to minority ethnic groups. She makes the further point that employers' recruitment practices may actively encourage such migration if job vacancies are filled through information channels that existing employees are able to direct toward their kin.

The connection between geographical proximity and common employment among kinsfolk is a recognized feature of established occupational communities such as longshoremen (Pilcher, 1972), dockers (Hill, 1976) and steelworkers (Harris, 1987). It is a cultural norm in such male-dominated occupations for sons to follow fathers into the job, and for wider networks of relatives to work alongside each other. In other industries such as textiles or pottery in which women were employed, oral historians have demonstrated that work was often secured by female relatives "speaking for" individuals seeking positions (Roberts, 1995: 192; Sarsby, 1988: 54). Morris (1990) suggests that this tradition continues to be important. The link between family and local residence may survive the demise of the industry on which it was originally founded, as has happened in dockside communities (Foster, 1999) and former coal-mining communities (Wight, 1993; Warwick and Littlejohn, 1992). Wight (1993) argues that finding work through relatives, particularly in the hidden economy, may even have gained in importance as the labor market has become less formally regulated. Almost a quarter of Warwick and Littlejohn's Yorkshire respondents indicated that they would seek help from local relatives when searching for work for themselves or other family members, and almost half said that they would rely on local relatives should they need to borrow money urgently. Over 80 percent of these respondents had kin living locally. These findings led the researchers to conclude that "kinship networks continue to be a very strong part of the social structure of our localities" (1992: 120), despite the demise of the area's mining industry.

It is significant that a higher percentage of women than men in Warwick and Littlejohn's study reported having relatives living in the same locality. This is consistent with the common finding that the social support provided by kin comes predominantly from women. Social support takes various forms, ranging from undertaking unpaid care to the provision of financial assistance, and from sharing information to the provision of moral support. Social support does not come exclusively from kin, and friends and neighbors can be important sources of assistance in people's everyday lives, but that involving kin tends to have a more enduring quality. This may be understood in terms of cultural norms, whereby kinship obliges individuals to participate in relationships even where they are highly unequal, whereas friendship and neighborliness are more likely to be characterized by balanced reciprocity and a greater degree of calculation (Crow and Allan, 2000). The assumption that social support is something that works to everyone's advantage is therefore questionable, as Oakley has noted: "[a]lthough we may be tempted to view social support as universally and intrinsically beneficial, such a definition . . . counters some of the evidence we already have that support both given and received may be experienced as more of a burden than a benefit" (1992: 27). Notions of duty and obligation figure prominently in the history of family support (Roberts, 1995: 180), and although it can be argued that family responsibilities have become more negotiable than they were (Finch and Mason, 1993), the constraining character of social support involving kin continues to be reported in a number of contexts, for example in studies of male unemployment in former mining areas (Dicks, Waddington, and Critcher, 1998) and of lone mothers in London and southern England (Duncan and Edwards, 1999).

## "Family Communities" and Social Order

The appeal of family relationships bears a strong resemblance to the attraction of community, and it is unsurprising to find close interconnections between the two. Dempsey's community study of the Australian settlement of Smalltown includes the telling observation that many of its residents liken it to "one big happy family," claiming that it is "a friendly and caring community where most people can and do feel at home" (1990: 55). What Dempsey found in practice often fell short of the ideal of a mutually supportive social environment, but there was nevertheless a strong commitment to the ideology of community members having obligations to the group that necessarily placed limits on individualistic behavior. The same picture emerges from several other community studies, including Rayside's (1991) study of Alexandria, Ontario in which the dominant culture celebrates harmony, caring, and cooperation, and Neville's (1994) research in the Scottish Borders, where the symbolism of the town as the "mother" of its residents again contrasts with the notion of the independent and self-sufficient individual. Communitarian philosophy also makes use of what Frazer calls "the rhetorical and political power of the link between 'family' and 'community'" (1999: 150) in its effort to bring together people who have the potential to be divided along lines of gender, age, social class, and other sociological variables.

The communitarian project of simultaneously revitalizing families and communities has been criticized as backward-looking and unworkable, with the implication that there is no place in modern societies for communities that are based on family values (e.g., Calhoun, 1995: 228), but it is not only in the realms of communitarian philosophy that the family–community connection has been pursued. Richards's (1990) study of the Melbourne, Australia suburb of Green Views found that people were attracted there by its promise of "a family community" constructed around nuclear families but with the potential for wider kinship support networks to be maintained. The scope for suburbanization to allow the conscious reshaping of family life has been taken further still in gated communities in which, as Aitken describes them, "'family orientation' and 'old-style' community values" (1998: 130) are made positive selling points. Aitken goes on to detail the numerous ways in which the "fantasies" of rich and rewarding family life promised by gated communities contrast with the more mundane realities of privatized lifestyles in safe but socially truncated environments. McKenzie argues that the "homogeneous communities" thus created "deprive people of social resources and thus stultify their lives; promote isolation and conflict between residents of the community and the rest of society; stunt children's ability to relate to people unlike themselves; and leave residents frozen in their present way of life" (1994: 189). Baumgartner's (1988) description of suburbia as a social order in which orderliness is achieved only by the deliberate avoidance of social relationships that might give rise to conflict suggests that it is not only in gated communities that idealized visions of family and community life prove elusive.

There is nothing new about the identification of a discrepancy between people's idealization of local social life and the more prosaic realities. Vidich and Bensman's study of Springdale in upper New York State made much of "the contrast between illusion and reality," whereby local people's beliefs that their town was characterized by "friendliness, neighborliness and mutual aid" were "at odds with the institutional realities of the community" (1968: 312, 320). Sennett cites this research as an example of a more widespread phenomenon, the pursuit of "the myth of a purified community" in which "people feel they belong to each other, and share together, because they are *the same*" (1971: 39, emphasis in original). He argues that people idealize what they have in common with other community members and deny their differences in order to reinforce their shared sense of identity when it comes under threat. In the process, the distinction with "outsiders," between "us" and "them," is heightened. Elias and Scotson's study of this process illustrates how local family networks can be central to the reproduction of this pattern of community. Sensing that the arrival of migrants from elsewhere in the British Isles threatened their position, the established residents of the English Midlands suburb of Winston Parva drew on their membership of families that had lived in the neighborhood for generations and expressed the belief "that they belonged there and that the place belonged to them" (1994 [1965]: 2). They also promulgated the "fantasy" that the "old families" were morally superior to the newcomers. Elias and Scotson account for their respondents' ability to stigmatize newcomers in terms of the dense local kinship network that they had and that the newcomers lacked. This kinship network supported family members provided that they conformed to the local cultural norms according to which claims to superiority were made. The newcomers acceded to the inferior position within local community relationships assigned to them because they lacked the solidarity as a group that would have been required to mount an effective challenge.

The situation described by Elias and Scotson is only one of many possible scenarios. In-migrants do not necessarily have to accept the equation of high community status with the ability to trace back family connections to a place over several generations. This is shown by Newby's (1980) account of middle-class ex-urbanites moving to the English countryside and by Wallman's (1984) research in an ethnically diverse area of inner London. Newcomers in such contexts are able to contest the association of prestige with length of residence and family connections to an area by pointing to other ways in which they contribute to community life, particularly where they form a majority. "Established" residents may thereby find themselves marginalized and retreat into a separate community (Crow, Allan, and Summers, 2001). That hierarchies within communities are subject to change is also illustrated by patterns of social evolution in new settlements. The planners of the mid-twentieth-century British New Towns experiment attempted to build communities that would be socially balanced and bring people from different social class backgrounds together. However, the types of community relationships that have emerged have tended to be at variance from the social engineers' blueprints, not least because patterns of everyday interaction at the local level have subverted the structures put in place to contain them (Crow and Allan, 1994: ch. 7). Finnegan's study of one of these New Towns, Milton Keynes, reveals that informal networks of social relationships have emerged, but they have done so along "pathways" created by residents themselves, in defiance of the planners' intention that people who shared the same space would develop a sense of belonging together. Finnegan's findings show the development of local music groups, to which people were prepared to travel beyond their immediate neighborhoods. Individuals were frequently introduced to these groups through kinship ties, giving rise to the comment that "[t]he local brass bands seemed to be full of relatives" (1989: 54). There was an orderliness to the social organization of these musical "communities," but it was something that the members themselves had created rather than being the expression of successful social engineering.

Families matter to local community hierarchies in other ways besides their positions in relation to each other as families. Contained within the notion of a "family community" is a set of ideas about gender relations, and in particular about the place of women. The social order of Dempsey's *Smalltown* (1990) is founded on gender inequalities that make it *A Man's Town* (1992). Local culture discourages women's employment by "making wifehood and motherhood so central that paid work can only be considered if it is in the interests of husband and children" (1992: 5), and obstacles to women taking jobs are particularly important in the reproduction of gender inequality. The idea of women's role as homemakers was also prominent in the Melbourne suburban housing estate studied by Richards (1990), but here the economic necessity for more than one income per household meant that there was a much higher rate of women's employment. One consequence of this was that it allowed a more explicit recognition of the contradictions inherent in the ideal of the "family community" as the discrepancies between wives' and husbands' perceptions were revealed: "Her dream of the home is very different from his, her idea of community from his, there are different meanings for her and him of privacy, security, the need for neighbours and their danger" (1990: ix). The growth of women's employment has been identified by some contemporary social theorists as a key factor in the decline of "traditional" family and community arrangements. Greater geographical mobility and globalization, the development of welfare-state programs, the growth of a more individualistic culture, and the shift away from the male breadwinner model of the family has meant, according to Beck, that "the relationship between community and locality has been transformed" (1998: 36) in an unsettling process of change that is irreversible. We prefer the alternative interpretation of the findings produced by researchers like Richards (1990), that people respond to the forces of change by regarding community as a potential source of material and emotional security in an uncertain world, and thereby are led to pursue involvement in community rather than to abandon it.

## Social Change in Family and Community Life

Bulmer (1986) is among a number of authors who have argued that the solidarity of community life in earlier generations had a forced quality, at least among the poorer parts of the population. Poverty necessitated the development of arrangements whereby material assistance from kin and neighbors could be drawn upon in times of particular hardship. In his discussion of traditional British working-class communities, Bulmer argues that "self-help networks at the local level were a realistic response to low incomes, economic adversity and unpredictable domestic crisis. In the absence of state support for the relief in the home of illness, old age or unemployment, the 'safety net' for most families was the neighborhood itself." Bulmer's judgment is that such arrangements are "a thing of the past, rapidly being eliminated by the forces of social change" (1986: 92), and that their disappearance is more of a matter for celebration than mourning. The development of the welfare state and the availability of more reliable and better-paid employment opportunities have brought a corresponding reduction in the degree of dependence on others beyond the household, and it is against this background that the emergence of "privatized" families is located. The ideal type of the privatized family was taken by Goldthorpe and his colleagues (1969) to be geographically and socially mobile. The ability to move away from wider kin networks was made possible by the availability of better-paid work. The prospect of affluent lifestyles provided a stronger pull than staying near kin, albeit that "[c]ouples had no doubt often approached the move with misgivings about its effects on their social lives" (1969: 97), involving as it often did migration over considerable distances. Other researchers suggested that people came to prefer "the mobile society" to "the cohesive society" on the grounds that the latter's stability and enduring character (that is, its traditions) also meant that it was experienced as "the stagnant society" (Rosser and Harris, 1965: 299). The embryo of Beck's (1992) more recent thesis concerning the impact of individualization on traditional community patterns and Giddens's (1991) arguments about the increasingly "disembedded" character of local activities can be detected in these ideas.

Another economic force for change has been the restructuring of industries around which occupational communities grew up. The restructuring of old, heavy industries in the UK such as coal-mining, steel-making and shipbuilding was particularly significant in that it dramatically reduced employment levels in the areas in which they were located. High levels of local unemployment appeared to make out-migration the most economically rational option for many individuals, but the actual numbers following this course turned out to be surprisingly small in Harris's (1987) study. He attributed this to the strength of the attachment to the area that the redundant steelworkers exhibited as a result of their long residence and their movement into the ranks of owner-occupiers, both of which militated against moving away. A more prominent effect of economic restructuring found by Harris and by others (Crow and Allan, 1994: ch. 3) was social polarization, the consequence of which was to deepen divisions between different sections of the local population and increase the reliance on local social networks of the more disadvantaged groups. Kin figured prominently in these networks, and Allatt and Yeandle suggest that the priority given to family members is underpinned by the philosophy that "in a poor labour market 'you first look after your own'" (1992: 2). Although rising living standards tend to loosen people's ties to local neighborhoods through the promotion of "mobility and choice," certain groups (e.g., young mothers and elderly people without their own transport) remain significantly dependent on local social support, even in periods of general prosperity (Bulmer, 1986: 95, 99). Studies of social polarization show that those in marginal labor-market positions have less mobility and choice than their more affluent counterparts, and may as a result find themselves leading lives that are "involuntarily home-centred" (Pahl and Wallace, 1985: 224), that is, forced into a rather different sort of privatized lifestyle. Such polarization has a spatial as well as a social expression, with more and less prosperous households being geographically separated (Byrne, 1999).

The unevenness of the effects of economic change on families and communities is also a theme in the literature on globalization. The nature of life in "the global city"

(Eade, 1997) varies significantly according to the extent to which people have choices over where they live. The options open to the cosmopolitan businessperson whose work involves travel to and residence in various global cities and other parts of the world are incomparably greater than those of the poor working-class tenant of an inner-city estate (Fennell, 1997). In contrast to those people who actively choose to live in the inner city because of the lifestyles that it allows to those with the resources to engage in them, "[t]he 'trapped' are the people who stay behind... because they cannot afford to move, or are otherwise bound to their present location.... Many of them are old people living out their existence on small pensions" (Gans, 1968: 100). Urban life has particular appeal to unmarried, childless people whose interests do not lie in the development of deep and enduring relationships with their neighbors; they are, as Gans describes them, "detached from neighbourhood life" (1968: 101). This social environment is one that people tend to leave in favor of the suburbs when they become parents. Gans's (1967) investigation of the process of suburbanization in his study of *The Levittowners* in New Jersey, USA, supported the general argument that relocation tends not to have the profoundly disruptive effect on people's social networks that some of the more pessimistic predictions of urban redevelopment had suggested.

One of the principal reasons why geographical mobility has not led to the breakdown of wider kinship networks is that developments in transport and communications allow the maintenance of contact. Wellman and colleagues found in their study of the East York area of Toronto, Canada, that cars and telephones were used to maintain active ties with kin, friends, co-workers and other members of people's "personal communities" in networks that extended well beyond their immediate neighborhoods. They found that "the lives of most are confined to home and cottage, neighbourhood, kin and work," and the resultant networks constituted "multiple, thinly connected circles" (Wellman, Carrington, and Hall, 1988: 175, 156) rather than a "community" in the traditional, locality-based sense. Wellman's more recent work on internet communities further illustrates the general point that technology can be used to overcome spatial distance, and the claim is made that "strong, intimate ties can be maintained online as well as face-to-face" (Wellman and Gulia, 1999: 181). Not all technological developments are interpreted as having a benign influence on families' links to wider kin and community. Putnam has attributed "reduced contacts with relatives, friends and neighbours" at least in part to the spread of "TV ownership and usage" (2000: 234), to cite an example of a study that is more skeptical of the view that networks of social support are readily adaptable. On the whole, however, generational change is associated with the emergence of new opportunities for community building.

Much of the debate about the capacity of families' relationships with their wider kin to survive geographical mobility hinges on the meaning that is attached to social contact. Social contact over geographical distance is less likely to involve the provision of care than it is to include other elements of social support and interaction. Finch and Mason found that "geographical distance is very commonly used to explain the inability to provide support" (1993: 109), and although exceptions were present among their respondents, the propensity to provide care decreased with the distance to be traveled. The literature on care in the community supports Mason's remark that "[l]iving near enough to provide... help can mean being expected always to be the first to help" (1999: 156), an expectation that applies particularly to women who are commonly regarded as "natural" carers. The migration patterns that produce such outcomes are complex, and include older people moving in order to be closer to their children and/or siblings (Wenger, 1984), and mothers of dependent children locating themselves within traveling distance of their mothers (Ribbens, 1994). The role of children themselves in facilitating community connections, whether by enabling adult family members to meet other adults locally or by increasing the likelihood of in-migrant families being accepted as "belonging," is also worthy of attention (Maclean, 2003). Phillipson and his colleagues' finding that the majority of elderly people in their recent British study lived in the same parish as at least one of their children allowed them to conclude that "[k]inship remains . . . central in terms of the ties of our respondents" (1999: 245), although the three urban areas studied did exhibit important variations in the detail of the patterns of contact. Local friends also figured in these older people's networks, as did neighbors, to a lesser extent.

The imagery of informal local community networks as "havens," as refuges and sources of support for people whose lives are otherwise dominated by large-scale, impersonal forces is something that is frequently invoked (Castells, 1997: 64; Jankowski, 1991: 193). Wellman and his colleagues report that most of their respondents "value the pastoral ideal of community: they prefer to be members of densely knit, local networks, filled with emotionally compatible persons exchanging a wide range of aid" (1988: 172), even though their actual situations fall short of this ideal. Part of the explanation of the appeal of local communities within which family relationships figure prominently is their apparent "naturalness" and authenticity (Bauman, 1990). Harris argues that shared place continues to be important in the creation of people's enduring personal relationships, even in an age of historically high levels of geographical mobility. His reasoning is that "[w]hile distance need not be a barrier to the *maintenance* of a relationship, it remains . . . a barrier to its *establishment*, since establishment requires face-to-face interaction, and that in turn requires proximity, i.e. location in the same place" (1990: 78, emphases in original). Thus although the equation of places with particular types of social relationships is untenable as a sociological proposition, the location within which social encounters unfold continues to exert an important influence on how they unfold. Macro-social forces do not eliminate the significance of where social relationships take place, and Robertson's argument about "glocalization," that is, about how "globalization has involved the reconstruction . . . of 'home', 'community' and 'locality'" (1995: 30), is one of a number of ways in which the unevenness of general trends has been captured. It is particularly instructive from the point of view of the argument that we are seeking to develop that Robertson refers to the reconstruction rather than the dissolution of local communities.

## Theoretical and Methodological Developments

Recognition of the complexity of the connections between local community and family relationships has required the development of more sophisticated approaches than those of community studies whose authors understood their work as an exercise in description, or who attempted to interpret the phenomena under investigation in terms of crudely deterministic theories. Elias and Scotson's contribution to the field took as its premise that "the nature of family ties and the structure of families cannot be understood and explained as if families existed in a communal vacuum or as if the structure of families determined by itself that of the communities in which they lived" (1994 [1965]: 44). The revitalization of community studies through the adoption of the more theoretically informed approach that Elias and Scotson called for necessitated a number of things, including an acknowledgment of the great diversity of family and community forms that exist, and an appreciation of the social, economic, and political forces that are responsible for this diversity. The essentially dynamic nature of family and community relationships and their creation and maintenance by their members has also had to be taken on board. Among the many different approaches that have incorporated these ideas into research in this field, the work of oral historians such as Roberts (1995) is particularly instructive for its demonstration of the enduring nature of gender inequalities in family and community relationships and of the interconnections between the two. The emphasis on the reproduction over time of patterns of social inequality and exclusion can also be found in Dempsey's *Smalltown* (1990), in which it is argued that the community context may temper pressure for change. Where people live, work, and play alongside each other, "a sense of shared identity and common fate are highly likely to take precedence over class-, age-, or gender-based rivalries and serve to encourage the disadvantaged as well as the advantaged... to remain" (1990: 4). The families and households within which people live are in turn part of wider configurations of community that can exercise powerful constraints on their range of options.

One new way in which attempts have been made to understand how families and communities are linked together is through the related concepts of social capital (Putnam, 2000) and local cultural capital (Warwick and Littlejohn, 1992). Family ties are at the heart of local traditions of community participation and mutual aid independent of the state, and the cause of the variation in the extent to which such patterns are found in different locations is an issue of obvious political relevance. Many of the contributors to this debate are critical of the assumption that the promotion of social capital brings only benefits. In addition to the point noted earlier about how social support may be experienced as constraining rather than empowering, there are also concerns about enthusiasm for social capital on the part of governments "seeking ways of transferring responsibility for both delivery and financing of welfare to the market, family, community and individuals" (Taylor, 1995: 99). Two things are of particular note about Putnam's account of social capital. He argues that what he describes as "the erosion of traditional family values" and the trend toward "civic disengagement" in recent decades (2000: 279) are not causes of this decline in social capital, contrary to the arguments made by at least some communitarians. The other point is that Putnam makes a distinction between "bonding social capital" and "bridging social capital" (2000: 23), the former tending to accentuate the exclusivity of different communities while the latter opens up possibilities for this often problematic exclusivity to be circumvented through the creation of links between communities. This approach offers a new angle on an issue that has long been a matter of debate in social network analysis, concerning the extension of connections beyond the boundaries of local communities. It also ties in with the greater emphasis on the fluid nature of family and community relationships in an era of extensive mobility.

The conventional wisdom is that social relationships in families and local communities are becoming ever more open as a result of increased mobility, but the image of the weakening of boundaries is questionable. The rise of gated communities is significant here because their rationale is the very opposite of openness. The image of community as "fortress" (Davis, 1990: ch. 4) betrays what Aitken refers to as "[a]spirations for territorial control and the establishment of real boundaries" (1998:167) that are rooted in mistrust of others. This development builds on older ideas about space in neighborhoods being a resource that can be deployed "defensively" (Amin and Graham, 1999), and it might be imagined that this theme would also figure prominently in Beck's (1992) account of living in what he terms "risk society." In fact, his argument is that the relationship between families and local communities highlights how individualization undermines people's attachments to others, despite their attempts to avoid the shallowness of fully individualized lifestyles. Taken to its logical extreme, individualization would produce a society composed of individuals "'unhindered' by a relationship, marriage or family" who would also be freed of ties to particular localities as "community is dissolved in the acid bath of competition" (Beck, 1992: 116, 94). The starkness of this prospect leads to the recognition that "individualization also fosters a longing for the opposite world of intimacy, security and closeness" (Beck-Gernsheim, 1998: 67) that bears more than a passing resemblance to Tönnies's (1955 [1887]) *Gemeinschaft*, although there is little optimism about the realization of such aspirations. Our own view is that local community relationships and the family relationships that are an important part of their composition are proving themselves to be far more resilient than Beck and like-minded theorists have predicted.

## Conclusion

The anticipation of the declining relevance of local community context for understanding family relationships has a long history, but it is a perspective that is constantly being confounded. The erosion of traditional community relationships like those of poor working-class communities in an earlier industrial period should not be equated with a general decline in the influence that local community contexts have on family life. People are unquestionably more mobile than was the case for previous generations, but migration strategies have the potential to re-create as well as to break links with wider kin and with place, as they always have done (Crow and Maclean, 2000). Furthermore, geographical distance is not necessarily a bar to the maintenance of supportive family networks, although this is something that varies with social class and access to the means of communication. It appears in addition to have different implications for women and men, and also for children, although the effect on children of movement away from local community networks has not been researched as fully as it has for adults. The general conclusion to emerge from recent research is that privatized families can never become wholly independent of their local surroundings and that, in fact, families do not tend to seek such independence. Rather, community in its local form continues to be positively valued by people.

### References

Aitken, S. (1998) *Family Fantasies and Community Space*. New Brunswick, NJ: Rutgers University Press.

Allatt, P., and Yeandle, S. (1992) *Youth Unemployment and the Family: Voices of Disordered Times*. London: Routledge.

Amin, A., and Graham, S. (1999) Cities of connection and disconnection. In J. Allen, D. Massey, and M. Pryke (eds.), *Unsettling Cities: Movement/Settlement*. London: Routledge.
Anderson, M. (1971) *Family Structure in Nineteenth Century Lancashire*. Cambridge: Cambridge University Press.
Bauman, Z. (1990) *Thinking Sociologically*. Oxford: Basil Blackwell.
Baumann, G. (1996) *Contesting Culture: Discourses of Identity in Multi-Ethnic London*. Cambridge: Cambridge University Press.
Baumgartner, M. (1988) *The Moral Order of a Suburb*. New York: Oxford University Press.
Beck, U. (1992) *The Risk Society: Towards a New Modernity*. London: Sage.
Beck, U. (1998) *Democracy Without Enemies*. Cambridge: Polity.
Beck-Gernsheim, E. (1998) On the way to a post-familial family: from a community of need to elective affinities. *Theory, Culture and Society*, 15, 53–70.
Bell, C., and Newby, H. (1971) *Community Studies: An Introduction to the Sociology of the Local Community*. London: George Allen & Unwin.
Bulmer, M. (1986) *Neighbours: The Work of Philip Abrams*. Cambridge: Cambridge University Press.
Byrne, D. (1999) *Social Exclusion*. Buckingham: Open University Press.
Caccamo, R. (2000) *Back to Middletown: Three Generations of Sociological Reflections*. Stanford, CA: Stanford University Press.
Calhoun, C. (1995) *Critical Social Theory: Culture, History and the Challenge of Difference*. Oxford: Blackwell.
Castells, M. (1997) *The Power of Identity*. Vol. 2 of *The Information Age: Economy, Society & Culture*, Oxford: Blackwell.
Crow, G., and Allan, G. (1994) *Community Life*. Hemel Hempstead: Harvester Wheatsheaf.
Crow, G., and Allan, G. (2000) Communities, family support and social change. In J. Canavan, P. Dolan, and J. Pinkerton (eds.), *Family Support: Direction from Diversity*. London: Jessica Kingsley.
Crow, G., Allan, G., and Summers, M. (2001) Changing perspectives on the insider/outsider distinction in community sociology. *Community, Work and Family*, 4, 29–48.
Crow, G., and Maclean, C. (2000) Community. In G. Pagne (ed.), *Social Divisions*. Basingstoke: Macmillan.
Davis, M. (1990) *City of Quartz: Excavating the Future in Los Angeles*. London: Vintage.
Dempsey, K. (1990) *Smalltown: A Study of Social Inequality, Cohesion and Belonging*. Melbourne: Oxford University Press.
Dempsey, K. (1992) *A Man's Town: Inequality Between Women and Men in Rural Australia*. Melbourne: Oxford University Press.
Dicks, B., Waddington, D., and Critcher, C. (1998) Redundant men and overburdened women. In J. Popay, J. Hearn, and J. Edwards (eds.), *Men, Gender Divisions and Welfare*. London: Routledge.
Duncan, S., and Edwards, R. (eds.) (1997) *Single Mothers in an International Context: Mothers or Workers?* London: UCL Press.
Duncan, S., and Edwards, R. (1999) *Lone Mothers, Paid Work and Gendered Moral Rationalities*. Basingstoke: Macmillan.
Eade, J. (ed.) (1997) *Living the Global City: Globalization as Local Process*. London: Routledge.
Elias, N., and Scotson, J. (1994[1965]) *The Established and the Outsiders: A Sociological Enquiry into Community Problems*. London: Sage.
Fennell, G. (1997) Local lives – distant ties. In J. Eade (ed.), *Living the Global City: Globalization as Local Process*. London: Routledge.
Finch, J., and Mason, J. (1993) *Negotiating Family Responsibilities*. London: Routledge.
Finnegan, R. (1989) *The Hidden Musicians: Music-Making in an English Town*. Cambridge: Cambridge University Press.
Foster, J. (1999) *Docklands: Cultures in Conflict, Worlds in Collision*. London: UCL Press.

Frazer, E. (1999) Unpicking political communitarianism. In G. Jagger and C. Wright (eds.), *Changing Family Values*. London: Routledge.

Gans, H. (1962) *The Urban Villagers*. New York: Free Press.

Gans, H. (1967) *The Levittowners: Ways of Life and Politics in a New Suburban Community*. New York: Vintage.

Gans, H. (1968) Urbanism and suburbanism as ways of life. In R. Pahl (ed.), *Readings in Urban Sociology*. Oxford: Pergamon.

Giddens, A. (1991) *Modernity and Self-Identity*. Cambridge: Polity.

Giddens, A. (1998) *The Third Way: The Renewal of Social Democracy*. Cambridge: Polity.

Goldthorpe, J., Lockwood, D., Bechhofer, F., and Platt, J. (1969) *The Affluent Worker in the Class Structure*. Cambridge: Cambridge University Press.

Grieco, M. (1987) *Keeping it in the Family: Social Networks and Employment Chance*. London: Tavistock.

Hareven, T. (1982) *Family Time and Industrial Time: The Relationship Between the Family and Work in a New England Industrial Community*. Cambridge: Cambridge University Press.

Harris, C. (1980) The changing relation between family and societal form in western society. In M. Anderson (ed.), *Sociology of the Family*. 2nd ed. Harmondsworth: Penguin.

Harris, C. (1987) *Redundancy and Recession in South Wales*. Oxford: Basil Blackwell.

Harris, C. (1990) *Kinship*. Milton Keynes: Open University Press.

Hill, S. (1976) *The Dockers: Class and Tradition in London*. London: Heinemann.

Hoggett, P. (ed.) (1997) *Contested Communities: Experiences, Struggles, Policies*. Bristol: Policy Press.

Jankowski, M. (1991) *Islands in the Street: Gangs and American Urban Society*. Berkeley: University of California Press.

Jasper, J. (2000) *Restless Nation: Starting Over in America*. Chicago: University of Chicago Press.

Maclean, C. (2003) Making it their home: In-migration, time, social change and belonging in a rural community. In G. Allan and G. Jones (eds.), *Social Relations and the Life Course*. Basingstoke: Palgrave.

Madge, J. (1970) *The Origins of Scientific Sociology*. London: Tavistock.

Mason, J. (1999) Living away from relatives. In S. McRae (ed.), *Changing Britain: Families and Households in the 1990s*. Oxford: Oxford University Press.

McKenzie, E. (1994) *Privatopia: Homeowner Associations and the Rise of Residential Private Government*. New Haven, CT: Yale University Press.

Morgan, D. (1996) *Family Connections: An Introduction to Family Studies*. Cambridge: Polity.

Morris, L. (1990) *The Workings of the Household: A US–UK Comparison*. Cambridge: Polity.

Neville, G. (1994) *The Mother Town: Civic Ritual, Symbol, and Experience in the Borders of Scotland*. Oxford: Oxford University Press.

Newby, H. (1980) *Green and Pleasant Land? Social Change in Rural England*. Harmondsworth: Penguin.

Oakley, A. (1992) *Social Support and Motherhood: The Natural History of a Research Project*. Oxford: Blackwell.

Pahl, R., and Wallace, C. (1985) Household work strategies in economic recession. In N. Redclift and E. Mingione (eds.), *Beyond Employment: Household, Gender and Subsistence*. Oxford: Basil Blackwell.

Phillipson, C., Bernard, M., Phillips, J., and Ogg, J. (1999) Older people in three urban areas. In S. McRae (ed.), *Changing Britain: Families and Households in the 1990s*. Oxford: Oxford University Press.

Pilcher, W. (1972) *The Portland Longshoremen: A Dispersed Urban Community*. New York: Holt, Rinehart, & Winston.

Putnam, R. (2000) *Bowling Alone: The Collapse and Revival of American Community*. New York: Simon & Schuster.

Rayside, D. (1991) *A Small Town in Modern Times: Alexandria, Ontario.* Montreal: McGill-Queen's University Press.
Rees, A. (1951) *Life in a Welsh Countryside: A Social Study of Llanfihangel yng Ngwynfa.* Cardiff: University of Wales Press.
Ribbens, J. (1994) *Mothers and Their Children: A Feminist Sociology of Childrearing.* London: Sage.
Richards, L. (1990) *Nobody's Home: Dreams and Realities in a New Suburb.* Melbourne: Oxford University Press.
Roberts, E. (1995) *Women and Families: An Oral History, 1940–1970.* Oxford: Blackwell.
Robertson, R. (1995) Glocalization. In M. Featherstone, S. Lash, and R. Robertson (eds.), *Global Modernities.* London: Sage.
Rosser, C., and Harris, C. (1965) *The Family and Social Change.* London: Routledge & Kegan Paul.
Sarsby, J. (1988) *Missuses and Mouldrunners: An Oral History of Women Pottery Workers at Work and at Home.* Milton Keynes: Open University Press.
Sennett, R. (1971) *The Uses of Disorder: Personal Identity and City Life.* London: Allen Lane.
Taylor, M. (1995) Community work and the state. In G. Craig and M. Mayo (eds.), *Community Empowerment: A Reader in Participation and Developmen.* London: Zed Books.
Tönnies, F. (1995) [1887] *Community and Association.* London: Routledge & Kegan Paul.
Vidich, A., and Bensman, J. (1968) *Small Town in Mass Society: Class, Power and Religion in a Rural Community. Revised Edition.* Princeton, NJ: Princeton University Press.
Wallman, S. (1984) *Eight London Households.* London: Tavistock.
Warwick, D., and Littlejohn, G. (1992) *Coal, Capital and Culture: A Sociological Analysis of Mining Communities in West Yorkshire.* London: Routledge.
Wellman, B., Carrington, P., and Hall, A. (1988) Networks as personal communities. In B. Wellman and S. Berkowitz (eds.), *Social Structures: A Network Approach.* Cambridge: Cambridge University Press.
Wellman, B., and Gulia, M. (1999) Virtual communities as communities. In M. Smith and P. Kollock (eds.), *Communities in Cyberspace.* London: Routledge.
Wenger, G. (1984) *The Supportive Network: Coping with Old Age.* London: George Allen & Unwin.
Wight, D. (1993) *Workers not Wasters: Masculine Respectability, Consumption and Employment in Central Scotland.* Edinburgh: Edinburgh University Press.

# II

# Life-Course Perspectives on the Family

# 6

# Generations, the Life Course, and Family Change

J. Beth Mabry, Roseann Giarrusso, and Vern L. Bengtson

The family as the focus for scholarly research, public policy, and social commentary too often has been limited to the "nuclear" family of people immediately related by blood and marriage (parents and their children). However, this isolated view neglects intergenerational family ties as well as the recent demographic and historical trends that have made multigenerational relationships increasingly important. Our purpose in this chapter is to review evidence about intergenerational relationships in technologically advanced and developing countries alike. This research supports the hypothesis that intergenerational family relationships will be increasingly important in the early twenty-first century, with families functioning as the basic institution of social life and as the primary source of care, nurturance, and well-being for individuals (Bengtson, 2001).

We begin this chapter with a description of the life-course theoretical perspective and how it assists our understanding of the ways that macro-level societal conditions shape contemporary family life. Then we discuss three sets of issues as they relate to multigenerational families: (1) the historic, economic, demographic, and social changes that occurred during the twentieth century to shape family lives; (2) the consequences of these changes for solidarity and conflict in intergenerational families today; and (3) whether these changes have led to a decline in the importance of families, as has been suggested by many social critics today, particularly with regard to the care and support of older family members. We conclude by arguing that, despite the significant historical changes in demography, economy, and family structure that have occurred over the past century, the intergenerational family will remain the principal source of support for elderly parents.

## Economic, Demographic, and Social Changes and the Intergenerational Family

### The life-course theoretical perspective

To understand reasons for the increasing importance of intergenerational relationships requires the application of theory. The life-course theoretical perspective, with its emphasis on multiple temporal and social contexts (Bengtson and Allen 1993; Elder 1994; Hareven 2001), focuses on the historical and social circumstances in which families are embedded. Examining families within these contexts suggests that the nature of intergenerational families, their patterns of interaction, and the quality of their relationships are closely linked to shifting economic, demographic, and social conditions that have occurred over time.

Four concepts are central to the life course perspective (Elder 1994). First is the *linkage between individual development and historical times*, which highlights both the impact of social change on the options and constraints people confront, as well as uniform change across age groups stemming from historical events and circumstances. Second, *the timing of life events* calls our attention to the incidence, duration, and sequence of roles and their normative or "off-time" social timing – which is not always in keeping with biological timing, as is the case with early or delayed marriage and childbearing. The principle of *linked lives* points to the importance of interactions in family and other relationships that link our lives and trajectories to those of others. For instance, whether and when a person becomes a grandparent depends upon the choices of an adult child, and those choices may be influenced by larger social forces such as the economy. Finally, the concept of *individual agency* suggests that the intentional choices individuals make from their available options help to shape and direct the course of their lives.

Taken together, the concepts of the life-course perspective illuminate how historical and social forces impinge upon family roles and relationships over time. We advocate the life-course perspective as a useful conceptual lens for viewing the influence of historic, economic, and demographic change, as well as social change, on families over time and particularly for intergenerational family relationships as they evidence "drifting apart and coming together" across several decades.

### The influence of economic change on intergenerational families

The sources of change in intergenerational families can be linked to processes of modernization, as argued by Ogburn (1933) and Cowgill (1974). With modernization, the economy makes the transition from an agricultural to an industrial base; fertility declines and longevity increases, leading to an "aging" of the population; and social values and practices change as the social structures are altered. The technological process of industrialization, its economic and cultural cousin globalization, and the related social processes of modernization profoundly affected intergenerational family relations; the effect of these transitions are apparent in many societies around the world.

As a result of worldwide modernization the age structure of societies, and therefore intergenerational families, has grown older with fewer children and more elders; work has shifted from being a family enterprise in the home to an altogether separate sphere that often requires younger generations to migrate from rural homelands into urban areas to seek work; and the values that reinforced traditional family roles and governed family relationships have changed to accommodate the new needs of different generations. In many developing nations, industrialization is more recent, and the transformation of family life began toward the second half of the twentieth century and continues today. These changes may have altered the family's relationship to the economy, as well as social values concerning family relationships (Bengtson and Putney, 2000).

## The influence of demographic change on intergenerational families

One of the most profound alterations of the family has occurred at the demographic level. Intergenerational family life depends on who is in the family – the family structure. The structure of a person's family might include parents, grandparents, a spouse or partner, siblings, children, grandchildren, other extended kin, step-relatives, and others. Family structures vary by gender, ethnicity, and social class. For example, men typically have a spouse throughout their lives because of their shorter life expectancy and their later average age at marriage compared with women. And as life expectancy extends to nearly 80 years while fertility hovers at or below replacement levels in the industrialized world (Eurostat, 2002), these demographic trends have resulted in increasingly aging populations for nations where older age groups (rather than children) become the fastest growing segment of the population and the average age of the society has shifted from early adulthood to midlife. These population-level patterns are replicated in the composition of intergenerational families. The shape of the contemporary intergenerational family looks more like a pillar, whereas it used to look more like a pyramid with many young members at the bottom and fewer older members at the top. Today's more verticalized, or "beanpole" intergenerational family (Bengtson, Rosenthal, and Burton, 1996) parallels the structure of an aging population resulting from declines in fertility (fewer members of each generation in a family) and increases in life expectancy (more generations are alive at the same time).

How fast are populations aging and families verticalizing? Consider for example the UK, Germany, and Japan. At the end of the twentieth century each of these countries had similar proportions of older people in their populations (about 16 percent), and the proportion of elderly in the US was only slightly smaller, at 13 percent. At the same time, developing nations like South Korea and China had smaller proportions of elderly, just 7 percent over age 65 (US Population Reference Bureau, 1999). Although the proportion of elderly in all nations is expected to increase in coming decades, the rate of population aging may be more rapid in Eastern nations than in Western nations because of more recent increases in longevity (Bengtson and Putney, 2000). For example, Japan's elderly population will increase from 16 percent to over 27 percent by 2025. According to projections, population aging around the world will stabilize only after the middle of the twenty-first century (US Population Reference Bureau, 1999).

A notable exception to the global demographic transition to aging populations is the case of sub-Saharan Africa. In many African nations, civil wars, famines, the AIDS epidemic, and persistent poverty have decimated several generations. These trends, coupled with comparatively high fertility rates (5.5 children per woman compared to less than 2 children on average for European and North American women), suggest that many south and central African nations have relatively young populations (UN Population Division, 1999).

The verticalization of families and longer years of shared lives for family members suggest greater opportunities for both intergenerational solidarity and conflict (see later parts of this chapter). But how is the verticalization of intergenerational families related to horizontal family relationships, especially with regard to elder care? Are elderly parents with only one child less likely to receive care than those with more than one child? In the US, elderly parents of "only children" are less likely than those with multiple children to receive assistance from a child (Kivett and Atkinson, 1984). Yet the greatest proportion of sons and daughters involved as primary caregivers to elderly parents are "only children" (Coward and Dwyer, 1990). Factors such as income, geographic proximity, and parental health are more important in determining whether "only children," compared to those with siblings, care for their elderly parents (Kivett and Atkinson, 1984). In Thailand, however, recent research suggests only a weak relationship between the number of children and caregiving for elderly parents. The character of the individual child is more important in the provision of care than is the number of children (Knodel, Saengtienchai, and Obiero, 1995). These findings suggest that declines in fertility in Third World countries will not necessarily result in declines in elder care.

One way to determine how verticalization of intergenerational families is related to horizontal family relationships is to use the technique of microsimulation (Laslett, 1988; Wolf, Soldo and Freedman, 1996). Microsimulation uses probabilistic methods to model kinship structures over time based on assumptions regarding behaviors such as marriage and childbearing. For example, using the observed distribution of births by parity and mother's age in Taiwan in 1985, researchers (Tu et al., 1993) have projected that continued dependence on children for elder care in the future will mean a large number of elders will have no source of support and adult children will have to shoulder a large financial burden. However, not all projections are negative. Although kin numbers are being reduced over time in China as a result of the one-child policy, leaving fewer adult children to care for their elderly parents, this trend is being offset by the increased longevity of elder kin at horizontal levels, such as spouses and siblings (Yang, 1992).

In addition to longer years of shared lives for family members at horizontal levels, another consequence of increased longevity is that grandparents can expect to see their grandchildren grow into adulthood (Uhlenberg, 1996). Today it is more the rule than the exception for grandparents to have at least one grandchild who has reached adulthood. In a study of intergenerational family structures in seven economically developed nations, Farkas and Hogan (1995) find that slightly more than half the population age 65 and older have a grandchild who is at least 18 years old. This percentage is consistent with a 1990 study of intergenerational relations conducted in the US, which shows that 56 percent of those 65 years of age and older have at least one adult grandchild (Bengtson and Harootyan, 1994). For children, then, it is now common to reach adulthood in families of three or more generations. Fewer than half of the US adolescents living in 1900 had two or more grandparents alive, but by 1976 that figure had grown to almost 90 percent (Uhlenberg, 1980). Still, we know relatively little about these increasingly common adult intergenerational relationships because they were so rare until recently.

## The influence of social change on intergenerational families

At the close of the twentieth century, changing social norms concerning family roles and relationships resulted in dramatic shifts in singlehood, cohabitation, divorce, and childlessness. Lifelong singlehood, which once was rare, is increasingly common among more recent cohorts of adults. Nearly one in ten Europeans and one in twelve Americans never marry. Today in the US more than one-quarter of married couples lived together before marriage (Smith, 1999), and in some European nations cohabiting is even more common and may be a substitute for marriage (Rothenbacher, 1995). A third of European marriages end in divorce (Rothenbacher, 1995), as do a similar proportion of American marriages (Smith, 1999), fueling projections of divorce among ever married people that reach 50 percent (Smith, 1999). An increasing proportion of households include few or no children. At the same time, the age at which children leave home is increasing, and more adult children are returning to their parents' homes for a time (Goldscheider and Goldscheider, 1993), or remaining longer (Schnailberg and Goldenberg, 1989). Thus, the structure and patterns of intergenerational family relations across the life course are changing around the world.

The last half of the twentieth century produced a greater diversity in intergenerational family structures and roles as well (Bengtson, Rosenthal and Burton, 1996). These new intergenerational structures and roles include: (a) both large and small age differences between generations, (b) non-marital childbearing, (c) an increase in step-relations, (d) gay and lesbian families, (e) matriarchal families, (f) differential acculturation of family generations, and (g) childlessness. Each of these structures and roles is discussed below. This diversity reveals there is no single type of intergenerational family.

### AGE CONDENSED/GAPPED INTERGENERATIONAL PATTERNS

In a minority of intergenerational families, there has been an increase in age-condensed intergenerational patterns resulting from "off-time" childbearing. Early childbearing often occurs across multiple generations which can result in age differences of just 15–18 years between each of five or six generations. On the other hand, age-gapped intergenerational patterns have also increased: delayed parenting creates extensions in the length of time between generations. In European Union nations, the average age at which women first give birth is now 29 (Eurostat, 2002). In the US, delayed childbearing is most prevalent among well-educated, professional women (Boyd and Treas, 1989), sometimes creating an age difference between generations as wide as 35–40 years. With the development of the science of endocrinology and improvements in fertility treatments, this trend may grow.

### NONMARITAL CHILDBEARING

Today, fewer people marry before having children. One third of children born in the US and in many European nations are born to unmarried mothers (Smith, 1999). While this does not necessarily mean fathers are absent from the lives of their children, it may make family ties more fluid and more ambiguous. This suggests that roles and responsibilities for family members across the life course, such as childrearing and caregiving, may be less clearly defined and more dependent on the nature and quality of individual relationships than on traditional family roles.

## STEP-PARENTING AND STEP-GRANDPARENTING

In the West, marriage remains popular, though it occurs increasingly later and is not particularly stable. Divorce rates that climbed in the 1960s, 1970s, and 1980s have stabilized, and most divorced people remarry (Bumpass, Sweet, and Martin, 1990). Of these, one in five will divorce again; many will marry for a third time. This pattern of serial marriage has important implications for intergenerational family life, including (1) greater uncertainty in establishing long-term ties between parents and their biological and stepchildren, and (2) the declining family role of divorced fathers who tend to not get custody of their biological children and who tend to remarry to become stepfathers to another set of children (Furstenberg and Cherlin, 1991).

## GAY AND LESBIAN FAMILIES

A growing literature documents alternative family forms in old age, such as gay and lesbian couplehood. Though the implications of these family types for aging only recently have begun to be investigated, it is clear that there will be a growing number of acknowledged gay and lesbian households (Peplau, 1991; Kimmel, 1992). This is likely due to increasing acceptance and recognition of these arrangements. The aging of these partnerships – some with children and most without (Stacey and Biblarz, 2001) – will be a focus for understanding how nontraditional families cope with intergenerational roles and aging members. However, some evidence suggests that gay and lesbian individuals develop social networks which produce extended-family-like structures, or "fictive kin," that may be quite functional for providing support and care in later life, whether or not traditional sources of family support are available (Kimmel 1992).

## MATRIARCHAL FAMILIES

Women-headed family patterns are increasingly common, particularly in light of growing nonmarital childbearing. In some ethnic groups, older women are often called on by their daughters and granddaughters to serve as surrogate parents for their offspring (Burton, 1995). When older women share a household with their daughters and grandchildren, they often assist with childrearing and help to relieve the economic pressures of single parenthood, thereby placing these older women in positions of power and responsibility.

## ACCULTURATION OF IMMIGRANT FAMILIES

Migrating from traditional, familistic cultures to Western, more individualistic societies can profoundly influence intergenerational family life. Successive waves of ethnic groups arriving in the Europe and in the US over the last century often successfully adapted to the norms of the dominant culture of their new countries. Newer immigrants to North America and Europe, many from Central and South (Latin) America, the Middle East, and Northern Africa, as well as Asia, are doing so, as well. However, acculturation may potentially disrupt intergenerational relations in the immigrant family by weakening the otherwise strong obligation that family members feel toward each other (Silverstein and Chen, 1999; Giarrusso et al., 2001).

In cohorts of immigrant families the process of acculturation typically intensifies with time as succeeding generations are increasingly exposed to and influenced by the mainstream culture. There are fears that when younger immigrants to Western countries achieve economic success, they are also more likely to adopt the more individualistic values of the mainstream culture that clash with the more traditional values of older generations. Some evidence supports the hypothesis that the offspring of immigrants display weaker norms of familism than their immigrant parents who were foreign-born, raising questions about the viability of family support for elderly family members in a culture that traditionally values such support. Evidence also suggests that the slow acquisition of the language of the new host nation may contribute to distress among older immigrants by increasing their risk of isolation from community members (Silverstein and Chen, 1999).

### CHILDLESSNESS

The most truncated intergenerational family form consists of the childless. Fertility in most European countries is below replacement level, suggesting that many adults are choosing to remain childless (Eurostat, 2002). Although childlessness is less common in the US, it is a growing trend there as well. Childlessness has special implications for later life. Compared to the old-old (people age 85 and older) and the middle-old (people age 75–84), the young-old (people age 65–74) tend to have lower rates of childlessness because they are the parents of the baby-boomers. However, due to changes in lifestyle choices (especially among women who have unprecedented access to contraception, education, and career opportunities) in the future, childlessness may increase among the elderly. Perhaps one in five American baby-boomers will reach old age without children. Since childlessness is a risk factor for institutionalization, people without children in this cohort will need to develop alternative family ties or plan and arrange for paid care services, especially in countries where the state does not provide for long-term care of chronic medical conditions or cognitive impairments.

### "THE FAMILY?," OR "TYPES OF FAMILIES?"

As economic, historical, and social changes have profoundly altered the structure of families, it has become increasingly more difficult to talk about "the family" as though a singular form and monolithic patterns exist in the family institution. It now makes sense to talk about "types of families." What the changes and evidence highlight is the rapidly increasing diversity of family forms. But how have these changes affected family relationships over the life course and the ways that families function in providing nurturance and support for their members?

## Intergenerational Family Solidarity and Conflict

### The co-survival of generations

Today's historically unprecedented situation of many individuals entering old age with their own parents still alive means that people will spend more years in family roles and relationships than ever before. The phenomena of more generations alive together is called the *co-survival of generations.*

What do we mean by *generations*? This term is employed frequently in both common vernacular (especially in the media) and in scholarly writing. But the meaning of the term may be unclear, especially if used interchangeably with *cohorts.* Sociologists usually reserve the term *generations* to refer to microsocial relationships in family lineages and kinship linkages. *Cohorts* are macrosocial categories based on year of birth and refer to groups of people who experience the same historical events and conditions at the same ages. Yet another term, *historical generations*, is sometimes used by social historians, such as Karl Mannheim, to denote age cohorts who, typically during their youth, develop distinct self-definitions and become agents of social change. The distinction between generations and cohorts is further blurred by political debates in many Western nations about *generational equity*, concerns regarding the distribution of resources and power in society among different age groups (cohorts) to the detriment of another (Bengtson et al., 1991). We use generations to refer to family relationships, and cohorts to refer to age groups in discussing the implications of changing demographics.

By 2020, most middle-aged adults will have a surviving parent, compared to less than one in five in the 1960s (Uhlenberg, 1996). Today, children and parents may share 50 or more years of life. This means that adults will spend more years as an adult child of an aging parent than as the parent of children under age 18 (Bengtson, Rosenthal, and Burton, 1996). In addition, women now at age 70 are twice as likely to have a husband alive than they would have 100 years ago. Grandparents typically live to know their grandchildren as adults (Uhlenberg, 1996). So, although child-rearing remains an important function and focus of families, an increasing proportion of the life course centers on relations among adult family members.

This has led many family researchers to examine the consequences of the co-survival of generations in terms of intergenerational family solidarity and conflict. For example, is there greater potential for solidarity across generations because of "longer years of shared lives," or is there an equal potential for having long-term conflicted relationships? Research suggests that the answer is not clear-cut. At any one time, intergenerational family relations typically reflect varying degrees of solidarity, conflict, and ambivalence (Bengtson et al., 2000).

## The solidarity model of intergenerational relations

Assessing the nature of intergenerational relationships to compare the strength of relationships – over time, across groups, and in relation to life-course events and transitions – requires a common set of dimensions and measures. The concept of *intergenerational solidarity* has become a paradigm for assessing the multifaceted aspects of family relationships over long periods of time and examining their consequences for the well-being of family members (Bengtson and Schrader, 1982; Silverstein and Bengtson, 1997).

Solidarity refers to the multiple dimensions of sentiment, interaction, and cohesion in intergenerational relations between parents and children or grandparents and grandchildren (Bengtson, Olander, and Haddad, 1976). The dimensions of solidarity are: (1) *affectual solidarity*, the sentiments and emotional evaluations of a relationship with a parent, child, or grandparent; (2) *associational solidarity*, the type and frequency of interaction between two family members of different generations; (3)

*consensual solidarity*, how closely the generations within a family agree on values, opinions, and orientations; (4) *functional solidarity*, the exchange of material and instrumental support and assistance between generations; (5) *normative solidarity*, the shared expectations about intergenerational support and filial obligations; and (6) *structural solidarity*, the opportunities the generations have for interaction based on the number, gender, and geographic proximity of intergenerational family members.

A growing body of research suggests that intergenerational solidarity has positive consequences for both younger and older generations. Positive memories of early childhood relationships with their parents are associated with greater concern and support for aging parents by adult children (Silverstein, Parrott, and Bengtson, 1995). Aging parents' solidarity with adult children also enhances their well-being and decreases their mortality risks (Silverstein and Bengtson, 1991; Wang, Silverstein, and Bengtson, 1999). In addition, rather than older individuals relying on younger generations for support, the improved economic security among many of today's aging cohorts makes it possible for some older family members to assist younger family members in need. These new intergenerational links may strengthen older adults' roles within the family while bolstering the economic welfare of younger generation and family cohesion (Kohli, 1999).

Research using the multidimensional solidarity model indicates that, rather than either being very cohesive or very distant, intergenerational family relationships vary considerably on this dimension. Silverstein and Bengtson (1997) found five general types of relationships between adult children and their parents in a nationally representative sample of Americans: (1) *tight-knit*, where children engage with parents on five dimensions of solidarity; (2) *sociable*, with interaction, proximity, shared values and closeness, but no exchanges of help and support; (3) *obligatory*, including frequent contact, proximity, and exchanges of assistance, but relations lack closeness and shared values; (4) *intimate but distant*, characterized by closeness and shared vales, but without proximity, frequent contact, or exchanges of assistance; and (5) *detached*, as children and parents are not engaged on any dimension of solidarity. In the US, more than half of all adult children have tight-knit or sociable relationships with their parents. About one in five adults experiences an intimate but distant or obligatory relationship with their parents. The detached type of relationship is rare between adult children and mothers, but up to 25 percent of adult children have detached relationships with fathers, usually due to the parents' divorce. Of course, family relationships differ tremendously and these categories do not capture all the variations, but these classifications are helpful in developing typologies of the complexity and contradictions of family life.

## Intergenerational family conflict

Disagreement, competition, and conflict can coexist with order, stability, and cooperation within the family and between generations (Bengtson, Rosenthal, and Burton, 1996). *Conflict* may emerge through a collision of individuals' agendas and interests, as a result of tactics or responses to the clash of interests, or because of one person's hostility toward others (Straus, 1979). Conflict is inherent in family relationships, and intergenerational families typically embody elements of both solidarity and conflict, rather than extremes representing either harmony and refuge or anger and abuse.

Research on intergenerational family conflict shows that adult children and their parents tend to disagree on a variety of issues. Clarke et al. (1999) identified six general sources of intergenerational conflict between aging American parents and their adult children: (1) differences in communication and interaction style; (2) personal habits and lifestyles; (3) child rearing practices and values, (4) politics, religion and ideology, (5) work orientations, and (6) household maintenance. These findings suggest that conflict is an integral part of ongoing intergenerational relationships, and differences in values, preferences, and attitudes may create friction between parents and adult children.

Intergenerational relationships involve solidarity and conflict, positive and negative feelings, tensions, and uncertainties. Some past research and popular portrayals tend to characterize the family either as harmonious and idyllic or as dysfunctional and abusive. Such extremes are inaccurate representations that ignore the complexities of families both past and present. Additional concepts have been established to capture the presence of both solidarity and conflict in intergenerational families; these include ambivalence and ambiguity.

## AMBIVALENCE

Family relationships typically involve both positive and negative sentiments – such as affection and resentment – as well as conflicts between family roles, such as being the mother of dependent children and the primary caregiver for aged parents. Luescher and Pillemer (1998) proposed "ambivalence" as a new perspective in the study of intergenerational relationships. Intergenerational ambivalence connotes contradictions in relationships both at the psychological level, where people experience contradictory feelings, motivations, and thoughts; and at the sociological level, where social norms, roles, and statuses come into conflict in intergenerational family relations. For instance, in rapidly changing Asian cultures, the traditional norm of filial piety is coming into conflict with opportunities and expectations for women to participate in the workforce rather than be caregivers to their parents-in-law, creating ambivalence about obligations to extended family members (Bengtson and Putney, 2000). Ambivalence stems from tensions between autonomy and dependence; conflicting norms and values about family, mutual dependency, and obligations; status transitions and their inherent gains and losses; and ambiguous expectations accompanying changes in family structures and roles. However, because ambivalence has proven difficult to operationalize and measure, research evidence in this area has as yet been limited. As a result, little is known about the extent of ambivalence in intergenerational relations, its causes and consequences, or how it differs from such constructs as role conflict and dimensions of solidarity (Bengtson et al., 2002).

## AMBIGUITY

Changes in intergenerational family structures and cultural norms surrounding family life also contribute to greater ambiguity in intergenerational relations. "Ambiguity" is reflected in undefined roles and uncertainty over expectations for relationships, such as contemporary stepparent–stepchildren relations. Given the increasing structural diversity of families today, new conceptual approaches to understanding intergenerational relations are needed. Pauline Boss (1999) explores the boundary ambiguity in intergenerational relations that also can occur when family members are physically present but psychologically absent (as in the case of family members with severe Alzheimer's disease), or when family members are physically absent but psychologically present (as in the case of some noncustodial divorced fathers living apart from their minor age children). The growing body of evidence about ambiguity and its consequences in families suggests that this will become a useful perspective in understanding intergenerational relationships as they are affected by trends in nonmarital childbearing, divorce, cohabitation, and remarriage.

## Parents and adult children

Despite persistent portrayals of the elderly as abandoned by their families, adult children and their parents demonstrate considerable solidarity (Bengtson and Harootyan, 1994). In addition, the parent–child tie appears to be increasingly important with the growing number of years of life the two generations share – currently, upwards of five decades. Parents and their adult children typically feel a great deal of affection for each other (Lye, 1996).

However, parents of all ages express greater affection toward their children than their children express toward them. This generational asymmetry in affection, called the *intergenerational stake phenomenon*, was originally attributed to the need of the younger generation to establish its independence and the need of the older generation for generational continuity and stability (Bengtson and Kuypers, 1971). The persistence of this pattern across the life course suggests that it may have more to do with asymmetrical patterns of intergenerational exchange: generations higher in the intergenerational chain invest more in the relationship than those lower in the intergenerational chain, leading parents to see the relationship in a more favorable light than children (Giarrusso, Stallings, and Bengtson, 1995).

Parents and adult children are in contact frequently, in person or by telephone. Mothers and daughters have more frequent contact than other parent–child pairs, perhaps reflecting women's traditional kin-keeping role. Widowed parents have more contact with their children than married or divorced parents, and unmarried children are in contact with their parents more often than married children. European and American parents and children usually do not share a household (Bengtson and Putney, 2000), although after age 75 co-residence with children is not uncommon among some minority ethnic groups in the US (Quadagno, 1999) and in many southern European nations (Pampel, 1992).

Parents and adult children also exchange various types of assistance. Emotional support is the type of help most frequently exchanged. However, when it comes to other types of assistance, each generation tends to provide the other with different kinds of help (Logan and Spitze, 1996). Parents are more likely to give their adult children help with child care, financial assistance, and advice than they are to receive such help. Adult children are more likely to give their parents instrumental assistance with household chores, repairs, and personal care. Parents tend to receive more help than they give after age 75, but until then they provide more help than they get from their children. Expectations about caring for older family members, or norms of filial responsibility, are another aspect of intergenerational solidarity. Although aging parents in Western societies generally do not expect their adult children to take care of them, most adult children today feel a high degree of filial responsibility (Bengtson and Harootyan, 1994).

Changes in living arrangements typically accompany population aging and changed family structures. The elderly in traditional, familistic societies are far more likely to live with their children, while elders in the modern, individualistic societies more commonly live alone or with a spouse only (Bengtson and Putney, 2000). However, industrialization often produces migration from rural communities to urban areas. For instance, although a traditional, familistic society, Korea has a large proportion of young people who have moved into cities, leaving many aging parents behind in rural areas. Co-residence is declining in Korea, China, and Japan contributing to an increase in the number of elderly living with spouse only or alone (Bengtson and Putney, 2000; Chen and Silverstein, 2000; Ujimoto, 1999). The traditional residence patterns of the elderly in Eastern and Western nations are different, but becoming more similar.

Household sizes have declined over the last several decades in Western nations, and more elderly live alone. Longevity, widowhood and divorce, and non-marriage among very elderly women contribute to the growth in the elderly living alone. However, this trend is mostly due to the preference of older individuals to remain independent and their ability to do so with the aid of public and private pensions (McGarry and Schoeni, 1995).

## Grandparents and grandchildren

The tie between grandparents and grandchildren appears to be meaningful to both generations, representing family continuity and linking the past with the future. Uhlenberg (1996) has pointed out that grandparent availability increased dramatically over the last century: only 24 percent of the 1900 birth cohort were born with all four of their grandparents alive, as contrasted with 68 percent today. As a result, grandparents represent a newly available resource for the family to rely upon in the event of a crisis or ongoing strains (Bengtson, 2001).

The grandparent role may take several forms, depending in part on the age and health of the grandparent, their geographic proximity to the grandchildren, and the grandparents' relationships with the grandchildren's parents (Bengtson, 1985). The solidarity model of intergenerational relationships also has been used to examine the quality of grandparent–grandchild relations. Although both grandparents and adult grandchildren report feeling close to one another, grandparents report a greater degree of closeness than do adult grandchildren (Bengtson et al., 2000). And, although affectual solidarity between grandparents and young grandchildren is influenced by the middle generation (Cherlin and Furstenberg, 1986), adult grandchildren feel close to grandparents after they leave their parental house (Kennedy, 1992). Further, young adult grandchildren report that close relationships with grandparents remain even when there is a divorce in the parental generation (Cooney and Smith, 1996).

Similarity in beliefs and values, or consensual solidarity, between grandparents and grandchildren is generally taken as evidence of successful socialization to the social structure of adult life (Troll and Bengtson, 1979). Grandparents in particular are considered as "wardens of culture" guarding against deculturation (Gutmann, 1975).

The grandparent–grandchild relationship is also influenced by structural solidarity: not only a variety of demographic and personal characteristics, such as the number of grandchildren in the family, the age, gender, and health of the grandparents (Bengtson, 1985), but also by how geographically close the grandparents are to the grandchildren's parents, and whether the grandchildren's parents are divorced (Cherlin and Furstenberg, 1986).

Regarding associational solidarity, grandparents and grandchildren do stay in regular contact (Kivett, 1985), at least when this is not impeded by the divorce of the parents. Divorce has a particularly harsh effect on the relationship between grandparents and grandchildren whose parents have not been given custody – usually the father.

Scholarly interest in grandparenting has grown in recent years, prompted by recognition of the valued role that grandparents, particularly grandmothers, play in caring for their grandchildren. Such care ranges from babysitting, allowing both parents to work, to being a full-time guardian for the grandchild when the parents are no longer willing or able to fulfill their parenting duties. Most striking is the steep increase in the percentage of American grandparents who are raising a grandchild. As many as one in ten American grandparents may care for a grandchild for at least six months at some time in their lives. While some of the extraordinary contribution by grandparents is involuntary (due to dysfunctions in the middle generation, such as drug addiction, unemployment, incarceration, and divorce), much of the supportive activities represent the fulfillment of a fundamental family obligation felt by grandparents toward their children and grandchildren (Giarrusso et al., 2001).

There is general consensus in the field of sociology that family disruptions, most significantly parental divorce, place many adolescents and young adults at risk of psychological, social, and economic distress (Amato and Booth, 1997; Furstenberg and Cherlin, 1991). Grandparents, especially grandmothers, can (and often do) provide resources that may serve to offset, or buffer, the negative consequences of divorce on their grandchildren. To the extent that single mothers and other distressed parents experience strains from both family and work obligations following divorce, the amount of time they have to spend with children will decrease. However, if grandparent involvement with children increases as parents' time with children declines, this may help to compensate for declines in parents' time with their children and may reduce the risk of negative outcomes for children in disrupted families (Bengtson, 2001).

Much of the research on grandparents has tended to categorize styles of grandparenting into a set of distinct types. Although these studies use different sampling frames, focus on different aspects of the relationship, and consider different family life-stages, they all point to substantial heterogeneity in the way that grandparent styles are adopted. In the most seminal of these studies, Cherlin and Furstenberg (1986) classified relationship styles between grandparents and their adolescent grandchildren into five types: (1) detached, (2) passive, (3) influential, (4) supportive, and (5) authoritative. Interestingly, they found that no one type of style constituted a clear majority. The absence of a modal type of grandparent style implies substantial variability in the ways that grandparents enact their roles, and suggests that there are few universal elements in this role. Indeed, there is evidence as well that grandparent roles have become more diverse over historical time; however, they will be no less important.

## The Debate about Families

### Changing family roles in caregiving

The demographic changes which have led to the co-survival of generations have implications for solidarity and conflict in intergenerational family relations over the life course. "Longer years of shared lives" may mean that adult children could spend more years caring for elderly parents than they spend in raising their own children (Bengtson, Rosenthal, and Burton, 1996). Will caregiving to older parents extend into the later life of the adult child? If so, how will that affect the quality of life of the elderly child in terms of retirement and financial planning? Will the empty-nest phase of life fade into the caregiving phase? Will retirement, as we have recently come to know it as a leisure-oriented time of life (Blaikie, 1999), become a time to care for very old parents?

In developed and developing countries, it is argued, there are now four phases of life: (1) childhood; (2) independence, responsibility, and earning; (3) retirement; and (4) dependence and death (Laslett, 1987). The third phase of life, which Laslett has termed the "Third Age," should be a time when individuals realize life goals. That is, retirement should not be a time of leisure but rather an time for older adults to be actively pursuing second careers, volunteering for social causes, continuing their education, and so on. Will caregiving responsibilities interfere with this Third Age freedom, and consequently diminish the quality of intergenerational family relations? Might adult children abandon their care of elderly parents?

## Is the family in decline?

In the West, population aging, delayed marriage and parenthood, divorce and remarriage, childbearing outside of marriage, and same-sex relationships produce an array of family forms and living arrangements. In the US, some social critics take these changes as indications of the declining importance of the family and its failure to perform its traditional functions of rearing children and caring for the elderly. In regard to older individuals, many believe that elderly Americans are isolated or abandoned by their families (Bengtson, Rosenthal and Burton, 1995). But other scholars contend that the evidence suggests that contemporary families have not declined in their importance or in valuing the roles and responsibilities that their members play in each other's lives. Although other social institutions, such as the state and formal education, have supplanted some traditional family functions typical in the early twentieth century, a growing body of research suggests that intergenerational family members are not isolated from one another, but maintain strong supportive bonds and provide emotional and instrumental support when needed (Bengtson, 2001). This support does not depend on co-residence or even residential proximity (Silverstein and Bengtson, 1997).

Much recent debate in family studies and family sociology has revolved around the issue of whether or not families are in decline as a central institution in social life, and thus the source of many societal ills such as the isolation of the elderly from their families (Bengtson, 2001). Much of the family decline thesis stems from the theoretical orientations deriving from the same stream of ideas that created disengagement theory (Cummings and Henry, 1961), which proposed that it was necessary for older people to be "left behind" for the younger generation of adults to achieve its greatest success. This position was held by sociologist Talcott Parsons (1949), who viewed the elderly as slowing economic progress because families were more adaptable and mobile when they were smaller. Goode (1970) noted that economic development of a nation was usually associated with the nuclearization of family structure, the change from households that were extended (that is, multiple adult generations and children) to families that were nuclear (only parents and their dependent children).

Most recently, the debate about family decline moved to moral and political terms as neo-conservatives, especially in the US, have used the term "declining family values" to capture what they see as the erosion of family life. They claim that the family is no longer equipped to nurture its members and care for their old. Proponents of the "family decline" hypothesis, such as conservative sociologist David Popenoe (1993), emphasize the negative consequences of changing family structure resulting from divorce and single-parenting for the well-being of dependent children and older adults.

Is the family declining in importance? Is this a useful and productive avenue of debate about the changes in contemporary family life? Proponents of the "family decline" thesis maintain that social norms legitimating the pursuit of individual over collective goals and the availability of alternative social groups for the satisfaction of basic human needs have fatally weakened the family as a source of nurturance for young and old alike (Bengtson, 2001). Earlier social theorists such as Ernest Burgess (1928) and William Ogburn (1933) noted that families in modern, urban societies were more reliant on public institutions, such as schools, hospitals, and transportation, to satisfy basic human needs. As a result, the family was reduced to fulfilling just two functions: emotional intimacy and procreation (Burgess, 1960).

With regard to the multigenerational family, decline proponents rely on several trends to portray a shift away from kinship as an important social institution for the aged. One focus is the residential independence of elderly parents from their adult children as a sign that the family has lost its earlier function of serving the needs of older, dependent members. According to the family decline thesis, the trend away from intergenerational co-residence and the tendency of children to live at far distances from their parents signal decline in the function of the family as a source of support and security for elders. But research shows that most elderly individuals remain in regular contact with their children, whether or not they live nearby (Lye, 1996).

A second social trend cited as eroding the family's role in caring for its older members is the increase in women's paid employment. Dual-earner families, in conjunction with expanded education and occupational opportunities for women, substantially increased the labor-force participation of women. While much evidence suggests that working mothers do no harm and may benefit children (Menaghan and Parcel 1990; Perry-Jenkins, Repetti, and Crouter, 2000), women's labor-force participation may strain the capacity of the family to provide for older generations, a stressor often added to existing child-caring responsibilities. The small percentage of women who provide care for both younger dependent children and older parents at the same time are known as "the sandwiched generation" of those squeezed between two generations of dependent family members. This trend is more common among professional women who tend to delay childbearing, and therefore are the most likely to have school-age children in the household when their parents are approaching an age that puts them at risk for physical impairments.

Some scholars also interpret the large geographic distances between adult generations in the family as evidence that the intergenerational family is in decline. The demands of long-distance caregiving to older parents is a growing multigenerational family issue in a geographically mobile society. With mobility increasing in developing nations, and members of younger generations leaving home for work in the industrialized cities, older individuals may be left without family to provide care – an especially dire circumstance in developing countries where formal (paid) care services to fill the gap are rare (Bengtson and Putney, 2000). Still, much research shows that regardless of distance, older parents and their adult children have regular contact and exchange social support (Lye, 1996). Further, in Western Europe and the US, more than half of adult children live within a one-hour drive of their parents (Kohli, 1999; Lawton, Silverstein, and Bengtson, 1994).

A third social trend that family decline proponents point to is a relative weakening of attitudes regarding responsibility to family that serve as the basis for maintaining strong intergenerational commitment. Some scholars have noted a slight decline in the strength of filial obligation since the 1970s in both the more individualistic Western societies and the more familistic and collective societies of the East (Bengtson and Putney, 2000). However, the sense of responsibility for the care of aged family members remains strong (Rossi and Rossi, 1990).

Finally, increases in the use of group living quarters and formal care, particularly long-term care services, are cited by some social critics as a sign that families have abandoned their responsibility for the elderly. In the US, rates of institutionalization of the elderly nearly doubled in the 30 years following the institution of limited government funding for nursing-home care in 1974. However, today less than 5 percent of US elderly are institutionalized (Maddox, 2001), and families in industrialized nations still provide more than 90 percent of needed care to the elderly (Rein and Saltzman, 1995). Around the world, families still provide most of their elderly members' long-term care needs. It does not appear that government policies undermine family care, as some conservative scholars suggest. Instead, perhaps formal care services and institutions fill existing needs of families who require alternative means for providing chronic care to older members that they are unable to supply.

## Resilience and adaptation in contemporary families

While the family decline debate has generated much heat, especially in the often oversimplified terms of political discourse, it has shed little light. The more important issue is not *whether* families are changing, but *how* they are changing in the context of profound economic, social, and technological shifts. By examining intergenerational family life along a number of dimensions, it becomes clear that families remain the central source of nurturance and support for young and old members alike.

### INTERGENERATIONAL CONTACT

Contemporary research documents that the extended family maintains cross-generational cohesion through modern communication and transportation technologies that allow contact in spite of social forces that distance family members. Studies of intergenerational family relations revealed that parents and adult children are not isolated but frequently interact even when separated by large geographic distances (Lye, 1996). One feature of the "modified-extended" family is the capacity to respond to the needs of its members despite geographic distance. This is exemplified in the "latent kin matrix" suggested by Riley and Riley (1993), with its emphasis on contingent family relationships which remain latent when not needed for support, and become quickly activated when required to provide help in a crisis involving a family member.

## NORMS OF FAMILISM

The strength of obligation and positive regard across generations is little diminished by geographic separation suggesting a pattern characterized as "intimacy-at-a-distance" (Rosenmayer and Kockeis, 1963). American and European surveys show that the strength of intergenerational responsibility for older parents, or norms of filial obligation, appears to be quite strong even among adult children who live at great distances from their aging parents (Silverstein et al., 1998; Kohli, 1999).

Norms of familism also govern the provision of care and support among family members as a central tenet of many traditional cultures around the world. The Confucian ethic of "filial piety" in Asian cultures requires respect and care for family elders and helps to maintain family order by promoting interdependence, responsibility, sacrifice, and harmony; and viewing oneself and others in relation to the family (Bengtson and Putney, 2000). Familism and its emphasis on the collective contrasts with Western individualism and its emphasis on independence, self-reliance, and self-fulfillment (Sung, 2000). Despite advancing industrialization, extended family patterns in Japan, Korea, and China remain more traditional and familistic than most Western industrialized societies (Kojima, 2000). Familism also is central to intergenerational relationships in Central and South America, where multigenerational households are more common than in North America and Europe (Cherlin, 1999).

Still, norms of familism and filial piety are changing in many traditional societies due to greater industrialization and urbanization (modernization) of these societies. In Korea and China, extensive migration patterns recently have made filial piety through co-residence more difficult; older parents expect to rely on their children less, and many now prefer to live separately from adult children (Yoon, Eun, and Park, 2000). In some rapidly aging societies, policies that promote respect for the elderly and preserve of traditional family care of the elderly reflect social concern over changes in filial piety and the impending cost of caring for an aging population (Bengtson and Putney, 2000; Sung, 2000). However, Chow (1999) predicts that long-held values of filial piety will govern behavior in Chinese families as long as the family remains the fundamental unit in society.

## INTERGENERATIONAL RELATIONSHIPS AND ECONOMIC WELL-BEING

The advent of pensions and state old-age support programs have endowed today's older cohorts with resources that make new exchanges between generations possible (Kohli, 1999). Adults now reach old age with different levels of personal and family resources than their parents and grandparents did. Economic solidarity between generations is strong, with the net transfers going down the generational ladder, from older to younger family members. Data from economically developed countries such as France and Germany (Kohli, 1999) and the US (McGarry and Schoeni 1995) demonstrate that the elderly have become net providers to, rather than depending upon, younger generations.

## HEALTH IMPROVEMENTS AND FAMILY SUPPORT

Recent studies indicate that health is improving among the elderly in many nations, resulting in a compression of morbidity into fewer years, at the very end of life.

Improvements in health habits and technological developments in health care have produced the healthiest older population in human history. This raises the possibility that, in the early twenty-first century, less family support for the aged will be required as the result of improved health and wealth in subsequent cohorts of elderly family members.

### KINSHIP EXPANSION AND THE INCREASING IMPORTANCE OF MULTIGENERATIONAL RELATIONSHIPS

Although nuclear families have been getting smaller in recent decades, Bengtson (2001) has proposed the hypothesis that in the twenty-first century multigenerational relationships will become increasingly important for the well-being of family members, for both younger and older generations. Testing the validity of this hypothesis will, of course, require data collected over the next several decades. The basis for the hypothesis is the increase in "shared lives" or co-survival of generations over time, such that (1) the increase in the number of generations alive at the same time potentially increases the amount of *time* generations will have to interact and exchange with others. In addition, (2) trends in divorce and remarriage will increase the sheer *number* of kin who feel a sense of responsibility to provide support for those identified as "family members." Consequently, (3) family relationships and the sense of responsibility to and rewards from them will increasingly depend on social, not biological, definitions of "family ties."

## Conclusion

Providing care and support to the elderly is a common concern for multigenerational families in nations around the world. Where government funding traditionally has provided high levels of support to elders, such as in the Scandinavian countries, today's aging populations are making it increasingly difficult to fund generous state welfare benefits (Pampel, 1998). In countries where elders traditionally have relied almost exclusively on their families to meet their financial and personal care needs, factors such as migration, geographic mobility, and more individualistic values mean that older people may not be able to depend solely on their families for their care. Nonetheless, around the world, families still provide most of the support that is required by their elders.

Thus, while the structure and interactions of intergenerational families have changed significantly in the last century, they remain important to their members, both young and old, and to society. Families continue to serve as the principal site of socialization and rearing of children and of support and care for the aged. The intergenerational family provides individuals with a sense of security, continuity, and identity. Social change greatly affected family life across the twentieth century. Yet the intergenerational family, in its increasingly diverse forms, appears to be a remarkably adaptive social institution that will remain crucial to the well-being of individuals and societies in the twenty-first century.

## References

Amato, P., and Booth, A. (1997) *A Generation at Risk: Growing Up in an Era of Family Upheaval*. Cambridge, MA: Harvard University Press.

Bengtson, V. L. (1985) Diversity and symbolism in the grandparent role. In V. Bengtson and J. Robertson (eds.), *Grandparenthood*. Beverly Hills, CA: Sage.

Bengtson, V. L. (2001) Beyond the nuclear family: The increasing importance of multigenerational bonds. Burgess Award Lecture. *Journal of Marriage and the Family*, 63, 1–16.

Bengtson, V. L., and Allen, K. (1993) The life course perspective applied to families over time. In P. G. Boss, W. J. Doherty, R. LaRossa, W. R. Schumm, and S. K. Steinmetz (eds.), *Sourcebook of Family Theories and Methods: A Contextual Approach*. New York: Plenum.

Bengtson, V. L., Giarrusso, R., Mabry, J. B., and Silverstein, M. (2002) Solidarity, conflict, and ambivalence: Complementary or competing perspectives on intergenerational relationships? *Journal of Marriage and the Family*, 64, 3, 568–76.

Bengtson, V. L., Giarrusso, R., Silverstein, M., and Wang, H. (2000) Families and intergenerational relationships in aging societies. *Hallym International Journal of Aging*, 2, 3–10.

Bengtson, V. L., and Harootyan, R. (eds.) (1994) *Intergenerational Linkages: Hidden Connections in American Society*. New York: Springer.

Bengtson, V. L., and Kuypers, J. A. (1971) Generational difference and the developmental stake. *Aging and Human Development*, 2, 249–60.

Bengtson, V. L., Marti, G., and Roberts, R. E. L. (1991). Age group relations: Generational equity and inequity. In K. Pillemer and K. McCartney (eds.), *Parent–Child Relations Across the Lifespan*. Hillsdale, NJ: Lawrence Erlbaum.

Bengtson, V. L., Olander, E. B., and Haddad, A. A. (1976) The generation gap and aging family members: Toward a conceptual model. In J. F. Gubrium (ed.), *Time, Roles, and Self in Old Age*. New York: Human Sciences Press.

Bengtson, V. L., and Putney, N. (2000) Who will care for the elderly? Consequences of population aging East and West. In K. D. Kim, V. L. Bengtson, G. C. Meyers, and K. S. Eun (eds.), *Aging East and West: Families, States, and the Elderly*. New York: Springer.

Bengtson, V. L., Rosenthal, C. J., and Burton, L. M. (1996) Paradoxes of families and aging. In R. H. Binstock and L. K. George (eds.), *Handbook of Aging and the Social Sciences*. 4th ed. San Diego: Academic.

Bengtson, V. L., and Schrader, S. S. (1982) Parent–child relations. In D. Mangen and W. Peterson (eds.), *Handbook of Research Instruments in Social Gerontology*, vol. 2. Minneapolis: University of Minnesota Press.

Blaikie, A. (1999) *Ageing and Popular Culture*. Cambridge: Cambridge University Press.

Boss, P. (1999) *Ambiguous Loss: Learning to Live with Unresolved Grief*. Cambridge, MA: Harvard University Press.

Boyd, S., and Treas, J. (1989) Family care of the frail elderly: A new look at women in the middle. *Women's Studies Quarterly*, 112, 66–73.

Bumpass, L. L., Sweet, J., and Martin, C. (1990) Changing patterns of remarriage. *Journal of Marriage and the Family*, 52, 747–56.

Burgess, E. W. (1928) The changing American family. *Religious Education*, 23, May, 408–15.

Burgess, E. W. (1960) Aging in Western culture. In E. W. Burgess (ed.), *Aging in Western Societies*. Chicago: University of Chicago Press.

Burton, L. (1995) Intergenerational patterns of providing care in African-American families with teenage childbearers: Emergent patterns in an ethnographic study. In V. L. Bengtson, K. W. Schaie, and L. M. Burton (eds.), *Adult Intergenerational Relations*. New York: Springer.

Chen, X., and Silverstein, M. (2000) Intergenerational social support and the psychological well-being of older parents in China. *Research on Aging*, 22, 43–65.

Cherlin, A., and Furstenberg, F. (1986) *The New American Grandparent: A Place in the Family, a Life Apart*. New York: Basic Books.

Cherlin, A. J. (1999) *Public and Private Families*. Boston: McGraw-Hill.

Chow, N. (1999) Diminishing filial piety and the changing role and status of the elders in Hong Kong. *Hallym International Journal of Aging*, 1, 67–77.

Clarke, E., Preston, M., Raskin, J., and Bengtson, V. L. (1999) Types of conflicts and tensions between older parents and adult children. *The Gerontologist*, 39, 261–70.

Cooney, T. M., and Smith, L. A. (1996) Young adults' relations with grandparents following recent parental divorce. *Journals of Gerontology: Series B: Psychological Sciences and Social Sciences*, 51B, S91–S95.

Coward, R., and Dwyer, J. (1990) Association of gender, sibling network composition, and patterns of parent care by adult children. *Research on Aging*, 12, 158–81.

Cowgill, D. (1974) The aging of populations and societies. *Annals of the American Academy of Political and Social Science*, 415, 1–18.

Cummings, E., and Henry, H. (1961) *Growing Old: The Process of Disengagement*. New York: Basic Books.

Elder, G. L. (1994) Time, human agency, and social change: Perspectives on the life course. *Social Psychology Quarterly*, 57, 4–15.

Eurostat (2002) People in Europe. *Eurostat Yearbook 2002*. Luxembourg: Office for Official Publications of the European Communities.

Farkas, J., and Hogan, D. (1995) The demography of changing intergenerational relationships. In V. L. Bengtson, K. W. Schaie, and L. M. Burton (eds.), *Adult Intergenerational Relations: Effects of Societal Change*. New York: Springer.

Furstenberg, F., and Cherlin, A. (1991) *Divided Families: What Happens to Children When Parents Part*. Cambridge, MA: Harvard University Press.

Giarrusso, R., Feng, D., Silverstein, M., and Bengtson, V. L. (2001) Grandparent–adult grandchild affection and consensus: Cross-generational and cross-ethnic comparisons. *Journal of Family Issues*, 22, 456–77.

Giarrusso, R., Silverstein, M., Feng, D., and Marenco, A. (2000) Primary and secondary stressors of grandparents raising grandchildren: Evidence from a national survey, *Journal of Mental Health and Aging*, 6, 4, 291–310.

Giarrusso, R., Stallings, M., and Bengtson, V. L. (1995) The "intergenerational stake" hypothesis revisited: Parent–child differences in perceptions of relationships 20 years later. In V. L. Bengtson, K. W. Schaie, and L. M. Burton (eds.), *Adult Intergenerational Relations: Effects of Societal Change*. New York: Springer.

Goldscheider, F. K., and Goldscheider, C. (1993) *Leaving Home before Marriage: Ethnicity, Familism, and Generational Relationships*. Madison: University of Wisconsin Press.

Goode, W. J. (1970) *World Revolution and Family Patterns*. New York: Free Press.

Gutmann, D. L. (1975) Parenting: A key to the comparative study of the life cycle. In N. Datan and L. H. Ginsberg (eds.), *Life-Span Developmental Psychology: Normative Life Crises*. New York: Academic.

Hareven, T. K. (2001) Historical perspectives on aging and family relations. In R.H. Binstock and L.K. George (eds.), *Handbook of Aging and the Social Sciences*. San Diego: Academic.

Kennedy, G. E. (1992) Quality in grandparent/grandchild relationships. *International Journal of Aging and Human Development*, 35, 83–98.

Kimmel, D. (1992) The families of older gay men and lesbians. *Generations*, 16, 37–8.

Kivett, V. (1985) Grandfathers and grandchildren: Patterns of associations, helping, and psychological closeness. *Family Relations*, 34, 565–71.

Kivett, V., and Atkinson, M. (1984) Filial expectations, association, and helping as a function of number of children among older rural-transitional parents. *Journal of Gerontology*, 39, 499–503.

Knodel, J., Saengtienchai, C., and Obiero, W. (1995) Do small families jeopardize old age security? Evidence from Thailand. *Bold*, 5, 13–17.

Kohli, M. (1999) Private and public transfers between generations: Linking the family and the state. *European Societies*, 1, 81–104.

Kojima, H. (2000) Japan: Hyper-aging and its policy implications. In K. D. Kim, V. L. Bengtson, G. C. Meyers, and K. S. Eun (eds.), *Aging East and West: Families, States, and the Elderly*. New York: Springer.

Laslett, P. (1987) Emergence of the Third Age. *Ageing and Society*, 7, 133–60.

Laslett, P. (1988) Kinship and its numerical history. *Annales*, 43, 5–24.

Lawton, L., Silverstein, M., and Bengtson, V. L. (1994) Solidarity between generations in families. In V. L. Bengtson and R. Harootyan (eds.), *Intergenerational Linkages: Hidden Connections in American Society* . New York: Springer.

Logan, J. R., and Spitze, G. D. (1996) *Family Ties: Relations between Parents and their Grown Children*. Philadelphia, PA: Temple University Press.

Luescher, K., and Pillemer, K. (1998) Intergenerational ambivalence: A new approach to the study of parent–child relations in later life. *Journal of Marriage and the Family*, 60, 413–25.

Lye, D. N. (1996) Adult child–parent relationships. *Annual Review of Sociology*, 22, 79–102.

Maddox, G. L. (2001) Housing and living arrangements: A transactional perspective. In R. H. Binstock and L. K. George (eds.), *Handbook of Aging and the Social Sciences*. San Diego: Academic.

McGarry, K., and Schoeni, R. F. (1995) Transfer behavior in the health and retirement study. *Journal of Human Resources*, 30, Supplement, S184–S226.

Menaghan, E. G., and Parcel, T. L. (1990) Parental employment and family life: Research in the 1980s. *Journal of Marriage and the Family*, 52, 1079–98.

Ogburn, W. F. (1933) The family and its functions. In the Report of the President's Committee on Social Trends, *Recent Social Trends in the United States*. Vol. 1. New York: McGraw-Hill.

Pampel, F. (1992) Trends in living alone among the elderly in Europe. In A. Rogers (ed.), *Elderly Migration and Population Redistribution*. London: Belhaven.

Pampel, F. (1998) *Aging, Social Inequality, and Public Policy*. Thousand Oaks, CA: Pine Forge.

Parsons, T. (1949) The social structure of the family. In R. N. Anshen (ed.), *The Family: Its Function and Destiny*. New York: Harper.

Peplau, L. A. (1991) Lesbian and gay relationships. In J. C. Gonsiorek and J. D. Weinrich (eds.), *Homosexuality: Implications for Social Policy*. Newbury Park, CA: Sage.

Perry-Jenkins, M., Repetti, R. L., and Crouter, A. C. (2000) Work and family in the 1990s. *Journal of Marriage and the Family*, 62, 981–98.

Popenoe, D. (1993) American family decline, 1960–1990: A review and appraisal. *Journal of Marriage and the Family*, 55, 527–55.

Quadagno, J. (1999) *Aging and the Life Course*. New York: McGraw-Hill.

Rein, M., and Saltzman, H. (1995) Social integration, participation and exchange in five industrial countries. In S. Bass (ed.), *Older and Alive*. New Haven, CT: Yale University Press.

Riley, M. W., and Riley, J. W. (1993) Connections: Kin and cohort. In V. L. Bengtson and W. A. Achenbaum (eds.), *The Changing Contract across Generations*. New York: Aldine de Gruyter.

Rosenmayer, L., and Kockeis, C. (1963) Propositions for a sociological theory of ageing and the family. *International Social Service Journal*, 15, 410–26.

Rossi, A., and Rossi, P. (1990) *Of Human Bonding: Parent–Child Relations across the Life Course*. New York: Aldine de Gruyter.

Rothenbacher, F. (1995) European family indicators. *Eurodata Newsletter*, 3, article 10.

Schnailberg, A., and Goldenberg, S. (1989) From empty nest to crowded nest: The dynamics of incompletely launched young adult. *Social Problems*, 36, 251–69.

Silverstein, M., and Bengtson, V. L. (1991) Do close parent–child relations reduce the mortality risk of older parents? *Journal of Health and Social Behavior*, 32, 382–95.

Silverstein, M., and Bengtson, V. L. (1997) Intergenerational solidarity and the structure of adult child–parent relationships in American families. *American Journal of Sociology*, 103, 429–60.

Silverstein, M., Burholt, V., Wenger, G. C., and Bengtson, V. L. (1998) Parent–child relations among very old parents in Wales and the US: A test of modernization theory. *Journal of Aging Studies*, 12, 387–409.

Silverstein, M., and Chen, X. (1999) The impact of acculturation in Mexican-American families on the quality of adult grandchild–grandparent relationships. *Journal of Marriage and the Family*, 61, 188–98.

Silverstein, M., Parrott, T. M., and Bengtson, V. L. (1995) Factors that predispose middle-aged sons and daughters to provide social support to older parents. *Journal of Marriage and the Family*, 57, 465–75.

Smith, T. W. (1999) *The Emerging 21st Century American Family*. General Social Survey Social Change Report No. 42. Chicago: National Opinion Research Center, University of Chicago.

Stacey, J., and Biblarz, T. J. (2001) (How) does the sexual orientation of parents matter? *American Sociological Review*, 66, 159–83.

Straus, M. A. (1979) Measuring intrafamily conflict and violence: The Conflict Tactics (CT) Scales. *Journal of Marriage and the Family*, 41, 75–88.

Sung, K. T. (2000) An Asian perspective on aging East and West: Filial piety and changing families. In K. D. Kim, V. L. Bengtson, G. C. Meyers, and K. S. Eun (eds.), *Aging East and West: Families, States, and the Elderly*. New York: Springer.

Troll, L., and Bengtson, V. L. (1979) Generation in the family. In W. Burr, R. Hill, I. Reiss, and I. Nye (eds.), *Theories About the Family*, Vol. 1. New York: Free Press.

Tu, E., Jow, C., Freedman, V. A., and Wolf, D. A. (1993) Kinship and family support in Taiwan: A microsimulation approach. *Research on Aging*, 15, 465–86.

Uhlenberg, P. (1980) Death and the family. *Journal of Family History*, 5, 313–20.

Uhlenberg, P. (1996) Mutual attraction: Demography and life course analysis. *The Gerontologist*, 36, 226–29.

Ujimoto, K. V. (1999) Technology and aging: international perspectives. Paper presented at the Multidisciplinary Research Colloquium Series in Aging, University of Southern California, Los Angeles, October.

UN Population Division (1999) *The State of World Population*. New York: United Nations.

US Population Reference Bureau (1999) *1999 World Population Data Sheet*. Washington, DC: US Government Printing Office.

Wang, H., Silverstein, M., and Bengtson, V. L. (1999) The linkage between parent–child relations and the mortality risk of older parents: Evidence from a longitudinal study over 13 years. Paper presented at the meeting of the Scientific Meetings of the Gerontological Society of America, San Francisco, CA, November.

Wolf, D. A., Soldo, B. J., and Freedman, V. (1996) The demography of family care for the elderly. In T. Hareven (ed.), *Aging and Generational Relations over the Life Course: A Historical and Cross-Cultural Perspective*. New York: Walter de Gruyter.

Yang, H. (1992) Population dynamics and kinship of the Chinese rural elderly: A microsimulation study. *Journal of Cross-Cultural Gerontology*, 7, 135–50.

Yoon, G., Eun, S. I., and Park, K. S. (2000) Demographic trends, sociocultural contexts, and public policy. In K. D. Kim, V. L. Bengtson, G. C. Meyers, and K. S. Eun (eds.), *Aging East and West: Families, States, and the Elderly*. New York: Springer.

# 7

# Children's Families

Jacqueline Scott

The focus of this chapter is on children's families in the context of rapid social change. In the literature, terms like "modern childhood" and "children of postmodernity" are used. The societal changes that have altered the shape of adult lives – secularization, urbanization, industrialization, individualization, and the like – also affect the lives of children. For children, many of the effects of social changes are played out in the context of family life. Families themselves have, as this volume shows, changed markedly in the modern era. The greater diversity of families associated with the increases in childbirth outside of marriage and the high rates of divorce are well known. Changes in maternal work patterns and the changing work–family balance have had consequences for the culture of care, in which children are both recipients and providers. Falling birthrates have resulted in smaller families with fewer siblings. Increased longevity has changed intergenerational relations in ways that are little short of revolutionary. All these changes to the structure of family life have important implications for what, from the child's point of view, is his or her own particular family.

We all tend to take our families for granted while, at the same time, regarding them as unique. When we fall in love, have kids, get divorced, we are bowled over by experiences that are intensely personal. Yet, as sociologists, we are all too aware of how even something as private as having a baby is a highly structured experience. The declining rate of childbirth in Europe, in one sense, is the sum of many individual choices. However, those choices are made in the context of socioeconomic opportunities and constraints which have led to the postponement and reduction of childbirth. Similarly, children's lives are structured in ways that reflect socioeconomic events and changes. Many of these changes are mediated through families because children's lives are codependent on parents and other family members. Yet children's own preferences and actions are also crucial. The study of children's families involves understanding the structure of childhood, the experiences and agency of children, and the dynamic processes that are associated with children's unfolding lives across time and place.

It is now taken as a given that "childhood" is a social construction. In 1960, the now classic book by Philippe Ariès, *Centuries of Childhood*, set the tone for the new sociological interest in children and childhood. The questions he addressed revolved around the origin of modern ideas about the family and about childhood. Ariès argued that before the seventeenth century a child was regarded as a small and inadequate adult; the concept of "the childish" as something distinct from adults is a creation of the modern world. The change involved far-reaching implications for the family, for education and for children themselves. "The concept of the family... is inseparable from the concept of childhood. The interest taken in childhood... is only one form, one particular expression of this more general concept – that of family" (1962 [1960]: 353). Ariès's work has had many critics but, for our purposes, it does not matter whether his historical interpretation is right or wrong. What Ariès succeeded in, beyond doubt, was demonstrating that childhood and family are social constructs that are rooted in time and place.

In nineteenth-century America, the increasing differentiation between economic production and the home transformed the basis of family cohesion. According to Zelizer (1985), between the late nineteenth century and early twentieth century there emerged the "economically worthless" but "emotionally priceless" child. Children are expensive and contribute relatively little to the household income or even to household chores. From the hard-nosed perspective of rational choice: "As soon as men and women... acquire the habit of weighing the individual advantages and disadvantages of any prospective course of action, they cannot fail to become aware of the heavy personal sacrifices that family ties and especially parenthood entails under modern conditions" (Schumpeter, 1988 [1942]: 501–2). The below-replacement population levels of fertility in many Western societies suggest that the wish for parenthood may indeed erode further under the pressures of competing opportunities for men and women.

However, the relationship between price and value is far from straightforward as Zelizer shows. There is a curious paradox in that the market price of an economically useless child far exceeds the money value of a nineteenth-century "useful" child. The very notion of a market price is an uncomfortable one when applied to children. But people pay huge sums for black-market babies. And childless women (and their partners) expend enormous amounts of money, time, and suffering in new fertility treatments to assuage their mounting "baby hunger" as the biological clock ticks by (Hewlitt, 2002). The value of children is not something that can be inferred, simply, from economic and demographic trends. If the value of children is hard to assess, so is any assessment of their instrumental worth.

Zelizer expressed great frustration at the limited knowledge about children. She writes:

> The information is amazingly limited, we simply don't know much about what children do. Feminist research on the relationship between women's housework and market work deals primarily with gender inequality within the family and the lack of public childcare facilities. Children remain spectators of an adult struggle, seldom considered as possible contributors to a solution. While there has been much concern to liberate boys and girls from traditional sex stereotypes, age stereotypes have seldom been examined. The limited available evidence suggests, however, that children of working mothers follow their father's reluctant footsteps into productive domesticity, increasing only slightly or not at all their participation in household chores. (1985: 225)

Zelizer was not the only one to note the surprising absence of knowledge about children in sociological research. In the 1980s a variety of authors began to bemoan the lack of research on children. Ambert (1986), for example, identified a near-absence of children in North American sociological research, and argued that this reflected the continuing influence of founding theorists whose preoccupations were shaped by the patriarchal values of the societies in which they lived (and hence paid little attention to children), and the nature of rewards in a discipline which favors research on "big issues" such as class, bureaucracies, or the political system. Feminist work challenging such patriarchal preconceptions was well under way when Thorne (1987) raised the question "Where are the children?" The notion that children or childhood should be accorded the same conceptual autonomy as other groups in society was novel. As Qvortrup notes: "Children are 'human beings', not only 'human becomings', they have not only needs, a fact which is recognized, they also have interests, that may or may not be compatible with the interests of other social groups or categories" (1994: 4).

Every parent knows that children are willful human beings who, from a very early age, play an active role in shaping their family environment. However, this view of the active child was not acknowledged by Durkheim, one of the founding fathers of sociology. In 1911, Durkheim wrote: "[Childhood is] a period of growth, that is to say, the period in which the individual, in both the physical and moral sense, does not yet exist, the period in which he is made, develops and is formed" (1979 [1911]: 150). This is quite a contrast to the way children are characterized in a text written 80 years later: "Children can be viewed as fully social beings, capable of acting in the social world and of creating and sustaining their own culture.... If we see children as actors... we can ask how their actions, constrain, facilitate and encourage and in a myriad of ways have implications for others, adults in particular" (Waksler, 1991). This amounts to nothing less than a transformation in sociological thinking about children and family life (Smart, Neale, and Wade, 2001). A similar transformation was seen with the rapid growth of a sociologically informed psychology of social development of children in the late 1960s and 1970s (Richards, 1974).

The emergence of new sociological thinking about childhood and children has gone hand in hand with new political and policy concerns about children's rights and well-being. Policy interests inevitably help shape research agendas – if only because the public purse is an important funder of social research. There are several major inter-related public concerns about children and families, at national and international levels (Brannen, 1999). The first theme relates to concerns about the "break-up" of the family life, parental responsibilities when marriage and childbirth are separated, and how children fare in the face of marital instability and family change. A second theme relates to concerns about growing levels of child poverty and its consequences. Other concerns involve children's rights and how they should be translated in law and practice; changing "work–life balance" that has put a time squeeze on families and has led to increasing pressures on family care; and demographic shifts that have changed the balance of generations and the ratio of children to elderly, with all that entails for the future of welfare.

These areas of policy concern are all bound up with the changing context of children's family lives. Childhood experience is inextricably linked to changes in the lives of women and the shifting boundaries of the public and private spheres. In the early twentieth century, the creation of a "family wage" cemented the notion of women and children as dependents. The traditional gender division of labor was taken as a given. "Family" meant a male breadwinner and a female carer who would look after the household needs and be responsible for the care of the children.

How times have changed. As Jensen (1994) argues, the shift to a "feminisation of childhood" has had dramatic consequences. The claim is that, as children have become increasingly economically useless, the incentive for men to marry and legalize their claim to children has been eroded. Whether the causal attribution that this implies is justified or not, the feminization of childhood is indisputable. There is a worldwide increase in the number of children living with single mothers. Single-mother families are disproportionately represented in lower-income households. The "feminisation of poverty" (Garfinkel and McLanahan, 1985) is therefore something of a misnomer. The women who are overrepresented among the poor are women with children. Feminization and pauperization of childhood go hand in hand.

Another change is the increasing diversity among children's families. In the US, as we enter the twenty-first century, even for the white middle class, family structure has become quite diverse. Not only is Mom more likely to be employed outside the home, but among married couples, dual-earner couples are now the modal family type. Families with same-sex parents have become more visible. One in three children born in the late 1990s have mothers who were not married at the time of their birth (US Bureau of the Census, 1998). While the majority of children currently live with married parents (including stepparents), divorce and single parenthood have changed the family experiences of many children. Children also experience family diversity from a very different vantage point from that of their parents.

In this chapter, we review some of the findings of the new sociological approach to children, that takes the viewpoint of the child. We also examine studies that use the life-course perspective to investigate how children's experiences are shaped by historical time and place and how childhood experience, in turn, shapes their various pathways through to adult life. One of the central arguments that we make is that the two perspectives are both needed. It is not a case of *either* approaching children as "beings" *or* approaching children as "becoming." It must be both.

In the next section we examine the new sociological perspective which views children as social actors. We show how social constructions of childhood have helped render aspects of children's activities invisible. One example concerns the "time-bind syndrome" (Hochschild, 1997), where the long work-hours culture changes children's experiences of family time and family care. Another example which, in some instances, may be a consequence of the time bind is "children's work." In the industrial West, the domestic work and informal labor of children has been ignored because work has been defined as "paid work." The subsequent section explores the implications of childhood as a "social category". Following Qvortrup (1990), we show why it is so important to make children visible, rather than being subsumed as part of the family or household, as is often the case. We examine what is known and what is lacking in current knowledge about the social economic conditions of "childhood" in general and children's families in particular. This "structural" approach to childhood is illustrated by reference to both family structure and child poverty, in the UK and the US.

The final section reviews what the life-course perspective has revealed about children and families in time and place. The life-course perspective is concerned with the way societal change impinges on individual lives. It also offers a dynamic view of how the codependencies of children and family members are changing in a rapidly changing world. In the conclusion we suggest that the sociological understanding of children and families has made rapid progress in the past few decades, but there are some glaring deficiencies in our knowledge. These reflect not only conceptual limitations in our understanding of children's families, but also ongoing divisions of methodologies. In addition, we suggest that research on children's families is hindered by the ideological baggage associated with "ideals" of childhood and family and value judgments concerning "family change" and "family decline."

## Children as Social Actors

The United Nations Convention on the Rights of the Child (United Nations, 1989) has had a wide-ranging impact on the way children are treated by the state, and their entitlement to representation in the judicial and administrative procedures that affect their lives. This includes their family relationships in the wake of divorce. The interest in children's rights has provided a receptive climate for social research that considers children the central focus. The emerging new sociological perspective on children takes seriously the notion that childhood and children's social relationships and cultures are worthy of study in their own right, and not just in respect to their social construction by adults. This new paradigm asserts that children should be seen as actively involved in the construction of their own social lives, the lives of those around them and the societies in which they live.

There has been a wealth of research in the last decade that belongs to this emerging paradigm. Strangely, there was some initial reluctance to study children in the context of family lives. For example, James and Prout (1996) recount how researchers working toward establishing the independent intellectual integrity of a sociology of childhood have wanted to wrestle the study of children out of the familial context of socialization, where it was traditionally located. This was because while children were seen within family sociology under headings such as child-rearing and other adult-centric activities, children were certainly not heard. Just as women had to be liberated from their families (conceptually speaking) in order to be seen and heard, this same consideration applied to children (Oakley, 1994). But the position that studying children in their family settings is inappropriate was clearly untenable. Families are the key context in which children's identities are formed. Moreover, changes that affect the life-world of parents, such as the long work-hours culture, have far-reaching implications for the experience of the child.

### Children's take on the time bind

How do children view the complex "culture of care" that is necessitated when parents work long hours? Even when only four years old, children can learn a great deal through eavesdropping on parental conversations. Hothschild (2001) points to how two children have very different "takes" on their care situations. One child clearly resented the parents' absence and was angry and difficult at dinnertime, which made it all the harder for the parents to come home (the time-bind syndrome). The other child didn't seem to feel any resentment, had ceased to look to the parents as exclusive caregivers, and made it less hard for the parents to reenter family life.

What explains the difference? Hothschild suggests that children are themselves sophisticated observers of their social worlds. They pick up on what their parents never say to them directly. From overheard conversations, they learn about the "problems" parents experience in finding care, the conflicts that result from different expectations of care, and whether the carers are doing the work for love, for money, or both. Children know the difference between care by Granny and the paid care worker. They know, in other words, if the care culture is one that draws on an integrated community of neighbors and kin who are involved in the child's life, or whether it draws on a market economy, where carers are "good with children," but in relation to *any* child. The former, Hothschild suggests, is getting rarer, but may work better from the child's point of view.

There is an ongoing and highly charged debate about the consequences of maternal employment for children. Recent studies have claimed that there has been surprising continuity in the amount of time children spend with their mothers, despite the dramatic changes in mothers' labor-market commitment (Bianchi, 2000). Yet, although mothers may be quite successful at juggling time to ensure that children's well-being is not adversely affected, children from a very young age are exposed to diverse forms of care that may be more or less beneficial, in terms of child outcomes.

The point is worth reiterating that what is "good care" from the adult perspective may not appear the same to the eyes of a child. Children's interests, mother's interests, and societal interests do not necessarily coincide. The change in maternal labor-force participation and the long work-hours culture is one example of the relation between social change and family life. Since family is not a monolith, it is necessary to differentiate between the different family members, whose acceptance, responses, and contributions to change will vary. Children's perspectives and contributions to family life are beginning to be taken seriously, but the long tradition of pervasive adultcentric bias in sociology means that there is a long way to go.

## Children's work

Childhood research has traditionally been located in sociology of family. By contrast, studies of "work" and children, until quite recently, focused almost exclusively on the impact of children on the labor-force participation of adults, mothers in particular. Of course, many children do work – in formal part-time employment, in casual informal work, in their family businesses, and in domestic labor. Yet children's labor outside of school in contemporary Western societies has been rendered relatively invisible by conceptions of children as dependent and nonproductive (Morrow, 1996). On both sides of the Atlantic there is mounting evidence that children do contribute to household labor in the form of routine daily tasks and child-care. The characterization of children as "priceless but useless" may understate their continuing contributions to the domestic economy, the division of labor, and family care. It may be the case that, because of exposure to family disruption and family diversity, children perform more emotional labor – for instance, in supportive roles such as parental confidante – at quite young ages. Certainly, the children of immigrants are often called on, in both routine and emergency situations, to act as "language brokers," on their parents' behalf.

In the US, nearly all adolescents do paid work at some point during high school and, perhaps for that reason, there has been a longer tradition of US research on adolescents' work than in the UK. An interesting study that contrasts the family and work relations of youth in a rural and urban community found that young people in rural communities are more likely than their urban counterparts to suggest that parents construe their work as "adultlike" (Shanahan et al., 1996). The researchers suggest that the rural–urban difference is because urban work opportunities are highly variable, whereas much of the available work in the rural community is integral to the shared agricultural way of life. These findings echo a study of the involvement of Norwegian children in the fishing industry, where children worked alongside adults in baiting fishing lines (Solberg, 1994). Children's temporary position as workers meant that restrictions associated with the status of "child" were frequently overridden.

Similarly, in a study of "homestaying" children in Norway (children who spend a good deal of time at home, unsupervised, while parents are at work), Solberg (1990) notes how by "looking after themselves" and by contributing to "homecare," children are able to negotiate an enhanced "social age." Solberg puts a positive spin on children spending more time by themselves, suggesting that children can benefit from parental acknowledgment of their autonomy. Hochschild, in her study of the time bind of work and family in corporate America, sees "home-alone" children in a less positive light. She suggests that rationalizing parental absence in the name of children's "independence" is yet another twist on the varied ways of evading the "time bind". Children, in this instance, are being asked in essence to "save time" by growing up fast (Hochschild, 1997: 229).

The child-focused research, described in this section looks at children as "beings-in the present." Viewing children as prospective adults – the workers, parents, citizens, or dropouts of the future – can inadvertently diminish the importance of children as children. Yet, rejecting "developmental" perspectives on childhood makes no sense, given that children's actions, family life, and the social and economic processes which are integral to family structure and change unfold over time. This is why the study of children's families also requires a life-course approach. Before examining the insights that can be gained from adopting a life-course perspective, we first consider what it means to examine childhood as a social category and why an understanding of children's families is not the same as the study of families with children.

## The Social Structure of Childhood

There is a case for arguing that childhood is a structural concept that is a permanent form, even if its members change continuously, and even if it varies considerably across historical time and place. This assumption is necessary for a comparative framework that examines conditions of childhood (e.g., poverty rates of "dependent children") across different societies, across different groups within societies, and across time. In this section, we examine how childhood has been affected by the revolutionary demographic shifts in family life in the West, in the latter part of the twentieth century, using examples from the US and the UK. One of the consequences of these changes is the increase in single-parent families, the vast majority being headed by women, and the related increase in child poverty.

### Children's family structures

Changes in demographic behavior have been so dramatic that they have been termed by some the "second demographic transition" (Lesthaeghe, 1995). This term contrasts the changes that have occurred since 1960 with those in the first half of the century. Underlying the more recent demographic shifts is an increased value placed on individual autonomy and the associated shifts in ideas concerning gender equality. These changes have been the subject of heated debate, with traditionalists believing that the family is collapsing, while modernists welcome the new opportunities for women and the wider choices for both sexes. However, among both camps, there are those who suggest that the greater choice for parents and equality gains for women may be at the expense of their children (Clarke, 1996). Whatever the truth in the judgments about the relative benefits for adults and children, these changes are unlikely to be reversed.

Patterns of family formation and dissolution have become markedly more frequent, less strictly patterned, and more complex since the 1960s. But, to a great extent, it is adults not children, who trigger these family changes. The evidence is beginning to be assembled on the relative (in)stability of different household forms, the frequency of household compositional change, and the amount of time, contact, and resources that flow between different family members, as they form, leave, and reform household groups (see Pryor and Trinder, chapter 19, this volume). But what has happened to the children?

Most data are analyzed and collected in relation to adult circumstances and are not focused on children. It is hard to get information from the official publications of the UK Office of National Statistics (ONS), for example, on children of different ages with working mothers. The information is, normally, the other way around, with the focus being on mother's employment status, by age of youngest child. Similarly, family-level statistics are rarely expressed in terms that take the child as the unit of analysis. For example, we may be told how many families have one, two, three, or more dependent children; but this does not tell us how many children have none, one, two, or more siblings. The percentage of dependent children having no siblings is usually far less than the percentage of families with only one child.

What difference does it make that the unit of observation is family and not child? Qvortrup (1990) is surely right when he claims that the obscuration of children in family or household statistics contributes to children's marginalization. Any recent textbook on sociology of families will contain numerous entries to the lone-parent family. Yet few have entries on the one- or two-child family. The adult-centric bias of family texts is striking. Children are often portrayed in terms of their consequences for parental earnings, time, satisfaction, etc. When siblings do figure, it is more from the perspective of parental resource allocation than from the perspective of children's family experience. Yet, as psychologists have shown, children can have very different experiences within the same family. Children notice and respond to differences in the way they are treated relative to their siblings. It has even been suggested that differential treatment by parents is more influential for children's development than the common characteristics of the family environment (Dunn and Plomin, 1990). Yet despite the glaring holes in what we know about children's family composition and experiences within families, statistical access is improving in both the UK and the US.

In the UK, there has been a marked decrease in the proportion of children under 16 living with both natural parents who are married to each other (from 83 percent of all children in 1979, to only 68 percent in 1991). In the same period, the proportion of children living with lone mothers doubled from 9 to 17 percent and those living with mother and "stepfather" from 5 to 10 percent (Clarke, 1996). There has been little change in the last decade and, in 2001, 18 percent of children lived in lone-parent households (UK Office of National Statistics (ONS), 2002b). Twelve percent of children were from a minority ethnic group in 2001–2, of which 6 percent were Asian or Asian British and 3 percent black (UK Office of National Statistics, 2002a). Unfortunately, even in the ONS's *Social Focus: Children 2002*, while the breakdown of couple and lone-parent families by ethnic group is presented, the proportion of children, by ethnic group, living with different family structures is not. In the US, there has been a similar decrease in the proportion of children living with two parents, although the shift toward other family structures began somewhat earlier than in the UK. In 1970, for example, 85 percent of American children were living with two parents. This dropped to 77 percent in 1980, and 68 percent in 1998 (Casper and Bianchi, 2002: 214). However, the living arrangements of children varies enormously by race and Hispanic origin. In 2000, 64 percent of children were white non-Hispanic; 16 percent were Hispanic, and 15 percent were black non-Hispanic. In 1998, whereas 74 percent of white children lived with two parents (married or cohabiting), the equivalent figures for Hispanics and blacks were 64 percent and 32 percent, respectively. In all race and ethnic groups the proportion of children in a father-only household was small (around 4 percent). However, lone-mother households varied from 18 percent of whites, to 51 percent of blacks and 27 percent of Hispanics (Federal Interagency Forum on Child and Family Statistics, 2002). Increasingly, children are also living in other non-nuclear family structures, including households of grandparents (Casper and Bryson, 1998) and lesbians or gays (see Treas, chapter 23, this volume).

Recent changes in patterns of family formation and dissolution have not only led to changes in the composition of children's families, but also to children's likely transit from one form of family to another, during their childhood years. One estimate suggests that, in Britain, the proportion of children born of married parents and staying with the same parents through childhood could be as low as 50 percent (Clarke, 1992). A rather different way of viewing the same issue leads American researchers to estimate that, on average, the American child will only spend 71 percent of his or her childhood years with both parents (Bumpass and Lu, 2000). Again, this varies hugely by race and ethnicity, with the most recent estimates (based on 1990s data) showing whites at 80 percent, blacks at 16 percent, and Hispanics at 67 percent of childhood years.

Does it matter that an increasing proportion of children experience a variety of family settings as they pass through childhood and adolescence? Current consensus is that it does (see also Pryor and Trinder, chapter 19, this volume). As we shall see, the evidence is more complex to evaluate than the media headlines acknowledge. To understand the very different experiences of children as they negotiate the complex family settings that can follow family disruption, qualitative methods can be invaluable. However, large-scale, longitudinal surveys are also crucial for following the lives of children over time, and unpacking the complex relationship between family structure and process and between the antecedents and consequences of children's attributes and actions. We review some of the survey findings in the section on the life-course perspective.

## Child poverty

The size and structure of children's families are important in determining child poverty. In the UK, despite a fall in the number of families with children and declining family size, the number of children living in households with below half the average income has risen rapidly in recent decades. By the end of the 1990s about one-fifth of all children were living in such households, representing a threefold increase over just two decades between 1979 and 1999. The rise in child poverty is closely linked to a growth in the number of children living in families without work. Sixty-one percent of all poor children live in a household where no one is in employment. Half of all poor children live in a lone-parent household. Three-quarters of poor children are white, but the risk of child poverty is higher in all minority ethnic groups, especially households of Bangladeshi or Pakistani origin (Bradshaw, 2002).

Poverty thresholds are a nightmare for the uninitiated (see also Walker and Collins, chapter 12, this volume). The definition of poverty as "households below median income" can be described as a measure of inequality, which conceptualizes poverty as relative. The US threshold is an absolute, specifying in dollars the annual income required to purchase the range of goods and services seen as constituting an acceptable way of life in America. On the relative measure, the UK and the US both have the shameful record of being among the worst four out of the twenty-nine OECD countries, for proportion of children in poverty (UNICEF, 2000). To show the scope of national variation, it is worth noting some of the relevant figures. For the UK, child poverty is 20 percent and for the US 22 percent, whereas in Germany child poverty stands at 11 percent, in Denmark 5 percent, and in Sweden 3 percent. Using the US absolute threshold the UK fares only marginally better in its standing relative to other OECD countries, while the US child climbs to midway in the league table with a child poverty level of 16 percent (figure for 2000) which is the lowest since 1979 (Federal Interagency Forum on Child and Family Statistics, 2002). The decrease in "absolute poverty" in the US was especially marked for black children in female-householder families, which dropped, for the first time, to fewer than half living in poverty in 2000 (ibid.).

In both the US and the UK, there has been an extraordinary output of work on the causes and consequences of child poverty. While much of the research is directly relevant to policy interventions and is couched in terms of "What works for children?" (e.g., Chase-Lansdale and Brooks-Gunn, 1995), it must be recognized that children's interests, family interests and societal interests, may well be different (Glass, 2001). For example, policies aimed to reduce poverty by raising family income through paid work may not necessarily be consistent with the desire to strengthen family ties or to prioritize parental care of young children. While sociological research can usefully inform policy initiatives, the role of sociology is not in constructing societal engineering blueprints. Rather, it consists of "careful analyses of social processes, awareness of their concealed and unintended manifestations, and sustained efforts to understand the participants' own reactions to their situation" (Portes, 2000).

There has been a great deal of work analyzing the complexity of social processes involved in "growing up poor." As family structure, parental characteristics, and household poverty are so interlinked, sorting out what is causing what, and with what consequences, is no easy task (Duncan et al., 1998). There has been much less work devoted to understanding children's own reactions to their family's poverty. Children's poverty is measured in terms of household income, but we know from a number of influential feminist studies that the household allocation of resources is often structured on gender and generational lines. The "black box" of household finances is very difficult to prize open. One of the few studies to look at household income from the child's perspective suggests that children, as young as seven are good tacticians in persuading parents to buy them the things they want. Nevertheless, although parents are often willing to make financial sacrifices to protect children from some of the more visible aspects of poverty, children, like adults, suffer from relative deprivation. Children's consumption ideas are shaped by affluent images portrayed in the media and comparisons with more fortunate peers (Middelton, Ashworth, and Walker, 1994).

## Children's Families: A Life-Course Perspective

One thing life-course research has demonstrated convincingly is that children's lives are not *determined* by historical circumstances, economic change, or family structures. Nevertheless, some children grow up in much more disadvantaged circumstances than others, which has clear knock-on effects for children's subsequent behaviors and achievements. A great deal of research has been devoted to understanding why some children's life courses are blighted by disadvantage; while others "beat the odds" and make a success of their lives, despite the risks. Fundamental to the idea of risk is the predictability of life chances from earlier circumstances (Bynner, 2001). There are clear patterns and associations between earlier circumstances and later outcomes. For example, persistent child poverty has a well-known detrimental effect on educational attainment. However, there is also considerable individual variation in children's developmental pathways. To understand children's life chances, we need to take seriously the way children act to select, shape, and respond to the great number of choices available in contemporary societies.

Studying children's lives in times of extreme social, economic or cultural upheaval can be a useful way of revealing the processes by which an external risk affects the vulnerability and resilience of children. It can also help identify factors that minimize or accentuate the risk. *Children of the Great Depression* was one of the first of this mould (Elder, 1999 [1974]). The study examined archival data on children born in Oakland, California in 1920–1. It showed that the impact of economic deprivation during the Depression was felt mainly through children's changing family experiences, including altered family relationships, different division of labor, and enhanced social strain.

Elder also undertook a comparison study, using a group of children from Berkeley, born just eight years later in 1928–9. This showed marked differences between the way economic deprivation affected the children of the two birth cohorts. The Oakland children encountered the Depression hardships after a relatively secure phase of early childhood in the 1920s. By contrast, the Berkeley group spent their early childhood years in families which were under extraordinary stress and instability. The adverse effects of the Depression were far more severe for the Berkeley group, particularly the boys. The Oakland cohort were old enough to take on jobs outside the home and, as we saw in the last section, children, by working, can enhance their status within families. This would have been particularly true under conditions of economic hardship, when children's earning money could be vital to their families' welfare.

The study underlines the need to recognize children as agents of their own family experience and to take account of the multiple relationships which define patterns of family adaptation in hard times. Such insights have helped shape the four principles that underpin the life-course perspective (Elder, 2001). First, the historical time and place of childhood leaves a lasting imprint on people's lives. Second, the timing of events, life transitions, and behavioral choices are critically important. Third, individual lives are inseparably linked to the lives of significant others, especially family members. Fourth human agency, including children's agency, must be recognized. We illustrate, in turn, how these insights have contributed to more recent studies of the interrelation of social change, families, and children's lives.

## THE IMPRINT OF CHANGING HISTORICAL TIME

One way of looking at the imprint of historical time on children's lives is to compare children's experiences across different societies or different socio-historical contexts (Wadsworth, 1991; Elder, Modell and Parke, 1993). With the increasing availability of longitudinal samples, it is possible to compare the diverse pathways from childhood to early adulthood, of children born at different points in time. One such study, comparing children born in 1958 and 1970 in Britain, found that the material circumstances of families had improved for the more recent cohort. The study also found that the accumulative disadvantages associated with children's socioeconomic background has become more marked over time (Schoon et al., forthcoming). This result brings little comfort to politicians who hope that, by raising the standard of living, without tackling inequality, they will improve children's life chances. Subjective assessments of economic well-being are not usually based on comparisons with the past, but on existing expectations for life. Children whose families are left behind in the overall improvement of standards of living continue to be at a disadvantage.

## THE TIMING OF EVENTS AND INTERLINKED LIVES

Research in both UK and the US has shown that family economic conditions in early childhood are more important than those of later childhood for predicting children's cognitive ability and educational achievement (Schoon et al., forthcoming; Duncan and Brooks-Gunn, 1997). It is also worth noting that family economic resources seem to matter far more than family structure in terms of children's cognitive development (Duncan and Brooks-Gunn, 1997; Joshi et al., 1999). Still, most research to date suggests that children experiencing lone parenthood or family disruption or both have, on average, tougher lives, more limited options and less desirable outcomes than those who don't (Rodgers and Pryor, 1998; McCulloch et al., 2000).

From the same 1958 British birth cohort study (the National Child Development Study), we know that girls who experienced family disruption between ages 7 and 16, are more likely than girls from intact families to experience "bad" outcomes (Bhrolcháin et al., 2000). These involve a range of premature transitions that can stifle young people's opportunities, including early school-leaving, leaving home early, teenage first partnership, early entry into parenthood, and extramarital childbirth. For these outcomes, for boys, family disruption only makes a difference in terms of forming a teenage partnership and leaving home before their eighteenth birthday.

Of these particular outcomes, leaving home early is the one most strongly associated with childhood family disruption. Yet even here, the large majority of children, regardless of family composition, had not left home by age 18. The risks were higher for those from disrupted homes: 19 percent of boys and 27 percent percent of girls had left compared with 10 percent of boys and 12 percent of girls from intact families. There are clear disparities in overall outcomes between children from two-parent intact families and those from other family types, including lone-parent or reconstituted families. Yet, it is far from clear that the differences are due to family structure or disruption per se (Furstenberg and Kiernan, 2001). Recent research has stressed the importance of the preceding family circumstances, particularly family conflict. It may be that families where there is a lot of conflict are more prone to disruption and more prone to unhappy outcomes for children. Even if family disruption itself causes adverse outcomes for children, it could be for a variety of different reasons. Disruption involves much more than a family composition change. What matters for children? Is it a fall in economic status? A loss of a father figure? An erosion of social contacts? A reduction in parental care? Do all of them matter? And is what matters different for different children?

We can glean some evidence from studies that go into greater detail about the context of childhood experiences and the process through to later outcomes. However, national longitudinal studies inevitably have to make trade-offs that sacrifice depth for breadth. In particular, they tend to have limited information about children's own actions, perspectives, and choices.

Until quite recently survey researchers, when investigating aspects of childhood, have preferred to ask adult respondents such as parents or teachers to report on children's lives, rather than to ask children themselves. In part this has been because of concerns about the cognitive ability of children to process and respond to structured questions about behavior, perceptions, opinions, and beliefs. Yet by including children as respondents in longitudinal surveys, social scientists can improve the theoretical understanding and empirical knowledge of the dynamics of social inclusion and exclusion as they affect childhood experiences and children's life-course trajectories.

Interviewing children does pose distinctive methodological problems that could impinge on the quality of data (Scott, 2000). In particular, survey techniques might not be appropriate for younger children because of cognitive and language limitations. However, by preadolescence (as young as 10), children are quite capable of providing meaningful and insightful information. Research on children as respondents lags behind research on adult respondents. Although child respondents do pose some special concerns (e.g., issues of power and ethics), when children are asked questions they are able and willing to answer, young age is no barrier to data quality.

## CHILDREN'S AGENCY

Children have an active role in shaping their own life course. Of course many childhood experiences, including poverty and family disruption, are not in the child's control. However, the process that links childhood experience and adult outcomes involves many chains of action that the child, himself or herself, initiates.

One chain of links was traced in a British study that followed a group of young people from age 10, through to their choice of first partner. The study demonstrated that childhood behavioral problems exacerbated the risk of young people choosing a first partner who was "deviant," in terms of antisocial behavior, persistent drug or alcohol misuse, or marked problems in interpersonal relations (Rutter et al., 1995).

Women were much more likely to have a deviant partner than were men. However, the things that helped reduce the risk were similar for both girls and boys. Children who showed forethought in planning life choices were at less risk; and those who had a nondelinquent peer group were less likely to form a "problem" partnership. A harmonious family environment also helped.

Children make choices among options that become building blocks of their evolving life courses. Often choices amplify tendencies already present. Problem peer groups enhance the chances of a child with deviant leanings going off the rails; whereas high achieving friends further motivate children's efforts to succeed. There is considerable individual variation in outcomes. Although family advantage, adversity, genes, and environment all tilt the odds, children's lives are their own and, to a great degree, are of their own making.

## Children and Families: Looking Back and Looking Forward

In this chapter we have taken it as a given that childhood, like family, is a social construct. The way childhood is conceived, in a particular time and place, frames our knowledge and understanding. In sociology, until quite recently, children were subsumed under family and households and not considered as actors in their own right. The new sociology of childhood rightly emphasizes that children are agents. Children are not passive victims of circumstance, they act and exert influence on the lives of others around them and they make choices, within the opportunities and constraints that contemporary life brings. Those opportunities and constraints are closely bound with the social positions that are reproduced and transmitted from one generation, to the next, within the family context. Yet children's fates are in no way determined. There is great variation in outcomes, with some children beating the odds and thriving despite childhood adversities, including poverty and family disruption.

We have insisted that family context is crucial for understanding children's contemporary well-being and future pathways. Children are agents, but agency is not individual, it is relational. Children's actions and choices are codependent on the lives of others, particularly their family members. Parents' lives are also codependent on the lives of their children. There are, of course, important power differences that age statuses bestow. However, as we saw both from examples of children's work and from children's responses to the time-bind syndrome, children, from a very early age, actively shape their family environment.

The study of children's families crosses the disciplinary divides and necessitates different methodologies for different purposes. In an early statement about "a new paradigm for the sociology of childhood," it was asserted that there was a need to break with the traditions of developmental psychology (Prout and James, 1990). It was also stated that ethnography is a particularly useful methodology for the study of childhood. Both claims are unfortunate. There is an ongoing divide between the mainly quantitative studies of children's families that use the developmentally informed life-course perspective, on the one hand; and the mainly qualitative research exploring children's perspectives, on the other. This divide needs to be broken down. It is not a matter of understanding children as beings or as becomings. We need both.

We have insisted that children must not be marginalized through seeing them only in terms of their family or household. This obscures the position of children. By making children visible in statistics, it becomes evident that children's interests can differ from those of women, parents, or other groups in society. The potential interest clash between children and other societal groups is clear when there are scarce resources to be distributed (e.g., in the case of child poverty). There may also be a clash between children's need for family stability and adults' desire for greater individual freedom and family choice.

The thorny issue of family change or family decline poses a particular challenge to the future study of children's families. Research on effects for children of family disruption, family diversity, changing work–family balance, and different care cultures, is often contentious. Ideology frequently colors interpretations and claims far exceed knowledge. Examples of ideology masking interpretation come from both liberal and conservative viewpoints. To use currently fashionable jargon, we need to "deconstruct" the literature on children's families to examine how ideals of childhood and family not only shape what questions are asked but also what answers are found.

## References


Ambert, A. (1986) The place of children in North American sociology. In P. and P. Adler (eds.), *Sociological Studies in Child Development*. Greenwich, CT: JAI.

Ariès, P. (1962) [1960] *Centuries of Childhood: A Social History of Family Life*. New York and Harmondsworth: Knopf and Penguin.

Bhrolcháin, M., Chappell R., Diamond, I., and Jameson, C. (2000) Parental divorce and outcomes for children: evidence and interpretation. *European Sociological Review*, 16, 67–91.

Bianchi, S. (2000) Maternal employment and time with children: dramatic change or surprising continuity? *Demography*, 37, 401–14.

Bradshaw, J. (2002) Child poverty and child outcomes. *Children and Society*, 16, 131–40.

Brannen, J. (1999). Reconsidering children and childhood: sociological and policy perspectives. In E. Silva and C. Smart (eds.), *The New Family?* London: Sage.

Bumpass, L., and Lu, H-H. (2000) Trends in cohabitation and implications for children's family contexts in the United States. *Population Studies*, 54, 29–41.

Bynner, J. (2001) Childhood risks and protective factors in social exclusion. *Children and Society*, 15, 285–301.

Casper, L., and Bianchi, S. (2002) *Continuity and Change in the American Family*. London: Sage.

Casper, L., and Bryson, K. (1998) Co-resident grandparents and their grandchildren: grandparent maintained families. *Population Division, Working Paper No.26*, Washington, DC: US Bureau of the Census.

Chase-Lansdale, P. L., and Brooks-Gunn, J. (1995) *Escape from Poverty: What Makes a Difference for Children?* Cambridge: Cambridge University Press.

Clarke, L. (1992) Children's family circumstances: recent trends in Great Britain. *European Journal of Population*, 8, 309–40.

Clarke, L. (1996) Demographic change and the family situation of children. In J. Brannen and M. O'Brien (eds.), *Children in Families: Research and Policy*. London: Falmer.

Duncan, G., and Brooks-Gunn, J. (1997) Income effects across the life span: integration and interpretation. In G. Duncan and J. Brooks-Gunn (eds.), *Consequences of Growing Up Poor*. New York: Russell Sage Foundation.

Duncan, G., Yeung, W. J., Brooks-Gunn, J., and Smith, J. (1998) The effects of childhood poverty on the life chances of children. *American Sociological Review*, 63, 406–23.

Dunn, J., and Plomin, R. (1990) *Separate Lives: Why Siblings are so Different*. New York: Basic Books.

Durkheim, E. (1979) [1911] Childhood. In W. F. Pickering (ed.), *Durkheim: Essays on Morals and Education*. London: Routledge.

Elder, G. H., Jr. (1999) (1974) *Children of the Great Depression*. Boulder: Westview.

Elder, G. H., Jr. (2001) Families, social change and individual lives. *Marriage and Family Review*, 177–92.

Elder, G. H., Jr., Modell, J. M., and Parke, R. D. (1993) *Children in Time and Place*. New York: Cambridge University Press.

Federal Interagency Forum on Child and Family Statistics (2002) *America's Children: Key National Indicators of Well-Being*. Washington, DC: Government Printing Office.

Furstenberg, F., and Kiernan, K. (2001) Delayed parental divorce: How much do children benefit? *Journal of Marriage and the Family*, 63, 446–57.

Garfinkel, I., and McLanahan, S. (1985) The Nature, Causes and Cures of the Feminization of Poverty. Paper delivered at the Annual Meeting of the Population Association of America, Boston.

Glass, N. (2001) What works for children? The political issues. *Children and Society*, 15, 14–20.

Hewlitt, S. A. (2002) *Baby Hunger: The New Battle for Motherhood*. London: Atlantic Books.

Hochschild, A. (1997) *The Time Bind: When Work Becomes Home and Home Becomes Work*. New York: Metropolitan Books.

Hochschild, A. (2001) Eavesdropping children, adult deals, and cultures of care. In R. Hertz and N. Marshall (eds.), *Working Families*. Berkeley: University of California Press.

James, A., and Prout, A. (eds.) (1990) *Constructing and Reconstructing Childhood: Contemporary Issues in the Sociological Study of Childhood*. London: Falmer.

James, A., and Prout, A. (1996) Strategies and structures: towards a new perspective on children's experiences of family life. In J. Brannen and M. O'Brien (eds.), *Children in Families: Research and Policy*. London: Falmer.

Jensen, A-M. (1994) The feminization of childhood. In J. B. Qvortrup, M. Bardy, G. Sgritta, and H. Wintersberger (eds.), *Childhood Matters: Social Theory, Practice and Politics*. Aldershot: Avebury.

Joshi, H., Cooksey, E., Wiggins, R., McCulloch, A., Verropoulou, G., and Clarke, L. (1999) Diverse family living situations and child development: a multi-level analysis comparing longitudinal information from Britain and the United States. *International Journal of Law and Social Policy*, 13, 293–314.

Lesthaeghe, R. (1995) The second demographic transition in western countries: An interpretation. In K. Mason and A-M. Jensen (eds.), *Gender and Family Change in Industrialized Countries*. Oxford: Clarendon.

McCulloch, A. Wiggens, R., Joshi, H., and Sachdev, D. (2000) Internalising and externalising children's behaviour problems in Britain and the US: relationships to family resources. *Children and Society*, 14, 368–83.

Middleton, S., Ashworth, K., and Walker, R. (1994) *Family Fortunes: Pressures on Parents and Children in the 1990s*. London: CPAG.

Morrow, V. (1996) Rethinking childhood dependency: children's contributions to the domestic economy. *Sociological Review*, 44, 58–77.

Oakley, A. (1994) Women and children first and last: Parallels and differences between children's and women's studies. In B. Mayall (ed.), *Children's Childhood Observed and Experienced*. London: Falmer.

Portes, A. (2000) The hidden abode: sociology as analysis of the unexpected. *American Sociological Review*, 65, 1–18.

Prout, A., and James, A. (1990) A new paradigm for the sociology of childhood? Provenance, promise and problems. In A. James and A. Prout (eds.), *Constructing and Reconstructing Childhood: Contemporary Issues in the Sociological Study of Childhood*. London: Falmer.

Qvortrup, J. (1990) A voice for children in statistical and social accounting: A plea for children's rights to be heard. In A. James and A. Prout (eds.), *Constructing and Reconstructing Childhood: Contemporary Issues in the Sociological Study of Childhood*. London: Falmer.

Qvortrup, J. (1994) Childhood matters: An introduction. In J. Qvortup, M. Bardy, G. Sgritta, and H. Wintersberger (eds.) *Childhood Matters: Social Theory, Practice and Politics*. Aldershot: Avebury.

Richards, M. (ed.) (1974) *The Integration of a Child into a Social World*. Cambridge: Cambridge University Press.

Rodgers, B., and Pryor, J. (1998) *Divorce and Separation. The Outcomes for Children*. York: Joseph Rowntree Foundation.

Rutter, M., Champion, L., Quinton, D., Maughan, B., and Pickles, A. (1995) Understanding individual differences in environmental risk exposure. In P. Moen, G. H. Elder, Jr., and K. Lüscher (eds.), *Examining Lives in Context: Perspectives on the Ecology of Human Development*. Washington DC: American Psychological Association.

Schoon, I., Bynner, J., Joshi, H., Parson, S., Wiggens, R., and Sacker, A. (forthcoming)The influence of context, timing and duration of risk experiences for the passage from childhood to early adulthood. *Child Development*.

Schumpeter, J. A. (1988) [1942] Decomposition. *Population and Development Review*, 14, 499–506.

Scott, J. (2000) Children as respondents: The challenge for quantitative methods. In P. Christensen and A. James (eds.), *Research with Children*. London: Falmer.

Shanahan, M., Elder, G. H., Jr., Burchinal, M., and Conger, R. (1996) Adolescent earnings and relationships with parents: the work-family nexus in urban and rural ecologies. In J. Mortimer and M. Finch (eds.), *Adolescents, Work and Family*. London: Sage.

Smart, C., Neale, B., and Wade, A. (2001) *The Changing Experience of Childhood: Families and Divorce*. Cambridge: Polity.

Solberg, A. (1990) Negotiating childhood: Changing constructions of age for Norwegian children. In A. James and A. Prout (eds.), *Constructing and Reconstructing Childhood*. Basingstoke: Falmer.

Solberg, A. (1994) *Negotiating Childhood: Empirical Investigations and Textual Representations of Children's Work and Everyday Lives*. Stockholm: Nordic Institute for Studies in Urban and Regional Planning.

Thorne, B. (1987) Revisioning women and social change: where are the children? *Gender and Society*, 1, 85–109.

UK Office of National Statistics (2002a) *Social Focus: Children 2002*. London: HMSO.

UK Office of National Statistics (2002b) *Social Trends*. London: HMSO.

UNICEF (2000) *A League Table of Child Poverty in Rich Nations*. Florence: Innocenti Research Centre.

United Nations (1989) *Convention on the Rights of the Child*. Treaty Series, vol. 1577, p. 3. New York: United Nations.

US Bureau of the Census (1998) *Current Population Reports*. Washington, DC: Government Printing Office.

Wadsworth, M. (1991) *The Imprint of Time: Childhood, History and Adult Life*. Oxford: Clarendon Press.

Waksler, F. (1991) *Studying the Social Worlds of Childhood: Sociological Readings*. London: Falmer.

Zelizer, V. (1985) *Pricing the Priceless Child: The Changing Social Value of Children*. New York: Basic Books.

# 8

# Aging and the Life Course

Chris Phillipson and Graham Allan

## Introduction: The Changing Life Course

Contemporary theorizing about late modernity highlights the degree to which different spheres of social and economic activity have become more fragmented and diversified than they were a generation ago. Frequently the changes in question are understood as having particularly profound consequences for younger cohorts who are usually perceived as being at the forefront of the emergent new order. In contrast, older cohorts brought up under the relatively stable social and economic conditions now seen as typifying the mid-twentieth century, are generally considered to be less influenced by and more resistant to the structures of late modernity. Such a view is, of course, open to considerable criticism. To begin with, the twentieth century can hardly be characterized as a period of economic, social or political stability. The lives the majority of people led at the beginning of the century were markedly different from those being led by its end, even though a sense of coherent transition, encapsulated by ideas of economic and social progress, dominated much of this period (Clarke, 1996; Thompson, Itzin, and Abendstern, 1990). But second, it is simply wrong to assume that social and economic developments in late modernity have had little impact on the experiences and lifestyles of older cohorts. Any significant transformations in the structuring of social and economic relationships are inevitably going to have consequences, albeit experienced differentially, across all segments of society (Riley and Riley, 1993).

This chapter focuses on some of the key changes affecting later life since the 1970s. Somewhat arbitrarily, we will concentrate principally on a particular cohort, broadly speaking those born between the late 1920s and the early 1950s. At times, we will refer to other ages, but our main concern will be with people aged between 50 and 75. In particular, we will explore how the family circumstances of this cohort have been altering over time, both as a consequence of their own aging and as a result of more wide-ranging changes in the ordering of social and economic relationships.

The term "family" is interpreted here in a broad sense to mean marital/partner ties as well as relationships across different generations (Allan and Crow, 2001). We will be particularly interested in the ways in which recent shifts in family and household formation and dissolution have had an impact on the family experiences of later-life cohorts. Throughout the chapter we will be drawing on data from Britain but with references as well to literature from the US. The circumstances of later life in other countries will inevitably vary from this, but given that the changes we are discussing are, to differing extents, affecting all Western countries, there will be commonalities across societies.

## The Life Course: Mid-Twentieth-Century Changes

The experience of aging has inevitably been influenced by shifts in the patterning of the life course during the twentieth century. Changes in the demography of aging and in patterns of work and retirement have been particularly important in shaping contemporary experiences of later life (Pillemer et al., 2001). On the first of these, improvements in life expectancy over the past 100 years have been crucial in routinizing both "middle" and "old" age as significant phases in the life course. In 1900 life expectancy at birth was around 44 years (for men) and 48 years (for women), with many people dying before they reached what would now be recognized as old age. With life expectancy at birth currently around 75 years for men and 80 years for women, survival past middle age is normal, even if frequently accompanied by a heightened awareness of the aging process and of future mortality (Warnes, 1996; National Statistics, 2002). This and other demographic shifts have also generated changes in familial responsibilities over the life course. For example, current cohorts of older people are experiencing far longer periods of "post-parental" life than earlier cohorts did. In 1900, women were likely to be in their mid-fifties/sixties when their last child married. Consequently, given lower life expectancy at this time, many women could expect to be widowed before their last child left home. With increased life expectancy, smaller family size and closer spacing of children, the average couple can now expect to live for some 20 years after the last child has moved out (Phillipson et al., 2001).

Moreover, despite the increasing propensity for divorce, the number of marriages lasting 20 or more years is far higher than in previous times. American research in the 1970s suggested that one marriage in five could expect to see its fiftieth anniversary. This contrasts sharply with the situation at the turn of the century, when most marriages were terminated during middle age by the death of a spouse (Sporakowski and Axelson, 1989). The significance of these changes is reinforced by earlier retirement (see below) and by changes in household composition. The former has meant an increase in the amount of time couples can choose to spend with each other, ahead of some of the health changes associated with late old age (Szinovacz, Ekerdt, and Vinick, 1992; Szinovacz, 2000). The latter has involved a decline of co-residence between elderly parents and their adult children, a change which gathered momentum in most Western countries from the late 1950s onward (Wall, 1992; Phillipson et al., 2001). Taken together, these changes have had quite profound implications for later life relationships and activities.

Changes in the organization of work have also been consequential in reshaping the life course. In general terms the period from 1945 to the mid-1970s confirmed the emergence of a "standardized" life course built around what Best (1980) termed the "three boxes" of education, work, and leisure. This period is associated with the creation of retirement as a major social institution, with the growth of entitlements to pensions and the gradual acceptance of an extended period of leisure following the ending of full-time work. Kohli and Rein summarize this development as follows:

> By the 1960s, retirement for men had become a normal feature of the life course, a taken-for-granted part of one's biography. The modern tripartition of the life course into a period of preparation, and one of "active" work, and one of retirement had become firmly established. Old age had become synonymous with the period of retirement: a life phase structurally set apart from "active" work life and with a relatively uniform beginning defined by the retirement age limit as set by the public-old age pension system. With the increasing labor-force participation of women, they too have increasingly been incorporated into this life-course regime. (1991: 21)

In fact, what Mayer and Muller (1986) refer to as the "institutionalisation of the life course" lasted a relatively short span of time in historical terms, with the period from 1945 to 1975 defining its outer limits. After the mid-1970s a number of changes can be identified arising from the development of more flexible patterns of work and the impact of high levels of unemployment. These produced what may be termed the reconstruction of middle and old age, with the identification of a "third age" in between the period of work and employment ("the second age") and that of a period of mental and physical decline ("the fourth age"). A characteristic feature of this new period of life is the ambiguity and flexibility of its boundaries, at both the lower and upper ends. Both these boundaries now involve complex periods of transition, with greater ambiguity associated with the move away from employment, and with the blurring of dependence and independence with physical and mental deterioration (Phillipson, 2002).

Thus, for men and women entering their fifties, in Britain the period since the 1970s has seen major changes in patterns of employment. Since that time, the number of men who were working fell from 93 percent in 1975 to around 77 percent at the end of the 1990s. For women, the percentage in work increased marginally from around 56 percent in 1996 to about 60 percent in 2000. In the case of the retirement transition, the template of previous generations – long work, short retirement – has undergone substantial alteration (Schuller, 1989). For many (mostly male) workers, the predictability of continuous employment is being replaced by insecurity in middle and late working life – an experience shared with the majority of female workers (Itzin and Phillipson, 1993). The retirement transition itself has become elongated and of greater complexity with the emergence of different pathways (e.g., unemployment, long-term sickness, redundancy, disability, part-time employment, self-employment) which people follow before they describe themselves or are defined within the social security system as "wholly retired" (Phillipson, 1998).

## The Life Course: Late Twentieth-Century Changes

The fragmentation of the life course, following the period of institutionalization between 1945 and 1975, has also seen significant transformations in family and household demography, particularly with regard to family constitution. Within Britain, as in many other countries in the Western world, increasing divorce rates were the first indicator of this development. In turn, and fueled further by births outside of marriage, the numbers of lone-parent households also rose. More recently, there has been a rapid decline in marriage rates, along with markedly higher levels of cohabitation and an increasing incidence of lone-person and non-familial households among the young (Allan and Crow, 2001). It seems unlikely that these shifts in patterns of family constitution will be reversed in the coming years. In large part, this is because they are rooted in the wider societal changes characteristic of late modernity, as theorists like Beck (1992; Beck and Beck-Gernsheim, 1995) and Giddens (1992) have suggested (see also Beck and Beck-Gernsheim, chapter 28, this volume). Put simply, emerging economic, technological, and social developments have fostered a process of individualization and an emphasis on rights of citizenship. These have had a particularly profound impact on women's lives, resulting in their having a good deal more freedom and choice than previous cohorts had. As a result, women are less dependent on men and are more able to challenge patriarchal forms of family and domestic control. Against this background, traditional modes of family living based around the close association of sex, marriage, and childbearing have lost their dominance, with previously standard practices now becoming matters of lifestyle choice rather than moral imperative.

While, given current child-care assumptions and continuing gender divisions in employment, it is easy to overemphasize the extent to which women really have become free of structural constraint inside and outside of the home (Jamieson, 1998, 1999; Smart and Neale, 1999), the changes there have been, especially in partnership and childbearing patterns, have nonetheless had a pervasive impact on people's experiences and expectations of family life. Two issues stand out. First, individuals now have far less certainty about the outcomes and future pathways of their own family lives than they did. Whereas previously most people had a clear and generally warranted vision of how their family and domestic life would be ordered, the sequencing of family life is now much more diverse and less predictable than once was the case. There is less uniformity about the timing and mode of partnership formation; even apparently stable relationships are liable to be dissolved; many will experience lone-parent and/or stepfamily living, as adults or children or both. Second, even those people whose own marital and childbearing experiences take a "traditional" form will be affected by "nontraditional" events and relationships in other people's lives. Thus parents whose own marriage continues intact may well have one or more children whose marriages end in divorce or who have children outside of marriage; increasing numbers of people have close relatives who are – or have been – involved in lone-parent families; and equally, a significant number now have direct or indirect experience of stepfamily relationships.

Most analyses of the impact of late modernity have concentrated on young people and those in early middle age. The consequences of these changes for the experiences of older people have received far less attention. However, the types of change discussed above have generated considerable diversity in the second half of the life course. At the lower levels of our age range, a once socially homogeneous fifties age group has become fragmented into various groupings reflecting different work, familial, and social experiences (Scales and Scase, 2001). At the upper end, there is increasingly a blurring of middle and old age, with gender, social class, and ethnicity important variables influencing the transition from one to the other (Phillipson,

2002). Here we seek to redress the dominant emphasis on youth a little and examine how the transformations of late modernity are altering the experiences of aging, particularly with regard to the character of family commitments and solidarities in later life. In the remaining sections of the chapter we explore these matters in greater depth, examining three main areas: the nature of partnerships and domestic organization; generational ties; and relationships beyond the immediate family.

## Partnerships and Domestic Organization

In Britain, the cohort we are considering – roughly those born between 1925 and 1950 – was one in which early marriage and childbearing were common. For example, between 1950 and 1975 – the primary years in which this cohort were marrying – average age at first marriage ranged between 26.5 and 24.4 for men and 24.2 and 22.4 for women. This compares with 30.1 and 28.0, respectively, for those marrying currently (*Marriage and Divorce Statistics*, 1976; *Marriage, Divorce and Adoption Statistics*, 1999). Similarly average age at first birth for married women was 25.8 in 1950, falling to 24.7 in 1975. In 1999, this was 29.3 (*Birth Statistics*, 1976, 1999). Moreover significantly less than 10 percent of children were born to unmarried women in this period, compared to nearly 40 percent in 1999. Furthermore, these marriages tended to last, though there were differences between those born earlier and later in the period. Thus, Haskey (1996) has estimated that some 7 percent of those marrying in 1951 had divorced by 1971, whereas 27 percent of those marrying in 1971 were divorced 20 years later. However, it is also clear that over time the propensity of each age group to divorce had itself increased. In other words, while those born before the 1940s were less likely to divorce than those born after this date, over time increasing numbers from both groups did so.

With hindsight, it can be recognized that significant shifts in understandings of marital commitment were being forged by the cohort born between 1925 and 1950. These changes have of course continued, as discussed earlier. But this cohort was in the vanguard of change, in which social understandings of marriage were developing from a view of marriage as a public institution, albeit based on companionate love (Finch and Summerfield, 1991), to a perspective in which personal happiness was prioritized. In Britain, this was encapsulated clearly in the Divorce Reform Act of 1967 – a time when the cohort we are examining was in young adulthood and early middle age – which for the first time placed relationship quality at the center of divorce proceedings rather than contractual rights (Gibson, 1994). At the same time, there were concomitant shifts in understandings of the impact of marital tension on children. Whereas up until the late 1960s, there had been an emphasis on the importance of sustaining marriage "for the sake of the children," this was gradually replaced by a different wisdom which emphasized the emotional damage children suffered when there was continual conflict between parents. One very important repercussion of this was a significant rise in the number of lone-parent families, in Britain, from 570,000 in 1971 to 1,600,000 in 1996.

Women's increased participation in employment, together with changing housing circumstances, also shaped the domestic experiences of this cohort. In 1951, only some 22 percent of married women were in any form of employment; by 1971 this had risen to 42 percent, of whom approximately half were in part-time employment

(Allan, 1985). Increasingly during this period there was an expectation that living standards required two incomes, albeit one generally markedly higher than the other. So too, post-1950 urban reconstruction, together with changing patterns of housing tenure, encouraged dual rather than single earning within marriage. In particular, the rapid rise of owner-occupation as the dominant form of housing often meant that a wife's income represented far more than "pin money" to the household. The desire for home improvement, itself fostered by the growth of owner-occupation, also played a part here.

As a result, women's experiences within the home and local community changed. Over time, far fewer were involved in the types of neighborhood relationships reported in "traditional" communities (Young and Willmott, 1957; Rosser and Harris, 1965; see Crow and Allan, 1994). However, the changes rarely resulted in any major restructuring of domestic relationships. Despite marital inequality becoming a highly contested issue within the feminist-inspired politics of domesticity, the underlying structure of the domestic division of labor appeared to change very little. In particular, notwithstanding the increased significance of wives' earnings for living standards, their employment was often defined as secondary. Their primary responsibility still lay within the domestic sphere, managing domestic organization and family relationships (Hunt, 1978; Allan, 1985). While rhetoric sometimes suggested otherwise, relatively few husbands actually participated equally in household or child-care tasks, though there was some movement in the overall balance of activities (Sullivan, 2000).

For many couples in the cohort we are considering, especially those who have remained married to each other since young adulthood, the patterns set in earlier life phases continue to frame later domestic organization. Research in this area has identified a number of important issues affecting the domestic lives of older couples. American research suggests that gender differentiation may diminish after retirement, with greater participation by husbands in traditionally "feminine" tasks such as cleaning and shopping (Sporakowski and Axelson, 1989). Such participation, however, is usually defined as "helping" wives and does not challenge the basic division of household tasks. Szinovacz (2000), for example, found little support for the common expectation that retired husbands take over a significant amount of household tasks. She concluded that: "They may help more [in the home] so as long as their wives are still employed, but they retrench from such help once their wives retire as well" (Szinovacz, 2000: 90).

British research by Mason (1987) reported very similar findings, arguing that retired couples had little incentive to renegotiate domestic relations in later life. If relatively successful – or at least acceptable – systems of household management have been established over time, why disrupt them in later life? Gender identities are also involved in this, with modes and divisions of paid and unpaid work established over the life course being key elements in individuals' definitions of masculinity and femininity. Mason also found that the men in her sample tended to encroach on their wives' personal time and space in the home, in the process creating additional forms of domestic work. In Britain, the impact of dual, as distinct from single, retirement on marriage has not yet received much research attention, though as Szinovacz, Ekerdt, and Vinick's (1992) research in the US has shown, the timing of a husband's and wife's retirement has consequences for marital relationships. Increasingly it will be important to examine couples retiring, rather than the return of a dominant breadwinner into the home – the overriding concern of existing research in this area.

The issue of the impact of early retirement on marital relationships is another area warranting further investigation (Cliff, 1989).

The changes there have been in women's employment also have the potential to alter material standards in retirement because of the possibility of "double" pensions. In reality, in Britain this is very much age- and class-linked. Because of the character of their occupational histories – typically involving low-paid, part-time, and fragmented employment – most women in the cohort under consideration have few pension entitlements. Only those who have been employed in professional occupations for significant periods of their adult life – and they are located mainly at the younger end of the 50–75 cohort – are likely to have acquired significant pension rights (Ginn, Street, and Arber, 2001). This has particular consequences for unpartnered women in retirement, many of whom will experience poverty in old age. The inadequacies of pension provision for both single women and widows has been a significant element in the growing feminization of poverty. Increases in levels of divorce among the 50–75 cohort will also play a part here, especially for divorces in Britain occurring prior to new legislation governing the division of pension rights. As table 8.1 indicates, the majority of women in this cohort are married but a significant minority are not. Some will repartner, though historically this has been far more likely for women under 40 than for women aged 50–75.

## Generational Relationships

The impact of changing family practices is not restricted to domestic or household matters. Relationships within and across generations are also responsive to social and economic change. On the one hand, much research evidence from different countries has shown that generational ties continue to be important across the life course. On the other, the growth of individualism, as identified by Beck (1992), Giddens (1992), and others, has almost certainly loosened some kinship ties, whilst making some other non-kin relationships more central, for older as well as younger people. What evidence can be cited to illustrate these changes, and what do they tell us about the nature of family life for middle-aged and older people? In the first place, research from a wide range of countries has demonstrated the significance of intergenerational ties in the family life of older people (Arber and Attias-Donfut, 2000; Bengston and Achenbaum, 1993; Finch and Mason, 1993; Phillipson et al., 2001). Attias-Donfut and Wolff's (2000) research in France is particularly relevant here for

**Table 8.1** Marital status of men and women aged 50–75, Great Britain, 2000 (%)

| *Marital status* | *Men* | | *Women* | |
|---|---|---|---|---|
| | *55–64* | *65–74* | *55–64* | *65–74* |
| Single | 8 | 8 | 5 | 5 |
| Married | 75 | 76 | 69 | 56 |
| Cohabiting | 3 | 1 | 2 | 1 |
| Divorced/separated | 10 | 5 | 12 | 7 |
| Widowed | 3 | 9 | 11 | 31 |

*Source*: General Household Survey (2001).

highlighting the role of the "pivot" (middle-age) generation in providing economic support to young people on the threshold of adulthood, as well as in providing flexible forms of care for the older generation as need arises. Importantly, these researchers also demonstrated the way in which public transfers have reinforced rather than weakened family solidarities. They present this interweaving of the public and the private as follows:

> Within the life course, individuals begin by receiving support from their mid-life parents which they in turn indirectly repay in their economically active years through their provision of pensions. During this period they also provide support to their adult children and receive private transfers from their elderly parents who in turn benefit from care as they enter later life. (Attias-Donfut and Wolff, 2000: 65)

The generations also continue to provide emotional support for one another. Longitudinal research reported by Bengston et al. (2000) tracked feelings of emotional closeness and support across generations. They found that emotional closeness stayed stable over a period of nearly two decades, with the maintenance of strong levels of affectual solidarity across generations. This is also reflected in intergenerational support, with adult children providing help to both mothers and fathers, although with the interesting finding that "The amount of support provided to mothers and fathers by adult children is higher when intergenerational affect is high. Further the amount of support provided to mothers is highest when mothers have greater need due to health problems" (Bengston et al., 2000: 6).

For the cohort we are focusing on in this chapter – those aged 50–75 – grandparent roles have also been refashioned, at least in part as a result of the demographic and other shifts discussed earlier. Thompson views grandparenting as a distinctively modern experience: "In the past, because they died earlier, two-thirds of children grew up without any significant memory of a grandparent" (1999: 476). Contrast this with the findings of the French study by Attias-Donfut and Wolff, where amongst the middle "pivot" generation: "Two out of three give care [i.e., spend time with their grandchildren in the absence of the parents] whether on a regular basis or occasionally during the entire year and also often during vacations" (2000: 35). Dench and Ogg's (2002) research, drawn from questions asked in the 1998 British Social Attitudes (BSA) Survey, confirmed the important role which grandparents continue to play in family life – particularly in relation to child-care and financial support. Minkler's (1999) research in the US has also highlighted the dramatic rise in grandparenting care through the 1980s and 1990s, with more than one in ten grandparents having primary responsibility for raising a grandchild at some point, with this care often lasting for several years.

These findings reflect the shift in the resources and prospects of the different generations. Bengston et al. (2000: 9) express the view that increasingly older people are the "donors, not the net recipients" of generational support. Furthermore, Kunemund and Rein have made the important observation that providing public resources to older people may assist in raising levels of emotional support within the family. They conclude that: "When elderly people have sufficient resources of their own, they are not forced by necessity to rely upon their families. Therefore interactions focused on intimacy and closeness have the potential to develop" (1999: 97). More generally, Bengston has proposed that given an increase in longevity, multigenerational ties have assumed greater importance within Western societies. He argues from this that: "for many Americans, multigenerational bonds are becoming more important than nuclear family ties for well-being and support over the course of their lives" (2001: 14).

At the same time, the diversity of family ties in the middle and later phases of the life course must also be acknowledged. Generational relationships remain important in anchoring people at different points of the life course; however, not everyone is involved to the same degree in these relationships. The extent to which people are depends on their individual circumstances, as well as those of the others in their kinship network. Moreover, each individual's personal network involves non-kin as well as kin. As we shall discuss more fully below, some of the social and economic changes that are currently occurring may well increase the significance of non-kin in people's lives. Irrespective of this, the kinship system itself is now more complex than it was for much of the twentieth century, as we indicated earlier. Riley and Riley (1993: 169) develop these points in producing their model of a latent matrix of relationships, which reflects the increasingly "fuzzy" edges and less distinct boundaries of contemporary kinship. The authors argue:

> the emerging boundaries of the kin network may become more influenced by gender or even by race and ethnicity, than by age or generation. Instead, the boundaries of the kin network have been widened to encompass many diverse relationships, including several degrees of stepkin and in-laws, single-parent families, adopted and other "relatives" chosen from outside the family, and many others . . . . (1993: 174).

The possibility of open or porous kinship boundaries is well established in the research literature. Stack's (1974) classic study of a black urban community in the US demonstrated how standard definitions of nuclear or extended families often failed to capture the complex way in which people lived their lives. Added to this are the demographic changes noted earlier, such as later age of marriage, delayed childbirth, cohabitation, and stepfamilies, all of which underline the significance of the view that there can be: "little doubt that the network of potentially significant relationships is becoming enlarged" (Riley and Riley, 1993: 187).

The growth of divorce, remarriage, and stepfamily formation provides a good illustration of how older people's kinship networks are becoming more complex and "fuzzy," sometimes directly, sometimes indirectly. Parental divorce, for example, can have a significant impact on relationships between the nonresidential parent and (usually) his child(ren) beyond childhood. Where a nonresidential parent has little consequent contact with a child, the relationship is unlikely to become particularly close in emotional or exchange terms as the parent enters later life. Similarly, it is unlikely that significant grandparental relationships will develop with any children the adult child may have. Divorce in later life, which, as noted above, is becoming more common, may not have the same impact as parental divorce in childhood, but depending on its circumstances and "natural history," can at times also lead to relationship tension and rifts between the generations, especially if one parent is judged to have treated the other unfairly. More obviously, an (adult) child's divorce often has repercussions on the parental generation, in particular with regard to relationships with grandchildren. While current policies encouraging continued parental involvement after separation are likely to alter this somewhat, divorce can often render relationships with grandchildren problematic. Interestingly, there is some evidence that nonresidential fathers are encouraged by their parents to sustain their relationships with their children, and in turn use their mothers especially (i.e., the child's grandmother) as a resource for managing contact periods (Burgoyne and Clark, 1984; Allan, Hawker, and Crow, 2001).

The increasing numbers of stepfamilies also has consequences for the cohort now aged 50–75, again particularly with respect to grandchild ties. The key issue here is the extent to which step-grandchildren – whether these be the children of stepchildren or the stepchildren of children – are seen as kin and regarded as part of "the family." There is a good deal of variation in the relationships people develop with step-grandchildren (Allan, Hawker, and Crow, 2001), in large part mediated through the tie developed and sustained between the stepchild and the stepparent. It is more likely that step-grandparents will treat a step-grandchild "grandparentally" where the stepchild lives with stepparent (i.e., the step-grandparents' son or daughter) and has some form of parental relationship with them. Further complexities are added, though, when there are natural as well as step-grandchildren living in the household, where the stepchild has active relationships with their natural grandparents on the nonresidential parents' side, and where the step-grandchildren are older rather than younger when the stepfamily is formed.

## Personal Communities

As we have indicated above, as well as having an impact on family and kinship structures, individualization and the other transformations associated with late modernity are also influencing the patterning of non-family ties to which individuals are party. Indeed increasingly an argument can be made that family and non-family ties need to be examined together; treating them in isolation may well result in the real processes and dynamics of family and community change being misrepresented. The concept of "personal communities" – the world of friends, neighbors, leisure associates, as well as family and kin – is particularly helpful here for capturing the interplay of the different kinds of social ties affecting people at various points of the life course. Wellman and Wortley define a "personal community network" as:

> a person's set of active community ties, [which] is usually socially diverse, spatially dispersed, and sparsely knit.... Its ties vary in characteristics and in the kinds of support they provide. Until now, community (and kinship) analysts have concentrated on documenting the persistence, composition, and structure of these networks in order to show that community has not been lost in contemporary societies. They have paid less attention to evaluating how characteristics of community ties and networks affect access to the supportive resources that flow through them. (1990: 560)

Placing people within the context of "personal communities" also bears upon an important sociological argument, namely, the development of a more "voluntaristic" element in personal relations. Instead of people locked into family groups, they may be more accurately perceived as "managing" a wide spread of relationships, with friends, kin, neighbors, and other supporters, exchanging and receiving help at different points of the life course (Pahl, 2000). Viewing people as "managers" of a network of relationships offers a different perspective to that commonly adopted within gerontology. Here, the traditional focus has been upon a preordained sequence starting with the family first, and leading outwards toward other sets of relationships (Shanas, 1979). However, an alternative approach is to view older people as active network participants, adopting a range of "strategies" in maintaining social ties.

Many of the changes we have been discussing clearly encourage such active participation in the construction of personal life, including in this the construction of personal communities. In comparison to the past when, as we have been arguing, people's experiences were more liable to be ordered in relatively "preordained" and standard fashions, there is now a greater sense of choice and "fluidity" over the manner in which they make lifestyle decisions. People's options in this are not as constrained as they previously were. This can be seen both in the demographic decisions which are altering the typical life course, especially those involving partnership formation and dissolution, and in the degree to which the exchange of resources between kinship generations is now understood as more a matter of give and take, where, in Segalen's terms, "the precondition of obedience has given way to a complex set of negotiations" (1997: 9).

Equally here different individuals – whether young or old – construct their personal networks in different ways. For the vast majority, family and kinship remain important, as Attias-Donfut and Wolff's discussion of the "pivot" generation clearly indicates. But equally non-kin relationships will be fostered to different degrees and be drawn on in different ways. Indeed, increasingly, friendships and other such ties may come to play a key role in people's social identity and their sense of who they are (Allan, 2001). In particular, for many of the cohort we have been concentrating on in this chapter, those currently aged 50–75, earlier retirement, together with a greater degree of economic security through occupational pension rights and owner-occupation, offers fresh possibilities for developing lifestyles in which friendships, leisure, and sociability are quite pivotal. Such possibilities were largely absent for previous cohorts of this age group.

While there is not space in this chapter to consider these issues fully, it is worth focusing briefly on one topic which highlights the relevance of analyzing both the operation of, and changes in, personal networks: the process of migration. This was the subject of a classic study by Karn (1977), who examined the movement of older people to the English "retirement resorts" of Bexhill and Clacton-on-Sea. Her research demonstrated a number of important changes affecting personal networks arising from migration. For example, contact with children tended to be reduced over time (although the proportion of migrants with no surviving children was higher than the national average). On the other hand, contact with siblings did not weaken as much as it did with children, and contacts with friends tended to be least adversely affected by the move. Marital status was, however, an important variable influencing social ties, with widows and widowers reporting the greatest difficulty in sustaining friendships. In this research, migration combined with the experience of living alone had the most impact on social networks in old age. Overall, however, the picture presented was one of positive adaptation to migration, an impression reinforced in a later study by King, Warnes, and Williams (2000) of British retirement migration to Mediterranean coastal resorts.

Studies such as these suggest that migration does not always lead to older people becoming more isolated from kin. Frequently, in later life people move to be closer to particular relatives, adopting a form of "chain migration" – a pattern whereby over time partial kin networks rather than just individuals relocate near one another (Ballard, 2001). Once the first migrants have "settled" into a new location, others in their kin network follow, either to be with them or to benefit from the relative advantages the "host" society offers. Such patterns are not restricted to "within-country" migration. Globalization processes have fostered high levels of international migration. While those who migrate typically tend to be from younger cohorts, such migration can result in some older people becoming marginalized from wider networks of support. In Britain, for example, Phillipson, Ahmed, and Latimer (2003) explored the experiences of women who had migrated from Bangladesh to the London borough of Tower Hamlets. The research documented tensions surrounding adaptation to life in an inner-city borough. On the one hand, most of the women had "chain-migrated" into well-established social networks built around common geographical locations. For example, of the 100 women interviewed close to two-thirds (60 per cent) could name a relative such as a sister, cousin, or niece within the borough. Neighborhood relationships in this context overlapped with kinship ties, a continuation of a longstanding tradition within the East End as reported by Ross (1983) and Young and Willmott (1957), amongst others. Virtually all the women interviewed reported having friends in their neighborhood, with most of these drawn from within the Bangladeshi community itself. However, 17 percent reported having friends from a variety of ethnic groups, these having been formed through contacts at school, work, education classes, and their own children (Phillipson, Ahmed, and Latimer, 2002). These networks provided support for immediate housing needs and in securing help with financial problems.

On the other hand, the women were often isolated from wider systems of support, notably in relation to public welfare and health services. The impact of racism in the immediate locality also reinforced the way in which first-generation migrant women were often divided about the benefits that migration had brought to their lives. For them it involved some degree of separation from close family (most had mothers, for example, still living in Bangladesh), but it represented opportunities as well – not least for their own children.

Overall, the globalization of family life is creating a major new research agenda in terms of tracking how generational and network-based ties are sustained across different nation states (Levitt, 2001). Some of the key questions that need to be considered include: are new means of contact and communication being developed to sustain traditional ties within families? What are the contrasting ways in which men and women respond to the pressures of migration? What are the distinctive types of reciprocity that might develop amongst families separated through time and space? What is the differential role of family and friends in providing help and support through the main stages of the life course, especially that of later life? The last question is a reminder that older migrants may have experienced a radically different life course in comparison to the majority, white population, with vastly different experiences and attitudes toward old age itself.

## Conclusion

This chapter has explored the complex relationship between aging, family relationships, and the life course. Aging, in its biological and physiological manifestation, has increased in importance given the impact of the growth in the number and proportion of elderly people in Western societies. But the extension of lives is also being changed by the reshaping of the life course, with the emergence of what

Gilleard and Higgs refer to as "the development of new later life identities" (2000: 29). One consequence of this is that the pathways into aging, followed by fresh cohorts of people entering their fifties and sixties, will almost certainly be less rigidly defined than was the case with their predecessors. Such pathways are likely to have a number of features in terms of the relationship between older people and their families. Social and demographic changes will almost certainly lead to the increased salience of multigenerational ties. Indeed, generally, there is likely to be a widening of the range of significant relationships upon which people draw for aid and support in times of crisis and need (Riley and Riley, 1993). Bonds of friendship may not replace kin ties, but they will almost certainly influence the range of help and support available (Pahl, 2000).

Thus, clusters of friends and neighbors may "crowd in" or "crowd out" family support (using the terminology of Kunemund and Rein, 1999), with the possibility of substitution and/or withdrawal of different types of help. Moreover, a broad range of social ties may well be required to cope with the pressures and conflicts affecting family relationships. Global changes associated with migration and increased mobility represent one important element in this. Of additional importance is the tension between work relations on the one side, and family support on the other. Richard Sennett (1998), for example, has argued that the new flexibility and mobility associated with paid work may have a corrosive effect on long-term ties to friends and family. His analysis suggests that family relationships may be compromised by the insecurities affecting people in employment (see also Taylor, 2002). This raises the important question of the extent to which the social environment appropriate for an aging society may conflict with the economic goals of global capitalism. Family groups and personal communities, as argued in this chapter, are traditionally associated with high levels of support to older people. However, this may be disrupted through work ties that encourage short-term forms of association rather the long-term connections characteristic of family ties.

The role of the family relationships within the life course is therefore likely to undergo modification, as new cohorts bring different experiences to the process of social aging. At the same time, the place of older people within the life course as a whole will develop in new ways as traditional sequences of work and family responsibilities are reorganized as a consequence of individual and structural change (Settersten, 2003). The key point to stress, however, is the dynamic process whereby older people both influence the shape of the life course, whilst themselves being affected by changes operating at an institutional level. Families, with their connecting intergenerational bonds, will remain at the center of this process, and will themselves contribute to what is likely be a major area for sociological research in the years ahead.

## References

Allan, G. (1985) *Family Life*. Oxford: Blackwell.

Allan, G. (2001) Personal relationships in late modernity. *Personal Relationships*, 8, 325–39.

Allan, G., and Crow, G. (2001) *Families, Households and Society.* Basingstoke: Palgrave.

Allan, G., Hawker, S., and Crow, G. (2001) Family diversity and change in Britain and Western Europe. *Journal of Family Issues*, 22, 819–37.

Arber, S., and Attias-Donfut, C. (2000) *The Myth of Generational Conflict*. London: Routledge.

Attias-Donfut, C., and Wolff, F-C. (2000) Complimentarity between private and public transfer. In S. Arber and C. Attias-Donfut (eds.), *The Myth of Generational Conflict*. London: Routledge.

Ballard, R. (2001) *The Impact of Kinship on the Economic Dynamics of Transnational Networks: Reflections on Some South Asian Developments. Working Paper 01-06b*. Princeton, NJ: Centre for Migration and Development, Princeton University.

Beck, U. (1992) *The Risk Society: Towards a New Modernity*. London: Sage.

Beck, U., and Beck-Gernsheim E. (1995) *The Normal Chaos of Love*. Cambridge: Polity.

Bengtson, V. L. (2001) Beyond the nuclear family: the increasing importance of multigenerational bonds. *Journal of Marriage and the Family*, 63,1–6.

Bengtson, V. L., and Achenbaum, W. A. (eds.) (1993) *The Changing Contract Across Generations*. New York: Aldine De Gruyter.

Bengtson, V. L., Giarrusso, R., Silverstein, M., and Wang, H. (2000) Families and intergenerational relationships in aging societies. *Hallym International Journal of Aging*, 2, 3–10.

Best, F. (1980) *Flexible Life Scheduling*. New York: Praeger.

*Birth Statistics* (1976) Series FM1, No 3. London: Stationery Office.

*Birth Statistics* (1999) Series FM1, No 28. London: Stationery Office.

Burgoyne, J., and Clark, D. (1984) *Making A Go of It*. London: Routledge & Kegan Paul.

Clarke, P. (1996) *Hope and Glory: Britain 1990–1990*. London: Allen Lane.

Cliff, D. (1989) Life After Work: An Investigation Of Men In Early Retirement. Doctoral dissertation, University of Huddersfield.

Crow, G., and Allan, G. (1994) *Community Life*. Hemel Hempstead: Harvester-Wheatsheaf.

Dench, G., and Ogg, J. (2002) *Grandparenting in Britain: A Baseline Study*. London: Institute of Community Studies.

Finch, J., and Mason, M. (1993) *Negotiating Family Responsibilities*. London: Routledge.

Finch, J., and Summerfield, P. (1991) Social reconstruction and the emergence of companionate marriage. 1945–59. In D. Clark (ed.), *Marriage, Domestic Life and Social Change*. London: Routledge.

General Household Survey (2001) *Living in Britain: Results from the 2000 General Household Survey*. London: The Stationery Office.

Gibson, C. (1994) *Dissolving Wedlock*. London: Routledge.

Giddens, A. (1992) *The Transformation of Intimacy: Sexuality, Love and Eroticism in Modern Societies*. Cambridge: Polity.

Gilleard, C., and Higgs, P. (2000) *Cultures of Aging*. London: Prentice-Hall.

Ginn, J., Street, D., and Arber, S. (2001) *Women, Work and Pensions*. Buckingham: Open University Press.

Haskey, J. (1996) The proportion of married couples who divorce: Past patterns and current prospects. *Population Trends*, 83, 25–36.

Hunt, P. (1978) Cash transactions and household tasks. *Sociological Review*, 26, 555–71.

Jamieson, L. (1998) *Intimacy*. Cambridge: Polity.

Jamieson, L. (1999) Intimacy transformed? A critical look at the pure relationship. *Sociology*, 33, 477–94.

Karn, V. (1977). *Retiring to the Seaside*. London: Routledge & Kegan Paul.

King, R., Warnes, T., and Williams, A. (2000) *Sunset Lives: British Retirement Migration to the Mediterranean*. Oxford: Berg.

Kohli, M., and Rein, M. (1991) The changing balance of work and retirement. In M. Kohli, M. Rein, A. M. Guillemard, and H. V. Gunsteren (eds.), *Time for Retirement*. Cambridge: Cambridge University Press.

Kunemund, H., and Rein, M (1999) There is more to receiving than needing: Theoretical arguments and empirical explorations of crowding in and crowding out. *Aging and Society*, 19, 93–121.

Levitt, P (2001) *The Transnational Villagers*. Berkeley: University of California Press.

*Marriage and Divorce Statistics* (1976) Series FM2, No 3. London: The Stationery Office.

*Marriage, Divorce and Adoption Statistics* (1999). Series FM2, No 27. London, The Stationery Office.
Mason, J. (1987) A bed of roses? Women, marriage and inequality in later life. In P. Allatt, T. Keil, A. Bryman, and B. Bytheway (eds.), *Women and the Life Cycle*. Basingstoke: Macmillan.
Mayer, K-U., and Muller, W (1986) The state and the structure of the life course. In A. B. Sorensen, F. Weinert, and L. Sherrod (eds.), *Human Development and the Life Course: Multidisciplinary Perspectives*. Hillsdale, NJ: Lawrence Erlbaum.
Minkler, M. (1999) Intergenerational households headed by grandparents. *Journal of Aging Studies*, 13,199–218.
National Statistics (2002) *Health Statistics Quarterly*. London: National Statistics.
Pahl, R. (2000) *On Friendship*. Cambridge: Polity.
Phillipson, C. (1998) *Reconstructing Old Age*. London: Sage.
Phillipson, C. (2002) *Transitions from Work to Retirement: Developing a New Social Contract*. Bristol: Policy Press.
Phillipson, C., Bernard, M., Phillips, J., and Ogg, J. (2001) *The Family and Community Life of Older People: Social Networks and Social Support in Three Urban Areas*. London: Routledge.
Phillipson, C., Ahmed, N., and Latimer, J (2003) *Women in Transition: A Study of the Experience of Bangladeshi Women Living in the London Borough of Tower Hamlets*. Bristol: Policy Press.
Pillemer , K., Moen, P., Wethington, E., and Glasgow, N. (2001) *Social Integration in the Second Half of Life*. Baltimore: Johns Hopkins University Press.
Riley, M. W., and Riley, J. (1993) Connections: kin and cohort. In V. L. Bengston and W. A. Achenbaum (eds.), *The Changing Contract Across Generations*. New York: Aldine De Gruyter.
Rosser, C., and Harris, C. C. (1965) *The Family and Social Change*. London: Routledge & Kegan Paul.
Ross, E. (1983) Survival networks: Women's neighbourhood sharing in the East End of London before World War One. *History Workshop*, Spring, 4–27.
Scales, J., and Scase, R. (2001) *Fit at Fifty*. Swindon: Economic and Social Research Council.
Schuller, T. (1989) Work-ending: Employment and ambiguity in later life. In B. Bytheway, T. Keil, P. Allatt, and A. Bryman (eds.), *Becoming and Being Old*. London: Sage.
Segalen, M. (1997) Introduction. In M. Gullestad and M. Segalen (eds.), *Family and Kinship in Europe*. London: Pinter.
Sennett, R. (1998) *The Corrosion of Character*. New York: W. W. Norton.
Settersten R. (2003*) Invitation to the Life Course: Toward New Understandings of Later Life*. New York: Baywood Press.
Shanas, E. (1979) The family as a social support system in old age. *The Gerontologist*, 19, 169–74.
Smart, C., and Neale, B. (1999) *Family Fragments?* Cambridge: Polity.
Sporakowski, M., and Axelson, L. (1989) Long-term marriages: a critical review. In L. Ade-Ridder and C. Hennon (eds.), *Lifestyles of the Elderly*. New York: Human Sciences Press.
Stack, C. (1974) *All Our Kin: Strategies for Survival in a Black Community*. New York: Harper.
Sullivan, O. (2000) The division of domestic labour: twenty years of change? *Sociology*, 34, 437–56.
Szinovacz, M (2000) Changes in housework after retirement: A panel analysis. *Journal of Marriage and the Family*, 62, 78–92.
Szinovacz, M., Ekerdt, D. J., and Vinick, B. H. (eds.) (1992). *Families and Retirement*. Newbury Park, CA: Sage.
Taylor, R. (2002) *Britain's World of Work: Myth and Realities*. Swindon: Economic and Social Research Council.

Thompson, P. (1999) The role of grandparents when parents part or die: some reflections on the mythical decline of the extended family. *Aging and Society*, 19, 471–503.

Thompson, P., Itzin, C and Abendstern, M. (1990) *I Don't Feel Old: The Experience of Later Life*. Oxford: Oxford University Press.

Wall, R. (1992) Relationships between generations in British families past and present. In C. Marsh and S. Arber (eds.), *Families and Households*. London: Macmillan.

Warnes, A. (1996) The demography of old age: Panic versus reality. In R. Bland (ed.), *Developing Services for Older People*. London: Jessica Kingsley.

Wellman, B., and Wortley, S. (1990) Different strokes by different folks: Community ties and social support. *American Journal of Sociology*, 93, 558–88.

Young, M., and Willmott, P. (1957) *Family and Kinship in East London*. London: Routledge & Kegan Paul.

# 9

# Parenting Practices

Duane F. Alwin

*Parenthood* is both a biological and social status. Viewed within a biological life-cycle framework, parenthood can be seen as a natural outcome of reproduction and regeneration. Viewed from a social and cultural perspective, the situation of parenthood conveys certain rights, responsibilities, obligations, and associated expectations regarding the care and nurture of children. While the role of parenthood viewed biologically has important consequences for children – particularly in the transmission of genetic information and predispositions that may have developmental consequences – our focus here is primarily on parenthood as a social and cultural phenomenon.

*Parenting practices* is a very broad term that includes the totality of attitudes, values, beliefs, and behaviors that parents bring to settings in which they interact with their child or children. While we recognize there may be some universal consequences that derive from the parent–child relationship, we must also indicate at the outset that the meaning of parenthood is quite diverse even within the same historical period and in the same society. The rights and obligations of parenthood depend on a host of parental and child characteristics. For example, what it means to be a *mother* versus what it means to be a *father* are generally quite different things in virtually all cultural settings. Also, what parents may try to achieve in parenting a newborn infant is something quite different from what they may aspire to in parenting an adolescent. The demands arising both from the parent–child relationship and from the social context in which the parental role is enacted are quite different across these life stages.

A central theme of this chapter is that what parents want for their children, and what they believe is the best approach to achieving their goals through their parenting practices will depend not only upon a host of parental and child characteristics but upon a number of historical, economic, demographic, cultural, ecological, and structural variables that shape parental approaches to child rearing.

## Social and Historical Perspectives

There has been quite a lot written in recent years about changes in the European and American family going back over the past three or four centuries. While many of the family's institutional functions have remained the same over such lengthy spans of time – e.g., the family has continued to be the *primary* agent for the care and nurture of children – the nature of parent–child relationships have experienced some significant changes (Greven, 1970; Vinovskis, 1987; French, 2002).

One does not have to look very far into the past to see some of the consequences of these changes for parental orientations to children. The recognition of this fact should help signify that the potential for change in parental practices over long spans of time can be great. Wrigley (1989) performed a content analysis of child-rearing manuals published in America over the twentieth century and found that the professional advice of child experts has changed from a preoccupation with such things as nutrition and toilet-training toward a greater emphasis on the need for cognitive development. These results are complemented by Alwin's (1996a) use of several different sources of survey data over the twentieth century that show significant changes have occurred in Western countries in the values parents emphasize in raising their children. There is a fairly clear pattern of increasing preferences for an emphasis that stresses the autonomy of children and a decline in the valuation of obedience. Over the periods and settings studied parental orientations to children had changed from a concentration on fitting children into society to one of providing for children in a way that would enhance their development.

Looking back even farther, the historical literature has suggested that there have been major changes in parental approaches to the socialization of children from medieval times onward. In one of the most highly cited works on the history of childhood Ariès (1962) [1960] argued that during the medieval period the boundaries between the household and the rest of society were relatively less rigidly defined than they are in their modern Western counterparts and that this had major implications for the parental responsibility in the socialization of children. Relationships within the nuclear family were not necessarily closer than those outside, and there was greater reliance on neighbors, relatives, and friends in the monitoring of children's behavior (see also Stone, 1977; Vinovskis, 1987). This may have been a consequence of the lack of privacy as much as anything else.

One needs to exact a certain degree of care in approaching the historical literature on the nature of the family and parent–child interactions, as historians often lack a direct empirical portal into the past. History is always written from the point of view of the present and of the writer. There is often a tendency to perceive different periods of time in terms of an evolution of stages, whereas in fact the temporal continuities and discontinuities may not be driven by any such evolutionary mechanisms.

Parenting practices depend (among other things) upon beliefs about the nature of children, and historians of childhood have debated the extent to which the nature of childhood itself may have undergone dramatic change over long periods of history. Ariès (1962) [1960] argued that in the Middle Ages, due in part to high rates of infant mortality, mothers were indifferent to their infants and did not display a great deal of grief if they died. He argued, additionally, that the discipline of children was often harsh and that this lack of affection for children continued until the sixteenth and seventeenth centuries. In the eighteenth and nineteenth centuries, according to Ariès (1962) [1960], there emerged the development of the idea of the individuality of children, the acceptance of their inherent worth, and an awareness of the innocence and purity of childhood. Not everyone agrees with the Ariès thesis (see Cunningham, 1991). For example, Pollock's (1983) examination of diaries among the educated classes of England across the sixteenth through nineteenth centuries casts considerable doubt on the assumption of maternal indifference to children during that period. Others (e.g., Shorter, 1975) have argued that the harsh treatment of children persisted into the eighteenth and nineteenth centuries among all social classes in Western Europe, and the harsh treatment of children continues to be associated with certain religious groups (see Greven, 1977; Ellison and Sherkat, 1993).

Without relying on *interpretations* of what parenting practices were likely to have prevailed in earlier historical periods, there are a number of important documented historical changes in Western society over the past two centuries that have produced concrete changes in the social and cultural conditions that affect parenting practices. Limitations of space prevent extensive discussion of these developments, but we can mention these briefly here.

First, there have been *major cultural changes* that have affected the ways in which parents interact with their children. Lesthaeghe (1983, 1995) points to the Enlightenment near the end of the eighteenth century, which he refers to as one of the most important ideational legacies of Western history, as redefining the position of the individual relative to society, "legitimizing the principle of individual freedom of choice" (p. 413). These changes have had a significant impact on parental orientations to children (see Alwin, 1988, 1996a; Zelizer, 1985).

Second, some of the historic change in parenting practices is linked to *demographic change*, given massive fertility declines have occurred throughout the Western world over the past two centuries (Davis, 1986; Alwin, 1996b). It has long been recognized that levels of fertility are relevant to parental orientations to children in several ways (Caldwell, 1976, 1982). One can view these demographic changes against the economic, cultural, and political changes mentioned earlier. Not only is declining fertility a reflection of the greater emphasis on individualism, but other changes in the family (e.g., the legitimation of non-marital cohabitation, rising ages of first marriage, voluntary childlessness, sexual freedom, rises in divorce, and the demand for abortion) can be seen as part of the larger picture of social change in the direction of religious secularization and the rise of individualism (Lesthaeghe and Meekers, 1986; Lesthaeghe and Surkyn, 1988; Westoff, 1986).

Third, *changes in social and economic organization* that accompanied the Industrial Revolution and the movement from a largely agrarian mode of production to an industrial one have led to important changes in the conditions under which children are raised (see Hernandez, 1993). Coleman (1990), for example, argued that the movement from forms of authority in which one person has authority over and responsibility for another toward organizations in which authority is delegated to specific realms or to the individual is one of the critical consequences of these massive technological transformations. This is a shift that clearly parallels the changes in parent–child relations, and Coleman (1990: 660) cites the evidence on changes in parental values as indicative of evidence in support of his argument (see Alwin, 1988).

Fourth, the Industrial Revolution also brought with it *the separation of work and the family.* In pre-industrial society both men and women worked near hearth and home, and both played an important role in the socialization of children. Given the nature of subsistence and agricultural modes of production, both men's and women's work was integrated into family activities and parental and child labor contributed to the economic well-being of the family. The economy and the home were essentially inseparable. The changing locus of economic production from the family to the factory eventually resulted in the "domestication" of women and the emergence of the role of "housewife" or "homemaker" (Lupri, 1983: 4). As a result of industrialization we have witnessed the *rise of the traditional nuclear non-farm family* which grew dramatically through World War II. In 1960 the non-farm "father breadwinner, mother homemaker" family was the dominant form experienced by children – nearly 60 percent – in American society (Hernandez, 1993, Figure 4.1: 103). Comparable figures in other Western democracies for this period are as high or higher.

Fifth, in the post-World War II period, due largely to increases in *women's labor-force participation*, the traditional non-farm "father breadwinner–mother homemaker" family form has declined dramatically, and we have seen the increase in the two-earner and single-parent families. Together these latter two types of families make up the vast majority of the families inhabited by children in American society today – upwards of 70 percent (ibid.). High rates of marital dissolution, the proliferation of nonmarital childbearing, and increases in women's labor-force participation have all contributed to this trend.

Sixth, the net result of all of these social forces means that more and more children are inhabiting what Furstenberg (1992) called the *neo-traditional family* – "a renovated model of the gender-based division of labor when women share a greater measure of economic responsibility and men may assume a greater share of domestic chores than was deemed appropriate in previous times." Employment in the paid labor force of women, especially those with young children, has been steadily increasing in virtually every country in Europe, as well as North America, although in Europe the changes are mainly seen in part-time work (see Hoffman, 1979, 1989; Rosenfeld and Birkelund, 1995; Rosenfeld, 1996; Dex, chapter 25, this volume). This *shift toward more egalitarian sex roles* has had major impacts on parenting practices, particularly sex-linked orientations of parents. Hoffman points toward research findings that daughters of working women are behaviorally more autonomous than those of nonworking women, and she speculates that fathers' increased participation in child rearing will facilitate the "development of independence and achievement in girls as well as boys, possibly lessening the sex differences that still seem to exist" (1977: 654). She argues further that the husbands of working women are less traditional than those whose wives do not work (see Alwin, Scott, and Braun, 1992) and the *combined* experiences of greater participation in childrearing and living with a working wife may "affect the father's childrearing behavior and his assumptions of what the adult roles are for which he is socializing his children" (Hoffman, 1977: 655).

Seventh, not only do these changes reflect the growing economic independence of women, they also suggest changes in the contexts of child-rearing which reflect growing *demands for the autonomy of children* (Alwin, 2001). With these post-World War II changes, along with the development of compulsory schooling in the early twentieth century in Western societies, some would argue that the responsibility for "parenting" has again shifted, or it at least is in flux. Children are now much more likely to spend time in institutions outside the family or on their own (see Hofferth and Sandberg, 2001).

## Social Class Differences

Life in an industrialized society was very difficult for children of the working classes, given their likely involvement in the labor force. By contrast, the lives of children of the elite classes were comfortable and relatively isolated from the ravages of working-class life. Some of these class differences can also be followed into the nineteenth and twentieth centuries. Zelizer (1985), for example, has argued that the "economically useful" child of nineteenth-century industrialized society was eventually replaced by the "economically worthless," but "emotionally priceless" child of the twentieth century. She contrasts these two views of childhood, as expressed in a variety of historical public documents in American society (child labor legislation, life insurance for children, compensation for the death of children, and patterns of adoption and foster care). The value conflicts inherent in the portraits Zelizer (1985) presents reflect important class differences. Working-class children were those exploited by the industrial economy and to some extent by the circumstances of their own families. But middle-class reforms against child labor eventually denied them access to income from jobs in factories and stores. The children of the elite and business classes were rarely involved in paid labor and were removed from public environments of day-to-day life. The promulgation of the "sentimentalized" view of children by middle-class reformers thus conflicted with working-class strategies to obtain optimal economic well-being for the family through the labor-force involvement of their children (see Alwin, 1996a).

It is important to stress that variation in parenting practices is often rooted in the material foundations linked to class formation, and any analysis of child-rearing that does *not* take into account differences among social classes is likely to draw an inaccurate picture of the tendencies of parenting practices in a particular society at any given time. Stone's (1977) vivid historical account of class differences in child-rearing during the seventeenth and eighteenth centuries in England and America presents a convincing case for this viewpoint. Among the upper classes during this period, he argued, a number of dramatic changes came about in child-rearing practices, indicating a more child-centered developmental orientation. But this change toward a "maternal, child-oriented, affectionate and permissive" mode did not occur in all social classes, and the working classes were less likely to adopt such a stance toward child rearing, if at all. A similar set of observations on class differences in child-rearing approaches during the same period in Germany were made by Schlumbohm (1980). Certainly with regard to the post-World War II period in American society, there is vast support for the view that socioeconomic factors have a profound effect on parental beliefs and behavior about optimal child-rearing approaches (see review by Alwin, 2001).

## Research on Parenting Practices

Despite its ubiquity, parenting as a focus of research is a relatively new activity among developmental scientists. It is becoming an established subfield that crosses several disciplinary traditions. There are several reasons why research on parenting practices is gaining momentum on the contemporary American scene (Zigler, 2002). First, it has had a nascent status in early scholarly concerns focusing on child and adolescent development, in that the (often unstated) assumptions of environmentalist approaches to development were that parents played an active role in child development (Bronfenbrenner, 1979). Second, post-World War II changes in the family have created a greater variety of family forms, and pervasive social concerns about the effects of family change on children's development has sparked greater interest in knowledge about the effects of such diverse environments and in providing social supports to parents. Third, although there has been governmental concern with child-rearing (as evidenced in the development of the US Children's Bureau in the early twentieth century), recent professional interest in parenting was spurred by the report of a committee of the National Research Council of the US Academy of Sciences that reinforced the view of the importance of early experiences for all types of development (Shonkoff and Phillips, 2000). Fourth, the federal statistical establishment has never in its history been better equipped to monitor the well-being of children, and although the development of indicators of child well-being may have been erratic in the past, there is now renewed interest among many social scientists in assessing the circumstances in which children are growing up (see Scott, chapter 7 this volume).

## Do Parents Affect How Their Children Turn Out?

It is important to stress the fact that the idea that parental inputs to early childhood experiences are important to later development *is not new*. It has long been held that the early years of a child's development are the most important, laying the groundwork for later experiences, and that effective parenting is an important component of those critical experiences.

Despite these widely shared views there have been some recent critics of the thesis that parents are consequential to the processes contributing to the children's development. In a recent popular book, *The Nurture Assumption: Why Children Turn Out the Way They Do*, Judith Harris (1998) argued that "very, very bad parents can cause irremediable harm to their children" (p. 390), but in the main how parents raise their children – their child-rearing practices – have little, if any, effect on how their children turn out. She bases her argument on a number of powerful pieces of evidence, including a famous review of the parental socialization literature from the early 1980s by Maccoby and Martin (1983) that reviewed intrafamilial correlations in personality characteristics among both biologically related and unrelated siblings. Their conclusion was that parental behaviors on the whole had no bearing on child characteristics (see also Maccoby, 1992; Scarr, 1992, 1995; Harris, 1995; Rowe, 1994; Loehlin, 1997; Pinker, 2002).

## Opportunities for Development

We should point out that Harris is *not* arguing that *environment* is unimportant to children's development. She has no evidence of that. Her argument is solely about that part of the family environment, which we here call *parenting practices*, that is, differences in the ways people raise their children, which she claims are unimportant. Some clarification of this may be useful. There are three broad categories of possible ways that differences among families – or "between-family" differences – can produce individual differences in child outcomes. By *child outcomes* I refer to any differences in well-being, personality, values, preferences, interests, skills, accomplishments, ways of behaving, and the like. These explanations are: (1) families can differ in the *opportunities* for development of particular outcomes; (2) families can differ in *genetic endowments* that contribute to the development of particular outcomes; or (3) families can differ in the way in which they nurture or socialize their children (Scarr, 1995). These three explanations do not address the possibility that there are "within-family" differences in parenting practices that contribute to child outcomes, a topic to which we return in the section on child effects on parenting, below.

The first explanation of "between family" differences is the standard sociological explanation for why some children do better in school, or achieve more socioeconomic status, than others – their families provide them with specific advantages or different opportunities for learning or success. The playing field is clearly not level, and children from different families turn out differently as a consequence of differential advantage/disadvantage (Sewell and Hauser, 1975; Jencks et al., 1979). Harris is presumably not disputing that such inequalities in opportunity exist, although some of her text could be mistakenly interpreted this way, e.g., when she says things like: "the evidence indicates that differences between one home and another, between one set of parents and another, do not have long-term effects on the children who grow up in those homes" (1998: 391), this gives the impression that she is including any and all differences among families and not just those having to do with socialization practices. There are a number of other examples, besides those having to do with educational and socioeconomic outcomes, which can be given for differential opportunities and child outcomes.

The problem with sorting out these various explanations is that the key explanatory factors highlighted by each category are correlated with one another. If genetic differences occur between families that have educational and socioeconomic consequences for children, then they are likely to be related, for example, to the factors that shape differential opportunity structures. Or, as we shall see below, parental socialization practices are linked to family differences in opportunities. They may not be adding anything independent to the explanation of individual differences in developmental outcomes, but their role may be one of mediating the effects of other (genetic and environmental) differences among families. We cannot resolve the intricacies for sorting out the truth or falsity of these various explanations here, but suffice it to say that the complexity of the issues should not prevent us from confronting them head-on.

## Behavioral Genetic Approaches

The field of behavioral genetics, which attempts to account for individual differences in terms of genetic variation, has recently gained considerable legitimacy among social and behavioral scientists (see Plomin, 1994, 1999; Rowe, 1994; Rowe and Teachman, 2001; Scarr, 1995; Shanahan, Hofer, and Shanahan, 2003). The claim is that individual differences in developmental outcomes arise, not from family differences in access to opportunities, nor from differences in socialization approaches, but from *genetically variable* attributes of families. The behavior genetic approach attempts to draw conclusions about the relative influences of genetic and environmental differences for specific traits in specific populations from genetically informed research designs (Scarr, 1995). Studies use multiple observations of individuals of specifiable degrees of biological relationship to draw inferences about genetic and environmental sources of variation. The classic example of such genetically informed designs involves the comparison of identical twins from the same home with identical twins raised in different homes, but there is a range of different possible comparisons. Adopted and biologically related siblings, identical and fraternal twins, reared in the same and different homes, and stepfamilies with full, half-, and unrelated siblings can be studied (see Reisset al., 2000). Genetically informed designs tackle a wide range of behaviors, including intelligence (Rowe, 1994; Scarr, 1995), personality (Plomin, 1994; Loehlin, 1997), physical attractiveness (Rowe, 1994), perceptions of parenting (Rowe, 1983, 1994), and delinquency (DiLalla and Gottesman, 1989), among other things.

There is still a great deal of controversy surrounding behavioral genetic approaches, due either to the belief that any such attempts to separate the influences of genes and environment are futile, or because of the view that the complexities of doing so outweigh the ability of our present scientific knowledge. Kagan suggests that the idea that such genetic and environmental influences can be separated is due to the "unprofitable and misleading dichotomy between biology and experience" (1984: 10). He argues that "we must never treat the biological and the experiential as separate, independent forces." It would be impossible, he suggests, to separate the independent influences of premature birth status and social class in the cognitive development of children. He uses the metaphor of water freezing in a pond and the futility of trying to explain the formation of ice by partitioning the causes of the event into one set of factors having to do with the inherent properties of water and another set of factors associated with the change in temperature.

The controversial features of the nature–nurture debates have forced behavioral geneticists to spell out the theoretical complexities of the ways in which genes and environmental contexts are correlated and interact to produce behaviors (see Shanahan, Hofer, and Shanahan, 2003). Genetic interpretations are routinely vulnerable to "selection bias" issues in that shared genes are often confounded with shared environments, even in studies of monozygotic twins reared apart. Also, given the possibility of gene–environment interactions – the unique expression of genotypic variation in behavior depends on the nature of the environmental context – the traditional meaning of *heritability* as a summary measure of the relative influence of genes and environment is no longer applicable in many cases (see Bronfenbrenner and Ceci, 1994). This has led to considerable elaboration of the ways in which environmental contexts and opportunity structures can moderate the influences of genetic potential on behaviors (Shanahan, Hofer and Shanahan, 2003).

In order to understand developmental outcomes in children it is no longer possible to phrase the question as an *either–or* question. The question is *not* one of nature vs. nurture, but one of how genes and environment interact to shape development – one of nature *and* nurture. Environments are essential for development to take place – genes cannot find their phenotypic expression without ecological or environmental settings within which to do so., and environments cannot function as facilitators of human behavior without the genetic potential to work with. In a variety of behavioral domains research on nature (genes) and nurture (environments) is converging (see, e.g., Mazur and Booth, 1998; Booth and Dabbs, 1993; Booth, Carver, and Granger, 2000; Booth, Johnson, and Granger, 1999; Booth and Osgood, 1993; Caspi et al., 2002; Udry, 1988, 1990, 1996, 2000; Plomin, 1994, 1999).

## Parenting Styles

A third explanation of family differences is found in socialization theories that propose that differences in child outcomes stem, not from family differences in opportunities afforded by favorable environments or genes, but from differences in parenting practices. For example, in one of the most persuasive efforts to specify relevant parenting practices Diana Baumrind (1989, 1991a, 1991b) contrasts parental behavior that is "authoritarian" (behavior that is demanding and directive, but not responsive, stressing obedience and respect for authority) with that which is "authoritative" (behavior that is both demanding and responsive, assertive, but not intrusive or restrictive). Baumrind (1989, 1991a, 1991b) defines several pure types of parental behavior in a fourfold classification based on the dimensions of parental demandingness and parental responsiveness, as follows:

> *Authoritative* – Parents who are both demanding and responsive. They impart clear standards for their children's conduct. They are assertive, but not intrusive or restrictive. Their disciplinary methods are supportive rather than punitive. They want their children to be assertive as well as socially responsible, and self-regulated as well as cooperative.
>
> *Authoritarian* – Parents who are demanding and directive, but not responsive. They are obedience and status-oriented, expecting their orders to be obeyed without explanation. They provide an orderly environment and a clear set of regulations, monitoring their children's activities carefully.
>
> *Permissive* – Nondirective parents, who are more responsive than they are demanding. They are lenient, do not require mature behavior, allow considerable self-regulation, and avoid confrontation.
>
> *Rejecting-neglecting* – Disengaged parents who are neither demanding, nor responsive. They do not structure and monitor their children's behavior, and are not supportive. They may be actively rejecting or neglect their child-rearing responsibilities altogether.

Although this scheme is intended to have broad applicability to the description of parents' behavior, Baumrind indicates that the "operational definitions of these four prototypes – authoritative, authoritarian, permissive, and rejecting–neglecting – differ somewhat depending on social context, developmental period, and method of assessment, but share certain essential features" (1991b: 62). One of the main contrasts in Baumrind's work in describing parenting behavior, which is of particular interest here is the contrast in the behavior of the *authoritative* vs. *authoritarian* parenting style. The former are more likely to instill *autonomy*, as an aspect of competence, in children. Her study of adolescent outcomes (Baumrind, 1991b) indicates that more than any other type, "the success of authoritative parents in protecting their adolescents from problem drug use and in generating competence should be emphasized" (p. 91). She suggests that "authoritative upbringing" consistently generates adolescent competence and deters problem behavior in both boys and girls at all developmental stages. Other researchers have reinforced this conclusion (see, e.g., Darling and Steinberg, 1993; Steinberg et al., 1995; Steinberg and Silk, 2002).

## Parental Control

Changes in the family, coupled with trend data on the declining well-being of children, have caused some observers to characterize the current state of family life as lacking in commitment on the part of parents to the parental role (Uhlenberg and Eggebeen, 1986). Others have gone even farther to argue essentially that the traditional family as we know it has lost its power to socialize children. Popenoe has, for example, argued that "family groups are becoming internally deinstitutionalized, that is, their individual members are more autonomous and less bound by the group…, and (among other things) family decline is occurring in the sense that familism as a cultural value is weakening in favor of such values as self-fulfillment and egalitarianism" (1988:8–9). He points to fertility declines, increasing rates of divorce, maternal employment, and the sexual revolution as strong indications that the traditional social control and socialization functions of the family are increasingly being given over to other social institutions.

It is true that over time in Western societies parental control over children has diminished (Vinovskis, 1987: 306–8). Whereas in earlier centuries parents exercised substantial control over children's lives – through the arrangement of marriages, the choice of careers and apprenticeships, and through the inheritance of land (see Greven, 1970) – in the modern era parents may sometimes wonder whether they have *any* control. Whether we should characterize this in terms of a reduced commitment on the part of parents to the parental role or in terms of the recognition of greater independence of children and youth is an open question. What is interesting in this regard is an emergence of research in the past several decades on variations in parental monitoring of children's behavior as a component of child development (Crouter and Head, 2002).

The assumption appears to be that parents can exercise a greater measure of control over their children's behavior if they know what they are doing. The key finding in what is a growing literature is that low levels of parental monitoring are linked to high levels of problem behavior. Parental monitoring in this literature is often indicated by parental knowledge of children's activities and whereabouts, and such knowledge "develops in the context of a trusting parent–child relationship and has more to do with the child's willingness to confide in the parent than in the parent's ability to track and monitor the child" (Crouter and Head, 2002: 461). Whatever the conceptual limitations of past research and the methodological problems attendant to the issue of "what parental monitoring is really about," the fact that there is a research literature on this topic is testimony to the fact that in modern society parental control and the monitoring of children's behavior are important issues of concern for the future.

## Child Effects on Parenting

A factor that is crucial but often missing from discussion of parenting is the role of the child in the way parents enact their role. Any parent who has had more than one child is likely to be aware of the subtle and sometimes striking differences among their offspring in the responses they call out in the parent. One of the recent trends in the parenting literature – the "child effects" movement – has rallied around the early observation made by R.Q. Bell (1968) that too often our unidirectional models of socialization – where the influence is assumed to run from parent to child – are overdrawn. Early work on child rearing (Sears, Maccoby, and Levin, 1957: 454-5) suggested there may be individual differences among children (they used the term *constitutional factors*) that affect parental behavior, but it has only been within the past few decades that researchers have taken up the challenge of isolating the nature and extent of child effects.

The sex of the child is an example of one obvious biological attribute that calls up a different response on the part of parents and society. The practice of swaddling newborns in blue vs. pink blankets is a practice that still has not gone out of style in many parts of North America, despite the "consciousness raising" that supposedly happened as a result of the feminist movement. There are many examples from the literature on *gender* socialization that attest to the differential treatment of children by parents and members of society on the basis of their sex. In addition, other physical and psychological attributes of children – their size (both weight and height), (right/left) handedness, skin color/complexion, abilities, disabilities, temperament, and personality – are all factors that are potentially relevant to how parents react to them. There are other differences among children that have to do with their social position and/or acquired characteristics – e.g., birth order, race, achievements, and interests – that produce differences in how they are treated by their parents and members of society, but the child effects literature emphasizes their biological and personality differences.

One literature on individual differences among very young children that has established a strong record for the consideration of child effects is research on *temperament*, although ideas about the phenomenon go back to ancient times. Recent research on temperament was stimulated by the early work of Thomas and Chess (1977), who argued that some aspects of human functioning may be quite stable from early childhood and that *behavioral individuality*, or the uniqueness of children's response to their environment, is a strong component of how parents respond. Models on which current research are based assume that child temperament and parenting are associated in part because child temperament influences parenting and in part because parenting influences the child.

An example of research that investigated the existence of such effects focused on how infant *difficulty* affected maternal caregiving behavior. The "difficult" child was one exhibiting such characteristics as "negative mood, withdrawal, low adaptability, high intensity and low rhythmicity," although the concept is sometimes defined differently (see Putnam, Sanson, and Rothbart, 2002: 256). A child who cries excessively is an example of such a child, and the original assumption of this literature was that child difficulty would be aversive to caregivers. Any parent who has experienced a child with colic (paroxysmal pain in the lower abdomen) can relate to this example. As Crockenberg's (1986) review of research indicated, however, the results were mixed. Some studies revealed the expected pattern, but other studies showed that highly irritable children often brought out increased sensitivity and understanding on the part of mothers (Crockenberg and Leerkes, 2001). She suggested that when mothers were at risk for less than optimal parenting (because of their own attributes or of the family environment in which she lived), the child's irritability would more frequently lead to maternal withdrawal, but when there were no such risk factors present, mothers of irritable infants reacted more positively (Crockenberg, 1986). She proposed that the relationship between child temperament and parenting therefore needs to be viewed within the framework of the family environment and an understanding of the relationship between children's temperament and parenting behavior must be sought in the context of other moderating factors.

## Parent–Child Relations Across the Life Span

By necessity we have emphasized discussions of parenting practices that are relevant to those stages of life in which parents have some direct responsibility for their children (see Mabry, Giarrusso, and Bengtson, chapter 6, this volume). But even here, it is not always easy to decide when parents and their children reach that stage. Zarit and Eggebeen (2002) discuss several critical issues in the study of parent–child relationships across the adult years, including both the assistance parents give their adult children and the reverse. In our discussion of declining fertility earlier we noted Caldwell's (1976, 1982) work on parental orientations to children. He posited a "theory of wealth flows" in which he argued that the fundamental issue in the transition from high-fertility to low-fertility regimes is "the *direction and magnitude of intergenerational wealth flows* or the balance of the two flows – one from parents to children and the other from children to parents – over the period from when people become parents until they die" (1976: 344; italics in original). In low-fertility societies there may be little of the latter, although there is much cultural variation in beliefs about whose responsibility it is to care for elderly family members. As Zarit and Eggebeen (2002: 145–52) point out, in American society parents are vastly more likely to give than to receive assistance from their children. It is only a minority of older parents that receive any routine assistance from their children, and while there are clear patterns of caregiving assistance provided by a minority of children, mostly daughters, the trends in modern society are clearly in the direction of increasing non-family supports for aging parents. With the present trend toward population aging (see Hayward and Zhang, 2001) and the rising affluence of the older population, these patterns are unlikely to reverse themselves anytime soon. These are issues that must be addressed by future research.

## Conclusions

In this chapter I have presented a brief introduction to the history and current status of the topic of parenting practices. A central idea is that parenting among humans occurs in a historical, demographic, cultural, and social organizational context. These forces help shape beliefs about children and constrain the nature of the parental role. I argue that except at a very abstract level it is not possible to discuss human parenting in universal terms that apply to all societies at all times, or even to all subcultures or social classes within a given society at a given time. An appreciation of the variation in the nature and meaning of parenting is a key to understanding the subject of parenting practices in contemporary society.

Even if it is ultimately established that parenting practices do not have any independent effects on child development, or even if their major role is determined to be one of *mediating* and *moderating* the effects of other differences in family environments (opportunities) or genetic differences among families, this does not render them uninteresting. Parenting practices are social behaviors that vary across societies, across time, and within societies in a given place and time, and are *of interest in their own right*, regardless of their direct consequences for their children's lives. The differences in the way parents rear their children is a key to understanding aspects of culture, social structure, and social change.

## Acknowledgment

Preparation of material presented here was supported by grants from the National Institute of Mental Health (MH37289 and MH39761), the National Science Foundation (SES-8712119), and the National Institute on Aging (AG04743). The author is grateful to Jacqueline Scott and Scott Hofer for helpful suggestions during the preparation of this chapter.

## References

Alwin, D. F. (1988) From obedience to autonomy: changes in traits desired in children. *Public Opinion Quarterly*, 52, 33–52.

Alwin, D. F. (1996a) Parental socialization in historical perspective. In C. Ryff and M. M. Seltzer (eds.), *The Parental Experience at Midlife*. Chicago: University of Chicago Press.

Alwin, D. F. (1996b) From childbearing to childrearing: The link between declines in fertility and changes in the socialization of children. *Population and Development Review*, 22, S176–S196.

Alwin, D. F. (2001) Parental values, beliefs, and behavior: A review and promulga for research into the new century. In S. J. Hofferth and T. J. Owens (eds.), *Children at the Millennium: Where Have We Come From, Where Are We Going?* New York: JAI.

Alwin, D. F., Scott, J. L., and Braun, M. (1992) The separation of work and the family: attitudes toward women's labor-force participation in Germany, Great Britain, and the United States. *European Sociological Review*, 8, 13–37.

Ariès, P. (1962) [1960] *Centuries of Childhood: A Social History of Family Life*. New York: Knopf.

Baumrind, D. (1989) Rearing competent children. In W. Damon (ed.), *Child Development Today and Tomorrow*. San Francisco: Jossey-Bass.

Baumrind, D. (1991a) Parenting styles and adolescent development. In R. M. Lerner, A. C. Peterson, and J. Brooks-Gunn (eds.), *Encyclopedia of Adolescence*. New York: Garland.

Baumrind, D. (1991b) The influence of parenting style on adolescent competence and substance use. *Journal of Early Adolescence*, 11, 56–95.

Bell, R. Q. (1968) A reinterpretation of the direction of effects in studies of socialization. *Psychological Review*, 75, 81–95.

Booth, A., Carver, K., and Granger, D. (2000) Biosocial perspectives on the family. *Journal of Marriage and the Family*, 62, 1018–34.

Booth, A., and Dabbs, J. M. (1993) Testosterone and men's marriage. *Social Forces*, 72, 463–77.

Booth, A., Johnson, D. R., and Granger, D. (1999) Testosterone and men's depression: The role of social behavior. *Journal of Health and Social Behavior*, 40, 130–40.

Booth, A., and Osgood, D. W. (1993) The influence of testesterone on deviance in adulthood: Assessing and explaining the relationship. *Criminology*, 31, 93–117.

Bronfenbrenner, U. (1979) *The Ecology of Human Development*. Cambridge, MA: Harvard University Press.

Bronfenbrenner, U., and Ceci, S. J. (1994) Nature–nurture reconceptualized in developmental perspective: a bioecological model. *Psychological Review*, 101, 568–586.

Caldwell, J.C. (1976) Toward a restatement of demographic transition theory. *Population and Development Review*, 2, 321–366.

Caldwell, J.C. (1982) *Theory of Fertility Decline*. New York: Academic Press.
Caspi, A., McClay, J., Moffitt, T.E., Mill, J., Martin, J., Craig, I.W., Taylor, A., and Poulton, R. (2002). Role of genotype in the cycle of violence in maltreated children. *Science*, 297, 851–4.
Coleman, J. S. (1990) *Foundations of Social Theory.* Cambridge, MA: Belknap Press of the Harvard University Press.
Crockenberg, S. (1986) Are temperamental differences in babies associated with predictable differences in caregiving? In J. V. Lerner and R. M. Lerner (eds.), *New Directions for Child Development: Temperament and Social Interaction in Infants and Children.* Vol 31. San Francisco: Jossey-Bass.
Crockenberg, S., and Leerkes, E. M. (2001) Infant temperament, caregiving, and family relationships. Paper presented at the National Symposium on Family Research, Pennsylvania State University, University Park, December.
Crouter, A. C., and Head, M. R. (2002) Parental monitoring and knowledge of children. In M. H. Bornstein (ed.), *Handbook of Parenting: Being and Becoming a Parent.* 2nd ed. Vol. 3. Mahwah, NJ: Lawrence Erlbaum.
Cunningham, H. (1991) *The Children of the Poor: Representations of Childhood Since the Seventeenth Century.* Cambridge, MA: Blackwell.
Darling, N., and Steinberg, L. (1993) Parenting style as context: an integrative model. *Psychological Bulletin*, 113, 487–96.
Davis, K. (1986) Low fertility in evolutionary perspective. In K. Davis, M. Bernstam, and R. Ricardo-Campbell (eds.), *Below-Replacement Fertility in Industrialized Societies.* Cambridge: Cambridge University Press.
DiLalla, L. F., and Gottesman, I. I. (1989) Heterogeneity of causes for delinquency and criminality: lifespan perspectives. *Development and Psychopathology*, 1, 39–349.
Ellison, C. G., and Sherkat, D. E. (1993) Conservative Protestantism and support for corporal punishment. *American Sociological Review*, 58, 131–44.
French, V. (2002) History of parenting: the ancient Mediterranean world. In M. H. Bornstein (ed.), *Handbook of Parenting: Biology and Ecology of Parenting.* 2nd ed. Vol. 2. Mahwah, NJ: Lawrence Erlbaum.
Furstenberg, F. F., Jr. (1992) Family change and the welfare of children: What do we know and what can we do Aaout it? Paper presented at the Seminar on Gender and Family Change in Industrialized Countries. Rome, January.
Greven, J., Jr. (1970) *Four Generations: Population, Land, and Family in Colonial Andover, Massachusetts.* Ithaca NY: Cornell University Press.
Greven, J., Jr. (1977) *The Protestant Temperament: Patterns of Child-Rearing, Religious Experience, and the Self in Early America.* New York: New American Library.
Harris, J. R. (1995) Where is the child's environment? a group socialization theory of development. *Psychological Review*, 102, 458–89.
Harris, J. R. (1998) *The Nurture Assumption: Why Children Turn Out the Way They Do.* New York: Simon & Schuster.
Hayward, M. D., and Zhang, Z. (2001) Demography of aging: a century of global change, 1950–2050. In R. H. Binstock and L. K. George (eds.), *Handbook of Aging and the Social Sciences* . 5th ed. New York: Academic Press.
Hernandez, D. J. (1993) *America's Children: Resources from Family, Government and the Economy.* New York: Russell Sage Foundation.
Hofferth, S. L., and Sandberg, J. F. (2001) How American children spend their time? *Journal of Marriage and the Family*, 63, 295–308.
Hoffman, L. W. (1977) Changes in family roles, socialization, and sex differences. *American Psychologist*, 32, 644–57.
Hoffman, L. W. (1979) Maternal employment: 1979. *American Psychologist*, 34, 859–65.
Hoffman, L. W. (1989) Effects of maternal employment in the two-parent family: A review of recent research. *American Psychologist*, 44, 283–92.

Jencks, C., Bartlett, S., Corcoran, M., Crouse, J., Eaglesfield, D., Jackson, G., McClelland, K., Mueser, P., Olneck, M., Schwartz, J., Ward, S., and Williams J. (1979) *Who Gets Ahead? The Determinants of Economic Success in America*. New York: Basic Books.

Kagan, J. (1984) *The Nature of the Child*. New York: Basic Books.

Lesthaeghe, R. (1983) A century of demographic and cultural change in Western Europe: An exploration of underlying dimensions. *Population and Development Review*, 9, 411–35.

Lesthaeghe, R. (1995) The second demographic transition in Western countries: An interpretation. In K. O. Mason and A-M. Jensen (eds.), *Gender and Family Change in Industrialized Countries*. Oxford: Clarendon Press.

Lesthaeghe, R., and Meekers, D. (1986) Value change and the dimensions of familism in the European Community. *European Journal of Population*, 2, 225–68.

Lesthaeghe, R., and Surkyn, J. (1988) Cultural dynamics and economic theories of fertility change. *Population and Development Review*, 11, 1–45.

Loehlin, J. C. (1997) A test of J. R. Harris's theory of peer influences on personality. *Journal of Personality and Social Psychology*, 72, 1197–201.

Lupri, E. (1983) *The Changing Position of Women in Family and Society: A Cross-National Comparison*. Leiden: E. J. Brill.

Maccoby, E. E. (1992) The role of parents in the socialization of children: an historical overview. *Developmental Psychology*, 28, 1006–17.

Maccoby, E. E., and Martin, J. A. (1983) Socialization and the context of the family: parent–child interaction. In E. M. Hetherington (ed.), *Socialization, Personality, and Social Development*. New York: John Wiley.

Mazur, A., and Booth, A. (1998) Testosterone and dominance in men. *Behavior and Brain Sciences*, 21, 353–63.

Pinker, S. (2002) *The Blank Slate: The Modern Denial of Human Nature*. New York: Viking.

Plomin, R. (1994) *Genetics and Experience: The Interplay Between Nature and Nurture*. Thousand Oaks, CA: Sage.

Plomin, R. (1999) Behavioral genetics. In M. Bennett (ed.), *Developmental Psychology: Achievements and Prospects*. Philadelphia: Taylor & Francis.

Pollock, L. A. (1983) *Forgotten Children: Parent–Child Relations from 1500 to 1900*. Cambridge: Cambridge University Press.

Popenoe, D. (1988) *Disturbing the Nest: Family Change and Decline in Modern Societies*. New York: Aldine de Gruyter.

Putnam, S., Sanson, A. V., and Rothbart, M. K. (2002) Child temperament and parenting. In M. H. Bornstein (ed.), *Handbook of Parenting*. 2nd ed. Vol. 1. Mahwah, NJ: Lawrence Erlbaum.

Reiss, D., Neiderhiser, J., Hetherington, E. M., and Plomin, R. (2000) *The Relationship Code: Deciphering Genetic and Social Patterns in Adolescent Development*. Cambridge, MA: Harvard University Press.

Rosenfeld, R. A. (1996) Women's work histories. In J. B. Casterline, R. D. Lee and K. A. Foote (eds.), *Fertility in the United States: New Patterns, New Theories*. New York: Population Council.

Rosenfeld, R. A., and Birkelund, G. E. (1995) Women's part time work: A cross-national comparison. *European Sociological Review*, 11, 111–34.

Rowe, D. C. (1983) A biometrical analysis of perceptions of family environment: A study of twin and singleton sibling kinships. *Child Development*, 54, 416–23.

Rowe, D. C. (1994) *The Limits of Family Influence: Genes, Experience, and Behavior*. New York: Guilford.

Rowe, D. C., and Teachman, J. (2001) Behavioral genetic research designs and social policy studies. In A. Thornton (ed.), *The Well-Being of Children and Families: Research and Data Needs*. Ann Arbor, University of Michigan Press.

Scarr, S. (1992) Developmental theories for the 1990s: development of individual differences. *Child Development*, 63, 1–19.

Scarr, S. (1995) How do families affect intelligence? Social environmental and behavior genetic predictions. In J. J. Hox, B. F. van der Meulen, J. M. A. M. Janssens, J. J. F. ter Laak and L. W. C. Tavecchio (eds.), *Advances in Family Research*. Amsterdam: Thesis.

Schlumbohm, J. (1980) "Traditional" collectivity and "modern" individuality: some questions and suggestions for the historical study of socialization: the examples of the German lower and upper bourgeoisie around 1800. *Social History*, 5, 71–103.

Sears, R. R., Maccoby, E. E., and Levin, H. (1957), *Patterns of Child-Rearing*. Evanston IL: Row, Peterson & Co.

Sewell, W. H., Sr., and Hauser, R. M. (1975) *Education, Occupation and Earnings: Achievement in the Early Career.* New York: Academic.

Shanahan, M. J., Hofer, S. M., and Shanahan, L. (2003) Biological models of behavior and the life course. In J. T. Mortimer and M. J. Shanahan (eds.), *Handbook of the Life Course.* New York: Kluwer Academic/Plenum.

Shonkoff, J. P., and Phillips, D. A. (eds.) (2000) *From Neurons to Neighborhoods: The Science of Early Childhood Development*. Washington, DC: National Academy Press.

Shorter, E. (1975) *The Making of the Modern Family.* New York: Basic Books.

Steinberg, L., Darling, N. E., and Fletcher, A. C., in collaboration with Brown, B. B. and Dornbusch, S. M. (1995) Authoritative parenting and adolescent adjustment: An Ecological Journey. In P. Moen, G. H. Elder, Jr., and K. Lüscher (eds.), *Examining Lives in Context: Perspectives on the Ecology of Human Development.* Washington, DC: American Psychological Association.

Steinberg, L., and Silk, J. S. (2002) Parenting adolescents. In M. H. Bornstein (ed.), *Handbook of Parenting*. 2nd ed. Vol. 1, Mahwah, NJ: Lawrence Erlbaum.

Stone, L. (1977) *The Family, Sex and Marriage in England, 1500–1800.* New York: Oxford University Press.

Thomas, A., and Chess, S. (1977) *Temperament and Development.* New York: Bruner-Mazel.

Udry, J. R. (1990) Biosocial models of adolescent problem behaviors. *Social Biology*, 37, 1–10.

Udry, J. R. (1988) Biological predispositions and social control in adolescent sexual behavior. *American Sociological Review*, 53, 709–22.

Udry, J. R. (1996) Biosocial models of low-fertility societies. *Population and Development Review*, 22, S325–S336.

Udry, J. R. (2000) Biological Limits of Gender Construction. *American Sociological Review*, 65, 443–57.

Uhlenberg, P., and Eggebeen, D. (1986) The declining well being of American adolescents. *The Public Interest*, 82, 25–38.

Vinovskis, M. A. (1987) Historical perspectives on the development of the family and parent–child interactions. In J. B. Lancaster, J. Altmann, A. S. Rossi, and L. Sherrod (eds.), *Parenting Across the Life Span – Biosocial Dimensions*. New York: Aldine de Gruyter.

Westoff, C. (1986) Perspective on nuptiality and fertility. In K. Davis, M. Bernstam, and R. Ricardo-Campbell (eds.), *Below Replacement Fertility in Industrialized Societies.* Cambridge: Cambridge University Press.

Wrigley, J. (1989) Do young children need intellectual stimulation? Experts' advice to parents, 1900–1985. *History of Education Quarterly*, 29, 41–75.

Zarit, S. H., and Eggebeen, D. J. (2002) Parent–child relationships in adulthood and later years. In M. H. Bornstein (ed.), *Handbook of Parenting*. 2nd ed. Vol. 1. Mahwah, NJ: Lawrence Erlbaum.

Zelizer, V. A. (1985) *Pricing the Priceless Child: The Changing Social Value of Children*. New York: Basic Books.

Zigler, E. (2002) Foreword. In M. H. Bornstein (ed.), *Handbook of Parenting*. 2nd ed. Vol. 1. Mahwah, NJ: Lawrence Erlbaum.

# 10

# Time, Through the Life Course, in the Family

Jonathan Gershuny

## Time and the Accumulation of "Capitals"

How we spend our time – our "time budget" – is a crucial determinant of our position in the social structure. This chapter discusses the way that individuals' time budgets are in turn influenced by changes in their family status and circumstances. It relies on data from a nationally sampled time-diary study and from a national household panel study. It uses a simple "data fusion" technique to combine these. And it uses the combined data set to show how time use is affected by changes in family statuses through the life course.

Time, as we know from sociologists from Adam (1990) to Zerubavel (1981), is made, a social product. All of human life relates itself to rhythms derived from more or less regular "time-givers." There are both natural and artificial time-givers: constellations, the sun and moon, church clocks, factory whistles, television programs, family rituals. The different time-givers are embodied in different structures of authority, domination, or reciprocation, producing a mixture of different time structures through which each individual must navigate during the day. And each person experiences the passage of time differentially according to context and circumstances, whether with an employer or with a lover, in flight from a predator, or in a complex collaboration with a co-worker. But notwithstanding the multiplicity of social times, and the complexity of individuals' experiences of them, it would be absurd to deny the existence of a single physicist's time, counted as, for example, oscillations of a pendulum or of a caesium crystal. Time of this sort is very strongly socially sanctioned, in the sense that any observer denying the regularity of the pendulum would be, in effect, also denying the whole of that body of scientific knowledge that underlies the last 300 years of world economic development. It would be perverse to consider this clock time as anything other than "objective time."

This chapter is not, however, about "objective time" itself but about the durations of various activities measured against its passage. We spend just so much time in work, in play, asleep, eating – what follows concerns how these activities vary through the life-course, and the consequences of this variation for people's acquisition of social positional characteristics.

The macro-sociological view summarized above sees time as produced by societies. But in this chapter we reverse the causal direction. In a micro-sociological context, individuals can be seen, in a recursive manner, as being produced by their own time allocation. We now (following the discussions in Bourdieu's *Distinction*) think of societies as structured by the distribution of different sorts of embodied "capitals" (the metaphor is perhaps inappropriate, we shall return to this in a moment) – in effect, aggregated past time devoted to particular sorts of activity, congealed or *cumulated experience* – to constitute various sorts of skills or capabilities.

The sociological legacy of nineteenth-century political economy is a view of society as structured by relationships of individuals and households to physical or financial capital. The time of individuals was located partly in the sphere of production (i.e., waged work) in which this capital operated directly, and partly in the sphere of reproduction (all other sorts of time). The patterns of domination associated with the ownership of capital in the production sphere were considered to carry over into consumption, particularly through the differentiation of gender roles, with men located mainly in the production sector interacting in a primary way with the structures of capital, and women located mainly in the reproductive sphere interacting with capital only indirectly through their family relationships with men.

Some remnant of this view remains, but in general the approach now seems inappropriate. We now have an alternative, fitting better what we know of the twenty-first century, across much of the richest parts of the world. Just as the old view took social structuration as a product of a single sort of resource, we may now think, in a Bourdovian manner, of multiple sorts of resource which in different combinations give different levels and qualities of access to the various institutions – and hence the different sorts of experience – afforded by our societies. We have various skills in different sorts of consumption and organizational participation – we play football, we arrange social events for the synagogue, church, or mosque, we cook food and give dinner parties, we listen to music. All of these activities give us different sorts of satisfaction, and different degrees of social status, depending on how fully and effectively we are able to participate in them. And in turn the effectiveness of these sorts of participation, and the extent of our engagement within the relevant institutions, depends in large part on the context, frequency, and duration of our previous engagement in these activities. Our past experiences – or at least some of them (since others simply evaporate, and have no further significance) – progressively congeal or cumulate to form personal resources, or capabilities. These congealed capabilities, all outcomes of our past time-budgets, are what Bourdieu called embodied "capitals."

"Capitals" in this sense fall into a wide range of different categories, classified both by their origin – e.g., deriving from the formal educational system, or informally from the practices of the individual's household-of-origin – or by their application – social, cultural or whatever. Indeed, it is the indefinite range and wide variety of these that makes the term "capitals" less than optimally useful for sociological purposes. But the key insight from this line of argument is that access to life-experiences is gained by combining various of these capabilities with each other, and with a distinct form of capability that goes under the misleadingly general-sounding category of "human capital"[1] – which describes the set of very specific skills which may be deployed within the labor market to obtain paid work and earn money. Human capital derives partly from experiences gained in the household of origin, partly from participation in the educational system, and finally from previous participation in paid work activities. Having a particular family and educational background, we acquire our first jobs, or arrange self-employment; subsequently, our record of performance in the labor-market context enables advancement (or otherwise) which in turn adds to our work record. Potential employers have requirements, which may be at one extreme strictly functional – evidence of diligence, skill, and specific knowledge – or at the other merely symbolic and related to abstract principles – such as a requirement for fairness – applied to the selection process. "Human capital" is the market valuation that emerges in the narrowly economic context of the distribution of these employer requirements, set against the distribution of relevant characteristics across the labor force.

Most social experiences require the combination of other embodied capitals, other personal resources of specific capabilities, with money payments which derive from human capital (or from wealth in the form of pensions, income from investments, and transfer payment rights, which in turn often derive from the deployment of human capital). To this extent – only – our twenty-first-century account corresponds to its nineteenth-century precursor. Labor income (now just one, though still an important one, of the elements in the money budgets of the general population) is a partial determinant – alongside the other sorts of capabilities – of the extent of participation in each of the activities of the society. But whereas the other capabilities are relatively specific to particular activities (i.e., sporting skills to the sports participation, cookery skills to the dinner parties, and so on), human capital deployed to produce money income has a direct or indirect influence on every one of these activities. So the old "dominance of the sphere of production" corresponds to the crucially important impact of this narrow category of human capital on life-chances.

Time allocation is thus central to the processes of social structuration. Differentiation of life chances is a function of the various accumulated capabilities that give access to various leisure, consumption, and sociable experiences. And our access to all or most of these different sorts of experiences has a common link to the accumulation of one specific class of capability, economically salient human capital. So, to understand differentiation of life-chances, it is necessary to investigate the processes through which time-allocation patterns are determined, and to be particularly concerned with those processes through which human capital accumulates. There is very little existing literature on this topic and this chapter, rather than providing an overview of an existing body of research, is setting out an agenda for the future.

The coverage of this chapter is limited. In what follows there is no discussion of processes of intergenerational inheritance and childhood socialization. There is no discussion of the accumulation of specific forms of cultural capacity through participation in particular leisure activities, no discussion of the formation of networks of acquaintance, familiarity, and obligation that is the subject of social capital. Instead, the focus is on empirical evidence of the operation of the single crucial impact of family processes through the adult life course, in differentiating individuals' access to the opportunities for accumulating labor market-related "human capital" – and hence determining future life-chances – between men and women.

What we do determines who we become. There are regularities, in the allocation of time between various broad categories of time use – paid work, unpaid work, sleep, and consumption time[2] – that are clearly related to current family circumstances, and to what we might think of as distinct stages in various cycles of family life. Differential specialization of individuals at one life-stage, in one or other of the tasks, has implications for their future options for participation in all of them. And in particular: differential levels of specialization in the different sorts of work (paid and unpaid) within households implies also differential rates of accumulation of human capital, and hence – of particular importance in a society in which household fission is the norm rather than the exception – differentiation in life chances. This chapter, therefore, focuses on the evidence of the relationship between family circumstances, and the allocation of time among the general categories of time use within the household.

## The Problem: Longitudinal Evidence

The conventional approach to studying time use through the life course considers time use by age. Figures 10.1 and 10.2 are drawn from a large time-diary study (sometimes alternatively described as a "time-budget" survey). In such a survey a large random sample of people are asked to complete a special questionnaire, and then to keep a diary detailing the continuous sequence of all activities, including their start and finish times, normally for a single day, but in the case of various British studies, including the Home-on-Line study ("HoL"; see Anderson and Tracey, 2001) used here, seven consecutive days. The approximately 1,400 diary weeks from two waves of the HoL study form the basis for the time-use estimates in this chapter (more about the HoL survey can be found in Appendix 10.1).

Clear, smooth, regular patterns of change in time-use through the life course are what emerge from these two figures. Paid work diminishes for women pretty continuously from youth to old age, increasing at first for men then again declining

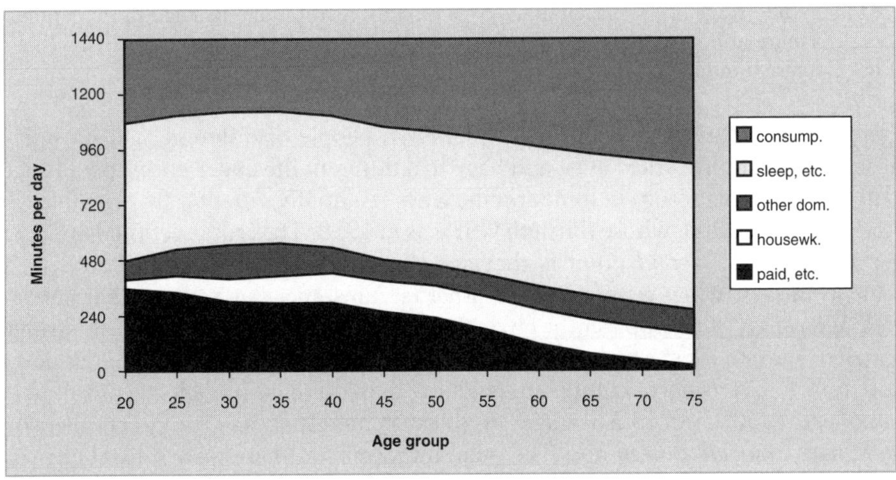


**Figure 10.1** Women's time use by age, UK, 1999–2000

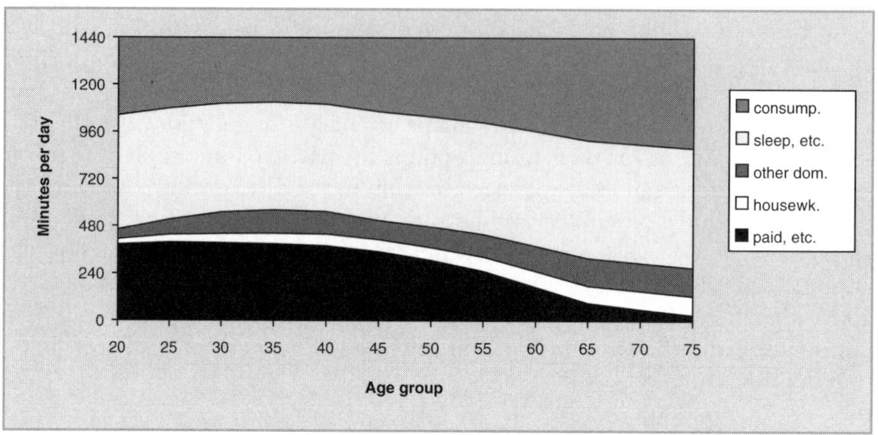


**Figure 10.2** Men's time use by age, UK, 1999–2000

from their mid-thirties. Housework and other unpaid domestic work increase sharply to a maximum for women between the ages of 25 and 35; the increases are more gradual for men but continue throughout most of the life course. Leisure/consumption time reaches a minimum for both sexes in their mid-thirties, and for both, increases steadily thereafter.

Or at least, these changes are what *seem* to emerge from the pictures. But if we think more carefully about them, we come to a rather different conclusion. They are drawn on the basis of a national survey conducted during 1999 and 2000. And they do not, in fact, tell us anything about *change* at all. They just tell us about *difference* between people of different ages. What we have presented here are "cross-sectional" data which allow us to compare different sorts of people, but never to detect change. In her conclusion to what is perhaps the only international comparative study of women's and men's time use over the life cycle, Lingsom wrote:

> in my opinion, the most serious shortcoming of the currently available data is that we cannot study transitions in the family cycle directly. . . . the stage reached in the family cycle is more important than age for understanding women's time use. This implies that our interest should be in the longitudinal analysis of the family cycle. (1995: 71)

There are two distinct issues of principle. *First*, people of different ages have lived through different historical eras, and have had different life experiences: people aged 30 in 2000 are, as a result, in some specific ways essentially *different* from people who were aged 50 in 2000, whose thirtieth year was in 1980. The cross-sectional approach ignores this. The *second* point is that age-change itself may not be the operative element: in fact, when we control for other circumstances, it appears that across a wide age range, even apparently physiologically limited activities are not strongly related to age (so, for example, Fisher (2002) shows that Britons in their sixties devote more time to sports participation and walking than do those in their twenties). In the case of figures 10.1 and 10.2, the age variable may merely act as a proxy for other sorts of changes *associated with* age. The most important of these prior causal elements associated with age is family status. What we see, in the first two figures may be, in fact, not the effect of people's *ages*, but of their family *stages*.

The first of the two principled objections to longitudinal interpretations from cross-sectional evidence is undoubtedly important. The correct response to it is the application of "pseudo-cohort analysis," in which cross-sectional studies from successive historical eras are compared, following the same birth cohorts. Thus, a group aged 10–20 in the 1960 survey would be 20–30 in the 1970 survey and 30–40 in that of 1980. Following the same group through successive surveys gives a genuine picture of life-course change. There is in fact time-diary data that would allow that sort of analysis in many countries – evidence of this sort from the US, Canada, the Netherlands, and Finland, among others, is discussed in Gershuny (2000) – but historical data was not collected on a very regular basis and the available evidence (with the exception of that for the Netherlands) is not entirely satisfactory for the purpose of this sort of analysis.

In this chapter, however, I shall simply ignore what is the evident fact that societies change, put the first objection aside, and take cross-sectional differences as a proxy for historical ones, in what Joshi and Davies (2002) call a "time warp." The focus will be on the second: on the effects of family status, and particularly on what Lingsom termed "transitions in the family cycle" – observations of what happens when particular individuals change from one family status to another. It is, after all, only by observing what happens to someone's time use when family circumstances change, that we can be sure that the shifts in time use relate specifically to the change in family circumstance, and not to some other characteristic of that same individual (such as the nature of her/his job, or ethnicity, or a response to a current fashion).

For this sort of analysis we need genuinely longitudinal data, repeated measurements of the same variables for the same respondent. The HoL Time Use study itself is a panel study with three annual waves of interviews and diary collection (for reasons explained in a moment, we do not, however, use it as a panel). In this chapter I use, as the basis for the exploration of family transitions, the much larger British Household Panel Study (Taylor et al., 2002) which involved interviews with all members of an initial 5000 households, and currently provides 10 annual waves of data (the BHPS is introduced in little more detail in Appendix 10.1).

The focus on the family-related changes in time use produces a major statistical problem: the *interesting* family transitions for the purpose of studying the relationship of family conditions to individuals' time use are also *rare* ones. Consider just the four distinct family statuses in table 10.1.

This is a "balanced sample" in which the same individuals appear in each of the waves (we start with wave 4 because some of the required variables were not collected in earlier waves). Over the seven years we observe them, the BHPS respondents get, of course, seven years older, and their family status changes accordingly. Fewer are partnered at the beginning of the period than at the end,

**Table 10.1** Family status distributions, BHPS adults, 1994–2000 (balanced sample waves 4–10, %)

| | *1994* | *1995* | *1996* | *1997* | *1998* | *1999* | *2000* |
|---|---|---|---|---|---|---|---|
| No partner, no co-resident child | 32.3 | 31.2 | 30.6 | 30.2 | 29.8 | 29.6 | 29.6 |
| Partner, no co-resident child | 41.6 | 42.8 | 43.7 | 44.2 | 44.8 | 45.6 | 45.5 |
| Partner, co-resident child(ren) | 23.0 | 22.7 | 22.7 | 22.3 | 22.4 | 21.8 | 21.9 |
| No partner, co-resident child(ren) | 3.1 | 3.3 | 3.0 | 3.2 | 3.0 | 2.9 | 3.0 |

fewer co-reside with their own child at the end than at the beginning of the period. Notice here that the changes are small. It is important to remember that these are "net" changes (i.e., change at aggregate, not individual, level). Part of the reason that in net terms fewer than 3 percent of the respondents move away from the "no partner no child" status is that, as well as gaining partners and children, people also frequently lose partners through divorce or death, and their children leave home. But it is also the case that not many of these transitions actually happen in any given year.

To investigate the rate at which these events occur in the population, we must use the panel *as* a panel. There are, including the 4 no-change "major diagonals", 16 possible transitions among these four states.

So as to get sufficiently large numbers, we adopt the frequently used panel analysis technique of "pooling" pairs of successive years – adding pairs of years from the same person into the same file – so that in the resulting "pooled file" seven successive observations of the same respondent will appear as six separate pair-of-year cases. This technique allows us to work as if we are using much bigger cross-sectional data sets. Table 10.2 and most of what follows is based on a file of just over 40,000 pooled cases. We see that, from one year to the next, only 10 percent of the younger, 6 percent of middle-age-group, and 2 percent of older people have *any* changes between the four broad family statuses. Despite the prevalence of family fission, most of these changes are on the what we might think of as the "main line" of stable partnership formation, followed by first child born within that partnership. Of the 10 percent of younger respondents who have one of these family changes over any

**Table 10.2** Year-on-year occurrence of family transitions in BHPS, 1994–2000 (% of all pairs of years, pooled pairs of waves, balanced sample waves 4–10, n of pairs = 42931)

| | *Men* | | | | *Women* | | | |
|---|---|---|---|---|---|---|---|---|
| | *20–40* | *41–60* | *>60* | *N* | *20–40* | *41–60* | *>60* | *N* |
| Joined partner | 3 | 1 | | 324 | 3 | 1 | | 325 |
| Single->partner + kid | 1 | | | 87 | | | | 18 |
| Keep partner, have kid | 3 | 1 | | 252 | 2 | | | 249 |
| Have kid, no partner | | | | 6 | | | | 27 |
| Lose partner, keep kid | | | | 22 | 2 | | | 184 |
| Keep partner, lose kid | 1 | 3 | | 283 | 1 | 3 | | 308 |
| Lose partner, no kid | 1 | 1 | 2 | 176 | 1 | 1 | 2 | 252 |
| Lose kid and partner | 1 | | | 87 | | | | 14 |
| Keep kid, gain partner | | | | 8 | 1 | | | 149 |
| Single parent→no kid | | | | | 17 | | 1 | 57 |
| *Total, any change* | *10* | *6* | *2* | *1262* | *10* | *6* | *2* | *1583* |
| Stay single | 33 | 12 | 22 | 4204 | 19 | 15 | 53 | 5651 |
| Stay partner/no kid | 19 | 63 | 75 | 8429 | 16 | 57 | 45 | 8086 |
| Stay partnered + kid | 38 | 18 | 1 | 4214 | 46 | 18 | | 5583 |
| Stay single parent | | 1 | | 75 | 8 | 3 | | 988 |
| Other | | | | 2 | | | | 9 |
| | 100 | 100 | 100 | | 99 | 99 | 100 | N |
| | 7849 | 6544 | 3793 | 18186 | 9283 | 7503 | 5114 | 21900 |

pair of years, more than half – 3 percent from single to partner, 3 percent having children in partnerships – lie on this main line. Among the middle-age group, around half of all the family transitions consist of grown-up children leaving home, again an event on the "main line." Among the older, virtually all of the events are the loss of a partner. The prevalence of main-line events means that some transitions are just too rare to study in general-purpose samples. So, for example, fewer than half of one percent of younger women move in successive years from having no partner to single parenthood – producing a barely viable cell-size for analysis even in a sample of over 9,000 young women. Very large data sets are clearly needed even to study the effects of even the least infrequent family transitions.

But the time-diary studies that provide the good time-use evidence are very expensive for researchers and onerous for respondents. It is difficult to produce time-diary data within a panel-study framework, since the diary-keeping activity is so burdensome, and we suspect that only rather special sorts of people might maintain this activity over extended periods of time. In fact the HoL study has a strong panel element, with around 1,200 pairs of diaries kept in successive years. But this is designed for a different purpose – estimation of time-use elasticities, exploring for example the time-use consequences of increased time devoted to Internet use, a relatively widespread phenomenon – and HoL's small scale means that it is not, in itself, appropriate for investigating the rare family transition events. Hence we have a requirement for *data fusion*: finding a way of attaching the evidence from the HoL diary study to the BHPS.

## Time-Use Consequences of Status Transitions

### Data fusion

Data fusion comes perilously close to getting something for nothing – without ever overstepping the boundary of good research practice. The regression approach to data fusion relies on identifying, in two separate surveys, identical good predictors of some variable or variables that occur in only one of the surveys. Regression coefficients derived from the "donor" survey with both the predictor and the target variables can be combined with the predictor variables in the "recipient" survey to estimate the target variable.

The HoL diary panel study was in fact designed by the same research team as is responsible for the BHPS, with exactly such a data-fusion exercise in mind. The BHPS carries (from wave 4, in 1994) a number of potential predictors of time use. There are "stylized-estimate" questions about normal weekly hours of paid and domestic work, and questions about participation in, and the distribution of, various unpaid work tasks within the household.[3] The HoL study also carried these variables, in most cases using the same question wording (the exception is that BHPS questions on paid work are more detailed). The imputed time-use values in the BHPS produced by fusion correspond well to the diary data in the HoL study (see Appendix 10.1). It is these imputed time-use estimates that we use in what follows.

### Activities by age by family transition – the "main line"

In figures 10.1 and 10.2 we looked just at age. But if we are to tell the whole story, we need to find some method of combining age with the family transition variables to show the sequence of time-use patterns that are experienced through the life course... without drowning in an uninterpretable sea of numbers! One way of doing this is to consider, for men and for women in separate age groups, changing patterns of time use on the "main line" through the traditional family formation sequence. Then (in the following section) we can turn to consider some of the alternative turnings off the main drag.

Table 10.3 shows the evolution of paid work through the traditional family formation stage. The table shows the mean time use in each of the separate pairs of years for each of the transitions. Where there is no change, both the first and the second years are included, to indicate the degree of annual change in time use that is associated with remaining in a given family situation. Where there is a family status transition, we have the patterns of time use in the year before, and in the year after, to indicate the change in time use that may be attributed to it.

So, in the case of paid work we see, for younger people who remain single, a small, questionably significant, annual increase in work time for both sexes, and not much difference between the sexes; there are similar small declines in work time for the two older groups. Young people acquiring partners reduce their paid work time, as do middle-aged women, though not middle-aged men. Young people who remain in partnerships do not change their paid work time in any consistent way. We might note, however, that these small changes do add up to what looks like a progressive change (or selection process), such that those young women in partnerships who then choose to have children (looking at the "before acquiring a child" column) do seem to have substantially less paid work than young single women, while younger men in partnerships who are just about to acquire a child seem to have substantially more paid work than young single men.

The big break, however, occurs at the acquisition of a child. Among the youngest group, both the new fathers and the new mothers reduce their work time. But the mothers' reduction is more than three times as large as the fathers'. And the mothers' reduction continues, as they remain with their partners and children (partly as a

**Table 10.3** Paid work (mins. per day)

| | *Stay single* | | *Acquire partner* | | *Stay partnered* | | *With partner, acquire child* | | *Stay partner + child* | | *Stay partnered, child leaves* | |
|---|---|---|---|---|---|---|---|---|---|---|---|---|
| | *Yr 1* | *Yr 2* | *Before* | *After* | *Yr 1* | *Yr 2* | *Before* | *After* | *Yr 1* | *Yr 2* | *Before* | *After* |
| *20–40* | | | | | | | | | | | | |
| Women | 365 | 374 | 382 | 370 | 367 | 363 | 354 | 289 | 261 | 264 | 286 | 292 |
| Men | 377 | 383 | 405 | 392 | 398 | 397 | 400 | 380 | 388 | 389 | 399 | 380 |
| *41–60* | | | | | | | | | | | | |
| Women | 249 | 242 | 266 | 240 | 216 | 208 | 206 | 200 | 255 | 251 | 262 | 239 |
| Men | 300 | 295 | 318 | 317 | 303 | 293 | 330 | 324 | 370 | 364 | 353 | 342 |
| *60+* | | | | | | | | | | | | |
| Women | 40 | 35 | 63 | 55 | 56 | 49 | | | 71 | 65 | 86 | 102 |
| Men | 61 | 56 | 65 | 52 | 86 | 76 | | | 73 | 71 | 150 | 143 |

result of acquiring further children), while by contrast, the fathers' paid work time returns, in subsequent years, to something like its pre-birth level. Even after the children leave home, even among the youngest group of women, paid work time hardly increases. At the start of the "main sequence" for young people, paid work time differed between men and women by hardly 3 percent; by the end of this phase, women do 30 percent less paid work. For middle-age-group men with partners and co-resident children, paid work time declines by around five minutes per day each year, and women continue to have just over two-thirds of men's total of paid work.

Note that the annual time-use changes for those in static family circumstances are generally small (though of course, a regular decline of only three minutes per day per year, cumulates to an hour's reduction if maintained continuously over two decades). And by contrast, the single-year working-time changes associated with the family status transitions are generally much more substantial, at least for women. There are, plainly, age effects, as we see by comparing the 20–40 age group single women with single women in the 41–60 age group. But much of this age-related difference in fact reflects change in the middle-age-group women's lives that occurred during previous family states, in partnerships which are now ended, and with children who have left home.

Patterns of change in routine housework mirror those in paid work (table 10.4). Again, we see periods of relative stability in time-use patterns while in an unchanging household, punctuated by rapid time-use changes associated with family events. Again we see young single men and women starting with not dissimilar levels, but with the small year-on-year increase for women that may reflect an age effect or alternatively, the consequence of previous partnerships. There is no substantial difference between the housework of young single people in general and that special group who are just about to form partnerships. Both young men and young women increase their housework at the time of partnering, but women increase it somewhat more than men, and a continuing three minutes per year increase during the partner-no children period means that in young couples just before acquiring a first child, men do

**Table 10.4** Cooking and cleaning (mins. per day)

| | *Stay single* | | *Acquire partner* | | *Stay partnered* | | *With partner, acquire child* | | *Stay partner + child* | | *Stay partnered, child leaves* | |
|---|---|---|---|---|---|---|---|---|---|---|---|---|
| | *Yr 1* | *Yr 2* | *Before* | *After* | *Yr 1* | *Yr 2* | *Before* | *After* | *Yr 1* | *Yr 2* | *Before* | *After* |
| *20–40* | | | | | | | | | | | | |
| Women | 34 | 37 | 38 | 64 | 79 | 82 | 80 | 97 | 123 | 125 | 133 | 128 |
| Men | 26 | 26 | 28 | 45 | 48 | 48 | 47 | 53 | 58 | 58 | 56 | 60 |
| *41–60* | | | | | | | | | | | | |
| Women | 103 | 104 | 102 | 122 | 146 | 147 | 141 | 144 | 149 | 149 | 145 | 145 |
| Men | 44 | 45 | 47 | 62 | 68 | 69 | 65 | 69 | 67 | 67 | 68 | 69 |
| *60+* | | | | | | | | | | | | |
| Women | 123 | 121 | 131 | 140 | 165 | 164 | | | 161 | 157 | 141 | 127 |
| Men | 79 | 79 | 93 | 85 | 93 | 94 | | | 97 | 95 | 75 | 82 |

approaching 60 percent as much housework as their partners, just after the child they do 55 percent, and in stable partnerships with children they do 46 percent. Middle-age-group single men and women have housework totals similar to those of younger people in partnerships – reflecting the fact that many of this group were previously partnered. The major family impact for this group is with the acquisition of a partner: as with the younger group, both show some increase in housework, but the woman's increase is larger than the man's, and continues to increase through the partnership period, with men's unpaid work at approximately 45 percent of women's. The older group shows even higher totals of paid work (though smaller differences associated with partnership formation). We should remember our earlier discussion of the "time-warp"; this group did acquire its primary socialization around or before the 1930s, a time when gender roles were more sharply divided: all the more striking, then, that this group has a more even gender division of housework than the younger, with men doing 55–70 percent of their partners' total – presumably reflecting the changes in paid work shown in table 10.3.

The other unpaid work activities, including child-care, as well as shopping, gardening, household repairs, and household management, shows quite the most remarkable pattern (table 10.5). Here again, for the youngest age group, we find the main changes, as previously, occurring around the points of family transition. But unlike the previous cases, these transitions are not the emergent points for gender differences. On the contrary, we see near-equality in the gender balance for persistent partnerships with no children. And though this slips considerably with the arrival of children, we still find men doing 83 percent of women's total in the continuing partnerships with children.

But the real contrast here is seen in the two older groups. Here the men do *more* unpaid work than women. The family transitions seem to have little impact and the totals do seem to increase progressively with age.[4] At no point do the higher proportional contributions of men to this category of unpaid work fully compensate in time terms for women's contribution to cooking and cleaning. But for the older

**Table 10.5** Other unpaid work (mins. per day)

| | *Stay single* | | *Acquire partner* | | *Stay partnered* | | *With partner, acquire child* | | *Stay partner + child* | | *Stay partnered, child leaves* | |
|---|---|---|---|---|---|---|---|---|---|---|---|---|
| | *Yr 1* | *Yr 2* | *Before* | *After* | *Yr 1* | *Yr 2* | *Before* | *After* | *Yr 1* | *Yr 2* | *Before* | *After* |
| *20–40* | | | | | | | | | | | | |
| Women | 57 | 56 | 55 | 65 | 67 | 70 | 80 | 188 | 186 | 180 | 146 | 85 |
| Men | 45 | 47 | 49 | 60 | 66 | 68 | 73 | 162 | 154 | 151 | 142 | 131 |
| *41–60* | | | | | | | | | | | | |
| Women | 75 | 76 | 73 | 81 | 91 | 91 | 90 | 95 | 120 | 114 | 102 | 91 |
| Men | 99 | 100 | 99 | 103 | 108 | 108 | 102 | 113 | 119 | 117 | 113 | 112 |
| *60+* | | | | | | | | | | | | |
| Women | 100 | 100 | 101 | 103 | 108 | 108 | | | 99 | 102 | 102 | 99 |
| Men | 140 | 140 | 147 | 143 | 138 | 139 | | | 143 | 143 | 136 | 139 |

**Table 10.6** Consumption (mins. per day)

| | *Stay single* | | *Acquire partner* | | *Stay partnered* | | *With partner, acquire child* | | *Stay partner + child* | | *Stay partnered, child leaves* | |
|---|---|---|---|---|---|---|---|---|---|---|---|---|
| | *Yr 1* | *Yr 2* | *Before* | *After* | *Yr 1* | *Yr 2* | *Before* | *After* | *Yr 1* | *Yr 2* | *Before* | *After* |
| *20–40* | | | | | | | | | | | | |
| Women | 385 | 379 | 371 | 354 | 347 | 347 | 345 | 287 | 295 | 296 | 304 | 362 |
| Men | 411 | 406 | 389 | 378 | 367 | 367 | 360 | 303 | 300 | 301 | 302 | 326 |
| *41–60* | | | | | | | | | | | | |
| Women | 424 | 428 | 412 | 407 | 404 | 408 | 413 | 413 | 342 | 351 | 357 | 388 |
| Men | 432 | 434 | 417 | 402 | 402 | 408 | 388 | 380 | 341 | 347 | 359 | 367 |
| *60+* | | | | | | | | | | | | |
| Women | 545 | 550 | 524 | 519 | 494 | 499 | | | 484 | 491 | 491 | 491 |
| Men | 559 | 564 | 544 | 554 | 522 | 528 | | | 523 | 528 | 494 | 489 |

age group the totals of the two sorts of unpaid work are at least *approaching* equality.

The younger adults' consumption time is most clearly affected by the acquisition of a child (table 10.6). Both men and women reduce their time devoted to consumption activities by just under an hour per day with the arrival of the first child, and their totals of leisure hardly recover throughout the early years that children are co-resident. Only when the last child finally leaves home does leisure time increase again, favoring particularly the youngest women. And as we see from the older age groups, the total of leisure time gradually increases as the children grow older and leave the household. It appears that older women have in general somewhat less leisure than men in equivalent family circumstances: this must be set against the totals of "sleep and personal care," where women show a reasonably regular excess over men, which reflects largely differences in personal care time. Women in the middle-age group show more leisure time than men, around the time of having a first child. The reason for this difference is not immediately apparent, but may reflect the gender-structured age difference between older couples having a first child.

## Off the main track

The remaining major transition that affects both sexes and each of the age groups is loss of a partner from a partnership with no children. This is most frequent for the oldest group, where the main reason is the death of the partner, but it occurs also with reasonable frequency among the younger groups, as a result of partnership dissolution.

Table 10.7 shows the effects for younger people to be, for both men and women, a small increase in paid work, using time freed as a result of reductions in the various categories of unpaid work. For the middle-age group, paid work shows small changes, but leisure time increases. For women in the oldest group, paid work and leisure both increase, while for older men, changes in each of the categories are relatively small.

**Table 10.7** Time-use effects – lose partner, no kids (mins. per day)

| | *Paid work* | | *Housework* | | *Other domestic* | | *Sleep* | | *Consumption* | |
|---|---|---|---|---|---|---|---|---|---|---|
| | *Before* | *After* | *Before* | *After* | *Before* | *After* | *Before* | *After* | *Before* | *After* |
| *20–60* | | | | | | | | | | |
| Women | 371 | 391 | 64 | 41 | 64 | 56 | 585 | 588 | 355 | 364 |
| Men | 409 | 431 | 41 | 24 | 55 | 49 | 561 | 561 | 374 | 376 |
| *41–60* | | | | | | | | | | |
| Women | 226 | 232 | 131 | 103 | 86 | 77 | 587 | 594 | 410 | 435 |
| Men | 339 | 332 | 55 | 42 | 97 | 97 | 553 | 557 | 395 | 413 |
| *61+* | | | | | | | | | | |
| Women | 26 | 40 | 159 | 123 | 111 | 100 | 623 | 632 | 522 | 545 |
| Men | 57 | 54 | 95 | 85 | 145 | 143 | 598 | 599 | 544 | 559 |

The final pair of changes is nonsymmetrical, each affecting just the two younger age groups, and applying to just one gender.

Of these, the first are changes that happen, with very few exceptions, just to women. The gender differential in expectations of child custody after partnership dissolution means that virtually all of those who lose a partner but maintain co-residence with their child are women. In these cases we see in the first panel of table 10.8, little change in paid work, and, perhaps surprisingly, reductions in

**Table 10.8** Time-use effects – dissolution and reformation with and without children (mins. per day)

| | *Paid work* | | *Housework* | | *Other domestic* | | *Sleep* | | *Consumption* | |
|---|---|---|---|---|---|---|---|---|---|---|
| | *Before* | *After* | *Before* | *After* | *Before* | *After* | *Before* | *After* | *Before* | *After* |
| *Lose partner, keep child* | | | | | | | | | | |
| Women 20–49 | 262 | 279 | 112 | 85 | 193 | 179 | 578 | 581 | 296 | 317 |
| Women 41–60 | 298 | 298 | 135 | 109 | 106 | 93 | 570 | 577 | 331 | 363 |
| *Gain partner, keep child* | | | | | | | | | | |
| Women 20–49 | 281 | 277 | 79 | 100 | 185 | 186 | 583 | 580 | 312 | 297 |
| Women 41–60 | 274 | 248 | 120 | 139 | 103 | 104 | 579 | 579 | 364 | 369 |
| *Lose partner and child* | | | | | | | | | | |
| Men 20–49 | 384 | 393 | 51 | 30 | 138 | 63 | 546 | 565 | 321 | 389 |
| Men 41–60 | 380 | 346 | 57 | 43 | 112 | 91 | 545 | 555 | 346 | 405 |
| *Gain partner and child* | | | | | | | | | | |
| Gen 20–49 | 410 | 386 | 24 | 47 | 64 | 159 | 566 | 546 | 376 | 302 |
| Men 41–60 | 397 | 385 | 33 | 59 | 85 | 105 | 546 | 543 | 379 | 349 |

unpaid work coupled with increases in leisure. The same differentials mean that virtually all cases of repartnering while continuing co-residence with an own child are also women. The second panel of table 10.8 shows the time-use consequences of re-partnering in this case to be a reasonably precise mirror-imaging of the first panel: the women increase their domestic work activities, seemingly, in those cases where they had a previous partnership, increasing toward the levels of domestic work in their previous partnerships, and reducing their leisure time to the previous levels.

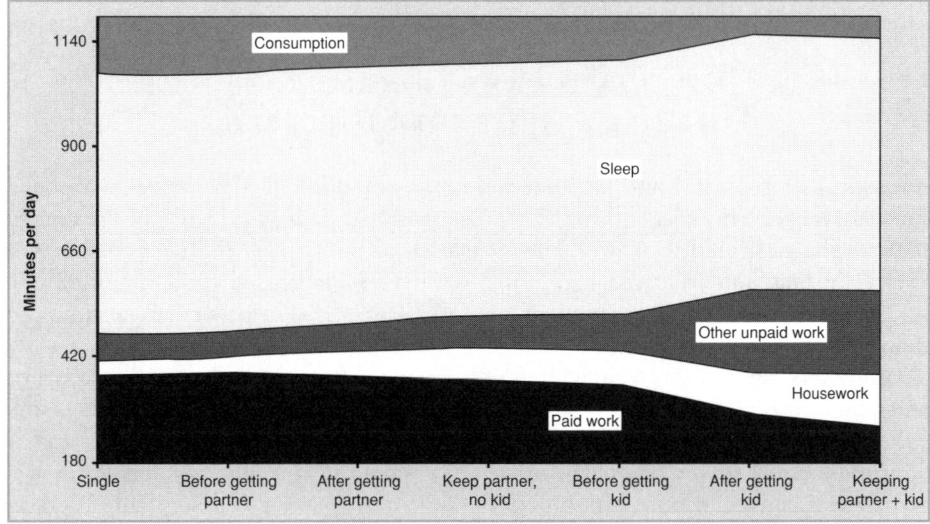


**Figure 10.3** Time-use consequences of status transitions, UK, women aged 20–40

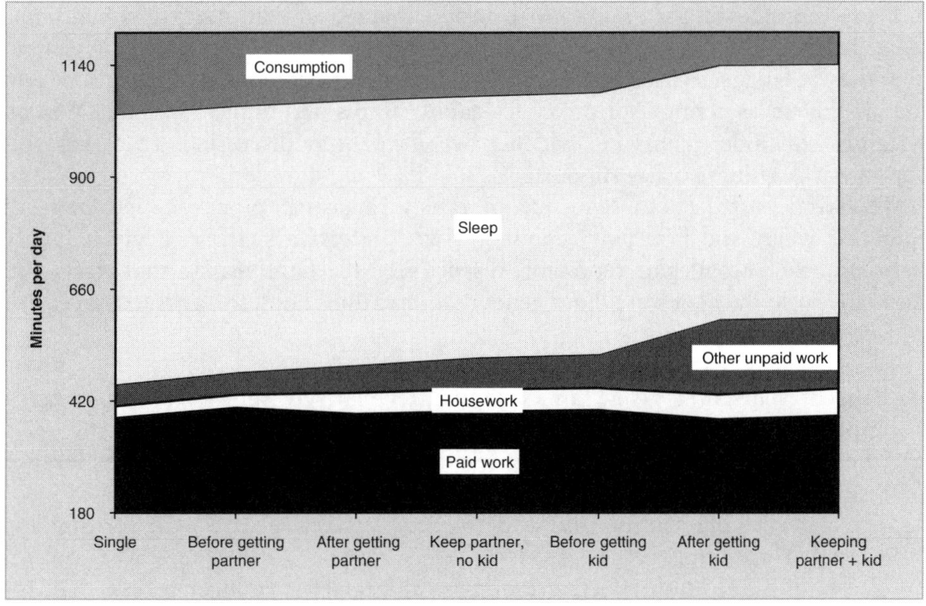


**Figure 10.4** Time-use consequences of status transitions, UK, men aged 20–40

Then there are the changes that apply – for just the same reasons – almost exclusively to men. In the third panel we see small increases in paid work for younger men losing both partners and children, and a substantial decline in paid work for middle-age-group men in this position, accompanied by substantial (if unsurprising) reductions in unpaid work, enabling substantial increases in both sleep and leisure time. And, just as in the parallel women's case, those men whose experiences are set out in the fourth panel of table 10.8, who are gaining both partners and co-resident children (and who in most cases are in fact again repartnering), pretty much reverse the pattern of changes in panel 3.

## Discussion and Conclusions: Time Use and Gender Difference

An important part of what has gone before is methodological argument. We have considered problems with interpreting cross-sectional data as evidence of life-course change, the desirability in principle of historical data so as to follow cohorts – advice, in fact, not followed here. And we have in fact used real "longitudinal" evidence – repeated measurement of the same subjects – to observe how time-use changes with family transitions.

Time-diary data is the technically correct source for this evidence. But it is not practicable (because of both financial cost and respondent burden) to collect the large-scale, time-diary materials needed to investigate the effects of family transitions, on a panel survey basis. The alternative is data fusion: since we have time-use predictor variables in both a donor (HoL time-diary) and a recipient (BHPS) data set, we use regression of predictors on time-diary evidence in donor data, imputing time use by multiplying resulting regression coefficients with predictor variables in the recipient data. What emerge are BHPS time-use estimates that make sense.

These estimates in turn allow us to produce important substantive conclusions. Lying behind the argument for the use of longitudinal data is in effect the general hypothesis that age, as used in conventional time diary-based discussions of time and the life course, is acting as a proxy for family status and family "events." We can certainly conclude, from the evidence we have been discussing, that that this hypothesis is quite strongly supported.

We have constructed a sequence of tables consisting of alternating pairs of columns, where the first pair represents two successive years in a given family state, and the second pair represent, respectively, the final year in that state, and the first year in the next state. Four general observations hold, to varying degrees, for tables 10.3 to 10.7:

1 Pairs of years in a given family status are relatively similar to each other – implying slow change in time use in each family state.
2 The average year in a given stable family state tends to show a similar level of time use to that of the year before a change in family state.
3 The largest changes in time use seem to occur between the two years surrounding a family transition.
4 The family transition effects are in general larger for younger people than for older.

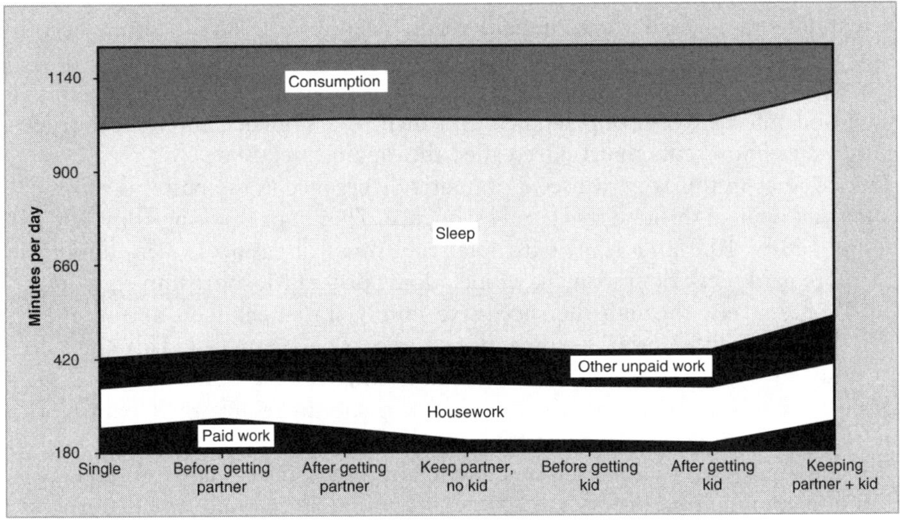


**Figure 10.5** Time-use consequences of status transitions, UK, women aged 41–60

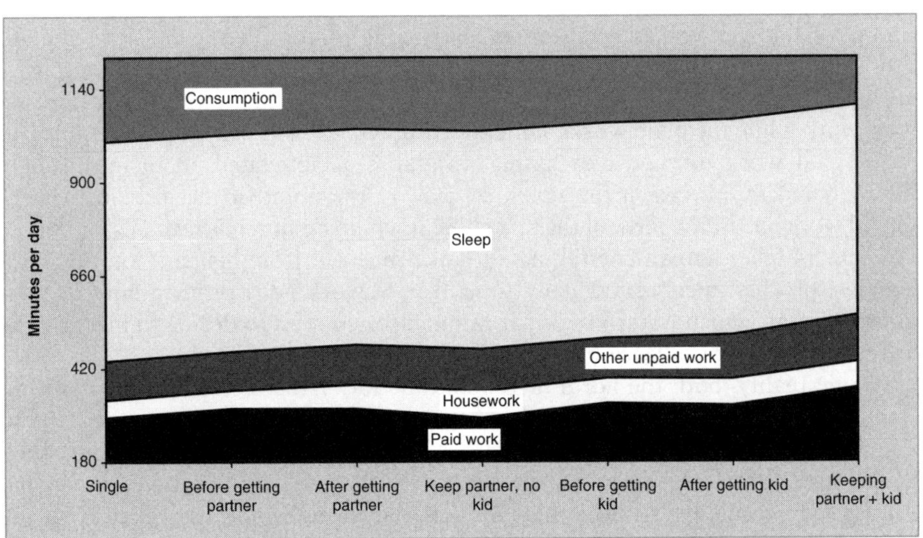


**Figure 10.6** Time-use consequences of status transitions, UK, men aged 41–60

In those cases where generalization 1 is strongly supported but 2 is not – as in the table 10.3 case of young women's paid work gradually increasing as the children grow up and leave home – we have in effect evidence of a small but steady time-use change, within a long-lasting family state. Where 1, 2, and 3 hold – as in table 10.5, 20–40 men and women's other unpaid work – we have time-use stability punctuated by brief changes associated with family transitions. And where all four hold, we have in addition the effect of an interaction of age with the family status and transition effects.

What remains is to fit together the various stories about the use of particular elements of time – paid work, unpaid work, sleep, and leisure – into a narrative about the effect of the family cycle, on the entire 1,440 minutes of the day; the impact of family life on time use as a whole. Figures 10.3 to 10.6 put together, for young and middle age-group women and men, the evidence for the sequence of family states and events that I have called the "main track."

Put together in this way, we see a dramatic divergence in the patterns of time use of men and women through this family sequence. They start (looking at the left-hand sides of figures 10.3 and 10.4) with relatively small differences, men doing just a little more paid work than women, women doing just a little more unpaid work than men. Progressively, through the successive family status changes, and as they get older, these two differentials become more and more pronounced. This effect could be explained by, for example, the differential impact of general social norms on particular family circumstances – e.g., "women should reduce their paid work to care for children" would have just this effect.

But equally, even if this norm were completely absent, the effect would emerge as a result of a combination of rational choices within family groups, and the process of accumulation of social-structural characteristics described in the first section of this chapter. The initial very small differentials in work time, with men having just slightly more paid work than women, may give the man a small excess of accumulated human capital (or alternatively, there may be a residual of workplace discrimination leading to somewhat lower women's wage rates). New couples, considering divisions of work responsibility when setting up house together, therefore decide that it is marginally advantageous (in total income terms) that the female partner specialize slightly in housework while the male works some overtime. As a result the proportions of paid and unpaid work diverge, and human capital is accumulated at an increasingly differentiated rate between the sexes, so that, at the point of the next increase in unpaid work needs, the birth of the first child, it would be simply irrational for the by-now-much-higher-human-capital male to take time out from his paid job. This is a recursive process: men's extra daily time in paid work adds differentially to their human capital, which in turn makes it rational for couples to decide to increase the degree of gender specialization in the different sorts of work.

Now in reality, both the norm-driven and the rationality-driven process work in parallel. We cannot really distinguish between these two. But it is important to remember that both operate together – because they are mutually reinforcing. Norms are, ultimately, what is perceived to be normal. So sometimes a rational process may result in a norm. But perhaps the more important effect is in the opposite direction. Over recent decades, expressed norms about women's special domestic responsibilities have been changing dramatically. Few British adults will now accede to the sorts of "women's place in the home" sentiments that were commonplace sixty years ago.[5] Yet, as we see from the final four figures, and despite the historical changes documented in Gershuny 2000, the gender differentials in paid and unpaid work remain dramatic. The norms have changed. But the rational process of recursive determination described above nevertheless provides an inertial effect that preserves the previous behavior.

Why is this important? Does it matter that men do less unpaid work and more paid work? In terms of the narrow time-use concerns of this chapter, it probably does not lead to any inequity, insofar as men's and women's totals of paid and unpaid work balance reasonably well, leading in turn to a quite equal overall balance of consumption time. But now consider what happens if the partnership dissolves. They have shared the income. He has built up the "human capital," she the domestic work skills and the stronger relationship with the children. Now they no longer share the income. He has the income from his high human capital, she has all that she can extract from her low human capital, constrained by the fact that she must also care for the children. Marketable work skills earn the income that gives the life chances. He wins, she loses.

## Notes

1 Economists led the discussion of these issues. Becker (1993) [1964] and Mincer and Polachek (1974) used the term "human capital" with this specific reference to the labor market. The same term is sometimes used in casual sociological discussions of what is referred to here as "embodied capital." It seems appropriate to follow Coleman (1988) here, who used the term in the economists' sense, but we may hope that a more satisfactory terminology emerges.
2 This corresponds precisely to Dagfin Aas's (1978) classification of four distinct time-use categories: contracted (paid work), committed (unpaid work), necessary (sleep and personal care), and discretionary.
3 Hoffman (1981) and Niemi (1983) argue that these stylized estimates are subject to systematic biases (though Jacobs, 1998 disagrees); the regression-based imputation will have the effect of reducing biases.
4 This unfamiliar result is not at all an artifact of the imputation methodology: just the same age/gender effect emerges from direct analysis of the HoL dataset:

*Other unpaid work: child-care, shopping, gardening, other domestic, UK, 1999—2000 (HoL diary study waves 1 and 2)*

| | *Mins./day* | | *No.* | |
|---|---|---|---|---|
| | *Women* | *Men* | *Women* | *Men* |
| All | 120 | 107 | 726 | 632 |
| Aged 20–40 | 152 | 92 | 290 | 251 |
| Aged 41–60 | 96 | 104 | 291 | 246 |
| Aged 60+ | 105 | 141 | 145 | 135 |

5 Dex (1988: 24) reports mid-1940s data showing in excess of 54 percent opposing married women's employment (except in wartime). BHPS in 1991 shows 27 percent of British adults agreeing with the proposition: "A husband's job is to earn money; a wife's job is to look after the home and family." By 1999, agreement with this proposition had fallen to 20 percent (BHPS Documentation Vol. 2; frequency distributions for variables aopfamf and iopfamf (Taylor et al., 2002.)

## References

Aas, D. (1978) Studies of time use: problems and prospects. *Acta Sociologica*, 15, 333–55.
Adam, B. (1990) *Time and Social Theory*. Cambridge: Polity.
Anderson, B., and Tracey, K. (2001) Digital living: the impact (or otherwise) of the internet on everyday life. *American Behavioural Scientist*, 45, 456–75.

Becker, G. (1993) [1964] *Human Capital*. Chicago: University of Chicago Press.
Bourdieu, P. (1984) *Distinction*. London: Routledge & Kegan Paul.
Coleman, J. (1988) Social capital in the creation of human capital. *American Journal of Sociology*, 94 (Suppl. 95), S95–S120.
Dex, S. (1988) *Women's Attitudes to Work*. Basingstoke: Macmillan.
Fisher, K. (2002) Chewing the Fat: the Story Time Diaries Tell About Physical Activity in the United Kingdom. *ISER Working Papers 2002–13*.
Gershuny, J. (2000) *Changing Times: Work and Leisure in Post-industrial Societies*. Oxford: Oxford University Press.
Hoffman, E. (1981) Accounting for time on Labour Force Surveys. *Bulletin of Labour Statistics* 1. Geneva: International Labour Organization.
Jacobs, J. A. (1998) Measuring time at work: An assessment of the accuracy of self reports. *Monthly Labor Review*, 121, 42–53.
Joshi, H., and Davies, H. (2002) Women's incomes over a synthetic lifetime. In E. Ruspini and A. Dale (eds.), *The Gender Dimension of Social Change*. Bristol: Policy Press.
Lingsom, S. (1995) Women's time-use over the lifecycle. In I. Niemi (ed.), *Time Use of Women in Europe and North America*. New York and Geneva: United Nations.
Mincer, J., and Polachek, S. (1974) Family investments in human capital: earnings of women. *Journal of Political Economy*, 82, 76–108.
Niemi, I. (1983) *Time Use Study in Finland*. Helsinki: Central Statistical Office.
Taylor, M. F. (ed.) (2002) (with J. Brice, N. Buck and E. Prentice-Lane) *British Household Panel Survey User Manual* Volume A: Introduction, Technical Report and Appendices. Colchester: University of Essex.
Zerubavel, E. (1981) *Hidden Rhythms*. Berkeley: University of California Press.

## APPENDIX 10.1 TWO PANEL DATASETS

### British Household Panel Study (BHPS)

Initial (1991) 5,000-household national random sample; all adults in household interviewed annually.
Questions on:

- work history, employment since last survey
- earnings, benefits, etc., since last survey
- family circumstances and history
- social attitudes, etc., etc.
- initial sample + descendants + current co-residents.

Wave 1 response rate 70%+, wave-on-wave >96%.

Additional samples selected in Scotland and Wales in 2000 and Northern Ireland in 2001: now 9,000 households, 16,000 respondents annually. Full documentation available online at www.iser.essex.ac.uk/bhps/index.php

### Home-on-Line ("HoL")

A three-wave time-diary panel study, funded by British Telecom during 1999–2001, based at the Institute for Economic and Social Research (ISER), University of Essex, UK. 1,000 households, national random sample, with over-sample for computer-owning households. First-wave personal interview for all adult members, leave-behind seven-day self-completion light diary for all aged 10+. First wave 60%+ questionnaire response rate, 50%-diary response. Specimen results available online at www.iser.essex.ac.uk/pubs/workpaps/2002-01.php

Diaries kept for 7 sequential days, with 15-minute recording period, and 35 fixed-activity categories.

HoL contains, *inter alia*, various BHPS-derived activity/participation questions:

- stylized estimate ("How much time . . . ?) questions:
- paid work
- housework
- "who does . . . ?

Shopping, cooking, cleaning, and clothes washing, used in fusion exercise.
DIY and child-care, not used in fusion.
Participation frequency on 10 leisure categories, not used in fusion.

# III

# Inequality and Diversity

# 11

# Inequality and the Family

Philip N. Cohen and Danielle MacCartney

Inequality is related to families and family structure in complicated ways. Family forms may be cause, or consequence, of various forms of inequality. In hard times, families may provide comfort or serve as resource pools to protect against scarcity. For the privileged, families are conduits for the intergenerational transmission of wealth and status. For others, the burden of caring for family members sometimes imposes impediments to economic mobility.

In this chapter, we describe four forms that the relationship between families and inequality may take. First, *families reflect inequalities*, because the unequal distribution of various resources – economic, social, and political – affects the availability or accessibility of some family forms. For example, low incomes increase the likelihood that poor people will find themselves living in extended families even when they would prefer the privacy of a smaller, nuclear family.

Even as inequality affects the forms that families take, however, it is also the case that *unequal outcomes result from different families and family forms*. This is the second relationship we discuss. This dynamic has both proximate and intergenerational components. A common example of the proximate effects is the disproportionate odds of poverty experienced by single mothers and their children. In terms of intergenerational effects, families remain perhaps the most important mechanism for the transmission of unequal life chances.

But families are not unitary subjects, experiencing the same consequences or impacts of the wider social world. Thus, our third observation is that *families contain and reproduce inequalities*, both personally intimate and economically pivotal. For example, the division of labor and resources within families usually privileges men, with women dominating unpaid housework and child-care while men hold privileged positions in the paid labor market. Further, children are subject to the often unchecked authority of their parents.

Thus, inequalities impose constraints on family forms, and the weight of each generation's troubles often falls on the shoulders of their children. And beyond these dynamics, the family is a cauldron of inequality in some ways all its own. However, we must not exclude the paradoxical reality that *family relationships offer responses to inequality and hardship* – our fourth dynamic. Without the cooperation and mutual support of individuals within families, survival itself would be compromised, at least for the poorest people. We address each of these relationships in turn.

## Families as Unequal Outcomes

In the modern era, it has been suggested, people use families for their personal instrumental, rather than collective, purposes. However, not everyone has equal access to the growing range of options regarding family forms. Unequal access to family forms is an expression of inequality that is often invisible, confounded by our belief that decisions about whom to marry, how many children to have, and with whom to live are deeply personal and individual. But these personal decisions are made in very unequal contexts.

### Family formation

One prominent explanation for the higher rate of single motherhood among African Americans in the US is that inner-city black women face a shortage of "marriageable" men (Wilson, 1987). Specifically, the combined effects of higher black mortality, incarceration, and chronic unemployment – all of which are concentrated in American inner cities – have greatly reduced the likelihood that a given Black woman will be able to find a man, or at least a man she wants to marry. In addition, Black couples are more likely to cohabit instead of marry than are white couples, which may reflect their decisions to postpone or forgo marriage under conditions of economic uncertainty (Raley, 1996). A shortage of available mates – for demographic, economic, or other reasons – can also run against men's odds of marriage. In China, for example, the historical practice of female infanticide, coupled with polygamy on the part of richer men, led to a shortage of available women, keeping many men, especially poor men, from ever marrying (Lee and Feng, 1999).

If a shortage of mates prevents the formation of some nuclear families, a lack of financial or other resources often leads to the growth of extended families. Asians, Latinos, and blacks in the US are all more likely to live in multigenerational households than are whites. Although culture and tradition play a role in these differences, it appears that such arrangements are more generally the result of economic or health conditions leading people to choose arrangements that run against their preference for more private family lives (Cohen and Casper, 2002). Low earnings, job insecurity, child-care expenses, health problems, and high housing costs may all contribute to the likelihood of living in extended households.

The poor are more likely to live in extended households, but extended family arrangements also reflect complicated patterns of intergenerational support. Older Americans are much more likely to have younger relatives move in with them than they are to move into the homes of others. To some degree, this reflects generational inequalities. Because of government support for middle-class homebuying after World War II, and partly because of Social Security support and other savings, older Americans are more likely to own homes than are their younger relatives. In a pinch, then, the younger generation may show up on the doorstep of their parents' or in-laws' homes. Additionally, difficulties finding jobs, connecting with marriage partners, and paying for college have led increasing numbers of young adults to delay forming their own households (Treas and Torrecilha, 1995). Multigenerational arrangements also reflect gendered patterns, as men are more likely than women are to live with their mothers (Cohen and Casper, 2002).

### Legal and social restrictions

The legally recognized formation of families also requires rights that not all enjoy. Family life therefore may be conditioned on inequalities in political power. Gay and lesbian couples, for example, have had to struggle for the right to have or adopt children and, in most places, are still prevented from legally marrying. Even the right to maintain familial relationships – such as visiting loved ones in hospital, making medical decisions for spouses, and passing on custody of children or property upon death – is often contested for gay and lesbian couples. On the other hand, the religious practice of polygamy among Mormons in the US has been legally curtailed as well. In these and other ways, state practices directly or indirectly affect the kind of families that may be formed or legally recognized. This is the case even though state affirmation is rarely visible to those making more mainstream family choices; married couples rarely, if ever, are asked to produce legal proof of their marriage.

Beyond the effects of state policy, there are strong social norms and taboos that support some family forms while condemning others to marginality or disparagement. These have been eroded in recent years, especially in some places – such as San Francisco, California – where advocates have been able to affect local policies and practices to explicitly protect unmarried couples. Nevertheless, informal enforcement of social expectations with regard to families remains quite strong, even though it may be subtle, as in the practice of paying married men higher wages or promoting them faster than single men.

Pierre Bourdieu writes:

> the family in its legitimate definition is a privilege instituted into a universal norm . . . Those who have the privilege of having a "normal" family are able to demand the same of everyone without having to raise the question of the conditions (a certain income, living space, etc.) of universal access to what they demand universally. (1998: 69)

Thus, the "normal" family is not accessible to everyone, for various reasons, but it is almost universally expected. And despite formidable barriers to this normalcy, those who fail to conform are generally considered to have made personal choices that cement their outsider status.

## Families Transmitting Inequality

As we have seen, there are many factors that determine what kind of family people are born into or live in. Equally important, however, are the effects that families and family forms have on their members, in the short run as well as intergenerationally. Family structure, background, and the resources available to children, including financial resources and education at home and in school, can affect children's lives and their future as adults.

## Family structure

Some kinds of families are at higher risk of poverty and other economic disadvantages, especially those headed by single women. In Britain, four out of five single-parent families qualify for poverty-level public assistance (Allan and Crow, 2001); in the US, about 40 percent of single-mother families live below the official poverty line (Casper and Bianchi, 2002). This is primarily because single women are often compelled to maintain families with one (woman's) earnings (Thomson et al., 1994). The increase in single-parent households in the US has been pronounced, and remains much higher for black families; only a third of African American children lived in two-parent families by the late 1990s, a decrease from two-thirds in 1960 (Sandefur et al., 2001). During that time, out-of-wedlock birth replaced divorce and widowhood as the predominant entry into single parenthood for women (Bianchi, 1995). Like other single mothers, never-married mothers have no male income to rely on. But divorced women have less difficulty obtaining child support because divorce procedures involve some court intervention (although many still do not receive adequate payments). Also, never-married mothers have lower average levels of education and are less often fully employed than divorced mothers, increasing the likelihood that they will have lower incomes and higher levels of poverty.

With at least 20 percent of all single-parent families headed by fathers, the implications of single-father families for children have also come under scrutiny. Single fathers usually have higher incomes and more material resources than single mothers, which allow the children of single-father families to gain some of the benefits accruing to the affluent. However, single fathers have fewer social resources and more difficulty with the parenting role than single mothers (Griffiths, 1999).

The conditions of life for poor families can have a significant immediate effect on children. Although conditions have improved among the poor in the US in recent decades, many still live in dilapidated homes, where walls, floors, and ceilings have open cracks or holes, and leaky roofs, exposed wires, and rodents, which all present health hazards (Mayer, 1997). Poor children are on average less healthy than other children, with higher rates of infant, child, or adolescent mortality and increased risk of infectious diseases. In addition to direct economic mechanisms, however, Guo and Harris (2000) found that some family-related factors, including cognitive stimulation and parenting style – along with physical environment and health at birth – contribute to developmental problems for poor children.

## Class mobility

Adherents of the benefits of modernity believe that with the spread of industrialization, and the bureaucratization that accompanies it, the effects of family background on children's futures should be gradually reduced as individual effort and natural ability are increasingly rewarded by the meritocratic system. Although there was evidence of declining father influence on sons' occupational standing in the 1960s and 1970s, more recent research shows a persistent and possibly increasing tendency for fathers to pass on their occupational standing to their sons. As Steven Rytina writes, "the apple lands as near the tree as it ever did, if not a little closer" (2000: 1270).

Most social scientists are not persuaded by the evidence for inherited intelligence as a powerful determinant of economic success later in life. But we know that families do affect their children's futures in many ways. Depending on the circumstances and measures used, it has been shown that the parental education and family income experienced as a child affect the odds of poverty as an adult. According to a multivariate analysis by Fischer et al. (1996), parents' income is the most important factor (although in the case of African Americans, parental education also plays an important role).

In general, families at the top and bottom of the economic hierarchy are most likely to produce children who replicate their families' social position. That is because the very rich have the most opportunity to advance their children's prospects, and the very poor have the least access to the kind of resources necessary to propel their children into a higher social position. There is considerably more fluidity in the middle of the economic distribution, which is more consistent with assumptions about modernity (Kerbo, 2000). So, although individual factors are clearly important, the reproduction of inequality takes place at least in part within families, and parental characteristics are among the most important predictors of adult outcomes.

The transmission of life chances from parents to children is complex, taking many forms. Outcomes for children of single-parent families, for example, are affected not just by income, but also by time spent with parents, parental help with schoolwork, and parental supervision (McLanahan and Sandefur, 1994). The mechanisms by which the children of single parents pay an economic penalty as adults are still contested. But it is safe to say that, at least for children of single mothers, lower income is probably the most important factor leading to poorer outcomes (Amato and Keith, 1991), including lower standardized test scores, lower levels of education, and lower income as adults (Downey, 1994). On the other hand, at least one major study has found that children from single-father families also grow up to attain lower socioeconomic status than children from married-couple families (Biblarz and Raftery, 1999).

Some family determinants of children's outcomes do not depend directly on the families' income, or on behaviors within families, but rather result from the areas or neighborhoods in which they live. Mary Corcoran suggests that the mechanisms by which neighborhood effects operate include a combination of "neighborhood poverty, neighborhood welfare use, an inadequate tax base, poor public services, neighborhood family structure, absence of middle class role models, or a host of other possibilities" (1995: 258), which may include local criminal activity and peer-group activities.

Certainly, where families live contributes to one major stratifying force for children: schooling. According to Alan Kerckhoff, "Especially in secondary school, there is an association between family social status and student access to favored educational locations – better schools, more academically challenging courses, and classes taught by the 'better' teachers" (1995: 328). Schools in more affluent areas have more resources, including more contemporary books, computer resources, or better staff, as well as advanced placement and honors courses. These advantages allow children from affluent families to have greater access to higher education and ultimately higher earnings. This may be one reason why children raised in poverty have lower incomes and lower educational attainment as adults – including a higher risk of dropping out of high school and a lower likelihood of attending college.

Less complicated, but no less important, is family transmission of wealth the old-fashioned way: inheritance. Affluent parents are able to leave wealth behind for their children when they die. They also pass on large sums of money at key life-course milestones, especially marriage and buying a home. These one-time investments in the next generation turn out to have important implications for future development. For example, in the US, these transfers play a very significant role in the widely divergent asset portfolios of whites and blacks with similar earned incomes (Oliver and Shapiro, 1995). In this way, family background can mean the difference between security and insecurity in early adulthood, influencing decisions about education, the accumulation of assets early in adulthood, and investments in children – which in turn affect the security of retirements and inheritances for future generations.

Children of affluent families also inherit less measurable but no less important assets from the formal and informal networks of their parents. Private schools and universities, for example, may give preferential admissions status to the children of alumni. Family connections among the wealthy also provide many opportunities for children. Because friendship networks among the wealthy are concentrated at the upper end of the class hierarchy, the casual intervention or assistance of friends is also highly stratified. Many young adults have a family friend help them get a summer job, for example, but who their parents are will affect the nature of those jobs. Family social networks, especially among the rich, also often bring young adults together in marriage (Domhoff, 2002).

## Inequality within Families

In some respects it is tempting to discuss families as functional units. By working together families increase efficiency; money and other resources are often shared, and decisions about how to deploy them often are made jointly. But as the age at marriage has increased, along with divorce rates, and more parents are raising children either alone or with unmarried partners, it has become increasingly obvious that people do not relinquish their individual interests when they cross the threshold of the family home. Like workplaces or other social arenas, families are themselves sites of negotiation and exchange, power and conflict, and inequality.

### Divisions of labor

In the majority of American married couples, both husband and wife are now in the labor force. Nevertheless, men still devote more time to paid work while women do more housework and child-care. As with any division of labor, whether mutual or coercive, the division of labor within couples – and the dynamic it sets in motion – have implications for inequality.

According to the US Census Bureau, the wife was the only spouse in the labor force in just 6 percent of all married couples in 2000. Among couples with children, that number fell to 3 percent of couples. On the other hand, 22 percent of couples send only the husband into the labor force, which rises to 28 percent in couples with children. Thus, in most couples, even most couples with children, both spouses are in the labor force. But the "traditional" breadwinner role is much more likely to be filled by the husband. Even without gender inequality in the labor market, then, we would expect husbands to earn more money than their wives. In fact, 59 percent of husbands have earnings $5,000 or more over their wives', compared to the mere 15 percent of wives who earn $5,000 more than their husbands. That gap is also wider in couples with children.

Despite substantial narrowing over the last several decades, the housework imbalance persists as well. In 1965, US married women spent 33.9 hours per week on all housework tasks, compared to 4.7 hours per week performed by husbands, a ratio of more than 7 to 1. By 1995, the ratio was below 2 to 1, as wives cut their hours down to 19.4, and husbands increased theirs to 10.4. However, there was little change in the 10 years after 1985, indicating that the convergence may be leveling off (Bianchi et al., 2000).

Female dominance of housework is by no means restricted to the US. An analysis of data collected in 22 industrialized countries in 1994 showed that no country approached equality in the division of housework between husbands and wives. The most egalitarian were the socially liberal countries – Norway, the US, Sweden, and Canada. The socially conservative and Catholic countries – Austria, Ireland, Italy, and Japan – had the most unequal divisions of labor. Great Britain, New Zealand, and Australia fell into the middle range (Batalova and Cohen, 2002).

A number of explanations have been offered for the persistence of the housework gap between husbands and wives (South and Spitze, 1994). The simplest is that wives do more housework because they have more time for housework, as the labor force consumes husbands' time. This explanation is problematic, however, because labor-force commitments have changed more rapidly than the division of housework has. This lends support to the second explanation, which is that the imbalance favors men because men bring greater resources – especially their incomes – to the family negotiation over housework. Housework is considered drudgery, so men use their stronger bargaining position to get out of it. Finally, it is clear that childhood socialization plays a role in the expectations that both men and women bring to marriages. Therefore, any change in the division of housework is likely to lag behind changes in the economy or other influences, as adults model behaviors they experienced decades earlier in their own families.

Even if the division of labor within couples were mutually agreeable – representing joint investment in the family unit – it would have consequences for inequality in cases where the marriage ends in divorce or widowhood. The time women spend out of the labor force takes a toll on their future earnings if they later choose, or need, to find full-time employment. However, even when work experience is taken into account, women who have had children suffer a wage penalty (Budig and England, 2001). It is possible that employers discriminate against mothers in hiring, or fail to promote them to positions with higher pay, because they believe mothers will be less reliable or committed to their jobs. That would fit with the considerable evidence that married men earn more than single men – even when differences in education, skill level, and experience are taken into account – perhaps because employers believe married men are more responsible, or will devote themselves more fully to their jobs (Cohen, 2002a). Thus, social norms and expectations about family life may magnify the effects of the gender division of labor within families, enhancing men's privilege and increasing women's dependence on men's earnings.

## Power, violence, and authority

Partly as a result of economic inequalities, the hierarchy within families generally ranks men at the top, followed by women and then children. Among children, there may be an additional hierarchy by age and gender, depending on the cultural and economic context. Thus, inequalities outside the family permeate families as well, contributing in turn to the reproduction of inequality in the wider social world.

Inequalities work through family relations to create hierarchies, partly through differential power among family members. Consider the role of children. They depend on parental support, supervision, and other resources in order to thrive. For example, in the US, children with more than one sibling on average attain lower levels of education than those with fewer siblings, presumably because of lower parental investments per child (Hauser and Kuo, 1998). The affect of parental decision-making is even more pronounced in many parts of Eastern and Southern Asia, where parents exhibit a strong preference for sons. This leads to sons getting more food and better health care at young ages. Also, if parents with a strong son preference stop having children only when they have reached the desired number of sons, girls on average will grow up in larger families, which itself is a disadvantage. Paradoxically, this also means that daughters will be more likely to live in families with a strong son preference, where they will be still further disadvantaged (Clark, 2000).

Despite its traditional overtones, however, the preference for sons is not just a fading feudal practice. Parents' preference for sons may be more common in societies with a dowry system, but son preference also results from calculation of the relative economic potential of boys versus girls, and thus reflects contemporary gender inequalities, regardless of their origins. And traditional son preferences interact with evolving state policy as well. Evidence from China suggests that girls living in communities that strictly enforce the government's one-child policy receive less parental care than girls living in other communities (Short et al., 2001).

Perhaps the clearest example of power relations within families, however, concerns sex and violence. The US Bureau of Justice Statistics, from data collected in the 1990s, reports that three-quarters of sexual assaults against children occur in a residence. The perpetrators of sexual assault against victims under 6 were family members in half the cases. The likelihood that a sexual assault will be perpetrated by family members decreases as children grow older and interact more outside the family, but even among children age 12 and over, 24 percent of sexual assaults are committed by family members. As with adults, girls are more likely to be sexually assaulted than boys, but at the youngest ages about 1 in 3 victims is a boy. Other violence within families usually but not exclusively targets women. In 1998, women comprised 72 percent of people killed by spouses and other intimates, and 85 percent of the victims in nonlethal, intimate violence. Sadly, for some, the family is a source of violence, degradation, and even death.

The patterns of family violence help illustrate the underlying power relationships, and how they interact with the hierarchies of the wider social world (Andersen, 2000). Despite difficulties in reporting, for example, it is clear that family violence extends up and down the economic spectrum and racial–ethnic hierarchy. However, stresses related to economic inequality, including unemployment, do contribute to incidences of family violence (Kimmel, 2000). Although both men and women may perpetrate family violence, there is some evidence that violence plays a different role for each. In keeping with men's more powerful positions, some research has shown that men's violence tends to be more instrumental, that is, men tend to use violence to gain obedience or acceptance of their dominant position within the household. Women, on the other hand, tend either to react defensively or to express immediate frustration or anger. Among same-sex couples – who overall experience similar levels of family violence as opposite-sex couples – violence may also be exacerbated by internalized homophobia, which provides a source of displaced anger, feelings of despair, or loss of control (Andersen, 2000).

## Families Resisting Inequality

For every story of hierarchy and domination within families, there is another that tells of families pulling together to make ends meet, support each other, and soldier on to produce the next generation in even the toughest of times. The centrality of the family as a social institution emerges when one observes that the family is so crucial both to the reproduction of inequality on the one hand, and to the resistance to inequality and hardship on the other. In this last section we outline some of the ways the family plays this latter role.

In recent years, careful longitudinal studies have been able to confirm some assumptions about the positive role that families can play, especially for children facing economic, health, or emotional hardship. For example, on the Hawaiian island of Kauai, a long-term study of vulnerable children showed that emotional support from family members, including extended family members, was an important factor in surviving and thriving into adulthood (Werner and Smith, 2001). For adolescents in American rural areas facing economic hard times, close relationships with grandparents and other extended family members provide an important source of support when parents cannot fulfill their protective roles, with positive effects on children's academic success and emotional well-being (Elder and Conger, 2000).

Similarly, the challenges single-mother families face, and the disadvantages in childhood that result, do not necessarily lead to reports of lower psychological well-being (Hilton, Desrochers, and Devall, 2001). Single parents do raise successful children, often by assuming both male and female role responsibilities, establishing extended care networks, serving as teachers, confidants, and role models for their children, and finding sources of income other than wages (Persaud, Gray, and Hunt, 1999; Tsushima and Gecas, 2001). Much of this activity escaped the attention of researchers, especially the use of informal networks to raise alternative sources of income (Edin and Lein, 1997).

Beyond support behaviors within families, two other strategies stand out as individual and adaptive responses to poverty and inequality. The first uses the family to go outside the family and household, building networks of support to create a social safety net, especially in the absence of adequate welfare support. New studies show that family networks – including related and nonrelated members – often contribute vitally to the educational success of children (Rosier, 2000). The second involves the actual form that families take. For example, with the onset of welfare reform in the US, new research has focused on the role of extended families in supporting the employment of single mothers, showing that those single mothers who live in extended households are more likely to be employed (Cohen, 2002b). One role for extended family members is taking care of children, especially since access to affordable day care is central to maintaining employment for single mothers (Manning and Smock, 1997).

Much of this research is part of a long history of interest in the central role played by family-support networks among African Americans (Stack, 1974). But recent scholarship emphasizes several limitations to this approach. First, one should not exaggerate the lifesaving capacity of kin networks. In fact, one of the vexing problems of inner-city decline for Black families has been the faltering of their networks – which remain only as strong as their members (Roschelle, 1997). Second, partly because family networks among the poor are so important for survival, reliance on such relationships is not always voluntary or even welcome. Katherine Newman has shown that, in the absence of sufficient earnings, social networks for the working poor preserve "a form of social capital that has all but disappeared in many an American suburb" (1999: 194). But while the middle class might regret the loss of such connections, these networks "remain tight, even oppressive at times, in poor communities."

## Conclusion

Families are formed and develop in a social context rife with inequality along many dimensions. We have seen the impact of these inequalities on the formation of families, but also how families are actors in the systems of inequality, transmitting inequalities to subsequent generations, reproducing inequalities within the confines of the family home and the networks of its members, but also resisting the effects of inequality and hardship. Like any major social institution, then, families are thoroughly intertwined with larger, structural forces in the cultural, economic, and political arenas. By examining the dynamics of families, we are able to learn not only some of the ways that inequality works its way into and through our lives, but also how inequality shapes our family environments, and how individual interaction both reflects and contributes to the inequalities we face.

### References

Allan, G., and Crow, G. (2001) *Families, Households, and Society.* Basingstoke: Palgrave.

Amato, P. R., and Keith, B. (1991) Separation from a parent during childhood and adult socioeconomic attainment. *Social Forces*, 70, 187–206.

Andersen, M. L. (2000) *Thinking About Women: Sociological Perspectives on Sex and Gender* (5th ed.). Boston: Allyn & Bacon.

Batalova, J., and Cohen, P. N. (2002) Premarital cohabitation and housework: Couples in cross-national perspective. *Journal of Marriage and the Family*, 64, 3, 743–55.

Bianchi, S. M. (1995) The changing demographic and socioeconomic characteristics of single parent families. *Marriage and Family Review*, 20, 71–97.

Bianchi, S. M., Milkie, M. A., Sayer, L. C., and Robinson, J. P. (2000) Is anyone doing the housework? Trends in the gender division of household labor. *Social Forces*, 79, 191–228.

Biblarz, T. J., and Raftery, A. E. (1999) Family structure, educational attainment, and socioeconomic success: Rethinking the "pathology of matriarchy". *American Journal of Sociology*, 105, 321–65.

Bourdieu, P. (1998) *Practical Reason: On the Theory of Action.* Stanford, CA: Stanford University Press.

Budig, M. J., and England, P. (2001) The wage penalty for motherhood. *American Sociological Review*, 66, 204–25.

Casper, L. M., and Bianchi, S. M. (2002) *Continuity and Change in the American Family.* Thousand Oaks, CA: Sage.

Clark, S. (2000) Son preference and sex composition of children: Evidence from India. *Demography*, 37, 95–108.

Cohen, P. N. (2002a) Cohabitation and the declining marriage premium for men. *Work and Occupations*, 29, 3, 346–63.

Cohen, P. N. (2002b) Extended households at work: Living arrangements and inequality in single mothers' employment. *Sociological Forum*, 17, 3, 445–63.

Cohen, P. N., and Casper, L. M. (2002) In whose home? Multigenerational families in the United States, 1998–2000. *Sociological Perspectives*, 45, 1–20.

Corcoran, M. (1995) Rags to rags: Poverty and mobility in the United States. *Annual Review of Sociology*, 21, 237–67.

Domhoff, G. W. (2002) *Who Rules America? Power and Politics*. 4th ed. Boston: McGraw Hill.

Downey, D. B. (1994) The school performance of children from single-mother and single-father families: economic or interpersonal deprivation? *Journal of Family Issues*, 15, 129–47.

Edin, K., and Lein, L. (1997) *Making Ends Meet: How Single Mothers Survive Welfare and Low-Wage Work*. New York: Russell Sage Foundation.

Elder, G. H., and Conger, R. (2000) *Children of the Land: Adversity and Success in Rural America*. Chicago: University of Chicago Press.

Fischer, C. S., Hout, M., Sanchez, M. J., Lucas, S. R., Swidler, A., and Voss, K. (1996) *Inequality by Design: Cracking the Bell Curve Myth*. Princeton, NJ: Princeton University Press.

Griffiths, J. (1999) Fathers as mothers: lone parenting for men. In G. Dench (ed.), *Rewriting the Sexual Contract*. New Brunswick, NJ: Transaction.

Guo, G., and Harris, K. M. (2000) The mechanisms mediating the effects of poverty on children's intellectual development. *Demography*, 37, 431–47.

Hauser, R. M., and Kuo, H. H. D. (1998) Does the gender composition of sibships affect women's educational attainment? *Journal of Human Resources*, 33, 644–57.

Hilton, J. M., Desrochers, S., and Devall, E. L. (2001) Comparison of role demands, relationships, and child functioning in single-mother, single-father, and intact families. *Journal of Divorce and Remarriage*, 35, 29–56.

Kerbo, H. R. (2000) *Social Stratification and Inequality: Class Conflict in Historical, Comparative, and Global Perspective*. 4th ed. Boston: McGraw-Hill.

Kerckhoff, A. C. (1995) Institutional arrangements and stratification processes in industrial societies. *Annual Review of Sociology*, 21, 323–47.

Kimmel, M. S. (2000) *The Gendered Society*. New York and Oxford: Oxford University Press.

Lee, J. Z., and Wang, F. (1999) *One Quarter of Humanity: Malthusian Mythology and Chinese Realities, 1700–2000*. Cambridge, MA: Harvard University Press.

Manning, W. D., and Smock, P. J. (1997). Children's living arrangements in unmarried-mother families. *Journal of Family Issues*, 18, 526–44.

Mayer, S. E. (1997) *What Money Can't Buy: Family Income and Children's Life Chances*. Cambridge, MA: Harvard University Press.

McLanahan, S. S., and Sandefur, G. D. (1994) *Uncertain Childhood, Uncertain Future*. Cambridge, MA: Harvard University Press.

Newman, K. S. (1999) *No Shame in My Game: The Working Poor in the Inner City*. New York: Knopf and the Russell Sage Foundation.

Oliver, M. L., and Shapiro, T. M. (1995) *Black Wealth/White Wealth: A New Perspective on Racial Inequality*. New York: Routledge.

Persaud, N., Gray, P. S., and Hunt, E. (1999) Raised by African-American single-parents to succeed: The perspectives of children. *International Journal of Sociology of the Family*, 29, 69–84.

Raley, R. K. (1996) Shortage of marriageable men? A note on the role of cohabitation in black-white differences in marriage rates. *American Sociological Review*, 61, 973–83.

Roschelle, A. R. (1997) *No More Kin: Exploring Race, Class, and Gender in Family Networks*. Thousand Oaks, CA: Sage.

Rosier, K. B. (2000) *Mothering Inner-City Children: The Early School Years*. New Brunswick, NJ: Rutgers University Press.

Rytina, S. (2000) Is occupational mobility declining in the US? *Social Forces*, 78, 1227–76.

Sandefur, G. D., Martin, M., Eggerling-Boeck, J., Mannon, S. E., and Meier, A. M. (2001) An overview of racial and ethnic demographic trends. In N. J. Smelser, W. J. Wilson, and F. Mitchell (eds.), *America Becoming: Racial Trends and Their Consequences, Vol 1*. Washington, DC: National Academy Press.

Short, S. E., Zhai, F., Xu, S., and Yang, M. (2001) China's one-child policy and the care of children: an analysis of qualitative and quantitative data. *Social Forces*, 79, 913–43.

South, S. J., and Spitze, G. (1994) Housework in marital and nonmarital households. *American Sociological Review*, 59, 327–47.

Stack, C. B. (1974) *All Our Kin: Strategies for Survival in a Black Community*. New York: Harper.

Thomson, E., Hanson, T. L., and McLanahan, S. S. (1994) Family structure and child well-being: Economic resources vs. parental behaviors. *Social Forces*, 73, 221-42.

Treas, J., and Torrecilha, R. (1995) The older population. In R. Farley (ed.), *State of the Union: America in the 1990s, Volume II: Social Trends*. New York: Russell Sage Foundation.

Tsushima, T., and Gecas, V. (2001) Role taking and socialization in single-parent families. *Journal of Family Issues*, 22, 267–88.

Werner, E. E., and Smith, R. S. (2001) *Journeys From Childhood to Midlife: Risk, Resilience, and Recovery*. Ithaca, NY: Cornell University Press.

Wilson, W. J. (1987) *The Truly Disadvantaged: The Inner City, the Underclass, and Public Policy*. Chicago: University of Chicago Press.

# 12

# Families of the Poor

Robert Walker and Claire Collins

To be poor in the post-industrial age is not simply to be without the resources necessary to meet social expectations. Being poor typically means active exclusion from the personal benefits of social integration and community. It means being denied access to public and privately provided institutions that create social and economic opportunity: good health care, education, insurance, credit, and transport. The effects of such exclusion can be long-term, scarring the aspirations and potential of young people and fostering destitution in old age.

Poverty frequently inhibits access to employment and with it a route to self-sufficiency and social standing. It limits participation as a consumer of choice in the marketplace and prevents people rejoicing in the tribalism of fashion and conspicuous consumption that has come to define identity in the modern world. The stigma that so often accompanies such curtailed autonomy is real, regardless of whether it is simply imagined or positively experienced. People in poverty often believe themselves to be failures in an achievement-orientated world, and are frequently perceived to be so by more affluent citizens and commentators who are apt to use the undifferentiated term "the poor" to label them.

In reality, people who are poor are extraordinarily heterogeneous in their circumstances and experience. Nor is their status immutably ascribed. Most spells of poverty are not permanent and, while very few poor people go on to enjoy real prosperity, enough do so to make real possibilities out of an optimistic myth. Likewise, of course, it is not unknown for the affluent to become poor. Both the twin engines of capitalism – fear of penury and greed for financial success – are fueled by real-world experience: the poor do change places with the non-poor. While this means that more people are cursed by poverty than simple, cross-sectional poverty statistics would suggest, it also demonstrates that society is not permanently divided into the same "haves" and "have-nots," and teaches that the life of the poor individual need not be without hope or purpose.

It follows that poverty is better conceptualized as a set of social processes rather than simply as a status or social state. Poverty is the experience lived out by families who are poor, one that they also help to shape. While the leverage that people in poverty can exert on their circumstances and life-chances is severely constrained – the power of social and economic forces seemingly stacked against them can be truly awesome, and to ignore the agency of people who are poor erodes their dignity, adds to their exclusion, and leads the observer to lose sight of the varied experience of being poor. Indeed, so different are the experiences of people in poverty that it may be apposite to talk of "poverties" rather than poverty, each, perhaps, with a different etiology and varying consequences.

The aim in this chapter is to integrate the rhetoric of this opening section, which by implication calls for a reconceptualization of poverty and policies designed to combat it, with recent empirical evidence drawn from advanced industrial societies. It moves from the more familiar measures of the incidence of poverty based on income shortfall, through evidence on dynamics that points out the differing experiences of poor people, to the least familiar, the worlds described and experienced by poor people themselves.

## The State of Poverty

While it is self-evident that poverty still exists in advanced industrial societies, consensus is lacking as to what poverty is. Some say that poverty can be defined behaviorally, arguing that people retreat from social participation once income falls below a particular threshold (Gordon and Townsend, 2000; Townsend, 1979). Others propose that poverty is no more than the bottom extreme of the income distribution, arbitrarily defined (LIS, 2001). Yet others suggest that poverty is primarily a rhetorical device; use of the term poverty is predicated on the assumption that something has to be done about it (Piachaud, 1983; Walker and Park, 1998).

### Definitions

Definitions are important. Ignoring them creates myth, fuels political rhetoric and distorts reality. Baulch's (1996) pyramid[1] (figure 12.1) links the conceptualization of poverty to both measurement and usage. At the top of the pyramid, poverty is portrayed in terms of a univariate concept of disadvantage: personal consumption, defined as expenditure plus home-produced products and services. In international comparative studies consumption is frequently measured indirectly via income, since information is easier to come by and money income is comparatively simple to measure in a standardized fashion.[2] This is the case in figures 12.2 to 12.7, discussed below.

Multidimensional conceptions of poverty of increasing complexity are found toward the base of the Baulch pyramid. These take account of the claims that people may or may not have on individual, communal, and government assets and services and take account of the loss of autonomy and dignity so frequently experienced by people when poor. It may be, certainly it is a testable hypothesis, that definitions

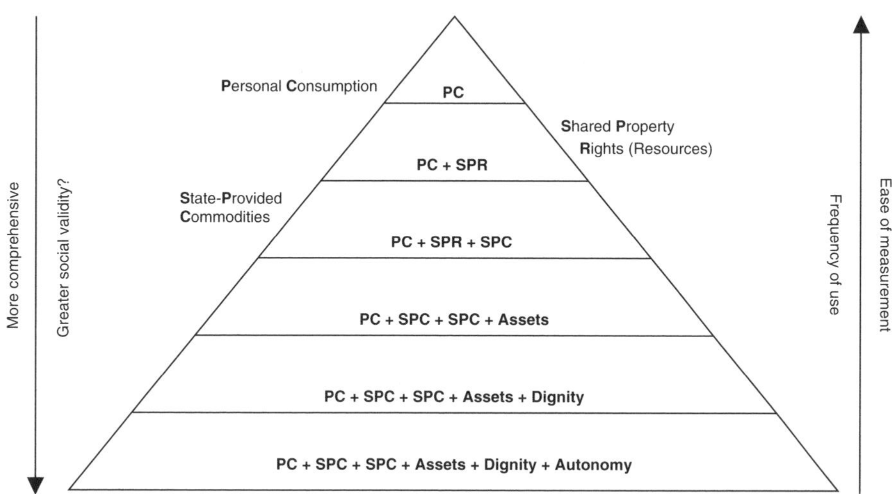


**Figure 12.1** Pyramid of Poverty Concepts

*Source*: Adapted from Baulch (1996).

closer to the base of the pyramid better approximate to the self-realization of people who would define themselves to be poor. Likewise, the challenges confronted by policymakers increase lower down the pyramid. If a lack of income is the root cause of poverty, then it can presumably be resolved by policies that make cash available to the poor. If poverty is multidimensional, policies need to be more creative and comprehensive.

Moreover, to the extent that Baulch's pyramid defines dimensions of poverty that are in varying degrees independent of each other, the implication is that there may well be many different kinds of poverty with different characteristics, etiologies, and solutions. The poverty suffered by some "asset-rich, income-poor" older householders could, for example, be contrasted with the situation of women with no independent access to resources living in ostensibly high-income families (Walker and Park, 1998).

Returning to the apex of Baulch's pyramid, the choice of income threshold below which people are counted as poor is essentially arbitrary.[3] Most international studies treat poverty as a relative rather than an absolute concept, with basic needs being defined in relation to the living standards currently prevailing in a society (e.g., OECD, 2001; Bradbury, Jenkins, and Micklewright, 2001; Goodin et al., 1999). This contrasts markedly with US domestic debates that use an absolute measure that ignores rising living standards.[4] By convention, the threshold for relative poverty is typically set as a percentage of median average income, often 50 percent, as in this chapter. This means that, in societies that experience prolonged economic growth, each generation of people in poverty will "enjoy" a higher standard of living than the preceding one. Relative measures also mean that the living standards of people who are defined as poor will differ from one country to another due to variations in national wealth, and hence in average per capita income.

Income is assessed for the household or family unit in which an individual resides, and the reference threshold, median household income, correspondingly takes account of differences in family size and needs by means of the application of equivalence scales (OECD, 2001).[5] Assessing poverty in this way presumes a degree of income-sharing within the family unit that may not always occur. This may mask real poverty as when, for example, women forgo expenditure on themselves to protect the living standards of their menfolk and children, but avoids the problem of children appearing to be destitute while their parents enjoy undue prosperity.

## Income poverty

Figure 12.2 reveals that the incidence of income poverty, both relative and absolute, varies markedly even among advanced industrial societies. It tends to be higher in Anglo-Saxon countries such as the US than in continental Europe or Scandinavia. So, for example, the US poverty rate in 1997, defined as household income of less than half the median when adjusted to take account of household size,[6] was 17.8 percent compared with 13.2 percent in the UK, 7.5 percent in Germany, and 5.5 percent in Finland. While these precise relativities vary over time according to the prevailing state of national economies, the rank order of countries is surprisingly constant (LIS, 2001).

Substantial international variation is also evident if a fixed poverty standard is used. The point estimates in figure 12.2 take the US Census Bureau definition and adjust it to take account of international variations in prices by using OECD purchasing-power parities. Data relate to 1994, the most recent year for which statistics are available, and record 13.6 percent of Americans as poor compared with 7.3 percent of Germans, 4.8 percent of Finns, and just 0.3 percent of people in

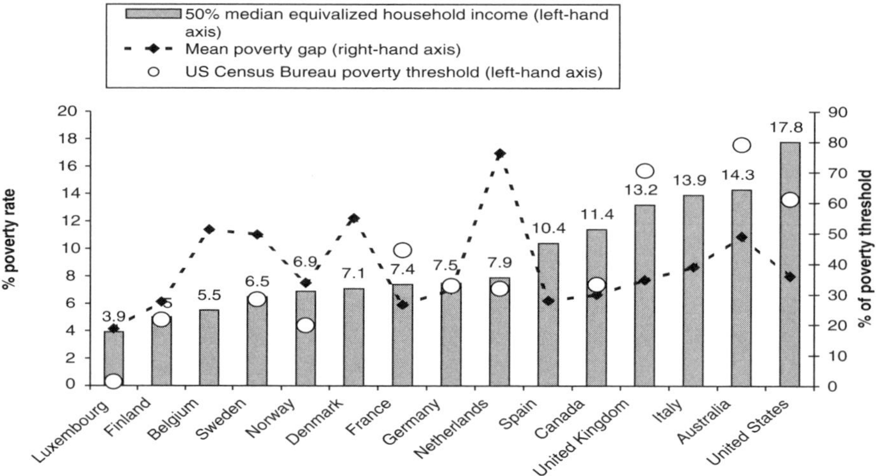


**Figure 12.2** Absolute and relative poverty rates and the poverty gap in selected countries, mid-1990s

*Source*: Smeeding, Rainwater, and Burtless (2000); and adapted from Brady (2001).

Luxembourg. The fact that poverty defined in this way was higher in Australia and the UK than in the US (the reverse was true using the relative measure) reflects the higher per capita incomes and the lower cost of living enjoyed by the average American.

At the turn of the nineteenth century, before the creation of the welfare state, a British social reformer, Seebohm Rowntree, observed that the incidence of poverty closely followed the life course (Rowntree, 1901). The risk of poverty was highest during childhood and child rearing, times when many mouths had to be fed but few family members were available to work, and in old age, when paid employment was no longer possible. Brief periods of comparative prosperity were enjoyed in youth and later in life after children had left home but before earning power was curtailed by poor health. This pattern is still evident in the UK and US but not in other developed countries, where the links between poverty and childhood and old age have been broken (figure 12.3[7]). In European and Scandinavian countries characterized by generally low rates of poverty, the risk of poverty in childhood is below average, often the result of universal income maintenance payments to children and plentiful, subsidized child-care. Rates of poverty among elderly persons, on the other hand, are comparatively high – the result of the failure of earnings-related social insurance schemes to protect those with a history of low wages or intermittent work.[8] In countries where poverty is much more prevalent even among people of working age, such as the US and UK, children tend to be disproportionately at risk of poverty (although this is not true in Australia).

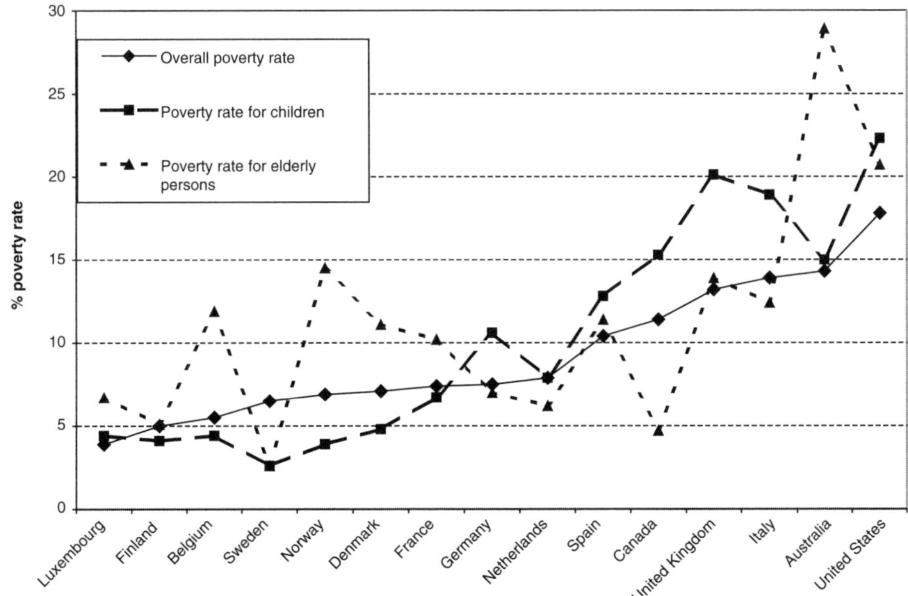


**Figure 12.3** Poverty rates for children and elderly persons (50% of median equivalised household income)

*Source*: Smeeding, Rainwater, and Burtless (2000).

Simple "headcount" measures of poverty provide no indication of the severity of poverty experienced by those who are poor. A measure that does is the mean poverty gap: the poverty gap is the amount by which a poor individual's income falls short of the poverty threshold expressed as a percentage of the threshold (figure 12.2[9]). In the mid-1990s, the average poor person in the US had an income that was 36 percent less than the poverty threshold, but the most severe poverty, as revealed by the poverty gap, was in the Netherlands, where the average poor person had an income that was 76 percent less than the poverty threshold. There is no evidence that poverty is particularly severe in countries like the US, where poverty rates are high (indeed, the Netherlands has only a moderate headcount poverty rate, while the statistical correlation between the poverty gap and the poverty rate is only 0.14). In the mid-1990s, the severity of poverty was also marked in Sweden, Belgium, and Denmark, which at the time had low poverty rates, and in Australia, which had a high poverty rate comparable with that of the US.

Of course, relative measures of poverty closely reflect the nature and degree of income inequality in a society and this, in turn, is likely to reflect the priority that countries give to reducing inequality and alleviating poverty.[10] The US and other Anglo-Saxon countries are often characterized as laissez-faire in terms of their response to these issues, relying heavily on the labor and capital markets to determine the resources available to individual families. In contrast, Scandinavian countries impose more progressive tax regimes to ensure more equitable disposable incomes, while countries in the Bismarckian tradition, such as Germany, seek to influence market incomes through national and sector-wide collective wage bargaining (Esping-Andersen, 1999; Walker, 2004).

Partial insight into the varying impact of these regimes is possible by comparing incomes before and after direct taxation and benefit transfers (figure 12.4[11]). Insight is partial because market incomes, that is, before tax and benefits, are themselves likely to reflect existing tax and benefit policies – employers in high-tax regimes may be tempted to pay higher salaries to boost the disposable incomes of their personnel.[12] In fact, it is not easy to account for the pattern of poverty based on market incomes. In the mid-1990s it was particularly high in Sweden, Denmark, Italy, and the UK but low in Luxembourg, Canada, and Finland. But what is clear is that poverty rates were much lower when based on incomes after tax and benefits than when based on market incomes; that is the impact of government transfer policies is to reduce poverty rates. However, it is also evident that the tax and benefit policies implemented by Anglo-Saxon countries, especially the US, and poorer southern European countries were much less effective in reducing poverty than those in northern continental Europe and Scandinavia. US tax and benefit polices succeeded in cutting the headcount rate by only 42 percent, compared with 79 percent in Germany and 88 percent in Luxembourg.

It is apparent, therefore, that while income poverty still exists on a large scale in several advanced industrial countries, notably Anglo-Saxon ones such as the US, others have succeeded in substantially reducing poverty levels, and most have eradicated the traditional association between poverty and childhood and old age.

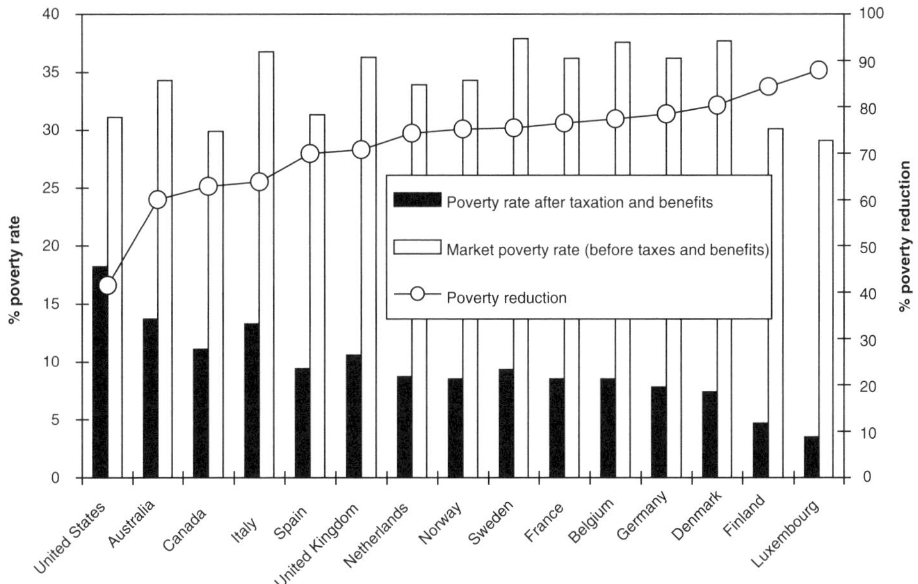


**Figure 12.4** Poverty reduction in selected countries, mid-1990s

*Source*: Adapted from Brady (2001).

## Poverty Dynamics

Static counts of the numbers of people who are poor reveal little about the nature and diversity of the poverty experienced by individuals and families (OECD, 1998; Oxley et al., 1997, 2000). Studies that expand the window of observation to take account of changes in people's circumstances are much more insightful. They show that more individuals suffer poverty than indicated by cross-sectional studies but that their experiences differ greatly. Most people are not poor for long, although many undergo repeated spells of poverty and a few endure poverty for considerable periods.

Take first the US and the period 1985–92 (OECD, 2001). Thirty-four percent of Americans were poor in at least three of these years, using equivalized household income of less than 50 per cent of the median as the measure of poverty. This figure is twice the prevailing annual poverty rate measured in the same way. Forty-seven percent of all spells of poverty lasted for less than a year but 52 percent of individuals who left poverty went on to experience another spell of hardship within six years. Indeed, 37 percent of all the people who were poor at any time between 1985 and 1992 – that is, 12.5 percent of all Americans – averaged incomes that fell short of half the median measured over the entire period (this index is called the permanent income ratio). Even so, "only" 4.5 percent of individuals were poor continuously throughout the eight-year period.

So Americans who live below the poverty line for long periods – a necessary but insufficient condition for the formation of an underclass[13] – constitute only a small minority even of the people who are ever poor. There is a much larger group of Americans who suffer repeated spells of poverty and who fail to acquire an income that is sufficient to lift them out of poverty in the longer term. However, the population of people who are poor at any one time is characterized by disproportionately high numbers of people suffering long or repeated spells of poverty.[14]

## National similarities and differences

This differentiated picture of transient, recurrent, and permanent poverty is repeated in all countries for which adequate data are available (OECD, 2001). But the balance between the types of poverty reflects national characteristics, including different policies and policy agendas (Goodin et al., 1999).

The way that poverty is distributed over time determines its distribution within the population and vice versa (Walker with Ashworth, 1994). If poverty is generally long-term, it will be visited on fewer people than if the same volume of poverty was experienced as predominately short spells. If the same people repeatedly suffer spells of poverty, an intermediate proportion of the population will ever experience poverty.

A simple index of the relative duration of poverty is provided by the ratio of the annual poverty rate to that observed over a longer time period. The lower the value, the greater the average duration. For the years 1993–5 this ratio (expressed as a percentage) was 47 percent for the US, which means that the number of people who experienced poverty increased by 47 percent as the window of observation was expanded from one year to three. Corresponding values for other countries were 59 per cent for Germany, 61 per cent for the UK, 73 percent for France, and 93 percent for Denmark (figure 12.5). These comparisons reveal the unusual permanence of

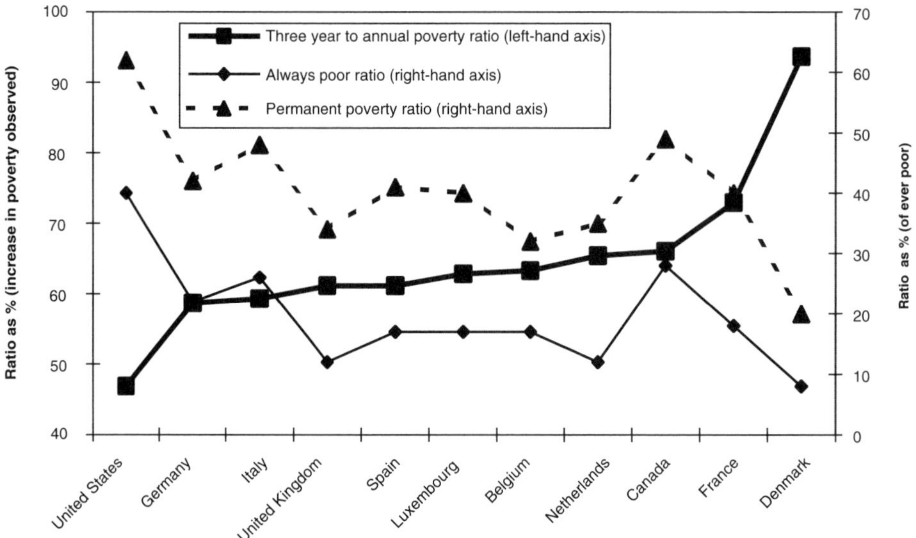


**Figure 12.5** Poverty dynamics in selected countries, 1993–1995

*Source*: OECD (2001).

poverty in the US relative to that found in Europe. Canada also appears to differ from Europe in terms of the types of poverty that are most prevalent. Large numbers of Canadians experience very short spells; many – though less than in the US – suffer long spells but comparatively few are poor repeatedly or for intermediate periods of time.

The unique pattern of poverties seen in the US is further emphasized by the fact that 62 percent of Americans who were poor at some time between 1993 and 1995 failed to accumulate sufficient resources to offset the shortfall in their income by the end of the three years (see the permanent income ratio in figure 12.5). This compares with a figure of 41 percent for Europe as a whole which, in turn, suggests that individuals who become poor in the US find it more difficult to earn or in other ways resource themselves out of poverty.

It would seem, then, that most spells of poverty are comparatively short but that in the same way that the poverty count varies by country, so some countries – notably the US and to a lesser extent the UK and Germany – exhibit a higher proportion of more persistent poverty. In proportional terms the burden of poverty in these countries is concentrated among fewer families than elsewhere, raising the prospect that they experience greater social exclusion.

## Demographic characteristics of poor families

Different families experience varying kinds of poverty and the relative risk of poverty faced by different types of family varies between one country and another. This international variation in the distribution or "shape" of poverty is captured in figure 12.6. The radar plots show the characteristics of individuals who experienced different kinds of poverty in the mid-1990s compared with individuals who were not poor (and who would, if plotted, have scored 1 on each radial axis). The larger the polygon, the greater the difference between the characteristics of poor and not-poor people; the more irregular the polygon, the more homogenous is the poverty population.

Families headed by women are more prone to poverty than those headed by men (figure 12.6).[15] In the US and continental Europe,[16] families that experienced poverty in the early 1990s were almost twice as likely to have female head of household than those that did not (in the UK the differential was marginally greater). The reasons for this are complex but include lower wage rates and job security for women, greater longevity – meaning women are more likely to live alone in old age, and lone parenthood – in most countries over 95 percent of lone-parent families are headed by a woman.

Lone-parent families are particularly exposed to poverty because of the necessary trade-off between earning and child-care. However, while lone parents in continental Europe were more likely to experience poverty in the mid-1990s than other families, they were only marginally more exposed to the risk of long-term poverty. This is in marked contrast to the US, where between 1993 and 1995 continuously poor families were 4.5 times more likely than non-poor ones to be headed by a lone parent. More needs to be known about the dynamics of lone parenthood, particularly the rate of repartnering in different countries, and about the pattern of benefit and child-care provision before these international differences can be adequately explained. But the evidence clearly shows that lone parenthood need not lead immutably to long-term poverty. While lone parents accounted for 30 percent of

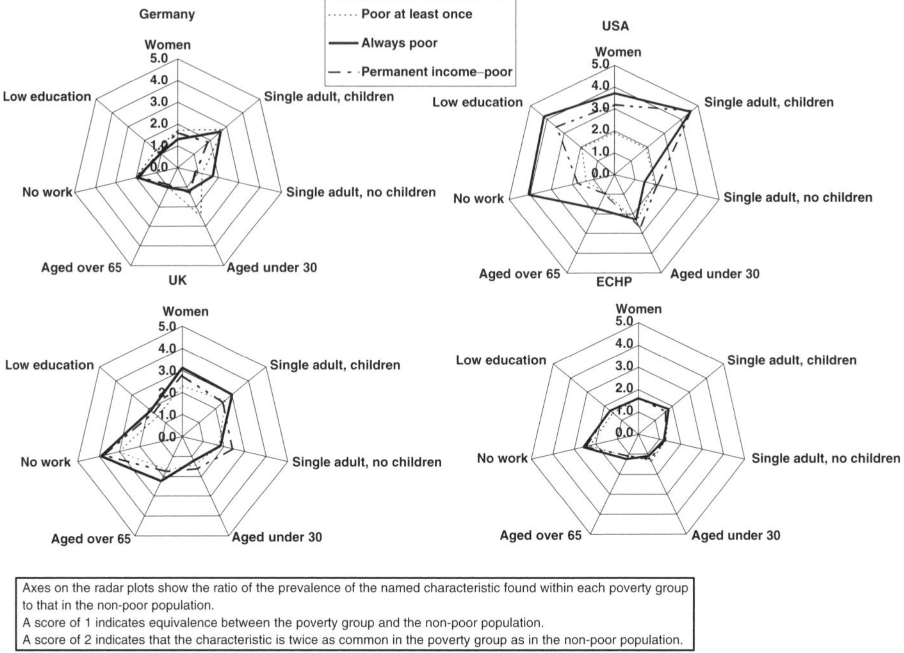


**Figure 12.6** The different shape of poverty

*Source*: Calculated from OECD (2001).

American families that were poor continuously between 1993 and 1995, they comprised only 15 percent in the UK and 9 percent in Europe as a whole (OECD, 2001).

Single adult households are also more prone to poverty than other types of family. This was most noticeable in the mid-1990s in the US and the UK, where people in poverty were twice as likely as more affluent ones to live alone. However, in the US, single adults who experienced poverty were, in marked contrast to lone parents, not greatly more at risk of suffering long-term poverty than other poor households. Individuals who live by themselves constitute a very diverse group, embracing, for example, young aspiring professionals, social outsiders, and housebound elders.

Whereas across much of Europe generous social insurance has broken the link between old age and poverty, this is not true in the UK or, in a different sense, in the US. In the UK in the mid-1990s, families headed by someone over 65 were both more likely than other families to suffer poverty and to remain poor for at least three years; most retired people without occupational pensions were reliant on social assistance. In the US, social insurance pensions generally succeeded in preventing retired households from slipping into poverty but, where this was not the case, poverty was likely to be long-term: 18 percent of spells lasted for six years or more compared with 7 percent in Germany and 8 percent in the UK (OECD, 2001).[17]

There is good reason to suspect that children are more at risk of poverty than adults, partly for reasons that Rowntree elucidated a century ago but also as a consequence of the growth of divorce. Measures of child poverty, however, are particularly sensitive to the choice of equivalence scale and inherent assumptions about the cost of children. Recent analyses, using equivalence scales that assume children have lower needs than adults, indicate that poverty rates are higher for children than adults in most OECD countries (OECD, 2001). However, figure 12.3, which applies an equivalence scale to Luxembourg Income Study data that does not directly distinguish children from adults, suggests that poverty rates for children are higher than for adults in countries, including the US and the UK, where overall poverty is high. A particular feature of childhood poverty is its potential long-term effect on individual development and well-being (Hills, 1999; Hill and Yeung, 2000).

While it is very difficult succinctly to summarize the demographic characteristics of poor families, figure 12.6 reveals that poor families differ markedly from other families in terms of age, family type, education, and employment and that those that suffer long-term poverty differ even more (i.e., the relevant polygons are larger). The distinctive and comparatively homogeneous characteristics of poor families in the US are also apparent.

## Triggers and causes of poverty

People become poor for a complex mix of structural and individualistic reasons. National poverty rates are statistically related to variations in income inequality and to differences in the level of public social expenditure and in the generosity of benefits.[18] The same is true of the duration of poverty. However, neither the poverty rate nor average duration is related to differences in national unemployment or employment rates or to variations in the dependency ratio or per capita GDP. This suggests that the redistribution policies adopted by governments are more important than either economic wealth or labor demand as structural determinants of the level and type of poverty found in a country.

Structural factors, be they targeted policies or features of a country's social and economic environment, can affect the likelihood of people experiencing events and circumstances that are prone to trigger poverty. They can also mediate the impact of such triggers by providing greater or lesser degrees of financial security. Therefore, while the absence of paid work is a factor associated with poverty in all advanced industrial countries, it is less important as a trigger of poverty in the US than in Europe. Indeed, in the US it is a less important cause of poverty than lone parenthood or poor education (figure 12.6). The reason is that relatively low wage rates in the US mean that employment provides less protection against poverty than in Europe, especially for those with limited education, while higher social benefits in Europe help more lone parents to escape poverty than in the US. The higher and more comprehensive unemployment benefits found in much of Europe – the UK is in this case an exception – also mean that the absence of paid work does not guarantee that families will be forced into long-term poverty, as it frequently does in the US.

An indication of the relative importance of family and employment events in triggering spells of poverty is given in figure 12.7. These two kinds of trigger are often closely intertwined, as when divorce or separation removes the principal breadwinner from a family. Therefore in the analysis reported in figure 12.7 changes in family structure are identified first and job-related events counted only for

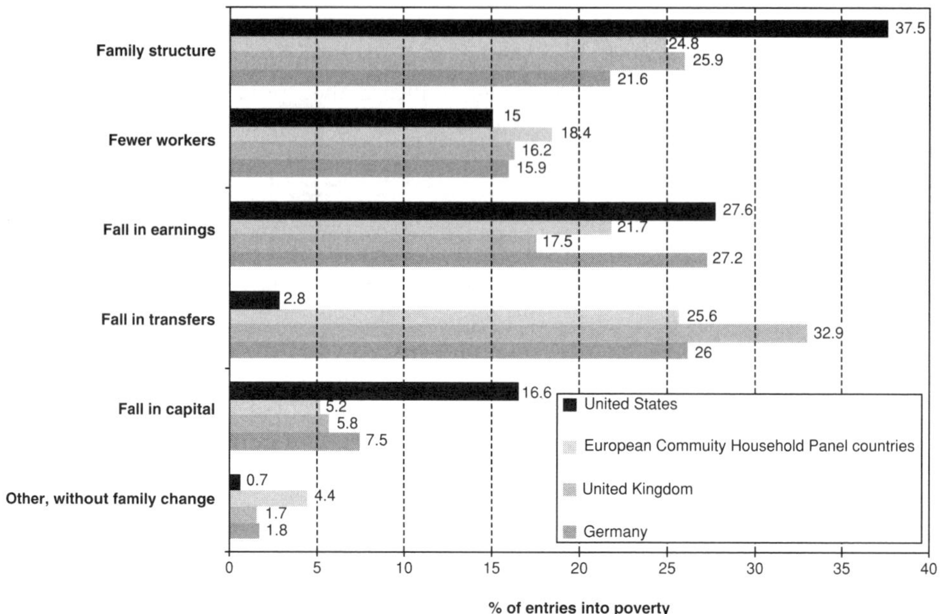


**Figure 12.7** Triggers of poverty in selected countries, 1993–1995

*Source*: OECD (2001).

those families that remained unchanged prior to a spell of poverty. This approach provides an upper limit to the number of spells of poverty triggered by family events between 1993 and 1995: 38 percent in the US and just 25 percent for Europe as a whole (OECD, 2001). Twenty percent of poverty spells in the US appear to have been caused by the break-up of a marriage or cohabiting relationship compared with less than 11 percent in Europe. And 9 percent were precipitated by the birth of a child – sometimes causing the mother to give up paid work – compared with only 3 percent in European countries. Again, the main reason for these differences is likely to be the more highly developed benefit systems found in Europe that are designed specifically to help with the cost of children.[19]

Twenty-eight percent of poverty spells in the US were caused by a fall in earnings, sometimes as the result of a decline in the number of hours worked, and 15 percent by people ceasing paid work due to unemployment and other reasons. In the mid-1990s unemployment was a much more important cause of poverty in some European counties, notably in Spain and Portugal, where unemployment insurance was not well developed and where unemployment triggered between 30 percent and 36 percent of all new spells of poverty. Across Europe as a whole, however, falls in earnings were marginally more important than unemployment as an immediate cause of poverty (linked to 22 percent and 18 percent of spells, respectively); this is because benefit replacement rates are typically high.

A notable irony is that well-developed social security systems can appear to be a direct cause of poverty: in Europe 26 percent of all spells of poverty were associated with a reduction in benefit income compared with just 3 percent of those in the US. It is likely that in most cases these movements into poverty were the result of a person exhausting their entitlement to social insurance benefits and transferring to social assistance, although in a few cases people may have experienced a fall in income on leaving benefits to take up low-waged work. In the US, most benefits are too low to hold families above the poverty line so that falls in benefit income take them deeper into poverty rather than being a prime cause of new spells (Dickens and Ellwood, 2003).

Routes out of poverty mirror the routes in. Thus, in Europe, receipt of benefit, increased earnings, and family members finding work are the three most important reasons why people escape poverty and together account for 78 percent of spells that end. In the US, increased earnings and changes in the family, notably people leaving home and remarriage, are the main factors.

Few studies have yet examined the etiology of different kinds of poverty. One that has (Walker with Ashworth, 1994) has considered the poverty experienced by children growing up in the US in the 1970s and 1980s. It showed that children who remained poor throughout childhood lived overwhelmingly in the rural South, were typically African American and lived mostly with one parent who had very limited earning power. Children who were repeatedly poor generally lived with two parents, although one-quarter to a third of these children spent time with only one adult. Their experience of poverty was shaped predominantly by low wages and, to a lesser extent, by unemployment. Children who were only briefly poor had more in common with never-poor children than they did with children who were poor for longer.

Poverty, then, is shaped by its distribution over time to such an extent that it may be best to think of different kinds of poverty defined in terms of the number, duration, and timing of spells.[20] This patterning reflects the distribution of poverty-inducing and poverty-ending events and the probability that the occurrence of such events will result in the beginning or ending of a spell of poverty. The risks and probabilities are much determined by structural factors, including welfare regimes and labor demand, but it is also important to take account of the agency of families themselves.

## Families Shaping Poverty

There is much still to be written on the balance between institutional factors and individual agency in determining the risk and distribution of poverty. However, for reasons of space the focus here is on how families cope with poverty when it occurs, mediate its worst effects and where possible, seek ways of boosting income.

### Coping strategies

The art of survival is to maximize the probability of having sufficient resources when needed.[21] This may involve attempts to increase the total resources available. It most certainly entails rationing demands on existing resources and shifting demand and resources over time by both deferring consumption and engaging in whatever means of saving and borrowing are possible. Poverty ratchets up the personal and social skills required successfully to undertake the basic tasks of domestic financial management.

Low income means that families have little choice but to plan budgets meticulously: setting priorities, hiding money for later, making lists even before benefits or wages are collected, tallying up the bill while in the store, and shopping frequently to avoid supplies at home being raided prematurely (Duerr Berrick, 1995, Kempson et al., 1994). Women usually take on these tasks, as Rowntree noted over a century ago (Rowntree, 1901; Pahl, 1989). They cut back first on luxuries and leisure, shop in discount stores, visit markets for end-of-the-day sell-offs, scour the neighborhood for bargains, and negotiate the trade-off between price and quality, especially in the case of clothing. Budgeting takes time, know-how, and patience. Food, though a priority expenditure, is often used to manage cash flows: food purchases are reduced to facilitate payment of important bills, notably the rent, electricity, and water. Women will go short of food better to feed their menfolk and children, and pay more to cater for individual tastes to ensure food is eaten rather than wasted. Cigarettes are knowingly used as hunger suppressants as well as rewards and as a means to lessen stress (Dobson et al., 1995). The elderly cut down on food and other expenditures to ensure that they protect their limited lifetime savings (Boaz, Hayden, and Bernard, 1999).

Budgeting strategies are universal but the pattern and harshness of the choices are influenced by welfare regimes. In Britain, mothers use the Child Benefit payments that they receive as a form of saving by not immediately cashing or claiming them; often they set them aside for future child-related expenditure, but such saving becomes impossible when financial pressures are extreme (Walker, Middleton, and Thomas, 1994). In the US, Food Stamps are sometimes traded to fund general expenditure but seldom remain unused, while Earned Income Tax Credit, paid annually, is reputedly frequently used to pay off credit-card debts (Duerr Berrick, 1995; Liebman, 1998).[22] Family budgeting in Britain is shaped by the two-week payment cycle for social assistance benefits, with expenditures being concentrated in the first week and food being eked out in the second. In Germany, monthly payments, together with more generous benefits, create a four-week cycle when resources are scarce in one week in four rather one week in two. Despite higher incomes, benefit recipients in Sweden and Germany still find saving difficult and confront hard choices. However, in these countries, they need to cut down on the length and number of holidays, for example, rather than foregoing them altogether, as in Britain and the US (Clasen, Gould, and Vincent, 1998).

Budgeting also involves managing demands on household resources from partners and children. Women typically accord their partners a disproportionate share of resources but couples still break up or fail to marry because of disputes over money (Kempson and Whyley, 1999; Edin, 2001). As far as children are concerned, parents typically give priority to expenditure connected with education. They are also often concerned to avoid their children being singled out as different by peers, especially in terms of clothing (Middleton, Ashworth, and Walker with Ashworth, 1994). Children themselves seem to share a common culture of acquisition, at least in the UK, irrespective of parental income, although those from poorer homes learn to limit, or at least to suppress, their economic demands (Middleton and Shropshire, 1999). Even so, they continue to use a repertoire of techniques to coerce expenditures from their parents, and there is some evidence that they may more often resort to confrontational techniques such as anger tantrums (Walker et al., 1994; McNeal, 1992). This may, in turn, reflect the fact that parents in poor families are, because of fluctuations in household finances, less able to give consistent responses to the demands of their offspring. The consequences of poverty can be particularly acute when a parent cannot afford to say "yes" to a child who refuses to take "no" for an answer.

An important additional strategy is to increase resources coming into the family. Nonmonetary exchanges between households are frequent, including informal assistance, bartering, gifts, discounted produce, second-hand clothes, and childminding. One constraint on informal exchange of this kind is that it often carries unstated and unpredictable obligations and expectations of reciprocity that may not be able to be met. Another is that certain kinds of exchange are limited to neighborhoods where home production is possible or where significant numbers of people have jobs (Nelson and Smith, 1999; Pahl, 1984). Cash normally exchanges hands only between relatives and even then, such is the sensitivity and similarity to charity, that they may only take the form of interest-free loans (Clasen, Gould, and Vincent, 1998). Charity itself is widely despised, perhaps especially in Europe, where the welfare state was initially created as a comprehensive alternative to charitable support, but necessarily used when more acceptable sources of support are not available.

A more dramatic strategy is to increase income or gain economies of scale through changing household composition. As noted above, this is a statistically significant factor in bringing spells of poverty to a close, especially in the US. There is evidence of young people returning to or not leaving home when out of work. Likewise, older people moving in with children frequently raises the living standard of the older person but the motivation is usually ill health rather than poverty per se (Burkhauser, Holden, and Myers, 1988). Likewise, although marriage or cohabiting can reduce poverty, financial need is rarely the trigger (Edin, 2001).

For lone parents extracting child support from former partners may be a more important, if sometimes very difficult, means of boosting income (McLanahan and Sandefur, 1994; Edin and Lein, 1997b; Marsh and Rowlingson, 2002). In a number of countries statutory agencies have been established to help recover child support, although the extent to which parents directly benefit financially from this assistance varies between jurisdictions. Seeking child support can be fraught with difficulties, especially where relationships were abusive or where matters of child access and custody are involved.

Welfare benefits are a major source of income. Indeed, some commentators have argued that people who are poor adapt their behavior in order to maximize their benefit income by, for example, reducing their paid employment and/or failing to report earnings; this, it is opined, creates a culture of dependency (Deacon, 2002; Field, 1995; Murray, 1984; Mead, 1993). However, the evidence that this happens on a large scale is limited and contested (Walker, 2001). In fact, there are significant costs attached to receiving welfare including, for example, stigma.

The extent to which benefit receipt adds to the stigma of poverty varies between countries and benefits. In the US, many welfare recipients accept the dominant ideology that work is good and welfare is bad but are forced to confront the dilemma that taking work (frequently merely to supplement welfare) might restrict their ability to live up to their ideal of good parenting (Scott et al., 2000; Duerr Berrick, 1995). Claimants in Germany and Sweden distinguish between insurance-based benefits, with entitlement linked to and legitimated by contributions, and locally based, means-tested assistance with eligibility determined on the basis of an intrusive assessment of need. Shame invoked by the latter causes some people not to claim benefit and others to keep their receipt a tight secret (Clasen, Gould, and Vincent, 1998). In Britain, too, the stigma attached to means testing has long been one factor associated with low benefit take-up (Craig, 1991).

Employment is a preferred strategy by which poor families seek to boost income. In countries such as Germany it also means access to insurance benefits and pensions, and hence the prospect of avoiding poverty and stigma in the future. However, employment is not without its risks, and people in poverty typically strive to reduce uncertainty as much as possible. The time to the first wage check has to be bridged and net take-home pay may be difficult to calculate in advance (Shaw, Kellard, and Walker, 1996). Work can mean the end of health coverage, as in the US, while uncertainty can be increased if eligibility for in-work benefits is unclear. Moreover, employment provides no guarantee against poverty: in the US 82 percent of people who suffer poverty work, as do 57 percent of those in Europe (OECD, 2001). Quite often people boost their incomes by working in a number of low-paying jobs, but while some people who gain a foothold in work progress rapidly, low-paid work typically offers little security and few prospects (Dickens, 2000; Holtzer and LaLonde, 2000; Holtzer, Stoll, and Wissoker, 2001). Indeed, it is likely that the pattern of recurrent spells of poverty is often shaped by a life spent on the margins of work (Walker with Ashworth, 1994).

But employment is not always possible. Loss of employment due to unemployment or sickness is, of course, an immediate cause of much poverty and long-term sickness, and disability, combined with slack labor demand, perpetuate it. Moreover, some lone mothers, when given a choice, prioritize personally caring for young children over paid work or at least wish to balance the roles of carer and worker more evenly than full-time employment allows.

Also, receipt of certain benefits, such as disability benefits and, in Britain, social assistance, is conditional on recipients not working. In other cases the rate of withdrawal of benefits with rising earnings may be so high as to discourage working creating a major conundrum. Claimants work but are penalized by high benefit withdrawal rates, or they work and do not report their earnings and so are criminalized. Or, else, they do not work, thereby confirming to themselves and others that they have joined the dependency culture (Mead, 1993).

The extent to which poor families and benefit recipients are engaged in illicit coping strategies is contested in most societies. That some are is indisputable. The need to support a family leads some people not to declare income to tax or welfare authorities, or to engage in other illegal means of raising income: theft, peddling drugs, prostitution, and robbery (Edin et al., 2000; Kempson, 1996). Crime tends to be concentrated in the poorest neighborhoods, although people in poverty are more often the victims rather than the perpetrators of such crime (Kling, Liebman, and Katz, 2001).

In some cases illicit activity is a symptom of the failure to cope. People who are financially desperate may be more vulnerable than most to swindles and fraud or to being drawn into criminal activity. Also, a proportion will be further burdened by illiteracy, disability, mental illness, and/or substance abuse and become trapped in a vicious cycle that demands ever-greater coping expertise from people who are the least able to cope (Ramey and Keltner, 2002; Kempson, 1996).

## Dignity

Even families that do not resort to antisocial behavior often experience poverty as personal failure in societies that rate success in terms of conspicuous consumption. People with low income are not only denied access to the purchases, possessions, and involvement that serve to define those who belong to the socially acceptable mainstream, they frequently live with shame or embarrassment (Beresford et al., 1999; Schwartz, 1997; Edin et al., 2000; Clasen, Gould, and Vincent, 1998). The American ideal is that the opportunity of success exists for all individuals of strong character who are prepared to work hard and persevere; therefore the demonstrable failure that poverty is widely perceived to be smacks of weakness and laziness. Even in Europe, where commitment to the work ethic is more muted, identity is very often defined in terms of occupation (Clasen, Gould, and Vincent, 1998). Feelings of worthlessness can be reinforced by the sense, real or imaginary, that other people, especially those in authority who act as gatekeepers, such as social workers, welfare officials, and employers, view people who are poor as feckless, scroungers, or dishonest. Only close relatives and true friends offer succor in times of financial adversity but even this may difficult to accept, being tempered by a sense of having failed one's nearest and dearest (Edin and Lein, 1997a; Edin et al. 2000; Middleton, Ashworth, and Walker, 1994).

Feelings of failure and rejection may be worst shortly after people experience a drop in income (Dobson et al., 1995). It takes time to learn how to accommodate to straitened circumstances, and early on some people are tempted to judge their new circumstances against their previous reference groups and lifestyle. They also carry forward the financial commitments incurred when finances were less restrictive. Moreover, as noted above, poverty is likely to be triggered by other life-wrenching events such as relationship breakdown, the birth of a child, or unemployment, that also have to be managed emotionally and socially (Leeming, Unell, and Walker, 1994; Duerr Berrick, 1995). It is during the early months of poverty, too, that former friends begin to drop away owing to embarrassment or in response to an inevitable lack of reciprocity. With growing experience many people acquire the skills with which to cope, possibly lower financial expectations, and find that their financial circumstances become more predictable and possibly more stable (Kempson, 1996; Leisering and Leibfried, 2000; Nelson and Smith, 1999).

Little research has yet been done on the social and psychological consequences of different forms of poverty. However, it is self-evident that poverty that lasts for a long time, and which is often also severe in terms of shortfall in income, drastically limits choice and opportunity. Analysis based on the US Panel Study of Income Dynamics over the period 1968–87 identified one million children who spent their entire childhood in families with income of less than one-third of the US poverty standard – such children experienced living standards little above those of not very prosperous families in the Third World (Ashworth, Hill, and Walker, 1994). Arguably their sense of relative deprivation, living in one of the richest of all nations, would have been extreme.

However, there is also a sense in which the very longevity of poverty may make life easier on a day-to-day basis, despite depleted savings and the depreciation of consumer durables, because of the acquisition of budgeting skills and experience. Indeed, it is at least possible that the experience of families subject to repeated spells of poverty is equally or even more traumatic because of the frustrated hopes and expectations that it entails and the need repeatedly to readjust to limited income. Even transient poverty, frequently dismissed by commentators as being inconsequential, may have profound consequences for those concerned. While some people, students, for example, may factor a temporary spell of poverty into a successful career plan with few ill effects (Buhr and Weber, 1998), the transitory nature of some poverty will only become apparent with hindsight. In the meantime, families will have to adjust to a fall in living standards and to the heightened uncertainty that characterizes life on a limited budget.

The experience of poverty is mediated by local environment. Living in a low-income neighborhood can help to ameliorate the individual trauma of long-term poverty. Networks of positive support and exchange may exist, based on the reciprocity of common circumstances that may not be available to these living in predominately prosperous areas (Kempson, 1996; Holman, 1998). Alternatively, concentrations of people living permanently in, or on the margins of, poverty may foster circumstances conducive to the development of an underclass (Katz, 1992; Wilson, 1997). Those residents who can tend to migrate out, and when this happens the individual interests and community norms of those left behind become detached from those of the wider society, with a significant minority adopting criminal activities as a means of funding and expressing their lifestyle.

When criminality is high in a low-income neighborhood, the threat and consequences of crime can be very real for residents, not only as direct victims but also in terms of the requirement psychologically and practically to defend homes and families from becoming directly affected by crime. Studies in high-poverty, inner-city neighborhoods in the US reveal – to a degree not yet reported in European cities – that parents spend inordinate amounts of time protecting their children from crime and danger and may do so at the cost of inhibiting their own advancement (Kling, Liebman, and Katz, 2000; Power and Tunstall, 1995; Kling, Katz, and Liebman, 2001).

Deprived communities where crime is rife acquire reputations as ghettos that serve to increase the stigma felt and experienced by law-abiding inhabitants (Wilson, 1997). Indeed, neighborhoods can acquire negative labels even in the absence of crime merely on account of the fact that they house disproportionate numbers of low-income families (Power and Tunstall, 1995). This may precipitate a spiral of disinvestment, causing retailers and employers to leave, thereby increasing local retail prices, reducing jobs, and eroding infrastructure and land values. Opportunities for advancement are curtailed and financial precariousness increased, in part because insurance and loan companies discriminate on the basis of address. This financial exclusion is growing in significance as society becomes increasingly "cashless" (Kempson and Whyley, 1999).

The psychological pressures imposed by poverty may be most severe for people of working age, particularly if they have children. Society expects people of "prime working age" to work and, through doing so, to provide adequately for their families, just as most people in poverty would like to do. Financial demands made by children can be relentless, even if these are tempered by an awareness of their family's financial circumstances (Walker, Middleton, and Thomas, 1994; Middleton and Shropshire, 1999). Many poor parents are hurt by their inability to provide and to exhibit model behaviors to their children (Edin et al., 2000). Lone parents additionally can carry the guilt of separation or premarital motherhood and feel the need to compensate their children for the loss of a parent (Leeming, Unell, and Walker, 1994). But elders are not immune to feelings of failure (Boaz, Hayden, and Bernard, 1999). Indeed, whereas younger people can grasp the hope that things may get better, such hope is denied to those beyond retirement age. In the evening of their lives they may contemplate a final failure, the equivalent of a pauper's funeral, and no inheritance to pass on.

Despair is not an inevitable consequence of poverty. Some people become resigned to their apparent fate, others rage in frustration against their situation (Duerr

Berrick, 1995). Most, though, actively try to make the best of life and to better themselves financially. Work for those who can offers the prospect of money, status, routine, and autonomy, although not necessarily an end to poverty. Those trapped in poverty by age, lack of skills, limited work experience, and health problems adopt other survival strategies.

## Agency and its consequences

The evidence assembled reveals neither the passivity nor the willfulness sometimes thought by the non-poor to characterize the behavior and attitudes of people in poverty. Since poverties are multifaceted and people who are poor are heterogeneous in their responses, it follows that some people in poverty will exhibit stereotypical characteristics. But merely to survive on a poverty-level income requires the individual ingenuity and agency documented by so many qualitative studies. Moreover, the existence of food cooperatives, credit unions, community banking, and community development initiatives demonstrates that collective agency can emerge spontaneously or be kindled in poor neighborhoods (Holman, 1998).

Some people in poverty who adopt antisocial coping strategies may well have negotiated a trajectory from income poverty toward social exclusion with increasingly high scores on a number of Baulch's dimensions of poverty, serving to constrain the options available. Perhaps, for example, unemployment reduces a person's income and lack of skills and slack labor demand make the objective chances of finding work remote. This may reduce morale, curtailing the search for work and increasing stress and depression, which adds impetus to a contraction of social networks that could have provided support. Continued lack of income may trigger creditors to repossess goods and the landlord to threaten eviction. Theft becomes an option but spells disaster if the person is caught. But even before this point, social welfare agencies may well have moved to more coercive, though not necessarily effective, policies and mainstream employers will have been deterred by inadequate personal references. The process toward exclusion will have become very hard to reverse.

Kempson, Bryson, and Rowlingson (1994) found that 12 out of 28 low-income families in Britain followed a downward trajectory over a two-year period. Likewise, Ludwig (1996) in Germany and Duerr Berrick (1995), Newman (1999), and Edin et al. (2000) in the US provide harrowing accounts of families caught in a socioeconomic downdraft. But, equally, all these authors tell of families who coped with chronic or recurrent bouts of poverty, variously helped and frustrated by welfare systems that were not necessarily well attuned to their varying circumstances, and of others who successfully negotiated a route out of poverty. The fact that 34 percent of Americans, 31 percent of Britons, and 17 percent of Germans experienced poverty between 1990 and 1997 without substantial social upheaval is testament to the ability of most poor families to keep their lives together – although at what long-term cost to their well-being is uncertain. It also reflects the effectiveness of welfare systems in holding most families' incomes at or above basic subsistence (although not, of course, above relative poverty thresholds). That so many poor families do cope may partly explain why societies continue to be content to let so many people suffer periods of poverty. To paraphrase Martin Rein, poverty exists politically only to the extent that it creates problems for the non-poor.

## Conclusion

Sociologically poverty is best conceptualized as the experience of living on a low income. So diverse is this experience that it is better to think of different types of poverty that are multidimensional by nature, forged by their incidence in time and shaped by institutions and through the agency of poor families themselves.

Mapping of the different kinds of poverty is still in its infancy. Most quantitative research focuses exclusively on income poverty[23] and only recently, with the arrival of panel data, have distinctions been drawn between transient, long-term, and recurrent kinds of poverty. These show that the extent and severity of relative poverty vary markedly between countries, that families headed by women, lone-parent families, and single-person households are particularly prone to poverty, but that in most continental European countries the historic links between poverty and old age and childhood have been severed. Most poverty is experienced in short spells, but repeated periods of poverty are very common and small numbers of families remain in poverty for long periods. Long-term poverty is particularly prevalent in the US, which also exhibits a higher incidence of poverty than most other advanced, postindustrial societies.[24]

Qualitative studies briefly reviewed in this chapter indicate that families with low incomes share common pressures and experiences irrespective of the country in which they live, but that these are molded by local institutions. They show, too, that dimensions other than income and time, notably those located at the base of the Baulch pyramid (figure 12.1), are important in shaping experiences of poverty. These include loss of dignity, choice, and control; limited access to social capital and to assets of other kinds; poor health; few opportunities; and an uncertain future.

Poverties are caused by the interaction of macro-structures and micro-processes. Structures help to determine the incidence and distribution of events that are likely to trigger the loss of income or perpetuate low income. Welfare systems, in particular, also influence the probability that such events will result in the occurrence of poverty. Micro-processes, behavioral choices made by individuals and families, affect the chances that particular individuals and families will be affected by a poverty-triggering event. Similar processes also help to determine whether the event will cause individuals and families to suffer poverty, whether the poverty will be prolonged, severe, and result in social exclusion.

But it is politics that labels periods of low income and social deprivation as "poverty" by defining the variables to be measured and the bifurcation thresholds to be set. Politics with a lower-case "p" comprises the research community that supplies theories, measures and sometimes, advice. The upper-case "P" in the political process determines the policy response, and sets the threshold and an agenda for action or inactivity.

### Notes

1 An iceberg is an alternative metaphor, suggested by figure 12.1. Traditional income-based measures reveal only a small part of the structure of poverty.

2 Use of income to define poverty as a surrogate for consumption can create distortion. The consumption of families often exceeds income as they draw down savings or supplement income by borrowing or home production (McGregor and Borooah, 1992). Equally,

though, people may choose a frugal lifestyle by spending little, in which case measures based on income may overstate consumption. Indeed, for this latter reason some have suggested that income is in fact a preferable index; available income provides a measure of the opportunities open to a person and is less sensitive than expenditure to the ramifications of individual choice (Atkinson et al., 2001; Atkinson, 1995; Citro and Michael, 1995). Annual income probably provides a closer approximation to consumption than monthly or weekly, since it is closer to the economist's ideal of "permanent" rather than current income.

3 Townsend (1979) and Gordon and Pantazis (1997) would dispute this, arguing that a step change in behavior coincident with a particular level of income can be identified and that this specifies the poverty between the poor and the non-poor.

4 Many US studies refer to variants of the official Census definition of poverty, which is derived from a basket of goods compiled in the 1960s that has subsequently been indexed to prices and not to rising average incomes (US Committee on Ways and Means, 2000; Rank and Hirschl, 2001).

5 The literature on deriving equivalence scales to adjust for the differing needs of men, women, and children is both large and technical (OECD, 1982; Hagenaars de Vos and Zaida, 1994; Sutherland, 1997; Triest, 1998). While the various approaches yield varying scales and the scales themselves need to be sensitive to cultural differences, the principal lesson is that like should be compared with like.

6 The equivalence scale used in this analysis is based solely on household size. Equivalized income (EI) is equal to unadjusted income (UI) divided by household size (S) raised to the exponential value (e), where $e = 0.5$, $EI = UI/S^e$.

7 See note 6 for a definition of the equivalence scale used.

8 An exception to this pattern is Sweden, where poverty rates for children and elderly people are both below average.

9 Poverty is defined as 50 percent median equivalized income, and the OECD equivalence scale is used, giving a weight of 1 for the head of household, 0.5 for additional adults, and 0.3 for children.

10 Eighty-one percent of the country-by-country variation in relative poverty (figure 12.2) is explicable in terms of income inequality (as indexed by the Gini coefficient).

11 See note 9 for a definition of the equivalence scale used.

12 See Goodin et al. (1999) for a thorough investigation of the impact of national policies on poverty rates.

13 For a further discussion of the underclass see below, Katz, 1992 and Wilson, 1997.

14 It turns out that the population of people who are poor at any one time contains a disproportionate number who are in the midst of a long spell of poverty (Walker with Ashworth, 1994). Drawing a cross-sectional sample, the poor people in the US at any time from 1985 to 1992 would have revealed about 36 percent in an episode of poverty that would last for seven years or more.

15 There is evidence that the extent of female poverty is understated in studies based on families or households, reflecting unequal allocation of resources between men and women within households (Sweating, 1998; Rodgers, 1995).

16 Countries belonging to the European Community Household Panel, namely Belgium, Denmark, France, Germany, Greece, Ireland, Italy, Luxembourg, the Netherlands, Portugal, Spain, and the UK. All Europe-wide analysis reported in this chapter relates to these 12 countries.

17 The long-term nature of poverty experienced by older Americans helps to explain why cross-sectional poverty rates are still higher among the elderly in America than among those aged below 65 (figure 12.3).

18 The independent effect of these factors is further supported by analysis of residuals from econometric analyses based on cross-national household surveys that take into account the individual level associations noted above, such as with youth and retirement age, worklessness, and family structure (OECD, 2001).

19 The pattern is maintained even in those European countries with divorce rates similar to those of the US.
20 A training as a geographer reminds one that poverty is also shaped by space. The space–time nexus that is poverty is discussed in Walker and Park (1998).
21 This section relies heavily on qualitative research conducted in Britain, the US, Germany, and Sweden. A systematic review of this material is in a preliminary stage.
22 In Britain, commercial considerations deny poor people access to credit cards and they are forced to rely on even more expensive forms of casual credit.
23 It is important to register that as part of the open method of coordination on social inclusion the European Commission has approved a set of over 30 indicators that will be compiled for each member state (Atkinson et al., 2001).
24 Poverty in the US has fallen markedly since the mid-1990s but there have also been falls in a number of other countries (Corbett, 2003).

## References

Atkinson, A. (1995) *Poverty and Social Security*. Hemel Hempstead: Harvester.

Atkinson, A., Cantillon, B., Marlier, E., and Nolan, B. (2001) *Indicators for Inclusion in the European Union*. Paper presented at a Conference on Social Inclusion hosted by the Belgian government, Antwerp, September.

Ashworth, K., Hill, M., and Walker, R. (1994) Patterns of childhood poverty: New challenges for policy. *Journal of Policy Analysis and Management*, 13, 658–80.

Baulch, B. (1996) The new poverty agenda: A disputed consensus. *IDS Bulletin*, 27, 1–10.

Beresford, P., Green, D., Lister, R., and Woodward, K. (1999) *Poverty First Hand: Poor People Speak for Themselves*. London: CPAG.

Boaz, A., Hayden, C., and Bernard, M. (1999) *Attitudes and Aspirations of Older People: A Review of the Literature*. London: Department of Social Security, Research Report 101.

Bradbury, B., Jenkins, S., and Micklewright, J. (2001) *The Dynamics of Child Poverty in Industrialized Countries*. Cambridge: Cambridge University Press.

Brady, D. (2001) *Rethinking the Sociological Measurement of Poverty*. Luxembourg: Luxembourg Income Study, Working Paper 264.

Buhr, P., and Weber, A. (1998) Social assistance and social change in Germany. In L. Leisering and R. Walker (eds.), *The Dynamics of Modern Society: Poverty, Policy and Welfare*. Bristol: Policy Press

Burkhauser, R., Holden, K., and Myers, D. (1988) Incidence, timing and events associated with poverty: a dynamic view of poverty in retirement. *Journal of Gerontology*, 43, 846–52.

Citro, C., and Michael, R. (1995) *Measuring Poverty: A New Approach*. Washington DC: National Academy Press.

Clasen, J., Gould, A., and Vincent, J. (1998) *Voices Within and Without: Responses to Long-term Unemployment in Germany, Sweden and Britain*. Bristol: The Policy Press.

Corbett, T. (2003) The new face of welfare in the US: From income transfers to social assistance? *Social Policy and Society*, 2, 2, forthcoming.

Craig, P. R. (1991) Costs and benefits: A review of research on take-up of income related benefits. *Journal of Social Policy*, 20(4), 537–65.

Deacon, A. (2002) *Perspectives on Welfare*. Milton Keynes: Open University Press.

Dickens, R. (2000) Caught in a trap? Wage mobility in Great Britain: 1975–1994. *Economica*, 67, 268, 477–97.

Dickens, R., and Ellwood, D. (forthcoming, 2003) Whither poverty in Britain and the US? The determinants of changing poverty and whether work will work. In R. Blundell, D. Card, and R. Freeman (eds.), *Seeking a Premier League Economy*.

Dobson, B., Beardsworth, A., Keil, T., and Walker, R. (1995) *Diet, Choice and Poverty*. London: Family Policy Studies Centre.

Duerr Berrick, J. (1995) *Faces of Poverty: Portraits of Women and Children on Welfare*. New York: Oxford University Press.
Edin, K. (2001) *Hearing on Welfare and Marriage Issues* -Testimony Before the Subcommittee on Human Resources of the House Committee on Ways and Means – www.gouse.gov/ways_means/humres/107cong/ 5-22-01/5-22edin.htm
Edin, K., and Lein, L. (1997a) *To Work or Not to Work? Reasons Women Give for Staying on Welfare* (from www.poverty.smartlibrary.org/segment.cfm?segment = 1850&table_of_contents = 14 . . . )
Edin, K., and Lein, L. (1997b) *Making Ends Meet: How Single Mothers Survive Welfare and Low-Wage Work*. New York: Russell Sage Foundation.
Edin, K., Lein, L., Nelson, T., and Clampet-Lundquest, S. (2000) *Talking to Low-income Fathers*, Joint Center for Poverty Research, University of Chicago, Newsletter, 4, 2.
Esping-Andersen, G. (1999) *Social Foundations of Postindustrial Economies*. Oxford: Oxford University Press.
Field, F. (1995) *Making Welfare Work*. London: Institute of Community Studies.
Goodin, R., Headey, B., Muffels, R., and Dirvan, H-J. (1999) *The Real Worlds of Welfare Capitalism*. Cambridge: Cambridge University Press.
Gordon, D., and Pantazis, C. (1997) *Breadline Britain in the 1990s*. Aldershot: Ashgate.
Gordon, D., and Townsend, P. (2000) *Breadline Europe*. Bristol: Policy Press.
Hagenaars, A. K. de Vos, and Zaida, A. (1994) *Poverty Statistics in the Late 1980s*. Luxembourg: Eurostat.
Hill, M., and Yeung, W-J. J. (2000) Behavior and Status of Children and Young Adults. *Generations and Gender Programme: Exploring future research and data collection options*, New York and Geneva: United Nations Economic Commission for Europe, United Nations Population Fund, 1-57 UNESCO children.
Hills, J. (ed.) (1999) *Persistent Poverty and Lifetime Inequality: The Evidence*. London: CASE/HM Treasury, CASE report 5.
Holman, B. (ed.) (1998) *Faith in the Poor*. Oxford: Lion Publishing.
Holtzer, H., and LaLonde, R. J. (2000) Employment and job stability among less skilled workers. In D. E. Card and R. M. Blank (eds.), *Finding Jobs: Work and Welfare Reform*. New York: Russell Sage Foundation.
Holtzer, H., Stoll, M., and Wissoker, D. (2001) *Job Performance and Retention Among Welfare Recipients*. Paper presented at the Annual Conference of the Association of Policy Analysis and Management, Washington, DC, November 1–3.
Katz, M. B. (ed.) (1992) *The Underclass Debate: Views from History*. Princeton: Princeton University Press.
Kempson, E. (1996) *Life on a Low Income*. York: York Publishing Services.
Kempson, E., Bryson, A., and Rowlingson, K. (1994) *Hard Times*. London: Policy Studies Institute.
Kempson, E., and Whyley, C. (1999) *Kept Out or Opted Out: Understanding and Combating Financial Exclusion*. Bristol: Policy Press.
Kling, J., Katz, L., and Liebman, J. (2001) Moving to opportunity in Boston: Early results of a randomized mobility experiment. *Quarterly Journal of Economics* 116, 2, 607–54.
Kling, J. R., Liebman, J. B., and Katz, L. F. (2000) Fear in the Ghetto and its Ramifications for Parents. Chicago: Joint Center for Poverty Research, University of Chicago, Policy Brief, 3, 10.
Leeming, A., Unell, J., and Walker, R. (1994) *Lone Mothers: Coping with the Consequences of Separation*. London: DSS Research Report No. 30.
Leisering, L., and Leibfried, S. (2000) *Time and Poverty in Western Welfare States: United Germany in Perspective*. Cambridge: Cambridge University Press.
Liebman, J. (1998) *Lessons About Tax-benefit Integration From the US Earned Income Tax Credit Experience*. York: York Publishing Services.
LIS (2001) Luxembourg Income Study website: www.lis.ceps.lu

Ludwig, M. (1996) *Armutskarrieren, Zwischen Abstieg und Aufstieg im Sozialstaat*. Opladen: Westdeutscher Verlag.

Marsh, A., and Rowlingson, K. (2002) *Low/Moderate-income Families in Britain: Changes in 1999 and 2000*. London: Department for Work and Pensions, Research Report 165, Corporate Document Services.

McGregor, P., and Borooah, V. (1992) Is low spending or low income a better indicator of whether a household is poor? *Journal of Social Policy*, 21, 53–69.

McLanahan, S., and Sandefur, G. (1994) *Growing Up With a Single Parent: What Hurts, What Helps*. Cambridge: Harvard University Press.

McNeal, J. U. (1992) *Kids as Consumers*. New York: Lexington Books.

Mead, L. M. (1993) *The New Politics of Poverty: The Nonworking Poor in America*. New York: Basic Books.

Middleton, S., Ashworth, K., and Walker, R. (eds.) (1994) *Family Fortunes: Pressures on Parents and Children in the 1990s*. London: Child Poverty Action Group.

Middleton, S., and Shropshire, J. (1999) *Small Expectations: Learning to Be Poor*. York:York Publishing Services.

Murray, C. (1984) *Losing Ground: American Social Policy, 1950–1980*. New York: Basic Books.

Nelson, M. K., and Smith, J. (1999) *Working Hard and Making Do: Surviving in Small Town America*. Berkeley: University of California Press.

Newman, K. S. (1999) *No Shame in My Game: The Working Poor in the Inner City*. New York: Vintage.

OECD (1992) *The OECD List of Social Indicators*. Paris: Organization for Economic Co-operation and Development.

OECD (1998) Low income dynamics in four OECD countries. *OECD Economic Outlook*, 64, 171–86.

OECD (2001) When money is tight: poverty dynamics in OECD countries. *OECD Employment Outlook*, June, 37–87.

Oxley, H., Dang, T.-T., and Antolin, P. (2000) Poverty dynamics in six OECD countries. *OECD Economic Studies*, 30, 7–49.

Oxley, H., Dang, T.-T., and d'Ercole, M. M. (1997) Income distribution and poverty in 13 countries. *OECD Economic Studies*, 29, 55–92.

Pahl, J. (1989) *Money and Marriage*. London: Macmillan.

Pahl, R. (1984) *Divisions of Labour*. Oxford: Oxford University Press.

Piachaud, D. (1987) Problems in the definition and measurement of poverty. *Journal of Social Policy*, 16, 147–64.

Power, A., and Tunstall, R. (1995) *Swimming Against the Tide: Polarisation or Progress on 20 Unpopular Council Estates*. York: Joseph Rowntree Foundation.

Ramey, S. L., and Keltner, B. (2002) Welfare reform and the vulnerability of mothers with intellectual disabilities (mild mental retardation). *Focus*, 22, 1, 82–6.

Rank, M., and Hirschl, T. (2001) The occurrence of poverty across the life cycle: Evidence from the PSID. *Journal of Policy Analysis and Management*, 20(4), 737–56.

Rodgers, H. R. (1995) *Poor Women, Poor Children: American Poverty in the 1990s*. Armonk, NJ: M. E. Sharpe.

Rowntree, S. (1901) *Poverty: A Study of Town Life*. London: Thomas Nelson and Sons.

Schwarz, J. E. (1997) *Illusions of Opportunity: The American Dream in Question*. New York: W. W. Norton.

Scott, J. (2000) Is it a different world than when you were growing up? Generational effects on social representations and child-rearing values. *British Journal of Sociology*, 51, 355–76.

Shaw, A., Kellard, K., and Walker, R. (1996) *Barriers, Bridges and Behaviour*. London: Department of Social Security In-house Report No 18.

Smeeding, T., Rainwater, L., and Burtless, G. (2000) *United States Poverty in a Cross-National Context*. Luxembourg: Luxembourg Income Study, Working Paper, 244.

Sutherland, H. (1997) Women, men and the redistribution of income. *Fiscal Studies*, 18, 1–22.

Sweating, C. (ed.) (1998) *Women and Poverty in the North*. Oxford: Oxfam.

Townsend, P. (1979) *Poverty in the United Kingdom*. Harmondsworth: Allen Lane.

Triest, R. K. (1998) Has poverty gotten worse? *Journal of Economic Perspectives*, 12, 97–114.

US Committee on Ways and Means (2000) Data on poverty. *2000 Green Book, Appendix H*, Washington, DC: Committee on Ways and Means, US House of Representatives.

Walker, R. (2001) Can work work? A preliminary assessment of the "welfare to work" strategy. *Zeitschrift für Sozialreform*, 47, 437–63.

Walker, R. (forthcoming, 2004) *Social Security and Welfare*, Milton Keynes: Open University Press.

Walker, R., with Ashworth, K. (1994) *Poverty Dynamics: Issues and Examples*. Aldershot: Avebury.

Walker, R., Ashworth, K., Kellard, K., Middleton, S., Peaker, A., and Thomas, M. (1994) "Pretty, pretty, please" just like a parrot: Persuasion strategies used by children and young people. In S. Middleton, K. Ashworth, and R. Walker (eds.), *Family Fortunes: Pressures on Parents and Children in the 1990s*. London: CPAG.

Walker, R., Middleton, S., and Thomas, M. (1994) How mothers use Child Benefit. In S. Middleton, K. Ashworth, and R. Walker (eds.), *Family Fortunes: Pressures on Parents and Children in the 1990s*. London: CPAG.

Walker, R., and Park, J. (1998) Unpicking poverty. In C. Oppenheim (ed.), *An Inclusive Society*. London: IPPR.

Wilson, W. J. (1997) *When Work Disappears: The World of the New Urban Poor*. New York: Vintage.

# 13

# Social Capital and the Family

Frank F. Furstenberg and Sarah B. Kaplan

## Introduction

While the term social capital has become fashionable only during the past decade or so, the concept is at the core of two strands of classical sociological thinking. Throughout his writings, Emile Durkheim (1951, 1961) observes that a cohesive social system, characterized by normative consensus, connectedness, and social control, promotes the welfare of its members. Durkheim argued that social life, itself, was a fundamental element that could not be reduced to its individual-level constituents. Alexis de Tocqueville (1945), the great political and social theorist, also recognized that vibrant social communities create a virtuous cycle of social life by generating trust that in turn promotes civic involvement and a commitment to the common good.

These attributes of normative consensus, social connectedness, trust, and a sense of the common good are popularly believed to be atrophying in contemporary society (Smith, 2002). Whether true or not, this perception helps to explain why the notion of social capital, a term that embodies in one form or another all of these elements, would command interest among social scientists, policymakers, and even the wider public. The pervasive concern that civic involvement is being eroded directs attention to the missing elements of social life. How have they been dissipated, and what would it take to recapture them, are questions that resonate in the social sciences as well as in political discourse.

Now it must be noted that the perception that vital social institutions – the family, the neighborhood, religion, and the polity – are in decline is hardly a novel one. Social theorists since Durkheim and de Tocqueville have worried about the weakening of social bonds, and they were not the first observers to have these apprehensions. Yet, whether justified or not, the fear of growing social disintegration is rampant, especially in the US but also throughout the Western world. Many observers believe the elementary forms of social life are dissolving, leaving in their wake unbridled individualism, low social and political trust, and weak, informal social controls – a formula that followers of Durkheim see as engendering malaise and misanthropy and followers of de Tocqueville fear may invite greater state control.

This chapter addresses a particular part of this broad concern with social disintegration. We focus almost exclusively on the institution of the family, which has long been an important source of social capital and, by many accounts, is becoming less cohesive, less embedded in the community, and hence less able to provide the necessary connections, normative control, and civic training that is required to prepare children for productive adult roles as workers, family members, and citizens. We need to examine closely the presumption that bonds are weakening within the family and parents are less connected to community institutions than they once were: that family-based social capital is less available to today's children than in the past. This set of suppositions poses a whole series of conceptual and methodological issues that expose some of the strengths and weaknesses of the concept of social capital. In addressing some of these problems, we will raise cautions about the empirical basis for more sweeping conclusions about the decline of social capital in the US.

Simply put, our argument is that the idea of social capital, while attractive, is being used so promiscuously that it is on the verge of becoming quite useless in empirical research. Unlike its conceptual cousin, human capital, social capital has achieved no common definition, much less a common measurement. In order to rescue this concept and ensure a meaningful long-term survival, we must rein in its uses and develop a reasonable way of measuring it empirically. Based on the record to date, we are not terribly sanguine about doing so. Nonetheless, our chapter is devoted to a discussion of what might be involved in studying family-based social capital more rigorously.

The initial section is devoted to examining the construct of family-based social capital. Doing so involves understanding the ways that social capital has been generated and deployed by families, and more broadly within kinship systems. We then review some of the extensive research on the consequences of mobilizing social capital by families for the welfare of children. This leads directly to the next part of the chapter – what has not been learned and needs to be investigated. This critical assessment suggests where researchers, particularly those interested in the role of family-based social capital in promoting success in later life, might profitably direct their attention in the future.

## Family-Based Social Capital: What Is It?

The theoretical traditions of Durkheim and Tocqueville have produced somewhat variant notions of social capital. James Coleman (1988), who was initially responsible for promoting the term in sociology, rooted his ideas in Durkheim's theory of social integration. (Coleman, in turn, borrows the term, itself, from Glen Loury, 1977.) Individuals, exposed to a normatively coherent system, receive the benefits of social control, connections, and sponsorship that can lead to more concerted efforts and greater compliance to social standards. The value of social capital is embedded in relations between actors and is defined by its function. As Coleman puts it: "the function identified by the concept of 'social capital' is the value of these aspects of the social structure to actors as resources that they can use to achieve their interests" (1988: S101).

Robert Putnam (1995, 1996), who has widely popularized the concept of social capital, draws more on the ideas of Tocqueville, who observed that social institutions play a critical role in generating the trust and civic involvement necessary to make democracy work. Consequently, Putnam is more concerned with the ways that association and social contact generate common civic values and emphasize the potential collective social benefits. He defines social capital as "features of social organization such as networks, norms, and social trust that facilitate coordination and cooperation for mutual benefit" (1995: 67).[1]

Obviously, these two ways of thinking about social capital have some overlap, but, as Portes (2000) observes in a review of the construct of social capital, Coleman sees it more as a property of groups or institutions to which individuals have access, while for Putnam it is an attribute that pervades the culture of political systems and even entire nations. In that respect, Coleman adheres more strictly to the concept of human capital. Much like financial or human capital, ongoing investments in social relationships can build a stock of resources upon which individuals may later draw to achieve their aims. According to this view, the advantages an individual gains from having greater amounts of social capital are inherently the result of interactions with other people. Or, within kinship systems, individuals may transfer these resources to other family members, especially as parents transfer to their children. Although its existence is acknowledged, Putnam provides no detail or explanation of an analogous notion of family-based social capital. To Putnam, the importance of social capital lies in the fact that it resides within societies and can be accessed by all citizens alike.

Yet a third notion of social capital has been referred to by Pierre Bourdieu (1973), who uses the term in conjunction with his theory of social reproduction. Along with material capital, Bourdieu refers to two other forms of capital: cultural capital is symbolic knowledge useful in understanding how the social world works, that can be passed on within families. Social capital, for Bourdieu, refers to the ability of families to manage successfully the material and symbolic resources that they possess for the benefit of its membership. Emphasizing the importance of the cultural capital necessary to activate social capital, Bourdieu suggests that *how* the social networks are used may be as valuable as (or even more valuable than) the existence of social networks themselves.

Bourdieu views the family as a "collective subject" – not a "simple aggregate of individuals" – that makes its members "feel required to act as a united body." Accordingly, the family makes choices that reflect "a solidarity of interests." He notes that the state reinforces, through the legal system and its policies, the social category of the family and its special rights and obligations to act on behalf of its members. The family is entitled to accumulate and allocate economic, cultural, and symbolic privileges. How effectively families exercise these privileges (whether it be in the choice of a home or a decision of where to send their children to school) reflects or reveals the amount of social capital that they possess. To Bourdieu, a family's possession of social capital is central to their activation of cultural capital and may subsequently influence a family member's success.

Bourdieu's notion of social capital subsumes many of the elements that Coleman identifies. The family's ability to mobilize on behalf of its members depends on: (1) its degree of solidarity (cohesiveness and mutuality of interests), (2) its resources (material and knowledge of the world), and (3) the reach of its connections or alliances with outside parties. However, Bourdieu establishes a virtual tautology:

families that succeed in mobilizing social capital are more successful (Bourdieu, 1986; Bourdieu and Passeron, 1977). Portes (2000) observes a similar problem in Putnam's notion that societies with more social capital have greater trust and civic involvement. In order to avoid this sort of tautology, Portes suggests that it is necessary to differentiate between the possessor's social capital, the sources of social capital, and the resources attributed to social capital. Thus, it makes more sense to view the generation and accumulation of social capital, its deployment, and its consequences as a set of distinct processes linked together, but not isomorphic.

Viewed this way, Bourdieu's theory of social capital poses an interesting set of empirical questions:

1 How is social capital generated and accumulated within families?
2 How do families possessing the elements of family-based social capital mobilize it in everyday life, that is, how is capital wisely or foolishly invested?
3 What are the consequences of the possession of family-based social capital for the long-term welfare of children as they grow up?
4 Why and how does social capital lead to certain forms of success?

As we shall see in the following sections, very little is known about these questions. Pieces of the theory of social capital have been tested, but the measurement issues often preclude drawing any firm conclusions about the validity of the theory. And the measurement issue requires some professional agreement on the construct of social capital itself.

For the purposes of this discussion, we regard social capital as *the stock of social good will created through shared norms and a sense of common membership upon which individuals may draw in their efforts to achieve collective or personal objectives*. How do we know whether social systems, whether they be families, communities, or larger social units, have high or low social capital? A system that has high social capital is one in which its members believe that they are indebted or obligated to respond to the needs of other members. In such a system members may feel entitled to draw upon the good will of others, but they are also equally compelled to respond to the requests for information, assistance, help, sponsorship, and the like. In a system with high social capital, most members are likely to feel that others contribute more than they do; and, conversely, members of a system with low social capital create the perception that others take more than they give. Social capital should not be confused with social solidarity, which emphasizes the importance of the larger collective rather than ongoing relationships operating among individuals within a social system that establishes claims and obligations.

Before moving to a review of the literature on family-based social capital, we must mention one issue lurking in the background of social capital theory. With few exceptions the studies carried out examine the success of families in achieving socially desirable goals consistent with normative expectations. However, clearly this need not be the case. The Cosa Nostra, the network of organized crime families, is a singularly apt example of a set of interlinked families with high social capital, though their greater objectives are not considered laudable. Thus, we must take care that we do not regard outcomes of success as if they were universally shared. If the theory of social capital has validity, it should operate equally well, regardless of the content or purpose of the objectives.

## The Generation of Family-Based Social Capital

How social capital is produced within families is a question that has been more assumed than examined by researchers. Following our discussion above, we must ask how a stock of good will is accumulated *both* within the family and within the communities in which families are embedded. Neither of these issues has been the subject of much research in studies that explicitly employ the concept of social capital, but researchers concerned with the question of the marital quality and the strength of family bonds have certainly concerned themselves with the sources of marital harmony, or the conditions that produce strong ties across the generations or between siblings. Similarly, family sociologists as well as community researchers have studied the strength of family ties to the community and the reciprocity established by families, within what Elizabeth Bott (1971) many years ago described as neighborhoods with densely and loosely constructed social networks. What follows is less a review than a distillation of some of the ideas that might be applied to the question of how families generate social capital both internally and within the larger community.

The literature on the sources of marital solidarity is vast and extends well beyond the borders of sociology into clinical psychology and psychiatry, economics, and anthropology. Followers of Durkheim have referred to the process of marriage as a "nomos-building" activity in which the couple constructs a common reality of rules and expectations and rituals and memories that bind the partners into a union (Berger and Berger, 1983; Furstenberg and Spanier, 1984; Vaughn, 1986). These shared understandings accumulate over time – sometimes hard earned through conflict and dissent – as the couple creates a tiny subculture. Marriages, and increasingly stable cohabitations, are the smallest unit in which social capital is generated.

Researchers in a wide range of fields have conducted numerous studies on how couples establish strong marital bonds, and many of the elements that produce common expectations and trust among the partners are well known. Sociologists have long recognized that a good many of the interactions leading to a building of trust and shared expectations occur in the courtship process, or what economists have dubbed a successful "search." Homophonous characteristics produce a higher likelihood of consensus because individuals enter the union with common constructions of the world. And the time shared before and during marriage leads to common "definitions of the situation." Skills related to human and cultural capital are also likened to the acquisition of social capital within unions such as communication skills, flexibility, and responsiveness. Thus, when individuals import high levels of human, cultural, and even psychological capital into the relationship, they are likely to foster consensus and trust. In a metaphorical sense, these personal attributes promote the efficient production of social capital within conjugal unions, contributing both to the stability of unions, and the benefits these unions confer in the forms of health and well-being. Social capital is a positive product of stable unions and presumably sets the stage for effective child rearing (Waite and Gallagher, 2000).

Children are incorporated into this subculture as if it were a natural entity and, if parents are successful in extending their shared understanding to their progeny, the children enter into the subcultural world of their parents. There is a remarkable paucity of information on the instantiation of family culture, considering how much research exists in developmental psychology and family sociology on patterns of parental socialization. The "nomos-building" process within family is, in fact, a study of the production of social capital. All too little ethnographic work exists on the ways that parents create family worlds: rules, rituals, and routines that regulate children's everyday behaviors and impart a sense of what is normal (see, for example, the classic studies by Bossard and Boll (1956), Hess and Handel (1959), and Gans (1962) on this topic, as well as the more recent work by Annette Lareau (2001)). Despite the increasing prevalence of alternative family forms, unfortunately, current research has not helped to expand the concept of social capital beyond the emphasized nuclear family norm. Interestingly, researchers have probably given more attention to discovering how families' worlds are shattered by marital dissolution and re-created when stepfamilies are formed than they have to the creation and maintenance of stable families (Furstenberg and Cherlin, 1994; Riessman, 1990).

A line of research, some of it quite old by now, has investigated the substantial differences in family cultures that occur across social classes (Bott, 1971; Hollingshead, 1949; Komarovsky, 1987). It is well established that pronounced social class differences exist in the ways that parents relate to their children regarding such matters as expectations of obedience and the questioning of authority, restrictive versus more liberal monitoring practices, and ways of expressing warmth and support (Alwin, 1996). It is an open question, however, whether these child-rearing practices have implications for the building of social capital within families. Do these practices, for example, create different levels of obligations or entitlements within families? Is there any reason to suspect that the generation of family-based social capital differs by social class? The answers to these questions depend on gaining better information on what goes on inside the family, a topic that requires close inspection of the daily life of parents and children, as well as how parents manage the interaction of the family with the world beyond the household.

Research examining social capital among families of different classes and cultures has also been limited. Yet given how characteristics such as race or class influence other types of social resources, it seems likely that access to and activation of social capital, too, varies by social location.

A burgeoning literature does exist on the family patterns of new immigrants. These groups increasingly have commanded the attention of social scientists in many Western nations, where the diversity of the population has grown rapidly over the past several decades (Portes, 1996; Rumbaut, 1996; Waters, 1996). It is widely believed that some immigrant groups have greater social capital both within the family and the community than others. However, it is less clear what specifically transpires within families to generate larger or lesser amounts of social capital. Part of the explanation may reside in the role of the extended kin and family systems beyond the immediate household, as well as the social organization of communities in which immigrant groups reside. Immigrants may feel that their new life is uncertain and therefore invest more in creating trusting relationships in their created communities (Loizos, 2000). Because a large proportion of the more recent immigrants do not come from Western societies, these different cultural traditions could contribute to the disparate amounts of social capital among various immigrant groups.

In Western societies, the nuclear family is widely regarded as the natural unit of society (Schneider, 1968). In fact, the parents and children are part of a larger system of kinship that differs in its cultural salience depending on the nation and social location of the family within nations. Even in many Anglophone countries that may downplay the extended family compared to Southern European nations, solidarity across generations is highly valued. Accordingly, nuclear units are embedded in larger kinship systems that share values and expectations and therefore may be sources of social capital. Social exchange across generations is surely one of the richest sources of social capital in Western society (Bott, 1971). Curiously, we know relatively little about the operation of the broader kinship system in the West. For example, we have few studies of exchanges among cousins or in-laws, not to mention relations between sets of in-laws, divorce and remarriage chains, and more distal sets of kin (Johnson 1988).

The relationship of families to their surrounding communities is one of the most promising areas for understanding the transactions that create social capital both within families and within communities. A family's integration or isolation from the neighborhood or broader community is perhaps the most central predictor of its ability to command social capital. However, we are just beginning to study the processes that lead to social isolation or integration. No doubt residential stability is among the most important of these: families that remain in place are more likely to acquire knowledge of community resources, be connected to other families through formal and informal associations, and have nearby kin who extend their outreach to neighbors and contacts in the wider world. At the same time, we know that upwardly mobile families who have the resources will strategically relocate in order to maximize opportunities for schooling or the acquisition of cultural capital through friends and neighbors. Observing how families acquire social capital through social mobility is a promising area for understanding how social capital is built outside of the household. How do parents invest in schools and communities that entitle them to make effective claims on their own or their children's behalf? And, how do children become incorporated in community-based institutions such as the school, church, or neighborhood so that they can gain the benefits of their parents' or their own investments?

Similarly, we need more research on the growing connections between families and the workplace. Growing maternal employment has been viewed by many as a source of erosion of women's commitment to the family by reducing their involvement in children directly and the community indirectly. In fact, it is not clear that either of these claims is true. Moreover, the connections of women to the workplace may confer benefits for children. As women increase their associations outside of their family, neighborhood, and immediate social circle, they may be able to increase their knowledge and draw on new information, useful to fostering their children's life chances. Whether we should refer to such information as social capital is questionable according to the definition that we proposed earlier. Portes (2000) has described such knowledge and contacts as "bridging social capital." We prefer to think of this greater access to information as "cultural capital," knowledge about the way that the world works.

Nonetheless, it is clear that contacts parents make in the workplace are an essential source for importing new information into the family. Although some sociologists suggest that women's participation in the paid labor market decreases the social capital available to their families (see Coleman, 1990), more recent arguments suggest that there are a number of reasons women's participation may actually bring relatively greater resources to the nuclear family unit, particularly numerous contributions compared to similar participation by men. Through workplace contacts, parents may expand their social networks and gain access to potentially valuable sponsors for their children, and mothers may be more likely than fathers to use these resources to benefit their children (Büchel and Duncan, 1998). Expanding social networks also provide emotional or instrumental support for mothers themselves, which will, in turn, benefit their children. Social resources gained through employment contacts may provide parents with role models, as well as positive and negative feedback regarding parenting practices (Cochran, et al., 1990). (But as Büchel and Duncan (1998) point out, increasing social contacts, as gained through the workforce, could have liabilities as well. The actual building of social capital is a time-consuming process which parents may undertake for their own enjoyment rather than for the benefit of their children.

Parents may also gain access to other forms of social capital because they work outside of the home. Although this point has yet to be fully explored, mothers' employment may also create new opportunities for building social capital through child-care arrangements. Depending on the individual situation, caregivers may provide both parents and children with additional information and social contacts, particularly valuable to those parents with fewer resources. Given the prevalence of mothers in the paid labor market, it is both timely and relevant to examine how the accrual of social capital at work affects the family. The trading of information and sponsorship is an important area to be studied in the growing area of family/workplace interchange.

In conclusion, researchers have only begun to scratch the surface in addressing how social capital is produced within families, themselves, and accessed by families within the communities in which they reside. Clearly, consensus or cohesion within the household and the broader community contribute to the generation of social capital by creating mechanisms that foster expectations, monitor and regulate behavior, establish obligations, and provide opportunities for sponsorship and patronage. We have argued that these processes occur within households, across households connected by kinship and friendship, and within broader communities sharing values and social connections. Children are born into families, kinship systems, and communities that contain varying levels of these resources. As a general proposition, the greater the social capital to which the child has access, the more benefits provided for the child. But access to social capital in resource-rich systems cannot be taken for granted, nor should we suppose that children in low-capital systems are necessarily shut out of the benefits of social capital. In part, access to social capital will vary by the skills of parents and children. It is important to give some attention to how parents and children "work the system," and activate those resources to which they might have access.

## The Management of Social Capital

Residing in a household with high social capital has been generally considered tantamount to possession of social capital and thereby its benefits for family members (a similar assumption is made about the residents of neighborhoods in which there is high social capital). Whether residing in a system with high social capital – be it a family, neighborhood, or nation – confers advantages to all members of the system in equal measure is an unexplored question. However, there is good reason to suspect that the individual benefits of social capital are not evenly distributed within families.

A number of conditions may influence the accessibility of social capital within social units. One of the most important of these is a member's ability to utilize the resources it possesses. There is a likely association between a family's ability to produce social capital and its ability to manage and deploy it: individuals who have more resources are more likely to spend them. Still, it is easy to see how some members in high social capital systems may not use what they have (misers); others may be profligate spenders and use up what they have (spendthrifts); and in systems with low social capital, individuals may be resourceful at making do with very little (thrifty managers). Wise use of social capital is not a topic that has been extensively investigated.

Little is known to our knowledge about the mismanagement of social capital that occurs through hoarding these resources. Surely, though, it is rather plausible that individuals build obligations without drawing upon them either because of a sense of virtue or because of the fear of incurring obligations to others. Consider the parent who refuses to ask for help from kin for a child in need of special assistance or even refuses aid when it is offered, feeling that the burden of reciprocal obligations will be too great. A failure to lay claim on available resources under-utilizes social capital, undercutting its potential benefits for members of a social system. Yet a person's ability to garner social capital is not invariably related to his or her social milieu. Individuals differently positioned in a high social capital system may also be more or less able to realize their natural advantages. Thus, while a kinship system may possess high social capital, some members may be more centrally located while others are more on the periphery. Therefore demographic or personal characteristics of individuals may influence their access to social capital within social systems. For example, an attractive or bright child may be more likely to derive benefit from a family, school system, or community than one who is less endowed by brains or appearance.

In a study of parents' management of social capital, the senior author of this chapter was able to show that parents possessed different levels of skills in deploying social capital for their children's behalf (Furstenberg et al., 1999). Parents displayed different levels of energy and determination in seeking out resources in systems with low social capital, that is, some parents were simply better managers than others or were less reserved about calling in their chips, or even in assuming that they possessed chips, what might be called the "chutzpah factor." In general, we found that more educated parents possessed skills that were better for accessing available resources. It is also important that these parents *felt* more entitled to employ these resources, so that a sense of entitlement can be influential in the accessing and activation of social capital. It seems that some of the same qualities that make individuals adept managers of money and time may also be related to the ways that individuals handle social resources.

Similarly, those who already have access to greater financial and social resources will get the most out of their activation of social capital. For example, McNeal (1999) finds that the presumed positive benefits of social capital on children's academic achievement and behavioral outcomes are greatest for those students from traditionally advantaged backgrounds, those who live with two parents, are white, and of middle to upper SES. Hofferth, Boisjoly, and Duncan (1998) find that the effects of social capital depend on a family's income – children from high-income families benefit from their parents' access to time and monetary assistance, whereas children from low-income families do not. The authors suggest that the networks in which low-income people participate may represent economic necessity and these cannot provide the rich resources that high-income networks do. In this respect, social capital may not compensate for a lack of income, but rather it may allow wealthier families to make better use of their incomes. In sum, a theory of social capital must allow for the possibility that personal and demographic qualities interact with properties of social systems to the benefit of some more than others.

It is also easy to see how poor managers of social capital may be cast either in the role of "spendthrifts" or "exploiters," as individuals who take advantage of the good will of others. In Carol Stack's (1974) classic work, *All Our Kin*, she describes how some members of the low-income community that she studied several decades ago violated the "norm of reciprocity" and became known as individuals who took far more than they gave. Such persons, Stack observed, burnt out their social systems by putting too heavy a load on their friends and neighbors for too long a period of time. In such situations, possession of social capital may become a burden to those who might have extensive kin obligations or for those who indulge others' exploitation of their generosity. The idea of social capital "exploiters" assumes a violation of obligational norms for a more egocentric purpose, but social capital can be asymmetrical such that exceptional situations (such as prolonged illness or unemployment) may tip the reciprocal balance of social capital for an extended period of time without avaricious intentions. Extrapolating from Stack's observations, it is easy to imagine how demanding children or highly dependent adolescents and young adults may exceed their families' or friends' capacity to offer assistance. The claims of such individuals may be rejected if individuals are unable to replenish the stock of resources drawn upon. Parents who are exploiters may exhaust the good will of their families or communities in ways that disadvantage their offspring.

In order to advance our understanding of how individuals manage family-based social capital, we need much more detailed studies of (1) how individuals in both capital-rich and capital-poor systems perceive their own level of capital possession. Individuals may feel poorer or richer in capital than they are perceived by others. (2) how individuals actually go about deploying capital – when and why they do make claims on others and how they go about doing it. Just as we pointed out that we know little about how family members generate capital, we also have all too little information on how and for what they spend their capital, both in terms of families and kin and within their immediate social settings. (3) Finally, we need to learn more about the repayment or regeneration of social capital within families and communities. Just as economists examine patterns of economic consumption, sociologists need to attend more to the ways that social capital is invested, consumed, and replenished in social systems.

## The Consequences of Social Capital for the Welfare of Family Members

The vast majority of studies that have examined features of family-based social capital have focused on the consequences of possessing varying levels of capital. In one way or another, researchers have examined the general proposition that children benefit when their families have high social capital or reside in a community with high social capital and are deprived of important social resources when they do not. As we said at the outset of this overview, the evidence in support of this theoretical assumption is mixed. However, since researchers have used such a wide variety of indicators to measure the construct of social capital and a range of different outcomes to measure the consequences, it is difficult to draw any firm conclusions about the impact of social capital on the welfare of family members.

In some respects, the methodological problems began with Coleman's initial article (1988), in which he used very crude indicators of social capital to test his theory. Coleman said that families had high social capital if they were intact (as opposed to headed by a single parent), held high educational expectations (as reported by one parent), had geographical stability, and if the child's parent knew the name of his or her friends. In later work, Coleman argued that students in parochial schools had higher social capital because parents possessed greater knowledge of the school community and shared a common belief system.

Coleman intended for social capital to be viewed as a resource residing in the connection between people that can be used to achieve a particular interest and can be accumulated and drawn upon when necessary. As this original definition concentrated on relationships, the indicators that other researchers have used have been especially creative or promiscuous. Teachman and his colleagues (1996, 1997) added communication between the family and school to Coleman's indicators. Others have used parent/child communication and quality of parent/child relationships (Pryor, 1999), monitoring children's behavior (Parcel and Menaghan, 1993), parental involvement in schoolwork (Parcel and Dufur, 2001), time spent with children (Bianchi and Robinson, 1997), size of the social network and the knowledge of other children's parents (Carbonaro, 1998), community involvement (Büchel and Duncan, 1998), involvement in the school (McNeal, 1999), perceived access to social aid from relatives and friends (Hofferth, Boisjoly, and Duncan, 1998), among other indicators, to tap the parents' level of social capital. And the list goes on to include the child's participation in classes outside of school, how much the child reads, and computer ownership (Powell and Parcel, 1999). Social capital's popularity extends to the field of medicine, where its measures include having only one or two children in a family and regular church attendance (Runyan et al., 1998).

Clearly, some of these indicators come closer than others to measuring the original intended construct of social capital (and some may even be considered cultural capital), but they all focus on the parent–child dyad without examining the greater interactions of a family unit. From the relationships with their parents, children gain knowledge, values, and skills, which according to Coleman, are all forms of social capital, resources which may help children to successfully navigate their life outside of the family. In Coleman's view, social capital within the family exists as the relationship between adults and children and is based on the time spent together, such that the absence of an adult "may be described as a structural deficiency in family social capital" (1988: S110). For instance, following Coleman's initial ideas, those families with one parent or two employed parents lack (to some extent) social capital specifically because these parents do not (in theory) have the same amount of time to spend with children as parents in traditional nuclear families.

Using presence of parents in the household as a measure of family-based social capital may also be problematic because it fails to take the quality of time that parents and children spend together into consideration, nor does it account for other familiar relationships, the influence of grandparents, aunts and uncles, or siblings. Few indicators of previous studies measure normative consensus within the family or the alignment of family and community expectations – the essential ingredients of any theory of family-based social capital. Instead, the indicators, at best, nibble at the edges of the theory without directly measuring the level of social capital, a task which requires measures of multiple members of the family unit, and/or the community in which the family resides.

In addition, the very indicators used as measures of social capital may themselves be very vague or value-laden. These indicators of social capital may lack the breadth and depth of what they were originally intended to measure and may often rely on undefined notions of quality or unrealistic standards of quantity. For example, most studies are based on large data sets which have preset questions that may not have been intended to measure social capital. Given that social capital can be seen as resources gained from social relationships, it would seem difficult to ascertain an accurate assessment of social capital's influence without greater understanding of the quality or nature of the relevant relationships. Because, at best, researchers have relied on indirect measures of social capital, it is impossible to tell whether or not the theory is being tested when positive or negative results are discovered. Positive results could be spurious or might be explained by numerous other theories. For example, it is not clear that the presence of two parents necessarily implies greater social capital in the family, especially if the parents do not share common expectations for their children. In any event, there are many other theories besides social capital that can explain how children might do better if they reside with both their parents. Similarly, high educational expectations, knowledge of a child's friends, involvement in the school, and most of the other indicators that have been employed to measure the level of social capital have long been used as indicators for various theories of educational attainment.

Educational attainment has been the outcome most extensively examined in empirical studies of family-based social capital, in part because of Coleman's interest and in part because of the accessibility of this quantifiable outcome in extant longitudinal data sets. Most researchers' emphasis on high school completion ignores some of the greater issues that social capital can affect leading to this outcome, such as rates of truancy and academic grades. The literature that does not look specifically at educational outcomes still uses various (and often nebulous) measures of children's development and behavior.

However, theories of social capital should be equally applicable to other positive outcomes such as employment, civic involvement, and perhaps marriage and marital stability as well as the absence of negative outcomes such as mental health problems or incarceration. As yet, there is not a large literature on these various measures of children's long-term welfare. Although there are a number of longitudinal data sets which may include the more standard and appropriate measures of social capital, they have not, as of yet, been used to explore these other immediate and long-term arenas of welfare.

Another limitation of the literature on the outcomes of varying levels of family-based social capital is that virtually all studies have focused on its impact on children's welfare, neglecting both the potential effects of other family members on children and possibly the influences of adult relatives on each other. This child-centered focus can be traced to Coleman's original statement of the theory. It is also possible that the concentration of social capital literature on child outcomes represents the theory's emphasis on the importance of the breadwinner father-homemaker wife family. We are unaware of any studies that examine how levels of capital within kinship systems affect marital stability, the strength of intergenerational ties among adults, relations among siblings, the benefits flowing to distant relations, or a range of other issues that go beyond children's developmental trajectories. Perhaps the lack of attention to these questions reflects the general indifference of sociologists to the operation of the family as a social system apart from its function as socializing agency for children. If common expectations and connections involving trust, obligations, and entitlements are the essential ingredients of social capital, then we might expect that families that possess high amounts of it establish different patterns of exchange, caregiving, sponsorship, outreach, and the like that could result in greater physical and mental health, for example, among the elderly or within marriages. We might suppose that social capital affects patterns of geographical mobility (as well as being affected by geographical mobility). And, we would expect that families with high amounts of social capital have a much broader pattern of exchange with kin beyond the immediate household. These topics invite further empirical investigation.

## Conclusions

This chapter has explored the notion of social capital within families with the aim of clarifying the construct and the theoretical assumptions that gave rise to it. We are not yet convinced, on the basis of the literature to date, that it will survive empirical scrutiny or endure over time. In order to do so, it must be applied more carefully, measured more precisely, and examined less mechanically. Specifically, most studies have employed a "states and rates" approach to social capital, that is, more of it produces better outcomes. We have argued that if the theory of social capital is to be developed and tested, it must be treated as a social process that occurs within families and more broadly within kinship systems as influenced by their greater social context.

We have raised a series of questions about how family-based social capital must be examined along certain theoretical dimensions. If by social capital we mean that family members are embedded in households and kinship systems that may be characterized by common expectations, claims and obligations, trust, and connectedness, then we should be looking at the ways that these features of families are produced and maintained, as well as how they become instantiated in everyday life. Of course, this examination involves closer scrutiny of how families and their members are connected to broader social communities and linked to institutions that foster and sustain social capital within families.

The assumption that the benefits of social capital are evenly distributed within families is a dubious one, in our view. Rather, we speculated that the skill of family members to garner and deploy social capital is likely to vary most by individuals' possessions of cultural capital. Consequently, we need to address the issue of how individuals manage social capital and deploy it to their advantage or the advantage of other family members. There is very little empirical work on this question.

Finally, we raised a series of issues regarding the likely consequences of social capital for family members. How social capital translates into social advantage, if it actually does, is not well understood. Moreover, the literature focuses exclusively on a narrow range of outcomes, particularly its effects on the educational attainment of children. If social capital is to remain a meaningful construct, it should be expanded to observe how families function to create and maintain advantage for their members. So, researchers should be considering how the creation and deployment of capital affects kin more broadly throughout the life cycle: in childhood, family formation, middle age, and into old age.

We believe that social capital theory has great potential for helping us to understand how the kinship system functions to reproduce social advantage and disadvantage. To realize that potential, however, requires a much more sophisticated approach to studying social capital's production, distribution, and effects both within the family and the surrounding community.

## Note

1 The definition is taken from Putnam (1995). In his book *Bowling Alone*, Putnam defines social capital as "connections among individuals, social networks and the norms of reciprocity and trustworthiness that arise from them" (2000: 19).

## References


Alwin, D. F. (1996) Parental socialization in historical perspective. In C. D. Ryff and M. Mailick Seltzer (eds.), *The Parental Experience in Midlife*. Chicago: University of Chicago Press.

Berger, B., and Berger, P. L. (1983) *The War Over the Family: Capturing the Middle Ground*. Garden City, NY: Anchor Press.

Bianchi, S. M., and Robinson, J. (1997) What did you do today? Children's use of time, family composition, and the acquisition of social capital. *Journal of Marriage and the Family*, 59, 332–44.

Bossard, J. H. S., and Stoker Boll, E. (1956) *The Large Family System*. Philadelphia: University of Pennsylvania Press.

Bott, E. (1971) *Family and Social Network: Roles, Norms, and External Relationships in Ordinary Urban Families*. 2nd ed. London: Tavistock.

Bourdieu, P. (1973) Cultural reproduction and social reproduction. In R. Brown (ed.), *Knowledge, Education, and Cultural Change*. London: Tavistock.

Bourdieu, P. (1986) The forms of capital. In J. C. Richardson (ed.), *Handbook of Theory and Research for the Sociology of Education*. New York: Greenwood.

Bourdieu, P., and Passeron, J. C. (1977) *Reproduction in Education, Society, and Culture*. London: Sage.

Büchel, F., and Duncan, G. J. (1998) Do parents' social activities promote children's school attainments? Evidence from the German Socioeconomic Panel. *Journal of Marriage and the Family*, 60, 95–108.

Carbonaro, W. J. (1998) A little help from my friend's parents: Intergenerational closure and educational outcomes. *Sociology of Education*, 71, 295–313.

Cochran, M., Larner, M,. et al. (1990) *Extending Families: The Social Networks of Parents and their Children*. Cambridge: Cambridge University Press.

Coleman, J. S. (1988) Social capital and the creation of human capital. *American Journal of Sociology*, 94, 95–121.

Coleman, J. S. (1990) *Foundations of Social Theory*. Cambridge, MA: Belknap Press.

Durkheim, E. (1951) *Suicide: A Study in Sociology*. Glencoe, IL: The Free Press.

Durkheim, E. (1961) *Moral Education: A Study in the Theory and Application of the Sociology of Education*. Glencoe, IL: The Free Press.

Furstenberg, F. F., and Cherlin, A. J. (1994) *Divided Families: What Happens to Children When Parents Part*. Cambridge, MA: Harvard University Press.

Furstenberg, F. F., Cook, T., Eccles, J., Elder, G. H., Jr., and Sameroff, A. (1999). *Managing To Make It: Urban Families in High-Risk Neighborhoods*. Chicago: University of Chicago Press.

Furstenberg, F. F., and Spanier, G. (1984) *Recycling the Family: Remarriage after Divorce*. Newbury Park, CA: Sage.

Gans, H. J. (1962) *The Urban Villagers*. New York: The Free Press.

Hess, R. D., and Handel, G. (1959) *Family Worlds: A Psychosocial Approach to Family Life*. Chicago: University of Chicago Press.

Hofferth, S. L., Boisjoly, J., and Duncan, G. J. (1998) Parents' extrafamilial resources and children's school attainment. *Sociology of Education*, 71, 246–68.

Hollingshead, A. de B. (1949) *Elmtown's Youth: The Impact of Social Classes on Adolescents*. New York: Wiley.

Johnson, C. L. (1988) *Ex Familia*. New Brunswick, NJ: Rutgers University Press.

Komarovsky, M. (1987) *Blue-Collar Marriage*. 2nd ed. New Haven, CT: Yale University Press.

Lareau, A. (2001) Embedding capital in a broader context: The case of family–school relationships. In B. Biddle and P. Hall (eds.), *Social Class, Poverty, and Education*. London: Falmer-Routledge.

Loizos, P. (2000) Are refugees social capitalists? In S. Baron, J. Field, and T. Schuller (eds.), *Social Capital: Critical Perspectives*. Oxford: Oxford University Press.

Loury, G. (1977) A dynamic theory of racial income differences. In P. A. Wallace and A. M. LaMond (eds.), *Women, Minorities, and Employment Discrimination*. Lexington, MA: Lexington Books.

McNeal, R. B,. Jr. (1999) Parental involvement as social capital: differential effectiveness on science achievement, truancy, and dropping out. *Social Forces*, 78, 117–44.

Parcel, T. L., and Dufur, M. J. (2001) Capital at home and at school: Effects on child social adjustment. *Journal of Marriage and Family*, 63, 32–47.

Parcel, T. L., and Menaghan, E. G. (1993) Family social capital and children's behavior problems. *Social Psychology Quarterly*, 56, 120–35.

Portes, A. (ed.) (1996) *The New Second Generation*. New York: Russell Sage Foundation.

Portes, A. (2000) The two meanings of social capital. *Sociological Forum*, 15, 1–11.

Powell, M. A., and Parcel, T. L. (1999) Parental work, family size and social capital effects on early adolescent educational outcomes: The United States and Great Britain compared. *Research in the Sociology of Work*, 7, 1–30.

Pryor, J. (1999) Waiting until they leave home: The experiences of young adults whose parents separate. *Journal of Divorce and Remarriage*, 32, 47–61.

Putnam, R. D. (1995) Bowling alone: America's declining social capital. *Journal of Democracy*, 6, 65–78.

Putnam, R. D. (1996) The strange disappearance of civic America. *The American Prospect*, Winter, 24, 34–48.

Putnam, R.D. (2000) *Bowling Alone: the Collapse and Revival of American Community*. New York: Simon & Schuster.

Riessman, C. K. (1990) *Divorce Talk: Women and Men Make Sense of Personal Relationships*. New Brunswick, NJ: Rutgers University Press.

Rumbaut, R. G. (1996) The crucible within: ethnic identity, self-esteem, and segmented assimilation among children of immigrants. In A. Portes (ed.), *The New Second Generation*. New York: Russell Sage Foundation.

Runyan, D. K., Hunter, W. M., et al. (1998) Children who prosper in unfavorable environments: The relationship to social capital. *Pediatrics*, 101, 12–18.

Schneider, D. (1968) *American Kinship: A Cultural Account*. Englewood Cliffs, NJ: Prentice-Hall.

Smith, T. W. (2002) The transition to adulthood and the generation gap: from the 1970s to the 1990s. Manuscript in progress.

Stack, C. (1974) *All Our Kin: Strategies for Survival in a Black Community*. New York: Harper.

Teachman, J. D., Paasch, K., and Carver, K. (1996) Social capital and dropping out of school early. *Journal of Marriage and the Family*, 58, 773–83.

Teachman, J. D., Paasch, K., and Carver, K. (1997) Social capital and the generation of human capital. *Social Forces*, 75, 1343–60.

Tocqueville, A.de (1945) *Democracy in America*. New York: Knopf.

Vaughn, D. (1986) *Uncoupling*. New York: Vintage Books.

Waite, L., and Gallagher, M. (2000) *The Case for Marriage: Why Married People Are Happier, Healthier, and Better Off Financially*. New York: Doubleday.

Waters, M. (1996) Ethnic and racial identities of second-generation black immigrants in New York City. In A. Portes (ed.), *The New Second Generation*. New York: Russell Sage Foundation.

# 14

# Family, the State, and Health Care: Changing Roles in the New Century

Ronald J. Angel and Jacqueline L. Angel

## Introduction

At the dawn of the twenty-first century, the nations of the developed world have achieved the longest life expectancies at birth in human history. For a period after the introduction of vaccines and antibiotics it was even possible to imagine that humanity might eventually defeat infectious disease completely, leaving medical science only the chronic diseases of old age with which to contend. Yet even in what must seem like health-care utopias from the perspective of the most impoverished nations, differences in health and access to health care persist. Those differences are often linked to race and ethnicity, and to other social factors that define citizenship. If the plagues of previous centuries that decimated entire nations are a distant memory, a plague of another sort is upon us. In both the developing and developed worlds, violence and social disruption blight the lives of millions of people and cause the death of countless others. Additionally, for poor nations, in which infectious disease continues to exact a high toll, aging populations bring the added burden of caring for the infirm old. If the nineteenth century ended with an exaggerated faith in the power of science and industry to cure human ills, the twentieth century ends on a more somber note, and with the realization that science cannot by itself eliminate pain and suffering. At the end of a violent century it is clear that the social problems that undermine the health of populations are immensely complicated and increasingly global.

For the majority of human history, the maintenance of health and the treatment of disease have been the responsibility of the family and the local healer. Even today, informal treatment and self-care are basic human activities. Most individuals engage in personal rituals, including exercise, diet, and the use of supplements to remain healthy or get well when they fall ill, and most turn to family members for help at such times. Anthropologists have documented the importance of the "lay referral network" in health care (Kleinman, 1986). This term refers to one's immediate social environment that consists of the strong interpersonal ties of spouse, children, and other family members. It extends out to the local community as well, but does not include formal institutions. Prior to the fairly recent domination of health care by modern scientific medicine, this lay network formed the core of the health-care system upon which most people relied and continue to rely today, especially in the developing world. The historical centrality of the lay network to the maintenance of health underscores the close tie between health and local social institutions, the most important of which is the family.

In most of the world today, though, traditional family forms and functions are changing rapidly. The increasing labor-force participation of women, international migration and internal displacement, lower fertility, and family disruption mean that the family units that provided care to their members in earlier eras are for many individuals no longer available. Today, older persons often have no family members who can provide emotional or instrumental support in the event of ill health. Children cannot count on aunts and other non-nuclear family members to care for them when their parents cannot. For many children, their biological father is not a part of their support network. As a result of the weakening of the family's support capacity, formal institutions and the state increasingly assume much of the responsibility for providing care to both the young and the old (Esping-Andersen, 1990, 1996, 1999). This shift in responsibility for vulnerable individuals from the family to formal organizations forces researchers and policy analysts to begin to document and understand how such formal structures operate and how they affect different groups of people (Weir, Orloff, and Skocpol, 1988). Today, health-care researchers examine inequities in the financing of care, inequalities among groups in access to care, and differences in the quality of care that individuals from different social groups receive. Changes in family forms, especially the dramatic rise in single-parent families that we have witnessed in recent decades, means that many of the institutional arrangements that make up the social welfare state, including those that finance and provide health care, are presented with new risk profiles for which they are not optimally designed (Esping-Andersen, 1999).

In this chapter we summarize what is known of the role of family in acute and long-term care, focusing on children, immigrants, and the aged. We compare the situations of developed nations to those of the developing world, and focus heavily on the US which, because it is unique among developed nations in not having universal publicly funded health care, faces unique problems of access for the most vulnerable groups. We end with proposals for a research agenda aimed at a better understanding of the increasing role of the state and formal institutions in providing care to citizens of all ages.

## The New Morbidity

In the developed world today the major threats to health increasingly consist of external, socially influenced health-risk factors such as violence, substance abuse, and family disruption, a set of social phenomena that have been labeled "the new morbidity" (Haggerty, Roghmann, and Pless, 1975). Ironically, the spread of democratic political practices to many parts of the world has been accompanied by the weakening of traditional social institutions, such as the family and local community, which exercised social control in previous eras. Today, problems such as learning disabilities, injuries, and emotional and behavioral disturbances associated with social and family disruption have replaced infectious disease as the major threats to children's physical and emotional well-being.

Yet even as diseases such as pertussus, tuberculosis, polio, and smallpox no longer threaten large numbers of children in the developed nations, they have not been vanquished. Several potentially dangerous childhood illnesses that are still common in the developing world and many that have become resistant to conventional drug therapies are making a comeback in the affluent nations. The fact that infectious disease remains common in the developing world presents those countries with many unique problems, including those that result from extreme differences in access to health care between the rich and the poor. Julio Frenk, former Executive Vice-President and Director of the Center for Health and the Economy of the Mexican Health Foundation, summarizes the plight of developing nations. He notes that,

> [a]s countries move along the path of transition, health inequalities, particularly those reflected in child mortality and communicable diseases, become more acute, producing what we have labeled as the epidemiological polarization.... Even though polarization may be present in all countries that undergo the epidemiological transition, for Latin America it is likely to be of paramount importance owing to the region's history of inequalities in the distribution of wealth. (Frenk, Bobadilla, and Lozano, 1996: 131)

This problem of polarization related to infectious disease in the developing world is compounded by the additional problem of aging populations. In Mexico, as elsewhere, the diseases associated with deep poverty exist in conjunction with growing numbers of older people who suffer from the diseases of affluence, including diabetes, heart disease, and cancer (Gwatkin, 2000). For instance, in Russia, heart disease is one of the leading causes of death and disability. A recent telephone survey of Muscovites between the ages of 25 and 64 found a high prevalence rate of behavioral risk factors related to chronic disease that included tobacco use, poor diet, inadequate physical activity, and excessive alcohol consumption (Zabina et al., 2001). Despite the urgent need to address these health problems in post-Soviet society, an eroding public health infrastructure has undermined the capacity of the Russian federation to care for its youngest and oldest citizens (Fox and Kassalow, 2001). In addition, developing countries, like those of the developed world, must contend with the mental, behavioral, and social health problems that are an increasing part of modern life (Desjarlais et al., 1995). All of these threats to physical and mental health are increasing in prevalence and severity just at a time when the family is often less able to carry out its traditional role of caring for its members in times of protracted need.

## Changing Family Forms and Children's Health Care in the US

During the last four decades of the twentieth century the developed world witnessed a dramatic change in the structure of the family. In the US, for example, by 1998 almost one-third of all children, and nearly two-thirds of black children, were living with only one parent (US Census Bureau, 2000a). In addition, the proportion of children living with neither biological parent has increased (Bryson and Casper, 1999). Approximately 1.5 million children in the US are currently in the care of grandparents or someone other than their biological parents (US Census Bureau, 2000b).

The causes and consequences of the increase in single parenthood, which almost always involves a single mother, will be debated for many years. A large fraction of single mothers in all parts of the world are young and have low levels of education (Angel and Angel, 1993; Kammerman, 1984; MacLanahan and Sandefur, 1994). Education itself is often used as an indicator of socioeconomic status and health knowledge (Bumpass and McLanahan, 1989). Parents with low levels of education are not only handicapped in their ability to obtain health care for themselves and their children, but they are less knowledgeable about preventive and curative measures. Low education is clearly a serious health-risk factor which is associated with poverty (Pappas et al., 1993). Much of the growth in single parenthood, however, reflects changing norms regarding marriage and fertility. In the US, Sweden, and the rest of the developed world a large fraction of all births are to unmarried mothers (Guyer et al., 1999; Popenoe, Elshtain, and Blankenhorn, 1996). In the past, teenage pregnancy accounted for the majority of unwed motherhood. Today a large fraction of unwed mothers are beyond their teenage years. Rather than representing the carelessness or reproductive ignorance of youth, these trends reflect a shift in norms and a growing acceptance of fertility outside of marriage. For certain groups, marriage seems less of an option or even an expectation, and for many the nuclear family has shrunk in membership to mother and children.

Although single motherhood per se cannot be shown definitively to harm children, the fact that many of these single-parent households experience serious economic hardship is indisputable (Angel and Angel, 1993). One of the major health risks associated with poverty is decreased access to health care. Although many poor single-parent families have access to Medicaid, many others do not, and both children and adults in such families often do without needed medical care (Holahan and Kim, 2000; Moffitt and Slade, 1997).

The poverty and parenting burden that many single parents experience has serious consequences for the health and morale of both adults and children (Dawson, 1991; McLeod and Shanahan, 1993; McGauhey and Starfield, 1993; Popenoe, 1988; Montgomery, Kiely, and Pappas, 1996; Wallerstein, 1991; Zill, Morrison, and Coiro, 1993). Single mothers who have no other adult present in the household are more likely than mothers in two-parent families or those in which some other adult is present to rate their children's health as poor (Angel and Worobey, 1988; Worobey, Angel, and Worobey, 1988). Sharing the economic and instrumental burdens of raising children seems to result in better health for both adults and children. The data also suggest that children in families in which a mother must bear the burdens of parenthood alone often experience both physical and emotional problems simultaneously (Angel and Angel, 1996a). Such findings provide strong evidence of serious physical and emotional health risks for women and children in single-parent households. Again, though, those risks are associated with the poverty in which many such families find themselves, and not to any negative effects of single parenthood itself (Angel and Angel, 1993).

## Citizenship and Health Care: The Plight of Migrant Families

In most of the developed world, full citizenship includes entitlement to the care provided by paternalistic states. All highly developed nations, other than the US, offer universal health-care coverage to their citizens. In the world today, though, the movement of people within and between nations gives rise to a new category of individual and family that do not have full access to the benefits of citizenship. Refugees, guest workers, illegal immigrants, and in some cases, even legal immigrants often do not have access to the full range of social services, including adequate health care. Families that are forced for economic or political reasons to migrate within or between nations are frequently torn apart and find that they are second- or third-class citizens in receiving areas in which they are often unwelcome.

In the US, race and Hispanic ethnicity historically have been associated with restricted access to many of the benefits of full citizenship. For African Americans such disadvantages arise from a history of slavery. For Americans of Hispanic origin, and today for Americans of Asian origin, migration plays an important role. Until the latter half of the twentieth century, immigration into the US originated primarily in Europe. Today, immigration streams originate primarily in Asia and Latin America. These new immigrants are an important source of the rapid growth in the Hispanic and Asian populations of the US and many new immigrants arrive as entire families.

In the US, as elsewhere, the citizenship status of these new arrivals is often uncertain or in transition. Although Puerto Ricans are citizens by birth, a large fraction of Cuban-origin individuals are foreign-born, and many, especially among the old, have not become citizens. A smaller fraction of Mexican-origin than Cuban-origin individuals are foreign-born, yet a substantial number of older Mexican Americans were born in Mexico. Asians differ greatly as well, not only in nation of origin, but the date of peak immigration for each group, factors that can affect eligibility for public health programs. One important aspect of recent immigration is that many of the new arrivals are undocumented and are in the US illegally (Fix and Tumlin, 1997). Because of their illegal status these individuals and their families are very wary of authority and many avoid formal bureaucracies, including those that provide health care.

The health risks and, consequently, the health-care needs of immigrants and their children are unique, as are the barriers that often keep them from receiving health care. Immigrants sometimes arrive in the host society with health problems that are rare in the developed world but more common in developing nations (Schulpen, 1996). Because of higher rates of infectious disease in the developing world, immigrant children from poor nations often experience higher morbidity and mortality from diarrheal diseases and acute respiratory infections, conditions that are exacerbated by malnutrition (Toole and Waldman, 1993). Because of genetic factors that are more common in sending areas, these children also suffer disproportionately from inherited disorders, such as sickle-cell disease and thalassemia major, a genetic disorder that causes metabolic problems (Rengelink-van Der Lee, Shulpen, and Beemer, 1995).

In addition to physical ailments, migrants to the developed world also experience serious acculturative stresses that can undermine their social and mental adjustment (Sam and Berry, 1995). The great social and cultural changes that migrants must endure, as well as the great physical distances they must often travel, increase the stresses they experience. Unfortunately, the family is often ill equipped to deal with mental illness. Conflicts and strife within the family can even be the source of emotional problems for both adults and children. These can be exacerbated by the stresses that migrants experience. The majority of adults and children with mental health problems receive no care at all and if they do, that care is likely to be provided by a general medical practitioner (Angel and Angel, 1996a). For immigrants who are unfamiliar with the mental health-care system of the receiving country, needed services are even more elusive.

Because they often do not know the language or cultural practices of the host society, foreign-born individuals are frequently socially isolated, a situation that can compromise health (Kossoudji, 1989). This isolation from the larger world increases the dependency of immigrants, and especially older immigrants, on their families. Both because of economic need and traditional cultural norms, immigrants are more likely than the native-born to live with family members (Angel et al., 1996, 1999; Angel, Angel, and Markides, 2000; Lee and Angel, 2002; Wilmoth, 2001; Wilmoth, DeJong, and Himes, 1997). Migration, therefore, can both undermine health and increase family dependency. Older foreign-born Mexican origin individuals, for example, report poorer health than the native born and are more likely to live with their family (Angel et al., 1996).

An immigrant family's ability to deal with ill health is directly affected by public policy (National Research Council, 1995). In the US, recent changes in welfare and immigration law place the entire burden of caring for a new immigrant on his or her sponsors, who are usually family members, for a period of five years (Angel et al., 2000). For an immigrant family struggling to move up the economic ladder in a new and strange country, such a burden can be onerous and the possibility of having to shoulder such a burden could discourage some families from bringing older relatives from the country of origin.

Restrictions in access to publicly funded health care represent a major health threat to immigrant families. Because of a lack of insurance, adults and children in these families usually have no regular source of care. For middle-class families with adequate coverage, a regular source of care increases the use of pediatric care for children and, in turn, increases the likelihood that they receive the specialist physical and mental health-care services they might need (Newacheck, Hughes, and Stoddard, 1996). Health care coverage, therefore, represents a tie to the medical care establishment that increases the likelihood of good health. Factors that disrupt this tie, therefore, represent serious health threats.

Voluntary migrants must endure the stresses associated with profound cultural change and the need to adapt to a new environment. Those forced from their homes and country of origin by civil war, natural disaster, or political upheaval face even more serious health threats. Many witness the loss of family members and experience serious post-traumatic stress disorders. Refugees often experience multiple forms of trauma as the result of political persecution, war, and detention. Their sense of safety is often undermined by armed attacks on refugee camps, forced recruitment of family members into military service, and sexual violence. Under such conditions, families are often separated and their supportive function undermined. Refugees face rejection in both intermediate and destination countries because of their number and the burden they represent. The human rights abuses committed against ethnic Albanian refugees from Kosovo in the former Yugoslavia provide unique testimony to the adverse public health consequences of political and civil disruption (Iacopino et al., 2001).

In 2001 nearly 22 million refugees had been forced to leave their native countries (United Nations High Commissioner for Refugees, 2002). In addition, an additional 20 million individuals were internally displaced (US General Accounting Office, 2001). These populations are in serious need of health care (Toole and Waldman, 1993). Given their irregular status and the often chaotic situations that force them to leave their homes, many of these individuals remain invisible or inaccessible to official international aid organizations. A large fraction of these refugees are children, who are scarred physically and mentally for life because they are often violently uprooted from their usual environments and forced to live in poverty and unhealthy conditions without adequate nutrition or medical care.

Although guest workers have provided labor to the nations of Western Europe since the end of World War II, the rapid increase in their number since the 1980s has led governments of the host countries to officially discourage new arrivals. The European Union estimates that over 500,000 illegal immigrants arrived in 2000, up from 40,000 in 1993 (Cohen, 2000). The response has been the introduction of restrictions to reduce what many Europeans perceive to be an excessive number of immigrants. These restrictions include reduced social benefits, detention of asylum seekers, and the application of narrow legal interpretations of who qualifies as a refugee. In Bonn, Germany, applicants receive assistance in kind rather than in cash, and at only 80 percent of the level of needy citizens (Kumin, 1999). Refugees in the Netherlands are housed in tents and placed on a waiting list for regular accommodation (ibid.). The physical and administrative barriers erected by host states make it increasingly difficult for the victims of persecution and violence to gain access to a normal life (United Nations High Commission for Refugees, 1997). Many spend years, or entire lifetimes, in camps and many others are forced back to unsafe homelands.

## The Family and the Care of the Elderly

As part of the changes that have affected the family, traditional intergenerational relationships are eroding. Increasingly, the local family-based social network is unable to provide basic material and emotional support to those who in the past were its responsibility. Today, the family is simply too small, the time demands of work and children too great, and aging parents and their adult children often too far apart to allow the family to assume the burden. Table 14.1 demonstrates the increasing labor-force involvement of women aged 45 to 64 between 1970 and 1995 in several countries. Traditionally, women of this age cared for their aging parents and, although in Japan and Spain many women in this age range are still housewives, in other countries, including the US and Sweden, the majority are employed outside the home. Although part-time work may still leave a woman time to provide care to older parents, it is clear that the care-giving resource represented by unemployed mature women is diminishing in large parts of the world.

In contemporary developed social welfare states the young no longer expect to provide economic support to their parents (Crystal, 1982). The socialization of basic economic support for the elderly through old-age public pension plans is both a response to the family's inability to assume the full responsibility for the elderly, and an added impetus to a shift in responsibility from the family to the state. One dilemma for long-term care policy relates to the extent to which the availability of family caregivers should be taken into account in the allocation of services (Wolf, 2001). Large families are more likely than smaller ones to be able to spread the burden of caring for infirm parents among many members. Older parents with children who live nearby can call on them more easily than parents whose children have moved far away. Smaller families are less able to share the care-giving burden, and providing for children's material needs and education means that even if they wish to, a family often

**Table 14.1** Labor-force participation by women aged 45–64 by selected nation, 1970 and 1995 (%)

| | *1970* | *1995* |
|---|---|---|
| Australia | 33.8 | 48.8 |
| Canada | 36.0 | 56.5 |
| Finland | 74.7 | 85.5 |
| France | 45.1 | 51.8 |
| Germany | 36.8 | 45.8[1] |
| Italy | 18.0 | 24.1 |
| Japan | 53.9 | 59.8 |
| Netherlands | 18.6[2] | 35.3 |
| Norway | 48.1[3] | 67.8 |
| Portugal | 38.2[4] | 47.4 |
| Spain | 23.9 | 27.7 |
| Sweden | 55.0 | 78.3 |
| UK | 49.3 | 58.6 |
| US | 48.7 | 61.8 |

Notes
[1]1991.
[2]1971.
[3]1972.
[4]1974.

*Source*: Organisation for Economic Co-operation and Development (1996), Table 1.A.7; US Census Bureau (2000d), Table 644.

cannot provide support to aging parents (Peterson 1999). A formal policy of taking the availability of family caregivers into account could lead to a system that is stratified on the basis of characteristics related to fertility. Latinos, for example, have larger families than non-Latinos, and if the availability of potential caregivers were considered in the allocation of resources, these groups might receive less since their supposed capacity to care for their own is greater (Mutchler and Angel, 2000).

Although many older individuals, especially recent immigrants and those with low incomes, live with their children, they do not necessarily do so by choice. In the US, it is clear that when they can afford it, most older persons prefer to live with a spouse, or alone once the spouse is gone. Certain studies indicate that even among fairly traditional groups, including some recent immigrants, many older individuals would prefer not to live with their families (Koh and Bell, 1987). For older immigrants, as for natives, living with children can result in intergenerational conflict, crowding, excessive housework, and unwanted child-care responsibilities. It is clear that, despite the possibility of a more familistic orientation, extended living arrangements are a necessity brought on by economic need and the inability to deal with a strange and foreign social environment (Goldscheider and Goldscheider, 1989). These families face multiple stresses at the same time that their capacities to deal with them are strained.

The elderly are, of course, at elevated risk of frailty and disability, and they use more medical services than younger people. Eventually, physical decline increases the likelihood that an older person requires long-term care. The family has traditionally provided that care, and even in the contemporary US the vast majority of the care needed by older persons is provided by kin (Angel and Angel, 1997). Yet the family and its ability to care for dependent elderly members are being undermined by demographic and economic forces, including migration, that are global in their nature (Spillman and Pezzin, 2000). The impact is particularly obvious in certain areas, such as the border region of Mexico and the US. For many Mexicans seeking a better life, the norm of family and community support for the elderly clashes with a new economic and demographic reality that forces younger family members to leave home in order to make a living (Angel and Angel, 1998; Becerra, 1988; Markides, Martin, and Gomez, 1983).

Lower labor costs in Mexico have attracted many assembly plants, known as "maquiladoras," to Mexico's northern states. This economic activity has brought much-needed income to Mexico and has encouraged migration from the interior to Mexico's northern border. Unfortunately, wage rates are too low to provide real economic security and, although identifiable communities continue to exist on both sides of the border, many are desperately poor and simply unable to provide support to the elderly. One serious consequence for Mexico is that many villages in the interior consist of the old who have been left behind (Soldo and Wong, 2000). In addition, the maquiladora industry generates a great deal of toxic waste and hazardous materials. The resulting environmental degradation results in air pollution and a seriously contaminated water supply which threatens human health. In one recent example of the extent of toxic danger children were intoxicated by toluene at a dump in Ciudad Juárez (Williams, 1996).

The changing family has created a new health-care environment for both the young and the old along the US/Mexico border, as it has in other parts of the world. Ecological areas that were once communities today have changed profoundly and no longer provide the same social control or support that they did in previous eras. Specific areas differ in their supportive capacities. For the Mexican-origin population, the availability of kin and formal community support varies greatly from the inner city, to more rural areas, to the unincorporated *colonias* that have sprung up outside of urban areas and in rural areas along the border (Ward, 1999).

The long-term care dilemmas faced by the US are becoming universal in the developed world, and increasingly in the developing world. As in the case of general health services, countries differ in how they deal with the problem. As their ability to care for the elderly is strained, families increasingly turn to the state for the care of elderly parents. Institutional care is relatively common in some advanced nations such as Japan, Canada, and Australia. These nations have extensive hospital systems for older patients. Conversely, some nations de-emphasize institutional care and strive to keep the frail and disabled in the community. A commitment to community care is particularly common in socialized countries such as Sweden, which has an extensive family income entitlement program (Organisation for Economic Cooperation and Development, 1996). The Nordic countries, France, and the UK top the list of nations in which a large fraction of the population receive long-term care from local authorities. In Denmark, in which home health care is free to older persons, home health care use by the elderly is particularly common (Holstein et al., 1991).

The changing role of the family is underscored by the recently expanded role of the state in providing long-term care for the elderly in Japan, a nation with a strong Confucian tradition that has had a formal policy of relying on the family. In response to a rapidly aging population and an increase in the number of very frail older persons, Japan has introduced a new mandatory long-term care insurance program (Campbell and Ikegami, 2000). As part of this program, everyone aged 40–64 pays a standard premium, and everyone over 65 is eligible to receive community-based care services. Japan provides the lesson that even in highly traditional and familistic cultures, the state must eventually assume the role of care insurer and provider for its most vulnerable citizens. In the US, the recent reauthorization of the Older Americans Act will for the first time provide critical and much-needed support to families who are caring for their ill and disabled loved ones. This new program provides support and respite care to hundreds of thousands of family members who are struggling to care for their older relatives at home.

Institutional care, and even formal community-based care, are extremely expensive and clearly not realistic options for poorer nations. Even in developed nations, for the poor and minorities such care is often not an option (Angel and Angel, 1998; Espino et al., 1988). In all nations, although many older individuals continue to live with their families, many others do not, and even when they become seriously infirm many continue to live alone (Angel, 1991; Worobey and Angel, 1990). In the developed world, an adequate income has made solitary living a possibility for older people (Myles, 1984). But even in the developing world, in which retirement incomes are not as secure as in the developed world, many older individuals live alone.

Table 14.2 presents the proportion of unmarried older population living alone in selected Latin American countries and the US. These data are extracted from Palloni's (2000) recent presentation at the United Nations conference on international aging. Because of lower retirement incomes, less available housing, and a more traditional family orientation, Latin Americans are less likely than non-Hispanic white Americans to live alone. In the more developed nations of Latin America, including Brazil, Chile, and Argentina, larger numbers of older individuals are living alone. In the US, older African Americans, Hispanics, and Asians are more likely than the majority of the population to live with others. Because of a more recent immigration history or because they continue to experience serious economic disadvantages, these groups remain more dependent on the family for the care of the elderly.

## Financing Long-Term Care

In the US one group is covered by a universal health-care financing system. Citizens over the age of 65 qualify for Medicare, a program that pays for hospitalization and many physician services. Although the program is universal, it is not completely free and requires that an older individual pay substantial premiums, co-payments, and deductibles. These can be quite onerous to an older individual on a fixed income. As citizenship entitlement, Medicare is not means-tested and is open to anyone receiving Social Security or other Federal cash assistance. Except for some short-term post-acute care, though, it does not cover the cost of nursing home or other long-term care. This fact leaves a serious gap in the overall health care safety net for the elderly that can adversely affect a family's long-term financial situation (Marmor, 1994).

In the US long-term care is the responsibility of the individual and his or her family. For those who cannot afford to pay for long-term care the cost is covered by Medicaid, the health care program for the poor. Unlike Medicare, though, Medicaid

**Table 14.2** Proportion of the older population living alone in selected nations, 1980–1994 (%)

| | |
|---|---|
| *Latin America* | |
| Argentina | 7 |
| Brazil | 20 |
| Chile | 8 |
| Mexico | 7 |
| *Western Europe* | |
| Belgium | 85 |
| France | 86 |
| Great Britain | 87 |
| Italy | 66 |
| Luxembourg | 73 |
| N. Ireland | 68 |
| Netherlands | 87 |
| W. Germany | 77 |
| *North America* | |
| USA | |
| White | 70 |
| Non-white | 49 |
| *Nordic countries* | |
| Denmark | 92 |
| Finland | 70 |
| *Asia* | |
| Japan | 35 |
| Taiwan | 23 |
| Thailand | 8 |

*Source*: Palloni (2000).

is means-tested, and requires that an individual have little income and few assets in order to qualify for long-term care. Although many older individuals qualify on the basis of little income and few assets initially, others with more assets are often forced to impoverish themselves before Medicaid takes over. Between 14 and 35 percent of older persons admitted to nursing homes as private pay patients eventually "spend down," a term that refers to the process whereby older persons deplete their assets to a level at which they qualify for Medicaid (Short et al., 1992). Among those who enter nursing homes as private pay patients, nearly 70 percent reach the poverty level after three months and 90 percent do so within one year. Since the income and asset limits apply to couples as well as individuals, a spouse whose partner must enter a nursing home can be left with very little to live on.

Although insurance coverage for long-term care is becoming more common and is offered as an employment benefit by some employers, relatively few individuals own such plans (Wiener, Illston, and Hanley, 1994). As a result, older individuals are at high risk of impoverishment in the event of a protracted illness that results in incapacity. The estimated average nursing home cost in the US is close to $50,000 per year (Health Insurance Association of America, 2000). Such expenditures can deplete even a substantial middle-class estate fairly quickly. The lack of long-term care insurance places the entire family at risk of loss. When a parent's assets must be used for long-term care, his or her estate cannot be passed on to children for the education of future generations or for the improvement of their lives. These families often find themselves with care giving responsibilities, even when an older parent finally qualifies for Medicaid.

## Barriers to Health Insurance for Families in the US

For nearly two-thirds of families in the US, employer-financed insurance is the dominant source of health care coverage (US Census Bureau, 2000c). After World War II, benefits such as health insurance and generous retirement plans have come to define what are considered good jobs. Large companies, the Federal and state governments, and public and private educational institutions offer generous retirement plans and health insurance to their employees. Small firms often do not (US Census Bureau, 2000c). As a result, nearly 16 percent of the population has no health insurance (ibid.).

Many families in the US face both financial and non-financial barriers to obtaining health insurance. These include factors that limit access to private or employer-based insurance including high costs, family structure, and employment in jobs that do not offer health insurance or only do so at a prohibitive cost to the employee. They also include factors that limit access to public insurance, including complicated application and renewal procedures, asset tests, and inadequate outreach efforts by agencies charged with administering health-related programs.

Certain groups face particularly serious financial barriers. In the US, the Mexican-origin population is seriously underinsured. Almost one-third of Mexican American women and nearly half of Mexican American men have no health insurance, and approximately one out of every three Hispanic children is uninsured (Cornelius, 1993; Santos and Seitz, 2000). This lack of insurance represents a clear health-risk factor for vulnerable individuals (Angel and Angel, 1996b). If health-care coverage remains elusive for native Mexican Americans, foreign-born Mexican origin individuals face even greater barriers to adequate health care coverage.

Other groups also face unique hurdles to health care coverage. In the US, with its focus on means-tested care for the poor, health insurance is often less available to two-parent families than it is to single-parent families. A poor single mother can frequently obtain Medicaid coverage for herself during pregnancy and for her children thereafter. Many two-parent families, though, are members of the working poor, and few jobs in the service sector, in which most recent employment growth has occurred, offer health insurance. Even when both parents work, such jobs can leave a family without enough money to purchase health insurance, and when they are available, many employer-sponsored policies cover only the employee and require substantial premiums to cover other family members. For a poor family struggling to make ends meet, the added expense can easily be prohibitive. Consequently, many families who have the option of employer-based health insurance often forgo it.

The lack of health insurance coverage places adequate medical care out of reach for many poor families in the US (O'Brien and Feder, 1998). Children in families that do not have employer-sponsored health insurance or Medicaid are less likely to have a usual source of care than children in families that are covered. On average, these children see the doctor less often for acute illnesses, and they are less likely to use prescription drugs than are children with insurance coverage. Although inequities in access to medical care between the rich and poor have been decreased by Medicaid, poor children are still far less likely to receive dental care than children in more affluent families.

Uninsured children are less likely than insured children to be treated for conditions such as asthma and ear infections that can lead to more serious health problems (Hoffman and Scholobohm, 2000). Uninsured children are also more likely than those with health coverage to be hospitalized for preventable illnesses and their consequences. Because they are less likely to have a regular source of care, uninsured children are more likely than insured children to receive care in emergency rooms, community and migrant health centers, and other publicly funded health facilities (Hernández and Charney, 1998). The lack of a usual source of care places these children at a high risk of undetected symptoms (Families USA, 1997). Routine care received in emergency rooms is excessively expensive and may be of lower quality than that received from a physician familiar with a child's overall health.

The health-care sector has experienced some of the most rapid inflation in costs in the economy, and employers have little choice but to pass along increases in the cost of health care to their employees. Employees are consequently forced to pay a larger share of their health insurance premium. Between 1988 and 1996 premiums for family coverage rose by 9.8 percent per year, while overall inflation increased by only 4 percent per year (O'Brien and Feder, 1998). As a result, many employees have stopped participating in employer-sponsored health insurance plans, and those who have kept their coverage are paying more for it.

At the same time that access to health insurance has increased for higher-income employees, those earning more than $15 an hour, it has decreased for workers who earn less than $7 an hour. Between 1987 and 1996, the proportion of high-paid workers with health insurance rose from 92 percent to 96 percent, while the proportion of lower-paid workers with insurance dropped from 60 to 55 percent (Kenny, Dubay, and Haley, 2000). The self-employed are also less likely than those who work for large companies or the government to have health insurance. Low-wage workers, a group commonly referred to as the working poor, present a particularly serious challenge to our system of health-care financing. The unemployed and the impoverished often have access to Medicaid, but those families with incomes too high to qualify for Medicaid often find themselves in a health-care limbo in which they earn too much for public means-based coverage, but too little to afford private or employer-sponsored plans. Since the Balanced Budget Act of 1997, states were allowed to expand financing of health insurance to low-income children under Title XXI of the Social Security Act (Health Care Financing Administration, 2000).

In the US the Federal government sets basic guidelines for the administration of most public programs, but US political culture is one that values states' rights. States, consequently, retain a great deal of autonomy in establishing eligibility criteria and coverage levels for programs like Medicaid, which is jointly funded by the Federal government and the state. The inevitable consequence of maximizing states' discretion in setting such criteria is great variation in who is covered, and to what level. Massachusetts has extended its Medicaid program for children well beyond what is required by Federal law and, consequently, that state covers nearly all eligible children. Texas, on the other hand, offers little beyond what is Federally mandated. As a consequence, the number of uninsured children in Texas is among the highest in the nation (Angel et al., 2001).

States differ not only in the extent and amount of coverage they offer. They also have different application procedures. Many states have traditionally had extremely long application and renewal forms, as well as stringent asset- and income-verification requirements for Medicaid and other social welfare programs. Applicants must provide documentation of income, both present and past, child-care costs, child support payments, and immigration status. They are usually required to present a child's birth certificate or school records and provide proof of residence and the names of everyone living in the household. They often must also provide an employment history, and if applicable, proof of any other insurance.

Federal Medicaid eligibility rules require that families have very few assets, which means that they can own very little in terms of cash, a home, or a car. A family cannot have an excess of $2,000 in assets, including money in the bank, savings, land, automobiles, and pension benefits, as well as other assets (exempted from this is a family home and one automobile). Although such information is clearly necessary to establish eligibility, this process is time-consuming and onerous. Often the applicant does not have the necessary information and must return to the welfare office several times. In addition to being onerous, though, the process is stigmatizing and demeaning. Often the application for Medicaid must be made at the same office at which one applies for cash assistance. In such a context, Medicaid is just another component of the welfare package that labels a family as dependent. Some families may be discouraged from applying because of a desire to avoid the stigma.

The drop in the Medicaid rolls during the second half of the 1990s was not an intended consequence of any policy action (Angel et al., 2001). In fact, the Federal government has attempted to increase eligible children's and families' participation in Medicaid. In order to insure maximum coverage, the major welfare reform legislation passed in 1996 specifically severed the tie between cash assistance and Medicaid, which means that eligibility for Medicaid does not depend on the receipt of cash assistance. Yet the Medicaid rolls continued to drop until 1999 (Pear, 2000). It appears that large numbers of families with eligible children do not know they qualify for Medicaid. In the absence of effective outreach efforts to inform families that they qualify for Medicaid, many remain uninformed. Many former recipients of cash assistance do not know that they are eligible for six months of transitional coverage, regardless of income, after they leave the welfare.

Those families that leave welfare are more likely than those who remain on Temporary Aid to Needy Families (TANF) to have unmet medical care needs. Recent analyses by the Urban Institute suggest that families leaving welfare may be "unintentionally and inappropriately" dropped from the Medicaid program (Garrett and Holahan, 2000). Federal law requires states to provide up to at least six months of Medicaid coverage when families leave welfare. States have the option of providing an additional six months of Medicaid for a total of twelve months of transitional coverage. The data show, though, that after leaving the welfare rolls, Medicaid coverage drops and is not compensated for by other forms of insurance (Garrett and Holahan, 2000; Moffit and Slade, 1997).

## Summary

The international economic crisis, large imbalances in economic growth between North and South, and large-scale international migration have led to the increasing globalization of social and health problems. These threaten economic growth and political stability in large parts of the world, and raise the possibility of the rapid transmission of disease around the globe (Murray, 1996). Within nations, differences among groups based on race, ethnicity, and citizenship are associated with inequities in access to basic social services and health care. The research on family and health that we have reviewed here makes it clear that, as yet, we do not fully understand how families cope with the illness of their members in different cultural, social, and political contexts. Nor do we know how much of a buffer the family represents in protecting its members, and especially its youngest members, from the health consequences of negative life events. Research on the family must identify the major threats to its role in protecting health and explore ways of enhancing its health protecting capacities.

In this chapter we have identified some of the major threats to the family and health in the world today. It is clear that social, economic, and political instability are among the major health threats that both adults and children face. Yet the family can play a protective role. Many immigrant groups enjoy very favorable morbidity and mortality experiences in their host countries. It appears that various aspects of their native culture and family support systems protect health even in the new environment (Angel and Angel, 1993; Bagley et al., 1995; Munroe-Blum et al., 1989). At the same time that we attempt to understand the health-risk factors faced by immigrants, it would benefit us all to identify those family factors that migrants carry with them that are health preserving. Such an understanding might help us to identify those aspects of community that we have lost that we might usefully attempt to resurrect.

At the same time that the developed nations must find ways to incorporate immigrants, large numbers of displaced families and children present the governments and health-care delivery systems of many developing nations with unique challenges that they are often ill prepared to address. In our increasingly globalized world, the health problems of these populations can quickly become international. The diversity of migrant populations and the racial and ethnic differences within nations compels us to increase our store of knowledge of how those differences affect health and access to health care. The great diversity in cultural beliefs and practices among migrant populations, differences in their motivations for migration, and the migration experience itself result in great diversity in the need for mental and physical health care. Children who migrate from developing nations to the developed world often arrive developmentally delayed, with inadequate immunization, and suffering from various infectious diseases. Many of those children may have spent some time as refugees and many have experienced severe trauma as the result of social and political turmoil. Researchers, policymakers, and advocates for the family must begin to understand the health consequences of early life events and family trauma in order that they may minimize their impacts. It is also important to understand the operation of barriers to health care, such as poverty, family structure, and lack of health insurance.

In the twenty-first century the care of the elderly presents the family and the state with unique challenges. Families will find it increasingly difficult to care for parents who are living longer and who have more serious health problems, at the same time that they provide for children and negotiate the labor market. The health consequences of the care-giving burden on the quality of lives of family members are potentially enormous, especially for those without extensive social networks. With the steady increase in both the number and proportion of minority elderly persons with disabilities in the US, and the soaring costs to both the government and to family caregivers, understanding the role of culture in health and care giving becomes essential.

Perhaps we can best sum up by noting that in the modern world all nations are faced with providing health care to individuals with different risk profiles than were typical of more settled times (Esping-Andersen, 1999). As the family finds itself less able to provide care directly, and where market solutions are not realistic alternatives, the state becomes the insurer of last resort. The poor, the disabled, the infirm elderly, and single-parent households are among the groups for whom the market fails (Stone, 2000). For them the paternalistic state is the only option. Each nation develops its own solutions for financing and distributing health care and other services based on its unique history and political culture. Yet everywhere the shift in responsibility to the state has resulted in rapidly increasing costs for social welfare, at the same time that traditional approaches to providing it have become increasingly obsolete (Esping-Andersen, 1999). The challenge for the world as a whole will be to provide health care and other services to ever larger populations of needy individuals in ways that optimize individual choices while taking advantage of the family's ability to protect the health of its members.

## References

Angel, J., and Angel, R. (1998) Caring for our elders: Latino America struggles with change. *Hispanic*, September, 18–26.

Angel, J. L. (1991) *Health and Living Arrangements of the Elderly*. New York: Garland.

Angel, J. L., Angel, R. J., and Markides, K. S. (2000) Late-life immigration, changes in living arrangements, and headship status among older Mexican-origin individuals. *Social Science Quarterly*, 81, 389–403.

Angel, J. L., Angel, R. J., McClellan, J. L., and Markides, K. S. (1996) Nativity, declining health, and preferences in living arrangements among elderly Mexican Americans: implications for long-term care. *The Gerontologist*, 36, 464–73.

Angel, R., Lein, L., Henrici, J., and Leventhal, E. (2001) *Health Care Coverage for Children and their Caregivers in Low-Income Urban Neighborhoods*. Policy Brief 01–02, Welfare Children & Families: A Three City Study, Baltimore, MD: Johns Hopkins University Press.

Angel, R. J., and Angel, J. L. (1996a) Physical co-morbidity and medical care use among children with emotional problems. *Public Health Reports*, 3, 140–5.

Angel, R. J., and Angel, J. L. (1996b) The extent of private and public health insurance coverage among adult Hispanics. *The Gerontologist*, 36, 332–40.

Angel, R. J., and Angel, J. L. (1997) *Who Will Care for Us? Aging and Long-term Care in Multicultural America*. New York: New York University Press.

Angel, R. J., Angel, J. L., Lee, G. Y., and Markides, K. S. (1999) Age at migration and family dependency among older Mexican immigrants: Recent evidence from the Mexican American EPESE. *The Gerontologist*, 39, 59–65.

Angel, R. J., and Worobey, J. L. (1988) Single motherhood and children's health. *Journal of Health and Social Behavior*, 29, 38–52.

Bagley, S. P., Angel, R., Dilworth-Anderson, P., Liu, W. and Schinke, S. (1995) Adaptive health behaviors among ethnic minorities. *Health Psychology*, 14, 632–40.

Becerra, R. M. (1988) The Mexican American family. In C. H. Mindel, R. W. Habenstein, and J. R. Wright (eds.), *Ethnic Families in America: Patterns and Variations*. New York: Elsevier.

Bryson, K., and Casper, L. M. (1999) Coresident grandparents and grandchildren. *Current Population Reports,* P23–198, 1–10.

Bumpass, L., and McLanahan, S. (1989) Unmarried motherhood: recent trends, composition, and black-white differences. *Demography,* 26, 279–86.

Campbell, J. C., and Ikegami, N. (2000) Long-term care insurance comes to Japan. *Health Affairs* 19, 26–39.

Cohen, R. (2000) Illegal migration rises sharply in European Union. *New York Times* Monday, December 25, A1.

Cornelius, L. J. (1993) Barriers to medical care for White, Black, and Hispanic American children. *Journal of the National Medical Association,* 85, 281–8.

Crystal, S. (1982) *America's Old Age Crisis*. New York: Basic Books.

Dawson, D. A. (1991) Family structure and children's health and well-being: Data from the 1988 National Health Interview Survey on Child Health. *Journal of Marriage and the Family,* 53, 573–84.

Desjarlais, R., Eisenberg, L., Good, B., and Kleinman, A. (1995) *World Mental Health: Problems and Priorities in Low-Income Countries*. New York: Oxford University Press.

Esping-Andersen, G. (1990) *The Three Worlds of Welfare Capitalism*. Princeton, NJ: Princeton University Press.

Esping-Andersen, G. (ed.) (1996) *Welfare States in Transition: National Adaptations in Global Economies*. Thousand Oaks, CA: Sage.

Esping-Andersen, G. (1999) *Social Foundations of Postindustrial Economies*. Oxford: Oxford University Press.

Espino, D. A., Neufeld, R. R., Mulvihill, M., and Libow, L. S. (1988) Hispanic and non-Hispanic elderly on admission to the nursing home: a pilot study. *The Gerontologist,* 28, 821–4.

Families USA (1997) *Unmet Needs: The Large Differences in Health Care Between Uninsured and Insured Children*. Available online at: http://www.familiesusa.org/media/reports/unmet.htm, last accessed June 6, 2002.

Fix, M. E., and Tumlin, K. (1997) *Welfare Reform and the Deevolution of Immigrant Policy*. Washington, DC: Urban Institute.

Fox, D. M. and Kassalow, J. S. (2001) Making health a priority of US foreign policy. *American Journal of Public Health,* 91, 1554–6.

Frenk, J., Bobadilla, J. L., and Lozano, R. (1996) The epidemiological transition in Latin America. In I. Timaeus, J. Chackiel, and L. Ruzicka (eds.), *Adult Mortality in Latin America*. New York: Oxford University Press.

Garrett, B., and Holahan, J. (2000) *Welfare Leavers, Medicaid Coverage, and Private Health Insurance*. Washington, DC: Urban Institute.

Goldscheider, F. K., and Goldscheider, C. (1989) The new family economy: residential and economic relationships among the generations. In F. K. Goldscheider and C. Goldscheider (eds.), *Ethnicity and the New Family Economy: Living Arrangements and Intergenerational Financial Flows*. Boulder, CO: Westview Press.

Guyer, B., Hoyert, D. L., Martin, J. A., Ventura, S. J., MacDorman, M. F., and Strobino, D. M. (1999) Annual summary of vital statistics: 1998. *Pediatrics*, 104, 1229–46.

Gwatkin, D. R. (2000) Health inequalities and the health of the poor: What do we know? What can we do? *Bulletin of the World Health Organization,* 2000, 78, 3–18.

Haggerty, R. J., Roghmann, K. J., and Pless, I. B. (1975) *Child Health and the Community*. New York: Free Press.

Health Care Financing Administration (2000) *The State Children's Health Insurance Program: Preliminary Highlights of Implementation and Expansion*. Washington, DC: US Department of Health and Human Services.

Health Insurance Association of America (2000) *Guide to Long-Term Healthcare*. Available online at: http://www.hiaa.org/cons/guideltc.html, last accessed February 22, 2001.

Hernández, D. J., and Charney, E. (eds.) (1998) *From Generation to Generation: The Health and Well-Being of Children in Immigrant Families.* Washington, DC: National Academy Press.

Hoffman, C., and Scholobohm, A. (2000) *Uninsured in America: A Chart Book* Washington, DC: Kaiser Commission on Medicaid and the Uninsured.

Holahan, J., and Kim, J. (2000) Why does the number of uninsured Americans continue to grow? *Health Affairs,* 19, 188–96.

Holstein, B. E., Almind, G., Due, P., and Holst, E. (1991) The Home-Help service in Denmark. In A. Jamieson (ed.), *Home Care for Older People in Europe: A Comparison of Policies and Practices.* Oxford: Oxford University Press.

Iacopino, V., Frank, M. W., Bauer, H. M., Keller, A. S., Fink, S. L., Ford, D., Pallin, D. J., and Waldman, R. (2001) A population-based assessment of human rights abuses committed against ethnic Albanian refugees from Kosovo. *American Journal of Public Health*, 91, 2013–18.

Kammerman, S. G. (1984) Women, children, and poverty: public policies and female-headed families in industrialized countries. *Signs: Journal of Women in Culture and Society*, 10, 249–71.

Kenny, G., Dubay, L., and Haley, J. (2000) Health Insurance, Access, and Health Status of Children, Findings from the National Survey of America's Families. Washington, DC: Urban Institute. Available online at http://newfederalism.urban.org/nsaf/child-health.html, last accessed March 22, 2003.

Kleinman, A. (1986) *The Social Origins of Distress and Disease.* New Haven, CT: Yale University Press.

Koh, J. Y., and Bell, W. G. (1987) Korean elders in the United States: Intergenerational relations and living arrangements. *The Gerontologist,* 27, 66–71.

Kossoudji, S. (1989) Immigrant worker assimilation: is it a labor market phenomenon? *Journal of Human Resources,* 24, 494–527.

Kumin, J. (1999) An uncertain direction. *Refugees Magazine, Europe: The Debate over Asylum* Issue 113. Available online at: http://www.unhcr.ch/pubs/rm113/rm11302.htm, last accessed February 22, 2001.

Lee, G.-Y., and Angel, R. J. (2002) Living arrangements and supplemental security income use among elderly Asians and Hispanics in the United States: The role of nativity and citizenship. *Journal of Ethnic and Migration Studies*, 28, 553–63.

Markides, K. S., Martin, H. W., and Gomez, E. (1983) *Older Mexican Americans: A Study in an Urban Barrio.* Austin: University of Texas Press.

Marmor, T. R. (1994) *Understanding Health Care Reform.* New Haven, CT: Yale University Press.

McGauhey, P. J., and Starfield, B. (1993) Child health and the social environment of white and black children. *Social Science and Medicine,* 36, 867–74.

McLanahan, S., and Sandefur, G. (1994) *Growing Up with a Single Parent: What Helps? What Hurts?* Cambridge, MA: Harvard University Press.

McLeod, J. D., and Shanahan, M. J. (1993) Poverty, parenting, and children's mental health. *American Sociological Review,* 58, 351–66.

Moffitt, R. A., and Slade, E. (1997) Health care coverage for children on and off welfare. *The Future of Children,* 7, 87–98.

Montgomery, L. E., Kiely, J. L., and Pappas, G. (1996) The effects of poverty, race, and family structure on US children's health: Data from the NHIS, 1978 through 1980 and 1989 through 1991. *American Journal of Public Health,* 86, 1401–5.

Munroe-Blum, H., Boyle, M. H., Offord, D. R., and Kates, N. (1989) Immigrant children: psychiatric disorder, school performance, and service utilization. *American Journal of Orthopsychiatry*, 59, 510–19.

Murray, C. J. L. (1996) Rethinking DALYs. In C. J. L. Murray and A. D. Lopez (eds.), *The Global Burden of Disease.* Cambridge, MA: Harvard University Press.

Mutchler, J. E. and Angel, J. L. (2000) Policy development and the older Latino population in the 21st century. *Journal of Aging and Social Policy,* 11, 177–88.

Myles, J. (1984) *Old Age in the Welfare State: The Political Economy of Public Pensions.* Boston, MA: Little, Brown.

National Research Council (1995) Immigrant children and their families: issues for research and policy. *Critical Issues for Children and Youths,* 5, 72–89.

Newacheck, P. W., Hughes, D. C., and Stoddard, J. J. (1996) Children's access to primary care: differences by race, income, and insurance status. *Pediatrics* 97, 26–32.

O'Brien, E., and Feder, J. (1998) *How Well Does the Employment-Based Health Insurance System Work for Low-Income Families?* Washington, DC: Kaiser Family Foundation.

Organisation for Economic Cooperation and Development (1996) *Caring for Frail Elderly People.* Social Policy Studies No. 19, Paris:OECD.

Palloni, A. (2000) Programmatic and Policy Aspects of Population Ageing and Living Arrangements. Paper presented at Technical Meeting on Population Ageing and Living Arrangements of Older Persons: Critical Issues and Policy Responses, United Nations, Population Division, New York.

Pappas, G., Queen, S., Hadden, W., and Fisher, G. (1993) The increasing disparity in mortality between socioeconomic groups in the United States, 1960 and 1986. *New England Journal of Medicine,* 329, 103–9.

Pear, R. (2000) Number of insured Americans up for first time since '87. *New York Times,* Vol. CL, No. 51,526, September 29, A15.

Peterson, P. G. (1999) Gray dawn: the global aging crisis. *Foreign Affairs*, January/February, 42–55.

Popenoe, D. (1988) *Disturbing the Nest: Family Change and Decline in Modern Societies.* New York: Aldine de Gruyter.

Popenoe, D., Elshtain, J. B., and Blankenhorn, B. (eds.) (1996) *Promises to Keep: Decline and Renewal of Marriage in America.* Lanham, MD: Rowman & Littlefield.

Rengelink-van Der Lee, J. H., Schulpen, T. W., and Beemer, F. A. (1995) Incidence and prevalence of hemoglobinopathies in children in the Netherlands (in Dutch). *Nederlands Tijdschrift voor Geneeskunde*, 139, 1498–1501.

Sam, D. L., and Berry J. W. (1995) Acculturative stress among young immigrants in Norway. *Scandinavian Journal of Psychology,* 36, 10–24.

Santos, R., and Seitz, P. (2000) Benefit coverage for Latino and Latina workers. In S. M. Perez (ed.), *Moving up the Economic Ladder: Latino Workers and the Nation's Future Prosperity.* Washington, DC: National Council of La Raza.

Schulpen, T. W. (1996) Migration and child health: the Dutch experience. *European Journal of Pediatrics,* 155, 351–6.

Short, P. F., Kemper, P., Cornelius, L. J., and Walden, D.C. (1992) Public and private responsibility for financing nursing home care: The effect of Medicaid asset spend-down. *Milbank Quarterly,* 70, 277–98.

Soldo, B., and Wong, R. (2000) Strategic Family Decisions and Remittances: Migration and Aging in Mexico. Paper presented at the annual meeting of the Gerontological Society of America, Washington, DC.

Spillman, B. C., and Pezzin, L. E. (2000) Potential and active family caregivers: changing networks and the "sandwich generation." *Milbank Quarterly,* 78, 347–74.

Stone, D. A. (2000) Reconsidering the role of competition in health care markets: United States. *Journal of Health Politics,* 25, 953–8.

Toole, M. J., and Waldman, R. J. (1993) Refugees and displaced persons: War, hunger, and public health. *Journal of the American Medical Association,* 270, 600–5.

United Nations High Commission for Refugees (1997) *The State of the World's Refugees: A Humanitarian Agenda.* Available online at: http://www.unhcr.ch/refworld/pub/state/97/intro.htm, last accessed December 30, 2000.

United Nations High Commissioner for Refugees (2002) *World Refugee Overview*. Geneva: UNHCR.

US Census Bureau (2000a) Children under 18 years old by presence of parents: 1980–1998. *Statistical Abstract of the United States*, Table 69, p. 58. Washington, DC: US Government Printing Office.

US Census Bureau. (2000b) Grandchildren living in the home of their grandparents: 1980–1998. *Statistical Abstract of the United States*, Table 71, p. 60. Washington, DC: US Government Printing Office.

US Census Bureau (2000c) Health Insurance Detailed Table: 1999. *Current Population Survey*, March 1999 and 2000. Washington, DC: US Government Printing Office. Available online at: http://www.census.gov/hhes/hlthins/hlthin99/dtable1.html, last accessed February 22, 2001.

US Census Bureau (2000d) Civilian labor force and participation rates with projections: 1970 to 2008. *Statistical Abstracts of the United States*, Section 13, Table 644. Washington, DC: US Government Printing Office. Available online at http://www.census.gov/prod/2001pubs/statab/sec13.pdf, last accessed March 22, 2003.

US General Accounting Office (2001) *Internally Displaced Persons Lack Effective Protection*. GAO-01-803. Washington, DC: US Government Printing Office.

Wallerstein, J. S. (1991) The long-term effects of divorce on children: A review. *Journal of the Academy of Child and Adolescent Psychiatry,* 30, 349-60.

Ward, P.M. (1999) *Colonias and Public Policy in Texas and Mexico: Urbanization by Stealth*. Austin,: University of Texas Press.

Weir, M., Orloff, A. S., and Skocpol, T. (1988) *The Politics of Social Policy in the United States*. Princeton, NJ: Princeton University Press.

Wiener, J. M., Illston, L. H., and Hanley, R. J. (1994) *Sharing the Burden: Strategies for Public and Private Long-term Care Insurance*. Washington, DC: Brookings Institution.

Williams, E. J. (1996) The Maquiladora industry and environmental degradation in the United States–Mexican borderlands. *St. Mary's Law Journal*, 27, 765–815.

Wilmoth, J. M. (2001) Living arrangements among older immigrants in the United States. *The Gerontologist,* 41, 223–8.

Wilmoth, J. M., DeJong, G. F., and Himes, C. L. (1997) Immigrant and non-immigrant living arrangements among America's white, Hispanic, and Asian elderly population. *Journal of Sociology and Social Policy,* 17, 57–82.

Wolf, D. A. (2001) Everything is Relatives: Individual, Familial, and Collective Roles in Elder Care. Paper presented at the Policy Roundtable *Aging in the Americas: Critical Social Policy Issues*. Austin: University of Texas at Austin.

Worobey, J. L., Angel, R. J., and Worobey, J. (1988) Family structure and young children's use of medical care. *Topics In Early Childhood Special Education,* 8, 30–40.

Worobey, J. L., and Angel, R. J. (1990) Functional capacity and living arrangements of unmarried elderly persons. *Journal of Gerontology,* 45, 95–101.

Zabina, H., Schmid, T. L., Glasunov, I., Potemkina, R., Kamardina, T., Deev, A., Konstantinova, S., and Popovich, M. (2001) Monitoring behavioral risk factors for cardiovascular disease in Russia. *American Journal of Public Health*, 91, 1613–14.

Zill, N., Morrison, D., and Coiro, M. J. (1993) Long-term effects of parental divorce on parent child relationships, adjustment and achievement in young adulthood. *Journal of Family Psychology,* 7, 91–103.

# 15

# Immigrant Families in the US

Karen Pyke

The stream of immigrants to the US since 1965 has contributed to a second great wave of immigration that continues today. Over 28 million foreign-born individuals currently reside in the country (Lollock, 2001). Never before has the US received immigrants from as wide an array of countries and from such differing social, economic, and cultural backgrounds as it does today. And never before have most of the arrivals been from non-European nations (Reimers, 1996).

The new immigration is challenging the racial and cultural hegemony of white, native-born Americans. White Americans now constitute a numeric minority in California, the gateway of the new immigration, and similar patterns will follow in other key immigrant states in the near future (Maharidge, 1996; Nelson and O'Reilly, 2000). Streams of immigrants are also transforming minority America with Latino Americans soon to replace African Americans as the leading racial minority (Zinn and Eitzen, 1996). The study of immigrant families is thus not a marginal concern, but at the very core of our understanding of the demographic and sociocultural dynamics of US society.

This chapter provides an overview of the research on today's immigrant families in the US. It begins with a look at their social diversity and follows with a discussion of the many different forms that immigrant families take, presenting challenges to popular assumptions of a unitary structure. As old theories of immigrant adaptation derived from the first wave of European immigrants have little applicability to today's immigrant families, this chapter also discusses the new approaches emerging in the field. Because gender dynamics in families affect patterns of migration and are also altered by conditions of immigration, this chapter summarizes the large literature on this topic. While most of the immigration literature focuses on the parental generation, scholars have recently begun to study the children of today's immigrants – the new second generation. Increasing attention is also being paid to family members at the end of the life course, including those who immigrated in late life as well as those who arrived earlier and are now growing old in America. This chapter describes these new areas of research and concludes with a discussion of the gaps in the current literature on immigrant families in the US.

## The Social Diversity of Today's Immigrant Families

Recent decades have witnessed a dramatic shift in the racial composition of immigrants with people of color from Asia, Latin America, and the Caribbean dominating the stream. As recently as the 1950s two-thirds of immigrants to the US came from Europe and Canada. This trend reversed in the 1960s and by the early 1980s, only 11 percent of immigrants to the US hailed from Europe (Mangiafico, 1988; Portes and Zhou, 1993). In 2000, 51 percent of the foreign-born population in the US had arrived from Latin America, 26 percent from Asia, and 15 percent from Europe (Lollock, 2001). Similar trends mark immigration in Canada (Badets and Chui, 1994).

The new immigration has spawned new ethnic groups in the US, including Korean Americans, Hmong Americans, and Vietnamese Americans. New immigrant groups, who do not have the benefit of longstanding ethnic enclaves with firmly established social networks to assist in successful adaptation, must create from scratch the meaning of their ethnicity. Unlike their European predecessors who were gradually incorporated into the stew of white ethnicities, today's immigrant families, most of whom come from countries where they were members of the racial/ethnic majority, must contend for the first time with a racial minority status and the forces of racism. The legal status of immigrants in the US also impacts their ability to adjust. Those who arrive without documents, mostly from Mexico and Central America, are restricted to the most menial types of low wage labor with few opportunities for upward mobility. Their lack of legal access to government supports and protections undermines their health and safety, and makes them easy prey for exploitation. The constant fear of detection and deportation limits their range of movement as they are forced to hide in the shadows (Chavez, 1991).

While earlier waves of immigrants from Europe were mostly manual laborers, there is greater diversity in the skill and educational levels among today's immigrants to North America, which includes manual laborers, the entrepreneurial middle class, and highly educated professionals (the latter arriving particularly from China, India, and the Philippines; Portes and Rumbaut, 1996). While some professionals are able to apply their skills in the new economy, (as is the case with immigrants from India and the Philippines who typically arrive knowing English) others find their credentials and work histories are not recognized by North American employers, thus relegating them to the low-pay service sector and prompting high rates of self-employment in small family-run businesses, most notably among Korean immigrants (Portes and Rumbaut, 1996). Earlier waves of immigrants to the US from Europe were able to find jobs in an expanding manufacturing economy that needed the unskilled labor they could provide. Today's lower skilled immigrants, on the other hand, find an economy reeling from global restructuring, the rapid decline of manufacturing jobs, and a growing gap in the wages and benefits of the professional class and the lower-skilled working class, where immigrants are disproportionately located (Portes and Zhou, 1993). This raises concern that the upward mobility enjoyed previously by children of European immigrants will not be replicated among today's children of immigrants in the US (Gans, 1992).

Despite their immense cultural and economic diversity, immigrant families to the US tend to share strong norms of familism (Fuligni, Tseng, and Lam, 1999) that contrast with the emphasis on individualism that has been a historically defining characteristic of American society (Bellah et al., 1985). Familism (also known as "collectivism") refers to a strong commitment and obligation to family over that of the individual, and is evident by high levels of contact, instrumental exchange, and geographic propinquity (Zinn and Wells, 2000). As a result family ties and one's role within the family shapes individual identity and destiny. Individualism, on the other hand, refers to an emphasis on individual needs and interests over that of the family group. It is marked by norms of independence, self-sufficiency, looser family ties, personal well-being, and the optional association of family members. The contrasting systems of familism and individualism structure other family dynamics as well. For example, familism tends to be associated with firm hierarchal family arrangements that require the devotion of women and children to men and elders. Individualism, on the other hand, has been associated with greater equality for women and children. So, despite their cultural diversity, immigrants to the US tend to share a collectivist family ideology that is in sharp contrast with the values and practices associated with mainstream US culture. The conflicting cultural systems of familism and individualism has been a dominant theme in scholarly attempts to explain immigrant experiences and adaptation outcomes (Zhou and Bankston, 1998).

## The Structural Diversity of Today's Immigrant Families

The popular image of the immigrant family in the US is a two- or three-generation unit held together by impenetrable bonds. In contrast, the families of native-born Americans are commonly regarded as diverse and even broken. This imagery distorts the wide-ranging diversity of immigrant families. Many families do immigrate as intact units and more do so today than in earlier waves of migration (Rumbaut, 1997b) but family patterns are often diverse and dynamic in sending societies, thus promoting a diversity of family structures among immigrants (Foner, 1997). Additionally, several other factors foster diversity in immigrant family structures and households, including the demographics of immigration, the criteria for admission, and conditions in both the home and host countries. For example, the prevalence of female-headed families in the Caribbean has contributed to an influx from those countries of female-headed families to the US (Waters, 1997), as well as to Britain where 50 percent of Caribbean mothers under age 35 are unwed (see Shaw, chapter 16, this volume). Similarly, political refugees arriving in the US from Indochina in the post-Vietnam era included high numbers of female-headed families who lost men to war and political prisons.

Economic conditions and processes of migration can generate entirely new family forms. Transnational families are created when one family member is sent ahead for the purpose of finding employment and housing to support the eventual arrival of other family members (known as "chain" or "family-stage migration"), or to earn income to be remitted to the family left behind (Boyd, 1989). This is a common and longstanding pattern among undocumented immigrants from Mexico and Central America, and those who arrive from Puerto Rico, the Dominican Republic, and elsewhere in the Caribbean (Chavez, 1991; Grasmuck and Pessar, 1991; Hondagneu-Sotelo, 1994; Toro-Morn, 1995). More recently, higher numbers of mothers, both single and married, have joined the flows arriving from the Caribbean, Mexico, and Central America, having left their children behind in the care of female kin or husbands. Transnational mothering has been attributed to the demand in the US for the low-cost labor of immigrant women, the need for women's higher earnings at home, difficulties in balancing work and child-care in a new country, concern about juvenile delinquency in the US, and a longstanding or newly evolving cultural acceptance of child fostering in the homeland (Hondagneu-Sotelo and Avila, 1997; Waters, 1997).

Not only do mothers immigrate without children but children also arrive without parents. These "parachute" children, who come in pursuit of educational opportunities not available in the homeland, constitute another form of transnational family, little studied by scholars but noted by school officials and journalists. Wealthy and professional parents in countries like Taiwan, Hong Kong, Korea, India, and the Philippines create satellite homes in the US for their children, aged 8–17, while they continue to work and reside in the homeland between visits to see their children (Zhou, 1998). Parachute children live on their own, or in the care of relatives, host families, servants, or older siblings and without day-to-day supervision or contact with parents. It is difficult to know how many parachute children reside in the US, but estimates suggest that 40,000 arrived in the 1980s from Taiwan alone, the largest origin of such children (Hamilton, 1993).

The condition of migration lead some immigrants to redefine the meaning of family to include groups previously excluded. For example, Vietnamese refugees who suffered a loss of kin from war and migration reconstructed the extended family structure of Vietnamese culture by redefining boundaries to include close friends, distant kin, kin by marriage, and kin of maternal as well as paternal descent (Kibria, 1993). Similarly, lone immigrants often form co-resident groups with unrelated immigrants as a strategy of coping with high rents, low wages, social isolation, and – in some cases – the insecurities of an undocumented status (Chavez, 1990; Kibria, 1993). Co-residence is usually a temporary strategy employed until enough money is saved for return migration or to sponsor the arrival of kin.

Family reunification is the predominant basis for immigration to the US. It is not uncommon, however, for many years to pass before transnational families are reunited through chain migration (Hondagneu-Sotelo, 1994). Extended as well as immediate kin are included in this chain migration, thus contributing to the higher occurrence of extended family households among immigrants than the native born (Duleep and Regets, 1996; Laguerre, 1994). When family reunification is complete, the years of separation contribute to bicultural households, with some family members having had more time to adapt to life in the US. The result can be a family of related strangers who have very different values, needs, and perspectives, and who may not even speak a shared language – particularly when children, who adapt more quickly, are among those who arrived first. Such differences can generate family tensions. Similarly, transnational marriages involving the importation of a spouse from the home country, as commonly occurs among Pakistanis in Britain, produce difficulties when spouses subscribe to different cultural expectations (see Shaw, chapter 16, this volume).

Immigrant families that arrive *in toto* or reunite through chain migration are often disrupted by the return migration of some family members. The difficulties of adjusting to a culturally and racially marginalized position in the US, social isolation, generational differences in acculturation, and shifting economic conditions of the host and sending society can prompt return migration. Such has been the case with large numbers of Korean immigrants who returned to their homeland in the 1980s leaving American-raised offspring behind (Min, 1998a). In some cases spouses do not share a desire to return, which can increase family tension and the risk of separation, divorce, and abandonment (Hondagneu-Sotelo, 1994). Return migrants also include those who arrived in late life to be reunited with adult children and to provide child-care and other services to their children's families, only to find that their children's long work hours and suburban lifestyle leave them isolated and unable to adjust to the social contours of the new society (Treas and Mazumdar, 2002). The ease of foreign travel in recent years also promotes return migration, particularly among Asian Americans who face no legal obstacles to re-entry and can afford regular visits (Min, 1998a).

As these examples demonstrate, immigrant families constitute a wide range of dynamic family types: the female-headed, the transnational, the extended, the nuclear, the reunited, and those forms, such as co-residence groups, that are newly constructed out of the conditions of immigration. Yet notions persist of a monolithic immigrant family based on an ideal collectivist form. While it is true that many immigrants bring traditional family ideology and strong norms of familism with them, they are also subject to changes prompted by conditions of the homeland, processes of migration, and circumstances in the receiving society. There has been a tendency for scholars to exclude from study those immigrant families that do not closely resemble the ideal nuclear and extended family models, often due to a substantive focus on dynamics in such family types, as between spouses (thus excluding single-headed families) or among intergenerational family members (thereby excluding transnational families). Narrow definitions of family that emphasize household co-residence among those tied by blood or legal marriage have rendered many immigrant families invisible (Ishii-Kuntz, 2000). As a result, the immigration literature has yet to fully examine the structural diversity of immigrant families and to be theoretically transformed by it.

## Theoretical Developments in the Study of Immigration and Immigrant Families

Because the post-1965 immigration trends differ tremendously from earlier waves of European immigrants in terms of their cultural diversity, racial composition, and the economic conditions they encounter, immigration scholars have had to revise existing theoretical frameworks that failed to capture the reality of today's immigrant families. Between the 1920s and 1960s assimilation theory and related cultural approaches dominated the immigration research. Based on the experiences of European immigrants at the end of the nineteenth century, the assimilation perspective assumes that, with time, immigrant families shed traditional "outdated" cultural values and structures while adopting patterns of the new "modern" culture. This "straight-line" assimilation model emphasizes a positive process of linear movement into mainstream American society accompanied by upward mobility (Park and Burgess, 1924) The expectation is that succeeding generations will be absorbed into a "melting pot" of mainstream culture.

Scholars initially made few adjustments in the assimilation framework when switching their analytic lens from earlier European immigrants to the new Third World immigrants. A variant of assimilation theory, the culture of poverty approach, gained popularity in the 1960s in the study of immigrant and poor families. Like assimilation theory, the culture of poverty approach centers on mainstream American culture, to which immigrants and their descendants (along with poor whites and African Americans) were expected to assimilate if they were to succeed. As a result, social problems among immigrant groups were attributed to a lack of assimilation, including the maintenance of traditional family patterns that were out of step with the demands of a "modern" society (Zinn, 1994). Problems among Mexican American families, such as poverty, were attributed to a cultural emphasis on familism and traditional patriarchal arrangements or "machismo" (Heller, 1966; Rubel, 1966). The strong family ties and instrumental exchanges with extended kin associated with Mexican American families were believed to contribute to permanent poverty by draining resources and limiting geographic and economic mobility. Implicit in this framework was a model of "normal" family life based on white, middle-class American standards against which immigrant families were judged (Pyke, 2000; Zinn and Wells, 2000). Families that deviated from this model were regarded as problematic. By emphasizing the internal cultural practices and structures of immigrant families, this approach placed blame for many social problems on the victims by ignoring the impact of larger forces, such as racism and the economic order, that limit opportunities for success and present barriers to assimilation.

Scholarly challenges to assimilation and culture of poverty approaches emerged in the late 1960s and 1970s, focusing on the top-down, white-centered approach that marginalized the experiences and perspectives of those studied (Boyd, 1989). Such challenges were bolstered by assimilation theory's inapplicability to the growing waves of immigrants of color to the US. At the same time, mounting evidence suggesting that familism is actually an important survival strategy among immigrants and the poor – a structural response to poverty rather than a cultural antecedent – contributed to a shift toward social structural approaches and away from models of cultural deviance (Alvirez and Bean, 1976; Hoppe and Heller, 1975).

As a result of these forces, in recent decades immigration and family scholars have focused on the effect of political, social, and economic conditions on the adaptation experiences of immigrants. One result is the emergence of segmented assimilation theory as an alternative to straight-line assimilation theory (Portes and Zhou, 1993; Rumbaut, 1994). This approach emphasizes the diversity of adaptation processes and economic outcomes of immigrant groups depending on variations in their place of settlement, regional resources, economic opportunities, community composition, and the human, political, and social capital they bring with them.

Segmented assimilation theory does not completely reject straight-line assimilation into the middle-class mainstream but acknowledges it as only one of many possible pathways. Further, it notes that assimilation into the middle class is a less traveled pathway for today's immigrant families whose non-white racial status marks them as "other" and prevents their complete amalgamation into the white-dominated mainstream. Indeed, recent research suggests some immigrant families face downward mobility in the US, with the second generation experiencing a decline in their economic (Gans, 1992; Portes and Zhou, 1993) and physical well-being (Rumbaut, 1997a), which is a reversal of the expectations of assimilation theory. Segmented assimilation theory suggests this pathway of downward mobility occurs predominately among immigrants of color who live in economically deprived communities, far from the resources and opportunities found in white, middle-class communities. For them assimilation into the local underclass community does not increase opportunities for success. A commonly provided example of this pathway is the children of Haitian immigrants living in the black inner city of Miami. Those who assimilate into the native-born community of black, inner-city youth tend to adopt the values of the local youth culture that are reactive to long-standing racism and denigrate academic achievement as "selling out" to the white world. In this scenario assimilation is not associated with educational success and upward mobility but long-term poverty (Portes and Zhou, 1993). Though segmented assimilation is primarily concerned with social structural forces, cultural factors also loom large. For example, in this instance the oppositional culture of poor native-born black youths, rather than the culture of the immigrants themselves, is blamed for negative outcomes in adaptation. Hence remnants of the culture of poverty approach are evident in the application of segmented assimilation theory.

A third pathway described by segmented assimilation stands straight-line assimilation theory on its head. It links positive outcomes among children of immigrants with the maintenance of ethnic practices. This pathway is characterized by the selective assimilation of immigrant families so as to accommodate mainstream society while holding on to ethnic cultural patterns. "Accommodation without assimilation" (Gibson, 1988) appears to provide resources from within the family and ethnic community, such as the support of ethnic organizations and the transmission of cultural values that promote hard work and academic achievement, while ethnic cultural practices are also adjusted to enable the acquisition of educational and economic resources from the mainstream society. Individuals alter their behavior to conform to mainstream expectations, but do not adopt the associated emotions or values. Rather, their maintenance of familism and strong ties to their ethnic community provides social capital that contributes to their success in the mainstream. This acculturative trajectory has been linked to the academic success of children of Vietnamese immigrants growing up in a predominately African American lower-income community (Zhou and Bankston, 1998), and children of Punjabi Sikh immigrants who academically outperform their white, native-born counterparts (Gibson, 1988).

Whereas scholars in the 1960s blamed familism and the maintenance of ethnic practices for poverty among immigrant families, today it is de rigueur to credit these very factors for economic and academic success among immigrants (Caplan, Choy, and Whitmore, 1991; Gibson, 1988; Valenzuela and Dornbusch, 1994). This is particularly the case in "model minority" depictions that exaggerate the level of success among Asian American immigrants. Yet such assertions suffer from a dearth of empirical research on Asian American families and the ambiguity surrounding the conceptualization of familism (Zinn and Wells, 2000). Although reliance on familism and ethnic continuity as explanations for adaptation have been joined by attention to external structural factors, such as race, economic opportunities, and class, they nonetheless remain of central importance in current theorizing. More theoretical work is needed to better understand the structural conditions in which familism and ethnic continuity are maintained, and those in which they are not, and in what situations they provide an adaptive advantage.

## Gender Dynamics

Immigrant research, influenced by the emergence of feminist theory in the 1970s, has provided overdue attention in recent decades to the contributions and experiences of women, which were previously encapsulated under those of men or buried in models of unitary household dynamics (Espiritu, 1997; Hondagneu-Sotelo, 1994; Morokvasic, 1983). Of particular focus in the study of immigrant families has been the impact of US immigration on gender dynamics, centered specifically on the wide-scale entrance of women into the wage labor system upon immigration. Despite the diversity of their cultural origins, contemporary newcomers to the US tend to share established patterns of patriarchal arrangements marked by rigid divisions in the labor of men and women, and the assignment of greater power and authority to male heads of households. Traditional gender arrangements that regard women's paid labor as undesirable are an integral component of the cultural and religious systems of immigrants from Asia, Latin America, the Caribbean, and the Middle East (Grasmuck and Pessar, 1991; Kar et al., 1995–6; Kibria, 1993). By contrast, the US experienced a rapid shift in gender arrangements with the post-1960 stream of middle-class married women into the labor force. Although the empirical record reveals that social relations in the US remain male-dominated, American women are portrayed as enjoying more autonomy, independence, and power than women in Third World countries from which most contemporary immigrants arrive, and having attitudes that are less supportive of patriarchal arrangements (Kim, 1994). Immigrants themselves are acutely aware of these differences and view the continuity of traditional gender arrangements as integral to the maintenance of ethnicity (Das Gupta, 1997). The adoption of more egalitarian gender arrangements is often regarded as a sign of Americanization, a loss of ethnic identity, the failure of men to fulfill their role, and the breakdown of the family unit. Although newcomers to the US are confronted with a mainstream culture that gives a great deal of lip service (if less structural support) to the notion of gender equality it is the new economic conditions rather than an altered gender consciousness that prompts a reconfiguration of gender relations within immigrant families (Foner, 1986; Kibria, 1993). Immigrant males often face difficulties in finding the kind of jobs that pay a family wage, resulting in unemployment, downward mobility, and an increased dependency on their wives' wage labor. Concurrently, immigrant women find their labor in demand by US employers who specifically target them for low-paying menial jobs (Bonacich, 1994). In fact, the greater demand for immigrant women's labor contributes to a female-dominated flow of immigrants, including married women who immigrate and secure employment prior to their husbands' arrival (Gordon, 1990). The movement of women into the labor force upon immigration is one of the most dramatic changes impacting upon immigrant families. In Korea, for example, only 25 percent of married women in urban areas were in the labor force in 1990 (National Statistical Office, Republic of Korea, 1993: 1), compared with 60 percent of married Korean women in the US (US Bureau of the Census 1993, Table 48). Other immigrant groups exhibit similar patterns of female labor-force participation (Grasmuck and Pessar, 1991).

Much of the immigrant research supports the notion that the greater economic resources, self-esteem, and independence that work provides immigrant wives results in a decline of patriarchal arrangements and male dominance, with husbands more likely to share household tasks, child-care, decision-making, and financial management with wives (Kibria 1993; Grasmuck and Pessar, 1991; Guendelman and Pérez-Itriago, 1987; Lim, 1997; Repack, 1997). In cases of serial migration where husbands arrive before wives – often against the wishes of women – the gender transformation occurs during the years of separation when wives take on the role of head of household in their husband's absence, which frequently involves breadwinning as the earnings husbands send home are typically insufficient (Hondagneu-Sotelo, 1994).

Meanwhile, men living independently in the US must manage their own domestic tasks. This leads to different expectations and more egalitarian practices when families are reunited (Hondagneu-Sotelo, 1994). Sometimes women use immigration as an opportunity to reduce their dependence on husbands through employment, to renegotiate gender arrangements, or to insist that husbands who immigrated previously assume their financial obligations (Grasmuck and Pessar, 1991; Hondagneu-Sotelo, 1994; Toro-Morn, 1995). In fact, the act of migrating can be an assertion of power by women when, as is often the case, they do so against the wishes of husbands.

Binary models that locate gender oppression in the family-centered worlds of the homeland and liberation in women's employment in the US have met with challenges (Alicea, 1997; Kibria, 1990). Many families maintain traditional arrangements despite the employment of wives. For example, the concentration of Korean immigrant women in small family-run businesses where they work alongside husbands and do not draw a separate salary seems to undercut the potential positive effects other types of employment have on immigrant women's family power (Min, 1998b). Though research on class differences is scant, some evidence suggests that middle-class, immigrant women have an easier time striking an egalitarian balance (Toro-Morn, 1995). In many immigrant families, men who fear losing their authority and status resist challenges to traditional arrangements, at times relying on abuse to maintain their power (Fernández-Kelly and García, 1990). Some immigrant wives attempt to bolster their husband's threatened self-esteem and the family's sense of tradition by maintaining a submissive stance. Women develop strategies within the patriarchal structure for maximizing their power and resources (Lim, 1997; Kandiyoti, 1988). Indeed, much of the empirical research suggests that immigrant women's economic resources and increase in power vis-à-vis their husbands does not undermine their commitment to a patriarchal structure. Rather, they remain committed to a traditional family structure as a means of preserving their parental authority, long-term economic security, and family networks that assist in the resistance of race and class oppression (Alicea, 1997; Kibria, 1990). In this scenario women's employment and increased independence are viewed as extensions of their traditional position prompted by the conditions of adaptation, and necessary only until the family can establish a firm footing on new soil. Several studies find that immigrant women view their paid employment and increased household power as temporary and aspire toward a middle-class lifestyle that involves their full time housewifery (Fernández-Kelly and García, 1990; Toro-Morn, 1995), though the unintended gains employed women experience in gender relations sometimes promote their commitment to paid labor (Grasmuck and Pessar, 1991). Hence the observed shifts in gender arrangements do not necessarily signal a profound challenge to the gender hierarchy, as some women do not use their power to press for permanently altered gender arrangements, but for the restoration of a traditional family structure.

Gender shifts in immigrant families are neither universal nor without contradictions across domains. Women who lead double lives by enacting independence in the workplace, and a submissive stance at home can experience tremendous emotional conflict and stress in the maintenance of contradictory personalities (Kar et al., 1995–6; Pyke and Johnson, 2003). Further, women's greater status vis-à-vis their husbands does not translate into an increase in their general social status. Indeed, such relative gains are propelled by their husband's loss of status in the class and race configurations of North America, which also constrains their own position in the larger society (Chai, 1987; Espiritu, 1997; Grasmuck and Pessar, 1991). Immigrant women still endure patriarchal arrangements in the workplace, as reflected in the low-wage labor reserved for them. Some suffer downward mobility as they move from higher-status occupations in their homeland to low-paying menial work upon immigration. Similarly, former homemakers whose husbands earned enough to support the family prior to immigration often experience the necessity of their employment, usually in menial jobs, as downward class mobility, and the juggling of both a paid job and domestic obligations as an added burden (Fernández-Kelly and García, 1990). Even if husbands "help out" more than before, the domestic workload is rarely truly shared and immigrant women face the stress of their work overload (Foner, 1986; Min, 1998a). And while immigration can provide women with some distance from controlling elders thereby increasing their autonomy and family power, it also denies them kin-based assistance with child-care and household chores (Chai, 1987). Similarly, immigrant women who relied on maids in the homeland typically find they can ill afford such services in the US (Fernández-Kelly and García, 1990).

The overall increase in power and economic opportunities for women upon immigration while that of men shrinks contributes to a gendered pattern of stated preference for return migration. Immigrant men who experience a marked loss of power both inside and outside of their families are more inclined to want to return than are their wives, who enjoy their new autonomy and power within the family domain (Hondagneu-Sotelo, 1994). Grasmuck and Pessar (1991) found that Dominican immigrant women used their new control of finances to invest family resources in furnishings and the establishment of a home, thereby strategically promoting settlement and draining the funds needed for return migration. Disagreement over return migration contributes to divorce rates in immigrant families.

## The New Second Generation

Scholarly neglect of immigrant children and the US-born children of immigrant parents accounts for a profound gap in our knowledge of the long-term adaptation processes and outcomes among immigrant families. Further, the largest growing segment of the child population in the US since the 1980s – those growing up in immigrant families – has been largely ignored. This began to change in 1994, with the publication of a special issue of the *International Migration Review* devoted to the "new" second generation, launching a massive effort to draw attention to this neglected group.

The growing research on today's second generation tells two distinct though reconcilable tales. On the one hand, strong ties to family and ethnicity have been associated with educational success among second-generation youth. This research, associated with segmented assimilation theory, stresses the role of the family and ethnic culture as an adaptive resource, and presents a somewhat harmonious view of immigrant family life (Caplan, Choy, and Whitmore, 1991; Gibson, 1988; Valenzuela and Dornbusch, 1994). Intensive investigation of the subjective experiences and emotional life of children of immigrants tells yet another tale. Regardless of their level of academic and social success, children in immigrant families tend to feel immense stress and tension in coping with their immigrant parents' expectations in the context of the contradictory pulls of the mainstream culture (Kibria, 1993; Pyke, 2000; Wolf, 1997; Zhou and Bankston, 1998). Glenn (1986) argues that both views of family life are accurate. Families provide a refuge from discrimination and the economic and cultural difficulties of the mainstream society. Families are also a site of conflict, particularly along axes of gender, generation, age, and acculturative differences. As a result the portrait that emerges of immigrant families fluctuates around the opposite poles of harmony and conflict. In this section I discuss the conflictual aspects of intergenerational relations centered around the different acculturative pathways of parents and children.

Immigrant children and children of immigrants tend to acculturate to the mainstream society much more rapidly than do their parents. The second generation gain fluency in English sooner than do parents, and tend to prefer English over the language of their parents (Rumbaut, 1997a; Zhou and Bankston, 1998). Hence, parents and children frequently lack fluency in a common tongue (Kibria, 1993). Further restrictions are placed on parent–child interaction by the long work hours of immigrant parents, with some children going for days without seeing one or both of their parents (Sung, 1987). These factors undermine the ability of parents to pass on to children their ethnic language and culture. Parent–child solidarity is also undermined by the limited applicability of parental experiences growing up in the homeland to those of their children in the US.

The gap between faster-changing children and slower-changing parents is further enhanced by the greater acculturative opportunities and pressures that children encounter via school, peers, and the media. Compared to the children of earlier waves of immigrants, today's children spend more time in the educational system and have greater interaction with non-immigrant peers. Adaptation processes have also been transformed by the advent of television. Fully 98 percent of all American households have one or more televisions, making it a tremendous assimilative force (Rumbaut, 1997a). The images and values disseminated by a high-tech media, non-immigrant peers, and the school system tend to reflect a narrow Euro-centric view of "normality." Given the weight of the mainstream culture, children of immigrants easily internalize these ideals and draw upon them as an interpretive frame in viewing their own family and ethnic practices as abnormal, deficient, and even pathological. For example, parents who stress instrumental aspects of love, rather than expressive displays, are often criticized as unloving, with children wishing their parents were more like "American" parents (Pyke, 2000). Relatedly, the practice of child fostering in the Caribbean and Mexico assumes new meaning once children immigrate and assimilate a more stigmatized interpretation of such practices (Waters, 1997).

Immigration is linked with a loss of parental authority, and parents tend to blame the permissiveness and individualism of US society (Kibria, 1993; Waters, 1997; Zhou and Bankston, 1998). However, it appears that the dependency of immigrant parents on children's English-speaking skills, often leading to their management of family finances, plays a big role in the transfer of power. The absence of parents who work long days or reside in the homeland further undermines their authority, while the power of older children who assume the supervision and care of younger siblings is enhanced (Pyke, forthcoming).

The divide between faster-changing children and slower-changing parents and the shift in intergenerational power are sources of conflict and tension in immigrant families. Suárez-Orozco and Suárez-Orozco (1995) report, however, that parent–child conflict is no greater among immigrant than native-born Latino families. Due to a lack of empirical research that compares immigrant families with those in the homeland or looks at the longitudinal changes that occur in families as they immigrate, it is difficult to gauge the extent to which immigration increases levels of family conflict. Nonetheless, intergenerational conflicts in immigrant families are shaped by clashes between American and ethnic practices, including issues of arranged marriage, dating, "going out" with friends, choosing a college major, academic performance, and independence versus dependency (Das Gupta, 1997; Kibria, 1993; Pyke, 2000; Wolf, 1997).

Daughters report more parent–child conflict than do sons (Rumbaut, 1994). The discrepancy between mainstream values of egalitarianism and the adherence to traditional gender hierarchies at home is a contributory factor. Daughters frequently complain of a parental double standard with males given more freedom and fewer household chores (Zhou and Bankston, 1998). Not surprisingly, sons are less likely to complain of gender arrangements. Tension also arises from the contradictory messages passed on to daughters who are told to succeed academically and pursue a career but forfeit attendance at distant, high-quality universities so as to stay close to home (Wolf, 1997). Females are often instructed to maintain traditional gender arrangements in the home at the same time they are pushed to compete with males in school and career. Hence the same gender contradictions that immigrant mothers face in the realms of work and family life are reiterated in the messages and conditions passed on to daughters.

Despite the challenges immigration presents to relations between parents and children, and the tendency of children to challenge ethnic practices, some aspects of ethnic culture are successfully transmitted to children. The most notable is a commitment to familism, including filial care, which is an important means by which children reaffirm their ethnic identity (Pyke, 2000). It is only the more assimilated who show weakened norms of familism (Silverstein and Chen, 1999).

## Elderly Immigrants

Most late-life immigrants arrive in order to join family members as permitted by family reunification allowances. Treas (1995) reports that two-thirds of elderly legal immigrants to the US in 1991 were parents of US citizens. The collectivist norms of the sending societies from which most elderly immigrants arrive emphasize the co-residence of elderly parents with adult children, contributing to such living arrangements in North America. However, diversity in living arrangements is related to the length of time that elderly immigrants have resided in the new society. Compared to the elderly who immigrated at younger ages, elderly newcomers are poorer and less likely to speak English (Treas and Mazumdar, 2002). They are thus more dependent upon family members for financial support and assistance in mediating the new culture, and more likely than native-born elders and those who immigrated at younger ages to live with kin in extended households (Boyd, 1991). However, a comparison of co-residence patterns among Asian Americans and white Americans found that Asian Americans, even those born in the US, display stronger patterns of co-residence. And children of Asian immigrants also express a commitment to filial care. Further, a study of Chinese immigrant families found that grown children feel a stronger sense of obligation to the filial care of their parents than their parents believed they should (Lin and Liu, 1993). This suggests that despite the waning of some ethnic practices with acculturation across time and generations, familism and a commitment to parental co-residence tend to persist over time (Kamo and Zhou, 1994). However, the geographic distance that often separates grown immigrant children from their elderly parents means that many are not actively engaged in filial care (Ishii-Kuntz, 1997). So while values of filial piety are important in shaping elder care among immigrants (Kamo and Zhou, 1994), structural factors such as geographical proximity also explain variations in immigrant caregiving.

Although immigrant norms tend to emphasize children's support and care of parents, in actuality immigrant elders provide high levels of assistance to their children through child-care and domestic tasks (Orleck, 1987; Treas and Mazumdar, 2002). Indeed, immigrant children who do not have parents residing nearby complain about the difficulties of raising children without their assistance (Tam and Detzner, 1998).

Even though traditional practices among most immigrant cultures assign greater authority and respect to elders than is the norm in the US, there is evidence that the dependency of immigrant elders on their grown children fosters their submissiveness and deference to the needs of their children and an unwillingness to challenge family arrangements (Treas and Mazumdar, 2002). This suggests that intergenerational dynamics do not conform as closely to immigrant cultural ideals as is often assumed. Departures from cultural expectations can create difficulties for elderly immigrants. The domestic obligations of elders who reside in the suburban homes of their employed children where social contact with coethnics is minimal report feelings of isolation, loneliness, and depression (ibid.). This is also the case among those elderly immigrants who expected to reside with children but instead live alone and feel cut off from an active role in day-to-day family life, undermining their sense of purpose and identity. These factors contribute to depression (Mui, 1998) and high suicide rates, such as among elderly Asian American female immigrants who are 65 percent more likely to kill themselves than elderly white American women (Pascual, 2000). However, many immigrant elders who have adapted to life in the US, particularly those who immigrated at younger ages, prefer to live independently (Min, 1998a). Their reasons include an intergenerational cultural gap, and the avoidance of domestic obligations in their children's home.

## Conclusions

Research on today's immigrant families has not yet attracted the sustained and organized attention of a large group of scholars. Hence the picture that emerges of immigrant families is at times fragmentary and contradictory. A lack of comparative research has resulted in the tendency to generalize across ethnic groups inadvertently contributing to the construction of monolithic family types. Much more research is needed that focuses on the differences among as well as within ethnic groups (e.g., comparisons across class, generational status, length of time in the US, and gender). Meanwhile, much of the immigrant research continues to focus on how and why immigrant families differ from the white-dominated mainstream ideal, even studies designed to revise earlier research that found immigrant families deficient. This focus on the white family standard has hindered a richer comparative understanding of differences and similarities among and within immigrant groups.

The ongoing shift in research from the post-1965 first-generation immigrants to their children highlights this group's strategic theoretical importance. The study of the second generation as they grow up, enter the occupational structure, marry, raise children, and respond to the needs of their aging parents can inform scholars about the long-term status and adaptative patterns of immigrant families. Will subsequent generations be incorporated into the higher echelons of the economic structure, or will they form permanently disadvantaged groups? How will assimilation, the maintenance of ethnic ties, racism, the loss of well-paid, blue-collar jobs in the current economy, and other factors, contribute to the economic futures of today's immigrant children? Answering these questions will contribute to the development of current theories of adaptation.

Research on immigrant families also needs to be integrated into the general stream of family studies as well as its subfields. For example, although there has been a growing interest in research on dynamics between gay, lesbian, and bisexual children and their parents, these dynamics have not been examined in immigrant families (Ishii-Kuntz, 2000). Similarly, immigrant families need to be included in studies of the divorced, remarried, and female-headed households. Doing so will expand our theoretical and empirical understanding of the diversity of family types, permit greater comparative analysis, and dramatically transform theoretical paradigms seeped in assumptions about "normal" family life that are derived from a white, middle-class model (Pyke, 2000).

While the current literature emphasizes the affect that contact with mainstream American society has on immigrant families, it is also necessary to examine the ways that mainstream American family practices are impacted by contact with immigrant cultures (Foner, 1997). As norms of familism appear to be maintained among immigrant families and their children, the question arises as to what extent, if any, familism will be incorporated or accommodated in the dominant society. How might immigrant practices of familism be affecting US policies and institutional practices? Or do structures of power and dominance create a hegemonic mainstream culture that is impervious to the influx of immigrant families? Further, to what extent can we attribute long-term patterns of familism among immigrant groups to social structural factors, immigration policies, and institutional practices in the US? These are important theoretical questions that family and immigration scholars have yet to address.

## References

Alicea, M. (1997) "A chambered nautilus": The contradictory nature of Puerto Rican women's role in the social construction of a transnational community. *Gender and Society*, 11, 597–626.

Alvirez, D., and Bean, F. D. (1976) The Mexican-American family. In C. H. Mindel and R. W. Habenstein (eds.), *Ethnic Families in America*. New York: Elsevier.

Badets, J., and Chui, T. (1994) *Canada's Changing Immigrant Population*. Ottawa: Statistics Canada.

Bellah, R. N., Madsen, R., Sullivan, W. M., Swidler, A., and Tipton, S. M. (1985) *Habits of the Heart: Individualism and Commitment in American Life*. Berkeley: University of California Press.

Bonacich, E. (1994) Asians in the Los Angeles garment industry. In P. Ong, E. Bonacich, and L. Cheng (eds.), *The New Asian Immigration in Los Angeles and Global Restructuring*. Philadelphia: Temple University Press.

Boyd, M. (1989) Family and personal networks in international migration: Recent developments and new agendas. *International Migration Review*, 23, 638–70.

Boyd, M. (1991) Immigration and living arrangements: elderly women in Canada. *International Migration Review*, 25, 4–27.

Caplan, N., Choy, M. H., and Whitmore, J. K. (1991) *Children of the Boat People: A Study of Educational Success*. Ann Arbor: University of Michigan Press.

Chai, A. Y. (1987) Freed from the elders but locked into labor: Korean immigrant women in Hawaii. *Women's Studies*, 13, 223–4.

Chavez, L. R. (1990) Coresidence and resistance: Strategies for survival among undocumented Mexicans and Central Americans in the United States. *Urban Anthropology*, 19, 31–61.

Chavez, L. R. (1991) *Shadowed Lives: Undocumented Immigrants in American Society*. San Diego: Harcourt Brace Jovanovich College Publishers.

Das Gupta, M. (1997) "What is Indian about you?" A gendered, transnational approach to ethnicity. *Gender and Society*, 11, 572–96.

Duleep, H. O., and Regets, M. C. (1996) Family unification, siblings, and skills. In H. O. Duleep and P. V. Wunnava (eds.), *Immigrants and Immigration Policy: Individual Skills, Family Ties, and Group Identities*. Greenwich, CT: JAI Press.

Espiritu, Y. L. (1997) *Asian American Women and Men*. Thousand Oaks, CA: Sage.

Fernández-Kelly, M. P., and García, A. M. (1990) Power surrendered, power restored: The politics of work and family among Hispanic garment workers in California and Florida. In L. A. Tilly and P. Gurin (eds.), *Women, Politics and Change*. New York: Russell Sage Foundation.

Foner, N. (1997) The immigrant family: Cultural legacies and cultural changes. *International Migration Review*, 31, 961–74.

Foner, N. (1986) Sex roles and sensibilities: Jamaican women in New York and London. In R. Simon and C. Brettell (eds.), *International Migration: The Female Experience*. Totowa, NJ: Rowman & Allanheld.

Fuligni, A. J., Tseng, V., and Lam, M. (1999) Attitudes toward family obligations among American adolescents with Asian, Latin American, and European backgrounds. *Child Development*, 70, 1030–44.

Gans, H. J. (1992) Second-generation decline: Scenarios for the economic and ethnic futures of post-1965 American immigrants. *Ethnic and Racial Studies*, 15, 173–92.

Gibson, M. A. (1988) *Accommodation Without Assimilation: Sikh Immigrants in an American High School*. Ithaca, NY: Cornell University Press.

Glenn, E. N. (1986) *Issei, Nisei, War Bride: Three Generation of Japanese American Women in Domestic Service*. Philadelphia: Temple University Press.

Gordon, M. H. (1990) Dependents or independent workers? The status of Caribbean immigrant women in the United States. In R. W. Palmer (ed,), *In Search of a Better Life: Perspectives on Migration from the Caribbean*. New York: Praeger.

Grasmuck, S., and Pessar, P. R. (1991) *Between Two Islands: Dominican International Migration*. Berkeley: University of California Press.

Guendelman, S., and Pérez-Itriago, A. (1987) Double lives: The changing role of women in seasonal migration. *Women's Studies*, 13, 249–71.

Hamilton, D. (1993) A house, cash – And no parents. *Los Angeles Times*, June 24.

Heller, C. (1966) *Mexican American Youth: Forgotten Youth at the Crossroads*. New York: Random House.

Hondagneu-Sotelo, P. (1994) *Gendered Transitions: Mexican Experiences of Immigration*. Los Angeles: University of California Press.

Hondagneu-Sotelo, P., and Avila, E. (1997) "I'm here, but I'm there": The meanings of Latina transnational motherhood. *Gender and Society*, 11, 548–71.

Hoppe, S. K., and Heller, P. L. (1975) Alienation, familism, and the utilization of health services by Mexican-Americans. *Journal of Health and Social Behavior*, 16, 304–14.

Ishii-Kuntz, M. (1997) Intergenerational relationships among Chinese, Japanese, and Korean Americans. *Family Relations*, 46, 23–32.

Ishii-Kuntz, M. (2000) Diversity within Asian American families. In D. H. Demo, K. R. Allen, and M. A. Fine (eds.), *Handbook of Family Diversity*. New York: Oxford University Press.

Kamo, Y., and Zhou, M. (1994) Living arrangements of elderly Chinese and Japanese in the United States. *Journal of Marriage and the Family*, 56, 544–58.

Kandiyoti, D. (1988) Bargaining with patriarchy. *Gender and Society*, 2, 274–90.

Kar, S. B., Campbell, K., Jimenez, A., and Gupta, S. R. (1995-1996) Invisible Americans: An exploration of Indo-American quality of life. *Amerasia Journal*, 21, 25–52.

Kibria, N. (1990) Power, patriarchy, and gender conflict in the Vietnamese immigrant community. *Gender and Society*, 4, 9–24.

Kibria, N. (1993) *Family Tightrope: The Changing Lives of Vietnamese Americans*. Princeton, NJ: Princeton University Press.

Kim, B. (1994) Value orientations and sex-gender role attitudes on the comparability of Koreans and Americans. In H. Cho and O. Chang (eds.), *Gender Division of Labor in Korea*. Seoul: Ewha Women's University Press.

Laguerre, M. S. (1994) Headquarters and subsidiaries: Haitian immigrant family households in New York City. In R. L. Taylor (ed.), *Minority Families in the United States*. Englewood Cliffs, NJ: Prentice Hall.

Lim, I. (1997) Korean immigrant women's challenge to gender inequality at home: the interplay of economic resources, gender, and family. *Gender and Society*, 11, 31–51.

Lin, C., and Liu, W. T. (1993) Intergenerational relationships among Chinese immigrant families from Taiwan. In H. P. McAdoo (ed.), *Family Ethnicity*. Newbury Park, CA: Sage.

Lollock, L. (2001) The foreign-born population in the United States: March 2000, Current Population Reports, 2001, pp. 20–534. Washington, DC: US Census Bureau.

Maharidge, D. (1996) *The Coming White Minority: California Eruptions and American's Future*. New York: New York Times Books.

Mangiafico, L. (1988) *Contemporary American Immigrants*. New York: Praeger.

Min, P. G. (1998a) *Changes and Conflicts: Korean Immigrant Families in New York*. Boston: Allyn & Bacon.

Min, P. G. (1998b) The Korean-American family. In C. H. Mindel, R. W. Habenstein, and R. Wright (eds.), *Ethnic Families in America: Patterns and Variations*. Upper Saddle River, NJ: Prentice Hall.

Morokvasic, M. (1983) Women in migration: beyond the reductionist outlook. In A. Phizacklea (ed.), *One Way Ticket: Migration and Female Labour*. Boston: Routledge & Kegan Paul.

Mui, A. (1998) Living alone and depression among older Chinese immigrants. *Journal of Gerontological Social Work*, 30, 147–8.

National Statistical Office, Republic of Korea (1993) *1990 Population and Housing Census Report, Vol. 6: Economic Activity*. Seoul: National Statistical Office, Republic of Korea.

Nelson, S. S., and O'Reilly, R. (2000) Minorities become majority in state, census officials say. *Los Angeles Times*, August, A1, A16.

Orleck, A. (1987) The Soviet Jews: Life in Brighton Beach, Brooklyn. In N. Foner (ed.), *New Immigrants in New York*. New York: Columbia University Press.

Park, R. E., and Burgess, E. W. (1924) *Introduction to the Science of Sociology*. Chicago: University of Chicago Press.

Pascual, C. (2000) Why more elderly Asian women kill themselves. *Los Angeles Times*, September 14, E1, E4.

Portes, A., and Rumbaut, R. G. (1996) *Immigrant America: A Portrait*. Los Angeles: University of California Press.

Portes, A., and Zhou, M. (1993) The new second generation: segmented assimilation and its variants. *Annals of the American Academy of Political and Social Science*, 530, 74–96.

Pyke, K. (forthcoming) "Generational deserters" and "black sheep": Acculturative differences among siblings in Korean and Vietnamese immigrant families. *Journal of Family Issues*.

Pyke, K. (2000) The normal American family as an interpretive structure of family life among grown children of Korean and Vietnamese immigrants. *Journal of Marriage and the Family*, 62, 240–55.

Pyke, K., and Johnson, D. (2003) Asian American women and racialized femininities: "Doing" gender across cultural worlds. *Gender and Society*, 17, 33–53.

Reimers, D. M. (1996) Third World immigration to the United States. In H. O. Duleep and P. V. Wunnava (eds.), *Immigrants and Immigration Policy: Individual Skills, Family Ties, and Group Identities*. Greenwich, CT: JAI Press.

Repack, T. A. (1997) New roles in a new landscape. In M. Romero, P. Hondagneu-Sotelo, and V. Ortiz (eds.), *Challenging Fronteras: Structuring Latina and Latino Lives in the U.S.* New York: Routledge.

Rubel, A. J. (1966) *Across the Tracks: Mexican Americans in a Texas City.* Austin: University of Texas Press.

Rumbaut, R. G. (1994) The crucible within: Ethnic identity, self-esteem, and segmented assimilation among children of immigrants. *International Migration Review*, 28, 748–94.

Rumbaut, R. G. (1997a) Assimilation and its discontents. Between rhetoric and reality. *International Migration Review*, 31, 923–60.

Rumbaut, R. (1997b) Ties that bind: Immigration and immigrant families in the U.S. In A. Booth, A. C. Crouter, and N. Landale (eds.), *Immigration and the Family: Research and Policy on U.S. Immigrants*. Mahwah, NJ: Lawrence Erlbaum.

Silverstein, M., and Chen, X. (1999) The impact of acculturation in Mexican American families on the quality of adult grandchild-grandparent relationships. *Journal of Marriage and the Family*, 61,188–98.

Suárez-Orozco, C., and Suárez-Orozco, M. (1995) *Transformations: Immigration, Family Life, and Achievement Motivation among Latino Adolescents*. Stanford, CA: Stanford University Press.

Sung, B. L. (1987) *The Adjustment Experience of Chinese Immigrant Children in New York City.* New York: Center for Migration Studies.

Tam, C., and Detzner D. (1998) Grandparents as a family resource in Chinese-American families. In H. I. McCubbin, E. A. Thompson, A. I. Thompson, and J. E. Fromer (eds.), *Resiliency in Native American and Immigrant Families*. Thousand Oaks, CA: Sage.

Toro-Morn, M. I. (1995) Gender, class, family, and migration: Puerto Rican women in Chicago. *Gender and Society*, 9, 712–26.

Treas, J. (1995) Older Americans in the 1990s and beyond. *Population Bulletin*, 50, 8–33.

Treas, J., and Mazumdar, S. (2002) Older people in America's immigrant families: Dilemmas of dependence, integration, and isolation. *Journal of Aging Studies,* 16, 243–58.

US Bureau of the Census (1993) *The 1990 Census of Population, General Population Characteristics, United States*. CP-2-1; Washington, DC: US Government Printing Office.

Valenzuela, A., and Dornbusch, S. M. (1994) Familism and social capital in the academic achievement of Mexican origin and Anglo adolescents. *Social Science Quarterly*, 75, 18–36.

Waters, M. C. (1997) Immigrant families at risk: Factors that undermine chances for success. In A. Booth, A. C. Crouter, and N. Landale (eds.), *Immigration and Family: Research and Policy on U.S. Immigrants*. Mahwah, NJ: Lawrence Erlbaum.

Wolf, D. L. (1997) Family secrets: Transnational struggles among children of Filipino immigrants. *Sociological Perspectives*, 40, 457–82.

Zhou, M. (1998) Parachute kids in Southern California: The educational experience of Chinese children in transnational families. *Educational Policy*, 12, 682–704.

Zhou, M., and Bankston, C. (1998) *Growing up American: How Vietnamese Children Adapt to Life in the United States*. New York: Russell Sage Foundation.

Zinn, M. B. (1994) Adaptation and continuity in Mexican-origin families. In R. L. Taylor (ed.), *Minority Families in the United States: A Multicultural Perspective*. Englewood Cliffs, NJ: Prentice Hall.

Zinn, M. B., and Eitzen, D. S. (1996) *Diversity in Families*. New York: HarperCollins.

Zinn, M. B., and Wells, B. (2000) Diversity within Latino families: New lessons for family social science. In D. H. Demo, K. R. Allen, and M. A. Fine (eds.), *Handbook of Family Diversity.* New York: Oxford University Press.

# 16

# Immigrant Families in the UK

Alison Shaw

## Introduction

This chapter focuses on families of relatively recent immigrant origins in Britain's former dependencies in South Asia and the Caribbean, because these immigrations represent the largest recent influx of non-white people to the UK. In the 1950s and 1960s, people from Pakistan, India, Bangladesh, and the Caribbean came to Britain in significant numbers in response to postwar labor shortages, and in the 1970s British subjects of South Asian origin came from Africa in response to the Ugandan and Kenyan governments' Africanization policies. Since then, the legal entry of unskilled, non-white people has been restricted to the dependants or spouses of these earlier immigrants. In consequence, Britain's contemporary immigrant-origin population mainly consists of these very specific groups of postwar immigrants and their descendants, in contrast to the greater social and ethnic diversity of recent immigrants to the US described by Pyke (chapter 15, this volume).

According to the 1991 UK Census, Pakistanis, Indians, and Bangladeshis numbered 1,480,000 people and comprised 4.5 percent of Britain's population, while black people, (identified in Census terms as Black Caribbean, Black African, and Black Other, with Caribbeans as the largest group) numbered 890,000 and comprised about 1.68 percent of the population; other ethnic groups including Chinese together numbered 2.4 percent (Coleman and Salt, 1996). The Caribbean and South Asian origin population is growing, as a consequence of its young age structure and the high fertility rates of some South Asian minorities, and numbers are expected to stabilize at about 9 percent (Ballard and Kalra, 1994). The presence of these numerically significant ethnic minorities and their descendants has challenged and continues to challenge conventional ideas about British identities and British culture.

Many young, British-born Caribbeans or South Asians would not consider themselves "immigrants," because they were born in Britain, or because their parents or grandparents were British citizens born in countries that were formerly part of the

British Empire. They are discussed here as members of "immigrant families" because, alongside their significant socioeconomic integration, some of their concerns and values, especially those relating to family forms and relationships, continue to reflect or be shaped by concerns derived from the social and cultural background of South Asia and the Caribbean. Moreover, families of immigrant origin are often assumed to be more traditional with respect to patterns of marriage, family formation, and relationships between the generations than the majority population. A focus on immigrant families therefore provides interesting case material for the exploration of changing family forms and relationships in Britain today. To what extent are forces for change in family forms and relationships affecting minority and majority groups with equal intensity, despite the diversity of immigrant origins? And to what extent do traditional patterns of family forms and relationships persist in the new context, especially among the second- and third-generation descendants of the pioneer immigrants?

This chapter explores these questions by examining the structure of kinship ties, patterns of household formation, and patterns of marriage among British families of Caribbean and South Asian origin. Recent survey-based evidence of ethnic difference in marriage trends and patterns of family formation suggests that social change is affecting all ethnic groups in much the same way. These changes have been interpreted as a trend towards "modern individualism." However, while the demographic evidence seems clear, it would be wrong to assume that the observed trend arises from identical processes and carries the same meanings in all ethnic groups. This chapter aims to refocus attention on the importance of socioeconomic and cultural differences *between* different ethnic groups, in particular between the different South Asian communities, in shaping patterns of marriage and family formation. It also stresses the importance for some ethnic groups of continuing transnational links in structuring patterns of marriage, shaping ideas about what constitutes "home" and "family," and motivating social interaction and support. From this perspective, outwardly similar family forms arise from very different processes and carry very different meanings for the participants, and socioeconomic pressures toward conformity seem likely to continue to be mediated by culturally shaped motivations and intentions that vary within and between ethnic groups. A review of research approaches to the social and cultural diversity of Britain's ethnic minority population provides a necessary starting point for this discussion.

## Assimilation, Integration, and Cultural Diversity

British people of South Asian and Caribbean origin tend to live in ethnically distinct though not ethnically exclusive areas within Britain's major towns and cities, although a substantial minority is more scattered across Britain, living in small towns and in villages. It is the main residential concentrations, however, that have attracted the most research interest, often with a focus on the development of particular immigrant "communities." In Brixton, South London, for instance, there is a strong Afro-Caribbean presence (Benson, 1981); Southall in West London is sometimes called Britain's "South Asian capital," in which Panjabi Sikhs comprise the dominant ethnic group (Baumann, 1996); London's East End has a distinctive Bangladeshi presence (Eade, 1990), and Pakistanis have settled in the Waltham Forest area (Jacobson, 1998). Outside of London, there are distinctive South Asian communities in the towns and cities of the Midlands and North, where pioneer migrants settled in response to the postwar need for factory labor. Leicester has a predominantly Gujarati presence, and Manchester, Leeds, Bradford, Sheffield, Rotherham, Birmingham, Huddersfield, Halifax, and Glasgow, for example, have distinct, inner-city areas of predominantly Pakistani Muslim settlement. These areas are distinctive also for their shops selling "ethnic" foodstuffs and other goods, and for their mosques, gurdwaras, or temples – many of them in converted former churches or public houses; some of them purposely built – to meet the religious and social needs of their communities.

The very existence of such settlements raises sociological questions about the degree of structural and cultural integration within British society. In the 1950s and 1960s scholars assumed that Britain's immigrant communities would follow the assimilation path taken by European immigrants in the US (Gordon, 1964). According to this model, the level of minority participation in the labor force and the educational system indicates the degree of structural integration, while the level of demographic conformity in patterns of marriage and family forms provides one indication of cultural integration. By the 1970s and 1980s, it was clear that measures of structural integration had failed to take into account the role of racial discrimination and structural disadvantage (Brown, 1984). It was also clear that significant structural integration in employment and education is not necessarily accompanied by cultural integration, because despite significant socioeconomic success, many minorities have continued to maintain distinct lifestyles, family forms, and patterns of marriage, differing from each other as well as from the host society, and this may be particularly visible in inner-city areas of high residential concentration. Scholars disagree about how far this follows from racial exclusion and socioeconomic disadvantage, and how far it indicates the strength and persistence of distinctive family and cultural traditions, but most accounts have replaced early models of assimilation with more complex accounts of cultural pluralism accompanied by varying degrees of socioeconomic integration.

Labor-force surveys conducted at intervals since the 1970s show that ethnic differences in employment, education, and housing have diminished with time, especially for men and women of Afro-Caribbean origin, although some significant divergences remain (see e.g. Model, Fisher, and Silberman, 1999). With respect to South Asians, a recent survey indicates that Indians have achieved greater socioeconomic mobility than Pakistanis and Bangladeshis, who have fared the least well of all ethnic groups in Britain, in terms of income, employment, and housing, and among whom unemployment is disproportionately high (Modood, 1997). There is also a marked gender difference: relatively few South Asian women have achieved parity with white or Caribbean women, and this is especially true of Pakistani and Bangladeshi women, whose participation in the labor force is low. In short, the survey data indicate a trend towards greater socioeconomic integration, but this is occurring at a much slower rate among Pakistanis and Bangladeshis than among other groups.

Explanations for these survey findings cite racism and structural disadvantage, but also require that attention is paid to the importance of socioeconomic and cultural differences between immigrant groups prior to migration, in the migration process, and in the subsequent resettlement. A fairly substantial ethnographic and anthropological literature, dating from the 1970s and given renewed emphasis in recent transnational perspectives, explores the significance of conditions in and interests and values derived from immigrants' areas of origin for understanding the diversity of the immigrant-origin presence in Britain (Watson, 1977; Pryce, 1979; Foner, 1979;

Jeffery, 1976; Ballard, 1994; Gardner, 1995; Shaw, 2000b). For instance, the literature on South Asian communities makes an important distinction between "direct migrant" and "twice migrants" that is often concealed by standard ethnicity data. Survey evidence of socioeconomic differences between Indians on the one hand, and Bangladeshis and Pakistanis on the other, could easily be attributed to religious difference, and to the influence of Islamic ideals that discourage female employment. However, standard ethnicity data generally fail to distinguish the migrants of the 1950s and 1960s, who came directly from South Asia, mainly from parts of rural Panjab (in India and in Pakistan), from Azad ("Free," or Pakistan-held) Kashmir, and from Bangladesh, and the "twice migrants" (Bhachu, 1985) of the 1970s who came via Africa following the Africanization policies of the Ugandan and Kenyan governments. Twice migrants are likely to identify themselves as Indian (if selecting from among conventional ethnic categories), and include mainly Hindus but also Sikhs and Muslims with origins in pre-Partition India, and a minority of mainly Hindu Indo-Caribbeans with more attenuated links with South Asia (Vertovec, 1994). Their socioeconomic status was generally high in comparison with the direct migrants, their English fluent, and many were professionals or had business experience from Africa (Bhachu, 1985). These qualities gave them a head start in the processes of resettlement in Britain, and continue to account for much of the contemporary socioeconomic difference between "Indians," "Bangladeshis," and "Pakistanis."

There is more ethnographic literature on British South Asian than on British Afro-Caribbean communities, perhaps because South Asians are generally regarded as culturally "more different," in their languages, religions, and patterns of kinship and marriage, and possibly as a result of an early academic prejudice that "Asians have culture, West Indians have problems" (Benson, 1996). The popular images of young Afro-Caribbeans in the 1970s and 1980s were that they were less law-abiding and more troublesome than the South Asians, particularly following the experience of "race riots" in some areas of London and Bristol, and the academic identification of an "expressive disreputable orientation" among a particular group of West Indian youth in Bristol (Pryce, 1979). The distinctive Caribbean pattern of kinship and cohabitation, characterized by women-centered, single-parent households originating in patterns of family life in the Caribbean, was often cited as the center of unstable and irresponsible childrearing, and thus as the prime source (rather than racism or socioeconomic disadvantage) of wider social problems. Recently, however, political and academic focus on "troublesome youth" has shifted to Pakistani and Bangladeshi Muslim males, especially following riots in the former mill towns of Bradford, Burnley, and Oldham in the summer of 2001. The ensuing public debates over integration and citizenship have focused on the persistence of traditional religious and cultural practices in explaining the "non-integration" of Pakistani and Bangladeshi Muslims, giving less emphasis to poverty, unemployment, and religious prejudice. But how far have "traditional" family forms persisted within Britain's immigrant communities? Recent survey data suggest that, contrary to the popular stereotypes, there is evidence of a trend toward demographic conformity for all ethnic groups.

## Toward Modern Individualism for All?

British society is experiencing major changes in patterns of household formation and marriage (Allan and Crow, 2001; McRae, 1999). These changes include a rise in cohabitation and marriage, a decline in conventional nuclear families comprising parents plus dependent children, and, in part associated with a rise in divorce, an increase in new family groupings comprising couples with children from previous relationships. Women's increased participation in the labor force is usually acknowledged as a major reason for these changes. There has also been an increase in single-parent families and in the number of elderly living alone.

But have these broad changes affected families of immigrant origin to the same extent? Survey data on marriage and family formation across ethnic groups have demonstrated some marked differences. For instance, almost all South Asians do get married, earlier or later, although second-generation South Asians are marrying later than their parents (though not as late as the white population), which suggests "some assimilation in marriage patterns... towards those of the white population" (Berrington, 1994: 530). There are also marked differences between South Asian groups: Pakistanis and Bangladeshis marry earlier than Indians, and are less likely to cohabit or divorce. By contrast, fewer Caribbean women marry, and rates of divorce, separation, and cohabitation are higher among Caribbeans than other groups (Berrington, 1994).

A more recent survey of rates of partnership, marriage, cohabitation, and child-rearing by ethnic origin (defined as Caribbean, South Asian, or white) since the 1970s indicates that *all* ethnic groups are moving toward lower rates of marriage and higher rates of single parenthood (and conventional nuclear household formation), though at different rates (Berthoud, 2000). This trend is most apparent among Caribbeans, because they are the least likely to be in a formal marriage, and Caribbean women are more likely to be single parents than white women. However, Caribbeans and whites are equally likely to be unmarried, divorced, or single parents. The survey also notes a significant proportion of ethnically mixed relationships: half of the British-born Caribbean men and one-third of the women were in relationships with white rather than Caribbean partners. As a result, only a quarter of so-called Caribbean children were living with two black parents. The trend away from the nuclear family toward single parenthood is much less apparent among South Asians, who are more likely to adhere to "old-fashioned values" and live in nuclear households. In fact, today's typical British nuclear family is more likely to be called Khan, Hussain, or Malik than Smith, Jones, or Wilson. The survey contends in conclusion that different ethnic groups have reached different stages in a single, one-directional process: "the objective fact is that white families are moving in a particular direction. Pakistanis and Bangladeshis (and to a lesser extent Indians) are behind.... Caribbeans are in front" (Berthoud, 2000).

Can we conclude, then, that despite the earlier evidence of cultural pluralism, distinctive cultural traditions and preferences ultimately count rather less than external socioeconomic pressures in shaping family forms and trends in marriage choices? The problem with relying on survey data such as age at marriage and household composition is that we do not know whether identical social and cultural processes have led to the observed trend, or whether these processes carry identical meanings for different ethnic groups. The rest of this chapter refocuses on these socioeconomic processes and their meanings for different groups within the immigrant-origin population. It considers the Afro-Caribbean experience with reference to recent research on the transnational character of Caribbean kinship in Britain. It then considers the significance of differences in socioeconomic background, marriage rules, gender conventions, and patterns of transnational kinship in accounting for differences *within* the category of direct migrants from South Asia, with reference to a comparison of Jullundri Sikhs and Mirpuri Muslims, and in conclusion draws out some implications and directions for further research.

## Caribbean Kinship: Transnational Links and Support

The so-called "Afro-Caribbean family pattern" encompasses various household forms, ranging from primarily conjugal to primarily consanguineous households of two or three generations of women with often absent men. In rural areas, young adults may remain living in their parents' household, contributing to the household economy, while forming extra-household sexual unions, and any children from these non-residential unions would live with their mothers (Foner, 1977). Although marriage is an ideal, circumstances often prevent couples marrying before having children, and couples with children may formally marry only in later life. A man who establishes his own household often does so after cohabiting with the mother of his most recent children for many years. Households are also commonly headed by a senior woman who has more authority than the men in the household and is the most stable presence, or are "consanguineal" households in which a woman lives with her children, and the children of her daughters. In such households, a mother might be the main breadwinner and also carry the main responsibility for children, or she might earn a wage while her mother cares for the household and children (Smith, 1988). Solien (1965) views the consanguineal household that accounted for 40 percent of the households in her field study as an adaptation to an economic system where recurrent male migration is the primary source of cash.

The majority of postwar Caribbean migrants to Britain came from Jamaica, with others from neighboring "small islands" such as Antigua, Barbados, St. Lucia, and St. Kitts/Nevis, at a time when local regional economies were in decline and people relied on remittances from relatives working away from home or overseas. The migrants to the UK were generally skilled, with the means to raise the fare (Philips and Philips, 1998), and most were fairly quickly followed by wives, common-law wives, or girlfriends. Children, however, stayed with their grandmothers at least until their parents had saved enough money for the additional fares (Foner, 1979; Olwig, 1999). This pattern of dispersed families, including leaving children with grandmothers, was a long-established response to socioeconomic circumstances.

Arrival in Britain initially brought a degree of conformity to English family patterns, because couples married earlier than in Jamaica, probably because their new economic circumstances enabled men to become reliable providers, and possibly also to avoid disapproval in a climate of racial hostility (Foner, 1977). Couples also spent more leisure time together, and were more likely to share domestic and child-care responsibilities than in Jamaica. Foner's speculation that this might prove but a short-term adaptation to new conditions, and that "there may be a partial return to 'old' patterns of family relations" (1977) has proved accurate. The current pattern of Caribbean household formation in Britain is reminiscent of complex and changing patterns in the Caribbean, with high rates of single motherhood, and close ties between women across generations, sometimes within three-generational households where grandmothers do more of the childrearing and domestic work than their daughters' male partners. The large proportion of children born to unmarried

Caribbean women and the relatively large proportion of Caribbean children living in lone-parent families has generated debates over the "problem" of black single motherhood (see Berrington, 1994; Song and Edwards, 1997).

A main problem with this focus on family forms, and in the Caribbean case especially, on rates of formal marriage, is that it overlooks the importance of strong and permanent ties with family beyond the household, in the UK and transnationally. Caribbean single parents usually have long-term, extra household partnerships, some of which are likely eventually to result in marriage, a process entirely consistent with earlier Caribbean patterns. Many Caribbean families also retain strong kinship and socioeconomic links with family in the Caribbean. These links facilitated their initial adaptation to life in Britain (Patterson, 1965: 261), and supported migrants' plans, shaped partly also in response to racism, to return to the Caribbean; over 50 percent of the adults in Foner's study planned to return to Jamaica (Foner, 1979; Chamberlain, 1977). Evidence of return migration is in fact inconclusive: the decrease in the number of Census returns from Caribbean-born people who are not recorded as dead may only mean that they have not completed their Census returns, not that they have returned to the Caribbean (Blakemore and Boneham, 1994: 64-5). Patterns of return migration are loosely linked with wealth, complicated by the fact that over time, migrants' links overseas have both contracted and widened (Byron, 1999).

Young, British-born people of Caribbean origin today may have in addition to grandparents extensive networks of aunts, uncles, cousins, and half-siblings in the Caribbean, whom they may visit at least every few years, or as often as finances permit. Many also have relatives in the US and Canada, which became the main destination of Caribbean emigrants after Britain closed the door to new immigrants the 1970s. These dispersed kinship ties have not brought about a decline in the emotional, spiritual, practical, and material support that family members can expect at times of need: on the contrary, Caribbean transnational kinship is sustained by a sense of duty and responsibility towards kin, especially siblings, and provides an important source of not only moral but also practical support (Goulborne, 1999). These values are grounded in a strong sense of the family's identity through its transnational networks, and this is being reproduced across the generations (Chamberlain, 1997, 1998; Goulborne, 1999).

## South Asian Families: Kinship within and beyond the Household

In South Asia, the "ideal" South Asian "joint" or "extended" household of the cities and the rural areas is a multigenerational unit (Vatuk, 1972), with external patrilineal links connecting it to a local descent group, known variously as *got*, *patti*, *qaum*, or *zat* (caste) or *biradari* (brotherhood). Marriage is preferentially arranged by parents and other relatives rather than by the couple themselves, is endogamous to the caste or descent group, and is motivated in part by concerns to preserve or enhance status and respectability. A bride goes to live in her husband's parents' household, under the authority of her mother-in-law, and is formally subordinate to her husband and his elder brothers and their wives. Relationships within the household are formally shaped by a hierarchy of gender, age, and status and ideally by a sense of loyalty to the group.

In practice, however, household composition changes over time and smaller nuclear households may be established within a particular locality, as sons marry, have children, and move out. While this is sometimes exacerbated by conflicts of interest between brothers or between couples, the process represents an expected development within the life cycle of a multigenerational household: the fact that a bride's dowry contains the goods necessary for establishing an independent household symbolizes this expectation (Ballard, 1990: 235). Each smaller household will then expand and may divide as sons marry and have children. Relationships between these smaller and larger households often remain of central importance in structuring networks of formal and informal exchange of goods and services (Vatuk, 1972).

Since the late nineteenth and early twentieth centuries, male labor migration has affected household structure in many parts of South Asia, particularly the Panjab, Azad Kashmir, and Bangladesh (from which men were initially recruited into army and navy service, and for railway construction in India and East Africa). A senior wife or widow often became the main decision-maker within such households, with junior wives eventually leaving to join husbands abroad – in East Africa earlier in the twentieth century, and in Britain from the 1960s onward. The households established abroad after the arrival of women and children were in many cases nuclear in form, but this was a necessary consequence of migration, and represented a stage in the development cycle of the joint family rather than a qualitative, long-term departure from the ideal of the extended family. Even then, it was not uncommon for two or more brothers, among Pakistani families at least, to establish two-generational, joint households when their wives and children arrived in Britain, and to continue to pool resources, and share the use of domestic space, for some years before establishing separate households of their own (see Shaw, 2000b: 102–6).

Today, among direct migrants of Pakistani, Bangladeshi, and Mirpuri Muslim origin, many households that comprised a man, his wife, and their children during the 1970s and 1980s are now larger, three-generational households, because sons have married and daughters-in-law have joined the households. Families have made creative use of domestic space in adapting the British terraced house to the needs of the extended family, through building extensions, or, if they can, by purchasing the house next door, and (in the minimal adaptation) building a gate into the fence that usually separates British terraced houses at the back. Alternatively, families establish ostensibly nuclear households in adjacent properties in the same street, or just a short auto-journey or walk away. Such households might be classified as nuclear in surveys of household composition, but are joint in both intention and use, and wages and household expenses may be paid into, and drawn from, a shared purse.

When married sons move out of the parental household to establish households of their own, they usually seek (within the constraints of council-house allocation) to live within the same neighborhood as their parents, and ties of consanguinity and marriage frequently remain central in importance in structuring networks of formal and informal exchange of goods and services (as in urban north India and in Pakistan). In areas of Pakistani, Azad Kashmiri, and Bangladeshi Muslim settlement, these networks are perhaps particularly important for young married women, who leave the parental home on marriage, but as a consequence of the preference for marriage within the *biradari*, are likely to marry a relative who is also likely to be first cousin, either raised here or from South Asia. The couple may initially live in the bride's parents' home, but even after establishing their own household (in a property perhaps purchased by the bride's family, or possibly obtained through the council) the wife's contacts with her natal family (probably now spread across several households) remain crucial, especially for child-care. Young married women often leave preschool children with their mothers, sisters, or sisters-in-law when they go to work. These local patterns of extra-household kinship are reminiscent of patterns of white, working-class kinship documented for East London in the 1960s (Young and Wilmott, 1957), but remain invisible in surveys of household composition.

An "East African effect" has been suggested in explaining differences in South Asian household patterns. One survey of a sample of elderly South Asians in Birmingham found that 71 percent lived in households of more than six people, while in a Coventry sample only 25 percent lived in such household, and suggested that this was because houses in Coventry are smaller and therefore less able to accommodate the extended family. While this might be true, Blakemore and Boneham observe that Birmingham's South Asians are mostly direct migrants, whereas Coventry's South Asians are predominantly East African Asians, who are more likely to live in nuclear households and to consider that a newly married couple should live independently of the groom's parents (1994: 81).

"Twice migrants" or "East African Asians" are also less likely to insist that marriages be conventionally arranged, and more likely to leave the choice of spouse to their son or daughter. This in turn is linked with their fewer socioeconomic ties in the Indian subcontinent. Women in these families are also more likely to be in paid employment outside of the home, and their daughters are more likely to become college or university graduates who will delay marriage and childbearing and choose their own spouses. These processes mark them out, to some extent, from "direct migrants." However, a preponderance of nuclear households may still mean that extra-household kinship ties are important, although the local networks of East African Asians may be less extensive than those of direct migrants, as a consequence of the circumstances of their migration. Ethnographic data suggest that in common with other South Asian immigrant groups, men and women tend to socialize within the ethnic group, and their patterns of expenditure and hospitality reflect traditional social and religious concerns, with young wage-earning women using their earnings to supplement their dowries (Bhachu, 1985). The implications for the elderly are also not straightforward, as elderly south Asians, whether direct or twice migrants, sometimes prefer to live separately from their children, choosing some independence, to visit and be visited, rather than to live jointly.

## Jullundri Sikhs and Mirpuri Muslims

There are also some marked differences in marriage patterns between different South Asian groups. The contrast between two direct-migrant populations, the Jullundri Sikhs, who comprise the majority of Britain's Indian Panjabi population, and Mirpuri Muslims, who comprise at least half of Britain's Pakistani population, provides a good example. This contrast is best drawn against a background of the socioeconomic conditions of the regions of origin, and the different circumstances of the migrations to Britain. Mirpur district is in Azad ("Free") Kashmir; Jullundur is about 170 miles away in Indian Panjab. Agriculturally and economically productive, Jullundur's fertile, irrigated plains have stimulated agricultural, economic, and industrial development since labor migration began in the late nineteenth century, and the remittance economy that accompanied the postwar migration has provided further impetus to both migration and local economic growth (Ballard 1983, 1990).

Mirpur, by comparison, is agriculturally and economically stagnant. It is situated in the northern plateau region of the Himalayan foothills where irrigation is difficult, agriculture is rainfall-dependent, and there is little industry. Families have for generations supplemented their income through male labor migration. Mirpuri men were seamen before World War I, and became munitions factory workers in the Midlands and North of England during World War II. The postwar demand for labor in Britain increased Mirpuri emigration, which accelerated in the 1960s when families were displaced during the construction of the Mangla dam. The region is heavily dependent on the remittance economy, which has not stimulated much local economic growth because the local infrastructure is poor, and money from abroad, if not left on bank deposit, is mostly used to construct stylish properties and establish small businesses to service the emigrant community. Young men pin their hopes of social advancement on going to England by marrying a relative there (Ballard, 1983).

A second set of differences concern the complexities of cultural motivation and religious rulings about appropriate marriage partners, the expectations and conventions of gender, and mortuary rites. Sikhs (and Hindus) generally expect marriage to be within the caste, and strict rules of exogamy prohibit marriage into the descent groups (*got*) of both parents, and of both grandmothers, and forbid the exchange of women between two families. As a result, brides move away from their natal village, to a family with whom they have no prior kinship ties. By contrast, the Muslim marriage rules permit first-cousin marriages. Moreover, in keeping with practice in many Muslim countries, Mirpuris actively prefer to arrange marriages between the offspring of siblings, a preference that almost has the force of a marriage rule. Parents expect to consider their siblings' claims over their offspring as spouses for their children, and rejecting such offers can cause deep offense, amounting to a repudiation of the obligations of kinship. Marriages also take place with more distant relatives and outside the *biradari*, but as many as half of Mirpuri marriages are with first cousins (Ballard, 1990: 231). In consequence, a bride's mother-in-law is frequently also her aunt and lives in the bride's natal village, and local kinship networks are dense, with relatives often related to each other in several different ways though overlapping agnatic and affinal ties.

Gender conventions govern relationships between men and women right across the Panjab: women are expected, for example, to cover their heads (with a *chunni* or *dupatta*) in the presence of senior male kin. However, the conventions of Muslim purdah tend to discourage female participation in public life, and require a woman traveling in public places to be concealed by a *chaadar* (shawl) or *burqa* (full-length veil), such that Mirpuri women's movements in general are more restricted that those of Panjabi Sikhs (and Hindus). A third difference concerns mortuary rituals. Ballard (1990) suggests that the Muslim custom of burying the dead in village graveyards roots Mirpuris in the particular localities of their villages of origin (the requirement for burial within 24 hours is suspended to allow bodies to be flown home from abroad). However, some Muslims are now being buried in Muslim cemeteries in the UK, because this is where their descendants are living. By contrast, the Sikh (and Hindu) practice of cremating the dead does not tie them to one place, for cremation, ideally within 24 hours of death, can be performed anywhere, and although ashes are ideally scattered in the Ganges, other rivers such as the Thames are acceptable substitutes.

Ballard (1990) suggests that the effect of these considerations is the creation for Mirpuri Muslims of locally focused, tight-knit kinship networks, within which women's physical mobility tends to be restricted, whereas the Jullundri Sikhs are less rooted locally. This has had a number of further consequences, played out in relation to the different political economies of the regions of origins. Jullundri Sikh migrants in Britain drew on their business and technical skills from the Panjab to escape factory work as soon as they could, establishing groceries, post offices, taxi services, and construction and other businesses, often with the help of kinsmen. Lacking close prior kinship ties with their in-laws, and freer from the constraints of purdah, their wives and children came to Britain as early as the 1950s – or as soon as men had purchased their own homes – and women readily took up paid employment. Ballard argues that both parents being better able early on to take advantages of opportunities in Britain, and to support their children's education, in large part explains why Sikh children have achieved educational parity with middle-class whites. Their upwardly mobile, middle-class lifestyles and aspirations also meant that they were better protected than the Mirpuris from the effects of the recession in the late 1970s and 1980s.

By contrast, Mirpuri men remained "international commuters" (Ballard 1990: 223) for much longer, periodically returning to Mirpur for lengthy respites from factory work, and remitting money to support their dependants in Mirpur rather than investing in property in the UK. This made them vulnerable to the effects of the recession, because by the 1970s an unskilled laborer who returned to Mirpur for several months risked losing his job, and was unlikely to obtain another. Mirpuri women and children began to arrive in Britain at this time, but family reunion was slow because immigration restrictions were now more stringent, with entry permits sometimes granted only after years of applications, appeals, and reapplication. Most families did not encourage women to work outside the home, though "homeworking" (sewing garments or assembling objects for local factories) to supplement a household's minimal income is common, particularly if husbands are unemployed. Women's generally more restricted access to public services, coupled with religious beliefs about the undesirability of family planning, has also meant that fertility has remained higher among the Mirpuris than the Jullundris, although there is evidence that this is changing with the second generation, and with later marriage. The relative socioeconomic disadvantage of Mirpuri Muslims in comparison with Jullundri Sikhs reflects these networks of political and economic factors and cultural and religious considerations.

## Contrasting Marriage Patterns

The contrasting experiences of these groups have influenced post-migration patterns of marriage and household formation. Pioneer-generation Jullundri Sikhs initially received and accepted marriage offers for their children from the Panjab, but now tend to arrange marriages within the UK, and sometimes the US or Canada. Increasingly, young British-born second- and third-generation adults take the initiative in the choice of spouse, and prefer to describe their marriages as "assisted," rather than "arranged." A newly married couple is likely to live independently of the groom's parents. Some couples have moved to Canada or the US, where there is an established diaspora community, and tend not to invest money in the Panjab because of its political instability.

Since Mirpuri family reunion occurred later, many second-generation, British-born Mirpuris are only now marrying and having children, and they are marrying relatives from Mirpur, especially first cousins. The rate of transnational marriage among both Mirpuris and Pakistanis generally is high, and there is evidence that rates of close consanguineous marriages has increased (Shaw, 2001). Analysis of Home Office referrals and Census data for Bradford shows that 57.6 percent of Pakistani marriages in 1992–4 were with spouses from Pakistan (Simpson, 1997: 104). Analysis of 70 Pakistani marriages in Oxford showed that 71 percent of marriages were with spouses from Pakistan, and 92 percent of these transnational marriages were with relatives (Shaw, 2001: 327). These are mostly conventionally arranged marriages, but parents consider a number of factors when arranging them, including, usually, the preferences of their children, who may themselves prefer spouses from Pakistan because they "know the culture." Parents also feel obliged to accept marriage proposals from siblings in Pakistan, because to refuse them is shameful and will cast doubt over the respectability *(izzat)* of the *biradari* at "home." This is an important consideration for relatives in Britain, who in most cases wish to maintain their strong socioeconomic links in the homeland. In fact, a proportion of retired or unemployed pioneer-generation men have returned to Pakistan and to Mirpur to reside in their remittance-built houses and live off their pensions, capital, or income from rented property; usually their wives remain in Britain, where their children and grandchildren are, often becoming the senior-status heads of three-generational households.

Transnational marriages have, however, proved problematic in some cases. The annual number of spouses arriving from South Asia has more than doubled since the Labour government waived the requirement that spouses prove their marriage is "genuine" (Home Office, 2002: 100). With this, the reported number of "forced" marriages – mainly of British girls of Mirpuri, Pakistani, and, to a lesser extent, Bangladeshi origin – has increased, received media attention, and been the subject of a specially commissioned enquiry. Sometimes, a daughter whose behavior is regarded as threatening to her family's reputation and damaging to her marriage prospects may be coerced into marriage in order to prevent the family being shamed. The "forced marriages" described in the media and involving girls taken to Pakistan and married unwillingly to cousins are usually contracted under such circumstances. Occasionally, too, girls run away, but by doing so they risk losing all future support from their families: this is a major consideration, given the close-knit character of the kinship system. Sometimes brothers, relatives, or paid "bounty hunters" may pursue the errant girl in an attempt to salvage the family's reputation. These incidents have generated debates over individual and civil rights in relation to minority cultural values, and it is in relation to such issues as "forced marriage" that the government has recently recommended "citizenship lessons" for new immigrants (*Guardian*, October 26, 2001).

Spouses from the Subcontinent – who are brides and grooms in roughly equal proportions – may not speak English fluently, and may find it difficult adapting to living within the household of their British relatives. Conventionally a bride moves to her husband's parents' household on marriage, but Pakistani and Mirpuri grooms from abroad usually join the households of their UK-raised brides (where at least one of their in-laws is likely to be an aunt or an uncle). This reinforces the pattern of joint living, but it can be humiliating for men to be even initially dependent on their wives (who may have had to demonstrate their financial independence and home-ownership to the Home Office in order to obtain entry permit for their husbands) and on their wives' relatives. Such wives often resent a husband's expectation that at least a proportion of the money he or his wife earns will be remitted to his parents and siblings in Pakistan, rather than used to improve the lifestyle of the family in Britain, and this is a common source of marital discord, as Dhanjal (1976) previously suggested for Sikh women in Southall who earn wages outside the home.

A second issue connected with South Asian Muslim marriage patterns concerns the biological risks of consanguineous marriage. A number of media reports have called for education about the risks of miscarriage, infant death, and childhood morbidity that are associated with the practice of cousin marriage, because epidemiological studies indicate a link between parental consanguinity and recessively inherited genetic disorders. In a five-year prospective study of the health of 5,000 Birmingham babies across ethnic groups, Pakistanis comprised only 20 percent of the study population but contributed to 40 percent of the observed disability (Bundey and Alam, 1993). Over 50 percent of the Pakistani infants had consanguineous parents, and adverse birth outcome was three times higher in this group, with consanguinity accounting for about 60 percent of the infant mortality and severe morbidity among the Pakistanis in that study. The precise contribution of parental consanguinity to adverse birth outcome in this population remains a matter of considerable debate, because of the close correlations also with social class, poverty, recent migration history, and women's generally restricted access to medical services (Ahmad, 1996; Proctor and Smith, 1997). How Pakistani-origin families are making decisions arising from genetic-risk information and the impact of this information may have on marriage patterns is a topic of current research (Shaw, 2000a, in press; Richards, chapter 27, this volume).

## Conclusions and Implications

An understanding of the process and circumstances of immigration and settlement for different minority groups shows how households apparently similar in composition may at a given point in time be the outcome of very dissimilar processes of marriage and household formation, that have quite different meanings for the participants. An Afro-Caribbean single-parent household may represent a stage toward the eventual establishment of a conjugal family, while a Pakistani nuclear family may represent a stage in the development cycle of a multigenerational household. Moreover, household survey approaches may reveal little about what life is like within particular households, about the nature of relationships between spouses and between other relatives, and about the nature of links beyond the household with kin and non-kin, including transnational links that may be important in times of crisis or in shaping the direction of marriage choices. An exploration of changing family forms and relationships needs to take account of these aspects of family life.

This chapter has drawn particular attention to observed differences between families of South Asian origin, between direct migrants and twice migrants, and between Jullundri Sikhs and Mirpuri Muslims, in order to suggest that these groups are following dissimilar routes of adaptation to life in the UK linked with dissimilar pre-migration starting points. This in turn helps to explain divergences in both levels of "assimilation" in UK terms, and in the strength of ties in South Asia. In describing these differences, however, it is important to avoid generating new stereotypes, because there are important divergences within the categories "Mirpuri Muslim" and "Jullundri Sikh," for example, with respect to *biradari* and caste identity (e.g., Jat Sikh, Ramgharia Sikh, etc.) and social class, discussion of which are beyond the scope of this chapter. Nevertheless, the distinctions shed light on other aspects of the South Asian experience. For instance, the experience of direct-migrant Jullundri Sikhs, sometimes described simply as "Panjabis" or "Indians," seems to parallel that of the East African and Panjabi Hindus more closely than that of the Mirpuri or Bangladeshi Muslims. Not surprisingly, then, one survey places "Indians and African-Asians" together in the same category with respect to their views of marriage, the domestic division of labor, and female paid work (Beishon, Modood, and Virdee, 1998). Many aspects of the Mirpuri Muslim experience, on the other hand, are paralleled in the migration pattern of Pakistani Panjabis and Bangladeshi Muslims, whose socioeconomic position is broadly similar to that of the Mirpuris, and who also delayed bringing wives and children to England. Thus, Pakistanis and Bangladeshis have been described as "the most traditional" in their views of household arrangements and marriage, stating a preference for multigenerational households (Beishon, Modood, and Virdee, 1998). Such a statement, however, overlooks the considerable internal differentiation among British Pakistanis, especially between those from the rainfall-dependent districts of northern Panjab such as Jhelum (bordering Mirpur), Rawalpindi, and Attock, and those from the irrigated *(nehri)* and more prosperous central districts of Faisalabad, Sargodha, and Sahival. Many UK Faisalabadis are from the Arain Muslim caste, with now attenuated pre-1947 roots in Jullundur district in India and their experiences are perhaps closer to those of the Julllundri Sikhs ("Panjabis") than to those of many other Muslim groups. They predominate in Manchester, Glasgow, Dewsbury, Huddersfield, and Oxford, where they are known to have become prosperous. While inter-*biradari* marriages have often enabled Arain to consolidate business interests and gain an economic foothold in Britain, a more outward pattern of marriage choices beyond first cousins may have facilitated their subsequent relative economic success (see Shaw, 2001; Werbner, 1990).

The account presented here cautions against placing undue emphasis on the extent to which the British-raised second- and third-generation descendants of pioneer immigrants have assimilated the values of the host society and are moving in the direction of "modern individualism" with respect to patterns of family form and marriage, by showing how these processes are governed by motives and pressures that may vary with ethnicity. Within many immigrant-origin families, distinctive patterns of kinship, obligations to siblings, and structures of authority and of gender are likely to shape marriage and family forms for some time to come, and these may in turn influence the extent to which migrants retain transnational links.

The dynamics of continuity and change in family forms and relationships and the nature of transnational links among the second- and third-generation descendants of South Asian and Caribbean immigrants are topics that warrant further detailed and comparative research. With respect to particular South Asian groups, it would be worth exploring the extent to which being married to a relative from South Asia will encourage the second generation to maintain close transnational links, which can now also be sustained by modern communications technology, and the extent to which the third generation will agree with parental choices of spouse, and feel bound by the obligations of kinship and *biradari*. How transnational kinship and family identities are sustained and communicated across generations, and the relationship between these processes and the socioeconomic and political conditions in the UK, South Asia, and the Caribbean also warrant further research.

## References

Ahmad, W. (1996) Consanguinity and related demons: Science and racism in the debate on consanguinity and birth outcome. In C. Samson and N. South (eds.), *The Social Construction of Social Policy: Methodologies, Citizenship and the Environment*. London: Macmillan.

Allan, G., and Crow, G. (2001) *Families, Households and Society*. Basingstoke: Palgrave.

Ballard, R. (1983) The context and consequences of migration: Jullundur and Mirpur compared. *New Community*, 11, 117–36.

Ballard, R. (1990) Migration and kinship: The differential effect of marriage rules on the processes of Punjabi migration to Britain. In C. Clarke, C. Peach, and S. Vertovec (eds.), *South Asians Overseas: Migration and Ethnicity*. Cambridge: Cambridge University Press.

Ballard, R. (ed.) (1994) *Desh Pardesh: The South Asian Presence in Britain*. London: Hurst.

Ballard, R., and Kalra, V. S. (1994) *The Ethnic Dimensions of the 1991 Census, A Preliminary Report*. Manchester: Census Dissemination Unit.

Baumann, G. (1996) *Contesting Culture: Discourses of Identity in Multi-Ethnic London*. Cambridge: Cambridge University Press.

Beishon, S., Modood, T., and Virdee, S. (1998) *Findings: Ethnic Minority Families*. Summary of Policy Studies Institute report. York: Joseph Rowntree Foundation.

Benson, S. (1981) *Ambiguous Ethnicity*. Cambridge: Cambridge University Press.

Benson, S. (1996) Asians have culture, West Indians have problems: Discourses of race and ethnicity in and out of anthropology. In T. O. Ranger, Y. Samad, and O. Stuart (eds.), *Culture, Identity and Politics: Ethnic Minorities in Britain*. Aldershot: Avebury.

Berrington, A. (1994) Marriage and family formation among the white and ethnic minority populations in Britain. *Ethnic and Racial Studies*, 17, 517–46.

Berthoud, R. (2000) *Family Formation in Multicultural Britain: Three Patterns of Diversity, a working paper*. Institute for Social and Economic Research: University of Essex.

Bhachu, P. (1985) *Twice Migrants: East African Sikh Settlers in Britain*. London: Tavistock.

Blakemore, K., and Boneham, M. (1994) *Age race and ethnicity: A Comparative Approach*. Buckingham: Open University Press.

Brown, C. (1984) *Black and White Britain: the third PSI Survey*. Aldershot: Gower.

Bundey, S., and Alam, H. (1993) A five year prospective study of the health of children in different ethnic groups, with particular reference to the effect of inbreeding. *European Journal of Human Genetics*, 1, 206–19.

Byron, M. (1999) The Caribbean-born population in 1990s Britain: Who will return? *Journal of Ethnic and Migration Studies*, 25, 285–301.

Chamberlain, M. (1997) *Narratives of Exile and Return*. University of Warwick Caribbean Studies Series. London: Macmillan.

Chamberlain M. (ed.) (1998) *Caribbean Migration: Globalised Identities*. London: Routledge.

Chamberlain, M. (1999) The family as model and metaphor in Caribbean migration to Britain. *Journal of Ethnic and Migration Studies*, 25, 251–66.

Coleman, D., and Salt, J. (1996) *Ethnicity in the 1991 Census, Volume One: Demographic Characteristics of the Ethnic Minority Populations*. London: HMSO.

Dhanjal, B. (1976) Sikh women in Southall. *New Community*, 5, 109–17.

Eade, J. (1990) *The Politics of Community: The Bangladeshi Community in East London*. Aldershot: Gower.

Foner, N. (1977) The Jamaicans. In J. Watson (ed.), *Between Two Cultures*. Oxford: Blackwell.

Foner, N. (1979) *Jamaica Farewell*. Berkeley: University of California Press.

Gardner, K. (1995) *Global Migrants, Local Lives: Travel and Transformation in Rural Bangladesh*. Oxford: Clarendon Press.

Gordon, M. M. (1964) *Assimilation in American Life*. Oxford: Oxford University Press.

Goulborne, H. (1999) The transnational character of Caribbean kinship in Britain. In S. McRae (ed.), *Changing Britain: Families and Households in the 1990s*. Oxford: Oxford University Press.

Home Office (2002) *Secure Borders, Safe Haven: Integration with Diversity in Modern Britain*. Parliamentary White Paper, London: HMSO.

Jacobson, J. (1998) *Islam in Transition: Religion and Identity Among British Pakistani Youth*. London: Routledge.

Jeffery, P. M. (1976) *Migrants and Refugees: Muslim and Christian Pakistani Families In Britain*. Cambridge: Cambridge University Press.

McRae, S. (1999) *Changing Britain: Families and Households in the 1990s*. Oxford: Oxford University Press.

Model, S., Fisher, G., and Silberman, R. (1999) Black Caribbeans in comparative perspective. *Journal of Ethnic and Migration Studies*, 25, 187–212.

Modood, T. (1997) *Ethnic Minorities in Britain: Diversity and Disadvantage*. London: Policy Studies Institute.

Olwig, K. F. (1999) Narratives of the children left behind: Home and identity in globalised Caribbean families. *Journal of Ethnic and Racial Studies*, 25, 267–84.

Patterson, S. (1965) *Dark Strangers: A Study of West Indians in London*. Harmondsworth: Penguin.

Phillips, M., and Phillips, T. (1998) *Windrush: The Irresistible Rise of Multi-Racial Britain*. London: HarperCollins.

Proctor, S. R., and Smith, I. J. (1997) Factors associated with birth outcome in Bradford Pakistanis. In A. Clarke and E. Parsons (eds.), *Culture, Kinship and Genes: Towards Cross-Cultural Genetics*. London: Macmillan.

Pryce, K. (1979) *Endless Pressure*. Harmondsworth: Penguin.

Shaw, A. (2000a) Conflicting models of risk: Clinical genetics and British Pakistanis. In P. Caplan (ed.), *Risk Revisited*. London: Pluto Press.

Shaw, A. (2000b) *Kinship and Continuity: Pakistani Families in Britain*. Amsterdam: Routledge/Harwood Academic.

Shaw, A. (2001) Kinship, cultural preference and immigration: Consanguineous marriage among British Pakistanis. *Journal of the Royal Anthropological Institute*, 7, 315–34.

Shaw, A. (in press) Negotiations of risk among Pakistani-origin users of the genetic services. In M. Unnithan-Kumar (ed.), *Reproductive Agency, Medicine and the State: Cultural Transformations in Childbearing*. Oxford: Berghahn Books.

Simpson, S. (1997) Demography and ethnicity: Case studies from Bradford. *New Community*, 23, 89–107.

Smith, R. T. (1988) *Kinship and Class in the West Indies: A Genealogical Study of Jamaica and Guyana*. Cambridge: Cambridge University Press.

Solien, N. (1965) The consanguineal household and matrifocality. *American Anthropologist*, 67, 1541–9.

Song, M., and Edwards, R. (1997) Comment: Raising questions about perspectives on black lone motherhood. *Journal of Social Policy*, 26, 233–44.

Vatuk, S. (1972) *Kinship and Urbanization: White Collar Migrants in North India*. Berkeley and Los Angeles: University of California Press.

Vertovec, S. (1994) Caught in an ethnic quandary: Indo-Caribbean Hindus in London. In R. Ballard (ed.), *Desh Pardesh: The South Asian Presence in Britain*. London: Hurst.

Watson, J. L. (ed.) (1977) *Between Two Cultures: Migrants and Minorities in Britain*. Oxford: Basil Blackwell.

Werbner, P. (1990) *The Migration Process: Capital, Gifts and Offerings among British Pakistanis*. Oxford: Berg.

Young, M., and Wilmott, P. (1957) *Family and Kinship in East London*. London: Routledge & Kegan Paul.

# IV

# Changing Family Forms and Relationships

# 17

# Religion, Romantic Love, and the Family

Bryan S. Turner

## Introduction: Body, Reproduction, and the Sacred

A sociological analysis of the general relationship between the family and religion as social institutions would be a large and problematic undertaking. In this chapter, it is important to make a number of basic assumptions in order to simplify the analysis. First, the definition of religion here is derived from Emile Durkheim (2001: 46), namely that religion is a system of belief and practice relating to the sacred. While the etymological roots of religion (*religiun*) are obscure, we might argue that *religio* is connected with the idea of rule and regulation. A religion is that which binds a people by its rituals and customs, and as a consequence religion forms a society. This notion of *religio* as constituting community through adherence to rituals that separate the sacred from the profane was the basis of the sociology of religion. Just as the swaddling bands of a child binds his or her body within the family, so religion binds the individual to society. In practice I am primarily concerned with the so-called Abrahamic religions – Judaism, Christianity, and Islam. By taking this approach to religion, I specifically exclude any discussion of magic and witchcraft, which are practices where women, particularly old women and widows, have suffered aggressive forms of social exclusion (Comaroff and Comaroff, 1993).

Secondly, this chapter avoids any engagement with the problem of how to define the family. For the sake of convenience, I shall define the family, as distinct from the couple, as a social unit that is primarily concerned with reproduction and the transmission of social values through socialization, and which normally involves common habitation in a household. It is obvious that even this minimalist definition could be criticized, but it will serve a convenient heuristic purpose (Turner, 1998). Finally, I assume that it is impossible to understand religion and the family in modern society without an adequate grasp of their historical development, and thus the analysis of institutions requires a comparative and historical sociology. My argument is therefore pursued through a historical study of key changes in romantic attachment and the family that have an "elective affinity" with transformations of religion, namely how ideas and interests converge historically (Weber, 1991: 280).

The Abrahamic religions were inextricably based on notions of family, generation and reproduction that occupy their core theology and cosmology. These religions were profoundly patriarchal, and hence the contemporary transformation of family life, sexuality, the sexual division of labor, and the status of women have had profound, and largely corrosive, effects on official religious teaching and practice. In modern secular societies, feminism, gay liberation, and other social movements have articulated a range of claims for social equality and access to alternative and sexual, familial, or coupling arrangements. Social and technological changes create the conditions for new modes of familial, sexual, and reproductive relationships that constitute a radical challenge to both traditional religion and conventional forms of the family. Although secularization has undermined the formal authority of the Christian churches in the control of family life, there is also evidence of the continuity of underlying religious values and assumptions. There is an important relationship or elective affinity between the growing emphasis in Christianity on subjectivity, emotions, and the individual, and in secular culture a parallel development of marriage as companionship and sexual satisfaction. Both religious and secular developments are manifestations of Romanticism.

There have been in the history of human societies a number of important, more or less permanent, connections between religion and the family. The core to these mythological, cosmological, and theological connections is the principle of generation and regeneration. Social struggles over the control of human reproduction have been reflected in controversies between matriarchy and patriarchy as forms of authority, and these political controversies can be discerned even in the historical origins of the tradition of a "high God." There is much disagreement, obviously, about the origins of human mythologies. For Mircea Eliade (1959: 17), in the development of agriculture, the symbolism and cults of Mother Earth and human fertility became dominant. An alternative view is that with the rise of agriculture, the plough breaks up the earth and makes it fertile. The plough is a phallic symbol that points to men taking gardening away from women and in Sumerian mythology Enki, the male god of water (semen), became the Great Father (Thompson, 1996: 162). However, the development of a high god and monotheism that challenged or replaced many of these fertility cults occurred simultaneously in a number of regions of the world. This creative religious period, from approximately 800 to 200 BC, has been defined as an "axial age," because it was the crucial turning point in the formation of civilizational complexes (Jaspars, 1968). Confucius, Buddha, Socrates, Zoroaster, and Isaiah, whose cosmological views had important common features, shaped the axial age of the emerging agrarian civilizations, within which city life began to emerge. It was the cultural basis from which sprang the ethical, prophetic leaders of monotheism, which resulted eventually in the so-called "religions of the book" in which divine revelation was recorded. The prophets of the axial age addressed human beings in the name of a supreme, moral being who could not be represented by an image and who could not be easily constrained or cajoled by ritual or magic. He was a God opposed to idols and idolatry, and who demanded unswerving commitment through a contractual relationship.

The emergence of belief in a high God and the creation of "confessional" states were the prelude to the subsequent construction of Judaism, Christianity, and Islam out of prophetic monotheism and ascetic criticism of worldliness. The prophets of the desert condemned the fleshpots of city life in the name of a jealous God, and the pre-exilic prophets, such as Jeremiah, in the middle of the seventh century BC, composed a catalog of sins (Weber, 1952). In Judaism, these ethical teachings were eventually assembled as the Decalog, within which filial piety, love of children, and the prohibition of adultery, incest, prostitution, and masturbation were central components of the Jewish paradigm of conjugal relationships.

Thus, the interconnection between divinity and fertility was extremely ancient, but when God as the Creator began to acquire the status of a Person, then He began to be conceptualized as a Father, specifically a Father to those tribes and communities that are loyal. There is therefore an important mythical role for a Father who is the patriarch of nations. In the Old Testament "Jacob" and "Israel" are used interchangeably. There is in the Old Testament an important division between the idea of creation in Genesis and the narrative account of the covenant between God as Father and the nation. This differentiation is important in understanding the division between God as the Creator of Nature and God as the Father of a nation, between an impersonal force and a personal God, between natural history and salvation history.

With the evolution of the idea of sacred fatherhood, there developed a range of problems about the body. How are bodies produced and reproduced? If they fragment and decay, then redemption is a problem (Bynum, 1991). There have been (and continue to be) major political and social issues about what we might call the authorship of bodies and authority over them. Matriarchy and patriarchy can be regarded as social principles for deciding on the legitimacy and ownership of bodies, especially parental ownership and control of children. As we will see, patriarchy has specific and important connections with religion as a principle of reproductive legitimacy. The rites and rituals that surround birth and rebirth are fundamental to all religions, and the notion of regeneration has been crucial to ancient cosmologies. In these cosmological schemes, there were common homologies between the reproductive work of a creator God, the creative force of nature, and reproduction with human families (Eliade, 1959: 167). As Victor Turner (1966: 82) has demonstrated, mythologies are often constructed upon these generative homologies to form systems of dichotomous classification between red menstrual blood as a symbol of transmission between generations, and white semen and milk as symbols of food, sustenance, and reproduction.

Given the salience of the problem of generation, family metaphors were also important in the basic theology of "salvation history." Trinitarian theology became important for a familial allocation of roles in the salvation of mankind, at the center of which stands the Holy Family. If the high God of the Old Testament was a remote and threatening figure, the God of the New Testament has been seen, at least by nineteenth-century Protestantism, as a loving Father. Christ's cry of anguish from the Cross, "Abba Father," was indicative of this sense of intimacy. The spiritual connections between God and humanity in the Abrahamic tradition were conceived as familial. It is necessary to recognize the diversity of views about women, marriage, and sexuality in the Jewish tradition (Biale, 1992). While the early Judeo-Christian teaching about women was not uniform, its legacy included a deeply negative understanding of women and sexuality. In the Genesis story, the original cooperative and companionate relationship between man and woman is replaced after the Fall by a relationship of domination in which man becomes the ruler of woman (Bird, 1974).

The Mosaic Law was addressed to a society in which women were components of household property and could not take decisions for themselves. The wife was the property of the husband and an adulterous wife was punished with death. Women thus appear with animals and children as chattels of the household. A wife who did not produce children was not fulfilling her duty and infertility was a legal ground for divorce. Barrenness in the Old Testament was a sign of divine disapproval, and polygyny, concubinage, and prostitution were tolerated as concessions to male sexual energy. Because menstruation and childbirth were ritually unclean, women were frequently precluded from participating in cultic activities. Israelite marriage was a contract between separate families, and thus wives were dangerous to men, not only because they could manipulate men with their sexual charms, but because they were recruited from outside of the husband's family. These negative images of women in the Old Testament have proved to be remarkably resilient historically.

## The Early Christian Church: Marriage as a Necessary Evil

Traditional religious teaching on the family in the West obviously depends on the theological view of sexuality, marriage, and reproduction in the Bible. In view of the authority of the New Testament, it is important to realize that Jesus had very little to say about marriage and his statements about sexual relationships were limited. By comparison with Jewish teaching at the time, Jesus appears to take little interest in the subject of family and marriage. The Gospels do not therefore contain a developed or systematic view of marriage and the family. In order to discover what was the teaching of the early Church on marriage and family life, we need to turn to St. Paul's New Testament theology. Paul's epistles to the early Christian communities, such as the letter to the Corinthians, were essentially ad hoc responses to specific local issues, but they have come to have a clear authority. Paul's teachings precluded divorce and if the couple did separate, they were not permitted to remarry. He also recognized that celibacy was superior to marriage. Because Paul was convinced that the end of the world was near, he had little to say about children and appears not to have regarded procreation as the main reason for marriage.

With the gradual erosion of the millennial vision of the early Church, Christians began to transform their view of the permanence and importance of the things of this world. The post-Pauline letters to Timothy and Titus, and the writings of St Augustine, began to fill out the gaps and silences in the Gospels with respect to how Christians should conduct themselves in this world. Post-Pauline theology can be regarded as a systematic philosophical attempt to come to terms with the Greco-Roman world. The early Church Fathers painted a picture of the Roman world as a licentious and decadent society in order to enforce the social division between Christian and pagan practice. They praised virginity over marriage, and Jerome, regarding virginity as the quickest road to paradise, encouraged women to enter religious orders, since marriage was no protection from lust (Reuther, 1974). In fact the historical evidence on the social life of Greco-Roman civilization indicates that marriage was regarded as a duty of citizens to uphold the empire, and the Roman ideal recognized loyalty and companionship as fundamental to marriage (Grubbs, 1999). The Christian denigration of Roman marriage customs was an ideological attack that sought to justify a new set of religious norms.

The underlying principles of Christianity were inevitably patriarchal in the sense that the structure of Christian theology required the concept of Jesus as the Son of God in order to make sense of "salvation history" as a redemptive act of sacrifice. God so loved the world that He gave His only Son that human beings could be saved from sin. If Christianity is fundamentally patriarchal, then we need to pay some attention to the ambiguous status of Mary (Warner, 1976). In theological terms, the virginity of Mary was necessary in order for Christ to be without sin, but Christ also had to be of woman born in order to achieve human status, and thus to experience our world. Over time, Mary herself was removed from the possibility of any connection with sin, and became detached from an association with the Fall of Adam and Eve. The doctrine of Immaculate Conception was declared in 1854, and she was exempt from original sin.

Mary was ambiguous in other ways. Mary became, in a patriarchal world, the great medieval symbol of motherhood. In the fourteenth century, the visions of St Bridget of Sweden pictured the Virgin, following the birth of Christ, on her knees in worshipful adoration of the Child, and by the fifteenth century paintings of the adoration of the mother were common. Commenting on this development, Simone de Beauvoir (1972: 160) saw this prostration of the mother as "the supreme masculine victory, consummated in the cult of the Virgin – it is the rehabilitation of woman through the accomplishment of her defeat." But the Virgin was also a vehicle in her own right of worship and adoration. The more she was exempt from sin, the more her status approximated that of Christ. In oppositional theology, she was often regarded as equal to Christ in the concept of co-redemption. Because she was spared from sin, she was also exempt from the physical experiences of the typical female – sexual intercourse, labor, and childbirth. She was removed from basic physical activities except for one – the suckling of the infant Jesus. As a result, a cult emerged around the breast of the Virgin and the milk that oozed from her teat. The theme of the nursing Virgin (the *Maria Lactans*) became an important part of medieval cultic belief and practice. In the absence of a powerful female figure in the Gospels, medieval Christianity elevated the spiritual status of Mary, who became the great champion of procreation and family life. This theological legacy continues to underpin much of the Catholic Church's teaching on procreation, contraception, abortion, and family life.

## Feudalism and Capitalism: Property and the Family

From the late twelfth century onward, there was a radical conflict between two models of marriage, the aristocratic and the ecclesiastical (Duby, 1978). The secular model expressed the view that marriage was an economic contract or treaty (*pactum conjugale*) between families in order to secure lawful property rights over land through a system of male primogeniture. Given a high rate of infant mortality, wives were expected to be fecund. These tensions between narrow primogeniture and high mortality rates were solved by various pragmatic arrangements. These included a tendency toward endogamy (including incest), a demand for premarital virginity, and exclusion of adultery. On the issues of female subordination and fecundity, the lay and ecclesiastical models were in complete harmony, but they departed over the questions of repudiation and divorce. The lay model required the option of repudiation in the case of sterile or barren wives in the interests of male succession, but the Church, regarding marriage as a necessary evil to protect society from the dangers of carnal lust, objected to divorce, repudiation, and remarriage.

The critical weakness in the Church's doctrine on marriage was the problem of endogamy. Because the feudal system required integrated estates, parents often preferred their children to enter endogamous marriages, for example with cousins. The Church abhorred any suggestion of incestuous union as an unnatural act, and hence any lord who "discovered" that he had unwittingly married a close relative, who turned out to be infertile, could safely repudiate her and remarry. Disputes about family genealogy were commonplace legal aspects of repudiation and divorce processes, and eventually the Church had to redefine the degrees of incest in order to combat these blatant abuses in the marriage system (Benson, 1976). In English ecclesiastical and political history, the most famous case of this struggle over religious regulation of the marriage and divorce was Henry VIII and the problem of succession. Henry employed a variety of legal devices to secure divorce in his attempts to secure male succession. While Henry's wives had produced viable offspring, his two daughters, Mary and Elizabeth, were declared illegitimate after he had divorced their mothers in 1533 and 1536, and his son Edward, who was born in 1537, died in 1553. Because the life expectancy of a Tudor male was 10.3 years at birth and 28 years at adolescence, the probability that his son would succeed Henry was low. Henry's divorces were in this context strategic rather than whimsical (Warnicke, 2000).

The Church was committed to the institution of monogamous marriage, but in reality there was a very high illegitimacy rate, and such illegitimate produce were not hidden or kept secret, but lived in the household alongside their legitimate siblings. This illegitimacy rate expressed the power differences between men and women because the feudal marriage contract only recognized the extramarital alliances of men. With the rise of the absolutist court society of the seventeenth and eighteenth centuries, the balance between the sexes was more equal, and husbands were less likely to control their wives by brute force than by the pressure of public opinion and moral restraint. The "civilizing process" meant that social restraints on sexual behavior were exercised through moral restraint on individuals. Marital relations, in a society where there had been some degree of liberation of high-status women, were subject to "the advance of the frontier of shame and embarrassment" (Elias, 2000: 155).

The Protestant Reformation and the origins of capitalist agriculture in the late seventeenth century ushered in the era of "possessive individualism" (Macpherson, 1962), which was in turn associated with the ideals of a bourgeois marriage system. The seventeenth century was the context of a major political struggle between patriarchalism and individualism, which had important consequences for the religious conceptualization of the nature of marriage. Royal privilege was challenged in the seventeenth century with the increasing power of merchants who attempted to defend their interests in Parliament and through the control of public opinion through the circulation of print. In a defense of tradition against the rise of Hobbesian contract theory, Sir Robert Filmer, in *Patriarcha* (written in 1640 and published in 1680), attempted to justify the "natural power of kings" against the "unnatural liberty of the people," and in the process reinvented the theory of patriarchy as an ideology of the modern state (Schochet, 1975). Through a set of contrived analogies and metaphors, he explained patriarchal power in terms of God and his people, the

Monarch and his kingdom, and the Father and his household. It was through these legal and political relationships that the connections between the domestic sphere and the state were secured.

Against the patriarchal theory of power, John Locke (1632–1704) developed his political theory of limited government, and in the two *Treatises of Government* (1690) argued that men were naturally free and that God did not appoint Adam and his descendants to rule over the world. While Locke did not deny the coercive nature of the state, his political theory of the social contract was based on consent and ownership of property. Locke rejected Filmer on the grounds that the obedience of children to their parents was based on consent, not on divine right. In the *Second Treatise*, Locke argued that human beings are born free, but children, who are vulnerable, need protection. The power that parents enjoy over their children "arises from the duty, which is incumbent upon them, to take care of their offspring during the imperfect state of childhood" (Locke, 1946: 29). This consent theory of government also had implications for his view of marriage, which exists primarily for "procreation, yet it draws with it mutual support and assistance, and a communion of interests" (Locke, 1946: 40). The problem with Locke's liberal theory of government was its presuppositions about the distribution of property (Macpherson, 1962), but it also reflected an important social departure from the aristocratic notions of government and family that had dominated medieval Europe. The transformation of religious justifications for the marriage union, however, owes more to Milton than to Locke.

The period from the Reformation to Locke's *Treatise* represented a major transformation of ideas and practice relating to religion and the family. Papal doctrines of the superiority of celibacy and the view of marriage as a property transaction without intimacy or love were rejected. However, we must not exaggerate these changes. The most radical sects of the seventeenth century adhered to the view that by nature women were inferior to men and that the Fall resulted from the temptation of Eve. It followed from this view that even in Paradise before the temptation woman was inferior to man. Even the Quakers accepted the view that a woman should not by freely and independently speaking usurp the authority of her husband. Although the natural subordination of women was assumed on religious grounds, the ideal Puritan marriage was premised on a small household in which the wife exercised authority over servants and was the companion or "helpmeet" of her husband (Hill, 1977). It was John Milton (1608–74), whose own marriage to Mary Powell in 1642 was a disastrous failure, who expressed these changes to the Puritan family in his *The Doctrine and Discipline of Divorce* (Milton, 1927) in 1642. For Milton, marriage was not a sacrament and could be dissolved by notification to a magistrate on grounds that were fairly liberal. In his divorce pamphlets, Milton maintained the household supremacy of the husband, but in *Paradise Lost* (Milton, 1953, ix: 908–12) he recognized a marriage of equals based on emotional, not rational bonds. Faced by loneliness with the loss of Eve after the Fall, Adam asks:

> How can I live without thee, how forgoe
> Thy sweet Converse and Love so dearly joyn'd,
> To live again in these wilde woods forlorn?

Milton's writings on marriage marked an important transition, but by the end of the century religious opinion had moved away from the bitter theological controversies of the Civil War, and the Cambridge Platonists emphasized human free will and perfectibility. The eighteenth century, with its key notions of sensibility and education, promoted the idea of the family as a training ground of human sentiment.

## Secularization, the Family, and Christian Fundamentalism

The Christian churches in Europe have, from the nineteenth century, been subject to a process of secularization in which religious life became a matter of private belief and practice (Wilson, 1966). The growth of an urban industrial society undermined the social, cultural, and intellectual conditions that sustained religious attachment and belief. While sects continue to flourish, there is incontrovertible evidence of an institutional decline of mainstream Christianity. Within this general pattern of decline, there are, however, discernible differences between the predominantly Roman Catholic and Protestant regions and states (Martin, 1978). While there has been erosion of church membership, adherence, and practice in Europe, the Christian churches in the US have remained relatively central to American culture and politics, and this resilience was reflected in the social impact of fundamentalism in the late twentieth century.

While there is much to support the secularization thesis, it is important not to confuse the decline of Christian institutions with the decline of religion. In other words, we must not equate "de-Christianization" with the decline of religious world-views. The importance of individual emotional attachment and loyalty in intimate relationships in a secular age can be taken as an indication of the continuity of religion in Western societies. From Protestantism, Western societies have acquired an emphasis on the individual and individualism through such phenomena as conversion, a personal relationship to Jesus, private devotion, and bible study. Conversion experiences emphasized the importance of experiencing a loving relationship with Jesus, where emotional intensity became a measure of spiritual intensity. Individualism in modern society has also become increasingly emotional and erotic. Beck and Beck-Gernsheim (1995s: 179) argue that love is now our "secular religion," and claim that as "religion loses its hold, people seek solace in private sanctuaries," but this interpretation fails to recognize that modern erotic, sentimental, and private love is itself part of the legacy of Protestant pietism. We can date this emotional component of religious experience in eighteenth-century England to the Methodist movement, specifically to the evangelical field preaching of John Wesley and the evocative hymns of Charles Wesley. With the routinization of the Methodist fellowship, hymn singing and extemporary prayer preserved a tradition of emotional expressivity. However, it was in German pietism that one finds the broad origins of this emotional trend in Christian spirituality. For example, Friedrich Schleiermacher (1768–1834) defended religion against the rationalist criticisms of the Enlightenment, and argued that religious feelings of dependency are the foundation of religious faith. Schleiermacher's "anthropology" recognized a common humanity that was articulated through feeling (Morrison, 1988: 250). From this religious tradition, one can derive the modern notion that private and intimate experiences are fundamental to our notion of the self, and that marriage is primarily about establishing satisfactory relations of intimacy. These ideas have been especially potent in the US in the New Age Movement (Heelas, 1996) and more generally in American approaches to marriage (Cancian, 1987).

In recent years, sociologists have turned to the more contemporary themes of romance and intimacy (Beck and Beck-Gernsheim, 1990; Giddens, 1992; Illouz, 1997; Luhmann, 1986). Romantic love in modern societies is equally contradictory because it requires or at least celebrates erotic, intense, fleeting, and contingent relationships, and enduring, permanent, and faithful relations of love. These transformations include the secularization of love, the growing prominence of love in film and advertising, the celebration of love in popular culture and its equation with personal happiness, the association of love with consumption, and the insertion of "fun" into the definition of marriage and domesticity. If Courtly Love expressed a feudalization of love in the Middle Ages, so the commercialization of love expresses the secularization of modern society.

While in the US emotional commitment had been since the eighteenth century regarded as a necessary component of a successful marriage, it was not until the development of a mass market and advertising, especially in the 1930s, that a new emphasis on expressivity, romantic attachments, and erotic adventure emerged in the marketplace. This process involves a romanticization of commodities, because there is a new aura of romance that is attached to commodities, an attachment that can take two forms. "Candid consumption" is the attachment of a romantic theme directly to the product; "oblique consumption" is the indirect connection between the activity of the couple, their setting, and the product. In particular, romantic couples are involved in lifestyle and the consumption of leisure, of which romantic love is an important ingredient. In the first half of the twentieth century, sexual love, in advertising and film emerged as a utopia, wherein marriage could also be exciting, romantic fun, especially if the couple could participate fully in leisure and consumption. The use of close-ups in film and photography and the employment of movie stars to advertise commodities created a social cosmology, in which consumer icons represented the new lifestyle.

The love utopia was based on the assumption of a democratization of love and the possibility of mass consumption. "Love for everyone" was combined with "consumption for all." However, social reality constantly brought the utopia into question. In the early decades of the twentieth century, marriage as an institution was in a profound crisis (Groves and Ogburn, 1928). The underlying factors were changes in matrimonial legislation, the entry of women into the labor force, unrealistic expectations about the romantic character of marriage, and conflicts over domestic expenditure. Marriage guidance experts began to devise a battery of practical solutions to inject fun into marriages, because it was assumed that the companionate marriage was no longer adequate unless it could find space for erotic love and enjoyment. The rise of the "dating system" also illustrates the new emphasis on youth culture, the cultural importance of intimacy and the private sphere, and the focus on "going out" and "dining out" as norms of both courtship and marriage. The commodification of love has become part of the American Dream. For example, romanticized advertisements rarely picture the couple at home with children, but emphasize instead the couple as tourists in a landscape, at a romantic restaurant or in an up-market hotel.

The paradigm of romantic love, sexual satisfaction, and youthfulness is now sufficiently powerful in popular culture to influence older generations who either expect to enjoy love and romantic attachment into old age, or wish to avoid growing old in order to maintain their romantic attachments (Riggs and Turner, 1999). These assumptions underpin popular commentaries on love and the aging woman in, for example, Betty Friedan's *The Fountain of Age* (1993). While the elderly are encouraged to sustain romantic love, there has been what we might call an "infantilization" of romance by which infants and teeny-boppers have been drawn into the complex of consumption and romance through popular music. These changes in expressiveness, romance, and youthfulness constitute what Talcott Parsons called the expressive revolution, a social change that he regarded as "a new religious movement of far-reaching importance" (1999: 316). This American religious revolution involved a shift from the cognitive-instrumental values of early capitalism to an affective-expressive culture. Perhaps in support of Parsons's argument one could refer to Madonna, whose popular songs "Like a Prayer" and "Open Your Heart" have been interpreted as aspects of popular religion, whose themes are often compatible with liberation theology (Hulsether, 2000: 92). For other sectors of American Christianity, her name and lifestyle represent a mocking travesty of religion and family values.

Christian fundamentalism in America is a direct response to secular humanism. A major feature of such fundamentalist movements is the desire to restore family values, improve Christian education, and protect children from lifestyles that are simultaneously anti-American and anti-Christian. This perception of the erosion of American values was at the heart of the Moral Majority, formed in 1979 under the leadership of Jerry Falwell. The original inspiration for this movement came from political groups that were frustrated with the Republican Party, and it included not only Protestants, but Roman Catholics, Mormons, and Pentecostalists. American domestic and foreign policy had to be based on the Bible, and in order to restore America to its true mission it was necessary to struggle against the "moral minority" that exercised power over the government. The New Christian Right, as they came to be known, were against abortion, gay rights, and drug liberalization. In fact, there was a significant emphasis on problems relating to sexuality (Armstrong, 2001: 311). Fundamentalists regarded feminism as a "disease" and equated homosexuality with pederasty. It was "secular humanism," a catchall phrase that included feminism, that had emasculated American men. In this respect, fundamentalism was able to address a range of popular anxieties about male impotence, high divorce rates, female self-assertion, and low birthrates.

American fundamentalism responded to this cultural and political crisis in a number of ways. From the late 1980s there were aggressive, and occasionally violent, campaigns against abortion clinics by so-called moral "rescuers." In the educational system, Christian creationists led an attack on evolutionary science and Darwinism in an effort to assert the literal truth of Genesis. In terms of family life, fundamentalists reasserted what they thought to be the biblical view of marriage, namely the importance of male headship. For example, the Southern Baptist Convention meeting in 1988 amended its *Baptist Faith and Message Statement* to declare that a woman should "submit herself graciously" to the leadership of her husband. The result of the amendment by the largest American Protestant denomination was to jettison the principle of an egalitarian family (Smith, 2000: 160). This assertion of male leadership was seen to be a necessary step in restoring the family that is seen to be fundamental to the continuity of Christianity and to the health of the nation. In practice, Christian interpretations of what leadership actual means in day-to-day terms are variable and pragmatic (Ammerman, 1987), but the influence of these fundamentalist ideas has been significant, as illustrated by President Clinton's eventual confession of sinfulness to a breakfast meeting of Christian leaders.

Although American fundamentalism has been predominantly a Protestant religious movement of the southern states, there has also been a remarkable convergence of opinion between fundamentalism, the political Right, Catholic conservatives and, ironically, components of the women's movement around pronatalism. These diverse movements have in various ways rejected liberal America in favor of the regulation of pornography, anti-abortion legislation, the criminalization of homosexuality, and the virtues of faithfulness and loyalty in sexual partnerships. In short, these values confirmed a religious view of sexual and marital relationships that transcended denominational affiliation.

## Fundamentalism and the Veil: Islam and Women's Rights in Marriage

There are important differences between the sociological origins of Christianity and Islam. It has been argued that the pre-Islamic Middle East had diverse forms of marriage and family life in which women enjoyed a considerable degree of power and freedom. Divorce and remarriage were common for both sexes. For example, the Prophet's first wife Khadija was a wealthy widow who, prior to her marriage, employed Muhammad to oversee her trading arrangements between Mecca and Syria. Her economic independence and influence over early Islam are taken as evidence of pre-Islamic opportunities for female independence. Islam arose in a society in transition where private property in trading centers like Mecca and Medina became important. With the growth of commercial wealth, women were increasingly regarded as aspects of individual prosperity and their status declined (Watt, 1953). However, because influential women, including the Prophet's wives, were early converts to Islam, women play an important role in the Qur'an, unlike women in the New Testament. Islam did not prescribe veiling or the seclusion of women, and proscribed the tribal custom of female infanticide.

Despite the fact that Qur'anic teaching and *hadith* protected women, the Orientalist literature has taken a critical view of Muhammad's relationship with women (Turner, 1974). While Jesus and Muhammad are both charismatic prophets, they are very different religious figures. Although Muhammad is a model of the perfect life, he is also an entirely human figure, and had a strong sexual appetite. Islam has never supported celibacy as a normative standard, and many Islamic texts, such as the theology of Abu Hamid al-Ghazali (d. 1111), advocate sexual relations as natural and healthy. Junayd of Baghdad, a renowned Sufi teacher, declared that he needed sexual intercourse as much as he required food, and that his wife was nourishment and a means of purifying the heart (Winter, 1995: 41).

The scholarly consensus is that early Islam protected women and gave them a definite role in the public functions of the community, but the ethical view of gender equality in the Qur'an was quickly submerged as Islamic expansion was consolidated into the empires of the Umayyad (661–750) and Abbasid (750–945) periods. The growth of a military elite and a slave economy also promoted widespread female domestic slavery, prostitution, and concubinage. Warfare and military expansion silenced the underlying religious view of human equality, and the earlier freedom of women to divorce and remarry was curtailed. The religious and ritualistic separation of the world of men and the world of women was increasingly rigid and formal.

During medieval Islam, these social patterns were generally reinforced, but we must take into account important regional and class variations. For example, polygamy and concubinage were typical of the ruling class, but not general in

Muslim society, where they were regarded as permissible rather than desirable. Because women need the protection of men, widows and divorcees, without kinship support, soon found themselves destitute. However, because women could inherit property, women of the middle class could avoid this fate of social exclusion. However, women's capacity to participate in economic activity was limited. The social seclusion of women was given expression in domestic architecture, where the *harem* or women's quarters of wealthy families was physically secluded and protected (Scarce, 1996).

The veil is the symbolic core of the issue of female emancipation in Islam, but veiling is only one component in a complex of religious and legal arrangements that include seclusion, polygamy, the unrestricted license of men to divorce, early marriage for girls, arranged marriages involving large disparities of age, and such practices as clitoridectomy (Ahmed, 1992). The veil presents a paradox for which there are no clear solutions. Veiling has been associated with religious prejudice and the social oppression of women, but it also has strong connections with Orientalism and Western colonial control of Muslim society. Various modernization movements have sought to undercut religious regulation of dress. In Turkey, under Mustafa Kemal Atatürk, the hat laws attempted to modernize men's headgear and to liberate women from the veil. However, with the spread of fundamentalism in the late twentieth century, women have been re-veiling. In some societies such as Java (Brenner, 1996), which have historically not had a history of veiling, recent adoption of the veil is associated with a redefinition of the female self. In other societies such as Egypt, the veil is deeply connected with colonial history. In *Modern Egypt* (1908), the Earl of Cromer concluded that, whereas the "Christian respects women; the teaching of his religion and the incidents of his religious worship tend to elevate them.... The Moslem, on the other hand, despises women; both his religion and the example of his Prophet, the history of whose private life has been handed down to him, tend to lower them in his eyes" (Baring, 2000: 157). His solution was that Islam would achieve successful modernization only when Muslim women had been liberated from ignorance and seclusion. His argument was hypocritical, since he simultaneously opposed the political liberation of women in England, where he was the president for the Men's League for Opposing Women's Suffrage. Of course, many Muslim reformers themselves had identified the veil with social and cultural backwardness, and had advocated the education of women, albeit in a limited and narrow curriculum, as the first step toward social modernization.

Cromer's contradictory attitudes in fact characterize the whole debate about the veil. Muslim women who want to de-veil appear to accept a Western critique of Islam as backward and patriarchal, and at the same time de-veiling has a powerful sexual meaning. Within their own societies, de-veiling is often closely associated with social class, because education and wealth are inversely related to the veil. Veiling for upper-class women has more to do with fashion than with religion. In defense of veiling, Muslim fundamentalists characteristically argue that sexual liberation for women in the West has resulted in their endless commercial and sexual exploitation. As a result, the seclusion and veiling of women cannot be separated from the history of colonialism, patriarchy, and social class (Arkoun, 1994: 60).

Egypt provides a useful case study to explore the historical development of women's status in the Middle East over the twentieth century (Botman, 1999). In the 1920s and 1930s, there was a period of rapid political and cultural development for women, with numerous women's associations and societies emerging such as the

Egyptian Woman, the Society of Mothers of the Future (1921), and the Society of the New Woman (1919). However, there was no success in the restriction of polygamy and divorce reform. Tunisia was the only country to prohibit polygamy (Charrad, 1997), and there were also no legal restrictions on the practice of clitoridectomy. In 1923, after Britain granted Egypt partial independence, the constitutional arrangements made no provision for women's political equality, and women who had been politically active were expected to return to domestic life in the private sphere, but women came to play a significant part in the development of Egyptian nationalism. World War II radicalized political consciousness in Egyptian society, and in 1944 the Egyptian Feminist Party was formed, with a political platform that included advocacy of birth control and abortion. Women were active in the rise of Egyptian nationalism and, through the Women's Committee for Popular Resistance, in 1951 supported the struggle against the British in the Suez crisis. Women enjoyed support from the Islamic modernists who argued that the Qur'an gave women equal social and political rights, and the nationalist government of Gamal Abd al-Nasser introduced a range of social reforms that enhanced women's status in post-colonial Egyptian society. While Nasser's "state feminism" undermined the power of husbands and fathers, it made women dependent on the state such that state patriarchy presupposed private patriarchy. In more recent times, the regimes of Anwar Sadat and Husni Mubarak have achieved political continuity by forging an alliance between fundamentalists, state officials, and the middle class (Hatem, 1994). In the 1980s many of the social advances of women were challenged by the politics of Islamism that sought to reestablish traditional values. The "politics of reversal" wants to enforce the *hijab* (curtain) as a potent symbol of the (re)domestication of women.

The complex cultural meanings of veiling and unveiling – a protest against Western imperialism, shelter in a patriarchal society, a statement of female egalitarianism, and an assertion of Islamic patriarchy – have given rise to many contested understandings of Muslim women and the family in particular, and sexuality more generally. What is less contested is the fact that, while many husbands would prefer their wives to stay at home, the Egyptian economy and rising consumerist expectations will keep women in the labor force. Female participation in education and in the labor market has expanded continuously, but with continuing high rates of unemployment, social frustration has also increased. There has been rapid demographic growth and an exodus of rural labor into the large cities. These social conditions, combined with the ultimate failure of Nasser's socialism, have been the breeding ground of Islamism and fundamentalism. The Muslim Brethren, founded by Hasan al-Banna (1906–49), were anti-British and anti-Western, although their ideas on social reform were close to the agenda of Muhammad Abduh. While their membership grew rapidly in the 1940s, they had little success in recruiting educated Egyptian women. The Society of Muslim Sisters was small, and the Brethren's plans for the emancipation of women were deeply conservative. As a result, the political history of women in Egypt shows clearly that the growth of citizenship is never a secure or certain movement of expansion. Social rights can only be sustained through constant and determined social struggle.

The recent history of women, the family, and reproduction in Islamic society is typically seen as a struggle between fundamentalism and modernism over the status of women. These political struggles, however, need to be seen in the context of the involvement of the state in the management of reproduction and its contribution to society. In the early twentieth century, most societies adopted eugenic strategies as components of systematic policies of modernization. Improving the nation required improvements to human breeding, involving, for example, compulsory and voluntary sterilization, contraception, abortion, laws that restricted marriage, and adoption. We need to see the struggle over women as a struggle over reproductive citizenship, where the state may often collaborate with fundamentalism to achieve a governance over women in the name of their social rights (Ong, 1990).

## Conclusion: The Problems of Religion and the Crisis of the Family

The principal debate about marriage and family life in the twentieth century has in retrospect revolved around the so-called romantic love complex, that is, the notion of love as the basic motivation for marriage and intimacy as the foundation of marital happiness. Through the Middle Ages, there was a tension between passionate love and the institution of marriage, because marriage was essentially a contract between families, which was designed to legitimize sexual intercourse in order to guarantee the continuous ownership and distribution of property through new generations. Modern marriages represent a revolutionary transformation of this traditional pattern, because they attempt to base marriage on romantic attachment and to define marriage in terms of companionship and intimacy. There is an increasing social emphasis on the importance of courtship and dating behavior in youth culture, and love rather than an economic partnership or a familial alliance becomes the sole justification for marriage, following a romantic courtship.

This emphasis on romantic love places major emotional burdens on the married couple, because they are committed to fulfilling high expectations of intimacy and sexual gratification. The norms of sincerity, trust, and emotional satisfaction have, paradoxically, consequences in widespread marital unhappiness and high divorce rates, because it is difficult to satisfy these expectations of romantic intimacy in a period where the majority of women have entered the labor force, where the grounds for divorce are very broad, and where early marriage and life expectancy combine to make multiple marriages in a single life-course demographically possible. The result is a paradoxical situation of high rates of marriage, a high incidence of adultery, high levels of remarriage, and extensive intrafamilial conflict across generations. The complexity of modern patterns of love, intimacy, and marriage have been described as "normal chaos" (Beck and Beck-Gernsheim, 1995).

This interpretation of the modern marriage as a "transformation of intimacy" has been a dominant theme of contemporary sociology, where the ideal of a "pure relationship" of love rather than calculation is seen to be the historical outcome of the rise of the romantic love complex, the quest for a democratic relationship in marriage by the women's movement, the critique of traditional double standards in marriage by feminism, and the emphasis on intimacy which is associated with gay and lesbian politics (Giddens, 1992). Although these features – equality, intimacy, and sincerity – are important values in modern marriage, it should be recalled that this account of the modern marriage has its antecedents in the notion of the "companionate" marriage from an earlier period. In the US, the companionate relationship was seen to be the emerging pattern of marriage in the 1930s (Nimkoff, 1934). It was defined as a state of lawful wedlock, which was entered into for the sake of intimate companionship rather than for the procreation of children. Such a relationship was associated with social and geographical mobility, with a leisure lifestyle referred to as "hotel living," and with social transience. Indeed such a relationship was termed the "hotel family" (Hayner, 1927). These companionate relations were assumed to be increasing, with the result that the family was evolving from an economic institution of contractual obligation to an intimate companionship.

The development of emotional intimacy and the pure relationship has been seen as part of the secularization of society, and in particular of the secularization of the traditional institution of marriage. Marriage as a means of stable procreation and the family as an institution for the socialization of children have been through a process of de-Christianization, but the new emphasis on love, eroticism, and companionship is also a radicalization of the Protestant tradition that had its origins in revolutionary debates about society in the seventeenth century. This illustration serves to remind us not to confuse the apparent transformation of contemporary institutions as irrefutable evidence of long-term cultural changes. The idea that modern love is chaotic because it is secular and individualized has become a fashionable component of contemporary sociology, but we need to take a deeper historical view of erotic and intimate relationships to grasp their enduring sacral character (Beck and Beck-Gernsheim, 2002). The roots of modern romanticism are to be found in the eroticism of religious enthusiasm and conversion that fathomed the unpredictable world of intimacy in the late eighteenth and early nineteenth centuries. The "modern romantic love complex" has to be seen as the contemporary heir of religious enthusiasm.

## References


Ahmed, L. (1992) *Women and Gender in Islam: Historical Roots of a Modern Debate*. New Haven, CT: Yale University Press.

Ammerman, N. T. (1987) *Bible Believers. Fundamentalists in the Modern World*. Brunswick, NJ: Rutgers University Press.

Arkoun, M. (1994) *Rethinking Islam: Common Questions, Uncommon Answers*. Boulder, CO: Westview.

Armstrong, K. (2001) *The Battle for God. Fundamentalism in Judaism, Christianity and Islam*. London: HarperCollins.

Baring, E. (2000) *Modern Egpt*. London: Routledge.

Beauvoir, S. de (1972) *The Second Sex*. Harmondsworth: Penguin.

Beck, U., and Beck-Gernsheim, E. (1995) *The Normal Chaos of Love*. Cambridge: Polity.

Beck, U., and Beck-Gernsheim, E. (2002) *Individualization. Institutionalised Individualism and its Social and Political Consequences*. London: Sage.

Benson, L. (1976) *Malory's Morte D'Arthur*. Cambridge, MA: Harvard University Press.

Biale, D. (1992) *Eros and the Jews. From Biblical Israel to Contemporary America*. New York: Basic Books.

Bird, P. (1974) Images of women in the Old Testament. In R. R. Ruether (ed.), *Religion and Sexism. Images of Woman in the Jewish and Christian Traditions*. New York: Simon & Schuster.

Botman, S. (1999) *Engendering Citizenship in Egypt*. New York: Columbia University Press.

Brenner, S. (1996) Reconstructing self and society: Javanese Muslim women and the "veil". *American Ethnologist*, 34, 673–97.

Bynum, C. W. (1991) *Fragmentation and Redemption: Essays on Gender and the Human Body in Medieval Religion*. New York: Zone Books.

Cancian, F. (1987) *Love in America*. Cambridge: Cambridge University Press.

Charrad, M. M. (1997) Policy shifts: State, Islam and gender in Tunisia. *Social Politics*, 4(2), 284–319.

Comaroff, J., and Comaroff, J. (eds.) (1993) *Modernity and its Malcontents. Ritual and Power.* Chicago: University of Chicago Press.

Duby, G. (1978) *Medieval Marriages. Two Models from Twelfth-century France.* Baltimore and London: Johns Hopkins University Press.

Durkheim, E. (2001) *The Elementary Forms of the Religious Life.* Oxford: Oxford University Press.

Eliade, M. (1959) *The Sacred and the Profane. The Nature of Religion.* New York: Harcourt Brace.

Elias, N. (2000) *The Civilizing Process. Sociogenetic and Psychogenetic Investigations.* Revised ed. Oxford: Blackwell.

Friedan, B (1993) *The Fountain of Age.* New York: Simon & Schuster

Giddens, A. (1992) *The Transformation of Intimacy. Sexuality, Love and Eroticism in Modern Societies.* Cambridge: Polity.

Groves, E. and Ogburn, W. F. (1928) *American Marriage and Family Relations.* New York: Henry Holt.

Grubbs, J. E. (1999) *Law and Family in Late Antiquity. The Emperor Constantine's Marriage Legislation.* Oxford: Oxford University Press.

Hatem, M. (1994) Egyptian gender discourse and political liberalisation: Do secularist and Islamic views really differ? *Middle East Journal*, 48(4), 661–76.

Hayner, N. S. (1927) Hotel homes. *Sociology and Social Research,* 12, 124–31.

Hill, C. (1977) *Milton and the English Revolution.* London: Faber & Faber.

Hulsether, M. D. (2000) Like a sermon: Popular religion in Madonna videos. In B. D. Forbes and J. H. Mahan (eds.), *Religion and Popular Culture in America.* Berkeley: University of California Press.

Illouz, E. (1997) *Consuming the Romantic Utopia. Love and the Cultural Contradictions of Capitalism.* Berkeley: University of California Press.

Jaspers, K. (1968) *The Origin and Goal of History.* New Haven, CT: Yale University Press.

Locke, J. (1946) *The Second Treatise of Government and a Letter concerning Toleration.* Oxford: Basil Blackwell.

Luhmann, N. (1986) *Love as Passion. The Codification of Intimacy.* Cambridge: Polity.

Macpherson, C. B. (1962) *The Political Theory of Possessive Individualism.* Oxford: Oxford University Press.

Martin, B. (1978) *A General Theory of Secularization.* Oxford: Basil Blackwell.

Milton, J. (1927) *Areopagitica and other Prose Works.* London: Dent.

Milton, J. (1953) *The English Poems of John Milton.* London: Macdonald.

Morrison, K. F. (1988) *"I am You". The Hermeneutics of Empathy in Western Literature, Theology and Art.* Princeton, NJ: Princeton University Press,

Nimkoff, M. F. (1934) *The Family.* Boston: Houghton Mifflin.

Ong, A. (1990) State versus Islam – Malay families, women's bodies, and the body politic in Malaysia. *American Ethnologist*, 17, 258–76.

Parsons, T. (1999) Religion in postindustrial America. In B. S. Turner (ed.), *The Talcott Parsons Reader.* Oxford: Blackwell.

Reuther, R. R. (1974) Misogynism and virginal feminism in the Fathers of the Church. In R. R. Ruether (ed.), *Religion and Sexism. Images of Woman in the Jewish and Christian Traditions.* New York: Simon & Schuster.

Riggs, A,. and Turner, B. S. (1999) The expectation of love in older age: towards a sociology of intimacy. In M. Poole and S. Feldman (eds.), *A Certain Age. Women Growing Older.* St Leonards: Allen & Unwin.

Scarce, J. (1996) *Domestic Culture in the Middle East.* Edinburgh: National Museums of Scotland.

Schochet, G. J. (1975) *Patriarchalism in Political Thought.* Oxford: Oxford University Press.

Smith, C. (2000) *Christian America? What Evangelicals Really Want*. Berkeley: University of California Press.
Thompson, W. I. (1996) *The Time Falling Bodies Take to Light. Mythologies, Sexuality and the Origins of Culture*. New York: St. Martin's Griffin.
Turner, B. S. (1974) *Weber and Islam. A Critical Study*. London: Routledge & Kegan Paul.
Turner, B. S. (1998) The origins of the sociology of the family. In B. S. Turner (ed.), *Readings in the Anthropology and Sociology of the Family*. London: Routledge/Thoemmes.
Turner, V. (1966) Colour classification in Ndembu ritual. In M. Banton (ed.), *Anthropological Approaches to the Study of Religion*. London: Tavistock.
Warner, M. (1976) *Alone of All Her Sex. The Myth and the Cult of the Virgin Mary*. New York: Vintage Books.
Warnicke, R. M. (2000) *The Marrying of Anne of Cleves. Royal Protocol in Tudor England*. Cambridge: Cambridge University Press.
Watt, M. (1953) *Muhammad at Mecca*. Oxford: Clarendon Press.
Weber, M. (1952) *Ancient Judaism*. New York: Free Press.
Weber, M. (1991) The social psychology of the world religions. In H. H. Gerth and C. Wright Mills (eds.), *From Max Weber: Essays in Sociology*. London: Routledge.
Wilson, B. (1966) *Religion in Secular Society*. London: Watts.
Winter, M. (1995) Islamic attitudes towards the human body. In J. M. Law (ed.), *Religious Reflections on the Human Body*. Bloomington and Indianapolis: Indiana University Press.

# 18

# Trends in the Formation and Dissolution of Couples

Joanne J. Paetsch, Nicholas M. Bala, Lorne D. Bertrand, and Lisa Glennon

Industrialized countries have experienced dramatic changes in values, attitudes, and behaviors related to couple formation and dissolution, particularly since the 1960s. People are marrying at a later age, and marriage rates fell significantly in the last decades of the twentieth century, while unmarried cohabitation increased at a very fast rate. Divorce rates rose over much of the twentieth century, but by the start of the new millennium they were starting to stabilize and even fall slightly in some countries. Some scholars believe that marriage as an institution is in crisis (Pollard and Wu, 1998). There has been a gradual trend toward the liberalization of divorce laws, and gradual social and legal recognition of nonmarital conjugal relationships – both opposite-sex and same-sex cohabitation – though there is substantial variation in trends between different jurisdictions.

This chapter briefly reviews the historical development of laws governing marriage and divorce, and presents current statistical information on marriage and divorce, unmarried opposite-sex cohabitation, and same-sex relationships. Socio-economic, demographic, and legal factors are examined to explain the recent trends in the formation and dissolution of couples, and comparisons are made between industrialized countries. Discussion focuses primarily on Canada, England, and the US, though some comparisons are also made with other countries. As there have been more legal developments in Canada in regard to many of these issues, that country is discussed more than the others.

## Marriage and Divorce

### The historical perspective

Within the past several decades, coincident with the rise of civil rights and feminism, marriage in industrialized countries has come to be viewed by many people as a partnership of equals. This was not always the case. Traditionally, many societies believed that a husband owned his wife, much as he could own property, and for this reason, his wife was expected to be subservient to him. A husband had the right to have sexual relations with his wife whether or not she consented, and he could not be convicted of raping her. Implicit in this patriarchal model was the notion that the husband was to be the "head of the household" and have primary responsibility for providing income, while the wife's role was to support him by maintaining the home, raising the children, and fulfilling her husband's needs. If the wife was employed outside of the home, the husband was entitled to her wages. While the family was the primary economic unit of pre-industrial society, romantic love and personal satisfaction were not considered important for marriage.

Religion also played a strong role in the structure of traditional marriages and provided norms and values that guided the behavior of married couples (Kurian, 1993). Foremost among these was the idea that marriage was permanent. Prior to the mid-nineteenth century, divorce in England could only be obtained by petitioning Parliament, a procedure that only the very wealthy could afford, though desertion without divorce was not unheard of, and an "innocent" wife deserted by a wealthy man might be able to claim alimony. In the late eighteenth and nineteenth centuries, there was a gradual move to permit divorce. In the late eighteenth century attitudes and laws about divorce were somewhat more liberal in some of the American states and Canadian colonies than in England, though a woman who was guilty of adultery, even after her husband deserted her, would lose custody of her children and had no claim to support.

In the twentieth century, with industrialization, urbanization, the decline of the influence of religion, and the recognition of greater rights for women in society, views about the nature of marriage changed. Improvements in birth control, the invention of labor-saving devices for the home, and the increased participation of women in the labor force all played a role in changing attitudes and behaviors related to marriage. Gradually marriage came to be viewed as a partnership of equals. Increasingly, people entered marriage from a sense of romantic love, in order to achieve companionship and personal fulfillment, rather than out of a sense of religious duty or economic necessity.

Along with changing perceptions of marriage, however, came the notion that if marriage is to be valued primarily for its personal satisfaction, then if the personal satisfaction derived from the relationship begins to wane, the marriage should be ended. "Gradually, the standard shifted from one which required couples to remain married even if they were not in love to one which virtually demanded divorce unless they remained in love" (Furstenberg, 1990: 380). While divorce was not common until the latter half of the twentieth century, after 1960 divorce laws began to change and divorce rates dramatically rose. Marriage was still generally viewed as the most desirable environment in which to raise children, but there was a growing acceptance and incidence of single parenthood.

## The changing legal framework for divorce

By 1970, almost every jurisdiction in the industrialized world had enacted a divorce law. The last two Canadian provinces to have legislative divorce were Quebec and Newfoundland, where the influence of the Roman Catholic Church prevented the enactment of this type of law until 1968. In the last third of the twentieth century, the only jurisdiction without divorce was the Republic of Ireland, where as a result of the influence of the Catholic Church, there was no divorce until 1996 when a referendum amended the Constitution to allow it. Legislation was subsequently passed that provided a no-fault divorce system in the Republic of Ireland, which means that a divorce can only be obtained if the parties have been separated for four years and there is no prospect of reconciliation (Shannon, 1999).

Until about 1960, divorce laws were fault-based, with the "innocent" spouse entitled to seek a divorce if the other spouse was guilty of a "matrimonial offense." Adultery was a ground for divorce in virtually every country, with some jurisdictions also recognizing cruelty, desertion, and other grounds.

In the late 1960s and 1970s attitudes toward divorce and legislation governing the divorce process went through a process of liberalization. In most industrialized countries, legislation was enacted to add "no-fault" grounds to the fault-based regimes, and in some cases to completely replace them. No-fault regimes allow either party to a marriage to seek legal dissolution of the marriage after a period of separation, ranging from a few weeks to five years. The existence of "no-fault" grounds signals a change in social and moral attitudes toward divorce, and is intended to encourage a less adversarial attitude toward the divorce process.

In Canada, legislation enacted in 1968 allowed for divorce based on three years' consensual separation, in addition to fault-based grounds; in 1986 there was a further liberalization, with the period of separation reduced to one year, and by the end of the century nine out of ten divorces were based on one year's separation. In 1969, California was the first state to enact a no-fault divorce law, and now about twenty American states allow a divorce only on the basis of the declaration of one or both parties that there has been an "irretrievable breakdown" of the marriage. Most American states have legislation allowing for divorce based on a period of separation, ranging from sixty days to three years, though the most common periods are six to eighteen months. New York and a couple of other states have retained essentially fault-based divorce regimes (Gregory, Swisher, and Wolf, 2001).

England has a mixed regime, allowing divorce either on fault-based grounds or two no-fault grounds: two years' separation with the respondent's consent to the divorce or five years' separation. Law-reform debates in the 1980s and 1990s in England focused on removing the concept of fault from divorce laws. This culminated in the passage of legislation in 1996 that removed the need to establish fault grounds in order to obtain a divorce. Instead, divorce was to be available to parties who had separated for at least eighteen months, provided that they went through a series of procedural steps, such as attending information meetings, which were intended to encourage the spouses to reflect more seriously on whether their marriage had irretrievably broken down (Eekelaar, 1999). This legislation was highly controversial as opponents expressed concern that it would undermine marriage. Part II of the Family Law Act 1996, which would have introduced no-fault divorce, has not been implemented because the government was not convinced that sufficient couples would save their marriage as a result of attending information meetings (Lord Chancellor's Department, 2001; Walker, 2001).

Laws governing divorce have also changed to reflect the more egalitarian nature of marriage. While there is a great deal of complexity and variation in property laws, at the same time as divorce laws were being liberalized, women were advocating adoption of property regimes that divided equally at least some of the assets acquired by either spouse during the marriage, based on a partnership model of marriage and as a recognition that domestic contributions should give rise to an entitlement to property claims. Spousal support laws have also gradually changed, and are now generally written in gender-neutral language, though almost invariably if a claim is made, it is by the woman, who is the partner most likely to have made career sacrifices and assumed a primarily domestic role. A woman is expected to take reasonable steps to become self-supporting after separation, and most women do not receive spousal support after they separate from their husbands. However, in most jurisdictions a woman is no longer automatically disentitled to support merely because she has committed a single act of adultery, but rather the focus is on the contributions and economic dependency in the relationship and how realistic it is for the woman to be self-supporting.

Along with the rise of no-fault divorce was an effort to reduce the adversarial nature of divorce. Increasingly, couples are looking to trained mediators to help them resolve disputes rather than to judges. There is increasing use of some form of "shared parenting" or "joint custody" after divorce, which in some jurisdictions is encouraged by legislative change and in others is simply a reflection of changing social and professional attitudes.

## Demographic Information on Marriage and Divorce[1]

### Marriage and divorce rates

The number of marriage ceremonies conducted in Canada peaked in 1972, and the crude marriage rate (i.e., number of marriages per 1,000 population) fell from 7.1 in 1987 to 5.1 in 1998. As marriage rates have fallen, cohabitation rates have soared. In Canada, the number of cohabiting couples (i.e., two persons of the opposite sex who are not legally married to each other, but live together as husband and wife in the same dwelling) increased by 28 percent between 1991 and 1996.

Marriage rates also fell in the last quarter of the twentieth century in other industrialized countries. In the US, the crude marriage rate fell by 23 percent from 10.9 in 1972 to 8.4 in 1998. In England and Wales, the crude marriage rate fell by 41 percent over the same period, from 17.3 in 1972 to 10.2 in 1998.

In Canada, the crude divorce rate (i.e., number of divorces per 1,000 population) peaked at 3.55 in 1987 following amendments to the Divorce Act, which allowed divorce after one year of separation instead of three. The crude divorce rate has been generally declining since 1987, although the number of divorces in 1998 was up slightly from that in 1997, resulting in a crude divorce rate of 2.28. Based on this rate, it is estimated that 36 percent of marriages will end in divorce within 30 years of marriage.

The crude divorce rate has also fallen in the US from a high of 5.3 in 1979 to 4.2 in 1998. In England and Wales, the crude divorce rate rose steadily from a low of 1.5 in 1971 to a high of 3.2 in 1993, and declined to 2.8 in 1998.

### Average ages at marriage and divorce

The average age of brides in Canada in 1998 was 31.1 years, up from 28.6 years in 1988, and the average age of first-time brides was 27.6 years. Men are also marrying later; the average age of grooms in Canada in 1998 was 33.7 years, up from 31.2 years in 1988, and first-time grooms averaged 29.6 years of age.

The average ages of women and men at marriage also increased over the years in other countries, although Americans tend to be younger at the time of marriage than in Canada or England. In the US, the median age of women at first marriage in 2000 was 25.1 years, up from 20.8 in 1970. The median age of men at first marriage in 2000 was 26.8 years, up from 23.2 in 1970 (Fields and Casper, 2001). While the age gap between men and women has narrowed, American men are still 1.7 years older than American women at the time of first marriage.

In England and Wales, the median age of women at first marriage in 1998 was 27 years, up from 21.5 in 1976, and the median age of men at first marriage in 1998 was 28.9 years, up from 23.7 in 1976.

Men and women are also divorcing at later ages. In 1998, the average age of Canadian women at divorce was 39.4 years old, while Canadian men were 42 years old. This is an increase of 2.6 years for both men and women since 1989. The same trend is seen in the other jurisdictions examined, although American men and women, in keeping with younger ages at marriage, are also younger at divorce. The median age at divorce for American women in 1996 was 29 years for divorce from a first marriage, and 37 years for divorce from a second marriage. For American men in 1996, the median age at divorce from a first marriage was 30.5 years, and 39.3 years for divorce from a second marriage (Kreider and Fields, 2001).

In England and Wales, the median age at divorce also increased for both men and women. In 1998, women were 36.3 years of age at divorce, compared to 33.1 years in 1976. Men were aged 38.7, up from 35.4 in 1976.

## The duration of marriages

The duration of marriages that end in divorce has also been increasing. Marriages that ended in divorce in 1998 in Canada lasted an average of 13.7 years, compared to 12.9 years in 1989. In England and Wales, the median duration of all marriages for divorcing couples in 1999 was 10.5 years, up from 9.7 years a decade earlier.

The median duration of marriage in the US is shorter, where most divorces occur within the first 10 years of marriage. In 1996, the median duration of first marriage for those whose first marriage ended in divorce was 7.9 years. The median duration of second marriages was even shorter, at 6.8 years for women and 7.3 years for men (Kreider and Fields, 2001). According to Bramlett and Mosher (2001), the duration of marriage is linked to a woman's age at first marriage. In a study of first marriage dissolution in the United States, they found that the older a woman is at first marriage, the longer that marriage is likely to last. Fifty-nine percent of marriages to brides under 18 ended in separation or divorce, compared to 36 percent of those married at age 20 or older.

## Repartnering

In two-thirds of the marriages in Canada in 1997, both partners were marrying for the first time. Both partners were previously divorced in 12 percent of the marriages, and in 18 percent, the marriage involved a first-time partner and a divorced partner. Less than 5 percent of the marriages in Canada in 1997 involved a widowed partner. Previously divorced women averaged 39.8 years at remarriage, and previously divorced men were 43.4 years old on average. Previously widowed women and men averaged 55.5 years and 62.1 years on average.

In a study of the decline of marriage in Canada, Nault and Bélanger (1996) found that while the number of marriages among divorced persons increased from 1981 to 1991, it was only because the population at risk, i.e., the number of divorced persons, increased rapidly. When looking at the variation in the marriage rate for divorcees, it decreased by 43 percent over the ten-year period, while the marriage rate for never-married persons decreased by 25 percent. Similarly, while the marriage rate for widowed persons was already much lower than that of never-married and divorced persons in 1981, by 1991 the rate had decreased by a further 29 percent.

According to Norton and Miller (1992: 5), high divorce rates in the US have created a "large pool of eligibles for remarriage." In 1991, 4 out of 10 marriages involved a second or higher-order marriage for the bride, the groom, or both. The data on remarriage after divorce show a decline in the percentage of women who remarried between 1975 and 1990. However, Bramlett and Mosher (2001) calculated that 75 percent of divorced women remarry within 10 years, and the probability of remarriage is significantly higher for women who were younger at divorce.

## Analysis of factors affecting trends in divorce

Marriage rates have fallen in Canada, the US, and Great Britain, as well as in Australia, New Zealand, and many other countries. While divorce rates increased dramatically between about 1960 and 1985, since 1990 they have stabilized and even gradually declined. Ages of first-time brides and grooms and women and men for all marriages have increased, although in the US they tend to be a little younger when compared to the other jurisdictions. Likewise, ages of men and women at divorce have increased.

Cohabitation rates are also increasing in the jurisdictions examined, and are usually cited as the main reason for declining marriage rates. Changing demographics, such as the aging "baby boomers," have also been suggested as causal factors affecting marriage rates. Nault and Bélanger (1996) acknowledge that the decline in the first-marriage rate in Canada is due, in part, to the aging of the never-married population, but argue that the effect is negligible. Likewise, Goldstein (1999) argues that compositional factors such as the age structure of the population (measured in terms of marital duration), age at marriage, and marriage order fail to account for the leveling of divorce rates in the US. The declining divorce rate is also likely in part due to the fact that fewer people are getting married, so the number of couples at risk of divorce is smaller.

Social characteristics appear to influence marriage and divorce rates. According to Bahr (2001), these include: (1) higher marital expectations; (2) the increasing economic independence of women; (3) the growing social acceptance of divorce; (4) no-fault divorce laws; and (5) increased individualism. Bahr (2001) suggests that, in American culture, the expectations of marriage for personal happiness have increased over time, while the protective, religious, educational, and recreational functions of the family have decreased, and may now be met by other institutions. If the expected fulfillment from the marriage is not achieved, then the major reason for being married no longer exists. This social characteristic is closely related to that of increased individualism. American culture emphasizes freedom, autonomy, and the pursuit of individual happiness. The civil rights and feminist movements of the 1960s and 1970s emphasized individual rights, and questioned traditional roles, responsibilities, and authority. A consequence is that Americans are less committed to marriage, and more likely to divorce, cohabit, or seek other alternatives to marriage.

Another major social change is the increasing economic independence of women. In the US, for example, the percentage of employed married women increased from 32 percent in 1960 to 62 percent in 1998. Bahr (2001) suggests that a woman who is employed may be more likely to leave an unhappy marriage than a woman who is unemployed. Likewise, an unhappy man may be more likely to leave a marriage if his wife is financially independent and there will be no spousal support obligation.

In Canada, enrolment in post-secondary education appears to be a major factor delaying first marriage, as it extends the period during which women are not viewed, or do not view themselves, as fully eligible for marriage (Pollard and Wu, 1998).

One of the controversial issues about divorce reform is whether the enactment of no-fault divorce laws has contributed to the decline in the stability of marriage. Some conservatives have criticized divorce reform, arguing that by facilitating divorce and allowing a spouse to terminate a marriage without establishing the fault of the other party, the no-fault regimes have contributed to a "culture of divorce" that undermines the family, leads to increased spousal abuse, and negatively affects children and their mothers (Wardle, 1999).

In the late 1990s, a few conservative American states with strong Christian influences, such as Louisiana and Arizona, enacted laws to allow "Covenant Marriages." Those who choose to enter this type of marriage are required to have premarital counseling from a minister or other person. Further, in the event of separation, a party to a Covenant Marriage must have a longer period of separation than if they have an ordinary marriage, typically having to wait two years instead of six months; an innocent spouse in a Covenant Marriage may still obtain a divorce based on such fault grounds as adultery or cruelty. It is still too early to assess the impact of Covenant Marriages on divorce rates, but relatively few couples are choosing this marital option, perhaps because of the more elaborate premarital process.

Liberals have responded that societal change has made divorce more acceptable, and reduced the number of women who are dependent on marriage for economic support. They argue that there is no evidence that no-fault divorce reform causes breakdown of marriages, but only that it facilitates the legal dissolution of marital relationships in which the parties have already separated (Ellman and Lohr, 1997). Glendon (1989) similarly notes that divorce is better understood as a symptom rather than a cause of marriage breakdown, and Rhode (1997) observes that making divorce harder does not keep couples together but simply makes the formal separation process more costly and acrimonious.

## Unmarried Opposite-Sex Cohabitation

### The growing incidence of unmarried opposite-sex unions

One of the most significant trends in couple formation in the last third of the twentieth century was the growing societal acceptance and incidence of unmarried opposite-sex cohabitation. The decline in religious influences, increased gender equality, and a decline in the sense of permanence of marriage all played a role in the increased popularity of cohabitation.

Cohabitation rates in Canada, the US, Great Britain, and Europe rose dramatically. The number of cohabiting couple families in Canada more than doubled between 1981 and 1991, and increased by a further 28 percent from 1991 to 1996, which was a rate of increase 16 times that for married-couple families. While the proportion of cohabiting couples increased in all age groups, the highest increase occurred among people aged 15 to 29. By 1996 approximately one conjugal opposite-sex couple in seven in Canada cohabited without marrying.

The cohabitation rate in Canada is higher than that of the US and England, though lower than that of the Scandinavian countries. In the US, census estimates indicate that the number of cohabiting couples increased from 1.1 million in 1977 to 4.9 million in 1997, almost 5 percent of all households. The increase in cohabitation occurred across all education levels, and among all racial and ethnic groups in American society. In England, cohabiting couples accounted for 7.3 percent of all households in 1996. It is estimated that the number of cohabiting couples in Great Britain, 1.56 million in 1996, will rise to 2.93 million in 2021, which would mean more than one in five of all couples cohabiting (Haskey, 2001).

There have also been increasing rates of cohabitation in Scandinavia, though the rates are significantly higher. By 1996, about one-quarter of all opposite sex unions were cohabiting rather than married in Sweden (22.7 percent), Denmark (27 percent) and Iceland (25.4 percent) (Wu, 2000).

## Factors influencing the formation of cohabiting relationships

The majority of Canadians cohabit in their first conjugal relationship. Between 1990 and 1995, over half (57 percent) of Canadians who entered their first conjugal union chose to live together rather than marry. Using data from the 1995 General Social Survey, Turcotte and Bélanger (1997) examined a variety of factors that influenced the formation of such unions. They found that the probability of living in a cohabitation relationship is significantly higher for women in more recent birth cohorts. The likelihood of cohabiting was 30 percent higher for women born between 1971 and 1980 (aged 15–24 at the time of the survey) than it was for women born between 1961 and 1970.

Women who attended weekly religious services were half as likely to cohabit in their first union as were women who attended services occasionally. Similarly, immigrants were half as likely to cohabit than were native-born Canadian women. The likelihood of cohabiting was not found to vary with different levels of educational attainment. However, women who were presently enrolled in school were 30 percent less likely to form a cohabitation relationship than were women who were not attending school. Women who were employed were twice as likely to opt for a cohabitation union than were women who did not work outside of the home.

## The instability of cohabiting relationships

Despite their popularity, cohabiting relationships tend to be short-lived unions. Data from the US (Forste, 2001) and Britain (Murphy, 2000) indicate that most cohabiting couples marry or separate within two years. An analysis of Canadian data reveals that starting conjugal life in a cohabiting relationship, as opposed to a marriage, sharply increases the probability of the first union ending in separation (Le Bourdais, Neill, and Turcotte, 2000). Moreover, the risk of separation is just as high whether or not the cohabiting partners eventually marry each other. For women aged 30 to 39, 63 percent of those whose first relationship was cohabitation had separated by 1995, compared to 33 percent of women who married first.

While marriage and cohabitation unions share many similarities (e.g., they both involve an intimate relationship, shared living quarters, and family environment), there are several important differences between cohabitation and marriage (Wu and Pollard, 2000). Although there is some mingling of economic resources in cohabitation unions, cohabitors are more likely to keep their finances separate from one another than are married couples. The likelihood of having children is lower in a nonmarital cohabiting relationship than in marriage, while the incidence of spousal abuse is higher. The better a woman's financial position, the less likely she is to marry her cohabiting partner and the more likely she is to separate. Likewise, increased social resources for women appear to decrease the probability of marriage. Wu and Pollard (2000) suggest that increased economic and social resources may make marriage less desirable, or may facilitate the dissolution of a bad union.

Full-time employment was also found to affect the instability of Canadian cohabitation relationships. Full-time skilled and semi-professional women were more likely to marry than unemployed women, but they were also more likely to separate. Wu and Pollard (2000: 324) suggest that increased women's labor-force participation may increase union instability because the "supply of attractive alternatives to current partners is increased." On the other hand, professional and full-time semi-professional men are more likely to marry than unemployed men. According to the authors, steady employment in high-level occupations makes men attractive as partners, and increases the pressure on them to legalize a nonmarital union.

The instability of cohabitation unions seen in Canada is also evident in other industrialized countries. A British study of marital dissolution among the 1958 birth cohort found that previous cohabitation with another partner and premarital cohabitation were both associated with higher rates of marital breakdown (Berrington and Diamond, 1999).

In a social demographic look at cohabitation in the US, Forste (2001) argues that there are two primary interpretations as to why cohabitation prior to marriage increases the risk of divorce. The first hypothesis is that people who choose to cohabit are different from people who choose to marry first, while the second is that the act of living together itself changes the relationship and encourages instability. Both of these positions have support in the literature. Wu (1999) suggests that cohabitational experiences delay marriage timing. He argues that cohabitors are reluctant to enter into a marital relationship because they have less conventional views of, and less commitment to, the institution of marriage. Forste (2001) concludes that because cohabitation is perceived as less permanent than marriage, cohabiting couples are less likely to engage in the activities that encourage commitment and longevity in the relationship.

## The legal recognition of cohabiting relationships

Until the last quarter of the twentieth century, nonmarital unions had no legal recognition. Women who lived with men outside of marriage would have no legal claims to property or support, despite living together for decades. Even if the parties made an agreement about their respective rights, the courts were likely to refuse to enforce it as it would be regarded as "contrary to public policy." While there might be a claim to child support if the couple had children together, the children were regarded as "illegitimate." The term "bastard" historically referred to a child born out of wedlock, a child who had an inferior legal status.

Canada is one of the countries that has gone the farthest in terms of the legal and social recognition of unmarried opposite-sex cohabitation. Starting in the late 1970s Canadian courts began to use trust and partnership doctrines to allow claims to a share in property acquired during a long-term cohabitation relationship, in order to recognize the contribution of one partner to the acquisition of property by the other and to prevent the unjust enrichment of one partner by the other. In the initial court cases, the contribution had to be in the form of direct labor on a joint enterprise, like a farm or business, but by the late 1980s the courts began to recognize that a domestic contribution, such as staying at home to look after a couple's children, could give rise to a claim.

Starting in the 1970s provinces also began to enact statutes to give unmarried partners the same right as married spouses to claim "spousal support" at the end of the relationship if they cohabited for a stipulated period of time (initially the legislation required relatively long periods of cohabitation – such as five years – but requisite periods of cohabitation are shorter now, often one year). These statutes are said to "ascribe" or impose a limited "spousal" status for specified purposes, regardless of the intent of the parties. The rationale for enacting this type of legislation was mainly to protect women who might become dependent in these marriage-like relationships, though the statutes are written in gender-neutral terms. This type of law also allowed the state to shift some women from social assistance to claiming support from their former partners.

As a result of a 1995 decision of the Supreme Court of Canada it has been held that, for purposes such as insurance claims, denying "spousal status" to a long-term unmarried partner is unconstitutional discrimination. A range of social and family legislation in Canada now recognizes the spousal status of an unmarried cohabiting partner, for such purposes as insurance, estate law, and taxation. For all issues related to children, the distinctions between marital and nonmarital relationships have been abolished in Canada.

In most provinces legislation still provides that for certain limited purposes, such as property law, married persons may have rights and obligations that the unmarried do not, but Canadian law has gone a long way toward equating the two types of relationships. Parties may choose to have an agreement to regulate aspects of their private relationship, such as in regard to property, and this is increasingly common. In 2002, the Supreme Court of Canada held because an unmarried person chose not to marry, it was not discriminatory to deny them access to matrimonial property statutes, though they may still make property claims based on agreements or to reflect contributions. (Bala and Bromwich, 2002).

In England, there is limited recognition of unmarried opposite-sex cohabitation, though it is clearly not fully equated to marriage. The courts are, for example, very reluctant to allow a property-based claim at the end of a nonmarital relationship in the absence of a clear agreement or direct financial contribution to the acquisition of assets. Some statutes recognize cohabitation relationships, for example, for succession law and responding to domestic violence, but for many purposes even long-term opposite-sex cohabiting relationships do not give rise to the same rights and obligations as marriage (Douglas, 2000). Even as regards children, a father of a child born out of wedlock will have fewer rights than if the child were born in a marital relationship (Pickford, 1999).

Although there is an increasing incidence of cohabiting relationships in the US, there is very limited legal recognition for these relationships, with the courts and legislatures expressing concern that the recognition of these relationships would undermine marriage. In most states agreements between cohabiting partners about sharing of property are now enforceable, though in a few states like Illinois the courts have held that enforcing such an agreement would still be contrary to public policy. An increasing number of municipalities have bylaws that recognize "domestic relationships" for such purposes as pension and health benefits. In many states the courts allow a nonmarital partner to make a claim for property acquired during a relationship, but it is generally necessary to establish that there was a contribution of money or labor, while domestic or child-care responsibilities will generally not give rise to a property claim. Apart from rare cases where there is an agreement, no state recognizes these relationships for purposes of establishing a support obligation after separation (Gregory, Swisher, and Wolf, 2001).

## Same-Sex Relationships

### From discrimination to growing legal recognition

Traditionally there has been great social and religious prejudice against homosexual relationships. Only a man and woman were entitled to marry, and only this type of conjugal relationship had legal, social, or religious sanction. In many countries engaging in homosexual acts was a crime. In Canada, for example, "sodomy" (anal intercourse) between consenting adults was a crime until 1969. In the US in 1986 the Supreme Court upheld the constitutional validity of criminalizing sodomy, at which time over a dozen states had this type of law.

As discussed above, with the rise in divorce rates in the last quarter of the twentieth century came a growing social and legal acceptance of unmarried opposite-sex cohabitation. It was, however, only in the last decade of the twentieth century that same-sex partners began to gain any legal recognition. The growing recognition of same-sex relationships is in a significant measure a reflection of the growing emphasis on human rights. Typically, the first efforts to gain rights for homosexuals were to prevent discrimination in such fields as employment, followed by claims for equal treatment in their intimate personal relationships.

Scandinavian countries, with their liberal social attitudes, were the first countries in the world to legally recognize same-sex relationships. The first legislation that explicitly acknowledged same-sex relationships was the Danish Registered Partnership Act 1989. This legislation provided that the legal implications of registering a partnership were the same as those of a marriage, with the main exception being a prohibition against adoption. This provision was amended in 1999 to provide that one member of a partnership can adopt the other member's child, as long as the child was not adopted from another country (New Zealand Law Commission, 1999).

Denmark's pioneering legislation became the model for other Scandinavian countries, and similar registered partnership legislation was enacted in Norway in 1993, Sweden in 1994, and Iceland in 1996. Other jurisdictions which have enacted legislation that to varying degrees recognizes same-sex partnerships include France, Germany, Spain, Hungary, Slovenia, and New Zealand.

In 1998, the Netherlands enacted what at the time was the most far-reaching legislation of any jurisdiction recognizing same-sex partnerships. This legislation provided for registered partnerships that could be either heterosexual or homosexual, and the differences between these partnerships and marriage were minimal (New Zealand Law Commission, 1999). In 2001, the Netherlands was the first country to pass legislation that allowed legal marriage among same-sex couples. This legislation provides full equality to opposite-sex married couples in terms of legal, economic, and social status. The only legal difference between same-sex and opposite-sex marriage deals with adoption rights: same-sex couples are not allowed international adoptions because of the concern that such adoptions would not be recognized in countries that do not allow same-sex marriage. Belgium also now allows same-sex partners to marry.

While by the early 1990s most governments in Canada had enacted human rights legislation prohibiting overt discrimination in such areas as employment, they were unwilling to enact laws to explicitly recognize same-sex relationships. The initial court challenges of gay and lesbian advocates claiming a violation of their constitutional rights because they were denied the right to marry were not successful. Since only those in a heterosexual relationship could have children, denial of the right to marry was not regarded as discriminatory. In the late 1990s, however, there were a series of successful challenges in which the Canadian courts accepted that it was a violation of the constitutional rights of gays and lesbians to deny them the same rights and obligations as arise under Canada's ascription statutes, which give limited spousal status to unmarried opposite-sex partners after a period of cohabitation.

The Federal government and several provincial governments responded to these decisions by enacting laws that have essentially given same-sex partners the same rights and obligations as unmarried opposite-sex partners who have cohabited for a specified period. For example, in 2000 the Federal Parliament enacted legislative changes to 68 Federal statutes that deal with such issues as pensions and taxation, to include same-sex partners within the definition that imposes rights and obligations on opposite-sex cohabiting couples based on one year's cohabitation.

In 2001 the province of Nova Scotia enacted legislation allowing same-sex couples to register their partnership and thus have some of the same benefits and obligations as the married, for example for purposes of provincial matrimonial property laws. A few other provinces have followed this lead.

Another response to the court challenges about the rights of same-sex partners has been a proposal to allow legal recognition of a relationship in which two adults are residing together in a "close personal adult relationship," regardless of whether the relationship has a conjugal or sexual nature. Some academics and policy analysts have proposed this as a logical and equitable way of treating relationships where two adults reside together with a significant degree of economic and emotional interdependence, without "privileging" marriage, heterosexual relationships, or even conjugal relationships (Law Commission of Canada, 2001).

The province of Alberta, traditionally one of the most conservative jurisdictions in Canada, has used this approach in its new Adult Interdependent Relationships Act. Under this law if one adult has "lived with" another adult for at least two years in a relationship in which they are "emotionally committed to one another and function as an economic and domestic unit," they will be deemed to be "adult interdependent partners" and have a number of rights and obligations imposed on them, including the possibility of claims for support and property at the end of the relationship. This type of legislation, unlike most Canadian laws dealing with spousal status, does not require a finding that the relationship is "conjugal," and hence a consideration whether there is a sexual relationship is theoretically irrelevant.

Some conservative politicians find this alternative more socially appropriate because it does not overtly recognize homosexual relationships. Critics, however, point out that this approach may include situations such as ones in which an elderly parent resides with an adult child, or a middle-aged adult agrees to allow an adult child or sibling to share a residence. Arguably the expectations and degree of commitment in these non-conjugal adult relationships is so different from those in which adults, whether heterosexual or homosexual, have a conjugal or spousal relationship, that there should be different legal treatment (Bala and Bromwich, 2002).

Despite granting significant recognition to same-sex relationships, Canada's Federal Parliament, which has jurisdiction over the law of marriage, has affirmed that marriage is "the union of one man and one woman." While public opinion polls suggest that a majority of Canadians are prepared to accept same-sex marriage, politicians who are concerned about offending voters have been unwilling to enact this type of law. A number of court challenges have been launched to the prohibition on same-sex marriage, with advocates hoping that the changed social and legal climate will result in a different outcome from similar challenges in the early 1990s.

Recent court decisions and legislation in Canada have recognized the rights of same-sex partners to jointly adopt children. Further, starting in the 1990s, Canadian courts have accorded long-term partners of lesbian and gay biological parents the rights and obligations of a "parent," applying Canadian statutes that had traditionally been used to give parental status to stepparents who "stand in the place of a parent" as a result of their marriage to a parent and are living with the child. Most recently, the Ontario Court of Appeal unanimously ruled that Canada's definition of marriage as being exclusively between a man and a woman is unconstitutional and two persons of the same sex should be permitted to marry. The issue of whether same-sex partners should be permitted to marry remains controversial in Canada, and will likely have to be resolved by the Supreme Court.

In England, legislation and case law generally do not recognize same-sex relationships, and there are currently no laws that allow for the acquisition of rights based on registration. In a 1999 decision, however, the House of Lords recognized that a long-term same-sex partner could be a member of the "family" of his partner for the purposes of landlord-tenant legislation. While this decision may be relevant for a limited range of other statutes that give rights to "family members," some commentators argue that it does not necessarily herald a general move toward a more inclusive legislative or judicial policy of giving same-sex couples greater legal recognition (Glennon, 2000).

In the US advocates for same-sex partners have challenged legislation in several states that allows only opposite-sex partners to marry on the basis that it discriminates because of sexual orientation, though the only successful constitutional challenges have been in Hawaii (1993) and Vermont (1999). In Vermont, the legislature responded by enacting "civil-union" legislation that allows same-sex partners to register a "civil union," with all of the rights and obligations of the marriage for state law purposes; these unions may not, however, have legal recognition in other states.

In Hawaii, the state responded by amending the state constitution to prohibit same-sex marriage, though the state has enacted a statute to allow same-sex couples to register as "reciprocal beneficiaries" for a limited range of purposes such as succession, and retirement and health benefits. Registration does not give rise to the right to make claims for support or property at the end of a relationship. A number of American cities have also enacted bylaws to allow same-sex partners to register and claim "spousal" benefits for such limited purposes as health insurance and pension eligibility.

American courts initially refused to recognize any rights or obligations for the lesbian partners of biological mothers, even if the partners jointly arranged for one woman to become pregnant by artificial insemination. In 1999, the courts in Massachusetts recognized that a woman could have parental rights toward the biological child of her former lesbian partner after separation, but courts in most states still do not follow this approach (Gregory, Swisher, and Wolf, 2001).

## Available data on formation rates of same-sex relationships

The US Census Bureau collects information annually from a representative sample of Americans through the Current Population Reports (CPR). According to the 2000 Census, approximately 1 percent of all cohabiting couples in the United States were reported to be same-sex partnerships.

In Canada, the 2001 census was the first decennial census to ask respondents to specify "same-sex partnership" as their marital status, with same-sex couples representing 0.5 percent of all couples. In New Zealand, the reported portion of same-sex couples was 0.6 percent in 2001. All these figures are likely to underrepresent the number of same-sex cohabiting couples, as there is great reluctance by many in these relationships to disclose their status.

## Note

1 Statistical data were obtained from Statistics Canada, National Center for Health Statistics (US), and the Office for National Statistics (England and Wales).

## References

Bahr, S. (2001) *Social Science Research on Family Dissolution: What It Shows and How It Might Be of Interest to Family Law Reformers.* Manuscript prepared for Symposium on the ALI's Family Dissolution Principles: Blueprint to Strengthen or to Deconstruct Families? Brigham Young University, February 1.

Bala, N., and Bromwich, R. (2002) Context and inclusivity in Canada's evolving definition of the family. *International Journal of Law, Policy, and the Family*, 16, 145–80.

Berrington, A., and Diamond, I. (1999) Marital dissolution among the 1958 British birth cohort: The role of cohabitation. *Population Studies*, 53, 19–38.

Bramlett, M. D., and Mosher, W. D. (2001) *First Marriage Dissolution, Divorce, and Remarriage: United States.* Advance data from vital and health statistics, no. 323. Hyattsville, MD: National Center for Health Statistics.

Douglas, G. (2000) Marriage, cohabitation and parenthood: From contract to status?" In J. Eekelaar, S. Katz, and M. MacLean (eds.), *Cross Currents: Family Law and Policy in the US and England*. Oxford: Oxford University Press.

Eekelaar, J. (1999) Family law: keeping us "on message". *Child and Family Law Quarterly*, 11, 387–96.

Ellman, I. M,. and Lohr, S. (1997) Marriage as contract, opportunistic violence and other bad arguments for fault divorce. *University of Illinois Law Review*, 3, 718–72.

Fields, J., and Casper, L. M. (2001) America's families and living arrangements: Population characteristics. *Current Population Reports*. Washington, DC: US Census Bureau.

Forste, R. (2001) *Prelude to Marriage or Alternative to Marriage? A Social Demographic Look at Cohabitation in the U.S.* Manuscript prepared for Symposium on the ALI's Family Dissolution Principles: Blueprint to Strengthen or to Deconstruct Families? Brigham Young University, February 3.

Furstenberg, F. J., Jr. (1990) Divorce and the American family. *Annual Review of Sociology*, 16, 379–403.

Glendon, M. A. (1989) *The Transformation of Family Law*. Chicago: University of Chicago Press.

Glennon, L. (2000) *Fitzpatrick v Sterling Housing Association Ltd* – An endorsement of the functional family? *International Journal of Law, Policy and the Family*, 14, 226–53.

Goldstein, J. R. (1999) The levelling of divorce in the United States. *Demography*, 36, 409–14.

Gregory, J. D., Swisher, P. N., and Wolf, S. L. (2001) *Understanding Family Law*. PLACE: Matthew Bender.

Haskey, J. (2001) Cohabitation in Great Britain: Past, present and future trends – and attitudes. *Population Trends*, 103, 5–25.

Kreider, R. M., and Fields, J. M. (2001) Number, timing, and duration of marriages and divorces: 1996. *Current Population Reports*. Washington, DC: US Census Bureau.

Kurian, G. (1993) Marital patterns in Canada. In G. N. Ramu (ed.), *Marriage and the Family in Canada Today* (2nd ed.) Scarborough, ON: Prentice Hall Canada.

Law Commission of Canada (2001) *Beyond Conjugality: Recognizing and Supporting Close Personal Adult Relationships*. Ottawa, ON: Law Commission of Canada.

Le Bourdais, C., Neill, G., and Turcotte, P. (2000) The changing face of conjugal relationships. *Canadian Social Trends*, 56, 14–17.

Lord Chancellor's Department (2001) *Divorce Law Reform – Government Proposes to Repeal Part II of the Family Law Act 1996*. London: Lord Chancellor's Department.

Murphy, M. (2000) The evolution of cohabitation in Britain, 1960–95. *Population Studies*, 54, 43–56.

Nault, F., and Bélanger, A. (1996) *The Decline in Marriage in Canada, 1981 to 1991*. Ottawa, ON: Minister of Industry.

New Zealand Law Commission (1999) *Recognising Same-Sex Relationships*. Wellington, New Zealand: Law Commission.

Norton, A. J., and Miller, L. F. (1992) *Marriage, Divorce, and Remarriage in the 1990's* Washington, DC: US Bureau of the Census.

Pickford, R. (1999) Unmarried fathers and the law. In A. Bainham, S. Day Sclater, and M. Richards (eds.), *What is a Parent: A Socio-Legal Analysis*. Oxford, Hart Publishing.

Pollard, M. S., and Wu, Z. (1998) Divergence of marriage patterns in Quebec and elsewhere in Canada. *Population and Development Review*, 24, 329–56.

Rhode, D. L. (1997) *Speaking of Sex: The Denial of Gender Inequality*. Boston: Harvard University Press.

Shannon, G. (ed.) (1999) *The Divorce Act in Practice*. Dublin: Round Hall.

Turcotte, P., and Bélanger, A. (1997) Moving in together: The formation of first common-law unions. *Canadian Social Trends*, 47, 7–10.

US Bureau of the Census (1998) *1998 Current Population*. Washington, DC: US Bureau of the Census.

Walker, J. (2001) *Information Meetings and Associated Provisions within the Family Law Act 1996*. London: Lord Chancellor's Department.

Wardle, L. D. (1999) Divorce reform at the turn of the millennium: Certainties and possibilities. *Family Law Quarterly*, 33, 783–800.

Wu, Z. (2000) *Cohabitation: An Alternative Form of Family Living*. Don Mills, ON: Oxford University Press.

Wu, Z. (1999) Premarital cohabitation and the timing of first marriage. *Canadian Review of Sociology and Anthropology*, 36, 109–27.

Wu, Z., and Pollard, M. S. (2000) Economic circumstances and the stability of nonmarital cohabitation. *Journal of Family Issues*, 21, 303–28.

# 19

# Children, Families, and Divorce

Jan Pryor and Liz Trinder

## Introduction

Perhaps the most fundamental aspect of families in the twentieth century is the increasing rate of family structural change as a result of parental separation and divorce. The transitions experienced by adults and children between two- and one-parent households, and into stepfamilies and often out again, reflect the widespread instability of family life in the twenty-first century. Households have become remarkably diverse in their structures, despite the lingering image of a family being constituted by two married parents and their biological children. In the UK, Canada, Australia, and New Zealand between 18 and 20 percent of children live in one-parent households at any one time, and in the US in the 1990s 27 percent lived with just one parent. The overwhelming majority of children will remain with their mothers, although there has been an increase in the number of father-headed homes. In New Zealand, for example, 17 percent of lone parents are fathers. However, parents are very likely to re-partner and it is estimated that 20 percent of children in the UK will become part of a stepfamily before age 16 (Haskey, 1994). In the US the numbers are even larger. Estimates are that, of those children born in the 1980s, 35 percent will live in a stepfamily before age 18 (Glick, 1989). The comparatively higher rate of breakdown of stepfamilies means that many children will go on to experience multiple family transitions. Nearly one in five children in a New Zealand cohort had experienced three or more households by age 9 (Fergusson, Horwood, and Shannon, 1984).

These two features, instability and diversity, exist in contexts that contribute to their pervasiveness, since they represent the often creative efforts by individuals to adapt to social and economic change. Accompanying structural diversity, too, are changes in internal family dynamics that both cause, and are a result of, social change. In this chapter we will consider first why family diversity has increased, emphasizing particularly the importance of the social, cultural, and legal context.

The second part of the chapter turns to the implications of family change for family members. This is a controversial and politicized area, and we begin by first considering some of the methodological and conceptual issues and assumptions that have characterized the research enterprise before moving on to present some of the key research findings addressing the implications of divorce and separation for adults and children. We conclude with a discussion of the ways in which further research and understanding of family change might inform family life and policies concerned with it.

## The Context of Family Change

Divorce is one of several major transitions that family members may experience. These transitions do not occur in a vacuum, but take place in legal, historical, cultural, and social contexts that form a framework within which they can be understood. It is important to remember that family structures and relationships have always been subject to change, and that children have always faced the risk of losing one or both parents. A major difference between now and 200 years ago, however, is that the main reason for losing a parent today is likely to be parental separation, whereas in earlier times it was most likely to be through death.

### Historic changes in families

There remains a tendency to see the nuclear family as the gold standard against which other family structures are compared. Yet a brief look at European history tells us that children have not always, or even predominantly, lived with two married biological parents and their siblings in one household. The nuclear family was a feature of the middle part of the twentieth century, when many but not all families were sufficiently affluent to afford to have one parent at home caring for children while the other earned a family wage in the workplace. In earlier times children were often sent to live in other households as apprentices, or in service, and families in those times constituted those individuals living under the same roof at any one time and usually headed by a father. Children were parented by a variety of adults who were not necessarily their biological parents. The diversity of households that we see today, then, is not a new phenomenon. It is probably true, however, that the rates of change are higher than in the past, and that the transitions undergone by children are less predictable in their timing and their nature.

Why have rates of family change risen? Skolnick (1997) suggests that current high levels of family transitions are similar to two earlier periods. The first was the move from a family-based economy to a wage-based economy with the advent of industrialization. This took place largely in the early nineteenth century, and meant that women increasingly ran households as men moved into the workplace. Accordingly, gender roles became more clearly defined, with women responsible for raising children and keeping the home as a "haven" for hardworking men, with men as sole providers for their families. Then, from the middle of the twentieth century, middle-class women moved increasingly into the paid workforce, impelled by the politicization of women and, increasingly, the inadequacy of the individual wages paid to men to support families. Again, family dynamics changed and marital relationships became more companionate. Gender roles became more equitable, in principle if not in fact. These changes varied by class; working-class women were far less likely than their sisters in middle-class households to have had the luxury of *not* going out into the workforce even in the heyday of the "nuclear" family. See Laslett and Gillis for accounts of the history of families (Gillis, 1985, 1997; Laslett, 1972).

Several factors contribute to the upheaval we see now and in particular to the vulnerability of marriages. One is the decreased economic dependence of women on their partners, brought about by their entry into the workforce. An implication of this is that unhappy couples are more easily able to separate rather than being held together by economic dependence. Another is that women spend more time in the workplace than at home and that children are often in child-care rather than in their homes after school. Linked to this is the demise of the home as the site of economic production, so that its raison d'être as a source of income ceases to exist.

Another factor is increased longevity. Couples can expect to live together after their children leave home for several decades in unions that might not survive for their own sakes. Furthermore, increased longevity means that their parents are more likely than in the past to be alive. Although grandparents provide an invaluable resource for families as children are growing up, in advanced old age they increasingly become dependent on their children for care and economic support, thus adding stress to households.

Perhaps the most significant changes in families are emotional and psychological. As the structures upholding marriage become based less on economic and institutional grounds, partnerships are more likely to be grounded in emotional and psychological underpinnings. From the late nineteenth century we can trace the growth of the "companionate" marriage in which principles of shared emotional and domestic lives were espoused if not upheld (see Harris, 1983) for an account of the complexities and contradictions in companionate marriages). As this concept has gained strength, it is likely that the demands on marriage are no longer economic but are for emotional fulfillment. Bernstein (1970) has described the transition from the *positional* family in which there are hierarchies, rules, and where obedience is expected; to the *personal* family where egalitarian roles are emphasized. This transformation of the basis of family relationships has been described by Finch and Mason (1993), who point out that obligations to family are no longer based on kinship and commitments of blood or legal relationships, but are individual negotiated commitments. Giddens (1992) has described what he calls the pure relationship that "exists for its own sake, for what can be derived by each person from a sustained association with another; and which is continued only in so far as it is thought by both parties to deliver enough satisfactions for each individual to stay within it" (p. 58). To the extent that partnerships are indeed based on negotiated commitments or characterized by pure relationship, the onus for stability rests predominantly on individuals themselves rather than factors outside themselves such as community or church-based constraints.

Changes in beliefs about childhood have contributed to the emotional and relational character of families. Until the end of the nineteenth century, comparatively few concessions were made to childhood, since children were an essential part of the family economy. By the end of that century, though, families had become child-oriented (Ariès, 1970; Cunningham, 1995). A major factor contributing to this was their removal from the workforce and their entry into state education, rendering them both economically dependent, and often better educated than their parents. It is likely that the latter contributed to the demise of the positional family and the rise of the personal one, as children were able to challenge their parents' views. Furthermore, children have increasingly become sources of emotional and psychological gratification to their parents, and in this sense there is a mutual dependency that has not existed in previous eras. Another factor adding to this process is the lowering of fertility rates, so that parents invest their emotional currency in fewer children than in the nineteenth century. Importantly for family transitions, there is an increasing recognition of children's rights and abilities to contribute to family decisions, including those associated with separation and divorce. Again, there are class differences in the ways in which family dynamics operate in terms of children's power, with middle-class families more likely to evince "democratic" parenting where children are consulted and involved in family decisions.

Some of these considerations may help to explain the intense feelings that accompany divorce and other family transitions. Children are no longer economic units in a family, and dramatically declining fertility rates have meant that there are not so many of them in a household as there were in the past. Rather, children have become precious emotional rather than economic assets – Cunningham has described the concept of the "priceless child." The accompanying increase in the centrality of the parent–child relationship and in parents' emotional dependence on their children has led to the possibility of the loss of that relationship as being deeply threatening. The separation of the parenting role from the partnership role that has occurred means, too, that parents expect to continue to be in a parenting relationship with their children even if their adult partnership fails. As young adults delay moving from the parental household because of extended education and other factors, the length of the proximal parent–child relationship has become extended. Added to this, individual's identities are associated with their personal relationships within families, rather than with their roles in communities so that changes in these can pose a significant threat to an individual's sense of self.

## Legal and demographic changes

The historic changes described above have taken place in parallel with demographic and legal transformations. Divorce rates in the UK and in North America have always been increasing. From the beginning of the twentieth century the rates increased incrementally, with a twentyfold increase in the UK between 1911 and 1960 (Pryor and Rodgers, 2001). In the US in the 1920s rates were about twenty times those of England and Wales over the same period, and in both countries there were sharp increases in rates following World War II. This has been attributed to the difficulties in sustaining marriages after wartime experiences, and the legalization of separations that had occurred during the war (Goode, 1993). At present, rates in the US are two to three times as high as in the UK, Australia, and New Zealand and in all countries there appears to be a recent slowing of rates of divorce. At the same time, however, a second feature of the postwar world has been the rapid expansion in cohabitation as both a prelude as well as an alternative to marriage. Although divorce rates appear to have stabilized, a significantly higher number of children are drawn into family transitions with the breakdown of their parents' cohabiting relationship.

The pace of change in family structures has prompted liberalization of hitherto highly restrictive divorce laws, leading to claims from some commentators that more relaxed legal frameworks were further fueling the breakdown of the family. The incidence of divorce and the legal framework does vary considerably internationally, with a marked difference between Catholic and Protestant countries. Most Protestant countries allowed divorce by the beginning of the twentieth century, whilst Ireland only permitted divorce at the end of the twentieth century and Malta still prohibits divorce. A more recent major change has been the introduction in some countries of no-fault legislation, where divorce could be obtained on the grounds of marital breakdown rather than on other factors such as infidelity. There is considerable debate about whether no-fault divorce laws have increased the incidence of divorce, or whether they simply made it easier for already estranged couples to formalize their separation. In fact, a majority of couples in the UK do not choose no-fault divorce but instead opt for fault-based divorce that can be granted in a relatively short time.

Recent legislation in the UK intended to put a more human face on to divorce, and to remove state intervention from the process as far as possible. It took the form of the Family Law Act (1996). The decision in 2001 not to implement the Act was based on the perceived failure of processes such as mediation to make a difference to the experiences of families.

The rise in cohabitation has not seen an accompanying conformity in legal regulation between it and divorce. In most European countries and in the US cohabiting and married couples are treated differently in regard to property and children's issues, although this is not the case in New Zealand.

To sum up, family transitions, including divorce, can be seen as responses to changes in the nature of families and family relationships, and to social and economic factors. Although family change has always been a feature of societies, both the reasons for it and the rates have changed. Whereas in the past changes were more likely to be a part of cultural and economic norms (such as children going into service in other families), today they are more often the result of the failure of relationships within families. The impact of these is intensified by the fact that parent–child relationships are highly emotionally imbued with meaning and that children take a more central role in family decision-making. Obligations and commitments are more likely now than in the past to be based on negotiation than on kinship. Considerable responsibility, then, falls on individual family members to arrange and sustain relationships. Family *processes*, rather than legal and biological considerations, have taken prominence.

## Understanding and Researching Divorce and Separation

The dramatic changes in family life over the last few decades have resulted in hotly contested debates among commentators and researchers (dubbed in the US as the "family wars") about their individual and societal significance. Broadly speaking, the debate is between those who see family change as symptomatic of wider societal decline and as inevitably harmful to children (e.g., Popenoe, 1996) and those who see it as a wider pattern of family change that reflects broad social forces and the attempts of families to adapt to their impact (e.g., Stacey, 1990). Empirical research can make some contribution to resolving these disputes; however, it is unlikely that researchers can provide answers to what are frequently moral or political questions. It is evident that the same data on demographic trends can be read as evidence of family decline or of family adaptation, depending upon one's perspective.

The role for empirical research is probably more modest than resolving the decline/adaptation question. Nonetheless, it is also critical to understand that researchers themselves are not inoculated against moral or political influences. Although this is true of all areas of research, it is likely that the intensely personal nature of family issues means that researchers are even less immune from coming to their work with a framework of values that may influence the questions asked and the answers gleaned. Just as the process and meaning of family change take place in a socio-historical context, so inevitably does the activity of researching family transitions. Research is not simply a technical matter (although the technical issues are themselves far from simple, as we point out below). Instead we consider that research also takes place from an implicit or explicit worldview where the questions asked and the means by which they are addressed are shaped to some extent by current social and political concerns.

## Intra-paradigm critiques: Methodological challenges

The rapid growth in divorce rates has sparked off in turn an impressive body of research on divorce and remarriage. As a result our understanding of the causes, processes, and consequences of divorce has advanced significantly over the last two decades. In particular a consistent message has emerged from studies undertaken in a range of countries that divorce is associated with a greater risk of adjustment problems for adults, and particularly for children. As a statement, however, this can only take us so far. How much of a risk is there, for how long, and for which children and adults? What is the linkage between divorce and outcomes, and what is it that "causes" enhanced risk? These more targeted questions have proved correspondingly difficult to answer with any degree of precision. Few studies have been conducted using large representative samples, with even fewer prospective studies. Although sampling strategies have become vastly more sophisticated over the last twenty years, for a process as complex and as common as family separation it remains a challenge to measure effects and disentangle causes. Income, social class, the level of conflict between parents, family size, and post-separation arrangements are just some of the factors that must be taken into account, presenting significant challenges for researchers. Whilst identifying the outcomes of divorce is methodologically challenging we should not underestimate the advances that have been made with the emergence of large, representative, community-based longitudinal studies, such as the ALSPAC (Dunn et al., 1998; O'Connor et al., 1999).

Another problem with research is that it deals with overall trends. It seems indisputable that in general terms divorce does have negative consequences for many children and adults. But research cannot predict how individuals will fare. Some individuals will experience little difficulty in adjustment or benefit from separation, some will struggle badly, and others will be "averagely" affected, but the aggregate approach of quantitative research generally blurs such distinctions.

A third issue is the comparative paucity of theory in divorce research. The focus on the need to discover causal links between independent variables and outcomes has diverted researchers from considering process models that might allow the complexities and nuances of family dynamics to be elucidated. There are some exceptions to this, including the work of Paul Amato in the US and Judy Dunn in the UK.

### Extra-paradigm critiques: Ontological challenges

Nonetheless, some of the implicit assumptions of the divorce adjustment literature have been challenged with arguments that better research requires more than just technical adjustments to methodologies, and instead a reassessment of the presumptions of the enterprise. Divorce research is a controversial area (see, e.g., Thompson and Wyatt, 1999). A cursory inspection of journal articles and books on divorce and separation over the last two decades will immediately reveal that researchers have been preoccupied with the consequences, and to a lesser extent on the causes, of family breakdown. Far less attention has been paid to the processes and meanings of family transitions, and as a result our understanding of this has developed less quickly. For some this focus stems from explicit or implicit moral concerns about "the decline of the family" (Demo, 1993). Furthermore, a common tactic has been to construct studies based on a comparison of divorced and non-divorced families, or stepfamilies versus intact families. Ganong and Coleman (1994) argue that this approach is based on an assumption of the nuclear family as the "gold standard," with the implication that other family structures are deviant or pathological, that is, a "deficit-comparison" approach. Grouping together family structures in this way limits the capacity of researchers to explore the variations within structures and focuses attention of problems and difficulties rather than strengths. Within-group comparisons, of for example, different types and processes within stepfamilies may be more instructive rather than inappropriate comparisons with intact families (Demo, 1993).

The vast majority of studies of divorce have been based on standardized measures administered to individual family members. This focus on what is measurable has a number of consequences. The model therefore is one based on atomized individuals rather than family members located in and engaging with interpersonal processes set in a wider social context. Scholars working from a systemic perspective have in particular pointed to the limited attention given to the critical role of interpersonal processes (e.g., Emery, 1994). At the same time the focus on what is measurable statistically has largely precluded attention to meanings of divorce. The "problem" focus of much of the divorce research has been subject to sustained critique from some feminist scholars, who have emphasized that for many women leaving a violent or otherwise difficult marriage may be preferable (Smart and Neale, 1999). Overall, despite some excellent studies of the tremendous diversity in how divorce is understood and processed by individuals, including the work on narratives of divorce of, for example Riesman (1990), this work has had a somewhat limited impact on the traditional body of divorce research.

## Adults and Divorce

Divorce or separation is a significant and stressful life event for the many adults who experience it. In overall terms a raft of studies undertaken in Western cultures have linked divorce to poorer outcomes for adults (for comprehensive reviews see Amato, 2000, and Kitson and Morgan, 1990). Adults who have divorced have heightened levels of mortality and morbidity compared with married people, and report lower levels of happiness and self-esteem and higher levels of psychological distress. Whilst these findings are worrying a closer examination of research suggests that the picture is somewhat more complicated. Although the overall message is that divorce is associated with poorer outcomes we must still ask more searching questions about what is harmful, for whom, by how much, and why. As we pointed out above there are methodological and theoretical issues that make finding straightforward answers to these complex questions quite difficult.

## Divorce as a process

One of the difficulties of identifying the outcomes of divorce is the increasing recognition that divorce is not a discrete thing or event that exists in isolation but instead is a process or sets of processes. The assessment of the processes associated with divorce or separation is not akin to a discrete experiment where a fixed quantity of a known chemical is added to another and the reaction measured. Disentangling cause and effect is highly challenging because it is almost impossible to separate the separation as an *event* from the prior relationship history. For many people some of the difficulties associated with poorer adjustment post-divorce clearly predate the actual separation or formal legal separation. Indeed, Amato's (2000) review reports a number of major studies that have found high or highest levels of distress predating the separation by a number of years. This raises the question, therefore, whether divorce is a cause of adjustment difficulties or whether those people who are more likely to divorce are also those who are more likely to experience adjustment difficulties. It may be that adjustment difficulties predate and therefore cause, or at least contribute to the likelihood of, separation. Amato concludes in his review that there is evidence for the divorce causation effect as well as for selection effects.

## What are the processes associated with well-being after divorce?

Researchers have increasingly sought to identify what it is about the divorce process that may lead to lower well-being for adults. As Amato points out, these mediators (or stressors) are short- or mid-term divorce-related factors contributing to long-term outcomes as well as being shorter-term consequences in their own right. The critical mediators identified fall into four major areas:

1 *Parenting*: the usual division of child-care responsibility post-divorce can be a source of stress for women adjusting to taking the primary burden of parenting. Non-residential fathers, on the other hand, can be adversely affected by a diminution of their fathering role.
2 *Conflict with spouse*: just as conflict can predate a separation so too can conflict continue post-divorce. It is typically centered on issues of property and child rearing, and may require adjudication.
3 *Loss of emotional support*: separation is likely to disrupt support networks in a number of ways, including the loss of the partner (who may have been more or less supportive) as well as possible changes in friend and kinship networks. This is a particularly important issue for men who are less likely than women to have their own support networks.
4 *Economic decline*: for women, in particular, one of the critical stressors is the loss of income following divorce. The division of assets that typically follows divorce almost inevitably reduces the resource available to each.

Divorce typically triggers a chain of reactions, each of which may lead to reduced well-being on a short- or long-term basis. Nonetheless, it should be pointed out that part of the difficulty with linking divorce and outcomes is that none of these socio-demographic and family process variables – parenting difficulties, conflict, support, and poverty are unique to the changes in family structure such as those which occur with separation and divorce. Nor are they confined to any one family form or household structure. The family processes we have indicated above account for adverse outcomes to a far greater extent than do structural differences or even structural change, and are often present before a separation occurs. For example, Demo and Acock's (1996) study of maternal well-being across a range of family types (never-married, married, and divorced) concluded that whilst married women had higher rates of well-being, "even the combined influence of family structure and socio-demographic variables is quite modest relative to the effect of family process variables."

## What are the protective factors?

There is not a single response to divorce. For some people divorce is characterized by a short-term period of adjustment to crisis, whilst for others chronic difficulties may endure over much longer periods (Amato, 2000). Attention is increasingly being giving to identifying what factors are associated with greater "resilience." Amato draws attention to the range of resources individuals are able to draw upon, including material and emotional resources. One significant issue is how individuals perceive or appraise the breakdown of the relationship and the other partner. Although the evidence for gender differences in adjustment is mixed, some researchers have suggested that women fare better emotionally after divorce as they are more likely to see themselves as the initiator (Braver, Whitley, and Ng, 1993).

Aside from feeling some sense of control over the divorce, researchers have also found that "moving on" and letting go of the past relationship is associated with better adjustment, whilst a continuing emotional attachment to the ex-spouse is associated with psychological and physiological symptoms. Johnston and Campbell's sample of highly conflicted parents post-divorce included individuals who were unable to tolerate the loss of the relationship by denying the reality of the separation, rationalizing the loss by denigrating the relationship and the former partner, being overwhelmed by anger, or adopting a position of complete severance and independence preventing all cooperation (Johnston and Campbell, 1988). Conversely Wang and Amato's (2000) study found that positive adjustment was associated with forming new intimate relationships and remarriage.

The research findings on what (generally) works for adults after divorce raise some interesting issues in terms of post-divorce parenting. As we shall see below, policy and practice in a wide range of jurisdictions have increasingly emphasized the importance of continued links between (nonresidential) parents and children after divorce which may at times be at odds with the desires of parents to move on emotionally. The high rates of remarriage coupled with increasing emphasis on and evidence of continued contact or visitation (Bradshaw et al., 1999; Maccoby and Mnookin, 1992), is leading to more complex patterns of family life and family boundaries.

## Outcomes for Children

There is now an extensive body of research that directly or indirectly addresses the consequences of family transitions for children, and it is possible to draw a long bow on these studies in order to gain an overall picture. Not surprisingly the findings are complex, reflecting the nature of families and family change. There are, though, several issues in considering the evidence. First, what do we mean by outcomes? For some, the focus is on educational factors such as school attendance and academic performance. For others, more important issues are social and emotional well-being. Yet others consider behavioral and mental health outcomes. Children are not necessarily going to have problems in all areas that we might consider as outcomes. For example, it is possible that a child may perform impressively in an academic sense yet suffer emotional problems.

Second, it is often difficult to determine what kind of family a child lives in and what his or her experiences have been. Many studies consider children living with one parent as being in a lone-parent household without, for example, identifying whether this is the result of the death of a parent, of parental separation, or whether they have never lived with two parents. Experiences in these three situations are likely to be very different. Similarly, children living in lone-parent households are unlikely to stay in that situation for a long period of time; Aquilino (1996) found in his study of children born to lone mothers that only one in five stayed in a lone-parent household until the age of sixteen, and recently twenty-one different marital status classifications were identified in the National Survey of Families and Households (Kim and McKenry, 2000). A third question is that of time since a transition occurred. Children's reactions and behavior change over time, and so short-term outcomes will not necessarily be the same as the risks faced in the medium and long term.

A more fundamental issue still is what comparisons should be made. Because the two-parent household is still both the most common family for children, and is seen as the desirable norm, outcomes for children who live in lone-parent families are usually compared with those in two-parent households where both parents are the birth parents of children. This implies a deficit model, as we mentioned earlier, and lone-parent households are not always distinguished according to the previous history of relationships. Comparisons of children in stepfamily households are even more ambiguous, since stepfamilies vary considerably in their composition and the relationships amongst their members. Again, they are usually compared with those living with both birth parents, but there is merit in comparing them with lone-parent children since both groups are likely to have experienced at least one family transition.

In the next section we will address the research findings that compare children in intact, lone-parent, and step-parent households, focusing on medium- and long-term outcomes. Short-term outcomes are rarely examined in large studies, so will be considered along with children's perspectives on family transitions.

### Medium and long-term outcomes for children after divorce

Almost all studies that have compared outcomes for children whose parents have separated with those whose parents have not, conclude that they are at risk for a range of adverse outcomes. There are several major reviews of the literature (see Amato, 2000; Rodgers, 1997 for Australia; Rodgers and Pryor, 1998 for the UK, and Pryor and Rodgers, 2001 for an international review of the literature). On average, children who experience divorce are between one and a half times and twice as likely to experience adversity as those who do not. The areas in which this is true include social and emotional problems, educational outcomes, aggressive and antisocial behavior, and substance abuse. In adolescence, people whose parents have separated are more likely than those whose parents have not to leave school early, to enter partnerships early, and to become parents early. In adulthood, the risks are greater in areas of socioeconomic attainment, alcohol and substance abuse, mental health including suicide and depression, and partnership formation and breakdown. Comparisons of findings from studies over several decades suggest, also, that the levels of risk did not change during the second half of the twentieth century despite the increasing prevalence of divorce.

What is important to recognize in this picture is that although there is a significant level of risk associated with parental separation, the majority of children who experience it do *not* go on to suffer adverse outcomes. The comparisons are of group means for individual outcomes, and although significant in a statistical sense do not imply that all or even most children suffer adverse consequences as a result of divorce.

## Outcomes for children in stepfamilies

When compared with children who grow up in intact families, those who live in stepfamilies are at about the same levels of risk as those who live in lone-parent families (Amato, 1994; Amato and Keith, 1991a; Pryor and Rodgers, 2001). When compared with those in lone-parent families, there are few differences. The most notable differences were reported by Kiernan (1992), who found that adolescents living in stepfamilies were very likely to leave home early, and to cite conflict in the family as a reason for leaving. They were also more likely to form partnerships before age 21 than those in lone-parent households. Overall, though, when risks for poor outcomes are considered, children in lone-parent and stepfamily households face similar levels.

## Multiple transitions

Children in lone-parent households are likely to have experienced at least one household transition when their parents separate, although as noted above some may have had none and others may have had several if their parents have had more than one partner. Similarly, those in stepfamily households are most likely to have experienced at least two transitions, out of an original two-parent home into a lone-parent household and then into a stepfamily. Again, studies often fail to take account of the fact that many will have gone through more than two transitions; however, recently increasing attention has been directed toward the outcomes for those who have experienced multiple family transitions.

In contrast to the few differences between those in stepfamilies and those who live in lone-parent families, children who have gone through multiple transitions are at a greater level of risk than either of these groups. Education appears to suffer; children report more school problems (Cockett and Tripp, 1994), and have lower grades if they have had more than two transitions. High levels of offending and disruptive behavior are more likely in these groups (Fergusson, Horwood, and Lynskey, 1992; Kurdek, Fine, and Sinclair, 1995), as are lower levels of well-being and poorer self-images (Cockett and Tripp, 1994). Early transitions to adult roles, such as entering the labor force and having a child are at higher levels of risk, and young people are less likely than those with one or two transitions to enter tertiary education (Aquilino, 1996; Wu and Martinson, 1993). In adulthood, the experience of multiple transitions while growing up increase the likelihood of having marital problems and marital instability, and of experiencing one's own divorce (Amato and Keith, 1991b). In sum, multiple transitions appear to put children at particularly high levels of risk for behavioral, emotional, and relational problems. This conclusion is supported by the finding that children who live in *stable* lone-parent households appear to do well (Ferri, 1976).

### Divorce as a process

For children, as for adults, divorce is a process that often begins a considerable time before one parent leaves the household. The risks for children that are associated with parental separation, then, are associated with factors that precede, accompany, and follow the event signaled by parents ceasing to live together, to the extent that to talk of the "effects" of divorce is mistaken. This is demonstrated by the finding, for example, that in children whose parents subsequently divorce levels of behavior problems and distress are elevated before the separation occurs (Cherlin et al., 1991; Elliott and Richards, 1991). Furthermore, children whose parents either stay together "for the sake of the children" or take a long time to separate and do so when they are young adults are also susceptible to risk for adverse outcomes (Furstenberg and Kiernan, 2001; Pryor, 1999). Factors that appear to be more important than the separation itself include conflict, both before and after separation (Amato and Booth, 1997; Hetherington, 1999; Jekielek, 1998); psychological well-being of residential parents (Simons, 1996); household income (McLanahan and Sandfur, 1994), and the quality of relationships with nonresidential parents (Amato and Gilbreth, 1999). Whether or not children enter a stepfamily household might also be an important factor. As we have seen above, the relative risks for poor outcomes are about the same for children in lone-parent and stepfamily households, despite the restoration of household income that takes place to some extent when a lone parent repartners, and the presence of two adults who are potential or actual parents in the family. The diversity of stepfamily dynamics, and the complex factors that appear to be important in determining children's well-being in them, make it difficult to pinpoint factors that explain how children fare. However, it is apparent that subsequent transitions beyond stepfamily formation, when they break down, for example, raise the levels of risks for children considerably, and the reasons for this are likely to be several, including some selection of adults into multiple transitions and the impact of making and breaking several relationships with family members.

## Children's Perspectives

Despite the impressive body of research that has addressed family transitions such as divorce and stepfamily formation, the majority of studies overlook the perspectives and experiences of children themselves, and have tended at least implicitly to take a caretaking, or welfarist, approach toward children (Archard, 1993; Trinder, 1997). In essence, it is held that children should be protected from making decisions relating to major family issues, since they lack the maturity to formulate valid opinions. Recently, however, we have seen increased attention directed toward children's views of families and family change, especially in the UK, Australia, and New Zealand. This has been driven to a significant extent by the United Nations Convention on the Rights of the Child (not yet signed by the USA), in which emphasis is placed on the rights of children to be heard in matters that concern them. Sociologists of childhood, too, argue that children have a right to be treated as autonomous individuals with the same rights as adults (James and James, 1999). In practice, children's rights to have information, to be heard, and to contribute to decisions made about their lives, are complex issues (see Pryor and Rodgers, 2001 for a discussion of these). In particular, their right to make or be involved in major decisions revolves around questions of competence (Freeman, 2001).

What do children think about family transitions? Like adults, their perspectives and the meanings that divorce and stepfamily living have for them are diverse. There are, though, some themes that emerge from studies that have asked them about their experiences. Children are usually sad and bewildered when parents separate, and long for reconciliation (Burns and Dunlop, 1999; Mitchell, 1985; Pritchard, 1998). Distress is not confined to young children; those who are adult at the time their parents separate also report high levels of unhappiness and shock (Pryor, 1999). Not all children report negative reactions to their parents' separation, however. In a New Zealand study 44 percent had neutral or mildly positive reactions (Smith et al., 1997).

In the majority of situations, children are not given adequate or even any explanations for the separation (Dunn et al., 2001; Neugebauer, 1989; Smith et al., 1997), yet both retrospective (e.g., Walczak and Burns, 1984) and more recent studies (Kim, Sandler, and Tein, 1997) suggest that adequate communication and information for children are linked with their ability to cope with parental divorce. In one instance, nearly half of children interviewed did not know why their parents had separated two years after it had happened.

To whom do children turn for support? Parents are often in states of distress that render it difficult for children either to turn to them or for them to support their children. and colleagues (Dunn et al., 2001) found that mothers were less likely to be used as intimate confidantes than extended family members and peers, and fathers were less often talked to than mothers. Children report talking to grandparents and other extended family members (Dunn et al., 2001; Gorrell Barnes et al., 1998). The importance of grandparents for children at times of family transitions is not adequately acknowledged, yet those in stepfamilies and lone-parent families often feel closer to grandparents than those in intact families, (Kennedy and Kennedy, 1993) presumably because they have spent significant amounts of time with them. Contact is maintained more with maternal than with paternal grandparents, probably because children are more likely to live with their mothers than with their fathers after separation. Children also turn to peers for support (Dunn et al., 2001; Smith et al. 1997), although for boys this may be more difficult, as their peers are less likely to be openly sympathetic.

Over time, children's distress over separation lessens, and some see positive aspects – for example feelings of competence and maturity (Amato, 1987; Kurdek and Siesky, 1980; Pritchard, 1998), closeness to mothers (Arditti, 1999), and for young adults, closeness to fathers (Pryor, 1999).

When parents part living arrangements for children are usually made by adults, and children are rarely consulted. The most common arrangement is for children to live with their mother and to visit their father, although many lose contact with their fathers over time, and the loss of day-to-day contact is often cited as the worst aspect of parental separation (Kurdek and Siesky, 1980; Neugebauer, 1989; Wallerstein and Kelly, 1980). When children and adolescents are asked, they are most likely to say that if their parents separated they would want to spend equal amounts of time with both parents (Derevensky and Deschamps, 1997; Kurdek and Sinclair, 1986; Pryor, 2001). And those who do experience co-parenting say that they are concerned about being fair to both parents, and that co-parenting arrangements fulfill their desire to maintain good relationships with mothers and fathers.

### Children's views of families

Young children take a conservative view of what constitutes a family, regarding two married adults living together with children as most likely to be a family (Gilby and Pederson, 1982; O'Brien, Alldred, and Jones, 1996). As they grow older they include lone-parent households and extended family members, and in adolescence and young adulthood non-legal arrangements and other less conventional groupings become included (Anyan and Pryor, 2002; Gilby and Pederson, 1982; O'Brien, Alldred, and Jones, 1996). At all ages, the presence of love and support is a crucial defining factor of family groupings (Smart, Neale, and Wade, 2001). They show, however, remarkable resilience in adapting to new household structures so long as contextual factors such as good communication and support are present.

## Conclusions and Implications

No longer is it the norm for children to spend their childhoods in one household, with both legally married birth parents. Yet the prevailing assumption that this is, and should be, the case continues to dominate the rhetoric and to a considerable extent the world-view adopted by researchers. Hence a deficit model is often used in regard to outcomes for adults and children in divorcing families, which precludes attention to the diversity of experience and meaning that might illuminate strengths rather than weaknesses in nontraditional families.

There is no doubting the message that large-scale, meta-analytic research gives us. On average, separation, divorce, and stepfamily living put individuals at risk in comparison with those who stay in "intact" family households. Those risks are sufficiently large that we should not ignore them. Household structure and separation in themselves, however, explain a small amount of variance in outcomes for both adults and children. More significant are the processes, diverse experiences, and the meanings of these for family members. Gillis has distinguished the families we live with from the families we live by. The first are the day-to-day realities for children and their parents, and often differ from the scripts provided for families by their communities and cultures. Morgan (1996) suggests that family is properly regarded as a verb; we "do" family as a set of social practices, rather than being family in a static sense. By considering families in this way, we can begin to identify what leads to optimal adaptation and enhances the likelihood of stability for family groups, without resorting to structure as the default independent variable. Not only are diverse household structures in all probability here to stay; it is also true that many work very well in nurturing the well-being and development of their members. Our task, then, is to understand those aspects of families that, regardless of structure, promote resilience and adaptability. This means, for example, taking a stronger focus on processes in families, and on meanings of transitions for individuals.

Change, and multiple change, is a different issue. The clear message from research is that chronic instability and multiple transitions put children at significantly increased risk. An understanding of the subtleties and complexities of processes and meanings may complement the broad-brush understandings offered by quantitative research, so that ways of promoting stability and fostering well-being can be found.

## References

Amato, P. (1987) Children's reactions to parental separation and divorce: the views of children and custodial mothers. *Australian Journal of Social Issues*, 22, 610–23.

Amato, P. (1994) The implications of research findings on children in stepfamilies. In A. Booth and J. Dunn (eds.), *Stepfamilies. Who Benefits? Who Does Not?* Mahwah NJ: Lawrence Erlbaum.

Amato, P. and Booth, A. (1997) *A Generation at Risk. Growing up in an Era of Family Upheaval.* Cambridge MA: Harvard University Press.

Amato, P. and. Gilbreth, J. G. (1999) Nonresident fathers and children's well-being: A meta-analysis. *Journal of Marriage and the Family*, 61, 557–73.

Amato, P., and Keith, B. (1991a) Parental divorce and the well-being of children: A meta-analysis. *Psychological Bulletin*, 110, 26–46.

Amato, P. R. (2000) The consequences of divorce for adults and children. *Journal of Marriage and the Family*, 62, 1269–87.

Amato, P. R., and Keith, B. (1991b) Parental divorce and adult well-being: A meta-analysis. *Journal of Marriage and the Family*, 53, 43–58.

Anyan, S., and Pryor, J. (2002) What is in a family? Adolescent perceptions. *Children and Society*, 16, 1–12.

Aquilino, W. (1996) The life course of children born to unmarried mothers: Childhood living arrangements and young adult outcomes. *Journal of Marriage and the Family*, 58, 293–310.

Archard, D. (1993) *Children, Rights and Childhood.* London: Routledge.

Arditti, J. (1999) Rethinking relationships between divorced mothers and their children: Capitalising on family strengths. *Family Relations*, 48, 109–19.

Ariès, P. (1970) *Centuries of Childhood.* Harmondsworth: Penguin.

Bernstein, B. (1970) A socio-linguistic approach to socialization. In J. Gumperz and D. Hymes (eds.), *Directions in Sociolinguistics.* New York: Holt, Rinehart & Winston.

Bradshaw, J., Stimson, C., Skinner, C., and Williams, J. (1999) *Absent Fathers?* London: Routledge.

Braver, S. L., Whitley, M., and Ng, C. (1993) Who divorced whom? Methodological and theoretical issues. *Journal of Divorce and Remarriage*, 20, 1–19.

Burns, A., and Dunlop, R. (1999) "How did you feel about it?" Children's feelings about their parents' divorce at the time and three and ten years later. *Journal of Divorce and Remarriage*, 31, 19–36.

Cherlin, A. J., Furstenberg, F. F., Chase-Lansdale, P. L., Kiernan, K. E., Robins, P. K., Morrison, D. R., and Teitler, J. O. (1991) Longitudinal studies of effects of divorce on children in Great Britain and the United States. *Science*, 252, 1386–9.

Cockett, M., and Tripp, J. (1994) *The Exeter Family Study.* Exeter: University of Exeter.

Cunningham, H. (1995) *Children and Childhood in Western Society since 1500.* Harlow: Longman.

Demo, D. H. (1993) The relentless search for effects of divorce: forging new trails or tumbling down the beaten path? *Journal of Marriage and the Family,* 55, 42–5.

Demo, D. H., and Acock, A. C. (1996) Singlehood, marriage, and remarriage. The effects of family structure and family relationships on mothers' wellbeing. *Journal of Family Issues*, 17, 388–407.

Derevensky, J. L., and Deschamps, L. (1997) Young adults from divorced and intact families: Perceptions about preferred custodial arrangements. *Journal of Divorce and Remarriage*, 27, 105–22.

Dunn, J., Davies, L. C., O'Connor, T. G., and Sturgess, W. (2001) Family lives and friendships: the perspectives of children in step-, single-parent and nonstep families. *Journal of Family Psychology,* 15, 272–87.

Dunn, J., Deater-Deckard, K, Pickering, K., and O'Connor, T. G. (1998) Children's adjustment and prosocial behavior in step-, single- and nonstep-family settings: Findings from a community study. *Journal of Child Psychology and Psychiatry,* 39, 1083-95.

Elliott, B. J., and. Richards, M. P. M. (1991) Children and divorce: Educational performance and behavior before and after parental separation. *International Journal of Law and the Family,* 5, 258–76.

Emery, R. E. (1994) *Renegotiating Family Relationships. Divorce, Child Custody and Mediation.* New York: Guildford Press.

Fergusson, D., Horwood, L. J., and Lynskey, M. T. (1992) Family change, parental discord and early offending. *Journal of Child Psychology and Psychiatry,* 33, 1059–75.

Fergusson, D., Horwood, J., and Shannon, F. (1984) A proportional hazards model of family breakdown. *Journal of Marriage and the Family,* 46, 539–49.

Ferri, E. (1976) *Growing Up in a One-Parent Family.* Windsor: NFER.

Finch, J,. and Mason, J. (1993) *Negotiating Family Responsibilities.* London: Routledge.

Freeman, M. (2001) The child in family law. In J. Fionda (ed.), *Legal Concepts of Childhood.* Cambridge: Hart.

Furstenberg, F. F., and Kiernan, K. E. (2001) Delayed parental divorce: How much do children benefit? *Journal of Marriage and the Family,* 63, 446–57.

Ganong, L. H., and Coleman, M. (1994) *Remarried Family Relationships.* Thousand Oaks, CA: Sage.

Giddens, A. (1992) *The Transformation of Intimacy: Sexuality, Love and Eroticism in Modern Societies.* Cambridge: Polity.

Gilby, R. L., and Pederson, D. R. (1982). The development of the child's concept of family. *Canadian Journal of Behavioral Sciences*, 14, 111–21.

Gillis, J. (1985) *For Better, For Worse: British Marriages 1600 to Present.* Oxford: Oxford University Press.

Gillis, J. (1997) *A World of Their Own Making: A History of Myth and Ritual in Family Life.* Oxford: Oxford University Press.

Glick, P. C. (1989) Remarried families, stepfamilies, and stepchildren: A brief demographic profile. *Family Relations*, 38, 24–7.

Goode, W. J. (1993) *World changes in divorce patterns.* New Haven, CT: Yale University Press.

Gorrell Barnes, G., Thompson, P., Daniel, G., and Burchardt, N. (1998) *Growing Up in Stepfamilies.* Oxford: Clarendon Press.

Harris, C. C. (1983) *The Family and Industrial Society.* London: Allen & Unwin.

Haskey, J. (1994) Stepfamilies and stepchildren in Great Britain. *Population Trends*, 76, 17–28.

Hetherington, E. M. (1999) Should we stay together for the sake of the children? In E. M. Hetherington (ed.), *Coping with Divorce, Single Parenting, and Remarriage. A Risk and Resiliency Perspective.* Mahwah, NJ: Lawrence Erlbaum.

James, A. L. and James, A. (1999) Pump up the volume. Listening to children in separation and divorce. *Childhood*, 6, 189–206.

Jekielek, S. M. (1998) Parental conflict, marital disruption and children's emotional well-being. *Social Forces*, 76, 905–36.

Johnston, J. R., and Campbell, L. (1988) *Impasses of Divorce. The Dynamics and Resolution of Family Conflict.* New York: Free Press.

Kennedy, G. E., and Kennedy, C. E. (1993) Grandparents: A special resource for children in stepfamilies. *Journal of Divorce and Remarriage*, 19, 45–68.

Kiernan, K. E. (1992) The impact of family disruption in childhood and transitions made in young adult life. *Population Studies*, 46, 213–34.

Kim, H. K., and McKenry, P. C. (2000) Relationship transitions as seen in the National Survey of Families and Households. *Journal of Divorce and Remarriage*, 34, 163–7.

Kim, L. S., Sandler, I. N., and Tein, J-Y. (1997) Locus of control as a stress moderator and mediator in children of divorce. *Journal of Abnormal Child Psychology*, 25, 145–55.

Kitson, G. C., and Morgan, L. A. (1990) The multiple consequences of divorce: A decade review. *Journal of Marriage and the Family*, 52, 913–24.

Kurdek, L., and. Sinclair, R. J. (1986) Adolescents' views on issues related to divorce. *Journal of Adolescent Research*, 1, 373–87.

Kurdek, L. A., Fine, M. A., and Sinclair, R. J. (1995) School adjustment in sixth graders: Parenting transitions, family climate, and peer norm effects. *Child Development*, 66, 430–45.

Kurdek, L. A., and Siesky, A. E. (1980) Children's perceptions of their parents' divorce. *Journal of Divorce*, 3, 339–78.

Laslett, P. (1972) *Household and Family Life in Past Time.* Cambridge: Cambridge University Press.

Maccoby, E. E., and Mnookin, R. H. (1992) *Dividing the Child: Social and Legal Dilemmas of Custody.* Cambridge, MA: Harvard University Press.

McLanahan, S., and Sandfur, S. (1994) *Growing Up with a Single Parent: What Hurts, What Helps.* Cambridge, MA: Harvard University Press.

Mitchell, A. (1985) *Children in the Middle. Living Through Divorce.* London: Tavistock.

Morgan, D. (1996) *Family Connections: An Introduction to Family Studies.* Cambridge: Polity.

Neugebauer, R. (1989) Divorce, custody and visitation: The child's point of view. *Journal of Divorce*, 12, 153–68.

O'Brien, M., Alldred, P., and Jones, P. (1996) Children's constructions of family and kinship. In J. Brannen and M. O'Brien (eds.) *Children in Families: Research and Policy.* London: Falmer.

O'Connor, T. G., Pickering, K., Dunn, J., and Golding, J. (1999) Frequency and predictors of relationship dissolution in a community sample in England. *Journal of Family Psychology*, 13, 436–49.

Popenoe, D. (1996) *Life Without Father.* New York: Free Press.

Pritchard, R. (1998) *When Parents Part. How Children Adapt.* Auckland: Penguin.

Pryor, J. (1999) Waiting until they leave home. The experiences of young adults whose children separate. *Journal of Divorce and Remarriage*, 32, 47–61.

Pryor, J. (2001) Adolescent attitudes to living arrangements after divorce. *Child and Family Law Quarterly*, 13, 1–13.

Pryor, J., and Rodgers, B. (2001) *Children in Changing Families. Life after Parents Separate.* Oxford: Blackwell.

Riessman, C. K. (1990) *Divorce Talk. Women and Men Make Sense of Personal Relationships.* New Brunswick, NJ: Rutgers University Press.

Rodgers, B. (1997) Social and psychological outcomes for children from divorced families: Australian research findings. In *Enhancing Children's Potential: Minimising Risk and Maximising Resiliency*. Dunedin: Children's Issues Centre.

Rodgers, B., and Pryor, J. (1998) *Divorce and Separation. The Outcomes for Children*. York: Joseph Rowntree Foundation.

Simons, R. L. (1996) *Understanding the Differences Between Divorced and Intact Families. Stress, Interaction, and Child Outcome*. Thousand Oaks, CA: Sage.

Skolnick, A. (1997) The triple revolution: social sources of family change. In S. Dreman (ed.), *The Family on the Threshold of the 21st Century*. Mahwah, NJ: Lawrence Erlbaum.

Smart, C., and Neale, B. (1999) *Family Fragments?* Cambridge: Polity.

Smart, C., Neale, B., and Wade, A. (2001) *The Changing Experience of Childhood*. Cambridge: Polity.

Smith, A. B., Taylor, N. J., Gollop, M., Gaffney, M., Gold, M., and Heneghan, M. (1997) *Access and other Post-Separation Issues*. Dunedin: Children's Issues Centre.

Stacey, J. (1990) *Brave New Families*. New York: Basic Books.

Thompson, R. A., and Wyatt, J. (1999) Values, policy and research on divorce. In R. A. Thompson and P. R Amato (eds.), *The Postdivorce Family. Children, Parenting And Society*. Mahwah, NJ: Sage.

Trinder, L. (1997) Competing constructions of childhood: Children's rights and children's wishes in divorce. *Journal of Social Welfare and Family Law*, 19, 291–305.

Walczak, Y., and Burns, S. (1984) *Divorce: The Child's Point of View*. London: Harper & Row.

Wallerstein, J. S., and Kelly, J. B. (1980) *Surviving the Breakup: How Children and Parents Cope with Divorce*. New York: Basic Books.

Wang, H., and Amato, P. R. (2000) Predictors of divorce adjustment: stressors, resources, and definitions. *Journal of Marriage and the Family*, 62, 655–68.

Wu, L., and Martinson, B. (1993) Family structure and the risk of a premarital birth. *American Sociological Review*, 58, 210–32.

# 20

# The Lesbian and Gay Family

JEFFREY WEEKS, BRIAN HEAPHY,
AND CATHERINE DONOVAN

## THE EMERGENCE OF "FAMILIES OF CHOICE"

Over the past generation there has been a highly significant movement amongst self-identified lesbian and gay people to define their own families: to create "families of choice" (Weeks, Heaphy, and Donovan, 2001). Everyone, a gay writer argues, has the right to shape family forms that fits his or her needs (Goss, 1997: 19). A proliferating library of books (e.g., Weston, 1991; Ali, 1996; Carrington, 1999; Weeks, Heaphy, and Donovan, 2001) simultaneously document these changes and circulate models for "doing family" (Morgan, 1996, 1999). Many homosexual people, traditionally seen as excluded from the scope of conventional family life, are simultaneously rethinking the meaning of same-sex relationships, and developing new meanings of family. Not everyone, of course, agrees that families can or should be created so readily. The defining moment in British engagement with the issue was the passing into law of the notorious Section 28 of the Local Government Act of 1988, which outlawed support by local authorities for the "promotion of homosexuality" and "the acceptability of homosexuality as a pretended family relationship" (Weeks, 1991: 137). A similar "touchstone moment" occurred in the United States in 1996 when Congress rushed into law the Defense of Marriage Act. In response to the Hawaiian Supreme Court's judgment in favor of same-sex marriages, this outlined states' rights not to recognize such marriages conducted in other states, and for the first time in federal law defined marriage as exclusively an arrangement between a man and a woman (Sullivan, 1997: ch. 6). But the fact that it was felt necessary to act so precipitately in both jurisdictions reflects a new international agenda, which has put the relationships of non-heterosexuals at the center of moral and political debate. Following the pioneering legislative changes in Scandinavia, France, the Netherlands, Germany, and elsewhere, which allowed the registration of same-sex partnerships, partnership rights, and issues relating to parenting, adoption, marriage, and family are now clearly of major concern, not only in the lesbian and gay world, but much more widely (see Sullivan, 1997; Strasser, 1997; Velu, 1999; Connolly, 2001: 19).

The language of "family" used by many lesbian and gay people can be seen as both a challenge to conventional definitions, and an attempt to broaden these; as a hankering for legitimacy and an attempt to build something new; as an identification with existing patterns, and a more or less conscious effort to subvert them (Weeks, Heaphy, and Donovan, 2001). The new narratives that many non-heterosexual women and men tell about families of choice and intimate life are creating a new public space where old and new forms jostle for meaning, and where new patterns of relationships are being invented (Plummer, 1995).

The emergence of non-heterosexual families of choice may be seen as a product of a double shift in the culture of intimacy in late modern societies. In the first place, campaigns for partnership recognition, same-sex marriage, and parenting rights are only the most public aspects of the growing maturity and complexity of the non-heterosexual world itself. But secondly, these shifts are also part of a wider transformation of intimate life, usually dramatized in terms of a "crisis of the family." The traditional family is indeed changing. But many of the values the family is supposed to represent are not necessarily in crisis. On the contrary, they are being reinvented in a variety of "experiments in living" through which new patterns of commitment are being enacted in everyday life (Giddens, 1992). The massive, and almost certainly irreversible social changes of the past generation are affecting heterosexual and non-heterosexual lives alike, but they have a special resonance for those who are defined, and define themselves, as different. In particular, women and men who have rejected what may be described as the dominant "heterosexual assumption" (Weeks, Heaphy, and Donovan, 2001) are creating ways of life that point to a more diverse culture of relationships than law and tradition have traditionally sanctioned. "Families of choice" may be seen as evidence of new relational patterns, made both possible and necessary by profound changes in Western societies.

## Why "Family"?

As Stacey (1996: 109) observes, what unifies non-heterosexual lives is the experience of institutionalized hostility toward homosexuality, and the complex social, psychic, individual, and cultural effects of this. The experiences of homosexual or bisexual men and women are shaped by their gendered histories, and by the linked but significantly different histories of lesbianism and male homosexuality. Ethnic, racial, class, geographical, and other social and cultural differences intersect and shape sexual identities and life patterns. But whatever the real and often searing differences and divisions, the climate in which non-heterosexual individuals are tested give rise to commonalities, to patterns, to regularities, shaped in a history of hostility toward homosexuality.

In such a history it is not surprising that the family, as the widely proclaimed cornerstone and "building block" of society, has often been seen as the antithesis of homosexuality. In Euro-American societies since at least the eighteenth century, and increasingly codified from the nineteenth century (Weeks, 1990 [1977]; Trumbach, 1998, 1999; Sedgwick, 1985, 1990), the category of "the homosexual" has served to define the boundaries of what it is to be "normal," that is, heterosexual. The fact that the divides between the two have always been permeable, as countless personal histories have revealed, made little difference to popular beliefs and prejudices or the legal realities. The divide between homosexuality and heterosexuality seemed rooted in nature, sanctioned by religion and science, and upheld by penal codes. It is not surprising, therefore, that distinctive social worlds emerged in which at first male and later female "homosexuals" developed different ways of life. These worlds were generally covert, and always vulnerable, but they provided the context for the solidification of distinctive sexual identities, and what Michel Foucault (1979) called a "reverse discourse." The hostile categorization became the starting point for positive identification.

Since the late 1960s, with the emergence of new forms of lesbian and gay activism, there has been a pronounced emphasis on the equal validity of non-heterosexual life choices. One of the most basic effects has been the assertion of identity and community: an affirmation of a positive sense of self and of the collective means of realizing this (see Weeks, 1995). Finding community, said one of the interviewees in Weston's book on "chosen families," means discovering "that your story isn't the only one in the world" (Weston, 1991: 123). The new stories – embodied in a library of "coming out" narratives – told of discovering the self, achieving a new identity, finding others like yourself, and gaining a new sense of belonging.

Since the early 1970s we have seen a vast expansion of distinctive sexual communities, and of what have been called quasi-ethnic lesbian and gay identities, and the proliferation of other distinctive sexual identities, from bisexual to sadomasochistic, and a catalog of subdivisions (Epstein, 1990). In this context, the transgressive element of lesbian and gay politics offered a sharp critique of the family as the forcing-house of hostility to homosexuality, and the subordination of women. For many lesbian and gay activists, "The very form of the family works against homosexuality" (London Gay Liberation Front, 1971: 2).

However, since at least the early 1980s a different emphasis has come to the fore, giving rise to new narratives of intimate relationships (see Altman, 1982). These new narratives focus attention on the values of everyday life, and form the basis of new claims to full citizenship for those hitherto on the margins, especially where relationships are concerned (Weeks, 1998). The achievements of the lesbian and gay movements have opened up possibilities for broader claims for validating a wide range of life experiences and relationships. The question of identity has not gone away, nor were issues about relationships absent from the early feminist and lesbian and gay movements. It is, nonetheless, surprising, on the surface at least, that the growing emphasis on the recognition of relational rights for non-heterosexuals should be expressed in the language of the family.

The usage is not in fact remarkably new, and can be traced through non-heterosexual narratives throughout the twentieth century, though often enclosed within the quotation marks of irony and self-mockery. Chauncey (1994) records its regular American use in his study of *Gay New York* during the first half of the twentieth century, and it also recurs in British testimonies (e.g., Weeks and Porter, 1998). Nor is the usage uncontested. Many strongly resist the use of the term, even as they describe very complex relationships with family of origin, friends, lovers, and offspring. People are uneasy with a term that is so clearly associated with an "institution" which has often excluded them, and which continues to suggest the perpetuation of an exclusively heterosexual mode of being.

Even the most passionate theoretical advocates of the rights of non-heterosexual people to form their own "families" are careful to emphasize the dimensions of difference. Goss writes: "The appropriation of the term *family* is not an assimilationist strategy of finding respectability in general society.... In fact, we are Queering the notion of family and creating families reflective of our life choices. Our expanded pluralist uses of family are politically destructive of the ethic of traditional family values" (1997: 12). For others, even the use of the term suggests a willingness to destroy the distinctive achievements of non-heterosexual history. Rofes argues "that our attempts to equate childless gay male social formations with even a liberal definition of 'family' runs the risk of intermingling constructs with very different values and tainting the creative interpersonal processes used by gay men in constituting relationships" (1997: 158–9).

For many others, however, like the conservative gay writer Andrew Sullivan (1995, 1997), the acceptance of lesbians and gays being allowed to marry, and create families in the traditional manner, is a key strategic goal in the road to full and equal citizenship. Clearly, this is an ongoing debate within the lesbian and gay social worlds through which friendships, partnerships, and intimate life are being defined, lived, and reshaped.

## Doing Family

What is at stake in these debates is the wider social acceptability, and recognition, of chosen patterns of relationships as "like," "akin to," or in fact identical with, the traditional notion of family life, whether or not children are present as part of the network of relationships. Part of the difficulty in generating such acceptance may well be a matter of language. The use of the term "family" underlines, perhaps, the poverty of our language in describing alternative forms of intimate life (Weeks, 1991). The language of familialism is all-pervasive in our culture, and it is difficult to escape it. We can begin to explain this usage, however, if we reflect on a wider shift in family politics over the past generation. The early polemics of gay liberation were concerned not only to critique but to outline *alternatives to* the family, which was seen as both an imprisoning and an outmoded institution. This reflected a wider challenge to the hegemony of the family, which was expressed both in theoretical critiques and in counter-cultural challenges to the existing order (Weeks, 1990 [1977]).

Since the 1970s, however, this rhetoric has almost completely gone. Increasingly, critics of the family have talked not of replacing the family but instead of recognizing *alternative families* (Weeks, 1991), an acknowledgment of the pluralization of forms of family life. There are various types of family, the argument goes, differentiated by class, ethnicity, geography, and simply lifestyle choices, but most fulfilling the basic purposes of family. If there are indeed so many types of family, why should same-sex families be ignored? As Stacey puts it, lesbian and gay families are

> Neither marginal nor exceptional, but rather represent a paradigmatic illustration of the "queer" postmodern conditions of kinship that we all now inhabit. Gays and lesbians who self-consciously form families are forced to confront the challenges, opportunities and dilemmas of the postmodern condition with much lower levels of denial, resistance, displacement or bad faith than most others can indulge. (1996: 15)

The appropriation of the language of the family by many non-heterosexuals can therefore be seen as one important way in which the sexually marginal are struggling to assert the validity of their own way of life. It is striking, for example, that the usage became much more common in Britain after the condemnation of "pretended family relationships" in Section 28 (Weeks, 1991). It is a classic example of "reversing the discourse": turning what was conceived of as derogatory into a resounding affirmation.

In doing this, non-heterosexual people are part of a wider struggle over meaning, both participating in and reflecting a wider crisis over family relationships. As Andrew Sullivan (1997) has argued, if the future of marriage is a critical ground of contestation in the wider world, it is hardly surprising that lesbians and gays should focus their demands on it. If parenting is perceived as in major need of rethinking, then why should non-heterosexuals be excluded from the debate? If families get ever more complex as a result of divorce, remarriage, recombination, or step-parenting, why should the chosen families of lesbians and gays, including with increasing frequency children, be denied a voice? (Weeks, Heaphy, and Donovan, 2001).

This has become even more important for many non-heterosexuals because of the changing cultural context in which homosexuality has been lived since the 1980s. One significant factor here has been the experience of premature illness and loss as a result of the dramatic emergence of the HIV/AIDS epidemic in the early 1980s. Weston has suggested that "Situated historically in a period of discourse on lesbian and gay kinship, AIDS has served as an impetus to establish and expand gay families" (1991: 183). The HIV/AIDS epidemic dramatized the absence of relational rights for non-heterosexuals in a climate of growing prejudice and enhanced need. The epidemic revealed how vulnerable non-heterosexuals were without full recognition of their significant commitments – without full citizenship (Watney, 1994: 159–68; Heaphy, Weeks, and Donovan, 1999).

Other developments – especially when children were involved – gave the same message. The first debates about the validity of non-heterosexual family type relations began in Britain and the US with controversies over the child-custody battles of lesbians in the 1970s (Hanscombe and Forster, 1982; Rights of Women Lesbian Custody Group,1986; Lewin, 1984, 1993). The so-called "lesbian baby-boom" (Weeks, Heaphy, and Donovan, 2001: ch. 7), and the claims by lesbians and gay men for equal rights in issues concerning fostering or adoption, further underlined the continuation of inequality, despite the gains that had been made over the previous decades. Not surprisingly, throughout Western countries, from Australasia to northern Europe, new demands for partnership rights, same-sex marriage, and recognition of new family forms developed throughout the last years of the twentieth century, often in relationship to child-care. As Nardi (1999) has observed, while the use of the term "family" may be little more than metaphorical when applied to adult friendships, it has a strong affinity with conventional uses when applied to units with children. All these factors have created a new agenda for non-heterosexual politics, in which the language of the family has become a key battleground.

A useful way of understanding what is at stake can be found by following Morgan (1996, 1999) in analyzing "the family" in terms of a set of social practices rather than an institution. From this perspective: "family" can be seen as less of a noun and more as an adjective or, possibly, a verb. "'Family' represents a constructed quality of human interaction or an active process rather than a thing-like object of social investigation," writes Morgan (1999: 16). This is an approach with important implications for understanding non-heterosexual lives. It displaces the idea that the family is a fixed and timeless entity, which one is either a member of, or excluded from. We may see it instead as a series of practical, everyday activities which we live: through activities such as mutual care, the division of labor in the home, looking after dependents and "relations," all practices in which lesbian and gay people regularly engage. "Family" is about particular sorts of relational interactions rather than simply private activities in a privileged sphere. Instead of being an objective phenomenon, "family" can be interpreted as subjective set of activities, whose meanings are made by those who participate in them. From this perspective, it is less important whether we are *in* a family than whether we *do* family-type things. In the term used by Judith Butler (1990) to talk about gender, family practices are "performative," and families are therefore constructed through their enactment. We live family rather than dwell within it.

This is an important way of thinking about what constitutes family today. It allows us to recognize and begin to understand the fluidity of everyday life practices, and the way doing family is related to the ways we do or perform gender, sexuality, work, caring, and the other activities that make up the totality of life experiences. Family life may therefore be seen as a historically specific, contextualized set of activities, intimately linked with other social practices. Using this approach, there is no theoretical reason to exclude non-heterosexual everyday practices from the pantheon of family and kin.

## The Friendship Ethic

What does distinguish lesbian and gay families from the traditional family, however, is the absence, or at least diminution, of the bonds of blood and the legal obligations entailed in marriage. The typical family of choice may include a range of people, including lovers and ex-lovers, members of families of origin, children in many cases, but above all friends. Non-heterosexual relationships, it is widely argued, are sustained by the intricately woven but durable strands of a "friendship ethic" in a "friends-as-family" model (Weeks, Heaphy, and Donovan 2001: ch. 3). Of all our relationships, claims Andrew Sullivan (1998: 176), "Friendship is the most common and most natural. In its universality it even trumps family."

Friendships exist in many forms, and have varying symbolic meanings in different places at different times (Allan, 1989, 1996; Rubin, 1985; Nardi, 1999; Pahl, 2000). They are especially important, however, in the circumstances that most lesbian and gay people find themselves in. Friendships particularly flourish when overarching identities are fragmented in periods of rapid social change, or at turning points in people's lives, or when lives are lived at odds with social norms (Weeks, 1995: 145–6). Friendships are portable, they can be sustained at a distance, yet they can allow individuals who are uprooted or marginalized to feel constantly confirmed in who and what they are through changing social experiences (Pahl, 2000). They offer the possibility of developing new patterns of intimacy and commitment. All these features give a special meaning and intensity to friendship in the lives of those who live on the fringes of sexual conformity. In the narratives of non-heterosexuals, friends provide emotional and material support, but also affirm identity and belonging (see, e.g., Nardi, 1999). As Altman noted: "what many gay lives miss in terms of permanent relationships is more than compensated for by friendship networks, which often become de facto families" (1982: 190).

Friendships, sometimes linked to couple relationships, but often not, provide the space for the exploration of who or what you are, and what you want to become. This is true at all stages of the life cycle, from the first tentative stages of coming out as "different," through the crises of relationships, to the potential loneliness of old age – those "fateful moments" (Giddens, 1991, 1992) of a life, which force individuals to reassess who and what they are, and to find ways of adapting to new situations.

Central to this reliance on friendship is the fact that friendships are chosen, and because of that offer a fundamental sense of equality, which can allow for greater emotional possibilities (Weeks, Heaphy, and Donovan, 2001: ch. 3). Choice, of course, implies selection and distinctions. No one chooses randomly, and there are limits to choice. In his study of friendship, Allan (1989) has argued that far from being simply a matter of personal or free choice, friendships are structured and patterned like all other social relations by factors that go beyond simple personal wish: by social class, social mobility, occupational status, leisure interests, gender differences, ethnic and racial categorizations, age, and so on. These are necessarily factors in non-heterosexual friendships also, and though a common sense of sexual identity often manages to bridge other divides, this does not happen automatically. Friendships are not given; they are based on a host of varying factors that shape the affinity circles that develop. Friendships have to be worked at.

Lesbian and gay friendship networks, like others, have fluid boundaries and varying membership, as friends work through the tensions and difficulties over a lengthy period (Weston, 1991). Friendships are necessarily dynamic, with members added or falling away as circumstances change. People do not consciously at any point decide that a given nexus of friends is close enough to be like family or not. Some speak of the gradual nature of developing relationships which involves shared experiences, an intertwined history, a sense of continuity, and some sense of permanence. The gradual process through which someone becomes a "family member" might only be realized in retrospect (Weeks, Heaphy, and Donovan, 2001: ch. 3). Individuals, therefore, may make distinctions amongst friends, those who are social friends and those who are "part of the family."

Sexual links add a particular element, which broadly differentiates non-heterosexual from heterosexual patterns. Many lesbians and gay men often include within their closest circles former lovers as well as current sexual partners (Weston, 1991; Blasius, 1994). This leads to highly intricate patterns. Weston speaks of "ties that radiated outwards from individuals like spokes from a wheel" (1991: 109). Friendship circles overlap, intersect, and move apart. But for many they provide, in Nardi's (1999) phrase, "invincible communities," through which both identity and belonging can be affirmed.

A strong feature is the tendency for close friendships to be homosocial, or single-sex, though this is by no means universal (cf. Weston, 1991; Nardi, 1999). While many lesbians and gays do intermingle in the same networks, for others there is an absolute barrier between the genders (see Dunne, 1997). A sense of difference, especially when shaped around gendered experience, helps produce different lesbian and gay male social worlds, and conversation across the divide becomes difficult. And yet, when faced by the power of the heterosexual assumption, a strong sense of common interests does occur. Rubin (1985) noted that lesbians and gay men established most of their close, supportive friendships among other non-heterosexuals, whether male or female, and this is confirmed by other accounts (e.g., Tanner, 1978;

Weeks, Heaphy, and Donovan, 2001). The accentuated separation of the homosexual and heterosexual worlds as self-identified lesbians and gays have developed quasi-ethnic identities (Altman, 1982; Lewin, 1998), have tended to shape a culture where friendship choices are often made entirely within homosexual circles.

Several commentators have observed that the emphasis on friendships within exclusively homosexual circles can limit the development of facets of the self that a broader range of friendships might encourage (Rubin, 1985; Blumstein and Schwartz, 1983). On the other hand, given that it is likely that most lesbians or gay men are likely to meet other people like themselves in non-heterosexual circles, friendships are likely to be formed around common emotional or sexual identifications. In this context it is hardly surprising that many friendships will transcend traditional divides. Blumstein and Schwartz (1983), for instance, have remarked that some couples at least are apparently mismatched in terms of social and class backgrounds because they met in places where the common denominator was sexual rather than shared leisure or intellectual pursuits. Far from being a disadvantage, this can be seen as a potential strength. As Stuart (1995: 43) puts it, "friendship can break rank," though inevitably there are different perceptions of how easy this is.

The experiences of people differ, of course, depending on their specific circumstances, needs, and other identifications. Non-heterosexuals, as much as heterosexuals, do usually live in more than one social world, and often choose friendships on the basis of their various identities, not simply on the basis of their homosexuality. This is especially true if they feel discriminated against on more grounds than simply their sexuality. Race and ethnicity are perhaps among the most crucial elements that cut across the possibilities of friendship. Many black feminists have long critiqued the early feminist (and gay) hostility to the traditional family (see Mirza, 1997) on the grounds that for minorities the family is an essential bulwark against oppression and a source of support (cf. Weston, 1991: 36). But even when black lesbians and gay men break with their family of origin to establish their own ways of life, racism is a constant presence, disrupting any sense of wider belonging to the non-heterosexual community, while also alienating you from your community of origin. Friendships inevitably have to weave in and through these complex social relationships, reflecting an increasingly diverse social world. This makes it all the more significant that despite differences, and whatever the barriers, many non-heterosexuals have constructed common values and commitments around friendship, which make meaningful lives possible for them.

## Mutuality

Friendship networks can be seen, in particular, as schools of values, especially those of reciprocity and mutuality. In friendship, Elizabeth Stuart (1995: 44) writes, "women and gay men experience mutuality," that is, a sense of involvement with others which goes beyond their isolated individual lives without diminishing their individuality. This is a delicate balancing act, which has to be constantly negotiated and renegotiated if friendship ties are to work and survive. This is not a peculiarly non-heterosexual challenge. As Finch and Mason (1993) have shown, it is precisely a similar challenge which shapes more conventional kin relationships, as family members try to balance a respect for the dignity and self-respect of individuals with a commitment to ongoing responsibilities to one another. In neither traditional kin relationships nor in non-heterosexual lives can anything be taken for granted. Relationships have to be worked at and worked out over time. Neither work to fixed rules (Finch and Mason, 1993: 166) – though heterosexual relationships do inevitably carry more latent assumptions – and individuals live by guidelines about the right way to proceed rather than a fixed list of "oughts" and "musts." And yet despite a high degree of fluidity, individuals do have a strong sense of moral agency and an implicit hierarchy of values in the way they conduct their everyday lives in interaction with others (Weeks, 1995; Weeks, Heaphy, and Donovan, 2001: ch. 3).

Many of these values are common to all forms of close friendship. There are, however, crucial differences between heterosexual and non-heterosexual friendships. Perhaps more important in this context is the lack of legitimacy in non-heterosexual relationships, however stable or fulfilling they may be, compared to the recognized legitimacy of kin interactions, however difficult or unsatisfying they may turn out to be. This puts an extra burden on non-heterosexual friendships because they combine both the traditional delights of friendship and the weight of emotional expectation.

As same-sex relationships are constructed and maintained outside of conventional institutional and legal support systems and structures, they are less likely to be characterized by predetermined assumptions and past histories than traditional family relationships. In the absence of either legitimation by blood or law, the key elements of family, alternative forms of legitimating commitment become necessary (Lewin, 1998). Inevitably, ideas of choice, trust, and love take on a new significance, and these are embodied in a strong sense of the value of "good friendship," which becomes a major legitimizing factor for non-heterosexual relationships.

Around the idea of good friendship a series of values have evolved, which involve balancing a strong sense of individual autonomy with ideals of reciprocity (Weeks, Heaphy, and Donovan, 1999). Weeks, Heaphy, and Donovan (2001: 69–76) found that terms such as duty and obligation tended to be rejected by interviewees in favor of concepts of responsibility, mutual care, and commitment. But these attitudes were seen by many lesbians and gay men not as weaknesses, but as strengths, because they were based on free choices. Distinctions are carefully made, especially with regard to aging parents, and particularly to dependent children. Parenting raises questions of obligation, commitment, and responsibility most sharply.

Many non-heterosexuals, both men and women, are involved in parenting in one way or another, as biological, adoptive, or social parents (Bozett, 1987; Lewin, 1993; Benkov, 1994; Drucker, 1998). A number of observers have commented on the extent of the "gayby" boom in recent years, as quite complex patterns both of conception (self-insemination, surrogacy, arrangements between gay men and lesbians) and parenting (single- and multi-parenting, "step" parenting) have developed (Weeks, Heaphy, and Donovan, 2001: ch. 7). It is apparent, however, that whatever the complexities of the emotional, sexual, and social arrangements, responsibility for the children becomes the focus for the negotiating of relationships. Obligation and duty – though the terms themselves may not always be used – here override the discourse of choice.

The emphasis on choice might lead the unwary to believe that lesbian and gay relationships are inevitably more fragile than relations based on blood or marriage. Yet it can equally be argued that the thinning of enforced obligations, a more sharply defined individualization, and the greater contingency of relationships that result, lead to a greater stress on making relationships work. Silva and Smart (1999: 6) have argued that for many people family ties have become more important for exactly this reason. Freely chosen relationships have the potentiality both to be free of imposed obligations, and, therefore, to be more intense (cf. Bronski, 1988; Plummer, 1995).

For many gay men, and lesbians also, the experience of the AIDS crisis has confirmed the importance of a commitment to mutual care and responsibility (cf. Adam, 1992). In the literature, AIDS has been widely located as a potential catalyst in expanding definitions of family to reflect the reality of contemporary life (e.g., Levine, 1991). It has also been argued that responses to the epidemic have made non-heterosexual caring relationships visible (e.g., Adam, 1992), and have allowed gay "extended families" to demonstrate their strength and durability (e.g., Bronski, 1988). But perhaps the most important legacy of the crisis has been to demonstrate the implications of friendship. As Sullivan has put it: "I don't think I'm alone in thinking that the deepest legacy of the plague years is friendship" (1998: 175).

This is an example of a response to an unexpected, and at first inexplicable, crisis. But the evidence suggests that this ethos underpins everyday life for many lesbians and gay men. A friendship ethic, based on notions of individual autonomy *and* mutual involvement, is the key feature of the contemporary non-heterosexual world.

## Reinventing Intimate Life

Lesbian and gay relationships are worked through at the intersection of two overlapping perceptions and experiences. On the one hand there is a strong sense in the non-heterosexual world of the continuation of institutionalized hostility. On the other, there is a widespread recognition that there are new opportunities for choice and self-invention.

The continuing institutional prejudice and discrimination against non-heterosexual forms of life have been variously theorized – as "compulsory heterosexuality" (Rich, 1983), the "heterosexual matrix" (Butler, 1990), the "heterosexual panorama" (Blasius, 1994), "heteronormativity" (Warner, 1993), or the "heterosexual assumption" (Weeks, Heaphy, and Donovan, 2001). Whatever the concept, it describes an all-encompassing institutional invalidation of homosexuality, and presumption in favor of heterosexuality. The idea recognizes the all-pervasive background noise which always privileges and shores up the heterosexual model as the norm, even as societies grow more formally accepting of difference. Much has changed over the past generation, and the broad result is a greater social toleration of non-heterosexuality, as the growing recognition of same-sex partnerships testifies. But the increasingly recognized fact of sexual diversity has not led to its full acceptance or validation.

The clearest expression of this can be seen in the nervousness with which even the most liberal of jurisdictions deals with non-heterosexual parenting. It was noticeable that the earliest attempts at formal recognition of same-sex partnerships explicitly excluded rights to adoption, and only since the turn of the millennium has this been modified, for example, in the Dutch acceptance of same-sex marriage in 2001 or of British liberalization of adoption laws in 2002 (see discussion in Domovan, Heapy and Wesks, 1999).

Given the resilience of the heterosexual assumption, it is not surprising that non-heterosexual people are thrown back on their own resources.

This has given rise to a strong narrative of self-invention amongst many lesbians and gay men, particularly in relation to self-identity and lifestyle. More generally, as Beck-Gernsheim has observed: "the normal life history is giving way to the do-it-yourself life-history" (1998: 57). Self-descriptions change as circumstances change, and new possibilities open up. The possibility exists for invention and reinvention. Lesbians and gays, however, have had to be arch-inventors (Giddens, 1992) – because the traditional narratives of family and marriage were frequently inapplicable.

But increasingly, it is clear, narratives of the self and narratives of chosen or invented families are being linked together. Weston argues: "When cast in narrative form, the shift from identification of gayness with the renunciation of kinship (no family) to a correspondence between gay identity and a particular type of family (families we choose) presents a kind of collective coming-out story: a tale of lesbians and gays moving out of isolation and into kinship" (1991: 212).

The freedom to choose is the necessary condition of responsible and reciprocal relationships, based on respect and care for others (Weeks, Heaphy, and Donovan, 2001).

This in turn requires a recognition that all relationships, but especially one-to-one partnerships, have to be based on an egalitarian system of values. The chosen nature of relationships, and the process of negotiation which that must involve, open unique opportunities, many lesbians and gay men argue, for more equal relationships than are available to heterosexuals (see Giddens, 1992; Weeks, Heaphy, and Donovan, 2001). A democratized, flexible model of couple relationships has, therefore, become the ideal. The reality, inevitably, is more complex: non-heterosexuals strive to achieve equality in terms of intimacy, sexual relations, and the division of labor in the household against all the inequalities which continue to structure our societies (e.g., see Dunne, 1997; Carrington, 1999). Many non-heterosexual women and men have consciously attempted to shape their relationships in opposition to assumed heterosexual models, with their inbuilt gendered divisions and assumptions.

Creativity and choice may be the leitmotifs of relationships, but there are very real limits to free choice and real equality. Non-heterosexuals have a realistic perception of the actuality of their everyday lives. While the percentages have varied dramatically across studies, some early North American work on same-sex relationships has suggested that only around 60 percent of lesbians (Peplau and Cochran, cited in Peplau, Venigas, and Miller Campbell, 1996) and of gay men (Harry and DeVall, 1978) describe their relationships as actually being fully "equal."

A large body of empirical research work has focused on the intimate and domestic lives of men and women, and suggests that relations, particularly within the home, continue to be marked and structured by inequalities with regard to labor and status (see Weeks, Heaphy, and Donovan, 2001: ch. 4). It is difficult to escape dichotomous ways of being. As Dunne says:

> Engagement with the everyday tasks and objects of the home is not simply about getting necessary work done, it is about engaging in the production of gender. . . . The domestic division of labor (one needs to add here – between women and men) is about linking the *musts* of work to be done with the *shoulds* of gender ideals. (1999: 69)

As Oerton (1997) points out, if gender is a social construction that is only contingently linked to bodily differences, then it is perfectly possible for same-sex relationships themselves to be reproduced in gendered terms.

Despite this, the absence of significant structural inequalities and the prevalence of the friendship ethic can provide some of the necessary conditions for greater intimacy. Various attempts to address the equality of same-sex male relationships suggest that they can be best understood as structured around "best-friend" models of relating (Harry and DeVall, 1978; Harry, 1984; Peplau, 1981; Kehoe, 1988). As Peplau, Venigas, and Miller Campbell suggest:

> A friendship script typically fosters equality in relationships. In contrast to marriage, the norms of friendship assume that partners are relatively equal in status and power. Friends also tend to be similar in interests, resources, and skills. Available evidence suggests that most American lesbians and gay men have a relationship that most closely approximates best friendship. (1996: 403)

Blumstein and Schwartz (1983), in their study of same-sex and heterosexual couples, have argued that lesbians and gay men appear to combine the need for friendship and romantic love in one person to a greater extent than heterosexuals. The research reported in Weeks, Heaphy, and Donovan (2001) confirms that for many lesbians and gay men friendship is seen as central to the operation of "successful" couple relationships.

Writers on marriage have used the term "intimate strangers" to refer to the different emotional goals that husbands and wives may have in traditional couple relationships (Mansfield and Collard, 1988). Perhaps a more accurate term to refer to non-heterosexual relations is the one used by Dunne (1997): "intimate friendships." It seems likely that the egalitarian ideals of same-sex relationships do indeed dissolve some of the boundaries between friendships and sexual/emotional commitments, making possible forms of intimacy that are difficult to attain amongst most heterosexual couples (cf. Giddens, 1992).

## Everyday Experiments

There can be no doubt of the powerful meanings attached to relationship networks by many lesbians and gay men. For many, these relationships have the potency of family relationships in either supplementing or displacing traditional forms. On the surface, at least, this lends credence to the idea that for many people friendships offer surrogate or "pretend" families: substitutes for the real thing. This is not, however, how non-heterosexuals see the significance of their relationships, nor how these relationships are characterized in the recent literature. Bozett (1987), for example, sees lesbian and gay relationships as having all the significant defining features of biological families. Weston (1991) has concluded that in creating chosen families lesbians and gays are neither involved in imitating heterosexual families, nor in necessarily replacing or substituting a family of choice for a family of origin: they have a reality in their own right.

Of course, using the language of family is not the same as saying that networks of non-heterosexual relations *are* families. Nardi, while acknowledging the potency of the language, is notably skeptical of the usage. He notes particularly the general absence of the age and status differentials which characterize most kin relations, and concludes: "Structurally, friendship circles do not look like families: they certainly do not have the legal, ceremonial, or religious attributes that characterize the family institutions in American society. To say they are like family may serve, then, as a shorthand form of communication" (1999: 68).

Families of choice are clearly different from traditional families. The frequent use of familial language amongst lesbians and gay men does, however, tell us something very important about contemporary relationships. The public emergence of "families we choose" signals an important shift in the preoccupations of the non-heterosexual world, which is part of a wider transformation of intimate life in which the idea of the family is itself changing. If we see family in terms of practices rather than institutional forms, of meanings rather than structures, many non-heterosexuals "do family" in ways which are parallel to heterosexual patterns. The growing preoccupation with parenting amongst many non-heterosexuals underlines rather than undermines these parallels (Weeks, Heaphy, and Donovan, 2001: ch. 7). The loaded term "family" may be a shorthand, but it is a useful one to signal a changing reality.

There are many historic echoes of the usage of family language, often by communities of marginalized or embattled people, which give rise to what has been described as "fictive kin" (Stack, 1974; Weston, 1991). Rapp (1982: 178) uses the phrase "continuous family" to describe such networks. There are obvious parallels with the lesbian and gay world, where friendship and sexual community provide some of the same elements of support as a working-class or ethnic neighborhood. However, the concept of "fictive kin" still assumes the blood family as the starting point, whereas for many non-heterosexuals it is precisely the ambiguous relationship with family of origin, especially when the fact of homosexuality leads to rejection from the family, that is the problem. Then friendships must become the core network of support.

The word "network" points us to the real significance of what is happening. A network is a complex system of interconnected strands. It also evokes today the dense lines of communication of the Internet, which has no single focus but rather a myriad of different points of information and communication, with an infinite possibility of juncture and disjuncture, apparently random, but able to resist practically any attack on its integrity (Weeks, Heaphy, and Donovan, 2001: 47–50). Using this metaphor, the family of choice can be seen as an example of the rise of "network families."

Such networks are the product both of changing patterns of communication, and of the dense interconnections that can exist between people. The new language of family amongst lesbian and gay people is an index of these changing social possibilities in a rapidly changing epoch. Clearly families of choice build on historical experience. But above all they can be seen as examples of the "everyday experiments in living" which theorists such as Giddens (1992) argue people are required to undertake in an ever-more complex world. Non-heterosexuals feel they have more open possibilities for two reasons: greater choice and openness in relationships, and the belief that they can escape many of the structural differences, especially those of heterosexuality, that limit traditional relationships. However difficult their achievement may be, these beliefs structure the everyday practices of many lesbian and gay people. When non-heterosexuals "do family" they are creating life patterns which give new meaning to their relationships in an increasingly complex world.

## Note

A fuller development of the themes discussed in this chapter can be found in the authors' book, *Same Sex Intimacies: Families of Choice and other Life Experiments* (Weeks, Heaphy, and Donovan, 2001).

## References

Adam, B. D. (1992) Sex and caring among men. In K. Plummer (ed.), *Modern Homosexualities: Fragments of Lesbian and Gay Experience*. London: Routledge.

Ali, T. (1996) *We are Family: Testimonies of Lesbian and Gay Parents*. London and New York: Cassell.

Allan, G. (1989) *Friendship: Developing a Sociological Perspective*. Boulder CO: Westview.

Allan, G. (1996) *Kinship and Friendship in Modern Britain*. Oxford: Oxford University Press.

Altman, D. (1982) *The Homosexualization of America, The Americanization of the Homosexual*. New York: St. Martin's Press.

Beck-Gernsheim, E. (1998) On the way to a post-familial family: from a community of need to elective affinities. *Theory, Culture and Society* 15, 53–70.

Benkov, L. (1994) *Reinventing The Family: The Emerging Story of Lesbian and Gay Parent*. New York: Crown.

Blasius, M. (1994) *Gay and Lesbian Politics: Sexuality and the Emergence of a New Ethic*. Philadelphia: Temple University Press.

Blumstein, P., and Schwartz, P. (1983) *American Couples*. New York: William Morrow.

Bozett, F. W. (ed.) (1987) *Gay and Lesbian Parents*. New York: Praeger.

Bronski, M. (1988) Death and the erotic imagination. In J. Preston (ed.), *Personal Dispatches: Writers Confront AID*. New York: St. Martin's Press.

Butler, J. (1990) *Gender Trouble: Feminism and the Subversion of Identity*. London: Routledge.

Carrington, C. (1999) *No Place like Home: Relationships and Family Life Among Lesbians and Gay Men*. Chicago and London: University of Chicago Press.

Chauncey, G. (1994) *Gay New York: Gender, Urban Culture, and the Making of the Gay Male World, 1890–1940*. New York: Basic Books.

Connolly, K. (2001) Germans flock to tie the knot after law change. *Observer*, July 22, 19.

Donovan, C., Heaphy, B., and Weeks, J. (1999) Citizenship and same sex relationships. *Journal of Social Policy*, 28, 689–709.

Drucker, J. (1998) *Families of Value: Gay and Lesbian Parents and Their Children Speak Out*. New York: Plenum.

Dunne, G. A. (1997) *Lesbian Lifestyles: Women's Work and the Politics of Sexuality*. London: Macmillan.

Dunne, G. A. (1999) A passion for sameness: Sexuality and gender accountability. In E. B. Silva and C. Smart (eds.), *The New Family?* London: Sage.

Epstein, S. (1990) Gay politics, ethnic identity: the limits of social constructionism. In E. Stein (ed.), *Forms of Desire: Sexual Orientation and the Social Constructionist Controversy*. New York and London: Garland.

Finch, J., and Mason, J. (1993) *Negotiating Family Responsibilities*. London: Routledge.

Foucault, M. (1979) *The History of Sexuality: Volume 1: An Introduction*. Harmondsworth: Penguin.

Giddens, A. (1991) *Modernity and Self-Identity*. Cambridge: Polity.

Giddens, A. (1992) *The Transformation of Intimacy: Sexuality, Love and Eroticism in Modern Societies*. Cambridge: Polity.

Goss, R. E. (1997) Queering procreative privilege: coming out as families. In R. E. Goss and A. S. Strongheart (eds.), *Our Families, Our Values: Snapshots of Queer Kinship*. Binghampton, NJ: Harrington Park Press.

Hanscombe, G., and Forster, J. (1982) *Rocking the Cradle: Lesbian Mothers. A Challenge in Family Living*. London: Sheba Feminist Publishers.

Harry, J. (1984) *Gay Couples*. New York: Praeger.

Harry, J., and DeVall, W. B. (1978) *The Social Organisation of Gay Male*. New York: Praeger.

Heaphy, B., Weeks, J., and Donovan, C. (1999) Narratives of love, care and commitment: AIDS/HIV and non-heterosexual family formations. In P. Aggleton, G. Hart, and P. Davies (eds.), *Families and Communities Responding to AIDS*. London: UCL Press.

Kehoe, M. (1988) Lesbians over 60 speak for themselves. *Journal of Homosexuality*, 16, 1–111.

Levine, C. (1991) AIDS and changing concepts of family. In D. Nelkin, D. P. Willis, and S. V. Parris (eds.), *A Disease of Society: Cultural and Institutional Responses to AIDS*. New York: Cambridge University Press.

Lewin, E. (1984) Lesbianism and motherhood: implications for child custody. In T. Dary and S. Potter (eds.), *Women-Identified-Women*. Palo Alto CA: Mayfield.

Lewin, E. (1993) *Lesbian Mothers: Accounts of Gender In American Culture*. Ithaca, NY and London: Cornell University Press.

Lewin, E. (1998) *Recognizing Ourselves: Ceremonies of Lesbian and Gay Commitment*. New York: Columbia University Press.

London Gay Liberation Front (1971) *Manifesto*. London: Gay Liberation Front.

Mansfield, P., and Collard, J. (1988) *The Beginning of the Rest of Your Life: A Portrait of Newly Wed Marriage*. London: Macmillan.

Mirza, H. S. (1997) *Black British Feminism: A Reader*. London and New York: Routledge.

Morgan, D. H. J. (1996) *Family Connections: An Introduction to Family Studies*. Cambridge: Polity.

Morgan, D. H. J. (1999) Risk and family practices: accounting for change and fluidity in family life. In E. B. Silva and C. Smart (eds.), *The New Family?* London: Sage.

Nardi, P. (1999) *Gay Men's Friendships: Invincible Communities*. Chicago: Chicago University Press.

Oerton, S. (1997) Queer housewives?: Some problems in theorising the division of labour in lesbian and gay households. *Women's Studies International Forum*, 20, 421–30.

Pahl, R. (2000) *On Friendship*. Cambridge: Polity.

Peplau, L. A. (1981) What homosexuals want in relationships. *Psychology Today*, March, 28–38.

Peplau, L. A., Venigas, R. C., and Miller Campbell, S. (1996) Gay and lesbian relationships. In R. C. Savin-Williams and K. M. Cohen (eds.), *The Lives of Lesbians, Gays, and Bisexuals*. New York: Harcourt Brace College.

Plummer, K. (1995) *Telling Sexual Stories: Power, Change and Social Worlds*. London: Routledge.

Rapp, R. (1982) Towards a nuclear freeze? The gender politics of Euro-American kinship analysis. In J. F. Collier and S. Yanagisako (eds.), *Gender and Kinship. Essays Toward a Unified Analysis*. New York: Stanford University Press.

Rich, A. (1983) On compulsory heterosexuality and lesbian existence. In A. Snitow, C. Stansell, and S. Thompson (eds.), *Desire: The Politics of Sexuality*. London: Virago Press.

Rights of Women Custody Group (1986) *Lesbian Mothers' Legal Handbook*. London: The Women's Press.

Rofes, E. (1997) Dancing bears, performing husbands, and the tyranny of the family. In R. E. Goss and A. S. Strongheart (eds.), *Our Families, Our Values: Snapshots of Queer Kinship*. Binghampton, NJ: Harrington Park Press.

Rubin, L. (1985) *Just Friends. The Role of Friendship in Our Lives*. New York: Harper & Row.

Sedgwick, E. K. (1985) *Between Men: English Literature and Male Homosocial Desire*. New York: Columbia University Press.

Sedgwick, E. K. (1990) *Epistemology of the Closet*. Berkeley and Los Angeles: University of California Press.

Silva, E. B., and Smart, C. (eds.) (1999) *The New Family?* London: Sage.

Stacey, J. (1996) *In the Name of the Family: Rethinking Family Values in the Postmodern Age*. Boston: Beacon.

Stack, C. (1974) *All Our Kin: Strategies for Survival in a Black Community*. New York: Harper.

Strasser, M. (1997) *Legally Wed: Same-Sex Marriage and the Constitution*. Ithaca: Cornell University Press.

Stuart, E. (1995) *Just Good Friends: Towards a Lesbian and Gay Theology of Relationships*. London: Mowbray.

Sullivan, A. (1995) *Virtually Normal: An Argument about Homosexuality*. London: Picador.

Sullivan, A. (ed.) (1997) *Same-Sex Marriage: Pro and Con – A Reader*. New York: Vintage.

Sullivan, A. (1998) *Love Undetectable: Reflections on Friendship, Sex and Survival*. London: Chatto & Windus.

Tanner, D. M. (1978) *The Lesbian Couple*. Lexington, MA: Lexington Books.

Trumbach, R. (1998) *Sex and the Gender Revolution, Volume 1: Heterosexuality and the Third Gender in Enlightenment London*. Chicago and London: Chicago University Press.

Trumbach, R. (1999) London. In D. Higgs (ed.), *Queer Sites: Gay Urban Histories Since 1600*. New York and London: Routledge.

Velu, C. (1999) Faut-il "pactiser" avec l'universalisme? A short history of the PACS. *Modern and Contemporary France*, 7, 429–42.

Warner, M. (ed.) (1993) *Fear of a Queer Planet: Queer Politics and Social Theory*. Minneapolis and London: University of Minnesota Press.

Watney, S. (1994) *Practices of Freedom: Selected Writings on HIV/AIDS*. London: Rivers Oram Press.

Weeks, J. (1977) [1990] *Coming Out: Homosexual Politics in Britain from the Nineteenth Century to the Present*. London: Quartet.

Weeks, J. (1991) *Against Nature: Essays on History, Sexuality and Identity*. London: Rivers Oram Press.

Weeks, J. (1995) *Invented Moralities: Sexual Values in an Age of Uncertainty*. Cambridge: Polity.

Weeks, J. (1998) The sexual citizen. *Theory, Culture and Society*, 15, 35–52.

Weeks, J., Heaphy, B,. and Donovan, C. (1999) Families of choice: autonomy and mutuality in non-heterosexual relationships. In S. McRae (ed.) (1999) *Changing Britain: Families and Households in the 1990's*. Oxford: Oxford University Press.

Weeks, J., Heaphy, B., and Donovan, C. (2001) *Same Sex Intimacies: Families of Choice and other Life Experiments*. London: Routledge.

Weeks, J., and Porter, K. (1998) *Between the Acts: Lives of Homosexual Men 1885–1967*. London: Rivers Oram Press.

Weston, K. (1991) *Families We Choose: Lesbians, Gays, Kinship*. New York: Columbia University Press.

# 21

# Couples and Their Networks

Eric Widmer

## Introduction

Conjugal dyads in the Western world, as the anthropologist Hsu pointed out, present an interesting paradox: They are at the same time prominent over all other interpersonal relationships and extremely unstable, as shown by the high divorce rates currently characterizing contemporary Western societies (Hsu, 1971). What, then, are the joint effects of the inherent centrality and fragility of conjugal dyads on the relational contexts in which those dyads are embedded? If couples are so central, their fragility is likely to have profound consequences beyond nuclear families. Likewise, the centrality and fragility of conjugal dyads means that network members may have strong concerns about what happens to them. Social networks may in various ways influence the trajectories of couples, while couples' trajectories may strongly affect social networks. Thus, we hypothesize that there is a duality between couples and their networks, which has profound consequences for the understanding of both relational realities.

This chapter focuses on the interconnections between couples and their networks, first in paying attention to conjugal network features, secondly in showing how they are linked with conjugal functioning. Two major types of variables have been considered by research dealing with the interdependence between couples and their networks. Some scholars have been mostly interested in exchanges taking place in conjugal networks. Supports and transactions of various forms – financial, material, psychological – characterize the embeddedness of couples in networks. This first set of variables is mostly quantitative and dynamic in nature, as they deal with the quantity of resources provided by networks to couples. They have a functional orientation, as they focus on how services provided by networks may or may not foster the adaptation of nuclear units. Other scholars, however, have emphasized structural dimensions of conjugal networks, that may be associated with conjugal functioning. Composition, connectivity, boundedness, and overlap of conjugal networks are structural features that were taken into consideration when asserting the interrelations between networks and conjugal functioning. This contribution underscores the interconnections existing between functional and structural features of conjugal networks and conjugal functioning.

One difficulty is the fact that for a long time empirical research specialized in either kinship or friendship relationships. This separation of empirical kinship and friendship studies was detrimental to the understanding of the interrelations between networks and couples, as it is very difficult to grasp the functional and structural features of one set of relationships without information on the other. Hopefully, more recent research has focused on conjugal networks as a whole. This chapter will show how various aspects of conjugal functioning are affected by conjugal networks formed by relatives and friends; it also shows how conjugal functioning affects various dimensions of friendship and kinship ties beyond nuclear units. The next pages do not constitute a full literature review on conjugal networks, but rather extract some of their most central features for the understanding of couples.

## Functional Features of Conjugal Networks

What are the main functional features of conjugal networks that may interplay with conjugal functioning? A large number of studies have identified the contribution of relational contexts to the functioning of nuclear families. As reported by Lee (1980) and Adams (1970), the primary focus of research on relational contexts of couples in the 1960s and 1970s was undoubtedly the issue of nuclear-family isolation from its kinship network. The theme that kin are not important to the functioning of the nuclear family (which is relatively "isolated" from them) was clearly enunciated in articles by Parsons (1943, 1949) and Linton (1949). Since then, empirical research has extensively documented the various ways in which nuclear families are embedded in larger family and nonfamily contexts. At first, research mostly focused on material exchanges linking couples and their kinship networks. More recently, scholars have underlined the import of psychological functions of conjugal networks. We consider these two sets of dimensions, focusing first on sociability and exchanges.

### Sociability

A first important result is that contrary to the thesis of the nuclear family's isolation, couples have regular contacts with both friends and relatives (Adams, 1970; Lee, 1980). If alternatives to face-to-face interactions, such as telephone calls or e-mails, are also considered, a large majority of couples do keep in touch with family members or friends. Whereas in earlier periods, personal networks were more localized, most couples today have networks in which neighborhood and locality play only a small part. Networks of friends and kin tend to be geographically dispersed rather than concentrated in particular places (Allan, 1998).

There are, however, great variations in the amount of interactions that couples develop with their networks. Some couples interact daily with relatives and friends, while the interactions of other couples are more casual. Some are more oriented toward relatives whereas others are more oriented toward friends. The number of kin in the area influences the number of regular interactions that one has with them (Fischer, 1982b). Also, men and women differ in their contacts with network members. Typically, women have a higher proportion of contacts with kin than do men (Fischer and Oliker, 1983; Mardsen and Lin, 1982; Treas and Cohen, in press). Women are more often in charge of sociability with kin, organizing special gatherings or more regular forms of contacts with relatives on both their own and their husbands' sides (Anspach and Rosenberg, 1972).

## Exchanges

Couples are not only embedded in interactions with friends and relatives; they are also functionally embedded in them. Many researchers since the 1960s have investigated material exchanges and support taking place in conjugal networks. They found that a large percentage of couples benefit from financial help, emotional support and help with children derived from their networks (Wellman and Wortley, 1989). In other words, interdependence, not isolation, is the rule, with only a small portion of the population being separated from relatives and friends.

If the thesis of functional isolation has proved to be inadequate, research has, however, emphasized the limits of exchanges between couples and their networks. In many cases, important exchanges concern the immediate kinship circle drawn from the couples' families of orientation (non-co-resident parents and siblings) and their own children (Fehr and Perlman, 1985). Most financial and domestic help is provided by relatives in direct ascending line. In other words, support mostly circulates from parents to children. Parents also provide tangible help with raising their grandchildren. Only a very limited proportion of exchanges within conjugal networks concern relatives beyond those genealogical limits. The assistance of horizontal relationships, either from siblings or from friends, is much less intense. Friendships are centered on leisure-time activities, informal sociability, companionship, and expressive support (Allan, 1979, 1998). As compared with parents, siblings do not support each other as much in terms of money or domestic tasks: they are mostly important in terms of emotional support (Coenen-Huther et al., 1994; Widmer, 1999a). In addition, normative imperatives to help are fairly low in friendship and kinship relationships as opposed to parent–child relationships. In other words, much of network support beyond parent–child ties is based on affinity rather than on status. Finally, it should be underscored that help provided by network members is mostly conjunctural rather than structural. The idea of a systematic cooperation between couples and their networks is not supported by empirical results. Kinship assistance is required mainly for coping with particular events or situations, such as the birth of a new child, temporary health and financial hardships, divorce, etc. (Coenen-Huther et al., 1994).

In reaction to the "isolation hypothesis," most research on kinship and friendship focuses on positive exchanges existing between couples and their relational context (Johnson, 2000). This focus has somehow obstructed the realization that conjugal networks may not only develop positive interactions for couples. Conflicts and social control are two other important contents of relationships (House, Umberson, and Landis, 1988). Conjugal networks are not only characterized by support and caring but also by problems and conflicts (Adams, 1970; Klein and Milardo, 2000; Coenen-Huther et al., 1994).

## Psychological support and cognitive significance

Another limit of research addressing the isolation hypothesis is the focus on material exchanges: relational contexts have also important cognitive functions for individuals and couples, in terms of emotional support and in the shaping of personal identities. In this regard, scholars have emphasized the import of "psychological networks," which are composed of people to whom individuals are committed emotionally and psychologically, who provide individuals with a concept of self, and who can sustain or alter one's self-definition through communication (Surra and Milardo, 1991). Interestingly, interactions and psychological significance do not fully overlap. In a direct comparison based on data collected for 25 wives and their husbands, only 25 percent of the network members identified were met on a regular basis *and* had psychological significance (Milardo, 1989).

What is the contribution of relatives to psychological networks? As underscored by Firth, the concept of family is of strong affective significance because "it expresses a sense of identity with specified persons who are members of one's kin universe" (Firth, Hubert, and Forge, 1970: 92). Families are ponds of *orientational others* (Kuhn, 1964), even in adulthood. Despite the fact that they live in different households and do not belong to the nuclear family of Ego anymore, parents and siblings of adults continue to have a great emotional and cognitive significance (Cicirelli, 1995; Fehr and Perlman, 1985, Goetting, 1986; Hoyt and Babchuk, 1983; Umberson, 1992). For instance, most siblings wish to keep in touch with each other and know in a general way what the other's overall situation is (Allan, 1979). Social comparison with close relatives, even in adulthood, is an extremely important component of family life (Adam, 1970). This dimension of orientation is of first importance during childhood and adolescence, where parents play a major role in shaping the identity of their children. The cognitive importance of family members is not ended when children leave the nest. As for friends, they are by definition people we feel psychologically connected to. However, there are again variations in the strength of cognitive import of friends, for instance, according to gender and social status (Allan, 1998).

## Ascription and achievement

Another issue of great functional import related to conjugal networks concerns the extent to which relationships constituting the relational contexts of couples are voluntary or imposed. In this sense, close relatives and friends represent the two extremes of a continuum from ascription to achievement. While friends can be chosen and abandoned, relatives are imposed, and presumably forever. In Western societies, ties of blood are taken as being much more durable than relationships based on other criteria (Schneider, 1980; Allan, 1979).

If there are few doubts that kinship ties are more ascriptive than friendship ties overall, the former are actually quite heterogeneous in that regard. Strong normative requirements to help or see one another only concern a very limited set of relationships, basically the family of orientation of both partners (Wellman and Wortley, 1989). Even within this immediate circle of family members, there is a great variety of normative expectations, for instance, between siblings and with parents, and negotiation rather than automaticity is the rule (Finch and Mason, 1993). As where parent–child relationships are characterized by a strong normative impetus toward helping, sibling support is based on liking, rather than on strong moral imperatives. Sibling relationships are grounded much more than parent–child relationships on the achievement dimension: sibling contact in adulthood is mostly voluntary and based on liking, except on certain ritual occasions such as weddings (Lee, 1990). Within the larger set of relatives, the impact of ascription is much weaker: personal liking, age, gender, stage in the life cycle, and frequency of contact are central to explaining the intimate and confidant kin chosen (Hoyt and Babchuk, 1983). Uncles and aunts, nephews and nieces, do not necessarily feel close to each other or help each other in any way. These relationships are achieved by personal activities pertaining to the work of "doing kinship," as Schneider put it (1980). Personal choices play a major role in this regard, and contacts are kept alive only if there is a history of positive relationships behind them. To summarize, beyond parents and children, kinship links become voluntary and selective (Fischer, 1982a).

At the same time, achieved relationships, such as friendship relationships, are in need of some underlying ascriptive structures that may reinforce them. As early as in 1969, Bellweg noted that 64 percent of the students he questioned used kin terms for at least one person who was not actually related to them (Bellweg, 1969). This may indicate that the solidarity and automaticity of kinship provide some advantages to couples. In picking an unrelated person and making him or her kin, one benefits from the freedom of choice associated with achieved relationships and the stability associated with ascriptive ones. This is especially true with fictive kin created out of non-kin relationships, such as godchildren or godparents, where the kin status has a normative, quasi-legal meaning.

This dimension is even reinforced in families "of choice" (Weston, 1991). Families are not formed solely upon the basis of blood and marriage. Affection and mutual interests play an increasingly important role in determining the basis for kinship formation. Families of choice seem to be especially active in nontraditional family forms, such as those of gay and lesbian couples which typically include friends and ex-lovers (ibid.). Such "social families" (Scanzoni and Marsiglio, 1993) resemble networks in the sense that they cross household lines and are based on ties that radiate "outward from individuals like spokes on a wheel" (Weston, 1991: 109). To deal with rejection by parents or siblings, gay and lesbian couples often give greater centrality to friends and to supportive kin even if they are not their closest relations on the genealogical chart (see Weeks, Heaphy, and Donovan, chapter 20 in this volume).

Does that mean that friends and kin are now interchangeable? Empirical research shows that closely related relatives provide a greater degree of support, and they do so in a wider variety of domains than friends; they are also more active in terms of social control. Friends are more active in terms of companionship (Rook and Ituarte, 1999; Wellman and Wortley, 1989). Thus, interchangeability of friends and relatives should be questioned, but there is undoubtedly today a need to make friends of relatives and to make relatives of friends. Relationships with in-laws present another case. As they are acquired indirectly and, in a sense, involuntarily, by marriage, they have a dimension of achievement and ascription. This mixture is associated with potential conflicts and tensions. Relations with parents-in-law are seen as more distant and tense than relations with parents (Fischer, 1983; Wish, Deutsch, and Kaplan, 1976).

## Summary

Contemporary couples are not isolated from their kinship and friendship networks. They keep regular contacts with relatives and friends, and various kinds of exchanges exist with them. Members of networks have very important psychological functions for couples. Those contacts and exchanges, however, should not be considered as indicators of profound interdependences between couples and their network members. Network support is limited in various ways. It only concerns a small number of persons, mostly drawn from the couple's families of orientation. It is more conjunctural than structural. That is, it becomes more and more voluntary and associated with personal liking, rather than norms of responsibility. When it is too strong, it triggers negative feelings.

On all these accounts, there is a primacy of the conjugal dyad over other interpersonal relationships included in conjugal networks, as normative expectations as well as actual solidarity are at their highest in conjugal relationships. Of course, what was just presented is an average profile of the functional features of conjugal networks. We will later see that variations of these features are associated with specific forms of conjugal functioning.

## Structural Features of Conjugal Networks

Investigating functional features of networks makes us focus on what network members provide to couples. This, of course, is an essential aspect of the interplay between couples and their networks, but it is not sufficient *per se*, as exchanges and interactions between network members and couples happen in larger webs of interpersonal relationships. Analyses of network structures precisely permit us to capture the influence of the network as a whole with properties that go beyond those of the connections that directly involve couples. In other words, they are based on the assumption that exchanges between couples and their networks not only have an impact on conjugal functioning because of their sheer amount, but also because they are part of larger configurations of relationships. Scholars interested in structural features of conjugal networks have mostly focused on network composition, network connectivity and boundedness, and overlap between personal networks of spouses or partners.

### Composition

Recent approaches have underscored that not all relationships composing conjugal networks have the same impact on conjugal functioning (Burger and Milardo, 1995; Milardo and Allan, 1997). In considering only overall functions of conjugal networks, we miss a fundamental feature of those networks, namely who composes them. Empirical research found that about four out of ten active network members are friends and another three are kin. Neighbors, co-workers, and acquaintances constitute only a minority of network members (Milardo, 1989; Wellman and Wortley, 1989). The proportion of friends and relatives that couples have in their networks is likely to have important effects on conjugal functioning as friends and relatives, as we have underscored above, do not contribute equally to exchanges with couples.

Another important dimension to consider is the sex ratio of conjugal networks. Contacts and exchanges with kin and friends are strongly influenced by gender. Women are more central in kinship relations than are men. They are more active in exchanges with kin (Johnson, 2000), communicate more often, and report more "close" kin than do men (Bahr, 1976; Booth, 1972; Hoyt and Babchuk, 1983). They play an important role as "kinkeepers" (Adams, 1970), even on their husbands' sides (Lee, 1980). Men interact with a wider range of people, in the context of larger, more heterogeneous groups (Ridgeway and Smith-Lovin, 1999). Those various tendencies lend support to the thesis that because women are much more active with kin than are men, the sex composition of conjugal networks is likely to have profound effects on couples' functioning.

Age and generation are a third important element of network composition. Because of the increase of life expectancy and the decrease in fertility that have characterized Western societies during the last two centuries, kinship ties have become more and more vertical: it is not unheard of to find kinship networks composed by five generations. At the same time, kinship networks have lost much of their horizontality: siblings are much less numerous than before and, consequently, cousins, aunts, and uncles represent a much smaller part of the kinship ties that are included in conjugal networks. Demographers have characterized this kind of network as "beanpole family structure," where the surviving lineage is tall and thin (Bengtson, Rosenthal, and Burton, 1996; Treas, 1995).

In a broader sense, heterogeneity of conjugal networks in terms of social status, age, religious affiliation, and so on is a central dimension of network composition. How similar are members of conjugal networks compared with each other? This question has received only a little attention from researchers, but it is likely to have great consequences for couples. In this regard, friendship and kinship ties may have quite different properties. Friendship ties, because of their achieved nature, are strongly biased toward homophily (McPherson, Smith-Lovin, and Cook, 2001), that is, they tend to link people with similar social characteristics. On the other hand, family ties, because of their strong affective bonds and ascriptive nature, often allow for much greater interpersonal heterogeneity. Thus, they can bridge differences in social and economic standing that would not normally be bridged if two people were not in the same family (Goldstein and Warren, 2000).

## Connectivity and boundedness

Connectivity refers to the extent to which network members know one another, or interact with one another. Technically, it is defined as the number of existing ties in a network compared with the number of ties potentially available, given the size of the network. Dense networks have specific functional properties: because ties are redundant in their case, social support and social control have a more collective nature, which reinforces their effects on individuals or couples (Coleman, 1988). For conjugal networks, Elisabeth Bott (1955, 1957) was the first to underscore the impact of network connectivity on conjugal functioning. Overall, the connectivity of conjugal networks is much lower than one would think. Individuals tend to concentrate their regular interactions and exchanges on a relatively small number of persons compared with the total of persons they happen to name as friends or relatives (Coenen-Huther et al., 1994). There are several reasons explaining this tendency, such as the geographical dispersion of kin, the fact that interactions with friends and family often occur separately, and the sheer logistical impossibility of maintaining regular interactions with great numbers of persons.

Associated with the issue of network connectivity is network boundedness. The boundaries of networks have always been of major import to understand their dynamics. It is rather straightforward that conjugal networks are "ego-centered" networks and not full networks (Scott, 1992): conjugal networks always refer to a single couple and no two couples have exactly the same network. Because of this feature, conjugal networks are rather unbounded by their very nature: individuals included in a couple A's network are themselves central in their own networks, which are constituted by other persons with only a partial overlap with couple A's networks. Therefore, conjugal networks open up to other conjugal or personal networks in an infinite and comprehensive web of interpersonal relationships. That said, one should also underscore that some conjugal networks are more bounded than others. The extent to which individuals included in a couple's network cite each other as significant members of their own network is variable. We shall later see that divorce and remarriage have profound effects on this dimension (Widmer, 1999b).

## Overlap

The low density and low boundedness of conjugal networks lend support to the idea that friendship and kinship networks are ego-centered sets of ties, i.e., many relationships are not shared by both spouses but are – quite to the contrary – specific to each of them. To address this issue, scholars have investigated the extent to which individuals in one partner's network are also members of the other partner's network (Milardo, 1986, Surra, 1988; Stein et al., 1992). This dimension is referred to as network overlap. In one of the very few studies that has empirically addressed the "shared versus specific" dimensionality of spouses' kinship networks (Stein et al., 1992), husbands listed an average of 4.3 separate family members and an average of 3 separate friends not listed by their spouses. Wives named an average of 5.7 separate family members and an average 4.8 separate friends. In comparison, on average, 7.7 family members and 1.5 friends were shared by both members of the couple. Overall, spouses reported fewer than half of their family members as shared. Such evidence confirms that many kinship ties are specific to egos.

Network-sidedness is only partially captured by network overlap. Two persons forming a couple may have not only different but quite unequal networks. In a typological approach of conjugal networks, it was found that in about four cases out of ten, spouses do not have equally present and supportive networks (Widmer, Kellerhals, and Levy, forthcoming). This proportion underlies two distinct situations. In couples with *patricentric networks*, men have a much larger number of relatives and friends than women. They meet with their relatives and friends more often and can get support from them much more easily than women do. Those couples can be described as asymmetrical or unicentric, because one side of the couple's network is predominant. Couples with *matricentric networks* stand in sharp contrast to couples with patricentric networks. In their case, the network of both relatives and friends on the woman's side is much larger and much more active than on the man's side, and support is more readily available on the woman's side than on the man's.

Couples who are characterized by non-overlapping personal networks may either have bicentric but fully segregated networks, or a unicentric network, a situation in which one spouse or partner is dominant in terms of network resources when compared with the other. Women's networks are more likely than men's to be in the latter case, as the kinship structures and small interconnected groups in which they are embedded are constituted more frequently by strong ties (Ridgeway and Smith-Lovin, 1999). Connectivity, therefore, is differently distributed within conjugal networks.

### Summary

Conjugal networks tend to be rather large, mostly constituted by friends and relatives, with a low density of relationships and a matrifocal organization. They are quite unbounded, expanding in all directions, and the overlap between spouses' networks is far from complete. They are more horizontal than vertical. Those structural features are deeply intertwined with functional features. Dense and overlapping conjugal networks are likely to increase support provided to couples but also social control (Milardo, 1988a), as interactions among alters have an impact on the interactions that alters develop with the couple.

## Conjugal Networks and Conjugal Dyads

Are functional and structural features of conjugal networks associated with conjugal functioning? In order to answer this question, we shall now consider the interrelations existing between conjugal networks and conjugal dyads by focusing on several central issues or moments for couples: the initiation of conjugal relationships, conjugal satisfaction, conjugal interactions, divorce, and remarriage. We do not imply that influence is unilateral, going only from networks to couples. As we shall see, networks receive some of their features from couples and couples get some of theirs from their inclusion in networks.

### Initiation of conjugal relationships

Interpersonal attraction and courtship happen in social contexts where personal networks play an important role. A result of research on the dynamics of relationships is that the creation of new dyadic relationships is not random but tends to foster a state of balance or "transitivity" within larger groups (Cartwright and Harary, 1956; Newcomb, 1961). Typically, this state is achieved when friends of friends become acquainted. Expressed another way, balance theory (Heider, 1958) predicts that there is a greater chance that two people become friends or intimates if they share mutual friends already, a result which is largely confirmed by empirical research (Parks, Stan, and Eggert, 1983; Parks and Eggert, 1991). Thus, a powerful collective and often unacknowledged influence is exerted on personal choices concerning the development of intimate relationships, including initiation of conjugal relationships. This influence has an interesting consequence: because personal networks are characterized by social homogeneity (friends, in particular, often are similar in age, educational background, social status, and religious or political orientation; see McPherson, Smith-Lovin, and Cook, 2001), conjugal relationships tend to pair persons with similar social traits (homogamy).

If networks influence the initiation of conjugal relationships, the creation of a new couple has important consequences for social networks. The strengthening of interdependencies between partners means the loosening of some ties, a process referred to as "dyadic withdrawal" (Parks and Eggert, 1991). Partners become less active with others as courtship progresses (Surra, 1985). In the later stages of courtship, dating individuals interact with fewer people, less often, and for shorter periods (Milardo, Johnson, and Huston, 1983). Some ties are severed in order for the couple to be able to affirm its primacy over other relationships: ex-lovers, formerly intimate relationships that might endanger couple intimacy, need to be put into a new perspective. In this regard, influence of networks may not always be a positive one for couples. For instance, network members may disapprove of a romantic relationship and speed its demise (Felmlee, 2001; Johnson and Milardo, 1984).

Usually, however, as two persons become closer, their network of mutual friends increases in size. Among dating couples, the absolute number of mutual friends and the ratio of mutual to separate friends increases as couples get more involved: in one excellent study, for example, Milardo (1982) found that couples in the later stages of courtship had roughly twice as many mutual contacts in their networks as couples in the earlier stages of courtship. Of course, the extent to which personal networks become joined is variable, and this variability has an important effect, as we shall see shortly, on couple functioning. Thus, courtship restructures various relationships in making new connections in response to the functional necessity for couples to have at least a few shared network members as well as in reducing older connections which may endanger conjugal privacy and conjugal primacy.

The development of interpersonal attraction and courtship shows the duality of couples and their networks. On the one hand, personal networks play a major role for the initiation of a new couple, in making joint interactions possible, in imposing social expectations toward pairing, in providing support and information, and in imposing barriers (Parks and Eggert, 1991). On the other hand, the emergence of couples as independent functioning entities implies profound changes in personal networks.

## Conjugal satisfaction

Do functional and structural features of conjugal networks matter for conjugal functioning? The few research studies that have empirically addressed this issue have focused on conjugal satisfaction. In general, it is found that spouses with more supportive networks report greater well-being and conjugal satisfaction (Bryant and Conger, 1999; Burger and Milardo, 1995; Felmlee, 2001). Associations between structural features of networks and conjugal satisfaction are assessed as well: spouses with denser and more overlapping networks report greater conjugal satisfaction, and more marital stability (Ackerman, 1963; Stein et al., 1992).

Some authors, however, have suggested that there may well be a curvilinear effect of network involvement (Holman, 1981; Johnson and Milardo, 1984, Widmer, Kellerhals, and Levy, forthcoming). In this regard, one major problem of couple-embeddedness in networks has been termed network interference, that is, network members perceived as trying to intrude into couple functioning. For instance, in a study of couples with children, 22 percent of women and 18 percent of men felt that their couple is controlled by their family (Widmer, Kellerhals, and Levy, forthcoming). When networks are too involved, they are seen as interfering in the couple's functioning, and as such, they become counterproductive in terms of conjugal quality. Likewise, it was shown that full overlap of personal networks of spouses is associated with lower marital satisfaction (Stein et al., 1992). Several mechanisms are likely to account for those results. The *interference model* (Johnson and Milardo, 1984; Julien et al., 1994) states that social networks and conjugal relationships might actually compete. Developing a relationship creates anxiety in social networks by challenging time and energy previously devoted to other relationships. Thus, social network members may try to hold or regain some influence on ego by interfering in his or her conjugal relationship. In this perspective, strong networks may not buffer the effects of conjugal conflict, but may actually increase it, because the emergence of conjugal problems opens doors to further interference from the network members in the couple's relationships. Those problems might stimulate and contribute to conflict between spouses, especially when interdependence among relatives is strong. Richly interconnected networks, in which some elements feud with other elements, become destructive for couple functioning (Broderick, 1988). For instance, intervention of third parties in an existing conjugal conflict reinforces partners' self-legitimacy (Klein and Milardo, 2000), thus making a consensual solution less likely. The fact that network support and network-connectedness are not linearly associated with conjugal satisfaction reveals the primacy of the conjugal dyad: Networks that are too strong may endanger it. In-laws and friends may be especially dangerous in this regard, because their absence of blood-relatedness means that no incest taboo bars a sexual relationship.

Effects of interactions with network members vary substantially according to their status. The processes underlying relations with kin and friends may be different for wives and husbands. In an exploratory study (Burger and Milardo, 1995), contact with kin, and especially brothers-in-law, was consistently associated with greater marital distress for wives, in the form of less love for their husbands and reports of greater conflict and ambivalence on the part of both spouses. Husbands also reported greater conflict and ambivalence when their wives interacted frequently with friends. Because of those variations, it has been hypothesized that the composition of the network (friends versus relatives) has an effect on conjugal outcomes.

Conjugal networks affect conjugal satisfaction in a variety of ways, which we are just starting to uncover. For instance, in a study with a North American sample, network perceptions of the conjugal dyad were more negative than those held by the couple and were successful at predicting relationship dissolution (Agnew, Loving, and Drigotas, 2001). Self-fulfilling prophecies of network members about a couple's fate may well have an impact. Other explanations for network effects on conjugal functioning are related to couples' preferred conflict management strategies (Klein and Milardo, 2000).

## Conjugal interactions

Conjugal quality is only one dimension of conjugal functioning. Other, more interactive than evaluative dimensions should also be taken into consideration when dealing with the interconnections existing between conjugal networks and conjugal functioning. In this regard, the seminal work of Elisabeth Bott has paved the way to a series of empirical studies addressing this issue. Briefly, Bott (1955, 1957) found that segregation of conjugal roles was related to the extent of network-connectedness. Couples with a high degree of segregation in the relationship between husbands and wife had a highly connected network. Couples where husband and wife had a joint and equalitarian division of labor (i.e., no role segregation) had low network density. Because it is not self-evident, this result has attracted the attention of scholars. As underlined by Milardo and Allan (1997), Bott explained this correlation between role differentiation and network-connectedness in two ways: First, dense networks are more apt, because of their interconnectedness, to impose norms concerning conjugal roles, compared with loosely connected networks. Second, in highly connected networks, mutual assistance among members is high and, as a consequence, spouses will have less need for one another's collaboration and companionship. Thus, segregated marital roles have a greater chance to emerge.

Although Bott's hypothesis has triggered considerable interest, there is little, if any, evidence that supports it. Milardo and Allan (1997) suggest that one problem lies in the fact that Bott equated density of networks with traditionalist views of network members concerning conjugal roles. This assumption was never tested and might be problematic. Highly interconnected networks might well be associated with weaker segregation of conjugal roles if their members hold progressive views about gender and the division of labor. In other words, structural features of conjugal networks may only make a difference when the content of values or norms that they support is also considered, i.e., when functional and structural features of groups are considered at the same time.

Bott's non-intuitive explanation of conjugal interactions has had enormous influence on sociological inquiries into conjugal networks. Other, maybe more intuitive, hypotheses should be put to the test. For instance, one may hypothesize that there is a connection between the level of role segregation within the couple and the segregation of gender roles in the couple's dealings with friends and relatives. The interest triggered by Bott's approach also lead researchers to focus entirely on the effects of conjugal networks on the division of domestic tasks. As a result, scant attention has been given to dimensions of conjugal functioning, such as conjugal cohesiveness (Olson and McCubbin, 1989), which capture the tension existing in contemporary couples between fusion and autonomy. Contemporary couples are confronted with the difficult tasks of reconciling the fusion ideals of conjugal life (in which "sharing" is considered a key to happiness) with the individualistic ideas of the "self," in which clearly establishing personal rights and autonomy are considered a sign of psychological maturity and relational success (Mansfield and Collard, 1988). The way in which couples construct their "we-ness" may be related with their embeddedness in specific conjugal networks. In couples in which there is a great emphasis on partnership and intimate closure, the value of spending time together outside of the home is increased (Allan, 1998). One may hypothesize that autonomy in marriage is associated with autonomy in networks. Couples with an individualistic orientation may develop less connected, less bounded, less overlapping, and more heterogeneous conjugal networks, which in turn may increase their tendency toward internal autonomy. Again, the duality of networks and couples seems to be a very crucial issue for the understanding of family realities in social contexts.

## Divorce and remarriage

When the process of divorcing has been activated, conjugal networks face many important changes (Feld and Carter, 1998; Milardo, 1987). The community aspects of divorce – that is, splitting friends, dismantling ties with former in-laws, and learning to live in social networks as a single person again – are a necessary stage in the process of divorcing (Bohannan, 1970). Typically, relationships with in-laws do not survive the dissolution of the marital dyad, especially when there are no children (Ambert, 1988; Spicer and Hampe, 1975). Divorce, therefore, hinders many personal ties. It is likely to shatter interpersonal ties for both former spouses, because couples participate as units in much of the sociability with friends in adulthood. But at the same time, divorce is an opportunity to rebuild strong ties with close family members or close friends. Differences between men and women seem to be significant in this regard. For men, personal friendships seem to be central in dealing with divorce effects. For women, bonds with kin remain very central after marriage while bonds with friends are only secondary (Milardo, 1988b). These circumstances lead women to networks that are dominated by kin, which are high in both exchanges of social support and interference (Hurlbert and Acock, 1990).

Remarriage brings the duality of networks and couples into full light. Interestingly, effects of remarriage on personal networks are very different from those of first marriage. This difference is associated with the presence of children from the previous union in conjugal networks stemming from remarriage. With remarriage, children gain centrality in their parents' networks, because the connections between children and their nonresident parents often remain strong, especially emotionally and cognitively (Coleman and Ganong, 1995; Furstenberg and Winquist Nord, 1985). Thus, children become bridges between their divorced parents. This structural change is likely to have the consequence of making the boundaries between couples and their networks quite difficult to delineate. As a matter of fact, many recomposed families are part of *divorce chains* or *remarriage chains* (Bohannan, 1970; Cherlin and Furstenberg, 1994), in which material, emotional and cognitive linkages exist among persons living in different households.

For a long time, research has considered the issue of family boundaries as settled, using either a predefined set of family roles or a common residence as valid criteria for defining what is the significant family unit. More recently, however, researchers interested in recomposed families have underlined that those boundaries are not obvious, because divorce and remarriage create ties among different households and extend the set of family roles (e.g., Cherlin and Furstenberg, 1994). Various typologies have been proposed to tackle the diversity of family structures stemming out of remarriage (Pasley and Ihinger-Tallman, 1987). The conceptualization of the family unit as a well-bounded, small group ("the nuclear family") with the conjugal dyad at its core does not enable us to deal with this diversity. Does this mean that conjugal primacy does not exist in conjugal networks stemming from remarriage? Goetting (1983) shows that the husband–wife dyad in reconstituted families still has priority over dyads consisting of a spouse and his or her children by a former marriage. Still, it is rather clear that decoupling of conjugality and parenting has an effect by making the boundaries of the nuclear family fuzzier and by placing the couple between contradictory claims from closely related (intimate) third parties.

Other structural and functional changes of networks stem from remarriage. First, the size of networks is often increased. A common source of expansion is the paternal grandmother who retains relationships with her former daughter-in-law and her relatives at the same time that she adds new relatives with her son's remarriage (Johnson and Barer, 1987). Adding new sets of ties to surviving ones increases the horizontality of conjugal networks, thus compensating for the verticalization of conjugal networks mentioned above. Second, connectedness of post-remarriage networks is lower than that of networks of first marriages. As a matter of fact, scholars have emphasized that relationships among stepparents and stepchildren are different in strength from relationships among parents and children (Coleman and Ganong, 1990; Ferri, 1984; Hobart, 1987). Because relationships among stepparents and stepchildren are perceived as less intimate and less supportive and are associated with more conflicts than relationships between parents and children (Coleman and Ganong, 1990), they tend to create low-density conjugal networks. That is, each remarried spouse is likely to have a larger proportion of unshared family members than in first marriage couples (Widmer, 1999a). Third, the matrifocality of conjugal networks tends to be reinforced: a solidary unit develops between mother and children as ties between father and children become weaker after divorce and remarriage (Cherlin and Furstenberg, 1994; Furstenberg and Winquist Nord, 1985). Finally, achievement may in many cases take precedence over ascription in networks of remarried couples. In her research on middle-class, suburban families with a divorce (Johnson, 1988, 2000), Johnson found that about one-third of couples were involved in networks where kinship categories from their serial marriages were blurred and where distance from or closeness to kin were established on the basis of liking, rather than from a sense of relatedness or responsibility.

## Conclusions

Structurally, networks of contemporary couples are characterized by relatively large size, vertical rather than horizontal depth, low density, low boundedness, and low overlap. Functionally, they are characterized by their secondary import compared with the conjugal dyad, specialization, the importance of members of the partners' families of orientation, and a mixture of ascription and achievement. Functional and structural dimensions of conjugal networks intertwine in their effects on conjugal functioning. Social control and social support are stronger in highly connected bounded and overlapping networks.

Couples do not function in isolation. The variation existing among couples concerning network features may explain much of variations in conjugal relationships. Networks have an impact on couples. First, they strongly influence mate selection by framing it in the homogeneity of social connections. Courtship takes place in networks in which transitivity is the basis for constituting new connections. When couples are formed, their functioning is influenced by network support and network structures, although we do not know as much on this issue as we need to know. Divorce and remarriage have distinct outcomes depending on network features. On all these accounts, relational contexts do play a major role for couples, even though this role is not by far always a positive one.

On the other hand, couples influence networks. Strong involvement in the courtship process can interfere with other ties, which mean that other personal networks may be shattered by the constitution of a new couple. This weakening of various ties due to couple formation is also to be seen in the fact that couples do not accept interference gladly. When couples divorce, conjugal networks are profoundly changed. When individuals remarry, this has implications for a large number of persons beyond the couple or their household. Courtship, conjugal functioning, divorce, and remarriage show that the centrality and fragility of couples in Western societies (Hsu, 1971) is intertwined with a great number of other relationships which they shape while being shaped by them.

Conjugality is thus highly embedded in larger relational contexts. Can conjugal embeddedness in networks be referred to a small set of principles? It is my opinion that two major relational structures are central in this regard. First, as we have underscored, conjugality is dominant and brittle in contemporary Western societies. This centrality and this frailty have significant consequences for conjugal networks, as we have seen. Marriage, much less cohabitation, exerts little pressure for network connectivity and boundedness. Divorce and remarriage surely exert an opposite pressure toward weak connectivity and unboundedness. Given only partial transitivity associated with sexual intimacy, spouses' personal networks virtually never fully overlap (Stein et al., 1992).

Second, as we have seen, parent–child relationships present a very distinct tendency: Although not dominant, in Hsu's sense (1971), in the Western system of interpersonal relationships, they have much more solidity than conjugal dyads. In a majority of cases, parents and children keep strong emotional connections even when they do not live together anymore, because of divorce or grown children leaving the parental home. Other relationships may only be positive externalities derived from the parent–child bond. For instance, aging parents play a central role in linking siblings together after they leave the parental home. By transitive closure, parent–child relationships create connections among relatives. Parent–child dyads have assumed an increased centrality in conjugal networks without, for the time being, having lost much of their solidity. With that in mind, future studies may wish to redirect their attention to networks of children, rather than to conjugal networks. Starting with children rather than with couples, we may learn more about family dynamics in contexts of interpersonal relationships, because parent–child relationships seem to be more and more the backbone of extended family relationships.

In any case, there is still much to learn on family embeddedness within larger interpersonal contexts.

## References


Ackerman, C. (1963) Affiliations: structural determinants of differential divorce rates. *American Journal of Sociology*, 69, 13–20.

Adams, B. N. (1970) Isolation, function and beyond: American kinship in the 1960s. *Journal of Marriage and the Family*, 32, 575–97.

Agnew, C. R., Loving, T. J., and Drigotas, S. M. (2001) Substituting the forest for the trees: Social networks and the prediction of romantic relationship state and fate. *Journal of Personality and Social-Psychology*, 81, 1042–57.

Allan, G. (1998) Friendship, sociology and social structure. *Journal of Social and Personal Relationships*, 15, 685–702.

Allan, G. (1979) *A Sociology of Friendship and Kinship*. London: George Allen & Unwin.

Ambert, A. M. (1988) Relationships with former in-laws after divorce: A research note. *Journal of Marriage and the Family*, 50, 679–86.

Anspach, D., and Rosenberg, G. S. (1972) Working-class matricentricity. *Journal of Marriage and the Family*, 34, 437–42.

Bahr, H. M. (1976) The kinship role. In: F. I. Nye (ed.), *Role Structure and Analysis of the Family*. Beverly Hills: Sage.

Bellweg, J. (1969) Extension of meaning and use for kinship terms. *American Anthropologist*, 71, 84–7.

Bengtson, V. L., Rosenthal, C., and Burton, L. (1996) Families and aging: diversity and heterogeneity. In R. Binstock and L. George (eds.), *Handbook of Aging and Social Sciences*. New York: Academic Press.

Bohannan, P. (1970) *Divorce and After: An Analysis of the Emotional and Social Problems of Divorce*. Garden City, NY: Anchor.

Booth, A. (1972) Sex and social participation. *American Sociological Review*, 37, 183–92.

Bott, E. (1955) Urban families: Conjugal roles and social networks. *Human Relations*, 8, 345–50.

Bott, E. (1957) *Family and Social Networks*. London, Tavistock.

Broderick, C. B. (1988) Healing members and relationships in the intimate network. In: R. M. Milardo (eds.), *Families and Social Networks*. Newbury Park, CA: Sage.

Bryant, C. M., and Conger, R. D. (1999) Marital success and domains of social support in long-term relationships: Does the influence of network members ever end? *Journal of Marriage and the Family*, 2, 437–50.
Burger, E., and Milardo, R. M. (1995) Marital interdependence and social networks. *Journal of Social and Personal Relationships*, 12, 403–15.
Cartwright, D., and Harary, F. (1956) Structural balance; A generalization of Heider's theory. *Psychological Review*, 63, 277–92.
Cherlin, A. J., and Furstenberg, F. F. (1994). Stepfamilies in the US: a reconsideration. *Annual Review of Sociology*, 359–81.
Cicirelli, V. G. (1995) *Sibling Relationships Across the Life Span*. New York: Plenum.
Coenen-Huther, J., Kellerhals, J., von Allmen, M., Hagmann, H.-M., Jeannerat, F., and Widmer, E. (1994) *Les Réseaux de Solidarité dans La Famille*. Lausanne: Réalités sociales.
Coleman, J. (1988) Social capital and the creation of human capital. *American Journal of Sociology*, 94, 95–121.
Coleman, M., and Ganong, L. H. (1990) Remarriage and stepfamily research in the 1980s: Increased interest in an old family form. *Journal of Marriage and the Family*, 52, 925–40.
Coleman, M., and Ganong, L.H. (1995) Family reconfiguring following divorce. In S. Duck and J. T. Woods (eds.), *Confronting Relationship Challenges*. Thousand Oaks, CA: Sage.
Fehr, B., and Perlman, D. (1985) The family as a social network and support system. In L. L'Abate (ed.), *The Handbook of Family Psychology and Therapy*. Homewood, IL: Dorsey Press.
Feld, F., and Carter, W. C. (1998) Foci of activity as changing contexts for friendship. In R. G. Adams and G. Allan (eds.), *Placing Friendship in Context*. Cambridge: Cambridge University Press.
Felmlee, D. H. (2001) No couple is an island: A social network perspective on dyadic stability. *Social Forces*, 79, 1259–87.
Ferri, E. (1984) *Stepchildren: A National Study*. Atlantic Highlands, NJ: Humanities Press.
Finch, J., and Mason, J. (1993) *Negotiating Family Responsibilities*. London: Routledge.
Firth, R., Hubert, J., and Forge, A. (1970) *Families and Their Relatives*. London: Routledge & Kegan Paul.
Fischer, C., and Oliker, S. (1983) A research note on friendship, gender and the life cycle. *Social Forces*, 62, 124–32.
Fischer, L. R. (1983) Mothers and mothers-in-law. *Journal of Marriage and the Family*, 45, 187–92.
Fischer, C. S. (1982a). The dispersion of kin in modern society: Contemporary data and historical speculation. *Journal of Family History*, 7, 353–75.
Fischer, C. S. (1982b) *To Dwell Among Friends. Personal Networks in Town and City*. Chicago: University of Chicago Press.
Furstenberg, F. F., and Winquist Nord, C. (1985) Parenting apart: Patterns of childrearing after marital disruption. *Journal of Marriage and the Family*, 47, 893–904.
Goetting, A. (1983) The relative strength of the husband-wife and parent-child dyads in remarriage: A test of the Hsu model. *Journal of Comparative Family Studies*, 14, 117–28.
Goetting, A. (1986). The developmental tasks of siblingship over the life cycle. *Journal of Marriage and the Family*, 48, 703–14.
Goldstein, J., and Warren, J. R. (2000) Socioeconomic research and heterogeneity in the extended family: contours and consequences. *Social Science Research*, 29, 382–404.
Heider, F. (1958) *The Psychology of Interpersonal Relations*. New York: John Wiley.
Hobart, C. (1987) Parent–child relations in remarried families. *Journal of Family Issues*, 3, 259–77.
Holman, T. B. (1981) The influence of community involvement on marital quality. *Journal of Marriage and the Family*, 143, 43–149.
House, J. S., Umberson, D., and Landis, K. R. (1988) Structures and processes of social support. *Annual Review of Sociology*, 14, 293–318.

Hoyt, D., and Babchuk N. (1983) Adult kinship networks: The selective formation of intimate ties with kin. *Social Forces*, 62, 84–101.

Hsu, F. (1971) *Kinship and Culture*. Chicago: Aldine.

Hurlbert, J. S., and Acock, A. (1990) The effects of marital status on the form and composition of social networks. *Social Science Quarterly*, 71, 163–74.

Johnson, C. L. (1988) *Ex-Familia: Grandparents, Parents and Children Adjust to Divorce*. New Brunswick, NJ: Rutgers University Press.

Johnson, C. L. (2000). Perspectives on American kinship in the later 1990s. *Journal of Marriage and the Family*, 62, 623–39.

Johnson, C. L,. and Barer B. M. (1987) Marital instability and changing kinship networks of grandparents. *The Gerontologist*, 27, 330–5.

Johnson, M. J., and Milardo, R. M. (1984) Network interference in pair relationships: A social psychological recasting of Slater's theory of social regression. *Journal of Marriage and the Family*, 46, 893–9.

Julien, D., Markman, H. J., Leveille, S., Chartrand, E,. and Begin, J. (1994) Networks' support and interference with regard to marriage: Disclosure of marital problems to confidants. *Journal of Family Psychology*, 8, 16–31.

Klein, R. C. A., and Milardo, R. M. (2000) The social context of couple conflict: support and criticism from informal third parties. *Journal of Social and Personal Relationships*, 17, 618–37.

Kuhn, M. H. (1964) The reference group reconsidered. *Sociological Quarterly*, 5, 5–21.

Lee, G. (1980) Kinship in the seventies: A decade review of research and theory. *Journal of Marriage and the Family*, 42, 923–36.

Lee, T. R. (1990) Sibling relationships in adulthood: Contact patterns and motivations. *Journal of Marriage and the Family*, 52, 431–40.

Linton, R. (1949) The natural history of the family. In R. A. Anshen (ed.), *The Family: Its Function and Destiny*. New York: Harper.

Mansfield, P., and Collard, J. (1988) The beginning of the rest of your life? A portrait of newly-wed marriage. *Sociology*, 23, 151–2.

Mardsen, P. V., and Lin, N. (1982) *Social Structure and Network Analysis*. Beverly Hills: Sage.

McPherson, M., Smith-Lovin, L., and Cook, J. M. (2001) Birds of feathers: Homophily in social networks. *Annual Review of Sociology*, 27, 415–44.

Milardo, R., and Allan, G. (1997) Social networks and marital relationships. In S. Duck (ed.), *Handbook of Personal Relationships*. Chichester: John Wiley.

Milardo, R. M. (1982) Friendship networks in developing relationships: Converging and diverging social environments. *Social Psychology Quarterly*, 45, 162–72.

Milardo, R. M. (1986) Personal choice and social constraint in close relationships: Applications of network analysis. In V. J. Derlega. and B. A. Winstead (eds.), *Friendship and Social Interaction*. New York: Springer Verlag.

Milardo R. M. (1987) Changes in social networks of women and men following divorce. *Journal of Family Issues*, 8, 78–96.

Milardo, R. M. (1988a) *Families and Social Networks*. Newbury Park: Sage.

Milardo, R. M. (1988b) Changes in social networks of women and men following divorce. *Journal of Family Issues*, 8, 78–96.

Milardo, R. M. (1989) Theoretical and methodological issues in the identification of the social networks of spouses. *Journal of Marriage and the Family*, 51, 165–74.

Milardo, R. M, Johnson, M. P., and Huston, T. L. (1983) Developing close relationships: Changing patterns of interaction between pair members and social networks. *Journal of Personality and Social Psychology*, 44, 964–76.

Newcomb, T. M. (1961) *The Acquaintance Process*. New York: Rinehart & Winston.

Olson, D. H., and McCubbin, H. I. (1989) *Families: What Makes Them Work?* Beverly Hills, CA: Sage.

Parks, M. R., and Eggert, L. L (1991) The role of social context in the dynamics of personal relationships. *Advances in Personal Relationships*, 2, 1–34.

Parks, M. R., Stan, C. M., and Eggert, L. L. (1983) Romantic involvement and social network involvement. *Social Psychology Quarterly*, 46, 116–31.

Parsons, T. (1943) The kinship system of contemporary United States. *American Anthropologist*, 45, 22–38.

Parsons, T. (1949) The social structure of the family. In R. N. Anshen (ed.), *The Family: Its Function and Destiny*. New York: Harper.

Pasley, K., and Ihinger-Tallman, M. (1987) *Remarriage and Stepparenting: Current Research and Theory*. New York: Guilford.

Ridgeway, C. L., and Smith-Lovin, L. (1999) The gender system and interaction. *Annual Review of Sociology*, 25, 191–216.

Rook, K., and Ituarte, P. (1999). Social control, social support, and companionship in older adults' family relationships and friendships. *Personal Relationships*, 6, 199–211.

Scanzoni, J., and Marsiglio, W. (1993) New action theory and contemporary families. *Journal of Family Issues*, 14, 105–32.

Schneider, D. M. (1980) *American Kinship. A Cultural Account*. Chicago and London: University of Chicago Press.

Scott, J. (1992) *Social Network Analysis*. Newbury Park. CA: Sage.

Spicer, J. W., and Hampe, G. D. (1975) Kinship interaction after divorce. *Journal of Marriage and the Family*, 37, 113–19.

Stein, C. H., Bush, E. G., Ross, R. R., and Ward, M. (1992) Mine, yours and ours: a configural analysis of the networks of married couples in relation to marital satisfaction and individual well-being. *Journal of Personal Relationships*, 9, 365–83.

Surra, C. A. (1985) Courtship types: variations in interdependence between partners and social networks. *Journal of Personality and Social Psychology*, 49, 357–75.

Surra, C. A. (1988) The Influence of the interactive network on developing relationships. In R. M. Milardo (ed.), *Families and Social Networks*. Newbury Park: Sage.

Surra, C. A., and Milardo, R. M. (1991) The social psychological context of developing relationships: Interactive and psychological networks. In J. Kingsley (ed.), *Advances in Personal Relationships*, 3, 1–36.

Treas, J. (1995) Beanpole or beanstalk? Comments on the demography of changing intergenerational relations. In V. L. Bengston, K. W. Schaie, and L. M. Burton (eds.), *Adult Intergenerational Relationships*. New York: Springer.

Treas, J., and Cohen, P. (in press) Maternal co-residence and contact: evidence from cross-national surveys. In H. A. Gauthier, C. Chu, and S. Tuljapurkar (eds.), *The Distribution of Private and Public Resources Across Generations*. Oxford: Oxford University Press.

Umberson, D. (1992) Relationships between adult children and their parents: psychological consequences for both generations. *Journal of Marriage and the Family*, 54, 664–74.

Wellman, B., and Wortley, S. (1989) Brothers' keepers: situating kinship relations in broader networks of social support. *Sociological Perspectives*, 32, 273–306.

Weston, K. (1991) *Families We Choose: Lesbian, Gays, Kinship*. New York: Columbia University Press.

Widmer, E. D. (1999a) *Les Relations Fraternelles des Adolescents*. Paris: Presses Universitaires de France.

Widmer, E. D. (1999b) Family contexts as cognitive networks: a structural approach of family relationships. *Personal Relationships*, 6, 487–503.

Widmer, E. D., Kellerhals, J., and Levy R. (forthcoming) Types of conjugal networks, conjugal conflict and conjugal quality. *European Sociological Review*.

Wish, M., Deutsch, M., and Kaplan, S. (1976) Perceived dimensions of interpersonal relations. *Journal of Personality and Social Psychology*, 33, 409–20.

# 22

# Men in Families and Households

David H. J. Morgan

## Introduction

One of the "growth areas" in the 1990s was the study of men and masculinities, a development reflected not only in general texts and more specific studies but also in journals, newsletters, courses, and conferences. What was relatively novel was not that such studies dealt with men, since studies about men have always been the norm, but that they specifically focused upon men and masculinities in such a way as to render such terms open to critical examination. Such a project had already been set in motion by feminist writings; clearly, concerns about patriarchy or male violence were centrally about the practices of men.

An influential early text was Andrew Tolson's *The Limits of Masculinity* (1977). Here Tolson clearly acknowledged the influence of feminist theory and practice, placing his analysis firmly within a framework of sexual politics. Tolson also, like several authors who came after him, identified a sense of tension or crisis in the practices of men in the late twentieth century. He sought to show the links and contradictions between the outward show and the inner psychic drama and to explore the limits of masculinity in modern times.

Many of the concerns highlighted by Tolson were to be taken up in other subsequent writings: these include the continuing influence of feminism (and also of gay studies); the sense of crisis in masculinities; the distinction and relation between the public and the private, and so on. Within these writings certain key themes were to emerge:

- *Patriarchy*. Even where there might have been some doubt about the usefulness of this term, an emphasis on power and inequality remained central.
- *Masculinities*. There was a stress on a plurality of masculinities rather than a single monolithic "Masculinity."
- *Hegemonic masculinity*. Connell's discussion of the way in which masculinities might be hierarchically organized within a given society proved to be highly

influential (1995). This concept highlighted both inequalities between men and women and between men and the complex ways in which these two inequalities might be related.

In this chapter I shall explore some of the ways in which these key ideas and concerns might inform a closer focus on the position of men within families. For some time, "men in families" has been largely equated with fatherhood, an emphasis which has perhaps unwittingly reinforced patriarchal representations. The involvement of men in families is complex and various and the studies of men and masculinities can be enriched through exploring these complexities. The framework deployed here is one that uses a broad notion of the life-course, moving from childhood through partnership and parenthood on to "caring," which is generally, although by no means exclusively, linked to old age. However, as the life-course in late modern society is increasingly complex, not everything fits neatly into this model. Divorce and domestic violence, with which I end this discussion, could take place at several points along this route.

Before proceeding with this investigation I should note the continuing uncertainties about the term "family," one which is complex and contested. In addition to the familiar contrast between "family" and "household," there is a contrast between the fluid way in which the family practices are understood and experienced by individuals themselves and a range of external, administrative or scientific, definitions. Further, definitions of "family" have particular relationships to understandings of men and masculinities. Thus the conventional model of the "nuclear family" was frequently given its identity and functional position through the identification of the male breadwinner or "head of household."

## Male Children in Family Life

Much of the recent discussion on men in families has focused upon fathers, sometimes forgetting, it would seem, that the identity "father" obviously also implies the reciprocal identity "child." Many recent studies seemingly focus on young men on the streets or in the classroom, rather than in the home. This contrasts with much social-psychological and psychoanalytical literature, where the processes of socialization and the troubled transitions to manhood are clearly a focus of attention. Further, social anthropologists have been concerned with the processes of achieving manhood within the family and wider social groups and the various rites of transition that frequently accompany this. In modern societies, in contrast, public concern has tended to focus on boys and young men only when, it would seem, the processes of socialization "go wrong." Under such circumstances the emphasis is upon the absence of an effective "father figure" and the worries around whether the young man was becoming too masculine or not masculine enough.

The developing "sociology of childhood" has some suggestions about the position of boys within families and households, although it is difficult to find a fully rounded picture emerging. There is a recognition that "adult understandings of gender structure children's experiences of being parented" (Mayall, 1996: 68), and the suggestion that men tend to remember less of their childhood than women might be seen as reflecting the tendency for men to be less involved in child rearing (ibid.: 3). In another recent British study (Brannen, Heptinstall, and Bhopal, 2000) gender seems to be a somewhat muted theme; in several aspects of children's perceptions of parenting and grandparenting, gender would seem to be relatively unimportant, although there was a tendency for children to see their fathers as the main link to the outside world (ibid.: 100) but not as confidants (ibid.: 105).

A sociological account of young men in families and households would need to look beyond the particular concerns of late modern societies and be aware of the wide range of ways in which boyhood is constructed and experienced within family life. One key set of questions would focus on the extent to and the ways in which boys come to occupy a different or, indeed, privileged position within family life. Throughout history and in a wide range of societies, the birth of a male child has been the occasion of special recognition and rejoicing, and such occasions seem to reflect a particular convergence of societal and familial expectations. One important set of questions, therefore, would be to do with the extent to which these near-universal patterns have been eroded under conditions of modernity. The logic would seem to suggest that the shifting of the basis of private property away from family-based to corporate-based entities, the development of more universalistic and achieved ways of recognizing status within the public sphere, and the increasing involvement of women in many or most key areas of public life would entail the loss of the privileged status accorded to the male infant. Further, it might be argued that more recent perceptions that boys constitute problems (educational underachievement, hooliganism, juvenile crime, and so on) might reduce this "patriarchal dividend" (Connell, 1995) even further.

Evidence for this seems, at present, to be difficult to find. It still appears to remain the case that boys and girls are treated differently by their parents in ways which go well beyond the more or less straightforward physical markers. At the same time this perception of "difference" does not usually encroach upon values to do with fairness and equal shares. There are some differences in the household tasks expected of boys and girls (Brannen, Heptinstall, and Bhopal, 2000; Morrow, 1996; Solberg, 1997) but the differences are often fairly subtle. Brannen et al.'s study finds some division of labor in household tasks: although girls do not seem to be more likely to engage in household tasks overall, they are more likely to do such tasks without being asked (Brannen et al., 2000: 160). Morrow (1996) found "clear gender stereotyping" (e.g., boys are more likely to do outdoor tasks) but there was also some overlap. Girls tend to do more in company with their mothers (Mayall, 1996: 90), but the general picture suggests that gender differences are not always straightforward and are shaped by many other factors.

Another important area is the differential perceptions of risk in relation to children. Some studies suggest that boys tend to be allowed more freedom outside the home than girls (Mayall, 1996: 138, 146). A recent US study looks at parents' fears for their children and argues that such fear tends to fall steadily as boys get older while, for girls, the fear falls until about the age of 11–15 and then rises again (Warr and Ellison, 2000). These practices on the part of parents, together with the more familiar aspects of childhood socialization, would seem to play an important part in the structuring of gendered identities.

A further set of questions deal with the ways in which or how far the transition from boyhood to manhood is especially marked within family life and beyond. There would seem, superficially at least, to be a fairly straightforward contrast between those social contexts where there are clear rituals which simultaneously celebrate the transition from boyhood to manhood and the differences between men and women and those social contexts, conventionally regarded as more "modern," where such rituals are nonexistent or muted or where there is relatively little overt difference between the treatment of boys and girls. Family practices may still be centrally involved in the special transition from boyhood to manhood within particular religious or cultural traditions (the bar mitzvah ceremony in Judaism, for example; Gilmore, 1990: 125), but generally the idea of a transition to manhood (as opposed to adulthood) may be relatively unimportant.

Linked to issues of the transitions from boyhood to manhood and the extent to which this has become blurred is the question of the move out of the parental home. Here again we find considerable variations; the extent to which young men remain in the parental home well into adulthood in Italy and Spain is well known and is a pattern which contrasts with most northern European countries (Corijn and Klitzing, 2001; Iacovou and Berthoud, 2001). Yet throughout most modern societies women are more likely to leave the parental home earlier than men and, increasingly, this is not simply a function of their getting married. Modern societies have also seen a tendency for both young men and women to remain longer in the parental home and for there to be increasing patterns of leaving and returning although, again, with considerable variations according to region, class, and ethnicity.

What is less clear is the extent to which the increasingly complex patterns of leaving the parental home influences the construction or the undermining of a clear sense of masculine identity. Modernity would seem to have entailed the achievement of full masculine identity with the departure from the parental home, obtaining a job, and the development of family responsibilities through marriage and parenthood. While these did not take place at once they were seen as part of the orderly transitions within the life-course. There were clear overlaps between ideas of adulthood, independence, and the assumption of responsibilities for others. It is now recognized that, for a variety of reasons, including changes in the structure of the labor market and in the development of higher education, this relatively clear set of interrelated transitions no longer happens in quite the same way and no longer clearly differentiates between the experiences of young men and young women. The reasons for leaving home become more diversified as the life-course itself becomes destandardized (Corijn and Klijzing, 2001).

Theoretically, the family has frequently been seen as crucially involved in the process of social and cultural, as well as physical, reproduction. Within this process, the reproduction of gender differences, differences between masculinity and femininity, was seen as central. What this account has suggested is that this process of the reproduction of gender differences and the place of family practices within it has becoming increasingly complex. This is partly a consequence of far-reaching changes in the labor markets and in education but also, one may speculate, of the growing reflexive monitoring of family practices. Clearly, family relationships remain very important in the understanding of the construction of masculinities. However, the emphasis would seem to be more or the plural nature of these identities and the blurring of familial boundaries in the process of reproducing gender differences over time.

## Men in Single-Person Households

Perhaps one of the most striking developments in Britain has been the growth in the proportion of single-person households (Hall, Ogden, and Hill, 1999). Thus *Social*

*Trends* for 2000 notes a rise from about one in twenty households in 1901, to just over 10 percent in 1961, to just under one in three by 1998–9 (Office for National Statistics, 2000: 34). Similar trends have been noted for other European countries and the US.

The generalized trends conceal a variety of different patterns according to both age and gender. Women of over pensionable age are currently more likely to be living alone than men, although this group is likely to be soon overtaken by men (Office for National Statistics, 2001b). The largest and most rapid increase, however, has been found among men under pensionable age. These trends have been attributed to the decline in marriage, the increase in late marriage, and the rise of separation and divorce (Office for National Statistics, 2001a: 44). These figures have led to speculation about the plight of younger men, returning to their apartments for solitary evenings of microwaved meals and a video. Other accounts have seen a deliberate lifestyle choice, reflecting the rising patterns of individualization highlighted by Beck and others (Hall, Ogden, and Hill, 1999). Care has to be made in reading off these experiences and interpretations from the statistics; figures of household composition can tell us nothing about actual social networks and relationships.

Thinking about men we may distinguish three different life circumstances:

1 Men of over pensionable age living alone but who may well have experienced married and family life and still be in regular contact with other family members. A sense of masculine identity here will arise out of the interaction between memories of past family, employment, and leisure experiences (together with such experiences as military service) and present living circumstances. Income, health, personal mobility, and social networks will all be relevant considerations.
2 Men in transition. These are men who have left the parental home and are living alone but with the expectation of marriage or cohabitation in the future. Similarly, there may be men who have left a particular relationship but who, again, anticipate entering a new one.
3 Men who have deliberately chosen a single and "living-alone" lifestyle and who do not necessarily see this as a transition to anything else.

This very preliminary list points to a range of life experiences within the general category. While the first two categories point to men who are at least partially defined by past or anticipated future family relationships, the third group suggests, but does not prove, a group who are weakly defined in terms of family ties and obligations. These men will frequently lead an urban lifestyle, possibly concentrating in particular parts of a city or part of a growing gay community. At the very least we can identify men whose capacity for domestic living does not depend upon partnership or family relationships and, while they may possibly be enjoying a good salary, whose masculinity does not depend upon the assumption of family responsibilities. Such experiences, although numerically small, point to the growing complexities of the links between men and family life. Also relevant is the growing interest in patterns of friendship between men and between men and women. Some of the earlier characterizations of men's friendships as being limited in depth or meaning are increasingly open to question (Pahl, 2000), and are being reassessed partly in light of the shifts in household composition discussed in this section.

## Men in Partnerships

The word "partner" has been increasingly used in recent years in order to capture a diversity of couple relationships. In this context I shall include men in formally recognized marriages but also cohabiting relationships, gay partnerships, and "living apart, living together" relationships.

"Marriage is still the usual form of partnership between men and women," notes *Social Trends* (Office for National Statistics, 2000a: 37), although marriage rates have been declining and people have been marrying later. There has been an increase in the proportion of childless married couples but the most striking development has been the increasing rates of cohabitation. In 1996, 1.6 million couples were to be found cohabiting in England and Wales, and the expectations are that this trend will continue and possibly double by 2021 (Office for National Statistics, 2001a: 45). This is not always a stage on the way to marriage. To some extent, these trends for the UK are reproduced in the US and many parts of Europe. In most parts of Europe, for example, marriage rates have been declining from the late 1960s and early 1970s and people have been marrying later (Kiernan, 1999). Cohabitation has also increased, although with considerable variation between the high rates in Nordic countries and the low rates in the south (ibid.). There has also been some widespread reporting of intimate relations with a person in a separate household, and some of these will be of the "living apart, living together" kind.

These trends may be part of a long-term process of the "de-institutionalization" of family life. They may signify the growth of "pure relationships"(Giddens, 1992) in late modernity or the trend toward individualization"(Beck and Beck-Gernsheim, 2002). All these arguments point to a steady loosening of formal and informal expectations and practices concerning marriage, once seen as the core adult relationship. Thus in a variety of countries we see formal recognition of cohabitation and, in some cases, single-sex partnerships (Kiernan, 1999).

Three questions suggest themselves:

1 To what extent do we see a growing participation of men in household tasks within heterosexual couples and a growing equality in terms of domestic labor, the control of money, and emotional labor?
2 What kinds of divisions of labor do we find within cohabiting and single-sex couples?
3 What are the implications of these trends for constructions and understandings of masculinities?

The first set of questions are the easiest to answer since we have a variety of detailed studies exploring sexual divisions of labor within the household and, to a lesser extent, changes over time. The British Household Panel Survey has been a particularly valuable resource here and, looking at this work and other surveys, Laurie and Gershuny conclude: "Wherever we find proper measurement, there is evidence of a long-term decline in women's unpaid work, and of a small increase in men's" (2000: 47).

The changes recorded have been small, but in the same direction, with attitudes changing more clearly than actual practices. In terms of money management we find relative stability, with most couples sharing the management of money and claiming to have an equal say in financial decisions. Yet, in most modern countries, we continue to find evidence of considerable disparities in domestic labor between women and men (Hochschild, for example, found that 80 percent of the men in her sample of two-job couples did not share housework or child-care (1990: 173) and most of the evidence, in the US, for example, seems to suggest little or only modest changes (Beck and Beck-Gernsheim, 2002: 101; Blair and Lichter, 1991; Shelton, 1990).

Thinking about emotional labor, we have to turn to more qualitative work, and here we find differences, sometimes subtle, between the practices of men and women. We see a persistence of the idea that women are the emotional specialists in intimate relationships, managing both their own emotions and the emotions of others such as partners or children (Langford, 1999; Mansfield and Collard, 1988). However, men may also engage in emotional labor (e.g., in suppressing tensions experienced at work in the context of the home), but in different ways and with different consequences (Duncombe and Marsden, 1998). Hochschild suggests that within many dual-earner households there is a tension between an ideology of equality within marriage and the reality in terms of day-to-day practices (1990). Both men and women experience this tension but it is likely that women are called upon to put more effort into managing it.

Taking all this together and adding questions to do with manifestations of power in relatively everyday practices such as watching TV and the use of the remote control (Walker, 1996), as well as intimate violence (see later section), we can see the persistence of inequalities within heterosexual marriages, despite some clear evidence of slow change. Recognizing evidence of mutual adjustment and accommodation, power differentials are still relevant in considering modern marriage (Blain, 1994).

As far as cohabiting couples are concerned the evidence seems to suggest some shifts in the direction of equality both in terms of a rejection of the traditional homemaker/breadwinner model and the divisions of actual tasks (Kiernan and Estaugh, 1993; Shelton and John, 1993). However, the differences seem to more or less disappear with the arrival or presence of children (Kiernan and Estaugh, 1993). There also seem to be some signs of greater equality among couples who are voluntarily childless (McAllister and Clarke, 1998). We know little specifically about the division of emotional labor in cohabiting couples except where these form part of a general sample of couples.

We know a little more about the practices of non-heterosexual couples. In a recent British study, the authors refer to such couples and relationships as "life-experiments" (Weeks, Heaphy, and Donovan, 2001). "Friendship" is the word most commonly used by the subjects themselves and they tend to reject notions of duty and obligation in favor of ideas of responsibility and mutual care. Considerable stress is given to egalitarian values and this, together with an emphasis on fluidity and complexity, is part of the way in which differences are established between these couples and heterosexual couples. However, some clearly recognize that there is still power within couple relationships, although this may be more to do with different access to resources and social capital.

What can we learn about the construction of masculinities through a consideration of couple relationships in modern societies? Here, Hochschild's idea of "gender strategies" may be of some help dealing with the interplay between discourses about masculinity and femininity and practices within the home and intimate relationships (1990: 15). In some cases these various elements may form a coherent whole and allow for the reproduction of gender divisions and inequalities over time. In some cases, and we may argue that this is increasingly likely, there may be discrepancies between, say, childhood experiences and experiences in later life or between the experiences and practices of men and women as they enter into intimate relationships. An understanding of gender strategies may help us understand not only how and why some practices are changing but also why the changes have been relatively slow. In the case of gay partnerships the circumstances of living an openly gay life within a predominantly heterosexual environment contributes not only to a sense of challenge to this dominant model but also to conventional notions of masculinity as well. At the very least we may suggest an interplay between a growing sense of fluidity, openness, and reflexivity in intimate relationships generally and a similar sense of fluidity or uncertainty with the gender order.

## Men As Fathers

One reason for the limitation of discussion about men in families to questions of fatherhood has been a growing public concern, in a number of countries, about this topic, a concern in part reflected in the growth of scholarly attention (Hobson, 2002; Marsiglio et al., 2000). While the emphasis differs in different welfare regimes, the main concerns would seem to be absent fathers or fathers who have little direct involvement in the day-to-day practices of being a father. There has also been some concern, from different quarters, about fathers as abusers (physical or sexual) within the family setting. Most discussion of fathers is about fathers with dependent children; interest in the topic seems to decline as the children get older, certainly by the time that they pass adolescence.

Several scholars have indicated a growing sense of difference, even polarization, between a concern with the positive aspects of fathering and how to encourage this and a concern (which is not itself necessary new, Lewis, 1986, 2002) with absent or non-involved fathers, the contrast between "good father/bad father" (Marsiglio, 1993). In reality, this simple opposition masks considerable diverse and complex patterns. Dowd, noting that "fatherhood is a common life experience for nearly all men" (2000: 22), suggests a threefold division:

1 "Men who father like mothers"; this includes some single-parent and some married fathers;
2 "Men fathering as a secondary parent";
3 Fathers who are "limited or disengaged nurturers"(ibid.: 4).

There are almost certainly many overlaps, partly as a consequence of variation in fathering practices over the life-course.

Concerns about the practices of fathers are not simply to do with economic provision and levels of public expenditure. They are also to do with what are supposed to be the adverse effects that follow from absent fathers or missing father figures. These include concerns about crime and delinquency, social exclusion and the development of an "underclass" and, more recently, the educational "underachievement" of boys in school. In Britain, for example, the development of a "laddish" culture might be in part attributed to the absence of a clear father figure.

The term "father" is ambiguous and this is not simply a question of the differences between the social and the biological father. The identification of the biological father is also a social process; given the difficulties associated with the firm establishment of paternity until quite recently, the biological father was conventionally assumed to be the man who was married to or had some similar long-term relationship, to the mother of the child. In more recent years, greater stress has been given to the identification of the biological father (Dowd, 2000; Smart and Neale, 1999), although, again, we need to explore in much greater detail the fluctuating meanings around the different ways of understanding the term "father."

One way of advancing this discussion is to distinguish between the terms "father," "fatherhood," and "fathering." In the case of the first term we are concerned with the process of identification, of linking a child or children to a particular man, identifying the biological or the social father or both. In the case of "fatherhood" we are concerned more with a social institution and the rights, duties, responsibilities, and statuses attached to being a father. We are also concerned with more general discourses (ideologies or representations) about the nature of fatherhood. The term "fathering" is the more recent term and is concerned more with the actual practices of fathers, of doing rather than being a father. These terms are linked, but their separation is a useful way of thinking about the range of different issues associated with fathers in a more comparative perspective (Hobson and Morgan, 2002). It might be noted that these distinctions are not simply to do with how individual fathers see themselves but also with the constructions of fathers, fatherhood, and fathering by social and political institutions and by significant others.

Despite the public concerns it remains the case that most fathers reside with their children; figures of 85 percent have been cited for Great Britain (Office for National Statistics, 2001a: 21). Various themes seem to be emerging from the literature relating to the US, Britain, and many other parts of Europe. The first is a sense of uncertainty about what is expected from fathers or how fathers see their own roles and practices. One small-scale American study found that fathers had difficulties in identifying role models; their own fathers only served as negative points of reference. They tended to have somewhat fragmented models of fathering, derived from a variety of persons, especially the women in their lives. They also saw that it was important to be a role model for their own children (Daly, 1993). Yet some patterns emerge, and Marsiglio claims to identify two core themes (1995). One is of univocal reciprocity (i.e., a sense of giving without expecting any immediate or direct return), and another is "generativity," which refers to a sense of a long-term commitment of involvement in the developing life of another person. Yet, in common with many other modern family practices, these general themes allow for a considerable range of interpretation and negotiation.

A second theme is to do with the continuing importance of "the provider" role. A British qualitative study found that "The most widely used term was simply that of 'provider' which was used no less than 135 times in the sample of 140 interviews. ... It arose spontaneously and repeatedly" (Warin et al., 1999: 13).

The idea of provider also emerged strongly in a survey of black, middle-class Americans (Haynes, 2000), and is clearly identified in the practices of the fathers that appear in a range of other studies. However, as the study by Warin et al. (1999) indicates, fathers do not *simply* see themselves as providers and combine this understanding with a range of other practices. Further, the term "provider" does cover a range of different themes (Christiansen and Palkovitz, 2001), and our understanding of it should not necessarily be limited to the simple and regular provision of cash.

A further important theme to emerge in the literature is that of continuing disparities in terms of the relative inputs of mothers and fathers. The often examined distinction between "helping" (feeding, playing with, changing diapers, or whatever) and "taking responsibility" is important here as it is in other areas of domestic life. Further, in most cases, men still have a considerable degree of choice about whether or not to participate in child-rearing tasks. At the same time, there is also evidence in a wide range of countries of increasing rates of participation on the part of fathers (Coltrane, 1995). Clearly, the increasing participation of married women and mothers in paid employment is a major contributory factor, but there is also some evidence to suggest that men actively wish to participate more in parenting.

The practices of fathers who are, in varying degrees, "present" in the home are often contrasted with the practices of nonresident fathers. This is where public concern has been focused, despite the fact that relatively little is known about them and they are often difficult to identify (Bradshaw et al., 1999). Increasing numbers of fathers are not living with their children, either as a result of the break-up of a marriage or cohabiting relationship or through fathering a child outside of a stable relationship. The picture here is often one of little or weak involvement, whether we are viewing this in either cash or care terms (Dowd, 2000). In some cases, Dowd reminds us, we can talk of "serial or multiple" fatherhood (ibid.: 28). In cannot, however, be assumed that all nonresident fathers have lost contact with their children, just as it cannot be assumed that all resident fathers have regular interaction with their children (Office of National Statistics, 2001b: 21). A variety of factors to do with employment, residence, and current relationships contribute to whether a nonresident father continues to have a relationship with his child or children but the general picture, in the US and Britain, suggests a serious attempt on the part of such fathers to maintain contact, often under quite unfavorable circumstances.

One important variation on the nonresidential father theme is to do with the increasing number of reconstituted households, following a divorce or its equivalent. This itself can allow for a variety of relationships between mother, father, and children, which Smart and Neale identify as co-parenting, custodial parenting, or solo parenting (1999). Hence all the considerations to do with nonresidential fathers – questions to do with the divisions of responsibilities and duties, the balance between cash and care, and the extent to which the mother assists in enabling the father to "do fathering" – apply in this important subgroup. However, other issues to do with the definition of the "real" father and the relationships between biological and social fatherhood also come to the fore. In some cases, these are clearly more than just abstract considerations: "What most fathers seemed to dread was the thought of another man punishing their children or their children calling another man, 'Dad'"(ibid.: 74–5).

Single fathers represent a minority of all single or lone-parent households, but they are increasing. The figure of 10 percent of all lone-parent households is often quoted for the UK, with something like 2 percent of all children being found in such households. In the US, a figure of 17 percent is provided for father-headed families as a percentage of all lone-parent households (Dowd, 2000: 23). While most of these are as a result of divorce, an increasing proportion are never married (Eggebeen, Snyder, and Manning, 1996). While the proportions are small, although increasing, their importance lies in the light that they throw upon fathering practices where there is no residential mother (Barker, 1994).

Yet another variation on the theme of fatherhood points to the intersections of gender and sexualities. Dowd quotes figures to the effect that some 20 to 25 percent of self-identified gay men are fathers (2000: 76). She argues that such men are at the margins of both conventional fatherhood and the gay male culture. Weeks, Heaphy, and Donovan (2001) find an increasing number of "nonheterosexual" couples opting for parenthood. They suggest that the very marginality of gay fathering allows for a greater degree of reflexivity in their parenting practices. They also consider the practices of gay men co-parenting with lesbian couples and the extent to which this too challenges certain conventional assumptions concerning the relationships between the biological and the cultural; and between parenthood and gender identity.

To conclude this section we should consider the relationship between fathers and masculinities. Here, the evidence from several modern societies suggests increasing complexities. Thus, biological fatherhood socially recognized and acknowledged might be taken as proof of masculinity. However, few societies would seem to be content simply with this construction. Fathers are conventionally expected to take on some of the responsibilities of fatherhood and the ability and willingness to assume these responsibilities was increasingly seen in modern societies as evidence of "manliness." This may be especially important as we see either the range of ways in which masculinity might be legitimately expressed diminishing or these expressions increasingly limited to the more successful or prestigious members of society (Furstenberg, 1995).

These expressions, in our terminology, relate to the identification of fathers and the rights and duties associated with fatherhood. In more recent years, however, it would seem that this emphasis on rights and duties attached to fatherhood have been supplemented, if not replaced, by more complex emphases on fathering practices. There would seem to be a reciprocal relationship between the development of more complex or more various ways of understanding masculinity, being a man, and a growing emphasis on the importance of fathering practices, involving all forms of caring and nurturing (Dowd, 2000: 43).

In some cases the argument might be that the separation of motherhood and fatherhood is no longer necessary and that a more generalized "parenting" and "parenthood" are more appropriate. In other cases, there may be some attempt to re-negotiate the identity of masculinity so that everyday fathering practices are not seen to be in contradiction with dominant ideas of what it is to be a man. Yet again, some men may experience a sense of conflict between a sense of masculinity rooted in work and employment and being a father. In yet further cases, "fathers' rights" movements may seek to reassert a more traditional, sometimes seemingly more aggressive, masculinity (Bertoia and Drakich, 1993). What we are seeing in a wide range of societies is the development of more complex, and sometimes more contradictory, relationships between men, masculinities, and fatherhood.

## Men and Other Family Identities

There are numerous other ways in which men have been involved in families, and while some of these identities have been discussed in classic anthropological literature it cannot be said that they make much of an appearance in recent sociological studies. One such identity is that of brother and brotherhood. Although there have been occasional calls to recognize the importance of sibling relationships, the amount of actual research is fairly sparse. Whereas the public rhetorics of brotherhood frequently deploy, at least implicitly, notions of male siblings, in actual families brothers are defined in relation to sisters as well as to male siblings. There are also the added complications of birth order and notions of younger or elder brother, differences which are smoothed over in public representations. Between the public representations and the relations within families lie practices where a fraternal relationship is assumed or where the rhetoric of brotherhood is used to describe actual practices (Liebow, 1967).

Another area where there has been some more sociological analysis has been the study of grandfathers. Here there has been some exploration of the interplay between the generational and the gendered, as in the title of Sarah Cunningham-Burley's article, "We don't talk about it" (1984). Despite the fact that grandfathers generally had less to say than grandmothers, there was little doubt that the grandfather status was important to the men she interviewed (Cunningham-Burley, 1987). A more recent study in the US (Roberto, Allen, and Blieszner, 2001), focusing specifically on grandfathers, found that the men spoke freely and showed a fair amount of knowledge while tending to incorporate the "good provider" aspect of fatherhood into their new roles. As grandparenthood (and great grandparenthood) becomes more widespread in lower age categories we may expect this to receive greater recognition in discussions of the family life of men.

More generally we may think of men in terms of kinship obligations. Again, kinship has usually been associated with women in modern societies, particularly focusing upon the role of women as "kin-keepers." Insofar as men have been considered it has been in terms of some kind of "deficit model," as being less involved in the everyday kin practices. A recent British study (McGlone, Park, and Roberts, 1999) repeated the familiar finding that women were more likely to see their relatives on a regular basis and were more likely to talk on the telephone. However, over a decade there had been a decline for both men and women. Another study of old people in three British communities found, again, that women tended to report larger networks than men (Phillipson et al., 2001). However, there were also some signs of a moving together in terms of the practices and experiences of older men and women and, for example, the active participation of sons in caring activities.

The problem of the simple "deficit" model of men in kinship is that it might smooth over considerable variations. Barbagli, for example, refers to the "relative dominance of matrilateral patterns" in a wide range of European countries (1997: 41). But parts of Italy where more patrilateral practices were in evidence proved to be an exception to this pattern. The work of Finch and Mason suggest that while we can see kinship obligations as being gendered, this is often in quite complicated ways or the result of long-term cumulative processes whereby women, rather than men, come to be especially identified with meeting particular family obligations (1993). However, as several of their cases show, this does not mean that men are excluded from expressing a belief in the importance of family obligations or in their realization in actual practices.

## Men As Carers – And Cared For

Much of the discussion of care, formal and informal, has focused upon the gendered character of this care, the fact that whatever aspect or context we are considering the care has a strong identification with the work of women in society. In some cases this might be linked to wider discussions of the ethical dimensions of care and the place of gender in discussions of moral philosophy.

Within the context of this general discussion of care, men often seem to be in an anomalous position. If there were a strong identification between women and the practice of care then men would seem to present difficulties when they are seen to enter these activities; the case of male nurses being a frequently discussed issue from the public and paid areas of caring. This is perhaps especially true when we consider later life and the care of the elderly. Here the fact that women, on average, live longer than men (a gap which has, in the UK, widened over the twentieth century (Arber and Ginn, 1991)) means that in later life men are more likely to be recipients rather than givers of care in family or informal settings. Curiously, however, we seem to know relatively little about the important questions raised by men as "cared-for." For example, in what ways can we go beyond an idea of being cared for as being at the receiving end of care and to move toward a more active understanding of the cared-for? Is it the case, as has been suggested (Rose and Bruce, 1995) that cared-for men still attempt to remain in control, or does the experience of being cared for contradict widely held notions of masculinity associated with independence and activity?

There is, however, a growing (if still quite small) literature on men as carers within family settings. This begins with a recognition that men can and do engage in caring practices. Women may live longer than men but they are more likely to suffer from health problems in old age. One informal carers' survey carried out in Britain in 1985 found that 12 percent of adult women were carers and 9 percent of adult men (Arber and Ginn, 1991: 131). An US survey of carers for the elderly found that roughly a quarter were men (Applegate and Kaye, 1993). Other studies suggest that where men are carers they may often do less caring work than women, may be less actively involved in the more intimate personal work, and may be more likely to receive formal or informal help.

However, when men are fully and actively involved in care of an elderly relative or spouse the picture becomes a little more blurred. Wilson argues that some reworking or reevaluation of gender roles is possible in advanced old age (1995), and Rose and Bruce found overlapping "rhetorics of coping" in their study of elderly carers in Britain (1995). Applegate and Kaye (1993) suggested a complex range of meanings and understandings on the part of male carers, ranging from attempts to renegotiate their caring work in terms of hegemonic masculinities to a recognition of a blurring of gender differences. They also pointed to a sense of "accomplishment and pride" on the part of male carers and this was also to be found in Rose and Bruce's British study. Men who were full-time carers tended to be seen as "coping wonderfully" and to be accorded greater esteem than women as a consequence. Perhaps this suggests that it is less a question of what tasks are performed or how carers themselves view and experience these tasks, and more in terms of the wider discourses which give meaning to these caring practices.

Men do not simply engage in caring responsibilities in relation to an elderly spouse but may be found engaging in the whole range of caring practices at different stages of the life-course. The theoretical implications of these understandings suggest a need to look more at the caring relationship, rather than focusing chiefly upon carers, and in exploring the ways in which gender might be defining and redefined in the process of caring over time. Further, if we are concerned with households which depart from the family-based model we shall also be concerned with the caring that takes place between men in gay partnerships or the care that is exchanged across households, say, between friends or neighbors.

## Men and Divorce

Clearly, divorce involves both men and women, although there are good reasons to suppose that there are differences in the meaning of divorce for husbands and wives. For one thing, it has long been noted that women are more likely to initiate divorce proceedings than men. In the UK around seven in ten decrees are granted to wives (Office for National Statistics, 1998: 14). These differences reflect a variety of factors, including the greater possibilities for women and lone mothers to develop a life outside of the marital home and the ways in which expectations concerning acceptable behavior within marriage have shifted over time. Women were more likely to be granted a divorce as a consequence of the unreasonable behavior of this husbands (ibid.), while the most common reason for husbands' divorcing was the adultery of their wives.

There is a considerable body of research that demonstrates that the economic disadvantages of divorce bear less heavily on men than on women (Kiernan and Mueller, 1999: 380). To some extent we may see these tendencies as both reflecting and contributing to a construction of masculinity which allows men greater freedom of movement and opportunities for self-determination. It also, of course, reflects on the fact that men tend to be more economically advantaged before and during marriage as well as after the dissolution.

It has also been found that, despite these economic factors, men are more likely to respond negatively to the experience of divorce. Emotions noted have included pained incomprehension, anger and resentment, and a general sense of loss (Ambrose, Harper, and Pemberton, 1983). As compared with women after divorce, the health of men is likely to deteriorate (Kiernan and Mueller, 1999). In part these may reflect the different ways in which men benefit from marriage, a theme initially raised by Durkheim in his discussion of suicide. In terms of masculinities these difficulties may be compounded by the supposed reluctance of men to talk about emotional difficulties within relationships or their relative lack of informal networks of support at times of personal crisis. Some of this may be exaggerated, but it is likely that divorce does have consequences for men's gendered identities. Again, these difficulties are exacerbated where children are concerned and where the man is not only an ex-husband but also, in most cases, a nonresident father.

Discussions of divorce and its impact are clearly based upon the presupposition of a legally recognized marriage. However, as has already been noted, many partnerships (including partnerships with children) are in unions which are not formally or wholly recognized by law. This includes both heterosexual and homosexual partnerships. What is important to consider is, first, whether there are significant differences in the consequences and meanings of the break-up of less formal partnerships as compared with marriage and, secondly, whether issues of gender are implicated in quite the same way as seemed to be the case in legally constituted marriages.

## Men and Domestic Violence

One of the most controversial aspects of the discussion of men in households and family life is to do with domestic violence. The controversies have to do with the incidence of domestic violence, the question of whether men commit more violent acts than women and the meanings for the partners involved. A question linking both these issues is the extent to which violence is strongly or weakly linked to gendered identities or structures of patriarchy.

To simplify, I shall consider violence between partners, married or cohabiting, and shall limit this analysis to heterosexual couples. Even so, it is important to ask the question as to what is meant by violence. Since the term "violence" is usually understood in negative terms, the application of the term to a particular set of acts or practices is itself a moral and political act. Social-scientific attempts to measure the incidence of violence can never fully escape from this wider evaluative framework. Here I shall take "violence" to refer to those acts or practices which are understood or defined in this way by either the recipient or an observer or both, and which are the object of a degree of moral condemnation. What is to be stressed here is the idea that we cannot be wholly indifferent to acts of violence; they involve pain, fear, a sense of a loss of autonomy and freedom, and often a breakdown of trust.

Within such a framework it obviously becomes very difficult to consider whether, in the context of adult heterosexual partnerships, men are more violent than women. What needs to be considered is the frequency of certain kinds of acts or practices, their severity, and whether they are repeated or more isolated. We also need to consider less tangible questions, such as the threat of violence and its perception.

Taking all this into consideration it does seem reasonable to suppose that men are more likely to be perpetrators of domestic violence than women (Dobash et al., 1992). What such a conclusion does not deny is the possibility that men may also be the victims of such violence. Further, it is very difficult to judge whether men have become relatively more or less violent in domestic situations over succeeding decades.

It seems likely that the incidence of domestic violence is too high to reduce it to questions of individual pathology reflecting, say, inadequate childhood socialization or alcohol or drug abuse. Hearn points to evidence that suggests that between 10 and 25 percent of British women have at some time been the victim of violence from a male partner (1998: 5), but considers this to be an underestimate. At the same time it seems inadequate to see all such acts as reflecting the persistence of patriarchal structures, institutions, and practices within the wider society. This is partly because of the presence of violence perpetrated by women, partly because there are differences in the character and meaning of acts of violence perpetrated by men, and largely because it does not seem theoretically helpful to see men and women as relatively passive victims of external structural forces. Rather than seeing patriarchy, or masculinity, as having a direct causal relationship to individual acts of violence within the home, it might be more helpful to see the gender order as providing the context for and giving meaning to these acts of violence and their consequences.

Some violent acts may be associated with particular notions of male power within the home, others with a sense of a loss or an erosion of masculine dominance. The role of alcohol in domestic violence may not be seen as an individual causal factor but as something which is bound up with the role in which alcohol plays in men's culture generally. Further, the gendered meaning of domestic violence does not stop with the act itself within the four walls of the home. It also extends to the responses of significant others, discussions in the media and, possibly, the intervention of police or other outside agencies.

Hearn's recent study of men's violences against female partners highlights some of these complexities. His analysis works on the distinctions and connections between the "violent self" and the "talking self" and between describing and accounting. For example, when a man in an interview says "I just slapped her," a sense of distance is established between the act and the present interview context, while the simple phrase contains a complex mixture of description and accounting. Hearn notes how many of the accounts focused on the violent incident rather than the "general social relation" (1998: 85) and how frequently the "violent self" is presented as being "somewhere else" (ibid.: 106). He stresses that such accounts cannot be detached from the real acts of violence (in other words, they are not simply texts or discourses), and that the wider context is one of gendered power revolving around constructions of heterosexuality.

There are further issues that need to be considered. One is to do with the perpetration of acts of violence (including sexual abuse) by men against children within the home. In the case of sexual abuse the links with issues of patriarchy and masculinities might seem to be relatively straightforward since, as far as we are able to tell, such acts are more frequently committed by men against children than by women. While the reasons at the level of individual motivation are undoubtedly complex, constructions of male sexual urges and male sexuality are almost certainly part of the explanation. Notions of male sexuality include, although are not confined to, notions of using the other (a woman, a child) as an object of physical gratification, whether reciprocated or not. In the case of physical abuse matters are more complicated in that women become more heavily involved. In part, this may well reflect the simple fact that women are more likely to be in the presence of children for longer periods of time than men.

We have relatively little information about violence between adults in single-sex couples. Similarly, we have relatively little understanding of men as victims of domestic violence although, again, it is the wider framework of interpretation and meaning that is important. Men are less likely to report being victims of domestic violence and are less likely to have their experiences taken seriously when these incidents are reported. While violence against wives is increasingly seen as illegitimate, this does not mean that violence against husbands is somehow seen as more acceptable or understandable.

The relations between masculinities and patterns of violence within the home are more complex than simple models would seem to suggest. Perhaps the most important fact is that such issues are now firmly on the agenda. The increasing condemnation and problematization of violence within the home may be less to do with the advancing civilizing process and more to do with the changing gender order and the role of feminism, in the broadest sense of the word, within this.

## Conclusion

What does such an analysis contribute to masculinity studies? The detailed exploration of any single site, or linked set of sites, must necessarily highlight complexities and tensions absent in more generalized analyses of patriarchies or gendered orders. Here we are reminded that the location of men within families and households is more than a question of the analysis of fatherhood, that it involves a variety of other family-based identities and that these vary over the life-course. Such a detailed exploration is necessary given the continuing tendency to locate masculinity studies within the more public spheres of work, leisure, and cultural representations. Further, it highlights the need to see masculinity as being constantly shaped and redefined in interaction with others – women, children, and other men.

What does such an analysis contribute to family studies? For some considerable while family studies have given particular focus to the experiences and identities of women within the home and household. Such an approach, emerging out of feminist scholarship, was both necessary and valuable. But it frequently allowed a limited role to men. To begin to explore their multiple involvements in family practices is not to diminish the contributions of feminist-inspired scholarship. Rather it is to round out and to enhance such an approach.

Finally, such an analysis, focusing upon men in family life, inevitably involves questions of wider social change. The changes have been mentioned at several points in this discussion and include changes in the structure of the labor market and work, other changes in the structured relationships between men and women in the public sphere and wider changes in the culture and the structure of expectations and life-chances. Such changes, whether or not we characterize them in terms such as "post-modernity," undoubtedly point to a greater sense of variation and openness in the organization of private and domestic life, with continuing importance for gendered identities. Gender, which clearly includes men as well as women, continues to be an important dimension along which we shall need to explore everyday family and household practices. But such an exploration must inevitably highlight tensions and ambiguities so that older gender divisions and inequalities coexist uneasily with a new sense of openness and experimentation.

### References

Ambrose, P., Harper, J., and Pemberton, R. (1983) *Surviving Divorce: Men Beyond Marriage*. Brighton: Wheatsheaf.

Applegate, J. S., and Kaye, L. W. (1993) Male elder caregivers. In C. L. Williams (ed.), *Doing "Women's Work": Men in Non Traditional Occupations*. Newbury Park, CA: Sage.

Arber, S., and Ginn, J. (1991) *Gender and Later Life: A Sociological Analysis of Resources and Constraints*. London: Sage.

Barbagli, M. (1997) Family and kinship in Italy. In M. Gullestad and M. Segalen (eds.), *Family and Kinship in Europe*. London: Pinter.

Barker, R. W. (1994) *Lone Fathers and Masculinities*. Aldershot: Avebury.

Beck, U., and Beck-Gernsheim, E. (2002) *Individualization*. London: Sage.

Bertoia, C., and Drakich, J. (1993) The fathers' rights movement: Contradictions in rhetoric and practice. *Journal of Family Issues,* 14, 592–615.

Blain, J. (1994) Discourses of agency and domestic labor: Family discourse and gendered practices in dual-earner families. *Journal of Family Issues,* 15, 515–49.

Blair, S. L. and Lichter, D. T. (1991) Measuring the division of household labor: Gender segregation of housework among American couples. *Journal of Family Issues,* 12, 91–113.

Bradshaw, J. S., Stimson, C., Skinner, C., and Williams, J. (1999) Non-resident fathers in Britain. In S. McRae (ed.), *Changing Britain: Families and Households in the 1990s.* Oxford: Oxford University Press.

Brannen, J., Heptinstall, E., and Bhopal, K. (2000) *Connecting Children: Care and Family Life in Later Childhood.* London: Routledge/Falmer.

Christiansen, S. L., and Palkovitz, R. (2001) Why the "good provider" role still matters: Providing as a form of parental involvement. *Journal of Family Issues*, 22, 84–106.

Coltrane, S. (1995) The future of fatherhood: Social, demographic and economic influences on men's family involvements. In W. Marsiglio (ed.), *Fatherhood: Contemporary Theory, Research, and Social Policy.* Thousand Oaks, CA: Sage.

Connell, R. W. (1995) *Masculinities.* Berkeley: University of California Press.

Corijn, M., and Klijzing, E (eds.) (2000) *Transitions to Adulthood in Europe.* Dordrecht: Kluwer Academic.

Cunningham-Burley, S. (1984) "We don't talk about it . . . ": Issues of gender and method in the portrayal of grandfatherhood. *Sociology,* 18, 325–38.

Cunningham-Burley, S. (1987) The experience of grandfatherhood. In C. Lewis and M. O'Brien (eds.), *Re-Assessing Fatherhood.* London: Sage.

Daly, K. (1993) Reshaping fatherhood: Finding the models. *Journal of Family Issues,* 14, 510–30.

Dobash, R. P., Dobash, R. E., Wilson, M., and Daly, M. (1992) The myth of sexual symmetry in marital violence. *Social Problems*, 39, 71–91.

Dowd, N. E. (2000) *Redefining Fatherhood.* New York: New York University Press.

Duncombe, J., and Marsden, D. (1998) "Stepford Wives" and "Hollow Men". Doing emotion work, doing gender and "authenticity" in intimate heterosexual relationships. In G. Bendelow and S. J. Williams (eds.), *Emotions in Social Life.* London: Routledge.

Eggebeen, D. J., Snyder, A. R., and Manning, W. D. (1996) Children in single-father families in demographic perspective. *Journal of Family Issues*, 17, 441–65.

Finch, J., and Mason, J. (1993) *Negotiating Family Responsibilities.* London: Routledge.

Furstenberg, F. F., Jr. (1995) Fathering in the inner city: Paternal participation and public policy. In W. Marsiglio (ed.), *Fatherhood: Contemporary Theory, Research, and Social Policy.* Thousand Oaks, CA: Sage.

Giddens, A. (1992) *The Transformation of Intimacy: Sexuality, Love and Eroticism in Modern Societies.* Cambridge: Polity.

Gilmore, D. D. (1990) *Manhood in the Making: Cultural Concepts of Masculinity.* New Haven, CT: Yale University Press.

Hall, R., Ogden, P. E., and Hill, C. (1999) Living alone: Evidence from England and Wales and France for the last two decades. In S. McRae (ed.), *Changing Britain: Families and Households in the 1990s.* Oxford: Oxford University Press.

Haynes, F. E. (2000) Gender and family ideals: An exploratory study of black middle-class Americans. *Journal of Family Issues,* 21, 811–37.

Hearn, J. (1998) *The Violences of Men.* London: Sage.

Hobson, B. (ed.), (2002) *Making Men into Fathers: Men, Masculinities and The Social Politics of Fatherhood.* Cambridge: Cambridge University Press.

Hobson, B., and Morgan, D. (2002) Introduction: Making men into fathers. In B. Hobson (ed.), *Making Men Into Fathers: Men, Masculinities and the Social Politics of Fatherhood.* Cambridge: Cambridge University Press.

Hochschild, A. (1990) *The Second Shift: Working Parents and the Revolution at Home.* London: Piatkus.

Iacovou, M., and Berthoud, R. (2001) *Young People's Lives: A Map of Europe*. London: Institute of Economic and Social Research.

Kiernan, K. (1999) *The Changing Demography of Partnership*. Working Paper 14. Leeds: Centre for Research on Family, Kinship and Childhood, University of Leeds.

Kiernan, K., and Estaugh, V. (1993) *Cohabitation: Extra-Marital Childbearing and Social Policy*. London: Family Policy Studies Centre.

Kiernan, K., and Mueller, G. (1999) Who divorces? In S. McRae (ed.), *Changing Britain: Families and Households in the 1990s*. Oxford: Oxford University Press.

Langford, W. (1999) *Revolutions of the Heart: Gender, Power and The Delusions of Love*. London: Routledge.

Laurie, H., and Gershuny. J. (2000) Couples, work and money. In R. Berthoud and J. Gershuny (eds.), *Seven Years in The Lives of British Families*. Bristol: Policy Press.

Lewis, J. (1986) Anxieties about the family and the relationships between parents, children and the state in twentieth-century England. In M. Richards and P. Light (eds.), *Children of Social Worlds*. London: Cambridge University Press.

Lewis, J. (2002) The problem of fathers: Policy and behaviour in Britain. In B. Hobson (ed.), *Making Men into Fathers: Men, Masculinities and the Social Politics of Fatherhood* Cambridge: Cambridge University Press

Liebow, E. (1967) *Tally's Corner*. Boston, MA: Little, Brown.

Mansfield, P., and Collard, J. (1988) *The Beginning of the Rest of Your Life? A Portrait of Newly-Wed Marriage*. London: Macmillan.

Marsiglio, W. (1993) Contemporary scholarship on fatherhood: Culture, identity and conduct. *Journal of Family Issues*, 14, 484–509.

Marsiglio, W. (1995) Fathers' diverse life course patterns and roles: Theory and social intervention. In W. Marsiglio (ed.), *Fatherhood: Contemporary Theory, Research, and Social Policy*. Thousand Oaks, CA: Sage.

Marsiglio, W., Amato, P., Day, R. D., and Lamb, M. E. (2000) Scholarship on fatherhood in the 1990s and beyond. *Journal of Marriage and the Family*, 62, 1173–91.

Mayall, B. (1996) *Children, Health and The Social Order*. Buckingham: Open University Press.

McAllister, F., and Clarke, L. (1998) *Choosing Childlessness*. London and York: Family Policy Studies Centre and the Joseph Rowntree Foundation.

McGlone, F., Park, A., and Roberts, C. (1999) Kinship and friendship: Attitudes and behaviour in Britain, 1986–1995. In S. McRae (ed.), *Changing Britain: Families and Households in the 1990s*. Oxford: Oxford University Press.

Morrow, V. (1996) Rethinking childhood dependency: Children's contributions to the domestic economy. *Sociological Review*, 44, 58–77.

Office for National Statistics/Equal Opportunities Commission (1998) *Social Focus on Men and Women*. London: Stationery Office.

Office for National Statistics (2000) *Social Trends*. London: Stationery Office.

Office for National Statistics (2001a) *Social Trends*. London: Stationery Office.

Office for National Statistics (2001b) *Social Focus on Men*. London: Stationery Office.

Pahl, R. (2000) *On Friendship*. Cambridge: Polity.

Phillipson, C., Bernard, M., Phillips, J., and Ogg, J. (2001) *The Family and Community Life of Older People*. London: Routledge.

Roberto, K. A., Allen, K. R., and Blieszner, R. (2001) Grandfathers' perceptions and expectations of relationships with their adult grandchildren. *Journal of Family Issues*, 22, 407–26.

Rose, H., and Bruce, E. (1995) Mutual care but differential esteem: Caring between old couples. In S. Arber and J. Ginn (eds.), *Connecting Gender and Ageing: A Sociological Approach*. Buckingham: Open University Press.

Shelton, B. A. (1990) The distribution of household tasks: Does wife's employment status make a difference? *Journal of Family Issues*, 11, 115–35.

Shelton, B. A., and John, D. (1993) Does marital status make a difference? Housework among married and cohabiting men and women. *Journal of Family Issues*, 14, 401–20.

Smart, C., and Neale, B. (1999) *Family Fragments?* Cambridge: Polity.

Solberg, A. (1997) Negotiating childhood: Changing constructions of age for Norwegian children. In A. James and A. Prout (eds.), *Constructing and Reconstructing Childhood* (2nd ed.). London: Falmer.

Tolson, A. (1977) *The Limits of Masculinity*. London: Tavistock.

Walker, A. J. (1996) Couples watching television: Gender, power and the remote control. *Journal of Marriage and the Family*, 58, 813–23.

Warin, J., Solomon, Y., Lewis, C., and Langford, W. (1999) *Fathers, Work and Family Life*. London and York: Family Policy Studies Centre and the Joseph Rowntree Foundation.

Warr, M., and Ellison, C. G. (2000) Rethinking social reactions to crime: Personal and altruistic fear in family households. *American Journal of Sociology*, 106, 551–78.

Weeks, J., Heaphy, B., and Donovan, C. (2001) *Same Sex Intimacies: Families of Choice and Other Life Experiments*. London: Routledge.

Wilson, G. (1995) "I'm the eyes and she's the arms": Changes in gender roles in advanced old age. In S. Arber and J. Ginn (eds.), *Connecting Gender and Ageing: A Sociological aApproach*. Buckingham: Open University Press.

## Further Reading

As indicated, the number of references on "Men" and "Masculinities" is already large and continues to grow. A useful, and recent, collection is Stephen M. Whitehead and Frank J. Barrett (eds.), *The Masculinities Reader* (Cambridge, Polity, 2001). An earlier but still useful collection is Mairtin Mac An Ghaill (ed.), *Understanding Masculinities* (Buckingham, Open University Press, 1996). Turning more specifically to men in families, Richard Collier's *Masculinity, Law and The Family* (London, Routledge, 1995) provides a theoretical and legal framework. Collections of articles directly or indirectly concerned with men in families include Jane C. Hood (ed.), *Men, Work and Family* (Newbury Park, CA, Sage, 1993); Robert A. Lewis and Robert E. Salt (eds.), *Men in Families* (Beverley Hills, CA, Sage, 1986), and Edward H. Thompson (ed.), *Older Men's Lives* (Thousand Oaks, CA: Sage, 1994). There are some references to gender and men in Linda McKie, Sophia Bowlby, and Susan Gregory (eds.), *Gender, Power and the Household* (Basingstoke, Macmillan, 1999). Jane Wheelock provides an interesting set of case studies in her *Husbands at Home: The Domestic Economy in a Post-Industrial Society* (London, Routledge, 1990). Readers who wish to explore this issue in historical context should look at Leonore Davidoff and Catherine Hall, *Family Fortunes* (London, Hutchinson, 1987) and John R. Gillis, *A World of Their Own Making* (Oxford, Oxford University Press, 1996).

# V

# Changing Social Contexts

# 23

# Sex and Family: Changes and Challenges

Judith Treas

Sex is central to our understanding of the family as a social institution. As the starting point for procreation, sex supplies new family members and sustains the family lineage across time and generations. Sexuality is the basis for mate recruitment and pair-bonding. Kinship roles – mother and son, brother and sister – are delineated, in part, by sexual taboos and prohibitions against incest. Because sexuality goes to the core of family relations, families have a stake in the regulation of sexual behavior. The community standing and economic welfare of family members long depended on restricting couplings to approved unions that had access to an adequate level of material resources. As Malthus observed, having too many mouths to feed mired unfortunate families in poverty. Historically, the most effective way to keep the family's consumption requirements in line with its resources was to limit births. In the absence of reliable contraception, this translated into two-pronged efforts to channel procreative sexual activity into marriage and to control which family members married and to whom.

In the face of the cultural trend toward greater permissiveness, it is easy to forget that socially sanctioned, sexual relationships used to be regarded as a demographic privilege. Marriage was an unequal life chance that differentiated the advantaged from the disadvantaged. Before the diffusion of birth-control practices made it possible to separate sexual pleasure from procreation, those who had the means to support a family were favored for marriage. Daughters who lacked a dowry and last-born sons who had no claim to the family farm lived out their lives without taking a mate, perhaps as dependents in the homes of married siblings on whom family fortunes were concentrated. In China, where female infanticide limited the supply of brides, many poor men never married, even as rich men took several wives and concubines (Lee and Feng, 1999). Thus, large segments of the population were denied routine access to sexual partners for their entire lives.

Just as differential access to economic resources meant unequal access to marital pleasures, gender inequality poses another obstacle to sexual parity. Women's sexuality has always been more strictly regulated than men's. Unfaithful wives have been more severely sanctioned by family, community, and the law than have adulterous husbands (Lawson, 1988). Parents have been more concerned about preserving the chastity of their daughters than discouraging the sexual adventures of their sons. Of course, a family's success in regulating sexuality depends on its social standing and economic circumstances. Poor parents who must work long hours have greater difficulty monitoring the sexual behavior of their adolescent children. Class and race define the limits of family control, if only because unequal power relations invite sexual exploitation. Calculated sexual exchanges with "social superiors" have a long history as a survival strategy (Quaife, 1979), poignantly among the most vulnerable and downtrodden. Family life has suffered from demoralizing, class-based sexual predations. Not being able to protect wives and daughters from sexual demands weighed heavily on subordinated men, whether they were Italian peasants (Schneider and Schneider, 1996) or American slaves (Patterson, 1998). Laws on sexual harassment demonstrate that the enduring problem of power-based sexual exploitation has followed middle-class women and female professionals into the contemporary workplace.

Once a demographic privilege, sexual relations, marriage, and parenthood have come to be widely regarded as individual rights, not family decisions. The drift of Western family law has been to remove the obstacles to marriage (Glendon, 1989). Parental approval is no longer required, except for the very young. Only the closest degree of blood kinship (e.g., brother–sister, parent–child) is considered too incestuous for marriage. Divorce is no longer an obstacle to a new match. Barriers to same-sex unions will undoubtedly be the next to fall. Cultural ideologies promoting self-determination and individual fulfillment have undermined popular support for the family control of marriage and sexuality (Frank and McEneaney, 1999). Unwed adolescents need not get their parent's permission to obtain contraceptives, and wives need not seek their husband's approval for an abortion. Just as family control over marriage has faded, fewer and fewer people regard sex outside of marriage as wrong. Except for lingering concerns about teenage motherhood, the stigma associated with nonmarital births has greatly diminished. Having removed some of the historical impediments to marriage and parenthood, contemporary social welfare states are now judged by their provision for female-headed families (O'Connor, Orloff, and Shaver, 1999). The upshot is intriguing patterns of consistency and change in public opinion and private behavior that shape the sex lives of young and old, married and single, heterosexual and nonheterosexual individuals.

## Youth Sex, Then and Now

Young people's sexuality has been the prime territory of family control. Generations of parents have struggled to help their offspring balance youthful desire and the need for pragmatic choices about marriage and childbearing. In law, these family concerns with youth are still embodied in parental-consent requirements for teen marriages (Glendon, 1989) as well as in minimum-age standards for sexual consent. Until fairly recently, there was widespread agreement that marriage should precede sex and childbearing. Today, families play an important role in the adolescent transition to adult sexuality, but formative sexual experiences increasingly occur at younger ages and outside of marriage. Responding to the potential threats of AIDS and teen pregnancy, schools and communities have stepped up their efforts to augment family responsibility for teen sexuality.

Over time, however, norms against premarital sex have lost their force. American women who were born after 1900 were more likely than their older sisters to engage in premarital petting, and even sexual intercourse (Kinsey et al., 1953). In the past, unmarried couples experimented quietly with sex, but there was still strong pressure from family and community to marry if a pregnancy resulted. If their first birth were conceived before marriage, couples were placed at a disadvantage, because they married at a younger age and obtained less schooling (Freedman and Thornton, 1979). Most of these couples, however, overcame early disadvantage and went on to become homeowners with middle-class incomes and money in the bank. Births out of wedlock were a different story. Motherhood without marriage was stigmatized and economically perilous. Many single women sought illegal abortions or gave up their babies, rather than raise children alone. When sex did not lead to marriage, sexual activities of single people were managed quietly so as not to come to public attention.

Despite the reservations of family-life educators (Ericksen and Steffen, 1999), the sexual mores and family formation patterns of young people underwent major changes in both the US (Cherlin, 1992) and Britain (Lewis and Kiernan, 1996). Once relatively circumspect about their sexual activities, youth in the 1960s flaunted premarital sex by openly cohabiting (Wilhelm, 1998). Bowing to the inevitable, public opinion came to accept sex before marriage. Beginning in the 1960s, American disapproval of premarital sex declined sharply (Smith, 1994). Slower declines followed. Between 1972 and 1998, the number of Americans who considered premarital sex to be "always wrong" dropped from 37 percent to 24 percent, as older, more conservative cohorts were replaced by younger, more permissive generations (Treas, 2002). Cohort succession also powered declines in Britain (Scott, 1998). With the exception of Ireland, where 35 percent say premarital sex is "always wrong," disapproval of premarital sex is very low elsewhere in the Western world (Widmer, Treas, and Newcomb, 1998). According to 1994 survey data, only 13 percent of Australians, 12 percent of the British, 12 percent of Canadians, 19 percent of New Zealanders, 7 percent of the Dutch, and 4 percent of Swedes think sex before marriage is "always wrong."

With cohabitation and premarital sex practiced widely among young adults, attention shifted to adolescents. Although premarital sex is increasingly accepted, teen sex is still seen as problematic. In 1994, fully 71 percent of Americans and 67 percent of the British said sex between young teens (ages 14–16) was "always wrong" (Widmer, Treas, and Newcomb, 1998). Elsewhere, disapproval ranged from high levels in Catholic populations to moderate levels in Scandinavian countries: 84 percent in Ireland, 81 percent in Northern Ireland, 71 percent in New Zealand, 61 percent in Australia, 58 percent in Italy, 55 percent in Canada, 45 percent in the Netherlands, and 32 percent in Sweden. This moral disapproval reflects practical concerns about the long-run ramifications of early sexual activity as well as cultural assumptions about teenagers' psychological immaturity, their irrationality, and their vulnerability to exploitation.

Since the 1950s in North America and Western Europe, age at first sex has declined by about three years for women (Teitler, 2002). The median age for males and females is somewhere between 17 and 18, except for southern Europe, where the median age for women is 19. The upshot of trends has been reductions in age-at-first-sex differences between countries, between social classes, between early and late initiators, and between genders (ibid.). In Canada, the historical double standard in sexual initiation between adolescent males and females virtually disappeared (Maticka-Tundale, Barrett, and McKay, 2000). Since time spent in romantic relationships before first sex also seems to have increased, young people may arrive at their sexual debuts better equipped to communicate and manage couple relations than in the past (Teitler, 2002). Nearly four out of five American women, 15–44, reported that their first sex was with a steady partner, a fiancé, or a husband (Abma et al., 1997).

Having had sex does not translate into a particularly high level of sexual activity for teenagers, since even sexually active males have relatively low frequencies of intercourse and long periods without a partner (Sonenstein, Pleck, and Ku, 1991). However, young people are more likely than their seniors to have multiple partners, in part because their relationships are of relatively short duration. In 1992, 15 percent of sexually active American women, ages 14–22, and 35 percent of their male counterparts reported having more than one sex partner just in the last three months – a risk that increases with the use of alcohol (Santelli et al., 1998). Sexual scripts are complex and changing. More adolescent males in the US report some sort of heterosexual genital contact than report having actually had vaginal sex (Gates and Sonenstein, 2000). Males, ages 15–19, were significantly more likely to have been masturbated by a female in 1995 than in 1988, but they were less likely to have had vaginal intercourse (ibid.). The likelihood that a black female adolescent had had sexual intercourse also declined in the 1990s while use of condoms by adolescents increased (Santelli et al., 2000). Teenagers, especially those who first have sex at younger ages, are less likely to have used contraception than those who postponed their sexual debuts. Although first sexual experiences are often spontaneous, contraceptive planning for first sex is on the rise in the US (Abma et al., 1997). More than three-quarters of American women who had first intercourse in the early 1990s reported using some contraceptive method as opposed to only half of those whose sexual debut was prior to 1980. Younger women were most likely to have used condoms, while slightly older women favored birth-control pills, a method requiring even more foresight.

## The Problem with Teenagers

There are certainly reasons for concern about teenagers who have sex. Sexually transmitted diseases (STDs) are prevalent among adolescents (although substantial cross-national differences suggest big gaps in the efficacy of education and prevention efforts). In the mid-1990s, gonorrhea infections reported per 100,000 young people, ages 15–19, numbered 596 in Russia, 572 in the US, 77 in England and Wales, 59 in Canada, and 2 in Sweden (Panchaud et al., 2000). Because early sex is sometimes coerced, teen sex raises concerns about sexual abuse of young people who are largely powerless and often unsophisticated. Fully 60 percent of American women who had first intercourse before age 15 reported they had been forced to have sex (Moore, Nord, and Peterson, 1989). The discovery that adult men sometimes fathered teenagers' babies (Males and Chew, 1996) made sexual abuse of minors a further justification for a public health war on teen sex and pregnancy in the US. Formative sexual experiences resonate across the life-course. American women who, as children, had sexual contact with an adult are at greater risk of sexually transmitted disease, teenage childbearing, and multiple sex partners as an adult (Browning and Laumann, 1997). In France, sexual precocity intrudes on the formation and maintenance of marital unions: those who are younger when they first have sex are less likely to marry, less likely to stay married, and more likely to have multiple sex partners (Bozon, 1996).

Of all the concerns with adolescent sexuality, however, teenage pregnancy receives the most attention, especially in the US. The difficulty is not so much that young women become pregnant as that they become single mothers. The 1950s' baby boom also had its share of teenage mothers, but they were usually married teenagers. Because age at first intercourse declined while age at first marriage rose, women have been exposed at younger ages and for longer periods to the risk of unmarried pregnancy. Where out-of-wedlock pregnancies once led to marriage, they increasingly result in either abortion (now legalized) or single motherhood. And, in contrast to Europe, unmarried mothers are less likely to have the support of a steady cohabiting relationship (Teitler, 2002). To be sure, early twentieth-century social reformers were also alarmed about sexually active girls (Nathanson, 1991). Their concern was the damage to a woman's marital prospects. Even during the Great Depression, a decade after the flappers of the 1920s first challenged premarital sex taboos, sexual propriety was still an asset in the marriage market: if she were conservative in her sexual behavior, an attractive, working-class girl stood a better chance of finding a middle-class husband (Elder, 1969). Today, having children outside of marriage reduces the chances a woman will marry (Upchurch, Lilliard and Panis, 2001), but high divorce rates demonstrate that marriage no longer offers women the security it once did. In fact, in California, a furor broke out over the revelation that social workers were trying to get men to marry their pregnant, underage partners, rather than sending these adult males to prison for statutory rape (Treas, 1999).

In keeping with the changes in women's roles, contemporary concerns with teenage motherhood focus on career consequences, not marriage-market penalties (Nathanson, 1991). Early motherhood, it is argued, consigns women to poverty by disrupting schooling and careers. The children of teen mothers are also a concern, because they are disadvantaged in terms of birth weight and cognitive development (Alan Guttmacher Institute, 1994). With US teen pregnancy in 1997 at its lowest level in 20 years, Jeffrey P. Koplan, Director for the Center for Disease Control, explained the broad benefits of this trend: "Few teens are ready for the challenges of parenthood. When they delay this responsibility, it enables them to gain the education and maturity they need to be good parents and good citizens" (National Center on Health Statistics, 2001).

Since the mid-1970s, teen childbearing has declined in Europe as well as the US, Canada, New Zealand, and Australia (Teitler, 2002). US rates remain markedly higher than those of other developed countries. Rates are higher still for African Americans (Singh, Darroch, and Frost, 2001). They are lower for immigrants, a pattern that also holds for Canada (Maticka-Tundale, Barrett, and McKay, 2000) and Britain (Singh, Darroch, and Frost, 2001). In the early and mid-1990s, there were 57 babies born to every 1,000 American women, ages 15–19, as compared to 29 in Britain, 11 in Germany, and 4 in Japan (Alan Guttmacher Institute, 1998). Since Americans disapprove of teen sex, their general lack of candor about sexual matters has been faulted for sending mixed messages that contribute to teen pregnancy (Jones et al., 1986). This cultural explanation may be insufficient, if only because teen-age childbearing in English-speaking countries closely tracks trends in adult fertility (Teitler, 2002). Disadvantage increases the likelihood of early childbearing in both the US and Britain (Singh, Darroch, and Frost, 2001). The US stands out in terms of teen pregnancy rates, in part, because it has proportionately more poor people than Britain does. Regardless of socioeconomic level, American teens are less likely to use contraceptives and more likely to have a baby than their British counterparts. This points to policy differences – less access in the US to contraception due to the lack of a national health system and less vigorous government efforts to reduce the socioeconomic disadvantages that shape the childbearing choices of young people (Singh, Darroch, and Frost, 2001).

Numerous antecedents of teen sexual activity and teen pregnancy have been identified, including psychological dispositions, hormone levels, partner dynamics, poverty, school problems, risk-taking (e.g., substance abuse), religious beliefs, and community context (Mott et al., 1996; Udry, 1988; Brewster, Billy and Grady, 1993; Sucoff and Upchurch, 1998; Singh, Darroch, and Frost, 2001; Kirby, 2001). Although peers are important, families remain powerful influences. Parents determine the broad circumstances of their children's upbringing, communicate and model their own values, and monitor their offspring's behavior. Through various pathways, family disruption leads to having sex at an earlier age (Kiernan and Hobcraft, 1997). Because low parental education and family disruption contribute to teen pregnancy, the ups and downs in teen birth rates in the US have been driven, in part, by demographic trends in broader family structure (Manlove et al., 2000).

At the intimate level of the household, however, teens are less likely to pursue risky sexual behavior when they have a good relationship with a parent who disapproves of such conduct. For example, positively perceived mother-child relationships, maternal disapproval of teen sex, and maternal discussion about birth control deter sexual activity and promote consistent contraceptive use among African American teens (Jaccard, Dittus, and Gordon, 1996). Perhaps because AIDS increased the urgency of parent–child communication about sex, 70 percent of young black and Hispanic adolescents say that parents have discussed STDs with them, but fewer report parent–child conversations about contraception and other aspects of sexuality (Miller et al., 1998). Teenagers talk about sex more readily with their mothers than with their fathers (ibid.), a finding that holds not only for heterosexuals, but also for gay, lesbian, and bisexual youngsters (D'Augelli, Hershberger, and Pilkington, 1998). Growing up in an unfavorable family environment (e.g., living apart from parents before age 14 or having parents who drink heavily or use illegal drugs) greatly increases the likelihood that women will have been sexually abused (Moore, Nord, and Peterson, 1989). On the other hand, parental support and monitoring reduce the number of sex partners, especially for teens with troubling histories of sexual abuse (Luster and Small, 1997).

Few people today view families as sufficient to prevent teen pregnancy or AIDS. Americans favor sex education in the schools by nearly seven to one (National Opinion Research Center, 2002), although parents can refuse to let their youngsters participate. Conservatives advocate "Just Say No" abstinence programs, but others support candid instruction about sexuality and safe sex. Evaluation studies show that abstinence-only programs do not deter sex, nor do discussions of contraception lead to a rise in sexual intercourse (Kirby, 1997). Effective programs give the facts about the risks of unprotected sex and methods of protection (ibid.). They have specific goals, such as changing behavioral norms (rather just giving students information on which to choose) (Kirby, 2001). They have teachers who are committed and trained, and they teach strategies for communicating, negotiating, and saying no to peer and partner pressure. Since teens facing poor schooling and job prospects are at high risk of pregnancy, youth development programs offering counseling, tutoring, and job placement can also affect adolescent sexual choices. Whatever its content and efficacy, sex education is a staple of American adolescence. Although only 51 percent of women ages 40–44 had had formal sex education by age 18, the figure stood at 96 percent for 18- and 19-year-olds in 1995 (Abma et al., 1997).

## From Procreation to Pleasure in Marriage

At least in Western societies, the marital sex act has been endowed with remarkable importance. Consistent with early Christianity's preoccupation with reproduction, the failure to consummate a marriage was sufficient grounds to annul the union. Marital sex, however, has been shrouded in privacy, despite its importance to pair bonding and the perpetuation of the family. Fortunately, demographers have been able to infer some changes in sexual practices across the centuries from declines in marital fertility. Separating sexual pleasure in marriage from its reproductive consequences stands as an important achievement in family life.

Besides the trend to smaller families, evidence of the marital fertility transition is seen in the fact that married women stopped having babies at younger ages and at lower parities. Birth control, once unthinkable and tainted by its association with illicit sex, ultimately found a place within the realm of conscious choice and domestic respectability. At the end of the eighteenth century, as Thomas Robert Malthus scolded about the improper arts employed to avoid the reproductive consequences of sexual relations, married couples in rural France were altering their sexual practices – using abstinence and withdrawal to prevent pregnancy. These demanding contraceptive methods required partners to cooperate and sacrifice sexual pleasure to reduce family size. Today's couples are the beneficiaries of a long political struggle to legalize the distribution of birth-control information as well as many scientific advances in contraceptive methods. Partners enjoy less obtrusive and more reliable means of contraception. As a consequence, married couples can and do have spontaneous, pleasure-oriented sex without giving much thought to the possibility of unwanted pregnancy.

At the beginning of the twenty-first century, there remain few, if any, differentials in contraceptive practice in the US. Whites and blacks, Catholics and Protestants, are equally and universally likely to use modern family planning. Nor is contraception just a stopping strategy that couples adopt after achieving their desired family size. Couples use contraception to prevent premarital pregnancy, to time the first birth, and to space later ones – in short, to synchronize biology with the complex timetables of family, work, and leisure. While couples once structured their sex lives to avoid pregnancy, they must now self-consciously reorganize their sexual practices in order to make babies.

## Making Marriage Erotic

The separation of sexual pleasure from procreation has eroticized partnered relationships. Coital frequency, for example, increased among married Americans in the 1970s when legal abortion and the pill reduced the fear of pregnancy (Ryder and Westoff, 1977). We know relatively little about the intimate details of married life in the more distant past. Victorian ideals of sexual restraint would have us believe that the marriage bed was a rather sedate place, where sexually inhibited women resigned themselves to thinking about God, country, and their wallpaper patterns. The surprising discovery of Clelia Mosher's unpublished sex questionnaires has challenged this view: the college-educated American wives whom she surveyed between 1892 and 1920 viewed nonprocreative sex in a generally favorable light, even if their cautious endorsements hinged on their spiritual aspirations, rather than on rapturous coital experience (Ericksen and Steffen, 1999). Without discounting the importance of marital sex to earlier generations, marriage has become more erotic in many ways. Husbands and wives hold high expectations for sexual aspects of their relationship.

The twentieth century saw the development of a new middle-class family norm – the companionate marriage. While previous generations had been content with an instrumental partnership dictating separate spheres for husband and wife, the modern companionate model called on married couples to find their satisfaction in the intimacy of their shared lives. Sex was a key component in this new marriage model. "Sexperts," including family-life educators, advice columnists, and marriage counselors, emphasized that sexual compatibility and mutual satisfaction were essential to marital happiness (Ericksen and Steffen, 1999). Americans took this advice to heart. A study of US college students over six decades reports that both men and women increasingly came to regard mutual attraction as important in mate choice (Buss et al., 2001).

Making marriage satisfyingly erotic called for instruction in sexual techniques. Given reigning ideas about gender differences in sexual responsiveness, pedagogical attention was devoted to discouraging the female inhibitions and male boorishness that were thought to impede orgasms for wives and sexual satiation for their husbands. Experts promoted this view of sex and marriage (Ericksen and Steffen, 1999). For example, *Ideal Marriage*, the bestselling marriage manual by the Dutch physician, Theodoor Van de Velde, was popular reading for American couples through most of the first half of the twentieth century (Bullough, 1994). Van de Velde's message was that wives, not just husbands, could enjoy sex, given good communication, patience, and a loving and skilled partner. Detailing ten coital positions, Van de Velde encouraged orgasms, preferably simultaneous ones, as well as noncoital sex and foreplay, to enhance the coital experience. The book's explicit discussion of marital sex illustrates the trend toward greater knowledge about sexual biology and greater candor about sexual behavior.

Each new generation of brides and grooms knows more about physiology, reproduction, and sexual practices than did their own parents. This is, in part, a consequence of the spread of family planning, which includes at least a rudimentary dose of sex education. However, there is also greater openness about sexual matters. In the 1930s, US decency codes dictated that movies show even married couples in separate beds. After the 1950s, sexually explicit material, ranging from birth-control information to pornography, became more widely available in the US due to court cases confirming Constitutional protections of free speech. Today, Van de Velde's legacy is evident in women's magazines where articles such as "How to Share His Secret Sex Dream" are sandwiched between domestic features on cooking and child rearing. Once considered only as erotica for men, sex videos are now marketed as education and entertainment for heterosexual couples.

Compared to their parents' generation, married couples not only know more about sex, but also have more first-hand sexual experience. The 1920s marked a watershed for premarital sexual experimentation in the US (Kinsey et al., 1953). While the honeymoon was once a momentous sexual initiation, 70 percent of men and 58 percent of women in recent US birth cohorts (i.e., 1963–74) report having had vaginal intercourse with their mate before marriage (Laumann et al., 1994). Sex is an integral part of courtship, as indicated by the fact that only 6 percent of male and 16 percent of female respondents in Britain reported that they first had sexual intercourse at marriage (Wellings et al., 1994). More and more newlyweds have shared a bed as cohabitors. By the late 1980s, half of recently married Americans had cohabited (Bumpass and Sweet, 1989). Increasingly, marriages involve a husband and/or a bride who has been married before. As the sexual practices of single and married people converged, sexual advice books stopped being called marriage manuals, because they had a much broader audience.

Married couples elaborate their sexual scripts to include more sexual practices than in the past. According to Kinsey and associates (1953), married women born after 1900 were more adventurous than their predecessors – fondling the male genitalia, making love in the nude, and being on top during sexual intercourse. The trend to a more diverse repertoire of sexual practices has continued. Although leveling off for recent cohorts, lifetime experience with oral sex increased sharply between the Great Depression cohorts (born 1933–7) and the cutting edge of the Baby Boom (1948–52). Among 25–29-year-old American women in the 1992 National Health and Social Life Survey (NHSLS), 76 percent reported ever having given oral sex as compared to 39 percent of women aged 55–59 (Laumann et al., 1994). British data from the National Survey of Sexual Attitudes and Life Styles confirm similar trends in experience with oral sex (Wellings et al., 1994). Rising living standards have abetted sexual experimentation, because married couples enjoy unprecedented privacy. While having preschool children can interfere with a couple's sex life (Donnelley, 1993), married people no longer face the constraints of earlier times when several family members often shared a room or even a bed.

To be sure, some groups remain relatively conventional in their sexual practices (Mahay, Laumann, and Michaels, 2001). Americans display greater variation in sexual behavior than do the British (Michael et al., 2001). Even controlling for factors such as age, marital status, and education, white Americans are significantly more likely to have oral sex than are Mexican Americans and African Americans. Within racial groups, college-educated Americans follow less conventional sexual scripts than do persons with less schooling. Similarly, in Britain, social class is positively associated with oral, anal, and nonpenetrative sex for both men and women (Wellings et al., 1994).

## The Sex Lives of Married People

While today's married couples may be more adventurous than earlier generations, most husbands and wives settle into fairly routine, if largely satisfying, sex lives. Among British informants who had vaginal sex in the past year, married people are less likely to report having oral, anal, and nonpenetrative sex than their cohabiting or unmarried counterparts (Wellings et al., 1994). In the US, married people are, if anything, *less* likely to have incorporated oral sex into their *last* sex act than are unmarried people (Laumann et al., 1994), perhaps because married people devote less time to their sexual encounters than singles do. Only 9 percent of married men said their last sexual event lasted an hour or more, compared to 38 percent of noncohabiting, never-married men (Laumann et al., 1994).

Married people have higher coital frequency than do singles. Having a regular sex partner, married people in Britain have sex more often than do the unmarried; the coital frequency of married persons is slightly lower than that of cohabitors, however, even controlling for the fact that cohabitors are younger (Wellings et al., 1994). There is not much evidence that married people have more physically pleasurable sex than other people, but married women do say that they derive more emotional satisfaction from their sexual relations than do cohabiting and single women (Waite, 2001). Is sex really the key to a happy marriage, as family life educators long argued? Affectionate ties and low conflict are associated with greater sexual attraction and frequency (Blumstein and Schwartz, 1983). About 16 percent of co-resident married people in the US (excluding those who were sick, had recently given birth or were pregnant) admitted that they had not had sex in the last month. Certainly, couples that never have sex tend to be unhappy and to have thought about separating (Donnelley, 1993). Coital frequency, however, is a poor gauge of marital quality, because high levels of sexual activity also occur in violent marriages, where husbands use physical threats to extort sex from their wives (DeMaris, 1997).

Coital frequency declines with duration of unions (Wellings et al., 1994), no doubt reflecting both habituation (i.e., novelty wears off) and the biological effects of aging. Older men report higher levels of sexual dysfunction (Laumann, Paik, and Rosen, 2001). Men aged 50–59 were three times more likely to say that they were disinterested in sex or had erection problems than were their counterparts aged 18–29. Women were less likely to report sexual problems with increasing age. Certainly, couples no longer take it for granted that menopause or advancing years mark the end of a sexual relationship. According to a US survey, half of married persons 60 and older had had sex in the last month – about four times a month, on average (Marsiglio and Donnelley, 1991). One-quarter of married people 76 and older were still sexually active. Until fairly recently, erotic interests among older people were regarded as humorous and unseemly, and their physical attractiveness and capacity for sex were discounted. Just as Viagra and hormone replacement therapy reduced the physical impediments to sex in later life, a host of popular sex books by physicians and scientists have offered up an enthusiastic prognosis for sex in middle age and beyond. Conveniently, *Love and Sex after 60* was published in a large-print edition (Butler and Lewis, 1996).

## Extramarital Sex

Most people believe that it is wrong for married people to have sexual relations with anybody except their marital partner. Fully 80 percent of Americans and 67 percent of the British say extramarital sex is "always wrong" (Widmer, Treas, and Newcomb, 1998). Similar views are voiced in Australia (59 percent), Canada (68 percent), Ireland (80 percent), Japan (58 percent), The Netherlands (63 percent), New Zealand (75 percent), Sweden (68 percent), and other Western countries. Although some people agree that extenuating circumstances can sometimes justify extramarital sex, virtually none of the respondents in this cross-national survey say that extramarital sex is "not at all wrong." In the US and Britain, only 2 percent saw nothing wrong with extramarital sex. Nor is there any evidence that moral judgments on extramarital sex are softening. British condemnation remains high (Scott, 1998). If anything, disapproval has increased in the US since the mid-1980s, perhaps in response to fears about AIDS (Treas, in press). Although women are more disapproving than men of extramarital sex, US data show that the gender gap narrowed after the mid-1980s when men adopted harsher views (Scott, 1998).

Despite a culture that accepts a wider range of sexual behavior, the importance of monogamy and sexual exclusivity in marriage is scarcely questioned. Fully 99 percent of married Americans say that they expect their partner to be sexually exclusive, as do 94 percent of cohabiting heterosexuals (Treas and Giesen, 2000). Among Europeans surveyed in the 1980s, 84 percent said that faithfulness was very important for a successful marriage (Harding and Phillips, 1986). In the late 1960s and early 1970s, "swinging" and "wife-swapping," a couple-oriented lifestyle of sexual adventuring, offered a brief, ideological challenge to sexual exclusivity. In the 1980s, this social innovation fell victim to sexual jealousies and fears of AIDS. Although some people may fall short of the ideal, the notion of limiting the sex lives of married people to marriage goes largely uncontested. Even though they are almost never enforced, laws against adultery remain on the books in many US states, because religious groups argue for their symbolic importance in supporting marriage and promoting sexual morality.

Men are more likely to be unfaithful than are women (Treas and Giesen, 2000). At elevated risk of infidelity are those married people who have greater interest in sex and greater sexual experience. Conservative sexual values and frequent attendance at religious services, on the other hand, buffer against the risk of infidelity. Having opportunities to meet potential sex partners outside of the company of one's spouse increases the likelihood of infidelity. Americans whose jobs place them in intimate contact with others are more likely to be unfaithful (ibid.). Similarly, British men and women who work away from home overnight are more likely to report having had multiple sex partners than do others (Wellings et al., 1994). Although social class may be positively associated with sexual infidelity among the British (ibid.), socioeconomic indicators have little effect on the extramarital behavior of Americans (Treas and Giesen, 2000).

Intimate social networks can promote sexual fidelity. In-laws, for example, monitor behavior, stabilize the union with support, and generally constitute a relationship-specific asset that would be put at risk by marital indiscretions. Individuals who know and enjoy their partner's family and friends are more likely to be sexually exclusive than are individuals without such intimate ties (ibid.). Although most cohabitors advocate sexual exclusivity just like married people, they are at higher risk of sexual infidelity, even controlling for the shorter duration of their unions and their more permissive sexual values (ibid.). This is generally attributed to the fact that cohabitors have lower investments in their unions – and less to lose – than do married people. Those who report lower subjective satisfaction with their relationship are also more likely to be unfaithful.

Sexual infidelity is seen as a danger to ongoing unions (Lawson, 1988), because it taps deeply held feelings of sexual jealousy and partner possession, diverts time and energy from the marital relationship, poses risks to health and reputation, and compromises sex as a basis for pair-bonding. Women, who tend to view affection as a requisite for sex, are more likely than men to describe extramarital sex as a threat to the relationship (Glass and Wright, 1992). By the same token, a married woman having an extramarital relationship is more likely to be perceived as being in love, committed, and ready to marry than is a man (Sprecher, Regan, and McKinney, 1998).

Despite clinical and anecdotal evidence, the nature of the association between extramarital sex and divorce remains uncertain. We do not know how frequently sexual infidelity figures in the breakdown of a marriage. Tellingly, 40 percent of recently divorced Americans said their spouse was involved with someone else before the marriage ended, but only 15 percent of these respondents admitted that they themselves were extramaritally involved (South and Lloyd, 1995). Neither is the link between extramarital sex and marital quality well understood. Although some studies report an association between infidelity and low marital satisfaction (Treas and Giesen, 2000), there is a lack of longitudinal data to assess the extent to which marital unhappiness causes infidelity as opposed to infidelity causing marital unhappiness. Although adultery may upset marital relationships, a new sexual relationship is also a strategy for exiting an unhappy marriage. Respondents' retrospective accounts of their relationships may be self-serving rationalizations. Divorced and separated persons who have had extramarital sex insist that their own infidelity was caused by marital problems, even as they maintain that their spouse's infidelity was a cause of their marital difficulties (Spanier and Margolis, 1983).

Although sexual infidelity is a private matter, it maintains a high cultural profile, as evidenced by the fact that extramarital sex is almost as common as marital sex on American television series (Lowry, 2000). Media preoccupation with adultery may explain why married Americans believe that other married people do not take fidelity as seriously as they do (Greeley, 1991). Despite adultery's high profile, empirical data do not show sexual infidelity run rampant. Recent US estimates for the percentage of married persons with a secondary sex partner in the last year range from 1.5 percent to 3.6 percent (Smith 1991; Choi, Catania, and Dolcini, 1994; Leigh, Temple, and Trocki, 1993). In Britain, 4.5 percent of married men aged 16–59 and 1.9 percent of comparable women reported two or more heterosexual partners in the last year (Wellings et al., 1994). While extramarital sex is underreported, these low figures are in keeping with public opinion about the importance of sexual exclusivity in marriage.

## Making Same-Sex Relationships Domestic

In Britain in the early 1990s, 1.1 percent of men and 0.4 percent of women reported having at least one same-sex partner during the past year (Wellings et al., 1994). In the US, the figures were 2.7 percent for men and 1.3 percent for women (Laumann et al., 1994), although large cities with established communities of gays and lesbians have higher concentrations. So long as gays and lesbians remained a marginalized minority pursuing closeted lives to avoid harassment and discrimination, the heterosexual public saw them largely in terms of exotic sexual practices, deviations from conventional gender roles, and presumed psychological pathology. Little thought was given to the possibility that gays and lesbians had families, much less confronted some of the same family challenges as heterosexuals. As acceptance of same-sex relations has increased, public discourse on gays and lesbians no longer revolves around their sexual lifestyles. Increasingly, nonheterosexuals are seen to share family and relationship concerns that resonate with heterosexuals. Gillian Dunne (2000: 31) points out that the presence of children in lesbian unions not only smoothes relations between women and their own parents, but more generally "helps make intelligible a lifestyle that can appear strange and 'other' to heterosexual observers." More widely appreciated by the general public, the domestic aspects of the lives of lesbians and gays have given rise to family policy initiatives and a growing research literature on nonheterosexuals as partners and parents.

The decriminalization of homosexual activity represents a legal revolution in values around the globe. This liberalization in the law has been attributed to the ideological trends favoring sex for pleasure over sex for procreative ends (Frank and McEneaney, 1999). Progress protecting private rights to sexual pleasure has been followed by political efforts to secure parity with heterosexuals in other domains, including housing, employment, and family. Public discourse has shifted from the sex lives of gays and lesbians to broader issues. Although coverage of nonheterosexuals in US news magazines of the 1980s focused on AIDS and sexual lifestyles, the top story in the early 1990s was a civil rights issue, the treatment of gays in the military service (Bennett, 2000). The defining concerns for lesbians and gays reach beyond sex and sexual orientation to embrace the broader family realm.

The AIDS crisis that integrated and mobilized the homosexual community brought to the fore the difficulties that confront caring relationships that do not conform to heterosexual family conventions. A spate of new legislation has recognized domestic partnerships and extended rights to nonheterosexual unions. This is a signal accomplishment, because until recently, lesbians and gays were regarded as irrelevant to the institution of marriage. In Europe and the US, there was no need for laws to bar marriages between gay men or between lesbians, because same-sex unions were conceived as being entirely outside of the scope of the marital institution (Glendon, 1989). Despite progress, nonheterosexuals have not achieved parity with heterosexuals when it comes to family life. As recently as 1990, 89 percent of respondents in the British Social Attitudes Survey did not think male homosexual couples should be allowed to adopt a baby under the same conditions as heterosexual couples; 81 percent voiced the same reservations about lesbian couples (Hayes, 1997). (Ironically, Americans preferred gays and lesbians to heterosexual men as babysitters, presumably because heterosexual males are not thought to be as well suited to nurturing activities (Regan and Ramirez, 2000).) To underscore the continuing resistance to incorporating nonheterosexuals into American family life, a politically conservative, highly religious social movement cites homosexuality's threat to families as a justification for opposing gay rights.

Despite resistance, gays and lesbians find greater acceptance today. Americans condemning same-sex relations as "always wrong" dropped from 77 percent in 1988 to 58 percent in 1998 (Treas, 2002). In Britain, disapproval also declined (Scott, 1998). While the growing tolerance of premarital sex was due to the replacement of conservative cohorts by more liberal ones, the greater acceptance of homosexual sex resulted because cohorts actually became more tolerant over time (Treas, in press). In a striking case of the diffusion of cultural innovations, less educated Americans moved closer to the permissive views of college graduates. Although conservative religious denominations oppose homosexuality, all but the most frequent American churchgoers softened their views on same-sex relations between 1988 and 1998. Men are less tolerant than women, no doubt because misogyny and homophobia are the cornerstones of hegemonic masculinity. Women's interest in the emotional content of relations may account for their greater sympathy for same-sex relationships (Scott, 1998). Not surprisingly, gender differences play out in families, where nonheterosexuals are more likely to disclose their sexual orientation to female than male relatives (D'Augelli, Hershberger, and Pilkington, 1998; Mays et al., 1998).

In part in response to rejection by kin, gays and lesbians have broadened notions of family to include voluntary ties of affection incorporating friends, lovers, ex-lovers, and others. As Weeks, Heaphy, and Donovan point out in chapter 20 of this volume, nonheterosexuals define family as "the families we choose," broad networks of supportive friendships that are forged not by blood and marriage, but out of affection and reciprocity (Weston, 1991; Nardi, 1999). The families-of-choice notion is part of a self-conscious effort by lesbians and gays not only to distinguish their family lives from those of their heterosexual counterparts, but even to argue for the superiority of their more voluntary and egalitarian relationships. There is a tension, of course, between constructions of family difference and efforts to define nonheterosexuals as just like heterosexuals, particularly in terms of parenting qualifications. An emerging research literature is beginning to clarify these assertions, pointing particularly to differences that emerge from the gender of partners, as opposed to their sexual orientation or practices.

Because they cannot rely on ready-made scripts based on gender differences to govern their relationships, gay and lesbian partnerships are organized along more egalitarian lines than heterosexual unions. While housework usually falls to women in heterosexual couples, gay and lesbian partners are more likely to split the chores (Kurdek, 1993; Sullivan, 1996). Lesbians often share the tasks, perhaps consistent with the high levels of relationship quality that they report (Kurdek, 2001). Same-sex partners have more autonomy than do heterosexual ones (Kurdek, 1998). For example, gay couples are less concerned with monogamy than are heterosexuals or lesbians (Blumstein and Schwartz, 1983). As studies of heterosexual cohabitors have suggested (Brines and Joyner, 1999), equality is not just an ideological commitment, but also the necessary precondition for stability in unions that lack the protection and presumed continuity of marriage. Without formal marriage, gay partners face fewer barriers to ending a union (Kurdek, 1998). They get less support from family members than do heterosexual couples without children (Kurdek, 2001), and the upshot is more frequent relationship break-ups, at least for gay men (Kurdek, 1998).

Other research has addressed outcomes for children raised by parents who are not heterosexual. Estimates for the US suggest that only 1 percent of children, ages 18 and younger, have a parent who self-identifies as nonheterosexual (Stacey and Biblarz, 2001). Scholarly accounts have focused on lesbians (but see Dunne, 2001), because gay men do not raise children as frequently. Although lesbians sometimes become mothers via donor insemination (Dunne, 2000), children of lesbians are usually the products of an earlier, heterosexual marriage (Stacey and Biblarz, 2001). Studies typically conclude that parents' sexual orientation is of little consequence for the development of offspring. Others charge that the interpretation of data has been colored by sympathetic reactions against the negative stereotyping of nonheterosexuals. The small but real differences observed between children raised by heterosexual and nonheterosexual parents, they argue, have been downplayed (Cameron, 1997; Stacey and Biblarz, 2001). A careful reading of more rigorous psychological research on child outcomes suggests that the nonbiological parent in a lesbian partnership is more intimately involved in the child's life than the typical father – although this is probably a function of the gender of lesbians, rather than their sexual orientation (Stacey and Biblarz, 2001). Despite their remarkable creativity in negotiating innovative ways of parenting (Dunne, 2000), it is testimony to heterosexual hegemony that even lesbian couples, who typically embrace egalitarian relationships, sometimes fall back on a conventional breadwinner-and-caregiver division of labor in order to give their children an "ordinary" family life (Sullivan, 1996). As for outcomes for nonheterosexuals' children, they come under less parental pressure to conform to rigid gender stereotypes and so they do not. They are also more open to homoerotic relationships (although they do not seem to be more likely to self-identify as gay or lesbian) (Stacey and Biblarz, 2001). Of course, sexual orientation and dyad gender composition may not be the only explanation for parenting differences between heterosexuals and nonheterosexuals. Lesbian mothers are apt to be older, more likely to live in an urban area, less politically conservative, and so on, and these differences may contribute to observed differences in parent roles or child outcomes.

## Conclusion and Discussion

Family control of sexuality once meant avoiding out-of-wedlock births and social disapproval by channeling sexuality into marriage. Norms about sexual behavior have changed, the lives of adolescents and young adults follow a less predictable course. Fewer and fewer young people fulfill the traditional expectation that marriage should occur before having sex, living together, siring children, becoming pregnant, or producing babies. Because age at first sex has declined and age at first marriage has risen, there is now a yawning gap of years that many young people fill by exploring various sexual practices with different sexual partners. This behavior is not without risks, especially in the US, where unprotected sex results in higher rates of teen pregnancy and sexually transmitted disease. Rather than discrediting the family's control of sexuality, these changes serve to highlight the importance of family structure, parent–child communication, and parental values for young people, who navigate their early sexual experiences more successfully when they have a positive family context.

Early sexual experience echoes through the life-course, affecting subsequent sexual behavior and even the likelihood of marriage and divorce. Premarital sex spills over into marriage. Given greater sexual sophistication, reliable contraception, and a companionate ideal of marriage, twentieth-century marriage became more erotic. Couples come to marriage with a much broader repertoire of sexual experience and practices than in the past. Committed – at least ideologically – to sexual fidelity, married couples today can expect to have mutually satisfying physical relations that will continue well into old age. Thus, most of the life-course – from early adolescence to the far side of old age – is sexualized. Disapproval of same-sex relations also declined. Paradoxically, as heterosexual unions became sexier, same-sex ones came to be seen as struggling with domestic concerns such as partnering and parenting that take their toll on the sex lives of married heterosexuals. Thus, heterosexual marriage has been eroticized, even as sex has receded as the defining characteristic of same-sex relationships.

### References

Abma, J. C., Chandra, A., Mosher, W., Peterson, L., and Piccinino, L. (1997) *Fertility, Family Planning, and Women's Health: New Data from the 1995 National Survey of Family Growth. Vital Health Statistics*. Washington, DC: National Center for Health Statistics, 23.

Alan Guttmacher Institute (1994) *Sex and America's Teenagers*. New York: Alan Guttmacher Institute.

Alan Guttmacher Institute (1998) *Into a New World: Young Women's Sexual and Reproductive Lives*. New York: Alan Guttmacher Institute.

Bennett, L. (2000) Fifty years of prejudice in the media. *Gay and Lesbian Review*, 7, 30–5.

Blumstein, P., and Schwartz, P. (1983) *American Couples*. New York: Morrow.

Bozon, M. (1996) Reaching adult sexuality: First intercourse and its implications: From calendar to attitudes. In M. Bozon and H. Leridon (eds.), *Sexuality in the Social Sciences*. Aldershot: Dartmouth.

Brewster, K. L., Billy, J. O. G., and Grady, W. R. (1993) Social context and adolescent behavior: The impact of community on the transition to sexual activity. *Social Forces*, 71, 713–40.

Brines, J., and Joyner, K. (1999) The ties that bind: Principles of cohesion in cohabitation and marriage. *American Sociological Review*, 64, 333–55.

Browning, C. R., and Laumann, E. O. (1997) Sexual contact between children and adults: A life course perspective. *American Sociological Review*, 62, 540–60.

Bullough, V. L. (1994) *Science in the Bedroom: A History of Sex Research*. New York: Basic Books.

Bumpass, L. L., and Sweet, J. A. (1989) National estimates of cohabitation. *Demography*, 26, 615-25.

Buss, D. M., Shackelford, T. K., Kirkpatrick, L., and Larsen, R. (2001) A half century of mate preferences: The cultural evolution of values. *Journal of Marriage and the Family*, 63, 491–503.

Butler, R. N., and Lewis, M. I. (1996) *Love and Sex after 60* (rev. ed.). Thorndike, ME: G. K. Hall.

Cameron, P. C. K. (1997) Did the APA misrepresent the scientific literature to courts in support of homosexual custody? *Journal of Psychology*, 131, 313–32.

Cherlin, A. J. (1992) *Marriage, Divorce, Remarriage*. Cambridge, MA: Harvard University Press.

Choi, K. H., Catania, J. A., and Dolcini, M. M. (1994) Extramarital sex and HIV risk behavior among American adults: Results from the National AIDS Behavior Survey. *American Journal of Public Health*, 84, 2003–7.

D'Augelli, A. R., Hershberger, S. L., and Pilkington, N. W. (1998) Lesbian, gay, and bisexual youth and their families: Disclosure of sexual orientation and its consequences. *American Journal of Orthopsychiatry*, 68, 361–71.

DeMaris, A. (1997) Elevated sexual activity in violent marriages: Hypersexuality or sexual extortion? *Journal of Sex Research*, 34, 361–73.

Donnelley, D. A. (1993) Sexually inactive marriages. *Journal of Sex Research*, 30, 171–9.

Dunne, G. A. (2000) Opting into motherhood: Lesbians blurring the boundaries and transforming the meaning of parenthood and kinship. *Gender and Society*, 14, 11–35.

Dunne, G. A. (2001) The lady vanishes: Reflections on the experiences of married and divorced non-heterosexual fathers. *Sociological Research Online*, 6, U113–U129.

Elder, G. H. (1969) Appearance and education in marriage mobility. *American Sociological Review*, 34, 519–33.

Ericksen, J. A., and Steffen, W. S. A. (1999) *Kiss and Tell: Surveying Sex in the Twentieth Century*. Cambridge, MA: Harvard University Press.

Frank, D. J., and McEneaney, E. H. (1999) The individualization of society and the liberalization of state policies on same-sex sexual relations, 1984–1995. *Social Forces*, 77, 911–44.

Freedman, D. S., and Thornton, A. (1979) The long-term impact of pregnancy at marriage on the family's economic circumstances. *Family Planning Perspectives*, 11, 6–13, 18–21.

Gates, G. J., and. Sonenstein, F. L (2000) Heterosexual genital sexual activity among adolescent males: 1988 and 1995. *Family Planning Perspectives*, 32, 295–7, 304.

Glass, S. P., and Wright, T. L. (1992) Justifications for extramarital relationships: The association between attitudes, behaviors, and gender. *Journal of Sex Research*, 29, 361–87.

Glendon, M. A. (1989) *The Transformation of Family Law: State, Law, and Family in the United States and Europe*. Chicago: University of Chicago Press.

Greeley, A. M. (1991) *Faithful Attraction*. New York: Tom Doherty Associates.

Harding, S., and Phillips, D. (1986) *Contrasting Values in Western Europe*. London: Macmillan.

Hayes, B. (1997) The influence of gender on public attitudes toward homosexual rights in Britain. *International Journal of Public Opinion Research*, 9, 361–85.

Jaccard, J., Dittus, P. J., and Gordon, V. V. (1996) Maternal correlates of adolescent sexual and contraceptive behavior. *Family Planning Perspectives*, 28, 159–65, 185.

Jones, E. M., Forrest, J. D., Goldman, N., Henshaw, S., Lincoln, R., Rosoff, J. I., Westoff, C. F., and Wulf, D. (1986) *Teenage Pregnancy in Industrialized Countries: A Study*. New Haven, CT: Yale University Press.

Kiernan, K. E., and Hobcraft, J. (1997) Parental divorce during childhood: Age at first intercourse, partnership and parenthood. *Population Studies*, 51, 41–55.

Kinsey, A. C., Pomeroy, W. B., Martin, C. L., and Gebhard, P. H. (1953) *Sexual Behavior in the Human Female*. Philadelphia, PA: W. B. Saunders.

Kirby, D. (1997) *No Easy Answers: Research Findings on Programs to Reduce Teen Pregnancy*. Washington, DC: National Campaign to Prevent Teen Pregnancy.

Kirby, D. (2001) Understanding what works and what doesn't in reducing adolescent sexual risk-taking. *Family Planning Perspectives*, 33, 276–81.

Kurdek, L. (1993) The allocation of household labor in gay, lesbian, and heterosexual married couples. *Journal of Social Issues*, 49, 127–39.

Kurdek, L. A. (1998) Relationship outcomes and their predictors: Longitudinal evidence from heterosexual married, gay cohabiting and lesbian cohabiting couples. *Journal of Marriage and the Family*, 60, 553–68.

Kurdek, L. A. (2001) Differences between heterosexual non-parent couples and gay, lesbian, and heterosexual-parent couples. *Journal of Family Issues*, 22, 727–54.

Laumann, E. O., Gagnon, J. H., Michael, R. T., and Michaels, S. (1994) *The Social Organization of Sexuality: Sexual Practices in the United States*. Chicago: University of Chicago Press.

Laumann, E. O., Paik, A., and Rosen, R. C. (2001) Sexual dysfunction in the United States: Prevalence and predictors. In E. O. Laumann and R. T. Michael (eds.), *Sex, Love, and Health in America: Private Choices and Public Policies*. Chicago: University of Chicago Press.

Lawson, A. (1988) *Adultery: The Analysis of Love and Betrayal*. New York: Basic Books.

Lee, J. Z., and Feng, W. (1999) *One Quarter of Humanity: Malthusian Mythology and Chinese Realities, 1700–2000*. Cambridge, MA: Cambridge University Press.

Leigh, B. C., Temple, M. T., and Trocki, K. F. (1993) The sexual behavior of U.S. adults: Results from a national survey. *American Journal of Public Health*, 83, 1400–8.

Lewis, J., and Kiernan, K. (1996) The boundaries between marriage, nonmarriage, and parenthood: Changes in behavior and policy in postwar Britain. *Journal of Family History*, 21, 372–87.

Lowry, B. (2000) Study: Sex Has Few Consequences in TV, Film. *Los Angeles Times*, March 29, F3.

Luster, T., and Small, S. A. (1997) Sexual abuse history and number of sex partners among female adolescents. *Family Planning Perspectives*, 29, 204–11.

Mahay, J., Laumann, E. O., and Michaels, S. (2001) Race, gender, and class in sexual scripts. In E. O. Laumann and R. T. Michael (eds.), *Sex, Love, and Health in America: Private Choices and Public Policies*. Chicago: University of Chicago Press.

Males, M,. and Chew, K. S. Y. (1996) The ages of fathers in California adolescent births, 1993. *American Journal of Public Health*, 86, 565–8.

Manlove, J., Terry, E., Gitelson, L., Papillo, A. R., and Russell, S. (2000) Explaining demographic trends in teenage fertility, 1980–1995. *Family Planning Perspectives*, 32, 166–75.

Marsiglio, W., and Donnelley, D. A. (1991) Sexual relations in later life: A national study of married persons. *Journals of Gerontology*, 46, S338–S344.

Maticka-Tundale, E., Barrett, M., and McKay, A. (2000) Adolescent sexual and reproductive health in Canada: A review of national data sources and their limitations. *Canadian Journal of Human Sexuality*, 9, 41–65.

Mays, V. M., Chatters, L. M., Cochran, S. D., and Mackness, J. (1998) African American families in diversity: gay men and lesbians as participants in family networks. *Journal of Comparative Family Studies*, 29, 73–87.

Michael, R. T., Wadsworth, J., Feinleib, J. A., Johnson, A. M., Laumann, E. O., and Wellings, K. (2001) Private sexual behavior, public opinion, and public health policy related to sexually transmitted diseases: A U.S.–British comparison. In E. O. Laumann and R. T. Michael (eds.), *Sex, Love, and Health in America: Private Choices and Public Policies*. Chicago: University of Chicago Press.

Miller, K. S., Kotchick, B. A., Dorsey, S., Forehand, R., and Ham, A.Y. (1998) Family communication about sex: What are parents saying and are their adolescents listening? *Family Planning Perspectives*, 30, 218–22, 235.

Moore, K. A., Nord, C. W., and Peterson, J.L. (1989) Nonvoluntary sexual activity among adolescents. *Family Planning Perspectives*, 21, 110–14.

Mott, F. L., Fondell, M. M., Hu, P. N., Kowaleski-Jones, L., and Menaghan, E. G. (1996) The determinants of first sex by age 14 in a high-risk adolescent population. *Family Planning Perspectives*, 28, 13–18.

Nardi, P. (1999) *Gay Men's Friendships*. Chicago: University of Chicago Press.

Nathanson, C. A. (1991) *Dangerous Passage: The Social Control of Sexuality in Women's Adolescence*. Philadelphia, PA: Temple University Press.

National Center on Health Statistics (2001) Teen Pregnancy Rate Reaches a Record Low in 1997.

National Opinion Research Center (2002) *General Social Survey 1972–2000 Cumulative Codebook*.

O'Connor, J. S., Orloff, A. S., and Shaver, S. (1999) *States, Markets, Families: Gender, Liberalism and Social Policy in Australia, Canada, Great Britain and the United States*. Cambridge: Cambridge University Press.

Panchaud, C., Singh, S., Feivelson, D., and Darroch, J. E. (2000) Sexually transmitted diseases among adolescents in developed countries. *Family Planning Perspectives*, 32, 24–32, 45.

Patterson, O. (1998) *Rituals of Blood: Consequences of Slavery in Two American Centuries*. Washington, DC: Civitas/Counterpoint.

Quaife, G. R. (1979) *Wanton Wenches and Wayward Wives: Peasants and Illicit Sex in Early Seventeenth Century England*. London: Croom Helm.

Regan, P. C., and Ramirez, C. (2000) Decisions on child care: do sex and sexual orientation matter? *Psychological Reports*, 86, 922–4.

Ryder, N. B., and Westoff, C. F. (1977) *The Contraceptive Revolution*. Princeton, NJ: Princeton University Press.

Santelli, J. S., Brener, N. D., Lowry, R., Bhatt, A., and Zabin, L. S. (1998) Multiple sex partners among U.S. adolescents and young adults. *Family Planning Perspectives*, 30, 271–5.

Santelli, J. S., Lindberg, L. D., Abma, J., McNeely, C. S., and Resnick, M. (2000) Adolescent sexual behavior: Estimates and trends from four national surveys. *Family Planning Perspectives*, 32, 156–65, 194.

Schneider, J. C., and Schneider, P. T. (1996) *Festival of the Poor: Fertility Decline and the Ideology of Class in Sicily, 1860–1980*. Tucson: University of Arizona Press.

Scott, J. (1998) Changing attitudes to sexual morality: A cross-national comparison. *Sociology*, 32, 815–45.

Singh, S., Darroch, J. E., and Frost, J. J. (2001) Socioeconomic disadvantage and adolescent women's sexual and reproductive behavior: The case of five developed countries. *Family Planning Perspectives*, 33, 251–9.

Smith, T. W. (1991) Adult sexual behavior in 1989: Number of partners, frequency of sexual intercourse and risk of AIDS. *Family Planning Perspectives*, 23, 102–7.

Smith, T. W. (1994) Attitudes toward sexual permissiveness: Trends, correlates, and behavioral connections. In A. S. Rossi (ed.), *Sexuality Across the Life Course*. Chicago: University of Chicago Press.

Sonenstein, F. L., Pleck, J. H., and Ku, L. C. (1991) Levels of sexual activity among adolescent males in the United States. *Family Planning Perspectives*, 23, 162–7.

South, S. J., and Lloyd, K. M. (1995) Spousal alternatives and marital dissolution. *American Sociological Review*, 60, 21–35.

Spanier, G. B., and Margolis, R. L. (1983) Marital separation and extramarital sexual behavior. *Journal of Sex Research*, 19, 23–48.

Sprecher, S., Regan, P. C., and McKinney, K. (1998) Beliefs about the outcomes of extramarital sexual relationships as a function of gender of the "cheating spouse". *Sex Roles*, 38, 301–11.

Stacey, J., and Biblarz, T. J. (2001) (How) Does the sexual orientation of parents matter? *American Sociological Review*, 66, 159–70.

Sucoff, C. A., and Upchurch, D. M. (1998) Neighborhood context and the risk of childbearing among metropolitan-area Black adolescents. *American Sociological Review*, 63, 571–5.

Sullivan, M. (1996) Rozzie and Harriet? Gender and family patterns of lesbian coparents. *Gender and Society*, 10, 747–67.

Teitler, J. O. (2002) Trends in youth sexual initiation and fertility in developed countries: 1960–1995. *Annals of the American Academy of Political and Social Science*, 580, 134–52.

Treas, J. (1999) Diversity in American families. In P. Moen, D. Dempster-McClain, and H. A. Walker (eds.), *A Nation Divided: Diversity, Inequality and Community in American Society*. Ithaca, NY: Cornell University Press.

Treas, J. (2002) How cohorts, education, and ideology shaped a new sexual revolution on American attitudes toward non-marital sex, 1972–1998. *Sociological Perspectives*, 45, 267–83.

Treas, J., and Giesen, D. (2000) Sexual infidelity among married and cohabiting Americans. *Journal of Marriage and the Family*, 62, 48–60.

Udry, J. R. (1988) Biological predispositions and social control in adolescent sexual behavior. *American Sociological Review*, 53, 709–22.

Upchurch, D., Lilliard, L. A., and Panis, C. W. A. (2001) The impact of nonmarital childbearing on subsequent marital formation and dissolution. In L. L. Wu and B. Wolfe (eds.), *Out of Wedlock: Causes and Consequences of Nonmarital Fertility*. New York: Russell Sage Foundation.

Waite, L. J. (2001) Emotional and physical satisfaction with sex in married, cohabiting, and dating unions: Do men and women differ? In E. O. Laumann and R. T. Michael (eds.), *Sex, Love, and Health in America: Private Choices and Public Policies*. Chicago: University of Chicago Press.

Wellings, K., Field, J., Johnson, A. M., and Wadsworth, J. (1994) *Sexual Behavior in Britain: The National Survey of Sexual Attitudes and Lifestyles*. London: Penguin.

Weston, K. (1991) *The Families We Choose: Lesbians, Gays, Kinship*. New York: Columbia University Press.

Widmer, E. D., Treas, J., and Newcomb, R. (1998) Attitudes toward nonmarital sex in 24 countries. *Journal of Sex Research*, 35, 349–58.

Wilhelm, B. (1998) Changes in cohabitation across cohorts: The influence of political activism. *Social Forces*, 77, 289–313.

# 24

# Feminism and the Family

Michelle Budig

> Patriarchy's chief institution is the family.
>
> – Kate Millett, *Sexual Politics*

> ...under patriarchy, female possibility has been literally massacred on the site of motherhood.
>
> – Adrienne Rich, *Of Woman Born*

> ...to suggest that mothers, by virtue of their mothering, are principally victims is an egregiously inaccurate account of many women's experience and is itself oppressive to mothers.
>
> – Sara Ruddick, *Maternal Thinking*

> It is the isolation and debasement of women under terms of male-dominated ideology that must be fought, not the activity, not the humanizing imperative, of mothering... too frequently mothering has been overassimilated into what feminists call "the shitwork".
>
> – Jean Elshtain, *Public Man, Private Woman*

To write an essay on feminism and the family requires a definition of each of those two terms and a statement of their relation to one another. What is feminism? What is the family? What do feminists think about the family and how it shapes women's lives? What impact has the feminist movement had on family life? Finally, how has feminism changed or challenged sociological analyses of the family?

As is typical in this modern and complex world, there is no simple definition of either feminism or family, nor is there any one feminist interpretation of the role of family in women's lives (as the opening four quotations from feminists exemplify). Liberal feminists have little to say about women's and men's home responsibilities, so long as women and men have equal opportunities in education and employment. Socialist and Marxist feminists advocate for socializing women's traditional family responsibilities to free them up for employment and political activism. Radical feminists debate whether the family is the source of women's oppression or the means to her liberation. Social/cultural feminists claim that the wisdom women gain through their traditional family roles can provide the antidote to patriarchy. The effects of feminist movements on family life have been interpreted positively (rape in marriage is now deemed illegal in most Westernized countries) and negatively (higher rates of divorce and single parenthood are sometimes attributed to "women's liberation").

Definitions of the family are as diverse as feminist positions on the family. Definitions of what constitutes a family are informed by social contexts that differ across history and geography. Factors that affect definitions of the family include the time period, level of industrialization, race and ethnicity, class, and cultural norms and values. In the US, images of the family differ dramatically across time: from the extended pioneering farm family of Laura Ingalls Wilder, to the nuclear family of Ward and June Cleaver in the 1950s, to the Murphy Brown mother-and-child dyad of modern times. Moreover, all of these relatively privileged European-descent families differ from matriarchal pre-Colonial Iroquois families and the forced severed relations of pre-Civil War slave families. Despite the great diversity of families – from those that incorporate extended kin to childless, dual-career couples of recent times – the family form that most feminists have taken to task has been the patriarchal, Westernized, middle- to upper-class nuclear family. Indeed, it is this family form – two heterosexual married adults and their children – that most social commentators and politicians take as the "natural" and "best" form, relegating other family forms as "broken" or inferior. It is precisely this isolated family unit that many feminists argue is the most oppressive for women.

In this chapter I discuss feminism's impact on the sociological analysis of the family, outline various feminist theories on the family, and discuss the impact of the feminist movement on family life. Specifically, I focus on what feminists say about the institution of the family, the meaning of marriage, the experience of motherhood, and the historic separation of women's family roles from employment and political activities. To demonstrate feminism's impact on sociological thinking, I will begin with a brief discussion of non-feminist thought on family structure and gender role assignments in the family.

## Nonfeminist Social Thought and the Family

### Industrialization and the doctrine of separate spheres

Since the age of industrialization, remunerated work has increasingly been performed outside of the family home. The separation of employment and family life is one example of the separation of private and public spheres. Prior to the Industrial Revolution, the home, or family farm, was frequently the site of economic production for the household. With the development of mass production during the industrial period, workers were drawn off the farm into factories. Typically, the adult male left the household for employment, and left behind the adult female to perform the domestic work of housekeeping and child rearing. While the sex division of labor was not new (even on the family farm women typically performed the clothes-making, cooking, and childminding along with the work in the fields), the separation of income generation from the home on a mass scale had major implications for the valuation of the work done by women, men, and children. As some feminists have argued, notably Joan Huber (1991), the level of women's economic contribution to the family has historically determined the degree of power and prestige women have in their families, and in society at large. Of course, many working-class families could not survive on one man's earnings alone, and women, and even children, worked in factories as well. However, even where women and children worked for pay, their earnings were considered secondary to the male breadwinner's both by male workers and by employers. Women and children were consistently paid less than adult men. To the extent that marital power is based on economic contributions, women's lower pay reifies their secondary status in the home.

Many social critics viewed industrialization, the rise of capitalism, and market society with apprehension. Sociologists such as Emile Durkheim and Ferdinand Tönnies fretted over the effects of increasing specialization on social solidarity and community well-being. A common response to this apprehension was to romanticize family life. Sociologists came to see the family as a haven in a heartless world. And women, as wives and mothers, were intended to be its guardian angels. In the US, social critics Catherine Beecher and Harriet Beecher Stowe argued that women must keep the values of hearth and home alive in an increasingly impersonal society. Their popular 1869 book, *The American Woman's Home*, claimed women were morally obligated to preserve family values of altruism and love in the face of a cold and selfish world. This line of reasoning claims that, to support the impersonal selfishness of capitalism, families must preserve altruism and love. Public and private spheres were to be kept separate, and the means of keeping them separate was to assign the public world to men and the private world to women.

## Early twentieth-century social thought on the family: Structural functionalism and home economics

Sociologists of the family, prior to the impact of feminist thought in the academy, argued that the doctrine of separate spheres – the assignment of family life and women's activities to the private world and income- and political power-producing activities to the male public world – was highly functional for industrialized societies.

American sociologists Talcott Parsons and Robert Bales (1955) argued that the role of the family in industrial, market societies was highly specialized; its primary function is the socialization of children and the stabilization of adult personalities. (This definition is still in use today; see, for example, Popenoe, 1993.) In modern societies, families are isolated, self-sustaining units, geographically separated from extended kin. To survive, argued Parsons and Bales, a family must bond as a small, solidaristic group, and garner sufficient material resources. Parson and Bales termed the needs for solidarity, socialization, and integration within the family "expressive" requirements, and the need for families to interface with society to obtain material resources "instrumental." Neatly, the sex division of labor in the home assigned the expressive role to women and the instrumental role to men. Parsons and Bales argued that these roles naturally align with sex because women are more tied to home and children through the activities of childbearing and breastfeeding (although this logic contradicts the widespread use of bottle feeding in the 1940s and 1950s). Men's assignment to the instrumental role results in their leadership position in the family because men are the pivotal family members who operate in both kinship and occupational spheres. Thus, the sex division of labor and the doctrine of separate spheres are functional in the sense that they efficiently meet the expressive and instrumental needs of families.

Parsons (1949) also argued that the sex division of labor is functional because it eliminates status competition between husband and wife. If women were to seriously compete in the occupational system, then they would be competing with their husbands, and such competition would undermine the solidarity of the family unit. The sex division of labor allows the family to procure the most material resources from the market via the husband's job. Having a wife frees a man from the demands of the expressive role and allows him to compete, unfettered, in the occupational sphere. Thus, Parsons argues that sex-role segregation is a functional necessity for marital stability and even for the viability of society itself (1949: 79–80).

The idea that the most functional family form is highly sex-segregated continued into successive decades and across social science disciplines. Like sociologists Parsons and Bales, economist Gary Becker agrees that families function best when spouses specialize in market and reproductive spheres. Again, this specialization happens to coincide with traditional sex roles for men and women. Ironically it is Becker, who, while criticized for his lack of attention to gender–power differentials within the family (England and Budig, 1998), is also credited with making economists recognize that families (and women's familial work) are sites of production. Emphasizing the productiveness of the domestic sphere has usually been the province of Marxist and Socialist feminists (discussed below). However, Becker also views child rearing as productive work. Parents invest time, money, energy, and love into raising children to be productive adult members of society. The fact that it is women who traditionally bear the responsibilities and costs of such child raising Becker attributes to women's biological advantage in rearing children (Becker, 1991). This advantage originates primarily in women's exclusive ability to breastfeed.[1]

Given women's initial comparative advantage in child rearing, and assuming that families are rational actors who logically follow the most efficient path in home economics, the sex division of labor arises where women specialize in home production and men specialize in market production. In this model, men altruistically share the earnings garnered from their market work with family members, just as women share the products of their home labor (well-raised children) with their husbands.

Like Parsons, Becker views specialization in market and domestic work by husbands and wives not only to be economically efficient, but to be a major motivation to become and remain married. And like Parsons, Becker views women's increasing employment to be a central factor in the decrease in marriage rates and the rise in divorce rates. Becker argues that the gains in productive efficiency from specialization that motivate marriage are reduced when women cease to specialize in domestic work. This reduces the gains from marriage and hence the attractiveness of the institution.

What Becker and Parsons ignore is the dimension of power in the family. Presumably, women's biological advantage in child rearing by virtue of being able to breastfeed was greatly reduced around 1910, when sterilization techniques enabled infants to thrive by being bottle-fed. This technological development did not result in an increase of men specializing in the domestic sphere, however. Why not? If, according to Beckerian thought, simple efficiency and comparative advantage fuel the sex division of labor, why don't specialization patterns change when comparative advantage is lost? This begs the question of relative power: whose needs are best met by traditional family structures? Parsons, Bales, and Becker do not focus on these questions, but feminists do.

## Families and Feminist Thought

While most feminists agree that the family is a central site of power struggles between women and men, there is no one feminist position on the family and its relation to women's oppression. This is largely due to the fact that there is no one feminist position on anything related to women's oppression. There are multiple schools of thought among feminists, and even within theoretical camps there is disagreement. Some have little to say about the family, others argue the family is the source of women's oppression, and still others claim the family is a source of resistance to sexism. In this section I will discuss feminism's critiques of the family as a social institution and its role in patriarchal society.

Recent feminist work recognizes the diversity of family forms and the class, race, and time variation in family structures. While the family has often been cast as a source of oppression for white, middle- and upper-class women, working-class women and women of racial and ethnic minority groups have also cited the family as a place of resistance to the oppression from capitalists and racist society (Collins, 1991). In the US, black feminists have exploded the myth of the American family structure assumed by the majority of feminists discussed above. White feminists have assumed a middle-class, nuclear family structure – a self-sustaining economic unit containing a heterosexual married couple with a male breadwinner and a female home and child caretaker. This has not been the reality for black working-class and poor families. Collins (1991) chronicles the long and unique history of black families in the US. The first African American families formed under the conditions of slavery were broken up when family members were sold to different slaveowners. Since children were often separated from parents, extended families consisting of kin and community relationships developed, and children were raised by what Collins calls "other-mothers." The tradition of community child-raising has extended to contemporary black families, where, "[i]n order to survive, the family network must share the costs of providing for children" (Collins, 1991: 47). The lack of jobs, fewer educational opportunities, and high rates of incarceration and of homicide have decimated the pool of marriageable black men. This has led to higher rates of unmarried motherhood among black women and the continued importance of extended networks of kin who fulfill the functions of middle-/upper-class nuclear families.

Despite the diversity of family forms, much of first- and second-wave feminism was concerned with middle- or upper-class white families of their times. The calls of the first feminist wave for women to pursue education and employment as the route to realizing their full potential as humans were clearly speaking only of upper-class, not working-class, women. As a result, in much of the following discussion, feminist theories of the family take the nuclear family form as the baseline and most patriarchal family structure.

## Family as a site of women's oppression

### LIBERAL FEMINISM AND THE FAMILY

Liberal feminism is rooted in liberal political thought, which developed during the Enlightenment and glorifies rationality. According to this intellectual tradition, what makes humans unique is our capacity to reason. According to liberal feminists, the confinement of women's roles to the family (as daughter, wife, and mother) restricts the development of their rational skills. In the end, the suppression of their capacity to reason prevents women from becoming fully human.

Often criticized as a "bourgeois" feminist movement (hooks, 1984), liberal feminism was primarily concerned with the plight of middle- and upper-class women and their families. The late 1700s and 1800s saw the rise of many notable liberal feminists in Britain. Three of the more influential include Mary Wollstonecraft, Harriet Taylor Mill, and John Stuart Mill. Wollstonecraft was troubled by the fate of what she called the "feathered race" of married, middle- and upper-class women. These women usually received a frivolous education and did not engage in productive work. The lack of meaningful work reduced these women to ornamental birds in gilded cages – prizes for their fathers and husbands to exhibit in drawing rooms. The education of such women in Wollstonecraft's time was usually limited to finishing school – where they were taught to play musical instruments and sing, to paint and appreciate fine art, to entertain and have impeccable manners – all of which increased their value as a potential drawing-room ornament (i.e., wife). The lack of a developed rational intellect and meaningful work lead to the "female" vices of vanity and envy, according to Wollstonecraft. She argued that women were not supercilious by nature (as many of the Enlightenment thinkers argued, most notably Rousseau), but that social constraints prevented them from developing higher capacities of rationality. Wollstonecraft argued that educating women would not only develop their rational capacities, but would enable them to be better mothers and wives. Although Wollstonecraft argued for women's education and productive employment, she did not think that such measures would revolutionize family life (nor was that her aim). Instead, she thought that improving women's minds and activities would lead to greater family harmony: "[W]ould but men . . . be content with rational fellowship instead of slavish obedience, they would find us more observant daughters, more affectionate sisters, more faithful wives, more reasonable mothers . . . in a word, better citizens" (1996 [1792]: 154).

Following on Wollstonecraft's heels were British intellectuals and feminists Harriet Taylor Mill and John Stuart Mill. Like Wollstonecraft, J. S. Mill argued, in his 1869 *Subjection of Women*, that women were potentially the intellectual equals of men. Furthermore, women should be given the same education, employment, and political-participation opportunities as men. Also, like Wollstonecraft, Mill's view of women's liberation did not seek to fundamentally change bourgeois family life, nor did he challenge the ideology of separate spheres. Upon marriage, Mill argued, the best sex division of labor remained that of the male breadwinner and female homemaker. Mill thought that women's *potential* to be the economic equivalents of their husbands would be sufficient to bring about greater equality in marriage. Interestingly, Mill's own wife had different views on this subject. In *The Enfranchisement of Women*, Harriet Taylor Mill argued that, no matter how little, a married woman should contribute to the earnings of her household. Only in this way can a wife "be raised from the position of a servant to that of a partner" (Mill, 1983 [1851]: 20).

Liberal feminists were most concerned with the rights and opportunities of women relative to men. Since these feminists mainly came from the middle and upper classes, they sought to obtain equal rights between men and women in this class. The liberal feminist movement of the nineteenth and early twentieth centuries, both in Britain and in the US, most actively sought the political enfranchisement of women, civil and legal rights for women (such as the ability to own and inherit property, enter into legal contracts, retain their own wages, establish credit in their own names, and initiate divorce proceedings), equal educational opportunities for men and women (including admitting women into all-male universities), and equal employment opportunities and equal pay for the same work for women and men. Many of the rights women take for granted in Westernized nations today result from the efforts of the liberal feminist movement.

Despite sweeping changes for women throughout society – increased labor-force participation, political and legal rights, reduced fertility, and increased education – the family is seen by some as the last bastion of male dominance. The sex division of labor in the family, and women's greater responsibilities for children and housework, persist despite women's political and economic gains. It is women's continued and almost exclusive responsibility for children that arguably lies behind the feminization of poverty (McLanahan and Kelly, 1999).

But what effect has this movement had on the family? While criticizing what they saw as the frivolity of women's nonproductive lives, liberal feminists did not fundamentally challenge the structure of the family. Even liberal feminists of the "second wave" in the US (such as Betty Friedan) who pushed for women's engagement in the public sphere did not challenge the role of men in the private family sphere, nor did they push for men to be fuller partners in housework and child-care. In a 2002 episode of the Oprah Winfrey talk show in the US, which highlighted feminists Gloria Steinem and Naomi Wolf, young women in their twenties and thirties said they were angry with these "older" liberal feminists for "ruining men." What they meant was that the liberal feminist push for women to enter the public sphere – to have careers – has not included a simultaneous call for men to enter the private sphere – to share home and family responsibilities. Instead, men are led to think that women can do it all – as an advertisement for women's perfume describes: "She can bring home the bacon, fry it up in a pan, and never, ever, let you forget you're a man."

Sociological research shows that working wives and mothers face a double bind in that they still carry the lion's share of housework and child-care at home in addition to performing paid work. Arlie Hochschild (1989) termed the homework and child-care women do at the end of a day's paid work the "second shift." In addition to retaining the bulk of the domestic workload, women find that men appear to create more housework than they do. South and Spitze (1994) compare the amount of housework done by men and women across marital statuses: never married/living alone, cohabiting, married, divorced, and widowed. They find that men do the least amount of housework when married, whereas women do the most amount of housework when married. This is true regardless of the presence of children in the home. In fact, upon marriage (with no children present), women's hours increase while men's hours decrease (South and Spitze, 1994; Hartmann, 1981).

Beyond liberal feminism's failure to call for greater male involvement in the domestic sphere, liberal feminism's solution to women's oppression has come under attack. Is paid employment the best route to liberation for women of all classes and races? The class bias of liberal feminists is clear when they assume that women are not already working for pay and that all paid work will develop women's talents. Whereas being a lawyer or doctor (the sort of occupations held by middle- and upper-class women's husbands) may be intellectually challenging and financially rewarding, flipping hamburgers at McDonald's would not be as rewarding. Women in low-paid service or manufacturing jobs may prefer homemaking to working. Similarly, liberal feminism has been accused of ignoring the experiences of nonwhite women, particularly in regard to paid employment. African American feminist bell hooks (1984) points out that, in the US, black women have always worked outside of the home. Post-slavery, black women frequently were maids or nannies for wealthier white families. This employment situation is arguably more oppressive than performing such work in one's own home and for one's own family. In sum, while the solutions to women's oppression offered by liberal feminists may be effective for white, middle-class and college-educated women, they are race- and class-bound. Furthermore, integrating women into the public sphere will not liberate women until men are equal participants in the private sphere.

## RADICAL FEMINISM AND THE FAMILY

Radical feminists agree on one radical claim: that sexism is the oldest and most pervasive form of discrimination in society, and it is learned from birth within the patriarchal family. Thus, it is the pattern upon which all other forms of discrimination (racism, ageism, etc.) are built. However, radical feminists do not all agree on whether the family is a source of oppression or of resistance to sexism for women. In this section I present radical feminist arguments that the reproductive family is inherently oppressive. The other view will be discussed later in the chapter.

Those radical feminists who see the family as a source of oppression have outlined two central ways through which traditional family structures oppress women: (1) through men's exploitation of women's domestic labor (housework and childcare) and (2) through men's control of women's sexuality and reproduction. Furthermore, radical feminists argue that the patriarchal family is the engine that perpetuates women's oppression. This is because it is within the family that children are socialized into limited sex roles and learn the cultural devaluation of all things associated with women. Bryson's discussion of radical feminism on the family sums up these ideas clearly:

> Far from being a "natural" arrangement based on mutual love and respect in which the emotional, sexual, and domestic needs of adult partners are met and their children cared for, it is a social institution in which women's labour is exploited, male sexual power may be violently expressed, and oppressive gender identities and modes of behaviour are learned. (1992: 198)

Radical feminists give many examples of Bryson's claims. Radical feminists argue that men benefit from women's assignment to the domestic sphere both by reaping the fruits of women's unpaid labor, and from the handicapping of women who attempt to compete with men in the public sphere (politics and paid employment). Research shows that male sexual power is too often violently expressed within families; it is estimated that marital rape accounts for approximately 25 percent of all rapes (Randall and Haskings, 1995; Resnick et al., 1991). The ideology of separate spheres protects men's power within the family. Governments have been hesitant to deny men their gender power by interfering in "private matters" like domestic violence. For example, while marital rape is illegal in Britain, by 1998, 33 US states still had some exemptions from prosecuting husbands for rape, usually with regard to the use of force. When governments have tried to regulate male power in the domestic sphere, efforts have not always been very profound. In old English common law, "rule of thumb" meant a man could legally beat his wife with a stick no larger than his thumb. Thus, not only is the family a site of men's oppression of women, but historically this oppression has been sanctioned by governing bodies.

What is the root of men's monopoly of power in the family? Shulamith Firestone argues it lies in biology. She contends that maternity and child-care are inherently oppressive, unfulfilling, and degrading: "The heart of women's oppression is her child-bearing and child-rearing role" (1970). Firestone claims that women and men's differing roles in reproduction lead to the fundamental division of power and labor in families and society. She argues that only by taking control of new reproductive technologies can women free themselves from their oppressive biological destiny. She also suggests that, through reproductive technology, babies could be conceived and gestated in a laboratory. Upon "birth," children could be raised in nonbiological families – including heterosexual and homosexual ones. In this scenario, women's roles in childbirth would no longer be any larger than men's roles. Firestone thought once men and women stopped playing different roles in reproduction, it would be possible to eliminate all sex roles and form an androgynous society.

Other radical feminists declare the root of men's power in the family resides in compulsory heterosexuality. For example, Rich (1976) claims that heterosexuality is not simply an expression of sexual desire, but a hegemonic political institution imposed on women for the benefit of men. How do men benefit from compulsory heterosexuality? One benefit is that men receive the free labor of women who maintain their homes, raise their children, and provide them with emotional and sexual services. The assignment of women to the private sphere and the definition of marriage as a relationship between one man and one woman ensures low-cost female labor. Another way men benefit from compulsory heterosexuality lies in sexual gratification. The common Western cultural definition of "having sex" can quite rigidly be limited to penile–vaginal coitus (as the hairsplitting rhetorical maneuvers of the 1998 Clinton and Lewinsky debacle poignantly made clear). This definition of sexual relations describes an act where men will usually achieve orgasm; however, coitus less frequently leads to orgasm for women. Research has shown many women do not receive enough clitoral stimulation during simple penetration to reach orgasm (Schwartz and Rutter, 1998). However, under patriarchy, women have been told that their sexual pleasure is of minor importance compared to men's. Freud even argued that an orgasm reached through direct clitoral stimulation (effective for women) is vastly inferior (even reflects a lack of maturity) in comparison to what he termed "vaginal orgasm" that occurs during coitus (effective for men).

In response to the repression of women's sexual fulfillment in many heterosexual families, the radical separatist movement called political lesbianism seeks to establish woman-centered sexuality and family life through the exclusion of men. For these feminists, rejection of heterosexuality for lesbianism is not simply a personal choice, but a political decision. It's also not simply about sex; lesbian feminism "is a threat to the ideological, political, and economic basis of male supremacy" (Bunch, 1986: 131). While not all radical feminists are separatists, the notions that heterosexual reproductive families are the source of women's oppression runs through many of their writings.

In sum, two of the unique contributions of radical feminists that are relevant to the family are: (1) their delineation of the ways that men attempt to control women's bodies and (2) their articulation of the ways that patriarchy constructs female sexuality to serve men's desires and self-interests. In the eyes of radical feminists, control over one's body is as essential to women's liberation as is the development of rational capabilities for liberal feminists. As Rosemarie Tong aptly states, "To the degree that a person is deprived of power over his or her own body, that person is deprived of his or her humanity" (1989: 72). The heterosexual family, the sex division of labor, and women's and men's roles in reproduction are the mechanisms through which men control women's bodies and sexuality. Regaining control over one's body is central to the radical feminist project. The impact radical feminism has had on the family is diffuse. In attempts to empower women, radical feminists have pushed for contraception and abortion rights, domestic and sexual violence legislation, and legitimization of a plurality of family forms: single-parent, lesbian, gay, and childless families.

## MARXIST AND SOCIALIST FEMINISM AND THE FAMILY

At first glance, it might not be obvious what the economic and political theories of Marxism and socialism would have to say about the family. Simply put, Marxist feminism argues that women's oppression is a result of capitalist exploitation of women *through* their roles in the family. Capitalists profit from the free provision of labor by women in their family roles. As wives, mothers, daughters, and sisters, women provide free care for the young, the old, the sick, and even the (male) able-bodied worker. Capitalists could not survive economically if they had to pay women for their work of reproducing the workforce.

In addition to capitalists, individual men profit from women's free labor and economic dependence under capitalism. One Marxist, Friedrich Engels, went as far as describing marriage as a form of prostitution. Engels argued that in a capitalist society, women lack access to paid employment and are thus forced to be economically dependent on men. Engels argued that the lack of access to the means of ensuring their own economic survival connects wives and prostitutes in the same enterprise of exchanging their only resource – their bodies – for subsistence. Engels argues the two are different only in a matter of degree: the wife differs from the prostitute "only in that she does not hire out her body, like a wage-worker, on piecework, but sells it into slavery once and for all" (1972: 63). However, wives are selling more than just sex; also included in the marriage bargain are housework, child-care, and emotional services. Marxist feminists argue that women's oppression will end with communism, where domestic work and child-care will be collectivized, and where women will have active roles in employment and politics. These roles will enable women to be economically independent and have a voice in the polity.

Whereas Marxist feminists think patriarchy is a product of capitalism and can be eradicated through communism, socialist feminists disagree. Socialist feminists argue that women are additionally oppressed due to a system of patriarchy. Patriarchy is separate from capitalism and persists in noncapitalist and communist societies. While women are oppressed by both systems, the interests of patriarchy and capitalism do not always coincide (Hartmann, 1979). Socialist feminists argue that women's oppression is determined both by their roles in production and reproduction.

Russian feminist and Bolshevik leader Aleksandra Kollontai extended Marxist theory to the family. She (1977) argued that the organization of reproduction through the traditional patriarchal family structure oppresses women and children and threatens the solidarity of the collective. Kollontai thought that the intimate exclusivity of the traditional marriage and family structure was inherently antisocial. She warned that restricting affection and care to the family reduces one's commitment to society. Isolation in the private sphere of the family also prohibits women's political involvement. Kollontai's solution to the isolation of women and children in the family is through communal child rearing. However, she does not mean that biological children should be removed from their mothers' care, as in Firestone's vision. Rather, she argues that mothers should care for all children of the collective together. Moreover, the benefits of mother-care should be unleashed on the whole collective itself by integrating women into the polity. Under communism, the greater solidarity shared by the collective raises the affection and care available to all; this reduces the need for love to be met through isolated family structures. In essence, the collective replaces the family. Love and care are shared among comrades who are equals. The collective-as-family ideal in Kollontai's vision does not imply "free-love" or promiscuous relationships; instead, the opposite is true: collectives that function as families heighten the individual responsibilities and duties of each member to the common good.

Where collectives function as families, the meaning and duty of motherhood is transformed. Rather than motherhood being the private choice of a woman and her partner, it becomes a contribution to the collective: "Society sees maternity as a social task ... in these months she no longer belongs to herself, she is serving the collective, 'producing' from her own flesh and blood a new social unit of labour, a new member of the labour republic" (Kollontai, 1977: 43–4).

The vision of motherhood as a social duty rather than an individual choice would strike terror into the hearts of radical feminists, for whom women's control over their own reproductive capacities is paramount. Kollontai believed, however, that if the hard work of motherhood was not the burden of individual women, but was collectivized, mandatory maternity need not be oppressive to women. Fortunately, the pragmatic side of Kollontai recognized that the early Russian communist state was far from achieving the necessary social supports for obligatory motherhood without it being oppressive for women. Thus, despite thinking that in the utopian society there would be no need for abortion, Kollontai supported the legalization of abortion in 1917 (Bryson, 1992: 144).

What effects have Marxism and Marxist feminism had on the family? Barbara Einhorne (1993) provides one account of the effects of state socialism in (the former) East Germany, Poland, Czechoslovakia, and Hungary on women's family and economic roles. Einhorne's analysis shows that under state socialism, government policies pushed women into employment and political spheres. As in Western democracies, the entrance of women into the labor force in large numbers was not accompanied by a parallel move of men into the private sphere. Thus, under state socialism women were left with the double burdens of public- and private-sphere responsibilities, just as their counterparts were in capitalist countries.

Einhorne (1993) finds that giving women access to economic resources did not challenge the historic power stratification within the home. By ignoring the other sources of power men hold over women, and by sending women to perform market work without addressing the power dynamics between men and women in the family, the socialist state created a double burden for women. This burden resulted from the gender assumptions built into social policies. For example, whereas the state recognized men as workers, women were recognized both as workers and as mothers in many socialist policies of Eastern Europe.[2] Legislation was designed to enable women to blend their two roles more easily, which reinforced their double burden. Women, not men, were allotted a periodic "household day" to catch up on housework. Similarly, women, but not men, were allotted paid sick leave for children; this reinforced women's role of primary child-care provider. While both women and men were given parental leave upon the birth of a child, because women generally earned less, they were almost universally the only parent to take advantage of parental leave. These kinds of policies served not only to reinforce women's double role as worker and mother, they also disadvantaged women in the workplace. Over time, women proved to be less desirable employees because they took more sick leave, exited and reentered the workplace with the addition of each child, and generally were more fatigued on the job because of their double burden (Einhorne, 1993).

## FAMILY AND/OR MOTHERHOOD AS A SOURCE OF RESISTANCE TO SEXISM

Not all feminists agree that the family is the seat of women's oppression. Some feminists claim that women's family roles are sources of power and wisdom that could be used to create a better society. They offer this intriguing thought: perhaps the reason the feminists discussed above see the family as a site of oppression is because they unwittingly buy into the sexist privileging of men's activities and devaluation of traditional women's work. Pro-family radical and socialist feminists have argued that women's family roles and their exclusion from politics and economics (and the selfishness, competitiveness, and individualism those entail in capitalist society) result in superior female virtues of cooperation, caring, and protecting learned in the domestic sphere. These feminists claim that the female virtues acquired through their family roles may provide the antidote to male-dominated culture.

## SOCIAL FEMINISM AND THE FAMILY

In *Public Man, Private Woman* (1981) Jean Elshtain, a socialist feminist, argues that women's experience as mothers gives them a type of moral superiority that could be used to govern society. In families, claims Elshtain, people experience the best of human relationships, such as long-term ties, obligations, responsibilities, intimacy, love, and attentiveness. Moreover, the family is the only place people can find love and comfort in a capitalist society, because it is the only place where profit is not the bottom line. Thus, the family is where individuals learn compassion, ethics, and responsibility. Elshtain argues that these qualities are imparted through good mothering. If the practice of mothering were extended to the social sphere, Elshtain argues, then the underlying system of rules, rights, and responsibilities for individuals would be radically changed. The family makes possible a morality of responsibility for civic society, rather than a morality based on individual freedoms. Elshtain claims that the practice of "social mothering" would fundamentally overturn our current system that prioritizes individual rights over community obligations. This would alter the feminist pursuit for gender equity. Rather than focusing on obtaining for women the same civil liberties and individual rights as men, social mothering would force men and women to focus on community welfare and responsibilities to others.

Elshtain attempts two radical moves in her theory of social mothering. First, she rejects the social privileging of men and male virtues over women and female virtues. Second, and here she distinguishes her theory, she rejects the privileging of the public realm over the private. In Elshtain's thinking, the separate spheres ideology that confined women to the private family sphere and men to the public sphere gives rise to superior, not inferior, virtues for women. The pattern of human relationships developed in the family – of compassion and responsibility – would be far more functional for society than the human relationships that have evolved in the public sphere that emphasize individual rights and independence.

What would the structure of the family look like in Elshtain's utopia? "Social mothering" refers to a practice that would change the underlying system of rules governing social interaction. It does not imply the communal parenting practices envisioned by radical or Marxist feminists in the previous section. In fact, Elshtain is explicitly against communal parenting. She thinks that children need intimate love with just two adults (parents) to best foster the development of family-based virtues.

Elshtain has been criticized for romanticizing family life. Mary Deitz (1985) charges that Elshtain ignores the fact that families can be neglectful, abusive, and even violent. Dysfunctional families are not rare and are unlikely to impart the values of responsibility and care that Elshtain praises as family virtues. Moreover, Deitz points out that not all women are good mothers; in fact, not all women are mothers at all. What is the role of these women in the society Elshtain envisions? If motherhood is the only source of women's perspectives and knowledge, are childless women inferior? For example, women's nonfamily experiences as workers, political and religious leaders, and even beggars could also provide a basis of female experience and knowledge. Elshtain's theory does not discuss these women's experiences in the public realm; in fact her theory reinforces the split between private and public spheres, and male and female dominions. A final criticism of Elshtain is that the mother–child relationship may not be the best model for social relationships in a democratic society (Deitz, 1985). Even healthy mother–child relationships require a power differential between the mother and the child. The mother is clearly the authority and the child is the ultimate dependent. Power-dependence relationships are the antithesis of a democratic relationship between equals. If power corrupts, might not mothers fall victim to the same selfish trappings of the public realm that men have?

Another feminist who argues that women have special values and insights due to their historic confinement to the motherhood role is Sara Ruddick. In contrast to Elshtain, Ruddick discusses the hard work and imperfection of mothering. She admits that mothers can be violent and neglectful. She also tackles the criticisms that connecting motherhood with governance and social justice can lead to the idealization and sentimentalizing of the reality of motherhood: "Because I am a mother, I know the demoralizing, mind-numbing effects of sentimental descriptions of good mothering" (1989: 31). Finally, Ruddick recognizes the danger of overgeneralizing and ignoring the differences among mothers and families.

Despite the potential pitfalls of mothering, Ruddick claims that the best maternal work is nonviolent and peacemaking. Mothers are not any more or less wonderful than other people – but mothers identify (if not always personify) virtues appropriate to the work of mothering. The work of mothers includes protecting, nurturing, and training children. Mothers are not naturally endowed with the skills necessary for good mothering; they develop them through thoughtful practice, or what Ruddick calls "maternal thinking." Ruddick argues that maternal thinking involves the strategies mothers use to create a safe and nurturant environment for their children. Maternal thinking is not effortless; in fact Ruddick claims it is a discipline in and of itself, like engineering. Unlike engineers, however, "mothers have been a powerless group whose thinking, when it has been acknowledged at all, has most often been recognized by people interested in interpreting and controlling rather than in listening" (ibid.: 26).

Thus the social value of good mothering has been limited to the family. Ruddick lobbies for an expansion of the principles of maternal thinking to greater society. She argues that a more peaceful society would result from the principles of maternal thinking and practice.

Is there any evidence to suggest that Elshtain's and Ruddick's arguments for using motherhood as a basis of social governance would be effective? Some research suggests that instead of women's family roles as wife and mother blocking them from participation in the public sphere, these roles can form the foundation of their civic and market participation. Two examples of motherhood motivating political action are found in Hondagneu-Sotelo's 1994 study of Mexican migrant women's civic engagement, and in El-Or and Aran's (1995) analysis of Jewish Israeli women's social protest.

El-Or and Aran (1995) show that maternal thinking led Israeli Jewish mothers to protest violence in the West Bank. Moreover, maternal thinking shaped the form of their protest. The mothers of El-Or and Aran's study felt pressed into political action out of their desire to keep their children safe. They had watched their husbands attempt to root out the violence by taking revenge on the terrorists. El-Or and Aran argue that the maternal ethics of care and nonviolence shaped the women's response to terrorist acts. The women in their study focused on transforming the conflict through peaceful protest. The protest took the form of creating a settlement named for a woman, Rachel, who had been the victim of terrorism. The female protesters camped in this settlement on the West Bank, where recent violence had occurred, and filled their days with studying the Torah. The peaceful and spiritual nature of their protest differed markedly from the response of the men in their community. El-Or and Aran contend that this was due to their different perspectives and skills as women and mothers.

A second example of motherhood motivating political action is found in Hondagneu-Sotelo's (1994) analysis of Mexican migrant women in the US. Hondagneu-Sotelo describes how, in Mexico, women are strongly defined through their motherhood status – an identity process called *marianismo*. While the status of mothers is high in Mexico, their roles are mostly confined to the family. When Mexican mothers migrate to work in the US, they and their families are subject to harsh migration and immigration policies that affect the well-being of their children. In Hondagneu-Sotelo's research, children's lack of access to good schools, medical assistance, and even nutritional food pushed these formerly very private mothers into political activism. Hondagneu-Sotelo shows how, on behalf of their children, migrant Mexican mothers engaged in American civic life by taking English language classes, seeking social assistance, and finding paid work to help support their family. While these public activities would not be appropriate for married mothers in Mexico, the need to ensure their children's well-being pushed women into the public realm as mother-activists. Thus women's roles as mothers propelled them into civic life.

Examples such as El-Or and Aran's (1995) and Hondagneu-Sotelo's (1994) research provide some evidence of women's family roles pressing them into political action. However, there is no way to evaluate whether this basis of political action is superior to, or produces better outcomes than, political action motivated by "male" values of individualism. The ideas that maternal thinking and social mothering are superior and would generate better societies are central to both Elshtain's and Ruddick's theories. The empirical proof for these arguments has yet to be found.

## RADICAL FEMINISM (AGAIN) AND THE FAMILY

Some radical feminists argue that motherhood itself is not the source of women's oppression, but patriarchy is. Thus, mothering *in a patriarchal society* is oppressive, but mothering per se is not. These feminists claim that the ability to create life from their own bodies is the source of women's power. While Firestone (1970) argued that women should abandon biological maternity for technological reproduction, other radical feminists think that asking women to give up their ability to create life is akin to asking women to give up the only power they have under patriarchy. Such a relinquishment would make men completely powerful because they would not need women at all, not even to reproduce.

The solution to end women's oppression, from this perspective, is not to abandon motherhood, but for women to reclaim its power. Adrienne Rich (1976) makes a useful distinction between two forms of motherhood: (1) the potential relationship between women and their reproductive power, and (2) the institution through which patriarchal control is exercised over this female power. In patriarchal societies, men control women's reproductive power through the patriarchal institutions of heterosexual marriage and motherhood. But what would motivate men to usurp women's reproductive independence and power? Rich argues that men fear women's reproductive power because if women can choose to give life, they can also choose to take it away. This fear is rooted in men's experience as being completely dependent on their own mothers in infancy.

Whether or not one agrees with Rich's argument about male fear of female reproductive power, she and others (Mitford, 1992; Wolf, 2001) have offered persuasive arguments that men, not women, have gained control of the childbirth process. According to Rich, men have sought to take control of childbirth and child-raising through the medicalization of childbirth and by acting as the authorities on how to "properly" raise children. Prior to the twentieth century, childbirth was considered a natural event. Typically, women gave birth in their homes with family members at hand, particularly female relatives who were already mothers. Midwives provided expertise and medical interventions were few. This arrangement was gradually eroded during the 1800s. French anthropologist Jacques Gelis (1991) meticulously documents the struggle over authority between midwives and the growing number of obstetricians in early modern Europe. In the US, pregnancy and childbirth became the province of the growing obstetrical branch of medicine during the early twentieth century. By the 1930s, women were increasingly giving birth in hospital settings in Westernized countries. Data from the National Vital Statistics System shows that in 1935, 37 percent of US births occurred in hospitals. By 1950 this percentage had increased to 88 percent, and by 1969 it reached 99 percent, where it remains today (NCHS, 1984, 2000). Feminists have pointed to the growing practices of inducing labor, using anesthetics, performing episiotomies, using a recumbent position for the laboring mother, using forceps, and performing Cesarean sections as evidence of childbirth being wrested from the mother's control to that of the (historically male) physician (Mitford, 1992; Wolf, 2001).

In addition to medicalization of childbirth, Rich (1976) and others argue that men have also exerted power over how to best raise a child. As the popular adage of the 1950s said, "Father knows best." Many women turned to the authority male psychologists, such as Dr. Spock, for instructions on child rearing. Rich outlines how, during this same era, male psychologists undermined women's confidence by blaming poor mothering for child problems ranging from poor self-esteem to juvenile crime. Ultimately, Rich claims, men's takeover has alienated women from childbirth and child-raising; it has undercut women's authority and participation. She argues that women need to take back more control of childbirth and child-raising in order to reclaim their reproductive power.

Since the 1960s, women have begun to regain control of childbirth and child rearing. In England, Sheila Kitzinger has greatly influenced the natural childbirth movement since the 1960s (Garcia, Kilpatrick, and Richards, 1990). In the US, the profession of midwifery has witnessed a renaissance (Mitford, 1992). Accredited programs in midwifery education have grown in number and in size. Insurance companies are increasingly reimbursing midwives for their work. Alternative birthing centers, where "natural" childbirth with a minimum of medical intervention is practiced in a more homelike setting, are a growing phenomenon. In addition to childbirth, feminists are examining the process of child rearing and recommending feminist ways of raising children. For example, Nancy Chodorow's (1978) landmark theory of mothering shows why women feel the need to mother and why the sex division of parenting produces misogyny and sexism in children. Chodorow contends that dual parenting, with equal investments from fathers and mothers, would produce psychologically healthier children. Naomi Wolf (2001) uncovers the patriarchal content of the advice literature on pregnancy and early infant care. Wolf contends women's experiences and knowledge are trivialized in much of this literature. Outside of the academy, individual women have formed feminist mothers' support groups to discuss how children can be raised to resist patriarchal values and practices. Such is the popularity of one such group, Feminist Mothers At Home, that it has had to close its Internet listserve to new members!

## When Public and Private Spheres Collide: Feminism and the Future of the Family

Despite the gains that women have made economically, politically, and in their familial relationships, much remains to be accomplished if the feminist project is to succeed. In the world's wealthiest nation, the US, the vast majority of the poor are women and children. Divorce leaves American women and children with severely reduced standards of living. In contrast to other Westernized nations like France, Sweden, or Denmark, the majority of working women in the US are without maternity leave and many women's jobs lack health insurance for themselves or their families (Clawson and Gerstel, 2002). Unlike many European countries, child-care is expensive and quality care is difficult to find in the US. Furthermore, child-care workers, mostly women, are among the lowest-paid workers in the American economy.

One important cause of these problems is the continued devaluation of work traditionally assigned to women. This work remains unpaid in the home, and is paid less than other forms of work in the marketplace (England, Budig, and Folbre,

2002). The work many women enter into is often similar to their work in families. Women's employment is largely concentrated in helping or service professions. These include nursing, social work, education, child-care, and clerical support occupations. Just as women's work in the family has long been devalued, so is the work they do in the market. Caring for children, the elderly, the ill, the disabled, and even for working adults is largely done by women at no or little cost to society. Those who perform this work face earnings penalties for doing so (ibid.). One solution to the impoverishment faced by those who perform caring labor is to perform a different kind of labor. Liberal feminists have long sought for women's access to more rewarding and prestigious occupations. But this solution neglects the fact that someone must care for children, the aged, and the ill.

In addition to being paid poorly for their work, women often find their employers also do not value women's commitments to their families. Parent-friendly jobs have not become institutionalized despite increases in women's employment. For women, the lack of child-care, inadequate wages, and restricted or nonstandard working schedules mean that mothers have a difficult time either being hired or finding a job that allows them to handle their family responsibilities. The difficulty in meeting both family and work demands may result in the earnings penalties suffered by mothers, as compared to women without children (Budig and England, 2001).

The task for feminists in the coming years will be to dismantle the legacy of the doctrine of separate spheres. It is not sufficient to grant women equal access to the male playing fields of paid work and politics. For real gender equality, individual men must play a greater role in the domestic sphere, just as women share in the burden of financially supporting the family. Workplaces must change to accommodate the family obligations of employees. No longer can firms assume each worker has a wife at home to free the worker from these obligations. Family-friendly work policies, such as fully paid family leave for men and women, must be instituted. But the greatest changes must come in how society distributes the costs of reproducing itself and supporting care work traditionally supplied from unpaid women. Should mothers (and fathers) alone bear the cost of raising children? If some of us elect to remain childless, are we not free-riding on the backs of parents who will produce the next generation of workers? Finding ways to value and support the important work of caring in the domestic sphere is an important challenge of future feminists.

## Notes

1 Becker also recognizes two other possible factors behind the sex division of labor. The first is socialization. Becker argues that parents invest in sex-specific human capital for their children. Because they assume that boys will grow up to specialize in market work, and girls in domestic work, parents teach boys market-relevant skills and girls, domestic-relevant skills. The second factor Becker recognizes in the 1991 edition of his *Treatise on the Family* is that sex discrimination in the labor force systematically lowers wives' earnings relative to their husbands'. Such discrimination may lie behind couples' decisions to specialize in market and domestic work in sex-traditional ways.

2 I do not mean to imply here that building social policy around employment relationships for men and familial relationships for women is by any means unique to socialism, central Europe, or the twentieth century.

## References


Becker, G. (1991) *A Treatise on the Family*. Cambridge, MA: Harvard University Press.

Beecher, C., and Stowe, H. B. (1869) *The American Woman's Home*. New York: J. B. Ford.

Bryson, V. (1992) *Feminist Political Theory*. London: Macmillan.

Budig, M. J., and England, P. (2001) The wage penalty for motherhood. *American Sociological Review*, 66, 204–25.

Bunch, C. (1986) Lesbians in revolt. In M. Pearsall (ed.), *Women and Values*. Belmont, CA: Wadsworth.

Chodorow, N. (1978) *The Reproduction of Mothering : Psychoanalysis and the Sociology of Gender*. Berkeley: University of California Press.

Clawson, D., and Gerstel, N. (2002) Caring for young children: The U.S. vs. Europe. *Contexts*, 1, 28–35.

Collins, P. H. (1991) *Black Feminist Thought: Knowledge, Consciousness, and the Politics of Empowerment*. New York: Routledge.

Deitz, M. G. (1985) Citizenship with a feminist face: The problem with maternal thinking. *Political Theory*, 13, 19–37.

Einhorne, B. (1993) *Cinderella Goes to Market: Citizenship, Gender, and Women's Movements in East Central Europe*. London: Verso.

El-Or, T., and Aran, G. (1995) Giving birth to a settlement: Maternal thinking and political action of Jewish women on the West Bank. *Gender and Society*, 9, 600–78.

Elshtain, J. (1981) *Public Man, Private Woman*. Princeton, NJ: Princeton University Press.

Engels, F. (1972) *The Origin of the Family, Private Property, and the State*. New York: International Publishers.

England, P., and Budig, M. J. (1998) Gary Becker on the family: His genius, impact, and blind spots. In D. Clawson (ed.), *Required Reading: Sociology's Most Influential Books*. Amherst, MA: University of Massachusetts Press.

England, P., Budig, M. J., and Folbre, N. (2002) Wages of virtue: The relative pay of care work. *Social Problems*, 49, 455–73.

Firestone, S. (1970) *The Dialectic of Sex*. New York: Bantam.

Garcia, J., Kilpatrick, R., and Richards, M. (eds.) (1990) *The Politics of Maternity Care*. Oxford: Oxford University Press.

Gelis, J. (1991) *History of Childbirth: Fertility, Pregnancy, and Birth in Early Modern Europe*. Boston: Northeastern University Press.

Hartmann, H. (1979) The unhappy marriage of Marxism and Feminism: Towards a more progressive union. *Capital and Class*, 8, 1–33.

Hartmann, H. (1981) The family as the locus of gender, class, and political struggle: The example of housework. *Signs*, 6, 366–94.

Hochschild, A. (1989) *The Second Shift*. New York: Viking Penguin.

Hondagneu-Sotelo, P. (1994) *Gendered Transitions: Mexican Experiences of Immigration*. Berkeley: University of California Press.

hooks, b. (1984) *Feminist Theory: From Margin to Center*. Boston: South End Press.

Huber, J. (1991) A theory of family, economy, and gender. In R. L. Blumberg (ed.), *Gender, Family, and Economy: The Triple Overlap*. Newbury Park, CA: Sage.

Kollontai, A. (1977) *Selected Writings*. (trans. A. Holt). London: Allison & Busby.

McLanahan, S. S., and Kelly, E. (1999) The feminization of poverty. In J. Chafetz (ed.), *Handbook of Gender Sociology*. New York: Plenum.

Mill, H. T. (1983) [1851] *The Enfranchisement of Women*. London: Virago.

Mill, J. S. (1869) *Subjection of Women*. New York: D. Appleton & Co.

Millett, K. (1970) *Sexual Politics*. Garden City, NY: Doubleday.

Mitford, J. (1992) *The American Way of Birth*. New York: Dutton.

National Center for Health Statistics (1984) *Midwife and Out-of-Hospital Deliveries, United States*. DHHS Publication No. (PHS) 84-1918. Hyattsville, MD: US Department of Health and Human Services.

National Center for Health Statistics (2000) *Vital Statistics of the United States, 1998, Volume I, Natality. Table 1-24*. Hyattsville, MD: US Department of Health and Human Services.

Parsons, T. (1949) Sex roles in American kinship systems. In T. Parsons, *Essays in Sociological Theory* Glencoe, IL: The Free Press.

Parsons, T., and Bales, R. (1955) *Family Socialization and Interaction Process*. Glencoe, IL: The Free Press.

Popenoe, D. (1993) American family decline, 1960–1990: A review and appraisal. *Journal of Marriage and the Family*, 55, 527–55.

Randall, M., and Haskings, L. (1995) Sexual violence in women's lives. *Violence Against Women*, 1, 6–31.

Resnick, H., Kilpatrick, D., Walsh, C., and Veronen, L. (1991) Marital rape. In R. T. Ammerman and M. Herson (eds.), *Case Studies in Family Violence*. New York: Plenum.

Rich, A. (1976) *Of Woman Born: Motherhood as Experience and Institution*. New York: Bantam.

Ruddick, S. (1989). *Maternal Thinking: Toward a Politics of Peace*. Boston, MA: Beacon.

Schwartz, P., and Rutter, V. (1998) *The Gender of Sexuality*. Thousand Oaks, CA: Pine Forge Press.

South, S. J., and Spitze, G. (1994) Housework in marital and nonmarital households. *American Sociological Review*, 59, 327–47.

Tong, R. (1989) *Feminist Thought: A Comprehensive Introduction*. Boulder, CO: Westview Press.

Wolf, N. (2001) *Misconceptions: Truth, Lies, and the Unexpected on the Journey to Motherhood*. New York: Doubleday.

Wollstonecraft, M. (1996) [1792] *A Vindication of the Rights of Woman*. Mineola, NY: Dover Publications.

# 25

# Work and Families

Shirley Dex

## Introduction

Families have been changing, as have workplaces, the distribution of paid work, the types of opportunities for individuals to be economically self-supporting and the gender composition of the workforce. The paid work side of this equation tends to get organized in labor markets through employers' decisions. Families supply their labor power to the market in exchange for money to support themselves, but also need to engage in unpaid work in the home, in part to reproduce themselves. On the supply side men and women have changed their participation in the labor market and their hours of work in response to opportunities offered, new preferences, and new constraints. However, the labor-market context in industrialized economies has also changed. Competitive pressures of the global economy have led to a growth in so-called flexible and insecure employment. Families have increasingly become two-earner although, in some cases, no-earner households are evident. The two-earner families have been faced with new issues and time schedules of combining the responsibilities of paid work and caring for both children and elderly relatives. Evidence has been mounting that families are under pressure either from having too much paid work, time poor – money rich, or having too little and insufficient income; time rich – money poor. Caring for children and elderly relatives have been increasing outsourced.

This chapter focuses on families of heterosexual couples and their changing relationships to the changing labor market and workplaces; other groups are given more specific focus in other chapters. The new relationships of families to the labor market are also mediated by and may contribute to other changes which are the subject of other chapters in this volume; for example, increases in cohabitation in preference to marriage commitments, and increases in marital breakdown. Workplaces are being forced to respond to some of these changes, although to varying degrees. As well as documenting the main dimensions of work and family change in this chapter, consideration is also given to explanations of why changes have occurred and the outcomes, interventions, and responses. Some elements of this complex picture are well charted; others are in the infancy of being researched.

This is a subject area ripe with sociological interest. Massive social change has been displayed in this area of social life, and this raises obvious questions about explanations: Why the changes? What are its drivers? Involved in these changes have been a challenge to earlier societal norms about gender relations and the gendered social structure. A new social structural map has been emerging in which women and mothers have a clear public as well as a private role. Norms of social life that used to be seen as neutral have been shown to have a male gender. Such views have then been challenged. This has had knock-on effects in a wide range of other societal institutions that have had to rethink their earlier rationale and modus operandi. In the history of sociological theorizing, families' functional role has been acclaimed, criticized, and rejected. However, at this interface between paid work and family life, the functional reproduction of the workforce or perhaps the population is undoubtedly a critical issue of public interest for societies. The quantity and quality of children produced will determine much of the future standard of living of our aging populations and make this area of study, and our understanding of the nature and reasons for change, a vital one.

## Overview of Changing Labor Markets

Labor-market restructuring has taken place alongside the process of industrialization and, more lately, with the move to post-industrial societies. The decline in full-time, male manufacturing employment and the rise in women's service-sector employment seen in the British figures is replicated in all industrialized countries (table 25.1). In some countries, including Britain, Germany, and Scandinavia, much of the increase in women's labor-force participation has been part-time hours, and in some countries, including Britain, in low-paid jobs. Some regions and communities have felt very severe effects from the decline of men's manufacturing jobs whilst others are relatively untouched. Britain has also seen an increase in so-called "flexible jobs" (Dex et al., 2000), where contracts are less secure (e.g., temporary, self-employed), or working conditions and benefits have traditionally been worse (e.g., part-time). The intensity of work and feelings of insecurity have also increased (Burchell et al., 1999).

Changes in the map of economic opportunities to support families have occurred for a number of reasons. Clearly employers have reorganized and restructured many jobs, in some cases, as part of a strategy to reduce costs and shift risk away from employers, more toward employees (Beck, 1992; Purcell, Hogarth, and Simm, 1999; Neathey and Hurstfield, 1995). In part this has been a response to competitive pressures from the global economy, declines in demand for outdated manufactured goods, and closures of companies in the face of these and macroeconomic pressures, excess supply, recession, or high interest rates. A notable decline in the influence of trade unions has taken place alongside the decline in male manufacturing jobs, their traditional stronghold, and sometimes in the face of new legislation or company pressures to curb trade-union power. Clearly, as well as the pressures employers have faced to reorganize, many have designed new jobs with the new women's labor

Table 25.1 Sectoral distribution of employment in Britain, 1983–1997

| | *1983* | | *1987* | | *1997* | |
|---|---|---|---|---|---|---|
| | *% total employment* | *000s* | *% total employment* | *000s* | *% total employment* | *000s* |
| *Manufacturing* | 24.5 | | 22.3 | | 18.0 | |
| Men | | 3,862 | | 3,547 | | 2,880 |
| Women | | 1,556 | | 1,502 | | 1,121 |
| Part-time women | | 336 | | 302 | | 204 |
| *Services* | 65.8 | | 69.2 | | 76.0 | |
| Men | | 6,110 | | 6,379 | | 7,197 |
| Women | | 7,060 | | 7,868 | | 9,696 |
| Part-time women | | 3,346 | | 3,774 | | 4,908 |
| *Public administration* | 7.1 | | 6.8 | | 5.9 | |
| Men | | 835 | | 831 | | 658 |
| Women | | 717 | | 746 | | 646 |
| Part-time women | | 218 | | 231 | | 192 |
| *Total (%)* | 97.4 | | 98.3 | | 100 | |
| *No. (000s)* | | 20,572 | | 21,080 | | 22,236 |

*Sources*: *Employment Gazette*, Historical Supplement, 100, 6, June 1992; *Labour Market Trends*, 106, 2, February 1998.

force in mind. The new labor force of mothers has proved an attractive reliable workforce to many service-sector employers compared with unqualified young male school-leavers and at the same, or sometimes lower, cost.

Families attempting to support themselves have been faced with a decline in the men's real earnings and job opportunities, an increase in risk attached to supporting the family, and a growth in opportunities for women's paid work. The growth in married women's and mothers' paid work has been attractive as a way of diversifying the family's financial support system and the associated risks, as well as offering the opportunity for a higher standard of living, and the potential for women to engage in public as well as private life. The overall addition to household income from having two earners has lowered the family risk attached to labor-market participation. Even though many of the jobs taken up by women have been in the higher risk and more vulnerable sector, the flexibility they offered has been welcomed by many mothers since it has allowed them to combine family responsibilities with income-generating activities. Elements of the changes can be explained, therefore, in terms of individuals' or family units' economic incentives; and from behavior under conditions of increasing risk. But, clearly, large-scale changes in attitudes and increased levels of education are also underpinning the new work – family relationships, and it is not always clear which was the chicken and which the egg.

## Earnings and wages

As well as the distribution of male earnings having become increasingly unequal (Gosling, Machin, and Meghir, 1996; Hills, 1995), there has been an increase in full-time, but not necessarily part-time women's earnings relative to those of men (Elias and Gregory, 1994; Harkness, Machin, and Waldfogel, 1995; Joshi, Davies, and Land, 1996; Paci and Joshi, 1996). Women's earnings were 80 percent of those of men by 1995 (Hakim, 1996; Joshi et al., 1995), an increase from less than two-thirds in 1970. The relative hourly wages of young male and female workers under 30 has now come close to equality. On the other hand, the gap has widened between women working full- and part-time, with wages experiencing a pay penalty from part-time hours of work (Joshi, Davies, and Land, 1996; Paci and Joshi, 1996). Research suggests that this disparity (between full- and part-time pay for women) is an influential explanatory factor in the lower earnings of mothers compared with women without children (Joshi, Macran, and Dex, 1996).

### Unemployment

Unemployment has fluctuated along with the business cycle. Unemployment affects family finances severely. Studies suggest that periods of unemployment can have a lasting effect on labor-market prospects (Dex and McCulloch, 1997). Where men have been unemployed and receiving means-tested benefit, this has had the effect of lowering the participation rate of their wives (Dex et al., 1995). The effect has varied across countries, depending on the details of the benefit regulations. What is also evident is that married women appear to be more likely to be unemployed than men in some countries. An examination of these differences suggests it is partly a product of the incentives to register as unemployed, the unemployment benefit rules, and the extent to which women see themselves as unemployed if they have other caring work in the home to carry out, or have been working part-time (Dex, 1996). There are effects on parents' health from unemployment (Warr, 1987) and it possibly increases the likelihood of marital breakdown (Lampard, 1994). There are also particular cohorts of young men whose potential for family formation and supporting children has been handicapped because they first entered the labor market at a time of severe recession (Ermisch and Francesconi, 1996).

## Families' Life Cycle of Involvement in the Labor Market

We can chart a snapshot picture of how many mothers and fathers are working, for how many hours at a point in time; how many have young or older children; where mothers, fathers, both parents, or neither are employed. But this hides elements of the social changes that have been taking place that can only be seen as we follow individuals over time, and we compare successive cohorts of parents passing through the same stages of their life-course. These two types of accounts are not in conflict, but both are needed to get the full picture of exactly which aspects of behavior have been changing.

### The snapshot picture

The snapshot picture at the turn of the twentieth century shows the majority of mothers and fathers in paid work in most industrialized countries. On the whole, mothers with younger children are less likely to be in paid work than mothers where the youngest child is older or a teenager. However, successive snapshot pictures do show that mothers with a young child have been progressively more likely to be in paid work since the mid-1980s in Britain. For married mothers with a child under 5, 58 percent were employed in 1997, compared with 45 percent in 1990; 78 percent with a youngest child aged 10 or over were employed in 1997. Compared with white-partnered mothers, Black-, Indian-, and Chinese-partnered mothers were more likely to be economically active in 1991 when they had a youngest child under 5 years old. The full-time/part-time split is most striking between couple mothers whose youngest child is under 5, of whom 21 percent were working full-time, and mothers whose youngest child was 10 or over, of whom twice as many were working full-time (36 percent) in 1997. While mothers in couples have dramatically increased their participation in the labor force, lone mothers' employment rates had hardly changed up to 1997 (Holtermann et al., 1999).

Econometric estimations suggest that the age of the youngest child is the single most important predictor of mother's labor-force participation (Joshi, Macran, and Dex, 1996), although the higher the woman's own potential wage the more likely she is to engage in paid work. These effects appear to be mediated by the extent of child-care and the state subsidy for child-care which exists in a society. So the depressing effect of children on women's labor-force participation is less where the extent of child-care for preschool children is greater (Dex, Walters, and Alden, 1993). The number of children is not a significant predictor of participation in Britain, although it is more important in other non-Scandinavian European counties. Levels of household income have also acted as a buffer for some couples, making it less likely that the mother will work where her partner's income level is higher. Over time, however, successive snapshots suggest that the influence of partners' income has been declining.

There has been a change in the structure of financial support in families; a move from one-earner to two-earner couples (see figure 25.1). However, the interaction with the unemployment benefit system in some countries has meant that where benefit is means-tested against the household income, there has been a disincentive for women married to unemployed men to take up paid work. This has helped to produce a small but significant percentage of no-earner households in Britain.

The same state support system has been responsible for some of the lower participation rates of lone parents. Their incentive to work has been dampened by a benefits system (including income support, housing benefit, and school-meals costs for children) that has had high marginal tax rates if mothers started to work. If the mother was only capable of low earnings either from a part-time job, or because of low skill levels, she would be worse off by taking a low-paid job and losing all the benefits.

There are fewer lone mothers in employment in Britain than in most European countries (apart from the Netherlands, Germany, and Ireland). The gap between the employment of lone mothers and married mothers in Britain has grown both from lone mothers decreasing and married mothers increasing their participation. However, part of the gap is due to British lone mothers being relatively young in age compared with all mothers (more than half of lone mothers are aged under 24). Another part of the gap is due to the fact that lone mothers are more likely than all mothers to have children under school age, and more than one child (Bradshaw et al., 1996). The presence of children in the family has made little difference to men's working patterns apart from a slight increase in weekly hours of work of fathers in Britain compared to other married men. Most fathers have a continuing commitment to

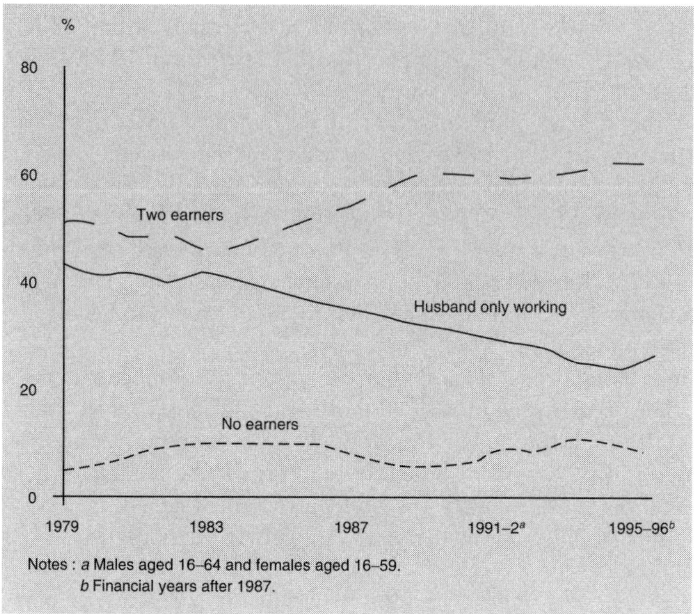


**Figure 25.1** Couples with dependent children by number of earners

*Source*: General Household Survey, in Office of National Statistics (1997).

full-time work through the arrival of children, and see themselves and their contribution to the family as the main breadwinner (Warin et al., 1999). The moving picture shows more of the dynamics and changes that have been occurring, mainly in mothers' behavior.

## The arrival of children and mothers' return to work

The arrival and then growing up of their children has had substantial effects on women's labor-force participation. In the mid-twentieth century it was common for mothers to stop work altogether to devote themselves to unpaid family work and care. A gradual move back into work occurred when children were older which gained momentum such that by 1980, 90 percent of mothers had eventually returned to work after having children. Cohort comparisons also started to see a progressive shortening of the period spent out of paid work. The combination of many mothers' preferences to keep contact with the labor market, and the income derived from it, coupled with changing legislation in the form of maternity leave, facilitated mothers' return to the same employer and helped to shorten the period spent out of work.

By 1988 in Britain, nearly half (45 percent) of women who were in work when they became pregnant were back at work within eight or nine months of having a baby. Even more marked was the increase in the number of mothers returning to full-time work. Over one-fifth of women who were working full-time when they became pregnant in 1988 returned to full-time work within eight or nine months of the birth, compared with 7 percent in 1979 (McRae, 1991). Other surveys also suggest that the proportion of women returning to work has continued to increase, particularly among the highly educated who delayed their first childbirth, and that a higher proportion are returning to full-time employment after only very short periods out of work (Macran, Joshi, and Dex, 1995; Callender et al., 1997).

## Partnership and the structure of employment

It is the case that the vast majority of parents are married couples, so in this sense parental status and legal marriage status overlap to a large extent. There are relatively few considerations of the effects of marriage per se (independently of children) on employment behavior. Some of the main findings, most extensively documented in US research, are summarized below:

- married men work longer and harder compared with other men (Akerlof, 1998);
- marriage has been shown to be associated with improvements in all measurable labor-market indicators for men, as well as with measures of health and well-being (summaries in Akerlof, 1998; Morgan, 1999);
- men's unemployment increases the likelihood of marital breakdown (Murphy, 1985; Cameron, 1995);
- mothers who work full-time and more continuously are more likely to divorce than mothers who do not work (Ermisch, 1991).

## Why do parents go out to work?

The main reason mothers go out to work is economic, and this has not changed since the 1970s (Martin and Roberts, 1984; Harkness, Machin, and Waldfogel, 1995). Other issues are relevant to the decision but less important overall; for example, the practicalities of child-care, and whether the mother actually *wants* to return to work (Thomson, 1995). Mothers clearly get more from being employed than just the money. For example, 71 percent of those working full-time reported that their job meant much more to them than simply a means of earning a living (Thomson, 1995). However, there is also evidence in Britain that many women would prefer to have more choice. One official survey (Department for Education and Employment, 1996) found that 87 percent of mothers of preschool children said they preferred to look after their own children; if money were not a problem, two-thirds of employed mothers with small children said they would prefer to stay at home.

A small qualitative study found that the arguments of mothers for staying at home were mainly linked to the care of children. Mothers who were working spoke of work as "a fall back in case anything happens" and "you can support yourself if you need to," as well as the need or wish to earn money (Spencer and Taylor, 1994). Mothers working part-time were found to enjoy the combination of part-time work and caring for a family (Watson and Fothergill, 1993), although clearly some work part-time involuntarily (Dex and McCulloch, 1997). The extent of employment amongst married women (especially in the US, but also in the UK) is consistent with the idea that they are taking out insurance against marital breakdown in the face of weakened divorce law (Parkman, 1992). Fathers' reasons for working have been studied less frequently. Recent research on a small sample of fathers in the northwest of England found that working for financial necessity to provide income for the family was the main reason fathers gave for working (Warin et al., 1999).

Many fathers saw this as integral to the role of being a father and, interestingly, mothers and teenage children all agreed. In some cases, there was pressure to provide clothes and other goods that teenagers demanded. This was in contrast to many of the women who cited "to give independence" as their reason for being employed.

### Working adolescent children and unpaid family workers

The issue of children at work had received relatively little attention from the research community and data sources have been limited. One national US study found that 61 percent of 10th-graders (15–16 years), 90 percent of 11th- and 12th-graders (ages 16–18) were employed at some time in the school year (Manning, 1990). A similar British nationwide survey found that 52 percent of 13–15-year-olds had worked at some time during the year compared with four-fifths of 16–18-year-olds. Most of the younger age group were working no more than a few hours a week, commonly in retail and service-sector jobs, and were doing so for financial reasons (Hibbett and Beatson, 1995). A further US study found that 47 percent of boys and 38 percent of girls were working more than 20 hours per week (reviewed in Mortimer and Finch, 1996).

There has been a concern in this literature with the extent of contravening legal restrictions on children's hours of work at given ages. Hibbert and Beatson's (1995) UK study found that contravention of legal restrictions was common. However, others have argued for the focus to be less on hours of work and more on the effects of the varying nature and quality of work (Mortimer and Finch, 1996). This change of focus was derived from learning in the study of the effects of work on adults. The findings from the subsequent programs of empirical research with children, based often on longitudinal data, have largely supported this differentiated view.

## Balancing Paid and Unpaid Work and Care – The Family's Perspective

Implicit in fulfilling the care responsibilities to children while sustaining the family financially is a division of labor within the household. Intact families can draw on the unpaid work of a father and a mother as well, possibly, as paid help to do the caring. Women's pay rates are often lower than those of men. This straight economic calculus would favor most mothers taking the caring responsibilities, with men being the breadwinner through paid work. However, for some women, it will be an investment decision where there are sufficient gains to their future income stream from staying in the labor market over childbirth. While this traditional pattern has been moderated by mothers also engaging in paid work, the evidence suggests that most mothers are still prepared to accept the major caring responsibility. They either work part-time and fewer hours than men, and in any case mothers tend to be the parent responsible for managing the care – work interface, arranging child-care, and attending to emergencies when children are sick, even when others are paid to contribute.

### Child-care

Mothers' increasing participation in the labor force has gone alongside a growth in outsourced child-care. The form this takes is very different across societies, even though the growth in mothers' employment rates has been common. In the social welfare regimes of Scandinavia, the state or regional authorities have provided extensive and subsidized formal institutional child-care for preschool children. At the other end of the spectrum, the relatively unregulated free-market economies of the UK and US have left market forces to resolve the care business, with the results that child-care is more disparate, ad hoc, costly, and less institutionalized. Comparisons across Europe in the mid-1990s found that British parents paid the highest child-care costs in Europe. On average, in Britain, 93 percent of child-care costs were met by parents. More latterly, and since 1997, the state has become partially involved with the provision of child-care in the UK, and a National Child Care Strategy has now been developed with targets for provision.

While the use of paid child-care provision has grown in Britain from 2 in 10 in 1989 to 4 in 10 child-care users in 1993 (Ford, Marsh, and McKay, 1995), the majority of British mothers who work make do with informal sources of care. In some cases, parents choose their shifts in order to cover the child-care between them (La Valle et al., 2002). In other cases, and more often for schoolage children, cover is arranged informally through a range of relatives, neighbors, and parents of other school peers, all contributing to a complicated patchwork that covers after school, early mornings, and school holidays. However, the choice by many mothers to work part-time and arrange child-care informally, typical in Britain, is not so typical in other countries. In France and the US, women are more likely to work full-time, and use their enhanced earnings to pay for formal child-care, or access state-subsidized child-care, as in France (Dex, Walters, and Alden, 1993; Dex and Shaw, 1986). There is evidence that the relative lack of formal child-care provision has been a factor in restricting a minority of women's economic activity in Britain (Thomson, 1995; Callender et al., 1997), more so in the past. But is also appears that British women differ in their attitudes toward nonmaternal care from mothers in some other countries.

The growth in outsourced care seems unable to carry on increasing in Britain. The gendered care workforce of women are now in short supply across nurses, child-care and social care workers. As job opportunities for women have grown, fewer women, the traditional carers both in unpaid and paid spheres, are wanting jobs that are relatively low-paid, sometimes at unsocial times of day. Childminders have seen notable falls in their numbers (Mooney et al., 2001). Care homes and the health service are experiencing severe shortages. The dynamics of these shortages would be predicted by economists to raise the wages of jobs in short supply. However, this means raising the costs of mothers taking up paid jobs. Also, where the jobs are paid for out of the public purse, this implies a tax rise for families which would affect the rewards from work and, therefore, the decision to engage in paid work. How these pressures and dynamics will work out is not clear.

## The division of paid and unpaid work

It is well established that domestic household work is rarely shared equally by women and men, even though men are doing more now than was once the case (Gershuny, 1995; Gershuny and Robinson, 1988; Ringen and Halpin, 1995). Women still tend to shoulder the lion's share while the decline in their domestic activity reflects the increasing time they are spending at work (Joshi, 1996). However, as a slight caveat about the figures which follow, Warin et al.'s (1999) small-scale, qualitative study suggested that survey and time-budget methods of noting who does what may underestimate men's contributions to domestic work.

An analysis of the time-use of parents in 1995 found that mothers spent more time than fathers doing cooking and housework. Fathers spent more time than mothers doing paid work. Where fathers are in employment, both mothers and fathers report that mothers do most of the core domestic activities of cleaning, laundry, shopping, and cooking, whether or not the mother herself is in paid employment. Although fathers are more inclined to say that domestic chores are shared, while mothers report that they do the most, there is more unanimity than disagreement between them about who does most of these central tasks. Parents are most likely to share domestic tasks when both are working full-time, while the share taken by mothers increases markedly for those working part-time, and this is little different from the share of mothers who are not employed outside of the home. Better-off, dual-earner families are also able to buy in domestic help and so ease home demands on them (Gregson and Lowe, 1993). Part of this disagreement may be due to the management role women often take on (Warin et al., 1999; Hochschild, 1990), and to women

**Table 25.2** Fathers' responsibility for domestic chores as reported in 1991 for 33-year-olds

| | *Dual worker* | | *Single worker* | |
|---|---|---|---|---|
| | *Wife f-t (%)* | *Wife p-t (%)* | *Wife works (%)* | *Wife home (%)* |
| *Preparing and cooking main meal* | | | | |
| I do most | 11 | 3 | 28 | 2 |
| Wife does most | 62 | 82 | 49 | 88 |
| Shared equally | 27 | 15 | 23 | 10 |
| *Shopping* | | | | |
| I do most | 9 | 5 | 33 | 6 |
| Wife does most | 51 | 67 | 49 | 66 |
| Shared equally | 40 | 28 | 18 | 28 |
| *Cleaning* | | | | |
| I do most | 2 | 1 | 17 | 1 |
| Wife does most | 63 | 83 | 58 | 88 |
| Shared equally | 35 | 16 | 25 | 11 |
| *Household repairs/DIY* | | | | |
| I do most | 72 | 79 | 76 | 77 |
| Wife does most | 2 | 3 | 5 | 5 |
| Shared equally | 26 | 18 | 19 | 19 |
| *Household money/paying bills* | | | | |
| I do most | 33 | 28 | 32 | 43 |
| Wife does most | 37 | 45 | 50 | 34 |
| Shared equally | 30 | 27 | 18 | 23 |

*Note*: Cohort fathers' report of their responsibility for domestic chores.

*Sources*: Ferri and Smith (1996), unpublished tables 3.15–3.20 available from the authors; National Child Development Study, Wave V.

**Table 25.3** Mothers' responsibility for domestic chores as reported in 1991 at age 33

| | *Dual worker* | | *Single worker* | |
|---|---|---|---|---|
| | *Mother f-t (%)* | *Mother p-t (%)* | *Mother works (%)* | *Mother home (%)* |
| *Preparing and cooking main meal* | | | | |
| I do most | 66 | 85 | 69 | 90 |
| Husband does most | 10 | 2 | 6 | 2 |
| Shared equally | 24 | 13 | 25 | 8 |
| *Shopping* | | | | |
| I do most | 57 | 74 | 62 | 72 |
| Husband does most | 10 | 4 | 8 | 5 |
| Shared equally | 32 | 23 | 30 | 23 |
| *Cleaning* | | | | |
| I do most | 66 | 87 | 69 | 91 |
| Husband does most | 3 | 1 | 9 | <1 |
| Shared equally | 31 | 12 | 22 | 9 |
| *Laundry* | | | | |
| I do most | 82 | 93 | 86 | 97 |
| Husband does most | 3 | 1 | 5 | – |
| Shared equally | 15 | 6 | 9 | 3 |
| *Household repairs/DIY* | | | | |
| I do most | 6 | 5 | 5 | 7 |
| Husband does most | 69 | 73 | 70 | 68 |
| Shared equally | 25 | 22 | 25 | 25 |
| *Household money/paying bills* | | | | |
| I do most | 44 | 48 | 42 | 40 |
| Husband does most | 23 | 27 | 20 | 35 |
| Shared equally | 33 | 25 | 38 | 25 |

*Note*: Cohort mothers' report of their responsibility for domestic chores.

*Sources*: Ferri and Smith (1996), unpublished tables 3.15–3.20 available from authors; National Child Development Study, Wave V.

feeling they are doing the emotion work (see Dunscombe and Marsden, 1993). Emotion work underpins the management role, wanting everything to run smoothly, sorting out changes to the schedule, and making sure relationships are maintained with the wider family, but it also extends to worrying when children have problems.

Just as the core domestic activities remain the responsibility of mothers, so household repairs and DIY remain overwhelmingly the responsibility of fathers (between 6 in 10 and three-quarters of families) as reported by both mothers and fathers.

Dealing with household money and paying bills are not reported as being tasks falling predominantly to either mothers or fathers; rather, there is more variation in how families assign these tasks. Between one-fifth and one-third reported that they share them equally.

Fathers appear to be fitting family commitments around their working lives and are able to be "*'single minded' in their focus on work*" (Spencer and Taylor, 1994, italics in original). For mothers, it is their labor-market activity which usually has to be fitted around their family responsibilities (Ferri and Smith, 1996; Spencer and Taylor, 1994). The effect is on the number of hours they worked rather than on the decision to be employed or not, but also on their level of seniority or the responsibility they felt able to cope with. On the other hand, women suggested that getting support from both employers and partners increased their ability to reconcile the conflicting demands of work and family life (Spencer and Taylor, 1994).

Other recent studies and reviews of fathers' roles confirmed that there was no evidence that men were signing up to the notion of being "new men" in large numbers (Lewis and O'Brien, 1987). It has long been recognized that there are competing forces on men's involvement in the home (McKee and O'Brien, 1982). Warin et al. (1999) found that fathering was constrained by the reluctance of both fathers and mothers to give up their traditional roles. Young single and non-residential fathers had some different perspectives on being fathers (Speak, Camerson, and Gilroy, 1997). They felt they were made to feel unimportant. In some cases, unemployment and the resulting lack of money prevented young men from being involved in the way they wanted to be.

Ferri and Smith's (1996) analysis of the relationship between family employment patterns and family activities found little difference in the activity patterns of families with either a sole-earner father or where both parents were in employment (whether or not the mother worked full- or part-time). LaValle et al.'s (2002) examination of the family activities of mothers or fathers working at atypical times of day, weekends, or long hours found that such working patterns did constrain parents from spending as much time or doing activities with their children and with each other. Dissatisfaction was expressed about the effects of working atypical hours on family life, with most dissatisfaction expressed about the effects of regular work on Sundays.

## The division of labor and its consequences

Some mothers have been happy with the earlier pattern of accepting almost full-time responsibility for looking after their own children. These are the relatively few single-earner families who have a clear-cut division of labor, the male partner doing paid work, the female partner doing unpaid caring. Consequences of this pattern are apparent in economic and sociological studies. These mothers experience a loss of lifetime earnings, and a loss in their potential hourly wage rate if they decide to return to work at a later date. The gap in working experience has a depreciating effect on the rate of pay they can expect on return, in proportion to the length of time out of paid work. However, in the US, there is evidence that former rates can be caught up because of a faster wage-rate growth on return (England, 1982). However, pensions, relying as they do on employment tenure and levels of contributions, are also lowered by periods out of employment, a factor many countries are now struggling to face up to as the populations age and require pension payments for longer than in the past. As well as the financial disadvantages, many mothers who have extensive gaps in employment also experience a loss of confidence about their labor-market skills and potential to contribute. Many of the jobs they finally return to are at a lower occupational status than jobs they did prior to childbirth (Dex, 1992). For those women who have given priority to caring for children over paid work, they also give priority to convenient work which implies short travel-to-work times, allowing for combining work and care responsibilities (Hakim, 2000). Such jobs also tend to be lower paid than if unconstrained job searches were thought possible. Some men's jobs clearly rely on the men having a stay-at-home wife who will take responsibility for all of the child-care and domestic management of the home, and while some occupations offer high earnings to make this division more acceptable, others do not (Finch, 1983). However, the mothers who put caring as a priority over work may experience advantages in their quality of life, although not in their income level, over those who work full-time.

Mothers who decide to return to work protect or improve their earnings potential, their retirement pension, and increase their lifetime earnings and household income. Other things equal, they are able to have a higher standard of living than couples where the mother does not work. They may also gain career benefits through promotion. However, there can be other disadvantages, that I will review later.

### Childlessness

While many women have been postponing having a first child, partly in order to establish their workplace career (Macran, Joshi, and Dex, 1995), some couples are responding to the conflicting demands of work and families by forgoing having children. The attractions to the woman of having a high-paid career have won over against the risks of losing this status that having children has generated.

The proportions of women remaining childless have increased. In Britain, more than one in six women born since 1950 (17 percent) were childless at age 40 compared with only 1 in 10 (10 percent) born a decade earlier. Current projections, based on extrapolating from the trends in each cohort and questions about family intentions in a large-scale official survey (GHS), suggest that as many as one-fifth of women born since 1974 and later will remain childless (McAllister and Clarke, 1998). This will mean there will be fewer families with children, assuming these women and men still marry or form coresidential partnerships. These families will be relatively advantaged in socioeconomic terms and in their ability to participate in work. A variety of reasons were given for remaining childless in one small-scale study. They included, for some, the desire to pursue a career, and for some, the feeling that they would not make good parents (McAllister and Clarke, 1998). This trend potentially has very serious consequences for supporting the aging population in future.

## The Changing Organization of Work

Balancing the demands of paid work and care since women entered the labor force in large numbers has become an important policy topic in most industrialized countries. As evidence of pressures and family breakdown have risen, the idea that those in work need to have greater flexibility to help them balance or integrate their work and family or personal lives has surfaced. Greater work–life balance is one of the planks politicians have been seizing on to help rescue us from declining populations, increasing work-related stress and ill health, the rising costs of care for the elderly, at the same time as moving towards greater gender equity. These may be somewhat conflicting aspirations.

Businesses throughout the industrialized world have been facing increased competition in the now global marketplaces and the 24/7 society. This has put pressures on businesses to be competitive and keep their costs and wage bill low, looking out for new efficiency gains and lean production processes that use the minimum of workers. For some employers, designing their jobs to facilitate the new, often lower-paid, women's labor supply has been their response. For others, expecting employees to work longer hours and harder has been an implicit strategy in their recruitment and reward systems. A proliferation of models of working-time arrangements have resulted from the same pressures operating in different product-market environments. Parents have got caught up in these trends and are more likely than other workers to be working nonstandard hours and arrangements.

It may not be surprising, therefore, to hear calculations of the costs of absence and stress to workplaces and the economy. One British government estimate put the costs of employee absence to cope with work and family at £11 billion to the British economy in 1999, an average of £500 per employee. Stress and ill health were estimated to cause between 4.4 and 8.5 million days lost and cost £360 million in the same year (DTI, 2000).

## Unsocial hours

Working "unsocial" hours – evenings, nights, and weekends – has been increasing (Hewitt, 1993; Mulgan and Wilkinson, 1995; Watson, 1994). According to the Labour Force Survey (LFS) in 1994, 1 in 6 of those in employment "usually work in the evening," 1 in 7 "usually worked shift work," and 1 in 17 "usually worked at night." Approximately 1,466,000 women and 2,414,000 men of working age did shift work as part of their job in 1994. Approximately one-third of the jobs which involved shift work were held by women and two-thirds were held by men. The LFS also reveals that a quarter of those in employment in the UK usually worked on Saturday in 1995 (Eurostat, 1996). Employees who usually work on Sundays increased from 10.8 percent in 1992 to 12.5 percent in 1998, and those who sometimes work on Sundays increased from 26.8 percent in 1992 to 30.3 percent in 1998. Since employment increased in total over this period, there has been a large increase in the numbers of employees working on Sundays.

Long hours of work are also very evident. Hogarth et al.'s (2000) survey found that 34 percent of men working full time and 17 percent of women worked more than 48 hours per week. British men worked the longest average hours in Europe (Moss, 1996). Ferri and Smith's analysis of the 1958 birth-cohort fathers in 1991 (Ferri and Smith, 1999) found that two-thirds of the fathers were working in the evening and 6 in 10 at the weekends. Almost a third were working nights between 10 PM and 4 AM and slightly more between 4 AM and 7 AM. Parents, and especially lone parents, increasingly work on Sundays and at other times when their children are at home. They are not happy about these working arrangements, especially having to work regularly on Sunday (LaValle et al., 2002). However, seen in a longer historical time frame, working hours for employees and male parents are now clearly considerably shorter than 100 years ago. The increased intensification of work and stress associated with working at the turn of the twenty-first century may say more about our attitudes and lifestyle than about the effects of changing hours of work (Wainwright and Calnan, 2002)

Other types of working arrangements on the increase have been working at home during normal working hours, annualized hours; shift work, early mornings and late evenings. Part-time, temporary, self-employment, some types of shift work, home-working and teleworking, often called flexible employment, are all more common among mothers than they are among other women (Dex 1999).

## Organizations' responses

There is a growing consideration of the work–family interface from the sociological and interdisciplinary perspectives embedded in management organizational behavior theory and empirical research. Leading-edge organizations have not been slow to recognize the issues their workforces face and to start to think about the implications for their organization's working arrangements, employment policies and practices, and even for organizational culture. These corporate initiatives led the way in the US, UK, and Australia, government policy interests following later in some cases. There are considerations of why some organizations and not others have taken strategic action to address these issues (Goodstein, 1994; Barringer and Milkovich, 1998; Dex and Smith, 2002); discussions of the business case for offering flexibility (reviewed in Dex and Scheibl, 1999); the management problems in facing these issues (Lewis and Lewis, 1996; Yeandle et al., 2002), unions' roles (Bond et al., 2002); focuses on small businesses (Dex and Scheibl, 2002); and action research projects introducing flexibility into organizations (Rapoport et al., 2002).

The action research projects have led to other interesting developments (Rapoport et al., 2002; Bailyn, 1993). The empirical work preceding such initiatives has uncovered underlying assumptions about how work should be organized, and what are the accepted ways of behaving, and theorizing about time and its organization (e.g., Perlow, 1999). Assumptions have come to light showing managers' and workers' assumptions that work is only efficient and productive if the worker is visible in the workplace, now called presenteeism; and that long hours of work show greater worker commitment than shorter hours. On these assumptions women can often appear to have lower productivity than men, whereas per hour spent they may even have higher productivity. Leading on from these findings, others have argued that the modern workplace, with its appraisal systems, feedback, structured individual reward systems, message of valuing the workforce, opportunities for socializing and friendship building, and social events have now taken the place of the home in workers' lives (Hochschild, 1997). The home, in contrast, is portrayed as a place of conflict between partners and children. The demands of workplace commitments impose a new rigid time-driven schedule on home and children, of getting to day care early and leaving late in order for parents to be at work, where the rewards make it seem worthwhile. While feminists used to argue for the higher valuation of home and care work (Oakley, 1974), this argument has been lost, being replaced by value accruing solely to paid and public work. Aided by the low societal valuation of home and domestic work, mothers feel more valued and appreciated by going out to paid work than they have done by staying home.

## Equal opportunities in the workplace

That there should be gender equity and equal opportunities in the workplace is now accepted by all industrialized societies and enshrined in legislation. Working through the reality of implementing and mainstreaming equal opportunities in organizations' recruitment, selection, training, and promotion procedures leaves much work to be done. But there is a still a debate to conclude over whose behavior patterns this is to be modeled on. Uncovering more of how organizational norms traditionally reflect men's behavior has led to the questioning of whether men's behavior (long hours of work, presenteeism, responsibility-free workers, macho styles, individualized promotion procedures) offers the model against which to judge women's progress in the workplace. A female model could be substituted (shorter hours, recognition of other responsibilities, less individualistic, more relational management styles), or alternatively some new hybrid negotiated to lie somewhere between the two. The outcomes of this issue are crucial to whether nonstandard and shorter-hours contributions to the labor market continue to be penalized and stigmatized. If we cannot reach a more equitable valuation of paid work that relates to the quality of work done per hour, we cannot hope to resolve the societal caring issues that are mounting from having two parents accepting long hours of work in order to protect and enhance their careers.

## The Influence of Paid Work on Family Life

There is now a substantial body of empirical work, much done by social psychologists, which has examined the various links between work and family, focusing on employed individuals who are also family members as the units of analysis. The reverse effects of family life on work are part of the same research considerations, using similar concepts, and in many studies cannot be distinguished one from the other. Many statistical associations can be shown, under a number of subheadings:

- there are spillover effects between the two domains, e.g., from mood or satisfaction, generating similarities between them;
- there are compensation effects, e.g., to offset dissatisfaction in one domain by seeking satisfaction in another;
- there are segmentation effects, where individuals separate the two domains in order to avoid them influencing each other;
- resource drain can occur if one domain is more demanding, leaving less energy to tackle the other domain;
- congruence is the similarity between work and family owing to a third common cause; and
- family-work conflict can occur, a form of inter-role conflict where the two domains become incompatible.

Studies under each of these headings are reviewed in Edwards and Rothbard (2000). However, these authors are also critical of much of this large body of empirical work which they describe as "ambiguous metaphor" rather than "formal theory" (p. 179). This judgment comes from the fact that much of the empirical associations have not clarified the signs, causal structure, or forces behind the statistical associations they have elaborated. Rather than throw out the decades of family–work research, Edwards and Rothbard offer a compromise that respecifies the causal relationships, the expected signs of those relationships, and whether there is individual intention behind the relationships, using the existing family–work concepts, as elaborated above. Under this more rigorous framework, the hard evidence on each strand of relationships is much less than the literature might imply, although there is some evidence under each heading. The gaps needing further research are also obvious.

On the effects of work on families, the main effects noted are mood, extent of feeling valued, and work satisfaction, which can affect the individual's family functioning. Also, extended work hours have been linked to work/family conflict and rigid work schedules to depression amongst women (Glass and Estee, 1997). The outcomes at work caused by family problems are lower productivity, higher turnover, higher absenteeism and sickness, and lower career achievement resulting from family problems (Glass and Estee, 1997). These reported effects have the problem that they often rely on self-reports by the workers or parents concerned. This field cries out for greater availability and collection of longitudinal data, which at least can chart the sequence in time of events and responses.

## Outcomes for children

One area where effects of work are being examined using longitudinal data is that of the outcomes for children of parents' employment. Outcomes for children from parents working cover a number of areas; their education and ability; their emotional development; and, to a lesser extent, the use of illegal substances and other criminal activity.

There has been a longstanding debate about the effect of parental employment on children's educational performance over a range of disciplines. The methods used to evaluate these effects are very varied, as are their conclusions (Haveman and Wolfe, 1995). A recent focus of concern has been with the relationship of mother's employment to the academic development of children. Research on teenagers in east London found that the best educational performance (as measured by attainment of GCSEs) of children arose where their mothers worked part-time (and fathers worked full-time) (O'Brien, 1997; O'Brien and Jones, 1999). These results outstripped those of their peers whose mothers were not in employment or worked full-time. Some earlier evidence found a positive relationship between the employment of mothers and children's educational achievement (Ermisch and Francesconi, 1997). However, recent British studies using longitudinal data found some negative effects on children's education from mothers having worked, especially full-time, when the child was of preschool age or a baby (Ermisch and Francesconi, 2000; Joshi, 2000). One of these studies used siblings within the same family to control for unobserved differences between families in how they bring up their children.

Gregg, Harkness, and Machin (1999) found that children growing up in households with financial hardship had significantly lower levels of educational attainment by age 23.

There has been a growing literature on the effects of lone-parent status on children. We are unable to review all of this material here since it is not particularly focused on work and family life. However, it is worth noting that a large part of this debate concerns the issues of whether poorer outcomes for children of lone parents arise because of lower incomes and resources of lone parents or from the fact of experiencing marital breakdown. Lone parents in Britain, and elsewhere are less likely to be employed than other parents and this contributes, in many cases, to their lower incomes. In this way, the lack of paid work of some lone parents may be contributing to the lower levels of outcomes for their children, as reviewed in Burghes (1994).

Alongside the increase in maternal employment has gone a discussion about the effects on children of different types of nonmaternal child-care arrangements. While strong claims are made that nonmaternal care is both inferior and superior, the evidence is in fact much weaker. It is mostly insufficiently detailed, representative, or longitudinal to draw firm conclusions. Most of the assessments of the effects of child-care have relied on cross-sectional studies and focused on development outcomes in early childhood (Mooney and Munton, 1997; Morgan, 1996). They are mixed in their findings (Waldfogel, 1999; Dex, 1999).

## Conclusions

While there have been dramatic changes in the employment status of mothers, the employment status of father has changed less. The division of domestic work within the home has not changed in proportion to the changes of partners' amounts of paid work. Neither has spending on child-care increased to match the increases in mothers' hours of work, since the many couples manage with informal arrangements for younger and older children, at least in unregulated market economies. The nature of these changes means that, compared with the mid-twentieth century, overlapping family time has been squeezed by the combination of growth in unsocial hours of work, long hours of work, weekend work, outsourced child-care, and parents taking shifts at caring for children. Surveys suggest that parents are not entirely happy about the current state of affairs. Changes in parents' structuring and valuation of time and the valuations of paid and unpaid activities have been occurring. The driver from the employer side has been increased global competition. The driving force from the family side has come from pressures to raise income partly from a decline in some men's real earnings and probably in part from aspirations for increased consumption. These changes have put pressures on many parents. For men, the changes have contributed to growing insecurity and worsening employment prospects, and for young men they are having implications for their family formation.

However, while there is much in common in the trends across countries, there are many differences in the way parents relate to the labor market, the hours of work they do, and how child-care is organized. The level of variation is such that we have only been able to touch on it in this chapter. Families are sometimes seen as essentially private units making decisions based solely on their own preferences. Fuller examinations of cross-national differences in work and family relationships show that family units and their members need to be viewed within a wider framework, one with four spheres; first, the context of a country's industrial structures; second, the context of labor-market conditions; third, in terms of their work-related regulation and organization policies; and fourth, in terms of a country's political economy of social reproduction, often reflected in the extent to which support while not in paid work is provided by the state or welfare system. This means that a full understanding of families' relationships to work, both paid and unpaid, has to be based on a consideration of the interactions between labor markets, public and private welfare provisions, legislation, and individual family support structures. While some elements of this complex framework are well understood, other parts remain to be investigated and linked to the rest.

## References


Akerlof, G. (1998) Men without children. *Economic Journal*, 108, 257–309.

Bailyn, L. (1993) *Breaking the Mould; Women, Men and Time in the New Corporate World.* New York: Maxwell Macmillan.

Barringer, M. W., and Milkovich, G. T. (1998) A theoretical exploration of the adoption and design of flexible benefit plans: a case of human resource innovation. *Academy of Management Review*, 23, 305–24.

Beck, U. (1992) *The Risk Society: Towards a New Modernity*, London: Sage.

Bond, S., Hyman, J. Summers, J., and Wise, S. (2002) *Family-Friendly Working? Putting Policy into Practice*. York: York Publishing Services for the Joseph Rowntree Foundation.

Bradshaw, J., Kennedy, S., Kilkey, M., Hutton, S., and Corden, A. (1996) *The Employment of Lone Parents – A Comparison of Policy in 20 Countries*. Family Policy Studies Centre: London.

Burchell, B., Day, D., Hudson, M., Lapido, D., Mankelow, R., Nolan, J., Reed, H., Witshert, I. C., and Wilkinson, F. (1999) *Job Insecurity and Work Intensification: Flexibility and the Changing Boundaries of Work*. York: York Publishing Services for the Joseph Rowntree Foundation.

Burghes, L. (1994) *Lone Parenthood and Family Disruption: The Outcomes for Children.* London: Family Policy Studies Centre.

Callender, C., Millward, N., Lissenburgh, S., and Forth, J. (1997) *Maternity Rights and Benefits in Britain 1996*. DSS Research Series, Report No. 67. London: Stationery Office.

Cameron, S. (1995) A review of economic research into determinants of divorce. *British Review of Economic Issues*, 17, 1–21.

Department of Education and Employment (1996) *Family and Working Lives Survey*. Data Source Book, Vol. 2, p. 236. London: Department of Education and Employment.

Department of Trade and Industry (2000) *Work and Parents: Competitiveness and Choice, A Research Review*. London: Department of Trade and Industry.

Dex, S. (1992) Labour force participation of women in Britain during the 1990s: occupational mobility and part-time employment In R. M. Lindley (ed.), *Women's Employment: Britain in the Single European Market*. London: HMSO.

Dex, S. (1996) Women's experience of unemployment. *Economic Affairs*, 16, 2, 6–10.

Dex, S. (ed.) (1999) *Families and the Labour Market*. London and York: Family Policy Studies Centre for the Joseph Rowntree Foundation.

Dex, S., Gustafsson, S., Callan, T., and Smith, N. (1995) Cross-national comparisons of the labour force participation of women married to unemployed men. *Oxford Economic Papers*, 47, 611–35.

Dex, S., and McCulloch, A. (1997) *Characteristics of the Unemployed: Secondary Analysis of the Family and Working Lives Survey*. DfEE Research Report RR32. London: Department of Education and Employment.

Dex, S., and Schiebl, F. (1999) Business performance and family-friendly policies. *Journal of General Management*, 24, 22–37.

Dex, S., Scheibl, F., Smith, C., and Coussey, M. (2000) *New Working Patterns*. London: Centre for Tomorrow's Company and Pertemps.

Dex, S., and Shaw, L. B. (1986) *British and American Women at Work*. Basingstoke: Macmillan.

Dex, S., and Smith, C. (2002) *The Nature and Patterns of Family-Friendly Employment Policies in Britain*. Bristol: Policy Press.

Dex, S., Walters, P., and Alden, D. (1993) *French and British Mothers at Work*. Basingstoke: Macmillan.

Dunscombe, J., and Marsden, D. (1993) Love and intimacy: the gender division of emotion and emotion work. *Sociology*, 27, 221–42.

Edwards, J. R., and Rothbard, N. P. (2000) Mechanisms linking work and family: clarifying the relationship between work and family constructs. *Academy of Management Review 2000*, 25,178–199.

Elias, P., and Gregory, M. (1994) *The Changing Structure of Occupations and Earnings in Great Britain, 1975–1990, An Analysis Based on the New Earnings Survey Panel Dataset.* Research Series No. 27. London Department of Employment.

England, P. (1982) The failure of human capital theory to explain occupational sex segregation. *Journal of Human Resources*, 17, 358–70.

Ermisch, J. (1991) *Lone Parenthood.* Cambridge: Cambridge University Press.

Ermisch, J., and Francesconi, M. (1996) Partnership Formation and Dissolution in Great Britain. ESRC Research Centre on Micro Social Change Working Paper series No.96–10. London: Economic Social and Research Council.

Ermisch, J., and Francesconi, M. (1997) Family matters. ESRC Research Centre on Micro-Social Change Working Paper 97–1. Colchester: University of Essex.

Ermisch, J., and Francesconi, M. (2000) The effects of parents' employment on children's educational attainment. ISER Working Paper 2000–31. Colchester: University of Essex.

Eurostat (1996) *Labour Force Survey Results 1995.* Luxembourg: Office for Official Publications of the European Communities.

Ferri, E., and Smith, K. (1996) *Parenting in the 1990s.* London: Family Policy Studies Centre.

Finch, J. (1983) *Married to the Job: Wives' Incorporation into Men's Jobs.* London: Allen & Unwin.

Ford, R., Marsh, A., and McKay, S. (1995) *Changes in Lone Parenthood.* Department of Social Security Research Report No. 40. London: HMSO.

Gershuny, J. (1995) Relationships between women's employment and other activities. In R. Bayley, A. Condy, and C. Roberts (eds.), *Policies for Families: Work, Poverty and Resources.* London: Family Policy Studies Centre.

Gershuny, J., and Robinson, J. (1998) Historical changes in the household division of labour. *Demography*, 25, 4, 537–52.

Glass, J. L., and Estee, B. S. (1997) Workplace support childcare and turnover intentions among employed mothers of infants. *Journal of Family Issues*, 17, 317–35.

Goodstein, J. D. (1994) Institutional pressures and strategic responsiveness; employer involvement in work-family issues. *Academy Management Journal*, 37, 350–82.

Gosling, A., Machin, S., and Meghir, C. (1996) The changing distribution of male wages in the UK. Paper No. 275. London: Centre for Economic Performance, London School of Economics.

Gregg, P., Harkness, S., and Machin, S. (1999) *Child Development and Family Income.* York: Joseph Rowntree Foundation.

Gregson, N., and Lowe, M. (1993) Renegotiating the domestic division of labour? A study of dual career households in north-east and south-east England. *Sociological Review*, 41, 475–505.

Hakim, C. (1996) *Female Heterogeneity and the Polarisation of Women's Employment, Key Issues in Women's Work.* London: Athlone.

Hakim, C. (2000) *Work-Lifestyle Choices in the 21*st Century: Preference Theory. Oxford: Oxford University Press.

Harkness, S., Machin, S., and Waldfogel, J. (1995) *Evaluating the pin money hypothesis: The relationship between women's labour market activity, family income and poverty in Britain.* Welfare State Programme 108. London: STICERD, London School of Economics.

Haveman, R., and Wolfe, B. (1995) The determinants of children's attainment: A review of methods and findings. *Journal of Economic Literature*, 33, 1829–78.

Hewitt, P. (1993) *About Time.* London: IPPR/Oram Press.

Hibbett, A., and Beatson, M. (1995) Young people at work. *Employment Gazette*, 103, 4, 169–72.

Hills, J. (1995) *Income and Wealth.* Vol.2. York: Joseph Rowntree Foundation.

Hochschild, A. (1990) *The Second Shift: The Revolution at Home. London: Piatkus.*
Hochschild, A. (1997) *The Time Bind: When Work Becomes Home and Home Becomes Work*. New York: Henry Holt.
Hogarth, T., Hasluck, C., Pierre, G., Winterbotham, M., and Vivian, D. (2000) *Work Life Balance 2000: Baseline Study of Work – Life Balance Practices in Great Britain*. Warwick: Institute for Employment Research, Warwick University.
Holtermann, S., Brannen, J., Moss, P., and Owen, C. (1999) Lone parents and the labour market: Results from the 1997 Labour Force Survey and review of research. Employment Service Research Department Report, ESR23. London: Department of Employment.
Joshi, H. (1996) *The Opportunity Costs of Childbearing: More than Mothers' Business*. Lecture to the British Society for Population Studies, St Andrews, September.
Joshi, H., Dale, A., Ward, C., and Davies, H. (1995) *Dependence and Independence in the Finances of Women Aged 33*. London: Family Policy Studies Centre.
Joshi, H., Davies, H., and Land, H. (1996) *The Tale of Mrs Typical*. Occasional Paper 21. London: Family Policy Studies Centre.
Joshi, H., Macran, S., and Dex, S. (1996) Employment after childbearing and women's subsequent labour force participation. *Journal of Population Economics*, 9, 325–48.
Joshi, H. E. (2000) *Maternal Employment and Child Outcomes*. London: Smith Institute.
Lampard, R (1994) An examination of the relationship between marital dissolution and unemployment. In D. Gallie, C. Marsh, and C. Volger (eds.), *The Social Consequences of Unemployment*. Oxford: Oxford University Press.
LaValle, I., Arthur, S., Millward, C., Scott, J., and Claydon, M. (2002) *Atypical Work and Family Life*. Bristol: Policy Press.
Lewis, C., and O'Brien, M. (1987) *Reassessing Fatherhood: New Observations on Fathers and the Modern Family*. London: Sage.
Lewis, S., and Lewis, J. (1996) *The Work-Family Challenge: Rethinking Employment*. London: Sage.
Macran, S., Joshi, H., and Dex, S. (1995) Employment after childbearing: a survival analysis. *Work Employment and Society*, 10, 273–96.
Manning, W. D. (1990) Parenting employed teenagers. *Youth and Society*, 22, 184–200.
Martin, J., and Roberts, C. (1984) *Women and Employment: A Life Time Perspective*. Department of Employment/Office of Population Censuses and Surveys, London: HMSO.
McAllister, F., and Clarke, L. (1998) *Choosing Childlessness*. London: Family Policy Studies Centre.
McKee, L., and O'Brien, M. (eds.), (1982) *The Father Figure*. London: Tavistock.
McRae, S. (1991) *Maternity Rights in Britain*. London: Policy Studies Institute.
Mooney, A., Knight, A., Moss, P., and Owen, C. (2001) *Who Cares: Childminding in the 1990s*. York: Family Policy Studies Centre for the Joseph Rowntree Foundation.
Mooney, A., and Munton, A. G. (1997) *Research Policy in Early Childhood Services: Time for a New Agenda*, London: Institute of Education.
Morgan, P. (1996) *Who Needs Parents?* London: Institute of Economic Affairs.
Morgan, P. (1999) *Farewell to the Family*, London: Institute of Economic Affairs.
Mortimer, J. T., and Finch, M. D. (1996) *Adolescents, Work and Family: An Intergenerational Development Analysis*. London: Sage
Moss, P. (1996) *Parental employment in the EU*, 1985–1993. *Labour Market Trends*, 104, 12, 517–22.
Mulgan, G., and Wilkinson, H. (1995) Well-being and time. *Demos Quarterly*, 5, 2–11.
Murphy, M. J. (1985) Demographic and socio-economic influences on recent British marital breakdown patterns. *Population Studies*, 39, 2, 235–58.
Neathey, F., and Hurstfield, J. (1995) *Flexibility in Practice: Women's Employment and Pay in Retail and Finance*. Equal Opportunities Commission Research Discussion Series No.16. London: Industrial Relations Services.

Oakley, A. (1974) *The Sociology of Housework*. Oxford: Martin Robertson.

O'Brien, M. (1997) She who sups with the media . . . . *Times Higher Educational Supplement*, February 14.

O'Brien, M. and Jones, D. (1999) Children in working-class families: Parental time, investment and educational outcomes. *Cambridge Economic Journal*, 23.

Office of National Statistics (1997) *Social Focus on Families*. London: HMSO.

Paci, P., and Joshi, H. (1996) *Wage Differentials Between Men and Women. Evidence from Cohort Studies*. Research Series No. 71. London: Department for Education and Employment.

Parkman, A. M. (1992) Unilateral divorce and the labor force participation rate of married women revisited. *American Economic Review*, 82, 671–8.

Perlow, L. (1999) The time famine: toward a sociology of work time. *Administrative Science Quarterly*, 44, 57–81.

Purcell, K., Hogarth, T., and Simm, C. (1999) *Whose Flexibility? The Costs and Benefits of Non-Standard Working Arrangements and Contractual Relations*. York: York Publishing Services for the Joseph Rowntree Foundation.

Rappoport, R., Bailyn, L., Fletcher, J., and Pruitt, B. (2002) *Beyond Work-Family Balance: Advancing Gender Equity and Workplace Performance*. San Francisco: Jossey Bass.

Ringen, S., and Halpin, B. (1995) *The Standard of Living of Children*. Oxford: Department of Applied Social Studies and Social Research, University of Oxford.

Speak, S., Camerson, S., and Gilroy, R. (1997) *Young Single Fathers. Participation in Fatherhood – Bridges and Barriers*. London: Family Policy Studies Centre

Spencer, L., and Taylor, S. (1994) *Participation and Progress in the Labour Market: Key Issues for Women*. Research Series No. 35. London: Department of Employment.

Thomson, K. (1995) Working mothers: Choice or circumstance? *British Social Attitudes, the 12th report*. Dartmouth: Social and Community Research Planning.

Wainwright, D., and Calnan, M. (2002) *Work Stress: The Making of a Modern Epidemic*. Buckingham: Open University Press.

Waldfogel, J. (1999) Early childhood interventions and outcomes. CASE/STICERD Discussion paper No. 21. London: London School of Economics.

Warin, J. Solomon, Y., Lewis, C., and Langford, W. (1999) *Fathers, Work and Family Life*. London and York: Family Policy Studies Centre and the Joseph Rowntree Foundation.

Warr, P. (1987) *Work, Unemployment and Mental Health*. Oxford: Clarendon Press.

Watson, G. (1994) The flexible workforce and patterns of working hours. *Employment Gazette*, 102, 239–47.

Watson, G., and Fothergill, B. (1993) Part-time employment and attitudes towards part-time work. *Employment Gazette*, 101, 213–20.

Yeandle, S., Wigfield, A., Crompton, R., and Dennett, J. et al. (2002) *Employers, Communities and Family-Friendly Employment Policies*. London and York: York Publishing Services for the Joseph Rowntree Foundation.

# 26

# Public Policy and Families

Wendy Sigle-Rushton
and Catherine Kenney

## Introduction

This chapter provides a comparative overview of one important aspect of public policy for families in the European Union (EU) – the development of governmental responses to the often-conflicting needs for parents to reconcile their work and caring responsibilities. While the range of laws, regulations, and policies that we could have examined in this chapter is extremely broad, we opt for a narrow policy focus so that we can provide a more comprehensive, comparative presentation. We choose this approach because we believe a thorough comparison of welfare-state policies and employment behaviors across countries can shed light on notable variations in cultural conceptions of the role of the family in society and inform our understanding of the changing interface between the family, the market, and the state. By understanding differences in the roles of individuals within families, as well as the roles of families in society, sociologists can develop a more robust theoretical conception of how families function and the way in which social policy influences, and is influenced by, their behavior. Nonetheless, it is important to keep in mind that our comparative overview will rely on aggregate data measures that may mask important differences among individuals (or groups of individuals) both within and across EU states. In our attempt to exploit important variances across states, we will necessarily obfuscate some of the potentially important differences within them.

We begin in the next section with an introduction to the post-industrial work–family problem and the ways in which emerging welfare states developed policies to support a male breadwinner–female carer division of labor within families. In the third section, we discuss how demographic and economic changes transformed the gendered division of labor and challenged prevailing assumptions concerning the structure and function of families. As a consequence of these changes, new governmental policies were required to support families in their economic and reproductive functions. In the fourth section, we discuss how ongoing work–family tensions in dual-earner families, along with a strengthening commitment to gender equality on the part of the EU, have begun to lead to the development of policies that offer a new solution to the balance of work and family.

## The Male Breadwinning Family

Problems reconciling the responsibilities of work and family emerged, in part, as a consequence of industrialization. As work moved increasingly outside of the home, it became less compatible with child rearing and other domestic tasks. The family became a more specialized arena of reproduction, socialization, and care, and time spent caring for children increasingly became time that could not be spent earning money to feed them. Families had to seek solutions that would allow them to combine their newly disparate economic and reproductive functions. The "solution" that emerged was a gendered division of labor in which men went out to trade their labor for wages and women took responsibility for the unpaid domestic and caring work – the male breadwinning family (Havas, 1995).

Although a specialized division of labor gained wide acceptance as the best possible resolution of competing demands, in reality few workers earned enough to support a dependent wife and children. Nonetheless, adherence to this ideal persisted well into the post-World War II period, when new sociological and psychological theories reaffirmed a "separate spheres" sexual division of labor, at least for families with children. American sociologist Talcott Parsons's functionalist perspective was particularly influential in idealizing a male breadwinner–female carer division of labor within the family, arguing that it was best suited to meeting the emotional needs of adults and the socialization needs of children (Parsons, 1949). In Parsons's ideal family, men assumed an "instrumental" role, providing the economic and emotional security that allowed women to stay at home, thus strengthening the bond between mother and child. These ideas were echoed in contemporaneous psychoanalytic theories of attachment that stressed the importance of the mother–child bond (Bowlby, 1952; Winnicott, 1957).

It is not inconsequential that the development and expansion of modern welfare states took place when this conception of family and society enjoyed generalized acceptance. Consequently, Lewis (1992) argues, all modern welfare regimes have, to some extent, supported the male breadwinning family (but Pfau-Effinger (1993) presents some convincing evidence that Finland may be an exception). However, since the degree of state support for the male breadwinning family has varied within countries and over time, she suggests that welfare regimes can be classified according to their level of adherence to the male breadwinning ideology, and that this previously overlooked factor cuts across other, preexisting welfare regime typologies like the one put forward by Esping Anderson (1990).

In a pure male breadwinner state, we would "expect to find married women excluded from the labor market, firmly subordinated to their husbands for the purpose of social security entitlements and tax, and expected to undertake the work of caring (for children and other dependents) at home without public support" (Lewis, 1992: 162). Using Ireland as an example of a strong male breadwinner state, she points to marriage bars prohibiting the civil service employment of married women that persisted until the late 1970s, to tax systems that discouraged the work of married women, and to low child-care provision.

Equally important, and often overlooked, is the way in which male breadwinning states perpetuated a definition of men that prioritized their role as economic provider and marginalized their domestic role to one of social support for the mother. Just as women were given unequal access to work and pay, men were given unequal opportunities to care for and nurture their children. Responsible fathers were expected to work long hours to provide for their families, and the level of absence this required was rarely considered to be problematic. What children needed was the continuous presence of their mother. Changes in custody rights from fathers to mothers reinforced this notion of what fathers should provide and what children required (Sarre, 1996).

Although there was substantial variation across European countries, most early welfare-state programs subsidized a gendered division of paid and unpaid labor. In an economy in which wages are set according to labor productivity and not family need, the gendered division of labor in the male breadwinning model is expensive to maintain. A married man faces greater economic challenges than an unmarried man earning the same wage. Sommestad argues that "there is no industrialized nation in which the male breadwinning system has been capable of carrying out the reproductive process without public support" 1977: 153). Consequently, one important source of support that governments provided to male breadwinning families was financial. Montanari (2000) demonstrates that by 1950, most European tax codes had introduced tax concessions for married couples with dependent spouses. She argues that the resulting marriage subsidy, along with family allowances and child benefits, contributed to the achievement of a "family wage" – a wage large enough for a single (male) earner to support a family. As long as the family wage was sufficient and social norms supported a specialized division of labor, financial redistribution to male breadwinning families was the way in which governments could support the reconciliation of paid and unpaid work.

## The Rise of the Dual-Earner Family

In the 1960s and 1970s, dramatic changes in both family structure and the economy began to transform the beliefs and reality surrounding the intra-family distribution of paid work. One particularly significant change was a drop in fertility levels, which meant both a reduction in the number of years a given family needed to devote to child rearing and, eventually, a shrinking population of young workers entering the labor market. Between 1960 and 1996, the total fertility rate had fallen from above to below replacement level in all EU countries (table 26.1). With fewer workers to support an aging population, countries increasingly needed high rates of employment among the entire working-age population.

At the same time, the evolution of the economy and the expansion of the service sector meant that women had increasing access to jobs that offered flexible hours and did not require physical strength (Pfau-Effinger, 1993). Although the transition began earlier in some European countries than others, between 1960 and 1999, all countries experienced a substantial increase in their rates of female labor-force participation (OECD, 2001). Over time, the dual-earner family became a common, if not normative, arrangement for European two-parent families.

Another important family change was the increase in the prevalence of lone-parent families, which resulted both from increases in family dissolution and in nonmarital

**Table 26.1** Changes in patterns of family formation and dissolution in the EU-15 countries

| | *Total fertility rate* | | | *% of live nonmarital births* | | | *Total divorce rate*[b] | | |
|---|---|---|---|---|---|---|---|---|---|
| | *1960* | *1998* | *change* | *1960* | *1998*[a] | *change* | *1975* | *1995* | *change* |
| Sweden (S) | 2.20 | 1.51 | −0.69 | 11.3 | 54.7 | 43.4 | 50 | 52 | 2 |
| Finland (FIN) | 2.72 | 1.70 | −1.02 | 4.0 | 37.2 | 33.2 | 26 | 49 | 23 |
| Denmark (DK) | 2.54 | 1.72 | −0.82 | 7.8 | 44.8 | 37.0 | 37 | 41 | 4 |
| Belgium (B) | 2.56 | 1.53 | −1.03 | 2.1 | 16.6 | 14.5 | 16 | 55 | 39 |
| France (F) | 2.73 | 1.75 | −0.98 | 6.1 | 40.7 | 34.6 | 16 | 38 | 22 |
| Germany (D) | 2.37 | 1.34 | −1.03 | 7.6 | 20.0 | 12.4 | 25 | 33 | 8 |
| Austria (A) | 2.69 | 1.34 | −1.35 | 13.0 | 29.5 | 16.5 | 20 | 38 | 18 |
| Luxembourg (L) | 2.28 | 1.68 | −0.60 | 3.2 | 17.5 | 14.3 | 10 | 33 | 23 |
| Netherlands (NL) | 3.12 | 1.62 | −1.50 | 1.4 | 20.8 | 19.4 | 20 | 37 | 17 |
| Italy (I) | 2.41 | 1.19 | −1.22 | 2.4 | 8.7 | 6.3 | 3 | 8 | 5 |
| United Kingdom (UK) | 2.72 | 1.72 | −1.00 | 5.2 | 37.6 | 32.4 | 32 | 45 | 13 |
| Ireland (IRL) | 3.76 | 1.93 | −1.83 | 1.6 | 28.3 | 26.7 | – | – | – |
| Greece (EL) | 2.28 | 1.30 | −0.98 | 1.2 | 3.8 | 2.6 | 6 | 17 | 11 |
| Spain (E) | 2.86 | 1.15 | −1.71 | 2.3 | 11.1 | 8.8 | – | 15 | – |
| Portugal (P) | 3.10 | 1.46 | −1.64 | 9.5 | 20.1 | 10.6 | 2 | 16 | 14 |

*Sources*: Eurostat (2000a, 2000b).

*Notes*: [a] Data for Belgium and Spain refer to 1995. Data for 1998 were not available.
[b] Data for Scotland and Northern Ireland are excluded.

birth ratios (table 26.1). Table 26.2 shows that in 1996, the percentage of households with children that contained a lone parent, most of which are headed by women, was, in most European countries, greater than 10 percent. Policies that redistributed economic resources to families through a male wage-earner would no longer reach many families with children, and women who specialized in domestic work often found that when their families dissolved, so did their access to social benefits.

Government interventions facilitated the transformation from male breadwinning to dual-earner families. Important policies include both those that granted women more equal access to the labor market and those that subsidized their entry – either by removing economic disincentives or by reducing the costs of child care. At an international level, the European Community has played a significant role in allowing married women and mothers greater access to the labor market. EU equal opportunity laws have been integral to dismantling the overt exclusionary and discriminatory employment policies in some member states. In fact, EU involvement extends back to Article 119 of the 1957 Treaty of Rome, which asserted that women and men should receive equal treatment in matters of employment and pay (Crompton and LeFeuvre, 2000). This treaty, along with the subsequent adoption of a series of Directives on equal treatment in the workplace, was an essential first step in the transformation of the male breadwinning family. Although some European states continued to embrace the male breadwinning ideal, EU equal opportunities polices began to lift marriage bars, equalize treatment within the labor market and social security systems, and allow for the greater inclusion of women into the labor force.

Unlike equal opportunities law, in which the EU took an active role from an early date, the implementation of work-support policies was, at least until the 1990s, left largely to the discretion of individual states. While the need for measures to address the reconciliation of work and family was repeatedly mentioned, the issue was delegated to "soft law" Communications and Recommendations that were not obligatory. Finally, in 1992, an EU directive on maternity leave was adopted – but as a health and safety measure. Except for this maternity leave Directive and a parental leave Directive several years later, most other aspects of EU work–family policy were non-binding. Consequently, national governments have been given a good deal of freedom to develop the policies they deem appropriate.

Despite the absence of binding policies at the EU level, there has been considerable convergence across states in some policies that would support the reconciliation of work and family responsibilities. The public provision of child care for 3–6-year-olds (generally preschool programs) is a good example. While public care for children under the age of 3 continues to vary across European countries, after the mid-1980s, public programs for children over the age of 3 were substantially expanded in those countries where, previously, they had been rare (the UK, Portugal, the Netherlands, and Luxembourg) (Randall, 1999). Furthermore, by the 1990s, maternity leave often became more similar across states (as well as longer and more generous) and parental leave more normative. As a consequence of the 1992 EU Directive, by 1997, all EU countries offered at least 14 weeks of paid and job-protected maternity leave to new mothers. Finally, in 1996, an EU Directive on parental leave was adopted – the first primary legislation to address the reconciliation of work and family. This Directive required member states to enact parental leave legislation that would allow parents at least three months of job-protected leave so that they could provide full-time care for a child (96/34/EC). While not requiring that the leave be paid, the 1996 Directive, like the earlier maternity leave Directive, ensured a minimum standard for all EU citizens.

**Table 26.2** Household characteristics and women's employment in the EU-15 countries, 1999

| | *Lone parent households (1996; %)* | *Couple families with a child aged 0–5 (1999; %)*[a, b] | | | | *Employment rates (1999)*[a, b] | |
|---|---|---|---|---|---|---|---|
| | | *Both partners work full-time* | *Man works full-time, woman works part-time* | *Man works full-time, woman doesn't work* | *Other* | *Lone parents* | *Mothers with child aged 0–5* |
| Sweden (S) | – | – | – | – | – | 64.6 | 77.8 |
| Finland (FIN) | 19% | – | – | – | – | 64.9 | 58.8 |
| Denmark (DK) | 14% | – | – | – | – | – | – |
| Belgium (B) | 14% | 26.6 | 27.7 | 19.0 | 26.7 | 49.2 | 69.5 |
| France (F) | 16% | 31.3 | 19.7 | 35.1 | 13.9 | 51.6 | 56.2 |
| Germany (D) | 14% | 20.9 | 26.3 | 41.6 | 11.2 | 49.7 | 51.1 |
| Austria (A) | 13% | 29.0 | 30.7 | 30.1 | 10.2 | 76.1 | 66.5 |
| Luxembourg (L) | 9% | 26.5 | 16.6 | 51.6 | 5.3 | 74.1 | 47.4 |
| Netherlands (NL) | 10% | 4.2 | 47.8 | 31.5 | 16.5 | 38.7 | 60.7 |
| Italy (I) | 10% | 32.6 | 9.5 | 47.5 | 10.4 | 72.2 | 45.7 |
| United Kingdom (UK) | 23% | 19.5 | 38.4 | 29.4 | 12.7 | 36.8 | 55.8 |
| Ireland (IRL) | 15% | 29.6 | 11.4 | 41.8 | 17.2 | 35.2 | 45.7 |
| Greece (EL) | 10% | 41.4 | 4.2 | 47.3 | 7.1 | 63.2 | 48.6 |
| Spain (E) | 9% | 31.0 | 6.9 | 52.1 | 10.0 | 64.9 | 41.8 |
| Portugal (P) | 12% | 60.7 | 5.9 | 25.9 | 7.5 | 82.9 | 70.6 |

*Sources*: First column, Chambez (2001); remaining columns, OECD (2000).

*Notes*:

– Data not available

[a]Data are restricted to families with no one over 60, and multi-family households are excluded.

[b]Data for Ireland are from 1997; for Finland, 1998, and from Sweden, 2000. Additionally the Swedish data refer to mothers aged 25–54 only.

Because standards have been set low, there continues to be substantial variation across EU states in the nature and extent of policies to help families combine their work and caring responsibilities.

## Gender Arrangements Across the EU

In the last decades of the twentieth century, many European countries, in response to dramatic changes in family life and the economy, developed a catalog of policies that support some form of dual-earner families. Nevertheless, there are substantial differences in policies, preferences, and in the rates and volume of employment across countries.

Drawing from the work of Pfau-Effinger (1993, 1998), we use a gender arrangement framework to characterize EU states. This framework assumes that government policies can reflect cultural norms as well as manipulate them. Beliefs regarding the appropriate division of labor between women and men and the allocation of responsibility for the care of children between the public and private spheres form the "gender culture" of a given country (Pfau-Effinger, 1993). Policy institutions are created within existing gender cultures and also interact with them. The result is a variety of "gender arrangements" for the division of paid and unpaid work (Pfau-Effinger, 1998). Based on the current state of their policies, patterns of employment and preferences, we would classify the EU nations into one of three "gender arrangements."

### The dual earner–state carer arrangement

According to Pfau-Effinger, this arrangement is characterized by the "full-time integration of both sexes into the employment system." (1998: 180). Full-time employment is the preference and the norm for both women and men. Child-care is effectively externalized because of active state involvement in its provision at an early age. Countries characterized by this gender arrangement are those countries that Hantrais and Letablier describe as having a "juxtaposition of family and employment with state support" (1996: 126). These countries include Denmark, Finland, and Sweden, all of which, for explicit reasons of gender equity, have introduced a range of universal support programs for working families. To encourage the labor-force participation of married mothers, all three of these countries changed, relatively early, from systems of joint taxation to independent taxation. With independent taxation and a progressive tax schedule, married families face the smallest tax burden when both spouses' earnings are roughly equal or, more precisely, fall within the same tax band. Whether as a cause or consequence of tax reform, labor-force participation of mothers with young children in these countries is high (table 26.2), and survey data collected from couples with at least one employed adult – the Employment Options for the Future Study – shows a strong preference for two full-time partners (table 26.3). Only 3 percent of individuals in these countries preferred a male breadwinning model (7–10 percent of those with a young child preferred male breadwinning).

France and Belgium have also, but in the context of different policy objectives, achieved high levels of full-time employment with a range of government-provided work supports (Hantrais and Letablier, 1996). In addition, both countries have stood out in their willingness to intervene in the labor market to limit hours and increase working-time flexibility. France, for example, mandated that a 35-hour

**Table 26.3** Preferred pattern of labor supply among couples where at least one is in paid employment and those with a child under 6, 1998 (%)

| | *Both partners work full-time* | *Both partners work half-time* | *Man works full-time, woman half-time* | *Man works, woman not employed* | *Other*[a] |
|---|---|---|---|---|---|
| *Dual earner–state carer* | | | | | |
| Sweden | | | | | |
| *Employed* | 36% | 30% | 26% | 3% | 5% |
| *Child under 6* | 67% | (in other category) | 22% | 7% | 4% |
| Finland | | | | | |
| *Employed* | 50% | 19% | 19% | 3% | 9% |
| *Child under 6* | 80% | (in other category) | 9% | 10% | 1% |
| Denmark | | | | | |
| *Employed* | 32% | 31% | 27% | 3% | 7% |
| *Child under 6* | | | unavailable | | |
| Belgium | | | | | |
| *Employed* | 29% | 11% | 33% | 21% | 7% |
| *Child under 6* | 55% | (in other category) | 29% | 13% | 3% |
| France | | | | | |
| *Employed* | 37% | 18% | 29% | 10% | 6% |
| *Child under 6* | 52% | (in other category) | 22% | 14% | 12% |
| *Modernized male breadwinner* | | | | | |
| Germany | | | | | |
| *Employed* | 26% | 15% | 37% | 17% | 5% |
| *Child under 6* | 32% | (in other category) | 43% | 6% | 19% |
| Austria | | | | | |
| *Employed* | 29% | 13% | 35% | 17% | 7% |
| *Child under 6* | 36% | (in other category) | 40% | 4% | 21% |
| Luxembourg | | | | | |
| *Employed* | 21% | 16% | 24% | 35% | 5% |
| *Child under 6* | 28% | (in other category) | 30% | 12% | 30% |

| | | | | | |
|---|---|---|---|---|---|
| Netherlands | | | | | |
| *Employed* | 12% | 31% | 40% | 14% | 3% |
| *Child under 6* | 6% | (in other category) | 70% | 11% | 14% |
| Italy | | | | | |
| *Employed* | 30% | 12% | 32% | 21% | 5% |
| *Child under 6* | 50% | (in other category) | 28% | 11% | 11% |
| United Kingdom | | | | | |
| *Employed* | 28% | 13% | 35% | 17% | 7% |
| *Child under 6* | 21% | (in other category) | 42% | 13% | 24% |
| Ireland | | | | | |
| *Employed* | 21% | 15% | 39% | 22% | 3% |
| *Child under 6* | 31% | (in other category) | 42% | 8% | 19% |
| *Dual earner–family carer* | | | | | |
| Greece | | | | | |
| *Employed* | 47% | 12% | 19% | 16% | 6% |
| *Child under 6* | 66% | (in other category) | 11% | 9% | 14% |
| Spain | | | | | |
| *Employed* | 55% | 10% | 17% | 15% | 3% |
| *Child under 6* | 60% | (in other category) | 12% | 20% | 9% |
| Portugal | | | | | |
| *Employed* | 63% | 13% | 15% | 6% | 3% |
| *Child under 6* | 84% | (in other category) | 8% | 4% | 4% |

*Sources*: Bielenski, Bosch, and Wagner (2001) for couples; OECD (2001) for couples with child under 6.

*Note*: [a] The other category includes situations where the woman works more hours than the man, and the woman only is employed. Additionally, the OECD report includes both working part-time in the residual category.

working week for all companies with more than 20 employees take effect by January 2000. Although gender equity issues have become more salient over time, the motivation for policies to support dual-earner families have been more broadly motivated than in the Scandinavian countries, where gender equity was the prime concern (Hantrais and Letablier, 1996). In the case of France, support for working mothers emerged, in part, out of pronatalist concerns (Gauthier, 1996). As a consequence, policies to support mothers have not included policies of positive action to bring about more equal outcomes in the labor market (Crompton and LeFeuvre, 2000). In both France and Belgium, as well, there are more remnants of the male breadwinning state. The tax systems in both countries continue to redistribute economic resources, often very generously, to male-breadwinning and large families (Shaver and Bradshaw, 1992). Table 26.3 shows that, compared to the Scandinavian countries, preferences for male-breadwinning families are somewhat stronger. Nonetheless, when the sample is restricted to couple families with a child under the age of 6, the majority would prefer to have two full-time earners. Because families with small children are also likely to be younger, this may reflect recent changes in attitudes about gender roles and the employment of mothers.

In all five of these dual-earner–state-carer countries, care for children is seen as a collective rather than a private responsibility (Daly and Lewis, 2000). Consequently, these countries have extensive programs of early childhood education and care that provide coverage for a high proportion of children. Moreover, as table 26.4 demonstrates, hours are set to accommodate the needs of working parents. The current

**Table 26.4** Publicly funded early childhood education and care in the EU-15 countries

| | *Year* | *Children under age 3 (coverage)* | *Children over age 3[a]* | |
|---|---|---|---|---|
| *Dual earner–state carer* | | | *Hours* | *Coverage* |
| Sweden | 1994 | 33% | full day | 72% |
| Finland | 1994 | 21% | full day | 53% |
| Denmark | 1994 | 48% | full day | 82% |
| Belgium | 1993 | 30% | full day | 97% |
| France | 1993 | 23% | full day | 99% |
| *Modernized male breadwinner* | | | | |
| West Germany[a] | mid-1990s | 2% | 1/2 day | 78% |
| Austria | 1994 | 3% | varies | 75% |
| Luxembourg[a] | mid-1990s | 3% | full day | 67% |
| Netherlands | 1994 | 8% | varies | 71% |
| Italy | 1993 | 6% | full day | 97% |
| United Kingdom | 1993 | 2% | varies | 60% |
| Ireland | 1993 | 2% | varies | 55% |
| *Dual earner–family carer* | | | | |
| Greece | 1993 | 3% | 1/2 day | 70% |
| Spain | 1993 | 2% | full day | 84% |
| Portugal | 1993 | 12% | 1/2 day | 48% |

*Sources*: Randall (1999); *a* Meyers and Gornick (2000).

Scandinavian model is an integrated system of early childhood education and care that falls under the authority of the social-welfare and educational systems. Access for working parents is nearly universal and waiting times are short or nonexistent. Both Sweden and Finland guarantee a place in publicly funded child-care from the first year. The French and Belgian model is a two-tiered system in which care for very young children is provided and regulated as a social welfare program. Between the ages of 2 and 3, children move into a (full-time) pre-primary school program that is offered through the educational system. When parents pay fees, the costs are generally subsidized and parental contributions are based on their level of income (Gornick and Meyers, 2001). Belgium has placed a great emphasis on the importance of providing and subsidizing after school programs of care as well.

The dual-earner–state-carer states were also among the first to offer generous parental leave options to new parents. The first parental leave policies were introduced in Sweden in 1974 (Bruning and Plantenga, 1999). Finland followed in 1980, France in 1985, and Denmark in 1992. Although Belgium's parental leave was not legislated until 1998, the country previously gave workers the right to "career breaks" which most new parents used as a form of paid, parental leave. Parental leave, by which we mean both parental and child rearing leave, can be taken by either parent or shared between them. In most cases, parental leave is provided as a supplement to maternity leave, and wage-replacement rates are less generous. Table 26.5 shows that compensation for parental leave in these states is generous relative to the rest of the EU, however.

## The modernized male breadwinning arrangement

This arrangement is one in which the economic role of women is secondary to their caring responsibilities (Pfau-Effinger, 1993). Child-care is viewed as a private and family responsibility, and it is expected that parents (mothers) will reduce their economic activity in order to provide care. For many, the preferred labor pattern is one in which men work full-time and women, mothers with small children in particular, work part-time (see table 26.3). This arrangement has emerged in states where there is active state involvement in family policy but little emphasis on the full integration of mothers into paid employment (Hantrais and Letablier, 1996). These include Germany, Austria, Luxembourg, the Netherlands, and Italy.

These countries all follow a continental model of child-care similar to France and Belgium, but without exception, programs for children under 3 are far less developed than in countries with dual-earner–state-carer arrangements (Randall, 1999; Kamerman, 2000b). Germany, Austria, and Luxembourg all have very poor coverage for small children, while the Netherlands and Italy both have moderate levels of coverage (table 26.4). Lower levels of coverage in these countries are often justified by lack of demand. In the case of the Netherlands, there is low supply because just "five percent of all women with children work at a full-time job. ... Most women stop working when they have their first child" (Schulze, 1999: 35–6). Preschool programs are more widely available but they are often open for short hours. In addition, primary schools frequently send children home for lunch. Only Italy offers meal provision and supervision during lunch breaks for those children who attend full days (European Commission, 1998a).

A modernized male breadwinning arrangement can also emerge as a result of non-intervention by the state. This has been the case in Ireland and the UK, where there

**Table 26.5** Leave policies in the EU-15 countries, 2001

| | *Maternity leave* | | *Parental leave* | | | *Part-time* |
|---|---|---|---|---|---|---|
| | *Duration* | *Replacement* | *Duration* | *Replacement* | *Right* | |
| *Dual earner–state carer* | | | | | | |
| Sweden | 102 days[e] | 80% | 263 days[e] | 80% | | |
| | | | 3 months | flat rate | mixed | yes |
| | | | 3 months | unpaid | | |
| Finland | 18 weeks | 70% | 26 weeks | 70% | mixed[f] | no |
| | | | until child is 3 | flat rate | family | yes |
| Denmark | 18 weeks | 60% | 10 weeks | 60% | family | |
| | | | 2 weeks | 60% | father | no |
| | | | 26 weeks | 90% UI benefit | mother | |
| | | | 26 weeks | 90% UI benefit | father | |
| Belgium | 15 weeks | 75–82% | 3 months | flat rate | mother | yes |
| | | | 3 months | flat rate | father | |
| France[b] | 16/26 weeks[b] | 84% | until child is 3 | unpaid/flat rate[b, c] | family | yes |
| *Modernized male breadwinner* | | | | | | |
| Germany | 14 weeks | 100% | 2 years | flat rate[c] | family | yes |
| | | | 1 year | unpaid | family | |
| Austria | 16 weeks | 100% | 18 months | partial | mixed[a] | yes |
| Luxembourg | 16 weeks | 100% | 6 months | flat rate | mixed | yes |
| | | | 6 months | flat rate | | |
| Netherlands | 16 weeks | 100% | 3 months | unpaid | mother | yes |
| | | | 3 months | unpaid | father | yes |
| Italy | 5 months | 80% | 6 months | 30%[d] | mixed | no |
| | | | 5/6 months | unpaid | | |
| United Kingdom | 6 weeks | 90% | 13 weeks | unpaid | mother | no |

| | | | | | | |
|---|---|---|---|---|---|---|
| | 12 weeks | flat rate | 13 weeks | unpaid | father | |
| Ireland | 14 weeks | 70% | 14 weeks | unpaid | mother | yes |
| | | | 14 weeks | unpaid | father | |
| *Dual earner–family carer* | | | | | | |
| Greece | 16 weeks | 70% | 3.5 months | unpaid | mother | no |
| | | | 3.5 months | unpaid | father | |
| Spain | 16 weeks | 100% | until child is 3 | unpaid | family | yes |
| Portugal | 6 months | 100% | 6 months | unpaid | mother | no |
| | | | 6 months | unpaid | father | |

*Notes*: [a]18 months are to be taken by one parent (either one); 6 months are reserved for other parent. [b] leave is longer for third + child, leave is paid for second + child. [c] benefit is income tested. [d] employers generally top off to 100%. [e] these are approximate – maternity leave begins 160 days before expected birthdate and ends 6 weeks after birth. [f] fathers have an individual right to 12 days.

*Source*: Kamerman (2000a), updated using European Commission (2001).

has been strong opposition to state interference in family life. The UK has often effectively opposed EU legislation on maternity leave, parental leave, work organization, and child-care, and the British and Irish governments have shown great reluctance to interfere with the rights of employers to negotiate contracts with their employees (Hantrais and Letablier, 1996). The Irish tax system (along with those in Germany and Luxembourg) redistributes relatively large amounts of income to families with a dependent spouse – an increase in net income (relative to a single person) of over 11 percent at average male earnings. In contrast, the UK tax system is one of the most family-neutral in all of the EU (Shaver and Bradshaw, 1995). In 2000, tax concessions for married couples of working age were eliminated, and most family instruments in the tax code are targeted toward low-income working families with children.

Similar to Austria, the former West Germany, and Luxembourg, child-care coverage rates for children under 3 are extremely low in Ireland and the UK. Moreover, existing programs tend to be targeted toward children at risk or in need. Unlike other countries with low coverage for 3–6-year-olds, Ireland's coverage rates remained static at moderately low levels throughout the 1980s and 1990s. In the late 1990s, the UK government set a goal of full coverage for 4-year-olds and a doubling of places for 3-year-olds. Nonetheless, as table 26.4 shows, coverage for 3–6-year-olds in the UK (60 percent) and Ireland (55 percent) are extremely low by European standards (Randall, 1999).

Countries with modernized male breadwinning arrangements can either use their parental leave policies to encourage women to stay home and care for their children, or they can, as a result of noninterference, give women few other options. Germany is an example of the former type. In Germany, women are given the option of caring for their children until they are 3 years old (table 26.5). Cash benefits are available, although means-tested, for the first two years. Because the benefits are made available to working and nonworking mothers, the policy operates more as a wage for mothering than a work support. The level of payments has, historically, been modest, but in 2001 the grant was substantially increased. Despite being offered on a gender-neutral basis, the right to leave is almost exclusively exercised by women, and the policy reinforces a traditional caring role of women (Bruning and Plantenga, 1999). In contrast, Ireland and the UK are examples of the latter type. By the mid-1990s, the UK and Ireland (and Luxembourg) had yet to legislate any form of parental leave. When it was finally legislated in the UK and Ireland, leave was both unpaid and of shorter duration compared to other European countries.

## The dual earner/ family carer arrangement

Mothers in Greece, Spain, and Portugal have been unique in their ability to combine high levels of full-time employment with minimal levels of government support. Compared to their European counterparts, these countries are economically underdeveloped and, as a consequence, social spending is meager. Even measured as a proportion of GDP, however, social expenditures in these countries are well below the European average. Low incomes and low levels of social protection mean that many families must work long hours. Indeed, table 26.2 shows that in 1999, over 60 percent of all couple families with a child aged 0–5 in Portugal had both partners working full-time. Although the rates are not quite as high, dual full-time employment patterns are also relatively common in Spain and Greece.

There is some evidence that constraints on employers have limited the supply of part-time jobs in both Portugal and Spain (Ruivo, do Pilar Gonzalez, and Varejaõ, 1998), but low family incomes have also limited the demand for part-time work. Table 26.3 shows that among respondents in the Employment Options for the Future Study, the majority in Spain and Portugal prefer a labor-supply pattern in which both partners work full-time. In Greece, just under a majority (47 percent) express the same preference. When the sample is further restricted to couples with a child under the age of 6, the preference for two full-time workers increases substantially. With 84 percent of these respondents expressing a preference for two full-time workers, Portuguese parents show a higher level of preference for equal, full-time employment than even Finnish parents. Preferences are not as pronounced in Spain and Greece, but nonetheless, 60 percent of Spanish and 66 percent of Greek respondents with a child under the age of 6 would prefer to have both partners working full-time. These percentages are much higher than those reported in the modernized male breadwinning states, where part-time work for women tends to be preferred.

In both Spain and Greece, there is very low provision of care for children under 3 (table 26.4). In Portugal, where the focus has been on educational programs for preschool children, rates of coverage for children under 3 are moderate and similar to those in Italy and the Netherlands (Randall, 1999). For children between the ages of 3 and 6, Spain stands out, with free and universal provision and coverage rates of 84 percent. Greece also has high rates of coverage at 70 percent, but care is generally provided only for half a day. Starting in 1996–7, Portugal instituted policies to expand care for children aged 3–6 (OECD, 2000a, 2000b), but rates of coverage are lower than the other countries at 48 percent. Like Greece, the programs are usually only half-day and so do not support, to any great extent, full-time dual earning.

Similar to the UK and Ireland, parental leave is minimal in these countries. In all cases, parental leave is unpaid, although Portugal provides a relatively generous six-month maternity leave, reimbursed at 100 percent of lost wages (table 26.5). Spain allows parents the option of staying home to care for a child under the age of 3, but because the leave is unpaid, this is not a viable option for many low-income families. Spain also grants parents the right to part-time leave, which may help parents combine work and family responsibilities. In the other countries, there is a large gap between the age at which parental leave ends and the age at which access to child-care (often for only half a day) begins. Portugal offers leave for a slightly longer period than Greece, but given the shortage of places for children under 3, it is unlikely that parental leave will effectively bridge the gap between birth and the availability of child-care.

In the absence of comprehensive government support, many parents have relied on family networks to provide care for young children (Lewis, 1993). This is made possible, to some extent, because of strong extended family ties and rapid changes in female labor-force participation. As young women moved into the labor force, often on the same terms as men, they redistributed some of their caring work to older female relatives, many of whom had no labor-market responsibilities. Unless trends change, this strategy will only work in the short-term, however. In a few decades, young women will not be able to rely on older women to provide care because they will likely be working as well. Moreover, it is not clear that this intergenerational redistribution of caring work is particularly effective at the moment. As table 26.1 makes clear, fertility rates in Spain, Greece, and Portugal are low both absolutely and relative to the European average. With a total fertility rate of 1.15, Spain has the lowest fertility in the EU. Comparing 1960 to 1998, women in Spain now average 1.71 fewer children. Similarly, total fertility fell by 1.64 children in Portugal. Only Ireland has experienced a bigger drop – from much higher initial levels – in total fertility since 1960.

## The Emergence of a Dual Earner–Dual Carer Family?

In the dual-earner family arrangements presented above, both men and women assume economic responsibilities and work for wages. Compared to the male breadwinning family, the dual-earner family represents a change in the allocation of responsibility to women. It is a family in which women engage in market work, but they usually also retain a higher level of responsibility for the home and child-care – with varying degrees of governmental support. Men are expected to work full-time regardless of their partner's employment level, and the role of men in the domestic sphere continues to be marginal. In describing Sweden as a dual-earner state, Lewis comments that "[women] have retained their responsibility for the unpaid work of caring; men's behavior has not been changed" (1992: 169).

Critics argue that the failure to generate any change in men's balance of paid work and caregiving makes the dual earner gender arrangements outlined above unsustainable (Hochschild, 1989). Women who work full-time and face a "second shift" of domestic work when their day is over simply cannot participate in the labor market on the same terms as men. In many cases, women attempted a three-tiered solution – they externalized some care, maintained responsibility for what they could, and left the rest undone (Bianchi, 2000). As a result, most European societies (excluding, perhaps, Ireland) have come to experience a "crisis of care" (Daly and Lewis, 2000).

The large deficits of time and care confronted by women and society suggest the need for a new family form and the kind of policies that would help make it a reality. One solution is to encourage men to move into the domestic sphere, creating a dual-earner–dual-carer family. In a dual earner-dual carer arrangement, both men and women would share equally in paid and unpaid family responsibilities. This model can only obtain when the labor market is reorganized to allow parents the flexibility to fulfill both their paid and unpaid responsibilities (Pfau-Effinger, 1998). While the radical changes necessary for this arrangement to become a reality are far from imminent, there is some evidence, at the European, country, and individual levels, to suggest that support for dual-earner–dual-carer families may be taking shape.

In the last decade, the EU has shifted its attention back to the domestic sphere and has expressed a growing interest in the responsibilities that men assume there. In a 1994 White Paper on social policy, the European Commission indicated that it would move forward on the issue of child-care legislation, and expressed a commitment to more direct legislative involvement in family policy at the European level. This same document stressed the importance of a more equitable sharing of parental responsibilities between men and women. With the formal adoption of "gender mainstreaming" in 1996, the EU endorsed a new approach to policymaking, one in which the gendered outcomes of *all* policies would be examined. The terms of the 1997 Treaty of Amsterdam solidify the EU's commitment to gender mainstreaming, making the incorporation of equal opportunities for men and women a fundamental aim of all EU policies.

As the EU moved toward a more comprehensive and broad approach to equal opportunities, it also began to establish primary legislation that would address the reconciliation of work and family. We have already mentioned the 1996 parental leave Directive, which was instrumental in extending job protection to new parents throughout Europe. The following year, an additional Directive laid the foundation for the eventual restructuring of the labor market. This Directive assured equal treatment to part-time and full-time workers, stressing that all employees should be able to request changes in their hours of work and that access to part-time work should be made available at all levels of a work establishment. Employment-related Communications and Green Papers repeatedly connected issues of work organization and family responsibilities. Despite early opposition, particularly by the UK, the EU appears poised to offer a new solution to the competing demands of paid and unpaid work that includes altering the structure of paid work and reassessing men's role in unpaid caring labor.

Since 1997, statements and policy changes at the state level have indicated a growing level of support for the dual-earner–dual-carer family, as well. Support has been particularly strong in countries that have strong state involvement in issues of gender equity. Sweden, for example, has issued policy statements maintaining that parents should have enough time to spend with their children and "women and men should be able to combine a meaningful working life with active parenting" (quoted in Kimbel, 1999). Not surprisingly, Sweden was one of the first countries to allow parents to work at 75 percent full-time hours (Lewis, 1992). By 2001, many countries had altered their parental leave arrangements to include the possibility of part-time leave (see table 26.5). In addition, recently enacted changes to parental leave entitlements have been implemented to encourage a greater level of father involvement in caring and domestic responsibilities.

In 1997, most EU countries offered parental leave to families rather than individuals. Only Greece, Denmark, and the Netherlands had adopted a system of parent-specific allotments to encourage fathers to take parental leave. Sweden, however, had introduced a combined system in which only part of the leave was transferable. Finland, as well, set aside 12 days that only the father could take (Bruning and Plantenga, 1999). Since then, there appears to have been a shift toward rules that encourage a more equitable split of leavetaking and caring responsibilities. In recent years, four countries adopted systems that encourage parents to share leave, either by assigning rights to each parent specifically or by introducing a mixed system in which some portion of the leave is set aside and the government stipulates who is allowed to take it. Belgium has adopted a system with parent-specific allotments, while Austria changed to a variant of the mixed system. After an initial 16 weeks of maternity leave, parents have a right to take up to two years of parental leave, the last 6 months of which can only be used by the other parent – usually the father (Kamerman, 2000a). Luxembourg's legislation, enacted in 1998, allows one parent the option to take 6 months' full-time leave or 12 months' half-time leave in the 12 months following birth. The other parent is granted the right to a similar leave until the child is aged 5. In 2000, Italy also set aside a portion of leave that can be used only by fathers. Table 26.5 demonstrates that by 2001, slightly more than half of the EU countries were making some attempt to encourage parents to share leave. Of these 8 countries, 5 (Belgium, Denmark, Greece, Luxembourg, and the Netherlands) offer parental leave in equal allotments. Because maternity leave is much longer than paternity leave, equal allotments of parental leave does not mean that parents are granted the same total number of leave days, however. In Belgium, for example, women can take 15 weeks of maternity leave and an additional 3 months of parental leave, while fathers can take 3 days of paternity leave and 3 months of parental leave (Bruning and Plantenga, 1999).

While data on takeup rates and leave durations within families is disappointingly incomplete, one study finds that, in the mid-1990s, the percentage of parental leave days taken by fathers was extremely low (Bruning and Plantenga, 1999). This is due to the fact that fathers are less likely to take parental leave, and when they do, they take fewer days. Even in countries like Sweden and Finland, where takeup among men is fairly high, their share of parental leave days remains low. On average, Swedish men account for just 16 percent of total leave days and Finnish men only 4 percent. In Finland, the average man takes just one day less than his 12-day, individual allotment. Interestingly, the same study shows that, although rates of uptake are lower, when Dutch and Danish fathers do take leave (generally middle-class, well-educated fathers), couples split their parental leave more equally. Both of these countries provide parent-specific allocations of parental leave that are equal and not transferable. In addition, in the Netherlands, in 1994, 13 percent of fathers with small children had temporarily reduced their working week to four days.

While the low rates of uptake suggest that men are not prepared to reduce their paid work responsibilities in order to spend more time in the home, many fathers report that employers' attitudes are part of the problem (European Commission, 1998b). Some fathers fear they will be labeled as uncommitted to their work and will not attain the same earnings and promotions as men who do not take leave. In order to address this issue, Sweden has initiated public campaigns to educate employers and unions about the benefits – to families and employers – of parental leavetaking by fathers (Gornick and Meyers, 2001).

The Employment Options for the Future study shows that in most countries, men would, in fact, like to reduce their work hours – even taking into account the lost earnings. In fact, if men and women could achieve their preferred work schedules, the gender gap in hours across the EU would decrease appreciably (Bielenski, Bosch, and Wagner, 2000). A significant minority of couples would prefer a situation in which each partner worked part-time – particularly in the Netherlands, Sweden, and Denmark (table 26.3). While dual part-time employment was only a reality among 3 percent of the couples interviewed, 16 percent stated that arrangement as their preference. At the same time, 47 percent of all those interviewed thought that part-time hours would be detrimental to their careers, and only 31 percent felt their employers would react favorably to a request for shorter hours (Gasparini et al., 2000).

While, at this point, changes in individual behavior have been modest, it does appear that there is a shift in attitudes taking place within EU countries. Both at the national and international level, men are being more strongly encouraged to be active parents as well as active laborers. Unions in some countries, like the Netherlands, are reinforcing the message with discussions of shorter working weeks so that men can be more involved as parents (Polatnick, 2000). Although at the moment, parental leave is taken mostly by middle-class and more highly educated men (OECD, 2001), there is evidence that many families in the EU would prefer a more equitable distribution of working hours between men and women. These trends suggest that, eventually, dual-earner states will begin to accommodate dual caring – particularly in countries like Denmark, Sweden, and the Netherlands, where there has already been some shift in preferences and priorities.

## Conclusions

In this chapter, we discussed the relationship between public policy and the allocation of responsibility for work and caring responsibilities within families. Originating at a time of consensus about the ideal roles of men and women within families, early welfare states all subscribed, both implicitly and explicitly, to the male breadwinning ideal. Over time, equal opportunities legislation began to weaken and modify the male breadwinner state. Today, the public policies of most EU countries support some form of dual-earner family, although some states provide stronger support for the externalization of child-care, while others tend to support policies that encourage mothers to take time off from work, or work part-time, to care for their children. Although some states have made greater strides toward gender equity in paid market work and unpaid caring work, few comprehensively support a caring role for men. In particular, the reluctance of the male breadwinning states to enter the private sphere has outlived the predominance of the male breadwinning family.

There is evidence of imminent change, however. Policy trends at both the EU and the country level, as well as preferences at the individual level, suggest a growing level of support for a dual-earner–dual-carer family. Important policy innovations are being devised with the expressed intention of promoting father involvement in child-care and the domestic sphere. But evidence of a large-scale shift to a new, intra-family distribution of paid and unpaid labor remains suggestive, at best. Although a number of countries have begun to move in the direction of supporting a dual-earner–dual-carer family, a great deal more will have to change before a more equal allocation of paid and unpaid work is achieved within families and encouraged in the policies that support them.

In these early stages, policies that encourage the more active involvement of fathers in the home are limited largely to innovations in parental leave policies and, to a lesser extent, working-time reforms. Women continue to retain responsibility for unpaid work, while men continue to perform only a small portion of it. Employers have not adapted their expectations so that neither women nor men are discouraged or penalized for taking leave. With the adoption of gender mainstreaming, the EU has already committed itself, and its member states, to considering the gendered outcomes of all policies. If taken seriously, this commitment has the potential to restructure governmental institutions so that policy incentives will encourage more equitable sharing of the rights, responsibilities, and fulfillments of paid and unpaid work between men and women. The extent to which these policy changes result in greater equality for men and women in the different countries of the EU will also depend, however, on concomitant changes in the economic and cultural institutions that have contributed to existing differences in behavior and policy among these countries.

### References

Bianchi, S. (2000) Maternal employment and time with children: Dramatic change or surprising continuity? *Demography*, 37, 401–14.

Bielenski, H., Bosch, G., and Wagner, A. (2001) *Employment and Working Time in Europe*. Dublin: European Foundation for the Improvement of Living and Working Conditions.

Bowlby, J. (1952) *Maternal Care and Mental Health*. Geneva: World Health Organization.

Bruning, G., and Plantenga, J. (1999) Parental leave and equal opportunities: Experiences in eight European countries. *Journal of European Social Policy*, 9, 195–209.

Chambez, C. (2001) Lone parent families in Europe: A variety of economic and social circumstances. *Social Policy and Administration*, 35, 658–71.

Crompton, R., and LeFeuvre, N. (2000) Gender family and employment in comparative perspective: The realities and representations of equal opportunities in Britain and France. *Journal of European Social Policy*, 10, 334–8.

Daly, M., and Lewis, J. (2000) The concept of social care and the analysis of contemporary welfare states. *British Journal of Sociology*, 51, 281–92.

Esping Anderson, G. (1990) *The Three Worlds of Welfare Capitalism*. Princeton, NJ: Princeton University Press.

European Commission (1998a) *Care in Europe: A Joint Report of the "Gender and Employment" and the "Gender and Law" Groups of Experts*. Brussels: European Commission.

European Commission (1998b) *Men within Family and Work, European Network on Family and Work, No. 2/98*. Luxembourg: European Commission.

European Commission (2001) *Social Protection in the EU Member States and the European Economic Area*. Luxembourg: European Commission.

Eurostat (2000a), *Living Conditions in Europe – Statistical Pocketbook*. Luxembourg: Office for Official Publications of the European Communities.

Eurostat (2000b) *European Social Statistics: Demography*. Luxembourg: Office for Official Publications of the European Communities.

Gasparini, G., Parent-Thiron, A., Latta, M., and de Nanteuil, M. (2000) *Full-Time or Part-Time Work: Realities and Options*. Dublin: European Foundation for the Improvement of Living and Working Conditions.

Gauthier, A. (1996) *The State and the Family: A Comparative Analysis of Family Policies in Industrialized Countries*. Oxford: Clarendon Press.

Gornick, J., and Meyers, M. (2001) Support for working families. *The American Prospect*.

Hantrais, L., and Letablier, M-T. (1996) *Families and Family Policy in Europe*. New York: Longman.

Havas, E. (1995) The family as ideology. *Social Policy and Administration*, 29, 1–9.

Hochschild, A. (1989) *The Second Shift: Working Parents and the Revolution of the Home*. New York: Viking.

Kamerman, S. (2000a) Parental leave policies: An essential ingredient in early childhood education and care policies. *Social Policy Report*, 14, 3–16.

Kamerman, S. (2000b) Early childhood education and care (ECEC): An overview of developments in the OECD countries. *International Journal of Education*, 33, 7–29.

Kimbel, G. (1999) *21^st^* Century Families. Chico, CA: Equality Press.

Lewis, J. (1992) Gender and the development of welfare regimes. *Journal of European Social Policy*, 2, 159–73.

Lewis, J. (ed.) (1993) *Women and Social Policies in Europe: Work, Family and the State*. Aldershot: Edward Elgar.

Meyers, M., and Gornick, J. (2000) Early childhood education and care (ECEC): Cross-national variation in service organization and financing. Paper presented to "A Consultative Meeting on International Developments in Early Childhood Education and Care," New York.

Montanari, I. (2000) From family wage to marriage subsidy and child benefits: Controversy and consensus in the development of family support. *Journal of European Social Policy*, 10, 307–33.

OECD (2000a) *Employment Outlook*. Paris: OECD.

OECD (2000b) *Early Childhood Education and Care Policy in Portugal, OECD Country Note*. Paris: OECD.

OECD (2001) *Employment Outlook*. Paris: OECD.

Parsons, T. (1949) The social structure of the family. In R. Anshen (ed.), *The Family: Its Functions and Destiny*. New York: Harper.

Pfau-Effinger, B. (1993) Modernization, culture, and part-time employment: The example of Finland and West Germany. *Work, Employment, and Society*, 7, 383–410.

Pfau-Effinger, B. (1998) Culture or structure as explanations for differences in part-time work in Germany, Finland and the Netherlands? In J. O'Reilly and C. Fagan (eds.), *Part-Time Prospects: An International Comparison of Part-Time Work in Europe, North America, and the Pacific Rim*. London: Routledge.

Polatnick, R. (2000) Working parents: Issues for the next decades. *National Forum*, 80, 1–4.

Randall, V. (1999) Childcare policy in the European states: Limits to convergence. *Journal of European Public Policy*, 7, 346–68.

Ruivo, M., do Pilar Gonzalez, M., and Varejão, J. (1998) Why is part-time work so low in Spain and Portugal?" In J. O'Reilly and C. Fagan (eds.), *Part-Time Prospects: An International Comparison of Part-Time Work in Europe, North America, and the Pacific Rim*. London: Routledge.

Sarre, S. (1996) A place for fathers: Fathers and social policy in the post-war period. In *The Welfare State Program, Discussion Paper No. 25*. London: London School of Economics.

Schulze, H-J. (1999) "*Netherlands*", *The Family Observer*. Vienna: Austrian Institute for Family Studies.

Shaver, S., and Bradshaw, J. (1995) The recognition of wifely labor by welfare states. *Social Policy and Administration*, 29, 10–25.

Sommestad, L. (1997) Welfare state attitudes to the male breadwinning system: The United States and Sweden in comparative perspective. *International Review of Social History*, 42, 153–74.

Winnicott, D. W. (1957) *The Child and the Outside World: Studies in Developing Relationships*. London: Tavistock.

# 27

# Assisted Reproduction, Genetic Technologies, and Family Life

Martin Richards

## Introduction

While the claim that we have entered the biotech century may be both a little premature and difficult to justify, it is undoubtedly true that the new genetic and reproductive technologies are increasingly playing a part in our daily lives. Those whose family medical histories suggest that they may be at risk of inheriting a genetic disease can, in many cases, take DNA tests which will tell them whether or not they are carrying the relevant gene mutation. In other contexts, the results of DNA tests are being used to determine liability to pay child support or settle issues of (biological) parentage, while others who thought they never would become parents have achieved this through the use of in vitro fertilization (IVF) or other reproductive technologies. On the day when I began to write this chapter the BBC news reported that, for the first time, a child in Britain had been treated, apparently successfully, by gene therapy for a potentially fatal genetic disease.

In this chapter I will discuss some of the ways in which genetic and reproductive technologies are being used, how they may influence family life and how our attitudes and assumptions about the family may, in turn, shape their development and use. The chapter begins with a discussion of DNA relationship testing and then considers some of the assisted reproductive technologies (ARTs). Attention is then turned to some of the medical genetic technologies, and the chapter concludes with a consideration of cultural assumptions and public attitudes to current and future technologies.

## Relationship Testing

Until 1987 paternity and other genetic relationship testing was carried out using blood-group proteins. Such tests, which were usually done in university laboratories, could rule out a child's potential father but a match only indicated a genetic relationship with a degree of probability. DNA tests are much more accurate than this. Apart from cases involving monozygotic ("identical") twins, DNA tests can establish parent–child genetic relationships with a degree of accuracy that amounts to certainty for all practical purposes. These tests analyze parts of our DNA which do not constitute our genes and which are relatively variable in sequence from family to family. Samples from a child and a potential father(s) are compared to see whether various sections of the DNA have the same sequence of the four "letters" that make up the genetic alphabet. Initially, these tests, which have been developed and provided commercially, used DNA extracted from the white cells in a blood sample, but today they may be based on hair follicles, cells collected from the inside of the mouth or, indeed, almost any tissue in our body or from the material we excrete. Do-it-yourself postal kits are available and the technology makes it easy for a sample to be collected without someone's knowledge or consent. In the UK the testing industry is regulated by government guidelines (Department of Health, 2001a), which require consent from interested parties and lay down technical standards for laboratories. But there is also an unregulated international trade which operates via the Internet.

In the UK about 10,000 tests were done in 2002, the majority on behalf of the state. The largest user was the Child Support Agency, for the purposes of settling contested paternity where there may be a liability to pay for child support. The second major government use is for the immigration control, when eligibility depends on family membership. Other use arises from a wide variety of familial situations where testing involves consenting adults and court sanctioned testing of children. A best-interests standard is used by the courts to decide whether children should be tested. Until very recently the judicial view was that testing was usually best avoided because it can potentially disturb established family relationships, but today there is more emphasis on a child knowing his or her genetic origins (Bainham, 2002). This shift in attitude may have been encouraged by both the easy availability of testing and cases where the results of offshore, unregulated testing have been used to bargain in the shadow of the law, as well as changing attitudes to an individual's need, or even right, to know the identity of their biological parents and the importance of this to their knowledge of their origins. In the child maintenance situation, there have been a number of cases where men have received repayment of child support payments after DNA testing has shown them not to be the genetic father of the relevant child. Such situations can lead to a child losing a social father without gaining access to or knowledge of their biological father. Similar disruptions of familial relationships have been reported as the result of using DNA testing for immigration control (Taitz, Weekers, and Mosca, 2002). In many countries there are categories for immigrants which depend on family relationships, and DNA testing is widely used to provide proof of such relationships.

As social scientists have often observed, while maternity is seldom in doubt, paternity can be much less certain. Indeed, functionalist explanations of marriage patterns, the seclusion of women, and much else have been based on this observation – as has a lot of speculation by sociobiologists and evolutionary psychologists. However, in the new moral order where a conscientious lawyer may suggest a DNA test as a sensible preliminary before a divorcing husband considers any child-support issues, we may be witnessing a cultural shift. Under English common law, there is a presumption that a child born to a married couple is a "child of the family" and both mother and father have the rights and duties of parents regardless of the biological origins of a child, unless one of them is able to prove nonpaternity.[1] A bill currently before the British Parliament will establish comparable arrangements for most children of unmarried parents. However, it can be argued that the existence of cheap and easily available DNA testing is shifting the situation to one in which parenthood becomes more or less coterminous with parentage and the latter is defined solely by shared DNA sequences.

The DNA techniques discussed thus far can establish whether or not there is a genetic link between two closely related people. Other techniques have been developed which can be used to trace family lineages. Male lines can be traced by investigating the degree of similarity of Y-chromosomes. Because the male's Y chromosome is unpaired, unlike all their other chromosomes, it is passed down over generations almost unchanged. This means that men with a common ancestor will have identical (or almost identical) Y-chromosomes. Y chromosome tests are available from several companies and are proving popular with genealogists and those interested in family history, as well as providing a powerful research tool. The test may be used, for example, to see if families with the same surname are biologically related. A use of the test which received wide publicity was in the case of the American President, Thomas Jefferson, and the longstanding accusation that he had fathered a child with Sally Hemings, one of his slaves. Jefferson did not have a legitimate male descendant, so Y-chromosome analysis was carried out on five male (living) descendants of his paternal uncle, Field Jefferson. These were compared with an analysis of DNA from Sally Hemings's great-great-great-grandson. The Y-chromosomes did match, so that we know that Jefferson (or a relative of Jefferson's) fathered Sally Hemings's child. DNA testing has the power to rewrite our family history – at least insofar as biological parentage is part of that history – and for some, revised family histories may cause discomfort and changed attitudes toward their forebears.

Similar analyses can be carried out on female lineages using mitochondrial DNA. Female X-sex chromosomes are paired, so would be unreliable for this kind of analysis. However, mitochondria, which are small cell organelles, are passed from a mother to her children in her eggs. Mitochondria have their own genome which can be analyzed and compared in the same manner as the Y chromosome and can be used to track female lineages. The best-known use of this technique was the identification of the remains of the Romanovs, who had been executed in 1918 during the Russian Revolution. Because the mitochondrial DNA of one female body recently exhumed exactly matched that of the Duke of Edinburgh, the body was identified as Nicholas II's tsarina, Alexandra. Her maternal grandmother was Queen Victoria who was also a direct ancestor of the Duke of Edinburgh.

Use of these techniques both by those interested in their family history or by researchers exploring connections of human populations, like DNA paternity and relationship testing, are likely to encourage ideas of genetic essentialism and the iconic status of DNA (Nelkin and Lindee, 1995). Necessarily they equate lineage and kin with a genetic connection and in confirming notions of the power of DNA, they also underpin a cultural concept of kinship which is biological, or perhaps more accurately, natural at root (Schneider, 1980).[2] Schneider describes how natural ties define identity and are a relationship of identity, while love provides a more diffuse familial solidarity. It is, of course, common ground for many theorists (e.g., Giddens, 1991) to point to the declining role of kinship as notions of individualism and independence have grown. But in this context it is worth drawing attention to the enormous growth in interest in family history in Western Europe and those parts of the world which have received immigrants from the region. Now the use of official and family records for genealogical enquiry can be supplemented and extended using DNA techniques. Clearly, interest in the connections of descent and kin remain strong and seem likely to receive reinforcement through the new possibilities of search and verification provided by DNA techniques.

## Assisted Reproduction Techniques (ARTs)

Assisted reproduction has a long history. The Old Testament (Genesis, 16: 2–3 and 30: 3–5) describes cases of what today would be termed partial surrogacy where the birth mother, rather than the commissioning couple, provides the egg.[3] The clinical use of artificial insemination by a husband (AIH) was recorded by John Hunter in about 1790, and the first insemination with donor sperm (AID[4]), "heterologeous insemination," followed in 1884[5] (Bartholomew, 1958). In the 1930s and 1940s this practice was encouraged by the Eugenics Movement as a method of providing "eutelegenesis" (Brewer, 1935) or "germinal choice" (Muller, 1963;[6] see also Blacker, 1958), for couples where the husband might be likely to transmit deleterious characteristics to his children or where a donor would be a better eugenic bet. But in Britain, at least, where in the 1930s there were a handful of clinics where AID was offered, the clientele were probably largely couples who were unable to conceive without help, rather than those driven by eugenic motives or trying to avoid passing on a genetic disease to their children (Jackson, 1945). However, the practice was widely condemned as a form of adultery. In 1948, for example, His Grace the Archbishop of Canterbury's Commission (1948) recommended that AID should be criminalized since it involved masturbation[7] and resulted in an illegitimate child.

The development of the "new" reproductive technologies may be dated from 1978 when the first IVF baby was born (Steptoe and Edwards, 1978), followed by the first case of a child conceived after egg donation in 1984. Since these events there has been a rapid development of the technologies and a widespread debate about ethics and regulation of their use. Opponents of the new technology ranged from feminists to religious conservatives. The latter argued that IVF would destroy marriage and the nuclear family while the former (or at least, some of them in FINRRAGE – Feminist International Network of Resistance to Reproductive and Genetic Engineering – and other groups, but not all, e.g., Stanworth (1987) saw assisted reproduction as an appropriation of the female body by means of "the great technological fuck" (Raymond, 1994) and its regulation merely an attempt to stabilize patriarchal social relations (Spallone, 1987). Others suggested that the technique would fragment women into womb, ovaries, and eggs and motherhood into segments of genetics, biology, and child rearing, making women's experience of reproduction as discontinuous as that of men (Hanmer, 1987).

In some countries (such as parts of the US) regulation is largely a matter of the market, while in others (such as the UK) there is legal control of the provisions of ART services, as well as of who may have access to them and the legal status of children created through their use.[8] There is wide variation between countries in the attitudes toward the development and use of ARTs, some of which reflect religious affiliations. In the US, for example, attitudes to research in this area are closely related to attitudes toward abortion (see Treas, chapter 23 in this volume). In other countries the situation has changed with party political shifts. So Italy, for instance, moved in 2002 from having a largely unregulated system ("The Reproductive Wild West of Europe") to proposed legislation which considerably restricts the techniques that can be employed.

In Britain, before the Family Law Act of 1987, DI children were regarded as the illegitimate children of the donor. The Human Fertilization and Embryology Act 1990 (Morgan, 1991) allows children produced with the use of donated sperm, eggs, or embryos to be registered on a birth certificate as the child of the couple or individual being treated in a (registered) clinic. In Britain, 18,000 such children have been born since 1991. Though this Act required clinics to take account "of the welfare of any child who may be born as the result of the treatment (including the need of that child for a father) and of any other child who may be affected by the birth," it takes a rather unusual approach to parentage. It allows men to become legal fathers in cases where donated sperm is used, simply by being involved in the treatment by accompanying a woman to the clinic, and in situations where a lone woman receives treatment, it creates the novel concept of a legally fatherless child. Donation of sperm,[9] eggs, or embryos is anonymous and the child has no access to information about their genetic parent. Nor does the donor get information about any child that may be born.[10] However, because of concerns of legislators about future unwitting incest, the HFE Act has the provision that those of 16 years or older may enquire of the Human Embryo and Fertilization Authority (HEFA), which holds data about those using licensed clinics and the donors, whether they are (genetically) related to someone they intend to marry.[11] In addition, it may be possible for a person conceived by the use of donated gametes or embryos, on reaching the age of 18, to request nonidentifying information[12] about their genetic parent(s) from the HEFA Register. However, the UK Government is currently consulting about this issue (Department of Health 2001b) and, as yet, it is unclear what information may be made available (see Haimes, 1998). The legislation treats gametes purely as a biological material necessary to achieve conception, or as "genetic material,"[13] as they are called in the Act. It has been suggested (e.g., Freeman, 1996) that this approach stems from the medical context in which these technologies were developed. In contrast, adoption, where children do have access to information about the birth parents and may be able to trace and contact them (Howe and Feast, 2000), has developed as a part of social-work practice leading to more attention to social and kin relationships.

There is now a considerable body of research on children born of DI and IVF and their families. Studies (e.g., Golombok et al., 2002b) indicate that most parents are concerned to normalize their ART families. Where children are conceived with donated gametes or embryos they are usually not told of their genetic origins. These "as-if" families are created by a systematic misrecognition (Bharadwaj, 2003) in which legislative regimes may collude with staff in clinics and parents to disguise a child's origins. This may be seen in the UK case, where legal parentage is created by the act of fertility treatment and clinic attendance. Donations of gametes and embryos are necessarily anonymous and donors and the recipient parents are "matched" on physical characteristics to facilitate the passing off of children as the parents' own. Openness with children is not encouraged by the clinical staff involved and is often held to be damaging for children (see Blyth, 1999). A similar situation involving secrecy has been described in very different cultures such as India (Bharadwaj, 2003). However, this pattern is not universal. A number of regulative regimes provide identifying information about donors (e.g., Austria, Sweden and Victoria, Australia). On the other hand, Italy has approved a draft law which would ban the use of donor sperm, eggs, or embryos in assisted reproduction on the grounds that it does not recognize the rights of the conceived children and can cause fragmentation of the parental figures with psychological and social consequences for the child (Reuters, 2002).

Some companies providing services in largely unregulated systems such as the US may give both donors (or more accurately, sellers) of gametes and the recipients the choice of secrecy or openness (Cook, 2002). Though research evidence remains limited, it seems that couples using such fertility services may use one of two approaches. All prefer to use their own gametes to conceive their children and only when it becomes clear that this is not possible do they resort to using gametes or embryos from others. At that point the majority continue to take the "as-if" route, matching their characteristics with those of anonymous donors and maintaining secrecy, while a smaller group are open with their children and, for them, there may be an expectation of a continuing relationship between themselves and their child and the donor (or birth mother, if another woman carries the pregnancy). In some cases this may be formalized in kinship terms, with the donor or birth mother becoming the child's godparent or a fictive aunt, uncle, or parent (Richards, 2002). This latter course is, not surprisingly, more commonly taken by same-sex couples[14] and where egg donation is used. It seems to bear out Haimes's (1993) contention that woman-to-woman donation of eggs (or embryos) is seen as asexual when compared with the man-to-woman donation of sperm which is seen as more intrusive, threatening, and potentially sexual. In a number of cultures the sisterly donation of eggs or embryos is seen as a primarily altruistic act, while the brotherly donation of sperm carries connotations of incest. Similarly, there may be differences in attitudes to a woman gestating an embryo produced by her daughter and partner, as compared with that of a son and his partner.

Ethnographic work in clinics in the US has described how the actors "do kinship" in order to realign biological and social accounts (Thompson, 2001). So, for example, a woman who used donor eggs from a friend stressed the small percentage of pregnancy spent at the gamete and embryo stage, so minimizing the biological contribution of the egg, while emphasizing the biological significance of her own gestational role. She also pointed out that she and her friend shared a common genetic pool as they came from the same ethnic background. The bonds of friendship between the donor and the mother allowed the donor's relationship to the baby to be seen as an enhancement of that friendship.

In another case where a husband's sister was the gestational surrogate, the surrogate was seen as having a custodial role only – providing a site and nurture for fetal development. "The children were fine with their auntie but could not wait to be reunited with their parents."

As mentioned earlier, many professionals involved in fertility treatment may regard openness about a child's genetic origin to be potentially damaging for a child. The little evidence available on the matter suggests that when children are brought up with knowledge of their origins, this can have a beneficial effect on parent–child relationships (Golombok et al., 2002a; see also Haimes, 1998). It is also worth pointing out that though most children may not know about their genetic origins, most parents tell other family members or friends about the manner of their conception (Golombok et al., 1996). This means, especially with easy access to DNA relationship testing and the growth of clinical genetic testing, that children are increasingly likely to discover their origins. Those who discover their origins (or are told) as teenagers or adults may be angry and resentful of the way they have been misled by their parents and the professionals involved (Donor Conception Support Group of Australia, 1997; Turner and Coyle, 2000, Richards, 2000).

As we have already noted, in the UK, as in many other countries, there are important differences in the ways in which the children of donor conception and those of adoption are treated. Almost all adopted children are told of their origins and given information about their birth parents. Increasingly, adoption is "open," with the possibility of continuing contact for children with their birth parents. Research suggests that adopted children benefit from openness (e.g., Grokevart and McRoy, 1998). In the UK, adopted children at 18, following counseling, have access to their birth certificates, and significant numbers use this information to try and trace their birth parents. The most common motive for doing this is for a sense of identity and connectedness with forebears (Howe and Feast, 2000). There also may be issues for them about self-worth related to the reasons why their birth parents gave them up for adoption and, for some, there is the possibility of a continuing relationship with the birth parent(s). In Howe and Feast's (2000) study, a third of those who tried to make contact were either rejected by the birth parents or found the contact unsatisfactory, but even these young people said they were glad to have made the search and to have "completed the jigsaw." Eight years after having made a satisfactory contact with a birth mother, more than half the adopted children maintained a relationship with her. Strathern (1992) suggests that kinship talk is about the manner in which social arrangements are based on and provide the cultural context for the natural processes of reproduction; and, we might add, also the less than natural arrangements that are made for the use of assisted or "artificial" reproductive technologies.

## Testing for Genetic Disease

Since the mid-1990s there have been intensive efforts, recently accelerated by the information from the Human Genome Project, to identify the genes with mutations that are associated with the Mendelian or single-gene diseases. Identification of the genes and their mutations opens up the possibility of genetic testing, which is now available for many of the 5,000 or so of these genetic diseases. All are rare, and many are only recorded from a handful of families but, taken together, they may effect up to 5 percent of the population. In terms of causation these diseases may be regarded as a genetic spanner in the works. A fault in the gene – a changed DNA sequence – which may be passed from parent to child, means that the protein which the gene is involved in producing is changed, so that it cannot perform its usual functions, and hence the disease. In the dominantly inherited Mendelian diseases, having a single faulty gene is usually sufficient to cause the disease. One of the first genes associated with a dominantly inherited disease to be identified is that associated with Huntington's disease. This is a degenerative disease of the central nervous system which generally develops in middle age,[15] (most dominantly inherited diseases are adult-onset).[16] After about 15 years of increasing physical and mental disability the disease is invariably fatal. Over the decade during which predictive genetic testing has been available for Huntington's disease, families with the condition have been intensively studied by social scientists (Marteau and Richards, 1996; Cox and McKellin 1999a, 1999b). These families have been called the "moral pioneers" of the new genetic era (Cox and Burgess, 2000; see also Kenen and Schmidt, 1978; Rapp, 2000), facing novel decisions about genetic testing, communicating test results to relatives and, more generally, living their lives in the shadow of a fatal genetic disorder which remains incurable. As with any dominantly inherited disorder, children of an affected parent have a 50 percent chance of inheriting the mutated form of the gene which leads to the disorder. Probably about 10 percent of those in that situation have chosen to take the genetic test which tells them whether or not they have the gene mutation (Marteau and Richards, 1996; Harper, Lim, and Craufurt, 2000). "While there is uncertainty, there is hope," is the way one family member described their decision about testing (Wexler, 1979). In these families, as those with other gene disease, communication about the disease is primarily undertaken by the women. They are the "kin-keepers" or "genetic housekeepers" and are more likely to use genetic testing than the men (Richards, 1996, 1998). Perhaps most surprising is the very limited use made of fetal genetic testing by affected parents. Here issues of genetic identity may be involved. To abort a fetus that has the gene mutation is to destroy an individual that has the same gene mutation as the affected parent.

With the recessively inherited diseases, only those with mutations in both their copies of the relevant gene develop the disease; those with a single copy are normal carriers. These are diseases which typically develop at or soon after birth. Better-known examples here are thalassemia (particularly common in Mediterranean and Middle Eastern populations), cystic fibrosis (northwest Europe), and Tay-Sachs disease (Ashkenazi Jewish populations). Carriers of recessive diseases may have an evolutionary selective advantage over noncarriers in these conditions. Thus carriers of thalassemia and sickle-cell disease have resistance to malaria, while cystic fibrosis carriers are thought to be resistant to typhoid. This evolutionary advantage (despite the likelihood of producing children with the disease) may account for the relatively high frequency in carriers in certain populations. In some of these cases population-screening programs have been set up. In Cyprus, where about a fifth of the population are carriers of thalassemia, couples are screened before marriage. When both are carriers, they then use prenatal diagnosis and abortion.[17] This has virtually eliminated the birth of affected children on the island. In parts of the UK, pregnant women are tested for cystic fibrosis-carrier status, if they test positive their partner is tested, and where both are positive, prenatal diagnosis with the possibility of an abortion of an affected fetus follows. But in most parts of the UK such screening is not offered and most carrier couples discover their status when a child with cystic fibrosis is born. This may then pose a profound dilemma for couples who want further children. Should they use prenatal diagnosis and abortion to avoid the birth of another child with the same condition as their existing child? In some orthodox Jewish communities in North America and elsewhere, where prenatal diagnosis and abortion are not acceptable, young people are screened for Tay-Sachs carrier status. To avoid the possible damage to self-esteem that knowledge of carrier status can bring, or of blighting marriage prospects, results are not given to the young person but to the matchmakers that some communities use, who then avoid coupling two carriers. Where matchmakers are not used there are schemes which offer young people a choice of receiving their own results or a personal identification number. This number then can be used together with that of a potential partner to determine whether or not both are carriers. In this way, young people avoid learning their carrier status except when both they and a potential partner are carriers.

Another way of avoiding the birth of affected children without the use of abortion is to employ pre-implantation diagnosis. This involves IVF and a genetic test is carried out on the embryos before implantation. Only those embryos not carrying the relevant gene mutation are then implanted. But, partly because of the low success of IVF programs (under 20 percent of treatments in infertile couples lead to a pregnancy)[18] and the high cost, this technology is not widely used.

The recessively inherited conditions also provide one of the very rare examples of a genetic disease for which there is a cure (more or less) brought about through environmental manipulation. This is phenylketoneurea (PKU). Those affected lack an enzyme which is necessary to digest a commonly occurring food component. This leads to accumulation of byproducts in the body which may cause permanent brain damage, especially during childhood while the brain is still developing. But by avoiding the relevant dietary constituent in childhood, brain development is largely normal. In many countries babies are screened at birth[19] (a Guthrie heel-prick blood test)[20] and affected children (approximately 1 in 10,000) are then put on a special diet.

The final category of Mendelian single-gene disease which should be mentioned are the X-linked diseases such as Duchenne muscular dystrophy or Fragile X syndrome. These diseases result from mutations from genes on the X-chromosome, one of the sex chromosomes. While women have paired X-chromosomes, men have an X and a Y. This means that if there is a gene with a potential disease producing on one of a woman's X-chromosomes, it is likely that she will have a normal copy of the gene on her other chromosome and hence no disease. But, if a man inherits an X-chromosome with a gene with the relevant mutation, he has no second X-chromosome to "balance" this, so disease results. Thus, X-linked conditions are generally confined to males but are inherited from their mothers. As has been reported in psychosocial studies of families which carry Duchenne muscular dystrophy, this gendering of the disease can produce difficult and complex dynamics in families (Parsons and Bradley, 1994).

The great increase in genetic testing using DNA techniques has led to much media discussion of diseases such as Huntington's disease or the inherited breast cancer syndrome and the family issues and dilemmas that genetic testing may raise. There have been claims by social scientists that genetic testing is leading to a geneticization of kinship and a new preoccupation with inherited disease; "DNA becomes a central repository of human memory by assuming agency and true ontological status with its alleged capacity to remember people's ancestry" (Finkler, 2001). However, this may be a rather ahistorical view (see the commentary published with Finkler, 2001). It is, of course, true that when a family member attends a genetic clinic and a family genetic history is taken, and perhaps a DNA genetic test is carried out, there may be implications for family members which emphasize matters of genetic relationship. Assembling a family history may involve enquiries about the health and diseases that distant family members may have suffered. But the assembling of such family histories is not new. The techniques, and indeed, the symbols used in the charts drawn up in genetic clinics today, were developed in the late nineteenth and early twentieth centuries by the social scientists and geneticists involved in the Eugenics Movement (Nukago, 2002). At that time these "pedigrees" often recorded the psychological and moral qualities which were central to the concerns of the eugenic movement as they waged a "jihad, or a holy war against customs and prejudices that impair the physical and moral qualities of our race" (Galton, 1907). It was assumed that qualities like intelligence, criminality, and drunkenness were inherited as Mendelian traits in the same manner as the single-gene diseases we have just been discussing (Paul, 1998). Family histories were often published to demonstrate this. Often these published pedigrees were designed to illustrate eugenic moral tales. For example, that of the woman who married twice. First, to a ne'er-do-well with whom she produced a string of children who themselves and whose descendants led lives of criminality and dissolution, and second to an upstanding man whose progeny were all pillars of society. Such propaganda was the stock in trade of the Eugenics Movement in North America, Europe, and elsewhere. It was not until the 1920s, when quantitative genetics was well established, that it was accepted that while such behavioral traits may be to a degree heritable, they were not transmitted as Mendelian traits "like the coat color of guinea pigs," as a poster of the American Eugenics Society had claimed.

These same concerns and interests in the inheritance of human qualities can be traced back to the nineteenth century and earlier. For example, common themes in nineteenth-century fiction concern inheritance in families and secrets of descent and forebears, as well as madness and other "bad blood." Contemporary preoccupations with inheritance may have developed new narratives and themes with development of DNA technologies (Nelkin and Lindee, 1995), but the metaphorical DNA, genes and chromosomes of the twenty-first century (Richards, 2001) resonate strongly with the good and bad blood of Victorian culture and ideology of eugenics in the twentieth century. Ethnographic studies (Atkinson, Parsons, and Featherstone, 2001) have described the process by which clinicians construct the family as both a social object and as a set of biological relationships. The professional work of geneticists is thus seen as traversing the boundaries of the natural and the social and the pedigree as a boundary object between these two discursive domains. This is a discussion to which I will return below.

Novas and Rose (2000) suggest that the key event in the development of genetic testing has been the creation of the person genetically at risk. This risk, it is argued, induces new and active relations to one's self and one's future as it generates new forms of "genetic responsibility" placing affected individuals and those at risk within new communities of obligation and identification. This may, it is claimed, transform the relations between patient and expert. "The birth of the person 'genetically at risk' is part of a wider reshaping of personhood along somatic lines and mutation in conceptions of life itself" (p. 486). Others have argued that a new kind of public health practice is being created based on a new concept of genetic risk (Petersen and Lupton, 1996; Petersen and Bunton, 2002).

Before leaving the topic of genetic testing, brief mention should be made of genetic testing in relation to the common "complex" diseases. With almost all common diseases, including infectious diseases, there are inherited differences which contribute to differential susceptibility. For some time a major research effort has been underway to find the gene variants that are responsible for these differences in diseases such as coronary heart disease, diabetes, and the common late-onset form of Alzheimer's disease. Unlike the mutation associated with the single-gene Mendelian diseases which were discussed earlier, these gene variants are common and will be carried by a significant proportion of the population. Rather than the spanner in the works that the mutations associated with Mendelian single-gene diseases may represent, these variants (or polymorphisms) are part of normal human variation. Because these gene variants only contribute a small part of the variation in susceptibility between individuals, it is unlikely that they will be useful in predictive testing. And for common diseases there are many such gene variants involved. These will

interact in complex ways with each other and environmental (dietary, lifestyle, etc) factors. The aim of identifying these gene variants is to provide new ways to dissect and analyze causal pathways involved in diseases[21] and to identify targets for drug development. Genetic variation may also be an important factor in the effectiveness of particular drugs and other treatments and there are already situations where patients are "stratified" in terms of gene variants to determine which drug, or particular drug dosage, is likely to be most effective.

As has been said, testing for particular gene variants may not be useful for prediction of common diseases. However, there are claims that by testing for many genetic variants at once – and technology to do this is already available – it is, or soon will be, possible to build up an individual's health profile which could be used to advise individuals about risk-reducing strategies. Indeed, a company has recently launched such a service. However, until many more gene variants associated with common diseases are identified (and research so far has not been very successful), and the very complex interactions between these and other factors are well understood (and that is a condition that is unlikely to be satisfied in the near future), most agree that such genetic approaches are unlikely to add much of value to current understanding of risk factors and risk prediction. The most likely way in which most of the population will be affected by these developments in the immediate future will be through involvement in the very large-scale studies of health, lifestyle, gene variation, and family relationships which are being used to search for genetic variants associated with common diseases. This includes the Icelandic database which involves the whole population (subject to an individual opt-out) and the planned Wellcome Trust–MRC Biobank UK, which will have half a million middle-aged volunteer participants. One of the features that made Iceland particularly attractive for the biotech company that bought access to the country's health records is that, typically, Icelandic families have very full and careful records of their family histories, in many cases going back to the first settlement (Árnason and Árnason, 2001).

## Biomedical technology: Deployment and cultural assumptions

Of course, biomedical researchers do not simply set out to understand our biological world, they also wish to change it. As current debates illustrate, public responses and attitudes to new developments are often complex (Gaskell and Bauer, 2001). In discussing attitudes to reproductive and genetic technologies, I want to argue that we are concerned with a particular set of values and a culture concerned with the maintenance of the boundary between the natural sphere of reproduction and the social sphere of family and kinship. Strathern (1992) and Edwards et al. (1999) have suggested that human reproduction is seen, at least in Europe and societies derived from these, as belonging to the domain of nature, not the domain of society, and the two are connected by concepts of kinship. It is important to note that the domain of nature referred to here is not the scientific world of biology but rather a cultural conception of nature (see Yanagisako and Delaney, 1995).[22] Where technologies threaten to shift this boundary and extend the reach of society into the domain of nature, there is unease and resistance. In the modern period, the first major assault on this boundary was the increasing use of contraception, or the *artificial* methods of birth control, as they were then termed, from the latter part of the nineteenth century onward. In 1877 there was the famous case in which Annie Besant and Charles Bradlaugh were convicted for distributing a book which described methods of birth control which was held to be obscene. After some initial hesitation that the availability of birth control might encourage the genetically well-endowed to have smaller families, eugenicists did much to increase the knowledge and availability of contraception in many countries. In Britain Marie Stopes set up her clinic for mothers in a poor part of London in 1921 as part of the activities of her Society for Constructive Birth Control and Racial Progress. Such efforts were swept along by the rising tide of eugenics, which, of course, also forcibly controlled the reproduction of those deemed unfit through the policies of institutional segregation and sterilization (Kevles 1985; Paul, 1998). However, there was continuing opposition from sections of the population that regarded (artificial) birth control as unnatural and against nature.[23] In Britain, it was not until 1974 that contraception, as it was now known, which by then included the pill, was generally available through doctors in the National Health Service. Today the right to "found a family" is included in the Human Rights Act of 1998 and there was a general acceptance of a notion of reproductive autonomy allowing individuals the freedom to choose to have or not to have children (Jackson, 2001).

From the 1950s onward the development of techniques for prenatal screening and diagnosis provided new methods for choosing what kinds of children to have or not have. There has been extensive research of attitudes toward the use of these techniques. In Britain, as elsewhere, there is strong endorsement for the availability of fetal tests and abortion for serious disease and disability (see Richards, 2002). But support falls off when conditions that develop later in life are involved, or those involving, for example, a restriction of growth. Table 27.1 shows data from the British Social Attitudes Survey where respondents were asked whether or not they thought it right for a woman to have a legal abortion in each of these situations.

Many opinion surveys on these issues have included questions about the use of techniques to select the sex of a baby.[24] These show that an overwhelming majority of both the public and professionals reject the use of such techniques for sex selection, and this is banned in many regulated systems (McMillan, 2002). Given that in countries such as the UK, where the predominant preference of parents is to have children of both sexes and the use of sex selection is unlikely to distort the sex ratio or be damaging in other ways (Steinbock, 2002), at first sight the strength of the opposition to this use of technology is perhaps surprising. However, here we are concerned with what are widely termed "designer babies."[25] Attitudes are very different toward the use of technology to avoid the birth of babies with serious

**Table 27.1** Attitudes about abortion with various hypothetical fetal conditions, Great Britain (%)

| *For women to have an abortion* | *Serious mental disability* | *Serious physical disability* | *Healthy but dies in 20s or 30s* | *Healthy but height of an 8-year-old* |
|---|---|---|---|---|
| Never right | 8 | 10 | 35 | 48 |
| Sometimes right | 39 | 45 | 42 | 32 |
| Always right | 49 | 41 | 18 | 16 |
| Don't know | 3 | 3 | 4 | 4 |

*Source*: Stratford, Marteau, and Bobrow (1999).

conditions and cases where the aim is in some way to enhance or choose a baby's characteristics. Overall, there is a strong public approval of the use of biotechnology to prevent or treat disease (Gaskell and Bauer, 2001). However, to use techniques to determine any attributes of an unborn child is seen as something quite different. Once again, it is the boundary between the social and the natural domains which is violated. Here using biotechnology is seen as "playing God," or being against "nature" or the natural order of things (Wagner et al., 2002). The other area of reproductive technologies where we find strong public and governmental opposition is with reproductive cloning.[26] Here again the natural order is disturbed. Cloning – assuming of course it becomes possible[27] – would permit a predictability of the reproductive outcome as well as the foregoing of the natural union of egg and sperm. An inherent characteristic of the natural processes of reproduction is a capricious uncertainty of the outcome. Broadly speaking, children show a mixture of the characteristics of their parents. They demonstrate familial traits. However, the combinations and mixtures lead to unpredictable and unique characteristics. When at birth a baby first enters the visible world, the same questions reoccur – "Is it a girl?", "Is it a boy?", "Is it all right?" – and mothers, as well as doctors and midwives, count fingers and toes. Of course, other technologies, first X-rays and now ultrasound, have made the unborn baby potentially visible (Oakley, 1984). But, interestingly, while these techniques are used to reveal physical abnormality as part of prenatal screening, in many situations parents do not learn the sex of their unborn child. This is either kept hidden from them or they do not choose to know it before the birth. And, of course, the personality and physical appearance of babies remain unseen until after birth. The social child remains invisible. So a boundary between the social world and nature remains intact. We may also notice that birth provides a boundary after which the enhancement of bodily and mental functions becomes commonplace, in contrast to the general rejection of such possibilities before birth. Even young children may be subjected to cosmetic surgery or have their height enhanced with growth hormone. We pin back ears, fix teeth, or even provide adolescents with breast enhancement. But modification before birth – except attempts to correct serious malformation – is not done, nor is any modification of the genes to be passed to future children permitted. Birth marks a boundary. We permit (in the UK, under license) genetic therapy of the already born – though, as yet, success in such experimental therapy has proved largely elusive – but modification of future children through germline therapy is not permitted. Yet it is difficult to see why there should be objections were we able to safely restore the function of the gene in devastating disorders such as Huntington's disease.[28]

We could argue that the commodification of gametes in IVF and DI is part of this same boundary maintenance. Reducing the reproductive processes of the production and donation of eggs and sperm to the provision of "genetic material" denies and excludes the social actions of donors from a part in the "natural" reproduction by the couple receiving treatment. They are effectively written out of the story of the origins of the child and so an apparently natural process of reproduction has taken place. Strategies for "naturalizing kinship" in IVF clinics may be seen in the same way (Thompson, 2001).

Of course, current boundaries may shift and, indeed, many have suggested that they will do so. In the end pragmatism may rule for many.[29] For example, Silver (1998) has suggested that we are heading for a world of the "GenRich" and the "naturals." The former will use all manner of genetic manipulation to enhance their capabilities and performance but the naturals, not least for economic reasons, will continue to rely on the natural and uncertain processes of reproduction. With an ever-increasing range of post-birth enhancements being used by those who have access to them, many predict that we are on a "slippery slope" toward the kind of future that Silver envisages. Cases like that of the English family who are using IVF and pre-implantation selection[30] to try to produce a genetically compatible child to provide stem cells for transplantation to treat an existing child who has thalassemia are cited as evidence of the slide. However, there may be a boundary which will prove robust. What is certain on the basis of current practice is that almost all parents, despite the possibilities of using gametes from all manner of desirable sources, prefer to have their "own" children, conceived by their own egg and sperm brought together through sexual intercourse (Richards, 2002).

## Conclusions

The new DNA technologies have not been with us for very long and we have only just begun to observe and analyze the ways in which they may play a part in family life. In the words of the old country song, "we are living in the future, where we have never been before," and it is not possible to see ways forward very clearly. DNA relationship testing allows a new explicitness in familial (genetic) connections and I have suggested that their use may serve to further emphasize, and indeed define, relationships in terms of shared DNA sequences. Here, as with the use of reproductive technologies, international markets become important. A country may attempt to regulate access to certain technology but its citizens are free to travel or to access global markets from their homes using the Internet. In the case of the UK, the use of ARTs has been controlled in line with past practice and, as far as possible, with the model of "natural" heterosexual reproduction. But medical tourism allows visits to the uncontrolled marketplaces, for example, gay men may seek egg donors (at a price) and birth mothers. Many travel from Europe[31] to the unregulated clinics of the US and the Far East; just as others surf the Net and travel to find babies for adoption, or sources where they can buy body parts for transplantation. These tourists may not be the GenRich but they need to be materially rich enough to indulge in this expensive medical and reproductive tourism.

I have suggested that we see resistance where new technologies threaten to change the boundary between the social world of human actions and activity and the unseen domain of nature. "Artificial" birth control has shifted that boundary, and what was once discouraged by law has been renamed contraception and has became part of conventional medical practice, commerce, and family life. With the exception of some minority religious dissent, contraception has become an accepted part of daily life. Perhaps we shall see a similar shift in the boundary which currently determines the acceptability of genetic and reproductive technologies. There is a wide acceptance of the genetic technologies which permit diagnosis and prediction of genetic disease and the possibility of avoiding the birth of affected children by using prenatal diagnosis and abortion or preimplantation diagnosis and embryo selection. Similarly, postnatal somatic gene therapy, while still largely a biotechnological aspiration, enjoys wide public support and encouragement. The current boundaries for resistance lie where prenatal selection (or treatment) moves from avoiding serious disease to the selection on the basis of social preference and prenatal enhancement. It is acceptable for parents to choose to select against a fetus with a serious genetic or congenital abnormality, but not for them to chose to use sex selection (or indeed, for deaf parents to choose to produce their desired deaf child).[32] Having avoided predictable abnormality, reproduction is left to the vagaries of natural uncertainty, but wherever possible using parental sperm and eggs. "Designing" a baby to have desired characteristics or replicating an individual by reproductive cloning (were this to become technically feasible) are seen as steps too far. Indeed, approaching this boundary is usually seen to be the beginning of the slide down a "slippery slope" which may lead to the boundary being shifted. However, if the history of contraception is any guide here, we may indeed be on a slippery slope and one day prenatal enhancement and the design of babies will become accepted social practice, assuming that there are widespread social pressures for these. When techniques become available which allow selection or modification of the unborn in ways that are seen to be socially desirable or useful, their use is likely to become acceptable. Then a further part of the natural world will have been successfully colonized by the social.

## Notes

1 There are complications to this situation where certain assisted reproductive technologies are involved, which will be discussed below.

2 These ideas have been refined and developed in a number of important ways. See Barnes (1973) and Franklin (2001), for example.

3 This was not an auspicious start. The first described case involving Sarah, Abraham, and Hagar was the origin of a family feud which continues to the present day, with tragic consequences.

4 Today the technique is generally referred to as donor insemination (DI). I shall comment below on the significance of the name change.

5 Secrecy ruled from the beginning. In this case it is reported that sperm from "the best-looking member" of a medical class was used, and neither the woman nor her husband were told what had taken place. Later, the doctor who carried out the insemination told the husband, but at his request the wife was never told (Achilles, 1992).

6 Muller, who was a Nobel prizewinning geneticist, was involved in setting up a sperm bank which provided sperm from insemination from Nobel laureates and others deemed to be of superior stock. Earlier in his career he spent some time in Russia, an experience which led him to remove Marx and Lenin from his list of those of superior breeding potential.

7 Indeed, the concern was sufficient for this body to consider a suggestion that semen might be collected from the donor's wife's vagina (see Haimes, 1993).

8 The situation for reproductive cloning is rather different. This potential technology had not been welcomed by the Eugenics Movement. "I think the idea of short-circuiting the genetic lottery and having a child with a pre-determined genotype with no contribution from either parent is decidedly unattractive; even if the child were to have an obviously superior genetic endowment" (Carter, 1983). On this issue, the eugenicists were ahead of the game. Following the birth of Dolly, the sheep, the first authenticated case of a cloned mammal, most industrialized countries have banned human reproductive cloning. We will return to the discussion of reproductive cloning later in the chapter.

We should also note that not all ethicists have supported the regulation of ARTs. Some (e.g., Harris, 1998) have argued for a reproductive autonomy which should leave parents free (more or less) to use any reproductive technology that is available. Others (e.g., O'Neill, 2002), however, draw a sharp distinction between an autonomy to decide whether or not to have children – the use of contraception, abortion, etc. – and that used to create children. Where a child may be produced there are considerations of their well-being and upbringing.

9 By this time, with wider acceptance of the technique, the "artificial" was dropped. AID became donor insemination. In a similar way, "artificial birth control" became birth control and, subsequently, contraception. As I will argue below, these rebrandings may indicate very significant cultural shifts.

10 British evidence suggests that most sperm donors are young, single students who are motivated by the modest payment they receive (Cook and Golombok, 1995). There are indications that such donors, especially after they have their own children, may regret what they have done and may become interested in the children they may have fathered (Baran and Pannar, 1989).

11 Interestingly, this too follows a much earlier suggestion for such arrangements by the Eugenics Society (Binney, 1949; Carter, 1983).

12 This consists of the height; weight; ethnic group; eye, skin, and hair color; occupation; and interests of the donor. The donor is also invited to give a "brief description of themselves as a person" (see Blyth and Hunt, 1998).

13 See Johnson (1999) for a discussion of this biologically misleading terminology.

14 See Weston (1996).

15 Huntington's disease is somewhat unusual among Mendelian diseases in that all those who carry the mutation will develop the disease (assuming they do not die of something else first). As a geneticist would put it, it is 100 percent penetrant. In most Mendelian diseases the penetrance is less than 100 percent, so that there are individuals who carry the mutation who do not develop the disease. This means that genetic tests (which identify those who carry the mutation) may be poor predictors of who will develop the disease.

16 If they had major effects early in life, they would effect reproduction so that there would be selective pressure operating against the gene mutation.

17 Two carrier parents have a one in four chance of producing an affected child.

18 But there are indications that the success rate may be slightly higher, presumably because couples using preimplantation diagnosis do not, in general, have fertility problems.

19 This test, which long predates the coming of DNA tests, is based on a biochemical anomaly in affected children. But the gene involved in the disease has now been identified and direct DNA tests are now possible.

20 This test has led to ethical dilemmas in a number of countries. Where there is screening of the whole population at birth, the cards with the blood spots used for the test could serve as a population DNA database. There are examples of the police using Guthrie cards to match DNA taken at a crime scene in New Zealand and some other countries.

21 This work may well lead to new biomarkers which may well be powerful predictors of disease development. So while there may not be a future with new usefully predictive genetic tests for common diseases, there may well be other physiological tests which are predictive.

22 My very brief remarks here do far less than justice to this important body of work. See, for example, Strathern (1999) and Franklin and McKinnon (2001).

23 We noted earlier the opposition to AID by groups such as His Grace the Archbishop of Canterbury's Commission. They termed the practice as *artificial* human insemination.

24 Currently the HFEA are carrying out a public consultation on the issue.

25 "Designer" in this context has two meanings; that which is deliberately made and artifacts that are part of the world of high fashion and consumer culture.

26 Stem-cell cloning is another matter. That has very strong commercial support, as it may lead to technologies for treatment of a wide range of degenerative diseases by providing tissues for implantation which would be genetically identical with the recipient and so avoid problems of rejection. Lines between stem-cell research and reproductive cloning

are carefully drawn, and in some countries such as the UK there is strong governmental endorsement of stem-cell cloning while in others both have been banned.

27 Human experimental reproductive cloning is banned in many industrialized countries. However, there are a number of countries where such research is unregulated and, indeed, is encouraged by governments interested in developing a biotech industry. This has led to patterns of long-distance commuting for some scientists and technologists from Europe and North America, largely to countries in the Far East.

28 The argument here would distinguish between the dominantly inherited conditions, such as Huntington's disease, and the recessively inherited conditions, such as cystic fibrosis, thalassemia, or Tay-Sachs disease. For the latter, avoiding the creation of children with these diseases or providing cures for them, if feasible, might be widely welcomed. However, as we have noted, carriers of the gene mutations associated with these diseases may have significant advantages in terms of disease resistance, and so there are reasons for maintaining their numbers in the population. We should also note that changing common gene variants will generally have multiple effects, so there may be little predictability of outcome.

29 An interesting example of this is demonstrated by stem-cell research. In several countries where stem-cell cloning has been banned, research proceeds with stem-cell lines which have been created elsewhere.

30 Under license from the Human Fertilization and Embryology Authority. Interestingly, the Authority did not permit another family to use the same approach in a situation where, unlike the embryos from the parents carrying thalassemia, the embryos would not be at risk of carrying a serious genetic condition and so would not also be subject to screening for genetic disease. That couple subsequently travelled to the USA, where these procedures were carried out, leading to the birth of a "saviour sibling" who is an appropriate HLA match for their affected child. However, it can be argued that added procedures of genetic screening for disease make no material difference and in both cases the key feature is the selection of embryos for implementation on the basis of the genetic compatibility with the potential stem-cell recipient.

31 There is also movement within Europe from the more regulated countries of the north-west to the currently largely unregulated clinics in Italy.

32 There are reports of this being done in unregulated markets in the US, but in the face of widespread social disapproval.

## Acknowledgments

I would like to thank all those who kindly provided comments on earlier drafts of this chapter. As ever, Jill Brown and Sally Roberts provided technical support. For sustenance while reading and writing I would like to thank the Flatlanders (that legend that was so briefly a band), James King, the Dry Branch Fire Squad, the Cox family, Alison Kraus, and Hazel Dickens.

## References

Achilles, R. (1992) *Donor Insemination: An Overview.* Ottawa: Royal Commission on New Reproductive on New Reproductive Technologies.

Árnason, V. and Árnason, G. (2001) Community consent, democracy and public dialogue: The case of the Icelandic health sector data base. *Politeia*, 17, 105–16.

Atkinson, P., Parsons, E., and Featherstone, K. (2001) Professional constructions of family and kinship in medical genetics. *New Genetics and Society*, 20, 5–24.

Bainham, A. (2002) Can we protect children and protect their rights? *Family Law*, 279–89.

Baran, A. and Pannar, R. (1989) *Lethal Secrets: The Psychology of Donor Insemination*. New York: Amistad.

Barnes, J. A. (1973) Genetrix: genitor : : nature : culture. In J. Goody (ed.), *Culture of Kinship*. Cambridge: Cambridge University Press.

Bartholomew, G. W. (1958) Development and use of artificial insemination. *Eugenics Review*, 49, 187–95.

Bharadwaj, A. (2003) Why adoption is not an option in India: The visibility of infertility, the secrecy of donor insemination and other cultural complexities. *Social Science and Medicine*, 56, 1867–80.

Binney, C. (1949) Legal and social implications of artificial insemination. *Eugenics Review*, 40, 199–204.

Blacker, C. P. (1958) Artificial insemination: The society's position. *Eugenics Review*, 50, 51–4.

Blyth, E. (1999) Secrets and lies. Barriers to the exchange of genetic origins information following donor-assisted conception. *Adoption and Fostering*, 23, 49–58.

Blyth, E., and Hunt, J. (1998) Sharing genetic origin information in donor assisted conception: Views from licensed centres on HFEA donor information form. *Human Reproduction*, 13, 3274–7.

Brewer, H. (1935) Eutelegenesis. *Eugenics Review*, 27, 121–6.

Carter, C. O. (1983) Eugenic implications of new techniques. In C. O. Carter (ed.), *Developments in Human Reproduction and their Eugenic, Ethical Implications*. London: Academic.

Cook, R. (2002) Villain, hero or masked stranger: ambivalence in transactions with human genetics. In A. Bainham, S. Day-Sclater, and M. Richards (eds.), *Body Lore and Laws*. Oxford: Hart.

Cook, R., and Golombok, S. (1995) A survey of semen donation: Phase 2 – the view of donors. *Human Reproduction*, 10, 951–9.

Cox, S. M., and Burgess, M. M. (2000) *Victims, Heroes or Pioneers; Moral Experiences of Hereditary Risk and Illness*. Paper presented at the Canadian Bioethics Society Conference, Quebec.

Cox, S .M., and McKellin, W. H. (1999a) "There's this thing in our family": Predictive testing and the social construction of risk for Huntington's disease. In P. Conrad and J. Gabe (eds.), *Sociological Perspectives on the New Genetics*. Oxford: Blackwell.

Cox, S. M., and McKellin, W. H. (1999b) "There's this thing in our family": Predictive testing and the construction of risk for Huntington's disease. *Sociology of Health and Illness*, 21, 622–46.

Department of Health (2001a) *Code of Practice and Guidance on Genetic Paternity Testing Services*. London: Department of Health.

Department of Health (2001b) *Donor Information Consultation. Providing Information About Sperm, Egg and Embryo Donors*. London: Department of Health. Available online at www.doh.gov.uk/gametedonors

Donor Conception Support Group of Australia (1997) *Let the Offspring Speak: Discussions on Donor Conception*. Genges Hill, NSW: Donor Conception Support Group of Australia.

Edwards, J. D., Franklin, S., Hirsch, E., Price, F., and Strathern, M. (1999) *Technologies of Procreation. Kinship in the Age of Assisted Conception*. 2nd ed. London: Routledge.

Finkler, K. (2001) The kin in the gene: The medicalization of family and kinship in American society. *Current Anthropology*, 42, 235–63.

Franklin, S. (2001) Biologization revisited: Kinship theory in the context of the new biologies. In S. Franklin and S. McKinnon (eds.), *Relative Values: Reconfiguring Kinship Studies*. Durham, NC: Duke University Press.

Franklin, S., and McKinnon, S. (eds.) (2001) *Relative Values: Reconfiguring Kinship Studies*. Durham, NC: Duke University Press.

Freeman, M. (1996) The new birth right? *International Journal of Children's Rights*, 4, 273–97.

Galton, F. (1907) *Probability, the Foundation of Eugenics. The Herbert Spencer Lecture.* Oxford: Clarendon Press.

Gaskell, G. and Bauer, M. W. (eds.) (2001) *Biotechnology 1996–2000.* London: Science Museum.

Giddens, A. (1991) *Modernity and Self-Identity: Self and Society in the Late Modern Age.* Cambridge: Polity.

Golombok, S., Brewaeys, A., Cook, R., Giavazzi, M. T., Guerra, G., Mantovanni, A., Van Hall, E., Crosignani, P. G., and Dexeus, S. (1996) The European study of assisted reproduction families. *Human Reproduction*, 11, 2324–31.

Golombok, S., Brewaeys, A., Giavazzi, M.T., Guerra, G., Mantovanni, A., Van Hall, E., Crosignani, P. G., and Dexeus, S. 1996. (2002a) The European study of assisted reproduction families: The transition to adolescence. *Human Reproduction*, 17, 830–40.

Golombok, S., MacCallum, F. M., Goodman, E., and Rutter, M. (2002b) Parenting and contemporary reproductive technologies. In M. H. Barnstein (ed.), *Handbook of Parenting*, 2nd ed. Vol. 3. Mahwah, NJ: Lawrence Erlbaum.

Grokevart, M. D., and McRoy, R. G. (1998) *Openness in Adoption. Exploring Family Connections.* New York: Sage.

Haimes, E. (1993) Issues of gender in gamete donation. *Social Science and Medicine*, 36, 85–93.

Haimes, E. (1998) The making of "the DI child": Changing representations of people conceived through donor insemination. In K. Daniels and E. Haimes (eds.), *Donor Insemination: International Social Science Perspectives.* Cambridge: Cambridge University Press.

Hanmer, J. (1987) Transforming consciousness. Women and the new reproductive technologies. In G. Cerea et al. (eds.), *Man-Made Women.* Bloomington: Indiana University Press.

Harper, P. S., Lim, S., and Craufurt, D. (2000) Ten years of pre symptomatic testing for Huntington's disease: The experience of the UK Huntington's disease consortium. *Journal of Medical Genetics*, 37, 567–71.

Harris, J. (1998) *Clones, Genes and Immortality: Ethics and the Genetic Revolution.* Oxford: Clarendon Press.

His Grace the Archbishop of Canterbury's Communication (1948) *Artificial Human Insemination.* London: Society for the Propagation of Human Knowledge.

Howe, D. and Feast, J. (2000) *Adoption, Search and Reunion.* London: Children's Society.

Jackson, E. (2001) *Regulating Reproduction. Law, Technology and Autonomy.* Oxford: Hart.

Jackson, M. H. (1945) A medical service for the treatment of involuntary sterility. *Eugenic Review*, 36, 117–25.

Johnson, M. (1999) A biomedical perspective on parenthood. In A. Bainham, S. Day-Sclater and M. Richards (eds.), *What is a Parent? A Socio Legal Analysis.* Oxford: Hart.

Kenen, R., and Schmidt, R. (1978) Stigmatization of carrier status: Social implications of heterozygote genetic screening programmes. *American Journal of Public Health*, 68, 1116–19.

Kevles, D. J. (1985) *In the Name of Eugenics.* New York: Knopf.

Marteau, T., and Richards, M. P. M. (eds.) (1996) *The Troubled Helix.* Cambridge: Cambridge University Press.

McMillan, J. (2002) Sex selection in the United Kingdom. *Hastings Center Report*, 32, 28–31.

Morgan, D. (1991) *Blackstone's Guide to the Human Fertilization and Embryology Act 1990.* London: Blackstone.

Muller, H. (1963) Discussion at international conference held by the Ciba Foundation. In G. Wolstenholme (ed.), *Man and His Future.* London: Churchill.

Nelkin, D., and Lindee, S. (1995) *The DNA Mystique.* New York: Freeman.

Novas, C., and Rose, N. (2000) Genetic risk and the birth of the somatic individual. *Economy and Society*, 29, 485–513.

Nukago, Y. (2002) Between tradition and innovation in new genetics: The continuity of medical pedigrees and the development of combination work in the case of Huntington's disease. *New Genetics and Society*, 21, 39–64.

Oakley, A. (1984) *The Captured Womb: A History of the Medical Care of Pregnant Women.* Oxford: Blackwell.

O'Neill, O. (2002) *Autonomy and Trust in Bioethics.* Cambridge: Cambridge University Press.

Parsons, E., and Bradley, D. (1994) Ethical issues in newborn screening for Duchenne muscular dystrophy. In A. Clarke (ed.), *Genetic Counselling, Practice and Principles.* London: Routledge.

Paul, D. B. (1998) *Controlling Human Heredity: 1865 to the Present.* Amherst, NY: Humanity Books.

Petersen, A., and Bunton, R. (2002) *The New Genetics and the Public's Health.* London: Routledge.

Petersen, A., and Lupton, D. (1996) *The New Public Health: Health and Self in the Age of Risk.* London: Sage.

Rapp, R. (2000) *Testing Women, Testing the Fetus: The Social Impact of Amniocentesis in America.* New York: Routledge.

Raymond, J. G. (1994) *Women or Wombs: Reproductive Technologies and the Battle Over Women's Freedom.* Melbourne: Spinifex.

Reuters (2002) June 11. Available online at www.reuters.com

Richards, M. (2002) Future bodies: Some history and future prospects for human genetic selection. In A. Bainham, S. Day-Sclater, and M. Richards (eds.), *Body Lore and Laws.* Oxford: Hart.

Richards, M. P. M. (1996) Families, kinship and genetics. In T. Marteau and M. P. M. Richards (eds.), *The Troubled Helix: Social and Psychological Implications of the New Human Genetics.* Cambridge: Cambridge University Press.

Richards, M. P. M. (1998) Annotation: Genetic research, family life and clinical practice. *Journal of Child Psychology and Psychiatry,* 39, 291–305.

Richards, M. P. M. (2000) *Unpublished Data.* Centre for Family Research, University of Cambridge.

Richards, M. P. M. (2001) How distinctive is genetic information? *Studies in the History of Biological and Biomedical Sciences,* 32, 663–87.

Schneider, D. (1980) *Kinship: A Cultural Account.* Chicago: University of Chicago Press.

Silver, L. M. (1998) *Remaking Eden. Cloning, Genetic Engineering and the Future of Human Kind.* London: Weidenfeld & Nicolson.

Spallone, P. (1987) Reproductive technology and the state: The Warnock Report and its clones. In P. Spallone and D. L. Steinberg (eds.), *Made to Order: the Myth of Reproductive and Genetic Progress.* Oxford: Pergamon.

Stanworth, M. (ed.) (1987) *Reproductive Technologies: Gender, Motherhood and Medicine.* Cambridge: Polity Press.

Steinbock, B. (2002) Sex selection. Not obviously wrong. *Hastings Center Report,* 32, 23–8.

Steptoe, P., and Edwards, R. G. (1978) Birth after the replacement of a human embryo. *Lancet,* ii, 366.

Stratford, N., Marteau, T., and Bobrow, M. (1999) Tailoring genes. In R. Jowell et al. (eds.), *British Social Attitudes. The 16$^{th}$* Report. Aldershot: Ashgate.

Strathern, M. (1992) *Reproducing the Future. Essays on Anthropology, Kinship and the New Reproductive Technologies.* Manchester: Manchester University Press.

Strathern, M. (1999) *Property, Substance and Effect. Anthropological Essays on Persons and Things.* London: Athlone.

Taitz, J., Weekers, J. E. M., and Mosca, D. T. (2002) DNA and immigration: The ethical ramifications. *Lancet,* 359, 794.

Thompson, C. (2001) *Strategic Naturalizing: Kinship in the Infertility Clinic. Relative Values. Reconfiguring Kinship Studies.* Duke, NC: Duke University Press.

Turner, J. and Coyle, A. (2000) What does it mean to be a donor offspring? *Human Reproduction,* 11, 2041–51.

Wagner, W., Kronberger, N., Gaskell, G. et al. (2002) Nature in disorder. The troubled public of biotechnology. In G. Gaskell and M.W. Bauer (eds.), *Biotechnology 1996–2000. The Years of Controversy.* London: Science Museum.

Weston, K. (1996) *Families We Choose: Lesbians, Gays, Kinship.* New York: Columbia University Press.

Wexler, N.S. (1979) Genetic "Russian roulette"; The experience of being "at risk" for Huntington's disease. In S. Kessler (ed.), *Genetic Counselling: Psychological Dimensions.* New York: Academic.

Yanagisako, S. and Delaney, C. (1995) Naturalizing power. In C. Delaney and S. Yanagisako (eds.), *Naturalizing Power.* New York: Routledge.

# 28

# Families in a Runaway World

Ulrich Beck and Elisabeth Beck-Gernsheim

## Introduction

Of all the changes shaking the world today, none affect us more directly than those at the core of our personal lives, at the very point where we experience the fundamental shifts in sexuality, marriage, parenthood, or divorce, and the ever-more complex forms of living together, living apart, or a mixture of the two. Already the question of what constitutes a family, where its frontiers are drawn, who does or does not belong to it at any given time and from whose point of view – triggers an avalanche of further questions. It also indicates a central problem that faces the sociology of the family – the fact that in a runaway world the basic categories themselves become unclear and unfocused. This happens not because of shortcomings in the research, but because the research reflects deep changes in the field of family sociology.

The difficulty of stabilizing elementary concepts and definitions in family research points to something that many contributions to this volume demonstrate: namely, that we find ourselves in the middle of a global revolution, in which people are taking apart and renegotiating the apparently eternal laws of what used to be straightforwardly known as "the family." The "nature" of intimacy, rights, and duties in relations between the sexes and generations, issues relating to collective and individual existence, solidarity and identity: these all become matters to be discussed and fought over.

It is undoubtedly true that the turbulence of the runaway world varies with the region and culture: it manifests itself differently in Europe or North America than in China, India, Africa, or South America. Nevertheless, the macrocosm of the runaway world is mirrored in the microcosm of the family. Much as, in a global and technological world, the boundaries between inner and outer, ourselves and others, war and peace, life and death, nature and society, subject and object, break down and have to be established anew, so too in family life the definitions of inner and outer, ourselves and others, death and life, men and women, fathers and mothers, are in a state of flux. It therefore also becomes necessary to map the many new concepts and new forms of relationships: egg donors and surrogate mothers, biological mothers or biological fathers, cohabitation, committed relationships, same-sex partnerships, patchwork families, conjugal succession, post-divorce families, and all the other forms that are constantly appearing. Of course, this scarcely solves the central question: what actually constitutes the sociological unit for "family research"? It merely makes the question all the more pressing.

Does the concept of household perhaps offer us a solution? That is certainly one way to go, which is often taken both in the analysis of social classes and in research into consumption habits, lifestyles, or milieux. But then the next question immediately arises: what is a "household" nowadays? For the aggregate changes taking place in society become visible precisely in the microcosm of the household. My, your, our children; nonmarital living together or living apart together; divorce and remarriage; commuter marriage and transnational migrant families: all these developments mean that a split has opened up between what used to thought of as belonging naturally together, the spatial, social, and economic dimensions of the household unit. These boundaries were once assumed to be identical in social science and empirical class analysis. That assumption, however, is no longer valid.

So, if neither family nor household denotes a unified category of research, what is it that sociologists study when they investigate "families"? The French sociologist Jean-Claude Kaufmann has given an exemplary answer to this question, by replacing family and household with *the couple* as the unit to be investigated. What is a couple, he asks, if it is no longer defined by a marriage certificate or by sexual relations? His answer is that a couple is when two individuals get one washing machine, not two. That is the start of a history of everyday entanglements, negotiations, speeches, and counter-speeches, which Kaufmann links to the turmoil of "laundry" (1992). What counts as dirty? Who washes when and for whom? Does it have to be ironed? What if he says yes and she says no? All this must be negotiated but may also not be negotiated, because intimate relationships presuppose what has to be reached through negotiation: the unquestioned certainty of a shared life together.

It follows from what has been said so far that social science which occupies itself with "families" must (like social science in general) discover again the bases of the familiar yet unknown realities in which we live. It must discover how these realities are produced, reproduced, and changed in people's lives together and in the ways they act, as well as how this can be understood, reconstructed, and explained in sociological terms.

This is a daunting task. In what follows we break this down by considering three questions. (1) What does "runaway world" signify in categories of sociological analysis? What is the theoretical framework in which the historical transformation of family life can best be represented? (2) How can this transformation be demonstrated by the example of the individualization of the family? At which levels and with what consequences does individualization operate within the family? (3) What points of departure does this framework offer for a new postfamilial sociology of the family?

## THEORETICAL PREMISES: THE "SECOND MODERNITY"

The "runaway world" metaphor (see Giddens, 1999) stands for radical social change – or, rather, for a *meta-change of modernity*, in which the foundations and coordinates of change themselves undergo change. We address this historical self-transformation of modernity within a theory of reflexive modernization (Beck, Giddens, and Lash, 1994; Beck, 1997; Beck, Bonss, and Lau, 2003). What is meant by this "reflexive modernization" or "second modernity"? And how, in this theoretical framework, should we understand the historical transformation of family life and of sociological categories of the family?

First, talk of a second modernity does not imply a division of epochs such that the first modernity lasted up to a certain point – say, the mid-1970s – and then the second modernity took over and everything that had constituted the first modernity came to an end and vanished. Talk of a second modernity refers to a different concept, one which has both a sting and a point. The sting is directed against many theorists of postmodernism who, though pursuing the deconceptualization of science, leave us in the lurch when it comes to its reconceptualization. What arises where modernity ends and postmodernity begins? The sociologist of postmodernity maintains, in much the same manner as conventional modernization theory, that there cannot be *another* future, *another* modernity; hence the future of postmodernity is postmodernity – a circular model of the eternal present of postmodernity. Now, this is where the theory of a second modernity comes in; this is precisely where it has its point. Insofar as the first and second modernity are distinguished from each other, modernity is retrospectively relocated in history and, at the same time, pluralized with regard to the future that is beginning to emerge; it thereby appears as contradictory, ambivalent and open-ended. This all assumes a community of "entangled modernities" (Randeria, 1999), which have to be transnationally defined in the confrontation between periphery and center, in the interplay of Asian, African, Chinese, South American, and North Atlantic experiences and modernization projects. Some of the assumptions of the first modernity are still present in this concept, while others undergo a category change. Within the framework of second modernity theory, there are four principal ideas that constitute its novelty.

(1) *Inner globalization*: One characteristic of the social science dominant today is what might be described as its "methodological nationalism." This approach, which equates societies with national societies or territorially distinct units, is deeply rooted in the sociological imagination. A sociology of the second modernity must radically change the point of view – away from the nation state as a basic unit of conceptualization and research, and away from the North Atlantic space in which, according to the prevailing legend, the future always first shows itself; forward to a global social cosmos in which the postcolonial voices of the so-called periphery play an important role (Beck, 2002a, 2002b). Thus, what used to be called society in the sense of national societies must be opened out to cover transnational areas and their experiences, crises, risks, ideas of justice, and so on. This brings into view, for example, the following phenomenon. The inner globalization of work, culture, and the economy, of personal experiences and biographies, escapes the territorial frontiers that were drawn in the first modernity as well as the self-understanding of those societies as national societies. For globalization means the removal of boundaries, including

between local and international, indigenous and foreign, and this manifests itself not least in the sphere of the family. An ever-increasing number of families are transnationally networked: they no longer live in just one place, are no longer rooted in just one country, but are developing into intricate wickerwork relationships spread over several countries or even continents.

(2) *Individualization*: The automatic equation of societies with collectives becomes questionable under conditions of "institutionalized individualization." This term denotes a twofold tendency (see Beck and Beck-Gernsheim, 2002). On the one hand, the traditional social ties, relations, and belief systems that used to shape people's lives in the narrowest way are today losing more and more of their significance. From family unit and village community through region and religion to class, occupation, and gender role – that which once gave a framework and rules to everyday life is continuing to crumble away. For the individual, this brings historically new free spaces and options: he can and should, she may and must, now decide how to shape their own life, within certain limits at least. For at the same time – and this is the other side of the individualization dynamic – people are linked into the institutions that arose with modern society, such as the labor market and citizenship, the education system, the legal system, social security, and so on. These produce their own rules – demands, instructions, requirements – which are typically addressed to the individual, not to the family as a whole. And the crucial feature of these new forms of regulation is that they call upon individuals to live a "life of their own," beyond the link to the family or other groups, and, indeed, actually urge them to break free of such ties and to act without regard for them. The creed of the new institutions is to promote and demand an active and self-directed conduct of life. But this immediately poses the question of what happens when the spiral of individualization gains ever more momentum. What then becomes of the family?

(3) *The economy of insecurity*: The "third industrial revolution" brings into the economy and labor market a political economy of insecurity which has domino effects in both the public and the private sphere. Things which complemented and reinforced one another in the first modernity – full employment, guaranteed pensions, high tax revenue, leeway in government policy – now become insecure and mutually threatening. Paid employment becomes flexibilized and precarious; basic principles of the welfare state cease to apply; the normal course of people's lives becomes fragile; risks are distributed so that they are no longer borne by the state and economy but shifted on to individuals and families. Consider, for example, the shape of the new labor market or the meaning of deregulation and flexibilization in the private sphere (e.g., Franks, 1999; Presser, 2000). Seven-day weeks and twenty-four-hour days, shift work and irregularly changing rhythms, training courses in a different city, weekend seminars, business trips, evening appointments: you can take that kind of life if you are young, healthy, and single. But what if there are two of you, maybe with children? How long can you discuss and agree on duty rosters or your place of residence? When does it become too exhausting? Who finds it all too much to cope with? How many relationships reach a point when they can no longer take the strain?

(4) *The intertwining of nature and society*: "Society" over here, "nature" over there – this opposition is one of the basic assumptions of the first modernity. But in the second modernity an ever-larger number of novel hybrids emerge which transcend that opposition. This may be seen in medical technology, for instance, especially in human genetics and reproductive medicine, where people are increasingly granted a creative role in relation to their own nature. The application of genetic

engineering to human beings produces completely new forms of intervention in the realm of reproduction, health and sickness (see, e.g., Andrews, 1999; Beck-Gernsheim, 1995; and Richards, chapter 27 in this volume), with the result that the natural basis of motherhood, fatherhood, family, or kinship – which went without saying in the first modernity – is transformed into a range of alternative options, decisions, and their side effects. The biological foundations of primary family relationships become increasingly open to planning and correction. That which, in the first modernity, was summarized in the notion of a biologically and socially inherited unity of the family is now broken down into a number of separate and independent situations: egg donor, surrogate mother, social and legal mother, sperm donor, social, legal, and economic father.

The question of who are the grandparents no longer has a "natural" answer in the brave new world of genetic options and pressures; instead, it becomes the object of rival claims and decisions and the material for human, social, and legal disputes, perhaps dependent on the biographical circumstances, financial staying-power, or social status of the relevant individuals and their interests. But this means that, whereas "family" and "relatives" used to be named and allocated to each individual with the self-evidence of a natural fact, they have now become a "both-and" – both allocated and open to choice.

If we summarize the criteria and perspectives just sketched out, we can outline what reflexive modernization means with regard to the family. The first modernity established certain foundations, boundaries, and models of the family, which were at once cultural, social, political, class-related, legal, and biological. Today, however, these are partly dissolving and giving way to optional choices, so that rival claims come into play and have to be negotiated and settled by various authorities, institutions, and individuals. This is the basic idea that we shall now develop in connection with "the family and individualization." In order to specify more clearly what is meant by meta-change of the family, it may be useful here to distinguish between *reflexion* and *reflexivity* (Beck, 1999), the idea being (as applied to our present theme) that meta-change of the family can be adequately described not in semantic but only in historical and social-structural categories. Thus, the second modernity arises when reflexivity triumphs over reflexion: that is, when the modernization process becomes reflexive and renders obsolete the self-images and models of modernity (in our case, of modern family life) that appeared with the first modernity.

With this in mind, we shall have to distinguish between self-description and description by others (Luhmann, 1995: 171–86). The thesis of a meta-change of the family will accordingly be developed and examined at three levels: the first refers to everyday lifeworlds, to people's models, expectations, and behavior, or in other words to *social self-description*; the second refers to politics and law, and the regulations and guidelines prevailing there, or in other words to *political description* by others; and the third refers to sociology and its interpretative models, categories, and research theories, that is, to the perspective of the *sociological observer* (description by others).

## Individualization of the Family

Individualization in a very general sense – that is, a process whereby people are released from pre-given ties, social relations, and belief systems – has undoubtedly existed in previous epochs. Earlier historical phases of individualization occurred in the Renaissance, in the courtly culture of the Middle Ages, in the inward asceticism of Protestantism, in the emancipation of the peasantry from feudal bondage and in the loosening of intergenerational family ties in the nineteenth and early twentieth centuries. European modernity has freed people from historically inscribed roles.

What, then, is new and distinctive about individualization processes in the second modernity? The answer is that they acquire not only a new scale but a new form, the form of *institutional individualization* (Beck and Beck-Gernsheim, 2002). Individualization means here a structural transformation of social institutions that establishes a new relationship between individual and society; in the second modernity the individual is for the first time in history the basic unit of social reproduction. Individualization in this sense does not denote a merely subjective phenomenon – for instance, a change in people's ideas, wishes, or hopes – over and against firmly established objective social structures such as classes, families, or gender roles. No, individualization *is* the paradoxical social structure of the second modernity. Central institutions of the Western world – e.g., basic civil, political, and social rights – are now addressed to the individual, not to the collective or to groups. The education system, labor-market trends, job careers, indeed, markets in general are individualizing structures, individualizing institutions, hence "engines" of individualization.

Under these conditions, individualization becomes an open-ended, highly ambivalent ongoing process. Individualization in a "non-linear mode" (Lash, 2002) is a structure which does not reproduce but transforms itself, enforcing biographies full of risk and precarious freedom. We shall show in a moment what this means for the sphere of the family. Our basic thesis is that, in the second modernity, there is not simply a change of the family but a meta-change – not change within given structures and models, but change *of* those structures and models.

## Family change in the first modernity

To make this thesis clear, let us begin by summarizing the family trends that were characteristic of the first modernity. Until the 1960s there was a generally accepted model of the family in Western societies, one to which people's lives approximated more or less closely according to their material circumstances, social class, religion, region, and so on. This *normal family* consisted of an adult couple and their own children; the adults were a man and a woman, never of the same sex; they were married and remained so until death did them part; and they operated a kind of division of labor whereby the husband-breadwinner went out to work and the wife took responsibility for the home and family. Even in those days, there were other lifestyles that individuals might either consciously choose, if they were especially daring, or find themselves forced into. Crucially, however, these were seen as *deviant* forms; people entered into them fairly seldom, usually without broadcasting the fact or by putting up some front. They were "indiscretions" or "aberrations," due to unfortunate circumstances or external constraints such as the madness of war and its ensuing upheavals.

Conditions did not, of course, remain static throughout the first modernity: many different processes of change were taking place in the private sphere. But we can see from the population figures that these processes remained within relatively narrow bounds – or, rather, they remained within the framework of the model.

> Throughout much of the twentieth century, trends in family and household composition in Britain and many other European countries followed a relatively predictable trajectory. Changes occurred, but they did so in ways that outside wartime were generally consistent. For example, in Britain between 1900 and 1970, the rate of marriage for single women increased from 45 per 1,000 unmarried women to 60 per 1,000, age at first marriage declined from 25.4 to 23.2 for men and from 24.0 to 21.3 for women, divorce rates remained relatively low, the number of children born within the average marriage declined from about four to less than two, and relatively few children were brought up by single parents. (Allan, Hawker, and Crow, 2001: 819).

Demographic change followed similar lines elsewhere in Western Europe, although of course there were national variations depending on welfare policy, religious education, and so on.

We can say, then, that although changes in the private sphere certainly did occur in the first modernity, the institutionalized structures, expectations, and models did not break down but remained in place. Broadly speaking, this was true at all three levels – self-description in the everyday life of family members, self-description in law and politics, and the language of the sociological observer. Insofar as images of the family at the different levels concurred, they could actually validate and reinforce one another.

## Family change in the second modernity

This is precisely what is different in the second modernity. The normal family, as we have described it, has not completely vanished, but it has many other forms alongside it and, above all, the norm itself has lost much of its force. In recent years changes have occurred "both in family behavior and in what is understood by a family," and now we see "different forms alongside one another, with equal rights being claimed for by all" (Lüscher, 1994: 19). Consequently, ideas of what is and is not normal are becoming relativized. This is, in fact, the decisive point. What characterizes the second modernity is not just that "deviations" occur ever more widely and with ever-greater frequency, but that formerly "deviant" forms of living together have now become normal and acceptable. This *model-shift* makes deviations the normal thing. It is a central feature (an operational criterion) of the second modernity.

In other words, what is now asserting itself is, much more than simple diversity, the *normalization of diversity*, whether in family law, the self-images of family members, or the observational viewpoint of sociology.

## Meta-change in the law

Let us start with family law. There can be no doubt that the state used to prescribe a clear order geared to the normal family in the sense described above; nor that such prescriptions have come under increasing attack and, more recently, often ceased to apply altogether. The rules that are taking their place acknowledge a wider range of family forms and lifestyles. This is true especially of relations between the sexes, where there has been a root-and-branch reform of the relevant legislation. Let us take the example of Germany.

| | *Original version of the Civil Code, in force since 1900* | *Reform of the laws governing marriage, in force since 1977* |
|---|---|---|
| § 1354 | The husband has the final say in all matters concerning married life, particularly in the choice of residence. | Revoked. |
| § 1355 | The wife receives the husband's surname. | As their marital name, the couple may decide either on the husband's name of birth or the wife's name of birth. |
| § 1356 | The wife . . . has a right and a duty to manage the common household. | The spouses shall conduct the housekeeping by mutual agreement. |

In Germany, as in other Western countries, many further reforms have operated in a similar direction (e.g., Mason, Fine, and Carnochan, 2001; Röthel, 1999). Just a few examples are: the greater ease of divorce; improvements in the legal position of cohabiting couples and children born out of wedlock; and the growing legal recognition of long-term homosexual relationships. The aim of legislation is less and less to prescribe a certain way of living, more and more to clear the institutional conditions for a multiplicity of lifestyles to be recognized.

One paradoxical yet predictable consequence of this trend is a new spiral of regulatory clauses. The more the old barriers set by legislation, tradition, or religion are relaxed, and the more choice there is in personal lifestyles, the more a new need for regulation emerges in the legal and social sphere. For society always requires rules and predictability in dealings among its members. If a divine or natural order no longer tightly prescribes how people live, then new laws and regulations must produce some order to prevent the multiplicity of lifestyles from leading to chaos. If gay or lesbian couples are able to marry or enter into officially recognized relationships, does this mean that they also have a right to parenthood through adoption or the latest achievements of reproductive medicine? If the wife no longer automatically takes her husband's name at marriage, which name should be given to the children? If more and more people marry twice or three times, what would be an equitable financial settlement among partners, ex-partners, ex-ex-partners, and their respective children? If, amid the changing family constellations, a child relates to several different persons as his or her adult references, which of the biological or social parents should have custody and which should have visiting rights? How should one handle new medical options of parenthood in situations without any precedent in human history – for example, deep-frozen embryos where the biological procreators suddenly die? Or, if a surrogate mother does not want to hand over the child after it is born, is she or those who ordered the pregnancy entitled to take it? Evidently, in reproductive medicine, "the increasing range of treatment options . . . creates pressure for the law to respond" (Mason, Fine, and Carnochan, 2001: 871). And the options that arise in other areas have similar consequences.

Wherever we look, then, the questions whirl around and provide more and more professionals with their daily bread. Whether politicians, judges dealing with family cases, divorce lawyers, experts on ethical matters, psychologists, or conciliation advisors, they all have to weigh up which of the new options are just and socially digestible. How can one mediate between the different parties and their respective claims, when there is not yet a generally recognized authority on such matters – when, instead, there is a discordant chorus in which commissions clash with organizations representing particular groups of individuals, spokesmen for science with spokesmen for the church, experts with counter-experts? Not only does this continually create new questions; the answers too are continually called into question.

## Meta-change in everyday life

The multiplicity of lifestyles is apparent not only in the law courts but also in everyday behavior. Today there is a "far greater degree of diversity in family and domestic arrangements than existed throughout most of the twentieth century" (Allan, Hawker, and Crow, 2002: 824; Beck-Gernsheim, 2002; Teachman, Tedrow, and Crowder, 2000). This is strikingly illustrated in the events out of which the so-called family cycle used to be made up. Let us recall that the model of a proper family used to include a clearly defined temporal sequence: "love – marriage – baby carriage"; first the meeting of hearts, then the union certified by the registry office and/or church, then, as the culmination of love, children. That was the norm, and most people more or less approximated to it – on pain of massive sanctions.

This picture of a "correct sequence" still exists in the minds of many people, and wide sections of the population still live it out. Ever more openly and frequently, however, different models are appearing alongside it. For example, love does not necessarily have to lead to the registry office: an increasing number of couples live together without a certificate. In Germany there were 2.2 million such cases in 2001 – which means that nearly every ninth couple was living together out of wedlock (Statistisches Bundesamt, 2003: 41). Parenthood is also increasingly separate from a marriage certificate. In 1960 the proportion of births outside of marriage in West Germany stood at 6.3 percent (Statistisches Bundesamt, 1995: 102); by 2000 it had risen to 25 percent for the whole of Germany (Statistisches Bundesamt, 2003: 38). And of those who sooner or later – usually later – decided to marry, many no longer kept to the old command that it should last for life. Meanwhile, every second couple in the US divorce, and every third in northern and Western Europe; the figure is lower in the Catholic countries of Europe, but it is clearly rising there too (Allan, Hawker, and Crow, 2001: 819). Many never marry; many do so a number of times in "successive polygamy," giving rise to complex, new family networks in which one finds marriage and divorce chains, ex-partners and part-life companions, serial marriages, patchwork families, serial parenting, and serial stepfamilies.

In other words, the clearly prescribed order of old has given way to a variety of trajectories and models. In everyday life, and in the branch of sociology concerned with it, the assignation of people involved in these different paths is becoming hard work and a source of ambiguity.

> Notions such as family and household can no longer be understood in as simple a manner as they once were. The whole question of who is a family member now raises substantial issues that were of minor consequence two generations ago. For example, when does a cohabiting partner become a member of your family, and when does he or she become a member of your children's, your parents', or your siblings' families? . . .

> With increasing separation and divorce, complicated further by repartnering, it is evident that many parents and children have different families in ways that were uncommon two generations ago. So too, the term *household* contains a range of elements that makes it necessary to recognize the permeability of household boundaries rather than assume membership can be categorized in an unproblematic way. Indeed, people may be thought of as members of different households for different activities or alternatively, be members or partial members of households for some periods of the day or week but not others. (Allan, Hawker, and Crow, 2001: 824)

Membership, like boundary lines, becomes uncertain or unsteady over time, at the mercy of the hopes and disappointments, interests, and claims of the people concerned. Who sees himself or herself as part of a couple, household or family, and of which family, at what stage of life and in what state of the emotions? How do the relevant others – partner, parents, children, sisters, brothers – view this at each stage of their lives and emotions? There is no longer one simple answer to these questions; different persons each have their own answers, which sometimes do and sometimes do not tally with those of others, perhaps do and perhaps do not remain the same over the years (Furstenberg and Cherlin, 1991; Schmitz and Schmidt-Denter, 1999; Seltzer, 2000; White, 1998). But this means that any collectively shared definition of relationships and individual positions is gone.

This individualization of interpretations must raise considerable methodological and conceptual problems for sociological research. For it becomes unclear what "objectively" constitutes the reference unit of family research and how it can be circumscribed; what should be ascertained and investigated, how and within which perspective. If men and women see themselves in the high plateau of their feelings as a cohabiting couple, but at the end of their love for each other describe their relationship as a short-term sexual affair (Trost, 1992: 102); if, to a simple question such as how many brothers and sisters they have, the same respondents give different answers over a period of time, because who figures as a brother or sister varies with the family constellation and the type of household or living arrangement (White, 1998) – how then does the researcher order, count and classify?

Where family relations are so ambivalent, sociological research is faced with a twofold challenge. On the one hand, it becomes ever more important that the researcher should consciously listen to the subjects, should deliberately open up to their interpretations.

> If we are to acknowledge noninstitutionalized family forms created by rising rates of nonmarital fertility, cohabitation, divorce, and remarriage, and if we are to recognize what Bourdieu (1977) has called kinship in practice, we must give credence to how respondents define their families. . . . We need to recognize that family structure has a larger subjective component than we have accorded it. (White, 1998: 732)

In other words, the distinction between family structures and family consciousness is no longer productive. What individualization of the family essentially means is that the perceived family *is* the family structure, and that consequently both the perception and the structure vary individually between members both within and between "families."

On the other hand, this is also the reason why family research itself must find a new framework – otherwise its field will be lost in the jungle of subjective viewpoints.

Unless the sociological observer is ultimately prepared to accept that "the family" is always what respondents take it to be, then a consensus becomes necessary that is not identical with the images that the actors have. How can we develop definitions, hypotheses, and concepts that allow us to probe the reality lying behind labels such as "family" or "quasi-family network," and to grasp the variety of antecedent, intermediate, and posterior forms emerging here?

## Meta-change in sociology

At the same time that diversity is spreading in the behavior and self-images of actors, greater diversity is also apparent in the perspective of the sociological observer. In other words, the new reflexivity of the modernization process is expressed in the fact that the classical self-images of modernity are becoming obsolete, from the viewpoint both of its actors and of the sociological observer. Thus, the functionalist language of observation in the sociology of the family (which goes back to Talcott Parsons) – together with its assumptions about functional prerequisites of male and female roles, parent–child relations, and so on – is deflated by the plural reflexivity of the sociology of the family. Whereas, in the first half of the twentieth century, it was exclusively men (white men) who carried out and set their stamp on sociological research into the family, what we find today is still mainly white men – but also, increasingly, other groups alongside them. The sociology of the family has had forced upon it a reflexivity that comprehends the diversity of lifestyles.

It was women who made a start. "By talking gender as a basic category of analysis, feminists have made important contributions to family theory" (Thorne, 1982: 2). Today many, if not quite all, family researchers would probably agree with that judgment. But what is now so evident was then nothing short of a revolution. When the feminists of the 1960s and 1970s began analyzing the family, they came up with a perspective radically questioning the then dominant view. Is the family a place of rest, emotion and intimacy? No – was now the militant answer. The family is also a place of work (women's work), and a place of everyday violence and oppression. As well as "history" there was now "herstory." Two marriages were discovered where there had been only one: the husband's marriage and the wife's marriage, partly overlapping but also partly diverging horizons (Bernard, 1976: 19ff.). Again and again the discussion turned to "experiences of inequality in everyday family life" (Rerrich, 1990).

> Because families are structured around gender and age, women, men, girls, and boys do not experience their families in the same way. Feminists have explored the differentiation of a family experience mystified by the glorification of motherhood, love, and images of the family as a domestic haven. Feminists have voiced experiences that this ideology denies: men's dominance and women's subordination within as well as outside of the family, and the presence of conflict, violence, and unequally distributed work within the "domestic haven." (Thorne, 1982: 2)

The critical reflexivity of feminist family research was immediately answered by a counter-movement of antifeminist research, which rediscovered the family as a "haven in a heartless world" (Lasch, 1977); the "war over the family" was soon in full swing (Berger and Berger, 1983). The next phase of reflexion and self-criticism began with the gradual rise of multiculturalism, especially in the US and Britain, as representatives of minority groups made their voices heard with increasing confidence. And the very reproach that women had made against male-dominated studies of female experience in society – that they were partial, one-sided, and distorted – was now turned around and raised against the women's movement. More, it was now raised by women – women from minority groups. White! Middle-class! Heterosexual! Such were the charges. Whereas it had previously been a question of "the" family, and then of the different experiences of women contrasted with those of men, now the "sisterhood" self-image began to break down and diversity among women came to the fore (Ang, 2001). Demands such as "White women, listen!" were raised (Carby, 2000), and representatives of "black feminism" explained why family had a quite different value for them than for white women:

> We would not wish to deny that the family can be a source of oppression for us but we also wish to examine how the black family has functioned as a prime source of resistance to oppression. We need to recognize that during slavery, periods of colonialism and under the present authoritarian state, the black family has been a site of political and cultural resistance to racism.... The way the gender of black women is constructed differs from constructions of white femininity because it is also subject to racism (ibid.: 83)

Not only feminist but multicultural observer perspectives: this is the second line of self-reflexion, whose effects have vigorously shaken the understanding that family research has of itself and of what seemed to be its empirical evidence. Because so-called minority groups (not least the numerous and heterogeneous families of a new batch of immigrants) have gradually come into focus, and because some of today's researchers themselves come from immigrant families or belong to minorities of another kind, old basic assumptions of family research are being devalued.

> More and more women, people of colour, lesbians and gays, and scholars from working-class backgrounds compose the academy. These scholars have challenged their exclusion by discourses that are presented as generic family reality, and some of us from the dominant groups who earlier saw families in a White, male, middle-class image have been listening and learning. (Marks, 2000: 611)

The image of the standard family as white and Anglo-Saxon has not entirely disappeared, but it has become much more brittle (McLloyd et al., 2000). Where the formulas used to reflect a self-assured consensus, doubts have begun to set in.

> Until we in the dominant group begin to "unpack (the) invisible knapsack" of privileges that accrue to our race, class, gender, and sexual orientation, our progress...will be retarded or stalled. We will slip back, without awareness, into White-think, middle-class-think, men-think, hetero-think or some combination of these, and the erasure of key components of the everyday experience of people in nondominant family arrangements will be inevitable. (ibid.: 614)

Two lessons should be drawn from this.

(1) The demand for objectivity is often used as a shield to decree certain definitions of what constitutes a "proper" family. In other words, a nonreflexive sociology of the family, which insists on the "objectivity" of its definitions and mass data, threatens to become ideology.

(2) In order to understand sociologically the changing self-images of members of various family-like constellations, and thereby to found a new "postfamilial" family research that is at once innovative and empirically aware, we need to include research into the subjective preferences and self-perceptions of the researchers themselves, instead of unthinkingly making them the foundation of categories of sociological observation.

Although many researchers still ignore them, it has become indispensable to ask a number of questions. How is a sociology of the family to be achieved that no longer concerns itself just with the indigenous majority and its male component? How can we design a family research whose framework, categories, and basic assumptions no longer ignore "other" groups but take in and give space to their everyday lives and their horizons of experience? The struggles and disputes over the "politics of recognition" (Taylor, 1992) have now come to family research. An irritating, uncomfortable question is in the air and cannot be avoided: "Theorizing diversity: Whose standpoint?" (Marks, 2000: 611).

## Prospects

Family research in the framework of a theory of second modernity opens up the questions pertaining to a "sociology of the family" without the security of a concept of the family, or, in other words, forces both the major and minor questions to be posed anew. The sociology of the first modernity was essentially a classificatory sociology, which conceptually sorted and tried to regularize conditions within the framework of methodological nationalism. In this discourse, the family was categorically defined and empirically grasped as the "nucleus of society" and the pillar of the state order. In the same process deviations from the norm were clearly marked. The key question of a postfamilial sociology of the family was ignored: what binds people together when interconnection and cohesion no longer rest upon inheritance, economics, and formal marriage? What binding quality characterizes marital ties and parent–child ties? How do these relate to ties of friendship, work obligations, or ethnic ties? How are the questions of justice and social inequality posed in relationships beyond the traditional heterosexual family? What ideas and obligations to children and partners develop in stepfamilies and serial marriages? Does legal divorce come up against limits in the indissolubility of the father–child and mother–child relationship, so that marriage but not parenthood can be dissolved? Should the emotions of family life be investigated anew in relation to emotional qualities of sexuality, partnership, maternity, and paternity, as well as to the emotional giving and taking of children within changing constellations of parenthood? How does the idea of inheritance change in postfamilial family constellations? Which morals, which obligations, and which traditions emerge under these conditions? What significance does religion have in this context? Do quasi-family relations perhaps emerge where living together is released from moral obligations and where people can leave without having to justify themselves?

What does everyday life together mean when, on the one hand, it heeds the ideals of partnership and "emotional democracy" (Anthony Giddens) but, on the other hand, faces a labor market where women are sucked into insecure employment, flexible working hours and the inequalities associated with them? What does it mean when, on the one hand, politicians invoke "family values," motherhood, and fatherhood but, on the other hand, demand and solemnly promise that everyone should be constantly and generally available on the labor market – a labor market, moreover, that offers ever fewer protected areas and long-term guarantees? What does it mean for couples when they have to bridge different national and ethnic origins in their daily lives? Is a society without established traditions a theology without God? Can there ever be a relationship between two egos without a conscious, deliberate transcendence of the ego? What can be the basis for such a relationship if it is based *only* on itself? Is there anything like an inherent limit to individualization, where the individualization of one becomes a problem for the other?

What are the political implications of the individualization and globalization of family constellations? Politics, understood as parliamentary and governmental politics, presupposes an aggregation of interests, and this in turn presupposes a relatively clear and stable (which has so far meant national) social structure together with corresponding parties and associations. The concept of interests (especially as it is posed in political theory) assumes the kind of collective society that is becoming questionable in the wake of individualization and globalization. Does reflexive modernization abolish the social preconditions of collectively binding decisions and state-political action? Or does a new form of politics arise, resting upon the norms and issues of a cosmopolitan society, and thus on recognition of the alterity of others rooted in human rights?

Individualized constellations of community and family can no longer be defined and integrated through pregiven norms, values, and hierarchies; rather, they must be defined through risky freedoms, and hence through *non*-integration. Accordingly, we must consider the constitutive legal, political, and economic norms of risky freedoms. But there is no longer any pregiven normative model that binds people together, no essentialist definition of human beings, men, women, Christians, Jews, blacks, Muslims, Americans, or Chinese. As Alain Touraine notes, culture becomes an experiment whose aim is to discover "how we can live together as equal but different." So what is it, in the process of individualization and globalization, which keeps alive an awareness that the bases of one's own life can be gained *only* in public and political interchange with others? How does it become possible for men and women, blacks and whites, Israelis and Arabs, Christians, and Muslims, to share a non-individualist and non-essentialist definition of the human condition?

## References

Allan, G., Hawker, S., and Crow, G. (2001) Family diversity and change in Britain and Western Europe. *Journal of Family Issues*, 22, 819–37.

Andrews, L. B. (1999) *The Clone Age. Adventures in the New World of Reproductive Technology*. New York: Henry Holt.

Ang, I. (2001) I'm a feminist, but . . . : 'Other' women and postnational identities. In I. Ang, *On Not Speaking Chinese: Living between Asia and the West*. London and New York: Routledge.

Beck, U. (1997) *The Reinvention of Politics*. Cambridge: Polity.

Beck, U. (1999) Knowledge or non-knowledge. In U. Beck, *World Risk Society*. Cambridge: Polity.

Beck, U. (2002a) The cosmopolitan society and its enemies. *Theory, Culture & Society*, 1–2, 17–44.

Beck, U. (2002b) *Macht und Gegenmacht im globalen Zeitalter.* Frankfurt: Suhrkamp.
Beck, U., and Beck-Gernsheim, E. (2002) *Individualization. Institutionalized Individualism and its Social and Political Consequences.* London: Sage.
Beck, U., Bonss, W., and Lau, Ch. (2003) *Theory of reflexive modernization. Theory, Culture and Society,* 20 (2), 1–33.
Beck, U., Giddens, A., and Lash, S. (1994) *Reflexive Modernization.* Cambridge: Polity.
Beck-Gernsheim, E. (1995) *The Social Implications of Bioengineering.* Atlantic Highlands, NJ: Humanities Press.
Beck-Gernsheim, E. (2002) *Reinventing the Family.* Cambridge: Polity.
Berger, B., and Berger, P. L. (1983) *The War over the Family. Capturing the Middle Ground.* Garden City, New York: Anchor Press/Doubleday.
Bernard, J. (1976) *The Future of Marriage.* Harmondsworth: Penguin.
Bourdieu, P. (1977) *Outline of a Theory of Practice.* Cambridge: Cambridge University Press.
Carby, H. V. (2000) White women listen! Black feminism and the boundaries of sisterhood. In K. Owusu (ed.), *Black British Culture and Society.* London and New York: Routledge.
Franks, S. (1999) *Having None of It. Women, Men and the Future of Work.* London: Granta.
Furstenberg, F. F., and Cherlin, A. J. (1991) *Divided Families. What Happens to Children when Parents Part.* Cambridge, MA: Harvard University Press.
Giddens, A. (1999) *The Runaway World: How Globalization Is Reshaping Our Lives.* London: Profile Books.
Kaufmann, J-C. (1992) *La Trame conjugale: Analyse du couple par son linge.* Paris: Nathan.
Lasch, C. (1977) *Haven in a Heartless World: The Family Besieged.* New York: Basic Books.
Lash, S. (2002) Individualization in a non-linear mode. In U. Beck and E. Beck-Gernsheim (eds.), *Individualization. Institutionalized Individualism and its Social and Political Consequences.* London: Sage.
Luhmann, N. (1995) Why does society describe itself as postmodern? *Cultural Critique* 30, 171–86.
Lüscher, K. (1994) Was heiβt heute Familie? In C. Brauns-Hermann, B. M. Busch, and H. Dinse (eds.), *Verlorene Liebe – Gemeinsame Kinder.* Reinbek: Rowohlt.
Marks, S. R. (2000) Teasing out the lessons of the 1960s: family diversity and family privilege. *Journal of Marriage and the Family,* 62, 609–22.
Mason, M. A., Fine, M. A., and Carnochan, S. (2001) Family law in the new millennium. For whose families? *Journal of Family Issues,* 22, 859–81.
McLloyd, V., Cance, A. M., Takeuchi, D., and Wilson, L. (2000) Marital processes and parental socialization in families of color: a decade review of research. *Journal of Marriage and the Family,* 62, 1070–93.
Presser, H. B. (2000) Nonstandard work schedules and marital instability. *Journal of Marriage and the Family,* 62, 93–110.
Randeria, S. (1999) Jenseits von Soziologie und soziokultureller Anthropologie. *Soziale Welt,* 50, 4, 373–82.
Rerrich, M. S. (1990) Ein gleich gutes Leben für alle? Über Ungleichheitserfahrungen im familialen Alltag. In P. A. Berger and S. Hradil (eds.), *Lebenslagen – Lebensläufe – Lebensstile. Soziale Welt.* Sonderband 7, Göttingen: Schwartz.
Röthel, A. (1999) Nichteheliche Lebensgemeinschaften – Neue Rechtsfragen und Regelungsaufgaben im In- und Ausland. *Zeitschrift für Rechtspolitik,* 12, 511–19.
Schmitz, H., and Schmidt-Denter, U. (1999) Die Nachscheidungsfamilie sechs Jahre nach der elterlichen Trennung. *Zeitschrift für Familienforschung,* 3, 28–55.
Seltzer, J. A. (2000) Families formed outside of marriage. *Journal of Marriage and the Family,* 62, 1247–68.
Statistisches Bundesamt (1995) *Im Blickpunkt: Familien heute.* Stuttgart: Metzler-Poeschel.
Statistisches Bundesamt (2003) Datenreport 2002. Zahlen und Fakten über die Bundesrepublik Deutschland. Bundeszentrale für politische Bildung.

Taylor, C. (1992) *Multiculturalism and the Politics of Recognition*. Princeton, NJ: Princeton University Press.

Teachman, J. D., Tedrow, L. M., and Crowder, K. D. (2000) The changing demography of America's families. *Journal of Marriage and the Family*, 62, 1234–46.

Thorne, B. (1982) Feminist rethinking of the family: an overview. In B. Thorne and M. Yalom (eds.), *Rethinking the Family. Some Feminist Questions*. New York and London: Longman.

Touraine, A. (1996) *Critique of Modernity*. Cambridge: Polity.

Trost, J. (1992) The last decades and matrimonial changes. In H. Birg and X. Kaufmann (eds.), *Bevölkerungswisenschaft heute. Kolloquium anläßlich des 10jährigen Jubiläums des Instituts für Bevölkerungsforschung und Sozialpolitik*. IBS-Materialien Nr. 33: Universität Bielefeld, 91–106.

White, L. (1998) Who's counting? Quasi-facts and stepfamilies in reports of number of siblings. *Journal of Marriage and the Family*, 60, 725–33.

# Bibliography


Aas, D. (1978) Studies of time use: problems and prospects. *Acta Sociologica*, 15, 333–55.

Abma, J. C., Chandra, A., Mosher, W., Peterson, L., and Piccinino, L. (1997) *Fertility, Family Planning, and Women's Health: New Data from the 1995 National Survey of Family Growth. Vital Health Statistics*. Washington, DC: National Center for Health Statistics, 23.

Achilles, R. (1992) *Donor Insemination: An Overview*. Ottawa: Royal Commission on New Reproductive on New Reproductive Technologies.

Ackerman, C. (1963) Affiliations: structural determinants of differential divorce rates. *American Journal of Sociology*, 69, 13–20.

Acock, A. C., and Demo, D. H. (1994) *Family Diversity and Well-Being*. Thousand Oaks, CA: Sage.

Adam, B. (1990) *Time and Social Theory*. Cambridge: Polity.

Adam, B. D. (1992) Sex and caring among men. In K. Plummer (ed.), *Modern Homosexualities: Fragments of Lesbian and Gay Experience*. London: Routledge.

Adams, B. N. (1970) Isolation, function and beyond: American kinship in the 1960s. *Journal of Marriage and the Family*, 32, 575–97.

Adelman, P. K., Chadwick, K., and Baerger, D. R. (1996) Marital quality of Black and White adults over the life course. *Journal of Social and Personal Relationships*, 13, 361–84.

Agnew, C. R., Loving, T. J., and Drigotas, S. M. (2001) Substituting the forest for the trees: Social networks and the prediction of romantic relationship state and fate. *Journal of Personality and Social-Psychology*, 81, 1042–57.

Ahlburg, D. A., and DeVita, C. J. (1992) *New Realities of the American Family*. Population Bulletin 47. Washington, DC: Population Reference Bureau.

Ahmad, W. (1996) Consanguinity and related demons: Science and racism in the debate on consanguinity and birth outcome. In C. Samson and N. South (eds.), *The Social Construction of Social Policy: Methodologies, Citizenship and the Environment*. London: Macmillan.

Ahmed, L. (1992) *Women and Gender in Islam: Historical Roots of a Modern Debate*. New Haven, CT: Yale University Press.

Aitken, S. (1998) *Family Fantasies and Community Space*. New Brunswick, NJ: Rutgers University Press.

Akerlof, G. (1998) Men without children. *Economic Journal*, 108, 257–309.

Alan Guttmacher Institute (1994) *Sex and America's Teenagers*. New York: Alan Guttmacher Institute.

Alan Guttmacher Institute (1998) *Into a New World: Young Women's Sexual and Reproductive Lives*. New York: Alan Guttmacher Institute.

Ali, T. (1996) *We are Family: Testimonies of Lesbian and Gay Parents*. London and New York: Cassell.

Alicea, M. (1997) "A chambered nautilus": The contradictory nature of Puerto Rican women's role in the social construction of a transnational community. *Gender and Society*, 11, 597–626.

Allan, G. (1979) *A Sociology of Friendship and Kinship*. London: George Allen & Unwin.

Allan, G. (1985) *Family Life*. Oxford: Blackwell.

Allan, G. (1989) *Friendship: Developing a Sociological Perspective*. Boulder CO: Westview.

Allan, G. (1996) *Kinship and Friendship in Modern Britain*. Oxford: Oxford University Press.

Allan, G. (1998) Friendship, sociology and social structure. *Journal of Social and Personal Relationships*, 15, 685–702.

Allan, G. (1999) *The Sociology of the Family: A Reader*. Oxford: Blackwell.

Allan, G. (2001) Personal relationships in late modernity. *Personal Relationships*, 8, 325–39.

Allan, G., and Crow, G. (2001) *Families, Households, and Society*. Basingstoke: Palgrave.

Allan, G., Hawker, S., and Crow, G. (2001) Family diversity and change in Britain and Western Europe. *Journal of Family Issues*, 22, 819–37.

Allatt, P., and Yeandle, S. (1992) *Youth Unemployment and the Family: Voices of Disordered Times*. London: Routledge.

Altman, D. (1982) *The Homosexualization of America, The Americanization of the Homosexual*. New York: St. Martin's Press.

Alvirez, D., and Bean, F. D. (1976) The Mexican-American family. In C. H. Mindel and R. W. Habenstein (eds.), *Ethnic Families in America*. New York: Elsevier.

Alwin, D. F. (1988) From obedience to autonomy: changes in traits desired in children. *Public Opinion Quarterly*, 52, 33–52.

Alwin, D. F. (1996) From childbearing to childrearing: The link between declines in fertility and changes in the socialization of children. *Population and Development Review*, 22, S176–S196.

Alwin, D. F. (1996) Parental socialization in historical perspective. In C. D. Ryff and M. Mailick Seltzer (eds.), *The Parental Experience in Midlife*. Chicago: University of Chicago Press.

Alwin, D. F. (2001) Parental values, beliefs, and behavior: A review and promulga for research into the new century. In S. J. Hofferth and T. J. Owens (eds.), *Children at the Millennium: Where Have We Come From, Where Are We Going?* New York: JAI.

Alwin, D. F., Scott, J. L., and Braun, M. (1992) The separation of work and the family: attitudes toward women's labor-force participation in Germany, Great Britain, and the United States. *European Sociological Review*, 8, 13–37.

Amato, P. (1987) *Children in Australian Families: The Growth of Competence*. Sydney: Prentice Hall.

Amato, P. (1987) Children's reactions to parental separation and divorce: the views of children and custodial mothers. *Australian Journal of Social Issues*, 22, 610–23.

Amato, P. (1994) The implications of research findings on children in stepfamilies. In A. Booth and J. Dunn (eds.), *Stepfamilies. Who Benefits? Who Does Not?* Mahwah NJ: Lawrence Erlbaum.

Amato, P., and Booth, A. (1997) *A Generation at Risk. Growing Up in an Era of Family Upheaval*. Cambridge MA: Harvard University Press.

Amato, P., and. Gilbreth, J. G. (1999) Nonresident fathers and children's well-being: A meta-analysis. *Journal of Marriage and the Family*, 61, 557–73.

Amato, P., and Keith, B. (1991) Parental divorce and the well-being of children: A meta-analysis. *Psychological Bulletin*, 110, 26–46.

Amato, P. R. (2000) The consequences of divorce for adults and children. *Journal of Marriage and the Family*, 62, 1269–87.

Amato, P. R. (2000) Diversity within single-parent families. In D. H. Demo, K. R. Allen, and M.A. Fine (eds.), *Handbook of Family Diversity*. New York and Oxford: Oxford University Press.

Amato, P. R., and Booth, A. (1991) Consequences of parental divorce and marital unhappiness for adult well-being. *Social Forces*, 69, 895–914.

Amato, P. R., and Keith, B. (1991) Parental divorce and adult well-being: A meta-analysis. *Journal of Marriage and the Family*, 53, 43–58.

Amato, P. R., and Keith, B. (1991) Separation from a parent during childhood and adult socioeconomic attainment. *Social Forces*, 70, 187–206.

Amato, P. R., and Sobolewski, J. M. (2001) The effects of divorce and marital discord on adult children's psychological well-being. *American Sociological Review*, 66, 900–21.

Ambert, A. (1986) The place of children in North American sociology. In P. and P. Adler (eds.), *Sociological Studies in Child Development*. Greenwich, CT: JAI.

Ambert, A. M. (1988) Relationships with former in-laws after divorce: A research note. *Journal of Marriage and the Family*, 50, 679–86.

Ambrose, P., Harper, J., and Pemberton, R. (1983) *Surviving Divorce: Men Beyond Marriage*. Brighton: Wheatsheaf.

American Academy of Pediatrics (2002) Coparent or second-parent adoption by same-sex parents. *Pediatrics*, 109, 339–40.

Amin, A., and Graham, S. (1999) Cities of connection and disconnection. In J. Allen, D. Massey, and M. Pryke (eds.), *Unsettling Cities: Movement/Settlement*. London: Routledge.

Ammerman, N. T. (1987) *Bible Believers. Fundamentalists in the Modern World*. Brunswick, NJ: Rutgers University Press.

Andersen, M. L. (2000) *Thinking About Women: Sociological Perspectives on Sex and Gender* (5th ed.). Boston: Allyn & Bacon.

Anderson, B., and Tracey, K. (2001) Digital living: the impact (or otherwise) of the internet on everyday life. *American Behavioural Scientist*, 45, 456–75.

Anderson, M. (1971) *Family Structure in Nineteenth Century Lancashire*. Cambridge: Cambridge University Press.

Andersson, G. (2001) Children's experience of family disruption and family formation: evidence from 16 FFS countries. *Paper presented at XXIV IUSSP General Population Conference, Session on Family Demography from a Children's Perspective*, Salvador, Brazil, August. Available online at www.demogr.mpg.de

Andrews, L. B. (1999) *The Clone Age. Adventures in the New World of Reproductive Technology*. New York: Henry Holt.

Ang, I. (2001) I'm a feminist, but . . . : "Other" women and postnational identities. In I. Ang, *On Not Speaking Chinese. Living Between Asia and the West*. London and New York: Routledge.

Angel, J., and Angel, R. (1998) Caring for our elders: Latino America struggles with change. *Hispanic*, September, 18–26.

Angel, J. L. (1991) *Health and Living Arrangements of the Elderly*. New York: Garland.

Angel, J. L., Angel, R. J., and Markides, K. S. (2000) Late-life immigration, changes in living arrangements, and headship status among older Mexican-origin individuals. *Social Science Quarterly*, 81, 389–403.

Angel, J. L., Angel, R. J., McClellan, J. L., and Markides, K. S. (1996) Nativity, declining health, and preferences in living arrangements among elderly Mexican Americans: implications for long-term care. *The Gerontologist*, 36, 464–73.

Angel, R., Lein, L., Henrici, J., and Leventhal, E. (2001) *Health Care Coverage for Children and their Caregivers in Low-Income Urban Neighborhoods*. Policy Brief 01–02, Welfare Children & Families: A Three City Study, Baltimore, MD: Johns Hopkins University Press.

Angel, R. J., and Angel, J. L. (1996) The extent of private and public health insurance coverage among adult Hispanics. *The Gerontologist*, 36, 332–40.

Angel, R. J., and Angel, J. L. (1996) Physical co-morbidity and medical care use among children with emotional problems. *Public Health Reports*, 3, 140–5.

Angel, R. J., and Angel, J. L. (1997) *Who Will Care for Us? Aging and Long-term Care in Multicultural America*. New York: New York University Press.

Angel, R. J., Angel, J. L., Lee, G. Y., and Markides, K. S. (1999) Age at migration and family dependency among older Mexican immigrants: Recent evidence from the Mexican American EPESE. *The Gerontologist*, 39, 59–65.

Angel, R. J., and Worobey, J. L. (1988) Single motherhood and children's health. *Journal of Health and Social Behavior*, 29, 38–52.

Anspach, D., and Rosenberg, G. S. (1972) Working-class matricentricity. *Journal of Marriage and the Family*, 34, 437–42.

Anyan, S., and Pryor, J. (2002) What is in a family? Adolescent perceptions. *Children and Society*, 16, 1–12.

Applegate, J. S., and Kaye, L. W. (1993) Male elder caregivers. In C. L. Williams (ed.), *Doing "Women's Work": Men in Non Traditional Occupations*. Newbury Park, CA: Sage.

Aquilino, W. (1996) The life course of children born to unmarried mothers: Childhood living arrangements and young adult outcomes. *Journal of Marriage and the Family*, 58, 293–310.

Arber, S., and Attias-Donfut, C. (2000) *The Myth of Generational Conflict*. London: Routledge.

Arber, S., and Ginn, J. (1991) *Gender and Later Life: A Sociological Analysis of Resources and Constraints*. London: Sage.

Archard, D. (1993) *Children, Rights and Childhood*. London: Routledge.

Arditti, J. (1999) Rethinking relationships between divorced mothers and their children: Capitalising on family strengths. *Family Relations*, 48, 109–19.

Ariès, P. (1962) [1960] *Centuries of Childhood: A Social History of Family Life*. New York and Harmondsworth: Knopf and Penguin.

Ariffin, J., and Louis, A. (eds.) (2001) *Family Well-Being: Learning From the Past for the Betterment in the Future*. Johor, Malaysia: Institute Sultan Iskandar (ISI) Publications.

Arkoun, M. (1994) *Rethinking Islam: Common Questions, Uncommon Answers*. Boulder, CO: Westview.

Armstrong, K. (2001) *The Battle for God. Fundamentalism in Judaism, Christianity and Islam*. London: HarperCollins.

Árnason, V. and Árnason, G. (2001) Community consent, democracy and public dialogue: The case of the Icelandic health sector data base. *Politeia*, 17, 105–16.

Aseltine, R. H., Jr., and Kessler, R. C. (1993) Marital disruption and depression in a community sample. *Journal of Health and Social Behavior*, 34, 237–51.

Ashworth, K., Hill, M., and Walker, R. (1994) Patterns of childhood poverty: New challenges for policy. *Journal of Policy Analysis and Management*, 13, 658–80.

Atkinson, A. (1995) *Poverty and Social Security*. Hemel Hempstead: Harvester.

Atkinson, A., Cantillon, B., Marlier, E., and Nolan, B. (2001) *Indicators for Inclusion in the European Union*. Paper presented at a Conference on Social Inclusion hosted by the Belgian government, Antwerp, September.

Atkinson, P., Parsons, E., and Featherstone, K. (2001) Professional constructions of family and kinship in medical genetics. *New Genetics and Society*, 20, 5–24.

Attias-Donfut, C., and Wolff, F-C. (2000) Complimentarity between private and public transfer. In S. Arber and C. Attias-Donfut (eds.), *The Myth of Generational Conflict*. London: Routledge.

Bachman, J. G., Wadsworth, K. N., O'Malley, P. M., Johnson, L. D., and Schulenberg, J. E. (1997) *Smoking, Drinking, and Drug Use in Young Adulthood*. Mahwah, NJ: Lawrence Erlbaum.

Bachu, A. (1999) Trends in premarital childbearing: 1930–1994. *Current Population Reports, P23-197*. Washington, DC: US Census Bureau.

Badets, J., and Chui, T. (1994) *Canada's Changing Immigrant Population*. Ottawa: Statistics Canada.

Bagley, S. P., Angel, R., Dilworth-Anderson, P., Liu, W. and Schinke, S. (1995) Adaptive health behaviors among ethnic minorities. *Health Psychology*, 14, 632–40.

Bahr, H. M. (1976) The kinship role. In: F. I. Nye (ed.), *Role Structure and Analysis of the Family*. Beverly Hills: Sage.

Bahr, S. (2001) *Social Science Research on Family Dissolution: What It Shows and How It Might Be of Interest to Family Law Reformers*. Manuscript prepared for Symposium on the ALI's Family Dissolution Principles: Blueprint to Strengthen or to Deconstruct Families? Brigham Young University, February 1.

Bailyn, L. (1993) *Breaking the Mould; Women, Men and Time in the New Corporate World*. New York: Maxwell Macmillan.

Bainham, A. (2002) Can we protect children and protect their rights? *Family Law*, 279–89.

Bala, N., and Bromwich, R. (2002) Context and inclusivity in Canada's evolving definition of the family. *International Journal of Law, Policy, and the Family*, 16, 145–80.

Ballard, R. (1983) The context and consequences of migration: Jullundur and Mirpur compared. *New Community*, 11, 117–36.

Ballard, R. (1990) Migration and kinship: The differential effect of marriage rules on the processes of Punjabi migration to Britain. In C. Clarke, C. Peach, and S. Vertovec (eds.), *South Asians Overseas: Migration and Ethnicity*. Cambridge: Cambridge University Press.

Ballard, R. (ed.) (1994) Desh Pardesh: The South Asian Presence in Britain. London: Hurst.

Ballard, R. (2001) The Impact of Kinship on the Economic Dynamics of Transnational Networks: Reflections on Some South Asian Developments. Working Paper 01-06b. Princeton, NJ: Centre for Migration and Development, Princeton University.

Ballard, R., and Kalra, V. S. (1994) *The Ethnic Dimensions of the 1991 Census, A Preliminary Report*. Manchester: Census Dissemination Unit.

Baran, A. and Pannar, R. (1989) *Lethal Secrets: The Psychology of Donor Insemination*. New York: Amistad.

Barbagli, M. (1997) Family and kinship in Italy. In M. Gullestad and M. Segalen (eds.), *Family and Kinship in Europe*. London: Pinter.

Baring, E. (2000) *Modern Egypt*. London: Routledge.

Barker, R. W. (1994) *Lone Fathers and Masculinities*. Aldershot: Avebury.

Barnes, J. A. (1973) Genetrix: genitor : : nature : culture. In J. Goody (ed.), *Culture of Kinship*. Cambridge: Cambridge University Press.

Barringer, M. W., and Milkovich, G. T. (1998) A theoretical exploration of the adoption and design of flexible benefit plans: a case of human resource innovation. *Academy of Management Review*, 23, 305–24.

Bartholomew, G. W. (1958) Development and use of artificial insemination. *Eugenics Review*, 49, 187–95.

Batalova, J., and Cohen, P. N. (2002) Premarital cohabitation and housework: Couples in cross-national perspective. *Journal of Marriage and the Family*, 64, 3, 743–55.

Baulch, B. (1996) The new poverty agenda: A disputed consensus. *IDS Bulletin*, 27, 1–10.

Bauman, Z. (1990) *Thinking Sociologically*. Oxford: Basil Blackwell.

Baumann, G. (1996) *Contesting Culture: Discourses of Identity in Multi-Ethnic London*. Cambridge: Cambridge University Press.

Baumgartner, M. (1988) *The Moral Order of a Suburb*. New York: Oxford University Press.

Baumrind, D. (1989) Rearing competent children. In W. Damon (ed.), *Child Development Today and Tomorrow*. San Francisco: Jossey-Bass.

Baumrind, D. (1991) The influence of parenting style on adolescent competence and substance use. *Journal of Early Adolescence*, 11, 56–95.

Baumrind, D. (1991) Parenting styles and adolescent development. In R. M. Lerner, A. C. Peterson, and J. Brooks-Gunn (eds.), *Encyclopedia of Adolescence*. New York: Garland.

Beauvoir, S. de (1972) *The Second Sex*. Harmondsworth: Penguin.

Becerra, R. M. (1988) The Mexican American family. In C. H. Mindel, R. W. Habenstein, and J. R. Wright (eds.), *Ethnic Families in America: Patterns and Variations*. New York: Elsevier.

Beck, U. (1992) *The Risk Society: Towards a New Modernity*. London: Sage.

Beck, U. (1997) *TheReinvention of Politics*. Cambridge: Polity.

Beck, U. (1998) *Democracy Without Enemies*. Cambridge: Polity.

Beck, U. (1999) Knowledge or non-knowledge. In U. Beck, *World Risk Society*. Cambridge: Polity.

Beck, U. (2001) Living your own life in a runaway world: individualization, globalisation and politics. In W. Hutton and A. Giddens (eds.), *On the Edge: Living with Global Capitalism*. London: Vintage.

Beck, U. (2002) The cosmopolitan society and its enemies. *Theory, Culture & Society*, 1–2, 17–44.

Beck, U. (2002) *Macht und Gegenmacht im globalen Zeitalter*. Frankfurt: Suhrkamp.

Beck, U., and Beck-Gernsheim, E. (1995) *The Normal Chaos of Love*. Cambridge: Polity.

Beck, U., and Beck-Gernsheim, E. (2002) *Individualization. Institutionalised Individualism and its Social and Political Consequences*. London: Sage.

Beck, U., Bonss, W., and Lau, Ch. (forthcoming) *Theory of Reflexive Modernization, Theory, Culture and Society*.

Beck, U., Giddens, A., and Lash, S. (1994) *Reflexive Modernization*. Cambridge: Polity.

Becker, G. (1991) *A Treatise on the Family*. Cambridge, MA: Harvard University Press.

Becker, G. (1993) [1964] *Human Capital*. Chicago: University of Chicago Press.

Beck-Gernsheim, E. (1995) *The Social Implications of Bioengineering*. Atlantic Highlands, NJ: Humanities Press.

Beck-Gernsheim, E. (1998) On the way to a post-familial family: from a community of need to elective affinities. *Theory, Culture and Society* 15, 53–70.

Beck-Gernsheim, E. (2002) *Reinventing the Family*. Cambridge: Polity.

Beecher, C., and Stowe, H. B. (1869) *The American Woman's Home*. New York: J. B. Ford.

Beishon, S., Modood, T., and Virdee, S. (1998) *Findings: Ethnic Minority Families*. Summary of Policy Studies Institute report. York: Joseph Rowntree Foundation.

Bell, C., and Newby, H. (1971) *Community Studies: An Introduction to the Sociology of the Local Community*. London: George Allen & Unwin.

Bell, R. Q. (1968) A reinterpretation of the direction of effects in studies of socialization. *Psychological Review*, 75, 81–95.

Bellah, R. N., Madsen, R., Sullivan, W. M., Swidler, A., and Tipton, S. M. (1985) *Habits of the Heart: Individualism and Commitment in American Life*. Berkeley: University of California Press.

Bellamy, C. (2000) *The State of the World's Children*. New York: UNICEF.

Bellamy, C. (2002) Speech to the World Summit on Sustainable Development. Johannesburg: UNICEF Press Centre, August 30.

Bellweg, J. (1969) Extension of meaning and use for kinship terms. *American Anthropologist*, 71, 84–7.

Bengtson, V. L. (1985) Diversity and symbolism in the grandparent role. In V. Bengtson and J. Robertson (eds.), *Grandparenthood*. Beverly Hills, CA: Sage.

Bengtson, V. L. (2001) Beyond the nuclear family: The increasing importance of multigenerational bonds. Burgess Award Lecture. *Journal of Marriage and the Family*, 63, 1–16.

Bengtson, V. L., and Achenbaum, W. A. (eds.) (1993) *The Changing Contract AcrossGenerations*. New York: Aldine De Gruyter.

Bengtson, V. L., and Allen, K. (1993) The life course perspective applied to families over time. In P. G. Boss, W. J. Doherty, R. LaRossa, W. R. Schumm, and S. K. Steinmetz (eds.), *Sourcebook of Family Theories and Methods: A Contextual Approach*. New York: Plenum.

Bengtson, V. L., Giarrusso, R., Mabry, J. B., and Silverstein, M. (2002) Solidarity, conflict, and ambivalence: Complementary or competing perspectives on intergenerational relationships? *Journal of Marriage and the Family*, 64, 3, 568–76.

Bengtson, V. L., Giarrusso, R., Silverstein, M., and Wang, H. (2000) Families and intergenerational relationships in aging societies. *Hallym International Journal of Aging*, 2, 3–10.

Bengtson, V. L., and Harootyan, R. (eds.) (1994) *Intergenerational Linkages: Hidden Connections in American Society*. New York: Springer.

Bengtson, V. L., and Kuypers, J. A. (1971) Generational difference and the developmental stake. *Aging and Human Development*, 2, 249–60.

Bengtson, V. L., Marti, G., and Roberts, R. E. L. (1991). Age group relations: Generational equity and inequity. In K. Pillemer and K. McCartney (eds.), *Parent–Child Relations across the Lifespan*. Hillsdale, NJ: Lawrence Erlbaum.

Bengtson, V. L., Olander, E. B., and Haddad, A. A. (1976) The generation gap and aging family members: Toward a conceptual model. In J. F. Gubrium (ed.), *Time, Roles, and Self in Old Age*. New York: Human Sciences Press.

Bengtson, V. L., and Putney, N. (2000) Who will care for the elderly? Consequences of population aging East and West. In K. D. Kim, V. L. Bengtson, G. C. Meyers, and K. S. Eun (eds.), *Aging East and West: Families, States, and the Elderly*. New York: Springer.

Bengston, V. L., Rosenthal, C., and Burton, L. (1990) Families and aging: diversity and heterogeneity. In R. Binstock and L. George (eds.), *Handbook of Aging and Social Sciences*. 4th ed. New York: Academic Press.

Bengtson, V. L., Rosenthal, C. J, and Burton, L. M. (1995) Paradoxes of families and aging. In R. H. Binstock and L. K. George (eds.), *Handbook of Aging and the Social Sciences*. 4th ed. San Diego: Academic Press.

Bengtson, V. L., and Schrader, S. S. (1982) Parent–child relations. In D. Mangen and W. Peterson (eds.), *Handbook of Research Instruments in Social Gerontology*, vol. 2. Minneapolis: University of Minnesota Press.

Benkov, L. (1994) *Reinventing The Family: The Emerging Story of Lesbian and Gay Parent*. New York: Crown.

Bennett, L. (2000) Fifty years of prejudice in the media. *Gay and Lesbian Review*, 7, 30–5.

Benson, L. (1976) *Malory's Morte D'Arthur*. Cambridge, MA: Harvard University Press.

Benson, S. (1981) *Ambiguous Ethnicity*. Cambridge: Cambridge University Press.

Benson, S. (1996) Asians have culture, West Indians have problems: Discourses of race and ethnicity in and out of anthropology. In T. O. Ranger, Y. Samad, and O. Stuart (eds.), *Culture, Identity and Politics: Ethnic Minorities in Britain*. Aldershot: Avebury.

Beresford, P., Green, D., Lister, R., and Woodward, K. (1999) *Poverty First Hand: Poor People Speak for Themselves*. London: CPAG.

Berger, B., and Berger, P. L. (1983) *The War Over the Family: Capturing the Middle Ground*. Garden City, NY: Anchor Press.

Bernard, J. (1976) *The Future of Marriage*. Harmondsworth: Penguin.

Bernstein, B. (1970) A socio-linguistic approach to socialization. In J. Gumperz and D. Hymes (eds.), *Directions in Sociolinguistics*. New York: Holt, Rinehart & Winston.

Berrington, A. (1994) Marriage and family formation among the white and ethnic minority populations in Britain. *Ethnic and Racial Studies*, 17, 517–46.

Berrington, A., and Diamond, I. (1999) Marital dissolution among the 1958 British birth cohort: The role of cohabitation. *Population Studies*, 53, 19–38.

Berthoud, R. (2000) *Family Formation in Multicultural Britain: Three Patterns of Diversity, a working paper*. Institute for Social and Economic Research: University of Essex.

Bertoia, C., and Drakich, J. (1993) The fathers' rights movement: Contradictions in rhetoric and practice. *Journal of Family Issues*, 14, 592–615.

Best, F. (1980) *Flexible Life Scheduling*. New York: Praeger.

Bhachu, P. (1985) *Twice Migrants: East African Sikh Settlers in Britain*. London: Tavistock.

Bharadwaj, A. (2003) Why adoption is not an option in India: The visibility of infertility, the secrecy of donor insemination and other cultural complexities. *Social Science and Medicine*, 56, 1867–80.

Bhrolcháin, M., Chappell R., Diamond, I., and Jameson, C. (2000) Parental divorce and outcomes for children: evidence and interpretation. *European Sociological Review*, 16, 67–91.

Biale, D. (1992) *Eros and the Jews. From Biblical Israel to Contemporary America*. New York: Basic Books.

Bianchi, S. (2000) Maternal employment and time with children: dramatic change or surprising continuity? *Demography*, 37, 401–14.

Bianchi, S. M. (1995) The changing demographic and socioeconomic characteristics of single parent families. *Marriage and Family Review*, 20, 71–97.

Bianchi, S. M., Milkie, M. A., Sayer, L. C., and Robinson, J. P. (2000) Is anyone doing the housework? Trends in the gender division of household labor. *Social Forces*, 79, 191–228.

Bianchi, S. M., and Robinson, J. (1997) What did you do today? Children's use of time, family composition, and the acquisition of social capital. *Journal of Marriage and the Family*, 59, 332–44.

Biblarz, T. J., and Raftery, A. E. (1999) Family structure, educational attainment, and socioeconomic success: Rethinking the "pathology of matriarchy". *American Journal of Sociology*, 105, 321–65.

Bielenski, H., Bosch, G., and Wagner, A. (2001) *Employment and Working Time in Europe*. Dublin: European Foundation for the Improvement of Living and Working Conditions.

Binney, C. (1949) Legal and social implications of artificial insemination. *Eugenics Review*, 40, 199–204.

Bird, C. E. (1997) Gender differences in the social and economic burdens of parenting and psychological distress. *Journal of Health and Social Behavior*, 33, 809–23.

Bird, P. (1974) Images of women in the Old Testament. In R. R. Ruether (ed.), *Religion and Sexism. Images of Woman in the Jewish and Christian Traditions*. New York: Simon & Schuster.

*Birth Statistics* (1976) Series FM1, No 3. London: Stationery Office.

*Birth Statistics* (1999) Series FM1, No 28. London: Stationery Office.

Blacker, C. P. (1958) Artificial insemination: The society's position. *Eugenics Review*, 50, 51–4.

Blaikie, A. (1999) *Ageing and Popular Culture*. Cambridge: Cambridge University Press.

Blain, J. (1994) Discourses of agency and domestic labor: Family discourse and gendered practices in dual-earner families. *Journal of Family Issues*, 15, 515–49.

Blair, S. L. and Lichter, D. T. (1991) Measuring the division of household labor: Gender segregation of housework among American couples. *Journal of Family Issues*, 12, 91–113.

Blakemore, K., and Boneham, M. (1994) *Age race and ethnicity: A Comparative Approach*. Buckingham: Open University Press.

Blasius, M. (1994) *Gay and Lesbian Politics: Sexuality and the Emergence of a New Ethic*. Philadelphia: Temple University Press.

Blumstein, P., and Schwartz, P. (1983) *American Couples*. New York: William Morrow.

Blyth, E. (1999) Secrets and lies. Barriers to the exchange of genetic origins information following donor-assisted conception. *Adoption and Fostering*, 23, 49–58.

Blyth, E., and Hunt, J. (1998) Sharing genetic origin information in donor assisted conception: Views from licensed centres on HFEA donor information form. *Human Reproduction*, 13, 3274–7.

Boaz, A., Hayden, C., and Bernard, M. (1999) *Attitudes and Aspirations of Older People: A Review of the Literature*. London: Department of Social Security, Research Report 101.

Bohannan, P. (1970) *Divorce and After: An Analysis of the Emotional and Social Problems of Divorce*. Garden City, NY: Anchor.

Bonacich, E. (1994) Asians in the Los Angeles garment industry. In P. Ong, E. Bonacich, and L. Cheng (eds.), *The New Asian Immigration in Los Angeles and Global Restructuring*. Philadelphia: Temple University Press.

Bond, S., Hyman, J. Summers, J., and Wise, S. (2002) *Family-Friendly Working? Putting Policy into Practice*. York: York Publishing Services for the Joseph Rowntree Foundation.

Booth, A. (1972) Sex and social participation. *American Sociological Review*, 37, 183–92.

Booth, A., and Amato, P. R. (1991) Divorce and psychological stress. *Journal of Health and Social Behavior*, 32, 396–407.

Booth, A., and Amato, P. R. (2001) Parental predivorce relations and offspring postdivorce well-being. *Journal of Marriage and the Family*, 63, 197–212.

Booth, A., Carver, K., and Granger, D. (2000) Biosocial perspectives on the family. *Journal of Marriage and the Family*, 62, 1018–34.

Booth, A., and Dabbs, J. M. (1993) Testosterone and men's marriage. *Social Forces*, 72, 463–77.

Booth, A., Johnson, D. R., and Granger, D. (1999) Testosterone and men's depression: The role of social behavior. *Journal of Health and Social Behavior*, 40, 130–40.

Booth, A., and Osgood, D. W. (1993) The influence of testesterone on deviance in adulthood: Assessing and explaining the relationship. *Criminology*, 31, 93–117.

Bosanquet, H. (1905) *The Family*. London: Macmillan.

Boss, P. (1999) *Ambiguous Loss: Learning to Live with Unresolved Grief*. Cambridge, MA: Harvard University Press.

Bossard, J. H. S., and Stoker Boll, E. (1956) *The Large Family System*. Philadelphia: University of Pennsylvania Press.

Botman, S. (1999) *Engendering Citizenship in Egypt*. New York: Columbia University Press.

Bott, E. (1955) Urban families: Conjugal roles and social networks. *Human Relations*, 8, 345–50.

Bott, E. (1957) *Family and Social Networks*. London, Tavistock.

Bott, E. (1971) *Family and Social Network: Roles, Norms, and External Relationships in Ordinary Urban Families*. 2nd ed. London: Tavistock.

Boulding, E. (1983) Familia faber: The family as maker of the future. *Journal of Marriage and the Family*, May, 257–66.

Bourdieu, P. (1973) Cultural reproduction and social reproduction. In R. Brown (ed.), *Knowledge, Education, and Cultural Change*. London: Tavistock.

Bourdieu, P. (1977) *Outline of a Theory of Practice*. Cambridge: Cambridge University Press.

Bourdieu, P. (1984) *Distinction*. London: Routledge & Kegan Paul.

Bourdieu, P. (1986) The forms of capital. In J. C. Richardson (ed.), *Handbook of Theory and Research for the Sociology of Education*. New York: Greenwood.

Bourdieu, P. (1998) *Practical Reason: On the Theory of Action*. Stanford, CA: Stanford University Press.

Bourdieu, P., and Passeron, J. C. (1977) *Reproduction in Education, Society, and Culture*. London: Sage.

Boushel, M., Fawcett, M., and Selwyn, J. (eds.) (2000) *Focus on Early Childhood, Principles and Realities*. Oxford: Blackwell.

Bowlby, J. (1952) *Maternal Care and Mental Health*. Geneva: World Health Organization.

Boyd, M. (1989) Family and personal networks in international migration: Recent developments and new agendas. *International Migration Review*, 23, 638–70.

Boyd, M. (1991) Immigration and living arrangements: elderly women in Canada. *International Migration Review*, 25, 4–27.

Boyd, S., and Treas, J. (1989) Family care of the frail elderly: A new look at women in the middle. *Women's Studies Quarterly*, 112, 66–73.

Bozett, F. W. (ed.) (1987) *Gay and Lesbian Parents*. New York: Praeger.

Bozon, M. (1996) Reaching adult sexuality: First intercourse and its implications: From calendar to attitudes. In M. Bozon and H. Leridon (eds.), *Sexuality in the Social Sciences*. Aldershot: Dartmouth.

Bradbury, B., and Jantti, M. (1999) *Child Poverty across Industrialised Nations*. Innocenti Occasional Papers: Economic and Social Policy Series, no. 71.

Bradbury, B., Jenkins, S., and Micklewright, J. (2001) *The Dynamics of Child Poverty in Industrialized Countries*. Cambridge: Cambridge University Press.

Bradford, J., Ryan, C., and Rothblum, E. D. (1994) National Lesbian Health Care Survey: Implications for mental health. *Journal of Consulting and Clinical Psychology*, 62, 228–42.

Bradshaw, J. (2002) Child poverty and child outcomes. *Children and Society*, 16, 131–40.

Bradshaw, J., Kennedy, S., Kilkey, M., Hutton, S., Corden, A., Eardley, T., Holmes, H., and Neale, J. (1996) *The Employment of Lone Parents: A Comparison of Policy in Twenty Countries*. London: Family Policy Studies Centre/Joseph Rowntree Foundation.

Bradshaw, J., Stimson, C., Skinner, C., and Williams, J. (1999) *Absent Fathers?* London: Routledge.

Bradshaw, J. S., Stimson, C., Skinner, C., and Williams, J. (1999) Non-resident fathers in Britain. In S. McRae (ed.), *Changing Britain: Families and Households in the 1990s*. Oxford: Oxford University Press.

Brady, D. (2001) *Rethinking the Sociological Measurement of Poverty.* Luxembourg: Luxembourg Income Study, Working Paper 264.

Bramlett, M. D., and Mosher, W. D. (2001) *First Marriage Dissolution, Divorce, and Remarriage: United States*. Advance data from vital and health statistics, no. 323. Hyattsville, MD: National Center for Health Statistics.

Brannen, J. (1999). Reconsidering children and childhood: sociological and policy perspectives. In E. Silva and C. Smart (eds.), *The New Family?* London: Sage.

Brannen, J., Heptinstall, E., and Bhopal, K. (2000) *Connecting Children: Care and Family Life in Later Childhood*. London: Routledge/Falmer.

Braver, S. L., Whitley, M., and Ng, C. (1993) Who divorced whom? Methodological and theoretical issues. *Journal of Divorce and Remarriage*, 20, 1–19.

Brenner, S. (1996) Reconstructing self and society: Javanese Muslim women and the "veil". *American Ethnologist*, 34, 673–97.

Brewer, H. (1935) Eutelegenesis. *Eugenics Review*, 27, 121–6.

Brewster, K. L., Billy, J. O. G., and Grady, W. R. (1993) Social context and adolescent behavior: The impact of community on the transition to sexual activity. *Social Forces*, 71, 713–40.

Brines, J., and Joyner, K. (1999) The ties that bind: Principles of cohesion in cohabitation and marriage. *American Sociological Review*, 64, 333–55.

Broderick, C. B. (1988) Healing members and relationships in the intimate network. In: R. M. Milardo (eds.), *Families and Social Networks*. Newbury Park, CA: Sage.

Bronfenbrenner, U. (1979) *The Ecology of Human Development*. Cambridge, MA: Harvard University Press.

Bronfenbrenner, U., and Ceci, S. J. (1994) Nature–nurture reconceptualized in developmental perspective: a bioecological model. *Psychological Review*, 101, 568–586.

Bronski, M. (1988) Death and the erotic imagination. In J. Preston (ed.), *Personal Dispatches: Writers Confront AID*. New York: St. Martin's Press.

Brown, C. (1984) *Black and White Britain: the third PSI Survey*. Aldershot: Gower.

Brown, S. (2000) The effect of union type on psychological well-being: Depression among cohabitors versus marrieds. *Journal of Health and Social Behavior*, 41, 241–55.

Brown, S. L., and Booth, A. (1996) Cohabitation versus marriage: A comparison of relationship quality. *Journal of Marriage and the Family*, 58, 667–8.

Browning, C. R., and Laumann, E. O. (1997) Sexual contact between children and adults: A life course perspective. *American Sociological Review*, 62, 540–60.

Bruner, J. (1994) *Four Ways to Make a Meaning*. Paper presented at the Annual Meeting of the American Educational Research Association, New Orleans, April 4–8.

Bruning, G., and Plantenga, J. (1999) Parental leave and equal opportunities: Experiences in eight European countries. *Journal of European Social Policy*, 9, 195–209.

Bryant, C. M., and Conger, R. D. (1999) Marital success and domains of social support in long-term relationships: Does the influence of network members ever end? *Journal of Marriage and the Family*, 2, 437–50.

Bryson, K., and Casper, L. M. (1999) Coresident grandparents and grandchildren. *Current Population Reports*, P23–198, 1–10.

Bryson, V. (1992) *Feminist Political Theory*. London: Macmillan.

Büchel, F., and Duncan, G. J. (1998) Do parents' social activities promote children's school attainments? Evidence from the German Socioeconomic Panel. *Journal of Marriage and the Family*, 60, 95–108.

Budig, M. J., and England, P. (2001) The wage penalty for motherhood. *American Sociological Review*, 66, 204–25.

Buhr, P., and Weber, A. (1998) Social assistance and social change in Germany. In L. Leisering and R. Walker (eds.), *The Dynamics of Modern Society: Poverty, Policy and Welfare*. Bristol: Policy Press

Bullough, V. L. (1994) *Science in the Bedroom: A History of Sex Research*. New York: Basic Books.

Bulmer, M. (1986) *Neighbours: The Work of Philip Abrams*. Cambridge: Cambridge University Press.

Bumpass, L., and Lu, H-H. (2000) Trends in cohabitation and implications for children's family contexts in the United States. *Population Studies*, 54, 29–41.

Bumpass, L., and McLanahan, S. (1989) Unmarried motherhood: recent trends, composition, and black-white differences. *Demography*, 26, 279–86.

Bumpass, L. L., Raley, R. K., and Sweet, J. A. (1994) *The changing character of stepfamilies: Implications of cohabitation and nonmarital childbearing*. NSFH working paper No. 63.

Bumpass, L. L., and Sweet, J. A. (1989) National estimates of cohabitation. *Demography*, 26, 615-25.

Bumpass, L. L., Sweet, J., and Martin, C. (1990) Changing patterns of remarriage. *Journal of Marriage and the Family*, 52, 747–56.

Bunch, C. (1986) Lesbians in revolt. In M. Pearsall (ed.), *Women and Values*. Belmont, CA: Wadsworth.

Bundey, S., and Alam, H. (1993) A five year prospective study of the health of children in different ethnic groups, with particular reference to the effect of inbreeding. *European Journal of Human Genetics*, 1, 206–19.

Burchell, B., Day, D., Hudson, M., Lapido, D., Mankelow, R., Nolan, J., Reed, H., Witshert, I. C., and Wilkinson, F. (1999) *Job Insecurity and Work Intensification: Flexibility and the Changing Boundaries of Work*. York: York Publishing Services for the Joseph Rowntree Foundation.

Burger, E., and Milardo, R. M. (1995) Marital interdependence and social networks. *Journal of Social and Personal Relationships*, 12, 403–15.

Burgess, E. W. (1928) The changing American family. *Religious Education*, 23, May, 408–15.

Burgess, E. W. (1960) Aging in Western culture. In E. W. Burgess (ed.), *Aging in Western Societies*. Chicago: University of Chicago Press.

Burghes, L. (1994) *Lone Parenthood and Family Disruption: The Outcomes for Children*. London: Family Policy Studies Centre.

Burgoyne, J., and Clark, D. (1984) *Making A Go of It*. London: Routledge & Kegan Paul.

Burkhauser, R., Holden, K., and Myers, D. (1988) Incidence, timing and events associated with poverty: a dynamic view of poverty in retirement. *Journal of Gerontology*, 43, 846–52.

Burman, B., and Margolin, G. (1992) Analysis of the association between marital relationships and health problems: An interactional perspective. *Psychological Bulletin*, 112, 39–63.

Burns, A., and Dunlop, R. (1999) "How did you feel about it?" Children's feelings about their parents' divorce at the time and three and ten years later. *Journal of Divorce and Remarriage*, 31, 19–36.

Burton, L. (1995) Intergenerational patterns of providing care in African-American families with teenage childbearers: Emergent patterns in an ethnographic study. In V. L. Bengtson, K. W. Schaie, and L. M. Burton (eds.), *Adult Intergenerational Relations*. New York: Springer.

Buss, D. M., Shackelford, T. K., Kirkpatrick, L., and Larsen, R. (2001) A half century of mate preferences: The cultural evolution of values. *Journal of Marriage and the Family*, 63, 491–503.

Butler, B. (ed.) (1997) *Ceremonies of the Heart: Celebrating Lesbian Unions*. Seattle: Seal Press.

Butler, J. (1990) *Gender Trouble: Feminism and the Subversion of Identity*. London: Routledge.

Butler, R. N., and Lewis, M. I. (1996) *Love and Sex after 60* (rev. ed.). Thorndike, ME: G. K. Hall.

Bynner, J. (2001) Childhood risks and protective factors in social exclusion. *Children and Society*, 15, 285–301.

Bynum, C. W. (1991) *Fragmentation and Redemption: Essays on Gender and the Human Body in Medieval Religion*. New York: Zone Books.

Byrne, D. (1999) *Social Exclusion*. Buckingham: Open University Press.

Byron, M. (1999) The Caribbean-born population in 1990s Britain: Who will return? *Journal of Ethnic and Migration Studies*, 25, 285–301.

Caccamo, R. (2000) *Back to Middletown: Three Generations of Sociological Reflections*. Stanford, CA: Stanford University Press.

Caldwell, J.C. (1976) Toward a restatement of demographic transition theory. *Population and Development Review*, 2, 321–366.

Caldwell, J.C. (1982) *Theory of Fertility Decline*. New York: Academic Press.

Calhoun, C. (1995) *Critical Social Theory: Culture, History and the Challenge of Difference*. Oxford: Blackwell.

Callender, C., Millward, N., Lissenburgh, S., and Forth, J. (1997) *Maternity Rights and Benefits in Britain1996*. DSS Research Series, Report No. 67. London: Stationery Office.

Cameron, P. C. K. (1997) Did the APA misrepresent the scientific literature to courts in support of homosexual custody? *Journal of Psychology*, 131, 313–32.

Cameron, S. (1995)A review of economic research into determinants of divorce. *British Review of Economic Issues*, 17, 1–21.

Campbell, J. C., and Ikegami, N. (2000) Long-term care insurance comes to Japan. *Health Affairs* 19, 26–39.

Cancian, F. (1987) *Love in America*. Cambridge: Cambridge University Press.

Caplan, N., Choy, M. H., and Whitmore, J. K. (1991) *Children of the Boat People: A Study of Educational Success*. Ann Arbor: University of Michigan Press.

Caplow, T., Bahr, H., Chadwick, B., Hill, R., and Holmes Williamson, M. (1982) *Middletown Families: Fifty Years of Continuity and Change*. Toronto: Bantam.

Carbonaro, W. J. (1998) A little help from my friend's parents: Intergenerational closure and educational outcomes. *Sociology of Education*, 71, 295–313.

Carby, H. V. (2000) White women listen! Black feminism and the boundaries of sisterhood. In K. Owusu (ed.), *Black British Culture and Society*. London and New York: Routledge.

Carrington, C. (1999) *No Place like Home: Relationships and Family Life Among Lesbians and Gay Men*. Chicago and London: University of Chicago Press.

Carter, C. O. (1983) Eugenic implications of new techniques. In C. O. Carter (ed.), *Developments in Human Reproduction and their Eugenic, Ethical Implications*. London: Academic.

Cartwright, D., and Harary, F. (1956) Structural balance; A generalization of Heider's theory. *Psychological Review*, 63, 277–92.

Casper, L. M., and Bianchi, S. M. (2002) *Continuity and Change in the American Family*. Thousand Oaks, CA: Sage.

Casper, L., and Bryson, K. (1998) Co-resident grandparents and their grandchildren: grandparent maintained families. *Population Division, Working Paper No. 26*, Washington, DC: US Bureau of the Census.

Caspi, A., McClay, J., Moffitt, T.E., Mill, J., Martin, J., Craig, I.W., Taylor, A., and Poulton, R. (2002). Role of genotype in the cycle of violence in maltreated children. *Science*, 297, 851–4.

Caspi, L., and Bianchi, S. (2002) *Continuity and Change in the American Family*. London: Sage.

Castells, M. (1997) *The Power of Identity*. Vol. 2 of *The Information Age: Economy, Society and Culture*. Oxford: Blackwell.

Chadwick, B. A., and Heaton, T. B. (eds.) (1999) *Statistical Handbook on the American Family*. 2nd ed. Phoenix, AZ: Oryx Press.

Chai, A. Y. (1987) Freed from the elders but locked into labor: Korean immigrant women in Hawaii. *Women's Studies*, 13, 223–4.

Chamberlain, M. (1997) *Narratives of Exile and Return*. University of Warwick Caribbean Studies Series. London: Macmillan.

Chamberlain M. (ed.) (1998) *Caribbean Migration: Globalised Identities*. London: Routledge.

Chamberlain, M. (1999) The family as model and metaphor in Caribbean migration to Britain. *Journal of Ethnic and Migration Studies*, 25, 251–66.

Chambez, C. (2001) Lone parent families in Europe: A variety of economic and social circumstances. *Social Policy and Administration*, 35, 658–71.

Charrad, M. M. (1997) Policy Shifts: State, Islam and gender in Tunisia. *Social Politics*, 4(2), 284–319.

Chase-Lansdale, P. L., and Brooks-Gunn, J. (1995) *Escape from Poverty: What Makes a Difference for Children?* Cambridge: Cambridge University Press.

Chauncey, G. (1994) *Gay New York: Gender, Urban Culture, and the Making of the Gay Male World, 1890–1940*. New York: Basic Books.

Chavez, L. R. (1990) Coresidence and resistance: Strategies for survival among undocumented Mexicans and Central Americans in the United States. *Urban Anthropology*, 19, 31–61.

Chavez, L. R. (1991) *Shadowed Lives: Undocumented Immigrants in American Society*. San Diego: Harcourt Brace Jovanovich College Publishers.

Chen, X., and Silverstein, M. (2000) Intergenerational social support and the psychological well-being of older parents in China. *Research on Aging*, 22, 43–65.

Cherlin, A., and Furstenberg, F. (1986) *The New American Grandparent: A Place in the Family, a Life Apart*. New York: Basic Books.

Cherlin, A. J. (1992) *Marriage, Divorce, Remarriage*. Cambridge, MA: Harvard University Press.

Cherlin, A. J. (1999) *Public and Private Families*. Boston: McGraw-Hill.

Cherlin, A. J., Chase-Lansdale, P. L., and McRae, C. (1998) Effects of divorce on mental health throughout the life course. *American Sociological Review*, 63, 239–9.

Cherlin, A. J., and Furstenberg, F. F. (1994). Stepfamilies in the US: a reconsideration. *Annual Review of Sociology*, 359–81.

Cherlin, A. J., Furstenberg, F. F., Chase-Lansdale, P. L., Kiernan, K. E., Robins, P. K., Morrison, D. R., and Teitler, J. O. (1991) Longitudinal studies of effects of divorce on children in Great Britain and the United States. *Science*, 252, 1386–9.

Children's Rights Development Unit (1994) *UK Agenda for Children*. London: Children's Rights Development Unit.

Chodorow, N. (1978) *The Reproduction of Mothering : Psychoanalysis and the Sociology of Gender*. Berkeley: University of California Press.

Choi, K. H., Catania, J. A., and Dolcini, M. M. (1994) Extramarital sex and HIV risk behavior among American adults: Results from the National AIDS Behavior Survey. *American Journal of Public Health*, 84, 2003–7.

Chow, N. (1999) Diminishing filial piety and the changing role and status of the elders in Hong Kong. *Hallym International Journal of Aging*, 1, 67–77.

Christiansen, S. L., and Palkovitz, R. (2001) Why the "good provider" role still matters: Providing as a form of parental involvement. *Journal of Family Issues*, 22, 84–106.

Cicirelli, V. G. (1995) *Sibling Relationships Across the Life Span*. New York: Plenum.

Citro, C., and Michael, R. (1995) *Measuring Poverty: A New Approach*. Washington DC: National Academy Press.

Clark, S. (2000) Son preference and sex composition of children: Evidence from India. *Demography*, 37, 95–108.

Clarkberg, M., Stolzenber, R. M., and Waite, L. J. (1995) Attitudes, values and entrance into cohabitational versus marital unions. *Social Forces*, 74, 609–32.

Clarke, E., Preston, M., Raskin, J., and Bengtson, V. L. (1999) Types of conflicts and tensions between older parents and adult children. *The Gerontologist*, 39, 261–70.

Clarke, L. (1992) Children's family circumstances: recent trends in Great Britain. *European Journal of Population*, 8, 309–40.

Clarke, L. (1996) Demographic change and the family situation of children. In J. Brannen and M. O'Brien (eds.), *Children in Families: Research and Policy*. London: Falmer.

Clarke, P. (1996) *Hope and Glory: Britain 1990–1990*. London: Allen Lane.

Clasen, J., Gould, A., and Vincent, J. (1998) *Voices Within and Without: Responses to Long-term Unemployment in Germany, Sweden and Britain*. Bristol: The Policy Press.

Clawson, D., and Gerstel, N. (2002) Caring for young children: The U.S. vs. Europe. *Contexts*, 1, 28–35.

Cliff, D. (1989) Life After Work: An Investigation Of Men In Early Retirement. Doctoral dissertation, University of Huddersfield.

Cochran, M., Larner, M., et al. (1990) *Extending Families: The Social Networks of Parents and their Children*. Cambridge: Cambridge University Press.

Cockett, M., and Tripp, J. (1994) *The Exeter Family Study*. Exeter: University of Exeter.

Coenen-Huther, J., Kellerhals, J., von Allmen, M., Hagmann, H.-M., Jeannerat, F., and Widmer, E. (1994) *Les Réseaux de Solidarité dans La Famille*. Lausanne: Réalités sociales.

Cohen, P. N. (2002) Cohabitation and the declining marriage premium for men. *Work and Occupations*, 29, 3, 346–63.

Cohen, P. N. (2002) Extended households at work: Living arrangements and inequality in single mothers' employment. *Sociological Forum*, 17, 3, 445–63.

Cohen, P. N., and Casper, L. M. (2002) In whose home? Multigenerational families in the United States, 1998–2000. *Sociological Perspectives*, 45, 1–20.

Cohen, R. (2000) Illegal migration rises sharply in European Union. *New York Times* Monday, December 25, A1.

Coleman, D., and Salt, J. (1996) *Ethnicity in the 1991 Census, Volume One: Demographic Characteristics of the Ethnic Minority Populations*. London: HMSO.

Coleman, J. S. (1988) Social capital and the creation of human capital. *American Journal of Sociology*, 94, 95–121.

Coleman, J. S. (1990) *Foundations of Social Theory*. Cambridge, MA: Belknap Press.

Coleman, M., and Ganong, L.H. (1995) Family reconfiguring following divorce. In S. Duck and J. T. Woods (eds.), *Confronting Relationship Challenges*. Thousand Oaks, CA: Sage.

Coleman, M., and Ganong, L. H. (1990) Remarriage and stepfamily research in the 1980s: Increased interest in an old family form. *Journal of Marriage and the Family*, 52, 925–40.

Collier, R. (1995) *Masculinity, Law and The Family*. London: Routledge.

Collins, P. H. (1991) *Black Feminist Thought: Knowledge, Consciousness, and the Politics of Empowerment*. New York: Routledge.

Coltrane, S. (1995) The future of fatherhood: Social, demographic and economic influences on men's family involvements. In W. Marsiglio (ed.), *Fatherhood: Contemporary Theory, Research, and Social Policy*. Thousand Oaks, CA: Sage.

Coltrane, S. (2000) Research on household labor: Modeling and measuring the social embeddedness of routine family work. *Journal of Marriage and the Family*, 62, 1208–33.

Comaroff, J., and Comaroff, J. (eds.) (1993) *Modernity and its Malcontents. Ritual and Power*. Chicago: University of Chicago Press.

Commaille, J. (1998) Family and democracy. In K. Matthijs (ed.), *The Family: Contemporary Perspectives and Challenges*. Leuven: Leuven University Press.

Compas, B. E. (1995) Promoting successful coping during adolescence. In M. Rutter (ed.), *Psychological Disturbances in Young People: Challenges for Prevention*. New York: Cambridge University Press.

Connell, R. W. (1995) *Masculinities*. Berkeley: University of California Press.

Connolly, K. (2001) Germans flock to tie the knot after law change. *Observer*, July 22, 19.

Cook, R. (2002) Villain, hero or masked stranger: ambivalence in transactions with human genetics. In A. Bainham, S. Day-Sclater, and M. Richards (eds.), *Body Lore and Laws*. Oxford: Hart.

Cook, R., and Golombok, S. (1995) A survey of semen donation: Phase 2 – the view of donors. *Human Reproduction*, 10, 951–9.

Cooney, T. M., and Smith, L. A. (1996) Young adults' relations with grandparents following recent parental divorce. *Journals of Gerontology: Series B: Psychological Sciences and Social Sciences*, 51B, S91–S95.

Coontz, S. (1997) The Way We Really Are: Coming to Terms with America's Changing Families. New York: Basic Books.

Corbett, T. (2003) The new face of welfare in the US: From income transfers to social assistance? *Social Policy and Society*, 2, 2, forthcoming.

Corcoran, M. (1995) Rags to rags: Poverty and mobility in the United States. *Annual Review of Sociology*, 21, 237–67.

Corijn, M., and Klijzing, E (eds.) (2000) *Transitions to Adulthood in Europe*. Dordrecht: Kluwer Academic.

Cornelius, L. J. (1993) Barriers to medical care for White, Black, and Hispanic American children. *Journal of the National Medical Association*, 85, 281–8.

Council of Europe (2001) *Recent demographic developments in Europe*. Strasbourg: Council of Europe.

Coward, R., and Dwyer, J. (1990) Association of gender, sibling network composition, and patterns of parent care by adult children. *Research on Aging*, 12, 158–81.

Cowgill, D. (1974) The aging of populations and societies. *Annals of the American Academy of Political and Social Science*, 415, 1–18.

Cox, S. M., and Burgess, M. M. (2000) *Victims, Heroes or Pioneers; Moral Experiences of Hereditary Risk and Illness*. Paper presented at the Canadian Bioethics Society Conference, Quebec.

Cox, S. M., and McKellin, W. H. (1999) "There's this thing in our family": Predictive testing and the social construction of risk for Huntington's disease. In P. Conrad and J. Gabe (eds.), *Sociological Perspectives on the New Genetics*. Oxford: Blackwell. Also in *Sociology of Health and Illness*, 21, 622–46.

Craig, P. R. (1991) Costs and benefits: A review of research on take-up of income related benefits. *Journal of Social Policy*, 20(4), 537–65.

Crockenberg, S. (1986) Are temperamental differences in babies associated with predictable differences in caregiving? In J. V. Lerner and R. M. Lerner (eds.), *New Directions for Child Development: Temperament and Social Interaction in Infants and Children*. Vol 31. San Francisco: Jossey-Bass.

Crockenberg, S., and Leerkes, E. M. (2001) Infant temperament, caregiving, and family relationships. Paper presented at the National Symposium on Family Research, Pennsylvania State University, University Park, December.

Crompton, R., and LeFeuvre, N. (2000) Gender family and employment in comparative perspective: The realities and representations of equal opportunities in Britain and France. *Journal of European Social Policy*, 10, 334–8.

Crouter, A. C., and Head, M. R. (2002) Parental monitoring and knowledge of children. In M. H. Bornstein (ed.), *Handbook of Parenting: Being and Becoming a Parent*. 2nd ed. Vol. 3. Mahwah, NJ: Lawrence Erlbaum.

Crow, G., and Allan, G. (1994) *Community Life*. Hemel Hempstead: Harvester Wheatsheaf.

Crow, G., and Allan, G. (2000) Communities, family support and social change. In J. Canavan, P. Dolan, and J. Pinkerton (eds.), *Family Support: Direction from Diversity*. London: Jessica Kingsley.

Crow, G., Allan, G., and Summers, M. (2001) Changing perspectives on the insider/outsider distinction in community sociology. *Community, Work and Family*, 4, 29–48.

Crow, G., and Maclean, C. (2000) Community. In G. Pagne (ed.), *Social Divisions*. Basingstoke: Macmillan.

Crystal, S. (1982) *America's Old Age Crisis*. New York: Basic Books.

Cummings, E., and Henry, H. (1961) *Growing Old: The Process of Disengagement*. New York: Basic Books.

Cunningham, H. (1991) *The Children of the Poor: Representations of Childhood Since the Seventeenth Century*. Cambridge, MA: Blackwell.

Cunningham, H. (1995) *Children and Childhood in Western Society since 1500*. Harlow: Longman.

Cunningham-Burley, S. (1984) "We don't talk about it . . . ": Issues of gender and method in the portrayal of grandfatherhood. *Sociology*, 18, 325–38.

Cunningham-Burley, S. (1987) The experience of grandfatherhood. In C. Lewis and M. O'Brien (eds.), *Re-Assessing Fatherhood*. London: Sage.

D'Augelli, A. R., Hershberger, S. L., and Pilkington, N. W. (1998) Lesbian, gay, and bisexual youth and their families: Disclosure of sexual orientation and its consequences. *American Journal of Orthopsychiatry*, 68, 361–71.

Daly, K. (1993) Reshaping fatherhood: Finding the models. *Journal of Family Issues*, 14, 510–30.

Daly, M., and Lewis, J. (2000) The concept of social care and the analysis of contemporary welfare states. *British Journal of Sociology*, 51, 281–92.

Darling, N., and Steinberg, L. (1993) Parenting style as context: an integrative model. *Psychological Bulletin*, 113, 487–96.

Das Gupta, M. (1997) "What is Indian about you?" A gendered, transnational approach to ethnicity. *Gender and Society*, 11, 572–96.

Davidoff, L., and Hall, C. (1987) *Family Fortunes*. London: Hutchinson.

Davis, K. (1986) Low fertility in evolutionary perspective. In K. Davis, M. Bernstam, and R. Ricardo-Campbell (eds.), *Below-Replacement Fertility in Industrialized Societies*. Cambridge: Cambridge University Press.

Davis, M. (1990) *City of Quartz: Excavating the Future in Los Angeles*. London: Vintage.

Dawson, D. A. (1991) Family structure and children's health and well-being: Data from the 1988 National Health Interview Survey on Child Health. *Journal of Marriage and the Family*, 53, 573–84.

de Jong Gierveld, J. (1998) Intergenerational relationships and solidarity within the family. In K. Matthijs (ed.), *The Family: Contemporary Perspectives and Challenges*. Leuven: Leuven University Press.

Deacon, A. (2002) *Perspectives on Welfare*. Milton Keynes: Open University Press.

Deitz, M. G. (1985) Citizenship with a feminist face: The problem with maternal thinking. *Political Theory*, 13, 19–37.

DeMaris, A. (1997) Elevated sexual activity in violent marriages: Hypersexuality or sexual extortion? *Journal of Sex Research*, 34, 361–73.

Demo, D. H. (1993) The relentless search for effects of divorce: forging new trails or tumbling down the beaten path? *Journal of Marriage and the Family*, 55, 42–5.

Demo, D. H., and Acock, A. C. (1996) Singlehood, marriage, and remarriage. The effects of family structure and family relationships on mothers' wellbeing. *Journal of Family Issues*, 17, 388–407.

Demo, D. H., and Cox, M. J. (2000) Families with young children: A review of research in the 1990s. *Journal of Marriage and the Family*, 62, 876–95.

Dempsey, K. (1990) *Smalltown: A Study of Social Inequality, Cohesion and Belonging*. Melbourne: Oxford University Press.

Dempsey, K. (1992) *A Man's Town: Inequality Between Women and Men in Rural Australia*. Melbourne: Oxford University Press.

Dench, G., and Ogg, J. (2002) *Grandparenting in Britain: A Baseline Study*. London: Institute of Community Studies.

Department of Education and Employment (1996) *Family and Working Lives Survey*. Data Source Book, Vol. 2, p. 236. London: Department of Education and Employment.

Department for Education and Employment (2000) Press release, September 14.

Department of Health (2000) *Protecting Children, Supporting Parents: A consultation document on the physical punishment of children*. London: Department of Health.

Department of Health (2001) *Code of Practice and Guidance on Genetic Paternity Testing Services*. London: Department of Health.

Department of Health (2001) *Donor Information Consultation. Providing Information About Sperm, Egg and Embryo Donors*. London: Department of Health. Available online at www.doh.gov.uk/gametedonors

Department of Trade and Industry (2000) *Work and Parents: Competitiveness and Choice, A Research Review*. London: Department of Trade and Industry.

Derevensky, J. L., and Deschamps, L. (1997) Young adults from divorced and intact families: Perceptions about preferred custodial arrangements. *Journal of Divorce and Remarriage*, 27, 105–22.

Desjarlais, R., Eisenberg, L., Good, B., and Kleinman, A. (1995) *World Mental Health: Problems and Priorities in Low-Income Countries*. New York: Oxford University Press.

Dex, S. (1988) *Women's Attitudes to Work*. Basingstoke: Macmillan.

Dex, S. (1992) Labour force participation of women in Britain during the 1990s: occupational mobility and part-time employment In R. M. Lindley (ed.), *Women's Employment: Britain in the Single European Market*. London: HMSO.

Dex, S. (1996) Women's experience of unemployment. *Economic Affairs*, 16, 2, 6–10.

Dex, S. (ed.) (1999) *Families and the Labour Market*. London and York: Family Policy Studies Centre for the Joseph Rowntree Foundation.

Dex, S., Gustafsson, S., Callan, T., and Smith, N. (1995) Cross-national comparisons of the labour force participation of women married to unemployed men. *Oxford Economic Papers*, 47, 611–35.

Dex, S., and McCulloch, A. (1997) *Characteristics of the Unemployed: Secondary Analysis of the Family and Working Lives Survey*. DfEE Research Report RR32. London: Department of Education and Employment.

Dex, S., and Schiebl, F. (1999) Business performance and family-friendly policies. *Journal of General Management*, 24, 22–37.

Dex, S., Scheibl, F., Smith, C., and Coussey, M. (2000) *New Working Patterns*. London: Centre for Tomorrow's Company and Pertemps.

Dex, S., and Shaw, L. B. (1986) *British and American Women at Work*. Basingstoke: Macmillan.

Dex, S., and Smith, C. (2002) *The Nature and Patterns of Family-Friendly Employment Policies in Britain*. Bristol: Policy Press.

Dex, S., Walters, P., and Alden, D. (1993) *French and British Mothers at Work*. Basingstoke: Macmillan.

Dhanjal, B. (1976) Sikh women in Southall. *New Community*, 5, 109–17.

Dickens, R. (2000) Caught in a trap? Wage mobility in Great Britain: 1975–1994. *Economica*, 67, 268, 477–97.

Dickens, R., and Ellwood, D. (forthcoming, 2003) Whither poverty in Britain and the US? The determinants of changing poverty and whether work will work. In R. Blundell, D. Card, and R. Freeman (eds.), *Seeking a Premier League Economy*.

Dicks, B., Waddington, D., and Critcher, C. (1998) Redundant men and overburdened women. In J. Popay, J. Hearn, and J. Edwards (eds.), *Men, Gender Divisions and Welfare*. London: Routledge.

DiLalla, L. F., and Gottesman, I. I. (1989) Heterogeneity of causes for delinquency and criminality: lifespan perspectives. *Development and Psychopathology*, 1, 39–349.

Dillaway, H., and Broman, C. (2001) Race, class, and gender differences in marital satisfaction and divisions of household labor among dual-earner couples: A case for intersectional analysis. *Journal of Family Issues*, 22, 309–27.

Dobash, R. P., Dobash, R. E., Wilson, M., and Daly, M. (1992) The myth of sexual symmetry in marital violence. *Social Problems*, 39, 71–91.

Dobson, B., Beardsworth, A., Keil, T., and Walker, R. (1995) *Diet, Choice and Poverty*. London: Family Policy Studies Centre.

Domhoff, G. W. (2002) *Who Rules America? Power and Politics*. 4th ed. Boston: McGraw Hill.

Donati, P. (1998) The new citizenship of the family. In K. Matthijs (ed.), *The Family: Contemporary Perspectives and Challenges*. Leuven: Leuven University Press.

Donnelley, D. A. (1993) Sexually inactive marriages. *Journal of Sex Research*, 30, 171–9.

Donor Conception Support Group of Australia (1997) *Let the Offspring Speak: Discussions on Donor Conception*. Genges Hill, NSW: Donor Conception Support Group of Australia

Donovan, C., Heaphy, B., and Weeks, J. (1999) Citizenship and same sex relationships. *Journal of Social Policy*, 28, 689–709.

Donzelot, J. (1979) *The Policing of Families*. London: Hutchinson.

Douglas, G. (2000) Marriage, cohabitation and parenthood: From contract to status?" In J. Eekelaar, S. Katz, and M. MacLean (eds.), *Cross Currents: Family Law and Policy in the US and England*. Oxford: Oxford University Press.

Douglas, M. (1993) The idea of a home: a kind of space. In A. Mack (ed.), *Home: A Place in the World*. New York: New York University Press.

Dowd, N. E. (2000) *Redefining Fatherhood*. New York: New York University Press.

Downey, D. B. (1994) The school performance of children from single-mother and single-father families: economic or interpersonal deprivation? *Journal of Family Issues*, 15, 129–47.

Drucker, J. (1998) *Families of Value: Gay and Lesbian Parents and Their Children Speak Out*. New York: Plenum.

Duby, G. (1978) *Medieval Marriages. Two Models from Twelfth-century France*. Baltimore and London: Johns Hopkins University Press.

Duerr Berrick, J. (1995) *Faces of Poverty: Portraits of Women and Children on Welfare*. New York: Oxford University Press.

Duleep, H. O., and Regets, M. C. (1996) Family unification, siblings, and skills. In H. O. Duleep and P. V. Wunnava (eds.), *Immigrants and Immigration Policy: Individual Skills, Family Ties, and Group Identities*. Greenwich, CT: JAI Press.

Duncan, G., and Brooks-Gunn, J. (1997) Income effects across the life span: integration and interpretation. In G. Duncan and J. Brooks-Gunn (eds.), *Consequences of Growing Up Poor*. New York: Russell Sage Foundation.

Duncan, G., Yeung, W. J., Brooks-Gunn, J., and Smith, J. (1998) The effects of childhood poverty on the life chances of children. *American Sociological Review*, 63, 406–23.

Duncan, S., and Edwards, R. (eds.) (1997) *Single Mothers in an International Context: Mothers or Workers?* London: UCL Press.

Duncan, S., and Edwards, R. (1999) *Lone Mothers, Paid Work and Gendered Moral Rationalities*. Basingstoke: Macmillan.

Duncombe, J., and Marsden, D. (1998) "Stepford Wives" and "Hollow Men". Doing emotion work, doing gender and "authenticity" in intimate heterosexual relationships. In G. Bendelow and S. J. Williams (eds.), *Emotions in Social Life*. London: Routledge.

Dunn, J., Davies, L. C., O'Connor, T. G., and Sturgess, W. (2001) Family lives and friendships: the perspectives of children in step-, single-parent and nonstep families. *Journal of Family Psychology*, 15, 272–87.

Dunn, J., Deater-Deckard, K, Pickering, K., and O'Connor, T. G. (1998) Children's adjustment and prosocial behavior in step-, single- and nonstep-family settings: Findings from a community study. *Journal of Child Psychology and Psychiatry*, 39, 1083-95.

Dunn, J., and Plomin, R. (1990) *Separate Lives: Why Siblings are so Different*. New York: Basic Books.

Dunne, G. A. (1997) *Lesbian Lifestyles: Women's Work and the Politics of Sexuality*. London: Macmillan.

Dunne, G. A. (1999) A passion for sameness: Sexuality and gender accountability. In E. B. Silva and C. Smart (eds.), *The New Family?* London: Sage.

Dunne, G. A. (2000) Opting into motherhood: Lesbians blurring the boundaries and transforming the meaning of parenthood and kinship. *Gender and Society*, 14, 11–35.

Dunne, G. A. (2001) The lady vanishes: Reflections on the experiences of married and divorced non-heterosexual fathers. *Sociological Research Online*, 6, U113–U129.

Dunscombe, J., and Marsden, D. (1993) Love and intimacy: the gender division of emotion and emotion work. *Sociology*, 27, 221–42.
Durkheim, E. (1951) *Suicide: A Study in Sociology*. Glencoe, IL: The Free Press.
Durkheim, E. (1961) *Moral Education: A Study in the Theory and Application of the Sociology of Education*. Glencoe, IL: The Free Press.
Durkheim, E. (1979) [1911] Childhood. In W. F. Pickering (ed.), *Durkheim: Essays on Morals and Education*. London: Routledge.
Durkheim, E. (2001) *The Elementary Forms of the Religious Life*. Oxford: Oxford University Press.
Eade, J. (1990) *The Politics of Community: The Bangladeshi Community in East London*. Aldershot: Gower.
Eade, J. (ed.) (1997) *Living the Global City: Globalization as Local Process*. London: Routledge.
Edgar, D. (1992) Childhood in its social context: The under-socialised child. *Family Matters*, 33, 32–6, Melbourne: Australian Institute of Family Studies.
Edgar, D. (1992) Conceptualising family life and family policy. *Family Matters*, 32, 28–37, Melbourne: Australian Institute of Family Studies.
Edgar, D. (1997) La famille Australienne comme expression de la modernité. In J. Commaille and F. de Singly (eds.), *La Question Familiale en Europe*. Paris: L'Harmattan.
Edgar, D. (1997) *Men, Mateship, Marriage*. Sydney: HarperCollins.
Edgar, D. (1999) Families as the crucible of competence in a changing social ecology. In E. Frydenberg (ed.), *Learning to Cope: Developing as a Person in Complex Societies*. Oxford: Oxford University Press.
Edgar, D. (2001) *The Patchwork Nation: Rethinking Government, Rebuilding Community*. Sydney: HarperCollins.
Edgar, D., and Glezer, H. (1994) Family and intimacy: family careers and the reconstruction of private life. *International Social Science Journal*, 46, 117–39.
Edin, K. (2001) *Hearing on Welfare and Marriage Issues* – Testimony Before the Subcommittee on Human Resources of the House Committee on Ways and Means – www.gouse.gov/ways_means/humres/107cong/5-22-01/5-22edin.htm
Edin, K., and Lein, L. (1997) *Making Ends Meet: How Single Mothers Survive Welfare and Low-Wage Work*. New York: Russell Sage Foundation.
Edin, K., and Lein, L. (1997) Work, welfare, and single mothers' economic survival strategies. *American Sociological Review*, 62, 253–66.
Edin, K., and Lein, L. (1997) *To Work or Not to Work? Reasons Women Give for Staying on Welfare* (from www.poverty.smartlibrary.org/segment.cfm?segment = 1850&table_of_contents=14 . . . )
Edin, K., Lein, L., Nelson, T., and Clampet-Lundquest, S. (2000) *Talking to Low-income Fathers*, Joint Center for Poverty Research, University of Chicago, Newsletter, 4, 2.
Edwards, J. D., Franklin, S., Hirsch, E., Price, F., and Strathern, M. (1999) *Technologies of Procreation. Kinship in the Age of Assisted Conception*. 2nd ed. London: Routledge.
Edwards, J. R., and Rothbard, N. P. (2000) Mechanisms linking work and family: clarifying the relationship between work and family constructs. *Academy of Management Review 2000*, 25, 178–99.
Eekelaar, J. (1999) Family law: keeping us "on message". *Child and Family Law Quarterly*, 11, 387–96.
Eekalaar, J. (2000) The end of an era? In S. Katz, J. Eekalaar, and M. Maclean (eds.), *Cross Currents: Family Law in the US and England*. Oxford: Oxford University Press.
Eggebeen, D. J., Snyder, A. R., and Manning, W. D. (1996) Children in single-father families in demographic perspective. *Journal of Family Issues*, 17, 441–65.
Ehrenreich, B., and English, D. (1979) *For Her Own Good: 150 Years of the Experts' Advice to Women*. London: Pluto.
Einhorne, B. (1993) *Cinderella Goes to Market: Citizenship, Gender, and Women's Movements in East Central Europe*. London: Verso.

Elder, G., Jr. (1978) Family history and the life course. In T. Hareven (ed.), *Transitions: The Family and Life Course in Historical Perspective*. New York: Academic Press.

Elder, G., Jr. (1981) History and the family: the discovery of complexity. *Journal of Marriage and the Family*, 43, 489–519.

Elder, G. H. (1969) Appearance and education in marriage mobility. *American Sociological Review*, 34, 519–33.

Elder, G. H., and Conger, R. (2000) *Children of the Land: Adversity and Success in Rural America*. Chicago: University of Chicago Press.

Elder, G. H. Jr. (1994) Time, agency, and social change: Perspectives on the life course. *Social Psychology Quarterly*, 57, 5–15.

Elder, G. H., Jr. (1999) (1974) *Children of the Great Depression*. Boulder: Westview.

Elder, G. H., Jr. (2001) Families, social change and individual lives. *Marriage and Family Review*, 177–92.

Elder, G. H., Jr., Modell, J. M., and Parke, R. D. (1993) *Children in Time and Place*. New York: Cambridge University Press.

Eliade, M. (1959) *The Sacred and the Profane. The Nature of Religion*. New York: Harcourt Brace.

Elias, N. (2000) *The Civilizing Process. Sociogenetic and Psychogenetic Investigations*. Revised ed. Oxford: Blackwell.

Elias, P., and Gregory, M. (1994) *The Changing Structure of Occupations and Earnings in Great Britain, 1975–1990, An Analysis Based on the New Earnings Survey Panel Dataset*. Research Series No. 27. London Department of Employment.

Elias, N., and Scotson, J. (1994[1965]) *The Established and the Outsiders: A Sociological Enquiry into Community Problems*. London: Sage.

Elliott, B. J., and. Richards, M. P. M. (1991) Children and divorce: Educational performance and behavior before and after parental separation. *International Journal of Law and the Family*, 5, 258–76.

Ellison, C. G., and Sherkat, D. E. (1993) Conservative Protestantism and support for corporal punishment. *American Sociological Review*, 58, 131–44.

Ellman, I. M., and Lohr, S. (1997) Marriage as contract, opportunistic violence and other bad arguments for fault divorce. *University of Illinois Law Review*, 3, 718–72.

El-Or, T., and Aran, G. (1995) Giving birth to a settlement: Maternal thinking and political action of Jewish women on the West Bank. *Gender and Society*, 9, 600–78.

Elshtain, J. (1981) *Public Man, Private Woman*. Princeton, NJ: Princeton University Press.

Emery, R. E. (1994) *Renegotiating Family Relationships. Divorce, Child Custody and Mediation*. New York: Guildford Press.

Engels, F. (1972) *The Origin of the Family, Private Property, and the State*. New York: International Publishers.

England, P. (1982) The failure of human capital theory to explain occupational sex segregation. *Journal of Human Resources*, 17, 358–70.

England, P., and Budig, M. J. (1998) Gary Becker on the family: His genius, impact, and blind spots. In D. Clawson (ed.), *Required Reading: Sociology's Most Influential Books*. Amherst, MA: University of Massachusetts Press.

England, P., Budig, M. J. ,and Folbre, N. (2002) Wages of virtue: The relative pay of care work. *Social Problems*, 49, 455–73.

Epstein, S. (1990) Gay politics, ethnic identity: the limits of social constructionism. In E. Stein (ed.), *Forms of Desire: Sexual Orientation and the Social Constructionist Controversy*. New York and London: Garland.

Erera, P. I. (2002) Family Diversity: Continuity and Change in the Contemporary Family. Thousand Oaks, CA: Sage.

Ericksen, J. A., and Steffen, W. S. A. (1999) *Kiss and Tell: Surveying Sex in the Twentieth Century*. Cambridge, MA: Harvard University Press.

Ermisch, J. (1991) *Lone Parenthood*. Cambridge: Cambridge University Press.

Ermisch, J., and Francesconi, M. (1996) Partnership Formation and Dissolution in Great Britain. ESRC Research Centre on Micro Social Change Working Paper series No.96–10. London: Economic Social and Research Council.

Ermisch, J., and Francesconi, M. (1997) Family matters. ESRC Research Centre on Micro-Social Change Working Paper 97–1. Colchester: University of Essex.

Ermisch, J., and Francesconi, M. (2000) The effects of parents' employment on children's educational attainment. ISER Working Paper 2000–31. Colchester: University of Essex.

ESCAP (1998) *Asia and the Pacific into the 21st Century: Prospects for Social Development.* Kuala Lumpur: ESCAP.

Esping-Andersen, G. (1990) *The Three Worlds of Welfare Capitalism.* Princeton, NJ: Princeton University Press.

Esping-Andersen, G. (ed.) (1996) *Welfare States in Transition: National Adaptations in Global Economies.* Thousand Oaks, CA: Sage.

Esping-Andersen, G. (1999) *Social Foundations of Postindustrial Economies.* Oxford: Oxford University Press.

Espino, D. A., Neufeld, R. R., Mulvihill, M., and Libow, L. S. (1988) Hispanic and non-Hispanic elderly on admission to the nursing home: a pilot study. *The Gerontologist*, 28, 821–4.

Espiritu, Y. L. (1997) *Asian American Women and Men.* Thousand Oaks, CA: Sage.

Eurobarometer (1991) *Desire for Children.* Eurobarometer, No. 32.

European Commission (1998) *Care in Europe: A Joint Report of the "Gender and Employment" and the "Gender and Law" Groups of Experts.* Brussels: European Commission.

European Commission (1998) *Eurobarometer No. 50.1.* ESRC Data Archive, Essex, England.

European Commission (1998) *Men within Family and Work, European Network on Family and Work, No. 2/98.* Luxembourg: European Commission.

European Commission (1999) *Eurobarometer No. 51.* ESRC Data Archive, Essex, England.

European Commission 2000) *Eurobarometer No. 53.* ESRC Data Archive, Essex, England.

European Commission (2001) *Social Protection in the EU Member States and the European Economic Area.* Luxembourg: European Commission.

Eurostat (1994) *Demographic Statistics 1994.* Luxembourg: Office for Official Publications of the European Communities.

Eurostat (1996) *Labour Force Survey Results 1995.* Luxembourg: Office for Official Publications of the European Communities.

Eurostat (1997) *Statistics in Focus: Population and Social Conditions No. 14.* Luxembourg: Office for Official Publications of the European Communities.

Eurostat (2000) *European Social Statistics: Demography.* Luxembourg: Office for Official Publications of the European Communities.

Eurostat (2000), *Living Conditions in Europe – Statistical Pocketbook.* Luxembourg: Office for Official Publications of the European Communities.

Eurostat (2002) People in Europe. *Eurostat Yearbook 2002.* Luxembourg: Office for Official Publications of the European Communities.

Families USA (1997) *Unmet Needs: The Large Differences in Health Care Between Uninsured and Insured Children.* Available online at: http://www.familiesusa.org/media/reports/unmet.htm, last accessed June 6, 2002.

Farkas, J., and Hogan, D. (1995) The demography of changing intergenerational relationships. In V. L. Bengtson, K. W. Schaie, and L. M. Burton (eds.), *Adult Intergenerational Relations: Effects of Societal Change.* New York: Springer.

Federal Interagency Forum on Aging-Related Statistics (2000*) Older Americans 2000: Key Indicators of Well-Being. Federal Interagency Forum on Aging-Related Statistics.* Washington, DC: US Government Printing Office, August.

Federal Interagency Forum on Child and Family Statistics (2002) *America's Children: Key National Indicators of Well-Being.* Washington, DC: Government Printing Office.

Fehr, B., and Perlman, D. (1985) The family as a social network and support system. In L. L'Abate (ed.), *The Handbook of Family Psychology and Therapy.* Homewood, IL: Dorsey Press.

Feld, F., and Carter, W. C. (1998) Foci of activity as changing contexts for friendship. In R. G. Adams and G. Allan (eds.), *Placing Friendship in Context*. Cambridge: Cambridge University Press.

Felmlee, D. H. (2001) No couple is an island: A social network perspective on dyadic stability. *Social Forces*, 79, 1259–87.

Fennell, G. (1997) Local lives – distant ties. In J. Eade (ed.), *Living the Global City: Globalization as Local Process*. London: Routledge.

Fergusson, D., Horwood, J., and Shannon, F. (1984) A proportional hazards model of family breakdown. *Journal of Marriage and the Family*, 46, 539–49.

Fergusson, D., Horwood, L. J., and Lynskey, M. T. (1992) Family change, parental discord and early offending. *Journal of Child Psychology and Psychiatry*, 33, 1059–75.

Fernández-Kelly, M. P., and García, A. M. (1990) Power surrendered, power restored: The politics of work and family among Hispanic garment workers in California and Florida. In L. A. Tilly and P. Gurin (eds.), *Women, Politics and Change*. New York: Russell Sage Foundation.

Ferri, E. (1976) *Growing Up in a One-Parent Family*. Windsor: NFER.

Ferri, E. (1984) *Stepchildren: A National Study*. Atlantic Highlands, NJ: Humanities Press.

Ferri, E., and Smith, K. (1996) *Parenting in the 1990s*. London: Family Policy Studies Centre.

Field, F. (1995) *Making Welfare Work*. London: Institute of Community Studies.

Fields, J., and Casper, L. M. (2001) America's families and living arrangements: Population characteristics. *Current Population Reports*. Washington, DC: US Census Bureau.

Finch, J. (1983) *Married to the Job: Wives' Incorporation into Men's Jobs*. London: Allen & Unwin.

Finch, J., and Mason, J. (1993) *Negotiating Family Responsibilities*. London: Routledge.

Finch, J., and Summerfield, P. (1991) Social reconstruction and the emergence of companionate marriage. 1945–59. In D. Clark (ed.), *Marriage, Domestic Life and Social Change*. London: Routledge.

Fine, M. A., McKenry, P. C., Donnelly, B. W., and Voydanoff, P. (1992) Perceived adjustment of parents and children: Variations by family structure, race, and gender. *Journal of Marriage and the Family*, 54, 118–28.

Finkler, K. (2001) The kin in the gene: The medicalization of family and kinship in American society. *Current Anthropology*, 42, 235–63.

Finnegan, R. (1989) *The Hidden Musicians: Music-Making in an English Town*. Cambridge: Cambridge University Press.

Firestone, S. (1970) *The Dialectic of Sex*. New York: Bantam.

Firth, R., Hubert, J., and Forge, A. (1970) *Families and Their Relatives*. London: Routledge & Kegan Paul.

Fischer, C., and Oliker, S. (1983) A research note on friendship, gender and the life cycle. *Social Forces*, 62, 124–32.

Fischer, C. S. (1982). The dispersion of kin in modern society: Contemporary data and historical speculation. *Journal of Family History*, 7, 353–75.

Fischer, C. S. (1982) *To Dwell Among Friends. Personal Networks in Town and City*. Chicago: University of Chicago Press.

Fischer, C. S., Hout, M., Sanchez, M. J., Lucas, S. R., Swidler, A., and Voss, K. (1996) *Inequality by Design: Cracking the Bell Curve Myth*. Princeton, NJ: Princeton University Press.

Fischer, L. R. (1983) Mothers and mothers-in-law. *Journal of Marriage and the Family*, 45, 187–92.

Fisher, K. (2002) Chewing the Fat: the Story Time Diaries Tell About Physical Activity in the United Kingdom. *ISER Working Papers 2002–13*.

Fix, M. E., and Tumlin, K. (1997) *Welfare Reform and the Deevolution of Immigrant Policy*. Washington, DC: Urban Institute.

Flaks, D. K., Fischer, I., Masterpasqua, F., and Joseph, G. (1995) Lesbians choosing motherhood: A comparative study of lesbian and heterosexual parents and their children. *Developmental Psychology*, 31, 105–14.

Folbre, N. (1994) *Who Pays for the Kids? Gender and Structures of Constraint*. London: Routledge.

Folbre, N. (2001) *The Invisible Heart: Economics and Family Values*. New York: The New Press.

Foner, N. (1977) The Jamaicans. In J. Watson (ed.), *Between Two Cultures*. Oxford: Blackwell.

Foner, N. (1979) *Jamaica Farewell*. Berkeley: University of California Press.

Foner, N. (1986) Sex roles and sensibilities: Jamaican women in New York and London. In R. Simon and C. Brettell (eds.), *International Migration: The Female Experience*. Totowa, NJ: Rowman & Allanheld.

Foner, N. (1997) The immigrant family: Cultural legacies and cultural changes. *International Migration Review*, 31, 961–74.

Ford, R., Marsh, A., and McKay, S. (1995) *Changes in Lone Parenthood*. Department of Social Security Research Report No. 40. London: HMSO.

Forehand, R., Bordy, G., Long, N., Slotkin, J., and Fauber, R. (1986) Divorce/divorce potential and interparental conflict: The relationship to early adolescent social and cognitive functioning. *Journal of Adolescence Research*, 1, 389–97.

Forste, R. (2001) *Prelude to Marriage or Alternative to Marriage? A Social Demographic Look at Cohabitation in the U.S.* Manuscript prepared for Symposium on the ALI's Family Dissolution Principles: Blueprint to Strengthen or to Deconstruct Families? Brigham Young University, February 3.

Fortin, J. (1998) *Children's Rights and the Developing Law*. London: Butterworth.

Foster, J. (1999) *Docklands: Cultures in Conflict, Worlds in Collision*. London: UCL Press.

Foucault, M. (1979) *The History of Sexuality: Volume 1: An Introduction*. Harmondsworth: Penguin.

Fox, D. M. and Kassalow, J. S. (2001) Making health a priority of US foreign policy. *American Journal of Public Health*, 91, 1554–6.

Frank, D. J., and McEneaney, E. H. (1999) The individualization of society and the liberalization of state policies on same-sex sexual relations, 1984–1995. *Social Forces*, 77, 911–44.

Franklin, S. (2001) Biologization revisited: Kinship theory in the context of the new biologies. In S. Franklin and S. McKinnon (eds.), *Relative Values: Reconfiguring Kinship Studies*. Durham, NC: Duke University Press.

Franklin, S., and McKinnon, S. (eds.) (2001) *Relative Values: Reconfiguring Kinship Studies*. Durham, NC: Duke University Press.

Franks, S. (1999) *Having None of It. Women, Men and the Future of Work*. London: Granta.

Frazer, E. (1999) Unpicking political communitarianism. In G. Jagger and C. Wright (eds.), *Changing Family Values*. London: Routledge.

Freedman, D. S., and Thornton, A. (1979) The long-term impact of pregnancy at marriage on the family's economic circumstances. *Family Planning Perspectives*, 11, 6–13, 18–21.

Freeman, M. (1996) The new birth right? *International Journal of Children's Rights*, 4, 273–97.

Freeman, M. (2000) Disputing children. In S. Katz, J. Eekalaar, and M. Maclean (eds.), *Cross Currents: Family Law in the US and England*. Oxford: Oxford University Press.

Freeman, M. (2001) The child in family law. In J. Fionda (ed.), *Legal Concepts of Childhood*. Cambridge: Hart.

French, V. (2002) History of parenting: the ancient Mediterranean world. In M. H. Bornstein (ed.), *Handbook of Parenting: Biology and Ecology of Parenting*. 2nd ed. Vol. 2. Mahwah, NJ: Lawrence Erlbaum.

Frenk, J., Bobadilla, J. L., and Lozano, R. (1996) The epidemiological transition in Latin America. In I. Timaeus, J. Chackiel, and L. Ruzicka (eds.), *Adult Mortality in Latin America*. New York: Oxford University Press.

Friedan, B (1993) *The Fountain of Age*. New York: Simon & Schuster

Friedman, L., Chiriboga, D. A., and Catron, L. S. (1991) Social supports in the context of divorce. In D. A. Chiriboga and L. S. Catron (eds.), *Divorce: Crisis, Challenge, or Relief?* New York: New York University Press.

Frydenberg, E., and Lewis, R. (1997) *Coping Scale for Adults*. Melbourne: Australian Council for Educational Research.

Fuligni, A. J., Tseng, V., and Lam, M. (1999) Attitudes toward family obligations among American adolescents with Asian, Latin American, and European backgrounds. *Child Development*, 70, 1030–44.

Funder, K. (1997) Children's rights: Setting the scene. In K. Funder (ed.), *Citizen Child, Australian Law and Children's Rights*. Melbourne: Australian Institute of Family Studies.

Furstenberg, F. F., and Cherlin, A. J. (1991) *Divided Families. What Happens to Children when Parents Part*. Cambridge, MA: Harvard University Press.

Furstenberg, F. F., and Cherlin, A. J. (1994) *Divided Families: What Happens to Children When Parents Part*. Cambridge, MA: Harvard University Press.

Furstenberg, F. F., Cook, T., Eccles, J., Elder, G. H., Jr., and Sameroff, A. (1999). *Managing To Make It: Urban Families in High-Risk Neighborhoods*. Chicago: University of Chicago Press.

Furstenberg, F. F., and Kiernan, K. E. (2001) Delayed parental divorce: How much do children benefit? *Journal of Marriage and the Family*, 63, 446–57.

Furstenberg, F. F., and Spanier, G.. (1984) *Recycling the Family: Remarriage after Divorce*. Newbury Park, CA: Sage.

Furstenberg, F. F., and Winquist Nord, C. (1985) Parenting apart: Patterns of childrearing after marital disruption. *Journal of Marriage and the Family*, 47, 893–904.

Furstenberg, F. F., Jr. (1992) Family change and the welfare of children: What do we know and what can we do About it? Paper presented at the Seminar on Gender and Family Change in Industrialized Countries. Rome, January.

Furstenberg, F. F., Jr. (1995) Fathering in the inner city: Paternal participation and public policy. In W. Marsiglio (ed.), *Fatherhood: Contemporary Theory, Research, and Social Policy*. Thousand Oaks, CA: Sage.

Furstenberg, F. J., Jr. (1990) Divorce and the American family. *Annual Review of Sociology*, 16, 379–403.

Galton, F. (1907) *Probability, the Foundation of Eugenics. The Herbert Spencer Lecture*. Oxford: Clarendon Press.

Ganong, L. H., and Coleman, M. (1994) *Remarried Family Relationships*. Thousand Oaks, CA: Sage.

Gans, H. (1962) *The Urban Villagers*. New York: Free Press.

Gans, H. (1967) *The Levittowners: Ways of Life and Politics in a New Suburban Community*. New York: Vintage.

Gans, H. (1968) Urbanism and suburbanism as ways of life. In R. Pahl (ed.), *Readings in Urban Sociology*. Oxford: Pergamon.

Gans, H. J. (1962) *The Urban Villagers*. New York: The Free Press.

Gans, H. J. (1992) Second-generation decline: Scenarios for the economic and ethnic futures of post-1965 American immigrants. *Ethnic and Racial Studies*, 15, 173–92.

Garcia, J., Kilpatrick, R., and Richards, M. (eds.) (1990) *The Politics of Maternity Care*. Oxford: Oxford University Press.

Gardner, K. (1995) Global Migrants, Local Lives: Travel and Transformation in Rural Bangladesh. Oxford: Clarendon Press.

Garfinkel, I., and McLanahan, S. (1985) The Nature, Causes and Cures of the Feminization of Poverty. Paper delivered at the Annual Meeting of the Population Association of America, Boston.

Garrett, B., and Holahan, J. (2000) *Welfare Leavers, Medicaid Coverage, and Private Health Insurance*. Washington, DC: Urban Institute.

Gaskell, G. and Bauer, M. W. (eds.) (2001) *Biotechnology 1996–2000*. London: Science Museum.

Gasparini, G., Parent-Thiron, A., Latta, M., and de Nanteuil, M. (2000) *Full-Time or Part-Time Work: Realities and Options*. Dublin: European Foundation for the Improvement of Living and Working Conditions.

Gates, G. J., and. Sonenstein, F. L (2000) Heterosexual genital sexual activity among adolescent males: 1988 and 1995. *Family Planning Perspectives*, 32, 295–7, 304.

Gauthier, A. (1996) *The State and the Family: A Comparative Analysis of Family Policies in Industrialized Countries*. Oxford: Clarendon Press.

Gelis, J. (1991) *History of Childbirth: Fertility, Pregnancy, and Birth in Early Modern Europe*. Boston: Northeastern University Press.

General Household Survey (2001) *Living in Britain: Results from the 2000 General Household Survey*. London: Stationery Office.

Gershuny, J. (1995) Relationships between women's employment and other activities. In R. Bayley, A. Condy, and C. Roberts (eds.), *Policies for Families: Work, Poverty and Resources*. London: Family Policy Studies Centre.

Gershuny, J. (2000) *Changing Times: Work and Leisure in Post-industrial Societies*. Oxford: Oxford University Press.

Gershuny, J., and Robinson, J. (1998) Historical changes in the household division of labour. *Demography*, 25, 4, 537–52.

Giarrusso, R., Feng, D., Silverstein, M., and Bengtson, V. L. (2001) Grandparent–adult grandchild affection and consensus: Cross-generational and cross-ethnic comparisons. *Journal of Family Issues*, 22, 456–77.

Giarrusso, R., Silverstein, M., Feng, D., and Marenco, A. (2000) Primary and secondary stressors of grandparents raising grandchildren: Evidence from a national survey. *Journal of Mental Health and Aging*, 6, 4, 291–310.

Giarrusso, R., Stallings, M., and Bengtson, V. L. (1995) The "intergenerational stake" hypothesis revisited: Parent–child differences in perceptions of relationships 20 years later. In V. L. Bengtson, K. W. Schaie, and L. M. Burton (eds.), *Adult Intergenerational Relations: Effects of Societal Change*. New York: Springer.

Gibson, C. (1994) *Dissolving Wedlock*. London: Routledge.

Gibson, M. A. (1988) *Accommodation Without Assimilation: Sikh Immigrants in an American High School*. Ithaca, NY: Cornell University Press.

Giddens, A. (1991) *Modernity and Self-Identity: Self and Society in the Late Modern Age*. Cambridge: Polity.

Giddens, A. (1992) *The Transformation of Intimacy: Sexuality, Love and Eroticism in Modern Societies*. Oxford: Polity.

Giddens, A. (1998) *The Third Way: The Renewal of Social Democracy*. Cambridge: Polity.

Giddens, A. (1999) *Runaway World: How Globalization Is Reshaping Our Lives*. London: Profile Books.

Giele, J., and Elder, G., Jr. (1998) *Methods of Life Course Research: Qualitative and Quantitative Approaches*. London: Sage.

Gilby, R. L., and Pederson, D. R. (1982). The development of the child's concept of family. *Canadian Journal of Behavioral Sciences*, 14, 111–21.

Gilleard, C., and Higgs, P. (2000) *Cultures of Aging*. London: Prentice-Hall.

Gillis, J. (1985) *For Better, For Worse: British Marriages 1600 to Present*. Oxford: Oxford University Press.

Gillis, J. (1997) *A World of Their Own Making: A History of Myth and Ritual in Family Life*. Oxford: Oxford University Press.

Gillis, J. R. (1996) *A World of Their Own Making*. Oxford: Oxford University Press.

Gilmore, D. D. (1990) *Manhood in the Making: Cultural Concepts of Masculinity*. New Haven, CT: Yale University Press.

Ginn, J., Street, D., and Arber, S. (2001) *Women, Work and Pensions*. Buckingham: Open University Press.

Glass, J. L., and Estee, B. S. (1997) Workplace support childcare and turnover intentions among employed mothers of infants. *Journal of Family Issues*, 17, 317–35.

Glass, J. L., and Estee, S. B. (1997) The family-responsive workplace. *Annual Review of Sociology*, 23, 289–304.

Glass, N. (2001) What works for children? The political issues. *Children and Society*, 15, 14–20.

Glass, S. P., and Wright, T. L. (1992) Justifications for extramarital relationships: The association between attitudes, behaviors, and gender. *Journal of Sex Research*, 29, 361–87.

Glendon, M. A. (1989) *The Transformation of Family Law: State, Law, and Family in the United States and Europe*. Chicago: University of Chicago Press.

Glenn, E. N. (1986) *Issei, Nisei, War Bride: Three Generation of Japanese American Women in Domestic Service*. Philadelphia: Temple University Press.

Glennon, L. (2000) *Fitzpatrick v Sterling Housing Association Ltd* – An endorsement of the functional family? *International Journal of Law, Policy and the Family*, 14, 226–53.

Glick, P. C. (1989) Remarried families, stepfamilies, and stepchildren: A brief demographic profile. *Family Relations*, 38, 24–7.

Goetting, A. (1983) The relative strength of the husband-wife and parent-child dyads in remarriage: A test of the Hsu model. *Journal of Comparative Family Studies*, 14, 117–28.

Goetting, A. (1986). The developmental tasks of siblingship over the life cycle. *Journal of Marriage and the Family*, 48, 703–14.

Goldscheider, F. K., and Goldscheider, C. (1989) The new family economy: residential and economic relationships among the generations. In F. K. Goldscheider and C. Goldscheider (eds.), *Ethnicity and the New Family Economy: Living Arrangements and Intergenerational Financial Flows*. Boulder, CO: Westview Press.

Goldscheider, F. K., and Goldscheider, C. (1993) *Leaving Home before Marriage: Ethnicity, Familism, and Generational Relationships*. Madison: University of Wisconsin Press.

Goldstein, J. R. (1999) The levelling of divorce in the United States. *Demography*, 36, 409–14.

Goldstein, J., and Warren, J. R. (2000) Socioeconomic research and heterogeneity in the extended family: contours and consequences. *Social Science Research*, 29, 382–404.

Goldthorpe, J., Lockwood, D., Bechhofer, F., and Platt, J. (1969) *The Affluent Worker in the Class Structure*. Cambridge: Cambridge University Press.

Golombok, S., Brewaeys, A., Cook, R., Giavazzi, M. T., Guerra, G., Mantovanni, A., Van Hall, E., Crosignani, P. G., and Dexeus, S. (1996) The European study of assisted reproduction families. *Human Reproduction*, 11, 2324–31.

Golombok, S., Brewaeys, A., Giavazzi, M.T., Guerra, G., Mantovanni, A., Van Hall, E., Crosignani, P. G., and Dexeus, S. 1996. (2002a) The European study of assisted reproduction families: The transition to adolescence. *Human Reproduction*, 17, 830–40.

Golombok, S., MacCallum, F. M., Goodman, E., and Rutter, M. (2002b) Parenting and contemporary reproductive technologies. In M. H. Barnstein (ed.), *Handbook of Parenting*, 2nd ed. Vol. 3. Mahwah, NJ: Lawrence Erlbaum.

Goode, E. (2002) Group backs gays who seek to adopt a partner's child. *New York Times*, February 4, pp. A1, A21.

Goode, W. J. (1970) *World Revolution and Family Patterns*. New York: Free Press.

Goode, W. J. (1993) *World changes in divorce patterns*. New Haven, CT: Yale University Press.

Goodin, R., Headey, B., Muffels, R., and Dirvan, H-J. (1999) *The Real Worlds of Welfare Capitalism*. Cambridge: Cambridge University Press.

Goodstein, J. D. (1994) Institutional pressures and strategic responsiveness; employer involvement in work-family issues. *Academy Management Journal*, 37, 350–82.

Gordon, D., and Pantazis, C. (1997) *Breadline Britain in the 1990s*. Aldershot: Ashgate.

Gordon, D., and Townsend, P. (2000) *Breadline Europe*. Bristol: Policy Press.

Gordon, M. H. (1990) Dependents or independent workers? The status of Caribbean immigrant women in the United States. In R. W. Palmer (ed.), *In Search of a Better Life: Perspectives on Migration from the Caribbean*. New York: Praeger.

Gordon, M. M. (1964) *Assimilation in American Life*. Oxford: Oxford University Press.

Gornick, J., and Meyers, M. (2001) Support for working families. *The American Prospect*.

Gorrell Barnes, G., Thompson, P., Daniel, G., and Burchardt, N. (1998) *Growing Up in Stepfamilies*. Oxford: Clarendon Press.

Gosling, A., Machin, S., and Meghir, C. (1996) The changing distribution of male wages in the UK. Paper No. 275. London: Centre for Economic Performance, London School of Economics.

Goss, R. E. (1997) Queering procreative privilege: coming out as families. In R. E. Goss and A. S. Strongheart (eds.), *Our Families, Our Values: Snapshots of Queer Kinship*. Binghampton, NJ: Harrington Park Press.

Goulborne, H. (1999) The transnational character of Caribbean kinship in Britain. In S. McRae (ed.), *Changing Britain: Families and Households in the 1990s*. Oxford: Oxford University Press.

Gove, W. R. (1973) Sex, marital status and mortality. *American Journal of Sociology*, 79, 45–67.

Graefe, D., and Lichter, D. (1999) Life course transitions of American children: Parental cohabitation, marriage, and single motherhood. *Demography*, 36, 205–18.

Grasmuck, S., and Pessar, P. R. (1991) *Between Two Islands: Dominican International Migration*. Berkeley: University of California Press.

Greeley, A. M. (1991) *Faithful Attraction*. New York: Tom Doherty Associates.

Gregg, P., Harkness, S., and Machin, S. (1999) *Child Development and Family Income*. York: Joseph Rowntree Foundation.

Gregory, J. D., Swisher, P. N., and Wolf, S. L. (2001) *Understanding Family Law*. USA: Matthew Bender.

Gregson, N., and Lowe, M. (1993) Renegotiating the domestic division of labour? A study of dual career households in north- east and south-east England. *Sociological Review*, 41, 475–505.

Greven, J., Jr. (1970) *Four Generations: Population, Land, and Family in Colonial Andover, Massachusetts*. Ithaca NY: Cornell University Press.

Greven, J., Jr. (1977) *The Protestant Temperament: Patterns of Child-Rearing, Religious Experience, and the Self in Early America*. New York: New American Library.

Grieco, M. (1987) *Keeping it in the Family: Social Networks and Employment Chance*. London: Tavistock.

Griffiths, J. (1999) Fathers as mothers: lone parenting for men. In G. Dench (ed.), *Rewriting the Sexual Contract*. New Brunswick, NJ: Transaction.

Grokevart, M. D., and McRoy, R. G. (1998) *Openness in Adoption. Exploring Family Connections*. New York: Sage.

Groves, E. and Ogburn, W. F. (1928) *American Marriage and Family Relations*. New York: Henry Holt.

Grubbs, J. E. (1999) *Law and Family in Late Antiquity. The Emperor Constantine's Marriage Legislation*. Oxford: Oxford University Press.

Guendelman, S., and Pérez-Itriago, A. (1987) Double lives: The changing role of women in seasonal migration. *Women's Studies*, 13, 249–71.

Guo, G., and Harris, K. M. (2000) The mechanisms mediating the effects of poverty on children's intellectual development. *Demography*, 37, 431–47.

Gutmann, D. L. (1975) Parenting: A key to the comparative study of the life cycle. In N. Datan and L. H. Ginsberg (eds.), *Life-Span Developmental Psychology: Normative Life Crises*. New York: Academic.

Guyer, B., Hoyert, D. L., Martin, J. A., Ventura, S. J., MacDorman, M. F., and Strobino, D. M. (1999) Annual summary of vital statistics: 1998. *Pediatrics*, 104, 1229–46.

Gwatkin, D. R. (2000) Health inequalities and the health of the poor: What do we know? What can we do? *Bulletin of the World Health Organization*, 78, 3–18.

Haas, L., Hwang, P., and Russell, G. (eds.) (2000) *Organisational Change and Gender Equity: International Perspectives on Fathers and Mothers at the Workplace*. Thousand Oaks, CA: Sage.

Hagenaars, A. K. de Vos, and Zaida, A. (1994) *Poverty Statistics in the Late 1980s*. Luxembourg: Eurostat.

Haggerty, R. J., Roghmann, K. J., and Pless, I. B. (1975) *Child Health and the Community.* New York: Free Press.

Haimes, E. (1993) Issues of gender in gamete donation. *Social Science and Medicine*, 36, 85–93.

Haimes, E. (1998) The making of "the DI child": Changing representations of people conceived through donor insemination. In K. Daniels and E. Haimes (eds.), *Donor Insemination: International Social Science Perspectives.* Cambridge: Cambridge University Press.

Hakim, C. (1996) *Female Heterogeneity and the Polarisation of Women's Employment, Key Issues in Women's Work.* London: Athlone.

Hakim, C. (2000) *Work-Lifestyle Choices in the 21st* Century: Preference Theory. Oxford: Oxford University Press.

Hall, R., Ogden, P. E., and Hill, C. (1999) Living alone: Evidence from England and Wales and France for the last two decades. In S. McRae (ed.), *Changing Britain: Families and Households in the 1990s.* Oxford: Oxford University Press.

Hamilton, D. (1993) A house, cash – And no parents. *Los Angeles Times*, June 24.

Hanmer, J. (1987) Transforming consciousness. Women and the new reproductive technologies. In G. Cerea et al. (eds.), *Man-Made Women.* Bloomington: Indiana University Press.

Hanscombe, G., and Forster, J. (1982) *Rocking the Cradle: Lesbian Mothers. A Challenge in Family Living.* London: Sheba Feminist Publishers.

Hantrais, L., and Letablier, M-T. (1996) *Families and Family Policy in Europe.* New York: Longman.

Harding, S., and Phillips, D. (1986) *Contrasting Values in Western Europe.* London: Macmillan.

Hareven, T. (1977) Family time and historical time. *Daedalus*, 106, 57–70.

Hareven, T. (1982) *Family Time and Industrial Time: The Relationship Between the Family and Work in a New England Industrial Community.* Cambridge: Cambridge University Press.

Hareven, T. (2000) *Families, History and Social Change; Life Course and Cross-Cultural Perspectives.* Oxford: Westview.

Hareven, T. K. (2001) Historical perspectives on aging and family relations. In R.H. Binstock and L.K. George (eds.), *Handbook of Aging and the Social Sciences.* San Diego: Academic.

Harkness, S., Machin, S., and Waldfogel, J. (1995) *Evaluating the pin money hypothesis: The relationship between women's labour market activity, family income and poverty in Britain.* Welfare State Programme 108. London: STICERD, London School of Economics.

Harper, P. S., Lim, S., and Craufurt, D. (2000) Ten years of pre symptomatic testing for Huntington's disease: The experience of the UK Huntington's disease consortium. *Journal of Medical Genetics*, 37, 567–71.

Harris, C. (1980) The changing relation between family and societal form in western society. In M. Anderson (ed.), *Sociology of the Family.* 2nd ed. Harmondsworth: Penguin.

Harris, C. (1987) *Redundancy and Recession in South Wales.* Oxford: Basil Blackwell.

Harris, C. (1990) *Kinship.* Milton Keynes: Open University Press.

Harris, C. C. (1983) *The Family and Industrial Society.* London: Allen & Unwin.

Harris, J. (1982) The political status of children. In K. Graham (ed.), *Contemporary Political Philosophy.* Cambridge: Cambridge University Press.

Harris, J. (1998) *Clones, Genes and Immortality: Ethics and the Genetic Revolution.* Oxford: Clarendon Press.

Harris, J. R. (1995) Where is the child's environment? a group socialization theory of development. *Psychological Review*, 102, 458–89.

Harris, J. R. (1998) *The Nurture Assumption: Why Children Turn Out the Way They Do.* New York: Simon & Schuster.

Harris, K. M. (1996) Life after welfare: Women, work, and repeat dependency. American *Sociological Review*, 61, 407–26.

Harry, J. (1984) *Gay Couples.* New York: Praeger.

Harry, J., and DeVall, W. B. (1978) *The Social Organisation of Gay Male.* New York: Praeger.

Hartmann, H. (1979) The unhappy marriage of Marxism and Feminism: Towards a more progressive union. *Capital and Class*, 8, 1–33.

Hartmann, H. (1981) The family as the locus of gender, class, and political struggle: The example of housework. *Signs*, 6, 366–94.
Haskey, J. (1994) Stepfamilies and stepchildren in Great Britain. *Population Trends*, 76, 17–28.
Haskey, J. (1996) The proportion of married couples who divorce: Past patterns and current prospects. *Population Trends*, 83, 25–36.
Haskey, J. (1999) Cohabitational and marital histories of adults in Great Britain. *Population Trends*, 96, 13–24.
Haskey, J. (2001) Cohabitation in Great Britain: Past, present and future trends – and attitudes. *Population Trends*, 103, 5–25.
Hatem, M. (1974) Egyptian gender discourse and political liberalisation: Do secularist and Islamic views really differ? *Middle East Journal*, 48(4), 661–76.
Hauser, R. M., and Kuo, H. H. D. (1998) Does the gender composition of sibships affect women's educational attainment? *Journal of Human Resources*, 33, 644–57.
Havas, E. (1995) The family as ideology. *Social Policy and Administration*, 29, 1–9.
Haveman, R., and Wolfe, B. (1995) The determinants of children's attainment: A review of methods and findings. *Journal of Economic Literature*, 33, 1829–78.
Hayes, B. (1997) The influence of gender on public attitudes toward homosexual rights in Britain. *International Journal of Public Opinion Research*, 9, 361–85.
Hayner, N. S. (1927) Hotel homes. *Sociology and Social Research*, 12, 124–31.
Haynes, F. E. (2000) Gender and family ideals: An exploratory study of black middle-class Americans. *Journal of Family Issues*, 21, 811–37.
Hayward, M. D., and Zhang, Z. (2001) Demography of aging: a century of global change, 1950–2050. In R. H. Binstock and L. K. George (eds.), *Handbook of Aging and the Social Sciences*. 5th ed. New York: Academic Press.
Health Care Financing Administration (2000) *The State Children's Health Insurance Program: Preliminary Highlights of Implementation and Expansion*. Washington, DC: US Department of Health and Human Services.
Health Insurance Association of America (2000) *Guide to Long-Term Healthcare*. Available online at: http://www.hiaa.org/cons/guideltc.html, last accessed February 22, 2001.
Heaphy, B., Weeks, J., and Donovan, C. (1999) Narratives of love, care and commitment: AIDS/HIV and non-heterosexual family formations. In P. Aggleton, G. Hart, and P. Davies (eds.), *Families and Communities Responding to AIDS*. London: UCL Press.
Hearn, J. (1998) *The Violences of Men*. London: Sage.
Heider, F. (1958) *The Psychology of Interpersonal Relations*. New York: John Wiley.
Heller, C. (1966) *Mexican American Youth: Forgotten Youth at the Crossroads*. New York: Random House.
Hemstrom, O. (1996) Is marriage dissolution linked to differences in mortality risks for men and women? *Journal of Marriage and the Family*, 58, 366–78.
Henry, L. (1968) Historical demography. *Daedalus*, 97, 385–96.
Hernández, D. J. (1993) *America's Children: Resources from Family, Government and the Economy*. New York: Russell Sage Foundation.
Hernández, D. J., and Charney, E. (eds.) (1998) *From Generation to Generation: The Health and Well-Being of Children in Immigrant Families*. Washington, DC: National Academy Press.
Hess, R. D., and Handel, G. (1959) *Family Worlds: A Psychosocial Approach to Family Life*. Chicago: University of Chicago Press.
Hetherington, E. M. (1999) Should we stay together for the sake of the children? In E. M. Hetherington (ed.), *Coping with Divorce, Single Parenting, and Remarriage. A Risk and Resiliency Perspective*. Mahwah, NJ: Lawrence Erlbaum.
Hetherington, E. M., and Kelly, J. (2002) *For Better or For Worse: Divorce Reconsidered*. New York: Norton.
Hetherington, E. M., and Stanley-Hagan, M. (2000) Diversity among stepfamilies. In D. H. Demo, K. R. Allen and M. A. Fine (eds.), *Handbook of Family Diversity*. New York: Oxford University Press.

Hewitt, P. (1993) *About Time*. London: IPPR/Oram Press.

Hewlitt, S. A. (2002) *Baby Hunger: The New Battle for Motherhood*. London: Atlantic Books.

Hibbett, A., and Beatson, M. (1995) Young people at work. *Employment Gazette*, 103, 4, 169–72.

Hill, C. (1977) *Milton and the English Revolution*. London: Faber & Faber.

Hill, M., and Yeung, W-J. J. (2000) Behavior and Status of Children and Young Adults. *Generations and Gender Programme: Exploring future research and data collection options*, New York and Geneva: United Nations Economic Commission for Europe, United Nations Population Fund, 1-57 UNESCO children.

Hill, S. (1976) *The Dockers: Class and Tradition in London*. London: Heinemann.

Hills, J. (1995) *Income and Wealth*. Vol.2. York: Joseph Rowntree Foundation.

Hills, J. (ed.) (1999) *Persistent Poverty and Lifetime Inequality: The Evidence*. London: CASE/HM Treasury, CASE report 5.

Hilton, J. M., Desrochers, S., and Devall, E. L. (2001) Comparison of role demands, relationships, and child functioning in single-mother, single-father, and intact families. *Journal of Divorce and Remarriage*, 35, 29–56.

Himes, C. L. (2001) Elderly Americans. *Population Bulletin*, 56(4). Washington, DC: Population Reference Bureau, December. Retrieved from: http://www.prb.org/Content/NavigationMenu/PRB/AboutPRB/Population_Bulletin2/Elderly_Americans.htm

His Grace the Archbishop of Canterbury's Communication (1948) *Artificial Human Insemination*. London: Society for the Propagation of Human Knowledge.

Hobart, C. (1987) Parent–child relations in remarried families. *Journal of Family Issues*, 3, 259–77.

Hobbs, S., and McKechnie, J. (1998) Children and work in the UK: the evidence. In B. Pettit (ed.), *Children and Work in the UK: Reassessing the Issues*. London: Child Poverty Action Group.

Hobcraft, J. N., and Kiernan, K. (1995) Becoming a Parent in Europe. Plenary paper for European Population Conference. In EAPS/*IUSSP Proceedings of European Population Conference* Milan, September, 27–65. Also available as LSE STICERD Discussion Paper No. 116, 58pp.

Hobfoll, S. E. (1988) *The Ecology of Stress*. New York: Hemisphere.

Hobson, B. (ed.), (2002) *Making Men into Fathers: Men, Masculinities and The Social Politics of Fatherhood*. Cambridge: Cambridge University Press.

Hobson, B., and Morgan, D. (2002) Introduction: Making men into fathers. In B. Hobson (ed.), *Making Men Into Fathers: Men, Masculinities and the Social Politics of Fatherhood*. Cambridge: Cambridge University Press.

Hochschild, A. (1989) *The Second Shift: Working Parents and the Revolution of the Home*. New York: Viking.

Hochschild, A. (1990) *The Second Shift: Working Parents and the Revolution at Home*. London: Piatkus.

Hochschild, A. (1997) *The Time Bind: When Work Becomes Home and Home Becomes Work*. New York: Henry Holt.

Hochschild, A. (2001) Eavesdropping children, adult deals, and cultures of care. In R. Hertz and N. Marshall (eds.), *Working Families*. Berkeley: University of California Press.

Hochschild, A. (2001) Global care chains and emotional surplus value. In W. Hutton and A. Giddens (eds.), *On the Edge: Living with Global Capitalism*. London: Vintage.

Hoem, J., and Hoem, B. (1988) The Swedish family: Aspects of contemporary developments. *Journal of Family Issues*, 9, 397–424.

Hofferth, S. L., and Sandberg, J. F. (2001) How American children spend their time? *Journal of Marriage and the Family*, 63, 295–308.

Hofferth, S. L., Boisjoly, J., and Duncan, G. J. (1998) Parents' extrafamilial resources and children's school attainment. *Sociology of Education*, 71, 246–68.

Hoffman, C., and Scholobohm, A. (2000) *Uninsured in America: A Chart Book* Washington, DC: Kaiser Commission on Medicaid and the Uninsured.

Hoffman, E. (1981) Accounting for time on Labour Force Surveys. *Bulletin of Labour Statistics* 1. Geneva: International Labour Organization.

Hoffman, L. W. (1977) Changes in family roles, socialization, and sex differences. *American Psychologist*, 32, 644–57.

Hoffman, L. W. (1979) Maternal employment: 1979. *American Psychologist*, 34, 859–65.

Hoffman, L. W. (1989) Effects of maternal employment in the two-parent family: A review of recent research. *American Psychologist*, 44, 283–92.

Hogarth, T., Hasluck, C., Pierre, G., Winterbotham, M., and Vivian, D. (2000) *Work Life Balance 2000: Baseline Study of Work–Life Balance Practices in Great Britain*. Warwick: Institute for Employment Research, Warwick University.

Hoggett, P. (ed.) (1997) *Contested Communities: Experiences, Struggles, Policies*. Bristol: Policy Press.

Holahan, J., and Kim, J. (2000) Why does the number of uninsured Americans continue to grow? *Health Affairs,* 19, 188–96.

Hollingshead, A. de B. (1949) *Elmtown's Youth: The Impact of Social Classes on Adolescents*. New York: Wiley.

Holman, B. (ed.) (1998) *Faith in the Poor*. Oxford: Lion Publishing.

Holman, T. B. (1981) The influence of community involvement on marital quality. *Journal of Marriage and the Family*, 143, 43–149.

Holstein, B. E., Almind, G., Due, P., and Holst, E. (1991) The Home-Help service in Denmark. In A. Jamieson (ed.), *Home Care for Older People in Europe: A Comparison of Policies and Practices*. Oxford: Oxford University Press.

Holt, J. (1974) *Escape from Childhood: the Needs and Rights of Children*. Harmondsworth: Penguin.

Holtermann, S., Brannen, J., Moss, P., and Owen, C. (1999) Lone parents and the labour market: Results from the 1997 Labour Force Survey and review of research. Employment Service Research Department Report, ESR23. London: Department of Employment.

Holtzer, H., and LaLonde, R. J. (2000) Employment and job stability among less skilled workers. In D. E. Card and R. M. Blank (eds.), *Finding Jobs: Work and Welfare Reform*. New York: Russell Sage Foundation.

Holtzer, H., Stoll, M., and Wissoker, D. (2001) *Job Performance and Retention Among Welfare Recipients*. Paper presented at the Annual Conference of the Association of Policy Analysis and Management, Washington, DC, November 1–3.

Home Office (2002) Secure Borders, Safe Haven: Integration with Diversity in Modern Britain. Parliamentary White Paper, London: HMSO.

Hondagneu-Sotelo, P. (1994) *Gendered Transitions: Mexican Experiences of Immigration*. Los Angeles: University of California Press.

Hondagneu-Sotelo, P., and Avila, E. (1997) "I'm here, but I'm there": The meanings of Latina transnational motherhood. *Gender and Society*, 11, 548–71.

Hood, J. C. (ed.) (1993) *Men, Work and Family*. Newbury Park, CA: Sage.

hooks, b. (1984) *Feminist Theory: From Margin to Center*. Boston: South End Press.

Hope, S., Power, C., and Rodgers, B. (1999) Does financial hardship account for elevated psychological distress in lone mothers? *Social Science and Medicine*, 49, 1637–49.

Hoppe, S. K., and Heller, P. L. (1975) Alienation, familism, and the utilization of health services by Mexican-Americans. *Journal of Health and Social Behavior*, 16, 304–14.

Horwitz, A. V., White, H. R., and Howell-White, S. (1996) Becoming married and mental health: A longitudinal study of a cohort of young adults. *Journal of Marriage and the Family*, 58, 895–907.

House, J. S., Landis, K., and Umberson, D. (1988) Social relationships and health. *Science*, 241, 540–5.

House, J. S., Umberson, D., and Landis, K. R. (1988) Structures and processes of social support. *Annual Review of Sociology*, 14, 293–318.

Houseknecht, S. K., and Sastry, J. (1996) Family "decline" and child well-being: A comparative assessment. *Journal of Marriage and the Family*, 58, 726–39.

Howe, D. and Feast, J. (2000) *Adoption, Search and Reunion*. London: Children's Society.

Hoyt, D., and Babchuk N. (1983) Adult kinship networks: The selective formation of intimate ties with kin. *Social Forces*, 62, 84–101.

Hsu, F. (1971) *Kinship and Culture*. Chicago: Aldine.

Huber, J. (1991) A theory of family, economy, and gender. In R. L. Blumberg (ed.), *Gender, Family, and Economy: The Triple Overlap*. Newbury Park, CA: Sage.

Hughes, J. (1996) The philosopher's child. In R. Ladd (ed.), *Children's Rights Revisioned, Philosophical Readings*. London, New York, and Belmont: Wadsworth.

Hulsether, M. D. (2000) Like a sermon: Popular religion in Madonna videos. In B. D. Forbes and J. H. Mahan (eds.), *Religion and Popular Culture in America*. Berkeley: University of California Press.

Hunt, P. (1978) Cash transactions and household tasks. *Sociological Review*, 26, 555–71.

Hurlbert, J. S., and Acock, A. (1990) The effects of marital status on the form and composition of social networks. *Social Science Quarterly*, 71, 163–74.

Hutton, W., and Giddens, A. (eds.) (2001) *On the Edge: Living with Global Capitalism*. London: Vintage.

Iacopino, V., Frank, M. W., Bauer, H. M., Keller, A. S., Fink, S. L., Ford, D., Pallin, D. J., and Waldman, R. (2001) A population-based assessment of human rights abuses committed against ethnic Albanian refugees from Kosovo. *American Journal of Public Health*, 91, 2013–18.

Iacovou, M., and Berthoud, R. (2001) *Young People's Lives: A Map of Europe*. London: Institute of Economic and Social Research.

Illouz, E. (1997) *Consuming the Romantic Utopia. Love and the Cultural Contradictions of Capitalism*. Berkeley: University of California Press.

*International Journal of Law, Policy and Family* (2001) special issue, *Unmarried Cohabitation in Europe*, 15, 1.

Ishii-Kuntz, M. (1997) Intergenerational relationships among Chinese, Japanese, and Korean Americans. *Family Relations*, 46, 23–32.

Ishii-Kuntz, M. (2000) Diversity within Asian American families. In D. H. Demo, K. R. Allen, and M. A. Fine (eds.), *Handbook of Family Diversity*. New York: Oxford University Press.

Jaccard, J., Dittus, P. J., and Gordon, V. V. (1996) Maternal correlates of adolescent sexual and contraceptive behavior. *Family Planning Perspectives*, 28, 159–65, 185.

Jackson, E. (2001) *Regulating Reproduction. Law, Technology and Autonomy*. Oxford: Hart.

Jackson, M. H. (1945) A medical service for the treatment of involuntary sterility. *Eugenic Review*, 36, 117–25.

Jacobs, J. A. (1998) Measuring time at work: An assessment of the accuracy of self reports. *Monthly Labor Review*, 121, 42–53.

Jacobson, J. (1998) Islam in Transition: Religion and Identity Among British Pakistani Youth. London: Routledge.

James, A., and Prout, A. (eds.) (1990) *Constructing and Reconstructing Childhood: Contemporary Issues in the Sociological Study of Childhood*. London: Falmer.

James, A., and Prout, A. (1996) Strategies and structures: towards a new perspective on children's experiences of family life. In J. Brannen and M. O'Brien (eds.), *Children in Families: Research and Policy*. London: Falmer.

James, A. L., and James, A. (1999) Pump up the volume. Listening to children in separation and divorce. *Childhood*, 6, 189–206.

Jamieson, L. (1998) *Intimacy*. Cambridge: Polity.

Jamieson, L. (1999) Intimacy transformed? A critical look at the pure relationship. *Sociology*, 33, 477–94.

Jankowski, M. (1991) *Islands in the Street: Gangs and American Urban Society*. Berkeley: University of California Press.

Jasper, J. (2000) *Restless Nation: Starting Over in America*. Chicago: University of Chicago Press.

Jaspers, K. (1968) *The Origin and Goal of History*. New Haven, CT: Yale University Press.

Jeffery, P. M. (1976) Migrants and Refugees: Muslim and Christian Pakistani Families In Britain. Cambridge: Cambridge University Press.

Jekielek, S. M. (1998) Parental conflict, marital disruption and children's emotional well-being. *Social Forces*, 76, 905–36.

Jencks, C., Bartlett, S., Corcoran, M., Crouse, J., Eaglesfield, D., Jackson, G., McClelland, K., Mueser, P., Olneck, M., Schwartz, J., Ward, S., and Williams J. (1979) *Who Gets Ahead? The Determinants of Economic Success in America*. New York: Basic Books.

Jensen, A-M. (1994) The feminization of childhood. In J. B. Qvortrup, M. Bardy, G. Sgritta, and H. Wintersberger (eds.), *Childhood Matters: Social Theory, Practice and Politics*. Aldershot: Avebury.

Johnson, C. L. (1988) *Ex-Familia: Grandparents, Parents and Children Adjust to Divorce*. New Brunswick, NJ: Rutgers University Press.

Johnson, C. L. (2000). Perspectives on American kinship in the later 1990s. *Journal of Marriage and the Family*, 62, 623–39.

Johnson, C. L., and Barer B. M. (1987) Marital instability and changing kinship networks of grandparents. *The Gerontologist*, 27, 330–5.

Johnson, M. (1999) A biomedical perspective on parenthood. In A. Bainham, S. Day-Sclater and M. Richards (eds.), *What is a Parent? A Socio Legal Analysis*. Oxford: Hart.

Johnson, M. J., and Milardo, R. M. (1984) Network interference in pair relationships: A social psychological recasting of Slater's theory of social regression. *Journal of Marriage and the Family*, 46, 893–9.

Johnston, J. R., and Campbell, L. (1988) *Impasses of Divorce. The Dynamics and Resolution of Family Conflict*. New York: Free Press.

Jones, E. M., Forrest, J. D., Goldman, N., Henshaw, S., Lincoln, R., Rosoff, J. I., Westoff, C. F., and Wulf, D. (1986) *Teenage Pregnancy in Industrialized Countries: A Study*. New Haven, CT: Yale University Press.

Joshi, H. (1996) *The Opportunity Costs of Childbearing: More than Mothers' Business*. Lecture to the British Society for Population Studies, St Andrews, September.

Joshi, H. E. (2000) *Maternal Employment and Child Outcomes*. London: Smith Institute.

Joshi, H., Cooksey, E., Wiggins, R., McCulloch, A., Verropoulou, G., and Clarke, L. (1999) Diverse family living situations and child development: a multi-level analysis comparing longitudinal information from Britain and the United States. *International Journal of Law and Social Policy*, 13, 293–314.

Joshi, H., Dale, A., Ward, C., and Davies, H. (1995) *Dependence and Independence in the Finances of Women Aged 33*. London: Family Policy Studies Centre.

Joshi, H., and Davies, H. (2002) Women's incomes over a synthetic lifetime. In E. Ruspini and A. Dale (eds.), *The Gender Dimension of Social Change*. Bristol: Policy Press.

Joshi, H., Davies, H., and Land, H. (1996) *The Tale of Mrs Typical*. Occasional Paper 21. London: Family Policy Studies Centre.

Joshi, H., Macran, S., and Dex, S. (1996) Employment after childbearing and women's subsequent labour force participation. *Journal of Population Economics*, 9, 325–48.

Julien, D., Markman, H. J., Leveille, S., Chartrand, E., and Begin, J. (1994) Networks' support and interference with regard to marriage: Disclosure of marital problems to confidants. *Journal of Family Psychology*, 8, 16–31.

Kagan, J. (1984) *The Nature of the Child*. New York: Basic Books.

Kamerman, S. (2000) Early childhood education and care (ECEC): An overview of developments in the OECD countries. *International Journal of Education*, 33, 7–29.

Kamerman, S. (2000) Parental leave policies: An essential ingredient in early childhood education and care policies. *Social Policy Report*, 14, 3–16.

Kammerman, S. G. (1984) Women, children, and poverty: public policies and female-headed families in industrialized countries. *Signs: Journal of Women in Culture and Society*, 10, 249–71.

Kamo, Y., and Zhou, M. (1994) Living arrangements of elderly Chinese and Japanese in the United States. *Journal of Marriage and the Family*, 56, 544–58.

Kandel, D. B., Davies, M., and Raveis, V. H. (1985) The stressfulness of daily social roles for women. *Journal of Health and Social Behavior*, 26, 64–78.

Kandiyoti, D. (1988) Bargaining with patriarchy. *Gender and Society*, 2, 274–90.

Kar, S. B., Campbell, K., Jimenez, A., and Gupta, S. R. (1995-1996) Invisible Americans: An exploration of Indo-American quality of life. *Amerasia Journal*, 21, 25–52.

Karn, V. (1977). *Retiring to the Seaside*. London: Routledge & Kegan Paul.

Katz, M. B. (ed.) (1992) *The Underclass Debate: Views from History*. Princeton: Princeton University Press.

Kaufmann, J-C. (1992) *Schmutzige Wäsche*. Konstanz: Universitätsverlag.

Kaufmann, J-C. (1992) *La Trame conjugale: Analyse du couple par son linge*. Paris: Nathan.

Kehoe, M. (1988) Lesbians over 60 speak for themselves. *Journal of Homosexuality*, 16, 1–111.

Kellerhals, J. (1998) The family and the construction of adult identity. In K. Matthijs (ed.), *The Family: Contemporary Perspectives and Challenges*. Leuven: Leuven University Press.

Kempson, E. (1996) *Life on a Low Income*. York: York Publishing Services.

Kempson, E., Bryson, A., and Rowlingson, K. (1994) *Hard Times*. London: Policy Studies Institute.

Kempson, E., and Whyley, C. (1999) *Kept Out or Opted Out: Understanding and Combating Financial Exclusion*. Bristol: Policy Press.

Kenen, R., and Schmidt, R. (1978) Stigmatization of carrier status: Social implications of heterozygote genetic screening programmes. *American Journal of Public Health*, 68, 1116–19.

Kennedy, G. E. (1992) Quality in grandparent/grandchild relationships. *International Journal of Aging and Human Development*, 35, 83–98.

Kennedy, G. E., and Kennedy, C. E. (1993) Grandparents: A special resource for children in stepfamilies. *Journal of Divorce and Remarriage*, 19, 45–68.

Kenny, G., Dubay, L., and Haley, J. (2000) Health Insurance, Access, and Health Status of Children, Findings from the National Survey of America's Families. Washington, DC: Urban Institute. Available online at http://newfederalism.urban.org/nsaf/child-health.html, last accessed March 22, 2003.

Kerbo, H. R. (2000) *Social Stratification and Inequality: Class Conflict in Historical, Comparative, and Global Perspective*. 4th ed. Boston: McGraw-Hill.

Kerckhoff, A. C. (1995) Institutional arrangements and stratification processes in industrial societies. *Annual Review of Sociology*, 21, 323–47.

Kevles, D. J. (1985) *In the Name of Eugenics*. New York: Knopf.

Kibria, N. (1990) Power, patriarchy, and gender conflict in the Vietnamese immigrant community. *Gender and Society*, 4, 9–24.

Kibria, N. (1993) *Family Tightrope: The Changing Lives of Vietnamese Americans*. Princeton, NJ: Princeton University Press.

Kiernan, K. (1989) The family: Fission or fusion. In H. Joshi (ed.), *The Changing Population of Britain*. Oxford: Basil Blackwell.

Kiernan, K. (1999) *The Changing Demography of Partnership*. Working Paper 14. Leeds: Centre for Research on Family, Kinship and Childhood, University of Leeds.

Kiernan, K. (1999) Childbearing outside marriage in Western Europe. *Population Trends*, 98, 11–20.

Kiernan, K. (1999) Cohabitation in Western Europe. *Population Trends*, 96, 25–32.

Kiernan, K. (2000) European perspectives on union formation. In L. Waite, C. Bachrach, M. Hindin, E. Thomson, and A. Thornton (eds.), *Ties that Bind: Perspectives on Marriage and Cohabitation*. Hawthorne, NY: New York: Aldine de Gruyter.

Kiernan, K. (2001) Non-marital childbearing: A European perspective. In L. Wu and B. Wolfe (eds.), *Out of Wedlock: Causes and Consequences of Nonmarital Fertility*. New York: Russell Sage Foundation.

Kiernan, K. (2002) Cohabitation in Western Europe: Trends, issues and implications. In A. Booth and A. Crouter (eds.), *Just Living Together: Implications of Cohabitation on Families, Children and Social Policy*. Mahwah, NJ: Lawrence Erlbaum.

Kiernan, K. (forthcoming) Divorce and cohabitation across nations and generations. In P. L. Chase-Lansdale, K. Kiernan, and R. Friedman (eds.), *Potential for Change across Lives and Generations: Multidisciplinary Perspectives*. Cambridge: Cambridge University Press.

Kiernan, K., and Estaugh, V. (1993) *Cohabitation: Extra-Marital Childbearing and Social Policy*. London: Family Policy Studies Centre.

Kiernan, K., and Mueller, G. (1999) Who divorces? In S. McRae (ed.), *Changing Britain: Families and Households in the 1990s*. Oxford: Oxford University Press.

Kiernan, K. E. (1992) The impact of family disruption in childhood and transitions made in young adult life. *Population Studies*, 46, 213–34.

Kiernan, K. E., and Hobcraft, J. (1997) Parental divorce during childhood: Age at first intercourse, partnership and parenthood. *Population Studies*, 51, 41–55.

Kim, B. (1994) Value orientations and sex-gender role attitudes on the comparability of Koreans and Americans. In H. Cho and O. Chang (eds.), *Gender Division of Labor in Korea*. Seoul: Ewha Women's University Press.

Kim, H. K., and McKenry, P. C. (2000) Relationship transitions as seen in the National Survey of Families and Households. *Journal of Divorce and Remarriage*, 34, 163–7.

Kim, L. S., Sandler, I. N., and Tein, J-Y. (1997) Locus of control as a stress moderator and mediator in children of divorce. *Journal of Abnormal Child Psychology*, 25, 145–55.

Kimbel, G. (1999) *21st Century Families*. Chico, CA: Equality Press.

Kimmel, D. (1992) The families of older gay men and lesbians. *Generations*, 16, 37–8.

Kimmel, M. S. (2000) *The Gendered Society*. New York and Oxford: Oxford University Press.

King, M. (1997) *A Better World for Children: Explorations in Morality and Authority*. London: Routledge.

King, R., Warnes, T., and Williams, A. (2000) *Sunset Lives: British Retirement Migration to the Mediterranean*. Oxford: Berg.

Kinnear, P. (2002) *New Families for Changing Times*. Canberra: Australia Institute.

Kinsey, A. C., Pomeroy, W. B., Martin, C. L., and Gebhard, P. H. (1953) *Sexual Behavior in the Human Female*. Philadelphia, PA: W. B. Saunders.

Kirby, D. (1997) *No Easy Answers: Research Findings on Programs to Reduce Teen Pregnancy*. Washington, DC: National Campaign to Prevent Teen Pregnancy.

Kirby, D. (2001) Understanding what works and what doesn't in reducing adolescent sexual risk-taking. *Family Planning Perspectives*, 33, 276–81.

Kitson, G. C., and Morgan, L. A. (1990) The multiple consequences of divorce: A decade review. *Journal of Marriage and the Family*, 52, 913–24.

Kivett, V. (1985) Grandfathers and grandchildren: Patterns of associations, helping, and psychological closeness. *Family Relations*, 34, 565–71.

Kivett, V., and Atkinson, M. (1984) Filial expectations, association, and helping as a function of number of children among older rural-transitional parents. *Journal of Gerontology*, 39, 499–503.

Klein, R. C. A., and Milardo, R. M. (2000) The social context of couple conflict: support and criticism from informal third parties. *Journal of Social and Personal Relationships*, 17, 618–37.

Kleinman, A. (1986) *The Social Origins of Distress and Disease*. New Haven, CT: Yale University Press.

Kling, J., Katz, L., and Liebman, J. (2001) Moving to opportunity in Boston: Early results of a randomized mobility experiment. *Quarterly Journal of Economics* 116, 2, 607–54.

Kling, J. R., Liebman, J. B., and Katz, L. F. (2000) Fear in the Ghetto and its Ramifications for Parents. Chicago: Joint Center for Poverty Research, University of Chicago, Policy Brief, 3, 10.

Knodel, J., Saengtienchai, C., and Obiero, W. (1995) Do small families jeopardize old age security? Evidence from Thailand. *Journal of Cross-Cultural Gerontology*, 5, 13–17.

Kobrin, F. E., and Hendershot, G. E. (1977) Do family ties reduce mortality? Evidence from the United States, 1966–1968. *Journal of Marriage and the Family*, 39, 737–45.

Koh, J. Y., and Bell, W. G. (1987) Korean elders in the United States: Intergenerational relations and living arrangements. *The Gerontologist*, 27, 66–71.

Kohli, M. (1999) Private and public transfers between generations: Linking the family and the state. *European Societies*, 1, 81–104.

Kohli, M., and Rein, M. (1991) The changing balance of work and retirement. In M. Kohli, M. Rein, A. M. Guillemard, and H. V. Gunsteren (eds.), *Time for Retirement*. Cambridge: Cambridge University Press.

Kojima, H. (2000) Japan: Hyper-aging and its policy implications. In K. D. Kim, V. L. Bengtson, G. C. Meyers, and K.S. Eun (eds.), *Aging East and West: Families, States, and the Elderly*. New York: Springer.

Kollontai, A. (1977) *Selected Writings*. (trans. A. Holt). London: Allison & Busby.

Komarovsky, M. (1987) *Blue-Collar Marriage*. 2nd ed. New Haven, CT: Yale University Press.

Kossoudji, S. (1989) Immigrant worker assimilation: is it a labor market phenomenon? *Journal of Human Resources*, 24, 494–527.

Kreider, R. M., and Fields, J. M. (2001) Number, timing, and duration of marriages and divorces: 1996. *Current Population Reports*. Washington, DC: US Census Bureau.

Kuczynski, A. (2001) Guess who's coming to dinner? *New York Times*, December 23, Section 9.

Kuhn, M. H. (1964) The reference group reconsidered. *Sociological Quarterly*, 5, 5–21.

Kumin, J. (1999) An uncertain direction. *Refugees Magazine, Europe: The Debate over Asylum* Issue 113. Available online at: http://www.unhcr.ch/pubs/rm113/rm11302.htm, last accessed February 22, 2001.

Kunemund, H., and Rein, M (1999) There is more to receiving than needing: Theoretical arguments and empirical explorations of crowding in and crowding out. *Aging and Society*, 19, 93–121.

Kurdek, L. (1993) The allocation of household labor in gay, lesbian, and heterosexual married couples. *Journal of Social Issues*, 49, 127–39.

Kurdek, L. A. (1998) Relationship outcomes and their predictors: Longitudinal evidence from heterosexual married, gay cohabiting and lesbian cohabiting couples. *Journal of Marriage and the Family*, 60, 553–68.

Kurdek, L. A. (2001) Differences between heterosexual non-parent couples and gay, lesbian, and heterosexual-parent couples. *Journal of Family Issues*, 22, 727–54.

Kurdek, L. A., Fine, M. A., and Sinclair, R. J. (1995) School adjustment in sixth graders: Parenting transitions, family climate, and peer norm effects. *Child Development*, 66, 430–45.

Kurdek, L. A., and Siesky, A. E. (1980) Children's perceptions of their parents' divorce. *Journal of Divorce*, 3, 339–78.

Kurdek, L., and. Sinclair, R. J. (1986) Adolescents' views on issues related to divorce. *Journal of Adolescent Research*, 1, 373–87.

Kurian, G. (1993) Marital patterns in Canada. In G. N. Ramu (ed.), *Marriage and the Family in Canada Today* (2nd ed.) Scarborough, ON: Prentice Hall Canada.

Ladd, R. E. (1996) *Children's Rights Re-visioned: Philosophical Readings*. London, New York, and Belmont: Wadsworth.

Laguerre, M. S. (1994) Headquarters and subsidiaries: Haitian immigrant family households in New York City. In R. L. Taylor (ed.), *Minority Families in the United States*. Englewood Cliffs, NJ: Prentice Hall.

Lampard, R (1994) An examination of the relationship between marital dissolution and unemployment. In D. Gallie, C. Marsh, and C. Volger (eds.), *The Social Consequences of Unemployment*. Oxford: Oxford University Press.

Land, H. (1975) The introduction of family allowances: an act of historic justice? In P. Hall, H. Land, R. Parker, and A. Webb (eds.), *Change, Choice and Conflict in Social Policy*. London: Heinemann.

Langford, W. (1999) *Revolutions of the Heart: Gender, Power and The Delusions of Love*. London: Routledge.

Lareau, A. (2001) Embedding capital in a broader context: The case of family–school relationships. In B. Biddle and P. Hall (eds.), *Social Class, Poverty, and Education*. London: Falmer-Routledge.

Lasch, C. (1977) *Haven in a Heartless World: The Family Besieged*. New York: Basic Books.

Lash, S. (2002) Individualization in a non-linear mode. In U. Beck and E. Beck-Gernsheim (eds.), *Individualization. Institutionalized Individualism and its Social and Political Consequences*. London: Sage.

Laslett, P. (1965) *The World We Have Lost*. London: Methuen.

Laslett, P. (1972) *Household and Family Life in Past Time*. Cambridge: Cambridge University Press.

Laslett, P. (1987) Emergence of the Third Age. *Ageing and Society*, 7, 133–60.

Laslett, P. (1988) Kinship and its numerical history. *Annales*, 43, 5–24.

Laslett, P., and Wall, R. (eds.) (1972) *Household and Family in Time Past: Comparative Studies in the Size and Structure of the Domestic Group over the Last Three Centuries in England, France, Serbia, Japan and Colonial America*. Cambridge: Cambridge University Press.

Laumann, E. O., Gagnon, J. H., Michael, R. T., and Michaels, S. (1994) *The Social Organization of Sexuality: Sexual Practices in the United States*. Chicago: University of Chicago Press.

Laumann, E. O., Paik, A., and Rosen, R. C. (2001) Sexual dysfunction in the United States: Prevalence and predictors. In E. O. Laumann and R. T. Michael (eds.), *Sex, Love, and Health in America: Private Choices and Public Policies*. Chicago: University of Chicago Press.

Laurie, H., and Gershuny. J. (2000) Couples, work and money. In R. Berthoud and J. Gershuny (eds.), *Seven Years in The Lives of British Families*. Bristol: Policy Press.

LaValle, I., Arthur, S., Millward, C., Scott, J., and Claydon, M. (2002) *Atypical Work and Family Life*. Bristol: Policy Press.

Law Commission of Canada (2001) *Beyond Conjugality: Recognizing and Supporting Close Personal Adult Relationships*. Ottawa, ON: Law Commission of Canada.

Lawson, A. (1988) *Adultery: The Analysis of Love and Betrayal*. New York: Basic Books.

Lawton, L., Silverstein, M., and Bengtson, V. L. (1994) Solidarity between generations in families. In V. L. Bengtson and R. Harootyan (eds.), *Intergenerational Linkages: Hidden Connections in American Society*. New York: Springer.

Le Bourdais, C., Neill, G., and Turcotte, P. (2000) The changing face of conjugal relationships. *Canadian Social Trends*, 56, 14–17.

Lee, G. (1980) Kinship in the seventies: A decade review of research and theory. *Journal of Marriage and the Family*, 42, 923–36.

Lee, G.-Y., and Angel, R. J. (2002) Living arrangements and supplemental security income use among elderly Asians and Hispanics in the United States: The role of nativity and citizenship. *Journal of Ethnic and Migration Studies*, 28, 553–63.

Lee, J. Z., and Wang, F. (1999) *One Quarter of Humanity: Malthusian Mythology and Chinese Realities, 1700–2000*. Cambridge, MA: Cambridge University Press.

Lee, R. D. (1980) Aiming at a moving target: Period fertility and changing reproductive goals. *Population Studies*, 34, 205–26.

Lee, T. R. (1990) Sibling relationships in adulthood: Contact patterns and motivations. *Journal of Marriage and the Family*, 52, 431–40.

Leeming, A., Unell, J., and Walker, R. (1994) *Lone Mothers: Coping with the Consequences of Separation*. London: DSS Research Report No. 30.

Leigh, B. C., Temple, M. T., and Trocki, K. F. (1993) The sexual behavior of U.S. adults: Results from a national survey. *American Journal of Public Health*, 83, 1400–8.

Leisering, L., and Leibfried, S. (2000) *Time and Poverty in Western Welfare States: United Germany in Perspective*. Cambridge: Cambridge University Press.

Lesthaeghe, R. (1983) A century of demographic and cultural change in Western Europe: An exploration of underlying dimensions. *Population and Development Review*, 9, 411–35.

Lesthaeghe, R. (1995) The second demographic transition in western countries: An interpretation. In K. Mason and A-M. Jensen (eds.), *Gender and Family Change in Industrialized Countries*. Oxford: Clarendon.

Lesthaeghe, R., and Meekers, D. (1986) Value change and the dimensions of familism in the European Community. *European Journal of Population*, 2, 225–68.

Lesthaeghe, R., and Surkyn, J. (1988) Cultural dynamics and economic theories of fertility change. *Population and Development Review*, 11, 1–45.

Levine, C. (1991) AIDS and changing concepts of family. In D. Nelkin, D. P. Willis, and S. V. Parris (eds.), *A Disease of Society: Cultural and Institutional Responses to AIDS*. New York: Cambridge University Press.

Levitt, P (2001) *The Transnational Villagers*. Berkeley: University of California Press.

Lewin, E. (1984) Lesbianism and motherhood: implications for child custody. In T. Dary and S. Potter (eds.), *Women-Identified-Women*. Palo Alto CA: Mayfield.

Lewin, E. (1993) *Lesbian Mothers: Accounts of Gender In American Culture*. Ithaca, NY and London: Cornell University Press.

Lewin, E. (1998) *Recognizing Ourselves: Ceremonies of Lesbian and Gay Commitment*. New York: Columbia University Press.

Lewis, C., and O'Brien, M. (1987) *Reassessing Fatherhood: New Observations on Fathers and the Modern Family*. London: Sage.

Lewis, J. (1986) Anxieties about the family and the relationships between parents, children and the state in twentieth-century England. In M. Richards and P. Light (eds.), *Children of Social Worlds*. London: Cambridge University Press.

Lewis, J. (1992) Gender and the development of welfare regimes. *Journal of European Social Policy*, 2, 159–73.

Lewis, J. (ed.) (1993) *Women and Social Policies in Europe: Work, Family and the State*. Aldershot: Edward Elgar.

Lewis, J. (2002) The problem of fathers: Policy and behaviour in Britain. In B. Hobson (ed.), *Making Men into Fathers: Men, Masculinities and the Social Politics of Fatherhood* Cambridge: Cambridge University Press

Lewis, J., and Kiernan, K. (1996) The boundaries between marriage, non-marriage and parenthood: Changes in behaviour and policy in post-war Britain. *Journal of Family History*, 20, 372–87.

Lewis, R. A., and Salt, R. E. (eds.) (1986) *Men in Families*. Beverley Hills, CA: Sage.

Lewis, S., and Lewis, J. (1996) *The Work-Family Challenge: Rethinking Employment*. London: Sage.

Liebman, J. (1998) *Lessons About Tax-benefit Integration From the US Earned Income Tax Credit Experience*. York: York Publishing Services.

Liebow, E. (1967) *Tally's Corner*. Boston, MA: Little, Brown.

Lillard, L. A., and Panis, C. (1996) Marital status and mortality: The role of health. *Demography*, 33, 313–27.

Lillard, L. A., and Waite, L. J. (1995) Till death do us part: Marital disruption and mortality. *American Journal of Sociology*, 100, 1131–56.

Lim, I. (1997) Korean immigrant women's challenge to gender inequality at home: the interplay of economic resources, gender, and family. *Gender and Society*, 11, 31–51.

Lin, C., and Liu, W. T. (1993) Intergenerational relationships among Chinese immigrant families from Taiwan. In H. P. McAdoo (ed.), *Family Ethnicity*. Newbury Park, CA: Sage.

Lingsom, S. (1995) Women's time-use over the lifecycle. In I. Niemi (ed.), *Time Use of Women in Europe and North America*. New York and Geneva: United Nations.

Linton, R. (1949) The natural history of the family. In R. A. Anshen (ed.), *The Family: Its Function and Destiny*. New York: Harper.

LIS (2001) Luxembourg Income Study website: www.lis.ceps.lu

Locke, J. (1946) [1690] *The Second Treatise of Government and a Letter concerning Toleration*. Oxford: Basil Blackwell.

Loehlin, J. C. (1997) A test of J. R. Harris's theory of peer influences on personality. *Journal of Personality and Social Psychology*, 72, 1197–201.

Logan, J. R., and Spitze, G. D. (1996) *Family Ties: Relations between Parents and their Grown Children*. Philadelphia, PA: Temple University Press.

Loizos, P. (2000) Are refugees social capitalists? In S. Baron, J. Field, and T. Schuller (eds.), *Social Capital: Critical Perspectives*. Oxford: Oxford University Press.

Lollock, L. (2001) The foreign-born population in the United States: March 2000, Current Population Reports, 2001, pp. 20–534. Washington, DC: US Census Bureau.

London Gay Liberation Front (1971) *Manifesto*. London: Gay Liberation Front.

Lord Chancellor's Department (2001) *Divorce Law Reform – Government Proposes to Repeal Part II of the Family Law Act 1996*. London: Lord Chancellor's Department.

Loury, G. (1977) A dynamic theory of racial income differences. In P. A. Wallace and A. M. LaMond (eds.), *Women, Minorities, and Employment Discrimination*. Lexington, MA: Lexington Books.

Lowry, B. (2000) Study: Sex Has Few Consequences in TV, Film. *Los Angeles Times*, March 29, F3.

Ludwig, M. (1996) *Armutskarrieren, Zwischen Abstieg und Aufstieg im Sozialstaat*. Opladen: Westdeutscher Verlag.

Luescher, K., and Pillemer, K. (1998) Intergenerational ambivalence: A new approach to the study of parent–child relations in later life. *Journal of Marriage and the Family*, 60, 413–25.

Luhmann, N. (1986) *Love as Passion. The Codification of Intimacy*. Cambridge: Polity.

Luhmann, N. (1995) Why does society describe itself as postmodern? *Cultural Critique* 30, 171–86.

Lupri, E. (1983) *The Changing Position of Women in Family and Society: A Cross-National Comparison*. Leiden: E. J. Brill.

Lüscher, K. (1994) Was heißt heute Familie? In C. Brauns-Hermann, B. M. Busch, and H. Dinse (eds.), *Verlorene Liebe – Gemeinsame Kinder*. Reinbek: Rowohlt.

Luster, T., and Small, S. A. (1997) Sexual abuse history and number of sex partners among female adolescents. *Family Planning Perspectives*, 29, 204–11.

Lye, D. N. (1996) Adult child–parent relationships. *Annual Review of Sociology*, 22, 79–102.

Lynd, R., and Lynd, H. (1929) *Middletown: A Study in American Culture*. New York: Harcourt & Brace.

Lynd, R., and Lynd, H. (1937) *Middletown in Transition: A Study in Cultural Conflicts*. New York: Harcourt & Brace.

Mac An Ghaill, M. (ed.) (1996) *Understanding Masculinities*. Buckingham: Open University Press.

Maccoby, E. E. (1992) The role of parents in the socialization of children: an historical overview. *Developmental Psychology*, 28, 1006–17.

Maccoby, E. E., and Martin, J. A. (1983) Socialization and the context of the family: parent–child interaction. In E. M. Hetherington (ed.), *Socialization, Personality, and Social Development*. New York: John Wiley.

Maccoby, E. E., and Mnookin, R. H. (1992) *Dividing the Child: Social and Legal Dilemmas of Custody*. Cambridge, MA: Harvard University Press.

Maclean, C. (2003) Making it their home: In-migration, time, social change and belonging in a rural community. In G. Allan and G. Jones (eds.), *Social Relations and the Life Course*. Basingstoke: Palgrave.

Macpherson, C. B. (1962) *The Political Theory of Possessive Individualism*. Oxford: Oxford University Press.

Macran, S., Joshi, H., and Dex, S. (1995) Employment after childbearing: a survival analysis. *Work Employment and Society*, 10, 273–96.

Maddox, G. L. (2001) Housing and living arrangements: A transactional perspective. In R. H. Binstock and L. K. George (eds.), *Handbook of Aging and the Social Sciences*. San Diego: Academic.

Madge, J. (1970) *The Origins of Scientific Sociology*. London: Tavistock.

Maharidge, D. (1996) *The Coming White Minority: California Eruptions and American's Future*. New York: New York Times Books.

Mahay, J., Laumann, E. O., and Michaels, S. (2001) Race, gender, and class in sexual scripts. In E. O. Laumann and R. T. Michael (eds.), *Sex, Love, and Health in America: Private Choices and Public Policies*. Chicago: University of Chicago Press.

Males, M., and Chew, K. S. Y. (1996) The ages of fathers in California adolescent births, 1993. *American Journal of Public Health*, 86, 565–8.

Mangiafico, L. (1988) *Contemporary American Immigrants*. New York: Praeger.

Manlove, J., Terry, E., Gitelson, L., Papillo, A. R., and Russell, S. (2000) Explaining demographic trends in teenage fertility, 1980–1995. *Family Planning Perspectives*, 32, 166–75.

Manning, W. D. (1990) Parenting employed teenagers. *Youth and Society*, 22, 184–200.

Manning, W. D., and Smock, P. J. (1997). Children's living arrangements in unmarried-mother families. *Journal of Family Issues*, 18, 526–44.

Mansfield, P., and Collard, J. (1988) The beginning of the rest of your life? A portrait of newly-wed marriage. *Sociology*, 23, 151–2.

Mansfield, P., and Collard, J. (1988) *The Beginning of the Rest of Your Life? A Portrait of Newly-Wed Marriage*. London: Macmillan.

Manting, D. (1996) The changing meaning of cohabitation. *European Sociological Review*, 12, 53–65.

Mardsen, P. V., and Lin, N. (1982) *Social Structure and Network Analysis*. Beverly Hills: Sage.

Markides, K. S., Martin, H. W., and Gomez, E. (1983) *Older Mexican Americans: A Study in an Urban Barrio*. Austin: University of Texas Press.

Marks, N. F. (1996) Flying solo at midlife: Gender, marital status and psychological well-being. *Journal of Family Issues*, 9, 917–33.

Marks, N. F., and Lambert, J. D. (1998) Marital status continuity and change among young and midlife adults. *Journal of Family Issues*, 19, 652–86.

Marks, S. R. (2000) Teasing out the lessons of the 1960s: family diversity and family privilege. *Journal of Marriage and the Family*, 62, 609–22.

Marmor, T. R. (1994) *Understanding Health Care Reform*. New Haven, CT: Yale University Press.

*Marriage and Divorce Statistics* (1976) Series FM2, No 3. London: Stationery Office.

*Marriage, Divorce and Adoption Statistics* (1999). Series FM2, No 27. London, Stationery Office.

Marsh, A., and Rowlingson, K. (2002) *Low/Moderate-income Families in Britain: Changes in 1999 and 2000*. London: Department for Work and Pensions, Research Report 165, Corporate Document Services.

Marsiglio, W. (1993) Contemporary scholarship on fatherhood: Culture, identity and conduct. *Journal of Family Issues*, 14, 484–509.

Marsiglio, W. (ed.) (1995) *Fatherhood: Contemporary Theory, Research, and Social Policy*. Thousand Oaks, CA: Sage.

Marsiglio, W. (1995) Fathers' diverse life course patterns and roles: Theory and social intervention. In W. Marsiglio (ed.), *Fatherhood: Contemporary Theory, Research, and Social Policy*. Thousand Oaks, CA: Sage.

Marsiglio, W., Amato, P., Day, R. D., and Lamb, M. E. (2000) Scholarship on fatherhood in the 1990s and beyond. *Journal of Marriage and the Family*, 62, 1173–91.

Marsiglio, W., and Donnelley, D. A. (1991) Sexual relations in later life: A national study of married persons. *Journals of Gerontology*, 46, S338–S344.

Marteau, T., and Richards, M. P. M. (eds.) (1996) *The Troubled Helix*. Cambridge: Cambridge University Press.

Martin, B. (1978) *A General Theory of Secularization*. Oxford: Basil Blackwell.

Martin, J., and Roberts, C. (1984) *Women and Employment: A Life Time Perspective*. Department of Employment/Office of Population Censuses and Surveys, London: HMSO.

Mason, J. (1987) A bed of roses? Women, marriage and inequality in later life. In P. Allatt, T. Keil, A. Bryman, and B. Bytheway (eds.), *Women and the Life Cycle*. Basingstoke: Macmillan.

Mason, J. (1999) Living away from relatives. In S. McRae (ed.), *Changing Britain: Families and Households in the 1990s*. Oxford: Oxford University Press.

Mason, M. A., Fine, M. A., and Carnochan, S. (2001) Family law in the new millennium. For whose families? *Journal of Family Issues*, 22, 859–81.

Masson, J. (2000) From Curtis to Waterhouse: state care and child protection in the UK 1945-2000. In S. Katz, J. Eekalaar, and M. Maclean (eds.), *Cross Currents: Family Law in the US and England*. Oxford: Oxford University Press.

Maticka-Tundale, E., Barrett, M., and McKay, A. (2000) Adolescent sexual and reproductive health in Canada: A review of national data sources and their limitations. *Canadian Journal of Human Sexuality*, 9, 41–65.

Mayall, B. (1996) *Children, Health and The Social Order*. Buckingham: Open University Press.

Mayer, K-U., and Muller, W. (1986) The state and the structure of the life course. In A. B. Sorensen, F. Weinert, and L. Sherrod (eds.), *Human Development and the Life Course: Multidisciplinary Perspectives*. Hillsdale, NJ: Lawrence Erlbaum.

Mayer, S. E. (1997) *What Money Can't Buy: Family Income and Children's Life Chances*. Cambridge, MA: Harvard University Press.

Mays, V. M., Chatters, L. M., Cochran, S. D., and Mackness, J. (1998) African American families in diversity: gay men and lesbians as participants in family networks. *Journal of Comparative Family Studies*, 29, 73–87.

Mazur, A., and Booth, A. (1998) Testosterone and dominance in men. *Behavior and Brain Sciences*, 21, 353–63.

McAllister, F., and Clarke, L. (1998) *Choosing Childlessness*. London and York: Family Policy Studies Centre and the Joseph Rowntree Foundation.

McCulloch, A. Wiggens, R., Joshi, H., and Sachdev, D. (2000) Internalising and externalising children's behaviour problems in Britain and the US: relationships to family resources. *Children and Society*, 14, 368–83.

McGarry, K., and Schoeni, R. F. (1995) Transfer behavior in the health and retirement study. *Journal of Human Resources*, 30, Supplement, S184–S226.

McGauhey, P. J., and Starfield, B. (1993) Child health and the social environment of white and black children. *Social Science and Medicine*, 36, 867–74.

McGlone, F., Park, A., and Roberts, C. (1999) Kinship and friendship: Attitudes and behaviour in Britain, 1986–1995. In S. McRae (ed.), *Changing Britain: Families and Households in the 1990s*. Oxford: Oxford University Press.

McGregor, P., and Borooah, V. (1992) Is low spending or low income a better indicator of whether a household is poor? *Journal of Social Policy*, 21, 53–69.

McKee, L., and O'Brien, M. (eds.) (1982) *The Father Figure*. London: Tavistock.

McKenzie, E. (1994) *Privatopia: Homeowner Associations and the Rise of Residential Private Government*. New Haven, CT: Yale University Press.

McKie, L., Bowlby, S., and Gregory, S. (eds.) (1999) *Gender, Power and the Household*. Basingstoke, Macmillan.

McLanahan, S., and Adams, J. (1989) The effects of children on parents' psychological well-being: 1957–1976. *Social Forces*, 68, 1124–46.

McLanahan, S., and Sandefur, G. (1994) *Growing Up with a Single Parent: What Helps? What Hurts?* Cambridge, MA: Harvard University Press.

McLanahan, S. S., and Kelly, E. (1999) The feminization of poverty. In J. Chafetz (ed.), *Handbook of Gender Sociology*. New York: Plenum.

McLanahan, S. S., and Sandefur, G. D. (1994) *Uncertain Childhood, Uncertain Future*. Cambridge, MA: Harvard University Press.

McLeod, J. D., and Shanahan, M. J. (1993) Poverty, parenting, and children's mental health. *American Sociological Review*, 58, 351–66.

McLloyd, V., Cance, A. M., Takeuchi, D., and Wilson, L. (2000) Marital processes and parental socialization in families of color: a decade review of research. *Journal of Marriage and the Family*, 62, 1070–93.

McMillan, J. (2002) Sex selection in the United Kingdom. *Hastings Center Report*, 32, 28–31.

McNeal, J. U. (1992) *Kids as Consumers*. New York: Lexington Books.

McNeal, R. B., Jr. (1999) Parental involvement as social capital: differential effectiveness on science achievement, truancy, and dropping out. *Social Forces*, 78, 117–44.

McPherson, M., Smith-Lovin, L., and Cook, J. M. (2001) Birds of feathers: Homophily in social networks. *Annual Review of Sociology*, 27, 415–44.

McRae, S. (1991) *Maternity Rights in Britain*. London: Policy Studies Institute.

McRae, S. (1999) *Changing Britain: Families and Households in the 1990s*. Oxford: Oxford University Press.

Mead, L. M. (1993) *The New Politics of Poverty: The Nonworking Poor in America*. New York: Basic Books.

Meintel, D., Labelle, M., Tircotte, G., and Kempineers, M. (1987) The new double workday of immigrant women workers in Québec. *Women's Studies*, 13, 273–93.

Menaghan, E. G., and Parcel, T. L. (1990) Parental employment and family life: Research in the 1980s. *Journal of Marriage and the Family*, 52, 1079–98.

Meyers, M., and Gornick, J. (2000) Early childhood education and care (ECEC): Cross-national variation in service organization and financing. Paper presented to "A Consultative Meeting on International Developments in Early Childhood Education and Care," New York.

Michael, R. T., Wadsworth, J., Feinleib, J. A., Johnson, A. M., Laumann, E. O., and Wellings, K. (2001) Private sexual behavior, public opinion, and public health policy related to sexually transmitted diseases: A U.S.–British comparison. In E. O. Laumann and R. T. Michael (eds.), *Sex, Love, and Health in America: Private Choices and Public Policies*. Chicago: University of Chicago Press.

Middleton, S., Ashworth, K., and Walker, R. (eds.) (1994) *Family Fortunes: Pressures on Parents and Children in the 1990s*. London: Child Poverty Action Group.

Middleton, S., and Shropshire, J. (1999) *Small Expectations: Learning to Be Poor*. York: York Publishing Services Milardo R. M. (1987) Changes in social networks of women and men following divorce. *Journal of Family Issues*, 8, 78–96.

Milardo, R. M. (1982) Friendship networks in developing relationships: Converging and diverging social environments. *Social Psychology Quarterly*, 45, 162–72.

Milardo, R. M. (1986) Personal choice and social constraint in close relationships: Applications of network analysis. In V. J. Derlega. and B. A. Winstead (eds.), *Friendship and Social Interaction*. New York: Springer Verlag.

Milardo, R. M. (1987) Changes in social networks of women and men following divorce: A review. *Journal of Family Issues*, 8, 78–96.

Milardo, R. M. (1988) Changes in social networks of women and men following divorce. *Journal of Family Issues*, 8, 78–96.

Milardo, R. M. (1988) *Families and Social Networks*. Newbury Park, CA: Sage.

Milardo, R. M. (1989) Theoretical and methodological issues in the identification of the social networks of spouses. *Journal of Marriage and the Family*, 51, 165–74.

Milardo, R., and Allan, G. (1997) Social networks and marital relationships. In S. Duck (ed.), *Handbook of Personal Relationships*. Chichester: John Wiley.

Milardo, R. M, Johnson, M. P., and Huston, T. L. (1983) Developing close relationships: Changing patterns of interaction between pair members and social networks. *Journal of Personality and Social Psychology*, 44, 964–76.

Mill, H. T. (1983) [1851] *The Enfranchisement of Women*. London: Virago.

Mill, J. S. (1869) *Subjection of Women*. New York: D. Appleton & Co.

Miller, K. S., Kotchick, B. A., Dorsey, S., Forehand, R., and Ham, A.Y. (1998) Family communication about sex: What are parents saying and are their adolescents listening? *Family Planning Perspectives*, 30, 218–22, 235.

Millett, K. (1970) *Sexual Politics*. Garden City, NY: Doubleday.

Milton, J. (1927) *Areopagitica and other Prose Works*. London: Dent.

Milton, J. (1953) *The English Poems of John Milton*. London: Macdonald.

Milward, C. (1992) Keeping in touch: extended family networks. *Family Matters*, 32, 14–19, Melbourne: Australian Institute of Family Studies.

Milward, C. (1995) Family networks in rural and urban settings. *Family Matters*, 41, 10–14, Melbourne: Australian Institute of Family Studies.

Min, P. G. (1998) *Changes and Conflicts: Korean Immigrant Families in New York*. Boston: Allyn & Bacon.

Min, P. G. (1998) The Korean-American family. In C. H. Mindel, R. W. Habenstein, and R. Wright (eds.), *Ethnic Families in America: Patterns and Variations*. Upper Saddle River, NJ: Prentice Hall.

Mincer, J., and Polachek, S. (1974) Family investments in human capital: earnings of women. *Journal of Political Economy*, 82, 76–108.

Minino, A. M., and Smith, B. L.(2001) Deaths: Preliminary data for 2000. *National Vital Statistics Reports*, 49(12). Hyattsville, MD: National Center for Health Statistics, October, 1–40. Retrieved from http://www.cdc.gov/nchs/data/nvsr/nvsr49/nvsr49_12.pdf

Minkler, M. (1999) Intergenerational households headed by grandparents. *Journal of Aging Studies*, 13, 199–218.

Minow, M. (1996) Rights for the next generation: a feminist approach to children's rights. In R. Ladd (ed.), *Children's Rights Revisioned, Philosophical Readings*. London, New York, and Belmont: Wadsworth.

Mirowsky, J. (1996) Age and the gender gap in depression. *Journal of Health and Social Behavior*, 37, 362–80.

Mirza, H. S. (1997) *Black British Feminism: A Reader*. London and New York: Routledge.

Mitchell, A. (1985) *Children in the Middle. Living Through Divorce*. London: Tavistock.

Mitford, J. (1992) *The American Way of Birth*. New York: Dutton.

Model, S., Fisher, G., and Silberman, R. (1999) Black Caribbeans in comparative perspective. *Journal of Ethnic and Migration Studies*, 25, 187–212.

Modood, T. (1997) *Ethnic Minorities in Britain: Diversity and Disadvantage*. London: Policy Studies Institute.

Moffitt, R. A., and Slade, E. (1997) Health care coverage for children on and off welfare. *The Future of Children*, 7, 87–98.

Montanari, I. (2000) From family wage to marriage subsidy and child benefits: Controversy and consensus in the development of family support. *Journal of European Social Policy*, 10, 307–33.

Montgomery, L. E., Kiely, J. L., and Pappas, G. (1996) The effects of poverty, race, and family structure on US children's health: Data from the NHIS, 1978 through 1980 and 1989 through 1991. *American Journal of Public Health*, 86, 1401–5.

Mooney, A., Knight, A., Moss, P., and Owen, C. (2001) *Who Cares: Childminding in the 1990s*. York: Family Policy Studies Centre for the Joseph Rowntree Foundation.

Mooney, A., and Munton, A. G. (1997) *Research Policy in Early Childhood Services: Time for a New Agenda*, London: Institute of Education.

Moore, K. A., Nord, C. W., and Peterson, J. L. (1989) Nonvoluntary sexual activity among adolescents. *Family Planning Perspectives*, 21, 110–14.

Morgan, D. (1991) *Blackstone's Guide to the Human Fertilization and Embryology Act 1990*. London: Blackstone.

Morgan, D. H. J. (1996) *Family Connections: An Introduction to Family Studies*. Cambridge: Polity.

Morgan, D. H. J. (1999) Risk and family practices: accounting for change and fluidity in family life. In E. B. Silva and C. Smart (eds.), *The New Family?* London: Sage.

Morgan, P. (1996) *Who Needs Parents?* London: Institute of Economic Affairs.

Morgan, P. (1999) *Farewell to the Family*, London: Institute of Economic Affairs.

Morokvasic, M. (1983) Women in migration: beyond the reductionist outlook. In A. Phizacklea (ed.), *One Way Ticket: Migration and Female Labour*. Boston: Routledge & Kegan Paul.

Morris, L. (1990) *The Workings of the Household: A US–UK Comparison*. Cambridge: Polity.

Morrison, K. F. (1988) *"I am You". The Hermeneutics of Empathy in Western Literature, Theology and Art*. Princeton, NJ: Princeton University Press,

Morrow, V. (1996) Rethinking childhood dependency: children's contributions to the domestic economy. *Sociological Review*, 44, 58–77.

Mortimer, J. T., and Finch, M. D. (1996) *Adolescents, Work and Family: An Intergenerational Development Analysis*. London: Sage

Moss, P. (1996) *Parental employment in the EU*, 1985–1993. *Labour Market Trends*, 104, 12, 517–22.

Mott, F. K. (1990) When is a father really gone? Paternal–child contact in father-absent homes. *Demography*, 27, 499–517.

Mott, F. L., Fondell, M. M., Hu, P. N., Kowaleski-Jones, L., and Menaghan, E. G. (1996) The determinants of first sex by age 14 in a high-risk adolescent population. *Family Planning Perspectives*, 28, 13–18.

Mui, A. (1998) Living alone and depression among older Chinese immigrants. *Journal of Gerontological Social Work*, 30, 147–8.

Mulgan, G., and Wilkinson, H. (1995) Well-being and time. *Demos Quarterly*, 5, 2–11.

Muller, H. (1963) Discussion at international conference held by the Ciba Foundation. In G. Wolstenholme (ed.), *Man and His Future*. London: Churchill.

Munroe-Blum, H., Boyle, M. H., Offord, D. R., and Kates, N. (1989) Immigrant children: psychiatric disorder, school performance, and service utilization. *American Journal of Orthopsychiatry*, 59, 510–19.

Murphy, M. (2000) The evolution of cohabitation in Britain, 1960–95. *Population Studies*, 54, 43–56.

Murphy, M., Glaser, K., and Grundy, E. (1997) Marital status and long-term illness in Great Britain. *Journal of Marriage and the Family*, 59, 156–64.

Murphy, M. J. (1985) Demographic and socio-economic influences on recent British marital breakdown patterns. *Population Studies*, 39, 2, 235–58.

Murray, C. (1984) *Losing Ground: American Social Policy, 1950–1980*. New York: Basic Books.

Murray, C. J. L. (1996) Rethinking DALYs. In C. J. L. Murray and A. D. Lopez (eds.), *The Global Burden of Disease*. Cambridge, MA: Harvard University Press.

Mutchler, J. E. and Angel, J. L. (2000) Policy development and the older Latino population in the 21st century. *Journal of Aging and Social Policy*, 11, 177–88.

Myles, J. (1984) *Old Age in the Welfare State: The Political Economy of Public Pensions*. Boston, MA: Little, Brown.

Nardi, P. (1999) *Gay Men's Friendships: Invincible Communities*. Chicago: Chicago University Press.

Nathanson, C. A. (1991) *Dangerous Passage: The Social Control of Sexuality in Women's Adolescence*. Philadelphia, PA: Temple University Press.

National Center for Health Statistics (1984) *Midwife and Out-of-Hospital Deliveries, United States*. DHHS Publication No. (PHS) 84-1918. Hyattsville, MD: US Department of Health and Human Services.

National Center for Health Statistics (2000) *Vital Statistics of the United States, 1998, Volume I, Natality. Table 1-24*. Hyattsville, MD: US Department of Health and Human Services.

National Center on Health Statistics (2001) Teen Pregnancy Rate Reaches a Record Low in 1997.

National Gay and Lesbian Task Force (2001) *Issues: Same-Sex Marriage*. Washington, DC: 2001. Retrieved from: http://www.ngltf.org/issues/issue.cfm?issueID = 10

National Marriage Project (2000) *The state of our unions, 2000: The social health of marriage in America*. New Brunswick, NJ: Rutgers University Press.

National Opinion Research Center (2002) *General Social Survey 1972–2000 Cumulative Codebook*.

National Research Council (1995) Immigrant children and their families: issues for research and policy. *Critical Issues for Children and Youths*, 5, 72–89.

National Statistical Office, Republic of Korea (1993) *1990 Population and Housing Census Report, Vol. 6: Economic Activity*. Seoul: National Statistical Office, Republic of Korea.

National Statistics (2002) *Health Statistics Quarterly*. London: National Statistics.

Nault, F., and Bélanger, A. (1996) *The Decline in Marriage in Canada, 1981 to 1991*. Ottawa, ON: Minister of Industry.

Neathey, F., and Hurstfield, J. (1995) *Flexibility in Practice: Women's Employment and Pay in Retail and Finance*. Equal Opportunities Commission Research Discussion Series No.16. London: Industrial Relations Services.

Nelkin, D., and Lindee, S. (1995) *The DNA Mystique*. New York: Freeman.

Nelson, M. K., and Smith, J. (1999) *Working Hard and Making Do: Surviving in Small Town America*. Berkeley: University of California Press.

Nelson, S. S., and O'Reilly, R. (2000) Minorities become majority in state, census officials say. *Los Angeles Times*, August, A1, A16.

Neugebauer, R. (1989) Divorce, custody and visitation: The child's point of view. *Journal of Divorce*, 12, 153–68.

Neville, G. (1994) *The Mother Town: Civic Ritual, Symbol, and Experience in the Borders of Scotland*. Oxford: Oxford University Press.

New Zealand Law Commission (1999) *Recognising Same-Sex Relationships*. Wellington, New Zealand: Law Commission.

Newacheck, P. W., Hughes, D. C., and Stoddard, J. J. (1996) Children's access to primary care: differences by race, income, and insurance status. *Pediatrics* 97, 26–32.

Newby, H. (1980) *Green and Pleasant Land? Social Change in Rural England*. Harmondsworth: Penguin.

Newcomb, T. M. (1961) *The Acquaintance Process*. New York: Rinehart & Winston.

Newman, K. S. (1999) *No Shame in My Game the Working Poor in the Inner City*. New York: Knopf and the Russell Sage Foundation.

Newman, K. S. (1999) *No Shame in My Game: The Working Poor in the Inner City*. New York: Vintage.

NGO Human Rights Watch (2002) Retrieved from http:www.hrw.wg/press/2002/05/UNchil dren qa 0502.html

Niemi, I. (1983) *Time Use Study in Finland*. Helsinki: Central Statistical Office.

Nimkoff, M. F. (1934) *The Family*. Boston: Houghton Mifflin.

Norton, A. J., and Miller, L. F. (1992) *Marriage, Divorce, and Remarriage in the 1990's* Washington, DC: US Bureau of the Census.

Novas, C., and Rose, N. (2000) Genetic risk and the birth of the somatic individual. *Economy and Society*, 29, 485–513.

Nukago, Y. (2002) Between tradition and innovation in new genetics: The continuity of medical pedigrees and the development of combination work in the case of Huntington's disease. *New Genetics and Society*, 21, 39–64.

Oakley, A. (1974) *The Sociology of Housework*. Oxford: Martin Robertson.

Oakley, A. (1984) *The Captured Womb: A History of the Medical Care of Pregnant Women*. Oxford: Blackwell.

Oakley, A. (1992) *Social Support and Motherhood: The Natural History of a Research Project*. Oxford: Blackwell.

Oakley, A. (1994) Women and children first and last: Parallels and differences between children's and women's studies. In B. Mayall (ed.), *Children's Childhood Observed and Experienced*. London: Falmer.

O'Brien, E., and Feder, J. (1998) *How Well Does the Employment-Based Health Insurance System Work for Low-Income Families?* Washington, DC: Kaiser Family Foundation.

O'Brien, M. (1997) She who sups with the media . . . . *Times Higher Educational Supplement*, February 14.

O'Brien, M., and Jones, D. (1999) Children in working-class families: Parental time, investment and educational outcomes. *Cambridge Economic Journal*, 23.

O'Brien, M., Alldred, P., and Jones, P. (1996) Children's constructions of family and kinship. In J. Brannen and M. O'Brien (eds.) *Children in Families: Research and Policy*. London:

FalmerOECD (1992) *The OECD List of Social Indicators*. Paris: Organization for Economic Co-operation and Development.
O'Connor, J. S., Orloff, A. S., and Shaver, S. (1999) *States, Markets, Families: Gender, Liberalism and Social Policy in Australia, Canada, Great Britain and the United States*. Cambridge: Cambridge University Press.
O'Connor, T. G., Pickering, K., Dunn, J., and Golding, J. (1999) Frequency and predictors of relationship dissolution in a community sample in England. *Journal of Family Psychology*, 13, 436–49.
OECD (1998) Low income dynamics in four OECD countries. *OECD Economic Outlook*, 64, 171–86.
OECD (2000) *Early Childhood Education and Care Policy in Portugal, OECD Country Note*. Paris: OECD.
OECD (2000) *Employment Outlook*. Paris: OECD.
OECD (2001) *Cities and Regions in the New Learning Economy*. Paris: Organization for Economic Cooperation and Development.
OECD (2001) *Employment Outlook*. Paris: OECD.
OECD (2001) When money is tight: poverty dynamics in OECD countries. *OECD Employment Outlook*, June, 37–87.
Oerton, S. (1997) Queer housewives?: Some problems in theorising the division of labour in lesbian and gay households. *Women's Studies International Forum*, 20, 421–30.
Office for National Statistics (2000) *Social Trends*. London: Stationery Office.
Office for National Statistics (2001) *Social Focus on Men*. London: Stationery Office.
Office for National Statistics (2001) *Social Trends*. London: Stationery Office.
Office for National Statistics/Equal Opportunities Commission (1998) *Social Focus on Men and Women*. London: Stationery Office.
Office of National Statistics (1997) *Social Focus on Families*. London: HMSO.
Ogburn, W. F. (1933) The family and its functions. In the Report of the President's Committee on Social Trends, *Recent Social Trends in the United States*. Vol. 1. New York: McGraw-Hill.
Oliver, M. L., and Shapiro, T. M. (1995) *Black Wealth/White Wealth: A New Perspective on Racial Inequality*. New York: Routledge.
Olson, D. H., and McCubbin, H. I. (1989) *Families: What Makes Them Work?* Beverly Hills, CA: Sage.
Olwig, K. F. (1999) Narratives of the children left behind: Home and identity in globalised Caribbean families. *Journal of Ethnic and Racial Studies*, 25, 267–84.
O'Neill, O. (1996) Children's rights and children's lives. In R. Ladd (ed.), *Children's Rights Re-visioned: Philosophical Readings*. London, New York, and Belmont: Wadsworth.
O'Neill, O. (2002) *Autonomy and Trust in Bioethics*. Cambridge: Cambridge University Press.Ong, A. (1990) State versus Islam – Malay families, women's bodies, and the body politic in Malaysia. *American Ethnologist*, 17, 258–76.
Orbuch, T. L., House, J. S., Mero, R. P., and Webster, P. S. (1996) Marital quality over the life course. *Social Psychology Quarterly*, 59, 162–71.
Organisation for Economic Cooperation and Development (1996) *Caring for Frail Elderly People*. Social Policy Studies No. 19, Paris:OECD.
Orleck, A. (1987) The Soviet Jews: Life in Brighton Beach, Brooklyn. In N. Foner (ed.), *New Immigrants in New York*. New York: Columbia University Press.
Otero, L. L. (1994) *Nature, Plurality and the Future of the Family Phenomenon*. New York: United Nations Organization, IYF94 Report.
Oxley, H., Dang, T.-T., and Antolin, P. (2000) Poverty dynamics in six OECD countries. *OECD Economic Studies*, 30, 7–49.
Oxley, H., Dang, T.-T., and d'Ercole, M. M. (1997) Income distribution and poverty in 13 countries. *OECD Economic Studies*, 29, 55–92.
Paci, P., and Joshi, H. (1996) *Wage Differentials Between Men and Women. Evidence from Cohort Studies*. Research Series No. 71. London: Department for Education and Employment.

Pahl, J. (1989) *Money and Marriage*. London: Macmillan.

Pahl, R. (1984) *Divisions of Labour*. Oxford: Oxford University Press.

Pahl, R. (2000) *On Friendship*. Cambridge: Polity.

Pahl, R., and Wallace, C. (1985) Household work strategies in economic recession. In N. Redclift and E. Mingione (eds.), *Beyond Employment: Household, Gender and Subsistence*. Oxford: Basil Blackwell.

Palloni, A. (2000) Programmatic and Policy Aspects of Population Ageing and Living Arrangements. Paper presented at Technical Meeting on Population Ageing and Living Arrangements of Older Persons: Critical Issues and Policy Responses, United Nations, Population Division, New York.

Pampel, F. (1992) Trends in living alone among the elderly in Europe. In A. Rogers (ed.), *Elderly Migration and Population Redistribution*. London: Belhaven.

Pampel, F. (1998) *Aging, Social Inequality, and Public Policy*. Thousand Oaks, CA: Pine Forge.

Panchaud, C., Singh, S., Feivelson, D., and Darroch, J. E. (2000) Sexually transmitted diseases among adolescents in developed countries. *Family Planning Perspectives*, 32, 24–32, 45.

Pappas, G., Queen, S., Hadden, W., and Fisher, G. (1993) The increasing disparity in mortality between socioeconomic groups in the United States, 1960 and 1986. *New England Journal of Medicine*, 329, 103–9.

Parcel, T. L., and Dufur, M. J. (2001) Capital at home and at school: Effects on child social adjustment. *Journal of Marriage and Family*, 63, 32–47.

Parcel, T. L., and Menaghan, E. G. (1993) Family social capital and children's behavior problems. *Social Psychology Quarterly*, 56, 120–35.

Park, R. E., and Burgess, E. W. (1924) *Introduction to the Science of Sociology*. Chicago: University of Chicago Press.

Parker, R. (1988) An historical background. In I. Sinclair (ed.), *Residential Care: The Research Reviewed*. London: HMSO.

Parkman, A. M. (1992) Unilateral divorce and the labor force participation rate of married women revisited. *American Economic Review*, 82, 671–8.

Parks, M. R., and Eggert, L. L (1991) The role of social context in the dynamics of personal relationships. *Advances in Personal Relationships*, 2, 1–34.

Parks, M. R., Stan, C. M., and Eggert, L. L. (1983) Romantic involvement and social network involvement. *Social Psychology Quarterly*, 46, 116–31.

Parsons, E., and Bradley, D. (1994) Ethical issues in newborn screening for Duchenne muscular dystrophy. In A. Clarke (ed.), *Genetic Counselling, Practice and Principles*. London: Routledge.

Parsons, T. (1943) The kinship system of contemporary United States. *American Anthropologist*, 45, 22–38.

Parsons, T. (1949) Sex roles in American kinship systems. In T. Parsons, *Essays in Sociological Theory*.

Parsons, T. (1949) The social structure of the family. In R. N. Anshen (ed.), *The Family: Its Function and Destiny*. New York: Harper.

Parsons, T. (1999) Religion in postindustrial America. In B. S. Turner (ed.), *The Talcott Parsons Reader*. Oxford: Blackwell.

Parsons, T., and Bales, R. (1955) *Family Socialization and Interaction Process*. Glencoe, IL: The Free Press.

Pascual, C. (2000) Why more elderly Asian women kill themselves. *Los Angeles Times*, September 14, E1, E4.

Pasley, K., and Ihinger-Tallman, M. (1987) *Remarriage and Stepparenting: Current Research and Theory*. New York: Guilford.

Patterson, C. J. (1992) Children of lesbian and gay parents. *Child Development*, 63, 1025–42.

Patterson, C. J. (2000) Family relationships of lesbians and gay men. *Journal of Marriage and the Family*, 62, 1052–69.

Patterson, O. (1998) *Rituals of Blood: Consequences of Slavery in Two American Centuries*. Washington, DC: Civitas/Counterpoint.

Patterson, S. (1965) *Dark Strangers: A Study of West Indians in London*. Harmondsworth: Penguin.

Paul, D. B. (1998) *Controlling Human Heredity: 1865 to the Present*. Amherst, NY: Humanity Books.

Pear, R. (2000) Number of insured Americans up for first time since '87. *New York Times*, Vol. CL, No. 51,526, September 29, A15.

Peplau, L. A. (1981) What homosexuals want in relationships. *Psychology Today*, March, 28–38.

Peplau, L. A. (1991) Lesbian and gay relationships. In J. C. Gonsiorek and J. D. Weinrich (eds.), *Homosexuality: Implications for Social Policy*. Newbury Park, CA: Sage.

Peplau, L. A., Venigas, R. C., and Miller Campbell, S. (1996) Gay and lesbian relationships. In R. C. Savin-Williams and K. M. Cohen (eds.), *The Lives of Lesbians, Gays, and Bisexuals*. New York: Harcourt Brace College.

Perlow, L. (1999) The time famine: toward a sociology of work time. *Administrative Science Quarterly*, 44, 57–81.

Perry-Jenkins, M., Repetti, R. L., and Crouter, A. C. (2000) Work and family in the 1990s. *Journal of Marriage and the Family*, 62, 981–98.

Persaud, N., Gray, P. S., and Hunt, E. (1999) Raised by African-American single-parents to succeed: The perspectives of children. *International Journal of Sociology of the Family*, 29, 69–84.

Petersen, A., and Bunton, R. (2002) *The New Genetics and the Public's Health*. London: Routledge.

Petersen, A., and Lupton, D. (1996) *The New Public Health: Health and Self in the Age of Risk*. London: Sage.

Peterson, P. G. (1999) Gray dawn: the global aging crisis. *Foreign Affairs*, January/February, 42–55.

Pfau-Effinger, B. (1993) Modernization, culture, and part-time employment: The example of Finland and West Germany. *Work, Employment, and Society*, 7, 383–410.

Pfau-Effinger, B. (1998) Culture or structure as explanations for differences in part-time work in Germany, Finland and the Netherlands? In J. O'Reilly and C. Fagan (eds.), *Part-Time Prospects: An International Comparison of Part-Time Work in Europe, North America, and the Pacific Rim*. London: Routledge.

Phillips, M., and Phillips, T. (1998) *Windrush: The Irresistible Rise of Multi-Racial Britain*. London: HarperCollins.

Phillips, R. (1988) *Putting Asunder: A History of Divorce in Western Society*. Cambridge: Cambridge University Press.

Phillipson, C. (1998) *Reconstructing Old Age*. London: Sage.

Phillipson, C., Ahmed, N., and Latimer, J (2002) *Women in Between: A Study of the Experience of Bangladeshi Women Living in the London Borough of Tower Hamlets*. Final Report to the Nuffield Foundation.

Phillipson, C., Bernard, M., Phillips, J., and Ogg, J. (1999) Older people in three urban areas. In S. McRae (ed.), *Changing Britain: Families and Households in the 1990s*. Oxford: Oxford University Press.

Phillipson, C., Bernard, M., Phillips, J., and Ogg, J. (2001) *The Family and Community Life of Older People: Social Networks and Social Support in Three Urban Areas*. London: Routledge.

Piachaud, D. (1987) Problems in the definition and measurement of poverty. *Journal of Social Policy*, 16, 147–64.

Pickford, R. (1999) Unmarried fathers and the law. In A. Bainham, S. Day Sclater, and M. Richards (eds.), *What is a Parent: A Socio-Legal Analysis*. Oxford, Hart Publishing.

Pilcher, W. (1972) *The Portland Longshoremen: A Dispersed Urban Community*. New York: Holt, Rinehart, & Winston.

Pillemer , K., Moen, P., Wethington, E., and Glasgow, N. (2001) *Social Integration in the Second Half of Life*. Baltimore: Johns Hopkins University Press.

Pinker, S. (2002) *The Blank Slate: The Modern Denial of Human Nature*. New York: Viking.
Plomin, R. (1999) Behavioral genetics. In M. Bennett (ed.), *Developmental Psychology: Achievements and Prospects*. Philadelphia: Taylor & Francis.
Plomin, R. (1994) *Genetics and Experience: The Interplay Between Nature and Nurture*. Thousand Oaks, CA: Sage.
Plummer, K. (1995) *Telling Sexual Stories: Power, Change and Social Worlds*. London: Routledge.
Polatnick, R. (2000) Working parents: Issues for the next decades. *National Forum*, 80, 1–4.
Pollard, M. S., and Wu, Z. (1998) Divergence of marriage patterns in Quebec and elsewhere in Canada. *Population and Development Review*, 24, 329–56.
Pollock, L. A. (1983) *Forgotten Children: Parent–Child Relations from 1500 to 1900*. Cambridge: Cambridge University Press.
Popenoe, D. (1988) *Disturbing the Nest: Family Change and Decline in Modern Societies*. New York: Aldine de Gruyter.
Popenoe, D. (1993) American family decline, 1960–1990: A review and appraisal. *Journal of Marriage and the Family*, 55, 527–55.
Popenoe, D. (1996) *Life Without Father*. New York: Free Press.
Popenoe, D., Elshtain, J. B., and Blankenhorn, B. (eds.) (1996) *Promises to Keep: Decline and Renewal of Marriage in America*. Lanham, MD: Rowman & Littlefield.
Portes, A. (ed.) (1996) *The New Second Generation*. New York: Russell Sage Foundation.
Portes, A. (2000) The hidden abode: sociology as analysis of the unexpected. *American Sociological Review*, 65, 1–18.
Portes, A. (2000) The two meanings of social capital. *Sociological Forum*, 15, 1–11.
Portes, A., and Rumbaut, R. G. (1996) *Immigrant America: A Portrait*. Los Angeles: University of California Press.
Portes, A., and Zhou, M. (1993) The new second generation: segmented assimilation and its variants. *Annals of the American Academy of Political and Social Science*, 530, 74–96.
Powell, M. A., and Parcel, T. L. (1999) Parental work, family size and social capital effects on early adolescent educational outcomes: The United States and Great Britain compared. *Research in the Sociology of Work*, 7, 1–30.
Power, A., and Tunstall, R. (1995) *Swimming Against the Tide: Polarisation or Progress on 20 Unpopular Council Estates*. York: Joseph Rowntree Foundation.
Presser, H. B. (2000) Nonstandard work schedules and marital instability. *Journal of Marriage and the Family*, 62, 93–110.
Prinz, C. (1995) *Cohabiting, Married, or Single*. Aldershot: Ashgate.
Pritchard, R. (1998) *When Parents Part. How Children Adapt*. Auckland: Penguin.
Proctor, S. R., and Smith, I. J. (1997) Factors associated with birth outcome in Bradford Pakistanis. In A. Clarke and E. Parsons (eds.), *Culture, Kinship and Genes: Towards Cross-Cultural Genetics*. London: Macmillan.
Prout, A., and James, A. (1990) A new paradigm for the sociology of childhood? Provenance, promise and problems. In A. James and A. Prout (eds.), *Constructing and Reconstructing Childhood: Contemporary Issues in the Sociological Study of Childhood*. London: Falmer.
Pryce, K. (1979) *Endless Pressure*. Harmondsworth: Penguin.
Pryor, J. (1999) Waiting until they leave home: The experiences of young adults whose parents separate. *Journal of Divorce and Remarriage*, 32, 47–61.
Pryor, J. (2001) Adolescent attitudes to living arrangements after divorce. *Child and Family Law Quarterly*, 13, 1–13.
Pryor, J., and Rodgers, B. (2001) *Children in Changing Families: Life after Parents Separate*. Oxford: Blackwell.
Purcell, K., Hogarth, T., and Simm, C. (1999) *Whose Flexibility? The Costs and Benefits of Non-Standard Working Arrangements and Contractual Relations*. York: York Publishing Services for the Joseph Rowntree Foundation.

Putnam, R. D. (1993) Bowling alone: America's declining social capital. *Journal of Democracy*, 6, 65–78.

Putnam, R. D. (1993) *Making Democracy Work: Civic Traditions in Italy.* Princeton, NJ: Princeton University Press.

Putnam, R. D. (1996) The strange disappearance of civic America. *The American Prospect*, Winter, 24, 34–48.

Putnam, R.D. (2000) *Bowling Alone: the Collapse and Revival of American Community.* New York: Simon & Schuster.

Putnam, S., Sanson, A. V., and Rothbart, M. K. (2002) Child temperament and parenting. In M. H. Bornstein (ed.), *Handbook of Parenting.* 2nd ed. Vol. 1. Mahwah, NJ: Lawrence Erlbaum.

Pyke, K. (2000) The normal American family as an interpretive structure of family life among grown children of Korean and Vietnamese immigrants. *Journal of Marriage and the Family*, 62, 240–55.

Pyke, K. (forthcoming) "Generational deserters" and "black sheep": Acculturative differences among siblings in Korean and Vietnamese immigrant families. *Journal of Family Issues.*

Pyke, K., and Johnson, D. (2003) Asian American women and racialized femininities: "Doing" gender across cultural worlds. *Gender and Society*, 17, 33–53.

Quadagno, J. (1999) *Aging and the Life Course.* New York: McGraw-Hill.

Quaife, G. R. (1979) *Wanton Wenches and Wayward Wives: Peasants and Illicit Sex in Early Seventeenth Century England.* London: Croom Helm.

Qvortrup, J. (1990) A voice for children in statistical and social accounting: A plea for children's rights to be heard. In A. James and A. Prout (eds.), *Childhood: Constructing and Reconstructing Childhood: Contemporary Issues in the Sociological Study of Childhood.* London: Falmer.

Qvortrup, J. (1994) Childhood matters: An introduction. In J. Qvortup, M. Bardy, G. Sgritta, and H. Wintersberger (eds.) *Childhood Matters: Social Theory, Practice and Politics.* Aldershot: Avebury.

Raley, R. K. (1996) Shortage of marriageable men? A note on the role of cohabitation in black-white differences in marriage rates. *American Sociological Review*, 61, 973–83.

Raley, R. K. (2001) Increasing fertility in cohabiting unions: Evidence for the second demographic transition in the United States? *Demography*, 38, 59–66.

Ramey, S. L., and Keltner, B. (2002) Welfare reform and the vulnerability of mothers with intellectual disabilities (mild mental retardation). *Focus*, 22, 1, 82–6.

Randall, M., and Haskings, L. (1995) Sexual violence in women's lives. *Violence Against Women*, 1, 6–31.

Randall, V. (1999) Childcare policy in the European states: Limits to convergence. *Journal of European Public Policy*, 7, 346–68.

Randeria, S. (1999) Jenseits von Soziologie und soziokultureller Anthropologie. *Soziale Welt*, 50, 4, 373–82.

Rank, M., and Hirschl, T. (2001) The occurrence of poverty across the life cycle: Evidence from the PSID. *Journal of Policy Analysis and Management*, 20(4), 737–56.

Rapp, R. (1982) Towards a nuclear freeze? The gender politics of Euro-American kinship analysis. In J. F. Collier and S. Yanagisako (eds.), *Gender and Kinship. Essays Toward a Unified Analysis.* New York: Stanford University Press.

Rapp, R. (2000) *Testing Women, Testing the Fetus: The Social Impact of Amniocentesis in America.* New York: Routledge.

Rappoport, R., Bailyn, L., Fletcher, J., and Pruitt, B. (2002) *Beyond Work-Family Balance: Advancing Gender Equity and Workplace Performance.* San Francisco: Jossey Bass.

Raymond, J. G. (1994) *Women or Wombs: Reproductive Technologies and the Battle Over Women's Freedom.* Melbourne: Spinifex.

Rayside, D. (1991) *A Small Town in Modern Times: Alexandria, Ontario.* Montreal: McGill-Queen's University Press.

Rees, A. (1951) *Life in a Welsh Countryside: A Social Study of Llanfihangel yng Ngwynfa*. Cardiff: University of Wales Press.

Regan, P. C., and Ramirez, C. (2000) Decisions on child care: do sex and sexual orientation matter? *Psychological Reports*, 86, 922–4.

Reimers, D. M. (1996) Third World immigration to the United States. In H. O. Duleep and P. V. Wunnava (eds.), *Immigrants and Immigration Policy: Individual Skills, Family Ties, and Group Identities*. Greenwich, CT: JAI Press.

Rein, M., and Saltzman, H. (1995) Social integration, participation and exchange in five industrial countries. In S. Bass (ed.), *Older and Alive*. New Haven, CT: Yale University Press.

Reiss, D., Neiderhiser, J., Hetherington, E. M., and Plomin, R. (2000) *The Relationship Code: Deciphering Genetic and Social Patterns in Adolescent Development*. Cambridge, MA: Harvard University Press.

Rengelink-van Der Lee, J. H., Schulpen, T. W., and Beemer, F. A. (1995) Incidence and prevalence of hemoglobinopathies in children in the Netherlands (in Dutch). *Nederlands Tijdschrift voor Geneeskunde*, 139, 1498–1501.

Repack, T. A. (1997) New roles in a new landscape. In M. Romero, P. Hondagneu-Sotelo, and V. Ortiz (eds.), *Challenging Fronteras: Structuring Latina and Latino Lives in the U.S.* New York: Routledge.

Rerrich, M. S. (1990) Ein gleich gutes Leben für alle? Über Ungleichheitserfahrungen im familialen Alltag. In P. A. Berger and S. Hradil (eds.), *Lebenslagen – Lebensläufe – Lebensstile. Soziale Welt*. Sonderband 7, Göttingen: Schwartz.

Resnick, H., Kilpatrick, D., Walsh, C., and Veronen, L. (1991) Marital rape. In R. T. Ammerman and M. Herson (eds.), *Case Studies in Family Violence*. New York: Plenum.

Reuters (2002) June 11. Available online at www.reuters.com

Reuther, R. R. (1974) Misogynism and virginal feminism in the Fathers of the Church. In R. R. Ruether (ed.), *Religion and Sexism. Images of Woman in the Jewish and Christian Traditions*. New York: Simon & Schuster.

Rhode, D. L. (1997) *Speaking of Sex: The Denial of Gender Inequality*. Boston: Harvard University Press.

Ribbens, J. (1994) *Mothers and Their Children: A Feminist Sociology of Childrearing*. London: Sage.

Rich, A. (1976) *Of Woman Born: Motherhood as Experience and Institution*. New York: Bantam.

Rich, A. (1983) On compulsory heterosexuality and lesbian existence. In A. Snitow, C. Stansell, and S. Thompson (eds.), *Desire: The Politics of Sexuality*. London: Virago Press.

Richards, L. (1990) *Nobody's Home: Dreams and Realities in a New Suburb*. Melbourne: Oxford University Press.

Richards, M. (ed.) (1974) *The Integration of a Child into a Social World*. Cambridge: Cambridge University Press.

Richards, M. (2002) Future bodies: Some history and future prospects for human genetic selection. In A. Bainham, S. Day-Sclater, and M. Richards (eds.), *Body Lore and Laws*. Oxford: Hart.

Richards, M. P. M. (1996) Families, kinship and genetics. In T. Marteau and M. P. M. Richards (eds.), *The Troubled Helix: Social and Psychological Implications of the New Human Genetics*. Cambridge: Cambridge University Press.

Richards, M. P. M. (1998) Annotation: Genetic research, family life and clinical practice. *Journal of Child Psychology and Psychiatry*, 39, 291–305.

Richards, M. P. M. (2000) *Unpublished Data*. Centre for Family Research, University of Cambridge.

Richards, M. P. M. (2001) How distinctive is genetic information? *Studies in the History of Biological and Biomedical Sciences*, 32, 663–87.

Ricketts, W., and Achtenberg, R. (1990) Adoption and foster parenting for lesbian and gay men: creating new traditions in family. In F. W. Bozett and M. B. Sussman (eds.), *Homosexuality and Family Relations*. New York: Praeger.

Ridgeway, C. L., and Smith-Lovin, L. (1999) The gender system and interaction. *Annual Review of Sociology*, 25, 191–216.

Riessman, C. K. (1990) *Divorce Talk: Women and Men Make Sense of Personal Relationships*. New Brunswick, NJ: Rutgers University Press.

Riggs, A., and Turner, B. S. (1999) The expectation of love in older age: towards a sociology of intimacy. In M. Poole and S. Feldman (eds.), *A Certain Age. Women Growing Older*. St Leonards: Allen & Unwin.

Rights of Women Custody Group (1986) *Lesbian Mothers' Legal Handbook*. London: The Women's Press.

Riley, M. W., and Riley, J. W. (1993) Connections: Kin and cohort. In V. L. Bengtson and W. A. Achenbaum (eds.), *The Changing Contract across Generations*. New York: Aldine de Gruyter.

Ringen, S., and Halpin, B. (1995) *The Standard of Living of Children*. Oxford: Department of Applied Social Studies and Social Research, University of Oxford.

Roberto, K. A., Allen, K. R., and Blieszner, R. (2001) Grandfathers' perceptions and expectations of relationships with their adult grandchildren. *Journal of Family Issues*, 22, 407–26.

Roberts, E. (1995) *Women and Families: An Oral History, 1940–1970*. Oxford: Blackwell.

Robertson, R. (1995) Glocalization. In M. Featherstone, S. Lash, and R. Robertson (eds.), *Global Modernities*. London: Sage.

Rodgers, B. (1997) Social and psychological outcomes for children from divorced families: Australian research findings. In *Enhancing Children's Potential: Minimising Risk and Maximising Resiliency*. Dunedin: Children's Issues Centre.

Rodgers, B., and Pryor, J. (1998) *Divorce and Separation. The Outcomes for Children*. York: Joseph Rowntree Foundation.

Rodgers, H. R. (1995) *Poor Women, Poor Children: American Poverty in the 1990s*. Armonk, NJ: M. E. Sharpe.

Rofes, E. (1997) Dancing bears, performing husbands, and the tyranny of the family. In R. E. Goss and A. S. Strongheart (eds.), *Our Families, Our Values: Snapshots of Queer Kinship*. Binghampton, NJ: Harrington Park Press.

Rook, K., and Ituarte, P. (1999). Social control, social support, and companionship in older adults' family relationships and friendships. *Personal Relationships*, 6, 199–211.

Roschelle, A. R. (1997) *No More Kin: Exploring Race, Class, and Gender in Family Networks*. Thousand Oaks, CA: Sage.

Rose, H., and Bruce, E. (1995) Mutual care but differential esteem: Caring between old couples. In S. Arber and J. Ginn (eds.), *Connecting Gender and Ageing: A Sociological Approach*. Buckingham: Open University Press.

Rosenfeld, R. A. (1996) Women's work histories. In J. B. Casterline, R. D. Lee and K. A. Foote (eds.), *Fertility in the United States: New Patterns, New Theories*. New York: Population Council.

Rosenfeld, R. A., and Birkelund, G. E. (1995) Women's part time work: A cross-national comparison. *European Sociological Review*, 11, 111–34.

Rosenmayer, L., and Kockeis, C. (1963) Propositions for a sociological theory of ageing and the family. *International Social Service Journal*, 15, 410–26.

Rosier, K. B. (2000) *Mothering Inner-City Children: The Early School Years*. New Brunswick, NJ: Rutgers University Press.

Ross, C. E. (1995) Reconceptualizing marital status as a continuum of social attachment. *Journal of Marriage and the Family*, 57, 129–40.

Ross, C. E., Mirowsky, J., and Goldsteen, K. (1990) The impact of the family on health: The decade in review. *Journal of Marriage and the Family*, 52, 1059–78.

Ross, C. E., and Van Willigen, M. (1996) Gender, parenthood, and anger. *Journal of Marriage and the Family*, 58, 572–84.

Ross, E. (1983) Survival networks: Women's neighbourhood sharing in the East End of London before World War One. *History Workshop*, Spring, 4–27.

Rosser, C., and Harris, C. C. (1965) *The Family and Social Change*. London: Routledge & Kegan Paul.

Rossi, A., and Rossi, P. (1990) *Of Human Bonding: Parent–Child Relations across the Life Course*. New York: Aldine de Gruyter.

Röthel, A. (1999) Nichteheliche Lebensgemeinschaften – Neue Rechtsfragen und Regelungsaufgaben im In- und Ausland. *Zeitschrift für Rechtspolitik*, 12, 511–19.

Rothenbacher, F. (1995) European family indicators. *Eurodata Newsletter*, 3, article 10.

Rowe, D. C. (1983) A biometrical analysis of perceptions of family environment: A study of twin and singleton sibling kinships. *Child Development*, 54, 416–23.

Rowe, D. C. (1994) *The Limits of Family Influence: Genes, Experience, and Behavior.* New York: Guilford.

Rowe, D. C., and Teachman, J. (2001) Behavioral genetic research designs and social policy studies. In A. Thornton (ed.), *The Well-Being of Children and Families: Research and Data Needs*. Ann Arbor, University of Michigan Press.

Rowntree, S. (1901) *Poverty: A Study of Town Life*. London: Thomas Nelson and Sons.

Roxburgh, S., Stephens, R. C., Toltzis, P., and Adkins, I. (2001) The value of children, parenting strains, and depression among urban African American mothers. *Sociological Forum*, 16, 55–72.

Rubel, A. J. (1966) *Across the Tracks: Mexican Americans in a Texas City.* Austin: University of Texas Press.

Rubin, L. (1985) *Just Friends. The Role of Friendship in Our Lives*. New York: Harper & Row.

Ruddick, S. (1989). *Maternal Thinking: Toward a Politics of Peace*. Boston, MA: Beacon.

Ruivo, M., do Pilar Gonzalez, M., and Varejão, J. (1998) Why is part-time work so low in Spain and Portugal?" In J. O'Reilly and C. Fagan (eds.), *Part-Time Prospects: An International Comparison of Part-Time Work in Europe, North America, and the Pacific Rim.* London: Routledge.

Rumbaut, R. G. (1994) The crucible within: Ethnic identity, self-esteem, and segmented assimilation among children of immigrants. *International Migration Review*, 28, 748–94.

Rumbaut, R. G. (1996) The crucible within: ethnic identity, self-esteem, and segmented assimilation among children of immigrants. In A. Portes (ed.), *The New Second Generation.* New York: Russell Sage Foundation.

Rumbaut, R. G. (1997) Assimilation and its discontents. Between rhetoric and reality. *International Migration Review*, 31, 923–60.

Rumbaut, R. (1997) Ties that bind: Immigration and immigrant families in the U.S. In A. Booth, A. C. Crouter, and N. Landale (eds.), *Immigration and the Family: Research and Policy on U.S. Immigrants*. Mahwah, NJ: Lawrence Erlbaum.

Runyan, D. K., Hunter, W. M., et al. (1998) Children who prosper in unfavorable environments: The relationship to social capital. *Pediatrics*, 101, 12–18.

Rutter, M., Champion, L., Quinton, D., Maughan, B., and Pickles, A. (1995) Understanding individual differences in environmental risk exposure. In P. Moen, G. H. Elder, Jr., and K. Lüscher (eds.), *Examining Lives in Context: Perspectives on the Ecology of Human Development.* Washington DC: American Psychological Association.

Ryder, N. B., and Westoff, C. F. (1977) *The Contraceptive Revolution*. Princeton, NJ: Princeton University Press.

Rytina, S. (2000) Is occupational mobility declining in the US? *Social Forces*, 78, 1227–76.

Sam, D. L., and Berry, J. W. (1995) Acculturative stress among young immigrants in Norway. *Scandinavian Journal of Psychology*, 36, 10–24.

Sandefur, G. D., Martin, M., Eggerling-Boeck, J., Mannon, S. E., and Meier, A. M. (2001) An overview of racial and ethnic demographic trends. In N. J. Smelser, W. J. Wilson, and F. Mitchell (eds.), *America Becoming: Racial Trends and Their Consequences, Vol 1.* Washington, DC: National Academy Press.

Santelli, J. S., Brener, N. D., Lowry, R., Bhatt, A., and Zabin, L. S. (1998) Multiple sex partners among U.S. adolescents and young adults. *Family Planning Perspectives*, 30, 271–5.

Santelli, J. S., Lindberg, L. D., Abma, J., McNeely, C. S., and Resnick, M. (2000) Adolescent sexual behavior: Estimates and trends from four national surveys. *Family Planning Perspectives*, 32, 156–65, 194.

Santos, R., and Seitz, P. (2000) Benefit coverage for Latino and Latina workers. In S. M. Perez (ed.), *Moving up the Economic Ladder: Latino Workers and the Nation's Future Prosperity*. Washington, DC: National Council of La Raza.

Sarre, S. (1996) A place for fathers: Fathers and social policy in the post-war period. In *The Welfare State Program, Discussion Paper No. 25*. London: London School of Economics.

Sarsby, J. (1988) *Missuses and Mouldrunners: An Oral History of Women Pottery Workers at Work and at Home*. Milton Keynes: Open University Press.

Scales, J., and Scase, R. (2001) *Fit at Fifty*. Swindon: Economic and Social Research Council.

Scanzoni, J., and Marsiglio, W. (1993) New action theory and contemporary families. *Journal of Family Issues*, 14, 105–32.

Scarce, J. (1996) *Domestic Culture in the Middle East*. Edinburgh: National Museums of Scotland.

Scarr, S. (1992) Developmental theories for the 1990s: development of individual differences. *Child Development*, 63, 1–19.

Scarr, S. (1995) How do families affect intelligence? Social environmental and behavior genetic predictions. In J. J. Hox, B. F. van der Meulen, J. M. A. M. Janssens, J. J. F. ter Laak and L. W. C. Tavecchio (eds.), *Advances in Family Research*. Amsterdam: Thesis.

Schlumbohm, J. (1980) "Traditional" collectivity and "modern" individuality: some questions and suggestions for the historical study of socialization: the examples of the German lower and upper bourgeoisie around 1800. *Social History*, 5, 71–103.

Schmitz, H., and Schmidt-Denter, U. (1999) Die Nachscheidungsfamilie sechs Jahre nach der elterlichen Trennung. *Zeitschrift für Familienforschung*, 3, 28–55.

Schnailberg, A., and Goldenberg, S. (1989) From empty nest to crowded nest: The dynamics of incompletely launched young adult. *Social Problems*, 36, 251–69.

Schneider, D. (1968) *American Kinship: A Cultural Account*. Englewood Cliffs, NJ: Prentice-Hall.

Schneider, D. (1980) *Kinship: A Cultural Account*. Chicago: University of Chicago Press.

Schneider, J. C., and Schneider, P. T. (1996) *Festival of the Poor: Fertility Decline and the Ideology of Class in Sicily, 1860–1980*. Tucson: University of Arizona Press.

Schochet, G. J. (1975) *Patriarchalism in Political Thought*. Oxford: Oxford University Press.

Schoon, I., Bynner, J., Joshi, H., Parson, S., Wiggens, R., and Sacker, A. (forthcoming) The influence of context, timing and duration of risk experiences for the passage from childhood to early adulthood. *Child Development*.

Schuller, T. (1989) Work-ending: Employment and ambiguity in later life. In B. Bytheway, T. Keil, P. Allatt, and A. Bryman (eds.), *Becoming and Being Old*. London: Sage.

Schulpen, T. W. (1996) Migration and child health: the Dutch experience. *European Journal of Pediatrics*, 155, 351–6.

Schulze, H-J. (1999) *"Netherlands", The Family Observer*. Vienna: Austrian Institute for Family Studies.

Schumpeter, J. A. (1988) [1942] Decomposition. *Population and Development Review*, 14, 499–506.

Schwartz, P., and Rutter, V. (1998) *The Gender of Sexuality*. Thousand Oaks, CA: Pine Forge Press.

Schwarz, J. E. (1997) *Illusions of Opportunity: The American Dream in Question*. New York: W. W. Norton.

Scott, J. (1992) *Social Network Analysis*. Newbury Park. CA: Sage.

Scott, J. (1998) Changing attitudes to sexual morality: A cross-national comparison. *Sociology*, 32, 815–45.

Scott, J. (2000) Children as respondents: The challenge for quantitative methods. In P. Christensen and A. James (eds.), *Research with Children*. London: Falmer.

Scott, J. (2000) Is it a different world than when you were growing up? Generational effects on social representations and child-rearing values. *British Journal of Sociology*, 51, 355–76.

Sears, R. R., Maccoby, E. E., and Levin, H. (1957), *Patterns of Child-Rearing*. Evanston IL: Row, Peterson & Co.

Sedgwick, E. K. (1985) *Between Men: English Literature and Male Homosocial Desire*. New York: Columbia University Press.

Sedgwick, E. K. (1990) *Epistemology of the Closet*. Berkeley and Los Angeles: University of California Press.

Seeman, T. E., Berkman, L. F., Blazer, D., and Rowe, J. W. (1994) Social ties and support and neuroendocrine function: The MacArthur studies of successful aging. *Annals of Behavioral Medicine*, 16, 95–106.

Segalen, M. (1997) Introduction. In M. Gullestad and M. Segalen (eds.), *Family and Kinship in Europe*. London: Pinter.

Seltzer, J. A. (1998) Men's contributions to children and social policy. In A. Booth and A. C. Crouter (eds.), *Men in Families: When do They Get Involved? What Difference Does it Make?* Mahwah, NJ: Lawrence Erlbaum.

Seltzer, J. A. (2000) Families formed outside of marriage. *Journal of Marriage and the Family*, 62, 1247–68.

Sennett, R. (1971) *The Uses of Disorder: Personal Identity and City Life*. London: Allen Lane.

Sennett, R. (1998) *The Corrosion of Character*. New York: W. W. Norton.

Settersten, R. (2003) *Invitation to the Life Course: Toward New Understandings of Later Life*. New York: Baywood Press.

Settles, B. (1998) Putting families in family policy and programs: local, regional, national and international options. In K. Matthijs (ed.), *The Family: Contemporary Perspectives and Challenges*. Leuven: Leuven University Press.

Sewell, W. H., Sr., and Hauser, R. M. (1975) *Education, Occupation and Earnings: Achievement in the Early Career*. New York: Academic.

Shanahan, M., Elder, G. H., Jr., Burchinal, M., and Conger, R. (1996) Adolescent earnings and relationships with parents: the work-family nexus in urban and rural ecologies. In J. Mortimer and M. Finch (eds.), *Adolescents, Work and Family*. London: Sage.

Shanahan, M. J., Hofer, S. M., and Shanahan, L. (2003) Biological models of behavior and the life course. In J. T. Mortimer and M. J. Shanahan (eds.), *Handbook of the Life Course*. New York: Kluwer Academic/Plenum.

Shanas, E. (1979) The family as a social support system in old age. *The Gerontologist*, 19, 169–74.

Shannon, G. (ed.) (1999) *The Divorce Act in Practice*. Dublin: Round Hall.

Shaver, S., and Bradshaw, J. (1995) The recognition of wifely labor by welfare states. *Social Policy and Administration*, 29, 10–25.

Shaw, A. (2000) Conflicting models of risk: Clinical genetics and British Pakistanis. In P. Caplan (ed.), *Risk Revisited*. London: Pluto Press.

Shaw, A. (2000) *Kinship and Continuity: Pakistani Families in Britain*. Amsterdam: Routledge/ Harwood Academic.

Shaw, A. (2001) Kinship, cultural preference and immigration: Consanguineous marriage among British Pakistanis. *Journal of the Royal Anthropological Institute*, 7, 315–34.

Shaw, A. (in press) Negotiations of risk among Pakistani-origin users of the genetic services. In M. Unnithan-Kumar (ed.), *Reproductive Agency, Medicine and the State: Cultural Transformations in Childbearing*. Oxford: Berghahn Books.

Shaw, A., Kellard, K., and Walker, R. (1996) *Barriers, Bridges and Behaviour*. London: Department of Social Security In-house Report No 18.

Shelton, B. A. (1990) The distribution of household tasks: Does wife's employment status make a difference? *Journal of Family Issues*, 11, 115–35.

Shelton, B. A., and John, D. (1993) Does marital status make a difference? Housework among married and cohabiting men and women. *Journal of Family Issues*, 14, 401–20.

Sherman, S. (ed.) (1992) *Lesbian and Gay Marriage: Private Commitments, Public Ceremonies*. Philadelphia: Temple University Press.

Shonkoff, J. P., and Phillips, D. A. (eds.) (2000) *From Neurons to Neighborhoods: The Science of Early Childhood Development*. Washington, DC: National Academy Press.

Short, P. F., Kemper, P., Cornelius, L. J., and Walden, D.C. (1992) Public and private responsibility for financing nursing home care: The effect of Medicaid asset spend-down. *Milbank Quarterly*, 70, 277–98.

Short, S. E., Zhai, F., Xu, S., and Yang, M. (2001) China's one-child policy and the care of children: an analysis of qualitative and quantitative data. *Social Forces*, 79, 913–43.

Shorter, E. (1975) *The Making of the Modern Family*. New York: Basic Books.

Silberman, L. (2000) The Hague children's conventions: The internationalisation of child law. In S. Katz, J. Eekalaar, and M. Maclean (eds.), *Cross Currents: Family Law in the US and England*. Oxford: Oxford University Press.

Silva, E. B., and Smart, C. (eds.) (1999) *The New Family?* London: Sage.

Silver, L. M. (1998) *Remaking Eden. Cloning, Genetic Engineering and the Future of Human Kind*. London: Weidenfeld & Nicolson.

Silverstein, M., and Bengtson, V. L. (1991) Do close parent–child relations reduce the mortality risk of older parents? *Journal of Health and Social Behavior*, 32, 382–95.

Silverstein, M., and Bengtson, V. L. (1997) Intergenerational solidarity and the structure of adult child–parent relationships in American families. *American Journal of Sociology*, 103, 429–60.

Silverstein, M., Burholt, V., Wenger, G. C., and Bengtson, V. L. (1998) Parent–child relations among very old parents in Wales and the US: A test of modernization theory. *Journal of Aging Studies*, 12, 387–409.

Silverstein, M., and Chen, X. (1999) The impact of acculturation in Mexican American families on the quality of adult grandchild-grandparent relationships. *Journal of Marriage and the Family*, 61,188–98.

Silverstein, M., Parrott, T. M., and Bengtson, V. L. (1995) Factors that predispose middle-aged sons and daughters to provide social support to older parents. *Journal of Marriage and the Family*, 57, 465–75.

Simons, R. L. (1996) *Understanding the Differences Between Divorced and Intact Families. Stress, Interaction, and Child Outcome*. Thousand Oaks, CA: Sage.

Simpson, S. (1997) Demography and ethnicity: Case studies from Bradford. *New Community*, 23, 89–107.

Singh, S., Darroch, J. E., and Frost, J. J. (2001) Socioeconomic disadvantage and adolescent women's sexual and reproductive behavior: The case of five developed countries. *Family Planning Perspectives*, 33, 251–9.

Skolnick, A. (1997) The triple revolution: social sources of family change. In S. Dreman (ed.), *The Family on the Threshold of the 21st Century*. Mahwah, NJ: Lawrence Erlbaum.

Smart, C., and Neale, B. (1999) *Family Fragments?* Cambridge: Polity and Blackwell.

Smart, C., Neale, B., and Wade, A. (2001) *The Changing Experience of Childhood: Families and Divorce*. Cambridge: Polity.

Smeeding, T., Rainwater, L., and Burtless, G. (2000) *United States Poverty in a Cross-National Context*. Luxembourg: Luxembourg Income Study, Working Paper, 244.

Smith, A. B., Taylor, N. J., Gollop, M., Gaffney, M., Gold, M., and Heneghan, M. (1997) *Access and other Post-Separation Issues*. Dunedin: Children's Issues Centre.

Smith, C. (2000) *Christian America? What Evangelicals Really Want*. Berkeley: University of California Press.

Smith, M. (1997) Psychology's under-valuation of single motherhood. *Feminism and Psychology*, 7, 529–32.

Smith, R. T. (1988) *Kinship and Class in the West Indies: A Genealogical Study of Jamaica and Guyana*. Cambridge: Cambridge University Press.

Smith, T. W. (1991) Adult sexual behavior in 1989: Number of partners, frequency of sexual intercourse and risk of AIDS. *Family Planning Perspectives*, 23, 102–7.

Smith, T. W. (1994) Attitudes toward sexual permissiveness: Trends, correlates, and behavioral connections. In A. S. Rossi (ed.), *Sexuality Across the Life Course*. Chicago: University of Chicago Press.

Smith, T. W. (1999) *The Emerging 21st Century American Family*. General Social Survey Social Change Report No. 42. Chicago: National Opinion Research Center, University of Chicago.

Smith, T. W. (2002) The transition to adulthood and the generation gap: from the 1970s to the 1990s. Manuscript in progress.

Solberg, A. (1990) Negotiating childhood: Changing constructions of age for Norwegian children. In A. James and A. Prout (eds.), *Constructing and Reconstructing Childhood*. Basingstoke: Falmer.

Solberg, A. (1994) *Negotiating Childhood: Empirical Investigations and Textual Representations of Children's Work and Everyday Lives*. Stockholm: Nordic Institute for Studies in Urban and Regional Planning.

Solberg, A. (1997) Negotiating childhood: Changing constructions of age for Norwegian children. In A. James and A. Prout (eds.), *Constructing and Reconstructing Childhood* (2nd ed.). London: Falmer.

Soldo, B., and Wong, R. (2000) Strategic Family Decisions and Remittances: Migration and Aging in Mexico. Paper presented at the annual meeting of the Gerontological Society of America, Washington, DC.

Solien, N. (1965) The consanguineal household and matrifocality. *American Anthropologist*, 67, 1541–9.

Sommestad, L. (1997) Welfare state attitudes to the male breadwinning system: The United States and Sweden in comparative perspective. *International Review of Social History*, 42, 153–74.

Sonenstein, F. L., Pleck, J. H., and Ku, L. C. (1991) Levels of sexual activity among adolescent males in the United States. *Family Planning Perspectives*, 23, 162–7.

Song, M., and Edwards, R. (1997) Comment: Raising questions about perspectives on black lone motherhood. *Journal of Social Policy*, 26, 233–44.

Sorrentino, C. (1990) The Changing Family in International Perspective. *Monthly Labor Review*, 113, 41–58.

South, S. J., and Lloyd, K. M. (1995) Spousal alternatives and marital dissolution. *American Sociological Review*, 60, 21–35.

South, S. J., and Spitze, G. (1994) Housework in marital and nonmarital households. *American Sociological Review*, 59, 327–47.

Spallone, P. (1987) Reproductive technology and the state: The Warnock Report and its clones. In P. Spallone and D. L. Steinberg (eds.), *Made to Order: the Myth of Reproductive and Genetic Progress*. Oxford: Pergamon.

Spanier, G. B., and Margolis, R. L. (1983) Marital separation and extramarital sexual behavior. *Journal of Sex Research*, 19, 23–48.

Speak, S., Camerson, S., and Gilroy, R. (1997*) Young Single Fathers. Participation in Fatherhood – Bridges and Barriers*. London: Family Policy Studies Centre

Spencer, L., and Taylor, S. (1994) *Participation and Progress in the Labour Market: Key Issues for Women*. Research Series No. 35. London: Department of Employment.

Spicer, J. W., and Hampe, G. D. (1975) Kinship interaction after divorce. *Journal of Marriage and the Family*, 37, 113–19.

Spillman, B. C., and Pezzin, L. E. (2000) Potential and active family caregivers: changing networks and the "sandwich generation." *Milbank Quarterly*, 78, 347–74.

Sporakowski, M., and Axelson, L. (1989) Long-term marriages: a critical review. In L. Ade-Ridder and C. Hennon (eds.), *Lifestyles of the Elderly*. New York: Human Sciences Press.

Sprecher, S., Regan, P. C., and McKinney, K. (1998) Beliefs about the outcomes of extramarital sexual relationships as a function of gender of the "cheating spouse". *Sex Roles*, 38, 301–11.

Stacey, J. (1990) *Brave New Families*. New York: Basic Books.

Stacey, J. (1996) *In the Name of the Family: Rethinking Family Values in the Postmodern Age.* Boston: Beacon.

Stacey, J., and Biblarz, T. J. (2001) (How) does the sexual orientation of parents matter? *American Sociological Review*, 66, 159–83.

Stack, C. B. (1974) *All Our Kin: Strategies for Survival in a Black Community.* New York: Harper.

Stack, S., and Wasserman, I. (1993) Marital status, alcohol consumption, and suicide: An analysis of national data. *Journal of Marriage and the Family*, 55, 1018–24.

Stanworth, M. (ed.) (1987) *Reproductive Technologies: Gender, Motherhood and Medicine.* Cambridge: Polity.

Statistisches Bundesamt (1995) *Im Blickpunkt: Familien heute.* Stuttgart: Metzler-Poeschel.

Statistisches Bundesamt (2003) Daten report 2002. Zahlen und Fakten über die Bundesrepublik Deutschland. Bundeszentrale für politische Bildung.

Steedman, C. (1990) *Childhood, Culture and Class in Britain: Margaret McMillan 1860–1931.* London: Virago.

Stein, C. H., Bush, E. G., Ross, R. R., and Ward, M. (1992) Mine, yours and ours: a configural analysis of the networks of married couples in relation to marital satisfaction and individual well-being. *Journal of Personal Relationships*, 9, 365–83.

Steinberg, L., Darling, N. E., and Fletcher, A. C., in collaboration with Brown, B. B. and Dornbusch, S. M. (1995) Authoritative parenting and adolescent adjustment: An Ecological Journey. In P. Moen, G. H. Elder, Jr., and K. Lüscher (eds.), *Examining Lives in Context: Perspectives on the Ecology of Human Development.* Washington, DC: American Psychological Association.

Steinberg, L., and Silk, J. S. (2002) Parenting adolescents. In M. H. Bornstein (ed.), *Handbook of Parenting.* 2nd ed. Vol. 1, Mahwah, NJ: Lawrence Erlbaum.

Steinbock, B. (2002) Sex selection. Not obviously wrong. *Hastings Center Report*, 32, 23–8.

Stephens, M. A. P., Townsend, A. L., Martire, L. M., and Druley, J. A. (2001) Balancing parent care with other roles: Interrole conflict of adult daughter caregivers. *Journal of Gerontology: Psychological Sciences*, 56B, P24–34.

Steptoe, P., and Edwards, R. G. (1978) Birth after the replacement of a human embryo. *Lancet*, ii, 366.

Stone, D. A. (2000) Reconsidering the role of competition in health care markets: United States. *Journal of Health Politics*, 25, 953–8.

Stone, L. (1977) *The Family, Sex and Marriage in England, 1500–1800.* New York: Oxford University Press.

Strasser, M. (1997) *Legally Wed: Same-Sex Marriage and the Constitution.* Ithaca: Cornell University Press.

Stratford, N., Marteau, T., and Bobrow, M. (1999) Tailoring genes. In R. Jowell et al. (eds.), *British Social Attitudes. The 16th* Report. Aldershot: Ashgate.

Strathern, M. (1992) *Reproducing the Future. Essays on Anthropology, Kinship and the New Reproductive Technologies.* Manchester: Manchester University Press.

Strathern, M. (1999) *Property, Substance and Effect. Anthropological Essays on Persons and Things.* London: Athlone.

Straus, M. A. (1979) Measuring intrafamily conflict and violence: The Conflict Tactics (CT) Scales. *Journal of Marriage and the Family*, 41, 75–88.

Stuart, E. (1995) *Just Good Friends: Towards a Lesbian and Gay Theology of Relationships.* London: Mowbray.

Suárez-Orozco, C., and Suárez-Orozco, M. (1995) *Transformations: Immigration, Family Life, and Achievement Motivation among Latino Adolescents.* Stanford, CA: Stanford University Press.

Sucoff, C. A., and Upchurch, D. M. (1998) Neighborhood context and the risk of childbearing among metropolitan-area Black adolescents. *American Sociological Review*, 63, 571–5.

Sullivan, A. (1995) *Virtually Normal: An Argument about Homosexuality*. London: Picador.

Sullivan, A. (ed.) (1997) *Same-Sex Marriage: Pro and Con – A Reader.* New York: Vintage.

Sullivan, A. (1998) *Love Undetectable: Reflections on Friendship, Sex and Survival.* London: Chatto & Windus.

Sullivan, M. (1996) Rozzie and Harriet? Gender and family patterns of lesbian coparents. *Gender and Society*, 10, 747–67.

Sullivan, O. (2000) The division of domestic labour: twenty years of change? *Sociology*, 34, 437–56.

Sun, Y. (2001) Family environment and adolescents' well-being before and after parents' marital disruption: A longitudinal analysis. *Journal of Marriage and the Family*, 63, 697–713.

Sung, B. L. (1987) *The Adjustment Experience of Chinese Immigrant Children in New York City.* New York: Center for Migration Studies.

Sung, K. T. (2000) An Asian perspective on aging East and West: Filial piety and changing families. In K. D. Kim, V. L. Bengtson, G. C. Meyers, and K. S. Eun (eds.), *Aging East and West: Families, States, and the Elderly.* New York: Springer.

Surra, C. A. (1985) Courtship types: variations in interdependence between partners and social networks. *Journal of Personality and Social Psychology*, 49, 357–75.

Surra, C. A. (1988) The Influence of the interactive network on developing relationships. In R. M. Milardo (ed.), *Families and Social Networks.* Newbury Park: Sage.

Surra, C. A., and Milardo, R. M. (1991) The social psychological context of developing relationships: Interactive and psychological networks. In J. Kingsley (ed.), *Advances in Personal Relationships*, 3, 1–36.

Sutherland, H. (1997) Women, men and the redistribution of income. *Fiscal Studies*, 18, 1–22.

Sweating, C. (ed.) (1998) *Women and Poverty in the North.* Oxford: Oxfam.

Szinovacz, M (2000) Changes in housework after retirement: A panel analysis. *Journal of Marriage and the Family*, 62, 78–92.

Szinovacz, M., Ekerdt, D. J., and Vinick, B. H. (eds.) (1992). *Families and Retirement.* Newbury Park, CA: Sage.

Taitz, J., Weekers, J. E. M., and Mosca, D. T. (2002) DNA and immigration: The ethical ramifications. *Lancet*, 359, 794.

Tam, C., and Detzner D. (1998) Grandparents as a family resource in Chinese-American families. In H. I. McCubbin, E. A. Thompson, A. I. Thompson, and J. E. Fromer (eds.), *Resiliency in Native American and Immigrant Families.* Thousand Oaks, CA: Sage.

Tanner, D. M. (1978) *The Lesbian Couple.* Lexington, MA: Lexington Books.

Tasker, F. L., and Golombok, S. (1997) *Growing Up in a Lesbian Family: Effects on Child Development.* New York: Guilford.

Taylor, C. (1992) *Multiculturalism and the Politics of Recognition.* Princeton, NJ: Princeton University Press.

Taylor, M. (1995) Community work and the state. In G. Craig and M. Mayo (eds.), *Community Empowerment: A Reader in Participation and Developmen.* London: Zed Books.

Taylor, M. F. (ed.) (2002) (with J. Brice, N. Buck and E. Prentice-Lane) *British Household Panel Survey User Manual* Volume A: Introduction, Technical Report and Appendices. Colchester: University of Essex.

Taylor, R. (2002) *Britain's World of Work: Myth and Realities.* Swindon: Economic and Social Research Council.

Teachman, J. D., and Heckert, A. (1985) The impact of age and children on remarriage. *Journal of Family Issues*, 6, 185–203.

Teachman, J. D., Paasch, K., and Carver, K. (1996) Social capital and dropping out of school early. *Journal of Marriage and the Family*, 58, 773–83.

Teachman, J. D., Paasch, K., and Carver, K. (1997) Social capital and the generation of human capital. *Social Forces*, 75, 1343–60.

Teachman, J. D., Tedrow, L. M., and Crowder, K. D. (2000) The changing demography of America's families. *Journal of Marriage and the Family*, 62, 1234–46.

Teitler, J. O. (2002) Trends in youth sexual initiation and fertility in developed countries: 1960–1995. *Annals of the American Academy of Political and Social Science*, 580, 134–52.

Thane, P. (1981) Childhood in history. In M. King (ed.), *Childhood, Welfare and Justice*. London: Batsford.

Thomas, A., and Chess, S. (1977) *Temperament and Development*. New York: Bruner-Mazel.

Thompson, C. (2001) *Strategic Naturalizing: Kinship in the Infertility Clinic. Relative Values. Reconfiguring Kinship Studies*. Duke, NC: Duke University Press.

Thompson, E. H. (ed.) (1994) *Older Men's Lives*. Thousand Oaks, CA: Sage.

Thompson, P. (1999) The role of grandparents when parents part or die: some reflections on the mythical decline of the extended family. *Aging and Society*, 19, 471–503.

Thompson, P., Itzin, C and Abendstern, M. (1990) *I Don't Feel Old: The Experience of Later Life*. Oxford: Oxford University Press.

Thompson, R. A., and Wyatt, J. (1999) Values, policy and research on divorce. In R. A. Thompson and P. R Amato (eds.), *The Postdivorce Family. Children, Parenting And Society*. Mahwah, NJ: Sage.

Thompson, W. I. (1996) *The Time Falling Bodies Take to Light. Mythologies, Sexuality and the Origins of Culture*. New York: St. Martin's Griffin.

Thomson, E., Hanson, T. L., and McLanahan, S. S. (1994) Family structure and child well-being: Economic resources vs. parental behaviors. *Social Forces*, 73, 221-42.

Thomson, K. (1995) Working mothers: Choice or circumstance? *British Social Attitudes, the 12th report*. Dartmouth: Social and Community Research Planning.

Thorne, B. (1982) Feminist rethinking of the family: an overview. In B. Thorne and M. Yalom (eds.), *Rethinking the Family. Some Feminist Questions*. New York and London: Longman.

Thorne, B. (1987) Revisioning women and social change: where are the children? *Gender and Society*, 1, 85–109.

Tocqueville, A.de (1945) *Democracy in America*. New York: Knopf.

Tolson, A. (1977) *The Limits of Masculinity*. London: Tavistock.

Tong, R. (1989) *Feminist Thought: A Comprehensive Introduction*. Boulder, CO: Westview Press.

Tönnies, F. (1995) [1887] *Community and Association*. London: Routledge & Kegan Paul.

Toole, M. J., and Waldman, R. J. (1993) Refugees and displaced persons: War, hunger, and public health. *Journal of the American Medical Association*, 270, 600–5.

Toro-Morn, M. I. (1995) Gender, class, family, and migration: Puerto Rican women in Chicago. *Gender and Society*, 9, 712–26.

Toulemon, L. (1997) Cohabitation is here to stay. *Population: An English Selection*, 9, 11–46.

Touraine, A. (1996) *Critique of Modernity*. Cambridge: Polity.

Townsend, A. (2002) Human rights, transnational corporations and the World Bank. In P. Townsend and D. Gordon (eds.), *World Poverty: New Policies to Defeat an Old Enemy*. Bristol: Policy Press.

Townsend, P. (1979) *Poverty in the United Kingdom*. Harmondsworth: Allen Lane.

Treas, J. (1995) Beanpole or beanstalk? Comments on the demography of changing intergenerational relations. In V. L. Bengston, K. W. Schaie, and L. M. Burton (eds.), *Adult Intergenerational Relationships*. New York: Springer.

Treas, J. (1995) Older Americans in the 1990s and beyond. *Population Bulletin*, 50, 8–33.

Treas, J. (1999) Diversity in American families. In P. Moen, D. Dempster-McClain, and H. A. Walker (eds.), *A Nation Divided: Diversity, Inequality and Community in American Society*. Ithaca, NY: Cornell University Press.

Treas, J. (2002) How cohorts, education, and ideology shaped a new sexual revolution on American attitudes toward non-marital sex, 1972–1998. *Sociological Perspectives*, 45, 267–83.

Treas, J., and Cohen, P. (in press) Maternal co-residence and contact: evidence from cross-national surveys. In H. A. Gauthier, C. Chu, and S. Tuljapurkar (eds.), *The Distribution of Private and Public Resources Across Generations*. Oxford: Oxford University Press.

Treas, J., and Giesen, D. (2000) Sexual infidelity among married and cohabiting Americans. *Journal of Marriage and the Family*, 62, 48–60.

Treas, J., and Mazumdar, S. (2002) Older people in America's immigrant families: Dilemmas of dependence, integration, and isolation. *Journal of Aging Studies*, 16, 243–58.

Treas, J., and Torrecilha, R. (1995) The older population. In R. Farley (ed.), *State of the Union: America in the 1990s, Volume II: Social Trends*. New York: Russell Sage Foundation.

Triest, R. K. (1998) Has poverty gotten worse? *Journal of Economic Perspectives*, 12, 97–114.

Trinder, L. (1997) Competing constructions of childhood: Children's rights and children's wishes in divorce. *Journal of Social Welfare and Family Law*, 19, 291–305.

Troll, L., and Bengtson, V. L. (1979) Generation in the family. In W. Burr, R. Hill, I. Reiss, and I. Nye (eds.), *Theories About the Family*, Vol. 1. New York: Free Press.

Trost, J. (1992) The last decades and matrimonial changes. In H. Birg and X. Kaufmann (eds.), *Bevölkerungswisenschaft heute. Kolloquium anläalich des 10jährigen Jubiläums des Instituts für Bevölkerungsforschung und Sozialpolitik*. IBS-Materialien Nr. 33: Universität Bielefeld, 91–106.

Trovato, F., and Lauris, G. (1989) Marital status and mortality in Canada: 1951–1981. *Journal of Marriage and the Family*, 51, 907–22.

Trumbach, R. (1998) *Sex and the Gender Revolution, Volume 1: Heterosexuality and the Third Gender in Enlightenment London*. Chicago and London: Chicago University Press.

Trumbach, R. (1999) London. In D. Higgs (ed.), *Queer Sites: Gay Urban Histories Since 1600*. New York and London: Routledge.

Tsushima, T., and Gecas, V. (2001) Role taking and socialization in single-parent families. *Journal of Family Issues*, 22, 267–88.

Tu, E., Jow, C., Freedman, V. A., and Wolf, D. A. (1993) Kinship and family support in Taiwan: A microsimulation approach. *Research on Aging*, 15, 465–86.

Tucker, K. H. (1998), *Anthony Giddens and Modern Social Theory*. London: Sage.

Turcotte, P., and Bélanger, A. (1997) Moving in together: The formation of first common-law unions. *Canadian Social Trends*, 47, 7–10.

Turner, B. S. (1974) *Weber and Islam. A Critical Study*. London: Routledge & Kegan Paul.

Turner, B. S. (1998) The origins of the sociology of the family. In B. S. Turner (ed.), *Readings in the Anthropology and Sociology of the Family*. London: Routledge/Thoemmes.

Turner, J. and Coyle, A. (2000) What does it mean to be a donor offspring? *Human Reproduction*, 11, 2041–51.

Turner, V. (1966) Colour classification in Ndembu ritual. In M. Banton (ed.), *Anthropological Approaches to the Study of Religion*. London: Tavistock.

Udry, J. R. (1988) Biological predispositions and social control in adolescent sexual behavior. *American Sociological Review*, 53, 709–22.

Udry, J. R. (1990) Biosocial models of adolescent problem behaviors. *Social Biology*, 37, 1–10.

Udry, J. R. (1996) Biosocial models of low-fertility societies. *Population and Development Review*, 22, S325–S336.

Udry, J. R. (2000) Biological Limits of Gender Construction. *American Sociological Review*, 65, 443–57.

Uhlenberg, P. (1980) Death and the family. *Journal of Family History*, 5, 313–20.

Uhlenberg, P. (1996) Mutual attraction: Demography and life course analysis. *The Gerontologist*, 36, 226–29.

Uhlenberg, P., and Eggebeen, D. (1986) The declining well being of American adolescents. *The Public Interest*, 82, 25–38.

Ujimoto, K. V. (1999) Technology and aging: international perspectives. Paper presented at the Multidisciplinary Research Colloquium Series in Aging, University of Southern California, Los Angeles, October.

UK Office of National Statistics (2002) *Social Focus: Children 2002*. London: HMSO.

UK Office of National Statistics (2002) *Social Trends*. London: HMSO.

Umberson, D. (1987) Family status and health behaviors: Social control as a dimension of social integration. *Journal of Health and Social Behavior*, 28, 306–19.

Umberson, D. (1992) Gender, marital status, and the social control of health behavior. *Social Science and Medicine*, 34, 907–17.

Umberson, D. (1992) Relationships between adult children and their parents: psychological consequences for both generations. *Journal of Marriage and the Family*, 54, 664–74.

Umberson, D., and Gove, W. R. (1989) Parenthood and psychological well-being: Theory, measurement and stage in the family life course. *Journal of Family Issues*, 10, 440–62.

Umberson, D., and Williams, K. (1999) Family status and mental health. In C. S. Aneshensel and J. C. Phelan (eds.), *Handbook of the Sociology of Mental Health*. New York: Kluwer Academic/ Plenum.

UN Committee on the Rights of the Child (2002) Press Release HR/ 4624, 04/ 10/ 2002. New York: United Nations.

UN Population Division (1999) *The State of World Population*. New York: United Nations.

UN Preparatory Committee for the Special Session of the General Assembly on Children (2001) *A World Fit for Children*, A/ AC.256/ CRP.6/ Rev.3. New York: United Nations.

UN Preparatory Committee for the Special Session of the General Assembly for the Follow-up to the World Summit for Children in 2001 (2000) *Emerging Issues for Children in the Twenty-first Century*, A/ AC.256/ 3. New York: United Nations.

UN Special Session of the General Assembly (2002) Agreed Text, A/S – 27/19/Rev.1. New York: United Nations.

UNDP (1999) *Human Development Report*. New York: United Nations Organization and Oxford University Press.

UNICEF (1997) *The Progress of Nations*. Paris: United Nations Children's Fund.

UNICEF (1998) *Indicators for Global Monitoring of Child Rights*. New York: UNICEF.

UNICEF (2000) *A League Table of Child Poverty in Rich Nations*. Florence: Innocenti Research Centre.

UNICEF (2001) *Children's Rights: A Second Chance*. New York: UNICEF.

UNICEF (2001) *The State of the World's Children: Early Childhood*. New York: United Nations.

United Nations (1989) *Convention on the Rights of the Child*. Treaty Series, vol. 1577, p. 3. New York: United Nations.

United Nations (1992) *Questionnaire and Codebook: Fertility and Family Surveys in Countries of the ECE Region*. New York: United Nations.

United Nations Children's Fund (1994) *The Progress of Nations*. New York.

United Nations Economic Commission for Europe (2000) *Women and Men in Europe and North America 2000*. New York and Geneva: United Nations.

United Nations Economic Commission for Europe 1996–2001 (2001) *Fertility and Family Surveys in Countries of the ECE Region*. Geneva: United Nations.

United Nations High Commission for Refugees (1997) *The State of the World's Refugees: A Humanitarian Agenda*. Available online at: http:/ /www.unhcr.ch/refworld/pub/state/97/ intro.htm, last accessed December 30, 2000.

United Nations High Commission for Refugees (2002) *World Refugee Overview*. Geneva: UNHCR.

UNO (2001) *The Nature and Evolution of Poverty, World Development Report*. New York: United Nations Organization.

Upchurch, D., Lilliard, L. A., and Panis, C. W. A. (2001) The impact of nonmarital childbearing on subsequent marital formation and dissolution. In L. L. Wu and B. Wolfe (eds.), *Out of Wedlock: Causes and Consequences of Nonmarital Fertility*. New York: Russell Sage Foundation.

US Bureau of the Census (1992) Marriage, divorce, and remarriage in the 1990s. *Current Population Reports, Series P23-180*. Washington, DC: US Government Printing Office.

US Bureau of the Census (1993) *The 1990 Census of Population, General Population Characteristics, United States.* CP-2-1; Washington, DC: US Government Printing Office.

US Bureau of the Census (1997) Marital status and living arrangements: March (Update). *Current Population Reports*, Series P20–506. Washington, DC: US Government Printing Office.

US Bureau of the Census (1997) *Statistical Abstract of the United States: 1997*, 117th ed. Washington, DC.

US Bureau of the Census (1998) *Current Population Reports*. Washington, DC: Government Printing Office.

US Bureau of the Census (1998) *1998 Current Population*. Washington, DC: US Bureau of the Census.

US Bureau of the Census (1998) *Household and Family Characteristics: March, 1997.* Washington, DC, pp. 20–509.

US Bureau of the Census (1998b) Marital status and living arrangements: March, 1998. *Current Population Reports*, Series P20–514. Washington, DC: US Government Printing Office.

US Bureau of the Census (1998c) *Statistical Abstract of the United States: 1998*, 118th ed. Washington, DC: US Government Printing Office.

US Bureau of the Census (1999) Poverty in the United States: 1998. Table 2. *Current Population Reports*, Series P60–207. Washington, DC: US Government Printing Office.

US Bureau of the Census (2001) America's families and living arrangements: Population characteristics 2000. *Current Population Reports*, Series P20–537. Washington, DC: US Government Printing Office.

US Census Bureau (2000) Children under 18 years old by presence of parents: 1980–1998. *Statistical Abstract of the United States*, Table 69, p. 58. Washington, DC: US Government Printing Office.

US Census Bureau (2000) Civilian labor force and participation rates with projections: 1970 to 2008. *Statistical Abstracts of the United States*, Section 13, Table 644. Washington, DC: US Government Printing Office. Available online at http:/ /www.census.gov/prod/2001pubs/statab/sec13.pdf, last accessed March 22, 2003.

US Census Bureau. (2000) Grandchildren living in the home of their grandparents: 1980–1998. *Statistical Abstract of the United States*, Table 71, p. 60. Washington, DC: US Government Printing Office.

US Census Bureau (2000) Health Insurance Detailed Table: 1999. *Current Population Survey*, March 1999 and 2000. Washington, DC: US Government Printing Office. Available online at: http:/ / www.census.gov/ hhes/ hlthins/ hlthin99/ dtable1.html, last accessed February 22, 2001.

US Committee on Ways and Means (2000) Data on poverty. *2000 Green Book, Appendix H*, Washington, DC: Committee on Ways and Means, US House of Representatives.

US Department of Health and Human Services (2002) *Women are having more children, new report shows, teen birth rate continues to decline*, Vol. 50. Washington, DC. Retrieved from: http:/ /www.hhs.gov/news/press/2002pres/20020212.html

US General Accounting Office (2001) *Internally Displaced Persons Lack Effective Protection.* GAO-01-803. Washington, DC: US Government Printing Office.

US Population Reference Bureau (1999) *1999 World Population Data Sheet*. Washington, DC: US Government Printing Office.

Valenzuela, A., and Dornbusch, S. M. (1994) Familism and social capital in the academic achievement of Mexican origin and Anglo adolescents. *Social Science Quarterly*, 75, 18–36.

van de Kaa, D. (1987) Europe's second demographic transition. *Population Bulletin*, 42.

VanLaningham, J., Johnson, D. R., and Amato, P. (2001) Marital happiness, marital duration, and the U-shaped curve: Evidence from a five-wave panel study. *Social Forces*, 79, 1313–41.

Vatuk, S. (1972) *Kinship and Urbanization: White Collar Migrants in North India.* Berkeley and Los Angeles: University of California Press.

Vaughn, D. (1986) *Uncoupling*. New York: Vintage Books.

Veevers, J. E. (1980) *Childless by Choice*. Toronto: Butterworth.

Velu, C. (1999) Faut-il "pactiser" avec l'universalisme? A short history of the PACS. *Modern and Contemporary France*, 7, 429–42.

Vertovec, S. (1994) Caught in an ethnic quandary: Indo-Caribbean Hindus in London. In R. Ballard (ed.), *Desh Pardesh: The South Asian Presence in Britain*. London: Hurst.

Vidich, A., and Bensman, J. (1968) *Small Town in Mass Society: Class, Power and Religion in a Rural Community. Revised Edition*. Princeton, NJ: Princeton University Press.

Vinovskis, M. A. (1987) Historical perspectives on the development of the family and parent–child interactions. In J. B. Lancaster, J. Altmann, A. S. Rossi, and L. Sherrod (eds.), *Parenting Across the Life Span – Biosocial Dimensions*. New York: Aldine de Gruyter.

Wadsworth, M. (1991) *The Imprint of Time: Childhood, History and Adult Life*. Oxford: Clarendon Press.

Wagner, W., Kronberger, N., Gaskell, G. et al. (2002) Nature in disorder. The troubled public of biotechnology. In G. Gaskell and M.W. Bauer (eds.), *Biotechnology 1996–2000. The Years of Controversy*. London: Science Museum.

Wainwright, D., and Calnan, M. (2002) *Work Stress: The Making of a Modern Epidemic*. Buckingham: Open University Press.

Waite, L. J. (2001) Emotional and physical satisfaction with sex in married, cohabiting, and dating unions: Do men and women differ? In E. O. Laumann and R. T. Michael (eds.), *Sex, Love, and Health in America: Private Choices and Public Policies*. Chicago: University of Chicago Press.

Waite, L. J., and Gallagher, M. (2000) *The Case for Marriage: Why Married People are Happier, Healthier, and Better Off Financially*. New York: Broadway Books.

Waite, L. J., and Nielsen, M. (2001) The rise of the dual-earner family, 1963–1997. In R. Hertz and N. L. Marshall (eds.), *Working Families: The Transformation of the American Home*. Berkeley and Los Angeles: University of California Press.

Waksler, F. (1991) *Studying the Social Worlds of Childhood: Sociological Readings*. London: Falmer.

Walczak, Y., and Burns, S. (1984) *Divorce: The Child's Point of View*. London: Harper & Row.

Waldfogel, J. (1999) Early childhood interventions and outcomes. CASE/STICERD Discussion paper No. 21. London: London School of Economics.

Walker, A. J. (1996) Couples watching television: Gender, power and the remote control. *Journal of Marriage and the Family*, 58, 813–23.

Walker, J. (2001) *Information Meetings and Associated Provisions within the Family Law Act 1996*. London: Lord Chancellor's Department.

Walker, R. (2001) Can work work? A preliminary assessment of the "welfare to work" strategy. *Zeitschrift für Sozialreform*, 47, 437–63.

Walker, R. (forthcoming) *Social Security and Welfare*. Milton Keynes: Open University Press.

Walker, R., with Ashworth, K. (1994) *Poverty Dynamics: Issues and Examples*. Aldershot: Avebury.

Walker, R., Ashworth, K., Kellard, K., Middleton, S., Peaker, A., and Thomas, M. (1994) "Pretty, pretty, please" just like a parrot: Persuasion strategies used by children and young people. In S. Middleton, K. Ashworth, and R. Walker (eds.), *Family Fortunes: Pressures on Parents and Children in the 1990s*. London: CPAG.

Walker, R., Middleton, S., and Thomas, M. (1994) How mothers use Child Benefit. In S. Middleton, K. Ashworth, and R. Walker (eds.), *Family Fortunes: Pressures on Parents and Children in the 1990s*. London: CPAG.

Walker, R., and Park, J. (1998) Unpicking poverty. In C. Oppenheim (ed.), *An Inclusive Society*. London: IPPR.

Wall, R. (1992) Relationships between generations in British families past and present. In C. Marsh and S. Arber (eds.), *Families and Households*. London: Macmillan.

Wallerstein, J., Lewis, J. M., and Blakeslee, S. (2000) *The Unexpected Legacy of Divorce: A 25-Year Landmark Study*. New York: Hyperion.

Wallerstein, J. S. (1991) The long-term effects of divorce on children: A review. *Journal of the Academy of Child and Adolescent Psychiatry*, 30, 349-60.

Wallerstein, J. S., and Kelly, J. B. (1980) *Surviving the Breakup: How Children and Parents Cope with Divorce*. New York: Basic Books.

Wallman, S. (1984) *Eight London Households*. London: Tavistock.

Walzer, S. (1998) *Thinking About the Baby: Gender and Transitions into Parenthood*. Philadelphia: Temple University Press.

Wang, H., and Amato, P. R. (2000) Predictors of divorce adjustment: stressors, resources, and definitions. *Journal of Marriage and the Family*, 62, 655–68.

Wang, H., Silverstein, M., and Bengtson, V. L. (1999) The linkage between parent–child relations and the mortality risk of older parents: Evidence from a longitudinal study over 13 years. Paper presented at the meeting of the Scientific Meetings of the Gerontological Society of America, San Francisco, CA, November.

Ward, P. M. (1999) *Colonias and Public Policy in Texas and Mexico: Urbanization by Stealth*. Austin,: University of Texas Press.

Wardle, L. D. (1999) Divorce reform at the turn of the millennium: Certainties and possibilities. *Family Law Quarterly*, 33, 783–800.

Warin, J., Solomon, Y., Lewis, C., and Langford, W. (1999) *Fathers, Work and Family Life*. London and York: Family Policy Studies Centre and the Joseph Rowntree Foundation.

Warner, M. (1976) *Alone of All Her Sex. The Myth and the Cult of the Virgin Mary*. New York: Vintage Books.

Warner, M. (ed.) (1993) *Fear of a Queer Planet: Queer Politics and Social Theory*. Minneapolis and London: University of Minnesota Press.

Warnes, A. (1996) The demography of old age: Panic versus reality. In R. Bland (ed.), *Developing Services for Older People*. London: Jessica Kingsley.

Warnicke, R. M. (2000) *The Marrying of Anne of Cleves. Royal Protocol in Tudor England*. Cambridge: Cambridge University Press.

Warr, M., and Ellison, C. G. (2000) Rethinking social reactions to crime: Personal and altruistic fear in family households. *American Journal of Sociology*, 106, 551–78.

Warr, P. (1987) *Work, Unemployment and Mental Health*. Oxford: Clarendon Press.

Warwick, D., and Littlejohn, G. (1992) *Coal, Capital and Culture: A Sociological Analysis of Mining Communities in West Yorkshire*. London: Routledge.

Waters, M. (1996) Ethnic and racial identities of second-generation black immigrants in New York City. In A. Portes (ed.), *The New Second Generation*. New York: Russell Sage Foundation.

Waters, M. C. (1997) Immigrant families at risk: Factors that undermine chances for success. In A. Booth, A. C. Crouter, and N. Landale (eds.), *Immigration and Family: Research and Policy on U.S. Immigrants*. Mahwah, NJ: Lawrence Erlbaum.

Watney, S. (1994) *Practices of Freedom: Selected Writings on HIV/ AIDS*. London: Rivers Oram Press.

Watson, G. (1994) The flexible workforce and patterns of working hours. *Employment Gazette*, 102, 239–47.

Watson, G., and Fothergill, B. (1993) Part-time employment and attitudes towards part-time work. *Employment Gazette*, 101, 213–20.

Watson, J. L. (ed.) (1977) *Between Two Cultures: Migrants and Minorities in Britain*. Oxford: Basil Blackwell.

Watt, M. (1953) *Muhammad at Mecca*. Oxford: Clarendon Press.

Waugh, B. (1897) Introduction to W. Clarke-Hall, *The Queen's Reign for Children*. London: Fisher Unwin.

Weber, M. (1952) *Ancient Judaism*. New York: Free Press.

Weber, M. (1991) The social psychology of the world religions. In H. H. Gerth and C. Wright Mills (eds.), *From Max Weber: Essays in Sociology*. London: Routledge.

Weeks, J. (1977) [1990] *Coming Out: Homosexual Politics in Britain from the Nineteenth Century to the Present*. London: Quartet.

Weeks, J. (1991) *Against Nature: Essays on History, Sexuality and Identity*. London: Rivers Oram Press.

Weeks, J. (1995) *Invented Moralities: Sexual Values in an Age of Uncertainty*. Cambridge: Polity.

Weeks, J. (1998) The sexual citizen. *Theory, Culture and Society*, 15, 35–52.

Weeks, J., Heaphy, B., and Donovan, C. (1999) Families of choice: autonomy and mutuality in non-heterosexual relationships. In S. McRae (ed.) (1999) *Changing Britain: Families and Households in the 1990's*. Oxford: Oxford University Press.

Weeks, J., Heaphy, B., and Donovan, C. (2001) *Same Sex Intimacies: Families of Choice and other Life Experiments*. London: Routledge.

Weeks, J., and Porter, K. (1998) *Between the Acts: Lives of Homosexual Men 1885–1967*. London: Rivers Oram Press.

Weir, M., Orloff, A. S., and Skocpol, T. (1988) *The Politics of Social Policy in the United States*. Princeton, NJ: Princeton University Press.

Wellings, K., Field, J., Johnson, A. M., and Wadsworth, J. (1994) *Sexual Behavior in Britain: The National Survey of Sexual Attitudes and Lifestyles*. London: Penguin.

Wellman, B., Carrington, P., and Hall, A. (1988) Networks as personal communities. In B. Wellman and S. Berkowitz (eds.), *Social Structures: A Network Approach*. Cambridge: Cambridge University Press.Wellman, B., and Gulia, M. (1999) Virtual communities as communities. In M. Smith and P. Kollock (eds.), *Communities in Cyberspace*. London: Routledge.

Wellman, B., and Wortley, S. (1989) Brothers' keepers: situating kinship relations in broader networks of social support. *Sociological Perspectives*, 32, 273–306.

Wellman, B., and Wortley, S. (1990) Different strokes by different folks: Community ties and social support. *American Journal of Sociology*, 93, 558–88.

Wenger, G. (1984) *The Supportive Network: Coping with Old Age*. London: George Allen & Unwin.

Werbner, P. (1990) *The Migration Process: Capital, Gifts and Offerings among British Pakistanis*. Oxford: Berg.

Werner, E. E., and Smith, R. S. (2001) *Journeys From Childhood to Midlife: Risk, Resilience, and Recovery*. Ithaca, NY: Cornell University Press.

Westoff, C. (1986) Perspective on nuptiality and fertility. In K. Davis, M. Bernstam, and R. Ricardo-Campbell (eds.), *Below Replacement Fertility in Industrialized Societies*. Cambridge: Cambridge University Press.

Weston, K. (1991) *The Families We Choose: Lesbians, Gays, Kinship*. New York: Columbia University Press.

Wexler, N. S. (1979) Genetic "Russian roulette"; The experience of being "at risk" for Huntington's disease. In S. Kessler (ed.), *Genetic Counselling: Psychological Dimensions*. New York: Academic.

Wheelock, J. (1998) *Husbands at Home: The Domestic Economy in a Post-Industrial Society*. London: Routledge.

White, L. (1998) Who's counting? Quasi-facts and stepfamilies in reports of number of siblings. *Journal of Marriage and the Family*, 60, 725–33.

Whitehead, S. M., and Barrett, F. J. (eds.) (2001) *The Masculinities Reader*. Cambridge: Polity.

Wickrama, K. A. S., Lorenz, F. O., Wallace, L. E., Peiris, L., Conger, R. D., and Elder, G. H. (2001) Family influence on physical health during the middle years: The case of onset of hypertension. *Journal of Marriage and the Family*, 63, 527–39.

Widmer, E. D. (1999) Family contexts as cognitive networks: a structural approach of family relationships. *Personal Relationships*, 6, 487–503.

Widmer, E. D. (1999) *Les Relations Fraternelles des Adolescents*. Paris: Presses Universitaires de France.

Widmer, E. D., Kellerhals, J., and Levy, R. (forthcoming) Types of conjugal networks, conjugal conflict and conjugal quality. *European Sociological Review*.

Widmer, E. D., Treas, J., and Newcomb, R. (1998) Attitudes toward nonmarital sex in 24 countries. *Journal of Sex Research*, 35, 349–58.

Wiener, J. M., Illston, L. H., and Hanley, R. J. (1994) *Sharing the Burden: Strategies for Public and Private Long-term Care Insurance*. Washington, DC: Brookings Institution.

Wight, D. (1993) *Workers not Wasters: Masculine Respectability, Consumption and Employment in Central Scotland*. Edinburgh: Edinburgh University Press.

Wilhelm, B. (1998) Changes in cohabitation across cohorts: The influence of political activism. *Social Forces*, 77, 289–313.

Williams, D. R., Takeuchi, D. T., and Adair, R. K. (1992) Marital status and psychiatric disorders among blacks and whites. *Journal of Health and Social Behavior*, 33, 140–57.

Williams, E. J. (1996) The Maquiladora industry and environmental degradation in the United States–Mexican borderlands. *St. Mary's Law Journal*, 27, 765–815.

Williams, K., and Umberson, D. (2001) Marital status stability, marital transitions, and physical health status: A life course perspective. Presented at the Annual Meeting of the Population Association of America, Washington, DC.

Wilmoth, J. M. (2001) Living arrangements among older immigrants in the United States. *The Gerontologist*, 41, 223–8.

Wilmoth, J. M., DeJong, G. F., and Himes, C. L. (1997) Immigrant and non-immigrant living arrangements among America's white, Hispanic, and Asian elderly population. *Journal of Sociology and Social Policy*, 17, 57–82.

Wilson, B. (1966) *Religion in Secular Society*. London: Watts.

Wilson, G. (1995) "I'm the eyes and she's the arms": Changes in gender roles in advanced old age. In S. Arber and J. Ginn (eds.), *Connecting Gender and Ageing: A Sociological Approach*. Buckingham: Open University Press.

Wilson, M. N. (1989) Child development in the context of the Black extended family. *American Psychologist*, 44, 380–5.

Wilson, W. J. (1987) *The Truly Disadvantaged: The Inner City, the Underclass, and Public Policy*. Chicago: University of Chicago Press.

Wilson, W. J. (1997) *When Work Disappears: The World of the New Urban Poor*. New York: Vintage.

Winnicott, D. W. (1957) *The Child and the Outside World: Studies in Developing Relationships*. London: Tavistock.

Winter, I. (ed.) (2000) *Social Capital and Public Policy in Australia*. Melbourne: Australian Institute of Family Studies.

Winter, M. (1995) Islamic attitudes towards the human body. In J. M. Law (ed.), *Religious Reflections on the Human Body*. Bloomington and Indianapolis: Indiana University Press.

Wiseman, P. (2002) China's future is awry as boys outnumber girls. *USA Today*, June 19, 1–2.

Wish, M., Deutsch, M., and Kaplan, S. (1976) Perceived dimensions of interpersonal relations. *Journal of Personality and Social Psychology*, 33, 409–20.

Wolf, D. A. (2001) Everything is Relatives: Individual, Familial, and Collective Roles in Elder Care. Paper presented at the Policy Roundtable *Aging in the Americas: Critical Social Policy Issues*. Austin: University of Texas at Austin.

Wolf, D. A., Soldo, B. J., and Freedman, V. (1996) The demography of family care for the elderly. In T. Hareven (ed.), *Aging and Generational Relations over the Life Course: A Historical and Cross-Cultural Perspective*. New York: Walter de Gruyter.

Wolf, D. L. (1997) Family secrets: Transnational struggles among children of Filipino immigrants. *Sociological Perspectives*, 40, 457–82.

Wolf, N. (2001) *Misconceptions: Truth, Lies, and the Unexpected on the Journey to Motherhood*. New York: Doubleday.

Wollstonecraft, M. (1992) [1792] *A Vindication of the Rights of Women*. Harmondsworth: Penguin.

Wollstonecraft, M. (1996) [1792] *A Vindication of the Rights of Woman*. Mineola, NY: Dover Publications.

Woodhouse, B. (2000) The status of children, a story of emerging rights. In S. Katz, J. Eekalaar, and M. Maclean (eds.), *Cross-Currents: Family Law in the US and England*. Oxford: Oxford University Press.

Worobey, J. L., and Angel, R. J. (1990) Functional capacity and living arrangements of unmarried elderly persons. *Journal of Gerontology*, 45, 95–101.

Worobey, J. L., Angel, R. J., and Worobey, J. (1988) Family structure and young children's use of medical care. *Topics In Early Childhood Special Education*, 8, 30–40.

Wrigley, E. (1966) Family limitation in pre-industrial England. *Economic History Review*, 2nd Ser., 19, 82–109.

Wrigley, J. (1989) Do young children need intellectual stimulation? Experts' advice to parents, 1900–1985. *History of Education Quarterly*, 29, 41–75.

Wrong, D. H. (1961) The oversocialised conception of man. *American Sociological Review*, 26,183–93; reprinted in P. I. Rose (ed.), *The Study of Society*. New York: Random House, 1970.

Wu, L., and Martinson, B. (1993) Family structure and the risk of a premarital birth. *American Sociological Review*, 58, 210–32.

Wu, Z. (1999) Premarital cohabitation and the timing of first marriage. *Canadian Review of Sociology and Anthropology*, 36, 109–27.

Wu, Z. (2000) *Cohabitation: An Alternative Form of Family Living*. Don Mills, ON: Oxford University Press.

Wu, Z., and Pollard, M. S. (2000) Economic circumstances and the stability of nonmarital cohabitation. *Journal of Family Issues*, 21, 303–28.

Wyke, S., and Ford, G. (1992) Competing explanations for associations between marital status and health. *Social Science and Medicine*, 34, 523–32.

Yanagisako, S. and Delaney, C. (1995) Naturalizing power. In C. Delaney and S. Yanagisako (eds.), *Naturalizing Power*. New York: Routledge.

Yang, H. (1992) Population dynamics and kinship of the Chinese rural elderly: A microsimulation study. *Journal of Cross-Cultural Gerontology*, 7, 135–50.

Yeandle, S., Wigfield, A., Crompton, R., and Dennett, J. et al. (2002) *Employers, Communities and Family-Friendly Employment Policies*. London and York: York Publishing Services for the Joseph Rowntree Foundation.

Yoon, G., Eun, S. I., and Park, K. S. (2000) Demographic trends, sociocultural contexts, and public policy. In K. D. Kim, V. L. Bengtson, G. C. Meyers, and K. S. Eun (eds.), *Aging East and West: Families, States, and the Elderly*. New York: Springer.

Young, M., and Willmott, P. (1957) *Family and Kinship in East London*. London: Routledge & Kegan Paul.

Young, M., and Wilmott, P. (1957) *Family and Kinship in East London*. Glencoe, IL: Free Press.

Young, M., and Wilmott, P. (1973) *The Symmetrical Family*. London: Penguin.

Zabina, H., Schmid, T. L., Glasunov, I., Potemkina, R., Kamardina, T., Deev, A., Konstantinova, S., and Popovich, M. (2001) Monitoring behavioral risk factors for cardiovascular disease in Russia. *American Journal of Public Health*, 91, 1613–14.

Zarit, S. H., and Eggebeen, D. J. (2002) Parent–child relationships in adulthood and later years. In M. H. Bornstein (ed.), *Handbook of Parenting*. 2nd ed. Vol. 1. Mahwah, NJ: Lawrence Erlbaum.

Zelizer, V. A. (1985) *Pricing the Priceless Child: The Changing Social Value of Children*. New York: Basic Books.

Zerubavel, E. (1981) *Hidden Rhythms*. Berkeley: University of California Press.

Zhou, M. (1998) Parachute kids in Southern California: The educational experience of Chinese children in transnational families. *Educational Policy*, 12, 682–704.

Zhou, M., and Bankston, C. (1998) *Growing up American: How Vietnamese Children Adapt to Life in the United States*. New York: Russell Sage Foundation.

Zick, C. D., and Smith, K. R. (1991) Marital transitions, poverty, and gender differences in mortality. *Journal of Marriage and the Family*, 53, 327–36.

Zigler, E. (2002) Foreword. In M. H. Bornstein (ed.), *Handbook of Parenting*. 2nd ed. Vol. 1. Mahwah, NJ: Lawrence Erlbaum.

Zill, N., Morrison, D., and Coiro, M. J. (1993) Long-term effects of parental divorce on parent child relationships, adjustment and achievement in young adulthood. *Journal of Family Psychology*, 7, 91–103.

Zinn, M. B. (1994) Adaptation and continuity in Mexican-origin families. In R. L. Taylor (ed.), *Minority Families in the United States: A Multicultural Perspective*. Englewood Cliffs, NJ: Prentice Hall.

Zinn, M. B., and Eitzen, D. S. (1996) *Diversity in Families*. New York: HarperCollins.

Zinn, M. B., and Wells, B. (2000) Diversity within Latino families: New lessons for family social science. In D. H. Demo, K. R. Allen, and M. A. Fine (eds.), *Handbook of Family Diversity*. New York: Oxford University Press.

# Index